"This prodigiously well-read, well-written, elegant, and accessible study has a passionate and serious treatise to expound. As its title hints, it is not another book on the history of interpretation, except in the sense that Professor Provan believes that the history of interpretation, especially in the time of the Fathers and the Reformers, has vital significance for the twenty-first century. So, we need to pay attention if we are to get interpretation on the right track five hundred years after Luther posted his theses. Aspects of Professor Provan's own thesis about literal interpretation are unfashionable and therefore need to be pondered with open minds."

—JOHN GOLDINGAY, David Allan Hubbard Professor of Old Testament, Fuller Theological Seminary

"Iain Provan has given us here a vigorous affirmation on how to read the Bible as a Protestant. An important and nuanced argument set in the context of the wider Christian tradition and recent hermeneutical developments, this book stands out among the welter of recent writings on the Reformation."

—TIMOTHY GEORGE, Dean, Beeson Divinity School at Samford University and general editor of the Reformation Commentary on Scripture

"I've been waiting years for a book such as this: a comprehensive treatment of the nature, history, and significance of the Bible's literal interpretation. Here is a sustained argument for the importance of reading with the Reformers, which in Provan's account means doing as they say, not exactly as they do. This is a brave book that sails against the prevailing winds of hermeneutical fashion, charting a 'fifth way' that avoids reductive historical, expansive postmodern, narrow literalistic, and unregulated spiritual ways of reading the Bible. Read literally, Scripture is not a wax nose that can be turned this way or that, but a divinely inspired, authoritative text with real bite."

—KEVIN J. VANHOOZER, Research Professor of Systematic Theology, Trinity Evangelical Divinity School

"Using the magisterial Reformation for his compass, Provan surveys the current landscape of biblical interpretation and seeks to chart a faithful path forward. His sprawling, historiographical cartography explores the trails taken by those he styles as inveterate historical critics, unrepentant fundamentalists, modish postmoderns, and fashionable post-Protestants, all so he can offer a timely affirmation of 'literal' reading, rightly understood. Provan's 'fifth way' entails a chastened, reframed use of critical methods, rather than capitulating to them or rejecting them. His ultimate destination is a renewed emphasis on 'the Great Biblical Story as a canonical whole.'"

—STEPHEN B. CHAPMAN, Associate Professor of Old Testament and Director of Graduate Studies in Religion, Duke University

THE REFORMATION
and the
RIGHT READING of SCRIPTURE

Iain Provan

BAYLOR UNIVERSITY PRESS

© 2017 by Baylor University Press
Waco, Texas 76798

All Rights Reserved. No part of this publication may be reproduced, stored in a retrieval system, or transmitted, in any form or by any means, electronic, mechanical, photocopying, recording, or otherwise, without the prior permission in writing of Baylor University Press.

Cover design by AJB Design, Inc.
Cover image: map of Wittenberg from vol. 12 of *Topographia Germaniae*, 30 vols., Frankfurt am Mayn, Zum Truck verlegt von denen Merianischen Erben (imprint varies), 1642–1688. Published by Matthaeius Marian and continued by his son. Text by Martin Zeiller.

Library of Congress Cataloging-in-Publication Data

Names: Provan, Iain W. (Iain William), 1957– author.
Title: The Reformation and the right reading of scripture / Iain Provan.
Description: Waco, Texas : Baylor University Press [2017] | Includes bibliographical references and index.
Identifiers: LCCN 2017003709| ISBN 9781481306089 (hardback: alk. paper) | ISBN 9781481306096 (pbk. : alk. paper) | ISBN 9781481307499 (ePub) | ISBN 9781481307505 (Mobi/Kindle) | ISBN 9781481306102 (web pdf)
Subjects: LCSH: Bible—Hermeneutics. | Bible—Criticism, interpretation, etc. | Reformation.
Classification: LCC BS476.P78 2017 | DDC 220.601—dc23
LC record available at https://lccn.loc.gov/2017003709

For Lynette
On Your Birthday

And Martin
On Your Anniversary

Fall 2017

Possible After All!

Contents

	Acknowledgments	ix
	Abbreviations	xi
1	Introduction *O Little Town of . . . Wittenberg*	1

I
Before There Were Protestants
Long-Standing Questions

2	Scripture and Canon in the Early Church *On Chickens and Their Eggs*	27
3	The Formation of the Christian Canon *The Pressure of the Twenty-Two*	55
4	On the Meaning of Words *The Literal, the Spiritual, and the Plain Confusing*	81
5	The Reading of Scripture in the New Testament *All That the Prophets Have Spoken*	107
6	Literal Reading, Typology, and Allegory in Paul *A Rose by Any Other Name*	131
7	Justin, Irenaeus, and Tertullian *False Economies and Hidden Treasure*	151
8	Origen, Theodore, and Augustine *The Fertility of Scripture*	173
9	How Shall We Then Read? *The Church Fathers, the Reformers, and Ourselves*	199
10	The Septuagint as Christian Scripture *It's All Greek to Me*	227

| 11 | The Vulgate, the Renaissance, and the Reformation
When in Rome . . . | 253 |

II
Now There Are Protestants
Scripture in a Changing World

12	The Perspicuity of Scripture Alone *A Lamp unto My Feet*	283
13	The Authority of Scripture *Thy Word Is Truth*	313
14	The Bible, the Heavens, and the Earth *The Beginnings of an Eclipse*	347
15	The Emergence of Secular History *The Way We (Really) Were*	383
16	On Engaging with a Changing World *Fight, Flight, and the Fifth Way*	415

III
Still Protesting
Scripture in the (Post)Modern World

17	Source and Form Criticism *Behind the Text*	455
18	Redaction and Rhetorical Criticism *The Persuasive Text*	487
19	Structuralism and Poststructuralism *Texts and Subtexts*	517
20	Narrative Criticism *Getting the Story Straight*	549
21	Social-Scientific and Feminist Criticism *Texts as Social Constructs*	577
22	The Canonical Reading of Scripture *The End of Criticism*	609
23	Postscript	641

Appendix: Modern Developments in Our Understanding of the Biblical Text — 643
Bibliography — 649
Index of Biblical References and Ancient Jewish Sources — 687
Index of Authors — 697
Index of Subjects — 711

Acknowledgments

I have numerous Regent College students and alumni to thank for helping me so generously in the production of this book. In its early stages, Stacey Van Dyk, James Smoker, and Margie McKerron worked hard on collecting sources. Amy Anderson spent a whole academic year as my research assistant, and as the major editor of part 1, and she was succeeded by Daniel Supimpa, with support from Henna Lehtonen, in parts 2 and 3. Zachariah Kahler came on board in the final six months as the über-editor of the entire manuscript. Ryan Carroll read part 1 and Rachel Toombs most of part 1 in its early final form, and both made excellent suggestions that helped to improve it. I am also grateful to the excellent Regent College library staff for their support throughout the project, and especially during the final months.

Various academic colleagues also reviewed sections of the book in draft form and provided valuable input: Stephen Chapman, Dennis Danielson, Ross Hastings, Bruce Hindmarsh, Phil Long, Archie Spencer, Sven Soderlund, Kevin Vanhoozer, and Rikk Watts. I thank each one, although the normal caveats apply concerning their lack of responsibility for what I eventually chose to write. I also need to thank Hans Boersma, for a different reason. My disagreement with Hans on a range of issues to do with Bible reading and theology, and on related matters like what we should think about modernity, will be clear throughout this book, and I have no desire to disguise it. The issues are too important. Yet the clarity that I have reached on these issues is itself the result of engaging extensively with Hans' thinking, both in print and in conversation at Regent College, in a broader Christian context in which we share much in common. I am very grateful for this.

Finally, I must thank the Alexander von Humboldt Foundation in Germany for the funding that allowed me to spend a sabbatical term in Erfurt in the fall of 2016, working on the heart of the book, and Christoph and Ursula Bultmann for the warm welcome that they gave us there. It was a wonderful thing to be able to write about the Reformation in the heart of Reformation country, and I am grateful for the opportunity to have done so.

Iain Provan
Advent 2016

Abbreviations

Unless noted in the list below, all the abbreviations in this book follow the form in the Society of Biblical Literature Handbook of Style (2nd ed.; Atlanta: SBL, 2014).

ACW	Ancient Christian Writers
AJP	*American Journal of Physics*
ANCTRTB	Ashgate New Critical Thinking in Religion, Theology and Biblical Studies
ANF	*Ante-Nicene Fathers*
ASPTLA	Ashgate Studies in Philosophy and Theology in Late Antiquity
AYBRL	Anchor Yale Bible Reference Library
BAC	Bible in Ancient Christianity
BSCH	Brill's Series in Church History
BSIH	Brill's Studies in Intellectual History
CalC	Calvin's Commentaries
CB	Clarendon Bible
CH	*Church History*
CI	*Critical Inquiry*
CIT	Current Issues in Theology
CJMRS	*Comitatus: A Journal of Medieval and Renaissance Studies*
CP	Commentaries on the Prophets
CPC	Church and Postmodern Culture
CS	*Christian Scholar*
CSBH	Chicago Statement on Biblical Hermeneutics
CSBI	Chicago Statement on Biblical Inerrancy
CSCT	Columbia Studies in the Classical Tradition
CSRT	Columbia Series in Reformed Theology
CTC	Christian Theology in Context
CTHP	Cambridge Texts in the History of Philosophy

DTIB	*Dictionary for Theological Interpretation of the Bible*. Edited by Kevin J. Vanhoozer et al. Grand Rapids: Baker, 2005.
ECCA	Early Christianity in the Context of Antiquity
FCI	Foundations of Contemporary Interpretation
FP	*Faith and Philosophy*
FRMC	Figurae: Reading Medieval Culture
HBOT	*Hebrew Bible / Old Testament: The History of Its Interpretation*. Edited by Magne Sæbø. Göttingen: Vandenhoeck & Ruprecht, 1996–2015.
HS	*History of Science*
IAHI	International Archives of the History of Ideas
ISPR	Indiana Series in the Philosophy of Religion
IST	Issues in Systematic Theology
IVPNTC	IVP New Testament Commentary
JPSSDS	JPS Scholar of Distinction Series
JSHJ	*Journal for the Study of the Historical Jesus*
JTI	*Journal of Theological Interpretation*
LW	*Luther's Works*. Edited by Jaroslav Pelikan et al. 75 vols. St. Louis: Concordia, 1955–.
LWW	Library of the Written Word
NLH	*New Literary History*
NPNF	*Nicene and Post-Nicene Fathers*
NSBT	New Studies in Biblical Theology
PBTM	Paternoster Biblical and Theological Monographs
PSCF	*Perspectives on Science and Christian Faith*
PTGRFP	Pew-Templeton Global Religious Futures Project
RR	*Renaissance and Reformation*
SASRH	St. Andrews Studies in Reformation History
SBLTCS	SBL Text-Critical Studies
SCES	Sixteenth Century Essays and Studies
SHCT	Studies in the History of Christian Traditions
TCH	Transformation of the Classical Heritage
UB	Understanding the Bible
UBW	Understanding the Bible and its World
VCSup	Supplements to Vigiliae Christianae
WA	*D. Martin Luthers Werke*, Kritische Gesamtausgabe
WesTJ	*Wesleyan Theological Journal*
WP	*Works of Philo*. Translated by C. D. Yonge. London: H. G. Bohn, 1854–1890.

1

Introduction
O Little Town of... Wittenberg

> ... this stinking hole, this barbaric underworld, this heretical new Rome.
> —Johannes Cochlaeus[1]

> Out of love and zeal for truth and the desire to bring it to light, the following theses will be publicly discussed at Wittenberg....
> —Martin Luther[2]

This is a book about biblical interpretation, or "hermeneutics"—but we cannot begin there. If we are to understand the questions that lie at its heart, we must necessarily begin with some European history.

The town of Wittenberg in what is now northeastern Germany has an interesting past, both real and imagined.[3] Founded in the twelfth century AD, it soon became the residence of the Ascanian dynasty under Albrecht II (1250–1298), the founder of the duchy of Saxe-Wittenberg. By the time that this dynasty had run its course in the early fifteenth century, the town had become a strong fortress, owning almost all of the surrounding land and most of the electoral privileges (e.g., the right to mint coins). In the late fifteenth and early sixteenth centuries, now the capital of the Wettin King Frederick III "the Wise" (1463–1525), Wittenberg gained a new castle complete with a castle church, a university, and (consequently) more and more housing for the accommodation of faculty and students.

---

[1] Heinrich Böhmer, *Road to Reformation: Martin Luther to the Year 1521* (trans. John W. Doberstein and Theodore G. Tappert; Philadelphia: Muhlenberg, 1946), 47.

[2] Martin Luther, *Ninety-Five Theses; or, Disputation on the Power and Efficacy of Indulgences* (1517), in *Luther's Works* (75 vols.; ed. Jaroslav Pelikan, Helmut T. Lehmann, and Christopher Boyd Brown; St. Louis: Concordia, 1955–), 31:25. This American compendium will hereafter be cited as *LW*.

[3] William Shakespeare tells us that Hamlet, a prince of Denmark, studied in Wittenberg, along with his friend Horatio—the fictional development of real events involving Christian II (1481–1559), the nephew of Frederick the Wise, who spent some time in Wittenberg as an exile.

The university, founded at Frederick's request in 1502 by Johann von Staupitz, who became the first dean of the theological faculty and also assumed a professorship in Bible there (1502/3–1512), was principally maintained from income deriving from the castle church, with which it was closely associated. This church still stands in Wittenberg, in some respects not looking very different in its exterior now than it did in the sixteenth century, albeit that its wooden door, destroyed by fire in 1760, was replaced in 1858 with a bronze one, and its current roof and spire are differently (and controversially) constructed.[4] At the time of writing, it is being thoroughly renovated, together with the castle itself, in preparation for the five-hundredth anniversary celebrations of the events that I shall shortly describe. Much of the town of Wittenberg has changed to a greater extent, as a result of developments both internal and external. During the Seven Years' War in the eighteenth century, Wittenberg was bombarded by the Austrian army, and during Napoleon's campaigns in the nineteenth, it was occupied by the French. In the twentieth, mercifully, it escaped destruction during the Second World War, unlike many other historic German cities, although it was again occupied in the aftermath of war—this time by the Russians. It became part of East Germany in 1949, and of a reunited Germany in 1990.[5]

Wittenberg remains an interesting town. Yet not even nowadays does it strike the visitor as a likely venue for the beginning of a revolution. Back in the sixteenth century AD, when the Protestant Reformer Martin Luther launched his own kind of revolution there, the absurdity of the idea was already apparent to some. One of Luther's opponents, Duke George of Saxony (1471–1531), once proclaimed that it was intolerable that "a single monk, out of such a hole, should undertake a reformation."[6] Luther himself was not much more complimentary about the "hole," at least on his bad days. He could refer to it as "a butcher's yard" (i.e., where the animal parts not for sale were located), found "on the far border of civilization."[7] It is this reference that Heinrich Böhmer picks up in the title of

---

[4] Some contemporary German Protestants see the construction, with its surrounding motto drawn from Luther's famous hymn, "A Mighty Fortress Is Our God," as a symbol of the appropriation of Luther by the forces of German nationalism in the nineteenth century, and would like to see it replaced by something less fraught with negative associations. See, e.g., Christoph Bultmann, "Wider 'Ein feste Burg' als faktisches Motto des Reformationsgedenkens 2017," *Pastoral-Theologie* 102 (2013): 219–38.

[5] For a description of Wittenberg in the time of Luther, see Helmar Junghans, "Luther's Wittenberg," in *The Cambridge Companion to Martin Luther* (ed. Donald McKim; Cambridge: Cambridge University Press, 2003), 20–35.

[6] Ernest G. Schweibert, *Luther and His Times: The Reformation from a New Perspective* (St. Louis: Concordia, 1950), 206.

[7] This comment is dated to 1532 in *D. Martin Luthers Werke*, Kritische Gesamtausgabe: *Tischreden* (6 vols.; Weimar: Hermann Böhlaus Nachfolger, 1912–1921), 2:2800b (p. 669). The translation is my own. On Luther and Wittenberg, see further vols. 3:2880a (p. 47) and 4:4681

the sixth chapter of his book *Road to Reformation* (1946) as he begins to describe Wittenberg—this town "on the outskirts of civilization"[8]—using the words of Luther's arch-enemy Johannes Cochlaeus (writing in 1524):

> It is a poor, wretched, filthy town, hardly worth a red cent in comparison with Prague. Indeed, it is not worthy of being called a town in Germany. It is a town with an unhealthy and disagreeable climate, without vineyards, orchards, or fruit-bearing trees, with an atmosphere like that of a beer-cellar, altogether uncouth and made unpleasant by smoke and frost. What would Wittenberg be if it were not for the castle, the chapter house, and the university? Without these one would see nothing but Lutheran—that is to say, filthy—houses, dirty streets, and all the roads, paths, and alleys filled with slop. One would find a barbarous people which trades only in beer and catchpenny merchandise. Its market is not peopled. Its town has no citizenry. The people wear small-town clothing, and there is great want and poverty among the inhabitants.[9]

Cochlaeus was keen, Böhmer tells us, "to have this 'stinking hole, this barbaric underworld, this heretical new Rome' wiped from the face of the earth" (see the first epigraph to the present chapter). It was the Nazareth of medieval Germany, out of which no good thing could come (John 1:46).

MARTIN LUTHER IN WITTENBERG

Yet it was from Erfurt to Wittenberg that the troubled young Augustinian monk and priest Martin Luther was transferred late in 1511 by his longtime superior and confessor von Staupitz, succeeding him in 1512 as a professor in Bible in the university.[10] And it was this same Martin Luther who did, in fact, launch a revolution only a few years later that shook the very foundations of medieval Europe, turning Nazareth (in the eyes of many) into more of a Bethlehem. It began on October 31, 1517, but the immediate events that provoked it have deeper roots going back to March 31, 1515, when Pope Leo X granted a "plenary [complete] indulgence ... which was intended to finance the building of the new St. Peter's Basilica in

---

(p. 429), and Martin Brecht, *Martin Luther: His Road to Reformation 1483–1521* (vol. 1 of *Martin Luther*; trans. James L. Schaaf; Philadelphia: Fortress, 1985), 107. The Weimar edition of *Luther's Works* will hereafter be cited in its various divisions as *WA*, and is not to be confused with the American edition mentioned in an earlier footnote.

[8] *Road to Reformation* is a translation of Böhmer's *Der Junge Luther*, whose sixth chapter is headed "An der Grenze der Zivilisation (1508–1509)."

[9] Böhmer, *Road to Reformation*, 47.

[10] While still pursuing his theological studies, Luther had already taught in Wittenberg during 1508–1509. Brecht, *Luther: His Road*, 92–93.

Rome."[11] Indulgences in this period were designed to distribute to those who received them the excess "merit" accumulated by Christ and the saints, such that they received forgiveness for their sins. By Luther's time, they had become a major instrument for financing the Church, and at the same time a problem for rulers who saw money flowing out of their territories that they would have preferred to retain. In 1514 the pope had nevertheless cleverly negotiated the right to sell his plenary indulgence in the Church provinces of Mainz and Madgeburg, whose (joint) archbishop was Albrecht of Brandenburg-Hohenzollern—a man financially beholden to Rome because of the way in which he had risen to power. So it was that, at the beginning of 1517, the selling of plenary indulgence letters finally took off in these provinces, under the supervision, in Magdeburg, of a Dominican monk from Leipzig, Johann Tetzel. Soon the people of Wittenberg began to travel to the province of Magdeburg in order to gain access to this important commodity, and this had an immediate impact on pastoral care in Wittenberg—since when they returned, they naturally expected absolution from their priests without repentance or the amending of their lives. It was Luther's reflections on these events during the spring and summer of 1517 that ultimately spurred him into fateful action.

On October 31, Luther sent a letter to Archbishop Albrecht expressing concern about the papal indulgence and the manner in which it was being administered; he also wrote to at least one other bishop, and possibly to more. Along with the letter to Albrecht he enclosed his famous ninety-five theses. Either on the same day, or more likely a few weeks later,[12] he left his residence in the Augustinian Monastery (also called the Black Monastery) at the east end of Wittenberg, walked up to the door of the castle church, and nailed his theses to it. In the popular imagination, this action has taken on overtones of a defiant and loud "statement," the hammer-wielding Luther pounding into the sturdy door nails that would ultimately pierce the heart of the bishop of Rome himself. More likely we should think of it as akin to posting an advertisement for an upcoming seminar in the town square: "The door of the Schlosskirche . . . , which lay conveniently between the university library and the law lecture rooms, was the logical site for the university bulletin board."[13] The ninety-five theses are in reality as much an invitation as they are a statement, as their introduction makes clear. Their public discussion will take place

---

[11] For more on the background to, and also the development of, the indulgences "crisis" as summarized below, see Brecht, *Luther: His Road*, 176–92 (178).

[12] For a discussion of the chronology, see Brecht, *Luther: His Road*, 199–202.

[13] Brian Cummings, *The Literary Culture of the Reformation: Grammar and Grace* (Oxford: Oxford University Press, 2002), 31.

under the chairmanship of the reverend father Martin Lutther [sic], Master of Arts and Sacred Theology and regularly appointed Lecturer on these subjects at that place. He requests that those who cannot be present to debate orally with us will do so by letter.[14]

At the heart of the ninety-five theses, of course, lies concern about "papal indulgences" (thesis 27), by means of which "inestimable gift" (some claimed) "man is reconciled to [God]" (thesis 33). Luther's proposal, to the contrary, is that "those who believe that they can be certain of their salvation because they have indulgence letters, will be eternally damned, together with their teachers" (thesis 32); that "they who teach that contrition is not necessary on the part of those who intend to buy souls out of purgatory or to buy confessional privileges preach unchristian doctrine" (thesis 35); and that "any truly repentant Christian has a right to full remission of penalty and guilt, even without indulgence letters" (thesis 36). Criticism of the pope himself is never far below the surface, even if it is typically represented as deriving not from Luther, but from others. In thesis 81, for example, we read: "This unbridled preaching of indulgences makes it difficult even for learned men to rescue the reverence which is due the pope from slander or from the shrewd questions of the laity." The "laity's" criticism is then described in thesis 82: "Such as: Why does not the pope empty purgatory for the sake of holy love and the dire need of the souls that are there if he redeems an infinite number of souls for the sake of miserable money with which to build a church? The former reasons would be most just; the latter is most trivial." At the same time, Luther is careful to distinguish the pope's real intentions from the practices actually occurring in Germany; "if, therefore, indulgences were preached according to the spirit and intention of the pope," he writes in thesis 91, "all these doubts [the ones Luther has identified in the document] would be readily resolved. Indeed, they would not exist." This careful avoidance of attacks on the pope characterizes Luther's writings in the immediately succeeding period as well, even as he begins to question in a more serious manner notions such as papal infallibility.

The ninety-five theses quickly became known throughout Europe. Translated from Latin into German by the end of 1517, and then printed and distributed widely, almost immediately they were being read throughout Germany, and within a few months they had reached the rest of Europe; they were sent by

---

[14] Luther, *Ninety-Five Theses*, LW 31:25; all the quotes from the theses in what follows are taken from this same translation. Luther's name is found written in various forms in the sources; the matriculation book of the Great College in Erfurt, e.g., knows him (in Latin) as "Martinus ludher ex mansfelt"—"Mansfeld" being the city to which his parents had moved in 1484 from the vicinity of Eisenach, by way of Eisleben, shortly before his birth. Brecht, *Luther: His Road*, 1:9–14, 29.

Erasmus of Rotterdam to Thomas More in England, for example, on March 5, 1518.[15] By the summer of that same year, Luther's thinking about the forgiveness of sin had further developed—forgiveness is promised to the one who believes in God's Word—and radical implications had begun to emerge for the Church's entire penitential system (and not only with respect to indulgences).[16] By this point Luther was in serious trouble with Rome, and in October he arrived in Augsburg in southern Germany to meet with Cardinal Thomas Cajetan. The two main points at issue in their various encounters were "the certainty of salvation as the heart of Luther's doctrine of justification and the teaching of the treasure of the church as the foundation for the papal power of indulgences."[17] Cajetan informed Luther that he "should return to the heart of the church, retract his errors, and in the future refrain from them and from everything else which could disturb the church."[18] Luther refused to do so, eventually fleeing in the night under threat of arrest and deportation to Rome. For the next twenty-eight years until his death in Eisleben on February 18, 1546, he continued to debate with opponents, to teach, and to write tracts in pursuit of his vision of a reformed Church. By the time of his death, not only had Luther been excommunicated by Pope Leo X for refusing to recant his mistaken views,[19] but also Western Christendom was divided between Protestant and Roman Catholic camps.[20]

THE REFORMATION, AUTHORITY, AND BIBLICAL INTERPRETATION

At the heart of this important story lie questions of authority and—intrinsically connected to these—biblical interpretation. These questions are nicely brought out in Luther's response to enquiries about his writings at the Diet of Worms in 1521.[21] Asked whether he stood by everything he had written, he responded (while apologizing for his harsh tone in dealing with some individual opponents):

> Unless I am convinced by the testimony of the Scriptures or by clear reason (for I do not trust either in the pope or in councils alone, since it is well known that they have often erred and contradicted themselves), I am bound by the Scriptures

---

[15] Brecht, *Luther: His Road*, 1:204–5.
[16] Brecht, *Luther: His Road*, 1:221–37.
[17] Brecht, *Luther: His Road*, 1:250, in the midst of a gripping account of the events in Augsburg and their immediate aftermath (1:246–65).
[18] Brecht, *Luther: His Road*, 1:253.
[19] Brecht, *Luther: His Road*, 1:426–27.
[20] Derek Wilson, *Out of the Storm: The Life and Legacy of Martin Luther* (New York: St. Martin's, 2007), 284.
[21] A "diet" was a meeting (somewhat like a parliament) of the various estates of the realm of the Holy Roman Empire.

> I have quoted and my conscience is captive to the Word of God. I cannot and I will not retract anything, since it is neither safe nor right to go against conscience. May God help me. Amen.[22]

Luther takes his stand on "the testimony of the Scriptures" as he understands them, and it matters not that the bishop of Rome or any other bishop considers his position untenable, for they themselves are only fallible readers. This same theme comes out clearly in Luther's earlier encounter in a public forum with the theologian John Eck (Leipzig, 1519), in the course of which Luther explicitly asserts that Matthew 16:18 (which begins "you are Peter, and on this rock I will build my church")[23] does not give the pope the exclusive right to interpret Scripture and then simply tell other Christians what it says. The issues at stake are clarified in the response of the presiding officer at Worms to Luther's refusal to recant:

> Martin, in the last resort you retreat and take refuge to the place where all heretics are wont to resort and have recourse. Of course, you say that you are prepared . . . to accept instruction from the Holy Scriptures from anyone at all. . . . Is it not the case that all the heretics have always behaved in the same manner? Is it not the case that you, just as they did, want Holy Scripture to be understood by your whim and your own ideas? . . . Many of the ideas you introduce are heresies of the Beghards, the Waldenses, the Poor Men of Lyons, of Wycliffe and Huss, and of others long since rejected by the synods.[24]

An appeal to Scripture by an individual over against the Church was not to be tolerated. Notorious heretics had attempted it before—exactly the company of Scripture readers to which Luther was assigned by the imperial Edict of Worms, issued a month after his defense, by which time Luther himself had left the city under a prior promise of safe conduct:

> [T]he said Martin Luther shall hereafter be held and esteemed by each and all of us as a limb cut off from the Church of God, an obstinate schismatic and manifest heretic . . . you shall refuse to give the aforesaid Martin Luther hospitality, lodging, food, or drink; neither shall any one, by word or deed, secretly or openly, succor

---

[22] Brecht, *Luther: His Road*, 1:460.
[23] All Scripture translations are from the NIV unless otherwise noted.
[24] James Atkinson, *The Trial of Luther* (New York: Stein & Day, 1971), 159–60. Confusingly, this presiding officer was also named Eck, so we must be careful to distinguish the two. Johann von der Eck was the official of the archbishop of Trier just mentioned in relation to the Diet of Worms (1521). The Leipzig disputant Johann Maier von Eck (1486–1543) was a professor at the University of Ingolstadt. For the sake of continuing clarity, I shall refer to the former as "Johann von der Eck" or "von der Eck" and to the latter as "John Eck" or "Eck." On the Ecks, Leipzig, and Worms, see Brecht, *Luther: His Road*, 1:299–322, 452–70.

or assist him by counsel or help; but in whatever place you meet him, you shall proceed against him; if you have sufficient force, you shall take him prisoner and keep him in close custody; you shall deliver him, or cause him to be delivered, to us or at least let us know where he may be captured. In the meanwhile you shall keep him closely imprisoned until you receive notice from us what further to do, according to the direction of the laws.[25]

Happily for Luther, he had been "kidnapped" on his journey back from Worms by servants of Frederick the Wise and hidden in the secluded Wartburg, a spectacular castle still sitting high above the town of Eisenach, where he was shortly to translate the New Testament (NT) into German. So it was that he returned to the town where, as a teenager, he had for several years attended school.[26]

It was out of the tumult of these events that there first began to emerge a "Protestant" approach to the Bible, as Luther and those who followed his lead developed their argument that Scripture, and not the bishop of Rome, should be the final authority in matters of faith and life. This argument is often referred to using the slogan *sola Scriptura* (the Latin for "Scripture alone"). The requirement that Christians should consult Scripture alone for guidance on doctrine and practice, in a historical context in which the tradition of the medieval Church was already being subjected to widespread scrutiny (as we shall see in subsequent chapters), inevitably led on to further questions that required good answers.

The Canon

First of all, *which* Scripture was to be read "alone"? As to the *extent* of the biblical canon, Reformers like Martin Luther and John Calvin—who are mainly but not exclusively in view (as "the greatest of the Reformers")[27] when I refer in this book to "the Reformers" or "Reformation thinkers"[28]—followed the lead of Christian writers in the first few centuries of the post-apostolic Church like Jerome (c. AD 347–420) and excluded the Apocrypha. These are books like the Wisdom of Solomon and Ecclesiasticus, which had occupied an important place in the life of the

---

[25] James H. Robinson, ed., *From the Opening of the Protestant Revolt to the Present Day* (vol. 2 of *Readings in European History: A Collection of Extracts from the Sources Chosen with the Purpose of Illustrating the Progress of Culture in Western Europe since the German Invasions*; Boston: Ginn, 1906), 87–88.

[26] Brecht, *Luther: His Road*, 1:17–21.

[27] Gerald Bray, *Biblical Interpretation: Past and Present* (Leicester: Apollos, 1996), 177.

[28] It is above all the ideas of Luther and Calvin in which I am interested as templates for future hermeneutical endeavor in this book, although I shall from time to time draw in other important figures like Martin Bucer, Philipp Melanchthon, and Huldrych Zwingli. I shall to a much lesser extent draw into my discussion the "radical Reformers," whose ways of approaching the Bible were often significantly different from the "magisterial Reformers" (who get their name from the ways in which they related to the secular authorities of their day).

early post-apostolic Church, but whose canonicity had always been a disputed matter.[29] This perspective is reflected in Luther's 1534 German translation of the Bible, in which the books of the Apocrypha appear in a separate, intertestamental section.[30]

The Text

As to the *text* of the canon, the Reformers shared the broadly held Renaissance Humanist opinion of their time that texts in their original biblical languages (mainly Hebrew and Greek) should form the basis for study of the Bible, and not the venerable Latin Vulgate deriving largely from Jerome. The Vulgate is only "the ancient interpreter," as Calvin frequently refers to it[31]—to be consulted, certainly, but also to be corrected as necessary. The very preservation of the gospel itself depends on competence in the original biblical languages, which "are the sheath in which this sword of the Spirit is contained . . . the casket in which this jewel is enshrined . . . the vessel in which this wine is held."[32] It was upon such original-language texts that Luther himself depended for the translations that ultimately came to make up his 1534 Bible. Other vernacular, original-text translations, in different European languages, began to appear in the same time period.[33] These translations were necessary, of course, since most people (then as now) could not read Hebrew or Greek. Scripture could function in a Protestant way for most Christian believers, then, only if translations in the vernacular were available.

The Perspicuity of Scripture

The Reformers believed that, equipped with Bible translations that faithfully represented the original texts, purified now from ancient corruptions, no one possessing some rudimentary rules of reading "would have undue difficulty in understanding the plain meaning of the sacred text"[34]—since as Luther once put

---

[29] See further my chapter 2 below.

[30] For an interesting account of the production of this epochal piece of European literature, see John L. Flood, "Martin Luther's Bible Translation in Its German and European Context," in *The Bible in the Renaissance: Essays on Biblical Commentary and Translation in the Fifteen and Sixteenth Centuries* (ed. Richard Griffiths; SASRH; Aldershot: Ashgate, 2001), 45–70.

[31] E.g., John Calvin, *Commentaries on the First Book of Moses Called Genesis* (CalC 1; ed. and trans. John King; London: Calvin Translation Society, 1847; repr., Grand Rapids: Baker, 1981), 113.

[32] Martin Luther, *To the Councilmen of All Cities in Germany That They Establish and Maintain Christian Schools* (1524), LW 45:360.

[33] Martin Brecht, *Martin Luther: Shaping and Defining the Reformation 1521–1532* (vol. 2 of *Martin Luther*; trans. James L. Schaaf; Minneapolis: Fortress, 1990), 46–47, 55. See Bray, *Biblical Interpretation*, 168, regarding other vernacular translations (briefly), and, further, my chapter 11 below.

[34] Bray, *Biblical Interpretation*, 190.

it, "[t]he Holy Spirit is the simplest writer and adviser in heaven and on earth."[35] Therefore (he asserts in *The Bondage of the Will*, 1525), "[t]ruly it is stupid and impious, when we know that the subject matter of Scripture has all been placed in the clearest light, to call it obscure on account of a few obscure words."[36] That is, Scripture is "perspicuous."

The Literal Sense

As to "rudimentary rules" of reading, the Reformers placed enormous emphasis on the "literal sense" of the biblical text. Such opinion rejected the common idea of the preceding medieval and patristic centuries that other levels of meaning in a text—sometimes summarized under the heading "allegorical," since they concern what is "other" (Gk. *allos*) than the literal, and what is allegedly hidden in the text rather than what is clear—were often or even normally more important than the literal sense, and indeed represented the "spiritual" sense of a text. There was widespread agreement among Reformation thinkers, to the contrary—and in this they also agreed with considerable Renaissance Humanist opinion—that the literal sense of Scripture, rooted in its historical context, is in fact also its spiritual sense. It is here that the "simple" sense is to be found—in what someone like Moses said and meant back in his own time. It is for this reason, for example, that Calvin disagrees with Augustine's reading of Genesis 1:1 as referring to Christ, since this is not what Moses wished to say.[37] The Reformers could be strident in their opposition to allegorical reading, most especially when it was premised on the idea that "the perusal of Scripture would be not merely useless, but even injurious, unless it were drawn out into allegories"—an error that Calvin claims has been "the source of many evils."[38]

The Analogy of Scripture

In the thinking of the Reformers, however, the literal sense is not to be found in individual biblical texts by themselves. The "Scripture alone" that Christians are to read for guidance concerning faith and life is the whole Scripture, stretching from Genesis to Revelation, which we should receive from God as a coherent

---

[35] Martin Luther, *Answer to the Hyperchristian, Hyperspiritual, and Hyper-learned Book by Goat Emser in Leipzig—Including Some Thoughts Regarding His Companion, the Fool Murner* (1521), LW 39:178.

[36] Martin Luther, *The Bondage of the Will* (1525), LW 33:26.

[37] Calvin, *Genesis*, 69–70. Note also references early in this commentary such as those to "the design of Moses" at Gen 1:6 and 2:4 (80, 108), and what "Moses intended to note" at Gen 2:18 (131).

[38] John Calvin, *Commentary on the Epistles of Paul the Apostle to the Corinthians* (CalC 20; GSC; ed. and trans. John Pringle; London: Calvin Translation Society, 1847; repr., Grand Rapids: Baker, 1981), 174—in a comment on 2 Cor 3:6.

message to the Church and to the world. Thus, individual texts must be read in the context of the whole unfolding covenantal story of Scripture. In particular, nothing should be inferred from a difficult or unclear passage that is not evident from other, clearer passages (whose existence is what provides Scripture overall with "perspicuity"). Again, in *The Bondage of the Will*, Luther remarks:

> I admit, of course, that there are many texts in the Scriptures that are obscure and abstruse, not because of the majesty of their subject matter, but because of our ignorance of their vocabulary and grammar; but these texts in no way hinder a knowledge of all the subject matter of Scripture.... The subject matter of the Scriptures, therefore, is all quite accessible, even though some texts are still obscure owing to our ignorance of their terms.... If the words are obscure in one place, yet they are plain in another.[39]

This principle is often referred to as "the analogy of faith" (Latin *analogia fidei*). This terminology carries with it the potential for confusion, however, since it is routinely used by Roman Catholics (in line with pre-Reformation tradition), along with the closely related "rule of faith" (*regula fidei*), to refer to a principle whereby biblical passages must not be set in opposition either to one another, or to the faith and teaching of the Roman Catholic Church. For this reason, others prefer the term "analogy of Scripture," which makes it clearer that the rule of faith—sometimes also referred to as the "rule of truth"—is Scripture itself, and not something external to it.[40]

THE INSPIRATION OF SCRIPTURE

That Scripture is indeed to be "received from God" brings us to a couple of final aspects of the developing Protestant approach to the Bible in the sixteenth century that need to be emphasized at this point in our discussion. They are both connected to the notion that the Bible is the final authority in matters of faith and life. The Reformers believed, along with Christians throughout the ages before them, that the Bible is inspired by God, who speaks through it to the Church and to the world; as John Chrysostom put it in the fourth century, in commenting on Isaiah 6, "[t]he mouths of the inspired authors are the mouth of God."[41] As such, the Bible is infallible, in the sense that it does not lead its faithful readers

---

[39] Luther, *Bondage*, LW 33:25–26.
[40] See H. Wayne Johnson, "The 'Analogy of Faith' and Exegetical Methodology: A Preliminary Discussion on Relationships," *JETS* 31 (1988): 69–80 (70). In a more recent article on Protestant hermeneutics, Henry Knapp discusses the analogy of faith and the analogy of Scripture under separate headings, but it is difficult to see what the real difference between them is. Henry M. Knapp, "Protestant Biblical Interpretation," *DTIB*, 633–38.
[41] Cited in Robert C. Hill, *Reading the Old Testament in Antioch* (BAC 5; Leiden: Brill, 2005), 30.

into spiritual error, albeit that its words were penned by people long ago, and that in various ways they reflect their own times and their places. This is certainly Calvin's view:

> In order to uphold the authority of the Scripture, [Paul] declares that it *is divinely inspired*; for, if it be so, it is beyond all controversy that men ought to receive it with reverence. This is a principle which distinguishes our religion from all others, that we know that God hath spoken to us, and are fully convinced that the prophets did not speak at their own suggestion, but that, being organs of the Holy Spirit, they only uttered what they had been commissioned from heaven to declare. Whoever then wishes to profit in the Scriptures, let him, first of all, lay down this as a settled point, that the Law and the Prophets are not a doctrine delivered according to the will and pleasure of men, but dictated by the Holy Spirit . . . we owe to the Scripture the same reverence which we owe to God.[42]

At the same time, not every reader of the Bible does in fact receive Scripture as "from God," even if it *is* perspicuous in its meaning, because understanding is not itself conviction as to truthfulness; it is possible to comprehend a text perfectly, and yet not believe a word of what it says. The work of the Holy Spirit is required in a person's heart if he or she is to become convinced that what the text *says* is also *true*. God must speak *to the individual* as well as *in the text*: "there are two kinds of clarity in Scripture, just as there are also two kinds of obscurity: one external and pertaining to the ministry of the Word, the other located in the understanding of the heart."[43]

Five Hundred Years on Contemporary Protestant Interpretation

Five hundred years have elapsed since Luther's publication of his ninety-five theses, and the Protestant Church that he (accidentally) founded in the subsequent years has grown at an astonishing rate since that time—most notably during the last one hundred and fifty years. Data from the Pew Forum suggest that in 2010 there were 804 million Protestant Christians worldwide, representing more than one-third of all Christians (37 percent).[44] This might suggest to the casual observer, among other things, that as we celebrate the beginnings of the Reformation in 1517, Protestant biblical interpretation remains alive and well—that

---

[42] John Calvin, *Commentaries on the Epistles to Timothy, Titus, and Philemon* (in CalC 21; GSC, also including *Galatians, Ephesians, Philippians, Colossians*, and *I & II Thessalonians*; ed. and trans. William Pringle; London: Calvin Translation Society, 1847; repr., Grand Rapids: Baker, 1981), 248–49.

[43] Luther, *Bondage*, LW 33:28.

[44] Conrad Hackett et al., *The Global Religious Landscape: A Report on the Size and Distribution of the World's Major Religious Groups as of 2010* (PTGRFP; Washington, D.C.: Pew Research Center, December 2012), 17–18.

Protestant hermeneutics continue to give an account of the Bible and of human experience that many people find compelling. The reality is, however, different. Probe just beneath the surface and you will find that, in reality, the contemporary field of Protestant hermeneutics, both at a scholarly and at a popular level, lies in some disarray. The situation may satisfactorily be summarized by describing four contemporary "ways" of reading.

THE FIRST WAY: HISTORICAL CRITICISM

Among the various scholarly heirs of the Reformation, we find among our contemporaries, first of all, those of a historical-critical mind-set. Dominant in many Western universities throughout most of the late nineteenth century and then the twentieth, historical critics have shown a consistent interest (in their source, form, and redaction criticism) in the written and oral traditions that underlie our biblical texts, and the editorial processes by which they have come down to us. These "first way" critics have displayed a strong commitment to establishing single, original, and literal meanings for biblical texts in their various historical contexts (and languages), and they have prioritized such intended authorial meanings in their reflection on theology and practice, often over against both traditional and prevailing norms of interpretation. For a biblical scholar like James Barr, for example, it is precisely the prioritizing of such academic work that Reformation principles require of us. We must above all seek to understand what biblical texts, in their original languages, first meant to those to whom they were written:

> Biblical authority on Protestant terms ... exists only where one is free, on the ground of scripture, to question, to adjust, and if necessary to abandon the prevailing doctrinal traditions. Where this freedom does not exist, however much the Bible is celebrated, its authority is in fact submitted to the power of a tradition of doctrine and interpretation. The Protestant approach to scripture can operate only if the actual datum of the biblical text, the *Wortlaut* to use the German term, the actual linguistic and grammatical datum of the text, its form with the semantic implications of that form, can in principle assert itself as against what is alleged to be the interpretation.[45]

"First way" scholarship tends at the same time to diminish the importance of, or ignore, interpretative questions that arise at the level of whole sections of biblical text, or of the biblical canon as a whole. It also tends greatly to problematize the ability of Scripture as a whole coherently to address the Church and the world at the present time. Indeed, it sometimes seems that the entire purpose of such scholarship is to *prevent* Scripture from addressing either the Church

---

[45] James Barr, *Holy Scripture: Canon, Authority, Criticism* (Philadelphia: Westminster, 1983), 31–32.

or the world, by complicating just as much as it can the question of how we can move from the past of the text to its present. The first way "movement" has been, to a significant degree, an "anti-perspicuity" movement—which has a lot to do with its point of origin, as we shall see later in the book. Correspondingly, even for scholars in this mode whose Protestantism is more than merely cultural, and who believe that God does *somehow* still speak through the Bible, it sometimes appears that any connection between their academic and their Church life is tenuous at best. In this respect, at least, "modernists" at this end of the spectrum are not very Protestant at all.

The Second Way: Postmodern Reading

These modernists remain more Protestant, however (and second), than many of those who adopt more recent, postmodern approaches to the Bible, emphasizing the independence of texts from their authors and the role of the reader in *constructing* meaning out of texts. In this "second way" of approaching biblical interpretation, readers and their communities play a decisive role in hermeneutics, affirming or resisting the theology explicit or implicit in biblical texts from their own standpoint within the larger story about reality that they hold to be true. The biblical text in itself as a historical artifact, or even as an objective reality in the present, becomes much less important in this way of thinking than those who encounter or even "create" the text as they read it. Unsurprisingly, biblical languages are often among the first casualties of such an approach, since questions of original textual meaning tend greatly to diminish in importance for its advocates. Further casualties include many theological and ethical perspectives that have long been regarded—because they have been understood to be rooted in Scripture—as central to Protestant Christian faith. This is arguably the inevitable consequence of embracing a consciously "weak theology" of the kind advocated by philosopher John Caputo (in dependence on the deconstructive thought of Jacques Derrida), in a book like *The Weakness of God*.[46] Here the emphasis lies on an undogmatic, perspectival approach to theology, in which an omnipotent God actively at work in the world is replaced by a weak God who does not intervene in nature—and this applies as much to the incarnation as anything else. The highest human virtues, correspondingly, are weak rather than strong (i.e., hospitality, and openness). If we ask about the meaning of the word "God" itself, in fact, it turns out not to refer to a person, but to represent "a call for justice,

---

[46] John D. Caputo, *The Weakness of God: A Theology of the Event* (ISPR; Bloomington: Indiana University Press, 2006)—"Derrida's American ambassador," according to James K. A. Smith, *Introducing Radical Orthodoxy: Mapping a Post-Secular Theology* (Grand Rapids: Baker, 2004), 59.

forgiveness, hospitality ...'calling upon what is best in us.'"⁴⁷ To *conceptualize* God in response to this call, as confessional faiths do, is (on this view) to miss the point. To read Scripture in pursuit of propositions rather than as poetry is, likewise, to miss the point.

Although it is difficult to see how much of this "second way" reading is at all congruent with Reformation perspectives, this has not prevented such postmodern thinking from making impressive inroads into contemporary Protestant communities, and shaping or influencing their hermeneutics. What is often called the "emergent church," in particular, has been significantly impacted by thinkers like Caputo, and by Protestant counterparts like Peter Rollins (in books like *The Fidelity of Betrayal* and *The Idolatry of God*).⁴⁸ The emergent church has in turn been welcomed in many quarters as good news for the Church at large.⁴⁹

THE THIRD WAY: THE CHICAGO CONSTITUENCY

A third group of scholarly heirs of the Reformation takes a very different view of Bible reading (and many other things), setting their face resolutely against both modernist biblical hermeneutics and its postmodern successors. This position finds its institutional home in conservative Christian churches, seminaries, and other institutions, especially in North America, and it is well represented not so much by a person as by a document: *The Chicago Statement on Biblical Hermeneutics (CSBH*, 1982).⁵⁰ "Third way" Bible readers flatly reject postmodern developments—any notion "that the 'horizons' of the biblical writer and the interpreter may rightly 'fuse' in such a way that what the text communicates to the interpreter is not ultimately controlled by the expressed meaning of the Scripture" (article 9). Their view of what is involved in the pursuit of "the expressed meaning of the Scripture" is very similar to that of modernist historical critics. They are looking for the "single, definite and fixed" meaning expressed in each

---

⁴⁷ Stefan Stofanik, "Introduction to the Thinking of John Caputo: Religion without Religion Is the Way out of Religion," in *Between Philosophy and Theology: Contemporary Interpretations of Christianity* (ed. Lieven Boeve and Christophe Brabant; Farnham: Ashgate, 2010), 19–25 (21). He is citing partially from Caputo, *Weakness of God*, 41.

⁴⁸ E.g., Peter Rollins, *The Fidelity of Betrayal: Towards a Church Beyond Belief* (Brewster, Mass.: Paraclete, 2008); and *The Idolatry of God: Breaking Our Addiction to Certainty and Satisfaction* (New York: Howard, 2012). For one indication of the impact, note the fulsome praise for Caputo's literary output offered by Brian McLaren in the foreword to Caputo's 2007 book, *What Would Jesus Deconstruct? The Good News of Postmodernism for the Church* (CPC; Grand Rapids: Baker, 2007); for another, note that both John Caputo and Peter Rollins were featured speakers at the Greenbelt Christian Festival in England in 2013.

⁴⁹ Phil Snider and Emily Bowen, *Toward a Hopeful Future: Why the Emergent Church Is Good News for Mainline Congregations* (Cleveland: Pilgrim Press, 2010).

⁵⁰ The *CSBH* is available in E. D. Radmacher and R. D. Preus, eds., *Hermeneutics, Inerrancy, and the Bible: Papers from ICBI Summit II* (Grand Rapids: Zondervan, 1984), 881–87.

biblical text (article 7)—the "grammatical-historical sense, that is, the meaning which the writer expressed" (article 15). However, they take it to be one aspect of Protestant orthodoxy that Bible readers should be careful only to allow "legitimate critical techniques" to be used "in determining the canonical text and its meaning" (article 16), and they urge caution with respect to particular methods, like form criticism (article 13). Indeed, they urge caution with respect to modern biblical scholarship in general, invoking the idea of the perspicuity of Scripture: while no one "should ignore the fruits of the technical study of Scripture by biblical scholars," yet "a person is not dependent for understanding of Scripture on the expertise of biblical scholars" (article 24). Their particular concern in all of this is not only to advance the idea that God does indeed speak clearly and trustworthily to both the Church and the world through Scripture, but also to defend a set of specific understandings of *what it is* that God has said. Following the lead of some Protestants in the late sixteenth century and then the seventeenth (whom I shall discuss in chapter 13), they interpret the "infallibility" of Scripture as involving its complete inerrancy concerning whichever subject it touches upon: "a statement is true if it represents matters as they actually are, but is an error if it misrepresents the facts" (article 6). This includes statements of an apparently scientific nature: "We affirm that Genesis 1–11 is factual, as is the rest of the book" (article 22). This kind of commitment to Reformation principles, then, leads "third way" Protestant Bible readers to reject modern and postmodern developments not only in biblical hermeneutics, but also in other spheres as well, including science: "We deny that . . . scientific hypotheses about earth history or the origin of humanity may be invoked to overthrow what Scripture teaches about creation" (article 22).

The Fourth Way: Counter-Reformational Protestantism

A similarly negative assessment of modernity and postmodernity is evident, fourth, among other Protestant thinkers who nevertheless propose a very different approach to biblical hermeneutics. These "fourth way" thinkers are sympathetic to some Roman Catholic and Orthodox critiques of the Protestant understanding of the Bible, which is perceived as problematic both in its often sharp distinction between Scripture and Christian tradition, and in its rejection of ways of reading the Bible that are deeply *rooted* in this tradition. Indeed, in line with a long history of Roman Catholic analysis—reflected most recently in significant books by Charles Taylor and Brad Gregory[51]—"fourth way" schol-

---

[51] Charles Taylor, *A Secular Age* (Cambridge, Mass.: Belknap, 2007); Brad S. Gregory, *The Unintended Reformation: How a Religious Revolution Secularized Society* (Cambridge, Mass.: Belknap, 2012). On Taylor's work as Catholic apologetic, see Günter Thomas, "The Temptation of Religious Nostalgia: Protestant Readings of *A Secular Age*," in *Working with* A Secular Age: *Interdisciplinary Perspectives on Charles Taylor's Master Narrative* (ed. Florian Zemmin, Colin Jager, and

ars hold the Reformation at least partially responsible for the rise of modern secularism, such that we should "regard the Reformation not as something to be celebrated but as something to be lamented."[52] They seek, then, to reconnect Protestant hermeneutics to a more distant past than they believe the Reformation represents. In doing so, they tend to dispute standard Protestant accounts of the emergence of the biblical canon, arguing that "[t]he church existed before the Bible"—that is, Scripture arose out of the Church.[53] The core tradition of the Church—the "Rule of Faith against which everything was measured in the second century"—is therefore the context in which all the Scriptures (including the writings of the developing NT) must be read.[54] A good example of this "rule of faith" (or its synonym, "rule of truth"—I shall use both terms in this book without intending a distinction between them) is provided by the second-century bishop Irenaeus of Lyons in Roman Gaul (c. AD 130–202), who writes of the Church believing (among other things)

> in one God, the Father Almighty, Maker of heaven, and earth, and the sea, and all things that are in them; and in one Christ Jesus, the Son of God, who became incarnate for our salvation; and in the Holy Spirit, who proclaimed through the prophets the dispensations of God, and the advents, and the birth from a virgin, and the passion, and the resurrection from the dead, and the ascension into heaven in the flesh of the beloved Christ Jesus, our Lord, and His [future] manifestation from heaven in the glory of the Father.[55]

Guido Vanheeswijck; Berlin: de Gruyter, 2016), 49–70. On Gregory's, see Ephraim Radner, "The Reformation Wrongly Blamed," *First Things*, June/July 2012, 47–52.

[52] Hans Boersma, *Heavenly Participation: The Weaving of a Sacramental Tapestry* (Grand Rapids: Eerdmans, 2011), 85. For a brief summary of Gregory's overall argument, in the context of the presentation of a number of "witnesses for the prosecution" with respect to the Reformation's allegedly baneful effects on the world (secularization, skepticism, schism), see Kevin J. Vanhoozer, *Biblical Authority after Babel: Retrieving the Solas in the Spirit of Mere Protestant Christianity* (Grand Rapids: Brazos, 2016), 10–12 (10).

[53] Craig D. Allert, *A High View of Scripture? The Authority of the Bible and the Formation of the New Testament Canon* (Grand Rapids: Baker, 2007), 76.

[54] Allert, *High View*, 125.

[55] I have reproduced here only part of what Irenaeus includes in his summary of Christian faith. The full text can be found in his *Adversus haereses* (*Against Heresies*), 1.10.1, in *The Apostolic Fathers with Justin Martyr and Irenaeus* (vol. 1 of *Ante-Nicene Fathers*; ed. Alexander Roberts and James Donaldson; Peabody, Mass.: Hendrickson, 1999), 330. The *Ante-Nicene Fathers* series will be referred to henceforth as *ANF*. NB: Ancient and medieval sources like this one, from the Church Fathers and other writers, are often cited only in an abbreviated Greek or Latin form. To make life easier for the reader of this book, however, they will be cited herein on their first footnoted appearance using their full Greek or Latin title, accompanied by its English translation. On subsequent appearances, only the abbreviated form of the English will be used.

On this view of the correct way of approaching Scripture, its literal reading is important, but we should not dismiss other levels of meaning in the text—especially when it comes to the Old Testament (OT)—as we seek to read the Bible in conformity with the rule of faith (now understood in a markedly non-Protestant manner). "Fourth way" Protestants like my esteemed Regent College colleague Hans Boersma, then, question the wholesale rejection of allegorizing among many modern heirs of the Reformation. They wish to retrieve a medieval "Platonist-Christian synthesis" marked by an emphasis on "participatory or sacramental ontology" (i.e., a theory about "being")—the idea that creation "subsists or participates in God."[56] Boersma shares this pursuit with the contemporary "movement" known as Radical Orthodoxy, for whom "participation [is] the only proper metaphysical model for understanding creation" and its recovery is the only antidote for the

> flatness and materialism that ultimately leads to [the] nihilism [of postmodernity] . . . only a participatory ontology—in which the immanent and material is suspended from the transcendent and immaterial—can grant the world *meaning*.[57]

In line once again, then, with certain ongoing streams of Roman Catholic thought—well represented in the contemporary context by Matthew Levering[58]—"fourth way" Protestants advocate for the retrieval of a "spiritual reading" of Scripture over against a modern Protestant "biblicism" that prioritizes literal and historical reading. They do so in the conviction that "linear-historical tools alone will not suffice" for the reading of Scripture in the Church; "instead the participatory-historical quest must be restored to its proper position."[59] Therefore, "fourth way" Protestants are assuredly not focused on the single, fixed textual meaning that is the target of modern scholars of the "first" and "third ways"— since "the literal sense . . . is [only] the starting point (*sacramentum*) of a search for the greater, more christological reality (*res*) of the gospel" and it is only a "sacramental hermeneutic [that] will allow evangelicals to retain the centrality of the Bible while they rediscover its hidden spiritual depths."[60] "Fourth way" Protestant

---

[56] Boersma, *Heavenly Participation*, 21, 24.

[57] Smith, *Radical Orthodoxy*, 74–75.

[58] Matthew Levering, *Participatory Biblical Exegesis: A Theology of Biblical Interpretation* (Notre Dame: University of Notre Dame Press, 2008). For an influential earlier essay on the virtues of spiritual reading, e.g., see David C. Steinmetz, "The Superiority of Pre-critical Exegesis," *ThTo* 37 (1980): 27–38; for further advocacy, Daniel H. Williams, *Evangelicals and Tradition: The Formative Influence of the Early Church* (Grand Rapids: Baker, 2005), 102–13. On Protestant "biblicism," e.g., see Christian Smith, *The Bible Made Impossible: Why Biblicism Is Not a Truly Evangelical Reading of Scripture* (Grand Rapids: Brazos, 2011).

[59] Levering, *Exegesis*, 64.

[60] Boersma, *Heavenly Participation*, 152–53.

advocacy in respect of biblical languages is therefore not typically enthusiastic, since their approach to Scripture does not require facility in such languages (at least among theologians). They are, in addition, typically critical of notions of the perspicuity of Scripture (the truth of which emerges, in fact, only in the conversation between Scripture and tradition).[61]

CONFUSION

Obviously I do not claim that this brief typology of contemporary Protestant approaches to Bible reading (and related matters) covers all the possibilities; much more could be said, and much more nuance could be offered. I hope that I have said enough, however, to illustrate my current point: there are multiple perspectives in contemporary Protestantism on "how to read the Bible," taught in universities and seminaries, and indeed in churches, and then filtering down in various ways to ordinary Christian people on the ground, whether directly or indirectly. Even graduate students who make it their business directly to enter the debate can get confused as a result, not to say overwhelmed. Needless to say, other kinds of Christians—to the extent that they encounter these very different opinions by way of their education in college or university, or their interactions on the Internet, or their reading, or sermons that they hear—are not likely to be less confused and overwhelmed. Can "Scripture alone" really speak to us clearly as from God, guiding us reliably as to what we should believe and how we should live—especially when our biblical texts are so very old? Which Scripture should we read, and how should we read it? Should I, after all, strive to read the literal sense of the text, and what does it mean to do so? Does such an objective "sense" really exist, or does not every reader simply interpret the text as seems right in his or her own eyes? What am I supposed to make of claims about infallibility and inerrancy, and do such claims require that I reject other commonly accepted truths about the world of the past and the present (e.g., about the age of the earth, or about the history of humanity)? Do they require that I adopt a sixteenth-century worldview? These are only some of the questions of our time.

It does not take too much exposure to the confusion, it seems, to sow serious doubts in many people's minds about the viability of the whole Protestant enterprise—to engender a loss of confidence in *sola Scriptura*, and in our ability to comprehend its meaning. It is such doubts that are in part responsible for the small but significant exodus (at least in North America) out of Protestant

---

[61] In this, too, they agree with standard, historic Roman Catholic critiques of Protestantism, more recently rearticulated by authors like Gregory (e.g., *Unintended Reformation*, 92–93) and Smith: "If the truth of the Bible is really sufficiently understandable to the ordinary reader, then why do so many of them ... find it impossible to agree on what that truth is?" (*Bible Made Impossible*, 39–40).

churches and into Roman Catholic or "Eastern" Orthodox ones (as Westerners like to call them). More commonly, it seems, these doubts lead many people who are still members of Protestant churches into solipsistic, subjective, quasi-Christian cultural religion, in which the Bible is still formally the authority for faith and life, but in reality it is contemporary culture that is shaping belief and practice—and woe betide any preacher who challenges those beliefs and practices on the basis of biblical teaching.

Both "departures" raise, in different ways, important questions. Was the Reformation a mistake? Did it propose something that is in fact impossible? Must we now abandon its fundamental perspectives on the place of Scripture in our lives, and return to the bosom of the church(es) from which we were so unfortunately ripped all those centuries ago? Or is the only alternative to this repentance to try and find our own way in the contemporary world as best we can, founding our lives on the opinions of the latest charismatic megachurch leader or dazzling public intellectual, or on the sage advice of the television or radio personalities who possess the greatest reach, or on the basis of what "most people think," or what is "self-evidently right," or what I find myself most deeply to desire?

THE ARGUMENT OF THE BOOK

The questions are pressing, and the five-hundredth anniversary of "the Wittenberg Affair" is a good moment in which to consider them. It is my intention in this book to do so. Its argument may be briefly stated here, along with a description of its various stages.

The Fifth Way

My own conviction is that it is possible in our Bible reading to be appreciative of, and to stand properly in continuity with, much of the pre-Reformation heritage, while at the same time by no means abandoning the attempt to read both tradition and Scripture in accordance with the principles of Reformation hermeneutics. It is possible at the same time to be appreciative of both modern and postmodern contributions to biblical hermeneutics, some aspects of which Reformation insights themselves can be understood as generating. It is possible thus to arrive at an approach to biblical interpretation for the twenty-first century that does not merely replicate the Protestant hermeneutics of the sixteenth century, but certainly stands in fundamental continuity with them. Such an approach holds fast, in particular, to the Reformation affirmation of the centrality of the literal sense of the text in right-minded biblical interpretation (and the importance of learning biblical languages in order to be able to accomplish this). This book commends, in fact, the "seriously literal interpretation" of Scripture.

I intend to chart in what follows, then, a "fifth way" of approaching the interpretation of Scripture in relation to the four I have already described—the *right* way (I propose), in contrast to wrong or deficient "ways." I shall sometimes refer to this "fifth way" simply as "reformed" reading, hermeneutics, or interpretation. The lowercase and the scare quotes are deliberate. They indicate biblical interpretation that is consistent with magisterial Reformation principles and practices, rather than being exclusively (or merely) Protestant, or indeed more narrowly Calvinist (Reformed). Indeed, I shall try to show the many ways in which these same principles and practices are both rooted in pre-Reformation biblical hermeneutics and embraced in post-Reformation, non-Protestant Christianity. It is such principles and practices (I propose) that should lie at the heart of "the right reading of Scripture" to which my book title refers. This is not a proposal only about the Protestant reading of Scripture, then, even though it was primarily my concern about the contemporary state of Protestant hermeneutics that first generated the project, and it is to Protestants that I am making my proposal in the first instance. The "fifth way" (I propose) is the right way for *all* Christian readers of Scripture to approach it.

There are of course many other interpretive travelers already troubled by at least certain aspects of the first four "ways." Some of them, too, do not agree with how "fourth way" Protestants tend to describe the normativity of the ancient Christian past. They recognize the importance of Christian tradition (especially the ecumenical creeds of the first number of Christian centuries) in defining the broad parameters of genuine Christian theology, but they affirm the "reformed" idea that Scripture stands above tradition as the canonical rule by which it must be measured. There are others whose convictions on this point are bound up, as my own are, with convictions about the status of the OT, in particular, as Scripture that *precedes* the Church, and about the necessity of "plain reading" of the OT (and then the NT as well) if this scriptural status is genuinely to be maintained. There are others again who, over against "second" *and* "fourth way" Protestants, are strong advocates of the learning of biblical languages, with a view to attaining the most accurate understanding possible of our original-language biblical texts. There are certainly others who are more open than many contemporary Protestants (including "third way" Bible readers) to finding positive features in both modern and postmodern biblical hermeneutics while at the same time being deeply alarmed by various aspects of the appropriation of both modernism and postmodernism in the contemporary Church. The reader will encounter many of these fellow travelers throughout this book, especially in the footnotes, as their judgments intersect with my own at various points.

The Plan

My plan in pursuing my argument is to explore the pertinent issues by way of a discourse that is historically focused, taking us from the earliest decades of the Christian Church, in its encounter with the OT Scriptures in its Hellenistic-Roman environment, down to the present moment, in its encounter with postmodernity. To be clear, this is not a book about the history of biblical interpretation as such, concerning which a vast mountain of literature has arisen even in the course of the past several decades. The need of the hour, in my judgment, is not to make that mountain bigger, but to help people to understand what the past means for the present. My aim in this book, then, is not primarily to *describe*, but to *prescribe*—not merely to inform the reader about how people have read the Bible in the past, but also to make a proposal about how best we should read it now. Yet this proposal is certainly *rooted* in the past, and its plausibility depends in part on how accurately I *describe* the past—albeit that we shall only meander around on the lower slopes of the literary "mountain" just mentioned, footnoting extensively for the sake of those who wish to explore further.

Before There Were Protestants

I first reexamine—in chapters 2 and 3—the idea, and the canon, of Scripture in the early Christian centuries: how and why did Christians come to have a Scripture containing an OT and a NT, and is the Protestant notion of an identifiable and stable Scripture that can function as a canonical rule coherent? What is the best way of conceiving of the relationship between Scripture and all that may be placed under the heading of early Christian "tradition," including the rule of faith and the early creeds?

Second, I subject to renewed scrutiny, in chapters 4 through 9, all the various arguments about how the early Christians and those who followed them in the Middle Ages *read* Scripture,[62] and what this might or might not authorize us to do now. Some of the questions discussed here are the following: How far do the NT authors read Scripture literally, and how far do they not? When they appear not to do so, what *are* they doing, and what does this mean for us? What does the spectrum of reading look like among the Church Fathers and their successors in the Middle Ages,[63] what was at stake for those who adopted different positions

---

[62] For a discussion of the nomenclature of "Middle Ages," see Magne Sæbø, "The Problem of Periodization of 'the Middle Ages': Some Introductory Remarks," *HBOT* 1/2:19–27.

[63] "Church Fathers" is a collective term commonly used to describe important, formative Christian authors who lived between the apostles and the beginning of the medieval period (broadly from the end of the first century to the end of the fifth, although in different parts of the Christian Church later writers can also be included in the number). The great majority wrote originally in either Greek or Latin, which subdivides them into "Eastern" and "Western" Fathers

(e.g., in Antioch and Alexandria), and how are we to *assess* what was happening? Should we read Scripture "literally," or "spiritually," or in both these ways?

In chapters 10 and 11, third, I ask: To which texts, in which languages, do we rightly refer when we refer to Scripture? Were the Reformers correct to set at the heart of their interpretative endeavors the predominantly Hebrew and Greek texts in which the biblical literature first appeared, and indeed to strive to reconstruct through textual criticism the best versions of those texts? What does this mean for contemporary readers as we, too, handle the biblical text?

THE REFORMATION UNTIL MODERNITY

In chapters 12 and 13 I address some of the questions raised by the leading Reformers to which I have not yet given full attention in the first eleven chapters. What did they really think about Scripture and tradition, what did they mean by *sola Scriptura*, and is their view defensible? What does it mean to claim that Scripture is perspicuous, and does this claim make sense? Which kind of authority did they ascribe to Scripture, and in relation to which kinds of knowledge? As I ask these questions, I reflect at the same time upon the quickly changing context in sixteenth- and seventeenth-century Europe in which these matters were being discussed, both by the Reformers themselves and by their immediate Protestant successors. I consider how to evaluate their responses in that context, and I ask what can be learned from all of this for a "reformed" hermeneutics in our own day. Chapters 14 and 15 subject the period from the middle of the seventeenth to the middle of the nineteenth centuries to similar scrutiny. Chapter 16 reviews this whole second section of the book in pursuit of articulating a viable Christian, biblical hermeneutic for our contemporary moment that is genuinely and deeply rooted in the past. It is in this chapter that I return explicitly to engage the third and the fourth hermeneutical "ways" described above, on the way to engaging the first and the second "ways" in chapter 17 to the end.

MODERN AND POSTMODERN CRITICISM

In the remainder of the book, finally, I bring the story of biblical interpretation down into the modern and postmodern periods, describing various important developments in biblical hermeneutics and criticism and asking what is genuinely problematic and what is genuinely useful about each of these. How far do these various modern and postmodern ways of reading biblical texts help us to read the Bible as Scripture, and how far do they hinder us in that task? Can we stand

---

according to a notional line that runs between Greece and Italy and down through Roman North Africa, setting Egypt (e.g., Alexandria) and Syria (e.g., Antioch) on the Eastern side and modern Tunisia and Algeria (e.g., Carthage and Hippo) on the Western side.

in continuity with earlier Christians in their faith without believing everything about the Bible that they might have believed, and without reading it in exactly the way that they did? With such questions in mind, I discuss source and form criticism (chapter 17), redaction and rhetorical criticism (chapter 18), structuralism and poststructuralism (chapter 19), narrative criticism (chapter 20), and social-scientific and feminist criticism (chapter 21). The final substantive chapter deals with canonical criticism (chapter 22), and it is followed in chapter 23 by some concluding comments.

The Overall Argument

My argument will establish that the Reformers' confidence about our ability to read Scripture "rightly" was well grounded, even if not everything that Protestant Bible interpreters have said about the Bible has itself been right, and even if there are dimensions to what a right reading of Scripture looks like that contemporary "reformed" readers must inevitably add to the reading tradition that precedes them. We still have good grounds, in particular, for thinking that Scripture is clear enough in what it says to be capable of "teaching, rebuking, correcting, and training in righteousness" (2 Tim 3:16). The "seriously literal interpretation" of Scripture is still well capable of discerning the word that God wishes to address to both the Church and the world.

With this introductory chapter now complete, then, we turn to part 1 of the book, entering as we do so the world "before there were Protestants."

I

BEFORE THERE WERE PROTESTANTS
Long-Standing Questions

In chapter 1, I shared my conviction that it is possible in our Bible reading as Christians to be appreciative of, and to stand properly in continuity with, much of our pre-Reformation heritage, while at the same time by no means abandoning the attempt to read both tradition and Scripture in a "reformed" manner. Part 1 of the book aims to demonstrate that this is so. In its ten chapters, I shall discuss three important areas of pre-Reformation debate, touching on questions of canon, text, and interpretative approach. In all three areas the Reformers were joining long-standing conversations within the Church. They were taking sides in discussions that were already ongoing "before there were Protestants." It was not a sixteenth-century Protestant novelty to argue for a shorter rather than a longer canon of Scripture, or for the fundamental importance of the literal sense of the biblical text, or for the reading of this text in its original languages. Reformation perspectives in these areas, I shall propose, are deeply rooted in both Scripture and tradition. Moreover, we can and should retain these perspectives as we ourselves engage with Scripture as twenty-first-century Bible readers—albeit that we are, indeed, twenty-first- and not sixteenth-century people.

2

SCRIPTURE AND CANON IN THE EARLY CHURCH
On Chickens and Their Eggs

> [W]hen I want to know something about the gospel message, I go to the church as the privileged interpreter because this is where the Bible grew and continues to live.
>
> —Craig Allert[1]

> Nothing... can be more absurd than the fiction, that the power of judging Scripture is in the Church, and that on her nod its certainty depends. When the Church receives it, and gives it the stamp of her authority, she does not make that authentic which was otherwise doubtful or controverted, but, acknowledging it as the truth of God, she, as in duty bound, shows her reverence by an unhesitating assent.
>
> —John Calvin[2]

Before there were Protestants, there was already a canon of Christian Scripture—a set of texts accepted by Christians (and in many cases, also by Jews) as "*authoritative for religious practice and/or doctrine, and whose authority is binding... for all generations.*"[3] But what was the extent of this canon, who decided which texts were canonical, and on what grounds? Such questions were already to some extent controversial in the early Church (which for the purposes of this book we shall define as the Church prior to the fall of the Western Roman Empire in AD 476), but they became particularly heated in the sixteenth century.

The Reformers, as we saw in chapter 1, drew a sharp distinction between the books of the Hebrew Bible, which they regarded as canonical, and various OT Apocrypha that had been widely regarded for a long time in the Western Church

---

[1] Allert, *High View*, 86.

[2] John Calvin, *Institutes of the Christian Religion* (2 vols.; trans. Henry Beveridge; Grand Rapids: Eerdmans, 1989), 1:69 (in Calvin's original four volumes, 1.7.2; the *Institutes* will henceforth be cited only in this latter way).

[3] Sid Z. Leiman, *The Canonization of the Hebrew Scripture: The Talmudic and Midrashic Evidence* (Hamden, Conn.: Archon, 1976), 14. Leiman is referring here to the Jewish definition of canon, but it stands as a valuable Christian definition as well.

in the same way, but were now to be rejected as such (even though they might represent edifying reading). This provoked the Counter-Reformational Council of Trent (1546) to produce a list of Scriptures that removed any distinction between these two groups of texts. Listing the books constituting each Testament (and including the OT Apocrypha), Trent announced that what was now the Roman Catholic Church "accepts and venerates with a like feeling of piety and reverence all the books of both the old and the new Testament" and anathematized all those who did not.[4]

The Reformers also argued that canonical Scripture was capable of standing in judgment of the beliefs and practices of the Church whose Scripture it is. Trent advised, on the other hand, that

> no one, relying on his personal judgment in matters of faith and customs which are linked to the establishment of christian doctrine, shall dare to interpret the sacred scriptures either by twisting its text to his individual meaning in opposition to that which has been and is held by holy mother church, whose function is to pass judgment on the true meaning and interpretation of the sacred scriptures; or by giving it meanings contrary to the unanimous consent of the fathers.[5]

Underlying this dispute about who has the authority to interpret Scripture is the question of the right way of thinking about the relationship between Scripture and Church. Does Scripture precede the Church, and provide the "rule" against which the teaching of the Church is to be measured, or does the Church precede Scripture, and provide the only context in which Scripture may rightly be understood?

A convenient way into this discussion is provided by Craig Allert's 2007 book, *A High View of Scripture?*, to which we shall turn in a moment. This will lead us, in the present chapter and the next, into a series of reflections first on the *relationship* between Scripture, canon, and Church, and then on the *formation* of the canon of Scripture prior to, and then in, the Church. *I shall argue in these chapters that Scripture does precede the Church and provide the "rule" against which the teaching of the Church is to be measured, and that the Reformers were justified in drawing a sharp distinction between the books of the Hebrew Bible as canonical and the Apocrypha as not—indeed, that they had the majority of the early Christian tradition behind them in drawing such a distinction.* Before we go any further, however, it may be helpful to clarify which *are* the texts that are typically referred to as "Apocrypha" in this context, and at the same time to introduce other ancient

---

[4] Norman P. Tanner, S.J., ed., *Decrees of the Ecumenical Councils* (2 vols.; London: Sheed & Ward, 1990), 2:663.

[5] Tanner, *Decrees*, 2:664.

Jewish texts (Pseudepigrapha) that must necessarily also enter into our discussion, as well as the major sources available to us as we proceed.

OF APOCRYPHA AND OTHER TEXTS

The Apocrypha "at issue" in the sixteenth century were Tobit, Judith, 1–2 Maccabees, the Wisdom of Solomon, Ecclesiasticus (also known as Sirach or Ben Sira), the Additions to Esther, Baruch, the Epistle of Jeremiah, the Song of the Three, Susanna, and Bel and the Dragon. Other writings not on this list can also sometimes be referred to as Apocrypha, because they are included in the canon of one or other branches of the Christian Church.[6] Among the more notable of these should be mentioned 1–2 Esdras, the Prayer of Manasseh, and 3–4 Maccabees. All such Apocrypha are of Jewish origin, and for the most part they date from the early second century BC through to the late first century AD. Some of them are not independent compositions: 1 Esdras is an expanded version in Greek of the books of Ezra and Nehemiah, and the Additions to Esther and the Song of the Three each originated as expansions to the Greek versions of Esther and Daniel, respectively. The same is probably true of the Prayer of Manasseh (an expansion within the Greek version of 2 Chronicles). Other apocryphal texts *were* probably once independent compositions, but they were typically already closely associated in ancient times with what are now indisputably canonical books. Susanna, and Bel and the Dragon, were already part of the Greek Daniel by the time that early Church Fathers like Irenaeus were reading that book in Greek, while Baruch and the Epistle of Jeremiah were closely associated with Jeremiah and could be read by the Church Fathers as parts of that book.[7] These facts must be borne in mind when assessing the extent to which various of the Fathers considered the early OT canon to be greater in extent than what is now the Protestant OT canon. We shall consider in chapter 3 the general question of what weight the citation (or indeed noncitation) of, or reference to, texts should rightly play in arriving at a judgment on this matter. For the moment we should simply note that, whatever the best answer to this general question may be, the mere citation of, or reference to, one of the *expanded* canonical books just mentioned is certainly not secure evidence in this respect. It may simply suggest not the acceptance of a larger canon, but only the use of a canonical text (e.g., Daniel) in the Greek version of that text that was known to the reader. *These* Apocrypha, then, are not the most important for our purposes at present, and I shall delay their further consideration until we

---

[6] For a helpful list of the canonical books in the Greek and Russian Orthodox traditions, see Lee M. McDonald, *The Biblical Canon: Its Origin, Transmission, and Authority* (rev. ed.; Peabody, Mass.: Hendrickson, 2007), 443–44.

[7] Roger Beckwith, *The Old Testament Canon of the New Testament Church, and Its Background in Early Judaism* (Grand Rapids: Eerdmans, 1985), 339–43.

turn to the question of texts and translations in chapters 10 and 11. Of far more value with respect to questions of canon are the remaining, "independent" Apocrypha, which is where we shall focus our attention in the present chapter.

The Pseudepigrapha represent a further category of ancient Jewish writings. These are books like *1 Enoch* (parts of which date from the third century BC); the *Letter of Aristeas*, the *Testament of Levi*, *Jubilees*, and further sections of *1 Enoch* (second century BC); the *Psalms of Solomon* (first century BC); and various other texts from either the late first century BC or the early first century AD (e.g., the *Assumption of Moses*; the *Martyrdom of Isaiah*).[8] They are important for our purposes because a number of them were highly valued in at least some parts of the post-apostolic Church and were arguably regarded as canonical by at least some Christian leaders. Like the independent Apocrypha, then, they have been of great interest when it comes to questions about Scripture and canon. Indeed, we need to realize that "[t]he line that divides the Old Testament Apocrypha from the Old Testament Pseudepigrapha is not clearly drawn";[9] for example, the Prayer of Manasseh and 3–4 Maccabees can sometimes be assigned to the Pseudepigrapha rather than the Apocrypha.

It may also be helpful to clarify which further sources are available to us as we ponder our questions. They comprise, first, manuscripts deriving from Qumran and the ancient, sectarian Jewish community that was based there, dating from the third century BC to the first century AD.[10] Second, there are various fragments from earlier Hellenistic authors like Aristobulus (fl. c. 160 BC), embedded now in later works that quote them.[11] These give us access to other earlier writers like Eupolemos (second century BC), as well as to the earliest extant translation of the OT, the Greek Septuagint (or LXX), translated in the course of the third to the first centuries BC.[12] Third, there are early translations of Hebrew books

---

[8] See Beckwith, *Canon*, 17–19, and footnotes, for details concerning these sources.

[9] Craig A. Evans, "Introduction," in *Exploring the Origins of the Bible: Canon Formation in Historical, Literary, and Theological Perspective* (ed. Craig A. Evans and Emanuel Tov; Grand Rapids: Baker, 2008), 15–29 (25).

[10] For a brief introduction to Qumran and its literature, see McDonald, *Biblical Canon*, 125–36.

[11] For a brief introduction to Aristobulus and his fragments, see Folker Siegert, "Early Jewish Interpretation in a Hellenistic Style," *HBOT* 1/1:130–98 (154–62).

[12] For a full description of the Septuagint (and the reason why it is abbreviated as "LXX"), see my chapter 10. "Some scholars prefer to use the term 'Old Greek' (OG) instead of 'Septuagint' for the earliest stage that can be reconstructed for any [OT] book [translated into Greek]." Jennifer M. Dines, *The Septuagint* (UBW; London: T&T Clark, 2004), 3. Others use "Old Greek" at least for the earliest versions of the translations of the OT books not found in the Pentateuch. I believe that it is simpler in the context of my book simply to use "Septuagint" (LXX) for the entire, earliest Greek translation of the OT.

into other languages (such as the Aramaic Targums).[13] Also important for our purposes are the Alexandrian Jewish writer Philo (c. 25 BC to AD 50),[14] various first-century AD Christian writings (the NT and *1 Clement*), and the Roman Jewish historian Flavius Josephus, who wrote important works in the closing decades of the first century AD.[15]

These further sources cast extensive light on issues of Scripture and canon in the period just before and during the emergence of the early Christian Church. Sources from the post-apostolic Church Fathers and from rabbinic Judaism then also cast light back on these periods, the latter of which should be further described, since they will not be familiar to many readers.[16] Jewish tradition is rooted in the early labors of the scribes who worked in the period of "the Great Assembly" in the later Persian and then the Hellenistic periods, who were succeeded by the "Tannaim" who first emerged toward the end of the scribal era and whose teachings are contained in the Mishnah and the Baraita (i.e., Tannaitic traditions not contained in the Mishnah). The Tannaim were succeeded by the "Amoraim," who worked during the third to the sixth centuries AD, and whose discussions of and elaborations on the Mishnah are contained in the Gemara. Mishnah and Gemara together constitute the Talmud, the basis of religious authority in Orthodox Judaism, which appears in two forms—the longer Babylonian and the shorter Palestinian Talmud. The former has traditionally been regarded as the more authoritative.

One final clarification is in order at this point. Like others who have written about such matters, I have on several occasions thus far used the word "book" in referring to various ancient writings, and I shall continue to do so below, throwing in here and there a word like "scroll." This accepted usage is, however, loose, and potentially misleading, because in the reality of technological development in the ancient world "scrolls" precede "books" (also known as "codices," of which the singular is "codex"). Codices do not begin to appear, it seems, until the latter half of the first century AD: none have been found at Qumran or Pompeii in the earlier part of that century, and there is no mention of them in our historical sources until the Roman poet Martial in AD 84.[17] We do not begin to find them outnum-

---

[13] For a brief and helpful introduction to the Targums—Aramaic translations and interpretations of Scripture made in the face of declining competence in Hebrew among Jews in the postexilic period onward—see Étan Levine, "The Targums: Their Interpretative Character and Their Place in Jewish Text Tradition," *HBOT* 1/1:323–31.

[14] For a helpful introduction to Philo's life and work, see Siegert, "Early Jewish Interpretation," 162–89.

[15] For an introduction to Josephus' contribution to the questions under discussion here, see Steve Mason, "Josephus on Canon and Scriptures," *HBOT* 1/1:217–35.

[16] See Beckwith, *Canon*, 17–19, and footnotes, for details on all of these sources.

[17] Martial, *Epigrams* (trans. Walter C. A. Ker; London: William Heinemann, 1968), 1.2.

bering scrolls in the historical record of the Roman world until around AD 300. I shall use "books" and "scrolls" interchangeably in this volume, nevertheless, unless something depends on the distinction, in which case I shall make this clear.

A HIGH VIEW OF SCRIPTURE?

Our necessary digression now complete, we return to Craig Allert's view of the biblical canon. Allert is critical of the way in which most evangelical Protestants (his target audience) "have ... a 'dropped out of the sky' understanding of the Bible," and he wants to draw their attention to the fact that Scripture "did not drop from heaven but was the result of historical and theological development."[18] In tracing this development, he is heavily dependent upon the work of Albert Sundberg.[19] According to Sundberg, the early Church received from Judaism two closed collections of Scripture and a further, open collection of revered religious texts. The first of the closed collections comprised the books still now found in the first section of the Jewish Bible, known as the Law (Genesis through Deuteronomy). The second comprised the books now found in the second section of the Jewish Bible, known as the Prophets: the historical books from Joshua through 2 Kings (the Former Prophets), and the prophetic books Isaiah, Jeremiah, Ezekiel, and Hosea through Malachi (the Latter Prophets). The open collection included the books that later made up the third section of the Jewish Bible as described in the Babylonian Talmud, known as the Writings: Psalms, Job, Proverbs, Ruth, Song of Songs, Ecclesiastes, Lamentations, Esther, Daniel, Ezra, Nehemiah, and 1–2 Chronicles. However, this open collection also included (in Sundberg's view) what are now commonly termed Apocrypha and Pseudepigrapha. It was not until the late first century AD, at the Council of Jamnia, that Judaism ultimately defined the third canonical section (restricted to the books now found in the Writings) of what now became for the first time the (completely closed) Hebrew canon. The Church remained unaffected by this closure of the Jewish canon, however, so that what Sundberg refers to as the "wide religious literature without definite bounds [that] circulated throughout Judaism as holy scripture before Jamnia" continued for some time to circulate as Scripture among Christians. At length the Church defined for itself what it came to know as the OT, embracing some of

---

[18] Allert, *High View*, 10, 14.

[19] Albert C. Sundberg, *The Old Testament of the Early Church* (Cambridge, Mass.: Harvard University Press, 1964). Other notable modern contributors to discussions of canon influenced by Sundberg include Lee McDonald, who holds that "[t]he biblical canon in the time of Jesus and before was not sharply defined, even though the Law and the Prophets were widely received as authoritative Scriptures in the early Christian churches along with a less well-defined category" that he then proceeds to discuss. McDonald, *Biblical Canon*, 104.

the Apocrypha that Judaism had rejected.[20] Early in its history, then (according to Allert), canon was not on the Church's mind, and this was true both of the OT and the NT: "[I]f the church did not inherit the idea of a delimited list of authoritative writings from Judaism, there is no clear reason to think that this would be on the minds of Christians for their own (uniquely Christian) writings."[21] On this view, canon-consciousness appears relatively late in the history of the early Christian church, and this "has direct implications for the [Protestant] argument that the early church appealed to the Bible and the Bible alone for its doctrine: one cannot properly speak of a Bible in the first several centuries of the church's existence."[22] In fact, the very criteria employed for the inclusion of NT books in the Christian canon involved already their conformity with the "rule of faith"— that is, with Christian orthodoxy. "Before there was even Scripture, there was the faith," and "[i]t was this Rule of Faith against which everything was measured in the second century—even the writings of the developing New Testament."[23] Therefore, "an appeal to the 'Bible' as the early church's sole rule for faith and life is anachronistic."[24] It is the Church that is actually "the privileged interpreter" of the Bible (see the first epigraph above to the present chapter).

I certainly agree with Craig Allert that the Christian Bible never "dropped out of the sky." However, his account of its "historical and theological development" is problematic, as we shall now begin to see.

OF OPEN AND CLOSED CANONS

At the heart of Allert's argument, first of all, lies an important confusion with respect to notions of "Scripture" and "canon." No biblical canon, he informs us, in the sense of "a delimited list of authoritative writings"—neither an OT nor a NT canon—existed in the early Christian centuries. Therefore, "one cannot properly speak of a Bible in the first several centuries of the church's existence."[25] The Bible, he claims, comes into being as a result of the teaching and practice of the Church, as expressed in the rule of faith and later the creeds; therefore, there is a problem with Christians appealing to it over against the teaching and the practice of the Church. The Bible itself cannot be regarded as the rule of faith, Allert proposes, because early Christians like Tertullian "did not know of a closed canon."[26]

---

[20] Sundberg, *Old Testament*, 102–3.
[21] Allert, *High View*, 48.
[22] Allert, *High View*, 51.
[23] Allert, *High View*, 79, 82, 125. For an example of what the rule of faith looks like, see Irenaeus, *Against Heresies*, 1.10.1 (ANF 1:330).
[24] Allert, *High View*, 145.
[25] Allert, *High View*, 48, 51.
[26] Allert, *High View*, 83.

All of this begs the question, however, as to whether it is possible to have a recognized Scripture that is functioning canonically (that is, authoritatively in respect of religious practice and/or doctrine), without yet possessing a finally "delimited list of authoritative writings" in a closed canon. Brevard Childs already addresses this question in his own writings about canon, which predate Allert's book by a number of years.[27] In turn, Childs has attracted criticism for his position from James Barr. Consideration of their exchange, largely about the OT canon, proves to be helpful when evaluating Allert's argument.

Scripture-Consciousness in Ancient Israel

Childs works against the background of a modern biblical scholarship that has tended to think of the concept of canon as an arbitrary and late imposition on the OT texts by religious authorities who have thereby distorted this literature's essence.[28] Childs argues, conversely, that canonization is not a moment in history, but a complex historical process that entailed the collecting, selecting, and ordering of emerging texts so that they could serve a normative function as Scripture within the continuing religious community of ancient Israel. Canon-consciousness, he tries to show, lies deep within the OT literature itself; the OT people of God were already aware of what they were doing in gathering texts and transmitting them together to subsequent generations.

James Barr's view, on the other hand, is that biblical faith was not, in essence, a scriptural religion: "In what we call 'biblical times'... there was as yet no Bible."[29] People back then related to God directly and personally, or through holy persons and institutions, and little or not at all through preexisting written and authoritative holy books. It is only in the later centuries BC that we find a clearly defined, written "book of the law" and other books of authoritative religious status, and only then that we encounter explicit references in a book like Daniel to other preexisting biblical books (in this case, to Jeremiah) as sources that need to be explained and interpreted. According to Barr, then, the idea of Scripture is a relatively late phenomenon in ancient Israel, and the idea of canon (in the sense of a precise definition of the Scriptures) is later still.

[27] E.g., Brevard S. Childs, *Introduction to the Old Testament as Scripture* (London: SCM Press, 1979); and *Biblical Theology of the Old and New Testaments: Theological Reflection on the Christian Bible* (Minneapolis: Fortress, 1993). For a fuller consideration of Childs' "canonical approach" to Scripture, see my chapter 22.

[28] A key player in introducing and developing this idea was Johann Semler, whose *Treatise on the Free Investigation of the Canon* (4 vols.; Halle: Carl Hermann Hemmerde, 1771–1776) argued that a theological approach to the Hebrew canon that was based on historical misconceptions should be replaced by a strictly historical approach that would reveal its true nature.

[29] Barr, *Holy Scripture*, 1; see also "Childs' Introduction to the Old Testament as Scripture," *JSOT* 16 (1980): 12–23.

The argument is problematic, however. Barr himself acknowledges that many of the traditions of Israel that later became Scripture were already central and authoritative in earlier times. He asserts that these traditions were not yet separable from the general life of all the traditions of the community, but in fact there is no evidence that this is so, and logic tells against it. It seems intrinsic to the careful preservation and passing on of OT prophetic traditions, for example, that these traditions were already regarded at their point of origin as especially important—already marked off from other texts that did not possess such status. This is presumably why they, and not others, were passed on. Thus demarcated, they were clearly brought into conversation with other texts that had been demarcated in the same way. We can see this in the extraordinarily high level of cross-referencing or intertextuality among the various texts in what later became the Law and the Prophets—the earliest parts of the OT, by common scholarly consent, to achieve canonical status. The very form in which each text is written invites reference time and again to other authoritative texts, such that together they comprise (in Stephen Chapman's words) "a cumulatively expanding, intertextually referential body of normative, communal religious writings."[30] This is an important reality to grasp when it comes to reading OT Scripture, since it implies that the reading of individual passages and even books "in themselves" is not going to do full justice to how the authors and editors who passed them down to us intended these passages and books to be read. We shall return to this matter in chapter 4, and again in chapter 22. For the moment, all that needs to be said is that Barr's case for the lateness of Scripture-consciousness in ancient Israel is unconvincing.

Scripture- and Canon-Consciousness

Nor is his case for a radical distinction between Scripture-consciousness and canon-consciousness. Barr understands the Law as having arrived at supreme and authoritative status in the time of Ezra (a kind of de facto canonization), but he believes that *both* the Prophets and the Writings existed in a somewhat more fluid state, and for longer, than Sundberg envisages.[31] Even supposing that he were

---

[30] Stephen B. Chapman, "Second Temple Jewish Hermeneutics: How Canon Is Not an Anachronism," in *Invention, Rewriting, Usurpation: Discursive Fights over Religious Traditions in Antiquity* (ed. Jörg Ulrich, Anders-Christian Jacobsen, and David Brakke; ECCA 11; Frankfurt am Main: Peter Lang, 2012), 281–96 (293).

[31] In NT times, "the category of 'Prophet' was not a closed one: any non-Torah book that was holy Scripture was a 'Prophet' . . . the boundary between the Prophets and other books was fluid, still vague, and possibly quite unimportant in the first century AD." Barr, *Holy Scripture*, 55–56. This kind of extension of the Sundberg "fluidity" argument to include the Prophets is also found in the work of John Barton; e.g., *Oracles of God: Perceptions of Ancient Prophecy in Israel after the Exile* (London: Darton, Longman & Todd, 1986), 35–95. He regards this extension as "following

correct about this extended fluidity, however (but see further below), does this mean that no canon-*consciousness* existed in earlier times? Is it not in fact implicit in the notion that a certain text is Scripture that another text is not (see my comments just above)? Is this implicit notion not seen precisely in the position ultimately attained, however it was attained, by the Law and the Prophets? The question is not whether everyone agreed in earlier times about exactly which texts were canonical Scripture and which were not. The question is whether the idea of Scripture itself implies the idea of limitation—of canon—even if people do not yet conceive that the limits have been reached. I believe that the idea of Scripture evidently does—and so, it seems, does Barr, at least in some moments in his book. For example, he is of the opinion in one place that there was

> back into early Old Testament times, a sort of core of central and agreed tradition, a body of writings already recognized and revered, which ... functioned ... in the same general way in which the canon of scripture functioned for later generations.... [T]he whole nature of Israelite religion was canonical ... it depended on the selection of a limited set of traditions which were accepted and were to be authoritative in the community.[32]

This certainly looks like the kind of early (at least exilic) canon-consciousness that various others biblical scholars also affirm.[33] The question of when and how the OT canon was formally closed is another matter, which is not immediately relevant to the question of canon-consciousness: "the margins of the emerging canon are less significant than the character and function of the canon (or 'core canon') itself."[34] This is the very point that Childs himself makes when discussing his use of the word "canon" in his *Introduction to the Old Testament as Scripture*. He rightly insists that it makes sense to speak of an "open canon," precisely because closure is only one element in the process of canon, and not constitutive of it. That process, he affirms, had already begun in Israel's preexilic period. Scripture and canon therefore cannot be sharply distinguished.

Sundberg's argument to its logical conclusion." John Barton, "The Significance of a Fixed Canon of the Hebrew Bible," *HBOT* 1/1:67–83 (69). That being said, "he largely confirms the existence and *authoritative status* of most, if not all, of the books of the Prophets and Writings at a very early date." Stephen B. Chapman, *The Law and the Prophets: A Study in Old Testament Canon Formation* (FAT 27; Tübingen: Mohr Siebeck, 2000), 57.

[32] Barr, *Holy Scripture*, 83.

[33] E.g., James A. Sanders, *Torah and Canon* (Philadelphia: Fortress, 1972); Joseph Blenkinsopp, *Prophecy and Canon: A Contribution to the Study of Jewish Origins* (Notre Dame: University of Notre Dame Press, 1977); and Rudolf Smend, "Questions about the Importance of the Canon in an Old Testament Introduction," *JSOT* 16 (1980): 45–51. See also various other scholars whose work is described in Chapman, *Law*, 20–44.

[34] Chapman, "Second Temple Jewish Hermeneutics," 294.

It should be obvious to the reader that if this is so, it is a problem for Allert's argument, which possesses a certain similarity in its style to Barr's. Both wish to argue that in what we call biblical times, there was as yet no Bible, but only holy persons and institutions, creating and handing on tradition. Scripture came later, and the idea of a canon (in the sense of a precise definition of the Scriptures) later still. It is on the basis of this understanding of historical reality that Allert then dismisses the idea that the Bible might be regarded as the Christian rule of faith, because the early Christians "did not know of a closed canon."[35] In reality, however, one does not need to have a *closed* canon in order to have an authoritatively functioning Scripture that is a "measuring stick" (the meaning of the Greek word *kanōn*), against which belief and practice may be assessed. One only needs to have a "mere" canon: a collection of texts, albeit not yet necessarily regarded as complete, that serves a normative function within the community—"a sort of core of central and agreed tradition, a body of writings already recognized and revered, which . . . functioned . . . in the same general way in which the canon of scripture functioned for later generations."[36]

CANON AND CHURCH

Did such "a body of writings" exist in the early Church? Here we must deal with one of the more surprising statements in Allert's book. "The church existed before the Bible," he claims; "[b]efore there was even Scripture, there was the faith."[37] As John Barton indicates, however, the opposite is the case—albeit that, like Allert, Barton favors the idea of a longer lasting fluidity in canonical matters: "By the first century CE there is not much doubt which books formed the core of [the] 'canon': more or less the books that are now in the Hebrew Bible," although "[t]here may have been a little doubt about a few of them."[38] The Bible self-evidently existed before the Church, then, and Scripture before (Christian) faith.

SCRIPTURE IN ANCIENT ISRAEL

Its prior existence is clearly indicated in the Gospels in what Jesus himself names on a number of occasions as "the Law and the Prophets" or close variants (like "Moses and the prophets"); in Luke 16:16, for example, he announces that the

---

[35] Allert, *High View*, 83.
[36] Barr, *Holy Scripture*, 83.
[37] Allert, *High View*, 76, 82.
[38] Barton, "Significance," 71. Similarly Timothy H. Lim, *The Formation of the Jewish Canon* (AYBRL; New Haven: Yale University Press, 2013), 180: "By the end of the first century CE, there was a canon that most Jews accepted." Neither author supports the idea of an early *closure* of the canon, but even so, both recognize the deep historical roots of notions of scriptural authority as attaching to most of the books that ended up *in* the canon.

"Law and the Prophets were proclaimed until John." There can be no doubt that this terminology refers *at the very least* to the OT books now found in the first two sections of the Jewish canon. As we shall see shortly, it may also refer to more than these. Minimally, however, it refers *at least* to these books, whose roots lie deep in Israel's history, as selected human words were recognized as representing at the same time the word of God and preserved for posterity.[39] That is to say, they were recognized as prophetic, in the broad sense; they were recognized as "inspired" (that is the technical term often used) by God. The OT itself identifies Moses as one of the earliest and the most important of these prophets, initiating the production of what later became canonical law.[40] In time, these traditions developed into the two broad collections of scriptural material that we are now discussing ("Law" and "Prophets").[41] By the sixth century BC, when the overarching story of the Former Prophets from Joshua through Kings was coming into its present form (cf. 2 Kings 25:27-30), "both mosaic law and mosaic prophecy are viewed as already-recognized authorities."[42] Late in that same century, Zechariah 7:12 speaks of those who "would not listen to the law or to the words that the LORD Almighty had sent by his Spirit through the earlier prophets." By the time we get to the late fifth and early fourth centuries, we find the latest of the books of the Latter Prophets, Malachi, concluding with an epilogue that "presupposes a collection of the latter prophets with Malachi at the end and with a collection of torah and former prophets preceding it."[43] This epilogue is probably integral to the book itself, but it also neatly serves as the conclusion to the whole prophetic corpus. That is to say, the work of producing a collection of Minor Prophets (typically regarded in ancient times as one scroll with twelve parts) was already taking place in the context of the larger project of producing a coherent prophetic corpus allied with a corpus of law:

> The individual prophets of the Three [Isaiah, Jeremiah, Ezekiel] and the Twelve are provided a history of prophecy in the DtrH [Joshua-Kings] that locates their activity in time-specific contexts and yet also seeks to understand prophecy as a uniform and coordinated phenomenon operating within the providential episodes

---

[39] Peter R. Ackroyd, *Continuity: A Contribution to the Study of the Old Testament Religious Tradition* (Oxford: Blackwell, 1962), 13–14.

[40] Leiman, *Canonization*, 16–20. "According to the biblical evidence, the Israelite notion of canonicity begins with appearance of canonical laws" (24).

[41] For a plausible reconstruction of the process, see Chapman, *Law*, 283–86, and all the material earlier in his book that undergirds the argument.

[42] Chapman, *Law*, 200.

[43] David L. Petersen, *Zechariah 9–14 and Malachi* (OTL; Louisville, Ky.: Westminster John Knox, 1995), 34.

of post-Mosaic leadership until the fall of Jerusalem and beyond. Prophecy and law are inseparable.[44]

Later in the fourth century BC, we find in the books of Chronicles and Ezra-Nehemiah what Stephen Chapman has called "the persistent pairing of law and prophets" as Scripture.[45] Indeed, "[t]he Chronicler works with a canon of scripture very much like the one we know, and he works within a conception of scripture which we can recognize as that of 'the Law and the Prophets.'"[46] The Law and the Prophets have by this point reached "a relatively stable form,"[47] soon to be translated into Greek in the LXX (probably beginning in the third century BC), and their authority is reflected in other early Jewish writings such as Tobit, the Prologue to Ben Sira (132 BC), and 1 Maccabees (c. 100 BC).[48] It is this canonical collection of Law and Prophets, then, closed already well before Jesus' time, which provides "the basic grammar of the God of Israel and his people."[49] I note again (as I did earlier) the importance of this understanding of canonical Scripture as the outcome of an *intentional* process for the question of how we should best read the biblical texts as a collection.

SCRIPTURE IN THE NEW TESTAMENT

It is also this canonical collection of Law and Prophets that in Jesus' own lifetime and in the history of the earliest Church "was viewed as a privileged, stable witness against which the claims of the gospel were tested and shown to have been established from of old"[50]—was understood, indeed, as "the very words of God" (Rom 3:2). In Matthew 7:12, for example, Jesus exhorts his hearers as follows: "In everything, do to others what you would have them do to you, for this sums up the Law and the Prophets." The Law and the Prophets still represent the "measuring stick" when it comes to the question, "how shall I live?" What is implied here about the continuing authority of these Scriptures is explicitly indicated in Matthew 5:17-20:

> Do not think that I have come to abolish the Law or the Prophets; I have not come to abolish them but to fulfill them. I tell you the truth, until heaven and earth

---

[44] Christopher R. Seitz, *The Goodly Fellowship of the Prophets: The Achievement of Association in Canon Formation* (Grand Rapids: Baker, 2009), 91–92. See further James D. Nogalski, *The Book of the Twelve: Hosea–Jonah* (SHBC; Macon, Ga.: Smyth & Helwys, 2011); and *The Book of the Twelve: Micah–Malachi* (SHBC; Macon, Ga.: Smyth & Helwys, 2011).
[45] Chapman, *Law*, 247.
[46] Chapman, *Law*, 230.
[47] Chapman, *Law*, 138, 254–56, 286.
[48] Chapman, *Law*, 253–54, 258–64.
[49] Seitz, *Goodly Fellowship*, 35.
[50] Seitz, *Goodly Fellowship*, 35.

disappear, not the smallest letter, not the least stroke of a pen, will by any means disappear from the Law until everything is accomplished. Anyone who breaks one of the least of these commandments and teaches others to do the same will be called least in the kingdom of heaven.

In line with this, we find Jesus again and again in the Gospels basing his teaching or arguments on these OT writings, sometimes prefacing what he is about to say with phrases like "it is written that" (e.g., Mark 14:27; Matt 11:10) and thereby drawing people's attention to the authority upon which he rests his case. After the resurrection, Jesus rebukes two of his confused and downhearted disciples for failing to take these same Scriptures sufficiently seriously when trying to understand their present experience:

> "How foolish you are, and how slow of heart to believe all that the prophets have spoken! Did not the Christ have to suffer these things and then enter his glory?" And beginning with Moses and all the Prophets, he explained to them what was said in all the Scriptures concerning himself. (Luke 24:25-27)

The central importance of the OT Scriptures is emphasized again shortly afterward, in Luke 24:44, when Jesus advises all the core disciples and others that "[e]verything must be fulfilled that is written about me in the Law of Moses, the Prophets, and the Psalms." To "the Psalms" we shall return shortly.

The remainder of the NT is likewise premised on the notion of an already-existing Scripture. This comes to expression very clearly in the famous words of 2 Timothy 3:16, where the notion of "inspiration" is once again patent: "every part of Scripture is God-breathed and useful one way or another—showing us truth, exposing our rebellion, correcting our mistakes, training us to live God's way." In the book of Acts, Christians share with Jews a commitment to hearing what "the Law and the Prophets" have to say (Acts 13:15) and believing it: "I believe everything that agrees with the Law and that is written in the Prophets," affirms the apostle Paul to Felix in Acts 24:14. Various of his letters to the Christian churches of the first-century Roman world illustrate the seriousness with which he took this idea. Everywhere in this correspondence he grounds his teaching in the pre-existing Scriptures (e.g., applying the Ten Commandments to the various ethical situations with which he is confronted in the emerging churches; Rom 7:7, 13:9; Eph 6:2-3). For Paul and the other apostles, it was impossible to speak of Christ without speaking of him "in accordance with the Scriptures" of Israel that already existed—Scriptures that "men spoke from God as they were carried along by the Holy Spirit" (2 Pet 1:20-21)—which the Church

> at its origin received . . . as the sole authoritative witness. . . . These Scriptures taught the church what to believe about God: who God was; how to understand

God's relationship to creation, Israel, and the nations; how to worship God; and what manner of life was enjoined in grace and in judgment.[51]

Indeed, the apostles largely spoke of Christ only *in* relation to the OT, as Martin Luther once astutely observed, noting "how little Paul and Peter report the individual acts of Jesus in their letters: Paul wrote gospel by making mighty sermons out of a very few passages of the Old Testament."[52]

SCRIPTURE IN THE POST-APOSTOLIC CHURCH

The generations of Christians who came immediately after the apostolic age unsurprisingly followed the apostolic example. They held stubbornly to the belief that it was the Scripture of Israel that gave the Church its fundamental orientation to reality—the fundamental story of which it found itself a part—and that their reception of this literature as *their* Scripture was intrinsically bound up with their acceptance of Jesus Christ as Savior and Lord. They could not have the one without the other. As Allert himself notes, "it is axiomatic that authoritative Scripture for the Apostolic Fathers [AD 95–150] were [sic] the Hebrew Scriptures," albeit that they usually read them in Greek translation, because so many of the early Christians could not read Hebrew.[53] This is already true of 1 *Clement*, which dates from the closing decade of the first century AD: "Approximately a fourth of the entire text consists of Old Testament citations"[54] The *Epistle of Barnabas*, which was written sometime during the opening decades of the second century AD, likewise understands "the corpus of the Old Testament, including its entire portfolio of texts, as a document of revelation in which are found valid propositions for the present."[55] From the pen of Justin Martyr (c. AD 100–165) we have two surviving "apologies" (defenses of the Christian faith), written in the middle of the second century AD, and in both of these the OT is likewise central: "Justin ... appealed to the Scriptures (the Old Testament) as a prophetic witness for the Messiah, Jesus Christ. ... The Old Testament in Justin is without question recognized as the Scripture of the Christians."[56] This is the case even though Justin, like others before him, knew some of the writings of the apostles that would eventually form the NT. Yet "the New Testament is not actually

---

[51] Christopher R. Seitz, *The Character of Christian Scripture: The Significance of a Two-Testament Bible* (STI; Grand Rapids: Baker, 2011), 17. See further Chapman, *Law*, 276–82.

[52] Heinrich Bornkamm, *Luther and the Old Testament* (trans. E. W. and R. C. Gritsch; ed. V. I. Gruhn; Mifflintown, Pa.: Sigler, 1997), 85.

[53] Allert, *High View*, 109.

[54] Henning G. Reventlow, *History of Biblical Interpretation, Volume 1: From the Old Testament to Origen* (trans. Leo Perdue; RBS 50; Atlanta: Society of Biblical Literature, 2009), 127.

[55] Reventlow, *Biblical Interpretation*, 1:120.

[56] Reventlow, *Biblical Interpretation*, 1:140, 146.

interpreted [in his work]. Its character as 'Scripture' does not appear to have been held.... Demonstrations of the Christian truth ... are capable of being obtained only from the Bible held in common with the Jews."[57] As to this "commonality," it is striking that even though significant Jewish-Christian disagreement surfaces in Justin's *Dialogue with Trypho* in a number of areas, this is not the case on the question of which *are* the books in the Bible. On that question, at least, they do not disagree.[58]

Twice in his *First Apology*, Justin mentions someone who did take a very different view of the OT: Marcion of Sinope, who centered his Bible on ten of the apostle Paul's letters and rejected the OT as Scripture in its entirety.[59] Marcion did this in broad companionship with others in the early Christian centuries who have come to be described by Christian writers as "the Gnostics" (we shall hear more about them in my chapter 7), and he has often been regarded as essentially a Gnostic himself. These Gnostics substituted for the OT's fundamental ontological distinction between the Creator and his good material creation a distinction, instead, between the spiritual (good) and the material (evil) world. They proposed that salvation involved not the redemption of the whole world, including the body, but the escape of the individual spirit from the material world (and centrally from the body). This being so, Gnostics had no place in their philosophy for an incarnate deity dying for the sins of the world and rising bodily again so that others could do the same. The gnostic analysis of the world, indeed, did not find sin to be the obstacle to salvation, but rather ignorance—from which elite and esoteric "knowledge" (Gk. *gnōsis*) would deliver the initiate. The marginalization of the OT that we find in Marcion's approach to Scripture greatly facilitated this kind of conforming of Christian faith to the norms of a certain type of Hellenistic philosophy. The move was widely understood in the post-apostolic Church to be wrongheaded, however, and to be certain, if accepted, to change the very character of apostolic Christian faith. The change is already illustrated in Marcion's own teaching on the basis of a slimmed-down collection of Scriptures that did not (and could not) include even apostolic writings (like the Gospel of Matthew) that indicated significant continuity between the OT and the NT. Marcion was therefore condemned as a heretic, and the great opponent of both Marcionism and Gnosticism in the second century, Irenaeus, deployed

---

[57] Reventlow, *Biblical Interpretation*, 1:146.

[58] This is not to suggest that in *Dialogus cum Tryphone* (*Dialogue with Trypho*) Justin and Trypho necessarily agree on which *text* of the Bible best represents the original content of the biblical books. Justin is convinced, to the contrary, that the Jews have deleted from the OT Scriptures material represented in the LXX translation of some of the books, but not found in the Hebrew. Justin Martyr, *Dialogue with Trypho*, 71–73 (ANF 1:234–35).

[59] Bruce M. Metzger, *The Canon of the New Testament: Its Origin, Significance and Development* (Oxford: Clarendon, 1997), 90–99.

OT Scripture extensively in his attempts to discredit their doctrines. It is not surprising that in mounting this assault, Irenaeus became the first Christian writer in history to cite and allude to more apostolic than OT documents.[60] Marcion and the Gnostics had explicitly put on the agenda the question, is there genuine continuity and coherence between the two sets of truth claims? This forced writers like Irenaeus into far greater citation of NT texts than anyone before him, in order to demonstrate the continuity and coherence. Indeed, we find in Irenaeus' *Against Heresies* (c. AD 180) about twice as many NT as OT citations.[61] The only writings now in our NT that he does not cite are 3 John, Philemon, and Jude.[62] It is around the same time that we find our first extant list of apostolic books, in the so-called Muratorian Fragment from Rome (c. AD 180–200).[63] All the Gospels except Matthew are listed here, and Matthew was assuredly present in the original—the beginning of the Fragment is missing. Also appearing here are Acts, all of Paul's epistles (including those to Philemon, Titus, and Timothy), Jude, and two of the letters of John. So it is that by the end of the second century AD we see "the development of the authority of these [NT] texts," as they begin to be cited alongside OT texts in ever greater numbers.[64]

The serious attention given to OT texts by Christian writers during the first two centuries AD continued all the way down through the succeeding ones, even as the final contours of the NT corpus were becoming firmly settled in the church. Both Clement of Alexandria (c. AD 150–215) and Tertullian (c. 160–240) continue in this line in the early part of the third century. Slightly later, so does Origen (c. 185–254), and after him in the fourth century come such important writers as the "Cappadocian Fathers" (Basil the Great, Gregory of Nazianzus, and Gregory of Nyssa), and in the fifth century Theodoret of Cyrus, for whom (even at this late stage) "commentary on the New Testament [remains] in a minor key."[65] Worthy of especial note as we move into the fifth century is Augustine (AD 354–430). Not a single one of these early Christians believed that "the church existed before the Bible," or faith before Scripture. All of them believed that Scripture and Bible preceded the Church,[66] as well as being produced *in* the Church, and

---

[60] Allert, *High View*, 119.

[61] It is significant that while this is true of a work explicitly directed against heretics, it is not true of his nonpolemical *Epideixis tou apostolikou kērygmatos* (*Proof of the Apostolic Preaching*, trans. Joseph P. Smith; ACW 16; New York: Newman, 1952), which proceeds in a more traditional manner. Reventlow, *Biblical Interpretation*, 1:157–58.

[62] Reventlow, *Biblical Interpretation*, 1:157.

[63] For this traditional and still most likely date, see Metzger, *Canon*, 191–201.

[64] Reventlow, *Biblical Interpretation*, 1:155.

[65] Hill, *Antioch*, 44.

[66] Hill describes the Antiochene commentators in general (Diodorus of Tarsus, Theodore of Mopsuestia, John Chrysostom), e.g., and not just Theodoret, in the following way: they "think

that the truth claims of the Church had to be grounded in prior Scripture, even as it was producing new Scripture. Thus Basil of Caesarea, for example, in a letter to Eustathius, rejects the idea that "custom is to be taken in proof of what is right," but insists that custom must be judged by Scripture: "let God-inspired Scripture decide between us; and on whichever side be found doctrines in harmony with the word of God, in favor of that side will be cast the vote of truth."[67] Augustine, likewise, has this to say:

> whether concerning Christ, or concerning His Church, or any other matter whatsoever which is connected with your faith and life.... "Though an angel from heaven preach any other gospel unto you than that which" ye have received in the lawful and evangelical Scripture, "let him be accursed."[68]

It is this same Augustine who provides such a powerful example of the post-apostolic Church's convictions concerning the unity of Scripture, OT and NT, when he remarks in *Against Adimantus* that

> in it [the OT] there is such strong prediction and preannouncement of the New Testament that nothing is found in the teaching of the Evangelists and the apostles, however exalted and divine the precepts and promises, that is lacking in those ancient books.[69]

SCRIPTURE, CANON, AND THE RULE OF FAITH

It is clear from everything described thus far, then, that the "Rule of Faith against which everything was measured in the second century,"[70] and also in succeeding centuries, was God-breathed (God-inspired) Scripture, even if the ultimate and precise boundaries of this Scripture (at least with respect to the NT writings) had not yet been defined. It was to this "body of writings already recognized and revered" that from its very point of origin the early Church constantly referred, as it articulated the truth of the gospel of Jesus Christ—and even as it gradually supplemented this same body of writings in the course of the first Christian centuries with apostolic texts:

---

that their canon is Jewish in origin and ... that all the books came to them from Judaism." Hill, *Antioch*, 23.

[67] Basil of Caesarea, *Letters*, in *Basil: Letters and Works* (vol. 8 of *Nicene and Post-Nicene Fathers, Second Series*; ed. Philip Schaff and Henry Wace; Peabody, Mass.: Hendrickson, 1999), 229. The *Nicene and Post-Nicene Fathers* series will be referred to henceforth as *NPNF* 1 and *NPNF* 2.

[68] Augustine, *Contra litteras Petiliani* (*Answer to the Letters of Petilian*) 3.6–7 (*NPNF* 1, 4:599).

[69] Augustine, *Contra Adimantum* (*Against Adimantus*) 3.4, as translated in David F. Wright, "Augustine: His Exegesis and Hermeneutics," *HBOT* 1/1:701–30 (714).

[70] Allert, *High View*, 125.

the *paradosis* [instruction, tradition] of the Church, faithful to that of the apostles, was precisely this transmission of the Christ-event, as based documentarily on the Old Testament writings and, at the same time, explaining the meaning of these writings.[71]

It is this "foundational role of the Scriptures (Law and Prophets) for the logic of the rule of faith," as Christopher Seitz rightly states, that "is overlooked entirely in [Craig Allert's] conceptuality."[72] This leads Allert, in company with others who approach the matter similarly, to misconstrue the nature of the rule of faith/truth. When these terms are used by early post-apostolic Fathers like Irenaeus and Tertullian, they typically refer simply to *summaries* of the grand biblical narrative and its leading themes, beginning in Genesis and ending with the apostolic teaching that is more fully unpacked in the writings that ultimately became part of the NT.[73] These summaries are not themselves independent "canons" against which the truthfulness of Scripture might be measured, and indeed, "[a]ny of the ancient church fathers would have been horrified to find their written legacy placed on a par with Holy Scripture."[74] The content of the summaries was instead understood to have been drawn from Scripture itself, "the ground and pillar of our faith":[75] "the church fathers saw [the rule of faith] as emerging from Scripture, as thoroughly in line with Scripture, and not as a plot imposed on Scripture to order what is disordered."[76] To the extent that these early Christian authors distinguish the two, then, it is only to make the point that one cannot simply read the various parts of Scripture in any way that one likes. Their summaries of the Great Story (as I shall sometimes call the biblical narrative from Genesis to Revelation, sometimes abbreviating simply to "Story"), referred to by the term "rule of faith," ensure that the basic shape of the biblical narrative will not be distorted as people engage in the reading of particular texts. They ensure that the parts of Scripture will be correctly read in the light of a correct understanding of the whole.

---

[71] Yves M.-J. Congar, O.P., *Tradition and Traditions: An Historical and a Theological Essay* (trans. Michael Naseby and Thomas Rainborough; London: Burns & Oates, 1966), 31.

[72] Seitz, *Goodly Fellowship*, 20n4.

[73] Earlier versions of such summaries are found in Ignatius and Polycarp, in what Greene-McCreight refers to as "kernels of the Rule of Faith." Kathryn E. Greene-McCreight, *Ad Litteram: How Augustine, Calvin, and Barth Read the "Plain Sense" of Genesis 1–3* (IST 5; New York: Peter Lang, 1999), 5.

[74] Williams, *Evangelicals and Tradition*, 60. Augustine, e.g., is explicit in distinguishing these, referring to "our writings, which are not a rule of faith or practice, but only a help to edification," and going on to say that "there is a distinct boundary line separating all productions subsequent to apostolic times from the authoritative canonical books of the Old and New Testaments." Augustine, *Contra Faustum (Reply to Faustus)*, 11.5 (*NPNF* 1, 4:180).

[75] Irenaeus, *Against Heresies*, 3.1.1 (*ANF* 1:414).

[76] Craig G. Bartholomew, *Introducing Biblical Hermeneutics: A Comprehensive Framework for Hearing God in Scripture* (Grand Rapids: Baker, 2015), 58.

Irenaeus and the Rule of Faith

Irenaeus, for example, in opposing both Marcion and the Gnostics in *Against Heresies*, was especially concerned to demonstrate the many ways in which the NT literature to which the Gnostics appealed, and the OT literature whose authority they could indirectly recognize but in practice ignored, were inseparable from each other, and must necessarily be read as one Bible. In order to be interpreted correctly, individual texts must be read with attention to their immediate contexts, and larger sections of text must be read with attention to the sweep of the biblical story as a whole. For example, one cannot make just what one wishes of Paul's declaration in 1 Corinthians 2:6 that "we speak wisdom among those that are perfect, but not the wisdom of this world," as the Gnostics do when "each one of them alleges [this wisdom] to be the fiction of his own inventing."[77] The question is, What does Paul's teaching elsewhere in that letter and in other places suggest that Paul meant by it? Similarly, one of the favorite expressions of the heretics is that "flesh and blood cannot inherit the kingdom of God" (1 Cor 15:50). However, in insisting that "this passage refers to the flesh strictly so called, and not to fleshly works," and in failing to take account of what else Paul says in this chapter—"without having perceived the apostle's meaning, or examined critically the force of the terms, but keeping fast hold of the mere expressions by themselves"—they miss the "manifest and clear" biblical teaching about the bodily resurrection.[78] These examples illustrate the entire heretical approach to Scripture, which Irenaeus portrays in this way:

> [C]ollecting a set of expressions and names scattered here and there [in Scripture], they twist them . . . from a natural to a non-natural sense. In so doing, they act like those who bring forward any kind of hypothesis they fancy, and then endeavour to support them out of the poems of Homer, so that the ignorant imagine that Homer actually composed the verses bearing upon that hypothesis, which has, in fact, been but newly constructed.[79]

The correct way to read Scripture, conversely, is to take all the biblical verses that the heretics have scattered and to restore each to its proper position, so that the entire scriptural mosaic once again portrays a king rather than a dog or a fox.[80] It is this entire Great Story to which Irenaeus refers on several occasions in *Against Heresies* as the "rule of truth" by which right reading of the various parts of

---

[77] Irenaeus, *Against Heresies*, 3.2.1 (ANF 1:415).
[78] Irenaeus, *Against Heresies*, 5.13.2–3 (ANF 1:539–40).
[79] Irenaeus, *Against Heresies*, 1.9.4 (ANF 1:330).
[80] Irenaeus, *Against Heresies*, 1.8.1; 1.9.4 (ANF 1:326, 330).

Scripture is to be measured.[81] "[A]s we follow for our teacher the one and only true God," he declares,

> and possess His words as the rule of truth, we do all speak alike with regard to the same things, knowing but one God, the Creator of this universe, who sent the prophets, who led forth the people from the land of Egypt, who in these last times manifested His own Son, that He might put the unbelievers to confusion, and search out the fruit of righteousness.[82]

The rule of truth is Scripture correctly read—the understanding of the Great Story that allows the Christian who stands in the apostolic tradition not to mistake the heretical fox for the orthodox likeness of the king.[83] "The sense of a biblical statement is hit upon correctly only when the meaning conforms to the entirety of the Scriptures."[84] For Irenaeus, the rule of truth can also refer to the correct understanding of particular parts of this biblical story, most notably the part with which Irenaeus is most concerned in *Against Heresies* (over against the Gnostics): "The rule of truth which we hold, is, that there is one God Almighty, who made all things by His Word, and fashioned and formed, out of that which had no existence, all things which exist. Thus saith the Scripture, to that effect."[85] As Henning Reventlow rightly says, "the existence of the Scriptures as the basis of faith is central to Irenaeus's thinking."[86] This is why, even though Irenaeus emphasizes the role of the Church in guiding the faithful in the correct interpretation of Scripture,[87] he spends so much time *arguing* what Scripture as a whole and in its parts says and means, rather than simply appealing to his own episcopal authority as a bishop standing in the apostolic succession[88]—for "[t]he rule of religious practice and truth is not the authority of the ministers as such, but rather that which they guard and transmit."[89]

---

[81] Irenaeus, *Against Heresies*, 2.27.1; 3.12.6 (ANF 1:398, 432).
[82] Irenaeus, *Against Heresies*, 4.35.4 (ANF 1:514).
[83] Irenaeus, *Against Heresies*, 1.9.4 (ANF 1:330).
[84] Reventlow, *Biblical Interpretation*, 1:173.
[85] Irenaeus, *Against Heresies*, 1.22.1; cf. 3.11.1 (ANF 1:347; cf. 426).
[86] Reventlow, *Biblical Interpretation*, 1:172.
[87] E.g., in *Against Heresies*, 4.26.1; 4.26.5; 4.32.1; 4.33.8 (ANF 1:496, 498, 505–6, 508).
[88] On some understandings of the rule of truth/faith, the volume, nature, and intensity of this argument in Irenaeus (or indeed in Tertullian) becomes incomprehensible, since on this view the role of the Scripture reader is only ever to discover what the Church or authoritative leaders within the Church teach about its meaning. I recall a particular conference I attended a number of years ago in the course of which the question arose about the best way in which to interpret Psalm 137 within a Christian frame of reference. One view expressed was that we did not need to discuss the matter, because St. Augustine had already told us how to read the psalm.
[89] Congar, *Tradition*, 28, who goes on to ask: "What is the content of the rule of faith?," answering that it is "the Scriptures and the creed" (29), with the latter comprising only "a résumé of

In this, Irenaeus' practice stands in stark contrast to many of those Church leaders who followed him in subsequent centuries, including those in charge of dealing with Martin Luther from 1518 onward, who displayed a strong preference for appeals to episcopal authority over *against* argument based on, or even involving, Scripture. These include Sylvester Mazzolini (known as Preirias), tasked by the pope in 1518 with preparing a theological opinion in advance of Luther's heresy trial. The pope is the infallible rule of truth when he speaks about faith and morals, Preirias maintained, and whoever does not adhere to the teachings of the Church as interpreted by the pope (including its teachings about indulgences) is a heretic. The authority of the Church stands explicitly above that of Scripture, and may not be questioned. Luther's response (in part) is to point out that Augustine, at least, would certainly not have agreed with such propositions, since he ascribed infallible authority only to Scripture. It is precisely the unwillingness of his opponents to argue their case on the basis of Scripture (or even on the basis of what the Church Fathers taught) that so vexes Luther in these early years of the Reformation, and in due course leads him to the conclusion that they are more interested in power than in truth.[90]

We shall return to the teaching of other Church Fathers on Scripture and the rule of faith/truth in chapter 12. In summation only of Irenaeus at present:

> If Irenaeus wants to prove the truth of a doctrine materially, he turns to scripture, because therein the teaching of the apostles is objectively accessible. Proof from tradition and from scripture serve one and the same end: to identify the teaching of the church as the original apostolic teaching. The first [tradition] establishes that the teaching of the church is this apostolic teaching, and the second [Scripture], what this apostolic teaching is.[91]

The rule of truth "is simply the understanding of the coherence proper to the scriptures that permits one to read them coherently"[92]—the understanding that excludes the kind of reading that (to quote Polycarp around AD 110) "perverts the oracles of the Lord to his own lusts, and says that there is neither a resurrection nor a judgment."[93] It is something intrinsic to Scripture itself, rather than

---

the apostolic faith testified to in the Scriptures" (30).

[90] Brecht, *Luther: His Road*, 1:240–65, on Preirias, and then also on Cajetan, at whose hands Luther learned something of an "arbitrary, unscriptural authority in the church" that sought to suppress those who raised legitimate theological questions, rather than to debate with them (256).

[91] Ellen Flesseman-van Leer, *Tradition and Scripture in the Early Church* (Assen: Van Gorcum, 1954), 144.

[92] Leonard G. Finn, "Reflections on the Rule of Faith," in *The Bible as Christian Scripture: The Work of Brevard S. Childs* (ed. Christopher R. Seitz and Kent H. Richards; Atlanta: Society of Biblical Literature, 2013), 221–42 (233).

[93] Polycarp, *Epistula ad Philippenses* (Letter to the Philippians), 7.1–2 (ANF 1:34).

extrinsic to it, as John O'Keefe and Russell Reno imply: "the rule is the principle or logic of scripture itself."[94] The rule is not brought *to* Scripture by the Church, even though it is certainly true that it *is* the understanding of the great narrative of Scripture that the Church has always held.[95]

Tertullian and the Rule of Faith

Tertullian, likewise, in writing *Against Marcion*—and asking whether Marcion innovated on the rule of faith by way of his separation of law and Gospel, or whether (as Marcion claims) he restored it after it had previously been adulterated—proposes that if there had been any dispute in the apostle Paul's time about the identity of the God of the OT and the God of the NT, this would be evident in the apostle's writings. In fact, it is not: "during the life of the apostles their teaching on this great article did not suffer at all."[96] Tertullian proceeds to remind his readers "to what rule *of faith* the Galatians were brought for correction," because they had become confused concerning in which story they found themselves, and they had departed from the Great Story.[97] It is this biblical story that Tertullian summarizes as the "rule of faith" in his *Prescription against Heretics*:

> Now, with regard to this rule of faith—that we may from this point acknowledge what it is which we defend—it is, you must know, that which prescribes the belief that there is one only God, and that He is none other than the Creator of the world, who produced all things out of nothing through His own Word, first of all sent forth; that this Word is called His Son, *and*, under the name of God, was seen "in diverse manners" by the patriarchs, heard at all times in the prophets, at last brought down by the Spirit and Power of the Father into the Virgin Mary, was made flesh in her womb, and, being born of her, went forth as Jesus Christ; thenceforth He preached the new law and the new promise of the kingdom of heaven, worked miracles; having been crucified, He rose again the third day; (then) having ascended into the heavens, He sat at the right hand of the Father; sent instead of Himself the Power of the Holy Ghost to lead such as believe; will come with glory to take the saints to the enjoyment of everlasting life and of the heavenly promises, and to condemn the wicked to everlasting fire,

---

[94] John J. O'Keefe and Russell R. Reno, *Sanctified Vision: An Introduction to Early Christian Interpretation of the Bible* (Baltimore: Johns Hopkins University Press, 2005), 120.

[95] In spite of the words just cited, O'Keefe and Reno proceed immediately to propose (puzzlingly, and without adequate argument) that it is a rule "extrinsically given" by the Church, without which "discernment of the intrinsic scriptural logic" is apparently impossible—thereby raising serious questions about whether it is actually intrinsic at all, as they appear just previously to have acknowledged. O'Keefe and Reno, *Sanctified Vision*, 120; and again, "the fathers ... do not 'find' the rule of truth in the text.... It is something brought to the material" (122).

[96] Tertullian, *Adversus Marcionem* (*Against Marcion*), 1.20–21 (ANF 3:285–86).

[97] Tertullian, *Against Marcion*, 4.5 (ANF 3:350).

after the resurrection of both these classes shall have happened, together with the restoration of their flesh.[98]

Again, this is nothing other than a summary of the biblical narrative and its leading themes, beginning in Genesis and ending with the apostolic teaching that is articulated in the NT. When Tertullian then proceeds in this same document to say that in dealing with heretics "[o]ur appeal ... must not be made to the Scriptures,"[99] it would be absurd to interpret him as saying anything other than that arguments with heretics about individual texts will prove futile when the heresy that is being confronted (as he has just described it)

> does not receive certain Scriptures; and whichever of them it does receive, it perverts by means of additions and diminutions, for the accomplishment of its own purpose; and such as it does receive, it receives not in their entirety; but even when it does receive any up to a certain point as entire, it nevertheless perverts even these by the contrivance of diverse interpretations.[100]

In spite of this warning, indeed, Tertullian himself in reality *constantly* appeals directly to Scripture in his own writings, even when dealing with heretics: "for Tertullian scripture is [in fact] the only means for refuting or validating a doctrine as regards its content."[101] It is the Scriptures that would have corrected you concerning the incarnation, he tells his opponent in *The Flesh of Christ*, "[i]f you had not purposely rejected in some instances, and corrupted in others, the Scriptures which are opposed to your opinion."[102] When you claim that angels take a body out of a material substance, he maintains, "there is no evidence of this, because Scripture says nothing."[103] And again, "I do not admit what you advance of your own apart from Scripture."[104] It is Scripture that is the "canon" that measures correct doctrine and practice,[105] and indeed Tertullian concludes

---

[98] Tertullian, *De praescriptione haereticorum* (*Prescription against Heretics*), 13 (ANF 3:249). Note also the shorter version in *De virginibus velandis* (*The Veiling of Virgins*), 1 (ANF 4:27): "The rule of faith, indeed, is altogether one, alone immoveable and irreformable; the rule, to wit, of believing in one only God omnipotent, the Creator of the universe, and His Son Jesus Christ, born of the Virgin Mary, crucified under Pontius Pilate, raised again the third day from the dead, received in the heavens, sitting now at the right (hand) of the Father, destined to come to judge quick and dead through the resurrection of the flesh as well (as of the spirit)."

[99] Tertullian, *Prescription*, 19 (ANF 3:251).

[100] Tertullian, *Prescription*, 17 (ANF 3:251).

[101] Flesseman-van Leer, *Tradition*, 184.

[102] Tertullian, *De carne Christi* (*The Flesh of Christ*), 3 (ANF 3:523).

[103] Tertullian, *Flesh*, 6 (ANF 3:527).

[104] Tertullian, *Flesh*, 7 (ANF 3:528).

[105] See, similarly, Clement of Alexandria, *Stromata* (*Miscellanies*), 7.16 (ANF 2:550–54). The chapter, headed "Scripture the Criterion by Which Truth and Heresy Are Distinguished," begins in this way: "But those who are ready to toil in the most excellent pursuits, will not desist from the

The Flesh of Christ by asserting that "proof enough has been adduced of the flesh in Christ having both been born of the virgin, and being human in its nature," contrary opinions having been challenged both as to "the arguments which sustain them, and . . . the Scriptures which are appealed to."[106] In this treatise, in other words, he responds to his opponents not with a summary of the Great Story, but with arguments about the correct exegesis of specific texts. The summarizing and the exegesis are two aspects of the one reality, for "wherever it shall be manifest that the true Christian rule and faith shall be, *there* will likewise be the true Scriptures and expositions thereof."[107] Whatever is not found in Scripture is not to be believed:

> I revere the fulness of His Scripture, in which He manifests to me both the Creator and the creation. In the gospel, moreover, I discover a Minister and Witness of the Creator, even His Word. But whether all things were made out of any underlying Matter, I have as yet failed anywhere to find. Where such a statement is written, Hermogenes' shop must tell us [it is against Hermogenes that Tertullian is writing in this text]. If it is nowhere written, then let it fear the *woe* which impends on all who add to or take away from *the written word*.[108]

This same recourse to Scripture when it comes to knowledge of God and all other important matters of faith and practice is also commended by Hippolytus: "There is . . . one God, the knowledge of whom we gain from the Holy Scriptures, and from no other source. . . . Whatever things, then, the Holy Scriptures declare, at these let us look; and whatsoever things they teach, these let us learn."[109]

Summation

In summation, then:

> The Rule [of Faith] is . . . a basic "take" on the subject matter and plot of the Christian story, which couples the confession of Jesus the Redeemer with the confession

---

search after truth, till they get the demonstration from the Scriptures themselves. There are certain criteria common to men, as the senses; and others that belong to those who have employed their wills and energies in what is true—the methods which are pursued by the mind and reason, to distinguish between true and false propositions."

[106] Tertullian, *Flesh*, 25 (ANF 3:542).

[107] Tertullian, *Prescription*, 19 (ANF 3:251–52). The line proceeds, "and all the Christian traditions," which are naturally to be understood, in the light of everything else that Tertullian has to say, as traditions consistent with Scripture.

[108] Tertullian, *Adversus Hermogenem* (*Against Hermogenes*), 22 (ANF 3:490). See also chap. 31 of the same treatise, where the statement "God made man of the dust of the ground" is said to have "the authority of Scripture itself" (ANF 3:495).

[109] Hippolytus, *Contra haeresin Noeti* (*Against the Heresy of One Noetus*), 9 (ANF 5:227).

of God the Creator, and thus "rules out" heretical statements that do not honor the content of the Rule.[110]

Scripture should be interpreted only in accordance with its own overall "plot"—what Herman Bavinck describes as "its own basic purport":

> This basic purport is for Irenaeus and Tertullian the *Regula* [Rule]. For the *Regula* is ... the fundamental tenor of the one message of scripture ... it is one and the same to explain scripture according to its inherent harmony and according to the *Regula*. This is the same as what the Reformation calls interpretation according to the analogy of faith. For in neither case is meant a formal principle outside of scripture, but the purport, intention of scripture itself.[111]

For both Irenaeus and Tertullian, indeed, to "appeal to revelatory truth apart from scripture is heretical gnosticism."[112]

CONCLUSION

Does Scripture precede the Church, then, and represent the "rule" against which the teaching of the Church is to be measured, or does the Church precede Scripture, and provide the only context in which Scripture may rightly be understood? Against the position of "fourth way" Protestant Bible readers like Craig Allert, I have argued in this chapter that Scripture does *indeed* precede the Church and represent its "rule." "The Christian Church was born with a Bible in its hands," as Stephen Dempster puts it,[113] and it always had one thereafter, looking for its guidance on faith and life to the prophets, and then to the apostles, on whose foundational teaching the Church had been built—looking to what the *Clementine Homilies* (in the second or third century AD) name as "the prophetic rule."[114] "[T]he church exists *for* this rule," asserts Leonard Finn. "It 'preserves it,' and through continued preaching and teaching, it 'enlightens all men that are willing to come to a knowledge of the truth' [quoting Irenaeus]."[115] As John Calvin rightly claims, then (in the second epigraph to the present chapter), "the power of judging Scripture" does not lie in the Church (even though the Church, at both

---

[110] Kathryn Greene-McCreight, "Rule of Faith," *DTIB*, 703–4 (704).

[111] Herman Bavinck, *Gereformeerde Dogmatiek* (4 vols.; Kampen: J. H. Bos, 1895–1901), 1:510–11, as translated in Flesseman-van Leer, *Tradition*, 194.

[112] Flesseman-van Leer, *Tradition*, 191.

[113] Stephen G. Dempster, "Canon and Old Testament Interpretation," in *Hearing the Old Testament: Listening for God's Address* (ed. Craig G. Bartholomew and David J. H. Beldman; Grand Rapids: Eerdmans, 2012), 154–79 (159). See also his essay "Torah, Torah, Torah: The Emergence of the Tripartite Canon," in Evans and Tov, *Exploring the Origins*, 87–127.

[114] *Clementine Homilies*, 2.15 (ANF 8:231).

[115] Finn, "Reflections," 237.

individual and corporate levels, must make judgments about what it means, as it is read). The Church lives its life, rather, within the unified Story that canonical Scripture was already unfolding long before the Church existed—commissioned, by the One who lies at that story's center, to write only its final chapters.

I shall return to this matter of the *priority* of Scripture in chapter 12, when we consider the Reformation idea of *sola Scriptura*. For the moment we turn our attention, in the next chapter, to the matter of the *formation* of the biblical canon.

3

THE FORMATION OF THE CHRISTIAN CANON
The Pressure of the Twenty-Two

Our books ... are but two and twenty.... We have given practical proof of our reverence for our own Scriptures. For, although such long ages have now passed, no one has ventured either to add, or to remove, or to alter a syllable.

—Flavius Josephus[1]

There are ... of the Old Testament, twenty-two books in number.... [T]here are other books besides these not indeed included in the Canon, but appointed by the Fathers to be read by those who newly join us, and who wish for instruction in the word of godliness.

—Athanasius[2]

We have established in chapter 2 that, *even if* the OT canon was not yet already closed in the earliest period of the life of the emerging Christian Church, the Church certainly possessed from the beginning an authoritatively functioning set of canonical Scriptures, shared with Judaism, that formed the "measure" of its belief and practice. But *was* the OT canon, after all, closed? Is it really true, as Sundberg and Allert claim, that beyond the Law and the Prophets there was in the Judaism of the first century AD only an open collection of religious texts, in which no clear distinction yet existed between the Apocrypha and Pseudepigrapha, on the one hand, and the texts that ultimately came to make up the Jewish "Writings," on the other?

THE MATTER OF METHOD

Here we must consider first the best way of discovering the answer to this question. One possible way of proceeding would be simply to note citations or

---

[1] Josephus, *Contra Apionem* (*Against Apion*), 1.38–42, in *Josephus, Volume 1* (trans. Henry St. John Thackeray; LCL 186; London: Heinemann, 1926), 179, 181.

[2] Athanasius, *Epistulae Festalis* (*Festal Letters*), 39.4, 7 (NPNF 2, 4:552).

references in first-century literature to texts now classified as part of the OT's Writings, or the Apocrypha, or the Pseudepigrapha, in the hope that by so doing we could build up a picture of which texts beyond the Law and the Prophets were regarded, at least by some groups, as canonical. The governing assumption here would be that texts cited or referenced *in certain ways* can safely be judged to have been canonical, while the remainder, whether cited in some way or not, fall outside that group. The caveat with regard to the "certain ways" is of course necessary, since it is generally understood that the *mere* citation of, or reference to, a text cannot be considered in itself to be significant. Acts 17:28 and Titus 1:12 cite, respectively, the Greek authors Aratus and Epimenides, because these writers are held to speaking truly in the passages cited; but in neither case do the NT authors intend to suggest that the works in question form part of canonical Scripture. Truthfulness does not equate to canonicity. The caveat, then, places certain constraints around the *manner* of the citation or reference, insisting that it must clearly indicate that the text in question is canonical—perhaps by the formula that is used in the introduction (e.g., "it is written that"). Even with this caveat entered, however, it is doubtful whether the governing assumption just described is justified.

First, can texts *not* cited or referenced in the first century AD in the ways noted safely be judged to have been *noncanonical* at that time? It is certainly not true in general terms that one could safely make this kind of move. Consider by way of analogy the contemporary situation in the Protestant churches of the West. It is quite possible to sit for years listening to sermons in church, and also to read widely in Christian literature, and yet not come across any references at all to certain books of the OT (in particular) as Scripture. This does not mean, however, that such books are absent from the Protestant canon of Scripture (whose contents we happen already to know). It means instead, perhaps, that there are favorite books that speakers or writers tend to prefer, and that they find no need to go beyond them in making or illustrating the points in which they are interested. Or perhaps it means that their *audiences* have favorite books, and that the contemporary communicators need to focus on these books in order to be more persuasive in their exhortations. Or perhaps their patterns of citation or reference are simply functions of the size of the books concerned: larger books like Isaiah have more content to *be* cited or referenced, and they might well be expected to turn up more often than smaller books like Obadiah, whose single chapter might well not turn up at all. These are not the only explanations as to why canonical texts might not be cited or referenced, but they are certainly important ones. Is there any reason to think that in the particular circumstances of the first century AD the reality was different, such that lack of citation or reference, back then, can be interpreted as infallibly signifying the absence of a text from the canon?

To the contrary, it is clearly the case that although the Law and the Prophets were certainly canonical Scripture for both first-century Jews and Christians, not every biblical book in those collections is cited or referenced in the Jewish and/or Christian literature of the period. As Sid Leiman notes, for example, Philo never cites the book of Ezekiel, nor does the NT cite the book of Judges.³ Obadiah, Nahum, and Zephaniah are also virtually, if not entirely, invisible in the NT. This cannot reasonably be taken to imply that these books were, after all, regarded by Philo or the NT writers as lying outside the canon of Scripture. It is simply that ancient authors, like modern ones, make use of prior texts only to the extent that they suit their particular purposes in writing particular compositions. The case of Philo is particularly interesting in this respect. He cites about forty times more texts from the Law as from the rest of Scripture combined. However, since the great majority of his work comprises allegorical exposition of the patriarchal and exodus narratives, this proportion is not in the least surprising. It certainly cannot be assumed that the numbers tell us anything about the relative weight that Philo attaches to different parts of Scripture in general, nor indeed about which texts he regarded as *being* Scripture.

Second, can texts that *are* cited or referenced "in certain ways" in the first century AD safely be judged to have been *canonical* at that time? Again, the answer is "no." The reason for the negative is that ancient Jewish and Christian authors in the general time period with which we are currently dealing can be shown routinely to have cited and referred to certain texts in ways that make them *appear* to possess the same kind of authority as core canonical texts, even though we know for sure that they did not actually regard them in this way. In fact, they distinguish sharply between these texts, on the one hand, and the core canonical Scriptures that ultimately serve as the "measuring stick" for what they should believe and how they should live, on the other. This is not necessarily immediately apparent, however, *in their manner of citation or reference*. As internal biblical examples should perhaps already have warned us, it does not follow that, just because an author introduces a text with some such formula as "it is written that," he believes that the text in question forms part of canonical Scripture.⁴ It does not follow that, just because a text is broadly prophetic, it is so in the same way that the core

---

³ Leiman, *Canonization*, 31.
⁴ "When, e.g., Josh. 10:13 and 2S. 1:18 cite the *Book of Jashar* or when Nu. 21:14 cites the *Book of the Wars of the Lord*, we can assert nothing concerning the canonicity of those two lost books. They are cited as references and not as guides for Israelite religious practice or doctrine." Leiman, *Canonization*, 25. This is so even though both references to the Book of Jashar speak of what "is written" there.

texts of Holy Scripture are prophetic: "While canonical Scripture was regarded as prophetic, prophetic writing did not necessarily become canonical."[5]

Consider, for example, the well-known and robust distinction found in rabbinic Judaism between prophetic writings of venerable age and authority, dating back at least to the Persian period, and more recent literature, which is not to be placed on the same level as these ancient Scriptures. The reason for the distinction is provided in the Talmudic tractate *Sotah*: "When the last prophets—that is, Haggai, Zechariah, and Malachi—died, the holy spirit ceased in Israel."[6] This is why, according to tractate *Yadayim*, "The books of Ben Sira and all other books written from then on do not defile the hands" (i.e., are not part of sacred, inspired Scripture).[7] They are "outside books" so far as the canon of Scripture is concerned, which is something of which the author of the Prologue to Ben Sira is already aware, characterizing Ben Sira as simply offering further help to those seeking to live in accordance with the Law.[8] So it is that Rabbi Akiba can even affirm that those who read Ecclesiasticus (and any of the apocryphal or pseudepigraphical literature, it seems) "have no share in the world to come."[9] Yet in spite of this belief about the qualitative distinction between earlier and later works, which is also strongly reflected in the first century in the work of Josephus (see the first epigraph at the head of the present chapter, and also further below), later works can nevertheless sometimes be cited or referenced in rabbinic Judaism in ways that make it *appear* that this distinction does not, after all, exist. Ecclesiasticus is itself frequently cited in this way: "the many Ben Sira citations in the Talmud and their introductory formulae, indicate that the book of Ben Sira was sometimes expounded much like any other biblical book."[10]

We find the same phenomenon in the Church Fathers. Origen, for example, is clear in listing the sacred Scriptures as twenty-two in number, and he explicitly differentiates these from "the Maccabees," which are "besides these."[11] Yet while he recognizes that in some churches books like Tobit that are "outside the number" (to quote the heading to the LXX Psalm 151) are being read,[12] Origen is prepared

---

[5] E. Earle Ellis, *The Old Testament in Early Christianity: Canon and Interpretation in the Light of Modern Research* (Grand Rapids: Baker, 1991), 5.

[6] *T. Sotah* 13.2. For the text, see Leiman, *Canonization*, 66 (§33).

[7] *T. Yadayim* 2.13. For the text, see Leiman, *Canonization*, 93 (§72).

[8] For the text, consult an ecumenical Bible translation like the NRSV.

[9] *M. Sanhedrin* 10.1; *J. Sanhedrin* 28a. For the texts, see Leiman, *Canonization*, 86–87 (§§68, 69), and for a thorough discussion of their likely meaning, see 86–102.

[10] Leiman, *Canonization*, 97.

[11] Cited in Eusebius, *Historia ecclesiastica* (*Church History*), 6.25 (NPNF 2, 1:272). For a brief introduction to this important work, see Andrew Louth, "Eusebius and the Birth of Church History," in *The Cambridge History of Early Christian Literature* (ed. Frances Young, Lewis Ayres, and Andrew Louth; Cambridge: Cambridge University Press, 2004), 266–74.

[12] Origen, *Epistula ad Africanum* (*Letter to Africanus*), 13 (ANF 4:391).

to regard at least some of these books as useful for Christians. He himself can cite from them (e.g., from 1 *Enoch*), using formulae that he also employs to introduce citations from canonical texts.[13] Jerome, similarly, distinguishes between a carefully defined number of canonical Scriptures (twenty-two or twenty-four, depending on how one counts) and books like the Wisdom of Solomon, Ecclesiasticus, Judith, and Tobit, which "are not in the canon."[14] These latter books (and others like 1–2 Maccabees) are read by the Church for "edification," but they are not "among the canonical Scriptures" and they do not "give authority to doctrines of the Church."[15] Yet like other ancient Christian authors,[16] Jerome can introduce noncanonical texts like the Wisdom of Solomon and Ecclesiasticus using formulae elsewhere employed in introducing canonical ones.[17] It does not seem at all likely that all these authors are simply contradicting themselves, unable to make up their minds about which texts are, and which are not, canonical. It seems clear, rather, that the mere citation of a text, implying that in some sense it possesses authority, cannot of itself be interpreted—even if the citation is introduced by a strong formula such as "it is written"—as an indicator that the author believes the text to comprise part of canonical Scripture.

Earle Ellis is worth quoting at length on this topic of citation and reference throughout the early centuries of Church history, and especially on the subject of "formulae." Formulae, he argues,

> may introduce both express citations of canonical writings and "rewritten" interpretive renderings of these texts. Equally, they may introduce citations of noncanonical documents that are regarded as correct commentary (midrash) on canonical books or as authoritative in some way. Even when they are employed in their technical reference to holy or religious writing, they sometimes have a broader connotation than canonical or covenantal writing. Ordinarily, then, introductory formulas do not in themselves constitute evidence for the canonical authority of the book cited.[18]

---

[13] Origen, *De Principiis* (*First Principles*), 4.35 (ANF 4:380). We must depend for the most part on Rufinus' sometimes not very reliable Latin translation of this text—only a few passages in Origen's Greek survive, because they were quoted by other authors. I shall use the English translations of the Greek from *ANF*, where available, otherwise depending on the *ANF* translations from the Latin.

[14] Jerome, *Prologus galeatus* (*Helmeted Preface to Samuel and Kings*) to his Vulgate translation of Samuel and Kings. For the text see Leiman, *Canonization*, 45–47.

[15] Jerome, *Prologus* (*Preface*) *to Proverbs, Ecclesiastes, and Song of Songs* (NPNF 2, 6:492).

[16] E.g., Gregory of Nazianzus also carefully differentiates the canonical from the noncanonical books, but can nevertheless be found citing texts like the Wisdom of Solomon and Judith. Ellis, *Old Testament*, 23n73.

[17] See further Ellis, *Old Testament*, 32n102.

[18] Ellis, *Old Testament*, 33–34.

It is for such reasons that Ellis insists that, in attempting to define the OT canon of the NT Church, we should focus our attention not only on citation and reference, but also on what ancient authors explicitly have to say about the extent and content of the canon. Indeed, we should give "priority to explicit canonical affirmations and [interpret] the usage of the writers in the light of them."[19] This is, in my view, the correct approach. Was the OT canon already closed in the first century AD? Was there already a clear distinction between the Apocrypha and Pseudepigrapha, on the one hand, and the texts that ultimately came to make up the Writings, on the other? In attempting to answer these questions, we should depend in the first instance on explicit early testimony about such matters.

THE LAW, THE PROPHETS, AND "THE REST OF THE BOOKS"

In chapter 2 I argued that the canon of Scripture as it existed in Jesus' time comprised at least the OT books that are now found in the first two sections of the Jewish canon. It is at least to these books that the language of "the Law and the Prophets" in the Gospels refers. Yet close attention to these same Gospels already reveals that the scope of "the Law and the Prophets" therein may in fact be greater than this. It is intriguing that in John 10:34 and 15:25, for example, the Psalms, at least, can also be described as part of "the Law." It is possible, then, that "the Law and the Prophets" is at least sometimes used in the NT as shorthand simply for "Scripture" (Gk. *graphē*; John 13:18; Gal 3:8), which includes the Law and the Prophets but also other texts as well (John 13:18 cites Ps 41:9).

The Gospel writers can also refer to this same Scripture using not a bipartite, but a tripartite designation, in which the Psalms seemingly comprise a third category (or part of a third category) in *addition* to the Law and the Prophets. In Luke 24:44 Jesus is recorded as saying: "Everything must be fulfilled that is written about me in the Law of Moses, the Prophets and the Psalms." Traces of this tripartite way of referring to Scripture are also found in other early texts. The Prologue to Ben Sira is the earliest of these (middle to later second century BC); it refers to "the Law and the Prophets and the others that followed them," as well as to "the Law and the Prophets and the other books of our ancestors," and to "the Law itself, the Prophecies, and the rest of the books."[20] From this Prologue, then, we learn that its author regards "the rest of the books" as being of venerable age (they come from the "ancestors"), and as having a status comparable to the

---

[19] Ellis, *Old Testament*, 33.

[20] Prologue to Ben Sira (NRSV). The Prologue implies—in acknowledging the differences between the Hebrew and Greek forms of the corpus—that a stable Hebrew form of "the Law, the Prophecies, and the rest of the books" from which Greek translations could be made must already have existed well before the second century. With thanks to Stephen Chapman (personal communication) for the observation.

Law and the Prophets.²¹ A slightly later text from Qumran, known as 4QMMT, may also add further texts to the Law and the Prophets, describing "the book of Moses, and the books of the prophets, and of David."²² David is associated with the Psalms, of course, but also with other texts that ended up in the Writings, like Ruth (which describes his ancestry) and 1 Chronicles (which expatiates upon his crucial role in developing Israel's worship system). Philo, similarly (writing during the first part of the first century AD), speaks of "laws and oracles delivered through the mouths of prophets, and psalms and anything else which fosters and perfects knowledge and piety." These "Holy Scriptures" he differentiates from the further "writings of men of old" treasured by the Egyptian Therapeutae sect.²³

It seems appropriate to deduce from all this evidence that for some time prior to the middle of the second century BC, Jews had regarded as Scripture not only the books that eventually came to compose the Law and the Prophets, but also the Psalms and at least some other texts as well.

The Evidence of Josephus

This is explicitly what Josephus claims toward the end of the first century AD in *Against Apion* (c. AD 95), the treatise cited in the first epigraph to the present chapter.²⁴ The number of the Jewish Scriptures is fixed, he claims, and it has been for some time: there are five books of Moses, thirteen of prophetic history from Moses to the Persian Emperor Artaxerxes, and four of hymns and precepts—that is, twenty-two books in total. This idea that the Scriptures total twenty-two (paralleling the number of letters in the Hebrew alphabet) may in fact be attested even earlier, in *Jubilees* (2:23), dating from around 104 BC.²⁵ As we have already seen, it is certainly attested later, in the third and fourth centuries AD, by the Christian scholars Origen and Jerome.²⁶ These twenty-two books, Josephus asserts, comprise *sacred* literature, inspired by God, and they always have been

---

²¹ As to which particular writings among "the rest of the books" are explicitly reflected in Ben Sira, Pancratius Beentjes lists Proverbs, Psalms, Lamentations, and possibly Chronicles. He notes a consensus "that Ben Sira does not mention, nor quote from, the books of Esther, Ruth, Daniel, Song of Songs, and the Book of Ezra." Pancratius C. Beentjes, "Canon and Scripture in the Book of Ben Sira (Jesus Sirach/Ecclesiasticus)," *HBOT* 1/2:591–605 (595).

²² Chapman, *Law*, 257. See, however, Lim, *Formation*, 127–28, who agrees that "[b]y the second half of the first century BCE the sectarians already had an implicit sense of authoritative scriptures in the form of a collection of writings attributed to Moses, another set of books of the Prophets, and one or more versions of the Psalter" (128), but thinks of the collection as "broadly bipartite" (131). "It is unlikely that the psalms were part of a third division" of Scripture (146).

²³ Philo, *De vita contemplativa* (*The Contemplative Life*), 3.25, 28, 29.

²⁴ Josephus, *Ag. Ap.* 1:37–43.

²⁵ Beckwith, *Canon*, 235–40.

²⁶ Eusebius, *Church History*, 6.25 (*NPNF* 2, 1:272); Jerome, *Helmeted Preface*.

treated as such by Jews: "no one has ventured either to add, or to remove, or to alter a syllable" and every Jew is ready, if need be, to die for this literature.[27] Here Josephus echoes Philo: the Jews "have not altered even a single word of what had been written by [Moses], but would rather endure to die ten thousand times, than yield to any persuasion contrary to his laws and customs."[28] The sanctity of these books is bound up with the time and the circumstances of their composition: they are *old, prophetic* books, deriving from the time before prophecy ceased in Israel in the period of the Persian Empire. They are to be sharply differentiated from the books that came later, which Jews do not consider to be on the same level as the earlier literature: "From Artaxerxes to our own time the complete history has been written, but has not been deemed worthy of equal credit with the earlier records, because of the failure of the exact succession of the prophets."[29] These sentiments are very much in line with those of the rabbis who have already been mentioned.

Josephus' reliability concerning what all Jews through time have believed has sometimes been questioned.[30] Yet what he writes is certainly consistent with the earlier evidence, and as Ellis notes, "Josephus was writing a closely reasoned polemic against *inter alia* the work of an erudite Alexandrian grammarian, and could not afford to indulge in careless misstatements that could be thrown back at him."[31] Leiman generalizes the point: "any Roman reader could inquire of the nearest Jew and test the veracity of Josephus' statement,"[32] at least as to what the majority of Jews *believed* about their Scriptures. Steve Mason agrees: "His claims to speak for all Judeans when he specifies the figure of twenty-two volumes would be vulnerable to immediate disconfirmation if it were merely an ad hoc invention."[33] In sum, it is not likely that Josephus in *Against Apion* is doing otherwise than articulating a more generally shared first-century view of Scripture. There are twenty-two books of sacred literature, inspired by God, and they have been regarded as such by Jews for a long time.[34]

---

[27] Josephus, *Ag. Ap.* 1.42–43.

[28] Philo, fragment of *Hypothetica*, preserved in Eusebius, *Praeparatio evangelica* (*Preparation for the Gospel*; trans. Edwin H. Gifford; Grand Rapids; Baker, 1981), 8.6 (1:357b–c).

[29] This does not mean, of course, that Josephus declines to use later books like 1–2 Maccabees in writing his own history, *Antiquitates judaicae* (*Jewish Antiquities*). Nevertheless, "he seems aware, though he does not advertise it, that [such] books ... are later and separate [from the canonical books]." Mason, "Josephus," 233.

[30] So, recently, Lim, *Formation*, 48–49, 180.

[31] Ellis, *Old Testament*, 39.

[32] Leiman, *Canonization*, 34.

[33] Mason, "Josephus," 229n38. See also Chapman, *Law*, 273.

[34] It is worth noting here, in connection with my earlier comments on correct method, that if we only knew how Josephus *uses* the Scriptures in his *Jewish Antiquities*, and did not also possess his explicit *statement* about them in the *Against Apion*, we might well regard him as offering "the

Further Jewish and Christian Evidence

Certainly a very similar set of ideas about Scripture is found in some manuscripts of 2 Esdras 14:44-48, dating from around the same time period (the end of the first century AD). In this text, the biblical Ezra is described as comprising ninety-four scrolls. Seventy are designed to be read only by "the wise," while the remainder are "public." Here again we seem to have old and sacred Scriptures of a fixed number (along with a larger number of other texts), except that the number on this occasion is twenty-four, which is precisely the number of the Scriptures that later consistently appears in rabbinic literature and in manuscripts of the Hebrew Bible. The Babylonian Talmud already uses this number in a Tannaitic tradition that dates from no later than the second century AD.[35] Both ways of counting (twenty-two and twenty-four) are reflected in what Jerome has to say in the fourth century about the Jewish definition of Scripture, and he offers an explanation for the difference.[36] In the preface to his Vulgate (Latin) translation of the Hebrew Samuel and Kings—a translation to which we shall return in chapters 10 and 11—Jerome counts the Scriptures as including five books of the Law, then Joshua, Judges-Ruth, Samuel, and Kings each as one book, along with Isaiah, Jeremiah (in which he includes Lamentations), Ezekiel, and the Minor Prophets (as one book), totaling eight Prophets. He follows these with Job, Psalms, Proverbs, Ecclesiastes, Song of Songs, Daniel, Chronicles (one book), Ezra-Nehemiah (one book), and Esther, totaling nine Writings.[37] These are the very books that also appear in Origen's earlier list, albeit differently ordered.[38] Jerome then notes a second tradition within Judaism, in which Ruth is distinguished from Judges, and Lamentations from Jeremiah, and both are included in the Writings, bringing the total number of books to twenty-four. This is the very way in which the books are positioned and counted in the Babylonian Talmud. From this it is clear that the second way of counting does not offer us a different reckoning as to the *content* of Scripture. It is only offering us a different way of *describing* the content.

There is no reason to think that Jews who for some time *before* Josephus' lifetime had not "ventured either to add, or to remove, or to alter a syllable" in the

---

clearest case for an open canon." Mason, "Josephus," 234. Happily, we do in fact have this explicit statement.

[35] B. Bava Batra 14b–15a. See Beckwith, *Canon*, 121–22; and Dempster, "Canon," 164n40.

[36] Beckwith, *Canon*, 118–27.

[37] Jerome, *Helmeted Preface*.

[38] Origen's list as we have it actually omits the Minor Prophets and numbers only twenty-one books, but this is undoubtedly merely a copying mistake on the part of a later scribe, since Origen himself explicitly describes them as twenty-two in number. Ellis, *Old Testament*, 13. Confusion often arises about one aspect of the remainder of Origen's list, because it mentions two books of "Esdras." These are probably not the Pseudepigrapha 1–2 Esdras, but rather the biblical books Ezra and Nehemiah. Ellis, *Old Testament*, 15–16.

sacred books would have taken a different view of the matter in the period immediately *afterward*. We are justified in assuming, then, that when Josephus writes of twenty-two of these books, they comprise the same twenty-two (or twenty-four) that we find in our later witnesses. We might then populate the categories following the "five books of Moses" as follows: his "thirteen" prophetic books that record "the events of their own times" would comprise Joshua, Judges-Ruth, Samuel, Kings, Chronicles, Ezra-Nehemiah, Esther, Isaiah, Jeremiah-Lamentations, Ezekiel, Daniel, the Minor Prophets, and Job. His "four" books of "hymns to God and precepts for human life" would then be Psalms, Proverbs, Song of Songs, and Ecclesiastes.[39]

The Ordering of the Books in the Jewish Canon

Taken together, then, all the evidence described in the present section of the chapter concerning the Law, the Prophets, and "the rest of the books" stands in favor of the existence of a closed canon prior to the time of Jesus (during "long ages" past) that already included all the books later found in the Jewish Writings, but excluded the Apocrypha and the Pseudepigrapha.[40] This is not to say that these "holy books" were always *listed* in the same way. Even though neither Josephus nor the Babylonian Talmud hints at the slightest degree of uncertainty in Judaism in the early centuries AD about which books compose the Jewish canon and which lie outside it, they nevertheless describe the biblical corpus in very different ways, no doubt because of the purpose that lies behind each description. Josephus is writing for a Gentile audience, and he understandably introduces his readers to the Jewish holy books in a topical way that is (for them) accessible and comprehensible, gathering together in one place all the books that touch on history.[41] It is not clear that he even means thereby to reflect a traditional Jewish order for the books, although he may. The Talmud, on the other hand, is explicitly intent on informing Jews what certain rabbis taught about the correct order of the books, which suggests that for some reason uncertainty had arisen in the second century AD concerning this question and that it needed to be addressed. Here the Prophets are clearly distinguished from the Writings, the precise ordering of the books in the latter category apparently reflecting for the most part beliefs about

---

[39] So also Leiman, *Canonization*, 32–33; and Ellis, *Old Testament*, 7n25.

[40] The precise date by which this closure might have occurred is of less importance than the fact that it did. Leiman, e.g., chooses a date "shortly after the death of Antiochus IV (164/163 B.C.)." Leiman, *Canonization*, 30.

[41] Beckwith, *Canon*, 123–27. "The distinction of genres, along with the two other criteria [authorship and chronology], simply help the gentile reader understand the various kinds of material within the twenty-two volumed official Judean record." Mason, "Josephus," 221.

the historical order of the biblical authors.[42] Here the description of the canon reflects an important distinction between the Prophets, which were read along with the Law each week in the synagogue service, and the Writings, which were largely not.[43] Even in later Jewish tradition we have evidence of different ways (for differing reasons) of describing the canon and the ordering of the biblical books within each section of the canon,[44] and Jerome strongly implies that this kind of diversity is not new, but traditional. He himself can list the biblical books in different ways in various of his own writings; in one of these, for example, he places Job between Deuteronomy and Joshua.[45] So the *listing and the ordering* may vary in the early Jewish and Christian documents (i.e., prior to the fourth century), but all of them can be read satisfactorily as referring to or implying the same canonical *content*. The only early list that causes any kind of difficulty in this regard is that of the second-century Christian bishop Melito of Sardis in Asia Minor.

Melito of Sardis

The difficulty here is not great, but it *is* interesting. Pressed by a friend to obtain "accurate facts about the ancient writings" in terms of number and order, Melito traveled to Palestine around AD 170 to do exactly that.[46] The difficulty with his account of these books is not great because, although his order differs from both Josephus and the Babylonian Talmud and he counts the number as twenty-five rather than twenty-two or twenty-four, the content of Scripture as he describes it is almost exactly the same as theirs.[47] The interest lies in the exception: Melito *appears* to have received information in the course of his trip that led him to omit

---

[42] Ellis, *Old Testament*, 12n36.

[43] Leiman, *Canonization*, 33 and 33n158, qualified by Stephen B. Chapman, "'A Threefold Cord Is Not Quickly Broken': Interpretation by Canonical Division in Early Judaism and Christianity," in *The Shape of the Writings* (ed. Julius Steinberg and Timothy J. Stone; Winona Lake, Ind.: Eisenbrauns, 2015), 281–309 (297n45).

[44] Ellis notes, e.g., that some later manuscripts of the Jewish Bible have four divisions rather than the Talmudic three: Law, Megillot (the five smaller scrolls each associated with an important Jewish festival: Ruth, Lamentations, Song of Songs, Ecclesiastes, and Esther), Prophets, and Writings. Ellis, *Old Testament*, 12n38. See further Beckwith, *Canon*, esp. 181–234.

[45] Ellis, *Old Testament*, 32n100.

[46] For the text, see Leiman, *Canonization*, 41–42.

[47] The order conforms closely to the LXX Codex Vaticanus (see further my chapter 10), in which law is followed by history and poetry, with prophecy coming last of all. It may reflect an early Jewish ordering different from the two described by Jerome, and it is the sequence followed later also by Origen (Ellis, *Old Testament*, 11–12, 15). The number twenty-five arises because Melito omits Esther (see below), splits Judges from Ruth (like the Babylonian Talmud), but then also splits 1 Samuel from 2 Samuel, 1 Kings from 2 Kings, and 1 Chronicles from 2 Chronicles. Nehemiah is no doubt counted with Ezra, and Lamentations with Jeremiah.

Esther from among the canonical OT books. Certainly Esther does not appear on his list as we now have it. This list in turn apparently influenced some later fourth-century Christian scholars when compiling *their* lists: Esther is not included, for example, in the catalogue of Athanasius that is found in one of his *Festal Letters*, dating from AD 367, nor in the list of Gregory of Nazianzus (c. 329–390).[48] The question is how to weigh this evidence, given the likely attestation to the book of Esther in Josephus in the first century, its explicit attestation in rabbinic sources in the second,[49] and its presence in the canonical lists of Origen and Jerome in the third and fourth (both of whom were very familiar with the Jewish heritage)—not to mention its appearance also in the lists of Hilary of Poitiers (315–367), Cyril of Jerusalem (c. 315–386), Epiphanius of Salamis (c. 315–403), and Rufinus of Aquileia (c. 344–410), and of the Councils of Laodicea (360), Hippo (393), and Carthage (397).[50] Whatever the doubts that some Christians may have had about Esther (including, perhaps, Melito's informants—whoever they might have been), it is not likely that these reflect doubts among Jews of the earlier period, and indeed none of the Christian writers who follow Melito in omitting Esther from their lists ever suggest otherwise (i.e., that Esther is not "one of the number" of the Jewish Scriptures). If the omission is not simply the result of a scribal mistake, similar to the mistake that later omits the Minor Prophets from Origen's list,[51] then perhaps it arises from the perception, not that Esther lay outside the number of the *Hebrew* books of the canon, but that it lay outside the number of the books of "the" original *LXX translation* of the OT that many Christians regarded as inspired.[52]

---

[48] The situation in nearby Antioch in the fourth century is unclear. Hill notes that none of the Antiochene commentators cites Esther directly from Scripture; Theodore cites it only from Josephus. Yet Hill also acknowledges that "[a]bsence of evidence . . . is not conclusive evidence of absence," and reminds us, first, that most of Diodore's and Theodore's commentary work is lost, and second, that (the later) Theodoret, who provides us with "the greatest number of extant Antiochene exegetical works," does not give "sustained attention" in his commentating to works "more marginal to the canon." Hill, *Antioch*, 23–24.

[49] Aside from B. Bava Batra 14b–15a, note the early affirmation of Esther as Scripture by Rabbi Simeon ben Johai, a student of Rabbi Akiba, in B. *Megillah* 7a (Leiman, *Canonization*, 106, §77).

[50] Ellis, *Old Testament*, 10–33.

[51] Ellis, *Old Testament*, 11n34.

[52] Leiman, *Canonization*, 48n239. On the question of the LXX as "inspired translation," see further my chapter 10.

CONTRARY INDICATIONS?

Is there compelling evidence that stands *against* this idea that an OT canon, including the books later found in the Jewish Writings but excluding the Apocrypha and Pseudepigrapha, was already closed in the early first century AD?

Rabbinical Disputes

It has sometimes been asserted, first, that later rabbinical disputes about some of the books now found in the Writings raise doubts about the settled boundaries of this body of literature at an earlier date.[53] There is no good reason to accept this assertion, however. It is true that some later rabbis did raise questions about certain books for various reasons. Sometimes they debated, for example, whether this or that text should be withdrawn from circulation because of problems that might arise from its public use.[54] Yet as Leiman persuasively argues, such withdrawal "in no way casts aspersions on the sanctity or canonicity of the books."[55] Canonicity was not at issue in these discussions. That this is so is confirmed by the fact that the rabbis discussed the book of Ezekiel in the same way, since "its words contradicted Torah" and it was regarded as dangerous to the immature.[56] By the time that these discussions were taking place, however, the presence of Ezekiel in the biblical canon was not in question.[57]

Sometimes the rabbis debated whether certain books really did "defile the hands" as a result of their composing part of sacred, inspired Scripture. Ecclesiastes lies at the center of an early first-century AD dispute on this point, for example,[58] and the Song of Songs, Ruth, and Esther are also mentioned in relation to this question.[59] None of this demonstrates, however, that any of these books had not long been widely regarded as Jewish Scripture—any more than Martin Luther's later questions in respect of Esther or James raise this question about *Christian* Scripture. In the case of the Song of Songs, indeed, Rabbi Akiba (d. AD 135) emphatically declares: "No man in Israel ever disputed the status of the

---

[53] This popular modern idea was first proposed in 1871 by the Prussian Jewish historian Heinrich Graetz.

[54] B. *Shabbat* 30b notes discussion of Ecclesiastes and Proverbs along these lines, e.g., because they contain internal contradictions. B. *Abot of Rabbi Nathan* 1:4 describes a time when Proverbs, Song of Songs, and Ecclesiastes *were* withdrawn for a while until their meaning had been clarified. Leiman, *Canonization*, 73–74 (§§49, 51).

[55] Leiman, *Canonization*, 79.

[56] B. *Shabbat* 13b; B. *Hagigah* 13a (Leiman, *Canonization*, 72–73, §§47, 48).

[57] "[The rabbis] attempted to withdraw the book of Ezekiel because it troubled them; but they never entertained doubts about its inspired origin." Yehezkel Kaufmann, cited in Leiman, *Canonization*, 72n318.

[58] M. *Eduyyot* 5.3 (Leiman, *Canonization*, 105, §75).

[59] B. *Megillah* 7a (Leiman, *Canonization*, 106, §77).

Song of Songs saying that it does not defile the hands... all the writings are holy, but the Song of Songs is the holiest of the holy."[60] It has now been established beyond reasonable doubt, in fact, that a so-called "Council of Jamnia" in the last decade of the first century, which used to be widely interpreted as incorporating these "disputed" books into the Jewish canon and closing it, did no such thing—which is exactly what we would expect if Josephus, writing around the same time, is to be trusted in what he says about the antiquity of all the Scriptures.[61] "The rabbis," Leiman convincingly proposes, "were questioning the inspired status of some of the books included in a biblical canon already closed."[62] They were not closing a hitherto open-ended canon. Just a few decades later, all the books concerned are included—although discussions about some of them are still ongoing in subsequent centuries—in Aquila's Greek translation of the OT (c. AD 130), which was designed to replace for Jews the LXX that was being widely used by Christians.[63] This is again consistent with what both Josephus and the Babylonian Talmud tell us.

An Alexandrian Canon?

It has sometimes been argued, second, that among Hellenistic Jews outside Palestine there was a "Hellenistic" or "Alexandrian canon" of greater extent than the Palestinian one, and that the former contained the Apocrypha.[64] This theory is premised, first of all, on the fact that the larger surviving LXX manuscripts of the OT include various of the Apocrypha. However, all these manuscripts are late, they are of Christian origin, and they diverge in which Apocrypha they include.[65] They are not reliable guides to the original situation among Hellenistic Jews in earlier times.[66] As we examine these earlier times themselves, there is no reason to think that Hellenistic Jews took a view of the boundaries between Scripture and other books that was different from their Palestinian counterparts, with whom they shared close "community of language and ideas."[67] Hellenistic Jews may have

---

[60] M. *Yadayim* 3.5 (Leiman, *Canonization*, 105–6, §76). B. *Megillah* 7a further affirms that Ruth and Esther defile the hands.

[61] Leiman, *Canonization*, 120–24: "The widespread view that the Council of Jamnia closed the biblical canon, or that it canonized any books at all, is not supported by the evidence and need no longer be seriously maintained" (124).

[62] Leiman, *Canonization*, 120.

[63] Beckwith, *Canon*, 277. On Aquila's revision of the LXX, see further my chapter 10.

[64] The theory is first associated with the names of Francis Lee, in the eighteenth century, and F. C. Movers, in the nineteenth. Beckwith, *Canon*, 3.

[65] Codex Sinaiticus and Codex Vaticanus (fourth century AD), e.g., both contain the Wisdom of Solomon, Ecclesiasticus, Tobit, and Judith, but they differ beyond that.

[66] Beckwith, *Canon*, 382–83.

[67] Beckwith, *Canon*, 31.

valued various books "outside the number" of the Scriptures in their Greek form, but there is no clear evidence that they considered any of these books to be part of their primary Scripture.[68] In sum, "[t]here is no evidence of an Alexandrian Canon as opposed to a Palestinian Canon."[69]

PATTERNS OF CITATION AND REFERENCE

It is with all this in mind that we must now return briefly to the question of the patterns of citation and reference that are evident in our early sources before and during the first century AD. Is it possible to offer a coherent account of what we find there, if we grant that there already existed in that time period the kind of closed canon that I have just described on the basis of other evidence?

At Qumran, first of all, evidence of all of the books in the Jewish canon has been discovered, with the exception of Esther.[70] There is also evidence of two of the Apocrypha (Ben Sira and Tobit, leaving aside the Epistle of Jeremiah for the reasons provided in chapter 2), and of numerous Pseudepigrapha (e.g., *Jubilees*).[71] Considering the overall pattern of citation and reference, there is little reason to believe that the Qumran sectarians, while valuing highly a whole range of texts, regarded any of the Apocrypha or Pseudepigrapha as Scripture alongside "the book of Moses, and the books of the prophets, and of David."[72] Among the Writ-

---

[68] Beckwith, *Canon*, 382–86.

[69] Johan Lust, "Septuagint and Canon," in *The Biblical Canons* (ed. J. M. Auwers and H. J. De Jonge; BETL 163; Leuven: Leuven University Press, 2003), 39–55 (55).

[70] The presence of Nehemiah has only recently been confirmed; see Lim, *Formation*, 121n3. For a possible explanation of the apparent absence of Esther, see Beckwith, *Canon*, 291–93. Leiman considers the absence merely fortuitous, noting that Ezra, Nehemiah, and 1–2 Chronicles (which is a vastly larger composition) are also scarcely represented at Qumran. Leiman, *Canonization*, 35. As one OT scholar has wittily said, "an additional hungry worm, and Chronicles, too, would have been missing." Frank M. Cross, *From Epic to Canon: History and Literature in Ancient Israel* (Baltimore: Johns Hopkins University Press, 1998), 225. Certainly the Qumran community appears to have known the *story* of Esther, since it is reflected in a number of scroll fragments. McDonald, *Biblical Canon*, 128–29n32. Eugene Ulrich actually includes Esther in his list of texts of "negligible" (i.e., not "no") importance at Qumran, along with Proverbs, Ecclesiastes, Ezra, Nehemiah, and Chronicles. Eugene Ulrich, "Qumran and the Canon of the Old Testament," in Auwers and De Jonge, *Biblical Canons*, 57–80 (72).

[71] Leiman, *Canonization*, 35.

[72] Beckwith, *Canon*, 407. The most striking case of what looks like "authoritative citation" of a nonbiblical text, and one that some have referred to as touching on issues of canon, is found in CD (the Damascus or Cairo Document) 16:1–4 (citing *Jubilees*). Yet the significance even of this example is disputed; see Johan L. Lust, "Quotation Formulae and Canon in Qumran," in *Canonization and Decanonization* (ed. Arie van der Kooij and Karel van der Toorn; SHR 82; Leiden: Brill, 1998), 67–77; and Lim, *Formation*, 131–35. Lim goes on to describe the distinction at Qumran between the Scriptures and the interpretative documents in terms of the possession of a "formal authority," on the one hand, and of a "contemporary authority," on the other (146).

ings, on the other hand, at least Psalms, Proverbs, Daniel, and Chronicles are cited or treated in ways that certainly imply an authoritative scriptural status.[73] Summarizing the evidence, Johan Lust concludes that "the community at Qumran appears to have given a special status, which we may call 'canonical,' to the books of the Hebrew Bible known to us, and to no other religious books."[74]

As we have already seen, Philo does not cite nearly as much from the Prophets and the Writings as he does from the Law: "there are approximately 2000 citations from the Torah and only 50 citations from the rest of Scripture."[75] Nevertheless, he cites from half the books in the Writings: Psalms, Job, Proverbs, Ezra, Nehemiah, and 1–2 Chronicles. He evidently knows Ben Sira, but "he never cites apocryphal books," even though he does so freely from various Greek philosophers.[76] Josephus cites all the texts in the Writings, with the exception of Ruth, the Song of Songs, and Lamentations, the last of which he nevertheless clearly regards in his *Jewish Antiquities* as Scripture.[77] He "was familiar with the Apocrypha" and borrowed significantly from them in his writings for various reasons,[78] but he never cites these books as Scripture.

In the NT, "the formal quotations of the Old Testament . . . are strikingly limited to the 'Hebrew Canon,' with only one *formal* quotation [in Jude 14–15, noted below] falling outside the canonical books."[79] The Psalms and Daniel are frequently cited as Scripture.[80] Job is cited by the apostle Paul when he writes to the Corinthian church (1 Cor 3:19), and Proverbs when he writes to the Romans (Rom 9:13; cf. also Jas 4:6). First-Second Chronicles may also be referenced.[81] The NT authors never quote from any of the Apocrypha, however, even though

---

[73] Beckwith, *Canon*, 74; Ulrich, "Qumran," 80 (and the discussion on 73–74). The Psalms are already known as a collection in something like their present form in the fourth century BC, when 1–2 Chronicles cite or allude to them in the course of proclaiming their message. Most significantly in the present context, 1 Chr 16:8-36 cites Ps 106:47-48, and verse 48 is the doxology that concludes book four of the Psalter. The Chronicler therefore shows knowledge of a collection of psalms that is already subdivided into at least four sections, and quite probably of the whole book of Psalms that we now possess. On the general importance of the evidence of 1–2 Chronicles for our understanding of the development of the OT canon, see further Chapman, *Law*, 218–31.

[74] Lust, "Quotation Formulae," 75.

[75] Leiman, *Canonization*, 31.

[76] Leiman, *Canonization*, 31, and 31n150.

[77] Beckwith, *Canon*, 79, referring to *Ant.* 10.5.1 and 10.78.

[78] Leiman, *Canonization*, 33.

[79] Oskar Skarsaune, "The Question of Old Testament Canon and Text in the Early Greek Church," *HBOT* 1/1:443–50 (445).

[80] E.g., Mark 12:36; Luke 4:10-11; Rom 3:4; 1 Cor 3:19-20; Eph 4:8; Matt 4:17; Mark 13:14, 14:62. First Macc 1:54, 6:7 (c. 100 BC) already regards Daniel as prophetic.

[81] If Matthew 23 does refer to 2 Chr 24:20-21, then the reference to a line of prophets from Abel (in Genesis) to Zechariah (in Chronicles) could also be taken to imply knowledge of a canon of Scripture that already begins with the first book of the Law and ends with what in later times

some of them display knowledge of apocryphal books, as they also display knowledge of various Greek authors, whom they do cite (as we have seen) without implying that they represent Scripture.[82] The NT authors *almost* never refer to the Pseudepigrapha either. The exceptions occur in 1 Peter and Jude. First Peter 3:18-20 alludes to 1 *Enoch* 10–16, and 1 *Enoch* 1:9 is quoted in Jude 14–15, which also (in v. 9) alludes to a story from the *Assumption of Moses*. Neither instance, however, provides us with evidence that these texts were regarded during the apostolic era as Scripture in the way that was true (for example) for the book of Psalms. Indeed, in the case of 1 Peter, 1 *Enoch* is apparently referenced only in order to contradict it.[83] Even in the post-apostolic Church, as we shall shortly see, where 1 *Enoch* was being read as a quasi-canonical text by some Christians, its status was under fierce attack from others—to such an extent that, according to Jerome, Jude's reference to 1 *Enoch* as even a broadly "prophetic" text was sufficient to create doubt in many Christian minds about Jude's own canonicity.[84] Augustine himself felt compelled to defend Jude from any impression of wrongdoing, distinguishing between the truth of what his pseudepigraphical source text said, on the one hand, and the question of the scriptural status of that source text itself, on the other: "it is not without reason that [the] writings [of Enoch] have no place in [the] canon of Scripture."[85]

There is nothing in any of this evidence that is problematic for the idea that the canon of OT Scripture was already closed as we arrive in the first century AD. We only need to imagine (and it does not require *much* imagination) that for all sorts of reasons the canon was only explicitly referenced as Scripture in part by our various early witnesses. The evidence is quite problematic, on the other hand, for those like Sundberg who posit "a wide religious literature without definite bounds" that "circulated throughout Judaism as holy Scripture before Jamnia."[86] If this were really true, we might then expect to see at least some of the Apocrypha, for example, being cited as Scripture by our various witnesses. There are no clear examples of this in Philo, Josephus, or the NT, however, nor any in "Ben Sira, the authors of Maccabees, Hillel, Shammai, and all the first century Tannaim."[87]

---

was routinely considered the last of the Writings. So Beckwith, *Canon*, 181–234. The matter is disputed, however; see Lim, *Formation*, 157–62, for a critique.

[82] Beckwith, *Canon*, 387n199.
[83] Beckwith, *Canon*, 402–3.
[84] Jerome, *De viris illustribus* (*Illustrious Men*), 4 (NPNF 2, 3:362): "because in it he [Jude] quotes from the apocryphal book of Enoch it is rejected by many."
[85] Augustine, *De civitate Dei* (*City of God*), 15.23.4 (NPNF 1, 2:305).
[86] Sundberg, *Old Testament*, 102–3.
[87] Leiman, *Canonization*, 39.

TOWARD THE (FINAL) CHRISTIAN CANON

A strong case can be made, then, that the content of what later became the Jewish Writings formed, along with the collections of the Law and the Prophets, the foundational Scripture of the Christian church right from its point of origin in the life and teaching of Jesus, and that other writings, however much they were revered, remained "outside the number" of the holy books. Of venerable age, some of the Writings (like Psalms and Proverbs) began their lives well before the sixth-century exile of the Israelites to Babylonia, and probably began to coalesce into a collection of their own already by the end of the Persian period, if not before,[88] such that this collection was already known in the Hellenistic period. Understood by Jews as texts that in various ways were deeply connected to various of the books in the Law and the Prophets (e.g., Psalms with 1–2 Samuel [David]), these connections could nevertheless be made differently, leading to differences in how the Scriptures overall were listed and even counted. Ruth could be listed with Judges in the Prophets, for example (where the story fits chronologically), or among "the rest of the books" (if the concern was more about use in the synagogue).[89] It is this reality that is still reflected in later times, as Jewish tradition settles down into what became the generally accepted view in Judaism about where books like Ruth rightly belong (i.e., in the Writings), while in the listings of canonical texts within the Christian Church, the books found in the Writings can and do "migrate toward other books with which they have intentional literary and theological affiliation"[90] (e.g., 1–2 Chronicles are placed next to 1–2 Kings). This demonstrates, however, *not* that we lack a stable set of twenty-two (or twenty-four) canonical books, common to both Jews and Christians in the first century AD, but only that stability of content should not be confused with stability in organization.[91]

---

[88] We perhaps already see a hint of this development earlier, in texts like Jer 18:18 ("Come, let's make plans against Jeremiah; for the teaching of the law by the priest will not be lost, nor will counsel from the wise, nor the word from the prophets") and Ezek 7:26 ("They will try to get a vision from the prophet; the teaching of the law by the priest will be lost, as will the counsel of the elders"), which could read as implying a distinction between law, prophets, and wisdom literature. Second Maccabees 2:13-14 can also plausibly be read as drawing back the veil on some of the processes involved, with their references to Nehemiah's creation of a library containing "the books about the kings and prophets, and the books of David, and letters of kings," and to Judas Maccabeus after the Maccabean Revolt of 167–164 BC "in like manner" gathering together "all those writings that had been scattered by reason of the war." Beckwith, *Canon*, 150–53.

[89] For a robust argument, nevertheless, for an early, settled order for the canonical OT books beneath and prior to later fluidity—"the earliest evidence is of a single, agreed order"—see Beckwith, *Canon*, 181–234 (quote on 222).

[90] Seitz, *Goodly Fellowship*, 101.

[91] "[T]here is stability, but this stability does not preclude shuffling and migrating. The 'Writings' are sufficiently individual works, sufficiently deferential to the core canon, and sufficiently

The Development of the New Testament Canon

It is on the foundation of this stable, authoritative OT witness that the remainder of the Christian canon is then subsequently built, as the Christian Church follows the logic of its own deep conviction that prophecy did not, after all, come to an end with Malachi, but was renewed among Jesus of Nazareth and his apostles.[92] So it is that in due course, beginning in the middle to late second century AD (as we saw in chapter 2), the NT literature rises to the same explicit level of authority in the Christian church as the OT had clearly enjoyed up to that point. Ultimately this NT literature comes to comprise twenty-seven books. The Muratorian Fragment from Rome (c. AD 180–200)[93] already lists twenty-two of them (along with two works not ultimately accepted as canonical—see below). These are the four gospels, Acts, thirteen letters of the apostle Paul, Jude, 1–2 John, and Revelation. This is not an exhaustive list of NT writings regarded as Scripture in the second century, however, since we know from other sources that 1 Peter was also so regarded at this time, as was Hebrews (at least in Egypt). The full sevenfold collection of the "Catholic Epistles" (James, 1–2 Peter, 1–3 John, and Jude) later referenced by Eusebius of Caesarea probably came into existence only at a slightly later time, in the third century.[94]

All these are the texts that ultimately stood the test of time, as the Church at large reflected on which texts should be added to its OT Scriptures, arriving eventually at a point in the fourth and fifth centuries when all of them together received final ratification. Along the way, other texts that at least some (perhaps many) Christians at some point regarded as Scripture fell away, including the popular *Apocalypse of Peter* (which is included in the Muratorian list), the *Shepherd of Hermas* (which is explicitly rejected there), *1 Clement*, and *Barnabas*. We gain extensive insight into this reality from Eusebius of Caesarea's *Church History*.

---

diverse and varied as works that the NT need not refer to them as a distinct canonical unit in order for them to be fully part of a stable 'OT', albeit in shifting orders." Seitz, *Goodly Fellowship*, 119.

[92] "[I]t is impossible to understand the person and work of Christ apart from the logic of accordance with the OT. The canonicity of the NT is an analogous and derivative phenomenon, taking its logic and bearings from the existence of an anterior witness in a given material form.... The New is not a phase of development that grounds the Old but rather a statement of the Old's abiding sense and final meaning, perceived now afresh within its own plain-sense deliverances and helping to interpret and ground the New's meaning and final purpose as well." Seitz, *Goodly Fellowship*, 131–32.

[93] For the date, see Metzger, *Canon*, 191–201.

[94] Eusebius, *Church History*, 2.23.25 (*NPNF* 2, 1:128). See further David R. Nienhuis and Robert W. Wall, *Reading the Epistles of James, Peter, John and Jude as Scripture: The Shaping and Shape of a Canonical Collection* (Grand Rapids: Eerdmans, 2013); and Carey C. Newman, "Jude 22, Apostolic Theology, and the Canonical Role of the Catholic Epistles," *PRSt* 41 (2014): 367–78, who sees the Catholic Epistles "as an intended collection, to be read alongside and in light of Acts, with its own decidedly theological agenda vis-à-vis the other collections within the New Testament" (377).

Writing in the opening decades of the fourth century, Eusebius distinguishes texts accepted by the Church as Scripture without qualification, on the one hand, from both disputed books (whose genuineness or authority is questioned) and heretical ones, on the other.[95] The texts accepted without qualification comprise the four Gospels, Acts, the fourteen letters of Paul (including Hebrews), 1 John, and 1 Peter. Eusebius is ambivalent about Revelation, reflecting unease in the Eastern Church for decades beforehand, even though in earlier times Revelation had been received in both the East and the West. In his "disputed" category Eusebius places James, Jude, 2 Peter, and 2–3 John, as well as some texts ultimately regarded as noncanonical: the *Acts of Paul*, the *Shepherd of Hermas*, the *Apocalypse of Peter*, *Barnabas*, and the *Didache*. However, Athanasius' slightly later fourth-century list (AD 367) admits of no dispute regarding Revelation, James, Jude, 2 Peter, and 2–3 John (which are canonical) and the remainder (which are not canonical), and it was this view that prevailed at the Councils of both Hippo (393) and Carthage (397)—albeit that Hebrews was extracted from among the letters of Paul and given its own place.

It was the twenty-seven books, then, that in the end were judged to meet the canonical criteria of apostolicity (authorship by an apostle, derivation from the time of the apostles, or agreement with apostolic teaching), catholicity (relevance to the wider Church), orthodoxy (conformity with Christian truth as rooted in the already-accepted Scriptures), and traditional usage (whether a book had been used from an early time and in most churches). It was these books that the Church agreed it must receive, on these grounds, as the NT Scriptures, now to be added to the OT Scriptures that preceded them and provided the foundation for their teaching. We should note in passing that the Church did in fact *add* them to the OT Scriptures. They did not *replace* the OT with the NT, nor did they *merge* the two collections of Scripture together. Nor, for that matter, did they create as a preface to the NT a compendium or summary of OT teaching (identifying, for example, the most important texts or themes), obliterating the distinctions between the different OT books within their various collections. The integrity of the OT as a library of separate books from the past was respected, even as OT Scripture was now supplemented by NT Scripture. It is, then, as a two-testament reality subdivided into individual (although associated) books, looking forward (OT) and then backward (NT) to Christ, that Christian readers encounter the Bible still to this day. Like other aspects of our discussion of Scripture and canon in chapters 2 and 3, this reality too must be taken seriously when we address in chapters 4 through 9 the question of how the Bible is best read.

---

[95] Eusebius, *Church History* 3.25 (NPNF 2, 1:155–57).

The Old Testament Apocrypha and Pseudepigrapha

As the Church was discerning in this way which of the many *Christian* (or quasi-Christian) texts that were highly regarded by at least some post-apostolic Christians should actually be viewed as Scripture, a parallel process was under way with respect to some *Jewish* texts from the Apocrypha and Pseudepigrapha. We have already encountered aspects of this process as we have moved through the present chapter. The NT authors themselves may never have ascribed scriptural authority to any of these texts, but among some of their post-apostolic successors, the line between core and other texts could become blurred, especially from the third century onward.[96]

This blurring was facilitated by the fact that already in the late second century AD a largely Greek-speaking Church had begun to find various of the Apocrypha included in their LXX codices—in their Bibles.[97] Such codices may well not reflect the scholarly and critical opinion across the Church at that time, but they do reflect popular usage and custom, and thus the broader context in which the scholars worked. Augustine was particularly sensitive to context, it seems, and this greatly influenced his approach to matters of both canon and text (as we shall see in chapter 10). It made him relatively unconcerned, in fact, about what was true about the Jewish canon and (Hebrew) text over against what he found in his Latin Bible (which was based on the Greek LXX).

Many held to the prevailing earlier view, nevertheless, that it was precisely the Scriptures that comprised the OT back in the originating moments of the Church, shared with the Jews, that ought still to comprise the Christian OT (even if the Hebrew must be translated). To the extent that they became "painfully aware" (as Leiman puts it)[98] of the differences between that Hebrew canon and their own, this knowledge created a problem for them. The pressure that this insistence on the common roots of Christianity and Judaism exerted on those who wished to regard as Scripture texts from outside the shared canon is often visible among post-apostolic writers, even when they choose to ignore it.

It is visible in the second century, for example, when the Muratorian Fragment lists the Wisdom of Solomon among the Scriptures but, significantly, places

---

[96] Prior to the third century, significantly (and if we disregard Clement of Alexandria), "there is [in the Church Fathers] an almost complete lack of quotations from the 'apocrypha' of the later LXX codices." Skarsaune, "Question," 445.

[97] The extant evidence comes from the earliest surviving codices of the LXX from the fourth century AD, but the practice appears to originate in earlier times, when the form of the LXX changed from scroll to codex. Ellis, *Old Testament*, 34–35. The Syriac translation of the OT (the Peshitta) appears to have grown in size over the same time period, also adding the Apocrypha by the fourth century. Ellis, *Old Testament*, 23n72, 24n74.

[98] Leiman, *Canonization*, 40.

it among the *NT*, not the OT Scriptures. We see it again when Tertullian is compelled "to defend at length his use of 1 Enoch" in his writings because this text is not found in the Jewish canon and is consequently not recognized by some Christians.[99] In the middle of the third century, Origen's use of the Pseudepigrapha can likewise be described only as cautious, as illustrated in a comment he makes on a section of *1 Enoch* in his *Commentary on John*: "if anyone cares to accept that book as sacred."[100] He is acutely aware (in his *Homilies on Numbers*) that *1 Enoch* does not appear "to have any recognized authority with the Hebrews," and (*Against Celsus*) that "the books which bear the name Enoch do not at all circulate in the Churches as divine."[101] The distinction that Origen thus draws between core and other texts (and it is also evident in his differentiation between Scripture and the apocryphal Maccabees, noted earlier) is then found in more stringent form in Cyril of Jerusalem (in the fourth century), who urges Christians preparing for baptism that with respect to OT Scripture they should "read the two and twenty books" (by which he means exactly those books now found in the Jewish canon), differentiating these from "apocryphal writings" with which they should have nothing at all to do.[102] Eusebius, likewise, distinguishes the twenty-two books of the OT that, according to Josephus, are "accepted without dispute among the Hebrews" from books like 1–2 Maccabees,[103] and Epiphanius acknowledges that Ecclesiasticus and the Wisdom of Solomon are not to be found among that number in the Jewish canon.[104] The pressure exerted by the idea of "the two and twenty" is also seen in Athanasius (even though he does not regard Esther as being one of the number, but counts Ruth and Judges separately to *make up* the number). He too is quite clear (note the second epigraph to the present chapter) about the distinction between the twenty-two and other books.[105] Then there is

---

[99] Beckwith, *Canon*, 397; Tertullian, *De cultu feminarum* (*The Apparel of Women*), 1.3 (ANF 4:15–16).

[100] Origen, *Commentarii in evangelium Joannis* (*Commentary on John*), 6.25 (ANF 9:371).

[101] Origen, *Homiliae in Numeros* (*Homilies on Numbers*), 28.2.1 (ed. Christopher A. Hall, trans. Thomas P. Scheck; Downers Grove, Ill.: IVP Academic, 2009), 184; *Contra Celsum* (*Against Celsus*), 5.54 (ANF 4:567).

[102] Cyril of Jerusalem, *Katēchēseis* (*Catechetical Lectures*), 4.34–35 (NPNF 2, 7:27). It is not likely that Cyril means absolutely to ban the reading of texts like the Wisdom of Solomon (Ellis, *Old Testament*, 20n64). Still, the sharp distinction between the twenty-two and the rest is striking.

[103] Eusebius, *Church History*, 3.9.5 (NPNF 2, 1:144).

[104] Beckwith, *Canon*, 252–53.

[105] The "other books" are the Wisdom of Solomon, Sirach, Esther, Judith, and Tobit, and "that which is called the Teaching of the Apostles, and the Shepherd." Nor is there any place in the canon, he continues, for "apocryphal writings [probably he means Pseudepigrapha]... they are an invention of heretics, who write them when they choose, bestowing upon them their approbation, and assigning to them a date, that so, using them as ancient writings, they may find occasion to lead astray the simple." Athanasius, *Festal Letters*, 39.7 (NPNF 2, 4:552).

Jerome, whose opinions we have already noted. Jerome was destined to become in later times one of the more influential Church Fathers to pronounce on the matter of the OT canon, because his opinions were embedded in the prefaces to his Vulgate translations of the Hebrew OT books.

This same pressure is evident even when it comes to Augustine in the late fourth and early fifth centuries. Like his predecessors, Augustine could certainly cite the Apocrypha. More important than his citations, however (for the general reasons I already provided earlier), is the list of the OT books that he provides in *On Christian Doctrine*. This list is often introduced into evidence in discussions about the early Christian Bible to promote the view that Augustine did not distinguish between the Apocrypha and the books of the Jewish canon. It reflects, it is claimed, a generalized North African perspective that is also evident in the position adopted by the Councils of Hippo (AD 393) and Carthage (397 and 419). However, the matter is by no means as simple as that, for "unlike the councils, the bishop himself did not [in reality] make an unqualified equation of canonical and apocryphal books."[106] What Augustine actually says in *On Christian Doctrine* is that the "whole canon of Scripture" he describes is an entity upon which "judgment is to be exercised." It is to be exercised

> according to the following standard: to prefer those that are received by all the catholic churches to those which some do not receive. Among those, again, which are not received by all, [the Christian] will prefer such as have the sanction of the greater number and those of greater authority, to such as are held by the smaller number and those of less authority. If, however, he shall find that some books are held by the greater number of churches, and others by the churches of greater authority (though this is not a very likely thing to happen), I think that in such a case the authority on the two sides is to be looked upon as equal.[107]

In other words, Augustine's listing of the biblical books does not remove the need for discrimination among the books that he lists. Elsewhere in his writings, indeed, he himself exercises precisely such discrimination, referencing the situation among the Jews, whom he frequently describes as "our librarians, our witnesses."[108] It is not surprising, then, that Brooke Westcott can say of Augustine

---

[106] Ellis, *Old Testament*, 29.

[107] Augustine, *De doctrina christiana* (*On Christian Doctrine*), 2.8.12 (NPNF 1, 2:538).

[108] Brooke F. Westcott, *The Bible in the Church* (London: Macmillan, 1877), 187. Augustine acknowledges in *City of God*, e.g., that among the Jews the books of the Maccabees are not found "in the Holy Scriptures which are called canonical," although they are held as canonical in the Church "on account of the extreme and wonderful sufferings of certain martyrs." Earlier he has described the canon of Scripture as that which "was preserved in the temple of the Hebrew people by the diligence of successive priests," and as "the Hebrew and Christian canonical Scriptures." Augustine, *City of God*, 15.23, 18.36 (NPNF 1, 2:305, 382).

with respect to the OT canon that in the end his teaching "if interpreted by his practice, does not differ essentially from that of Jerome except in language."[109] Earlier Protestant authors thought the same:

> We, with Jerome and many other fathers, deny these books to be canonical. Augustine, with some others, calls them canonical. Do, then, these fathers differ so widely in opinion? By no means. For Jerome takes this word "canonical" in one sense, while Augustine, Innocent, and the fathers of Carthage understand it in another. Jerome calls only those books canonical, which the church always held for canonical; the rest he banishes from the canon, denies to be canonical, and calls apocryphal. But Augustine calls those canonical which, although they had not the same perfect and certain authority as the rest, were wont to be read in the church for the edification of the people. Augustine, therefore, takes this name in a larger sense than Jerome.[110]

In other words, we need to be careful about what the word "canonical" means in different contexts. It is not always used in the same way in the patristic literature.

It is not surprising that this "pressure of twenty-two"—the pressure exerted by age-old tradition concerning the original nature of the OT back in apostolic times—should ultimately have led (as it did) to the profound marginalization of the Pseudepigrapha in the life of the Church after the third century AD.[111] The Apocrypha proved somewhat more resilient thereafter, especially in the East, but doubts about even the most accepted of these among educated people in the West—Augustine's catalogue of books notwithstanding—were continually expressed all the way through the succeeding centuries down to the period of the Reformation. Few unequivocally pronounced them to be canonical, and there was a significant current of opinion that was patently hostile to them. It is against this background that we must understand Luther's response to Eck in the course of their Leipzig dispute of 1519, when the latter referred to 2 Maccabees in support of the doctrine of purgatory. Luther replied that this text had no binding authority because it was found outside the canon of Scripture. It is against this same background that we must also understand the relegation of the Apocrypha in general, during the Reformation, to the status of secondary but helpful writings at best.

---

[109] Westcott, *Bible*, 188.

[110] William Whitaker, *A Disputation on Holy Scripture: Against the Papists Especially Bellarmine and Stapleton* (trans. William Fitzgerald; Cambridge: Parker Society, 1849; repr., Morgan, Pa.: Soli Deo Gloria, 2000), 45.

[111] Beckwith, *Canon*, 398.

CONCLUSION

What, then, was the extent of the canon of the early Christian church? In the first instance, in the first century AD, it certainly comprised the OT books in the Law and the Prophets. In my view, it almost certainly also comprised all those OT books that ultimately became the Jewish "Writings."[112] In the subsequent centuries, the canon came progressively to include the books now found in the NT, even as the authority of other texts valued by at least some, and sometimes many, Christians (or at least those who self-identified as such) came to be denied, or at least widely doubted.

Who decided which books were canonical, and on what grounds? In the first instance, with respect to the OT, no Christian "decided." The point was to *receive* the OT Scriptures, as from God in Christ. Marcion wished to "decide," and he was excommunicated. With respect to the NT, it is also true that to "decide" was not, in the most important sense, the point. As the second chapter of the Roman Catholic Church's *Dogmatic Constitution on the Catholic Faith* (1870) says about all of Scripture:

> These books the church holds to be sacred and canonical not because she subsequently approved them by her authority after they had been composed by unaided human skill, nor simply because they contain revelation without error, but because, being written under the inspiration of the Holy Spirit, they have God as their author, and were as such committed to the church.[113]

The point was not to "decide." The point was to receive new Scripture from the apostles who had been appointed by Christ, and who represented a new and authoritative prophetic "stream" in history, in continuity with the OT prophets.

Were the Reformers justified in drawing a sharp distinction between the books of the Hebrew Bible as canonical and other texts as not—even if some of the latter had been so regarded by many for a long time? Yes, they were so justified. Indeed, they can be said to have had the majority of the early Christian tradition behind them in drawing such a distinction.

Does it matter very much in the end, though, whether many Christians now still hold to a slightly larger biblical canon than the Protestant one? We live in a time, of course, when far from worrying about which parts of their Bibles their congregants are reading, many leaders across all the branches of the Christian Church would be delighted if they were to be found reading their Bibles very

---

[112] So also Bartholomew, *Biblical Hermeneutics*, 277.
[113] Cited in Stephen B. Chapman, "The Canon Debate: What It Is and Why It Matters," *JTI* 4 (2010): 273–94 (289).

much *at all*. Still, the question is worth asking. How important is the issue of the precise boundaries of the canon?

On the spectrum of issues of importance to Christian faith, the answer may well be "not very important." It all depends on whether readers of the Apocrypha (still) wish to hang anything of doctrinal or ethical importance upon them, in a way that is plainly out of step with what the core, shared texts of the Christian Church teach us. This is something that many of the Church Fathers (e.g., Origen, Rufinus, and Jerome) would themselves have resolutely forbidden Bible readers to do.[114] If we can assume that Apocrypha readers will always be minded to heed this patristic advice, then perhaps James Barr is correct:

> No one could reasonably suppose that the self-identity of the Roman Catholic Church would be materially affected if it dropped the Book of Ecclesiasticus from its canon, or even if it dropped all the books which Protestants have traditionally counted as Apocrypha. Nor would Protestant communities be materially changed if Ecclesiasticus or Wisdom were to be read in them as Old Testament lessons.[115]

Whether we can always depend on Bible readers heeding good advice, however, is open to question—even if that advice comes from very ancient authorities.

---

[114] Ellis, *Old Testament*, 17, 27, 32.
[115] Barr, *Holy Scripture*, 42.

4

On the Meaning of Words
The Literal, the Spiritual, and the Plain Confusing

> [S]cripture has depth, which consists in its having many mystical understandings.
>
> —Bonaventure[1]
>
> [I]t was very difficult for me to break away from my habitual zeal for allegory, and yet I was aware that allegories were empty speculations and the froth, as it were, of the Holy Scriptures. It is the historical sense alone which supplies the true and sound doctrine.
>
> —Martin Luther[2]

Before there were Protestants, there was already a canon of Christian Scripture (chapters 2 and 3) that was regarded as gifted to the Church by God so that people would know what they should believe and how they should live. But how was Scripture to be read? This, too, was a matter of controversy in the sixteenth century. It had become customary in the Church in the centuries beforehand to distinguish four "senses" that Scripture might be held to possess. These senses are briefly described in a Latin poem attributed to the early monk and theologian John Cassian (c. AD 360–435), which in English translation reads: "the letter teaches events; allegory, what you should believe; tropology, what you should do; anagogy, where you should aim." The Italian medieval theologian Bonaventure (1221–1274) writes at greater length:

> Besides its literal meaning, in many places [Scripture] can be interpreted in three ways: allegorically, morally, and anagogically. Allegory occurs when by one thing is indicated another which is a matter of belief. The tropological or moral understanding occurs when, from something done, we learn something else that we

---

[1] Timothy J. Johnson, *Bonaventure: Mystic of God's Word* (New York: New City, 1999), 39. The words come from the prologue to his *Breviloquium* or "brief discourse" on theology (c. 1257).

[2] Martin Luther, *Lectures on Genesis* (1535–1536), LW 1:232–33.

should do. The anagogical meaning, a kind of "lifting upwards," occurs when we are shown what it is we should desire, that is, the eternal happiness of the blessed.[3]

At the first of these four levels (the literal sense) the word of God was conceived of as being expressed in the ordinary human words and their ordinary communicative intent. Collectively, the last three levels (the allegorical, the tropological, and the anagogical) could be regarded as comprising "the spiritual sense" of the text, in which what God was understood to be saying could be rather different from what any human author originally meant. A strong preference for this spiritual sense, grounded in allegorical rather than in literal reading of Scripture (especially OT Scripture), had developed in many parts of the Church in the course of the Middle Ages—even though noted theologians like Thomas Aquinas (among others) came to insist in the thirteenth century, in line with important streams of earlier Christian thought, that the literal sense should be regarded as the primary sense, and as the most important when it came to matters of Christian doctrine.[4] The prevailing view, nevertheless—as one contemporary scholar has put it—was that "spiritual meanings . . . were the golden hoard contained in the casket of the literal."[5]

Leading Reformers like Luther and Calvin sided more with Aquinas than with others on the central point here, although they went further than he did. In conformity with broadly held Renaissance Humanist opinion of their time, they were committed to the "literal" or "historical" sense of the biblical text, and they rejected the idea that other levels of meaning, extracted by allegorical reading, were often or even normally more important. Unlike some of their contemporaries,[6] neither Luther nor Calvin has left us any systematic account of his hermeneutical method, and indeed neither necessarily always abides in his own writings by the principles that he elsewhere does articulate or hint at concerning correct and incorrect ways of interpreting the Bible. Their overall perspectives with regard to these principles are nevertheless clear in their many statements

---

[3] Johnson, *Bonaventure*, 39. For a brief account of Bonaventure's life and work, see Karlfried Froelich, "Christian Interpretation of the Old Testament in the High Middle Ages," *HBOT* 1/2:496–558 (546–54).

[4] "[N]othing necessary to faith is contained under the spiritual sense which is not elsewhere put forward by the Scripture in its literal sense." Thomas Aquinas, *Summa theologiae* (trans. Fathers of the English Dominican Province; New York: Benziger Brothers, 1947), 1.1.10 (p. 7). For a brief account of Aquinas' life and work, see Froelich, "Christian Interpretation," 538–46.

[5] Lesley Smith, "Nicholas of Lyra and Old Testament Interpretation," *HBOT* 2:49–63 (55–56).

[6] E.g., Philipp Melanchthon, *Erotematum Dialectices*, book 1 (first published in 1520); Martin Bucer, *Quomodo S. Literae pro Concionibus tractandae sint Instructio* (published in 1531).

that touch upon the subject.[7] Luther could be fierce, for example (as we see in the second epigraph to the present chapter), when it came to allegorical reading, to which in his earlier life as a monk he had been very much attached. He had come to believe that such reading, in its conviction that the ordinary words of the biblical text were only metaphors hiding a deeper meaning, had led its proponents to miss the sense of Christ in Scripture even as they believed they had penetrated right to it. Recognizing that this approach had significant roots in the post-apostolic church, Luther nevertheless believed that

> the allegorical methods with which Origen or Jerome sought to bring the Old Testament to the level of Christian taste and spirit in reality gave it the *coup de grace*: the allegorical interpretation killed the spiritual sense of the Old Testament.[8]

For Luther, the true spiritual sense was none other *than* the literal sense. The Word of God has "a sure, simple, and unequivocal meaning upon which our faith may build without wavering";[9] it is "the one simplest meaning which we call the written one, or the literal meaning of the tongue."[10]

John Calvin shared Luther's distaste for the allegedly nonliteral senses of the Bible, criticizing Origen and others who

> have seized the occasion of torturing Scripture, in every possible manner, away from the true sense. They concluded that the literal sense is too mean and poor, and that, under the outer bark of the letter, there lurk deeper mysteries, which cannot be extracted but by beating out allegories. And this they had no difficulty in accomplishing; for speculations which appear to be ingenious have always been preferred, and always will be preferred, by the world to solid doctrine.[11]

---

[7] Luther's theology as a whole "was not expressed in works of a systematic nature and character, but in polemical works, books and treatises . . . and in biblical commentaries. . . . This fact makes it understandable why there was among Martin Luther's followers far more disagreement about his teaching than, say, among the followers of John Calvin." Hans J. Hillerbrand, "The Legacy of Martin Luther," in McKim, *Cambridge Companion to Martin Luther*, 227–39 (230). Calvin provides us in various of his writings with glimpses into a more systematically worked-out approach to biblical interpretation. See, e.g., Institutes 1.6–9; 2.9–11.

[8] Bornkamm, *Luther and the Old Testament*, 89–90.

[9] Martin Luther, *On the Papacy in Rome against the Most Celebrated Romanist in Leipzig* (1520), LW 39:83.

[10] Martin Luther, *Answer to Goat Emser*, LW 39:178.

[11] John Calvin, *Commentaries on the Epistles of Paul to the Galatians and Ephesians* (trans. William Pringle; Grand Rapids: Eerdmans, 1948), 135—in a comment on Gal 4:22. See further on Calvin's hermeneutical method in general, Hans-Joachim Kraus, "Calvin's Exegetical Principles," Int 31 (1977): 8–18; Richard C. Gamble, "Brevitas et Facilitas: Toward an Understanding of Calvin's Hermeneutic," WTJ 47 (1985): 1–17; and David C. Steinmetz, "John Calvin as an Interpreter of the Bible," in *Calvin and the Bible* (ed. Donald K. McKim; Cambridge: Cambridge University Press, 2006), 282–91.

Calvin believed that Bible readers ought to have more reverence for the text than was displayed in such readings by "empty-headed creatures ... [who in reading allegorically] change dogs into men, trees into angels, and convert the whole of Scripture into an amusing game."[12] They ought to pay more careful attention to the language, grammar, syntax, and historical context of its various passages, as well as to the various rhetorical devices employed therein as part of various authors' efforts to communicate with their intended audiences. They ought to attend, indeed, to what modern writers would call plot-development in the biblical narrative.[13] This attention to the rhetoric of a text in the course of literary analysis in pursuit of "the writer's central arguments and concerns"[14] also characterizes the more systematically worked-out Protestant approaches of Philipp Melanchthon and Martin Bucer, the latter of whom once famously referred to allegorical reading as turning Scripture into "a wax nose that can be twisted in any direction."[15]

The Reformers, then, sought to sweep away all the other "senses" of the biblical text in favor of the literal or literal-historical sense, which could also be referred to as the "simple," or "genuine," or "natural" sense. This has come to be referred to in many quarters in modern times as the "plain" sense (to which terminology we shall return in chapter 12). It did not matter, said the Reformers, if notable Church Fathers had lent their authority to "spiritual" reading; the search for "deeper mysteries" beneath the surface of the biblical text had resulted only in the distortion of its message.

On the other side, the Roman Catholic Church pushed back, just as it did on questions of canon. Its view is exemplified in the work of the Jesuit theologian (and soon to be Cardinal) Robert Bellarmine (1542–1621), writing in the aftermath of the Council of Trent.[16] Bellarmine reiterated the medieval model of the four senses in the course of arguing that while in a human document words and sentences could have only one meaning (the one intended by the author), words and sentences in the Bible could have many meanings. The question of which of these many meanings was authorized by the Holy Spirit could be decided only by the Church. Only the Church, we recall the Council of Trent asserting

---

[12] John Calvin, *The First Epistle of Paul the Apostle to the Corinthians* (trans. John W. Fraser; Edinburgh: Saint Andrew Press, 1960), 187—in a comment on 1 Cor 9:8-9.

[13] Note, e.g., his attentiveness to such detail in his Genesis commentary, as described in Greene-McCreight, *Ad Litteram*, 107–18.

[14] John L. Thompson, "Calvin as a Biblical Interpreter," in *The Cambridge Companion to John Calvin* (ed. Donald McKim; Cambridge: Cambridge University Press, 2004), 58–73 (61).

[15] R. Gerald Hobbs, "Pluriformity of Early Reformation Scriptural Interpretation," *HBOT* 2:452–511 (461).

[16] Robert Bellarmine, *Disputations about the Controversies of the Christian Faith against the Heretics of This Time* (Ingolstadt, 1586–1593).

(chapter 2), could be the judge of "the true meaning and interpretation of the sacred scriptures."[17] Whereas the Reformers could be critical of Church Fathers like Origen, moreover, for the churchmen gathered at Trent they were examples to be followed. The Church Fathers, in turn, had claimed to be following the apostles only in the way that they approached biblical interpretation—merely exploring the implications of the apostle Paul's comment in 2 Corinthians 3:6 that "the letter kills but the spirit gives life." Origen, in particular, frequently claimed to find in the apostle Paul's use of the verb *allēgoreō* in Galatians 4:24, and in his general hermeneutical practice elsewhere, justification for his own allegorical reading of biblical narrative.[18] Augustine, later, in the course of commending literal reading, nevertheless states that

> if there is no way in which we can understand what has been written in a manner that is pious and worthy of God without believing that these things have been set before us in figures and in enigmas, *we have the apostolic authority* . . . to explain all those figures of things according to the Catholic faith.[19]

Literal reading is good—but other ways of reading are certainly permissible, and sometimes necessary.

How is this controversy to be adjudicated? Were the Reformers justified in their prioritizing of the literal sense of the biblical text, their rejection of other "senses," and their criticism of Church Fathers like Origen for their fondness for these? Did the Reformers thereby step out of line with a Christian tradition of biblical interpretation that goes all the way back to the apostles, and even to Jesus himself? Should we still read the Bible in pursuit of its literal sense? Our reflections on these important questions will occupy the next five chapters. In chapters 5 and 6 I shall ask what kind of Scripture reading can best be said to characterize both Jesus and the apostles. In chapters 7 and 8 we shall compare dominical and apostolic with patristic interpretative practice, on the way to offering in chapter 9 both an evaluation of the Reformers' historical position on reading the Bible properly (and a commentary on their actual reading practice), and a proposal about the "reformed" future with respect to right Bible reading. Before I can sensibly attempt any of this, however, I need to define some terms and, in particular, to ask: What does it mean to read Scripture "literally"? *My argument, in the present chapter, will be that to read Scripture "literally," in line with Reformation perspectives*

---

[17] Tanner, *Decrees*, 2:664.
[18] Peter W. Martens, *Origen and Scripture: The Contours of the Exegetical Life* (OECS; Oxford: Oxford University Press, 2012), 156–60.
[19] Augustine, *De Genesi contra Manichaeos* (*On Genesis against the Manicheans*), 2.2.3, in *Saint Augustine on Genesis* (ed. Thomas P. Halton et al.; trans. Roland J. Teske; FC 84; Washington, D.C.: Catholic University of America Press, 1991), 96 (emphasis added).

on this topic, means to read it in accordance with its various, apparent communicative intentions as a collection of texts from the past now integrated into one Great Story, doing justice to such realities as literary convention, idiom, metaphor, and typology or figuration.

THE LITERAL... AND THE LITERALISTIC

The word "literal" has been and continues to be employed in various ways, often without much or any discussion,[20] and since we do not wish as modern readers (I am sure) accidentally and without reflection to impose on previous generations our own definition, a discussion is necessary.

Consider, first, the following statement: "I was literally glued to my seat throughout the entire performance." What the writer means, of course, is that she was *metaphorically* glued to her seat throughout the entire performance (she had no desire to leave her seat), and she evidently wishes to state this emphatically (which is how "literally" is actually functioning in this sentence). Had she been *literally* glued to her seat, she might well have found great difficulty in leaving it, even had she wished to do so. The addition of the word "literally" to this sentence is therefore unhelpful, if the author's purpose is one of clear communication. She would have been better advised to leave it out, or to substitute a less confusing alternative—as a small contribution to the much-to-be-desired general elimination of this emphatic use of "literal" from current English usage. Certainly the Reformers were never tempted, so far as we can tell, to use the word (or more precisely, its Latin, German, and French equivalents) in this manner.

Of course, the omission of the word "literally" in this particular case would not necessarily prevent a communication problem arising. It would still be open to this author's readers to *read* her as referring to the stickiness of the seat, rather than to her absorption in the performance. Such readers might well pride themselves, in fact, exactly in their determination to read texts "literally"—to take them at "face value" (as they might say), paying attention to what they "obviously" say. "She *says* she was glued to her seat," they might say; "we need to take her at her word." These are the kinds of readers that Peggy Parish has in mind in her popular "learn to read" series of stories concerning "Amelia Bedelia." These stories

> involve Amelia repeatedly misunderstanding various commands of her employer by always taking figures of speech and various terminology literally, causing her to perform incorrect actions with a comical effect.... Much of her employment is as

---

[20] This remains just as true among readers of the Bible as among any other kind, in spite of James Barr's expression of surprise back in 1989 that "within the world of biblical scholarship, comparatively little discussion seems to take place about literality and the meaning of the literal." James Barr, "Literality," *FP* 6 (1989): 412–28 (412).

a maid for a wealthy couple known as the Rogers, who are astute enough to realize her literalism and write their requests as "undust the furniture" and "put the wet towels in the laundry and replace them with clean dry ones," as opposed to simply "change the towels."[21]

The point is that if they ask Amelia to change the towels, very likely she will go out and buy new ones. If they ask her to "dust" the furniture, she will add dust. After all, when she makes a sponge cake, she puts in real sponges, and when she pitches a tent, she throws it into the forest.

Here, then, the word "literal" refers to a kind of reading that misses the point of a communication through failing to understand how language is being used. The reader misunderstands what the author means to say, just as might happen in any other communicative situation in which people "talk past each other." In truth, however—as Kevin Vanhoozer suggests—this kind of reading does not deserve to be called "literal" at all, precisely because it does *not* attend carefully to the "letter" of the text on the page, and to the communicative intent of the person who put it there. Vanhoozer proposes instead (and I concur) that we call it "literalistic" reading,[22] since literalistic reading is, in truth, "less than fully 'literal'— insufficiently and only 'thinly' literal—insofar as it ignores the role of authorial intentions and communicative acts."[23] It focuses only on the words in themselves, whereas a truly literal reading pays attention to the "speech acts" of the author, and not just to words themselves:

---

[21] Online: https://en.wikipedia.org/wiki/Amelia_Bedelia (accessed December 9, 2015). I feel moved to apologize for citing Wikipedia at this point, but it has proved necessary for want of a better alternative.

[22] Kevin J. Vanhoozer, *Is There a Meaning in This Text? The Bible, the Reader, and the Morality of Literary Knowledge* (Grand Rapids: Zondervan, 1998), 310–12. Some more recent writers seem to prefer the term "biblicist," although *Merriam-Webster* defines "biblicism" as "adherence to the letter of the Bible," which is exactly where literalistic reading fails. Those who suspect that this suggests a degree of confusion among the population that likes to use "biblicism" in discussing biblical interpretation will quickly and easily uncover plenty of confirmatory evidence in the literature. It is possible even to encounter the confusion in the same book: see, e.g., Smith, *Bible Made Impossible*, who cannot make up his mind about what biblicism is and is not (cf. the two definitions on pp. viii and 4–5), nor about who is guilty of it (or not), and whose critique of its evils is often less than convincing (not least because of his tendency to generalize). Biblicism can be summarized in ten points, it seems, and yet it "is not a comprehensively formalized position always explicated in exactly these ten points. . . . Different people . . . emphasize and express a variety of these points somewhat differently. Some may even downplay or deny particular points" (5). I struggle to see how such a notably blunt diagnostic tool can be of much use in helping us toward a constructive analysis of what is good and bad in biblical interpretation. "Biblicism" is not a word, then, that I shall use in this chapter.

[23] Vanhoozer, *Meaning*, 311.

> The literal meaning of Jesus' statement "I am the door" is a function of his speech act (a metaphorical assertion), not of the words taken individually (and thus out of context)... it is only at the level of the sentence act that we can speak of an actual literal sense.[24]

The literal sense of a text is discovered, then, not only by consulting a dictionary about what a word like "door" typically means in the language spoken by the author (which is indeed important), but also by paying attention to how that word is used in a particular speech act. An author might well use a word like "door" metaphorically, but nevertheless intend to communicate "literal truth" (e.g., about Jesus) in the process. Literal reading makes room for this possibility. Literalistic reading, on the other hand,

> short-circuits the literal sense insofar as it fails to appreciate the author's intention to give his or her utterance a certain kind of force... [it] generates an unlettered, ultimately *illiterate* reading—one that is incapable of recognizing less obvious uses of language such as metaphor, satire, and so forth.[25]

If this is so, then in addition to avoiding the emphatic use of "literal" mentioned above, we should also avoid using it as an antonym (opposite) to words like "metaphorical," as in sentences like this one: "She failed to understand the metaphorical language in the poem and interpreted it literally." We should rather write: "In failing to understand the metaphorical language in the poem, she failed to interpret it literally." She missed the point of the literary communication.

"Literalistic" is of course a modern, and not an ancient term, but the distinction I am drawing in using it is one that the Reformers certainly considered to be important. Luther is very interested in the ways that the biblical authors are "artists and poets," for example, and he is attentive to phenomena in the text like Hebrew parallelism, metaphors, and metonymy.[26] "Like earlier commentators in the tradition of Augustine's *De doctrina christiana*... Calvin [likewise] regularly identified metaphor, allegory, personification, metonymy, synecdoche, and other tropes [i.e., figures of speech]."[27] He is impatient with those who fail to grasp that a faithful reading of Scripture must be attentive to such phenomena—an impatience well illustrated in the comments in his *Institutes of the Christian Religion* about "fanatical men" whose commitment to reading Scripture literally (as they see it) threatens to open the door to "a boundless barbarism [that] will

---

[24] Vanhoozer, *Meaning*, 311.
[25] Vanhoozer, *Meaning*, 311.
[26] Bornkamm, *Luther and the Old Testament*, 35–37.
[27] William J. Bouwsma, *John Calvin: A Sixteenth-Century Portrait* (Oxford: Oxford University Press, 1988), 123.

overwhelm the whole light of faith."[28] It was necessary, rather, for the biblical exegete to possess a sound knowledge of rhetoric, without which, as Calvin observed, "many supervacuous contentions will arise."[29] The Reformers could sometimes disagree about *which* texts were meant to be read metaphorically, or in accordance with some other figure of speech—most famously, perhaps, they disagreed about how to interpret Scripture concerning Christ's body and blood with respect to the Eucharist—but that the literal sense included such phenomena was widely understood. They were not the first to grasp the point, as we shall see when we discuss ancient Christian writers like Augustine in chapters 7 and 8.

THE LITERAL AND THE HISTORICAL SENSE

In the hypothetical case of just a moment ago, it so happens that our literalistic reader was guilty of "failing to understand the metaphorical language" specifically in a *poem*. However, such readers are more than capable of fixing their bleary eyes on other genres as well. So it is that a parable might easily be read as history, and so might an allegory—in neither case in line with the communicative intent of the author. The literal sense, then, is not to be equated with historical reference: "Reference to historical or empirical reality is only one of the things language does. . . . Literal interpretation . . . is more than a univocally descriptive and exact presentation of historical factuality."[30] It is important to underline this point precisely because of the frequency with which we find the terms "literal sense" and "historical sense" in close proximity to each other, and even virtually equated with each other, in discussions of biblical hermeneutics.

This is an unproblematic association if the intention is to underline that what authors mean they always mean in historical contexts. They mean what they mean in the context of the commonly received meanings of words in particular languages, of accepted literary conventions, and so on, which may (like definitions of words) change over time. The Reformers' emphasis on the importance of reading biblical texts in their original languages and not in Latin translation (to which we shall return in chapters 10 and 11) presupposes this kind of commitment to "historical" reading. They were attentive, for example, to the nature of the grammar and syntax in the Hebrew and Greek texts that lay before them. "I leave

---

[28] R. M. Frye, "Calvin's Theological Use of Figurative Language," in *John Calvin and the Church: A Prism of Reform* (ed. Timothy George; Louisville, Ky.: Westminster John Knox, 1990), 172–94 (181), citing Calvin, *Institutes* 4.17.23.

[29] Cited in Frye, "Figurative Language," 189. Confusingly for his later readers, Calvin can sometimes refer to metaphor using the language of allegory, seeing the latter as extended metaphor—even though he "more often . . . treats [allegory] as a hermeneutical aberration and sets it in opposition to simple truth and edification." Greene-McCreight, *Ad Litteram*, 150n8.

[30] Vanhoozer, *Meaning*, 307–8.

allegories alone," Luther tells his readers at one point in his writings; "Become a text critic and learn about the grammatical sense, whatever grammar intends, which is about faith, patience, death, and life."[31] What God says in Scripture is said in the ordinary language of those who lived in the past, and were conditioned by that past—people like Moses, who had a "design" in writing Genesis and used his own literary craft to further that design, which happens also to be the design of the Holy Spirit who "has spoken by his mouth."[32] In a way the Reformation begins (if we can date its beginning to Luther's actions in Wittenberg in 1517) with this issue already front and center, since the famous ninety-five theses open with a reference to the proper meaning of a biblical word:

1. When our Lord and Master Jesus Christ said, "Repent!" [Matt 4:17], he willed the entire life of believers to be one of repentance.
2. This word cannot be understood as referring to the sacrament of penance, that is, confession and satisfaction, as administered by the clergy.[33]

Just a few years later Luther tells Erasmus in *The Bondage of the Will* (1525) that "we must everywhere stick to the simple, pure, and natural sense of the words that accords with the rules of grammar and the normal use of language as God has created it in man."[34] The same idea is often expressed in Calvin's writings. In his search for the mind of God in the writings of Paul, for example, Calvin keeps firmly in view that "Paul was a first-century thinker who was conditioned by the cultures in which he moved and taught."[35] In fact, the full use that Calvin makes of contextual interpretation (in this respect and in others) is one of the obvious ways in which he demonstrates "his allegiance to humanistic ideals concerning the interpretation of texts."[36]

Understood in this way, an insistence on the "historical sense" can be taken as an encouragement to the reader not to read anachronistically, as if an ancient author were writing in a much more recent (and culturally distant from the

---

[31] Martin Luther, *A Brief, Yet Clear Exposition of the Song of Songs* (1530–1531), as cited in Bornkamm, *Luther and the Old Testament*, 92.

[32] Calvin, *Genesis*, 59. Just how seriously Calvin takes the rootedness of biblical authors in particular historical contexts is illustrated by his comments on 1 Cor 11:14, concerning what Paul means there by "natural": "Paul . . . sets *nature* before them as the teacher of what is proper. Now, he means by 'natural' what was accepted by common consent and usage at that time, certainly as far as the Greeks were concerned. For long hair was not always regarded as a disgraceful thing in men." Calvin, *First Corinthians*, 235.

[33] Luther, *Ninety-Five Theses*, LW 31:25.

[34] Luther, *Bondage*, LW 33:162.

[35] R. Ward Holder, *John Calvin and the Grounding of Interpretation: Calvin's First Commentaries* (SHCT; Leiden: Brill, 2006), 106.

[36] Holder, *Grounding*, 108.

original) idiom, or were more generally operating as a "modern" person. "Historical interpretation refers, in the context of the Reformation, to respecting the sense that words would have had for their authors," as Vanhoozer succinctly puts it, quoting Calvin's comment that "the more [the interpreter] leads away from the author's meaning so the more he leaves his own purpose and is certain to wander from his goal."[37] Understood in this way, an insistence on the "historical sense" can also be taken as encouragement to the reader to seek the mind of God in the mind of the human authors of Scripture, and not somewhere else. As Ward Holder says of Calvin's approach to Scripture, "when Calvin seeks to uncover the mind of the author in scripture, he is attempting to have access to the divine mind, the Holy Spirit's intention. He does so, however, through the medium of the mind of the human author," to which we have "direct and immediate access" (through the author's writings) in a way that can never be the case with the divine mind.[38]

So far, so good. However, in terms of what historically rooted texts understood in this manner mean to *say*, we must be careful. First, the possibility of historical reference in a text is only one of the things that a reader interested in its literal sense must consider. Texts may well be concerned with historical "facts," as with all kinds of other "facts" (e.g., about the nature of the world in which we live), but this may also *not* be the case. The literal cannot be reduced to the historical, the empirical, and the factual. To consider a nonbiblical example: I may well need a considerable amount of historical background information in order fully to understand John Bunyan's *A Pilgrim's Progress* (including knowledge of the state of the English language in his day), but this book was surely not intended to be read as a historical narrative. That was not the point. Likewise, the famous "Allegory of the Cave" in Plato's *Republic*, when read literally, is to be read allegorically, and not historically (in the sense of "as a historical narrative").[39] In both cases, the communicative intent of the author is clear, and a commitment to literal reading requires that we attend carefully to it. *This* kind of allegorical reading, then, is not at all to be contrasted with literal reading, since it is actually *in line with* the literal sense of the text. The point is important, not just with respect to allegory, and it was well understood by Reformation writers. Commenting on the parable of the Good Samaritan, for example—a parable often read allegorically in earlier times (see my chapter 8 for an example from Augustine)—Calvin insists that "we should have more reverence for Scripture than to allow ourselves to transfigure

---

[37] Vanhoozer, *Meaning*, 305.
[38] Holder, *Grounding*, 67–68.
[39] Plato, *Republic*, 514a–520a.

its sense so freely"; we should instead attend to "the mind of Christ."[40] The communicative intent is crucial.

There is an even more important way, however, in which the literal cannot be reduced to the historical, the empirical, and the factual. A text may well mean to refer, descriptively, to the past—such an event happened in such a way, involving these actions and words. Yet the purpose of the author in describing this past may not simply be to report upon it, but also to draw out significance from it—to teach something on the basis of it. That is to say, the heart of the communicative intent of the author may lie not in *description* of the past, but in *prescription* for the present; there is a message that he wishes to address to the reader in relation to what happened "back then." Prior to the eighteenth century, this was in fact the primary reason why historiography was valued: as an art that had close links to the ancient art of rhetoric, and had as its purpose to teach (as well as to delight) the reader. The ancient words of Dionysius of Halicarnassus, written during the reign of the Roman emperor Augustus, capture this reality well: "History is philosophy teaching by examples."[41] It is only in the late eighteenth century and then the nineteenth that we find a general move away from this position, with the rise of an allegedly scientific approach to history in which historiography tends to become (at least in principle) a search for "mere" facts. Even in this period, of course, it is clear that while striving for a kind of objectivity about the past, historians in fact told their stories about it always with an eye to what should be believed and enacted in the present. It was inevitable that they did. People always write about the past—albeit with varying degrees of self-consciousness—because they wish to communicate some kind of truth to their readers, or to advocate some kind of virtue (or vice).[42]

Certainly this is true of the *biblical* books that tell us about the past. They are profoundly interested in the past, but not for its own sake. They tell their story about it in order to persuade us of certain truths and to advocate certain ways of living. We shall miss the point, then, if we dwell only on the facts (or events) themselves.[43] We shall fail to read the biblical texts *literally*, in terms of the full communicative intent of our biblical authors—precisely because our understanding of "the literal" has become too closely identified with a faulty view of the historical (as "mere" fact or event).

---

[40] John Calvin, *A Harmony of the Gospels Matthew, Mark, and Luke, Volume 3, and the Epistles of James and Jude* (CalC; trans. A. W. Morrison; Edinburgh: Saint Andrew, 1972), 39.

[41] Marionos Yeroulanos, ed. *A Dictionary of Classical Greek Quotations* (London: I. B. Tauris, 2016), 210.

[42] For an extensive discussion, see Iain Provan, V. Philips Long, and Tremper Longman III, *A Biblical History of Israel* (2nd ed.; Louisville, Ky.: Westminster John Knox, 2015), 38–58.

[43] With respect to the OT historical books on this point, see further Iain Provan, "Hearing the Historical Books," in Bartholomew and Beldman, *Hearing the Old Testament*, 254–76.

One consequence of this kind of "literal" (but actually literalistic) Bible reading is all too often that it is indeed satisfied simply with establishing that the facts are indeed the facts, before (as it were) retiring to its intellectual or devotional bed for the night—none the wiser as to what these inert "facts" *mean*. "First way" historical-critical reading of the Bible has often been charged with inadequacy in this respect, and not without reason. However, the same is true (ironically, given its often-overt hostility to "first way" scholarship) of a considerable amount of "third way" historical-grammatical reading. The appreciation of the biblical text as *literature*, in each case, can be remarkably shallow, and sometimes nonexistent.

Another consequence of such literalistic reading is that a further interpretive "move" is then required by those who wish to render the "mere" facts (or events) spiritually useful in some way—as if the biblical authors had not already done so. "Fourth way" spiritual reading appears to be designed to overcome the perceived "problem" here. It aims to compensate for the presumed deficiencies of the text in its literal-historical sense. Just such a view is expressed, for example, by Michael Graves:

> Research into the *ad litteram* [literal] sense alone cannot uncover the contemporary significance of Scripture. The results of "literal" biblical exegesis can only be past-tense claims, such as, "This is what Jeremiah said to the Judeans," or "This is what Peter said to the first-century church."[44]

It is simply untrue, however, to say that the results of literal exegesis "can only be" the ones that Graves describes. Literal exegesis can and *must* involve much more than he thinks it does—or else it is simply not paying attention to the communicative intent of the biblical literature, in which case it is not literal exegesis at all. It is unfortunate to what a great extent historical critics, Chicago types, and contemporary "spiritual readers," for all that they tend to define themselves over against each other, are thus joined in intellectual matrimony (or polyamory) by their common failure to grasp this simple point—by their inability to think well about the "literal." The consequence is that "spiritual readers," rightly reacting to the deficiencies of much "first" and "third way" reading, all too often set out to solve a problem whose nature they have not fully analyzed. They desire to help the biblical text speak out of the past and into our contemporary concerns—but so focused are they on this quest that they fail to notice that the text is already doing this, and that it does not need our help. It was only ever their readerly opponents on the "first" and "third ways" who needed help, because of their inattention to all that the text was aiming to accomplish, literally and (at the same time) spiritually. The biblical text itself was always doing just fine.

---

[44] Michael Graves, *The Inspiration and Interpretation of Scripture: What the Early Church Can Teach Us* (Grand Rapids: Eerdmans, 2014), 134.

So it is that we come to understand the need for greater clarity, in discussions about biblical hermeneutics, not only about what we mean by "literal," but also about what we mean by "historical."

LITERALLY BEYOND THE SENTENCE

The kind of attentiveness to the communicative intent of an author that is thus required if a literal reading of any text is to be achieved is necessary not just with respect to sentences, but also to paragraphs, to sections of books, to whole books, and to whole collections of books. There is more than one way of taking words "out of context" (to quote Vanhoozer). Words mean what they mean in sentences, but also in larger contexts; as Roland Barthes once put it, "a narrative is [but] a large sentence."[45] This is a reality to which modern biblical scholarship has sometimes been blind, insisting on an atomistic style of reading that frequently proceeds as if the parts of any particular biblical book had little to do with the whole, and as if whole biblical books had little to do with others in the same canonical collection. In this "first way" of proceeding, the literal sense is conceived predominantly in terms of the meaning of small units of text that emerge out of particular historical contexts, divorced from the larger literary contexts in which they now find themselves. Little attention is paid to the ordinary words of the biblical text, as they reflect ordinary grammar and syntax or rhetorical device, within whole biblical books that form part of the unfolding covenantal Story of Scripture. This is, in truth, a bizarrely narrow and unhistorical idea of the literal, involving "isolating and freezing in time texts that historically were read and transmitted together,"[46] and it is one with which the Reformers would have had no sympathy. The literal reading of texts *requires* our attention to larger as well as to smaller literary contexts.

Joshua 10:40 in Context

The reader of the book of Joshua, for example, might at first misunderstand what is said in Joshua 10:40, in itself, where we are told that "Joshua subdued the whole region" (in the course of the Israelite settlement in Canaan) and "left no survivors. He totally destroyed all who breathed." It might well be "obvious" to the reader, at first, that we are being told here straightforwardly (and "factually") about the subjugation of an entire territory and the annihilation of all its inhabitants. However, Joshua 10:40 does not presently exist "in itself," and it probably never has done; it exists only as part of the book of Joshua. Reading further in

---

[45] Roland Barthes, "An Introduction to the Structural Analysis of Narrative," *NLH* 6 (1975): 256.

[46] Chapman, "Second Temple Jewish Hermeneutics," 294.

this book, we discover that neither the subjugation of an entire territory *nor* the annihilation of all its inhabitants has, in fact, earlier occurred. This should lead us to reconsider what we have read in Joshua 10, and to ponder its nature as (very probably) a hyperbolic account of military success in the well-established idiom of the ancient world, the detail of which cannot be pressed.⁴⁷ That is: the passage is, in its literal sense, hyperbolic. This becomes clear, if it was not so already, as we read the passage in its literary context.⁴⁸

Psalm 2 in Context

A different kind of example will establish my point, and at the same time complicate somewhat the question of the "literal." What is the literal sense of Psalm 2? In itself as an individual composition (which it is, marked out from both the preceding Ps 1 and the following Ps 3), we might well imagine—as many modern biblical scholars have done—that at one time it functioned in ancient Israel as a royal coronation psalm, celebrating the moment when God "installed" his king "on Zion, my holy hill," adopted him as a "son," and gave him the world as his "inheritance" (Ps 2:6-8). This is a perfectly reasonable hypothesis about what the psalm, in itself, once meant in preexilic Israel. It formed part of the Israelite liturgy of that period. Yet we must recognize that the psalm as we encounter it now is not "in itself." Although it is marked off as an *independent* entity, it is at the same time not an *isolated* entity. It has a literary context, within the book of Psalms, and in its present form this book dates from the postexilic period (note Ps 137, which looks back on the exile)—long after the period of the historical monarchy of Israel. So what is this "royal" psalm doing as one of two introductory compositions in the book of Psalms? In an era when there are no Israelite or Judean kings, why retain in this literature any psalms that speak of the king? It can only be because such texts are now intended as anticipatory of a kingdom that is yet to come. They are intended to speak about a son of David who has not yet arrived:

> [A]lthough the royal psalms arose originally in a peculiar historical setting of ancient Israel . . . they were treasured in the Psalter [i.e., the book of Psalms] for a

---

⁴⁷ Modern biblical scholarship has now helped us to understand that this kind of hyperbole is routinely found throughout ancient Near Eastern conquest accounts. See K. Lawson Younger Jr., *Ancient Conquest Accounts: A Study in Ancient Near Eastern and Biblical History Writing* (JSOTSup 98; Sheffield: JSOT Press, 1990).

⁴⁸ Of course, readers who already anticipate finding hyperbole in biblical texts might well suspect it in the case of Joshua 10 even without the confirmation of context. Perhaps some earlier readers of Scripture were more astute in such matters, however, than their modern counterparts: see Martin Luther, *Table Talk*, LW 54:452.

different reason, namely as a witness to the messianic hope which looked for the consummation of God's kingship through his Anointed One.[49]

That is their literal meaning within the context of the book of Psalms; that is how they are intended to be read—not so much as liturgy (or at least, not *only* as liturgy), but also as prophecy. This is indeed how these psalms evidently *were* being read already in the pre-Christian centuries that followed the composition of the book.[50] So it is that Psalm 2 comes to speak in this context of an anointed king who will (one day) be opposed by the nations.

In this example from the book of Psalms, we discover that there are two ways of reading the text literally, depending on which author(s) we are considering as possessing communicative intent. Is it the author of Psalm 2 as an *individual* composition, or is it the author of the *whole book* of Psalms?[51] There is here, in effect, what could happily be described—using the terminology of the fourteenth-century Christian author Nicholas of Lyra—as a double literal sense.

The Reformers and Contextual Reading

The Reformers were not modern biblical scholars, of course, and they did not write in a modern idiom, or as the possessors of modern knowledge. Neither they nor Nicholas of Lyra would have described the complexity of "the literal sense" of the books of Psalms in exactly the way that I have just attempted. We shall begin to consider in chapter 9 what all this means for a "reformed" hermeneutics for the twenty-first, as opposed to the sixteenth, century. For the moment, it is important only to notice two aspects of the Reformers' treatment of the literal sense.

---

[49] Childs, *Introduction*, 517. See further (e.g.) David C. Mitchell, *The Message of the Psalter: An Eschatological Programme in the Book of Psalms* (JSOTSup 252; Sheffield: Sheffield Academic, 1997); and Stephen G. Dempster, *Dominion and Dynasty: A Theology of the Hebrew Bible* (NSBT 15; Downers Grove, Ill.: InterVarsity, 2003), 199n14: "the importance of the Davidic king in the overall structure of the Psalter ... at a time when there was no Davidic king on the throne points to a pervasive eschatological orientation and messianic expectation."

[50] We see evidence of this in the LXX translation of the Psalms, as illustrated in the case of Psalm 2. Already by the time that this text was being translated into Greek, "a pre-exilic royal psalm had, through a long-going process of reinterpretation, become a messianic hymn." Joachim Schaper, *Eschatology in the Greek Psalter* (WUNT 2/76; Tübingen: Mohr Siebeck, 1995), 72–76 (75), who also refers more generally to "the 'messianization' of Jewish religious thought as documented in the Septuagint" (126).

[51] This is an important point that the modern historical-critical mind does not typically understand very well, even if it is intent on reading Scripture theologically. Thus: "if we are to preach Christ with confidence from the Royal Psalms, we must have ground for so doing in the historical consciousness of the *Psalmist*." S. H. Russell, "Calvin and the Messianic Interpretation of the Psalms," *SJT* 21 (1968): 37–47 (45) (emphasis added).

First, they were certainly interested—as modern scholars are—in reading the psalms as individual compositions rooted in historical contexts. Even in his early lectures on the Psalter, for example (1513–1516)—when he was still much more a "medieval" than a "Reformation" exegete—we find Luther asking questions about the nature and scope of whichever individual psalm lies before him, and (especially in the case of the later psalms) we discover an emerging sensitivity to questions about the original context.[52] This is even more evidently the case in Calvin's work on the book of Psalms (published in 1557), in which he commonly interprets them in their original context, and only then reads them in wider contexts.[53] The same interest in historical context can be found in both writers' approach to other biblical books—the book of Isaiah, for example, as illustrated in Luther's lectures of 1527–1530 and Calvin's commentary of 1551 (expanded in 1559).[54]

---

[52] Henning G. Reventlow, *History of Biblical Interpretation, Volume 3: Renaissance, Reformation, Humanism* (trans. James O. Duke; RBS 62; Atlanta: Society of Biblical Literature, 2010), 71. This is true, e.g., of Luther's comments on Psalm 90 (*First Lectures on the Psalms II, LW* 11:195–207). His sensitivity to questions of context is even more marked in a later treatment of Psalm 94 (dating from 1526), where a composition previously said simply to speak "against those who thought that Christ was neither God nor avenger, namely, the Jews" (*LW* 11:242) is now described as "clearly a prayer that is common to all the pious children of God and members of His spiritual people, to be prayed against all their persecutors. Therefore it can be prayed from the beginning of the world to its end by all pious and devout people, be they Jews, Christians, or patriarchs." In this second reading an analogy is drawn between past and present contexts, with the prayer articulating true faith in both. Martin Luther, *Selected Psalms III, LW* 14:243. Even in the case of "core" messianic psalms, we see similar development over time in Luther's exegesis, as they are increasingly read for "instruction and encouragement to the church" rather than as "literal prophecies of Christ." G. Sujin Pak, *The Judaizing Calvin: Sixteenth-Century Debates over the Messianic Psalms* (Oxford: Oxford University Press, 2010), 36.

[53] Note, e.g., that Psalm 45 is first about "the grace and beauty of Solomon, his virtues in ruling the kingdom, and also his power and his riches." Certainly "there can be no doubt, that under this figure the majesty, wealth, and extent of Christ's kingdom are [also] described and illustrated by appropriate terms." It is interesting and significant, nevertheless, just how much of the exegesis focuses on Solomon himself. John Calvin, *Commentary on the Book of Psalms*, vol. 2 (in CalC 5; trans. James McLean; London: Calvin Translation Society, 1847; repr., Grand Rapids: Baker, 1996), 173–94 (173).

[54] Luther begins his exposition of Isaiah 7, e.g., by insisting that "[t]o understand the prophet, one must first of all carefully ponder the historical situation," and his reading of the chapter extensively reflects this commitment (e.g., in his explanation of the water conduit in Isa 7:3)—although admittedly his treatment of the sign of Immanuel (7:14) in its original context is weak. Martin Luther, *Lectures on Isaiah Chapters 1–39, LW* 16:78–87 (78). Calvin is much more aware of the exegetical challenges at this point, acknowledging that for Isaiah to promise Ahaz the Messiah in the original context certainly looks like "an unseasonable transition to a very remote subject," and understanding very well the difficulty of reading verse 14 in this manner given the content of verse 16. His solutions in both cases are nevertheless unconvincing. John Calvin, *Commentary on the Book of the Prophet Isaiah*, vol. 1 (trans. William Pringle; Grand Rapids: Eerdmans, 1958), 244–51 (246).

Yet second, both Luther and Calvin would have regarded as incomplete any efforts of theirs to read "literally" any discrete section of a biblical book, had they not then proceeded to read it in its larger context. Calvin, for example, "always believed that each book of the scripture represented a coherent effort at expression by its author."[55] We routinely find in his commentaries, therefore, attention to the nature of the whole as well as to the parts of a particular book—not least in the *argumentum* that appears at the beginning of each of his commentaries on Paul's letters. He always tries to provide "an overall sense of [a letter's] general meaning."[56]

Both Reformers would have regarded anything less than such efforts to read contextually as a failure to make the attempt to read "literally"—and they would surely have been right to believe so. The literal sense should *not* be conceived of predominantly in terms of the meaning of small units of text that emerge out of particular historical contexts, divorced from the larger literary contexts in which they are now embedded.

THE LITERAL AND THE TYPOLOGICAL

In the example just cited from the book of Psalms, the Davidic king no longer stands for himself alone, but also points beyond himself to someone in David's line who is still in the future of the book's final compiler(s). This kind of "now and not yet" perspective in biblical texts has often been referred to under the heading of "typology," especially as it appears in narrative texts. (The term "figuration" is sometimes regarded as a synonym for "typology": earlier chapters of the biblical Story "prefigure" the later.)[57] The word "typology" picks up on the Greek terms *tupos* and *antitupos*, which are found in numerous NT contexts of relevance to our present discussion, where they refer to models or examples that have been, or are to be, followed. In constructing the tabernacle, Moses followed a "model" (*tupos*) that he had seen (Acts 7:44; Heb 8:5); Adam is a "model" in respect of Christ (Rom 5:14); various things that happened to the Israelites occurred as "examples" to which Christians would be well advised to pay attention (1 Cor 10:6; see also the adverbial *tupikos* in 10:11); Christian believers have functioned or ought to function as "models" for others to imitate (Phil 3:17; 1 Thess 1:7; 2 Thess 3:9; 1 Tim 4:12; Titus 2:7; 1 Pet 5:3). In the same way, baptism is like the waters of the flood in Noah's day, new life emerging out of death (*antitupos*, 1 Pet 3:21), and the earthly tabernacle is like the heavenly one (Heb 9:24). *Resemblance* within the context of the whole biblical Story is the key idea in all these passages. Within

---

[55] Holder, *Grounding*, 75.

[56] Holder, *Grounding*, 75–78 (76); also 98–99.

[57] E.g., Hans W. Frei, *The Eclipse of Biblical Narrative: A Study in Eighteenth and Nineteenth Century Hermeneutics* (New Haven: Yale University Press, 1974), 2n1.

that narrative (into which Christian believers are now to "read" themselves), certain persons or entities are, or ought to be, like each other in certain ways.

Shadows and Realities

On one occasion another Greek word, *skia* (shadow), is associated with this vocabulary, bringing a particular nuance to the passage in question (Heb 8:5): the tabernacle resembles the heavenly sanctuary as a shadow resembles a reality. Hebrews 10:1 goes on to refer to the OT law itself as a "shadow" in respect of NT realities. The apostle Paul uses this same word on one occasion himself, in respect of "a religious festival, a New Moon celebration, or a Sabbath day," which represent "a shadow of the things that were to come; the reality, however, is found in Christ" (Col 2:16-17). This language emphasizes not just that there are "resemblances" in various parts of the Great Story, but that the Story itself moves ever onward, such that we may characterize at least some of the resemblances as involving a "lesser" and a "greater." It is this that justifies a description of a typological (figurative) reading as one that "relates the past to the present in terms of a historical correspondence *and escalation* in which the divinely ordered prefigurement finds a complement in the subsequent and greater event."[58] At the same time, it would be a mistake to assume that "escalation" is always or even normally in view when typological connections are present. For this reason, Daniel Treier's more neutral definition of typological reading is preferable. He proposes that we think of it simply as "iconic" mimesis, which preserves "a 'narrative coherence' between referents."[59] The main point here is to resist the idea that there is in the NT any generalized notion that God's dealings with Israel in the OT are any less real, or any less important in themselves, than his dealings with the Church in the NT. It was exactly because of the tendencies of some typological reading in this direction that Luther can be found criticizing the approach,[60] even though he himself made typological connections between biblical texts—so long as it was understood that these connections were between real people of faith and their institutions in the OT, and real people of faith and their institutions in the NT. For Luther, God did not reveal himself in the OT through figurative hints, nor did that body of literature merely provide "images for a later Christ event." The Israelites lived their own substantive life of faith in response to God's revelation in OT events, *and then they also* prefigured NT realities.[61] Likewise, however much the OT is

---

[58] Ellis, *Old Testament*, 106 (emphasis added).
[59] Daniel J. Treier, "Typology," in *DTIB*, 823–27 (825).
[60] Bornkamm, *Luther and the Old Testament*, 187, 250, 256.
[61] See, e.g., Luther's "Sunday after Christmas" sermon in *Sermons on Gospel Texts for Advent, Christmas, and Epiphany* (formerly vol. 10 of *The Precious and Sacred Writings of Martin Luther*; Minneapolis: Lutherans in all Lands, 1905; repr. as vol. 1 of *Sermons of Martin Luther*, ed. John

considered in the NT to "point beyond itself," this is not at the cost of the reality or importance of God's relationship with his OT people. As Hans Frei puts it, in typology, "[w]ithout loss to its own literal meaning or specific temporal reference, an earlier story (or occurrence) [becomes] a figure of a later one."[62]

The Literal in the Typological

This being so, we should not drive a wedge between the literal and the typological, as "atomistic" modern readers tend to do when they reserve the vocabulary of "the literal" only for the meaning of smaller units of biblical text. The literal and the typological (figurative) are best understood not as two different ways of reading, but as two aspects of the same way of reading. The latter comes into its own not so much at the level of a sentence or a paragraph, but at the level of larger entities like whole books and even collections of books. In Frei's words, typological reading involves "literalism at the level of the whole biblical story"; figuration should not be conceived of as

> being in conflict with the literal sense of biblical stories, [but as being] . . . at once a literary and a historical procedure, an interpretation of stories and their meanings by weaving them together into a common narrative referring to a single history and its patterns of meaning.[63]

"Literal" and "typological" should not be considered as antonyms, then—at least insofar as the "weaving" that Frei has in mind follows the prompts of the authors and compilers of Scripture themselves, and is governed in its interpretation by what appears to be the communicative intentions of the people who handed their texts down to us in the form that they now possess.

The "form" that a book like Psalms now possesses certainly encourages its reader to read "David" typologically or figuratively in this way—a good example of the phenomenon in nonnarrative biblical texts. The same kind of encouragement to "make connections" is also widely found in narrative texts. Those responsible for transmitting the Former Prophets (Joshua through Kings), for example, have evidently embedded in their texts all sorts of typological connections between different parts of the story, and also between the Former Prophets

---

Nicholas Lenker; trans. John Nicholas Lenker et al.; Grand Rapids: Baker, 1983), 255–307. So also Calvin, who refers to "madmen" who think that "all that God promised [the Israelites] or gave them . . . only prefigured what had to be brought to full reality with the coming of Christ"—"a most damaging piece of nonsense." To the contrary, "those people foreshadowed the Christian Church in such a way that they were at the same time a genuine Church." Calvin, *First Corinthians*, 211—in a comment on 1 Cor 10:11.

[62] Frei, *Eclipse*, 2 (emphasis added).
[63] Frei, *Eclipse*, 2.

and the Torah, which are designed to draw out the fuller significance of the events and persons described and to reinforce the claim that the disparate parts of the story are indeed parts of *one* Story.

One main example will suffice. When we first meet Jeroboam in 1 Kings 12, he is presented to us in a way that reminds us of Moses. The people's complaint as the chapter opens is that under King Rehoboam they are no longer the people set free to live in the Promised Land. They have become once more a people under harsh labor, as they were in Egypt (Exod 1:14; 2:23). They toil like oxen under a heavy yoke. Jeroboam leads them out of this bondage. His similarity to Moses in this situation extends in the Hebrew text to a certain reluctance to take on such a role (cf. Exod 4:1-17): he remains in Egypt and has to be sent for. Rehoboam takes a hard line in response to his people's complaints (1 Kgs 12:8-11). He behaves exactly as Pharaoh behaved before him: he increases the oppression (cf. Exod 5:1-21). It is divinely ordained that he does so (1 Kgs 12:15): in the midst of all the human decisions, God's decision is being carried through. Echoes of the hardening of Pharaoh's heart (e.g., Exod 4:21; 7:3-4, 13) are distinctly audible. No sooner has the new exodus taken place in 1 Kings 12, however, than it leads to apostasy (as the first exodus also did)—specifically, to the worship of golden calves. King Jeroboam, like Aaron (Exod 32:1-35), makes gods for the people to worship in defiance of the Lord's words at Mount Sinai (Exod 20:4). Indeed, his words to them in 1 Kings 12:28 ("Here are your gods, O Israel, who brought you up out of Egypt") are almost exactly the words with which the people greet the construction of the first calf in Exodus 32:4. His subsequent actions also recall Aaron—Aaron, too, having made a golden calf, built an altar, and announced a festival on a date of his own choosing (cf. Exod 32:5). It was the Levites who on that occasion were also to be found distanced from the celebrations (Exod 32:26).

The story that is told in 1 Kings 12, then, is narrated in such a way that it evokes other stories with which it might usefully be compared or contrasted. This is not an isolated instance in 1–2 Kings. The kings of Judah are compared and contrasted with David; Elijah recalls Moses; both Manasseh and Josiah, in their own ways, remind us of Ahab; and so on.[64] This kind of compositional technique is a recurring feature of OT narrative literature more generally, and it represents one significant way in which the high levels of intertextuality now found particularly in the Law and the Prophets were attained, as they developed into their canonical form (as described in my chapters 2 and 3). We are not dealing in OT narrative with isolated texts, or even with isolated books. We are dealing with texts and books transmitted together by people who were already reflecting upon

---

[64] On David as pattern for the kings, see further Iain W. Provan, *1 and 2 Kings* (UB; Grand Rapids: Baker, 1995), 47, 124–25, 216, 235, 252–53, 270. On Moses as pattern for Elijah, see 145–46, 150, 178–79; and on Ahab as pattern for others, see 266–69, 272, 277.

them together, as sections of a larger, unfolding Story—one reality, described in individual segments. Any reading of Scripture that does not attend to these evident literary realities surely does not deserve the label "literal," however literate in other respects the reader may be. To read literally is to read biblical texts not only as they were first uttered or written by their originators, but also as they have been placed in larger literary entities and in conversation with other texts that are also part of the whole canonical collection of Scripture. There is communicative intent in all of this, and it must be attended to.

The Reformers and Typological Reading

Again, the Reformers were not modern biblical scholars. They would not have written about the literal and the typological in exactly the ways that I have just done. However, in their reading of biblical texts in their larger scriptural contexts, the Reformers were certainly attentive to the kinds of literary reality that I have just described. Calvin's commitment to this kind of large-scale contextual reading is well illustrated in his commentaries on Paul's letters. For example, he is interested in reading Romans not only as an entire book in itself, but also within the context of the entire corpus of the Pauline literature, and then of the entirety of Scripture.[65] In general, his conviction is that "the story of Israel repeats itself in the life of the (Christian) reader, and thus the words of the text are addressed not only to the characters in the story but also to Calvin and all readers."[66] With respect to typological reading specifically—"the pre-figuring in the Old Testament of more revealed events and persons and realities in the New Testament"[67]—Calvin understands the Sabbath (for example) both as "commanded to men from the beginning that they might employ themselves in the worship of God" and as continuing to have this function "to the end of the world," yet also as pointing forward to Christ and as foreshadowing eschatological rest.[68] Then again, what happens to Abraham's family in Genesis 21:1-20 after the birth of Isaac foreshadows typologically—is analogous to—the birth of the Christian church in the NT. This is Calvin's understanding of how the apostle Paul reads the Genesis passage in Galatians 4:21-31, employing "mystical interpretation" that is "not inconsistent with the true and literal meaning," since "the house of Abraham was then a true Church."[69]

---

[65] Holder, *Grounding*, 75–80.
[66] Greene-McCreight, *Ad Litteram*, 111–12.
[67] Holder, *Grounding*, 130.
[68] Calvin, *Genesis*, 107.
[69] Calvin, *Galatians and Ephesians*, 136.

TYPOLOGY, FIGURATION, AND ALLEGORY

Although we are not yet ready for a substantive discussion of allegorical reading in relation to literal reading, one terminological question does need to be discussed at this point, not least because in the example just cited from Galatians 4, what Calvin refers to as anagogue/typology is described by the apostle Paul using the Greek verb *allēgoreō*. Calvin himself also uses the word "allegory" in the course of his comments on the passage, even while insisting that it "does not involve a departure from the literal meaning."[70] We shall return later (in chapter 6) to the question of what Paul meant by *allēgoreō* in Galatians. The question of the moment is a broader one: Is there a legitimate basis for a distinction between "literal reading" that embraces typological/figurative reading as I have just described it, on the one hand, and "allegorical reading," on the other?

The question needs to be asked, because there have always been those (whether in ancient or modern times) who have wished to blur the distinction between allegorical and the typological/figurative reading, representing all of it together simply as "spiritual reading." John O'Keefe and Russell Reno, for example, in adopting the term "typology" in their book on early Christian interpretation of the Bible, "do so without assuming a sharp distinction from allegory. For us, it designates a ubiquitous patristic interpretive practice that discerns patterns within and between discrete events depicted within scripture."[71] Allegory, they claim,

> is not conceptually or essentially distinct from typology. It is an extension of the typological strategy that does not limit itself to discerning patterns of and between events. Allegory is more fluid and ambitious. It seeks patterns and establishes diverse links between scripture and a range of intellectual, spiritual, and moral concerns.[72]

The attentive reader will note, however, that O'Keefe and Reno here deny a sharp distinction at one moment, only to reinforce its reality in the next. Typological reading is *indeed* best thought of as discerning "patterns within and between events [and I would add 'persons' and 'entities'] depicted within scripture." On the other hand, allegorical reading is *indeed* "more fluid and ambitious," moving

---

[70] Calvin, *Galatians and Ephesians*, 136.
[71] O'Keefe and Reno, *Sanctified Vision*, 20. Coming at the question from a rather different, modernist Protestant point of view, James Barr is also skeptical about distinguishing typology from allegory. James Barr, *Old and New in Interpretation: A Study of the Two Testaments* (London: SCM Press, 1982), 103–48.
[72] O'Keefe and Reno, *Sanctified Vision*, 21.

beyond (and often well beyond) "patterns... depicted within scripture."[73] It is for this reason that Treier, having defined typological reading as "iconic mimesis, which preserves a narrative coherence between referents" (see above), defines allegorical reading as *"symbolic"* mimesis, "which arbitrarily imposes a thoroughly ahistorical connection."[74] No doubt some will wish to quibble with the word "arbitrary," since allegorical reading can possess method.[75] What is clear, however, is that the two kinds of reading described by O'Keefe and Reno are very different from each other. And whatever we may think of either, it does not help us in speaking and writing clearly about the rights and wrongs of various approaches to biblical hermeneutics if we already fudge distinctions by the language we use in describing them. *Typological reading is literal reading in a sense that we cannot plausibly ascribe to allegorical reading.* This is precisely because the former makes connections that internally illuminate the Bible as a coherent Story, presenting its own distinctive view of the world, whereas the latter obscures those connections in making "sense of texts that have been *resituated* within alien cultures and conceptual frameworks."[76] To put this in a different, but overlapping way:

> Typology emerges from the relationship between the two Testaments and centers in Christ as the fulfillment of the Old Testament. Allegory emerges from a flattening of the Scriptures into an atemporal whole, in which the same truth is to be found throughout. In this it reveals the vertical dualism of Platonism rather than the eschatological vision of Scripture.[77]

We shall return to the Greeks in relation to allegory in chapter 6. For the moment it is sufficient to note that the Reformers certainly distinguished typology from

---

[73] "Unlike typologies, allegories require significantly more interpretive investment capital.... Allegory involves so much interpretive ambition that it can create the impression that the real source of meaning is in the reader's imagination and not in the text itself." Indeed! O'Keefe and Reno, *Sanctified Vision*, 90.

[74] Treier, "Typology," 825 (emphasis added).

[75] With respect to Origen, e.g., Young says this: "Origen was happy to decode symbols without worrying about textual or narrative coherence, and the symbols were tokens. His procedures were not entirely arbitrary, for two reasons: the symbols were consistent ... and there was an underlying spiritual coherence, guaranteed by the unity of scripture." Frances M. Young, *Biblical Exegesis and the Formation of Christian Culture* (Cambridge: Cambridge University Press, 1997), 184. Richard Hanson distinguishes typology from allegory without any explicit reference to "arbitrariness" in the latter, although it is implied: "Typology is the interpreting of an event belonging to the present or the recent past as the fulfilment of a similar situation recorded or prophesied in Scripture. Allegory is the interpretation of an object or person or a number of objects or persons as in reality meaning some object or person of a later time, with no attempt made to trace a relationship of 'similar situation' between them." Richard P. C. Hanson, *Allegory and Event: A Study of the Sources and Significance of Origen's Interpretation of Scripture* (Louisville, Ky.: Westminster John Knox, 2002), 7.

[76] Vanhoozer, *Meaning*, 114 (emphasis added).

[77] Bartholomew, *Biblical Hermeneutics*, 145.

allegory. For example, "there is clearly a distinction in Calvin's mind between a valid and useful figurative reading and one which is a violation of proper interpretation. He does use the term allegory to indicate this violation and distinguishes this from 'genuine sense.'"[78] I shall retain the language of allegory in maintaining this same distinction, while fully recognizing that "allegory" and "typology" have (unhelpfully) been used in varying and sometimes overlapping ways by various authors throughout history.

CONCLUSION

What does it mean to read Scripture "literally," then, in line with Reformation perspectives on this topic? In essence it means to read it in accordance with its apparent communicative intentions as a collection of texts from the past, whether in respect to smaller or larger sections of text. It means to do so taking full account of the nature of the language in which these intentions are embedded and revealed as components of Scripture's unfolding covenantal Story—doing justice to such realities as literary convention, idiom, metaphor, and typology or figuration. To read literally is, in other words, to try to understand what *Scripture* is saying to us in just the ways in which we seek to understand what other *people* are saying to us—taking into account, as we do so, their age, culture, customs, and language, as well as the verbal context within which individual words and sentences are located. This is what it means to read "literally," in pursuit of the communicative intent of God—in search of what to believe, how to live, and what to hope for. It is always, at the same time, to read "canonically" by way of reading "figurally," which Christopher Seitz (as I noted in chapter 1) describes as "an effort to hear the two-testament witness to God in Christ, taking seriously its plain sense, in conjunction with apostolic teaching."[79] As such, to read literally is to read Scripture in ways significantly different from many "first" and "third way" Protestants (historical critics and Chicago types), who often claim to be reading literally but in reality are often not. It is also to read in ways significantly different from many "second way" (postmodern) Protestants, to the extent that these readers are uninterested in authors and in communicative intent (other than their own). To the extent that "fourth way" readers share with "first" and "third way" readers their understanding of the literal, moreover, the kind of "fifth way" engagement with Scripture that I have just described is also very different from theirs.

This is not everything that needs to be said about "reading literally" in a "reformed" manner, but it is enough, hopefully, to clarify the heart of the matter,

---

[78] Greene-McCreight, *Ad Litteram*, 103. The particular context of this comment is her discussion of Calvin's treatment of the serpent in Genesis 3.

[79] Christopher R. Seitz, *Figured Out: Typology and Providence in Christian Scripture* (Louisville, Ky.: Westminster John Knox, 2001), 10.

and it is sufficient to move us into the next segment of our discussion (chapters 5 and 6), in the course of which the question of "authority" will begin to occupy our attention. The Church Fathers, as we have seen, claimed to be following the apostles in the way that they approached biblical interpretation; it was upon this apostolic authority that they depended, in particular, when departing from what they thought of as the literal sense of Scripture and reading it in other ways. Those who have followed their example in more recent times—the "fourth way" Protestant readers just mentioned, along with their Roman Catholic counterparts—have in turn proposed that the Reformers, in critiquing aspects of the patristic approach, have stepped out of line with the apostolic tradition. Who is in the right? The next step in arriving at an answer to this question is obviously to ask: how *did* the apostles (and indeed Jesus himself) read Scripture?

5

The Reading of Scripture in the New Testament
All That the Prophets Have Spoken

> *The God of Abraham, Isaac and Jacob, the God of our fathers, has glorified his servant Jesus. You handed him over to be killed, and you disowned him before Pilate, though he had decided to let him go. . . . You killed the author of life, but God raised him from the dead. We are witnesses of this.*
>
> —Acts 3:13-15

> *The whole story of Israel builds to its narrative climax in Jesus. That is what Jesus tries to teach them on the road [to Emmaus].*
>
> —Richard Hays[1]

In this chapter and the next, I shall propose that Jesus and his apostles read Scripture (i.e., the OT) predominantly, perhaps even entirely, literally. That is to say, they pay attention to the apparent communicative intention of Scripture as a collection of texts from the past, taking full account of the nature of the language in which these intentions are embedded and revealed as components of Scripture's unfolding covenantal Story. They do not read it "spiritually," if that term is meant to distinguish a certain kind of reading as nonliteral. They certainly do not read it allegorically.

I cannot of course ground this proposal about how the NT reads the OT in a discussion of every instance. Much has been written on how inner-biblical interpretation works, and there are many detailed analyses of particular NT books, and even of small sections of those books, along such lines. My own project, possessing much wider scope, can only afford this particular topic a fraction of the space that these other analyses allow it. I intend, then, simply to illustrate with reference to a number of NT writings, first, the evident way in which the NT offers a substantively literal reading of the OT—an uncontroversial contention to

---

[1] Richard B. Hays, *Reading Backwards: Figural Christology and the Fourfold Gospel Witness* (Waco, Tex.: Baylor University Press, 2014), 14.

a very large degree, with respect to many of the texts that I shall cite. I shall then proceed to give focused attention to some of the NT texts that some or many biblical scholars have understood as exemplifying a nonliteral reading of the OT (whereas I do not). In this way I hope at least to provide the reader with sufficient coverage that the overall shape of the NT's reading of the OT is clear.

THE SCOPE OF THE CHAPTER

Before we get to the NT literature itself, however, it is important to be clear that in the ensuing discussion I shall remain focused on the question of how the early *Christians* were reading Scripture, with the intention of comparing this in chapters 7 and 8 to how later Christians were doing so. I am not interested, in the current context, in the question of how Scripture was being read in early Judaism.[2]

This is a complicated question all on its own, not least because it is bound up with its own problems of definitional clarity.[3] For example, should the term *peshat* ("straight" reading) be restricted in the early period of Jewish exegesis to literal interpretation, or should it be allowed a broader sense? How often is *peshat* actually literalistic rather than literal reading? How should we conceive of the connection between *peshat* and *midrash*, some of which could be considered simply as reading texts in their broader scriptural context (which to my mind would count as literal reading), and some of which certainly could not? Then again, how is *midrash* to be conceived of in relation to the *pesher* exegesis evident in the Dead Sea Scrolls, or in relation to allegorical reading—if indeed it is even correct to refer to *midrash* and *pesher* as hermeneutical techniques rather than genres?

The complications are not only terminological, however. There are questions to be asked, for example, about how far rabbinic literature, "codified, in the main, during the period from the end of the second century through the sixth century C.E.,"[4] allows us access to early Jewish exegetical practice prior to the second century AD.[5] Therefore, there are questions about our actual knowledge of the extent to which first-century Jewish reading practice was (for example)

---

[2] In other contexts I am very interested in both—e.g., in my *Discovering Genesis: Content, Interpretation, Reception* (London: SPCK, 2015).

[3] For a readable and brief introduction to the terminological issues, see Richard N. Longenecker, *Biblical Exegesis in the Apostolic Period* (2nd ed.; Grand Rapids: Eerdmans, 1999), 6–35.

[4] Longenecker, *Biblical Exegesis*, 10.

[5] "Detailed knowledge of the origins of the rabbinic system of exegesis remains elusive ... rabbinic documents ... manifest a much wider array of exegetical concerns and techniques than can be documented in the earlier literature.... The bridge, then, is narrow and shaky." Jay M. Harris, "From Inner-Biblical Interpretation to Early Rabbinic Exegesis," *HBOT* 1/1:256–69 (268–69). See also David Kraemer's comment that "whatever the traditions of reading of the Rabbis' more direct predecessors may have been, we have no means of recovering them." David Kraemer, "Local Conditions for a Developing Rabbinic Tradition," *HBOT* 1/1:270–84 (275).

"midrashic," if indeed we are clear about what we mean by this term.[6] It is of course not impossible, nevertheless, to make judicious proposals based on careful method about which aspects of rabbinic literature do reflect early Jewish tradition on this and other matters.[7] It is simply that "such dating of rabbinic traditions is often difficult."[8]

These various realities represent a challenge for those who want to be able to say (and to say precisely and with clarity) that this or that NT writer engages in this or that contemporary Jewish exegetical practice—in the apparent belief, it sometimes seems, that we can really understand what an early Christian writer (or Jesus himself) was doing only when we are able to attach to it a label (such as *peshat* or *midrash*) that is borrowed from Judaism. My own view, on the other hand, is that while the various Jewish backgrounds to the NT sometimes provide helpful descriptive parallels to NT hermeneutical practice, they do not prescribe what the NT authors must have been doing in their own writings. We need to look and see, rather, what they *were* actually doing. Otherwise—and even when we are arguing from Jewish texts that without question reflect contemporary hermeneutical practice—we run the risk of misreading the biblical text even as we bring its Jewish background to bear in an attempt to understand it.

It is arguable that Richard Longenecker, for example (in his *Biblical Exegesis in the Apostolic Period*), falls into this trap in his reading of Jesus' treatment of Psalm 110:1, as recorded in Matthew 22:41-46, Mark 12:35-37, and Luke 20:41-44. He has earlier described the *pesher* interpretation of the Qumran community as distinctively involving an approach to certain OT prophecies that "did not think of [them] ... as the message of God that was significant in an earlier period and now, *mutatis mutandis*, also relevant to them," but instead "looked on these selected passages as being exclusively concerned with them."[9] The emphasis at Qumran lies upon what is hidden in the text, sealed up until the end times in which the Qumran community is living, and only now revealed and understood because of the coming of the Teacher of Righteousness whom the Dead Sea Scrolls describe. This Teacher holds the key to what is "cryptic and enigmatic"

---

[6] For several pages of work providing a "brief definition of midrash," and some critical observations about the way in which the terminology has been used in NT studies, see Philip S. Alexander, "Midrash and the Gospels," in *Synoptic Studies: The Ampleforth Conferences of 1982 and 1983* (ed. C. M. Tuckett; JSNTSup 7; Sheffield: JSOT Press, 1984), 1–18 (11).

[7] Note, e.g., the kind of approach proposed by David Instone-Brewer in *Traditions of the Rabbis from the Era of the New Testament, Volume 1: Prayer and Agriculture* (Grand Rapids: Eerdmans, 2004), 28–40.

[8] David Instone-Brewer, "Rabbinic Writings in New Testament Research," in *The Handbook of the Study of the Historical Jesus* (4 vols.; ed. Tom Holmén and Stanley E. Porter; Leiden: Brill, 2011), 2:1687–1721 (1721), at the end of a very helpful, detailed discussion of the whole matter.

[9] Longenecker, *Biblical Exegesis*, 24.

in the OT texts.[10] Longenecker then proposes that such *pesher* interpretation represents Jesus' "most characteristic use of Scripture,"[11] employing the Gospel passages mentioned above as an example. He characterizes Psalm 110:1 as "a somewhat enigmatic passage" and Jesus as engaging "in a creative interpretation of Scripture that explicated the enigmatic" in relation to the Messiah. Indeed, "that those who heard [Jesus] . . . understood him" to be doing exactly this is "evident" from their reactions as reported in the Scripture passages in question.[12] By "creative" Longenecker means, I believe, that Jesus' interpretation is not one that is patent in the OT text when read in a "plain" manner (it is, instead, "hidden").

When one actually looks at the Gospel passages in question, however, it is not at all evident that those who heard Jesus on this occasion regarded his interpretation of Psalm 110 as "creative," or considered the psalm to be "enigmatic." Luke does not record their response at all, Mark tells us only that they "listened to him with delight," and Matthew that "no one could say a word in reply"—which is strange, when the obvious response (on Longenecker's theory) might have been, "that is a novel and creative approach to the psalm, and surely not what it means at all." We certainly read about this kind of push-back against Jesus' exegesis of the OT in *other* Gospel passages. Yet Longenecker himself provides the reason why the crowd might *not* have responded in such a way on this occasion, when he acknowledges (quoting another scholar) that "it seems fair to suppose that in the NT era a messianic interpretation of Ps 110 was current in Judaism"[13]—which would certainly not be at all surprising, in view of what I have already said in chapter 4 about the communicative intent of the postexilic book of Psalms (at a literal level). Jesus works with the grammar of the psalm in this larger context, which includes his audience's assumptions about the psalm's authorship. At least in this case, then, the desire to characterize a section of an early Christian writing using a "label" borrowed from (sectarian) Judaism—and a particular understanding of how texts labeled in such a manner "work" in that world—appears to have led to a misreading of the Christian writing in question.

In this present chapter, then, I shall attend only to the question of how Jesus and his apostles (with the exception of the apostle Paul, whose letters will be the focus of chapter 6) read OT Scripture. Clarity about this topic is in any case the necessary prerequisite for useful comparative work with respect to early Jewish and Christian hermeneutics. "Labeling" will inevitably make an appearance below, nevertheless, in some of the secondary material that I quote—at which

---

[10] Longenecker, *Biblical Exegesis*, 29. I pass over in the present context the question of whether this is an accurate description of *pesher* at Qumran.
[11] Longenecker, *Biblical Exegesis*, 54.
[12] Longenecker, *Biblical Exegesis*, 57.
[13] Longenecker, *Biblical Exegesis*, 57n56.

points readers will glimpse for themselves the unhelpful variety of ways in which the meaning of the labels is construed in contemporary scholarly usage.

LITERAL READING IN THE BOOK OF ACTS

As a way into our discussion of the NT reading of the OT, consider first of all Stephen's speech to the Jewish Sanhedrin in Acts 7—just as the early Church is starting out. This will lead us into a discussion of the remainder of Acts in more general terms, and then a brief consideration of the reading of the Psalms therein.

Stephen's Speech to the Jewish Sanhedrin in Acts 7

Required because of accusations made against him to give an account of his preaching of the gospel, Stephen launches here into a long retelling of the OT narrative. He reminds his hearers how Abraham was called by God to leave Mesopotamia and travel to Canaan, and he briefly mentions Abraham's immediate descendants, Isaac and Jacob. He reminds them of the way in which Jacob's sons got into conflict, with the result that Joseph was sold as a slave in Egypt, where God was with him, so that he rose to a position of power. The way in which Jacob's whole family later followed Joseph to Egypt is then rehearsed, and the subsequent exodus of the Israelites from Egypt is described, under the leadership of Moses who encountered God at the burning bush. The rebellion of Israel against God in the wilderness follows, and it is related to the general theme of rebelliousness that often appears in the Prophets (Acts 7:42-43, referencing Amos 5:25-27). Stephen next describes the tabernacle, constructed under Moses' guidance, taken up into the Promised Land by Joshua, and remaining there in the time of David, until Solomon built the temple in Jerusalem, which Stephen reminds his hearers cannot contain God (Acts 7:49-50, in line with what is said in Isa 66:1-2). The theme of Israel's rebellion against God is then dramatically brought to bear on Stephen's audience, in what "could be described in classical rhetorical terms as the 'peroration,' where the speaker applies the lessons learned from the previous material in his speech."[14] Stephen's listeners, he claims, are like their ancestors in the biblical story: a "stiff-necked people, with uncircumcised hearts and ears" (Acts 7:51, recalling OT passages like Exod 33:3-5; Lev 26:41; Deut 10:16) "who resist the Holy Spirit" (just like the people in Isa 63:10). They have received God's Law but have not obeyed it, and have now killed "the Righteous One" (Jesus) whom God has sent, just as their ancestors killed the prophets who predicted his coming (Acts 7:52). Accused of speaking against Moses and God (Acts 7:11) and against both temple and Law (Acts 7:13), Stephen proposes that it is in reality his listeners who are the opponents of God and the breakers of the Law.

---

[14] John B. Polhill, *Acts* (NAC 26; Nashville: Broadman & Holman, 1992), 205.

The Narrative of Acts More Generally

In Acts 7, we note, the lessons that are to be learned derive from the biblical story told in the Law and the Prophets, read in an entirely straightforward manner. There is a shared history that lies behind both the speaker and his audience, and Stephen invites the "readers" (in this case "listeners") to read themselves into the story according to its literal sense. The same is true of the beginning of Peter's earlier address to the crowd in Acts 2:14-39. To explain the events of Pentecost, he cites the prophet Joel, who anticipates in his ordinary words a future day when God "will pour out my Spirit on all people," and "everyone who calls on the name of the Lord will be saved" (Joel 2:28-32; Acts 2:16-21). This day has now arrived, proclaims Peter, in the aftermath of Jesus' resurrection from the dead (Acts 2:24). Later, in Acts 3, Peter heals a crippled beggar, and he contextualizes this event, too, within Israel's long narrative history with "the God of Abraham, Isaac and Jacob" (Acts 3:13). Moses himself had plainly said that "the Lord your God will raise up for you a prophet like me from among your own people; you must listen to everything he tells you," warning that "anyone who does not listen to him will be completely cut off from among his people" (Acts 3:22-23, cf. Deut 18:15, 18, 19). Peter's audience are now receiving the promise attached to God's covenant with Abraham in Genesis (Acts 3:25): "Through your offspring all peoples on earth will be blessed."

Later, in Acts 8, Philip meets an Ethiopian man on the road from Jerusalem, who is reading Isaiah 53:7-8, but without comprehension. The passage speaks in its ordinary words about a "servant" figure who takes the suffering of God's people upon himself, and is punished in death for their sins. Philip interprets these ordinary words as applying to Jesus. In Acts 13, in the synagogue of Pisidian Antioch, and after hearing readings from the Law and the Prophets, Paul stands up and rehearses the biblical Story once again, beginning with the Patriarchs and the exodus. He moves on to Israel's period in the wilderness and their entry into the Promised Land, then speaks about the time of the judges and the prophet Samuel, and then about Saul and David, "a man after [God's] own heart" (Acts 13:22). All of this provides the platform for Paul to speak in verse 27 about Jesus, in whose condemnation "the people of Jerusalem and their rulers ... fulfilled the words of the prophets that are read every Sabbath." In Acts 15, the question arises as to whether Gentile believers "must be circumcised and required to obey the law of Moses" (Acts 15:5). The experience of Peter, Paul, and Barnabas with respect to the Gentile mission suggests that this is not necessary and James then points out that Scripture itself (read according to its ordinary words) agrees, since Amos looks to a future time in which Gentiles will bear God's name (Acts 15:15-18; Amos 9:11-12, LXX).

The Reading of the Psalms in Acts (and Hebrews)

The overall direction of the reading of Scripture in the book of Acts is clear. It is read literally. It is within this general context that we must now place the reading of some of the Psalms, which has appeared to some to move in a different direction. After all, in Acts 4:25-28, Psalm 2 is said to speak of "Herod and Pontius Pilate [meeting] together with the Gentiles and the people of Israel in this city [Jerusalem] to conspire against your holy servant Jesus, whom you anointed." The "king" of Psalm 2 is, on this reading, Jesus; his enemies are people of Jesus' time. The psalm is considered to speak prophetically of these later events, and this corresponds to how Luke-Acts deals with the psalms generally: "That the author of the psalms was a prophet is axiomatic for Luke."[15] As we read Psalm 2 in itself, it is not evident that it has any intention of referring to these later events.

The fact is, however—as we have already seen—that Psalm 2 as we encounter it now in the OT canon is not "in itself." It forms part of a book in which the royal psalms are anticipatory of a kingdom that is yet to come in Israel's future. That is their literal meaning in their literary context; that is how they are intended to be read. Peter does not, therefore, read Psalm 2 "against the grain" in Acts 4; he simply illuminates the events of his own time, as they center upon Jesus of Nazareth, by citing the psalm in its prophetic nature within the whole book of Psalms, anticipating as it does a future Davidic king.

Context also helps to explain the use of Psalm 16 in Acts 2:25-31. Psalm 16 has David referring to himself, and not to someone else, when he utters the words that are cited in Acts 2: "you will not abandon me to the grave, nor will you let your Holy One see decay." Yet within the postexilic book of Psalms, "David" already stands for much more than simply the historical figure of David, who is *long* dead (abandoned to the grave and decayed) by the time the book develops into its current form. "David" is already caught up in a vision of the future in which a son of David will one day come to bring in God's kingdom. So it is that Peter is led to deduce, in the light of Jesus' resurrection, that Psalm 16 is actually speaking most importantly about Jesus, and not about David.[16] In the same way, Psalm 110—however it once functioned during the period of the Israelite monarchy—now looks ahead (in the *book* of Psalms) to the ascension of a future son of David to God's right hand. As such, this psalm is straightforwardly applied to Jesus in Acts 2:32-35. The words of Psalm 118, likewise, conceived as a Davidic composition, come by the same procedure to apply to the son of David in Acts 4:11 (cf. Ps 118:22).

---

[15] Luke T. Johnson, *The Acts of the Apostles* (SP 5; Collegeville, Minn.: Liturgical Press, 1992), 51.

[16] See also Acts 13:32-37, where Pss 2 and 16 are further associated with Isa 55:3.

All of this counts as "literal reading." The apostles are still paying attention to the apparent communicative intentions embedded in the texts that lie before them, in their literary contexts. It is the same kind of reading of the Psalter, incidentally, that we find in various other NT books, and perhaps most notably in the letter to the Hebrews (note, e.g., the reading of Psalm 2 in Heb 1:5).[17] Neither in Acts nor in Hebrews can we accurately characterize this reading as a "spiritual reading" that moves beyond the literal sense of the book of Psalms to another, different kind of sense. It is at this point that Longenecker's "labels" once again muddy our hermeneutical pond, although he is not the only NT exegete to succeed in this endeavor. He sharply (and rightly) distinguishes the author of Hebrews from Philo of Alexandria in their overall hermeneutical approaches—for instance, "Philo treated biblical history allegorically, setting aside the obvious meaning of a narrative in search of a deeper spiritual significance signaled by the verbal symbols," whereas "the writer to the Hebrews spells out typological correspondences existing within the framework of redemptive history."[18] Longenecker nevertheless regards the use of the psalms and other OT texts in Hebrews as representing *pesher* interpretation, which (we recall) he has previously differentiated from literalist and midrashic exegesis,[19] emphasizing the former's "creative" nature.[20] In Hebrews as in Acts, however, the truth is that God speaks through the ordinary human words of the text. "Creativity" in interpretation is not required. As to Philo, we shall return to him in the next chapter.

LITERAL READING IN THE GOSPEL OF MATTHEW

"Jesus Christ," Matthew's Gospel begins, is "the son of David, the son of Abraham" (Matt 1:1), whose family tree includes people like Jacob's son Judah (Matt 1:3; cf. Gen 38), Ruth (Matt 1:5), Solomon (Matt 1:6; cf. 1 Kings 1–11), and Josiah (Matt 1:10-11; cf. 2 Kgs 22–23). His coming was foretold by the prophet Micah, who foresaw that a king would one day be born in Bethlehem and become the shepherd of his people (Matt 2:6; cf. Mic 5:2). Jesus, tempted by the devil in Matthew 4, responds to him with quotations from Scripture, read in accordance with the normal sense of the scriptural words (Matt 4:3-11, referencing Deut 8:3, 6:16, and 6:13).

---

[17] "The framework of much of our author's argument is supplied by quotations from the Psalter ... more than once he starts a phase of his argument with a psalm quotation." F. F. Bruce, *Commentary on the Epistle to the Hebrews* (London: Marshall, Morgan & Scott, 1964), li.

[18] Longenecker, *Biblical Exegesis*, 154–55. See also Bray, *Biblical Interpretation*, 72.

[19] Longenecker, *Biblical Exegesis*, 50–54.

[20] Longenecker, *Biblical Exegesis*, 57 (specifically with respect to Ps 110).

The Fulfillment of the Law and the Prophets

In Matthew 5, Jesus announces that he has not come "to abolish the Law or the Prophets... but to fulfill them" (Gk. *plēroō*, v. 17). In Matthew's Gospel this verb "plays a prominent role, most notably in its ten occurrences in the formula quotations" (e.g., in Matt 1:22, "All this took place to fulfill what the Lord had said through the prophet").[21] What does it mean in Matthew 5:17? Judging by what follows, it means that Jesus has come to confirm, authoritatively, the true meaning of the Law and the Prophets—he has come to provide "the full picture" concerning what they have to say, which will remain authoritative until "heaven and earth disappear."[22] The remainder of Matthew 5–7 exemplifies this, as Jesus challenges inadequate contemporary understandings of certain aspects of Scripture by drawing attention to other parts of Scripture with which he expects them to be consistent. For example, Scripture teaches that we should not murder.[23] But it also teaches that "anger resides in the lap of fools" and that "a wise man keeps himself under control,"[24] and it exhorts the reader to "refrain from anger and turn from wrath," since "it leads only to evil."[25] It can lead, indeed, to murder.[26] So, "in your anger do not sin," exhorts Psalm 4:4; "when you are on your beds, search your hearts and be silent." It is against the background of such literally read Scripture that we must understand Jesus' words in Matthew 5:21-24. Likewise, in remembering that adultery is forbidden by Scripture,[27] we should not forget that the lust that precedes it is also a problem (Matt 5:27-30),[28] nor forget that although divorce is permitted,[29] God nevertheless regards marital breakdown as a serious matter. The fact that Scripture permits divorce does not mean that it reflects God's deepest will (Matt 5:31-32).[30] In all these ways Jesus, throughout the Sermon on the Mount, affirms the Scripture that he discusses but simultaneously exposes "a shallow and inadequate understanding of what the commandment

---

[21] Richard T. France, *The Gospel of Matthew* (Grand Rapids: Eerdmans, 2007), 182.

[22] Note the same verb in Matt 13:48, where the fishermen's net is "full"; Rom 8:4, where the requirements of the Law are "fully met"; and Phil 4:18, where Paul has received "full payment."

[23] Exod 20:13.

[24] Eccl 7:9; Prov 29:11.

[25] Ps 37:8.

[26] Gen 4:5-8.

[27] Exod 20:14.

[28] Cf. Exod 20:17; 2 Sam 11:2-4; Job 31:1-4.

[29] Deut 24:1.

[30] Cf. Mal 1:16. Jesus' view of this matter is more fully explained in Matt 19:3-9, where the law permitting divorce is described as an accommodation by God to the hardness of people's hearts, which must be read in the context of the whole biblical Story that begins by establishing lifelong marriage as God's will.

entails."[31] Along the same lines, if people are going to make oaths, they should certainly keep them,[32] but people of integrity should not need to make them in the first place (Matt 5:33-37). Integrity is the fundamental requirement in speech, as in all areas of moral life, and those who are wise choose their words carefully:[33] "The absolute reliability of one's word renders an oath superfluous"; a promise should simply be a promise.[34] Moreover, in remembering that appropriate justice is specified in various circumstances in Torah along the lines of "eye for eye, and tooth for tooth,"[35] we should not forget general scriptural imperatives to treat other people compassionately and mercifully, just as God does even in respect of those who are his enemies and whom he is said to "hate" (Matt 5:38-48).[36]

So it goes on. In Matthew 19, for example, a man asks Jesus about what is good (v. 16). Jesus tells him to obey the commandments, according to the straightforward meaning of the words: "Do not murder, do not commit adultery, do not steal, do not give false testimony, honor your father and mother" (Exod 20:12-16) and "love your neighbor as yourself" (Lev 19:18). He follows this up by reminding the man of the scriptural imperative concerning generosity (e.g., Deut 15:7-11). There is more to the righteous life than avoiding such offenses as murder, adultery, and stealing. In Matthew 23:23 the "teachers of the law and Pharisees" are blamed for a faulty assessment of the weight of biblical injunctions about righteousness; they pay attention to tithing while neglecting "the more important matters of the law—justice, mercy and faithfulness." This kind of contextualization of religious observance by larger moral imperatives is already found in the Prophets. Consider, for example, Amos 5:22-24: "Though you bring choice fellowship offerings, I will have no regard for them. Away with the noise of your songs! I will not listen

---

[31] Donald A. Hagner, *Matthew 1–13* (WBC 33A; Dallas: Word, 1993), 112.

[32] E.g., Lev 19:12.

[33] E.g., Prov 2:12, 16; 7:21; 10:19; 12:6, 18-19; 17:27; 18:6-8.

[34] Hagner, *Matthew 1–13*, 128, who notes (127) that "it seems to be assumed [in Matthew 5] that oath taking is in practice more often a means of avoiding what is promised than of performing it (cf. the polemic specifically against the Pharisees in 23:16-22)."

[35] Exod 21:24; Lev 24:20; Deut 19:21.

[36] "You hate all who do wrong" (Ps 5:5; cf. 11:4), and yet, "Who is a God like you, who pardons sin and forgives the transgression of the remnant of his inheritance? You do not stay angry forever but delight to show mercy" (Mic 7:18). This leads to the biblical imperative that the one who loves God rightly should "hate those who cling to worthless idols" (Ps 31:6) and are "double-minded men" (Ps 119:113) who "hate you, O Lord" (Ps 139:21). At the same time he or she is required in imitating God "not [to] gloat when your enemy falls" (Prov 24:17), nor rejoice "at [the] enemy's misfortune" (Job 31:29). Rather, "If your enemy is hungry, give him food to eat; if he is thirsty, give him water to drink" (Prov 25:21). Indeed, "When a man's ways are pleasing to the Lord, he makes even his enemies live at peace with him" (Prov 16:7). The "neighbors" whom we are to love (Lev 19:18) include, in the OT, our enemies.

to the music of your harps. But let justice roll on like a river, righteousness like a never-failing stream!"

It is a mistake, therefore, to understand the *plēroō* language in Matthew 5:17, and the content that follows it in the Sermon on the Mount, as implying that because Jesus has come, the interpretation of the Law and the Prophets, as Richard France puts it, "can no longer be merely at the level of the literal observance of regulations, but must operate at the deeper and more challenging level of discerning the will of God which underlies the legal rulings of the Torah"[37]—as if the canonical Law and Prophets had never before insisted on such discernment, and Jesus were now introducing an entirely new way of reading them ("a radically new understanding of what it means to live under the rule of God").[38] The "righteousness . . . of the Pharisees and the teachers of the law" that Jesus references in Matthew 5:20 was not perfectly acceptable up until the Saturday prior to the beginning of Jesus' ministry (at which point a "new regime" was introduced, in which "different standards apply"),[39] and thereafter, suddenly, completely inadequate. In terms of what Scripture requires, such righteousness was *already* inadequate beforehand, even though many failed to understand this. Scripture *already* required "radical openness to knowing and doing the underlying will" of God.[40] France himself perceives this in other sections of his commentary on the Sermon on the Mount, acknowledging (for example) that Jesus' dialogue partner in these various sayings "is not the OT law as such but the OT law as currently (and sometimes misleadingly) understood and applied."[41]

John Nolland is much nearer the mark, then, when he writes about Matthew 5:17 and what follows that

> [t]he fulfilment language represents a claim that Jesus' programmatic commitment, far from undercutting the role of the Law and the Prophets, is to enable God's people to live out the Law more effectively. . . . Matthew holds that Jesus offered, in part by drawing on the insights of the Prophets, a new depth of insight into what the Law requires over against what he (Matthew) considered to be a general superficiality, a foreshortened perspective, in the reading of the Law.[42]

---

[37] France, *Matthew*, 183.
[38] France, *Matthew*, 188.
[39] France, *Matthew*, 190.
[40] France, *Matthew*, 190.
[41] France, *Matthew*, 196.
[42] John Nolland, *The Gospel of Matthew: A Commentary on the Greek Text* (Grand Rapids: Eerdmans, 2005), 219. My only point of concern about this statement is the potentially misleading word "new" (see my earlier comments on what the Prophets were already doing), which seems to open up a gap between Matthew's and Jesus' views about the Law.

To be clear, however—not that Nolland would disagree—Jesus not only *teaches* this scriptural righteousness, but he also *lives it out*. In this way, too, he fulfills (provides "the full picture" in respect of) the Law and the Prophets, which together look for exactly the ideal and virtuous reader who will respond appropriately and fully, as Jesus does, to what they teach. (On "ideal readers," see further my chapters 19 and 22.)

Fulfillment More Generally

It is within the overall context of Matthew's literal reading of Scripture that we must now consider some particular verses in his Gospel where his reading of the OT may at first appear not to be "literal" at all. Perhaps the most famous of these is found in Matthew 1:22-23 where, as noted earlier, the birth of Jesus is said to "fulfill what the Lord had said through the prophet," namely that "the virgin will be with child and will give birth to a son, and they will call him Immanuel" (Isa 7:14).

If we read this prophecy in its immediate literary and historical context (Isa 6–9), we find that it is addressed to the untrusting King Ahaz of Judah as he faces the combined armies of Aram and northern Israel back in the eighth century BC. Isaiah's words look ahead to the year 733 BC, in fact, when the Assyrian emperor Tiglath-Pileser III absorbed most of northern Israel into his empire. Isaiah is evidently referring to a royal child who is to be born in the very near future, for before he is very old, "the land of the two kings you dread will be laid waste" (v. 16) and "the LORD will bring on you and on your people and on the house of your father a time unlike any since Ephraim broke away from Judah—he will bring the king of Assyria" (v. 17). "The" virgin in the prophecy is evidently a particular, identifiable person who is known to both Ahaz and Isaiah—perhaps a young woman who either is, or will shortly become, married to Ahaz, and will conceive her first child. We may well be intended to understand her as being, at the time of Isaiah's prophecy, an unmarried (but betrothed, and therefore identifiable) "virgin"—which is how the LXX understands the Hebrew *'almāh* (translating it with Gk. *parthenos*). However, the Hebrew also permits us to regard her (less specifically) simply as a "young woman" of childbearing age (in line with other Gk. translations).[43] The most natural candidate for her child, in this context, is Hezekiah, who in Isaiah 36–39 is all but overwhelmed by the Assyrian assault but survives, because God is "with" him (cf. the description in Isa 8:8). There can be little doubt, then, about what the eighth-century Isaiah was himself referring to in Isaiah 7:14, in general terms and according to the literal sense, when he first uttered these words to Ahaz—even if some of the detail remains obscure.

---

[43] Cf. the use of *'almāh* in Gen 24:43; Exod 2:8; Ps 68:25; Prov 30:19; Song 1:3, 6:8.

How do these words come to be attached to Jesus in Matthew's Gospel? Some commentators have argued that this move is best explained in terms of

> [a] hermeneutical method... [which] allowed verses to be separated from their contexts. Verses or individual words were understood to have esoteric meanings whose significance could be revealed to an inspired teacher or writer. Thus the entire Scripture was viewed as a prophecy intended to interpret the moment in which the reader lived.[44]

However, the first two sentences of this quotation represent a poor description of Matthew's hermeneutical method. Matthew evidently pays very *careful* attention to the context of Isaiah 7:14—but not only to its immediate context in Isaiah 6–9. He is also attentive to its broader context in the remainder of the book of Isaiah.

The whole book of Isaiah no doubt developed into its present form long after the lifetime of the prophet who gave it its name (i.e., it is the eventual product of the postexilic period). By that time, Ahaz and Hezekiah were long dead, and Judah itself, having miraculously survived the Assyrian invasion of 701 BC because God was "with" its king, had been absorbed into the Babylonian and then the Persian Empire. The first part of Isaiah (chapters 1–39) is now structured around narratives about these two kings: Isaiah 6:1–9:7 (concerning the king who did not trust in God) is balanced by Isaiah 36:1–39:8 (concerning the king who did).[45] Much of its second part (chapters 40–55), recognizing that the remainder of Israel's story in the Promised Land was not characterized by the "peace and security" that marked Hezekiah's lifetime (39:8, the last words of the chapter), casts its eyes to the future rather than the past. These later chapters look for renewed signs that "God is with us." Isaiah's oracle about exile and Hezekiah's response in Isaiah 39:5-8 lead directly, in fact, into "Comfort, comfort my people" in Isaiah 40:1. In looking to the future in this way, the second part of Isaiah (as Brevard Childs has noted) has become "fully eschatological," testifying to Israel's future with God.[46] In this context, Childs argues, the preceding chapters (Isa 36–39) "have assumed a... metaphorical role as a commentary on the death and rebirth of the nation."[47]

Going further than this, we should note the way in which the figure of Hezekiah himself is drawn into this vision of the nation's future by the structuring

---

[44] John D. W. Watts, *Isaiah 1–33* (WBC 24; Waco, Tex.: Word, 1985), 141.
[45] Peter R. Ackroyd, *Studies in the Religious Tradition of the Old Testament* (London: SCM Press, 1987), 105–20, building on the work of Roy F. Melugin, *The Formation of Isaiah 40–55* (BZAW 141; Berlin: de Gruyter, 1976).
[46] Childs, *Introduction*, 326.
[47] Childs, *Introduction*, 333.

of the book that makes his reign so central.⁴⁸ It is not just that Hezekiah's reign is presented in Isaiah 36–39 as the occasion for Isaiah's words of consolation in Isaiah 40–55.⁴⁹ More than this, the immediate juxtaposition of "There will be peace and security in my lifetime" (Isa 39:8) with the beginning of these words of consolation—and indeed the absence of any note of Hezekiah's death and burial, such as is found in this position in the narrative in 2 Kings 20—implies that Isaiah's promises will come to pass, in some sense, during "Hezekiah's" reign. Within the literary context of the book of Isaiah, in other words, the figure of Hezekiah has *himself* become "eschatological." Isaiah 8:23–9:6 plays its own part in this move because of its portrayal of the future king as one who possesses divine attributes, ushering in the reign of God. The total effect of all this is to identify Hezekiah as a paradigmatic king who points beyond himself to another Davidic monarch still to come. This helps to explain why, even though Hezekiah does not appear by name in the NT except in the genealogy of Jesus in Matthew 1:1-17, we hear so many echoes in the NT of the OT narratives about his reign.⁵⁰ Indeed, it is possible that he was already read "messianically," to some extent, in pre-Christian Judaism.⁵¹

There are "many clear indications" in the book of Isaiah itself, then, that the sign of Immanuel "was [already] understood messianically by the tradents of the Isaianic tradition, and shaped in such a way both to clarify and expand the messianic hope for every successive generation of the people of God."⁵² Hezekiah (the "son" of Isa 7:14) already points beyond himself to another Davidic descendant

---

⁴⁸ Much of what follows in this paragraph summarizes the larger argument found in my early essay "The Messiah in the Book of Kings," in *The Lord's Anointed: Interpretation of Old Testament Messianic Texts* (ed. Philip E. Satterthwaite, Rick S. Hess, and Gordon J. Wenham; Carlisle: Paternoster, 1995), 67–85. It is now most easily accessed in my *Against the Grain: Selected Essays* (ed. Stacey L. Van Dyk; Vancouver: Regent, 2015), 29–50.

⁴⁹ So Ackroyd, *Studies*, 105–20.

⁵⁰ See further Provan, *Kings*, 282–84.

⁵¹ According to the Babylonian Talmud (*Sanhedrin* 99a), the great Jewish teacher Hillel, who died in the early years of the first century AD, already associated Hezekiah with the Messiah, albeit only to deny that the Messiah was still to come: "There shall be no Messiah for Israel, because they have already enjoyed him in the days of Hezekiah." This may imply that some of Hillel's contemporaries already linked Hezekiah with a *future* Messiah, which is certainly a view attributed to Johanan ben Zakkai at the end of the first century AD: "Remove the vessels so that they shall not become unclean, and prepare a throne for Hezekiah the king of Judah who is coming" (*Berakhot* 28b). The link between Hezekiah and the Messiah is also explored around the end of the second century by Bar Kappara. He suggests that Hezekiah was destined to be the Messiah but that this was considered unfair to David, who sang so much about the glory of God, whereas Hezekiah did not (*Sanhedrin* 94a). There is also some evidence that the closely allied passage Isa 9:5-6 was already understood messianically at Qumran in the first century BC (1QHᵃ 11.9–10, with its reference to a "wonderful counsellor"), as it certainly was in later Judaism (e.g., in the Targum on Isaiah).

⁵² Brevard S. Childs, *Isaiah* (OTL; Louisville, Ky.: Westminster John Knox, 2001), 69.

who will represent the reality that "God is with us."⁵³ It is this idea that Matthew develops, signaling that in Jesus "the full picture" of God's work with David's line is finally visible. It is in this sense that Isaiah's prophecy is "fulfilled" in the events that Matthew describes in his first chapter, using the same Greek verb (*plēroō*) as he does in Matthew 5:17.

Matthew makes similar moves in other places where he uses the same verb. In Matthew 2:15, for example, he cites Hosea 11:1, not to suggest "that Hosea had some hidden additional meaning to 'son' only now revealed in Christ . . . [but to declare] that Hosea's hope of God's accomplishing his initial purposes in Israel is now eschatologically fulfilled in Jesus, his truly obedient son."⁵⁴ In Matthew 2:17-18 he reads Jeremiah 31:15, similarly, not according to some "esoteric" sense of the text, but in its literary context. The book of Jeremiah, like other prophetic books in the OT, looks forward to a great ingathering of Israel by God, as a result of which the scattered exiles "will come and shout for joy on the heights of Zion; they will rejoice in the bounty of the LORD . . . I will give them comfort and joy instead of sorrow" (Jer 31:12-14). Israel's return from exile in Babylon in the sixth century BC (the same prophetic corpus informs us) did not deliver this reality, but Matthew understands this new day now to be dawning. The correlation of the time of distress represented by the mass murder described in Matthew 2:16 with Jeremiah 31:15 ("a voice is heard in Ramah . . . Rachel weeping for her children") reminds the reader of where Jeremiah 31 goes next: "there is hope for your future. . . . Your children will return to their own land" (Jer 31:17).⁵⁵

These are just two examples of a number of readings of the OT in the Gospel of Matthew that we could discuss.⁵⁶ From all of them we see that, for Matthew, there are many places in the redemptive story of the NT, besides the section that concerns the birth of Jesus, where God has acted in ways similar to those in the OT redemptive story and has already intimated in Scripture that he will act in these same ways again. Notice these, Matthew urges his readers, and understand the bigger picture—how the NT "fulfills" the OT, enabling us to trace, as France puts it, "lines of correspondence and continuity in God's dealings with

---

⁵³ France, *Matthew*, 57.

⁵⁴ Rikk E. Watts, "How Do You Read? God's Faithful Character as the Primary Lens for the New Testament Use of Israel's Scriptures," in *From Creation to New Creation: Biblical Theology and Exegesis* (ed. D. M. Gurtner and B. L. Gladd; Peabody, Mass.: Hendrickson, 2013), 199–220 (209–10).

⁵⁵ As Richard Hays puts it, "the echo of Jeremiah 31 offers comfort, beckoning God's people to lean forward into the hope of the days that are surely coming when God—in the person of Jesus—will have *mercy*, bring back the exiles, and write the Law on their hearts." Hays, *Reading Backwards*, 43.

⁵⁶ See further, e.g., those examples where Matthew introduces the OT/NT connection with the same formula that we find in Matt 1:22 (Matt 2:23, 4:14, 8:17, 12:17, 13:35, 21:4, 27:9).

his people, discerned in the incidental details of the biblical text as well as in its grand design."⁵⁷

Reading Backward?

France himself appears to believe that these "patterns of fulfillment [are] not necessarily [to be found] in what the original authors of the OT texts had in mind but in what can be perceived in their writings with Christian hindsight."⁵⁸ He therefore shares a particular view of "typological reading" with (it seems) many other NT scholars—namely, that at least in some cases, typological reading is "out of joint" with what the OT itself wishes to say. If this is correct, then—at least at these points—the NT authors are not reading the OT literally (in pursuit of its communicative intent) after all.

It is not clear to me, however, that these scholars *are* correct. It is in fact my impression that modern NT scholars often tend greatly to underestimate the full extent and nature of the communicative intent of the various books of the OT, in part because so many continue to work with an inadequate notion of what the term "original authors" should rightly be understood to mean. The consequence is that they do not read the OT texts sufficiently contextually, but too often and too quickly make the assumption that what was "perceived . . . with Christian hindsight" to be present in the OT was not, as it were, originally "there." (This is also true, incidentally, of their reading of contemporary non-Christian Jewish texts in terms of their "Jewish hindsight.") They assert this, even though the ancient Christian writers cited in respect of their "hindsight" give every impression that *they* believe the meaning in question already to have been "there," and even though modern scholarship pertaining to the canonical shaping of the OT has uncovered voluminous evidence that should encourage *us* to believe that it was already there.

The pervasiveness of the assumption is such that even Richard Hays (in his wonderfully rich book, *Reading Backwards*)—a NT scholar who is refreshingly and deeply interested in what is actually "there" in OT Scripture, as we read its texts in context, and who is convinced of OT Scripture's importance in guiding us to read the Gospels rightly⁵⁹—can nevertheless write about the same Gospels helping us to see in the OT "latent figural meanings unsuspected by the original author and readers."⁶⁰ He does not mean by this only that the Gospel writers make connections between the OT and the events of their time people living in earlier times could not have suspected they would make. He means that "[r]eading

---

⁵⁷ France, *Matthew*, 12.
⁵⁸ France, *Matthew*, 12–13.
⁵⁹ Hays, *Reading Backwards*, 4.
⁶⁰ Hays, *Reading Backwards*, 15.

the OT anew in the light of the story of Jesus' death and resurrection opens both text and reader to new, previously unimagined, possibilities."[61]

The NT passage cited in support of this contention is Luke 24:13-35—the story of Jesus' meeting with two disciples, after the resurrection, on the road to Emmaus. Part of Hays' treatment of this passage is cited above, in the second epigraph to the present chapter, because I think it captures well what the apostles believed about the OT Scriptures they were reading: "The whole story of Israel builds to its narrative climax in Jesus." It is important to notice, however, what Hays says about how these two disciples come to hold this "integrative interpretation" of the OT, and what it is that they understand beforehand. The "interpretation," he believes, is only now given to them, by the resurrected Jesus, on the road. Before they receive it from him,

> the puzzled Emmaus disciples have all the facts but lack the pattern that makes them meaningful.... Somehow Jesus' exposition of Israel's Scripture will have to undertake the task of reading backwards: it will have to show *retrospectively* the pervasive presence of [the theme that the Messiah had to suffer before entering into his glory]—which had never been perceived by anyone in Israel prior to the crucifixion and resurrection.[62]

The obvious problem with this interpretation of Luke 24, however, is that before Jesus even begins to offer these disciples the "integrative interpretation" without which they allegedly lack "the pattern that makes [the facts they know] meaningful," he explicitly blames them for not already grasping the truth of what the OT has to say about the theme in question: "How foolish you are, and how slow of heart to believe all that the prophets have spoken! Did not the Christ have to suffer these things and then enter his glory?" (vv. 26-27). The disciples ought already to have been in possession of the right "integrative interpretation" of the OT! Lacking it, they are "fools and slow of heart of believe." In other words, to see the pattern in question never required their "reading backwards" after an encounter with Jesus (although they were in any case the beneficiaries of this encounter). It only ever required their "reading forwards" from "all that the prophets have [*already*] spoken." Certainly these disciples had not hitherto noted the pervasive presence in OT Scripture of the theme in question—but the point is that they *should* have done so, because it was there to be found.[63] Luke 24 is a poor passage

---

[61] Hays, *Reading Backwards*, 15.
[62] Hays, *Reading Backwards*, 14.
[63] Some other Jews were certainly already reading Scripture as pointing toward intense suffering in general prior to the great deliverance that was to come, and as concerning the important role of individual sufferers in birthing that deliverance. N. T. Wright, *Jesus and the Victory of God* (Minneapolis: Fortress, 1996), 576–92.

to choose, then, if the intention in appealing to it is to open up a gap between the communicative intent of the various books of the OT, on the one hand, and (in France's words) "what can be perceived in their writings with Christian hindsight." "Christian hindsight" in Luke 24 only sees, now, what was already there to be seen, had the readers not been quite so dense.

Hays then proceeds to provide throughout his book many excellent examples of figural connections between the OT and the Gospels. These examples *also* do not require us to believe that a great gulf is fixed between the communicative intent of the OT passages in question and their interpretation in the NT. In fact, quite the reverse is often explicitly the case. For example, Hays proposes that in Matthew 2:15 the writer "transfigures" Hosea 11:1 in making a connection between the two "sons of God" in these passages. His actual discussion of Matthew's reading, however, strongly emphasizes exactly what it is *in the meaning of OT text read in its OT context* that the evangelist draws upon in making this connection.[64] The pattern of fulfillment is comprehensively grounded in this instance "in what the original authors of the OT texts had in mind."[65] I question, therefore, whether "transfigures"—a word that does not imply merely development or even fulfillment, but a more radical reordering of meaning—is the correct word for what is happening here. The people who put together the book of Hosea might well have been "unsuspecting" as to *exactly* how Matthew would draw his analogies from their text in his much later situation, but whether they would have regarded him as indulging in the exploitation of their text's "unimagined possibilities" is quite another question.

Some critical reflection is required, then, on the common assumption that the typological "patterns of fulfillment" found in Matthew's Gospel (and also elsewhere in the NT) have more to do with "Christian hindsight" than with "what the original authors of the OT texts had in mind."[66] Reflection is required not least because of the strong internal evidence within the OT itself that much of what occurred in the canonical process was far from "unsuspecting." Matthew's reading of Scripture, typological or not, is highly constrained by the literal sense of the OT texts in their scriptural contexts. He is very far from practicing "[a] hermeneutical method . . . [which] allowed verses to be separated from their contexts," permitting "verses or individual words [to be assigned] . . . esoteric meanings."[67]

---

[64] Hays, *Reading Backwards*, 39–41.
[65] France, *Matthew*, 13.
[66] France, *Matthew*, 12–13.
[67] Watts, *Isaiah 1–33*, 141.

He is very far from offering us, over against a literal reading of the text, a "spiritual" reading of the kind that could only be generated by "an inspired teacher or writer."[68]

LITERAL READING IN THE GOSPEL OF JOHN

Characterized by Clement of Alexandria (ca. AD 150–215) as "a spiritual gospel" in contradistinction to the earlier ones that laid bare "the external facts,"[69] the Gospel of John certainly "contains one of the most artistically complex and sophisticated combinations of theological themes and ideas found anywhere in the Bible."[70] Yet like Matthew, Mark, and Luke, John is still fundamentally reading the OT in its literal sense as the background text that explains who Jesus is—not only "the Lamb of God who takes away the sin of the world" (John 1:29), but also "the actual human embodiment of the Godhead on earth."[71] The evidence for this assertion lies both in the direct quotations from the OT that are found in John's Gospel (which are in fact relatively few in number when compared to the other Gospels),[72] and in the more indirect ways in which the OT is constantly evoked.

In John 1:1-3, for example, Jesus is read against the background of both Genesis 1 and Proverbs 8, which speak not only of God creating the world by his word, but also of having "a craftsman at his side" as he did so (Prov 8:30; cf. also Ps 33:6). John proceeds then to correlate the appearance of Jesus *in* the world of the first century AD with God's promise in Ezekiel 37:24-27 that in the future, when the exile is over and a son of David rules over Israel once again as their shepherd, "[m]y dwelling place will be with them; I will be their God, and they will be my people" (Ezek 37:27). So it is that "the Word became flesh and made his dwelling ['tabernacled'] among us" (John 1:14, with allusions to Exod 33–34). Jesus is not to be confused with John the Baptist, who identifies himself only as "the voice of one calling in the desert, 'Make straight the way for the Lord,'" referencing the figure in Isaiah 40:3 who cries out in anticipation of the time when "the glory of the LORD will be revealed, and all mankind together will see it" (Isa 40:5; cf. John 1:14, 23). It is this Baptist who goes on shortly afterward to identify Jesus as the Lamb of God who takes away the sin of the world, perhaps alluding not only to the Passover lamb but also to the prophecy in Isaiah 53, where we encounter a mysterious servant of God who is "led like a lamb to the slaughter" (Isa 53:7) and in his death bears "the sin of many" and makes "intercession for the transgressors"

---

[68] Watts, *Isaiah 1–33*, 141.
[69] Eusebius, *Church History*, 6.14.5–7 (*NPNF* 2, 1:261).
[70] Gerald L. Borchert, *John 1–11* (NAC 25A; Nashville: Broadman & Holman, 1996), 24.
[71] Borchert, *John 1–11*, 31.
[72] There are 27 direct quotations in John's Gospel—significantly fewer than in Matthew (124), Mark (70), and Luke (109). Hays, *Reading Backwards*, 78.

(53:12).⁷³ According to Peter's brother Andrew in John 1:41, picking up on the language of the anointed son in Psalm 2 (already discussed above), Jesus is also "the Messiah . . . the Christ." The same OT text (Ps 2) is alluded to in the words of Nathanael in John 1:49. There, a line from the story of Jacob in Genesis 28 is cited by Jesus (John 1:51; Gen 28:12) to indicate that Nathanael will live to see something as astonishing as Jacob did in his famous dream.

In John 2:13-25 Jesus clears the temple in Jerusalem of merchants and moneylenders, calling to the disciples' mind the righteous man of Psalm 69 for whom "zeal for your house consumes me" (Ps 69:9). In John 3 he has a conversation with Nicodemus, in the course of which he tells him (v. 5) that "no one can enter the kingdom of God unless he is born of water and the Spirit"—alluding to the promise of God through Ezekiel that at a future time God would "sprinkle clean water on you, and you will be clean . . . give you a new heart and put a new spirit in you . . . put my Spirit in you and move you to follow my decrees" (Ezek 36:25-27). Jesus also alludes to Ecclesiastes 11:5 in the course of this dialogue (John 3:8), and to the incident in Numbers 29:4-9 involving Moses and the snake (John 3:14). Later, in John 6, Jesus responds to those who are grumbling about his statement that he is the "bread of heaven" by reminding them of Isaiah 54:13, which looks forward to a time in which God's "unfailing love" for Israel (v. 10) will be manifested in the fact that "[a]ll your sons will be taught by the LORD, and great will be your children's peace" (cf. John 6:45). John 7:38 borrows from Proverbs 18:4 the description of the wise man who possesses "the fountain of wisdom [that] is a bubbling brook" in order to characterize the wise person who believes in Jesus: "Whoever believes in me, as the Scripture has said, streams of living water will flow from within him."

In John 8, the question of the validity of Jesus' testimony comes up for discussion. In the ensuing dialogue, Torah is read straightforwardly by both Jesus and his opponents: all agree that "it is written that the testimony of two men is valid" (8:17). The question is, can anyone corroborate Jesus' testimony about himself? Yes, he tells them (8:18): "I am one who testifies for myself; my other witness is the Father, who sent me." In John 10:1-21 he extensively develops the metaphor of the shepherd, which is already an important feature of the way in which both God and his messianic king are described in the OT.⁷⁴ He will soon develop

---

⁷³ "[T]he Lamb of God brings deliverance through submission to death as the Passover Lamb . . . it is . . . possible that other elements of Jewish and Christian tradition will have been linked with the figure, notably the submissive lamb of Isa 53 (cf. Acts 8:32-35) and the lamb provided by God at the intended sacrifice of Isaac (Gen 22:10-13)." George R. Beasley-Murray, *John* (WBC 36; Dallas: Word, 1987), 25.

⁷⁴ E.g., Pss 23:1-4; 80:1; 95:7; Ezek 34; 37:24-28.

the already heavily used OT metaphors of the way and the vine (John 14–15).[75] Later in John 10 (vv. 22-39), Jesus' opponents are angry because Jesus calls himself God's "son." Jesus' response turns on the precise language of Psalm 82:7, in which kings are referred to as "gods" and "sons of the Most High." If those people can be described using such language, Jesus asks, what is the problem with his using the same—especially since he is not merely any king, but "the one whom the Father set apart as his very own and sent into the world" (John 10:36)?

As we come to the closing chapters of Jesus' life in this Gospel, we find John reminding us (12:15), in the context of the events surrounding Jesus' entry into Jerusalem, of Zechariah's prophecy about the king who would one day come to Zion "gentle and riding on a donkey, on a colt, the foal of a donkey" (Zech 9:9). That this triumphal entry did not lead on to an initially happy ending to the Jesus story may best be understood on the analogy of Isaiah's audience (John 12:37-40; cf. 6:10; Isa 53:1)—blind to reality, and the possessors of dead hearts. In John 13:18, Jesus himself identifies his betrayer in language drawn from Psalm 41:9, in which the righteous man is betrayed by a close friend. The language of "fulfillment" already encountered in Matthew's Gospel is once again deployed here in John in respect of the people in general and Judas in particular, and to similar effect. If Jesus' words and actions often remind us of other places in the redemptive Story of the Bible where God has already spoken and acted in similar ways, the same is true of those who fail to believe in Jesus and oppose him. Notice all the ways in which this is true, our gospel writers urge upon us, and understand the bigger picture.

So it is that Judas, in particular, appears in the Gospels as the "fulfillment" of the opponent of the righteous person who is so often described in the OT's lament psalms, and Jesus appears as the "fulfillment" of the righteous person also described therein—as the ultimate example of one who suffers unjustly at the hands of those who fail to walk in God's ways. This is certainly true of the Gospel of John, which deliberately draws attention to the connections between what happens to the righteous in the Psalms and what happens to Jesus during Passion Week (John 19:22-24 and Ps 22:18; John 19:33-35 and Ps 34:19-20). All of this comes rightly under the heading of literal, contextual reading of Scripture. It is not of itself problematic, of course, to refer to it at the same time as a spiritual reading of Scripture—but John's Gospel is, in this sense, no more or less "spiritual" than the other three.

---

[75] Cf., e.g., Ps 1; Isa 40:1-5; Ps 80:9-17; Ezek 15:1-8.

LITERAL READING IN THE LETTERS OF JAMES AND PETER

James writes of a "royal law found in Scripture" (Jas 2:8), which is "love your neighbor as yourself" (Lev 19:18). He expects his readers to keep it. He refers to Abraham's offering of Isaac on the altar in Genesis 22 in a straightforward way as illustrating faith in action (Jas 2:21-23), citing (like Paul) Genesis 15:6—"Abraham believed God, and it was credited to him as righteousness." This "illustrating" is signified by the same Greek verb (*plēroō*) that we discussed earlier in relation to Matthew's Gospel. The story in Genesis 22 "fulfills" the statement about Abraham's faith in Genesis 15 in the sense of contributing to a fuller picture of his faith as displayed in what Abraham *does*.[76] The story of Rahab in Joshua 2 is also straightforwardly referenced in the second chapter of James (2:25). James' strictures concerning the tongue in chapter 3 (vv. 5-12) are consonant with advice already found in Proverbs,[77] and in chapter 4 (v. 4) he applies the specific advice of Proverbs 3:34 directly to his readers. The ephemeral nature of life as described in James 4:14 is very much a favorite topic of OT Scripture (e.g., Isa 40:6-7; Ps 103:15-16), as is the economic oppression described in James 5:1-6 (e.g., Mic 3:9-12). Job is directly referenced in James 5:10-11 "as an example of patience in the face of suffering," and Elijah in James 5:17-18 as "a man just like us" who is a model of earnest prayer.

Peter, in his first letter, identifies his Christian readers as the "elect" of God just like Israel, and urges them as worshippers of the same God to "be holy, because I am holy" (1 Pet 1:15-16; Lev 11:44). *His* reflections on the ephemeral nature of life are grounded specifically in Isaiah 40:6-8 (1 Pet 1:24-25). Christ is the "precious cornerstone" that God says he will lay in Zion (Isa 28:16), such that "the one who trusts will never be dismayed" as God's judgment falls (1 Pet 2:4-8). Christians, like the ancient Israelites, are "a chosen people, a royal priesthood, a holy nation, a people belonging to God" (1 Pet 2:9). They need to follow Christ's example in suffering—one who "committed no sin, and no deceit was found in his mouth" (1 Pet 2:22, citing the prophecy of Isa 53:9 about the suffering servant). Sarah is recalled in 1 Peter 3:5 as one of "the holy women of the past" whom Peter's female readers are encouraged to imitate in being submissive to their husbands. In general, his readers are encouraged to follow their Christian calling as directly described in Psalm 34:12-16 (1 Pet 3:9-12).

Like the other NT writers already discussed, then, both James and Peter invite their readership to read themselves into the OT story according to its literal

---

[76] "What we have here is not a prophecy-fulfillment scheme ... but a use of Gen 15:6 to show that this OT verse ... is confirmation of what James has been saying [about faith and action]." Ralph P. Martin, *James* (WBC 48; Waco, Tex.: Word, 1988), 93.

[77] Prov 10:19, 31; 11:12; 12:18-19; 15:2, 4; 17:20; 18:21; 21:6, 23; 25:23; 26:28.

sense. They do not look beneath or behind the OT for a hidden, spiritual sense; the spiritual sense is found *in* the text, read in a literal and contextual manner.

CONCLUSION

As we reflect on our discussion in this chapter, then, concerning the way in which Jesus and his apostles read OT Scripture, it is clear (thus far) that there is abundant evidence in support of my proposal that they are reading it literally. That is, they are paying attention to the apparent communicative intention of Scripture as a collection of texts from the past, taking full account of the nature of the language in which these intentions are embedded and revealed as components of Scripture's unfolding covenantal Story. They are not to be found reading it "spiritually." Our discussion is not yet complete, however. We must still consider, in chapter 6, the apostle Paul.

6

LITERAL READING, TYPOLOGY, AND ALLEGORY IN PAUL
A Rose by Any Other Name

> *It is a weighty and damaging charge that heaven brings against Homer for his disrespect for the divine. If he meant nothing allegorically, he was impious through and through, and sacrilegious fables, loaded with blasphemous folly, run riot through both epics.*
>
> —Heraclitus of Alexandria[1]

> *Contrary to [normal] usage, [Paul in Galatians 4] calls a type an allegory; his meaning is as follows; this history not only declares that which appears on the face of it, but announces somewhat farther, whence it is called an allegory. And what hath it announced? No less than all the things now present.*
>
> —John Chrysostom[2]

In chapter 5 I proposed that throughout the NT, in the non-Pauline literature, we are invited to read ourselves into the OT story according to its literal sense; the spiritual sense is found *in* the text, read in a literal and contextual manner. The same emphasis on the literal sense is widely found in the Pauline literature. This is true, first, in one of his most famous letters, addressed to the church in Rome. As this letter opens, Paul immediately reminds his readers that a long history lies behind them in which God has already been known and worshipped (Rom 1:1-3). The Gospel was "promised beforehand through his prophets in the Holy Scriptures regarding his Son, who as to his human nature was a descendant of David." Both the Christians in Rome and Paul's fellow Jews can and must learn important lessons from the literature that describes this history, read in a normal manner. Addressing Jews, Paul challenges them about whether they really keep the law given them by God ("You who preach against stealing, do you

---

[1] Heraclitus, *Homeric Problems*, 1.1–3 (ed. Donald A. Russell and David Konstan; WGRW 14; Leiden: Brill, 2005), 3.

[2] John Chrysostom, *Commentary on Galatians*, 4.24 (*NPNF* 1, 13:34).

steal?"; Rom 2:21), accusing them of being just like the people described in Isaiah 52:5 who cause God's name to be "constantly blasphemed" (cf. Rom 2:24). A man is a Jew, Paul proposes, if he possesses a circumcised heart, not merely because he has been circumcised physically (Rom 2:28-29)—as Deuteronomy 10:16-20, addressed to the physically circumcised, already suggests.[3] But in fact all people, both Jew and Gentile, have sinned, in accordance with the sentiments of Psalm 14:1-3 and other Scriptures (Rom 3:10-18). All people need the righteousness that comes only from God through faith in Jesus Christ, "to which the Law and the Prophets testify" (Rom 3:21). They testify to it above all in what they narrate about Abraham, the father of both Jew and Gentile (Rom 4:16-17; Gen 17:5), of whom the Scriptures say that he "believed God, and it was credited to him as righteousness" (Rom 4:3; Gen 15:6)—and this was before Abraham was circumcised (Rom 4:10; cf. Gen17:24). Later, in Romans 9–11, Paul returns directly to the question of what this means for Jews, the possessors of "the divine glory, the covenants, the receiving of the law, the temple worship and the promises" (Rom 9:4)—the people from whom is traced "the human ancestry of Christ" (Rom 9:5). Recalling the stories of Isaac, Jacob, Esau, and the exodus, and drawing in many other (mainly prophetic) texts, he ponders the mystery of God's choices throughout the biblical Story and down to his moment of writing.

Other Pauline letters reflect this same literal hermeneutical commitment. For example, in 1 Corinthians 6:12-20, Paul reads Genesis 2:24 according to its literal sense when dealing with issues of sexual immorality. He reads Deuteronomy 19:15 similarly when announcing in 2 Corinthians 13:1 his third visit to Corinth, when he will begin to enact judgment on recalcitrant church members. In Galatians he returns to Abraham, and the importance of the fact that he, as the one in whom "all nations will be blessed" (Gen 12:3), "believed God, and it was credited to him as righteousness" (Gal 3:6-8). Those "who rely on observing the law" instead of relying on God (like Abraham) "are under a curse, as it is written: 'Cursed is everyone who does not continue to do everything written in the Book of the Law'" (Gal 3:10, referencing Deut 27:26)—and of course, no one has perfectly kept the Law. Everyone needs Christ, who "redeemed us from the curse of the law by becoming a curse for us" (Gal 3:13), for as Scripture teaches us, "cursed is everyone who is hung on a tree" (Deut 21:23).

The apostle Paul clearly reads the OT Scriptures at the very least in a *predominantly* literal manner. Whether we may replace *predominantly* with *entirely* then depends above all on how we understand six particular Pauline passages—passages that have routinely been characterized (and sometimes in strong terms)

---

[3] See also Deut 30:6; Jer 4:4; 9:25-26; Ezek 44:9, all of which pursue the same point.

as departing from the literal sense.⁴ I shall deal with five of these relatively briefly, and then with the sixth more extensively, because of its particular importance in the history of biblical interpretation.

ROMANS 10:6-9

Romans 10:6-9 makes use of Deuteronomy 30:12-14 in a manner that suggests to one commentator that Paul's reading of the OT at this point in his argument is "purely fanciful."⁵ Another accuses him of "drastic and unwarrantable allegorizing."⁶ These are questionable assessments. The context in Deuteronomy 30 concerns the blessings and curses that God has set before the Israelites, and the necessity of obeying God and turning to him "with all your heart and with all your soul" if they are to know his blessing (v. 10). What Moses thus commands, he tells them,

> is not too difficult for you or beyond your reach. It is not up in heaven, so that you have to ask, "Who will ascend into heaven to get it and proclaim it to us so we may obey it?" Nor is it beyond the sea, so that you have to ask, "Who will cross the sea to get it and proclaim it to us so we may obey it?" No, the word is very near you; it is in your mouth and in your heart so you may obey it.

Similarly, Paul declares in Romans 10:6-9 that gaining the blessing of salvation in gospel terms is very simple: it is a matter of confessing with your mouth that "Jesus is Lord," and believing in your heart that God raised him from the dead. There is no need to worry about ascending to heaven or descending to the deep in order to find "the righteousness that is by faith" (v. 6). That would be to undo the work of Christ, who has been raised from the dead already, and has already ascended into heaven. None of this is "fanciful" or "allegorizing." Paul is simply

---

⁴ These six are simply some of the more prominent examples of passages generally considered to require particular attention when it comes to Paul and "the literal sense" of the OT. Not least because of how they think of "the literal," some scholars would provide a much longer list, and some a shorter one. Longenecker (*Biblical Exegesis*, 109), e.g., who considers Paul normally to offer "literalist and midrashic exegesis" of Scripture, believes that only on two occasions does the apostle interpret the OT "allegorically, subordinating the literal sense and elaborating an additional meaning" (1 Cor 9:9-10 and Gal 4:21-31). For Reventlow (*Biblical Interpretation*, 1:63) "Allegory ... is found only three times in Paul" (1 Cor 9:9, 10:4; and Gal 4:21-31). Bray agrees with Longenecker in his count of occasions of allegorical exegesis (1 Cor 9:9-10 and Gal 4:21-31), but also finds three occasions upon which Paul "quotes Scripture out of context" (Rom 10:6-8; Gal 3:16; Eph 4:8). Bray, *Biblical Interpretation*, 66.

⁵ Charles H. Dodd, *The Epistle of Paul to the Romans* (London: Fontana, 1959), 177.

⁶ K. E. Kirk, *The Epistle to the Romans in the Revised Version with Introduction and Commentary* (CB; Oxford: Clarendon, 1950), 225.

drawing an analogy between the uncomplicated nature of faith in OT times and now in NT times.

FIRST CORINTHIANS 9:9-10

In 1 Corinthians 9:9-10, Paul defends his right as a minister of the gospel to receive material support from the Christians in Corinth—a right that he has not in fact insisted upon (v. 12). The general principle that those who work deserve to derive legitimate benefit from their work is illustrated with reference to "the Law of Moses" as it is articulated in Deuteronomy 25:4, which commands: "Do not muzzle an ox while it is treading out the grain." Paul's conviction is that the principle enunciated here applies not (merely) to oxen,[7] nor indeed to "the plowman" and "the thresher"—who do their work "in the hope of sharing in the harvest" (1 Cor 9:10)—but also to Christian workers. The principle is emphasized again in his first letter to Timothy (5:18), which characterizes Scripture as teaching *both* that people should not "muzzle the ox while it is treading out the grain," *and* that "the worker deserves his wages." It is important to be clear about whence this conviction derives, given the common idea that Paul here "ignore[s] Scripture's literal sense and resort[s] to allegorizing to extract a higher, spiritual meaning from the text."[8] Paul's conviction derives, first, from reading the Deuteronomy passage in its immediate context in Deuteronomy 24–25, whose laws "almost all serve to promote dignity and justice for human beings."[9] The reader of Deuteronomy is already invited not to make a sharp distinction between doing right by human beings and doing right by animals. It derives, second, from reading the passage in the context of what is said elsewhere in the Law and the Prophets about treating both workers and animals fairly.[10] It is not a "higher, spiritual" meaning in Scripture that Paul presses upon the Corinthian Christians, but an ordinary (and spiritual) one. What Scripture has to say about fair recompense for work applies to the Corinthian case as much as to any other.

FIRST CORINTHIANS 10:1-4

First Corinthians 10:1-4 forms part of a passage (vv. 1-13) in which Paul draws on the OT narratives concerning Israel's escape from Egypt and her subsequent

---

[7] It is most unlikely that Paul intends to say that God is not concerned about oxen at all, given not only the importance that the OT attaches in general to the care of animals (e.g., Prov 12:10), but also Jesus' own concern for them (e.g., Matt 12:11).

[8] David E. Garland, *1 Corinthians* (BECNT; Grand Rapids: Baker, 2003), 409, referencing scholars like Barrett and Longenecker.

[9] Richard B. Hays, *First Corinthians* (Interpretation; Louisville, Ky.: Westminster John Knox, 1997), 151.

[10] E.g., Exod 20:10; Lev 25:6-7; Isa 58:1-7; Prov 12:10.

wanderings in the wilderness to illustrate the need among the Christians in Corinth to persevere in their faith, and specifically to avoid idolatry. The first four verses are "often regarded as an a-contextual 'midrashic' or allegorical reading of Israel's exodus experience."[11] Yet as Rikk Watts has rightly said, "these assessments... fail to attend closely enough to the original text and its context and hence miss the deep symbolism already inherent in the original account."[12] All the Israelites, Paul reminds the Corinthians, were "baptized" like them with water, in their own way—they passed through the sea. Escape from threatening waters already symbolizes in the OT escape from death and entrance into new life, not least in the exodus story itself. "The Corinthians' baptism into Christ... is the eschatological new exodus equivalent of passing from death to life... to which the prophets themselves pointed."[13] These same Israelites also shared in "spiritual" food and drink, that is, food and drink that God himself miraculously provided—in the Corinthian case, the Eucharistic meal.

The Israelites' drink, specifically, is said to have derived from "the spiritual rock that accompanied them" (v. 4). This is a strange thing to say if the intended reference is to the physical rock out of which the water flowed for the Israelites in Exodus 17:5-7, since nothing in the OT narrative implies that this rock moved around with the Israelites—unless we are to read this implication into the later story in Numbers 20:2-13, where water gushes from a rock for a second time. It seems much more likely, however, that Paul intends by "spiritual rock" to refer to God. Not only is God already closely associated with the rock in Exodus 17 in his standing "upon" it (not "by" it, NIV) at the point when it is struck by Moses and produces its life-giving water, but it is also true that God is often represented metaphorically in the OT as a rock. This is most importantly the case in two particular locations. The first is Psalm 78, where we already find in the same context, first, a reference to God striking the rock so that "water gushed out" (v. 20), and, second, a reference to the Israelites remembering, after their rebellion, "that God was their Rock, that God Most High was their Redeemer" (v. 35). The second reference is in Deuteronomy 32, which begins by celebrating that God "is the Rock, his works are perfect, and all his ways are just" (v. 3), remembering God's ample provision for Israel—which includes nourishing Israel with "honey from the rock" (v. 13)—before also recalling Israel's rejection of "the God who made him... the Rock his Savior" (v. 15). Israel's idolatry is described here in terms of deserting "the Rock, who fathered you," and forgetting "the God who gave you birth" (v. 18). Thus, it is already the case in various OT contexts that "rock" alludes both to physical and metaphysical reality. It is this that explains Paul's easy transition

---

[11] Watts, "How Do You Read?" 210.
[12] Watts, "How Do You Read?" 210.
[13] Watts, "How Do You Read?" 211.

into the important statement about Christ in 1 Corinthians 10:4—"that rock was Christ." Jesus Christ is Yahweh, present with the Israelites back then and present now with the Corinthians—which is why they had better pay attention, because "God was not pleased with most of [the Israelites]; their bodies were scattered over the desert" (1 Cor 10:5).

GALATIANS 3:16

Galatians 3:16 references a number of passages in Genesis about the promise of God to Abraham that he and Sarah would have a son (Gen 12:7, 13:15, 24:7). Paul's argument turns on the very precise point that this promise refers to the "seed" of Abraham in the singular, and not to "seeds" in the plural. The "seed" of Abraham is one person, and that person is Jesus Christ. Paul is not unaware in saying this, of course, that this word "seed" in Genesis possesses both a collective as well as an individual sense. In itself, it can refer to Isaac (Gal 4:28; cf. Rom 9:7, 10), but also to all those descended from Isaac (Gal 3:29; cf. Rom 4:13-18). Nevertheless, at this point in his argument Paul wishes to emphasize the singular aspect, and to draw an immediate line of connection between Isaac and Jesus—for he is not reading the Genesis texts "in themselves," but within the whole context of OT Scripture. As Timothy George writes of Paul's overall approach to the OT in Galatians (in the context of his teaching about God's law in particular):

> [B]y bringing into view not just an isolated verse or even the five books of Moses but instead the entire corpus of sacred writings, that is, Holy Scripture, Paul showed that only from the perspective of the whole scope of scriptural revelation can the specific role of the law be assessed.... [I]n the final analysis the Bible is not merely a collection of disparate documents written across several millennia in various languages of antiquity. No, it is the rule of faith, the deposit of truth, a definitive canon, a sure word of promise. From beginning to end Scripture presents one coherent theme: the sovereign unfolding of God's eternal purposes in Jesus Christ, to the praise of his glory. This is the staggering overview Paul had in mind when he wrote "the Scripture declares."[14]

Similarly, as we read the promise to Abraham in the larger scriptural context, it is clear that this promise was never fulfilled in OT times. As Scripture is emerging into its canonical form in the postexilic period, the fulfillment of this promise is still anticipated—in a coming time when "You [God] will be true to Jacob, and show mercy to Abraham, as you pledged on oath to our fathers in days long ago" (Mic 7:20), and when the blessing of God on all nations will become a reality (e.g., Isa 19:23-25). Paul is reading the Abraham promise "from the perspective of the whole scope of [this] scriptural revelation," and that is what leads him to

---

[14] Timothy George, *Galatians* (NAC 30; Nashville: Broadman & Holman, 1994), 262.

identify the "seed" of Abraham ultimately (but not exclusively) as Jesus—the one in whom the promise is actually delivered. So whereas "Paul's emphasis on the singular nature of Abraham's seed is often described as an atomistic exegesis that survives only if 'seed' is examined in isolation," the opposite is in fact the case: "it reflects a solid awareness of the larger narrative."[15]

EPHESIANS 4:7-10

The fifth Pauline passage often characterized as departing from a literal reading of the OT is Ephesians 4:7-10, which might be viewed as a case of the apostle "creating an *ad hoc* text form to support his conclusions."[16] Here Paul tells the Christians in Ephesus that "to each one of us grace has been given as Christ apportioned it" (v. 7), referencing (in v. 8) Psalm 68:18. The Psalms passage envisages God ascending to his dwelling place after achieving a victory over his enemies that results in his possession of both "captives" and "gifts" (i.e., tribute from the conquered). Paul relates this passage analogically to Christ who, as God, has also "ascended on high" after winning a mighty victory over his enemies and has redistributed the gifts he received. He does not depart from the literal sense of the OT passage in drawing this analogy, although he does substitute third-person for second-person pronouns in order to integrate the OT text into his particular argument, and it is possible that he extends the picture that it paints beyond the receipt of the "gifts" to their redistribution. Even this is not certain, however: it is possible that the text of Psalm 68 that Paul had before him (or was remembering) already spoke of God "giving" gifts to men rather than "receiving" them.[17]

GALATIANS 4:21-31

There remains for discussion, then, the important passage in Galatians 4:21-31. Here Paul addresses Gentile Christians in Galatia who apparently desire to be "under the [OT] law" (4:21). He seeks to persuade them, instead, that "it is for freedom that Christ has set us free" (5:1). As one aspect of his argument, he reminds them of what "the law" (i.e., the whole Pentateuch, including its narrative sections) says about Abraham's two sons, Ishmael and Isaac ("one by the slave woman and the other by the free woman," v. 22). The first of these "was born in the ordinary way," but the second "as the result of a promise" (v. 23). "These things," Paul goes on to say in verse 24, "may be taken figuratively" (as the NIV translates

---

[15] Watts, "How Do You Read?" 212.
[16] Longenecker, *Biblical Exegesis*, 108—although he disputes the idea.
[17] Both the Syriac Peshitta translation and the Targum on the Psalms may reflect such a reading. For a brief discussion, see Andrew T. Lincoln, *Ephesians* (WBC 42; Dallas: Word, 1990), 242–43. Longenecker writes of the "likelihood" that "Paul is using . . . a variant reading that was then extant of Ps. 68:18" (*Biblical Exegesis*, 108).

his words), and he then proceeds to suggest how this may be the case, since "the women represent two covenants." As noted earlier, the Greek verb behind "taken figuratively" is *allēgoreō* (whose noun form is *allēgoria*), from which we derive the English "allegory" and "allegorize." Other English translations render it along these very lines, as in the old KJV: "which things are an allegory . . ." (cf. NRSV; ESV). Still others share the NIV's decision to avoid this English word: NLT has the women serving "as an illustration of God's two covenants" (cf. *The Message*), NKJV as "symbolic" in relation to the covenants, and NCV as "like" them. Behind these different translations lies an important interpretative question: what is it, exactly, that Paul is doing with his Genesis text? A practical question then follows: what is the best way of translating *allēgoreō* so as to make it *clear* what Paul is doing, and avoid leading Bible readers astray in appreciating this?

These questions are not new. They have been around for a long time, precisely because ancient Christian writers like Origen appealed to Galatians 4:21-31 in the course of defending his own allegorical approach to the biblical text, which owes a significant amount to his Jewish Alexandrian predecessor Philo, who was a contemporary of the younger Paul. In response, other ancient writers like John Chrysostom (cited in the second epigraph to the present chapter) argued that in Galatians 4 Paul pursues a customary typological approach to the OT while *referring* to it (unhelpfully, as it turns out) using the verb *allēgoreō*. That is to say, *allēgoreō* does not signify in Paul what it signifies in other ancient authors like Philo and his later fellow Alexandrians (such as Origen). It signifies rather the kind of typological/figurative reading that I suggested (in chapter 4) is best considered as one aspect of what is involved in the literal (and canonical) reading of Scripture. As Shakespeare's Juliet will later underline, what an entity is named does not necessarily communicate what it truly is: "What's in a name?" she asks; "that which we call a rose by any other name would smell as sweet."[18]

What's in a name? Is Chrysostom's opinion about the true nature of Paul's reading in Galatians 4 correct? In order to make a sound judgment on the matter, we first of all require clarity about how Philo did in fact read Scripture, and why he did so—which in turn requires a little knowledge about the history of allegorical reading in the ancient world.

Homer and the Birth of Allegorical Reading

The allegorical reading of literature is first documented in ancient Greece, where it arises out of a quest to find "mystical truths and cultic significance embedded in

---

[18] William Shakespeare, *Romeo and Juliet*, in *The Plays and Sonnets of William Shakespeare* (ed. William G. Clarke and William A. Wright; Great Books 26; Chicago: Encyclopedia Britannica, 1952), 2.2.43–44 (on p. 294 of this edition).

the poetic language and the figures of myth."[19] This quest was especially important with respect to the poetry of Homer, whom many felt must at all costs be defended against the charges of impiety and impropriety that began to be levelled at him from the sixth century BC onward. It is important to understand why so many Greeks considered the defense to be essential:

> Homer held a privileged place in Greek and Athenian culture ... [his was] the text first learnt and most studied at all levels of Greek education, and any educated Athenian could be expected to have a knowledge of it.... Homer was also a prime source of authority for knowledge, behavior, ethics ... the Homeric texts were essential not only to the actual process of teaching and to the festival institutions of Athens, but also to the make-up of Athenian social attitudes and understanding.... Even though Athenian religion did not have "sacred texts," it is with some justification that Homer has been called the Greek Bible—especially if one thinks, for example, of the use of the Bible in Victorian Britain: read after dinner, used in schools, a subject of heated academic debate, a cultural background widely diffused through different échelons of society, a much quoted source of moral and social guidance etc.[20]

The Homeric literature was very important to Greek culture. To be a Greek was to live life in Homer's shadow, to be immersed in his writings, and to look to him as an authority. The problem was that Greek society in the fifth and fourth centuries BC, and particularly Athenian society, had already moved on since Homer's time, and his poetry, while retaining its cultural authority, had become to some degree problematic. Increasingly, educated Greeks found his portrayals of the gods in both the *Iliad* and the *Odyssey* troubling. These deities appeared to be very similar to human beings, and—as measured by the standards of the times in which Homer's critics lived—not necessarily very virtuous characters.

The ideal solution, in Plato's mind, was to ban the reading of the Homeric epics.[21] Another, more practical solution was to encourage people to read them in a different way. Perhaps they could be read, not in accordance with their literal sense, but in some other way, so as to retain "their status as a kind of Scripture."[22] Perhaps they could be read as concerning physics and psychology (Theagenes

---

[19] Rita Copeland and Peter T. Struck, eds., *The Cambridge Companion to Allegory* (Cambridge: Cambridge University Press, 2010), 3.

[20] Simon Goldhill, *Aeschylus: The Orestia* (2nd ed.; Cambridge: Cambridge University Press, 2004), 41–42.

[21] Plato, *Republic*, 2.377–78. The myths of both Homer and Hesiod "are to be rejected not simply because they are lies ... but because they are *ugly* lies ... that distort that about which they speak, just as the bad painter distorts his subject." Robert Lamberton, *Homer the Theologian: Neoplatonist Allegorical Reading and the Growth of the Epic Tradition* (TCH 9; Berkeley: University of California Press, 1986), 16–17.

[22] Siegert, "Early Jewish Interpretation," 133.

of Rhegium), or ethics (Anaxagoras), or history (Euhemeros), or even geography (Strabo).[23] When the gods fought with each other, for example, perhaps this referred, in reality, to the opposition between the various elements in the world. The names of the gods could perhaps be read as dispositions of the soul (e.g., Aphrodite as desire).[24]

This, then, is where allegorical reading begins and first develops in the ancient world. It arises out of the shared conviction among its advocates that Homer's work in particular cannot be impious or improper. If it appears so, then the correct meaning of the text (which might well lie well under its surface, only hinted at by the poet) cannot yet have been attained. This perspective is then picked up in the fourth and third centuries BC by the early Stoics, and then by later ones such as Heraclitus of Alexandria, who is responsible for one of two late first-century AD definitions of *allēgoria*: "[t]he trope [i.e., the figurative or metaphorical use of a word] that says one thing but signifies something other than what is said." His fellow Alexandrian, Tryphon, defines it as "an enunciation which while signifying one thing literally, brings forth the thought of something else."[25] In due course, as we move into the third and fourth centuries, Neoplatonists and others become involved in the same Homeric project.[26] So it is that in the aftermath of the Emperor Constantine's conversion in the early fourth century, Homer is ultimately "rescued" for largely Christian posterity. As read allegorically by this long line of readers, he could safely be transmitted into the Middle Ages by Christian scholars for the benefit of Christian readers. The Roman writer Virgil, one of Rome's greatest poets and the author of the epic *Aeneid* (which purports to tell the story of the founding of Rome), passed through a similar "handling" process, on the way ultimately to his starring role in Dante's *Divine Comedy* in the fourteenth century as the guide who is capable of taking Dante through Hell and much of Purgatory, albeit not any further on his journey to Paradise.

Just how embarrassing and problematic in its literal sense the Homeric literature had become for many within "the Hellenistic tradition of reading" by the first century AD, specifically, is well illustrated by Heraclitus in the opening lines of his *Homeric Problems* (cited in the first epigraph to the present chapter), where his disdain for Homeric literature read literally is quite evident. Heraclitus holds strong beliefs about the true nature of the world, the gods, and the virtuous life,

[23] Reventlow, *Biblical Interpretation*, 1:33–40.

[24] See further Siegert, "Early Jewish Interpretation," 130–35; and J. F. Procopé, "Greek Philosophy, Hermeneutics and Alexandrian Understandings of the Old Testament," *HBOT* 1/1:451–77 (462–69).

[25] Both ancient writers are cited from Steven Di Mattei, "Paul's Allegory of the Two Covenants (Gal 4.21–31) in Light of First-Century Hellenistic Rhetoric and Jewish Hermeneutics," *NTS* 52 (2006): 102–22 (105–6).

[26] See further Procopé, "Greek Philosophy," 469–76.

and Homer does not measure up. Heraclitus' allegorical reading of Homer is designed to help the latter improve himself.

Philo and the Allegorical Reading of Scripture

Little is known about the life of Philo other than that he lived from about 20 BC until about AD 40 in the city of Alexandria in Egypt, which was at that time home to the largest Jewish community outside of Palestine. That being said, the very name "Alexandria" alerts us to one of the most important realities concerning his context. In the late fourth century BC, Alexander the Great had conquered much of the known world, making it Greek—not only politically, but also culturally, intellectually, and linguistically (in the sense that Greek replaced Aramaic as the lingua franca of empire). "Hellenism" came to permeate everything, which is to say (from the perspective of those who did not welcome it) that it came to *threaten* everything—including indigenous understandings of religion and traditional religious observance. Among the Jews of the Greek Empire, tensions arose in the centuries following Alexander's death between those who embraced this Hellenism and those who did not. For some Jews, to be at all Hellenistic in terms of culture, whether this involved dress, leisure activities, or enthusiasm for Greek philosophy, was at the same time to abandon Judaism. Others, however, freely adopted Greek culture and thought, while asserting that they had not given up on their essential Jewishness. Of all the cities in the ancient world where this Hellenistic Judaism took root and flourished, Alexandria was perhaps the most notable. This, then, is where Philo, the Hellenistic Jew, lived and worked, and attempted in his own particular way to bring Greek culture and Jewish faith into some kind of harmony with each other.

His challenge, as he did so, was not the one faced by writers like Heraclitus. It was not the challenge of reading *Homer* in a way that made sense to, and did not offend, educated Greek opinion. It was the challenge of reading *the Jewish Scriptures* in such a manner—and most especially Torah (as we saw in chapter 3), which in Alexandria, in Greek translation, "would have played a very similar role in Jewish education to that of Homer in Greek."[27] The Jews of Alexandria, albeit Hellenized to a great extent, were still noticeably different from their non-Jewish neighbors—their customs strange, and their religious observance a matter of amusement or derision. Non-Jewish Egyptian observers had been known in the course of the preceding centuries to adopt a hostile stance toward Judaism, sometimes slandering the Jews in the process; in the third century BC, for example, this had been true of the Egyptian priest and historian Manetho. It was an ongoing problem in the first century AD as well, as illustrated later in the century

---

[27] Sebastian P. Brock, "The Phenomenon of the Septuagint," *OtSt* 17 (1972): 23–77 (16).

by Josephus' confrontation with the Egyptian grammarian Apion (*Against Apion*, c. AD 95), who also happened to be a commentator on Homer. This was the broader context in which Philo operated. The more specific context is illustrated by the destruction of most of the synagogues in Alexandria in AD 39, and Philo's subsequent journey to the imperial court in defense of Jewish rights.[28] His problem was, as I say, not Heraclitus' problem. His *solution* to his problem, however, was the tried and tested Greek solution to which Heraclitus also resorted.[29] It was to subject his revered and authoritative (but now unfortunately difficult and embarrassing) traditional texts to allegorical reading, in order to reveal to the contemporary detractors of Judaism all the many ways in which Jewish scriptural teaching was, against all appearances, consistent with prevailing Greco-Roman philosophical and ethical norms.

What does Philo find Scripture to say as he reads it in this way? It concerns the spiritual life, understood in terms of intellectual contemplation, with which is to be contrasted a life that is preoccupied with earthly concerns—with the material world and the physical body. The latter is both evil and dead,[30] and it is an enemy of the soul that has descended into the material realm only for a time and must one day escape it again.[31] It must leave its "tomb" and once again "live according to its proper life ... released from the evil and dead body to which it is bound."[32] Therefore, the wise should gradually detach themselves from what is physical, and focus their minds on eternal realities. They should aim at achieving the "knowledge of the true and living God,"[33] and indeed union with God—although only the souls of philosophers are eventually able to escape this present world and return to the heavenly realm.[34] It is all this that Torah "truly" reveals and inculcates. Its author, Moses, himself reached the very summit of philosophy, and learned "from the oracles of God the most numerous and important of the principles of nature."[35] The ethics associated with this contemplative life center on the imitation of God, who is impassible (incapable of feeling); therefore, the

---

[28] For more details about Philo's apologetic context, and the consequent "necessity of coming to a practical arrangement with Hellenistic culture" in Alexandria, see Siegert, "Early Jewish Interpretation," 141–43 (143), 163–64.

[29] "The methods and vocabulary of Philo's exegesis are for the most part those of the earlier tradition of Homer commentary." Lamberton, *Homer*, 48. See further David Dawson, *Allegorical Readers and Cultural Revision in Ancient Alexandria* (Berkeley: University of California Press, 1992).

[30] Philo, *Legum allegoriae* (*Allegorical Interpretation*), 3.72–74, WP, 58; *De gigantibus* (*On Giants*) 15, WP, 153.

[31] Philo, *Alleg. Interp.*, 3.69, WP, 57–58; *Giants*, 12–15, WP, 152–53.

[32] Philo, *De opificio mundi* (*On Creation*), 67–69, WP, 10–11; *Alleg. Interp.*, 1.108, WP, 37.

[33] Philo, *De decalogo* (*On the Decalogue*), 81, WP, 525; *De Abrahamo* (*On the Life of Abraham*), 58, WP, 416.

[34] Philo, *De posteritate Caini* (*On the Posterity of Cain*), 12, WP, 133; *Giants*, 12–15, WP, 152–53.

[35] Philo, *Creation*, 8, WP, 3.

wise man should seek to attain a state of *apatheia*—that is, he should be free of irrational emotions like desire and sorrow and possess instead rational ones like joy. Serenity will follow.

Philo's treatment of the serpent in Genesis 3 provides a good example of the kind of reading of Scripture that permits him to say such things about its meaning:

> [T]hese things are not mere fabulous inventions, in which the race of poets and sophists delights, but are rather types shadowing forth some allegorical truth, according to some mystical explanation. And anyone who follows a reasonable train of conjecture, will say with great propriety, that the aforesaid serpent is the symbol of pleasure, because in the first place he is destitute of feet, and crawls on his belly with his face downwards. In the second place, because he uses lumps of clay for food. Thirdly, because he bears poison in his teeth, by which it is his nature to kill those who are bitten by him. And the man devoted to pleasure is free from none of the aforementioned evils; for it is with difficulty that he can raise his head, being weighed down and dragged down, since intemperance trips him up and keeps him down. And he feeds, not on heavenly food, which wisdom offers to contemplative men by means of discourses and opinions; but on that which is put forth by the earth in the varying seasons of the year, from which arise drunkenness and voracity, and licentiousness. . . . Owing to which conduct, he too, carries about poison in his teeth, no less than the serpent does; for his teeth are the ministers and servants of his insatiability, cutting up and smoothing everything which has a reference to eating, and committing them, in the first place to the tongue, which decides upon, and distinguishes between the various flavours, and, subsequently, to the larynx. But immoderate indulgence in eating is naturally a poisonous and deadly habit.[36]

There is just a hint here of the same kind of cultured disdain that we encountered earlier in Heraclitus for the traditional text in its literal sense. Were Genesis 3 not to be read allegorically along Philo's lines, its various aspects would require to be regarded as "mere fabulous inventions" of the kind that delight "poets and sophists" (who are assuredly not well regarded). Read in the "correct" way, however, the passage functions as a warning to those who pursue the pleasures of the body rather than the "heavenly food" offered by wisdom to "contemplative men."

What are we to make of Philo's reading of Scripture? Evidently it departs in a serious manner from anything that could reasonably be described as the literal sense of the text. This is so not just at the level of the individual text (e.g., what Gen 3 has to say about the serpent), but at the level of the biblical literature as a whole. That is to say, it is not simply that Philo allegorizes this or that detail of Scripture, in line with and constrained by the canonical shape of the literature as

---

[36] Philo, *Creation*, 157–59, *WP*, 22.

a whole read in a broadly literal way. He allegorizes it almost in toto, in line with Greek philosophical and ethical norms. It is these norms, whether borrowed from Plato, or the Stoics, or whoever, that drive the entire enterprise. Philo radically reshapes Scripture in conformity with what is considered rational and virtuous by the Greeks. For example, it is not from his Scriptures that Philo derives the idea that the body is "an evil and dead thing"; it is from Plato. It is, likewise, from Plato and not from his Scriptures that Philo gets the ideas that human souls once descended into the material realm are designed to fly back to an immaterial realm, and that philosophical contemplation is the key that unlocks the prison door to allow the soul's escape. Philo's ethics, likewise, owe considerably more to Stoic than to biblical doctrine, not least in the centrality of *apatheia*. These ethics are in turn bound up with a view of God's impassibility that is impossible convincingly to ground in Scripture. It is fundamentally the Greeks whom Philo is reading in his "reading" of the Bible. It is not really Scripture at all, which represents merely an obstacle that must be overcome.

Philo, Paul, and Scripture

Is Philo doing anything remotely similar in his reading of Scripture to what the apostle Paul is doing in Galatian 4:21-31? A recent essay by Steven Di Mattei answers this question in the affirmative, as others have done in the past.[37] In this essay, Di Mattei rests much weight on the definitions of *allēgoria* from Tryphon and Heraclitus. "We need not construct or postulate other sources than these definitions, which were a part of Hellenistic rhetorical education," he asserts, "to properly understand Paul's methodology."[38] Paul speaks of a slave woman and a free woman, "but intends something other than what is said, two covenants."[39] In so doing, he differs not at all from Philo in the literary "move" that he makes. Providing a number of examples from Philo, Di Mattei claims that in all of them, "the allegorical principle is identical, and it is precisely this principle which properly defines these authors' allegories as allegory. Paul's allegory is no different; it also displays this same rhetorical this-for-that: Hagar and Sarah are allegorically two covenants."[40] In both Philo and the Stoics, Di Mattei acknowledges, "allegorical exegesis served as an apologetic tool which allowed the exegete to claim that the text under examination in its entirety was one big allegory containing hidden philosophical doctrines."[41] This is admittedly not what Paul is about, he concedes;

---

[37] Di Mattei, "Paul's Allegory," 105.
[38] Di Mattei, "Paul's Allegory," 106.
[39] Di Mattei, "Paul's Allegory," 106.
[40] Di Mattei, "Paul's Allegory," 108–9.
[41] Di Mattei, "Paul's Allegory," 105.

Paul's apologetic aims are quite different. Yet at the level of the rhetorical trope, "allegory in Philo... is exactly the same as allegory for Paul."[42]

This is a bold attempt to narrow the gap that is often perceived between Paul and Philo when it comes to exegetical method, but it is unconvincing. It is clearly in their essential approaches to the biblical text that they differ—in the context of radically different cosmologies, and hence epistemologies and anthropologies—and not merely in their apologetic aims. Di Mattei's own examples reveal the extent to which this is so. Philo's approach to the text does indeed assume that while the text "says one thing" it actually "signifies something other than what is said" (Heraclitus). For Philo (as for Heraclitus, in his reading of Homer), this "something other" does indeed typically have little or nothing to do with reading the text in question in its literary context. Thus Moses can be conceived of as *saying* "heaven, camp, and helper" but as *meaning* "intellect, body, and the faculty of sensation." "This" is entirely unconstrained by "that," which is merely a convenient starting point for philosophical speculation. This is very far from describing Paul's approach.

The extent to which Philo differs from Paul is especially clear in the former's various treatments of Sarah and Hagar. For example:

> When, therefore, you hear that Hagar was afflicted by Sarah, you must not suppose that any of those things befell her, which arise from rivalry and quarrels among women; for the question is not here about woman, but about minds; the one being practised in the branches of elementary instruction, and the other being devoted to the labours of virtue.[43]

In these Philonic treatments, Hagar represents the academic disciplines that certainly must be attended to while the soul is journeying onward toward wisdom and truth, but thereafter—after "the birth of Isaac" (i.e., the attainment of enlightenment)—can be dispensed with. Sarah represents "virtue," the wife of Abraham, who is "the mind."[44] Nothing in the OT story itself justifies such interpretative "moves." Nor is the OT story important in itself as these moves are being made. Sarah and Hagar, as characters in this story, are themselves unimportant.

How does Paul approach the story of Hagar and Sarah, on the other hand, in Galatians 4:21-31? This passage draws an analogy between what was true back in the time of the patriarchs and what is true in the present; it is not so much interested in correlating "this" and "that" as it is correlating "then" and "now." The temporal nature of the connection is particularly clear in Galatians 4:29, which speaks of what happened "at that time" ("the son born in the ordinary way

---

[42] Di Mattei, "Paul's Allegory," 108.
[43] Philo, *De congressu eruditionis gratia* (*On the Preliminary Studies*), 180, WP, 320.
[44] Philo, *Alleg. Interp.*, 3.244, WP, 78; *De cherubim* (*On the Cherubim*), 3–8, WP, 80.

persecuted the son born by the power of the Spirit") and what is happening now ("it is the same now"). "Now" is the moment when "these things are now being interpreted allegorically" (this is the precise sense that the Greek present passive participle appears to suggest).[45] It is not that for Paul the Genesis story is "really" about something other than the lives of Abraham's family members—the journey of the individual soul, perhaps, or even the present experience of the Galatian church. On the contrary, the Genesis story is about Abraham's family members, but it is *also* of relevance to the Galatians, because the two women who stand at the center of Paul's interest are each associated in Genesis with promises that God makes about offspring.[46] In Sarah's case this promise is explicitly connected in Genesis with the language of "covenant" through her marriage to Abraham (e.g., Gen 15:1-20). In Hagar's case it is not, but the language in which the promise is articulated certainly invites the reader to make that same connection.[47] It is quite in line with the Genesis story's own narrative shape, then, to say that these two women "represent two covenants" (Gal 4:24), and that these covenants concern sons—born, first, in the normal way (Ishmael), and second, in accordance with God's promise and miraculously (Isaac). The relevance of the Genesis story to the Galatian Christians is that "those who believe are children of Abraham [and Sarah]" (Gal 3:7), and such believers should not become confused about their identity as "children ... of [this] free woman" (Gal 4:31)—that is, "children of the promise" (Gal 4:28). Therefore, the Galatians are encouraged to act like Abraham their father in his response to Sarah's instruction to him to "get rid of the slave woman and her son" (Gen 21:10; Gal 4:30).

---

[45] Richard N. Longenecker, *Galatians* (WBC 41; Dallas: Word, 1990), 197–219.

[46] It is this that is so clearly perceived not only by Chrysostom, but also by Theodore and Theodoret, when they insist that Paul's use of Genesis here is typological rather than allegorical. "They do so, first, because they do not see Paul dismissing the history of the Genesis narrative. Second, they hold it to be typology, because Paul by theoretic exegesis perceived in the plotlines a significant comparison. One of the plotlines was that of Genesis 16 and 21. The other plotline ... was in the circumstances of the Galatians, who were undergoing mistreatment by the Judaizers." Richard J. Perhai, *Antiochene Theōria in the Writings of Theodore of Mopsuestia and Theodoret of Cyrus* (Minneapolis: Fortress, 2015), 429–30.

[47] Note, e.g., the parallel between Gen 15:5 ("Look up at the heavens and count the stars—if indeed you can count them ... so shall your offspring be") and Gen 16:10 ("I will so increase your descendants that they will be too numerous to count"), and between Gen 12:2 ("I will make you into a great nation") and Gen 17:20/21:18 ("I will make him into a great nation"). The parallels are noted by, among others, Gordon Wenham. E.g., "'I shall so greatly multiply your descendants' is a regular ingredient of the promises to the patriarchs.... Abram has been told his descendants will be too many to count ... and now Hagar learns that her offspring are included in that promise." And again: "as the son of Abraham, [Ishmael] is to enjoy the blessing of multiplication and fruitfulness.... Indeed, he will become 'a great nation' just as had originally been promised to Abraham." Gordon J. Wenham, *Genesis 16–50* (WBC 2; Dallas: Word, 1994), 10, 27.

In the course of reaching this injunction, Paul reinforces his strong distinction between the chosen line of Abraham and Sarah and all those who stand outside it with reference to OT passages that anticipate a New Jerusalem—specifically, to Isaiah 54:1 (Gal 4:27). This verse stands at the beginning of a section of Isaiah that responds to Jerusalem's complaint in Isaiah 49:14 (as a woman both "bereaved and barren," v. 21) that "the LORD has forsaken me, the Lord has forgotten me." Isaiah 54 envisages a time when this same woman will have many children. The Galatian Christians, says Paul, are the children of this New Jerusalem, just as they are also the children of Abraham and Sarah. Hagar, on the other hand, represents both Sinai and the old Jerusalem. These are the Jewish descendants of Abraham who do not accept the reality of the moment in biblical salvation history in which they find themselves—a moment in which many aspects of the Law have fulfilled their purpose and are no longer to be observed by God's people (Gal 3:25).

What is Paul doing here? He is doing nothing other than what he does everywhere else in his letters. He is reading the OT Scriptures that lie before him literally, allowing the larger context always to inform his reading of the particular text, which in this case leads him to bring together two OT ways of speaking about God's chosen people over against outsiders: they are the children of Abraham and Sarah and of Mother Zion. The Galatian Christians need to remember in which Story they find themselves, and of which family they are members—the family of Abraham and Sarah and not Hagar, and the inhabitants of the New Jerusalem and not the old. Paul is reading literally; he is indeed reading "typologically" and "figuratively," in terms of the understanding of those terms that I articulated in chapter 4. He is engaging (in Frei's words, cited in that chapter) in "literalism at the level of the whole biblical story," interpreting the OT texts as "a common narrative referring to a single history and its pattern of meaning," without detriment to the "literal meaning or specific temporal reference" of an earlier biblical text, even as it functions analogically in respect of a later reality.

The Translation of Galatians 4:24

Is Paul doing anything remotely similar to Philo, then, in his Bible reading? In spite of Di Mattei's assertions to the contrary, he is not—not even at a methodological level underneath the apologetic one. How is it best, then, to render *allēgoreō* in Galatians 4:24?

It is interesting that, even among scholars who are quick to distinguish Paul's approach from both Philo's and that of later (especially Alexandrian) writers, there is an evident desire to retain the term "allegory" for at least some of what Paul is doing in Galatians 4. Walter Hansen, for example, understands very clearly that "Paul . . . is not using the text [here] as Philo did." Philo saw the Old Testament as primarily a book of symbols that have hidden meaning beyond the literal, historical sense. His allegorical interpretation of these symbols was guided not by the constraints of the text but by his desire to demonstrate that the Jewish Scriptures contained the essence of Greek philosophy.[48]

Yet Hansen insists on seeing allegorical method at work at least in the apostle's treatment of Hagar, Mount Sinai, and Jerusalem. Richard Longenecker, similarly, tells us that Paul's approach differs markedly from Philo's, and indeed (later) from Origen's.[49] He cites a passage from Richard Hanson in this regard, which in the original runs as follows:

> Paul is not here trying to emancipate the meaning of the passage from its historical content and transmute it into a moral sentiment or a philosophical truth, which is the almost invariable function of Alexandrian allegory.... He is envisaging [rather] a critical situation which took place under the Old Covenant (or, to be strictly accurate, before it but in prefiguration of it) as forecasting and repeated by a situation under the New Covenant.[50]

Yet at the same time, Longenecker cites with approval Hanson's comment that Paul's treatment of the Hagar-Sarah story "is explicitly and undisguisedly allegorical."[51]

How are we to explain this commitment to the language of "allegorizing" in the midst of all these caveats (and indeed contradictions)? To some extent it seems to arise from a desire not "to undermine what Paul actually wrote" (as Di Mattei puts it)—to retain the actual apostolic language.[52] If so, it is surprising to find such a commitment at work among interpreters (and indeed translators) who are well versed in the realities of working with foreign languages, and who would normally embrace without question the imperative to pay attention not only to what an author *says*, but to what he *means* by it. After all, what matters in this discussion is not what Philo certainly means by *allēgoreō/allēgoria* in writing for an educated Hellenistic readership at large in the Roman Empire during the early first century AD—nor indeed how other Alexandrian sources define this term numerous decades after Philo's (and Paul's) death. What matters is what *Paul* means by the term in Galatians 4, on the single occasion of its use in the NT literature, as he writes in the middle of the first century to some of the Christians in Asia Minor. The evidence suggests that he means something quite different

---

[48] G. Walter Hansen, *Galatians* (IVPNTC; Downers Grove, Ill.: InterVarsity, 1994), 142–43.
[49] Longenecker, *Galatians*, 209.
[50] Hanson, *Allegory and Event*, 82.
[51] Longenecker, *Galatians*, 209, citing Hanson, *Allegory and Event*, 80.
[52] Di Mattei, "Paul's Allegory," 103.

from "the Alexandrians," as they are sometimes in shorthand (and somewhat misleadingly) described.⁵³

Connected with this puzzling "stick to the words on the page" approach to Galatians 4—"let us retain 'allegory,' even though Paul means by it something very different from Philo"—is apparently a belief that Paul is indebted in Galatians 4 to another kind of allegorical reading tradition. Hanson refers to this as "allegory in a Palestinian rather than an Alexandrian tradition,"⁵⁴ and others describe it simply as "rabbinic" tradition. Given this "debt," some consider it appropriate (it seems) to name what is happening in Galatians 4 as "allegorizing," even though this has nothing to do with how Philo is reading Scripture in Alexandria. In response, I certainly recognize that the rabbinic interpretation of Scripture as it emerged in the first half of the second century AD embraced two broad approaches that had roots already in the preceding centuries—those of Rabbis Akiva and Ishmael—and that the latter was more closely associated with a literal approach to the text than the former. Whether it helps at all with our comprehension of the products of Akiva's approach to describe them as "allegory" is, however, open to question. Both Longenecker and Hanson stress, in using this terminology, just how *different* is this "Palestinian" tradition from the "Alexandrian" one. How does it promote clarity, then, to use the same term for both—even leaving aside the question about how far Paul's approach owes something to rabbinic reading method (which takes us back to near the beginning of chapter 5)?

I propose that, in all the circumstances, using the language of "allegory" in Galatians 4 is unhelpful. Those who have translated *allēgoreō* using other words, then, have been right to do so, in line with Louw and Nida's full definition in their lexicon of the semantic range of this verb: "to employ an analogy or likeness in communicating—to speak allegorically, 'to employ an analogy, to use a likeness.'"⁵⁵ I can imagine a world in which "allegorical interpretation" had not predominantly come to mean "the kind of interpretation engaged in by Philo and the later Christians influenced by him." In such a world it might be possible, without confusion inevitably arising about what Paul meant, to render *allēgoreō* in Galatians 4

---

⁵³ The problem with this term (or related terms, like "Alexandrian school"), as applied to Philo, Clement, Origen, and those who followed their general hermeneutical example, is that it tends to disguise the reality, first, that not all Jews or Christians in Alexandria in their time periods agreed with their approach and, second, that there were significant differences among those who did, even in the midst of marked similarity. Siegert, "Early Jewish Interpretation," 189–98; J. N. B. Carleton Paget, "The Christian Exegesis of the Old Testament in the Alexandrian Tradition," HBOT 1/1:478–542 (482–84).

⁵⁴ Hanson, *Allegory and Event*, 83.

⁵⁵ Johannes P. Louw and Eugene A. Nida, eds., *Greek-English Lexicon of the New Testament: Based on Semantic Domains* (2nd ed., 2 vols.; New York: United Bible Societies, 1989), 1:391.

using the English verb "allegorize." In the real world, however (as Di Mattei says), "[w]hen we think of allegory, we quite naturally envision the brand of allegory practiced by Philo and the Stoics."[56] In this real world, confusion *inevitably* arises when "allegory" is used for what Paul is doing in Galatians 4. The confusion is indeed rife, and of great posterity.

CONCLUSION

Neither Paul nor any of the other NT writers read OT Scripture remotely in the manner of Philo of Alexandria. They read it predominantly literally—entirely so, if the "six cases" discussed earlier in this chapter truly represent the best potential counter-examples. That is to say, all the NT writers are attentive to the apparent communicative intentions of Scripture as a document from the past, taking full account of the nature of the language in which these intentions are embedded and revealed as components of Scripture's unfolding covenantal Story. Writers like Philo built "their edifices of exegesis and scriptural allegory," upon the "ancient foundation of esoteric reading" that was already popular among the Greeks, developing "a hermeneutic aimed at the transcendent truths which are concealed in language."[57] The apostles, on the other hand, were not interested in truth that is *concealed* in OT language, but in truth that is *revealed* there. They did not regard the spiritual sense of the OT text as being located somewhere other than in its literal sense. They regarded the one sense as intrinsically connected to the other.

In all of this, the apostles were (unsurprisingly) following the lead of Jesus himself, as illustrated in passages like Luke 24:13-35. Here it is evident that Jesus' postresurrection words to the two disciples are *not*, "I can now tell you what the prophets really meant, underneath the veil of their ordinary language, which you were quite understandably unable to penetrate by yourselves." What he says, instead, is—as we have seen—"how foolish you are, and how slow of heart to believe all that the prophets have spoken!" They should have known. The meaning of the prophetic words was not difficult to discern. We shall return to this theme, and other sayings of Jesus and the apostles that pertain to it, in chapter 12.

---

[56] Di Mattei, "Paul's Allegory," 105.
[57] Copeland and Struck, *Allegory*, 3.

7

Justin, Irenaeus, and Tertullian
False Economies and Hidden Treasure

> *There existed, long before this time, certain men more ancient than all those who are esteemed philosophers. . . . They are called prophets. These alone both saw and announced the truth to men . . . being filled with the Holy Spirit.*
>
> —Justin Martyr[1]

> *What . . . has Athens to do with Jerusalem? . . . Our instruction comes from the "porch of Solomon," who had himself taught that "the Lord should be sought in simplicity of heart." Away with all attempts to produce a mottled Christianity of Stoic, Platonic, and dialectic composition! . . . With our faith, we desire no further belief.*
>
> —Tertullian[2]

In case any of my readers has become lost among the many trees of the argument in chapters 4 through 6 about the NT reading of Scripture, and has forgotten the purpose of exploring the forest, let me summarize where things stand. We are in the midst of a discussion of the question of authority. The Church Fathers, as we saw in chapter 4, understood themselves to be following the apostles in the way that they approached biblical interpretation. The question is, were they justified in this appeal to apostolic authority? This question is, in turn, one of a larger set concerning whether the Protestant Reformers were justified in their own approach to biblical interpretation (and in their criticism of the Fathers), and whether contemporary Christians should still read the Bible "literally," as the Reformers proposed.

Having discussed in chapters 5 and 6 how Jesus and the apostles read Scripture, in the next three chapters we shall, first of all, compare this with patristic interpretative practice, on the way, second, to addressing the larger set of questions about Reformation reading that I have just described. It is not my intention

---

[1] Justin, *Dialogue*, 7 (ANF 1:198).
[2] Tertullian, *Prescription*, 7 (ANF 3:246).

in pursuing the first goal to offer an exhaustive account of patristic exegesis throughout the first few centuries of the life of the Christian Church; that would obviously be impossible within the confines of this particular book. I shall restrict myself, as in the earlier discussion of the NT's reading of the OT, only to a number of exemplary cases: Justin Martyr, Irenaeus, and Tertullian (in chapter 7), and Origen, Theodore of Mopsuestia (c. AD 350–428), and Augustine (in chapter 8). Even in these cases, I shall focus on particular works, and not on each writer's entire corpus. My argument in these chapters will be that the Church Fathers were only partially justified in their appeal to apostolic authority with respect to their own biblical hermeneutics, that the Reformers were right to criticize them for at least some aspects of their approach to biblical interpretation and to insist that the Bible should be read literally, and that contemporary Christians should still strive to read Scripture in this way—albeit that our contemporary understanding of what this involves may differ from that of the Reformers.

JUSTIN MARTYR

Justin Martyr was born in Palestine around the beginning of the second century AD. His three surviving works date from the middle of that century: a *First Apology* (i.e., apologetic writing) addressed to Romans elites, including the emperor Antoninus Pius (AD 138–161); a *Second Apology* addressed to the Roman Senate; and a *Dialogue* with a Jewish man named Trypho.[3] Originally a convinced Platonist, with a history behind him of studies in Stoicism, Aristotelianism, and Pythagoreanism, Justin was nevertheless converted to Christian faith through an encounter with a man who spoke to him about the OT as ancient prophecy. It was as texts from the distant past that speak of events in their future, then, that Justin first encountered the OT Scriptures, and this reality dominated his thinking and writing from that moment onward—particularly as these Scriptures (he believed) predicted Christ and the realities of the Christian era (see the first epigraph to the present chapter).[4]

Justin and the Literal Sense

As he reads the OT Scriptures from this point of view, Justin displays a notable interest in the literal sense of the text. In *First Apology* 32, for example, he quotes

---

[3] For a brief introduction to the writings of Justin, Irenaeus, and Tertullian, see Richard A. Norris Jr., "The Apologists" and "Irenaeus," in Young, Ayres, and Louth, *Early Christian Literature*, 36–44, 45–52; also Ronald E. Heine, "The Beginnings of Latin Christian Literature," in Young, Ayres, and Louth, *Early Christian Literature*, 131–41.

[4] Justin, *Apologia I* (*First Apology*), 31 (*ANF* 1:173). For a detailed but nevertheless brief account of Justin's approach to the OT, see Oskar Skarsaune, "Scriptural Interpretation in the Second and Third Centuries," *HBOT* 1/1:373–442 (389–410).

Genesis 49:10 as promising a future Davidic king, whom he understands to be Christ: "The scepter shall not depart from Judah, nor a lawgiver from between his feet, until He comes for whom it is reserved."[5] In *First Apology* 34, he cites Micah 5:2 as a prophecy about where this Davidic ruler will be born: "And thou, Bethlehem, the land of Judah, are not the least among the princes of Judah; for out of thee shall come forth a Governor, who shall feed My people."[6] In *First Apology* 39, Justin correlates Isaiah 2:3 ("[f]or out of Zion shall go forth the law ... nation shall not lift up sword against nation, neither shall they learn war any more") with the events after Pentecost, when

> from Jerusalem there went out into the world, men, twelve in number, and these illiterate, of no ability in speaking: but by the power of God they proclaimed to every race of men that they were sent by Christ to teach to all the word of God; and we who formerly used to murder one another do not only now refrain from making war upon our enemies, but also, that we may not lie nor deceive our examiners, willingly die confessing Christ.[7]

In many similar cases Justin also reads the OT texts with careful attention to their apparent communicative intent in their contexts. Even when his particular readings fail to convince, the extent of his interest in reading them literally is nevertheless plain to see. We may note, for example, the precise attention given in *First Apology* 35 to the wording of a translation of Isaiah 9:6 known to Justin, which reads, "Unto us a child is born, and unto us a young man is given."[8] He deploys this verse in support of the contention that Christ's true identity was concealed from others until he was an adult—an argument unlikely to be persuasive to the modern reader who understands how parallelism in Hebrew poetry works, with both parts of the line typically referring to the same reality. Then again, in *First Apology* 33, reflecting on Isaiah 7:14, Justin states that

> Isaiah in express words foretold that [Christ] should be born of a virgin; ... For things which were incredible and seemed impossible with men, these God predicted by the Spirit of prophecy as about to come to pass.... "Behold, a virgin shall conceive," signifies that a virgin should conceive without intercourse. For if she had had intercourse with any one whatever, she was no longer a virgin; but the power of God having come upon the virgin, overshadowed her, and caused her while yet a virgin to conceive.[9]

---

[5] Justin, *First Apology*, 32 (ANF 1:173). The translation in this case, interestingly, does not come (as it typically does) from the LXX.
[6] Justin, *First Apology*, 34 (ANF 1:174).
[7] Justin, *First Apology*, 39 (ANF 1:175–76).
[8] Justin, *First Apology*, 35 (ANF 1:174).
[9] Justin, *First Apology*, 33 (1:174).

This argument is not very convincing. Even if the LXX's interpretation of the Hebrew *'almāh* as "virgin" (rather than simply "young woman") is correct[10]—and it is the LXX that Justin is reading—it does not necessarily follow (in terms of grammar and syntax) that someone who is now, at the time of the original prophecy, a virgin, will still be a virgin later, at the point of conception. However, it is not the quality of Justin's argument that is important here, but its nature: it is an argument grounded very precisely in the words of the text in their (perceived) literal sense. Moreover, it is important to notice the general direction that Justin takes when challenged in his reading of this verse by his Jewish counterpart Trypho in *Dialogue* 67:

> And Trypho answered, "The Scripture has not, 'Behold, the virgin shall conceive, and bear a son,' but, 'Behold, the young woman shall conceive, and bear a son,' and so on, as you quoted. But the whole prophecy refers to Hezekiah, and it is proved that it was fulfilled in him, according to the terms of this prophecy."[11]

We shall return later to some of the detail in Justin's long response to Trypho at this point in the *Dialogue*, in the course of which he introduces other OT texts that he considers relevant to the general case he is attempting to make about Christ fulfilling the OT Scriptures and also discusses other matters at issue between the two men. At the moment it is important only to notice *how* Justin responds. His overall response is not, "well, literally, you are correct, but at a spiritual level Isaiah 7:14 says something else." It is, instead: "I shall show that this prophecy of Isaiah refers to our Christ, and not to Hezekiah."[12] The demonstration itself contains arguments of dubious quality, but that is beside the point at present. What matters is that Justin considers it important to establish, with rational argument, that the literal sense of Isaiah 7:14 is as he claims it to be, and not otherwise.

Justin and All-Consuming Prophecy

Justin shares with the apostles themselves this general conviction that the OT read literally speaks in various ways about Christ—that it means to refer to him. Indeed, Justin follows the apostolic example closely when it comes to *where*, in the main, to look for Christ: "[e]specially the book of Isaiah and the Psalms offered the most scriptural proofs for him."[13] At the same time, he goes significantly *further* than the apostles in pursuing this prophetic theme. Writing about *First Apology*, 30–60, in particular, Henning Reventlow observes that

---

[10] See my chapter 4 above.
[11] Justin, *Dialogue*, 67 (ANF 1:231).
[12] Justin, *Dialogue*, 68 (ANF 1:232).
[13] Reventlow, *Biblical Interpretation*, 1:146.

long before Justin Christians had read certain statements of the Old Testament as predictions of Christ. In their center are passages that already had been understood as messianic prophecies in Jewish exegesis.... Nowhere [in the NT], however, [do we encounter] the argument from prophecy that is made with the same frequency that it occurs in this section of Justin's 1 Apology.[14]

George Gilbert, along similar lines, speaks of the "germs" of Justin's approach being found already in the NT, but he notes that Justin "emphasized [the OT's predictive element] and established it as a principle of interpretation." It was axiomatic for Justin that "the work of God—that which most clearly reveals his activity—is to tell of a thing before it happens, and his greatest interest in the Old Testament was to find in it predictions of Christ. These he discovered everywhere."[15] In other words, where the NT writers are restrained in looking for Christ in the OT, and attentive to context in doing so, Justin is much less restrained.

In this he continues a trend already markedly present in the slightly earlier *Barnabas*, which "regards the entire Old Testament as prophecy."[16] In pursuing this theme, *Barnabas* is already prone to move away in its OT reading from what could reasonably be described as the literal sense of the text. It is one thing to propose, for example, that the promise of Micah 5:2 regarding the birthplace of a future ruler refers to Christ, or even that he is the Davidic king anticipated by the book of Psalms. It is quite another to characterize as a "type" of Christ (as *Barnabas* does) Moses' stretching out his arms during a battle described in the book of Exodus,[17] or to claim that the numbers of Abraham's servants in Genesis 14:14 and 17:23 represent advance "knowledge given unto [Moses]" of the name "Jesus" and of the crucifixion.[18] The NT writers select "large sections of the Old Testament scriptures, especially from Isaiah, Jeremiah and certain minor prophets, and from the Psalms," and quote "particular verses or sentences from them rather as pointers to the whole context than as constituting testimonies in and for themselves."[19] The kind of exegesis just described in *Barnabas*, on the other hand, all but makes the OT into a series of disconnected examples of "pious

---

[14] Reventlow, *Biblical Interpretation*, 1:137.

[15] George H. Gilbert, "Interpretation of the Bible by the Fathers," *BW* 38 (1911): 151–58 (152).

[16] Reventlow, *Biblical Interpretation*, 1:121.

[17] Exod 17:8-13; *Barn.* 12:2 (*ANF* 1:144–45).

[18] *Barn.* 9:8 (*ANF* 1:142–43).

[19] Charles H. Dodd, *According to the Scriptures: The Sub-structure of New Testament Theology* (Welwyn: James Nisbet, 1952), 126–27. Dodd is later ably defended against criticism by I. Howard Marshall, "An Assessment of Recent Developments," in *It Is Written: Scripture Citing Scripture. Essays in Honour of Barnabas Lindars SSF* (ed. Don A. Carson and H. G. M. Williamson; Cambridge: Cambridge University Press, 1988), 1–21. For some of the detail concerning Justin's expansion (in relation to apostolic practice) of the number of OT "proof-texts," see Skarsaune, "Scriptural Interpretation," 389–410.

fortune-telling."²⁰ Justin, similarly, is so intent on finding the OT to be prophetic of Christ and of the realities of the Christian era that he, too, often proposes readings that display significant inattention to the question of what the OT writers meant to say.

Having begun in the fortieth chapter of his *Dialogue*, for example, by making a well-grounded typological connection between the paschal lamb and Christ in terms of blood sacrifice, Justin proceeds much less plausibly to associate the two goats of Leviticus 16 with the two comings of Christ. There is nothing in the Leviticus passage concerning how these two animals function within ancient Israel's ritual system that even remotely invites this analogy.²¹ In similar vein, the twelve bells attached to the robe of the high priest in Exodus 28:4 are said to symbolize the twelve apostles, "who depend on the power of Christ, the eternal Priest," and the red rope of Rahab in Joshua 2 is taken as a symbol of the blood of Christ by which all are redeemed.²²

In the midst of his argument with Trypho about the literal sense of Isaiah 7:14, moreover—where Justin claims with justification that it cannot be said of Hezekiah "that before he knew how to call father or mother, he received the power of Damascus and the spoils of Samaria"²³ and that Trypho "cannot prove that such a thing ever happened to any one among the Jews"²⁴—Justin develops a reading of Isaiah 8:4 that moves well away from its literal sense. Wishing to argue that the story of the infant Christ and the Magi who worshipped him fits the Isaianic prophecy much better than the story of Hezekiah, he proposes that King Herod is found in the Isaiah passage under the title of "king of Assyria on account of his ungodly and sinful character." He offers equally creative interpretations of both "Damascus" and "Samaria" in the same verse.²⁵

What is it that allows or even encourages Justin in such instances to depart so far from a literal and contextual reading? It is his conviction not only that the OT Scriptures foretell Christ, but in fact that Christ is widely (perhaps even *everywhere*) foretold in the OT. Indeed, one *must* find him foretold all across these Scriptures, even if it means positing (without any substantive justification in the OT text in context) that the text contains what Justin calls "parables and similitudes" that conceal Christ's presence there. Prophecy here becomes a kind of thematic, theological "Pac-Man" from the old computer game, where a hungry pursuer tries to gobble up everything else around him, and the game player

---

²⁰ Dodd, *According to the Scriptures*, 127.
²¹ Justin, *Dialogue*, 40 (ANF 1:214–15).
²² Justin, *Dialogue*, 42, 111 (ANF 1:215, 254).
²³ Cf. Isa 8:4, understanding "the child" as the same one as in Isa 7:14.
²⁴ Justin, *Dialogue*, 77 (ANF 1:237).
²⁵ Justin, *Dialogue*, 77–78 (ANF 1:237–38).

must try to escape his clutches. In just such a way, prophecy in Justin becomes an all-consuming reality with respect to explaining the relationship between the OT and the NT, threatening to displace all others possibilities. His error here, as Bertrand de Margerie puts it, is "the exaggeration of a truth, anticipating a tendency later characteristic of the Alexandrian school. That the Word is speaking throughout the Bible does not mean that he is speaking at every moment of himself."[26]

The Voice of the Author and the Voice of God

It is "parables and similitudes" of the kind just described, for example, that Justin explicitly invokes in his reading of Assyria, Damascus, and Samaria in Isaiah 8:4. For Justin, these are realities placed in the text, not by its human author, but rather by the Holy Spirit, who "oftentimes announces" future events by such means.[27] The Holy Spirit can also speak of future events even when the biblical text is written in the past tense. The "Divine Word" who inspires the OT authors only "sometimes ... declares things that are to come to pass, in the manner of one who foretells the future."[28] He can also describe

> things that are about to come to pass as if they had already taken place.... The things which He absolutely knows will take place, He predicts as if already they had taken place. And that the utterances must be thus received, you will perceive, if you give your attention to them.[29]

The immediate occasion of these words is Justin's reading of Psalm 96 as a "prophecy ... [that] intimated that Christ, after He had been crucified, should reign."[30] It is not sufficient for Justin, it seems, to make a broad connection within the context of the whole book of Psalms (and then within the context of the whole biblical Story) between a psalm in which the reign of God is announced as a present reality, and the reign of Christ that he later takes up after his ascension. No, there must be an explicit prophetic connection between the individual psalm and Christ—the psalm directly speaks of the future Christ—even if this means ignoring the grammar and syntax of the psalm.

A significant gap begins to open up in Justin's thinking, then, between what God is saying in a biblical text and what any human author could be conceived of as saying. Here, too, Justin anticipates later Alexandrian authors like Clement

---

[26] Bertrand de Margerie, S.J., *An Introduction to the History of Exegesis, Volume 1: The Greek Fathers* (trans. Leonard Maluf; Petersham, Mass.: St. Bede's Publications, 1993), 44.
[27] Justin, *Dialogue*, 77 (ANF 1:237).
[28] Justin, *First Apology*, 36 (ANF 1:175).
[29] Justin, *First Apology*, 42 (ANF 1:176–77).
[30] Justin, *First Apology*, 41 (ANF 1:176).

and Origen, for the latter of whom "the intent of scripture lay not at the level of the literary author but at the level of the inspiring Spirit."[31] Such a gap is not implied in apostolic Scripture reading practice, even though the apostles also acknowledge that "in the past God spoke to our forefathers through the prophets at many times and in various ways" and "prophecy never had its origin in the will of man, but men spoke from God as they were carried along by the Holy Spirit" (Heb 1:1; 2 Pet 1:21). In Justin's conception of the inspiration of Scripture, however, "the human agent in the production of the sacred writings [possesses] only a mechanical value." The soul of the prophet is no more than "a lyre which is struck by the *plectrum* of the Spirit."[32]

Justin, Prophecy, and Marcion

It is not improbable that Justin, in his determination to read the OT in such a thoroughgoing manner as "prophetic" of Christ, was already partly driven by the activities of a man whom he twice mentions in his *First Apology*, Marcion of Sinope—whom he accuses of "teaching men to deny that God is the maker of all things in heaven and on earth, and that the Christ predicted by the prophets is His Son, and preaches another god besides the Creator of all, and likewise another son."[33] Among his many faults, Marcion apparently had a tendency toward literalistic, wooden reading—which is all too often referred to in our modern secondary literature, unfortunately, as "literal" reading.[34] (On the importance of not confusing the two, see my chapter 4.) Marcion deployed this manner of reading heavily in pursuit of his "big idea," that the God of the OT (the creator God) has nothing in common with the God of the NT (the savior God), and that law has nothing to do with gospel. The OT cannot be Christian Scripture, in fact, "because the law of the Creator God . . . is morally inferior, foolish, and absurd."[35] For Marcion, the prophets speak on behalf of this deficient Creator God, and therefore not about Christ; in fact, they predict another Messiah altogether—one who is yet to come in the last days. With respect to the Isaiah prophecies, for example, Marcion's position (according to Tertullian) was, first, that Christ was not in fact named "Emmanuel" (Isa 7:14), and second, that Christ never "engaged in any warlike enterprise" (of the kind envisaged in Isa 8:4).[36] We shall return to Tertullian's response to Marcion on these points presently.

---

[31] Young, *Biblical Exegesis*, 184.
[32] Gilbert, "Interpretation," 151–52.
[33] Justin, *First Apology*, 58 (ANF 1:182).
[34] E.g., Reventlow, *Biblical Interpretation*, 1:152.
[35] Reventlow, *Biblical Interpretation*, 1:151.
[36] Tertullian, *Against Marcion*, 3.12 (ANF 3:331).

For the moment let it simply be noted that Marcion's attack on the prophetic connection between the OT and the NT provides us with one backdrop (aside from Jewish-Christian dialogue, and apologetics in respect of the empire) against which to understand Justin's robust development of his prophecy-fulfillment schema. At the same time, Marcion's proposal that particular verses like Isaiah 8:4 provide strong evidence for his own position helps to explain why an apologist like Justin might try so carefully to connect this verse with Christ, even though the attempt forces him to such a strained reading of the text. The deep connection between God's dealings with the people of God in the OT and his dealings with his people now (i.e., in Justin's time) must at all costs be maintained, lest the very character of the Christian faith be altered.

The danger that is front and center here is that "Christianity would no longer be understood in the sense of the fulfillment of the Old Testament ... so it would lose its roots in history and become an ancient mystery religion."[37] The danger that is perhaps not so clearly identified is that—in the pursuit of a simplistic, atomistic prophecy-fulfillment schema—the true and complex nature not only of the relationship between the two testaments that make up the Christian Bible, but also of the OT itself, might be obscured. There is, after all, no good reason to believe, on the basis of the teaching of Jesus and his apostles in the NT, that Christ is everywhere foretold in the OT. The attempt to impose such an idea on the OT regardless can only do violence to the texts that resist this imposition, and can indeed only discredit the more modest (and credible) claim that Christ is foretold in *some* of the OT texts. This second danger was already clearly understood by some of those writing in the patristic period:

> Those who wish to apply the Old Testament in its entirety to Christ are far from correct. In doing so, they provide arguments to the pagans and heretics who reject this principle. They do violence to the texts in attempting to extract from them a Christological sense they do not have, and in so doing they end up throwing into discredit the texts that speak quite clearly of Christ. There is a truth that seems evident to me: if the Old Testament does not always speak of Christ, it does at least sometimes refer to him.[38]

IRENAEUS

Irenaeus, who grew up in Asia Minor in a Christian family and later became bishop of Lyons in Roman Gaul, took the same view as Justin with respect to these "deep connections" between God's dealings with people in the OT and

---

[37] Reventlow, *Biblical Interpretation*, 1:153.
[38] The early fifth-century Isidore of Pelusium, *Letter* 195, cited in de Margerie, *Introduction*, 110.

the NT. In the decades following Justin's martyrdom, in fact, and in the face of ongoing attempts to undermine both the connections and some vital Christian truths bound up with them, Irenaeus found it necessary to write extensively as their advocate. His opponents were exactly those proponents of Christianity as "an ancient mystery religion" alluded to just moment ago; as we saw in chapter 2, they are usually referred to collectively as "Gnostics." Gnosticism "accommodated widespread ideas of Hellenistic late antiquity,"[39] and it was highly derivative in particular of Platonic thought.[40] Its proponents, however—like Marcion before them, whom some would also describe as a Gnostic—self-identified as Christians. Like him, the Gnostics appealed for their authority to the NT, and especially to the letters of Paul, who in the end "alone knew the truth . . . to him the mystery was manifested by revelation."[41] In *Against Heresies*, therefore, Irenaeus is especially concerned to demonstrate the many ways in which the NT literature is in fact inseparable from the OT literature, and in particular to defend the unity of God as revealed in the whole of Scripture. Like Justin, this involves among other things "the traditional Christian 'proof from prophecy' [which] had to be repeated and strengthened in debate with Marcion."[42]

The Unity of God and the Unity of Scripture

Marcion and the Gnostics claimed that the God of the OT could not possibly be identified with the God of the NT; these were different divinities. Irenaeus strongly affirms, on the other hand, that there is one God who is the creator of all, one Son of God who became the incarnation of the divine Word, and one Scripture that testifies to all of this:

> neither the prophets, nor the apostles, nor the Lord Christ in His own person, did acknowledge any other Lord or God, but the God and Lord supreme: the prophets and the apostles confessing the Father and the Son; but naming no other as God, and confessing no other as Lord: and the Lord Himself handing down to His disciples, that He, the Father, is the only God and Lord, who alone is God and ruler of all;—it is incumbent on us to follow, if we are their disciples indeed, their testimonies to this effect.[43]

---

[39] Reventlow, *Biblical Interpretation*, 1:155.

[40] For some further information about Platonism and Gnosticism in relation to biblical faith, see Iain Provan, *Seriously Dangerous Religion* (Waco, Tex.: Baylor University Press, 2014), 125–26, 242–44, 153–55.

[41] Irenaeus, *Against Heresies*, 3.13.1 (ANF 1:436).

[42] Skarsaune, "Scriptural Interpretation," 377; and, further on Irenaeus' approach to the OT, 422–29.

[43] Irenaeus, *Against Heresies*, 3.9.1 (ANF 1:422).

This is the simple truth of the matter, and there is no "hidden truth" waiting to be discovered underneath it:

> For if the apostles had known hidden mysteries, which they were in the habit of imparting to "the perfect" apart and privily from the rest, they would have delivered them especially to those to whom they were also committing the Churches themselves.[44]

This the apostles have not done. Paul himself spoke the same truth as the other apostles, and "taught with simplicity what he knew."[45] Had he possessed other, hidden truth, his companion Luke would surely have known about it, and "if Luke ... learned nothing different from him ... how can these men [Irenaeus' opponents], who were never attached to Paul, boast that they have learned hidden and unspeakable mysteries?"[46] The problem with the heretics is that they consider themselves "wiser not merely than the presbyters, but even than the apostles"—"purer [in doctrine], and more intelligent"—and as alone being able to discern "the hidden mystery" that lies concealed in Scripture.[47] Believing so, they are beyond correction, because when

> they are confuted from the Scriptures, they turn round and accuse these same Scriptures, as if they were not correct, nor of authority, and [assert] that they are ambiguous, and that the truth cannot be extracted from them by those who are ignorant of tradition.[48]

In pursuit of their own interpretation, the heretics apparently also allege that the apostles allegorize in the statements they make about God, and even propose that Jesus' words do not necessarily come from God.[49]

For Irenaeus, the Scriptures are not in the least ambiguous in what they teach, and it would be folly to turn away from them and listen instead to those who speak nonsense: "For what sort of conduct would it be, were we to forsake the utterances of the prophets, of the Lord, and of the apostles, that we might give heed to these persons, who speak not a word of sense?"[50] There are many truths communicated "clearly and unambiguously in express terms ... in the Sacred Scriptures,"[51] and indeed "the entire Scriptures, the prophets, and the Gospels, can be clearly, unambiguously, and harmoniously understood by all, although all

---

[44] Irenaeus, *Against Heresies*, 3.3.1 (ANF 1:415).
[45] Irenaeus, *Against Heresies*, 3.14.2 (ANF 1:438).
[46] Irenaeus, *Against Heresies*, 3.14.1 (ANF 1:438).
[47] Irenaeus, *Against Heresies*, 3.2.2; 3.12.12 (ANF 1:415, 434).
[48] Irenaeus, *Against Heresies*, 3.2.1 (ANF 1:415).
[49] Irenaeus, *Against Heresies*, 3.2.2; 3.12.11 (ANF 1:415, 434).
[50] Irenaeus, *Against Heresies*, 2.2.5 (ANF 1:362).
[51] Irenaeus, *Against Heresies*, 2.27.1 (ANF 1:398).

do not believe them."⁵² The crucial thing is to read individual biblical texts in context. We have already encountered in chapter 2 examples of what this meant for Irenaeus, as we considered his understanding of "the rule of truth." To read contextually is in fact to read Scripture no differently from any other book, since in that other reading, too, comprehension arises from first identifying the book's "hypothesis"—"the gist of a literary work"—and its "economy"—the "structure or plot that allows us to discern the flow of the narrative."⁵³ It is particularly important, then—on Irenaeus' understanding of things—to place the small number of unclear statements in Scripture within the larger scriptural context, seeking to understand them in line with "those statements the meaning of which is clear," in the confidence that "all Scripture, which has been given to us by God ... [is] perfectly consistent."⁵⁴ If we cannot understand unclear statements even then,

> yet let us not on that account seek after any other God besides Him who really exists. For this is the very greatest impiety. We should leave things of that nature to God who created us, being most properly assured that the Scriptures are indeed perfect, since they were spoken by the Word of God and His Spirit; but we, inasmuch as we are inferior to, and later in existence than, the Word of God and His Spirit, are on that very account destitute of the knowledge of His mysteries.⁵⁵

It is this whole scriptural story in its given, perfect, and perspicuous state—the Great Story that "can be clearly, unambiguously, and harmoniously understood by all"—that Irenaeus refers to as the "rule of truth," by which right reading of the various parts of Scripture is to be measured.⁵⁶

Irenaeus and Literal History

How exactly does Irenaeus conceive of this Great Story? What is his view of its "hypothesis" and its "economy"? He thinks of it as a history of salvation. Taking his lead from the apostle Paul in Romans 5, he understands human history, as exemplified by the history of Israel, to have been on the wrong track ever since the

---

⁵² Irenaeus, *Against Heresies*, 2.27.2 (*ANF* 1:398).
⁵³ O'Keefe and Reno, *Sanctified Vision*, 34, 37.
⁵⁴ Irenaeus, *Against Heresies*, 2.28.3 (*ANF* 1:400).
⁵⁵ Irenaeus, *Against Heresies*, 2.28.2 (*ANF* 1:399).
⁵⁶ Irenaeus, *Against Heresies*, 2.27.1; 3.12.6 (*ANF* 1:398, 432). So also Tertullian, *Against Marcion*, 1.21 (*ANF* 3:286), with its claims that in apostolic teaching ("the rule of sacred truth") there has never been any "other God ... than the Creator"; 4.5 (*ANF* 3:350), with its reminder as "to what rule of faith [as Tertullian typically calls it] the Galatians were brought for correction" (since they had become confused about which story they found themselves in); and 1.20 (*ANF* 3:285–86), with its idea that Marcion "innovate[d] on the rule (of faith) by ... separation of the law and the gospel," thereby distorting the scriptural story. In *Against Marcion*, 3.17 (*ANF* 3:336), Tertullian explicitly refers to the "rule" as "the rule of Scripture."

first Adam's sin. The second Adam, Jesus Christ, "repeats" or "recapitulates" the earlier narrative, but this time perfectly, returning the Great Story to its original trajectory:

> the Son of God ... was made man, [and] commenced afresh the long line of human beings, and furnished us, in a brief, comprehensive manner, with salvation; so that what we had lost in Adam—namely, to be according to the image and likeness of God—that we might recover in Christ Jesus.[57]

Crucial to Irenaeus' perspective here is the idea that God was working out his salvation-project in human history before Christ as well as in Christ—albeit accommodating himself to the condition of human beings as he found them in the particular moments of history. The one God of the Great Story, then, did not address himself to ancient Israel in the past as he now addresses himself to the Church, but he took account of the former's historical location.

Irenaeus' opponents' failure to grasp the genuine movement of the biblical Story through time is indeed one of the fatal mistakes they make in their approach to Bible reading, he believes. It leads them (as we have seen) to characterize OT law as "morally inferior, foolish, and absurd." They have missed the true hypothesis of Scripture, and in consequence they have constructed false economies in describing its structure and plot. In response, Irenaeus characterizes them as "those who are of a perverse mind ... judging [the law] to be dissimilar and contrary to the doctrine of the Gospel," while not applying themselves "to investigate the causes of the difference of each covenant."[58] The important point is that the Israelites were the Israelites and not the Church; certainly "[God] elected the patriarchs on account of their salvation; however, he formed the nation as he taught the unteachable to give obedience to God."[59] In the background here lie Paul's comments in Galatians 3:24 about the law being a "schoolmaster" (KJV) to bring people to Christ.

It is worth noting the contrast here between Irenaeus and Philo when it comes to their responses to the OT's critics. Philo's response is in the main to save the appearances of the OT law by "translating" it into Hellenistic categories of thought. He loses in the process the connection between the original text and both its historical and its literary context. Irenaeus, also faced with Hellenistic critique, responds by insisting on interpreting the OT law within *both* its historical and its literary context. Christian faith "continued to be bound to the

---

[57] Irenaeus, *Against Heresies*, 3.18.1 (ANF 1:446). "Recapitulation" in ancient rhetoric meant "final repetition, summing up, drawing to conclusion." O'Keefe and Reno, *Sanctified Vision*, 39.
[58] Irenaeus, *Against Heresies*, 3.12.12 (ANF 1:434).
[59] Reventlow, *Biblical Interpretation*, 1:163.

world and to history, both of which were fields of divine action of the one God."[60] Throughout his work, in fact, Irenaeus is intent on reading Scripture to a very great extent literally, historically, and contextually, and this is evident in many different ways.[61]

IRENAEUS AND FIGURAL READING

At the same time, even as he pursues so vigorously his demonstration of the coherence of the entire biblical Story, we do find in Irenaeus' work a tendency (similar to that in Justin Martyr) to move beyond the literal sense. He may not read the OT law, for example, through the lens of the kind of ahistorical Platonic dualism between flesh and spirit that is so beloved by Philo, but he does maintain that it can be read "figuratively" as predicting certain realities of the NT "economy" (as he refers to the NT age). This "figurative reading" can be quite unconstrained by the literal meaning of the text in the OT economy. Thus, it is true that "spiritual men shall not be incorporeal spirits," and that it is "the union of flesh and spirit, receiving the Spirit of God, [that] makes up the spiritual man."[62] Yet there are such persons as spiritual men, nevertheless, and these are distinguishable from "carnal" men who "are the slaves of fleshly lusts."[63] The OT law "has figuratively predicted all these, delineating man by the [clean and unclean] animals."[64] Here Irenaeus refers to Leviticus 11. Nothing about this passage read in its context, however, encourages one to make such a connection.

Then again, *Against Heresies* 4.31 begins with the proposition that when it comes to characters in the OT story who are far from being paragons of virtue (thereby offending the sensibilities of the Gnostics) and are blamed in Scripture for their misdeeds, we should "give thanks to God in their behalf, inasmuch as their sins have been forgiven them through the advent of our Lord." In cases where they are not explicitly blamed we should take the view that since the "Scriptures pass no censure... we ought not to become the accusers... for we are not more exact than God, nor can we be superior to our Master."[65] We might well imagine

---

[60] Reventlow, *Biblical Interpretation*, 1:207.

[61] Notice, e.g., his argument in *Against Heresies*, 3.7 (ANF 1:420–21) about the way in which the apostle Paul uses grammar—just one example of his attention to questions of authorial communicative intent. Notice further his reading of Dan 2:34-35 in *Against Heresies*, 3.21.7 (ANF 1:453), which Reventlow wrongly describes as "allegorical" (Reventlow, *Biblical Interpretation*, 1:169). Here the Daniel text anticipates that the kingdom of God will arrive miraculously ("not by human hands"). It is not "allegorizing" when Irenaeus cites this text in relation to Matthew's account of Jesus' birth.

[62] Irenaeus, *Against Heresies*, 5.8.2 (ANF 1:534).

[63] Irenaeus, *Against Heresies*, 5.8.2 (ANF 1:534).

[64] Irenaeus, *Against Heresies*, 5.8.4 (ANF 1:534).

[65] Irenaeus, *Against Heresies*, 4.31.1 (ANF 1:504).

that Irenaeus would leave the matter there, given his emphasis elsewhere on due humility in pursuing the questions we have about the Bible and his opposition to looking for what is allegedly hidden in the text. In fact, however, he goes on to propose that in the latter cases "we should search for a type ... For not one of those things which have been set down in Scripture without being condemned is without significance."[66] The example he chooses is the story of Lot (in Gen 19), whose two daughters he reads as speaking of Church and synagogue. Again, nothing about this OT passage encourages the reader to make such a connection.

At these points and others in Irenaeus' writing we find considerable evidence that for all his commitment to the literal and contextual reading of Scripture, deployed with great erudition and attention to detail in the course of his opposition to the Gnostics and their own various forays into the "spiritual reading" of the text, he himself does to some extent engage in nonliteral reading. He is convinced, in fact, that although Christ is found in Scripture "clearly and unambiguously in express terms," he is also the "treasure ... hid in the field":

> If any one, therefore, reads the Scriptures with attention, he will find in them an account of Christ, and a foreshadowing of the new calling.... For Christ is the treasure which was hid in the field, that is, in this world ... but the treasure hid in the Scriptures is Christ, since He was pointed out by means of types and parables.[67]

On this view, at least certain things that are true of Christ "could not be understood, prior to the consummation of those things which had been predicted."[68] For although "the entire Scriptures, the prophets, and the Gospels, can be clearly, unambiguously, and harmoniously understood by all," it is also true that "every prophecy, before its fulfilment, is to men [full of] enigmas and ambiguities."[69] To this extent, the truest meaning of Scripture is to be found not in what lies upon its surface, but on what is allegedly hidden beneath it.

TERTULLIAN

As we move into the early years of the third century AD we find Marcion and his views receiving still further focused attention from another of the early Church Fathers, Tertullian. Born in Carthage in Roman North Africa around the middle of the second century, Tertullian was converted to Christian faith around 197. In 208 (or thereabouts) he wrote a five-volume work titled simply *Against*

---

[66] Irenaeus, *Against Heresies*, 4.31.1 (ANF 1:504).
[67] Irenaeus, *Against Heresies*, 2.27.1, 4.26.1 (ANF 1:398, 496).
[68] Irenaeus, *Against Heresies*, 2.27.1, 4.26.1 (ANF 1:398, 496).
[69] Irenaeus, *Against Heresies*, 4.26.1, 2.27.2 (ANF 1:496, 398).

Marcion—although as Tertullian tells us, this was not the first time he had taken up his apologetic pen against this notable heretic.[70]

AGAINST MARCION, BOOK 1

Tertullian's target as he begins is Marcion's belief in two gods, "one judicial, harsh, mighty in war; the other mild, placid, and simply good and excellent."[71] Tertullian's recourse to Scripture at this point in his refutation is limited, because he is "for the most part engaged in preparing the way, by means of common sense and fair arguments, for a belief in the future support of the Scriptures also."[72] Yet even in book 1, Tertullian does refer to Scripture.

For example, he objects to Marcion's reference to an isolated biblical verse like Isaiah 45:7 ("I am He that creates evil") in support of his argument about his first god,[73] noting that Isaiah elsewhere speaks of one God with whom none can be compared ("To whom will you liken me?"; Isa 44:7).[74] He insists, referring to the Pentateuch, that this one true God was known to humanity from of old, and he challenges Marcion to read the text in accordance with its narrative order: "Do not, O barbarian heretic, put Abraham before the world."[75] A number of prophetic texts are invoked in relation to the apostle Paul's insistence that Christians are not required to practice Jewish rituals like circumcision. Here Tertullian draws on passages that describe God's ancient rejection of ritual observance in the context of OT promises about a new covenant,[76] in order to show continuity between the OT and NT writings: "Permanent still ... stood faith in the Creator and in His Christ; manner of life and discipline alone fluctuated."[77] Indeed, the OT command about loving one's neighbor as oneself, "although coming from the Creator's law, even you ought to receive, because, so far from being abrogated by Christ, it has rather been confirmed by Him."[78]

The true God is perfect, as Matthew 5:48 tells us; Marcion's Savior God is far from perfect, and this is seen not least in the fact that he "saves but few, and so rather leans to the alternative of not saving."[79] What is more, in Marcionite thinking the fortunate few "are saved only so far as the soul is concerned, but lost

---

[70] Tertullian, *Against Marcion*, 1.1 (*ANF* 3:271). For an overview of Tertullian's place within the Christian exegetical tradition, see Skarsaune, "Scriptural Interpretation," 429–34.
[71] Tertullian, *Against Marcion*, 1.6 (*ANF* 3:275).
[72] Tertullian, *Against Marcion*, 1.16 (*ANF* 3:283).
[73] Tertullian, *Against Marcion*, 1.2 (*ANF* 3:272).
[74] Tertullian, *Against Marcion*, 1.4 (*ANF* 3:273).
[75] Tertullian, *Against Marcion*, 1.10 (*ANF* 3:278).
[76] Tertullian, *Against Marcion*, 1.20 (*ANF* 3:285–86).
[77] Tertullian, *Against Marcion*, 1.21 (*ANF* 3:286).
[78] Tertullian, *Against Marcion*, 1.23 (*ANF* 3:288).
[79] Tertullian, *Against Marcion*, 1.23 (*ANF* 3:289).

in their body, which, according to [Marcion], does not rise again." But "what else is man than flesh," Tertullian asks, citing Genesis 2:7, since "it was the corporeal rather than the spiritual element from which the Author of man's nature gave him his designation?"[80] Marcion's hostility to the body is also seen in his proscription of marriage, which Tertullian holds to be a "disparagement of the Creator."[81] Here he cites OT texts like Genesis 1:28, insisting that it is within such a context that we must read other biblical texts like 1 Corinthians 7:29 ("they who have wives [should] be as though they had none").

Against Marcion, Book 2

Tertullian's reading of Scripture to this point (in book 1) is straightforwardly literal, and he continues in this manner as we turn to book 2, which opens with a catena of biblical texts concerning the nature of God and true knowledge about him.[82] He then proceeds in the same vein to discuss the biblical story of creation and fall, in the course of critiquing the Marcionite view of it. Even when advancing the curious argument that the prophecy of Ezekiel about the ruler of Tyre (in Ezek 28) actually refers "in the person of the prince of Tyre" to Satan, it is evident just how much Tertullian focuses on the words on the page in coming to this conclusion, "for none among human beings was either born in the paradise of God . . . nor placed with a cherub upon God's holy mountain."[83] The text does not "fit" the prince of Tyre, in Tertullian's judgment—it must therefore refer to someone else. It is indeed his precise attention to the words on the page, in their context, that allows him to dispute Marcion's reading of Isaiah 45:7, noting that "evil" in this context refers to God's punishment (cf. NIV's "disaster"), not to moral evil.[84] Both biblical narrative and prophecy, read in such a literal manner, testify to the goodness of God.[85] So does the OT law, which Tertullian understands as accommodated to some extent to the character of the people to whom God was good, in their own time and place:[86]

> It was not in severity that its Author promulgated this law, but in the interest of the highest benevolence, which rather aimed at subduing the nation's hardness of heart, and by laborious service hewing out a fealty which was (as yet) untried in obedience.[87]

---

[80] Tertullian, *Against Marcion*, 1.24 (*ANF* 3:290).
[81] Tertullian, *Against Marcion*, 1.29 (*ANF* 3:294).
[82] Tertullian, *Against Marcion*, 2.2 (*ANF* 3:297–98).
[83] Tertullian, *Against Marcion*, 2.10 (*ANF* 3:305–6).
[84] Tertullian, *Against Marcion*, 2.14 (*ANF* 3:308); see also 2.24 (*ANF* 3:315–16).
[85] Tertullian, *Against Marcion*, 2.17–19 (*ANF* 3:310–12).
[86] Tertullian, *Against Marcion*, 2.17–19 (*ANF* 3:310–12).
[87] Tertullian, *Against Marcion*, 2.19 (*ANF* 3:312).

This demonstration of God's goodness (and indeed his true divinity) in the OT, over against Marcionite attacks upon both, continues all the way through the latter part of book 2. Throughout, Tertullian resolutely sticks to literal reading and "purposely abstain[s] from touching on the mysterious senses of the law, considered in its spiritual and prophetic relation, and as abounding in types of almost every variety and sort."[88] Of the healing serpent described in Numbers 21:8-9, for example, he says "nothing of what was figured by this cure."[89]

AGAINST MARCION, BOOKS 3 THROUGH 5

This is not to say that Tertullian has no place for the typological and the figurative, as he makes clear in book 3, where he turns his attention to the nature of "the Scriptures of the Creator" as "prophetic announcement."[90] Here he maintains both that "future events are sometimes announced [in the OT] as if they were already passed," since God, being eternal, does not take account of time, and that "very many events are figuratively predicted by means of enigmas and allegories and parables, and ... they must be understood in a sense different from the literal description."[91] I have already proposed (in chapter 4) that the phenomena to which Tertullian refers in the immediate context of the second statement should be understood under the heading of the literal sense: metaphor (e.g., "a land flowing with milk and honey"), and typology (e.g., the case of the two women and their sons in Galatians 4). If they are indeed understood in this way, then to a significant extent Tertullian does not in fact move beyond the literal sense in what follows in books 3 through 5. Indeed, his attention to words in their contexts in the OT remains evident.

For example, in meeting Marcion's objection that the Immanuel prophecy in Isaiah 7:14, along with the close-by Isaiah 8:14—commonly read at the time as referring to the same child—do not "fit" when applied to Jesus, Tertullian suggests that Marcion "ought to look into the contexts of the two passages." Jesus might never have been named Immanuel, but he was certainly (and substantively) "God with us." Christ is "properly implied in the meaning of the name."[92] Likewise, Marcion is "equally led away by the sound of names" when he understands

---

[88] Tertullian, *Against Marcion*, 2.19 (ANF 3:312).

[89] Tertullian, *Against Marcion*, 2.22 (ANF 3:314). He does briefly mention in 2.26 (ANF 3:318), however, the way in which Moses appears as a type of Christ in Exodus 32, having previously indulged in 2.20 (ANF 3:312–13) in a throwaway ad hominem comment about the Marcionites being "'saucy cuttles' ... under the figure of whom the law about things to be eaten prohibited this very kind of piscatory aliment."

[90] Tertullian, *Against Marcion*, 3.5 (ANF 3:324).

[91] Tertullian, *Against Marcion*, 3.5 (ANF 3:324).

[92] Tertullian, *Against Marcion*, 3.12 (ANF 3:331).

"the riches of Damascus, and the spoils of Samaria, and the king of Assyria, as if they portended that the Creator's Christ was a warrior." For in Isaiah 8 itself it is a *young child* who takes away these riches and this spoil. This surely raises questions about the best way of understanding the passage, unless we are to imagine (as Tertullian cuttingly proposes) that the warrior mentioned "might be about to sound the alarm of war not with a trumpet, but with a little rattle."[93] It is obviously not a "real" warrior who is described in Isaiah 8, Tertullian suggests; his weapons are "allegorical" (by which, on both occasions of its use here, he clearly means "metaphorical"), and his spoils are figurative.[94]

At the same time, on many occasions Tertullian does significantly set aside what may reasonably be supposed to be the literal sense of the text. Like Justin, for example, he reads the two goats presented on the Day of Atonement in Leviticus 16 as figures of the two comings of Christ, and it is very difficult to see anything in the OT passage in question that justifies this kind of move.[95] It requires exactly the kind of distinction between "bare prophecy" and prophecy that is "obscur[ed] . . . in shadow" that Tertullian introduces in *Against Marcion* 3.18. This allows him to read the OT Joseph as a type of Christ, not on the more obvious ground that "he suffered persecution for the cause of God from his brethren," but on the much less obvious one that Joseph's "glory is that of a bullock; his horns are the horns of a unicorn," while Christ is "a bullock in respect of both His characteristics: to some as severe as a Judge, to others gentle as a Saviour, whose horns were the extremities of His cross."[96]

Tertullian, Athens, and Jerusalem

In sum, a thoroughly literal reading of Scripture provides the framework for Tertullian's argument in *Against Marcion*. Within that framework, other sorts of reading designed to discover what is hidden rather than plain also flourish, with the overall goal of undergirding Tertullian's defense of the whole Bible as unified in testifying about the one true God. However, for all that he is

---

[93] Tertullian, *Against Marcion*, 3.13 (*ANF* 3:331).
[94] Tertullian, *Against Marcion*, 3.14 (*ANF* 3:333). Since these are two of only three references to allegory in book 3—following the first one just noted ("enigmas and allegories")—they represent a reliable guide to what Tertullian has in mind in using the term here. See further 5.18 (*ANF* 3:467–70). In 5.4 (*ANF* 3:435–38), Tertullian returns to the question of Paul's use of Genesis in Gal 4:21-31, and here it is clear that what he means by "allegory" is what I have earlier suggested should be placed under the heading "typology," since he glosses "allegorized" with "that is to say, they presaged something *besides* the literal history" (436; emphasis added)—not "other than."
[95] Tertullian, *Against Marcion*, 3.7 (*ANF* 3:327).
[96] Tertullian, *Against Marcion*, 3.18 (*ANF* 3:336), with further examples of "types" following.

ready to acknowledge as legitimate the practice of allegorizing Scripture in the Church of his day, and will occasionally have recourse to it himself, he often rejects the practice and his writings leave a general impression that he was suspicious of allegory.[97]

This is not surprising, given how suspicious Tertullian generally is of Hellenistic thought and practice, and how trenchant he is in drawing attention to the gulf that separates these from biblical thought and practice. In *The Soul*, for example, Christians must clear away "[w]hatever noxious vapours ... exhaled from philosophy, obscure the clear and wholesome atmosphere of truth."[98] In *Against Marcion*, he lambasts Greek thinkers like Thales and Plato, who divinize the natural world, as "those very professors of wisdom, from whose genius every heresy derives its spirit."[99] Again, he notes that "[w]e are taught God by the prophets and by Christ, and not by the philosophers nor by Epicurus." We Christians, he states,

> who believe that God really lived on earth, and took upon Him the low estate of human form, for the purpose of man's salvation, are very far from thinking as those do who refuse to believe that God cares for anything. Whence has found its way to the heretics an argument of this kind: If God is angry, and jealous, and roused, and grieved, He must therefore be corrupted, and must therefore die. Fortunately, however, it is a part of the creed of Christians even to believe that God did die, and yet that He is alive for evermore. Superlative is their folly, who prejudge divine things from human.[100]

For Tertullian, it is to Scripture that we must fundamentally go, in order to discover what is true, and not to Greek philosophy—as indicated by his famous comments about Athens and Jerusalem (in the second epigraph to the present chapter). Tertullian was quite clear about the threat that Hellenistic ideas posed to authentic Christian faith, and he drew a prominent line in the sand between these two. It is not surprising that someone who was so insistent that "instruction comes from the porch of Solomon" and not from the world of the Greeks should have been reserved in his embrace of Greek ways of reading Scripture.

---

[97] Richard P. C. Hanson, "Notes on Tertullian's Interpretation of Scripture," *JTS* 12 (1961): 273–79 (274). In general, Tertullian's interpretation of Scripture is marked by "common sense, realism, and restraint" (275).

[98] Tertullian, *De anima* (*The Soul*), 3 (ANF 3:184).

[99] Tertullian, *Against Marcion*, 1.13 (ANF 3:280).

[100] Tertullian, *Against Marcion*, 2.16 (ANF 3:309).

CONCLUSION

Looking back on chapter 7, then, it is clear that all three of the exemplary Church Fathers examined thus far share a common desire to defend the unity of Scripture. Individual texts must be read within their larger biblical contexts, and ultimately within the context of the Great Story as a whole. Literal reading is fundamental to their work in this regard, as they present to their readers and interlocutors the unfolding biblical account of the one true God, who in the first instance predominantly revealed himself to and worked with the ancient Israelites, and then later created a more diverse people, on the way toward the ultimate consummation of history in the future. Within this framework, other reading "moves" are to a lesser or greater extent also made by our three Fathers, as a way of underscoring the coherence of the whole Story. In many of these cases we may with justification say of all three what de Margerie says of Justin: they do not "give enough consideration to the literal sense of the Old Testament Scriptures.... In certain respects ... [the] exegesis does not sufficiently value history, or the peculiar content and immediate sense of Old Testament data."[101] Yet although they are certainly in dialogue with the surrounding culture as they proceed in this way, the account of "life, the universe, and everything"[102] that they thereby proclaim is very different from others available in the first two centuries AD. This includes the accounts offered by Marcion and the Gnostics, with their indebtedness to those "widespread ideas of Hellenistic late antiquity" that we earlier noted. This is not so clearly the case in the work of the next subject of our attention, in chapter 8: Origen of Alexandria.

---

[101] de Margerie, *Introduction*, 44–45.
[102] This useful phrase is a favorite in Douglas Adams, *The Hitchhiker's Guide to the Galaxy* (London: Pan Books, 1979).

8

Origen, Theodore, and Augustine
The Fertility of Scripture

The design of that divine power which gave us the sacred Scriptures is, that we should not receive what is presented by the letter alone (such things being sometimes not true in their literal acceptation, but absurd and impossible).

—Origen[1]

Scripture, they say, is fertile, and thus produces a variety of meanings . . . I deny that its fertility consists in the various meanings which any man, at his pleasure, may assign . . . the true meaning of Scripture is the natural and obvious meaning; and let us embrace and abide by it resolutely.

—John Calvin[2]

When we turn to the writings of Origen, who was born around AD 185 in the markedly Hellenistic city of Alexandria and educated there in Greek literature, grammar, and philosophy, we encounter a very different attitude toward Hellenistic culture and belief and, connected with this, a very different approach to Scripture.[3] It is not that Origen was entirely uninterested in the letter of the biblical text. On the contrary (as we shall see in chapter 10), he devoted a considerable amount of time to text-critical work designed to establish what the letter of the text actually was. If Eusebius of Caesarea is to be believed, moreover, Origen castrated himself in accordance with a very straightforward (and many

---

[1] Origen, *First Principles*, 4.18 (ANF 4:367, from the Greek).
[2] Calvin, *Galatians and Ephesians*, 135–36—in the course of commenting on Gal 4:22.
[3] As with every topic covered in this book, I am aware that in discussing Origen's biblical hermeneutics I am entering contested territory, and I must acknowledge this even as I remain convinced of my own reading and its implications. No doubt those who appeal to books like the following will be dissatisfied with the first part of this chapter: Henri de Lubac, *History and Spirit: The Understanding of Scripture According to Origen* (1950; repr., San Francisco: Ignatius Press, 2007). Less dissatisfied will be those who appeal to books like Karen Jo Torjesen, *Hermeneutical Procedure and Theological Method in Origen's Exegesis* (PTS 28; Berlin: de Gruyter, 1986), and Joseph W. Trigg, *Origen: The Bible and Philosophy in the Third-Century Church* (1998; repr., London: Routledge, 2012).

would say literalistic) reading of Matthew 19:12, which tells us that some have "made themselves eunuchs for the kingdom of heaven's sake" (KJV).[4] Perhaps it is such realities that Christopher Seitz has in mind when he offers the (surprising?) judgment that "in many ways no one read the Bible more literally than Origen."[5]

ORIGEN AND HIS *FIRST PRINCIPLES*

However that may be, in the fourth book of *First Principles*, written in Alexandria probably between 219 and 230,[6] it is readily apparent just what kind of commitment Origen has to the literal sense. He certainly recognizes that it is present in Scripture as its "flesh," and that it is capable of edifying "the simple man."[7] However, he has already told us in the preface to the whole work that the Scriptures as authored by the Spirit of God "have a meaning, not such only as is apparent at first sight."[8] He develops this idea in book 4, claiming that—just like a human being—Scripture comprises body, soul, and spirit.

Body, Soul, and Spirit

Bodily meaning is found on the surface of the text, in its human art. The "soul" of Scripture exists for the edification of those who have "ascended a certain way" in their spiritual journey, and the "spiritual law" exists for the edification of those who are "perfect."[9] Subsequently, these two are apparently collapsed simply into "the spiritual" meaning, which lies *buried* in the text, even if we ourselves might be unable "to discover in every expression the hidden splendour of the doctrines veiled in common and unattractive phraseology."[10] This is true of both the OT and the NT.[11] What we have in the "body" of Scripture in both cases—albeit that

---

[4] Eusebius, *Church History*, 6.8 (*NPNF* 2, 1:254). The story may not be true, however; it is interesting that in his commentary on this verse in Matthew, Origen certainly does not offer a literalistic reading of this same verse, suggesting prayer (not self-harm) as the means of chastity: "God therefore will give the good gift, perfect purity in celibacy and chastity, to those who ask Him with the whole soul, and with faith, and in prayers without ceasing." Origen, *Commentary on Matthew*, 14.25 (*ANF* 9:512).

[5] Seitz, *Figured Out*, 7. For Origen, "there is nothing superfluous in Scripture, and even the most minor detail ... can carry a resonant theological meaning." Carleton Paget, "Christian Exegesis," 510.

[6] Gale Heide, *Timeless Truth in the Hands of History: A Short History of System in Theology* (PTMS 178; Eugene, Ore.: Pickwick, 2012), 28–29.

[7] Origen, *First Principles*, 4.11; cf. 4.19 (*ANF* 4:359; 368; from the Greek).

[8] Origen, *First Principles*, Preface at 8 (*ANF* 4:241).

[9] Origen, *First Principles*, 4.11 (*ANF* 4:359, from the Greek).

[10] Origen, *First Principles*, 4.7 (*ANF* 4:354–55, from the Greek).

[11] "[W]ho, on reading the revelations made to John, would not be amazed at the unspeakable mysteries therein concealed, and which are evident (even) to him who does not comprehend what is written? And to what person, skillful in investigating words, would the Epistles of the Apostles

it is "capable of improving the multitude, according to their capacity"—is only a "covering ... of the spiritual truths,"[12] whose very imperfections point us to deeper realities. These imperfections are not accidental. Had Scripture at the level of its literal sense been capable of coherent reading, we would not have believed that anything lay beneath its surface. For this very reason God arranged that it is not capable of coherent reading.[13] Indeed, in pursuit of incoherence at the level of the literal and the historical, the Holy Spirit has often inserted into the OT narrative certain things "that did not [even] take place, sometimes what could not have happened; sometimes what could, but did not."[14] This is also true of NT narrative: "[The Spirit] did the same thing both with the evangelists and the apostles ... in the histories that are literally recorded, circumstances that did not occur are inserted."[15]

Summarizing all this, Origen proposes "that the whole of [Scripture] has a 'spiritual,' but not the whole a 'bodily' meaning, because the bodily meaning is in many places proved to be impossible."[16] "[T]he treasure of divine meaning," as he will later put it, "is enclosed within the frail vessel of the common letter."[17] The "soul" of the text is what the reader should above all seek.[18]

The Deficiencies of the Letter

The far-reaching scope of Origen's search for "the hidden and secret meaning" in scriptural words becomes particularly clear as book 4 of *First Principles* moves to

---

seem to be clear and easy of understanding, since even in them there are countless numbers of most profound ideas, which, (issuing forth) as by an aperture, admit of no rapid comprehension?" Origen, *First Principles*, 4.10 (ANF 4:358, from the Greek).

[12] Origen, *First Principles*, 4.14 (ANF 4:363, from the Greek).

[13] In fact, God made it so that "certain stumbling-blocks, as it were, and offenses, and impossibilities, should be introduced into the midst of the law and the history, in order that we may not, through being drawn away in all directions by the merely attractive nature of the language, either altogether fall away from the (true) doctrines, as learning nothing worthy of God, or, by not departing from the letter, come to the knowledge of nothing more divine." Origen, *First Principles*, 4.15 (ANF 4:364, from the Greek).

[14] Origen, *First Principles*, 4.15 (ANF 4:364, from the Greek). The case of OT law is similar (same section): there is "often to be found what is useful in itself, and appropriate to the times of the legislation; and sometimes also what does not appear to be of utility; and at other times impossibilities are recorded for the sake of the more skilful and inquisitive, in order that they may give themselves to the toil of investigating what is written, and thus attain to a becoming conviction of the manner in which a meaning worthy of God must be sought out in such subjects."

[15] Origen, *First Principles*, 4.16 (ANF 4:364–66, from the Greek).

[16] Origen, *First Principles*, 4.20 (ANF 4:369, from the Greek).

[17] Origen, *First Principles*, 4.26 (ANF 4:375).

[18] "All [Alexandrian] exegesis was a quest for this soul," in pursuit of "the ultimate vision of truth." Carleton Paget, "Christian Exegesis," 481.

its conclusion.[19] Grounding himself in Paul's reference "somewhere" (1 Cor 10:18) to "Israel after the flesh," and in other NT texts that distinguish between a physical and a spiritual Israel and between an earthly and a heavenly Jerusalem, Origen proposes that the "'corporeal' Israelites" in Scripture are "types" of the "'spiritual' Israelites," and that "whatever . . . is predicted of Jerusalem" refers to "the heavenly city." By extension, the prophecies concerning the foreign nations (e.g., Egypt or Babylon) "are spoken not only of these 'bodily' Egyptians, and Babylonians . . . but also of their 'spiritual' (counterparts)."[20] This move opens up the whole OT narrative, in its detail as much as its generalities, to the search for "the hidden treasures of wisdom and knowledge" that have been "concealed in the histories"— "not visible to all, but buried."[21] This is especially the case when the move is allied to Origen's injunction to the person who cares about truth that he should be "little concerned about words and language . . . but let him rather direct his attention to the meaning conveyed by the words."[22] Among the truths revealed in this way (given that the OT law is only "a shadow of good things to come") is that Deuteronomy, a second version of the law delivered with "greater clearness and distinctness than in those books which were first written," foreshadows the second coming of Christ.[23] In the end, and to a very great extent, for Origen the literal sense of Scripture is not of great value. Its various statements should not "be judged . . . according to the worthlessness of the letter, but according to the divinity of the Holy Spirit, by whose inspiration they were caused to be written."[24]

It should be obvious by this point just how unlikely it is that we shall find in Origen's other work the kind of prolonged attention to the literal sense of Scripture that is so evident in earlier writers like Irenaeus and Tertullian. For both of these earlier Fathers it was fundamentally important to demonstrate the coherence of Scripture at a literal level, and they both believed that much of what God has to say is said at this level. The Word of God exists, not in what is allegedly hidden in the human words in a "spiritual" sense, but in what is patent in them in their ordinary sense. Indeed, both Irenaeus and Tertullian have some scathing commentary to offer concerning claims that Scripture is less than perspicuous and that its meaning is only discernible to elite interpreters possessing the appropriate "wisdom." They are also critical concerning claims about any part of Scripture being morally inferior, foolish, or absurd. For Origen, on the other hand, what the Holy Spirit has to say is frequently not to be found at the literal level of

---

[19] Origen, *First Principles*, 4.20–37 (ANF 4:369–82).
[20] Origen, *First Principles*, 4.21–22 (ANF 4:370–72, from the Greek).
[21] Origen, *First Principles*, 4.23 (ANF 4:372–73, from the Greek).
[22] Origen, *First Principles*, 4.27 (ANF 4:376).
[23] Origen, *First Principles*, 4.25 (ANF 4:375).
[24] Origen, *First Principles*, 4.27 (ANF 4:376).

meaning, but in the hidden depths of the text, detached from any human communicative intent. These depths can be plumbed only by wise or "perfect" readers who transcend the masses; the latter are incapable of seeing what is there.[25] The depths of the text *must* be plumbed precisely because of the many deficiencies of Scripture encountered when one surveys only its surface. If the sufficiency of Scripture at the level of the literal sense is later one of the great themes of the Reformation, in Origen we find only a marked conviction of its insufficiency.[26]

ORIGEN, THE GREEKS, AND THE TRADITION

In all of this Origen is a true disciple of Philo, his Alexandrian predecessor, and of the kind of Hellenistic allegorical reading that Philo had brought to bear on Scripture a couple of centuries earlier.[27] Philo's writings had indeed probably only been "rescued from the debris of Jewish-Alexandrian culture after the disastrous happenings in the century after [his] death"[28] because of the efforts of people like Origen's older Alexandrian colleague, Clement—a Christian deeply influenced by Hellenistic philosophy (and most particularly by Plato).[29] Clement had already developed his own allegorical approach to Scripture in pursuit of the divine voice that he believed spoke in biblical (and indeed in nonbiblical) literature. In searching for this voice, Clement is relatively uninterested in the literal sense of particular texts or of literary works as a whole.[30] The literal sense functions (as it does in Philo)[31] as little more than a starting point for his endeavors:

> [B]y using a divine voice rather than a specific text as the basis for revisionary reading, Clement can include direct quotations from competing literature as well as titles of works and names of authors. He can do this precisely because the

---

[25] Interestingly, Origen's preaching (to the masses!) did not necessarily reflect this theory. See Reventlow, *Biblical Interpretation*, 1:182–83, regarding some of Origen's homilies on Jeremiah, preached while he was in Caesarea.

[26] In this conviction he was followed by medieval scholars like Bede, for whom "the figures of the letter in the Jewish way" were also not up to the task of providing "consoling spiritual teaching." Henning G. Reventlow, *History of Biblical Interpretation, Volume 2: From Late Antiquity to the End of the Middle Ages* (trans. James O. Duke; RBS 61; Atlanta: Society of Biblical Literature, 2009), 113.

[27] David T. Runia, *Philo and the Church Fathers: A Collection of Papers* (Leiden: Brill, 1995), 117–25.

[28] Runia, *Philo*, 57. For a good account of Clement, his Alexandrian context, and his biblical interpretation see Carleton Paget, "Christian Exegesis," 482–99.

[29] Philo has left hardly any trace of himself in the literature either of Judaism ("[the] Rabbis... do not even record his name") or paganism. His name and work survive only because he "soon became one of the Church Fathers," and thereby exercised enormous influence on important later Christian thinkers like Ambrose and Augustine. Siegert, "Early Jewish Interpretation," 187–88.

[30] For the extent to which he *is* interested, see Carleton Paget, "Christian Exegesis," 494–95. "Like Philo before him," however, "Clement is primarily an allegorist" (498).

[31] In Philo's writings it "is mentioned, only to be ignored." Bray, *Biblical Interpretation*, 101.

textual or authorial specificity of his precursors is irrelevant to the fact that when subjected to his revisionary reading, they express the same underlying voice or meaning.[32]

That is to say, Clement's allegorizing strips texts of their original contexts in pursuit of his larger goals, thereby opening up a much larger gap than any of his Christian predecessors—who display a palpable "reticence to engage in allegory"[33]—between the voice of the human authors of Scripture, on the one hand, and the divine voice, on the other. Clement does this in the conviction that "[a]ll ... who have spoken of divine things, both Barbarians and Greeks, have veiled the first principles of things, and delivered the truth in enigmas, and symbols, and allegories, and metaphors, and such like tropes."[34] He does it, too—like all allegorical readers of Scripture in ancient Alexandria—in pursuit of defined social and political goals: they all "sought to convince their audiences that they were interpreting the text itself, [but in fact] they were actually seeking to revise their culture through their allegorical readings."[35] In pursuit of these goals, Clement subordinates "all texts, including scripture, to another criterion of meaning as the product of a divine voice or *logos*."[36]

Origen the Platonist

Origen follows Clement in endorsing "an essentially philosophical hermeneutic with Plato playing a prominent role."[37] He takes the project further, however, attempting what no one of Platonist persuasion prior to him had ever attempted—"a sustained allegorical reading" of a text, in this case Scripture.[38] As with Philo (and Clement), it is not simply that Origen allegorizes this or that detail of Scripture in line with, and constrained by, the canonical shape of the literature as a whole, read in a broadly literal way. The direction in which his thoroughgoing allegorizing takes him is in reality markedly *away* from the canonical shape of the biblical literature as a whole. It conforms biblical truth to a significant extent (similarly to Philo and Clement before him) to philosophical and ethical ideas that derive from elsewhere.[39] The "real" or most important mean-

---

[32] Dawson, *Allegorical Readers*, 206.
[33] Reventlow, *Biblical Interpretation*, 1:203.
[34] Clement of Alexandria, *Miscellanies*, 5.4 (ANF 2:449).
[35] Dawson, *Allegorical Readers*, 235.
[36] Dawson, *Allegorical Readers*, 239.
[37] Carleton Paget, "Christian Exegesis," 532.
[38] Mark J. Edwards, "Origen," *The Stanford Encyclopedia of Philosophy* (Spring 2014 ed.; ed. Edward N. Zalta), http://plato.stanford.edu/entries/origen/, accessed February 23, 2016.
[39] There is, e.g., "a perceptible gnostic contamination in some of Clement's writings." de Margerie, *Introduction*, 79.

ing of the text in Origen is often found to reflect what Greek philosophers, and especially Plato, have to say, rather than what Scripture (in either the OT or the NT) has to say. This is not to suggest that Origen can never be found disagreeing with Plato.[40] It is simply to note that it is Platonism (or more precisely, a Middle Platonism already mixed with Aristotelian, Pythagorean, and Stoic ideas)[41] that is often "found" in the Bible as a result of (or more properly as the basis for) Origen's allegorical exegesis, and that Plato plays a much more significant role in Origen's hermeneutics than simply as "the most prominent of the dead pagans who assisted him in the exegesis and harmonisation of this infallible text."[42]

In *First Principles*, for example, Origen advances the idea that God's first creation comprised disembodied minds that became souls, designed for endless contemplation of the divine, whose weariness with this task led to their "fall" and subsequent embodiment. He does not get this idea from Scripture, even though many biblical texts are quoted in conjunction with it. It derives from Hellenistic philosophy, and it is "an idea that can in no way be assimilated by Christian thought."[43] Nor is it from Scripture that Origen's related notion derives, that the saved soul must ascend by degrees once again to a state of pure mind—the notion that drives Origen's exposition, for example, of the biblical narratives concerning Israel's exodus and wilderness wanderings.[44] This notion, too, comes from the Hellenistic philosophy that formed "the foundation of education throughout the [third and] fourth century, even for educated Christians"—the philosophy that for Alexandrian theologians in particular "seems to play a role nearly as large as Paul and the New Testament" in their work. "The environing culture, still basically pagan," as Henning Reventlow concisely puts it, "had an influence on Christianity and its understanding of the Bible that is not to be underestimated."[45]

---

[40] E.g., in *Against Celsus*, 4.17 (ANF 4:503).

[41] For a helpful, brief introduction to Middle Platonism, see Procopé, "Greek Philosophy," 453–62; for a longer account, Robert M. Berchman, *From Philo to Origen: Middle Platonism in Transition* (BJS 69; Chico, Calif.: Scholars Press, 1984). "The Platonism of the Middle and Neo-Platonists was derived not only from Plato himself, but from a more eclectic blend of the more mystical elements of Plato's thought with Aristotelian logic and theology and to some extent with Stoicism, but the Aristotelian and Stoic elements were introductions into what was in essence a metaphysical structure derived from Plato." David S. Wallace-Hadrill, *Christian Antioch: The Study of Christian Thought in the East* (Cambridge: Cambridge University Press, 1982), 97.

[42] Edwards, "Origen," in his conclusion.

[43] de Margerie, *Introduction*, 108; see, e.g., Origen, *First Principles*, 2.8 (ANF 4:286–89), and further Martens, *Origen and Scripture*, 227–34. The truly authoritative texts for Origen here are such as Plato's *Republic*, 10.611b–612a; *Timaeus*, 41a–d; *Phaedrus*, 246a–248b; and *Phaedo*, 76c–84d.

[44] Mark S. M. Scott, *Journey Back to God: Origen on the Problem of Evil* (AARAS; Oxford: Oxford University Press, 2012), 104–15.

[45] Reventlow, *Biblical Interpretation*, 2:26—where he is focusing on Origen's successor, Didymus the Blind.

This "influence" causes great difficulty for Origen when it comes to articulating doctrine that *is* rightly drawn from Scripture, such as the resurrection of the body. Although he can be found affirming this doctrine, it is ultimately incompatible with his overall understanding of the cosmos, and indeed of the human spiritual journey. On that journey, according to Origen, we return in the end to the beginning[46]—our souls ascend once again to God. He routinely imposes this idea on Scripture in his writings, as when he finds in the OT's wisdom literature three stages of knowledge on the journey—ethics (Proverbs), physics (Ecclesiastes), and metaphysics (Song of Songs)—leading the pilgrim soul "from the sphere of the apparent along the path to the unseen, heavenly, and eternal."[47] On this understanding of the story of the cosmos, there can be no true and lasting place for a resurrected body as apostolic teaching describes it.[48] This being so, we may certainly say that Origen articulated "a drama of salvation." Whether he was justified in thinking of this as a "Christian drama of salvation" (to use Peter Martens' language) is another matter—"matter," indeed, being one of the main points of contention.[49] Richard Hanson takes a very different view of things:

> [Origen's] concept of the "spiritual gospel" seems to me to be, not a Platonized form of genuine Christian eschatology, but an alternative to eschatology, indeed an evasion of it.... Origen accepts *ex animo* all the apparatus of Christian doctrine.... But so strong is the Platonic strain in his thought ... that he must regard this apparatus as no more than the outward expressions of eternal and unchangeable truths which are more important than those expressions.... I do not think that anybody who has examined Origen's thought on this subject carefully could maintain that his eschatology was consistent with the eschatology of the New Testament.[50]

---

[46] This idea that "what transpired at the beginning would be mirrored at the end" is articulated on several occasions in *First Principles*. Martens, *Origen and Scripture*, 228.

[47] Reventlow, *Biblical Interpretation*, 1:188.

[48] Scott, *Journey*, 120–26, 129–60, who persuasively argues that "the logic of [Origen's] eschatology necessarily entails the end of corporeality ... all souls will be forever united with the divine.... God is incorporeal [and] when the soul unites with God, it, too, will become incorporeal" (126). This is the hidden meaning of the biblical texts on this matter, accessible only to the "wise."

[49] Martens, *Origen and Scripture*, 227. As interesting and important as it may be to discover in Mark Edwards' robust defense of Origen in *Origen against Plato* (2002) all the ways in which Origen was not a Platonist (which should be granted), the question still remains at the end of that book whether some of the things that Origen did believe (and Edwards lists them) make him more of a pagan than a Christian. Mark J. Edwards, *Origen against Plato* (ASPTLA; Aldershot: Ashgate, 2002), 159–61. E.g.: "every rational creature is incorporeal" and human souls preexist "in the hand of God before embodiment" (169—whether for a longer or a shorter period of time seems beside the point); and "[t]he goal of our Christian strife is ... that soul and body may be subsumed in spirit" (161).

[50] Hanson, *Allegory and Event*, 354–56.

Origen and Apostolic Hermeneutics

In pursuing this hermeneutical program Origen claims only to be exploring the implications of a number of things that Scripture itself has to say about the reading of Scripture. Analysis of the biblical texts that he mentions, however, reveals that this claim rests on very shaky foundations. Indeed, it is based on a reading of Scripture that is just as inattentive to the literal sense of the biblical text in *these* cases as it often is in others.

Origen's reading of 2 Corinthians 3:6 ("the letter kills but the spirit gives life") is an important case in point. Here he "understands letter and spirit primarily in a hermeneutical sense," encouraging us to move beyond a literal to a spiritual reading of Scripture.[51] However, as we read the text in the context both of 2 Corinthians and of Paul's other letters (notably Rom 2:29, 7:6, where the other two pairings of "letter" and "spirit" occur), it is difficult to imagine that this is what the apostle meant. Paul distinguishes, rather, between the new covenant that brings life, fulfilling the promise of the old, and the old covenant itself, which has passed away and can only bring death to the Corinthians if they insist on living under it.[52] It is not that the literal sense functions as a "veil" over the spiritual sense of the text (2 Cor 3:12-18), as some exegetes have wished to argue. Rather, the veil is one "of hard-heartedness which hides not the meaning of the Bible, but the glory of God"—an obstacle that is removed when an individual is spiritually transformed and can see God's glory (3:18).[53] In 2 Corinthians, "[t]he Spirit denotes a divine power that gives life rather than a divine inspiration that opens the true meaning of Scripture."[54] In this case and in others, it is all too apparent that Origen brings even to the apostolic writings (and not just to the OT) an interpretative lens that prevents him from reading carefully what they actually have to say.

Origen and the Tradition

Origen also claims for his program the support of the whole Church. The Church teaches, he asserts, that the Scriptures were composed by the Holy Spirit, and therefore possess a meaning that most readers do not notice. There is, in fact "one

---

[51] Paul S. Fiddes and Günter Bader, eds., *The Spirit and the Letter: A Tradition and a Reversal* (London: Bloomsbury T&T Clark, 2013), 4.

[52] Cf. C. E. B. Cranfield, *The Epistle to the Romans* (ICC; 2 vols.; Edinburgh: T&T Clark, 1975), 1:339–40, who sees "the letter" as representing an understanding of the law as an end in itself, rather than as something that leads to Christ: "'Letter' is ... what the legalist is left with as a result of his ... misuse of the law ... the letter of the law in isolation from the Spirit is not the law in its true character, but the law as it were denatured."

[53] Thomas E. Provence, "'Who Is Sufficient for These Things?' An Exegesis of 2 Corinthians 2:15–3:18," *NovT* 24 (1982): 54–81 (64).

[54] David E. Garland, *2 Corinthians* (NAC 29; Nashville: Broadman & Holman, 1999), 164.

opinion" throughout the Church on the matter—"that the whole law is . . . spiritual; but that the spiritual meaning which the law conveys is not known to all, but to those only on whom the grace of the Holy Spirit is bestowed in the word of wisdom and knowledge."[55] Leaving aside the dubious nature of another appeal to Scripture here (Rom 7:14) that appears to be poorly grounded in apostolic communicative intent,[56] Origen's substantive claim in this passage is also questionable. There is every reason to believe that Irenaeus and Tertullian, in particular, would have taken exception to a significant amount of what Origen has to say. There is every reason to think that they would have questioned, in general, both his conclusions and his method, pressing him about his "excessive use of allegory . . . [that] imputed to the authors of the [biblical] texts intentions in absolute contrast to the character of their works."[57] With respect to Origen's view of the OT Scriptures, in particular, it is likely that they would have asked how far it was compromised by the "strong ideological binding to the Greek worldview" that he shared with Marcion and the Gnostics.[58] Irenaeus had already noted that "it is characteristic of Gnostic exegesis to employ biblical expressions, but to invest them with a meaning derived from a system that is foreign to their authentic sense."[59] With respect to the NT writings, both he and Tertullian might well have asked Origen whether he really believed, like Marcion and the Gnostics, that he knew better than the apostles. This is especially likely if they had been able to read the Preface to *First Principles*, where Origen tells us that the apostles

> delivered themselves with the utmost clearness on *certain points* which they believed to be necessary to everyone, even to those who seemed somewhat dull in the investigation of divine knowledge; leaving, however, the grounds of their statements to be examined into by those who should deserve the excellent gifts of the Spirit, and who, especially by means of the Holy Spirit Himself, should obtain the gift of language, of wisdom, and of knowledge: while on other subjects they merely stated the fact that things were so, keeping silence as to the manner or origin of their existence; clearly in order that the more zealous of their successors, who should be lovers of wisdom, might have a subject of exercise on which to display

---

[55] Origen, *First Principles*, preface, 8 (*ANF* 4:241).

[56] It is evidently Paul's intention here not to encourage a "spiritual reading" of the law, but to assert that although the law (which is in itself good, v. 16) "derives from the Spirit (given by inspiration), embodies the Spirit, manifests the Spirit, [and] was intended to address at the level of the Spirit," he (Paul) is unable in his sinful nature to obey it. James D. G. Dunn, *Romans 1–8* (WBC 38A; Dallas: Word, 1988), 387.

[57] Reventlow, *Biblical Interpretation*, 1:203.

[58] Reventlow, *Biblical Interpretation*, 1:208. "Where there existed a strong ideological binding to the Greek worldview, one usually discovers that the heretics, Marcion and the gnostics, could not accommodate this to the Old Testament but rather ascribed this text to a lower deity."

[59] de Margerie, *Introduction*, 107.

the fruit of their talents,—those persons, I mean, who should prepare themselves to be fit and worthy receivers of wisdom.[60]

This sounds suspiciously similar to the kind of gnostic approach to the discovery of "wisdom" that Irenaeus and Tertullian were so concerned about. Its elitism (quite apart from anything else) would certainly have outraged Tertullian in particular.[61] It is very difficult to imagine him being at all enthusiastic about Origen's "depths" that can only be plumbed by perfect readers. At the end of the day, after all, there is a significant difference between believing that Scripture is fundamentally perspicuous, with a few "puzzles" or "problems" embedded within, and believing that it is fundamentally obscure. We shall return to this significant difference later, in chapter 12, when we discuss the debate between the Reformers and their sixteenth-century opponents about the perspicuity of Scripture.

There are real questions to be asked, then, about Origen's solidarity with the Christian writers who preceded him. Certainly some of those who followed shortly afterward found reason to distance themselves strongly from his approach, even as he was also lauded and embraced by many.[62] Already in the early fourth century, for example—or perhaps in the late third—we find Methodius, bishop of Olympus in Lycia, writing several works against Origen, including a treatise *On the Resurrection*. Slightly later in the fourth century, Eustathius, bishop of Antioch in Syria—the first to speak at the Council of Nicaea in AD 325—also opposes him. In fact, Eustathius' only surviving work is an attack on Origen and his followers for an approach to Scripture that detaches the words of the text from their moorings in history.[63] With this mention of Antioch we now turn to consider in more detail another of Origen's fourth-century critics, whose approach to biblical interpretation was very different from his: Theodore of Mopsuestia.

---

[60] Origen, *First Principles*, preface, 3 (ANF 4:239) (emhasis added).

[61] Although Tertullian makes some use of allegorical reading, he "certainly is no supporter of the idea that there are different meanings of Scripture for different classes of men, after the manner of the Gnostics and the Alexandrian theologians. Whatever is plain narrative is such for all men, and where a figurative meaning is to be discovered it is open to all." Robert E. Roberts, *The Theology of Tertullian* (London: Epworth Press, 1924), 19.

[62] E.g., Pamphilus composed, along with Eusebius, a six-volume apology for Origen, and Didymus the Blind composed a work to explain and justify the teaching of *First Principles* in particular. Gregory of Nazianzus, in collaboration with Basil of Caesarea, published a volume of selections from Origen's work; Gregory of Nyssa was "much more obviously Origenist in his assumptions than his brother Basil" (Carleton Paget, "Christian Exegesis," 541). Among writers in Latin, the work of Hilary of Poitiers, Ambrose of Milan, and Jerome is evidently indebted to Origen. Christoph Jacob, "The Reception of the Origenist Tradition in Latin Exegesis," HBOT 1/1:682–700.

[63] Hill, *Antioch*, 3n7, 6, 136.

THEODORE OF MOPSUESTIA

Antioch had been a notable early site of Gentile Christianity (Acts 11:19-30), whose church by the beginning of the fourth century had risen to a level of esteem granted otherwise only to Rome and Alexandria, but was soon to be eclipsed by Constantinople.[64] It was in this city of long Christian tradition, then, that Theodore was born around AD 352. In 370 he entered the monastic community established there by Diodore of Tarsus—also a fierce critic of Origenists—which had been founded in part to foster study of the Bible. Widely regarded as "the most learned scholar of the Antiochenes,"[65] Theodore eventually became bishop of Mopsuestia in Cilicia in 392, remaining in that position until his death in 428 or 429. During his lifetime he was well regarded as a defender of orthodox Christian faith, although in the long run he suffered from his writings being associated with heretical positions that became a matter of concern to the Church in the sixth century.

Theodore on Allegorical Reading

Our understanding of Theodore's view of allegorical reading would be greatly enhanced if we possessed his five-volume work *Concerning Allegory and History against Origen*, which unfortunately no longer exists. His opposition to the practice is nevertheless clear:

> There are people who have great zeal for overturning the meaning of the divine scriptures, and by breaking up everything placed there they fabricate from themselves certain foolish fictions and give their folly the name of allegory.... I should like to say to them that by breaking up the narrative they no longer have a narrative... if their view is true and what is written does not preserve an account of what really happened but points to something else profound and that must be understood intellectually—something spiritual, as they want to say, which they can discern since they are themselves spiritual people—where have they acquired this knowledge?[66]

For Theodore, the literal sense of Scripture is fundamental. To be clear, this literal sense includes such phenomena as metaphor, hyperbole, and synecdoche (referring to the whole by way of the part). For the Antiochenes generally, Beryl Smalley reminds us, "[t]he literal sense... covered the whole meaning of the

---

[64] Hill, *Antioch*, 2–7.
[65] Anthony Thiselton, *Hermeneutics: An Introduction* (Grand Rapids: Eerdmans, 2009), 111.
[66] Theodore of Mopsuestia, *The Commentaries on the Minor Epistles of Paul* (ed. John C. Cavadini and John T. Fitzgerald; trans. Rowan A. Greer; WGRW 26; Atlanta: Society of Biblical Literature, 2010), 113–15.

writer, including his metaphors and figures."⁶⁷ Such an understanding of the literal arises directly from Theodore's "classical-philological schooling" in Antioch.⁶⁸ It is also reflected in the work of his teacher Diodore, and of Diodore's other famous pupil, John Chrysostom. Chrysostom states in the case of the NT parables, for example, that they "must not be explained throughout word for word, since many absurdities will follow," advocating attention to the overall message of the author.⁶⁹ The mind of the author, on this view, is discovered above all by attending to his theme (connected with his setting), his purpose, and his meaning, focusing on the general thrust of the material as well as its detail.⁷⁰ Reading texts in their contexts is an important aspect of this endeavor.⁷¹ The Antiochenes were not generally "literalistic" readers, then (in the sense discussed in my chapter 4). Of course, they were just as capable as anyone else throughout history of individual readings that were somewhat wooden in nature.⁷² Their clear intention, however (even if they sometimes failed) was to read literally, taking deeply seriously not only the divine inspiration of the Scriptures but also the full involvement of the human authors in their composition. These human authors are not at all like Plato's divinely possessed seers, on the Antiochene view. They work with understanding.⁷³

THE MEANING OF THE WRITER

It is the "meaning of the writer," thus understood, that is fundamentally important to Theodore—the literal sense, directing the reader to God's actions in this world of historical truth, and not to another world of symbolic truth. To play "fast and loose" with this authorial meaning risks the entire understanding of biblical faith as a historically rooted faith. It is this, above all, that leads Theodore, in company with Diodore and John Chrysostom (and to a lesser extent the later Syrian writer Theodoret, who was more comfortable with what he called "the

---

⁶⁷ Beryl Smalley, *The Study of the Bible in the Middle Ages* (Notre Dame: University of Notre Dame Press, 1964), 14.
⁶⁸ Reventlow, *Biblical Interpretation*, 2:7.
⁶⁹ John Chrysostom, *Homily 47* (on Matt 13:34, 35; *NPNF* 1, 10:292).
⁷⁰ Hill, *Antioch*, 107–33.
⁷¹ E.g., Hill, *Antioch*, 40n41, 143–44, 154.
⁷² Theodore's reading of Jonah, whose reputation he clearly feels he needs to defend, is a case in point. Hill, *Antioch*, 76–77, 116–17; see Theodore, *Commentary on the Twelve Prophets* (trans. Robert C. Hill; FC 108; Washington, D.C.: Catholic University of America Press, 2004), 185–205. Theodore shares here a patristic tendency in general to treat biblical characters as models of virtue. It is an unconvincing reading, but not (as Hill seems to imagine, 153) evidence of a lack of intention on Theodore's part to read literally and in line with what he says about such reading elsewhere.
⁷³ Hill, *Antioch*, 32–35, albeit noting that on occasion both Theodore and Chrysostom flirt with the idea of mantic possession. On this matter see further my chapter 13.

norms of allegory"),[74] to criticize the Origenists. Biblical texts might well have "an elevated sense" (according to Diodore), as they are read within the whole scriptural context. It is entirely inappropriate, however, to understand this elevated sense in a way that overthrows the "underlying sense,"[75] which we arrive at (as Diodore had learned from his philosophical and rhetorical studies in Athens) by "concentration of mind upon observable facts."[76] The Antiochenes laid great emphasis, in fact, on

> the "reality" of the overarching narrative from creation through fall to incarnation and redemption ... [which] meant that spiritualising away the body, the material world, the "flesh" of Christ in the story of his birth, life or passion, or indeed in the eucharist, had to be deemed heretical. The symbolic allegory of Origen seemed to undermine the core by encouraging such spiritualising.[77]

Indeed, writes Theodore, Scripture itself gives no warrant for what others describe as "spiritual reading." In the particular case of Galatians 4, he argues, Paul's interpretation of Genesis builds on what Theodore regards as a historical account in its own right, and the apostle *then also* draws an analogy between the Genesis story and the later situation in which Christians find themselves. We saw in chapter 6 how Chrysostom also resists the idea that Galatians 4 is truly an example of "allegorical reading." Theodoret would later agree: Paul wrote what he wrote "not to exclude the factual basis, but to compare the type to the reality."[78] For Theodore, the nature of the Great Story as a salvation history is fundamentally important, and although Christ stands at the center of this history, its different phases must each be allowed their own integrity. This comes out clearly in the introduction to his commentary on Amos, for example, where he is at pains to emphasize that the prophet speaks very much to the circumstances of his own times, even though in a broader sense he points forward to Christ:

> It is quite obvious, on the one hand, that the blessed prophet Amos ... speaks in almost all his prophecy of the fate that would befall the people.... On the other hand, it is not without purpose that reference to this was made by the prophets;

---

[74] Hill, *Antioch*, 7n19, 140n20, and (for examples of Theodoret allegorizing), 158 (on the ruler of Tyre and Pharaoh). Chrysostom could also sometimes use allegory (146, 155–56), and even Theodore himself did so (156n62), but the whole tenor of Antiochene biblical interpretation ran against it (and not just among the scholars: Hill, *Antioch*, 155–56, where Chrysostom appears nervous about his congregation's reaction to allegory).

[75] Hill, *Antioch*, 138.

[76] Wallace-Hadrill, *Christian Antioch*, 96. "The Antiochene characteristically thought in terms of history and Scripture ... [paying] close attention to *phenomena* and to detailed examination of the facts of each matter" (102–3).

[77] Young, *Biblical Exegesis*, 296–97.

[78] Cited in Hill, *Antioch*, 157.

it was because God devoted complete attention to the people with a view to the manifestation of Christ the Lord, which would occur at a time of his choosing for the common salvation of all human beings. The reason, in fact, that he also marked them off from the nations, gave them in circumcision a mark of distinction, caused them to have a country of their own, and instructed them in provisions of the Law to conduct worship of him in isolation on Mount Zion was that when Christ the Lord came, he would make clear on the basis of such events, in keeping with the prophetic revelations and in addition to them the above provisions made for the people, the fact that God was not at some late stage making a new arrangement for the salvation of all people. Instead, at the outset and from the far distant past, he had of his own accord predetermined this.[79]

In Theodore's work, then, we find the same kind of pronounced emphasis on the history of salvation that we encounter in the Church Fathers prior to Clement and Origen.[80]

The Importance of the Literal Sense

Theodore is not only pushing back against Alexandrian allegorizing, however. He is pushing back against all Scripture reading that moves beyond the literal sense, and this includes what he regards as excessive recourse both to typology and to prophecy in biblical interpretation.[81] He is convinced in general, and not just in the case of Amos, that the prophets speak in almost all their prophecy about events that take place within the confines of OT history. This leads him time and again to dispute readings of prophetic texts that apply them directly to Christ. Thus Micah 5:2, he insists, concerns Zerubbabel, a Davidic descendant of Israel's postexilic period.[82] He regards the Psalms as authored by David, who is himself a prophet, but he looks for the historical occasion for each psalm, and when he comes to the conclusion that it dates from after David's time, he typically views the king as speaking in the voice of other OT characters in their own time.[83] In fact, so far as we can tell from Theodore's writings, he only clearly regarded three

---

[79] Theodore, *Twelve Prophets*, 126.
[80] For both Theodore and Theodoret, the book of Zechariah (e.g.) "is primarily a window onto the events Zechariah is alluding to, not a mirror in which the commentator may see himself and the life of his contemporaries reflected, not to mention a series of further layers of meaning rising upwards from the text." Hill, *Antioch*, 137.
[81] Hill, *Antioch*, 161: "typology ... is only infrequently invoked by Theodore."
[82] Theodore, *Twelve Prophets*, 226–27.
[83] See, e.g., Theodore's analysis of Psalm 34, in which he suggests that David "prophesies things in accord with the psalm before this, taking the part of Hezekiah in offering up this psalm as some sentiments of thanksgiving to the Lord." Theodore of Mopsuestia, *Commentary on Psalms 1–81* (ed. Rowan A. Greer; trans. Robert C. Hill; WGRW 5; Atlanta: Society of Biblical Literature, 2006), 315.

psalms as directly speaking of Christ prophetically (Pss 2, 8, 45)—although it is likely, in the light of the overall evidence, that he thought the same about a couple more.

Once their primary horizon has been established, both the prophetic writings and the psalms can then be seen *also* to concern Christ. This is the case not least because, in their poetic style, they often express themselves metaphorically and hyperbolically. In this way they "outstrip" their OT fulfillments, such that Jesus fulfills the prophecy in a fuller way than ever before. Yet Theodore is restrained in his appeal to such realities, largely limiting this kind of reading of the OT texts to examples where the NT itself reads in the same way (e.g., Mic 5:2; Ps 16). In his commentary on John's Gospel, for example, "[o]nly where John himself speaks of fulfilled prophecy is Theodore ready to acknowledge it."[84]

The literal sense is even more important to Theodore, then, than it is to writers like Irenaeus and Tertullian,[85] for although

> he did acknowledge the presence of typical/archetypal relation between the two [testaments] . . . [nevertheless] he insisted that both the type and the archetype had to be historical realities and that their mutual relation had to be also explicitly approved within the New Testament. He believed that the Scriptures themselves had to confirm God's inspired intent. As a result, he rejected allegorical interpretations as being the imaginative speculations of the exegete.[86]

So committed is he to the literal sense, indeed, that it can even lead him to relegate certain OT books to a secondary status, because he cannot read them literally and at the same time as inspired Scripture. Proverbs and Ecclesiastes are "human teachings"—Solomon possessed no prophetic gift—while the book of Job deviates in various respects from what we might expect from a scriptural composition.[87] The Song of Songs is a secular love poem—"Solomon's homage to pharaoh's daughter, meant to defend his marriage with her."[88]

It is interesting to compare Theodore's approach in the latter case with Origen's. Both agree that the Song, read according to its literal sense, is unworthy of inclusion in the canon. Theodore's solution is to exclude it. Origen's solution is

---

[84] Reventlow, *Biblical Interpretation*, 2:20.

[85] This is not, of course, to suggest that all his individual attempts to describe the literal are convincing. In fact, and despite his stated commitment to the literal sense, he can be found (like his teacher Diodore) playing "fast and loose" with it in his own way (e.g., Hill, *Antioch*, 76–77, 111, 116–17).

[86] Frederick G. McLeod, *The Roles of Christ's Humanity in Salvation: Insights from Theodore of Mopsuestia* (Washington, D.C.: Catholic University of America Press, 2005), 209n11.

[87] Reventlow, *Biblical Interpretation*, 2:9–10.

[88] Othmar Keel, *The Song of Songs* (trans. Frederick J. Gaiser; CC; Minneapolis: Fortress, 1994), 9.

to read it, verse by verse, allegorically. Unfortunately for Theodore, "it was Origen who wrote the commentary whose influence was all-pervasive" in the succeeding centuries,[89] and this influence is perceptible in the proceedings of the Second Council of Constantinople in 553, in the course of which Theodore and his writings were subject to extensive and critical review.

Theodore, Constantinople, and Judaizing

The charges were various, but Theodore's resistance to the allegorical reading of Scripture in general, and his rejection of it in the case of the Song of Songs in particular (characterized at the council as "an attack against tradition and the Holy Spirit"),[90] were certainly among the aspects of his literary output that offended the council's participants. So too was his refusal to countenance anything more than a minimal degree of direct prophetic prediction of Christ in the Psalms; "[h]e dismissed the prophecies about Christ," the council maintained, "and he vilified, as far as he could, the great mystery of the arrangements that have been made for our salvation."[91] His "detestable" writings were condemned as containing "unbelievable folly and ... disgraceful utterances,"[92] and he was accused of having a Jewish creed.

This charge of "Judaizing" interpretation was one that other Bible readers committed to the literal sense of the OT throughout the centuries also had to endure. According to Shaye Cohen, Clement of Alexandria was the first to use the slur, in his now almost completely lost work *Canon Ecclesiasticus, or Against the Judaizers*.[93] Origen picks up the idea, accusing those "who do not wish to think that 'the law is spiritual'" of failing to take heed of "the leaven of the Pharisees."[94] Later, Gregory of Nyssa, in *Against Eunomius*, "argues that if a Christian 'judaizes' by relying on the bare text of Scripture ... incorrect theology will be the result."[95] In the period of the Reformation, John Calvin was accused by Lutherans of

[89] J. Robert Wright, ed., *Proverbs, Ecclesiastes, Song of Solomon* (ACCS [OT] 9; Downers Grove, Ill.: InterVarsity, 2005), xxv.
[90] McLeod, *Christ's Humanity*, 209n12.
[91] Tanner, *Decrees*, 1:109.
[92] Tanner, *Decrees*, 1:109, 113.
[93] Shaye J. D. Cohen, *The Beginnings of Jewishness: Boundaries, Varieties, Uncertainties* (Berkeley: University of California Press, 1999), 190.
[94] Cited in Cohen, *Beginnings*, 190.
[95] Cited in Cohen, *Beginnings*, 190. It is interesting, however, that Gregory praises in extravagant language the *Hexaemeron* of his brother Basil of Caesarea (his homilies on the six days of creation), in which Basil says (among other things) that "I know the laws of allegory, though less by myself than from the works of others. There are those truly, who do not admit the common sense of the Scriptures ... who change the nature of reptiles and of wild beasts to suit their allegories. ... For me grass is grass; plant, fish, wild beast, domestic animal, I take all in the literal sense.'For I am not ashamed of the gospel.'" Basil, *Hexaemeron (Six Days)*, 9.1 (*NPNF* 2, 8:101).

"Judaizing" because of his typological interpretation of psalms that had traditionally been considered as messianic.[96] Calvin, in turn, accused both Roman Catholics and Radical Reformers of the same "Judaizing" sin.[97] It is an ugly accusation, reeking of implicit or overt anti-Semitism (scarcely concealed in a comment like Bonaventure's in the thirteenth century about "the Jew, who always gravitates toward the literal sense").[98] Its appalling deployment throughout history has only ever served, by way of imputing strong guilt through association, to release its users from the obligation to conduct sustained and reasoned argument with their opponents about hermeneutics. "To call a Christian practice 'judaizing' is to label it, not to explain it."[99]

AUGUSTINE

We come, finally, to Augustine, born in Thagaste in Roman North Africa in AD 354. In his teens he studied rhetoric in Carthage, subsequently adding to this expertise "a comprehensive knowledge of ancient philosophy and the other liberal arts."[100] Attracted for a while by Manichaeism (a sect founded by the third-century AD heretic Mani), with its Marcionite and gnostic overtones, and later by Neoplatonism, Augustine was ultimately baptized as a Christian in 387, and soon afterward became bishop of Hippo (around 396). He remained in that position until his death in 430. Augustine is the channel through which all the streams of thought among the earlier Church Fathers flowed out into the Western world, and indeed he is "the first Western theologian to develop a systematically organized theory of interpreting the Bible"—a sustained and reasoned argument about hermeneutics.[101] He was widely cited in later centuries as the great authority on both doctrine and interpretative practice, his influence "all-pervasive ... on Christian thought and writing in the medieval West."[102] It is fitting, then, that Augustine should be the final patristic exemplar studied in chapters 7 and 8. I shall focus our attention, in the first instance, on his great four-volume work, *On Christian Doctrine*.

---

[96] Pak, *Judaizing Calvin*, 103–24, who notes the stated intention of Calvin's critic Giles Hunnius "to 'pierce through the impious glosses of Calvin' by which Calvin 'darkens with Jewish darkness' many biblical passages that reveal and confirm Christ's divinity" (105).

[97] Greene-McCreight, *Ad Litteram*, 123.

[98] Reventlow, *Biblical Interpretation*, 2:210–11.

[99] Cohen, *Beginnings*, 196.

[100] Reventlow, *Biblical Interpretation*, 2:77.

[101] Reventlow, *Biblical Interpretation*, 2:76. This is not to diminish the importance of other mediating Christian thinkers in the transitional phase between the patristic and medieval periods, most notably Gregory the Great. See Stephan Ch. Kessler, "Gregory the Great: A Figure of Tradition and Transition in Church Exegesis," *HBOT* 1/2:135–47.

[102] Wright, "Augustine," 727.

On Christian Doctrine, Books 1 and 2

For Augustine, Scripture exists to foster in our hearts love for the eternal and unchanging Triune God and also for our neighbor.[103] There is such a thing in the biblical text as "the precise meaning which the author ... intended to express in that place," and the reader who fails to comprehend this meaning is to be corrected, since "faith will totter if the authority of Scripture begin to shake."[104] Yet in itself an individual error is not necessarily a huge problem, so long as the meaning that is drawn from the text is "used for the building up of love."[105] Faith, hope, and love lie at the heart of the Christian religion, and the one "who keeps a firm hold upon these" does not in fact need Scripture any more.[106] The reason is that Scripture will already have accomplished its goal as the bringer of a "remedy for the terrible diseases of the human will."[107] In the meantime, Scripture readers "seek nothing more than to find out the thought and will of those by whom it was written, and through these to find out the will of God, in accordance with which they believe these men to have spoken."[108] Those who seek will find, because although there are obscurities in Scripture, "almost nothing is dug out of those obscure passages which may not be found set forth in the plainest language elsewhere."[109] However, the seeker will do well first of all to know the content of the canonical books, and then to focus on "those matters that are plainly laid down in them, whether rules of life or rules of faith." It is only then, having "made ourselves to a certain extent familiar with the language of Scripture," that we should "proceed to open up and investigate the obscure passages."[110] Obscurity should be handled in the context of clarity, the more difficult texts in Scripture in the light of what is plain.

In addressing the challenges facing Scripture readers, Augustine turns first to what he calls "unknown" as opposed to "ambiguous" signs in Scripture.[111] "The great remedy" in respect of the former, he proposes, is "knowledge of languages." Latin speakers "need two other languages for the knowledge of Scripture, Hebrew and Greek"—not only to help them with idiom, but "on account of the diversities among translators. For the translations of the Scriptures from Hebrew into

---

[103] "Whoever, then, thinks that he understands the Holy Scriptures, or any part of them, but puts such an interpretation upon them as does not tend to build up this twofold love of God and our neighbour, does not yet understand them as he ought." Augustine, *On Christian Doctrine*, 1.36 (NPNF 1, 2:533).

[104] Augustine, *On Christian Doctrine*, 1.36–37 (NPNF 1, 2:533).

[105] Augustine, *On Christian Doctrine*, 1.36–37 (NPNF 1, 2:533).

[106] Augustine, *On Christian Doctrine*, 1.39 (NPNF 1, 2:534).

[107] Augustine, *On Christian Doctrine*, 2.5 (NPNF 1, 2:536).

[108] Augustine, *On Christian Doctrine*, 2.5 (NPNF 1, 2:536–37).

[109] Augustine, *On Christian Doctrine*, 2.6 (NPNF 1, 2:537).

[110] Augustine, *On Christian Doctrine*, 2.9 (NPNF 1, 2:539).

[111] Augustine, *On Christian Doctrine*, 2.10 (NPNF 1, 2:539).

Greek can be counted, but the Latin translators are out of all number,"[112] and they are often "deceived by an ambiguity in the original language" to such an extent that they impose upon a biblical text "a construction that is wholly alien to the sense of the writer."[113]

However, the Scripture reader requires not only linguistic but also historical and cultural knowledge in order to read well: "Anything ... that we learn from history about the chronology of past times assists us very much in understanding the Scriptures."[114] The "science of reasoning is of very great service in searching into and unravelling all sorts of questions that come up in Scripture,"[115] and knowledge of the arts is also helpful, so "that we may not be wholly ignorant of what Scripture means to convey when it employs figures of speech derived from these arts."[116] Later, in book 3, Augustine will emphasize the general importance of understanding "figures of speech" (tropes), in light of the fact that

> the authors of our Scriptures use all those forms of expression which grammarians call by the Greek name *tropes*, and use them more freely and in greater variety than people who are unacquainted with the Scriptures ... can imagine or believe.[117]

All such learning contributes greatly to Scripture comprehension, although the reader will also find in abundance therein "things that are to be found nowhere else, but can be learnt only in the wonderful sublimity and wonderful simplicity of the Scriptures."[118] Approaching Scripture in this way, the reader will find that "unknown signs" no longer hold him back.[119]

ON CHRISTIAN DOCTRINE, BOOKS 3 AND 4

Having read books 1 and 2, Augustine believes that the student of the Bible is now in a position to consider "ambiguous signs" in Scripture.[120] When he finds Scripture to be ambiguous (and now we are in book 3), he must first of

---

[112] Augustine, *On Christian Doctrine*, 2.11 (NPNF 1, 2:539–40).

[113] Augustine, *On Christian Doctrine*, 2.12 (NPNF 1, 2:540).

[114] Augustine, *On Christian Doctrine*, 2.28 (NPNF 1, 2:549), at the end of a long discourse on both linguistic and cultural matters in 2.13–27.

[115] Augustine, *On Christian Doctrine*, 2.31 (NPNF 1, 2:550).

[116] Augustine, *On Christian Doctrine*, 2.30 (NPNF 1, 2:550).

[117] Augustine, *On Christian Doctrine*, 3.29 (NPNF 1, 2:567).

[118] Augustine, *On Christian Doctrine*, 2.42 (NPNF 1, 2:555).

[119] He will not be "stopped by unknown words and forms of speech, [but will possess] the knowledge of certain necessary objects, so as not to be ignorant of the force and nature of those which are used figuratively; and [will be] assisted, besides, by accuracy in the texts, which has been secured by skill and care in the matter of correction." Augustine, *On Christian Doctrine*, 3.1 (NPNF 1, 2:556).

[120] Augustine, *On Christian Doctrine*, 2.42 (NPNF 1, 2:555).

all—considering the possibility of his own carelessness—check that there is nothing wrong with respect to his punctuation or pronunciation. As he does so, he should consult "the rule of faith which he has gathered from the plainer passages of Scripture, and from the authority of the Church," and thereafter he should pay attention to the context.[121] Ambiguities that do not relate either to punctuation or pronunciation must be examined in the same way.[122]

All of this is a matter of "ordinary care and diligence." This is not the case where "metaphorical words" are concerned.[123] Here the reader must be careful not to take a figurative expression literally—for example, thinking of "Sabbath" as "nothing but the one day out of seven which recurs in constant succession."[124] To read in such a way is "to follow the letter, and to take signs for the things that are signified by them," and it is "a mark of weakness and bondage."[125] On the other hand, it is also wrong "to take a literal form of speech as if it were figurative."[126]

How are we to tell the difference? Augustine notes that it frequently happens that "if Scripture either enjoins what is opposed to the customs of the hearers, or condemns what is not so opposed . . . they think that the expression is figurative."[127] In the same way, "if an erroneous opinion has taken possession of the mind, men think that whatever Scripture asserts contrary to this must be figurative."[128] In other words, readers all too often appeal to the figurative in order to evade what Scripture commands in its literal sense about what to believe and how to live. Their reading is self-serving.

Augustine's solution is that "[w]hatever there is in the word of God that cannot, when taken literally, be referred either to purity of life or soundness of doctrine, you may set down as figurative."[129] Therefore, although we must "consider carefully what is suitable to times and places and persons, and not rashly

---

[121] Augustine, *On Christian Doctrine*, 3.2–3 (*NPNF* 1, 2:556–58). See also 3.25–27 (*NPNF* 1, 2:566–67), where (however) the immediate context is mentioned *first* as the guide in discerning whether an expression is being used "metaphorically" in a good or a bad sense (3.25; *NPNF* 1, 2:566), and only then the broader context of the plainer passages of Scripture, with no reference at all to the authority of the Church: "if a man in searching the Scriptures endeavors to get at the intention of the author through whom the Holy Spirit spake, whether he succeeds in this endeavor, or whether he draws a different meaning from the words, but one that is not opposed to sound doctrine, he is free from blame so long as he is supported by the testimony of some other passage of Scripture" (3.27; *NPNF* 1, 2:567).

[122] Augustine, *On Christian Doctrine*, 3.4 (*NPNF* 1, 2:558).
[123] Augustine, *On Christian Doctrine*, 3.5 (*NPNF* 1, 2:559).
[124] Augustine, *On Christian Doctrine*, 3.5 (*NPNF* 1, 2:559).
[125] Augustine, *On Christian Doctrine*, 3.9 (*NPNF* 1, 2:560).
[126] Augustine, *On Christian Doctrine*, 3.10 (*NPNF* 1, 2:560).
[127] Augustine, *On Christian Doctrine*, 3.10 (*NPNF* 1, 2:561).
[128] Augustine, *On Christian Doctrine*, 3.10 (*NPNF* 1, 2:561).
[129] Augustine, *On Christian Doctrine*, 3.10 (*NPNF* 1, 2:560).

charge men with sins" (e.g., people in the OT), yet "sayings or . . . actual deeds, which appear to the inexperienced to be sinful, and which are ascribed to God, or to men whose holiness is put before us as an example, are wholly figurative."[130] However, if a biblical text, when read in its literal sense, "at once gives a meaning" that "tends to establish the reign of love," it is *not* to be read figuratively.[131] So if a sentence "is one of command, either forbidding a crime or vice, or enjoining an act of prudence or benevolence, it is not figurative" (albeit that "some commands are given to all in common, others to particular classes of persons"). If, however, a sentence "seems to enjoin a crime or vice, or to forbid an act of prudence or benevolence, it is figurative" (e.g., the statement "except you eat the flesh of the Son of man and drink His blood, you have no life in you").[132] In general, "the transactions recorded in the Old Testament are to be taken not literally only, but figuratively as well."[133] Yet when the reader

> reads of the sins of great men, although he may be able to see and to trace out in them a figure of things to come, let him yet put the literal fact to this use also, to teach him not to dare to vaunt himself in his own good deeds, and in comparison with his own righteousness, to despise others as sinners, when he sees in the case of men so eminent both the storms that are to be avoided and the shipwrecks that are to be wept over.[134]

These sins were recorded, in fact, in order to foster humility, reminding us that God resists the proud and gives grace to the humble.

In all, then, we must "walk by the light of Holy Scripture" itself when we are dealing with ambiguity, settling the controversy caused by "metaphorical expressions" in Scripture "by the application of testimonies sought out in every portion of the same Scripture."[135] Scripture must interpret Scripture.

Having dealt in this way in books 1 to 3 with the question of how to ascertain the proper meaning of Scripture, Augustine turns finally, in book 4, to the question of how to communicate this meaning. The authors of Scripture themselves, he proposes, are our best models in this endeavor, combining wisdom with eloquence,[136] albeit that Christian teachers should imitate them in their clarity and not "in those passages where . . . they have expressed themselves with a useful and wholesome obscurity."[137] The eloquent man, according to Cicero, "must speak so

---

[130] Augustine, *On Christian Doctrine*, 3.12 (NPNF 1, 2:561–62).
[131] Augustine, *On Christian Doctrine*, 3.15 (NPNF 1, 2:563).
[132] Augustine, *On Christian Doctrine*, 3.16–17 (NPNF 1, 2:563).
[133] Augustine, *On Christian Doctrine*, 3.22 (NPNF 1, 2:565).
[134] Augustine, *On Christian Doctrine*, 3.23 (NPNF 1, 2:565).
[135] Augustine, *On Christian Doctrine*, 3.28 (NPNF 1, 2:567).
[136] Augustine, *On Christian Doctrine*, 4.6 (NPNF 1, 2:577).
[137] Augustine, *On Christian Doctrine*, 4.8 (NPNF 1, 2:581).

as to teach, to delight, and to persuade.... To teach is a necessity, to delight is a beauty, to persuade is a triumph." Augustine agrees, and adds that the teacher "should not suppose that he has said what he has to say as long as he is not understood; for although what he has said be intelligible to himself, it is not said at all to the man who does not understand it."[138]

ON CHRISTIAN DOCTRINE: OVERVIEW

In *On Christian Doctrine*, then, Augustine lays out an approach to reading Scripture that is deeply and fundamentally rooted in the literal sense of the text—"the precise meaning which the author ... intended to express."[139] Beryl Smalley goes so far as to say that "[a]s an original Christian thinker he gave the 'letter' a concrete chronological reality which it never had before."[140] To discover the will of God in Scripture we must discover "the thought and will" of the human authors who wrote it, and this requires attention to the original languages in which they wrote, their rhetorical style, and as much background historical and cultural knowledge as we can accumulate. Establishing by such means what is plainly said in Scripture, we shall then be able to deal satisfactorily with what is not, reading individual passages within their immediate contexts, but also in the context of the whole unfolding biblical Story. This will enable us to grasp among other things not only what the OT Scriptures in themselves teach in their literal sense, but also how they foretell and foreshadow what is taught in the NT. In all of this, attending to the literal sense is of primary importance, not least because recourse to the figurative can mute Scripture's authoritative voice. In this proposal Augustine is evidently leading us back to a much closer connection between the voice of God and the voice of the human author in the biblical text than we find in Alexandrian authors like Clement and Origen, and even in earlier authors like Justin Martyr.

THE LITERAL MEANING OF GENESIS

This same commitment to the literal sense is clearly evident in Augustine's other works, and most notably in *The Literal Meaning of Genesis*, which dates from shortly after the composition of the majority of *On Christian Doctrine* (i.e., it was written between 404 and 420). Writing about an earlier work on Genesis directed against the Manicheans (388/389)—who, like Marcion, read the OT in what some have characterized as a "literal" manner, and had little time for it—Augustine tells us that he was already intent in that work on offering a literal reading of Genesis, but could not see how to do it. The theoretical primacy of the

---

[138] Augustine, *On Christian Doctrine*, 4.12 (*NPNF* 1, 2:583).
[139] Augustine, *On Christian Doctrine*, 1.36 (*NPNF* 1, 2:533).
[140] Smalley, *Study of the Bible*, 23.

literal sense to Augustine is indeed already seen in that earlier composition—even though it is also packed with allegorical interpretation to an extent that Augustine later came to regret. The literal sense is paramount, he maintains therein, but "if there is no way to understand what is written in a devout manner worthy of God without believing it to be set forth figuratively and enigmatically, we have the authority of the apostles . . . to explain all these figures of things in accord with the catholic faith."[141]

In *Literal Meaning of Genesis* Augustine now hopes "to show how the Book of Genesis has been written with a proper rather than an allegorical meaning in view."[142] He is interested in "the plain meaning of the historical facts, not . . . [the] future events which they foreshadow"[143]—albeit that the rendering of the literal sense (as we might expect, on the basis of what we have read in *On Christian Doctrine*) must take account of what is metaphorical. Thus, even though we are told in Genesis 3:7 that the eyes of the human beings in the garden were "opened," they could not previously have been closed in the normal sense of the word.[144] Likewise, God does not possess physical hands, no matter what Genesis 2:7 might be taken to imply.[145] The literal can contain the figural, but, for all that, the literal can certainly be distinguished from the allegorical. Literal reading (as we might also expect on the basis of *On Christian Doctrine*) also takes account of the larger context in which biblical texts appear, searching for "the literal sense while reading the texts in light of each other."[146] One way or another, however, seeking the literal sense of Scripture is the first and most important thing for Augustine in this work, and "spiritual reading" must not be allowed to obliterate this literal sense.[147] The rivers in Genesis 2, for example, are "true rivers, not just figurative expressions without a corresponding reality in the literal sense, as if the names would signify something else and not rivers at all."[148] The reader of Scripture must pay attention to such realities first of all, only later "searching for any further meaning they may have."[149]

---

[141] Augustine, *On Genesis against the Manicheans*, 2.2.3.

[142] Augustine, *De Genesi ad litteram* (*The Literal Meaning of Genesis*) (2 vols.; trans. John H. Taylor; ACW 41–42; New York: Newman, 1982), 8.2.5 (ACW 42:36).

[143] Augustine, *Literal Meaning*, 1.17.34 (ACW 41:39).

[144] Augustine, *Literal Meaning*, 11.31.40–41 (ACW 42:162–64).

[145] Augustine, *Literal Meaning*, 6.12.20 (ACW 41:192).

[146] Greene-McCreight, *Ad Litteram*, 60.

[147] "The biblical text is not to be read simply as containing ciphers which point to realities other than what they appear to be on the surface. On the contrary, the surface or 'letter' of the text can be trusted to speak of the world in which we live. The letter of the narrative can prefigure realities yet to come, but these realities do not destroy the power of the letter of the narrative to speak meaningfully of and refer to the world of 'material reality.'" Greene-McCreight, *Ad Litteram*, 63.

[148] Augustine, *Literal Meaning*, 8.7.13 (ACW 42:43).

[149] Augustine, *Literal Meaning*, 8.7.13 (ACW 42:43).

Augustine in Theory and in Practice

This is not to say that Augustine's hermeneutical practice in his various writings consistently reflects the principled approach outlined in *On Christian Doctrine*. To some degree, Augustine was not in fact capable of following his own sage advice in that treatise, because he knew almost no Hebrew, and only a little Greek.[150] So even in his *Literal Meaning of Genesis*, his interpretation "often seems far from what we might otherwise understand to be literal."[151] More broadly, his other surviving works are often heavily marked by allegorical reading. The Good Samaritan in Luke 10, for example, is Christ, and the beaten victim stands for human beings in general.[152] Jesus, risen from the dead, is able to take care of those (ourselves) who are "half dead." He is "refreshing" us even now in the "stable" (inn), which is the Church. Here Augustine builds on an interpretation of the parable that goes back to Irenaeus, Clement of Alexandria, and Origen. There is, however, nothing in the literal sense of Luke's text to suggest (as Augustine proposes) that "[i]n this Samaritan the Lord Jesus Christ wanted us to understand himself"[153]—nothing to make us think that Augustine is actually reading the parable as Jesus (or Luke) wishes it to be read. Jesus is not speaking about saving sinners as they recuperate in the Church; he is speaking explicitly about the identity of the neighbor whom I should love in accordance with the commandments. The parable concerns ethics—not ecclesiology, or soteriology. Augustine himself notes this in passing, telling his hearers about "the occasion of this narrative," but the text in its literal sense, in this instance—at least in the homiletical context (if not in his scholar's study)—is of little interest to him.

CONCLUSION

In 1529, in his workshop in Wittenberg, Lucas Cranach the Elder—court painter to the Electors of Saxony, whose portraits of their family members and associates are still to be found in art galleries and museums all over Germany—unveiled to the world one of several portraits of Martin Luther that he painted in the course of his lifetime. It now hangs in St. Anne's Church in Augsburg.[154] Luther is

---

[150] Greene-McCreight, *Ad Litteram*, 38.

[151] Greene-McCreight, *Ad Litteram*, 48.

[152] Augustine, "Sermon 171," in *Sermons 148–183* (ed. John E. Rotelle; trans. Edmund Hill; vol. 5 of *Sermons*, part III of *The Works of Saint Augustine: A Translation for the 21st Century*; New York: New City, 1992), 247. See also *Quaestiones Evangeliorum* (*Questions on the Gospels*), 2.19, in *New Testament I and II* (ed. Boniface Ramsey; vols. 15 and 16 of *The Works of Saint Augustine: A Translation for the 21st Century*; New York: New City, 2014), 388–89.

[153] Augustine, "Sermon 171," 248.

[154] Those who do not know the painting can see it online at https://commons.wikimedia.org/wiki/File:Martin_Luther,_1529.jpg.

dressed all in black, and stands against a light blue background—an unambiguous man, one feels, standing over against much of the culture of his time, with an unambiguous message to proclaim about the Christian faith.

By a curious coincidence, it was also around 1529 that the Italian Mannerist artist Parmigianino (Girolamo Francesco Maria Mazzola, 1503–1540) completed his *Madonna of the Rose*, which now hangs in the Zwinger museum in Dresden, about two hundred and eighty miles to Augsburg's northeast. *The Madonna of the Rose* is anything but unambiguous.[155] An artist whose mature style was marked by "affected elegance and thinly veiled eroticism,"[156] Parmigianino presents us with a woman whom we might well at first glance consider to be the biblical Mary, but whose right breast is visible through the thin veil of her garment, and whose pose overall reminds us more, in the end, of the pagan goddess Venus. It was with Aphrodite/Venus that the rose was associated in classical pagan myth and ritual. The child in the painting, for his part, has his left hand on a globe, suggesting Christ's role as savior of the world. Yet overall, he reminds us much more of Cupid than of the infant Jesus. This is a Christ child of "langorous pose, conspiratorial gaze, and prominent genitals," all conspiring together to "give the work its almost unhealthy intensity of mood."[157] So what are we looking at in this painting? Is it a Christian Madonna and Child, with ancient pagan allusions embedded within it? Or is it a pagan Venus and Cupid, whose Christian elements are only superficial and residual? It is far from clear, but the balance of probability favors the latter.

We do not encounter this kind of deep ambiguity with respect to Christianity and paganism in Justin, Irenaeus, or Tertullian, nor in Theodore and Augustine. Their "painting" of Christian faith and practice, for all its flaws, presents it in black and blue (if not black and white). We do find exactly this ambiguity in Origen, however—to such an extent that we wonder if we are dealing in this instance with a Christian making use of pagan forms, or a pagan making use of Christian ones.[158] For all that he claims to be standing in solidarity with his forebears, and inhabiting the same tradition, the two perspectives often seem in reality—like our two paintings—to be miles apart.

---

[155] This painting can be viewed at http://skd-online-collection.skd.museum/de/contents/showSearch?id=365254#longDescription.

[156] Rachel H. Smith, "Parmigianino," in *Renaissance and Reformation, 1500–1620: A Biographical Dictionary* (ed. Jo E. Carney; London: Greenwood, 2001), 279–80.

[157] David Ekserdjian, *Parmigianino* (New Haven: Yale University Press, 2006), 78.

[158] "The fact is that Origen's particular theological system, with its bias towards the intellectual, its disinclination towards taking history and event seriously and its allegorism twining like ivy round every branch of this theological structure, gives a peculiar and individual twist to every regular and traditional element in the Christian faith.... We see the familiar features there, but we can perceive that they are blurred." Hanson, *Allegory and Event*, 332.

9

How Shall We Then Read?
The Church Fathers, the Reformers, and Ourselves

> *Whoever takes another meaning out of Scripture than the writer intended, goes astray. . . . He is to be corrected . . . and to be shown how much better it is not to quit the straight road, lest, if he get into a habit of going astray, he may sometimes take cross roads, or even go in the wrong direction altogether.*
>
> —Augustine[1]

> *[A]ll the senses are founded on one—the literal—from which alone can any argument be drawn, and not from those intended in allegory . . . nothing of Holy Scripture perishes on account of this, since nothing necessary to faith is contained under the spiritual sense which is not elsewhere put forward by the Scripture in its literal sense.*
>
> —Thomas Aquinas[2]

We are now in a good position to draw conclusions about the Church Fathers' corporate appeal to apostolic authority in their approach to biblical interpretation, and to set these conclusions within the larger context of the argument of chapters 4 through 8 about the Reformation. I shall argue in the present chapter that the Church Fathers were only partially justified in their appeal to apostolic authority. The Reformers were right to criticize them for at least some aspects of their approach to biblical interpretation and to insist that the Bible should be read literally. Modern Christians should still strive to read it in this way—albeit that the contemporary "reformed" reading of Scripture will not simply duplicate that of our forebears.

APOSTOLIC WARRANT AND LITERAL READING

Insofar as the Church Fathers read Scripture literally, attending to its unfolding nature as one Great Story told by human authors inspired by the Holy Spirit—a

---

[1] Augustine, *On Christian Doctrine*, 1.36 (*NPNF* 1, 2:533).
[2] Aquinas, *Summa*, 1.1.10.

story in which God redeems first his OT and then his NT people, and gives them laws to live by—they have good reason for their confidence that they reflect apostolic hermeneutical practice. When Justin insists that the OT read in its literal sense means to speak about a coming Messiah, who is Jesus Christ; when Irenaeus labors so greatly to establish the unity of the biblical Story as a history of salvation, marked throughout its length, in its literal sense, by God's salvific work; and when Tertullian pays such careful attention to context in interpreting biblical texts, not least in interpreting the OT law—all three stand in line with the apostles. When Theodore emphasizes the way in which Scripture directs the reader's gaze toward God's actions in the world of historical truth, and not a world of symbolic truth, and when Augustine advises his readers, in judging the significance of a passage, to take account of where it sits within the whole biblical Story taken in its literal sense—both men stand in line with the apostles. Even Origen, as we have seen, possesses his own kind of commitment to the literal sense of the biblical text. Had he not, he would not have expended so much energy in establishing what he believed to be the correct text of Scripture (text-critically speaking). The literal sense of Scripture was, for the Church Fathers, the foundational sense, even if it was sometimes only a matter of clarifying which were the correct words that (in Origen's case) should almost immediately be read nonliterally. One of the great indications of the extent to which this was the case is that (as Gerald Bray notes) "the great doctrinal debates of the fourth and fifth centuries were conducted mainly at the level of literal exegesis."[3]

LITERAL READING IN THE MIDDLE AGES

The literal sense remained foundational for Christian thinkers throughout the succeeding centuries. The influence of Augustine's *On Christian Doctrine* on hermeneutical matters is everywhere to be seen.

The early ninth-century writer Alcuin, for example, commenting on how to read Genesis 49, states that "[t]he foundation in history must be laid first, so that the roof of allegory can be built more suitably on the first-established structure."[4] Three centuries later, Rupert of Deutz insists that "[s]ince the Bible is the only reliable report of God's works, its literal sense must be taken seriously in every instance."[5] Also in the twelfth century, Hugh of St. Victor teaches the necessity of first establishing "that original sense of the narrative that is expressed in the truly literal sense," before moving on to any other kind of endeavor.[6]

---

[3] Bray, *Biblical Interpretation*, 104.
[4] Cited in Reventlow, *Biblical Interpretation*, 2:123.
[5] Reventlow, *Biblical Interpretation*, 2:155.
[6] Cited in Reventlow, *Biblical Interpretation*, 2:165.

In the following century, the Dominican Thomas Aquinas—no doubt painfully aware of the way in which recent history had demonstrated that it was not only the orthodox, but also heretics, who could effectively deploy the allegorical reading of Scripture in defense of their prior convictions[7]—agrees that the literal sense is fundamental (note the second epigraph to the present chapter). Thomas therefore devotes considerable space to the literal sense in his commentary on Romans, for example, paying great attention to Paul's overall argument as well as to details of grammar, syntax, style, and historical background.[8] For Thomas, "it is the literal sense [which includes the metaphorical] that is normative and the basis for all theological argumentation."[9] For his Franciscan contemporary Bonaventure, no one can be a competent interpreter of Scripture who is not familiar with "the letters of the Bible."[10]

Finally, Nicholas of Lyra in the fourteenth century (c. 1270–1349) asserts that any further meanings of Scripture presuppose "the literal sense as . . . the foundation" of the interpretative building, and that "a mystical interpretation that deviates from the literal sense is to be judged inappropriate and inadequate."[11] He is indeed concerned that the literal sense of the biblical text has, over time, become "buried under so many mystical interpretations [as to be] nearly smothered."[12] This leads him to focus strongly in his own commentary work on the literal sense. In doing so in the case of the OT, Nicholas draws notably on a knowledge of Hebrew and of Jewish exegesis—specifically the exegesis of the eleventh-century French Jewish author Rashi (1040–1105)—that was unusual for his time. He often favors Rashi even over the esteemed Jerome.[13]

---

[7] Only a few decades had elapsed since the Church's suppression in the "Albigensian Crusade" (1209–1229) of the Cathars or Albigensians—dualist sectarians who read the Scriptures in a "spiritual" manner that led them to conclusions often diametrically opposed to those of the Church with respect to both doctrine and ritual practice. Part of the Church's response to this and other "spiritualist" movements was precisely to launch a campaign, centered in the universities, to restore to prominence reading Scripture in its literal sense. For some broader background, see Nicholas M. Healy, "Introduction," in *Aquinas on Scripture: An Introduction to His Biblical Commentaries* (ed. Thomas G. Weinandy et al.; London: T&T Clark, 2005), 1–20 (6–10).

[8] Bray notes in the subsequent period "the rise of the literal sense of interpretation to undisputed prominence in the schools where the Thomists taught." Bray, *Biblical Interpretation*, 153. In Thomas' own commentary work, "the use of the spiritual sense is relatively infrequent." Reventlow, *Biblical Interpretation*, 2:200.

[9] Healy, "Introduction," 8.

[10] Cited in Reventlow, *Biblical Interpretation*, 2:210.

[11] Cited in Reventlow, *Biblical Interpretation*, 2:250.

[12] Cited in Reventlow, *Biblical Interpretation*, 2:252.

[13] For more on Rashi and his school, see Avraham Grossman, "The School of Literal Jewish Exegesis in Northern France," *HBOT* 1/2:321–71.

Literal Reading in the Renaissance

The emphasis on the literal meaning of a text in its original language that we find in Nicholas of Lyra was shortly to become the mainstay of an entire cultural movement of the fourteenth to the sixteenth centuries. Often referred to as Renaissance Humanism, the slogan that came to characterize its ethos (although the ethos preceded the slogan) was *ad fontes*—"back to the sources."[14] These were often Greco-Roman sources, retrieved and reexamined with a view to renewing European culture on the basis of what they truly had to say once the accretions of tradition had been removed. However, study of the Bible was inevitably carried along to a certain extent by these same currents, not least because among the gifts that washed up on the shores of Western Europe at this time was a more widespread facility in biblical languages. Knowledge of Greek had never completely disappeared in the West, but the Renaissance saw its full recovery as a language there, in part because of an influx of refugee Greek scholars fleeing the sack of Constantinople by the Turks in 1453. Knowledge of Hebrew among Western Christians had been in short supply throughout the Middle Ages, although some scholars had found ways of learning it[15]—but it, too, experienced a renaissance in the late fifteenth century, not least because of the teaching career of the Jewish scholar Elias Levita (1469–1549), who taught the language to a number of Christian scholars in different European cities and also wrote a Hebrew grammar and dictionary. The first complete Hebrew Bible was in fact published during Levita's lifetime, at Soncino in 1488. I shall have much more to say about the significance of these developments in chapter 11. For the moment it is important only to note the way in which they contributed to the ongoing literal reading of Scripture as we move beyond the Middle Ages and into the period of the Reformation.

Literal Reading in the Reformation and the Counter-Reformation

What is clear, then, is that the Reformers stood at the far end of a long Christian tradition of attending to the literal sense of Scripture as its foundational sense.[16] They looked back upon it, and they explicitly depended upon it. Both they and their predecessors, including the Church Fathers, possessed ample apostolic warrant for regarding this sense as fundamental, and they were surely fully

---

[14] For some background on the Renaissance, see Trond Berg Eriksen, "Some Sociopolitical and Cultural Aspects of the Renaissance," and Jeremy Catto, "The Philosophical Context of the Renaissance Interpretation of the Bible," *HBOT* 2:94–105 and 106–22.

[15] Reventlow, *Biblical Interpretation*, 2:251.

[16] For a helpful description of Renaissance approaches to the reading of Scripture, see Reventlow, *Biblical Interpretation*, 3:5–63.

justified in deploying all the resources at their disposal in attempting to elucidate it—even if, for various reasons, posterity has not necessarily accepted all of their judgments on what the literal sense *is*, and what it entails.[17] They were not the only ones attempting the elucidation. Many Roman Catholic writers in the early Reformation period themselves continued to emphasize the literal sense of the biblical text even while remaining in "the old faith." Even though they

> continued to maintain the old distinction between the literal and the spiritual (allegorical) senses . . . they were under considerable pressure to minimize this as much as possible. In most cases, allegory was defended either because it was used in the New Testament, or because it had been consecrated in certain special cases by the consensus of the fathers of the church, not because it was an acceptable method in itself.[18]

In this period these Roman Catholic writers approached the biblical text in much the same way as their Protestant counterparts and, as they did so, they frequently came to similar conclusions about it.[19] "Until the 1540's, it was [also] possible for them to borrow extensively from Protestant writers, which many of them did."[20] After the Council of Trent, however, the Roman Catholic Church took a distinctively antihumanistic turn that was to have important consequences for its approach to biblical studies, and indeed to the modern world, for centuries thereafter. Not until 1943 did the Catholic Church officially begin to make peace once again with its own humanistic past in respect of Bible reading, with the publication by Pope Pius XII of the important papal encyclical *Divino afflante Spiritu*. This document exhorts the Roman Catholic exegete, "[b]eing thoroughly prepared by the knowledge of the ancient languages and by the aids afforded by the art of criticism," to

---

[17] E.g., the Antiochene emphasis on interpreting texts against not only a general but also a specific historical background leads to some less than satisfactory readings of the Psalms (Hill, *Antioch*, 74–76, 139–42), and connected with this is a questionable dismissal of the whole book of Psalms (and not only the individual compositions) as *possessing* a literal sense (Hill, *Antioch*, 29, 88).

[18] Bray, *Biblical Interpretation*, 192.

[19] One thinks here, e.g., of the important Roman Catholic humanist Tommaso de Vio (Cajetan, 1469–1534). Jared Wicks, "Catholic Old Testament Interpretation in the Reformation and Early Confessional Eras," *HBOT* 2:617–48 (617–23); and Michael O'Connor, "A Neglected Facet of Cardinal Cajetan: Biblical Reform in High Renaissance Rome," in Griffiths, *Bible in the Renaissance*, 71–94. Jenkins and Preston note in Cajetan's commentaries on the Pentateuch, e.g., an "emphasis on literal interpretation . . . the intention to expound the Hebrew text, not some translation of it . . . [and his] declared readiness to prefer if necessary his own judgement to that of the Holy Doctors of the church." Allan K. Jenkins and Patrick Preston, eds., *Biblical Scholarship and the Church: A Sixteenth-Century Crisis of Authority* (ANCTRTB; Aldershot: Ashgate, 2007), 154–55.

[20] Bray, *Biblical Interpretation*, 208.

undertake the task, of all those imposed on him the greatest, that namely of discovering and expounding the genuine meaning of the sacred Books. In the performance of this task let the interpreters bear in mind that their foremost and greatest endeavor should be to discern and define clearly that sense of the biblical words that is called "literal." Aided by the context and by comparison with similar passages, let them therefore by means of their knowledge of languages search out with all diligence the literal meaning of the words. All these helps indeed are wont to be pressed into service in the explanation also of profane writers so that the mind of the author may be made abundantly clear.[21]

Who the biblical author is and "what he wishes to express by his writing,"[22] is front and center here, and in pursuit of the author and his intended meaning the interpreter,

> with all care and without neglecting any light derived from recent research, [must] endeavor to determine the peculiar character and circumstances of the sacred writer, the age in which he lived, the sources written or oral to which he had recourse, and the forms of expression he employed.[23]

It is not without reason, then, that this encyclical has been described within Roman Catholic circles themselves as "a Magna Charta for biblical progress" after centuries in which that church was moving in a different direction.[24]

Divino afflante Spiritu was followed in 1965 by the Dogmatic Constitution *Dei Verbum*, proceeding from the Second Vatican Council. Here, too, we find a strong emphasis on the fundamental importance of the literal sense in hearing God's word through Scripture:

> Now since in Sacred Scripture God has spoken through human agents and in human fashion, the interpreter of Sacred Scripture, in order to ascertain what God himself wished to communicate to us, should carefully search out what the sacred writers truly intended to express and what God thought well to manifest by their words.[25]

Among other things, the Bible reader must therefore "search for what meaning the sacred writer, in his own historical situation and in accordance with the condition

---

[21] Pope Pius XII, "Encyclical Letter Promoting Biblical Studies, *Divino afflante Spiritu*," in *The Scripture Documents: An Anthology of Official Catholic Teachings* (ed. Dean P. Béchard; Collegeville, Minn.: Liturgical Press, 2002), 115–39 (125).

[22] *Divino afflante Spiritu*, 128.

[23] *Divino afflante Spiritu*, 128.

[24] Raymond E. Brown and Thomas A. Collins, O.P., "Church Pronouncements," *NJBC*, 1166–74 (1167).

[25] Second Vatican Council, "Dogmatic Constitution on Divine Revelation, *Dei Verbum*," in Béchard, *Scripture Documents*, 24.

of his time and culture, intended to express and did in fact express with the help of literary forms that were in use during that time." Attention must also be given "to the customary and characteristic modes of perception, speech, and narrative that prevailed at the time of the sacred writer, and to the customs that people of that time generally followed in their dealings with one another."[26]

We may note finally, along this line of enquiry, the Pontifical Biblical Commission's document, "The Interpretation of the Bible in the Church" (1993), which tells us that since Scripture is the word of God in human language,

> Catholic exegesis freely makes use of the scientific methods and approaches which allow a better grasp of the meaning of texts in their linguistic, literary, sociocultural, religious and historical contexts, while explaining them as well through studying their sources and attending to the personality of each author.[27]

In doing so, Roman Catholic exegesis makes it clear that it does not possess any particular (scientific) method of its own. It begins its task by recognizing exactly what our Christian ancestors often recognized, whether in the patristic and medieval periods or during the Renaissance and the Reformation: "that one of the aspects of biblical texts is that they are the work of human authors, who employed both their own capacities for expression and the means which their age and social context put at their disposal."[28]

These quite modern documents from the Roman Catholic tradition, taken together, represent precisely the kind of renewed commitment to the literal reading of Scripture that was already embraced in the Reformation. They are substantially "reformed." This being so, they speak to the truth of the Reformation claim that the Reformers stood squarely within the mainstream of Christian tradition going back to the apostles when they adopted the hermeneutical stance that they did and insisted on the literal sense of Scripture as its fundamental sense.[29]

APOSTOLIC WARRANT AND NONLITERAL READING

The patristic appeal to apostolic authority with respect to the *nonliteral* reading of Scripture is, on the other hand, far from persuasive. The Church Fathers do

---

[26] *Dei Verbum*, 25.

[27] Pontifical Biblical Commission, "The Interpretation of the Bible in the Church," in *The Interpretation of the Bible in the Church* (ed. J. Leslie Houlden; London: SCM Press, 1995), 3–98 (58).

[28] Pontifical Biblical Commission, "Interpretation," 58.

[29] This does not mean, of course, that there have been no attempts within the modern Roman Catholic Church to raise the profile once again of "spiritual reading," albeit that this often involves the promotion of a version of the ancient *lectio divina* that actively incorporates the insights of modern and postmodern reading strategies. See, e.g., Raymond Studzinski, *Reading to Live: The Evolving Practice of Lectio Divina* (Collegeville, Minn.: Liturgical Press, 2009), 177–219.

possess apostolic warrant for reading the OT, to a certain extent, as prophesying of Christ. The way in which this notion of prophecy is then so extensively developed in authors like Justin Martyr, however—finding Christ in OT texts lacking in any kind of human intention to be prophetic—is another matter. All that this excessive recourse to the idea of prophecy achieves in the end is a distortion of the true, multifaceted nature of the relationship between the two testaments of the Christian Bible. To a degree, similarly, there is apostolic warrant for reading the OT typologically in relation to the NT. However, some of the ways in which typology is then developed among patristic authors like Irenaeus or Tertullian—finding illustrations of life in the NT kingdom of God in the most unlikely of OT texts (e.g., the two goats of Lev 16, or clean and unclean animals in general)—move well beyond any such warrant. These developments flow, in fact, in the direction of the kind of allegorical reading to which the influential Origen so extensively resorted in the third century—and that kind of reading should not rightly be considered even to represent a *questionable* development of a genuinely apostolic approach to Scripture. Origen is up to something else entirely. What typological readings of this nature accomplish, once again, is a distortion of the true, complex nature of the relationship between the two testaments of the Christian Bible.

On Trains, Deep Water, and the Purpose of Allegorical Reading

Apostolic authority cannot convincingly be appealed to, then, in respect of nonliteral (including allegorical) patristic exegesis. Indeed, this kind of exegesis, in which the reader consciously sets his face against the verbal sense of a passage while claiming the leading of the Holy Spirit in his reading, threatens in the end to undermine the very apostolic authority to which it appeals—as well as the authority of the OT Scriptures that the apostles presuppose. (The Reformers themselves well understood this.)[30] For if we are to conceive of a significant gap opening up between the communicative intention of a human author and the communicative intention of God—for example, if the Holy Spirit really can speak of future events even when a biblical text speaks in the past tense (Justin)—how then are we to gain reliable access through those texts to what God is saying? Moreover, if the Holy Spirit can operate in this way in *those* texts, why not also in others? Why not in all the Scriptures, including the apostolic writings? Perhaps what God really wishes to say is hidden beneath the surface of all of them and cannot be grasped by attention to ordinary human language *at all*. Perhaps what

---

[30] Martin Bucer, e.g., writes that he has refrained in his work on the Psalms from "anagogical interpretations" that bring with them "the danger of undermining the authority of Scripture." Hobbs, "Pluriformity," 461. We recall his "wax nose" comment also from chapter 4.

God really wishes to say looks quite different from what appears on the surface of the human text *everywhere*.

The further we press the agenda of this "spiritual" Bible reading, the more we recognize the seriousness of the threat to what we came to believe on the basis of literal reading in the first place—and who is to say how far the agenda is to be pressed? Once the *allegorical* train, in particular, leaves the station and starts running along its tracks, where will it be forced to stop, and by whom? The author of the text cannot fulfill this role, since he was never informed about the departure of the train in the first place. He is powerless to prevent any manner of "deep water" (to change the metaphor briefly) being found in his text, and he is equally powerless to rescue the drowning reader from its embrace once she has plunged in.[31] Certainly if the train runs far enough without interference—to catch my previous connection—any text, however authoritative it might once have been, will inevitably end up "saying" what another, newly authoritative text is saying. About this new text, incidentally, one thing can be said with complete certainty, even before it is written: this new text, at least, will be subject only to literal reading. Not a breath of allegory will disturb its literal tranquility. For throughout history and down to the present time, one never finds readers allegorizing genuinely authoritative texts to which they ascribe primary authority, even if they pretend otherwise. (The same is true of modern deconstructionists in their deconstruction—see chapter 19.) Such a fate only befalls texts that require domesticating—texts that need to be made to say something, against their grain, in an important narrative that is alien to them. Allegorizing occurs "when the literal meaning of a text is seen to run in a wrong or unhelpful direction . . . [when] the reader is unhappy with the literal meaning"[32]—and "wrong or unhelpful" are of course measured in terms of an authority that lies elsewhere. So it was in the beginning, when allegorical reading was first invented in order to subjugate an old text (Homer) to a new one (largely Plato). So it is now:

---

[31] The metaphor is borrowed from Julian Barnes, who comments in an entirely different context with respect to Gustave Flaubert's parrot that "[w]e can, if we wish (and if we disobey Flaubert), submit the bird to additional interpretation . . . [but h]ow submerged does a reference have to be before it drowns?" Barnes, *Flaubert's Parrot* (London: Bloomsbury, 1992), 12–13.

[32] O'Keefe and Reno, *Sanctified Vision*, 103. They would not themselves say that this "saving the sense" is the *only* reason for reading allegorically—they try to distinguish it from "making sense of nonsense" and "adding to the sense" (93–107). However, the reader will have a hard time understanding how the examples provided by O'Keefe and Reno in these two "categories" are not simply providing further illustrations of readers who are unhappy with the literal sense of the text and would like it to say something different.

to construct an allegory or to read allegorically is certainly also to express one's own ideology and worldview in conscious or unconscious dialogue with—or, perhaps, in opposition to—the text from which one's allegory is ostensibly drawn.[33]

Allegory, says David Dawson, "is not so much about the meaning or lack of meaning in texts as it is a way of using texts and their meanings to situate oneself and one's community with respect to society and culture."[34]

Plato himself has been subjected to the same kind of treatment at different points in history; he too has been "interpreted" so as to remove the inconvenient edges that disturb his readers. Basilius Bessarion (of whom we shall hear more in chapter 11) did it during the fifteenth-century Italian Renaissance, for example, so as to make Plato's *Republic* say what he wished it to say about politics, in harmony with Aristotle.[35] Aristotle had been making something of a philosophical comeback in the Christian West since his rediscovery, with the help of Muslim scholars, in the twelfth and early thirteenth centuries.[36] Renaissance thinkers like Bessarion were more than "willing to reinterpret Platonic doctrines," when faced with those who understood him "in a crudely literal sense,"[37] in order to save Plato's appearances in respect of prevailing norms of thought and behavior. The Church Fathers have themselves been allegorized in modern times for similar reasons. Feminist writer Virginia Burrus, for example, proposes that "[t]he fathers are talking about God and salvation at the literal level, but at the allegorical level, they are really talking about gender and authority."[38] No one is safe from the speeding train of allegory, once it is given permission to run.

Patristic Awareness of the Problem

So any "interpretive move that directs attention away from the literal sense is ... a dangerous game. Allegorical readings, especially of obscure or offensive texts, are prone to spin out of control."[39] A certain degree of awareness of the threat

---

[33] John L. Thompson, *Writing the Wrongs: Women of the Old Testament among Biblical Commentators from Philo through the Reformation* (Oxford: Oxford University Press, 2001), 243—in the course of describing Gale Yee's opinion, but apparently agreeing with her.

[34] Dawson, *Allegorical Readers*, 236.

[35] James Hankins, *Plato in the Italian Renaissance* (CSCT 17; 3rd impression; Leiden: Brill, 1994), 226–28.

[36] This rediscovery was not universally acclaimed: "The spirit of Christ," one medieval abbot opined, "does not rule where the spirit of Aristotle dominates." Cited in Froelich, "Christian Interpretation," 520.

[37] Hankins, *Plato*, 241.

[38] O'Keefe and Reno, *Sanctified Vision*, 110. The book to which they refer is Virginia Burrus, *Begotten Not Made: Conceiving Manhood in Late Antiquity* (FRMC; Stanford: Stanford University Press, 2000).

[39] O'Keefe and Reno, *Sanctified Vision*, 93.

thus posed to the authority of Scripture by "spiritual reading" is already apparent in patristic times. It is apparent *even though* so many of the Christian leaders in those early centuries had been educated in classically Hellenistic ways, and *even though* the appropriateness of at least some degree of allegorical reading of ancient literature seemed to them self-evident.[40] We encounter it, for example, in Theodore's negative comments about "spiritual" interpretation, which he sees as rendering the Scriptures incomprehensible and meaningless. Even Didymus the Blind, a devoted follower of Origen who allegorizes constantly in his teaching, recognizes the threat, insisting that the cross of Christ (at least) cannot be subject to this treatment: "if the cross is allegorized, the resurrection has to be allegorized, too. But if the resurrection is allegorized, everything that took place is like a dream"[41] The later Jerome likewise insists that "spiritual interpretation must follow the sequence of the history."[42]

It is against this background, toward the end of a patristic period in which not a few writers give the impression of deciding on such matters arbitrarily, that Augustine's *On Christian Doctrine* seeks to formulate guidelines for Scripture reading —the first of the Fathers systematically to attempt to devise rules about where the allegorical train should begin and end its journey. As we have seen in chapter 8, Augustine is a strong advocate of reading Scripture according to its literal sense. Readers should resist the temptation to evade the imperatives of the text read literally by appealing to a nonliteral sense. Only when it proves impossible to read individual texts literally in line with the thrust of the whole biblical Story (and its major injunctions to love both God and neighbor), he proposes, should the text be read in a different manner. Here a strong intuition about the potentially injurious effects of "spiritual reading" on the authority of Scripture results in a serious attempt to rein it in.

One senses (but I speak allegorically) in these various comments from the Fathers the merest glimpse, on the far horizon, of the mystical chorus in the final scene of Goethe's *Faust*—"all that is transitory is only an allegory."[43] One senses a patristic awareness of what any concession to such a thoroughgoing hermeneutical Platonism will mean for historic Christian faith—namely, its end.

---

[40] Reventlow, *Biblical Interpretation*, 1:33–40; 2:5–6, 26.
[41] Cited in Reventlow, *Biblical Interpretation*, 2:31.
[42] Cited in Reventlow, *Biblical Interpretation*, 2:44.
[43] "Alles Vergängliche ist nur ein Gleichnis" (my own translation). Johann Wolfgang Goethe, *Faust: Erster und Zweiter Teil* (Munich: Deutscher Taschenbuch Verlag, 1997), Act V, Chorus mysticus, last sentence.

The Unseen Depths of the Problem

The Church Fathers were *somewhat* aware of the problem. However, it is only with the benefit of hindsight—as readers who do not share directly in the pagan Greco-Roman inheritance into which the Fathers were all inducted by way of upbringing and education[44]—that we can fully recognize its seriousness. It is only now that time has passed that we can look back and see the numerous ways in which Scripture's ability to function authoritatively, both in patristic times and in the Middle Ages, was not merely threatened but actually compromised by "spiritual" reading. Handled in such a manner, Scripture could not effectively challenge its readers. The literal sense could all too easily be ignored where it conflicted with favored prevailing ideas and ethical norms, and a "spiritual reading" could all too easily be found that conformed to them. Under such circumstances, Scripture could not function as an entity that is "God-breathed and ... useful for teaching, rebuking, correcting and training in righteousness, so that the man of God may be thoroughly equipped for every good work" (2 Tim 3:16-17)—even though this is what its Christian readers sincerely believed it to be accomplishing. Thomas Aquinas may well wish to claim in the thirteenth century, then, that "nothing necessary to faith is contained under the spiritual sense which is not elsewhere put forward by the Scripture in its literal sense" (the second epigraph to the present chapter).[45] But the fact is that a significant amount of what is represented as authentic Christian belief in the patristic literature and afterward is not obviously grounded in Scripture read in its literal sense at all. Irenaeus' mosaic may still portray a king rather than a fox—but it is a king sometimes so heavily clothed in Hellenistic dress that the Palestinian Jewish original is all but obscured.

Consider, for example, the question of the nature of the human body, and its relation to the soul. In general terms, comments David Wallace-Hadrill,

> the Platonic tradition envisaged the soul of man as a purely spiritual entity, uncreated and eternal, which enters the human body either in obedience to universal cosmic law or through its decline from its original destiny. There is no true harmony between body and soul, the body constituting a tomb or prison from which it is the object of the soul to be freed.[46]

---

[44] "[A] pagan rhetorical education was still a matter of course even for Christians in the fourth century" (Reventlow, *Biblical Interpretation*, 2:33). This is not, of course, to suggest that there was anything intrinsically bad about many aspects of such an education, nor indeed that it influenced all the Church Fathers in exactly the same way. The Antiochenes, e.g., were much indebted to its grammatical, rhetorical, and historical aspects as they sought to do justice to the literal sense of biblical texts, but they were not much influenced by Greek *philosophy* as such (Hill, *Antioch*, 7–10, 27–28).

[45] Aquinas, *Summa*, 1.1.10.

[46] David S. Wallace-Hadrill, *The Greek Patristic View of Nature*, (Manchester: Manchester University Press, 1968), 66–67.

In chapter 8, we saw exactly how this idea is reflected in Origen's *First Principles*. However, the same general conception of the body in relation to the soul is regularly presupposed, or actually articulated, in other patristic writings as well—even if their commentary does not often approach the extremes of bodily denigration found in Plato and among the Gnostics (and for that matter, in Philo). Tertullian can attack Marcion for his hostility toward the body as revealed in his proscription of marriage; yet marriage, if not proscribed by the Fathers, was certainly widely regarded as a less spiritual vocation than the monastic, single life. The early John Chrysostom, for example, excoriates his friend Theodore in uncompromising terms for his decision to leave the monastic life and to marry. He portrays this as a relapse from a spiritual to an unspiritual mode of existence:

> He who had already mounted to the sky, who was laughing to scorn the vanity of this life, who regarded bodily beauty no more than if it had been in forms of stone, who despised gold as it had been mud, and every kind of luxury as mire, even he, having been suddenly overwhelmed with the feverish longing of a preposterous passion, has ruined his health, and manly strength, and the bloom of his youth, and become a slave of pleasure. Shall we not weep then, I pray you, for such a man and bewail him, until we have got him back again?[47]

Augustine, writing *On the Good of Marriage* against the background of the condemnation by his mentor Ambrose of the fourth-century monk Jovinian—who had taught that marriage and celibacy were to be valued equally—is considerably more affirming than Chrysostom of marriage. "Marriage and continence are two goods," he asserts. Yet he immediately goes on to say that "the second is better."[48] This is a theme to which he returns in *Holy Virginity*. Although he had by this point in his life left behind the stark Manichean idea that all sexual relations, even for the purposes of procreation, are evil—which was not very far from the view of many Christians, who held that sexual relations became an aspect of human life only after the Fall—Augustine remained deeply uncomfortable with the sexual aspects of bodily functioning, even within marriage. He found it difficult to see how erotic desires and passions could be part of God's original plan for human sexual lives. The first humans lived in Paradise as virgins, he thought; even the OT patriarchs "used sexual intercourse" only out of "the duty of conservation" (i.e., procreation).[49]

---

[47] John Chrysostom, *Ad Theodorum lapsum* (*Letters to the Fallen Theodore*), 1.3 (NPNF 1, 9:92–93).

[48] Augustine, *De bono conjugali* (*On the Good of Marriage*), 8 (NPNF 1, 3:403). In the interests of fairness, it is important to note that Chrysostom is also far more positive about the institution in his later writings—e.g., in his homilies on Ephesians.

[49] Augustine, *On the Good of Marriage*, 18 (NPNF 1, 3:407).

Augustine was by no means alone in this view, which is why both Theodore and Origen—very different in other respects in their approach to biblical interpretation—can simply assume that the Song of Songs *cannot* be part of the canon of Scripture and at the same time a book that celebrates not only marriage, but also erotic love.[50] If the book is "spiritual" it cannot at the same time be "bodily." Therefore, the only way in which Origen can read the Song of Songs spiritually is to read it as not relating to bodies at all. We should not "interpret in a vicious and carnal sense the things the ancients wrote with good and spiritual intent,"[51] he writes, but understand them to pertain instead to the ascent of the soul to God. His reading of the Song of Songs, therefore, places it within an ascending series of OT wisdom books in which, in an "essentially Platonic schema, Proverbs represents ethics, Ecclesiastes physics, and the Song of Songs . . . the contemplation of divine things."[52]

This entire bundle of ideas—that the body is less important than the soul, and marriage less worthy than celibacy; that erotic desire and passion are problematic, and are to be suppressed; and that the goal of existence is the ascent of the soul to God—was then bequeathed by the Fathers to the medieval Church, and it profoundly shaped its character. It is not the literal reading of Scripture that drives the creation of this bundle. It is not from Scripture, which teaches us that it was when God formed bodies out of the dust of the ground and breathed into them the breath of life that human beings became living souls (Gen 2:7), that the patristic body-soul dichotomy arises. It is not from Scripture that there arise the principled hierarchies of soul and body, celibacy and marriage, or indeed spiritual and literal reading that we encounter in so much pre-Reformation Christian literature. It is not from Scripture that we get the notion of the spiritual life as a staged ascent of the soul to God. For these ideas to flourish, Scripture must be read in ways that its human authors (not being Greeks themselves) cannot be shown to have intended. Neoplatonic patriarchs must be found who, in spite of a deafening lack of textual evidence on the point, allegedly never delighted in sexual intercourse with their wives. Patriarchs must be found, indeed, who correspond to Neoplatonist ideals in every respect—even if it means portraying Jacob (as Ambrose did) as a wise man living a happy life because he pursued

---

[50] Theodore's thinking on this issue is partially shaped, interestingly enough, by precisely the overdevelopment of the prophetic idea in Scripture, relative to how the apostles read it, that we noted earlier in Justin and other early Christian authors. For Theodore the OT is *fundamentally* prophetic, and that is how and why it is also *inspired*. This is how he was led to his negative view not only of Song of Songs, but also of all the OT wisdom literature: it is all merely human wisdom. Reventlow, *Biblical Interpretation*, 2:9–10.

[51] Origen, *Commentarius in Canticum* (*Commentary on the Song of Songs*) (trans. R. P. Lawson; ACW 26; New York: Newman, 1957), prologue, part 2 (ACW 26:24).

[52] Carleton Paget, "Christian Exegesis," 528.

reason and possessed a clear conscience (since "the happiness of life does not lie in bodily pleasure, but in a conscience pure of every stain of sin").[53] Above all else, on this kind of view, it must never be considered for a moment that a text like the Song of Songs should be interpreted as challenging the correctness of any of the preconceptions held by Scripture readers about sex and marriage. It must never be considered possible that Scripture might be "useful for teaching, rebuking, correcting and training in righteousness" on *such* matters. Nor *was* it widely considered, for hundreds of years after Origen, even though the Song of Songs was one of the most-read biblical texts in medieval Europe. The reason? Everyone already "knew" that the Song should not be read literally.

Dogs That Cannot Bite

Into the significant "gap," then, between the voice of the human author and the voice of God in Scripture that was opened up by Bible readers in the post-apostolic Church came a considerable number of ideas that cannot be grounded in the literal sense of the biblical text—even though the literal sense was widely agreed to be the foundational sense. Scripture resists these ideas, but they entered into mainstream Christian discourse nevertheless, because whereas texts read literally can, like dogs, "bite back" at the reader—challenging his or her current ideas—texts read "spiritually" cannot.

The ideas in question are not, moreover, marginal or trivial. In the examples cited, they go right to the heart of what it means to be a human being, and how best to live our lives in pursuit of God-ordained goals. This is a fairly central matter of concern in Scripture, as it is in religious and philosophical writings

---

[53] Ambrose, *De Jacob et vita beata* (*Jacob and the Happy Life*), in *St. Ambrose: Seven Exegetical Works* (ed. Bernard M. Peebles et al.; trans. Michael P. McHugh; FC 65; Washington, D.C.: Catholic University of America Press, 1985), 137. It never seems to have occurred to most of the Church Fathers that God might have a message to communicate in the moral *failures* of biblical characters—a point that Luther and Calvin later *did* understand, although many medieval writers, whether Jewish or Christian, did not. For Calvin, e.g., with his commitment to the literal sense of the text, the patriarchs are not "laudable exceptions to the normal rules of Scripture, but ... perverse illustrations thereof." John L. Thompson, "The Immoralities of the Patriarchs in the History of Exegesis: A Reappraisal of Calvin's Position," *CTJ* 26 (1991): 9–46 (46). On Luther, see briefly Bornkamm, *Luther and the Old Testament*, 18. In general, patristic presuppositions about what the Genesis narrative *ought* rightly to say often lead them very quickly away from the literal sense, so that a good question they do ask about the text fails to lead to a convincing answer. In the second of his *Homilae in Genesim* (*Genesis Homilies*), e.g., Origen confesses that he cannot see any reason why Gen 9:20-27 describe Noah's drunken antics. This is fair enough as a starting point, but there is no satisfactory conclusion, because Origen is already deeply convinced that reading the text literally is like eating the paschal lamb raw (Vanhoozer, *Meaning*, 114). For a longer discussion of another place in which Origen would have benefited from some humility and patience before the text (his discussion of Lot's wife), see Provan, *Discovering Genesis*, 20–22.

generally throughout history. Particularly on such crucial matters pertaining to Christian faith, then—and others like them—one would indeed have hoped (to quote Aquinas) that more of the Church Fathers might have found in Scripture "contained under the spiritual sense" only that which is "elsewhere put forward . . . in its literal sense." One would have hoped that, even had they believed that the apostles indulged to some small degree in the nonliteral reading of Scripture, they would have been alert to the dangers of attempting more of it. Evidently, however, this was often not the case; and to that extent, wittingly or not, the Church Fathers undermined the authority of Scripture, including the authority of the apostles, even as they appealed to it. So did many of those who followed them in the Middle Ages, often unaware of the extent to which a significant gulf had now opened up between Scripture and tradition—unaware, because they had limited access both to Scripture in its original languages and context, and to the Fathers themselves, whom they frequently encountered only in heavily edited form.[54] Even the great Renaissance scholar Erasmus of Rotterdam, in the sixteenth century (c. 1466–1536)—a confessed admirer of Origen—"knew of no other way than allegory to gain meaning from large parts of the Old Testament"; he found the literal meaning of the text "senseless . . . repulsive and ridiculous."[55]

The absurdity of the hermeneutical approach that produced such significant distortions of biblical theology while destroying Scripture's ability to address the problem was not lost on one of patristic Christianity's earliest and fiercest critics, the late third-century Neoplatonist philosopher Porphyry:

> Some persons, desiring to find a solution of the baseness of the Jewish Scriptures rather than abandon them, have had recourse to explanations inconsistent and incongruous with the words written, which explanations, instead of supplying a defense of the foreigners, contain rather approval and praise of themselves. For they boast that the plain words of Moses are "enigmas," and regard them as oracles full of hidden mysteries; and having bewildered the mental judgment by folly, they make their explanations.[56]

To demonstrate the absurdity of providing such "explanations inconsistent and incongruous with the words written," Porphyry proposes applying the Christian allegorical method "to the struggle between Achilles and Hector in the *Iliad*, [portraying] this as the struggle between Christ (Achilles) and Satan (Hector), in the

---

[54] Reventlow, *Biblical Interpretation*, 2:137–43.

[55] Bornkamm, *Luther and the Old Testament*, 252. His dissatisfaction sometimes even with what he sees as the literal sense of the NT comes to expression in his debate with Luther about free will; see Cummings, *Literary Culture*, 144–83, for a good discussion of their hermeneutical disagreements. For a helpful, brief introduction to the life and work of Erasmus overall, see Erika Rummel, "The Textual and Hermeneutic Work of Desiderius Erasmus of Rotterdam," *HBOT* 2:215–30.

[56] Porphyry, *Against the Christians* (c. AD 270), cited from Eusebius, *Church History*, 1:265–66.

manner of Christian commentators."⁵⁷ Indeed, why not? In Porphyry's view, Origen had "foisted Greek conceptions on foreign myths."⁵⁸ Why *not* foist Christian conceptions on Greek ones?

Conclusion

The Reformers well understood that the long Christian tradition of reading Scripture nonliterally lacked apostolic warrant. They also comprehended how it undermined the authority of Scripture. Scripture could all too easily come to be understood, not as the very word of God (as the apostles believed)—"the loftiest and noblest of holy things," in Luther's words⁵⁹—but as an embarrassing problem to be solved by subtle hermeneutical manoeuvers. By the beginning of the sixteenth century the Reformers had indeed accumulated many more examples of the ways in which this was the case than were even conceivable by the end of the fifth. In the fifth century the full potential of the "spiritual reading" of Scripture's "enigmas" for validating all sorts of beliefs and practices in the Church that were not justifiable on the basis of the literal sense had not yet been realized. The Reformers perceived clearly that the very nature of Christian faith was at stake in this question of "how should we read," as well as general access to this faith. Could anyone other than elite Bible readers possessing esoteric knowledge, capable of penetrating "those labyrinths in which others show off their talents" (Melanchthon), grasp hold of biblical truth?⁶⁰ In these respects, the Reformers were in general perhaps a little more astute than some of their Protestant successors, who have managed to give the impression that it is a matter of relative indifference whether or not "reformed" Christians should engage in the nonliteral reading of the Bible.⁶¹ The Reformers were surely correct to reject such reading, and in doing so they rightly drew on much of what earlier writers like Theodore and Augustine had already said about it—even if their patristic *practice* did not necessarily follow through on the implications of their more *theoretical comments*. It was not the Reformers, in taking up such a position, but others before them in

---

⁵⁷ Aryeh Kofsky, *Eusebius of Caesarea against Paganism* (Leiden: Brill, 2002), 29.
⁵⁸ Procopé, "Greek Philosophy," 476.
⁵⁹ Hays, *Reading Backwards*, 1, quoting the preface to the German translation of the Pentateuch (1523).
⁶⁰ Cited in Hobbs, "Pluriformity," 496.
⁶¹ These include Gerald Bray, in his essay on "Allegory" in *DTIB*, 34–36: "[a]llegorical interpretation is often fanciful but seldom harmful because it is generally based on theological truths that can be proved from the clearer parts of Scripture" (36). Yet our preceding chapters suggest that this is an overly "sunny" reading of the history of interpretation, and it is particularly surprising that Bray should offer it, when he himself identifies elsewhere notable examples of "dogmas ... with little scriptural basis other than an allegorical interpretation of texts which have no literal bearing" on the matters at hand. Bray, *Biblical Interpretation*, 103.

taking up theirs, who in some measure or another stepped away from the apostolic tradition.

On this matter of nonliteral reading, too, the Roman Catholic Church has, over the course of time, moved officially and significantly in a "reformed" direction. One of the stated purposes of *Divino afflante Spiritu* in urging renewed theological interpretation of Scripture based on the literal sense was in fact to

> reduce to silence those who, affirming that they scarcely ever find anything in biblical commentaries to raise their hearts to God, to nourish their souls or promote their interior life, repeatedly urge that we should have recourse to a certain spiritual and, as they say, mystical interpretation.[62]

It is true, the encyclical goes on, that there is prefiguration in the OT, and this kind of "spiritual sense" must be attended to by Roman Catholic exegetes, "provided it is clearly intended by God."[63] However (and this is emphatically stated), Catholic exegetes must at the same time "scrupulously refrain from proposing as the genuine meaning of Sacred Scripture other figurative senses."[64] A degree of figuration may be useful in preaching, "provided this be done with moderation and restraint."[65] Yet even here, it must "never be forgotten that this use of Sacred Scripture is, as it were, extrinsic to it and accidental, and ... not free from danger."[66] *Divino afflante Spiritu*—to put it mildly—does not offer a ringing endorsement of ways of reading Scripture that depart from its literal sense.[67]

THE REFORMERS AND SCRIPTURE: LOOKING BACKWARD AND FORWARD

The implication of everything discussed thus far in the present chapter is naturally that contemporary "reformed" Christians should still read the Bible "literally," as their forebears proposed. They should not read it in the manner that "fourth way," "spiritually reading" Protestants now propose (nor, indeed, in the

---

[62] *Divino afflante Spiritu*, 125.
[63] *Divino afflante Spiritu*, 126.
[64] *Divino afflante Spiritu*, 126.
[65] *Divino afflante Spiritu*, 126.
[66] *Divino afflante Spiritu*, 126.
[67] Its cautionary tone is replicated in the closing remarks of a more recent essay from a Catholic scholar, Brian Daley, which pertain to the contemporary usefulness of patristic exegesis: "Early Christian interpretation, grounded in its strong sense of God's long involvement with humanity, can offer us at least parallels and models for reviving our exegetical imagination.... [It] may ... stimulate [readers] to develop new strategies for reading [the Bible]." A modest proposal indeed. Brian E. Daley, S.J., "Is Patristic Exegesis Still Usable? Some Reflections on Early Christian Interpretation of the Psalms," in *The Art of Reading Scripture* (ed. Ellen F. Davis and Richard B. Hays; Grand Rapids: Eerdmans, 2003), 69–88 (88).

way that "second way" postmodern readers propose). However, the "reformed" reading of Scripture as we move deeper into the twenty-first century should not look exactly as it did in the sixteenth century, for at least two reasons.

Theory and Practice in the Reformation

First, the Reformers were far from consistent in their own handling of Scripture. They emphasized the literal sense, and they used strong words about "pretended expositions which lead us away from the literal sense."[68] They themselves could depart from it, however.

Martin Luther, for example, never entirely left behind the fondness for allegorizing that he confesses as a habit difficult to break in the second epigraph to my fourth chapter. Formally turning away from John Cassian's "fourfold scheme" for reading Scripture after his lectures on Romans in 1516–1517, and thereby rejecting "allegorization as a significant key to Scripture,"[69] Luther can nevertheless be found indulging in the practice throughout his life, albeit that he perhaps "became more cautious" as time went on.[70] He could, sometimes, regard some small degree of allegorizing as a relatively harmless if unscholarly pastime, so long as it did not take up too much of the interpreter's time and was not regarded as establishing anything important about the nature of Christian faith. Faith could "play with symbols, as Luther did himself in his allegories, but only because faith [had] become confident on the basis of historical experience."[71] In his lectures on Isaiah (1527–1530), for example, Luther advises that

> playing games with the Sacred Scriptures has the most injurious consequences if the text and its grammar are neglected. From history we must learn well and much, but little from allegory. You use allegory as an embellishment by which the discourse is illustrated but not established. Let history remain honest. It teaches, which allegory does not do.... Allegory does not pertain to doctrine, but to doctrine already established it can be added as color.[72]

Certainly it is true, as we see here, that Luther places very significant constraints around the kind of allegorical reading he has in mind, only considering it "permissible if used according to the 'analogy of faith' and directed to a goal which was clearly and unequivocally determined by the literal sense of other Scripture passages."[73] Even so, his relaxed attitude to the allegorical approach at these points in

---

[68] Calvin, *Galatians and Ephesians*, 136.
[69] Bornkamm, *Luther and the Old Testament*, 88–89, 249.
[70] Bornkamm, *Luther and the Old Testament*, 94–95, 208.
[71] Bornkamm, *Luther and the Old Testament*, 256.
[72] Martin Luther, *Lectures on Isaiah* (1527–1530), 13.22, *LW* 16:136–37.
[73] Bornkamm, *Luther and the Old Testament*, 92.

his writings stands in some tension with his stern comments about it elsewhere. Those stern comments are in turn well justified in the light of what allegorizing has "achieved" for the Church historically, encouraging Christian Bible readers to read their core beliefs into biblical texts that do not evidently endorse them. Luther surely does this himself when, as a theologian looking all the time in his reading of the OT for wisdom about "household and labor, marriage and education . . . civic wisdom,"[74] he rejects Erasmus' reading of the Song of Songs as a love song, and offers his own allegorical interpretation of it as a description of the true social system. When he reads Ecclesiastes (over against monastic interpretations based on Jerome) as portraying the politics or economics of Solomon, he is proceeding in the same manner.[75] In offering such readings of Scripture, Luther was surely setting a bad example for those who came after him and claimed to represent his "Lutheran" tradition.[76] Some of these were already sixteenth-century followers—like Giles (Aegidius) Hunnius (1550–1603), "who bitterly attacked Calvin for his refusal to accept allegory as a valid form of biblical interpretation."[77] However, Gerald Bray sees Hunnius as representing a more general tendency among the later Reformers "to return to a spiritualizing exegesis of the Bible, which subsequently became a prominent feature of 'orthodox' Protestant commentaries," like the one published by Matthew Henry between 1704 and 1714.[78]

Then again, one of Luther's most important convictions was that the Triune God acted and was known in history by the ancient Israelites. This is where much of his antagonism toward the use of allegory and of at least some kinds of typology had its roots, in that both made the OT a world of shadow rather than of historical reality.[79] The precise way in which this played out in Luther's inter-

---

[74] Bornkamm, *Luther and the Old Testament*, 18.

[75] Bornkamm, *Luther and the Old Testament*, 16, 91–92.

[76] The same might be said of the Swiss Reformer Huldrych Zwingli in relation to those who followed him. Like Luther, Zwingli heavily emphasized the literal sense and warned against allegorical exegesis and its capacity to undermine the authority of Scripture. In relation to the food for the soul that literal reading provided, allegorical interpretation could only be a "spicy sauce as an added ingredient to the meal." Yet Zwingli could himself offer readings of Scripture that have little to no grounding in the literal sense of the biblical text, believing allegorical reading to be acceptable so long as it was clearly labeled as such. Peter Opitz, "The Exegetical and Hermeneutical Work of John Oecolampadius, Huldrych Zwingli and John Calvin," *HBOT* 2:407–51 (esp. 423–28; quotation on 426). Calvin was not impressed by Zwingli's wanderings away from the literal sense in his work on Isaiah: Zwingli "takes too much freedom," he complains, and strays "far from the meaning of the prophet." Opitz, "Exegetical and Hermeneutical Work," 433.

[77] Bray, *Biblical Interpretation*, 184.

[78] Bray, *Biblical Interpretation*, 184–85. For more detail, see Johann A. Steiger, "The Development of the Reformation Legacy: Hermeneutics and Interpretation of the Sacred Scripture in the Age of Orthodoxy," *HBOT* 2:691–757 (732–40).

[79] As Bornkamm points out, Luther could criticize the Antiochenes for precisely this failing: that although their approach did give OT events and persons their own contemporary importance,

pretation of Scripture, however, inevitably created problems for his insistence on reading Scripture literally, since he wanted to say that Christ "was himself present everywhere" in the OT in its literal sense, imparting himself to his OT people wherever his promise was believed.[80] Christ was everywhere to be found in the OT, and was everywhere prophesied in it.[81] Luther may have rejected the discovery of Christ everywhere in the OT by way of allegorizing, then—but he did insist on finding him everywhere in the literal sense! Many of his efforts along these lines, however, measured by the very standards that he himself sets for literal reading elsewhere in his work, must be judged a failure. Such is his passion for finding the reality of the Triune God throughout the length and breadth of the Scriptures that he frequently cuts across the communicative intent of the text. What drives him to this end is, quite simply, that although he has largely cut himself off from the exegetical tradition of the early and medieval Church in its allegorical mode, he is still wedded to this tradition in its prophetic/Christological mode—which I have argued represents, in its scope, an unwarranted development from apostolic tradition.

John Calvin is much more consistent with his stated hermeneutical principles when reading the OT prophetically and Christologically. We have already seen how his commitment to these principles with respect to the book of Psalms, which he is generally reluctant to read for messianic content,[82] led to the charge of "Judaizing" against him by Lutheran theologians. What this "Judaizing" consisted in was in reality nothing more than a refusal to go where the words on the scriptural page did not themselves lead—albeit that Calvin was more than ready to agree that some psalms spoke not only about their own times but also about Christ.[83] Calvin himself strongly distinguished this restrained typological approach from an allegorical approach.

Yet even Calvin can be found reading Scripture in ways that depart from the principles of (literal) interpretation that he elsewhere commends. As John Thompson puts it, Calvin's "seemingly absolute dismissal of allegory" in his

---

it was still too much about the "[s]hadowy anticipation of that which was to come." Bornkamm, *Luther and the Old Testament*, 250.

[80] Bornkamm, *Luther and the Old Testament*, 200, 202.

[81] The Church, as those who have believed, was already to be found in the OT as well—"the hidden community of saints, the people of God living from the Word of God." Bornkamm, *Luther and the Old Testament*, 217.

[82] Thompson, "Calvin as a Biblical Interpreter," 69.

[83] It is perhaps inevitable that the accusation displays just as much contempt for the long tradition of the Church in affirming the literal reading of Scripture as foundational as it does for the apostolic teaching concerning "Judaizing" (e.g., in Paul's letter to the Galatians), which has nothing to do with reading the biblical text literally, but everything to do with failing to understand where, in the literally read biblical story, the people of God now stand.

theoretical work is in fact "heavily modified in the field."[84] His practice does not entirely "conform to the expectations raised by his more theoretical statements."[85] It is possible to adopt a cynical view of this reality, and to propose that Calvin's distinction between typology and allegory is only a matter of useful polemic and "does not actually reflect a distinction in his exegetical methodology."[86] I see no reason to accept this cynical view. It seems much more likely that Calvin believed firmly in the rightness of his stated hermeneutical method, but then sometimes failed to follow it through in practice. He would not be the first scholar to have failed in this way.

What is unquestionably true, in any case, is that there is an evident gap between hermeneutical theory and practice in the Reformers' writings. For this very reason, "reformed" reading of Scripture in the future should not look exactly as it did in the sixteenth century. It should, instead, strive to be more fully literal.[87]

It is not, after all, that the passing of time since the Reformation has indicated that nonliteral reading has lost any of its potential for undermining scriptural authority—such that we need no longer be concerned about it. Quite the opposite is true. The temptation persists to divorce the words of God from the words of the prophets and the apostles, and even from the words of Jesus himself, so that the Holy Spirit can be found affirming what the reader wishes to have affirmed. Perhaps all Christian readers of Scripture, in all times, have had their "favorite things" in terms of beliefs or moral positions, or even entire theological systems, which they would be sorry to find unsupported by the Bible. It is only natural to want to resist this discovery—even if it means reading Scripture "spiritually" in a way that they would never dream of reading other authoritative texts, including ancient texts penned by Plato, Aristotle, Origen, or Augustine, or modern ones penned by the latest religious guru advocating beliefs that sound more friendly, or ethics that sound more compatible with prevailing norms. It is a great mistake to underestimate the extent to which even contemporary Bible readers who know in principle that Scripture ought to function as the canon of faith and life are all too often found, nevertheless, in active search of personal autonomy in these realms—preferring to stick with what God is allegedly saying to them in the Bible rather than worrying too much about what the human author might have meant. After all, literal reading requires hard work. It might even require

---

[84] Thompson, "Calvin as a Biblical Interpreter," 64.
[85] Thompson, "Calvin as a Biblical Interpreter," 70.
[86] Greene-McCreight, *Ad Litteram*, 98.
[87] I take it for granted that this involves opposition not only to "spiritual reading," but also to the wooden, literalistic reading of Scripture that has all too often been its close companion (and indeed precursor) throughout the history of biblical interpretation.

(God forbid!) the learning of Hebrew and Greek—as we shall see in chapters 10 and 11. In the end, it might cause inconvenience, and even pain.

There being so many good reasons for avoiding the literal reading of Scripture, the last thing that the Church needs to do, looking ahead, is to allow any impression to remain among its members that literal reading is unnecessary, and that some other kind of approach is equally or more legitimate. Christians have not always noticed the ways in which Hellenistic (and other foreign) ways of looking at the world, ungrounded in the literal sense of Scripture, have been integrated into their own theological perspectives—obscuring the clarity of the distinction between biblically grounded perspectives and those of competing religious and philosophical systems. It will remain ever necessary to continue the "reformed" work of retrieving what Scripture really has to say from underneath the tradition that has buried it, so that it can speak afresh to the Church and to the world.[88]

Literal Dissent

There is another important reason, however, why contemporary "reformed" reading of Scripture should not look exactly as it did in the sixteenth century—or in the fourth, or the fifth. It is not simply that the Reformers sometimes departed from the literal sense; it is also that sometimes their description of it, even if it was persuasive in their own time, may no longer be persuasive to us. There are many reasons why this might be so. The Reformers urge upon us expertise in the reading of the biblical languages, so that we can better read the original texts—and knowledge of the biblical languages has greatly increased since their times, as it has since patristic times.[89] They propose that we attempt to grasp hold of the art and rhetoric of our biblical texts—and modern knowledge of such matters is also greater than it was in the sixteenth century (and in patristic times).[90] Again, the Reformers press upon us the necessity of understanding the ancient past out of which our biblical texts emerged—its geography and chronology, for example—and we are vastly better informed than they (or the Church Fathers) about the ancient past, and especially about the centuries BC.[91] As counterintuitive as it

---

[88] For an extended attempt of my own to help contemporary Christians recover the distinctive voice of the OT, in particular, over against other voices that in their own ways attempt to describe reality, see Provan, *Seriously Dangerous Religion*.

[89] See further my chapters 10 and 11, and the appendix toward the end of this book.

[90] The Antiochenes, who placed such an emphasis on the literal sense of the biblical text, nevertheless "came to their task with a less than perfect preparation and without some skills necessary for exegesis [especially] of obscure material." Hill, *Antioch*, 40.

[91] As for Luther's understanding of the ancient world, e.g., "he knew some of its individual features, but not the vitality which is only vaguely revealed by the struggle of biblical faith against pagan piety. . . . It is only recent study of Hellenistic Near Eastern religions which has disclosed

seems at first sight, twenty-first-century biblical scholars, as a consequence of a combination of persistent hard work and some outrageous good luck on the part of their predecessors, mainly in the nineteenth and twentieth centuries, really do know much more about the ancient world out of which the Bible emerged (especially in OT times) than did their forebears. More generally, finally, modern people have a very different understanding of the world and how it works than the prevailing understanding in the sixteenth century, and this causes us to ask different questions of the biblical text, and sometimes to come up with different answers, even about how its literal sense might rightly be construed. For all these reasons and more, and even though we are as committed as the Reformers were to the literal reading of Scripture, our perception of how the literal is best articulated will sometimes differ from theirs.[92] Sometimes we may come to think that the arguments they adduce in support of particular ideas of the literal sense are simply not very good arguments.

Two examples will suffice, both from Calvin's commentary on Genesis (1554). Consider, first, Calvin's insistence on reading the garden in Eden in Genesis 2–3 as "a particular region, not extended over all the earth . . . a specific place in which the things narrated in Genesis 2 and 3 took place."[93] Calvin's argument is that "unless it had been a region of our world, it would not have been placed opposite to Judea, towards the east."[94] Yet there are good internal reasons in Genesis 1–11 to believe that "Eden" *is* actually meant to stand for the whole earth, not least because otherwise the command in Genesis 1:28 to "be fruitful and increase in number; fill the earth and subdue it" comes to depend upon human sin for its fulfillment, by way of the expulsion from the garden. Indeed, the very fact that Genesis 2:8 places the garden "in the east" is problematic—if we are dealing with "normal" geography—in the context of a story that presupposes constant human movement from the west *to* the east (ending up in Mesopotamia in Genesis 11). Knowing what we know nowadays about the conjunction in the ancient Near East between accounts of creation and accounts of the building of temples (with

---

the meaning of New Testament references to them. Luther was not able to share this knowledge." Bornkamm, *Luther and the Old Testament*, 45–46.

[92] It will also inevitably differ somewhat from that of the Antiochenes. Few modern readers, e.g., would imagine (with Diodore and Theodore) that the literal reading of a composition like Psalm 41 must involve tying it closely to a particular historical circumstance (Hill, *Antioch*, 139–42). Here "literal" and "historical" have certainly been connected with each other in an unhelpful manner (see my chapter 4). For further examples where the Antiochenes should probably not function as guides for the modern reader as to literal sense, see Hill, *Antioch*, 29, 88 (the compilers of the Psalter are "mere" compilers whose work is "haphazard"); and 76–77, 94–95 (where Theodore "defends" Jonah, "rewriting the text where necessary to preserve his credibility").

[93] Greene-McCreight, *Ad Litteram*, 127.

[94] Calvin, *Genesis*, 114.

their gardens), it does not in fact seem very likely at all that in its literal sense Genesis 2–3 is to be interpreted as Calvin proposes.⁹⁵

Then again, Calvin gives some attention to the meaning of the vocabulary in Genesis 3:16 relating to the "pain" that the woman will endure as a consequence of human sin. His treatment here is illustrative not only of the general truth that in this commentary "no translation, regardless of its authority ... is embraced without scrutiny," but also of his general habit of pointing out "rhetorical devices in the text of Genesis and [using] these observations in coming to exegetical conclusions"—in this case the hendiadys, "pains and conception."⁹⁶ Like many before and after him, Calvin interprets this "pain" in terms of the travails of pregnancy and childbirth. His work is careful, and based on the Hebrew text; his knowledge of Hebrew is extensive, and certainly vastly greater than commentators like Augustine before him. Even so, further modern study of the Hebrew vocabulary, as well as the hendiadys, strongly suggests that in its literal sense Genesis 3:16 concerns the generally difficult circumstances in which women bring children into the world and raise them, and not the pains of either pregnancy or childbirth as such. The possibility that this might be the case came as welcome news to women living in the nineteenth century, when medical doctors gained for the first time a greatly increased ability to reduce physical female pain and discomfort during both pregnancy and childbirth—and found themselves the subjects of inquisition and opposition by people who believed that Genesis 3:16 mandated women's suffering.⁹⁷

History, being history, is constantly moving on; perspectives change, and knowledge (at least in some respects) increases. In both the above examples this very fact plays its part in raising questions about the way in which the literal sense of Scripture has been construed in the past, and whether this is necessarily the best way in which to construe it now. A sober second look may well suggest otherwise. John Calvin himself is already reading Scripture along these lines in the sixteenth century. He allows the new scientific knowledge of his day, for example, to inform his proposals about what Genesis teaches in its literal sense. Writing about the "lights" in the sky in Genesis 1:15, for example, he proposes that this verse is not to be read as teaching that the moon dispenses light all by itself. He already knows that the moon, unless light is "borrowed from the sun," does not possess

---

⁹⁵ For an extended set of reflections on such matters, see Provan, *Seriously Dangerous Religion*, 31–40.

⁹⁶ Greene-McCreight, *Ad Litteram*, 107, 157n70, who also preserves the French original of Calvin's text (108), left untranslated by King because (apparently) it offended his sensibilities (149–50n5).

⁹⁷ Iain Provan, "Pain in Childbirth? Further Thoughts on 'An Attractive Fragment' (1 Chronicles 4:9–10)," in *Let Us Go Up to Zion: Essays In Honour of H. G. M. Williamson on the Occasion of His Sixty-Fifth Birthday* (ed. Iain Provan and Mark Boda; VTSup 153; Leiden: Brill, 2012), 285–96.

"sufficient brightness to enlighten the earth."[98] In the background here, of course, stand the beginnings of the scientific revolution in Europe, which from the sixteenth century onward would supply ever-increasing volumes of new, empirically grounded knowledge with which biblical exegetes would need to contend, since this knowledge often stood in significant tension with traditional interpretations of Scripture. We shall return in chapters 12 through 16 to the question of how, and how well, they handled this challenge.

On Honoring the Past by Turning to the Future

A "reformed" reading of Scripture in the twenty-first century, then—even as it remains committed to the literal reading of Scripture advocated by the Reformers—should not look exactly as it did in the sixteenth century. It is the Reformers' commitment to reading Scripture according to its literal sense that should be honored, and not necessarily their articulation of exactly what that involves. Time moves on, and the "reformed" reading of the Bible must take account of this reality.

This is a truth articulated in the modern Roman Catholic tradition. Already in *Divino afflante Spiritu*, for example, it is acknowledged that "not a few things, especially in matters pertaining to history, were scarcely at all or not fully explained by the commentators of past ages, since they lacked almost all the information that was needed for their clearer exposition." Moreover, "a more profound knowledge of antiquity" in modern times "has given rise to new questions on the basis of which the point at issue may be more appropriately examined." It is quite wrong, then, when some, "not rightly understanding the conditions of biblical study," maintain "that nothing remains to be added by the Catholic exegete of our time to what Christian antiquity has produced." On the contrary, "these our times have brought to light so many things that call for a fresh investigation and stimulate not a little the practical zest of the present-day interpreter."[99]

CONCLUSION

Were the Reformers justified in their prioritizing of the literal sense of the biblical text, their rejection of other "senses," and their criticism of Church Fathers like Origen for their fondness for them? Yes, they were. Did they thereby step out of line with a Christian tradition of biblical interpretation that goes all the way back to the apostles, and even to Jesus himself? No, they did not. Should Christians still read the Bible in pursuit of its literal sense? Yes, we should—rejecting not only "second way," postmodern skepticism about authorial communicative intent

---

[98] Calvin, *Genesis*, 86.
[99] *Divino afflante Spiritu*, 127–28.

(to which we shall return in much more depth in chapter 19), but also proposals from "fourth way" Protestants that we should retrieve from our deeper Christian past a "spiritual reading" that pursues Scripture's nonliteral in addition to its literal sense. However, this does not necessarily mean that "reformed," "fifth way" Christians will always understand the literal sense of Scripture in precisely the manner of the Reformers. We need to conduct our own modern and literal reading—not merely duplicate the reading of the past.

How much does this issue matter? Unlike the issue of the precise boundaries of the Christian canon discussed in chapter 3, but very much like the issue of the priority of Scripture over Church addressed in chapter 2, it matters a great deal. At stake is whether the canon of Scripture as described in my second and third chapters can in reality effectively fulfill its function as our rule of faith and life, challenging as well as affirming the beliefs and practices that we bring to Scripture for "measurement." Every reader of Scripture is a hopefully recovering heretic, with respect to belief; as to practice, every reader is a prodigal son, hopefully on the way back from a life gone astray. How shall we continue to disentangle the false from the true, and the good from the bad, as we strive to perceive truth and goodness a little more clearly each day, and to embrace both? Twenty-first-century reality can present itself to us just as ambiguously as fourth- or sixteenth-century reality did to our forebears. Embroiled already in culture by way of our upbringing and education, we (as they) can find it difficult to see the ways in which genuine Christian faith has already been mixed, in ourselves and in others, with unhelpful and perhaps even destructive contemporary ideas and norms. We look at *The Madonna of the Rose* (my chapter 8), and we cannot tell if we are looking at a Christian worldview lightly clothed in alien dress, or at an alien worldview lightly clothed in Christian dress. We need biblical texts that can decisively cut through the confusion, addressing us bluntly and directly in plain language, and bringing light out of darkness. We need texts that can bite back. We shall not discover such texts as allegorical readers, any more than as postmodern readers, of Scripture. We shall encounter them only as readers who are devoted to the letter.

10

THE SEPTUAGINT AS CHRISTIAN SCRIPTURE
It's All Greek to Me

If Chaldaeans [i.e., Hebrew speakers] were to learn the Greek language, and if Greeks were to learn Chaldaean, and if each were to meet with those scriptures in both languages, namely, the Chaldaic and the translated version, they would admire and reverence them . . . as one and the same both in their facts and in their language.

—Philo of Alexandria[1]

Since it becomes Christians . . . to make good use of the Holy Scriptures as their one and only book and it is a sin and a shame not to know our own book or to understand the speech and words of our God, it is a still greater sin and loss that we do not study languages.

—Martin Luther[2]

Before there were Protestants, there was already a canon of Christian Scripture that was regarded as given to the Church by God so that people would know what they should believe and how they should live. That it should be read, foundationally, in its literal sense, was widely accepted. But *which texts* of the Bible should be read, in which languages, and how were differences between the various texts to be handled? These were questions less easily answered. Already among the NT authors OT books can be cited directly from existing Hebrew forms of the text,[3] but also (and in fact predominantly) from Hebrew texts that had been translated into Greek—the lingua franca of the Hellenistic world. Before long (and perhaps already in the first century AD), Latin translations both of

---

[1] Philo, *De vita Mosis* (*On the Life of Moses*), 2.40, WP, 494.
[2] Martin Luther, *To the Councilmen*, LW 45:364.
[3] A very small proportion of the OT (sections of Daniel and Ezra) is written in Aramaic, but the constant use of "Hebrew and Aramaic" in a chapter like this, for the sake of those few texts not written in Hebrew, would quickly become tiresome for the reader. The reader should simply mentally supply "and Aramaic" to "Hebrew" where appropriate (and where I do not explicitly mention the former).

Greek translations of the OT and of the Greek NT also appeared. These older Latin translations were increasingly necessary for Bible readers and hearers in the Roman Empire who were more comfortable in Latin than in Greek (especially in regions like Gaul or North Africa)—just as Syriac translations became necessary in the region of Antioch by at least the second century, and Coptic ones in Egypt by the third.[4] In due course the older Latin versions were largely superseded by Jerome's translations of the OT directly from the Hebrew into Latin in the late fourth and early fifth centuries, along with his revisions of the Gospels on the basis of the Greek. Together, these formed the basis for the Latin Vulgate, which within only a few centuries became the authorized version of the Bible in the West.[5] In his own time, however, Jerome's work on the OT was controversial, and it attracted criticism from no less prominent a Church leader than Augustine, who did not view favorably (at least initially) Jerome's departure from what Augustine regarded as inspired Greek originals. He feared that "if Jerome's translation gained widespread acceptance, it would cause a rift between the Western and the Eastern Church, because Greek-speaking Christians would hold to the Septuagint."[6] His fears proved to be justified—although we obviously cannot lay entirely at Jerome's door the blame for the increasing distance between East and West throughout the succeeding centuries—and to this day the LXX remains the base original-language text for the OT Scriptures in the Eastern (as Westerners like to call it) Orthodox Church.

In the West, the Vulgate itself came under serious scrutiny from the High Middle Ages onward, and the Reformers came to share the widespread Renaissance concern about its accuracy. Instead, they set at the heart of their interpretative endeavors the predominantly Hebrew (OT) and Greek (NT) texts in which the biblical manuscripts were first written. They strove along with Renaissance scholars more generally to reconstruct, through textual criticism, the best versions of those early texts, insisting that the Vulgate must be viewed in their light. They strongly insisted, moreover, that competence in the biblical languages was essential to faithful biblical interpretation, and they advocated for language learning. Indeed, Luther appears to think that the Reformation would not have occurred had he not known these languages (see the first epigraph to my chapter 11). The Counter-Reformational Council of Trent (1546) took a very different view. It defended the Vulgate fiercely (note the *second* epigraph to my chapter

---

[4] Dines, *Septuagint*, 10–11; Hill, *Antioch*, 7–8, 50–51n14. In each of these cases, the translations were necessary in order to allow access to Scripture outside the urban environments where people spoke Greek.

[5] Reventlow, *Biblical Interpretation*, 2:36–45.

[6] Reventlow, *Biblical Interpretation*, 2:38.

11),[7] as did those who abided by its pronouncements in succeeding generations. They defended it not only on account of its lengthy usage in the Church, but also because they believed that it was more accurate than the Hebrew and Greek texts.[8] This was already a line of argument pursued prior to Trent in response to early Reformation ideas. The Vatican librarian Agostino Steuco (1497–1548) offered significant commentary along these lines in 1529, albeit that he himself was not above correcting the Vulgate on the basis of Hebrew and Greek texts.[9] Routinely, nevertheless, the Counter-Reformational party explained differences between the Latin, on the one hand, and the Hebrew and Greek, on the other, in terms of deficiencies in the latter two textual traditions caused by the carelessness of scribes, or by the need among Jews and heretics to possess texts that confirmed their wrong opinions. They regarded the Vulgate, on the other hand, as inspired by the Holy Spirit. Competence in the biblical languages was certainly not essential to faithful biblical interpretation, then, on this Tridentine view.

Who was right, who was wrong, and why? Related to this question, should contemporary Christians insist that the foundational scriptural texts against which all articulations of Christian doctrine and ethics should be measured, and in the light of which all Bible translations should be made, are texts in the original biblical languages? And should we seek competence in Hebrew (with Aramaic) and Greek in order to understand them? Our starting point in the present chapter in pursuing convincing answers to these questions will be to look at how the early Church viewed the relationship between the Greek translations of the OT books they possessed and their Hebrew precursors. This will provide the foundation for the argument of this chapter and the next, which is that the Reformers were right to insist on the primacy of the biblical texts in their original languages, and that contemporary Christians should still hold to this primacy, regarding the learning of biblical languages as centrally important in seeking to understand, translate, and communicate these texts.

HEBREW TEXTS AND JEWISH GREEK TRANSLATIONS

At least a century before there was a Greek translation of any part of the OT, there was already in Athens a Greek tradition of gathering together traditional literary texts with a view to producing authorized editions of them. The most

---

[7] For a helpful description of the proceedings of the Council on the matter of the Vulgate, see Wicks, "Catholic Old Testament Interpretation," 627–29.

[8] Note, e.g., Bellarmine's defense of the Vulgate against charges of inaccuracy laid by the Protestant writer Martin Chemnitz (1522–1586). Wicks, "Catholic Old Testament Interpretation," 647.

[9] R. Gerald Hobbs, "Translation of the Bible," in *The Oxford Encyclopedia of the Reformation* (4 vols.; ed. Hans J. Hillerbrand; Oxford: Oxford University Press, 1996), 1:164.

famous of these is the official copy of the tragic poets Aeschylus, Sophocles, and Euripides that was produced in Athens in 338–326 BC and deposited in the public archives there. Actors were thereafter forbidden to depart from the authorized script.[10] Whether there was an early official edition of Homer of a similar type is disputed. Later, after the death of Alexander the Great and the division of his extensive empire among some of his erstwhile generals, an important Greek kingdom was established in Ptolemaic Egypt under Alexander's friend and biographer Ptolemy I Soter. Its capital was Alexandria, and this city's new library quickly became the focus of frenetic literary activity. With an eye to its propaganda value in proclaiming through "the universal gathering of books" their universal rule as Alexander's successors,[11] the Ptolemies set about "endowing their library not only with as many texts as possible, but with the best editions of these texts."[12] These included official ("civic") copies of the Homeric epics, the *Iliad* and the *Odyssey*. These texts were collected from every possible city in the belief that, subject to proper method, the original text of Homer could be reconstructed from the variously corrupted manuscripts—albeit that corrupt versions would (and did) inevitably continue to circulate at the same time in this early period of critical work.[13] The standardization of the text of Homer was ultimately completed in Egypt by the middle of the second century BC. It is associated with Aristarchus of Samothrace, the librarian in Alexandria at the time. At this point divergent ("unauthorized") papyri of the Homeric poems began to disappear.

THE SEPTUAGINT

It is against this background that we must consider the case of the first part of the OT to be translated from Hebrew into Greek: the Pentateuch. This translation is probably to be dated to the early part of the third century BC,[14] and it has long been referred to as the "Septuagint" (or LXX, the Latin numeral for seventy) because of the claim in a second-century BC text, the *Letter of Aristeas*, that it was translated by approximately seventy (precisely, seventy-two) Jewish elders. These elders, it was said, traveled to Alexandria for this very purpose, taking with them an authoritative Hebrew scroll from Jerusalem—the "best edition"—that would form its basis.[15] The reliability of *Aristeas* has been the subject of much debate, but Sylvie Honigman makes good use of it in the course of constructing a plausible

[10] Sylvie Honigman, *The Septuagint and Homeric Scholarship in Alexandria: A Study in the Narrative of the Letter of Aristeas* (London: Routledge, 2003), 121.
[11] Honigman, *Septuagint*, 116–17.
[12] Honigman, *Septuagint*, 43.
[13] Honigman, *Septuagint*, 44, 122.
[14] See Honigman, *Septuagint*, 96–97, for the evidence; also Dines, *Septuagint*, 41–42.
[15] For an extensive introduction to *Aristeas*, see Honigman, *Septuagint*, 1–91.

scenario for the LXX translation. She envisages that it was first requested by the Jewish community in Alexandria for their own reasons, and then supported by royal patronage—in pursuit of the general political advantage described just above, but also with the specific goal of bolstering Ptolemaic claims, disputed by their rivals, the Seleucids, to Syria-Palestine. Translated by a small team of *Egyptian* Jewish translators (and not by seventy-two elders from Palestine), the LXX was shortly thereafter placed in the library of Alexandria, and was also used in copied forms by both Jews and Egyptian elites—among Jews, certainly in educational and possibly in legal contexts. Honigman's thesis is that gradually Egyptian Jews came to regard the LXX as sacred, and it is this sentiment that *Aristeas* reflects, and also aims to support, with respect to the mid-second-century authoritative version of the translation that the author knew. Perhaps this was the copy in the library in Alexandria, or perhaps it was a revised edition of that original—a revision arising out of dissatisfaction with the original translation, or with the corrupt state (already) of many of the local copies that were circulating.[16]

There is much about this reconstruction that remains uncertain,[17] but for my present purposes only one fact requires to be emphasized: already at the point when we first encounter a Greek translation of part of the OT, we do so in an environment in which it is customary to measure the authority of texts in relation to their precursors, and ultimately to their originals. *Aristeas* reflects such beliefs, and that is why its author goes to such lengths to emphasize the need both for a flawless Hebrew scroll (a canonical scroll) from Jerusalem, and for translators "of the most exemplary lives and mature experience, skilled in matters pertaining to their Law," who could translate the scroll with perfect accuracy so that the outcome would be "an outstanding version."[18] Both the quality of the manuscript and the quality of the translators are crucial. Otherwise, the translation will not faithfully represent the original text—and this matters greatly.

At some time later (mainly in the second century BC, it seems),[19] the other books that make up the OT were also translated into Greek, and the whole Greek Bible (not just the Pentateuch) soon came to be described (not quite in line with the tradition of seventy-two elders in *Aristeas*) as the work of "the Seventy." In the aftermath of this development, as early as the first century AD, we find further evidence of a pre-Christian, Jewish conviction about the importance of the close connection between the original and the translation, in significant

---

[16] Honigman, *Septuagint*, passim, and in her summary on 136–39.
[17] See Dines, *Septuagint*, 41–45.
[18] Honigman, *Septuagint*, 45.
[19] Dines, *Septuagint*, 16–24, 45–46; the translations of Ruth, Song of Songs, Ecclesiastes, and perhaps Esther are to be dated to the first century BC.

Jewish attempts to produce Greek translations that are more closely in line with the authoritative Hebrew text that lies before the translators—whether they are revising the LXX or attempting fresh translations.[20] The text in question is what later came to be known as the Masoretic Text (MT)—the sole authoritative Hebrew text in Judaism in the aftermath of the Roman devastation of Judea in AD 70.[21] In the conviction that a Greek translation ought to match the Hebrew original, efforts were made to address divergences where they had arisen.

It is in the first century AD that we encounter, for example, the so-called *kaige* revisions in the LXX, designed to make the Greek text "an exact reproduction of the Hebrew."[22] It is here, too, that we encounter the mysterious "Theodotion," whose name is attached mainly to scattered phenomena in later manuscripts of the LXX and to various readings in the NT and in patristic writers. This version, too, leans in the direction of the MT.[23] In the first half of the second century AD (c. 130), Aquila then develops the *kaige* style of his predecessors in producing a fresh Greek version of the MT, of which "only fragments and isolated readings" remain.[24] Aquila's translation is very close to the Hebrew, often at the expense of good Greek style. For Greek-speaking Jews, it soon became the most popular alternative to the LXX, which by this point had become firmly identified with the Christians. Aquila was followed in the late second or early third century by Symmachus (c. 170), whose work also reflects the MT but with more attention to good Greek style. This style is "so distinctive that, more than with the other two versions [Theodotion and Aquila], it can be described as a new translation rather than a revision."[25] Fragments of other Jewish Greek versions of the OT have also survived in early Christian literature, including a so-called "fifth

---

[20] The process possibly began in some degree earlier, but the significance of the evidence is disputed. Honigman, *Septuagint*, 123–27.

[21] The precursors of this medieval text are often referred to as the proto-Masoretic "family" of texts, although the early copies of texts in the family "differ little from each other and from the medieval text of MT with regard to the latter's consonantal text." I shall sometimes use this same nomenclature ("proto-Masoretic") where the context appears to require a focus on the distinction between earlier and later forms of the text. As we shall see later in the chapter, the MT was probably already "the standard text of the Pharisees" in pre-Christian times, originating and being very carefully transmitted "in the spiritual and authoritative center of Judaism," possibly in temple circles where scribes were entrusted with its copying and preservation. Emanuel Tov, "The History and Significance of a Standard Text of the Hebrew Bible," *HBOT* 1/1:49–66 (63–64).

[22] Dines, *Septuagint*, 81–84 (83).

[23] Theodotion's name is also attached to a version of the book of Daniel (perhaps a revision, perhaps a fresh translation) that is much closer than the LXX to the MT, and was known to the NT writers along with the LXX version. However, "readings attributed to Theodotion do not necessarily come from the same source." Dines, *Septuagint*, 84–87 (87).

[24] Dines, *Septuagint*, 88, 87–89 (88).

[25] Dines, *Septuagint*, 89–90 (90).

translation" (the "Quinta," counting the LXX and "the Three"—Theodotion, Aquila, and Symmachus—as the four preceding).[26] All this work is testimony to an ongoing Jewish belief in the first two Christian centuries that, while translations of Scripture into Greek are necessary, their validity depends entirely on their close connection to the authoritative Hebrew text that they claim, in this new language, to represent.[27]

PHILO OF ALEXANDRIA AND THE SEPTUAGINT

It is within this context that we must hear an important Jewish voice whose sentiments to some extent lead in a different direction—a voice we have encountered already in different contexts in chapters 2 through 9. Philo of Alexandria, where the LXX originated, certainly believed that the Hebrew Scriptures ought to be treated with admiration and reverence.[28] However, he also believed that the LXX (he is apparently thinking mainly of the Pentateuch/Torah) should be treated with the same degree of respect. It should be regarded as the product of divine inspiration, created not just by translators, but by prophets—in the Platonic sense, of those who "say many fine things, but know none of the things they say."[29] That is, the translators simply responded in a trance-like state to the divine voice that interpreted the Hebrew for them.[30] They neither added anything to the Hebrew, nor took anything away from it, nor changed it in any way.[31] This would be evident, maintained Philo, to anyone who knew both Greek and Hebrew, if he were to consider both texts together (note the first epigraph to the present chapter).

On the one hand, then, Philo makes a strong claim here for the LXX as inspired Scripture in its own right, independently of the Hebrew text that lies behind it. He might well be suspected of knowingly taking a stand against exactly the kind of revisionary work that is now preserved in the *kaige* revisions and in Theodotion. In this respect as in others—as we shall see—Philo was destined to become an important influence on the later Christian tradition. On the other hand, it clearly remains important to Philo that the LXX *does* precisely reflect the Hebrew text, to such an extent that he all but invites his readers empirically to test his strong claim about its absolute accuracy. He himself would not have

---

[26] Dines, *Septuagint*, 90–92.
[27] For the ongoing importance of the LXX (and indeed of Greek translation in general) within Judaism after this period, see Dines, *Septuagint*, 73–75.
[28] Philo, *Moses*, 2.40, WP, 494.
[29] Philo, *Moses*, 2.37, WP, 494; cf. Plato, *Apologia* (*Apology*), 22c.
[30] Philo, *Moses*, 2.37, WP, 494. On the language of this passage see Dines, *Septuagint*, 67–69.
[31] Philo, *Moses*, 2.34, WP, 494.

been able to do so, because "his knowledge of Hebrew was probably rudimentary."³² Those fellow Jews in the first two Christian centuries whose Hebrew was not rudimentary, and who worked to revise the LXX or even to offer alternative Greek translations of it, clearly disagreed with him, in empirically reviewing the question. They, too, became an important influence on the later Christian tradition, particularly to the extent that Christians were themselves familiar with Hebrew, and not just with Greek.

HEBREW TEXTS AND GREEK TRANSLATION IN EARLY CHRISTIANITY

Given that they were writing in Greek to an audience in which knowledge of Greek was widespread (see below), the apostles unsurprisingly used the LXX as a major source in citing the OT Scriptures.³³ There is no evidence that, like Philo, they believed the LXX to be inspired in itself. Paul, for example, appears to translate directly from the Hebrew on at least six occasions where the LXX does not agree with it; on at least twenty-eight occasions his citation reflects neither the MT nor the LXX. He and the other apostles were not bound to the LXX; rather, Paul "cited it when it suited him."³⁴ Nevertheless, they clearly must have regarded it as a sufficiently reliable translation of the Hebrew Scriptures for many of their purposes.

In the course of the second century AD, however, fierce disputes arose between Jews and Christians about what the Scriptures really said, and whether they supported Jewish or Christian beliefs. The reliability of the LXX became an issue in these disputes. Did it, or did it not, accurately reflect the Hebrew from which it had been translated?

The Reception of the Septuagint in Early Post-Apostolic Thought

In this ongoing debate, *Aristeas* as interpreted and embellished by Philo became particularly important. It was utilized by Christian apologists to defend the inspired nature of the LXX, and at the same time to suggest that the texts cited by their Jewish opponents against Christian interpretations were corrupt.

---

³² Dines, *Septuagint*, 70.

³³ On one recent calculation with respect to the apostle Paul (e.g.)—omitting Ephesians and 1–2 Timothy because of the calculator's doubts about their Pauline authorship—Paul's citations agree with the LXX on fifty-eight occasions out of a total of ninety-two. Lim, *Formation*, 165. For a slightly different count, including Ephesians and 1–2 Timothy, see Moisés Silva, "Old Testament in Paul," in *Dictionary of Paul and His Letters* (ed. Gerald F. Hawthorne, Ralph P. Martin, and Daniel G. Reid; Downers Grove, Ill.: InterVarsity, 1993), 630–42 (631).

³⁴ Lim, *Formation*, 168.

So it is, for example, that in the course of his *Dialogue* with his Jewish interlocutor Trypho, Justin Martyr accuses Trypho's teachers of having "altogether taken away many Scriptures from the translations effected by those seventy elders who were with Ptolemy."[35] The form of Justin's argument is significant. In defending the Greek, he is not at all indifferent to the question of its agreement with the original Hebrew. It is simply that, in his view, Trypho is working from a text that does not reflect that original.

Irenaeus is of the same opinion, referencing both Theodotion and Aquila in their translation "young woman" in Isaiah 7:14 instead of the LXX's "virgin" (Gk. *parthenos*). The latter, Irenaeus claims, is found in the "unadulterated Scriptures" preserved in Egypt, and Theodotion and Aquila are "impudent and presumptuous" to offer a different translation.[36] The LXX accurately preserves the meaning of the original Hebrew, whereas Theodotion and Aquila do not.

Tertullian, too, is evidently very conscious of the importance of maintaining that the LXX is an entirely accurate rendition of its Hebrew precursor, and in doing so he emphasizes the scholarly credentials of those who initiated and carried through the translation. He essentially even tells the readers of his *Apology* where to go if they would like to follow through on Philo's proposal about empirical testing: "To this day, at the temple of Serapis, the libraries of Ptolemy are to be seen, with the identical Hebrew originals in them."[37]

It is evident in all of this that the LXX is held in very high esteem by the early Church Fathers. Yet it is also evident that the LXX is regarded as a *translation* of an original, authoritative Hebrew text, and that its conformity with that Hebrew text must necessarily be asserted. In chapter 3 I wrote about the "pressure" placed on Christians in the patristic period, in respect of the question of canon, by their awareness of their shared heritage with the Jews, and I discussed a related conviction: that it was precisely the ancient Scriptures deriving *from the Jews* that ought still to compose the *Christian* OT—even if the Hebrew must necessarily be translated into Greek. This same "pressure" is palpable in patristic literature with respect to the language, and not only the canon issue. The early Church Fathers could not simply ignore the problems arising from divergent Hebrew and Greek texts, since they were potentially fatal to their appeals to authoritative Scripture in respect of at least some of their views. The Fathers had to address these problems; they had to show that they were not problems at all—at least, not for *them*.

---

[35] Justin, *Dialogue*, 71 (ANF 1:234).
[36] Irenaeus, *Against Heresies*, 3.21.1–3 (ANF 1:451–52).
[37] Tertullian, *Apologeticus* (*Apology*), 18 (ANF 3:32).

Origen, the Hexapla, and the Lucianic Recension

Nor could the third-century Alexandrian Christian scholar Origen avoid the reality that "the status of the Septuagint as a translation meant that it was in an important sense unoriginal and that the Hebrew form of [the] scriptures demanded some attention."[38] By this time it had become apparent—at least to those who had access to a sufficient amount of the necessary information—not only that the LXX diverged from (for example) Aquila, but that "the" LXX was no longer a simple unity. It was, rather, a collection of manuscripts marked by both textual corruption and revision within their own respective regional domains. This situation is still reflected, in the fourth and fifth centuries, in the "uncial" manuscripts (that is, texts written in capital letters) that are the first manuscripts to contain both the OT and the NT in Greek. These are Codex Vaticanus ("a prime textual witness to the original LXX"); Codex Sinaiticus ("often a reasonably reliable witness to an unrevised LXX," where it is extant); and Codex Alexandrinus ("idiosyncratic, and marked by revisions, but ... often an important witness to very early readings").[39] In addition to parallel text-critical work on the NT books,[40] therefore, Origen undertook the huge task of trying to bring some order to this unsatisfactory OT situation. Probably during the decade from 235 until 245 "[h]e set about correlating all available textual material in a six-column synopsis which for that reason came to be called the Hexapla ('six-fold')."[41] The original of this massive work was for a long time after its composition kept in the important library in Caesarea in Palestine.

From what we can tell from later accounts of the Hexapla (which is not itself extant), Origen's columns contained, in order: (1) unpointed Hebrew (that is, the consonantal text without the vowel points); (2) a Greek transliteration;[42] (3) Aquila; (4) Symmachus; (5) the LXX; and (6) Theodotion—the sixth column probably also contained readings from other available sources.[43] Origen himself can be read as implying that the fifth column in the original Hexapla already contained an LXX text that had been critically corrected in the light of the other columns—the proposed additions and deletions from his main text

---

[38] Edmon L. Gallagher, *Hebrew Scripture in Patristic Biblical Theory: Canon, Language, Text* (VCSup 114; Leiden: Brill, 2012), 2.

[39] Dines, *Septuagint*, 6–7.

[40] Martens, *Origen and Scripture*, 43n8.

[41] Dines, *Septuagint*, 97–98.

[42] As to the nature of the Hebrew text, none of the extant fragments of the Hexapla display column one, but "[r]etroversions [from column 2], where they can be made, result in something very close to the MT" (Dines, *Septuagint*, 100), and of course the MT also lies behind column three in particular.

[43] The alternative is to posit further columns in some biblical books. Martens, *Origen and Scripture*, 45–46.

being indicated by established (Alexandrian) critical marks as described below. Some scholars believe, however, that Origen's comments (reproduced below) refer to a subsequent phase of his work, and not to the composition of the Hexapla itself:

> We have been able, with God helping us, to repair the difference between the copies of the Old Testament, by using the remaining version [of the OT] as a criterion. Based upon these remaining versions, we made a judgment about the uncertainties in the Septuagint due to the difference in its copies. We kept what is in agreement with these [versions]. We marked some passages with an obelus that are not in the Hebrew (we did not dare to completely strike these out); but we added others with asterisks in order to make it clear that what we supplied was not in the Septuagint but from the remaining translation harmonious with the Hebrew.[44]

Whatever the exact process involved, a critically revised LXX more in line with the Hebrew underlying the Jewish Greek translations certainly did ultimately emerge from Origen's hexaplaric work. It inevitably involved more than simply dealing with the limited additions and deletions just mentioned.[45]

Whenever the corrected LXX text ultimately emerged, its production was already an important part of Origen's purpose, as he explains to his friend Julius Africanus in a letter dating from around 248–250, "lest in my controversies with the Jews I should quote to them what is not found in their copies."[46] As we shall see in a moment, it is not that Origen disagrees with his predecessors that corrupt Jewish texts exist.[47] Nor is he incapable in some of his other work of ignoring the Hebrew text in favor of different Greek readings, often without giving a reason.[48] Indeed, he appears in his various writings to be conflicted about "whether it is preferable to have a LXX corrected according to the Hebrew or a 'pure' LXX"— unsure about how far to follow through on particular text-critical insights.[49] In all, nevertheless, the Hebrew exerts "pressure" on Origen with respect to text, just as it does with respect to canon: "just as Origen advocated the Hebrew criterion for the OT canon, so also he generally endorses a Hebrew criterion for the OT

---

[44] Origen, *Commentary on Matthew*, 15.14, as translated in Martens, *Origen and Scripture*, 47. For doubts about his description of the fifth column in this respect, see Dines, *Septuagint*, 100–103.

[45] "Origen also had to cope with places where the word order was different, whole passages were transposed … or omitted … or with paraphrastic translations." Dines, *Septuagint*, 101.

[46] Origen, *Letter to Africanus*, 5 (ANF 4:387).

[47] Note his implicit agreement, e.g., in his sarcastic comments to Africanus about convincing them "to give us copies which shall be untampered with, and free from forgery!" Origen, *Letter to Africanus*, 4 (ANF 4:387).

[48] Martens, *Origen and Scripture*, 48n30.

[49] Gallagher, *Hebrew Scripture*, 180, 182. See further, on the complexity of Origen's attitude toward the LXX, Carleton Paget, "Christian Exegesis," 502–8.

text."⁵⁰ The very existence of the Hexapla and the revised LXX associated with it are notable testimony to this reality, and the fact that Origen's LXX "circulated widely, and became extremely popular" confirms that he was not alone in feeling this pressure.⁵¹ A striking example of its effects is found in the case of the book of Daniel. Origen favored Theodotion's text, which is much closer than the LXX to the MT. This had the consequence of entirely displacing the LXX Daniel in the Church in the second half of the third century, in an environment in which it was widely believed that Origen's "hexaplaric" LXX was the genuine LXX precisely because of its closeness to the Hebrew.⁵²

This did not, however, prevent a rival LXX revision, associated later by Jerome with Lucian of Antioch (c. 250–312), from emerging in that city, albeit heavily utilizing the "hexaplaric" LXX in the process.⁵³ Lucian himself was a Syrian who knew Greek and possibly a little Hebrew and who at one point in his life had studied in Caesarea, the home of the original Hexapla. The Antiochenes strongly defended the text associated with Lucian's name, over against claims (in Jerome, for example) that the hexaplaric text was the more scientific and accurate of the two. The way in which they defended it is well exemplified in Pseudo-Chrysostom's assertion that Lucian's text was the more faithful to the Hebrew, accompanied by Theodore's claim that Jerome had "no business overturning the translation of the Seventy," because of his allegedly poor *grasp* of Hebrew.⁵⁴ The implicit and explicit Antiochene appeal is again to the Hebrew text, which Theodore and colleagues like John Chrysostom simply assume is accurately (albeit not perfectly) reflected in the LXX—which in turn is accurately reflected in the Antiochene (Lucianic) text form.⁵⁵ The importance of the Hebrew to Theodore is also revealed in his negative comments about the translator of the (Syriac) Peshitta, whose understanding of Hebrew (he asserts) cannot possibly have been

---

⁵⁰ Gallagher, *Hebrew Scripture*, 183.

⁵¹ Dines, *Septuagint*, 101.

⁵² Dines, *Septuagint*, 86, 102.

⁵³ For a helpful, brief discussion of this "Lucianic recension" and its relationship to similar "proto-Lucianic" readings from earlier centuries, see Dines, *Septuagint*, 103–6; also Hill, *Antioch*, 57–60. "Lucian's" text is one of three that Jerome in the late fourth century describes as dominating various regions of the Church in his day. To the south, in Palestine, there was the text of Pamphilus (i.e., Origen's hexaplaric LXX). In Egypt and its surrounds, there was the text of Hesychius—although it is not in fact clear that this "text" amounts to anything more than "sporadic local textual characteristics." Dines, *Septuagint*, 95–96 (95).

⁵⁴ Dines, *Septuagint*, 94; Gallagher, *Hebrew Scripture*, 204.

⁵⁵ Hill, *Antioch*, 54–57. These general assumptions, along with the absence of much ability in Hebrew among the Antiochenes, help to explain why there was no great enthusiasm for consistent text-critical work in Antioch, even though someone like John Chrysostom often *refers* to textual variants. Hill, *Antioch*, 64–73.

the equal of that of the Seventy.⁵⁶ Recent research on the Lucianic revision itself suggests that it "had as its aim to fill in the gaps in the LXX in respect of the Hebrew text, to improve on mere transliteration of obscure terms by a puzzled LXX, to supply clarifying items, and in short to come up with a full text with no omissions.'"⁵⁷

THE HEBREW CRITERION AND THE APOCRYPHAL ADDITIONS

The importance of "the Hebrew criterion" when thinking about the text of the OT in the post-apostolic Church is well illustrated, further, by the main theme of the correspondence already mentioned between Origen and Africanus—which conveniently allows me to pick up some loose threads still hanging from my chapter 2. In that chapter I announced my intention of delaying consideration, until this point in the book, of the apocryphal expansions to canonical biblical compositions—expansions like Susanna (as opposed to independent apocryphal compositions like Tobit). It so happens that the letter to which Origen is responding when he makes his comments to Africanus about the purpose of the Hexapla (see above) is precisely about Susanna. Its contents, along with Origen's response, make for fascinating reading. Africanus expresses astonishment that his friend does not realize that the story of Susanna in the LXX of Daniel, to which Origen had previously referred, is a "modern forgery." Part of Africanus' reasoning is that "this section, along with the other two at the end of it [i.e., the Song of the Three, and Bel and the Dragon], is not contained in the Daniel received among the Jews." More importantly for our present purposes, "all the books of the Old Testament have been translated from Hebrew into Greek," whereas Susanna was evidently *composed* in Greek.⁵⁸ The first part of this statement, as Edmon Gallagher notes, is offered simply as an assertion: Africanus "simply assumes that informed Christians generally acknowledge the Hebrew criterion for the OT canon."⁵⁹ That is, Africanus assumes that only OT texts possessing Hebrew originals can function as Scripture and, moreover, that Origen will agree with him on this point. Origen certainly does agree, as is clear both from the nature of his response to Africanus and from comments elsewhere in his writings.⁶⁰ He deals with the problem of the

---

⁵⁶ Hill, *Antioch*, 56–57.
⁵⁷ Hill, *Antioch*, 61, quoting N. Fernández Marcos, *The Septuagint in Context: Introduction to the Greek Versions of the Bible* (Leiden: Brill, 2001), 230.
⁵⁸ Julius Africanus, *Epistula ad Origenem (Letter to Origen)* (ANF 4:385).
⁵⁹ Gallagher, *Hebrew Scripture*, 68.
⁶⁰ See Origen's *Stromata (Miscellanies)* as transmitted by Jerome, and cited in Gallagher, *Hebrew Scripture*, 69–73. As to his response to Africanus, the crucial point is that Origen expends considerable energy in trying to show that Africanus has no basis for his skepticism about a Hebrew original. Gallagher, *Hebrew Scripture*, 73–78.

omission of Susanna from the Hebrew book of Daniel, therefore, using a fairly typical early Christian argument: "they [the Jews] hid from the knowledge of the people as many of the passages which contained any scandal against the elders, rulers, and judges, as they could."[61] The point is that for Origen there simply *must* have been a Hebrew original of Susanna, already included in the OT texts translated by the Seventy. If we could not suppose that there were such an original, we could *indeed* not accept such a text as part of Scripture. The whole exchange implies, of course, that this is not simply a belief that Origen and Africanus share, but "that the Hebrew criterion was generally accepted in the Church of their day."[62]

This same belief is reflected in other post-apostolic writings. "All the sacred books of the Old Testament were originally composed in Hebrew," asserts John Chrysostom in the fourth century; "everybody would agree with us on this."[63] The scriptural authority of a text in the LXX ultimately depends upon this direct connection with an authoritative Hebrew original. It is the absence of evidence for such a connection, in respect of the apocryphal expansions to Daniel, Esther, and Jeremiah, which will shortly lead Jerome in his own Bible translation work generally to avoid making fresh Latin translations of this and other deuterocanonical material, and even to avoid revising earlier Old Latin translations of it. Where he does offer such translation, it is only with evident discomfort. Under pressure from friends, for example—and with the help of a native Aramaic speaker—he does translate Tobit from Aramaic into Latin, but he makes a point of noting that "the Hebrews [excise it] from the catalogue of Divine Scriptures."[64] He does the same, reluctantly, with Judith.[65] Without much enthusiasm, he also translates into Latin the Greek additions to Daniel (from Theodotion) and Esther (from the LXX), again making sure to advise readers "that [these additions] are not to be found in the Hebrew" and marking them with what he calls "their 'death-warrant,' the obelus."[66] His justification for his translation of the "additions" to Daniel is nervousness about the reaction of the "uninformed" should he leave them out. Therefore, he tells us, he has contented himself with "form[ing] them into an appendix, prefixing them to an obelus, and thus making an end of them, so as not to seem to the uninformed to have cut off a large portion of the volume."[67] The

---

[61] Origen, *Letter to Africanus*, 9 (ANF 4:388).

[62] Gallagher, *Hebrew Scripture*, 784.

[63] John Chrysostom, *Homiliae in Genesim* (*Homilies on Genesis*), 4.94, in *Saint John Chrysostom: Homilies on Genesis 1–17* (ed. Thomas P. Halton et al.; trans. Robert C. Hill; FC 74; Washington, D.C.: Catholic University of America Press, 1986), 56.

[64] Jerome, *Prologus (Preface) to Tobit*, as translated in Edmon Gallagher, "Why Did Jerome Translate Tobit and Judith?," *HTR* 108 (2015): 356–75 (374–75).

[65] Jerome, *Prologus (Preface) to Judith*, as translated in Gallagher, "Tobit and Judith," 375.

[66] Gallagher, *Hebrew Scripture*, 98.

[67] Jerome, *Prologus (Preface) to Daniel* (NPNF 2, 6:493).

point is that such writings have no real business being regarded as part of Scripture at all. Jerome would much rather not have to deal with them.

Jerome and the Vulgate

As we move into the fourth and early fifth centuries we discover that Origen's LXX itself has suffered significant textual corruption, even as it is widely regarded as close to the Hebrew and (therefore) the correct text.[68] The confused state of affairs to which this contributes in these centuries—not least because once again, significant gaps have opened up between the readings of the Hebrew texts that are reflected in the three major Jewish Greek translations (Theodotion, Aquila, and Symmachus) and the readings in what Christians in different parts of the Roman Empire think of as "the" LXX—produces two kinds of responses.

On the one hand, the view is expressed that the contemporary, extant (and inspired) LXX matches the original Hebrew more closely than any other Greek translation. The "Three" (over against the far more impressive "Seventy") reflect a corrupt (and sometimes intentionally corrupted) Hebrew text. We find this view articulated, for example, in Eusebius of Caesarea, Gregory of Nyssa, and Epiphanius of Salamis.[69] The LXX was translated "from ancient and uncorrupted copies of the Hebrew," according to Eusebius; the Jews have silenced the text of the book of Psalms, claims Gregory, through unbelief and willful misunderstanding.[70]

We also encounter the strong opinion, on the other hand (or at the same time), that the LXX is far from being a flawless translation of an ultimately authoritative Hebrew text, even if it remains the best text available. Here the names of Eusebius of Emesa, Diodore of Tarsus, and Theodore of Mopsuestia are worthy of mention.[71] Theodoret of Cyrus stands somewhat between these two groups of Christian authors, allowing for corruption at least in the LXX manuscript tradition.

For all the differences among these writers, however, they share a general agreement with their predecessors among the Church Fathers that the question of the original Hebrew text very much matters. Evidence that the LXX diverges from the Hebrew cannot simply be dismissed, but requires in some way to be addressed. This brings us to Jerome.

Much more than any other Christian before him, including Origen, Jerome invested great time and effort to researching into the text of Scripture.[72] Among

---

[68] Dines, *Septuagint*, 102.
[69] See the helpful discussion in Gallagher, *Hebrew Scripture*, 189–94.
[70] Cited in Gallagher, *Hebrew Scripture*, 191.
[71] Gallagher, *Hebrew Scripture*, 195–96.
[72] For more on this investment, see Adam Kamesar, *Jerome, Greek Scholarship, and the Hebrew Bible: A Study of the Quaestiones Hebraicae in Genesim* (Oxford: Clarendon, 1993), 41–72.

the many notable indications of his commitment, he claims to have read Origen's massive Hexapla twice, from cover to cover, in Caesarea.[73] Jerome also made it his business as a Western, Latin-speaking Christian, while in Antioch and its environs around 373–376, to take "systematic instruction in Greek" by way of improving his grasp of that language, and to begin learning Hebrew.[74] Origen's knowledge of Hebrew had probably been slight; among the Church Fathers, Jerome's ultimately became "exceptional, if not unique."[75]

His early critical work on the Bible followed shortly thereafter back in Rome, where "he undertook at the Pope's prompting [i.e., Damasus I] ... a thorough revision and standardization of the numerous Latin biblical translations" of at least the Gospels, based on the Greek texts in current circulation (often these are texts allied to Codex Vaticanus).[76] Pope Damasus himself evidently understood clearly the importance of biblical translations conforming to their source texts. Whether Jerome also revised the other NT books that are associated with his name, and ultimately came to form part of the Vulgate, is uncertain, but not improbable. In this period, too, Jerome revised the book of Psalms in accordance with a LXX manuscript containing Lucianic readings.[77]

Returning to the East a few years later, Jerome eventually settled in Bethlehem (386), where he remained for the rest of his life. There he attempted a thoroughgoing revision of the current Latin versions (the "Old Latin") of the entire OT corpus,[78] with the Hexapla in nearby Caesarea as his aid. Most of this work is now lost, but his revision of Psalms in this period (the *Gallican Psalter*, because it was first used for worship services in Roman Gaul) was destined to become an important text, rivalling the popularity of Jerome's later Latin translation

---

[73] Dines, *Septuagint*, 98.

[74] Reventlow, *Biblical Interpretation*, 2:34.

[75] Martens, *Origen and Scripture*, 43n9; Hill, *Antioch*, 51. Jerome himself, however, credits Epiphanius not only with Greek but also Hebrew, as well as Syriac, Egyptian, and some Latin. Gallagher, *Hebrew Scripture*, 126n73. See also Reventlow, *Biblical Interpretation*, 2:37, on unwarranted modern skepticism with respect to Jerome's Hebrew competence. Dines (*Septuagint*, 96, 99) is of the opinion that Origen, on the other hand, was "probably never very proficient" in Hebrew, but could at least write it, or call as necessary on "Jewish expertise."

[76] Reventlow, *Biblical Interpretation*, 2:34.

[77] This revision was used widely in Italy until the sixteenth century and to a certain extent also thereafter.

[78] The "stylistic and translational quality" of these versions "was markedly inferior to that of the Greek translation, presumably because the first Latin translations developed from oral rendering *ad hoc* during the worship service." Eva Schulz-Flügel, "The Latin Old Testament Tradition," *HBOT* 1/1:642–62 (643). The first extant traces of Latin translations of the OT are found in Tertullian (645).

(below).⁷⁹ Around 390, however, Jerome changed course and began to translate into Latin directly from Hebrew. He had come to believe that the LXX could no longer serve as the basis for further translation work.

This settled opinion is clear in the preface to Jerome's new translation of Job, where he protests against those who accuse him of inappropriately "censur[ing] the Seventy" (i.e., the translators of the LXX). He observes that he is not the first to note defects in the LXX; Origen precedes him. Even so, Origen's work is insufficient, and Jerome's own labor is necessary in order "to recover what is lost, to correct what is corrupt, and to disclose in pure and faithful language the mysteries of the Church." His object is

> not to censure the ancient translation, but that those passages in it which are obscure, or those which have been omitted, or at all events, through the fault of copyists have been corrupted, might have light thrown upon them by our translation.⁸⁰

The problem is not just that the LXX has become corrupt, however—a truth that Jerome often thinks his opponents fail to grasp, as illustrated in their assumption that "their" LXX is simply "the" LXX.⁸¹ The problem is that in its ancient, original form, the LXX was already less than perfect. This perspective is clear, for example, in the preface to Jerome's translation of Isaiah, where he envisages "the Seventy interpreters to have been unwilling at that time to set forth clearly" certain realities of the text. It is equally plain in the preface to the Ezekiel translation, where Jerome notes that "in some [OT books] they translated the same things, in others, different things," advising his readers to read his own translation instead because "it gives a clearer meaning to readers."⁸² The first producers of the LXX, the evidence suggests, were only translators, and not prophets. Jerome wonders, indeed, where the latter idea ever came from, since *Aristeas* and Josephus tell us only that the men involved assembled in one place where they "consulted together,

---

⁷⁹ Reventlow, *Biblical Interpretation*, 2:37. On the character of Jerome's "hexaplaric recension," see Schulz-Flügel, "Latin Old Testament," 650–52.

⁸⁰ Jerome, *Prologus (Preface) to Job* (NPNF 2, 6:491). This is not to say that Origen did not do important work: his use of asterisks, in particular, "makes what had previously been defective to beam with light." Jerome, *Prologus (Preface) to Genesis*, quoted in his *Adversus Rufinum (Apology)*, 2.25 (NPNF 2, 3:515–16).

⁸¹ Jerome, *Preface to Job* (NPNF 2, 6:491).

⁸² Jerome, *Prologus (Preface) to Isaiah*, trans. Kevin P. Edgecomb, *The Tertullian Project*, http://www.tertullian.org/fathers/jerome_preface_isaiah.htm (accessed March 23, 2016); Jerome, *Prologus (Preface) to Ezekiel*, trans. Edgecomb, *Tertullian Project*, http://www.tertullian.org/fathers/jerome_preface_ezekiel.htm (accessed March 23, 2016).

and did not prophesy. For it is one thing to be a prophet, and another to be a translator."[83]

One way or another, Jerome had come to believe that a new approach to the problem of the biblical text was required. Christian tradition already agreed concerning the authority of the original Hebrew text. If it was now much clearer than ever before that the LXX, for whatever reason, did not accurately represent the original text, then Jerome's proposal was a logical one. A translator should go directly to the Hebrew text—of whose fundamental stability as the *Hebraica veritas* ("Hebrew truth") Jerome was convinced, just as much as he was generally *unconvinced* that the Jews had engaged in falsification of it.[84] It was to this Hebrew text, in fact, that the apostles themselves referred in the NT (he maintained), as well as using the Greek where it did not deviate from the Hebrew.[85] The "pressure of the Hebrew text" now demanded, then, direct recourse to it, around the back (as it were) of an LXX text that was unsatisfactory. This was important for Jerome not least so that Christians could answer their Jewish critics more persuasively, on the basis of a text that they had always (in its original form) shared. From now on, as a result of this new translation work, "Christians would ... be able to refer to a text that was without doubt correct but nonetheless plainly spoke of Christ's coming."[86] That Jerome believed that this "move" was in line with already established Christian beliefs about the authority of the Hebrew text is evidenced in his frequent invitations to his opponents to compare his own translations with the Hebrew by way of asking Jews about it. (The great majority of his opponents knew no Hebrew of their own.)[87] Such invitations make no sense unless it was widely assumed in the Church at the time that the conformity of biblical translations to the original Hebrew text greatly mattered.[88]

---

[83] Jerome, *Preface to Genesis*, quoted in *Apology*, 2.25 (NPNF 2, 3:516).

[84] Some of the comments in his work reveal that he was aware of minor differences between Hebrew manuscripts and did not entirely dismiss the possibility of falsification. Gallagher, *Hebrew Scripture*, 199–200.

[85] Jerome, *Apology*, 2.34 (NPNF 2, 3:517); "To Pammachius on the Best Method of Translating," in *Epistulae (Letters)*, 57.11 (NPNF 2, 6:118); *Preface to Genesis*, quoted in his *Apology*, 2.25 (NPNF 2, 3:515–16).

[86] Reventlow, *Biblical Interpretation*, 2:40.

[87] E.g.: "Wherever in translation I seem to you to go wrong, ask the Hebrews, consult their teachers in different towns." Jerome, *Preface to Genesis*, quoted in *Apology*, 2.25 (NPNF 2, 3:515–16).

[88] Gallagher, *Hebrew Scripture*, 202–3.

Jerome and Augustine

The correspondence that ensued between Jerome and Augustine on the matter of Latin translations from the Hebrew is illuminating.[89] Augustine initiated it, writing to his elder colleague both in 394 and 403 with concerns about the latter's project. Although Augustine is by no means opposed to correcting faulty texts in general,[90] he confesses to Jerome that he finds it difficult to believe that "anything should at this date be found in the Hebrew manuscripts which escaped so many [ancient] translators perfectly acquainted with the language."[91] "For my part," he writes, "I would much rather that you would furnish us with a translation of the Greek version of the canonical Scriptures known as the work of the Seventy translators." This is, he maintains, "the one which the apostles used." It would be too easy otherwise (he warns) for critics in the future to undermine Jerome's new Latin version simply by producing "the original in Greek, which is a language very widely known."[92] Trouble has already ensued in Augustine's own region upon the reading in a church of Jerome's version of Jonah—and when this new translation was shared with local Jews (in line with Jerome's frequent invitation), they responded negatively. This raised questions about Jerome's competence in Hebrew. The problem is only with Jerome's OT translations on the basis of the Hebrew, Augustine reassures his colleague; he himself is very happy (having personally checked them) with Jerome's revisions of the Gospels in line with the original Greek.

The restrained but pointed tone of Jerome's reply to these letters (in 404) will be familiar to any older (but patient) person who has been questioned or criticized by a younger colleague who really knows very little about the subject upon which he is speaking. "You must pardon my saying that you seem to me not to understand the matter" of the transmission of the Greek text, Jerome tells Augustine, before illuminating him as to the meaning of Origen's critical marks in the Hexapla. A touch of sarcasm follows, aimed at Augustine's comments about the "original" Greek text: "I am surprised that you do not read the books of the Seventy translators in the genuine form in which they were originally given to the world, but as they have been corrected, or rather corrupted, by Origen"—on the basis of a text, it should be noted, deriving from "a Jew and a blasphemer"

---

[89] Augustine, *Letters*, 28, 71, 82 (*NPNF* 1, 1:251–53, 326–28, 349–61); Jerome, *Letters*, 112 (summary found at *NPNF* 2, 6:214).

[90] "[V]ery often a translator, to whom the meaning is not well known, is deceived by an ambiguity in the original language, and puts upon the passage a construction that is wholly alien to the sense of the writer ... we must learn not to interpret, but to correct texts of this sort." Augustine, *On Christian Doctrine*, 2.12 (*NPNF* 1, 2:540–41).

[91] Augustine, *Letters*, 28.2 (*NPNF* 1, 1:251).

[92] Augustine, *Letters*, 71.4–5 (*NPNF* 1, 1:327).

(Theodotion). Jerome then proceeds to defend both his competence in Hebrew and the necessity of his new Latin translations, even though they *are* new and not ancient. He concludes by politely asking Augustine to leave him alone.

Augustine's reply to Jerome (in 405) assures him that "you have now convinced me of the benefits to be secured by your proposal to translate the Scriptures from the original Hebrew." Augustine wishes to be sure, however, that Jerome does in fact possess the original Hebrew, and not merely later texts that have suffered deliberate corruption by the Jews. As welcoming as he now is of Jerome's new work, he still holds firmly to the belief that the authentic LXX displays the wisdom of the Seventy, and that "the seal of approbation was given [to this translation] by the apostles themselves."[93]

Augustine's mature thought on this issue is reflected in his *City of God* (written between 413 and 426). He clearly accepts by this point that Jerome's translation from the Hebrew is a good one: he is "a man most learned, and skilled in all three languages [Hebrew, Greek, and Latin]," and "the Jews acknowledge [his translation] to be faithful."[94] Augustine further acknowledges that the idea that the Jews have plotted to corrupt the Hebrew text is foolish,[95] and now also admits the significant differences between the original LXX and the Hebrew. This same admission is found in book 4 of *On Christian Doctrine* (composed in the same time period), where Augustine states that in writing about "the eloquence of the [OT] prophets" he will not

> follow the Septuagint translators, who . . . seem to have altered some passages with the view of directing the reader's attention more particularly to the investigation of the spiritual sense. . . . I shall [instead] follow the translation made from the Hebrew into Latin by the presbyter Jerome, a man thoroughly acquainted with both tongues.[96]

In Augustine's opinion, therefore, Jerome's translation is the more accurate of the two; he has not introduced matters into the text that were not originally present.

Yet Augustine also wishes to maintain that the LXX, even where it plainly disagrees with the Hebrew, represents an authoritative rendering of Scripture; it possesses an "authority . . . not . . . human but divine."[97] His resolution of the

---

[93] Augustine, *Letters*, 82.34–35 (*NPNF* 1, 1:361). See further on the dialogue Annemaré Kotzé, "Augustine, Jerome and the Septuagint," in *Septuagint and Reception: Essays Prepared for the Association for the Study of the Septuagint in South Africa* (ed. Johann Cook; Leiden: Brill, 2009), 245–60.

[94] Augustine, *City of God*, 18.43 (*NPNF* 1, 2:386).

[95] "[F]ar be it from any prudent man to believe . . . that the Jews, however malicious and wrong-headed, could have tampered with so many and so widely dispersed manuscripts." Augustine, *City of God*, 15.13 (*NPNF* 1, 2:293).

[96] Augustine, *On Christian Doctrine*, 4.7 (*NPNF* 1, 2:579–80).

[97] Augustine, *City of God*, 18.42 (*NPNF* 1, 2:386).

dilemma that he now faces comes by way of a strong affirmation of what Jerome had denied: the divine inspiration of the LXX translators. Even though Theodotion, Aquila, Symmachus, and indeed Quinta exist, "yet the Church has received this Septuagint translation just as if it were the only one."[98] Jerome, albeit "a man most learned," is just one man, and "the churches of Christ judge that no one should be preferred to the authority of so many men" (the Seventy), who were so evidently inspired by God in their work. Because they were inspired, it must necessarily be that "if any other translator of their Scriptures from the Hebrew into any other tongue is faithful, in that case he agrees with these seventy translators." The Seventy may not always have represented the words of the Hebrew exactly, and they may even have added things in and left things out. Authorized meaning nevertheless emerges in the LXX, since the translators "are justly believed to have received the Spirit of prophecy; so that, if they made any alterations under His authority, and did not adhere to a strict translation, we could not doubt that this was divinely dictated."[99]

For example, Jonah 3:4 in the MT says that Nineveh shall be overthrown after forty days. The LXX tells us that the city shall be overthrown after three. Augustine proposes that "the Seventy, interpreting long afterward, could say what was different and yet pertinent to the matter, and agree in the self-same meaning, although under a different signification." Christ Himself is signified both by the forty and by the three—"by the forty, because He spent that number of days with His disciples after the resurrection, and then ascended into heaven, but by the three days, because He rose on the third day."[100] The reader may in this way "be aroused from his sleep by the Septuagint interpreters," seeking Christ in both his ascension and his resurrection. According to Augustine, there are many other similar instances "in which the seventy interpreters may be thought to differ from the Hebrew, and yet, when well understood, are found to agree." Both the Hebrew and the LXX should be considered authoritative along these lines: "both should be used as authoritative, since both are one, and divine."[101]

Conclusion

We have just observed an astonishing development. The Church to this point has existed within the Roman Empire for several centuries, throughout which time it has routinely accepted as fundamentally important the identity of the LXX with

---

[98] Augustine, *City of God*, 18.43 (NPNF 1, 2:386).
[99] Augustine, *City of God*, 15.23 (NPNF 1, 2:305). See also *On Christian Doctrine*, 4.7 (NPNF 1, 2:579–80), where it is LXX translators under the guidance of the Holy Spirit in their translation who "seem to have altered some passages."
[100] Augustine, *City of God*, 18.44 (NPNF 1, 2:387).
[101] Augustine, *City of God*, 18.44 (NPNF 1, 2:387).

the Hebrew text from which it was first translated. Now, just as the empire is fragmenting and collapsing, and just as it has become clear how problematic is the claim that the LXX is identical to the Hebrew, Augustine suddenly announces (adopting what one Church historian has rightly called "a remarkable position")[102] that the question of identity does not matter after all. He adopts an entirely novel position, even as he produces arguments from ancient tradition and practice to support it. There emerges "the first sustained attempt" in Christian history "to divorce the authoritative biblical text from dependence on the Hebrew,"[103] albeit somehow holding on to the Hebrew at the same time. The LXX in itself (leaving aside the question of manuscript errors) has now been protected from any kind of criticism. This comes potentially at great cost, however, to the Church's ability to engage in public discourse about the reliability of its text. For this kind of argument from "divine inspiration" (developed, it should be noted, from an initial source text that does not even *refer* to divine inspiration)[104] is immune from possible contradiction on the basis of evidence. It is this kind of deployment of the doctrine of inspiration with a view to avoiding evidence that we shall unfortunately all too often encounter in the later history of biblical interpretation as it is described in the remainder of this book—beginning shortly, as we turn in the next chapter to the reception of the Latin Vulgate in the Church.[105] Before we do that, however, we must consider the position of the Hebrew language in the early post-apostolic Church.

HEBREW LANGUAGE AND THE READING OF SCRIPTURE

The earliest Church came into being in a multilingual environment in Palestine, "with Hebrew, Aramaic, and Greek each being spoken by a significant number of people, and other languages (e.g., Latin) represented as well."[106] At least some ability in Greek had become essential for many Palestinian Jews in the Hellenistically shaped world in which they lived, even though Aramaic was the primary Semitic language, with Hebrew (which the NT identifies as "the language of Jesus and his contemporaries") significant at a secondary level.[107] In Egypt, Jews were almost

---

[102] Wright, "Augustine," 719.

[103] Gallagher, *Hebrew Scripture*, 208.

[104] Dines, *Septuagint*, 63. The "divine inspiration" theme originates with Philo's *Moses*.

[105] Given the weight that Augustine carried in the medieval Church, it is not surprising to find his arguments repeated in this later era also with respect to the LXX; witness, e.g., Bishop John Fisher's response to Richard Pace's criticism of the LXX's inaccuracies in the early sixteenth century, "that the Greek text of the Septuagint was, as much as the Hebrew original, the product of divine inspiration." Richard Rex, "Humanism and Reformation in England and Scotland," *HBOT* 2:512–35 (522).

[106] Gallagher, *Hebrew Scripture*, 106.

[107] Gallagher, *Hebrew Scripture*, 136.

entirely Greek-speaking, possessing little facility in Hebrew—which is why the LXX translation was necessary in the first place. Not even the educated Philo possessed much, if any, Hebrew. Beyond Egypt, in the remainder of the Roman Empire, knowledge of Hebrew (so far as we can tell) was likewise limited among Jews, who tended to know Greek, and then perhaps Latin. Greek was the international language of the Eastern empire at the level of ordinary life, and was widely known also in the West (especially among the educated and governing classes). Latin was the native language of the Romans, and therefore the language of government and bureaucracy throughout the empire. Local languages also persisted, as Luke's description of the day of Pentecost illustrates (Acts 2:4-6).

The survival of Hebrew as a significant language in Palestine into the first century AD, in a situation where it was not even the first Semitic language of most Jews, can be explained only in terms of its importance as the ancestral holy language in which the Scriptures—so central to Jewish identity—were largely written.[108] It is as such that someone like the apostle Paul (who was also fluent in Greek)[109] would have learned Hebrew (if indeed he was not raised in it).[110] In Paul and the other apostles, knowledge of the Scriptures in their Hebrew form would therefore have coexisted with knowledge of them in Greek. They inevitably mainly used the Greek, however, in communicating the gospel to a world in which knowledge of that language was widespread but knowledge of Hebrew (even among Jews) was not.

It is this close connection between the Hebrew and Greek forms of Scripture that is to a very great extent lost as the apostolic generation gives way to its successors. Even in Palestine, "[i]t is generally believed that the fortunes of Hebrew declined . . . a few generations after the Second [i.e., Bar Kokhba] revolt (132–135 CE), and its revival took place only after the close of the ancient period."[111] Outside Palestine, a predominantly Gentile Church found itself living in a world in which, even had many Christians wished to learn Hebrew, they would have found it challenging to discover members of the Jewish communities known to them who could teach it. It is indeed a question whether the social, religious, and political circumstances of the times allowed for much meaningful

---

[108] Gallagher, *Hebrew Scripture*, 111–23.

[109] Apart from the obvious point that all his letters are written in Greek, note his ability to read Greek in Acts 17:23, 28; 1 Cor 15:33; Titus 1:12, and the fact that in Acts 21:37–22:2 he speaks in Greek to a Roman officer.

[110] In Acts 21:37–22:2 Paul addresses his Jewish audience in Jerusalem in Hebrew, and in Acts 26:14 he reports God speaking to *him* in Hebrew. Modern translations often translate "Hebrew" in these instances as "Aramaic," but the grounds for doing so are not strong, although in *later* centuries when writers refer to "Hebrew" they *can* mean "Aramaic." Gallagher, *Hebrew Scripture*, 123–31.

[111] Gallagher, *Hebrew Scripture*, 108.

Jewish-Christian conversation in the first place.[112] This was the de facto situation. When we discover, then, that not many Christians knew much Hebrew throughout the post-apostolic period, we must be careful about how we interpret this fact. Of itself, it might be taken to imply that Christians had simply ceased to care very much about the OT Scriptures in their original Hebrew form. Yet our discussion to this point in the chapter has already suggested that this is not the case, and it is a simple matter to identify other evidence that points in the same direction.

Origen, for example, who "probably knew very little about the Hebrew language,"[113] *evidently* cared about what the original Hebrew of the OT had to say, and indeed about whether a particular text like Susanna was composed in Hebrew or not. Unable to respond to his friend Africanus on aspects of this important question, he turned for help to Jewish acquaintances.[114] He cared about the issue, but his competence was limited. His successor in the Alexandrian tradition, Didymus the Blind, can also be found deferring to those who understand Hebrew.[115] The Antiochenes, for their part, frequently reference Hebrew idiom, grammar, and syntax in their work, sometimes even blaming the LXX for misunderstanding such matters.[116] Theodoret possessed "an impressive array of textual resources" for his research, including a lexicon of Hebrew terms.[117] Theodore's valuing of Hebrew competence is clearly revealed in his comments on Jerome's translation work—he blames him not for learning the language, but only for learning it from "a second-rate teacher."[118] In retrospect, it is easy to see that the Antiochenes claim far too much for themselves with respect to *their* Hebrew comprehension. Diodore of Tarsus was "unable [even] to detect the alphabetic structure of certain psalms, despite sensing the effect this can have on the psalmist's movement of thought,"[119] while "Theodore's knowledge of Hebrew seems to have been somewhat limited."[120] Even though they were not very competent, however, the significant fact in our present context is the extent to which they strove toward the goal. Augustine, finally—as we saw in chapter 8—knew almost no Hebrew (and for

---

[112] For a discussion of some aspects of this problem, see Günter Stemberger, "Exegetical Contacts between Christians and Jews in the Roman Empire," *HBOT* 1/1:569–86.

[113] Gallagher, *Hebrew Scripture*, 138.

[114] Origen, *Letter to Africanus*, 6 (ANF 4:387–88).

[115] Reventlow, *Biblical Interpretation*, 2:29.

[116] Hill, *Antioch*, 50–54, 107–33.

[117] Hill, *Antioch*, 73.

[118] Gallagher, *Hebrew Scripture*, 204.

[119] Hill, *Antioch*, 51.

[120] Rowan A. Greer, *Theodore of Mopsuestia: Exegete and Theologian* (London: Faith Press, 1961), 98. "As far as can be established from the preserved writings, the Antiochenes have virtually no knowledge of Hebrew." Sten Hidal, "Exegesis of the Old Testament in the Antiochene School with Its Prevalent Literal and Historical Method," *HBOT* 1/1:543–68 (553).

that matter, only a little Greek). He is adamant, nevertheless—in the course of a discourse about Christian education *in general*, no less—about the importance for accurate Bible reading of the knowledge of biblical languages.[121]

CONCLUSION

The general lack of facility in Hebrew in the patristic period should not be taken to imply any generalized conviction about its lack of importance. Of course, there was bound to be a lack of urgency on the matter of Hebrew learning so long as it was widely believed that the LXX represented a perfect rendering of the original Hebrew text of the OT. It is not surprising that "few Christians of the patristic period troubled themselves to learn Hebrew,"[122] when so many believed that they already possessed in the LXX a perfect representation of the original Hebrew Scriptures. It must be admitted, on the other hand, that it was only ignorance of (or limited competence in) Hebrew that "allowed the Fathers to champion the LXX as the most accurate representation of the Hebrew text in Greek" for so long in the first place.[123] With the work of Jerome, two paths opened up before the Church. Now that the facts were more fully known, would its historic embrace of the authority of the Hebrew text of OT Scripture lead to a fresh commitment to this text as the foundational text from which further translations would hitherto be made—which would imply a stronger commitment than before to the learning of Hebrew? Or would the Church continue to champion the LXX as the inspired, authoritative text, even though it could now be seen to diverge significantly from the Hebrew, with the almost inevitable result in the cultural circumstances of the time—and despite Augustine's novel idea of retaining both Hebrew and Greek texts as somehow authoritative—that the Hebrew text along with its language would become an irrelevance? In the aftermath of the final disintegration of the Roman Empire in the fifth century, the Church in the East, where Greek had always had the linguistic upper hand, followed the second path. It is to the Latin-speaking Church in the West that we now turn.

---

[121] Augustine, *On Christian Doctrine*, 2.11–12 (*NPNF* 1, 2:539–40).
[122] Gallagher, *Hebrew Scripture*, 137.
[123] Gallagher, *Hebrew Scripture*, 173.

11

THE VULGATE, THE RENAISSANCE, AND THE REFORMATION
When in Rome . . .

I too could have lived uprightly and preached the truth in seclusion; but then I should have left undisturbed the pope, the sophists [i.e., scholastics], and the whole anti-Christian regime. The devil does not respect my spirit as highly as he does my speech and pen when they deal with Scripture. For my spirit takes from him nothing but myself alone; but Holy Scripture and the languages leave him little room on earth, and wreak havoc in his kingdom.

—Martin Luther (1524)[1]

[T]he . . . holy council . . . decides and declares that the old well known Latin Vulgate edition which has been tested in the church by long use over so many centuries should be kept as the authentic text in public readings, debates, sermons and explanations; and no one is to dare or presume on any pretext to reject it.

—The Council of Trent (1546)[2]

Although Jerome's Latin translations from the Hebrew OT aroused significant disquiet in the fifth-century Church, they nevertheless gradually gained ground in the West. They did so along with the revisions of the Old Latin NT (from the Greek) that were also associated with his name and the translations that he had reluctantly made (from Aramaic or Greek) of some of the Apocrypha. By the seventh century all of these Latin texts were widely in use throughout the Latin-dominant world in what I shall now call for ease of reference "the Vulgate."[3] However, the reader should be aware that this title, deriving from the Latin

---

[1] Martin Luther, *To the Councilmen*, LW 45:366.
[2] Tanner, *Decrees*, 2:664.
[3] The collapse of the Western Roman Empire in AD 476 was later followed, of course, by the loss to the Christian West of North Africa, Egypt, Syria, and most of Spain, which fell to Islam—by which time all hope for the restoration of Empire had evaporated. Even so, "Latin remained the cultural language of western Europe." Bray, *Biblical Interpretation*, 130. For a convenient overview of the

editio vulgata ("the regularly used edition"), was only attached to that version of the Bible in much later times. When it later appears, moreover, the "Vulgate" to which it refers includes further Old Latin translations of some of the Apocrypha for which Jerome bears no responsibility. In the earlier period—we must be clear—the (proto-)Vulgate was "regularly used" only up to a point, and often alongside various Old Latin translations of OT books from the Greek that offer alternatives to Jerome's translations from the Hebrew.

THE EARLY HISTORY OF THE VULGATE

By the seventh century, nevertheless, the Vulgate has already begun to dominate the scene, and Isidore, the bishop of Seville in Spain from 599 until 636,[4] claims specifically that Jerome's OT translation "is deservedly preferred over the others, for it is closer in its wording [to the original texts], and brighter in the clarity of its thought."[5] In the eighth century, the Northumbrian monk Bede makes almost exclusive use of the Vulgate in his own scholarly work, recognizing "the importance of Hebrew for a proper understanding of the Bible."[6] He embraces the imperative, therefore, of following the *Hebraica veritas* (a term he actually uses) as translated by Jerome, rather than the LXX (to which, in later life, Bede had independent access). Comments like these in the early Middle Ages concerning the Vulgate OT have little to do with the writers' competence in Hebrew—Isidore appears to have known some, Bede probably only a few words—but they continue to demonstrate the status of the Hebrew text as the authoritative text underlying what is widely agreed (on the basis of what others have said) to be a reliable Latin translation of it. It is this reputation for reliability that leads to a situation by the ninth century in which the Frankish Benedictine monk and archbishop of Mainz, Hrabanus Maurus, can say that Jerome's translation is in

---

whole period, see Aryeh Grabois, "Political and Cultural Changes from the Fifth to the Eleventh Century," *HBOT* 1/2:28–55.

[4] For a description of Isidore's life and work, see Reventlow, *Biblical Interpretation*, 2:106–10; also Claudio Leonardi, "Aspects of Old Testament Interpretation in the Church from the Seventh to the Tenth Century," *HBOT* 1/2:180–95 (181–85).

[5] Isidore of Seville, *Etymologies* (trans. Stephen A. Barney et al.; Cambridge: Cambridge University Press, 2006), 6.4.5.

[6] Peter Hunter Blair, *The World of Bede* (2nd ed.; Cambridge: Cambridge University Press, 1990), 233–34. The entire book is a classic on the life and work of Bede; for a briefer overview, see Leonardi, "Aspects," 185–88.

general use in the Church everywhere.⁷ It has become "the most widely used Latin Bible in western Christendom."⁸

However, as a student of Alcuin of York, Hrabanus would also have been well aware of the extent to which Jerome's work—not just in the OT, but overall—had already by the ninth century suffered significant textual corruption in different regions of the West. Charles I (Charlemagne), the first Holy Roman Emperor in Europe, had recruited Alcuin in 781 to help him with the reformation and reorganization of the educational system in his empire, the controlling goal of which was "study of the Bible as the highest form of wisdom."⁹ One of Alcuin's tasks was to produce a revised text of the Vulgate. Precisely as a result of its coexistence with Old Latin texts throughout the preceding centuries (with different translations of different biblical books coexisting even in the same manuscripts), Jerome's Vulgate had been corrupted as copyists would accidentally or deliberately introduce older, familiar readings into his text.¹⁰ Alcuin's revision, completed by 801, was of a good quality and it circulated widely (unlike the revision by Theodulf of Orleans in the same time period), yet this Alcuinian text also became corrupt within a relatively short period of time. In the volatile period of European history that followed the demise of the "Carolingian Renaissance" that had provided the context for its production, other efforts to stem the ongoing tide of textual corruption in the Vulgate proved ineffective. It was not until the twelfth and thirteenth centuries that further serious and sustained attempts were made to restore the Vulgate to its original form. By this point, the extent to which it reflected either the *Hebraica veritas* of the OT or indeed the *Graeca veritas* (the Greek original)¹¹ of the NT was seriously questioned in scholarly Church circles. This, too, was probably not because most scholars knew the biblical languages well enough to offer independent judgments. It was simply because of the confusion in the Vulgate tradition itself.¹² However, the grave nature of the crisis inevitably raised the question once

---

⁷ Hrabanus Maurus, *De institutione clericorum* (*On the Institution of the Clergy*), 2.54.40, in *De institutione clericorum libri tres: Studien und Edition von Detlev Zimpel* (Frankfurt: Peter Lang, 1996), 417. For a brief account of Maurus, see Reventlow, Biblical Interpretation, 2:125–26.

⁸ Frans van Liere, *An Introduction to the Medieval Bible* (Cambridge: Cambridge University Press, 2014), 82. The entirety of 80–109 provides a helpful introduction to the Latin Bible, from the period of the Old Latin translations through to the period after the Reformation.

⁹ Reventlow, *Biblical Interpretation*, 2:120.

¹⁰ Frederic Kenyon, *Our Bible and the Ancient Manuscripts* (5th ed.; London: Eyre & Spottiswoode, 1958), 250–64.

¹¹ This is already a term used by Jerome in *Prologus* (*Preface*) *to the Gospels*, 4 (NPNF 2, 6:487). *Chaldaica veritas* ("the Chaldee original") also appears in relation to the Aramaic of Daniel in *Commentariorum in Danielem* (*Commentary on Daniel*), 5.11. *Jerome's Commentary on Daniel* (trans. Gleason L. Archer Jr.; Grand Rapids: Baker, 1977), 58.

¹² We must be careful here, however. Leaving aside the question of Greek, "[e]vidence for Christian Hebraism in the Middle Ages is steadily growing, and the more it grows, the more one

again of the (lack of) knowledge of Hebrew and Greek in Church and society, and this question began to be asked with increasing urgency.

THE CRISIS OF THE THIRTEENTH CENTURY: ROGER BACON

This concern about linguistic ignorance is well illustrated by three essays sent to the reigning Pope Clement IV in 1267–1268 by the English Franciscan monk Roger Bacon (c. 1214–1292). Within the context of a sustained and generalized lament about the state of education in the thirteenth-century world, Bacon gives considerable attention in these essays (*Opus maius, Opus minus,* and *Opus tertium*) to the question of biblical text and languages.

In terms of the big picture, first, Bacon's contemporaries (he claims) possess defective knowledge of the subjects they value, arising from a lack of knowledge of ancient languages and therefore a lack of proper access to the authors from whom they draw their knowledge. These "valued subjects" Bacon identifies as Latin grammar, logic, natural philosophy, and some aspects of metaphysics. The problem is that their teachers have their heads full of errors and misconceptions about at least the last three of these subjects, *because* they only know Latin. Latin simply does not suffice for true scholarship; people need to be reading at least Greek, Hebrew, and Arabic as well, if they really want to understand the world properly. Bacon's own commitment to ancient languages is reflected in the fact that he himself wrote both Hebrew and Greek grammars.

Second, and worse than this, the four "valued subjects" just mentioned are in any case not very important for theologians in comparison to others that are being thoroughly neglected. Besides foreign languages, Bacon discusses subjects such as mathematics, alchemy, chemistry, physics, experimental sciences, and moral philosophy. All these are ignored, he complains, in favor of speculative philosophy. He himself is thoroughly interested in such subjects as astronomy, the laws of gravity, agriculture, and medicine. He is a genuine experimental scientist, researching into the reflection of light, explaining the composition and effects of gunpowder, and discussing and affirming the possibility of later inventions such as steam vessels, microscopes, and telescopes. He is interested in new knowledge—in discovery. His contemporaries, he asserts, are not.

---

realizes that the return to Scripture in its original languages at the time of the Reformation and Renaissance was less of a bolt from the blue than used to be thought." Philip Alexander, "Reflections on the Christian Turn to the *Hebraica Veritas* and its Implications," in *Studies on the Text and Versions of the Hebrew Bible in Honour of Robert Gordon* (ed. Geoffrey Khan and Diana Lipton; VTSup 149; Leiden: Brill, 2012), 353–72 (361).

Bacon expresses his concern, third, about Bible reading and Church practice.[13] A particular target here is Peter Lombard's twelfth-century *Book of Sentences*—a four-volume work that follows the method of Lombard's teacher Peter Abelard (the preeminent Christian philosopher of twelfth century, 1079–1142).[14] *Sentences* seeks to integrate arguments from authority, derived from the Bible and from selected Church Fathers (especially Augustine), with reasoning about Christian dogma. This book was in fact one of the chief sources whence many medieval theologians drew their knowledge of the Fathers, and down to the sixteenth century it was a central textbook in the newly founded European universities.[15] Dependence upon this text, suggests Bacon, not only results in a poor education in the Fathers (especially those writing in Greek, who get limited exposure therein), but it also leads to neglect of the Scriptures themselves—not just in private life, but also in the educational curriculum. For Bacon, such a way of proceeding is inexplicable.

Bacon wants to see biblical exegesis given more weight. More than this, he wants to see it improved, since he evaluates the quality of what is generally being done quite negatively. The language issue lies once again at the heart of his concern. Few scholars, he claims, have more than an elementary knowledge of Hebrew and Greek. They depend upon the Latin, and the Latin texts of the Vulgate they favor are exceedingly corrupt—not least the version currently being used in the University of Paris and spread by its students over the whole world.[16] As a result of all this, Bacon argues, the literal sense of the biblical text has fallen into doubt, and therefore there must also be doubt about its spiritual meaning.

---

[13] See especially Roger Bacon, *The Opus Majus of Roger Bacon* (trans. R. B. Burke; Philadelphia: University of Pennsylvania Press, 1928), pt. III (75–115).

[14] See further on Peter Lombard, Froelich, "Christian Interpretation," 500–504.

[15] For the rise of the medieval university, including its earlier exemplars Paris and Oxford, and its place in the overall educational framework of Christendom, see Ulrich Köpf, "The Institutional Framework of Christian Exegesis in the Middle Ages," *HBOT* 1/2:148–79; and Köpf, "The Institutional Framework of Theological Studies in the Late Middle Ages," *HBOT* 2:123–53. For the kinds of Bible-reading typically conducted in the differing educational spheres in the Middle Ages, see Gilbert Dahan, "Genres, Forms and Various Methods in Christian Exegesis of the Middle Ages," *HBOT* 1/2:198–236; and G. R. Evans, "Masters and Disciples: Aspects of Christian Interpretation of the Old Testament in the Eleventh and Twelfth Centuries," *HBOT* 1/2:237–60.

[16] As we consider the question of which particular targets Bacon has in his sights in these three essays, it is worth noting that Thomas Aquinas studied and taught at the University of Paris for significant periods of time from 1252 onward, wrote a huge commentary on Lombard's sentences, and knew little Greek and virtually no Hebrew. In 1265 he was called to Rome by Pope Clement IV to serve as papal theologian, and it was while he was in Italy that he began his *Summa*, before being called back to Paris in 1268, where he immediately became entangled in disputes with important Franciscans like Bonaventure.

For where an understanding of the literal sense is wrong, the spiritual sense cannot rightly be grasped; the one is necessarily based upon the other.

Roger Bacon's strong call in the thirteenth century, then, is for a renewed commitment to genuine Christian scholarship involving (centrally) a renewed commitment to Scripture in its original languages (among which he explicitly includes Aramaic, differentiated from Hebrew). It will give serious attention, then, to the state of the Latin biblical text, which must be corrected with reference to the Hebrew/Aramaic and Greek originals.

Looking backward, Bacon's concerns reflect those of earlier scholars in the twelfth century such as Hugh of the royal monastery of St. Victor (in Paris), who like Bacon emphasized the importance of the original biblical languages and in particular the deficiencies of the LXX when compared to the *Hebraica veritas*. Hugh certainly knew some Hebrew himself, and he was also familiar with the work of Jewish scholars like Rashi (1040–1105) and his grandson Rashbam (Hugh's contemporary, 1080–1160). Hugh's student Andrew of St. Victor (1110–1175) "relied on the Hebrew original text of the Old Testament [even] more strongly than his master and recommended knowledge of Hebrew to his students."[17] Andrew appears to have been the first Western Christian scholar, in fact, to study Jewish texts systematically.[18]

Looking forward, Bacon anticipates in his comments on text and language the fourteenth-century work of the French Franciscan scholar Nicholas of Lyra (1270–1340), most famous for his *Commentary Notes (Postillae)* on the literal and moral senses of the Bible (c. 1322 to 1339), which often cite both Rashi and Andrew of St. Victor.[19] These *Notes* became widely available in the libraries of Western Christendom shortly after Nicholas' death, and they greatly influenced later writers like John Wycliffe and Martin Luther. In the second prologue to the *Notes*, Nicholas expresses the view that the Vulgate "frequently deviates from the Hebrew wording of the Old Testament," proposing (in accordance with Jerome's view) that we must defer to the latter.[20] Nicholas himself knew Hebrew, and was in a good position to follow through personally on his proposal, "in consultation with, and on the advice of people who were expert" in the language.[21] His consul-

---

[17] Reventlow, *Biblical Interpretation*, 2:170.

[18] For more on Hugh and "the Victorines," see Smalley, *Study of the Bible*, 83–195; Evans, "Masters and Disciples," 254–60; and Rainer Berndt, "The School of St. Victor in Paris," *HBOT* 1/2:467–95.

[19] See further Reventlow, *Biblical Interpretation*, 2:247–59; and Smith, "Nicholas of Lyra," 49–63.

[20] Reventlow, *Biblical Interpretation*, 2:251.

[21] Reventlow, *Biblical Interpretation*, 2:251.

tation was apparently not only with a written Jewish tradition of exegesis based on the literal sense of the text, but also with Jews personally known to him.[22]

THE RENAISSANCE AND ANCIENT TEXTS AND LANGUAGES

The question that now arose in the fifteenth and sixteenth centuries was how far this kind of proposal was to be taken, especially considering a context in which the scholarly ability to access the biblical text in its original languages was steadily improving.[23] Was it to be a continued matter, now, of revising corrupt Vulgate manuscripts, perhaps with more careful attention than before to the original biblical-language texts? Or was it to be a matter of following Jerome's *example*, rather than his *text*, and translating afresh from the originals?

REVISION OF THE VULGATE

Revision of the Vulgate certainly continued in the fifteenth and sixteenth centuries, as the first printed Bibles began to appear and were often found to be perpetuating a corrupt text.[24] One of the most famous of these is the Complutensian Polyglot, begun in 1502 under the auspices of Cardinal Francisco Ximenes de Cisneros—the founder in 1508 of the University of Alcalá (Latin, Complutum) in Spain, whose curriculum included both Hebrew and Greek.[25] This ambitious printing project was completed in 1517 and published (after awaiting papal sanction) in 1522. It presented to its readers the OT in Hebrew, Greek, and Latin, and the NT in Greek and Latin, as well as giving them access to the (Jewish) Aramaic Targum on the Pentateuch. Each page of the OT provides three parallel columns of text, with Jerome's Vulgate in the middle and the Hebrew and the Greek on either side. This arrangement consciously represents the Church's ongoing commitment to the Latin text, since the preface tells us that just as Jesus was crucified between the two thieves, so the Roman Catholic Church is set between the Jews

---

[22] For a helpful, brief account of the history of a medieval Jewish approach to Scripture that emphasized the literal sense of the text, beginning with the work of Saadiah Gaon (AD 882–942) in the tenth century, see Reventlow, *Biblical Interpretation*, 2:219–46.

[23] A conscious intention to improve is already discernible in the fourteenth century, e.g., in the deliberations of the Council of Vienne in southern France (1311–1312). Here resolutions were passed to establish teaching positions in Hebrew, Aramaic, and Arabic "wherever the Roman curia happens to reside" and also at the universities of Paris, Oxford, Bologna, and Salamanca. Robert Irwin, *For Lust of Knowing: The Orientalists and Their Enemies* (London: Allen Lane, 2006), 47–48; Tanner, *Decrees*, 1:379.

[24] For some reflections on the broader cultural significance of the invention of the printing press, see Eriksen, "Sociopolitical and Cultural Aspects," 103–5.

[25] Stephen G. Burnett, *Christian Hebraism in the Reformation Era (1500–1660): Authors, Books, and the Transmission of Jewish Learning* (LWW 19; Leiden: Brill, 2012), 28.

and the Eastern Church.²⁶ These words do not exactly communicate a high regard for the value of the original Hebrew and Greek texts overall. Nor does much of the discussion surrounding *ongoing* textual work within the Roman Catholic Church in the sixteenth century, after the Council of Trent had reaffirmed the authority of the Vulgate (note the second epigraph to the present chapter), and there continued a need to establish an official Latin text.²⁷

THE CULTURAL TIDE

By the opening decades of the sixteenth century, however, the cultural tide in many quarters had been running for some time in a way that was not favorable to the Vulgate. As we saw in chapter 9, Renaissance Humanism was marked by a movement *ad fontes*—"back to the sources." The fifteenth century saw developments that helped to make this more than a theoretical program, and not just because of the greater knowledge of biblical languages that now existed in the Christian West. A major goal of Renaissance scholarship was a recovery of ancient manuscripts that would allow exhaustive text-critical work to be carried out in order to establish the original versions of ancient texts. The importance of this goal is already evident in the life of Francesco Petrarch (1304–1374), who arguably initiated the Humanistic movement. Italian "revivalists" like Petrarch were soon followed by a generation of itinerant teachers and their students who journeyed from city to city throughout Europe, generating in ever-widening circles an enthusiasm for antiquity that promoted the quest for ancient manuscripts. Under the Medici rulers Cosimo (1429–1464) and Lorenzo the Magnificent (1469–1492), Florence became preeminently the seat of this new learning, boasting a Platonic academy (founded in 1459) that included among its members all the more prominent citizens of the city. Plato once again began to displace Aristotle in popularity in Italy. Among the notable humanists associated with Florence before this time and afterward were Poggio Bracciolini (1380–1459), who in 1417 rediscovered the *De rerum natura* of Lucretius; Ambrogio Traversari (1386–1439), the teacher of

---

[26] James P. R. Lyell, *Cardinal Ximenes: Statesman, Ecclesiastic, Soldier and Man of Letters with an Account of the Complutensian Polyglot Bible* (London: Grafton, 1917), 28–29, 35.

[27] Wicks, "Catholic Old Testament Interpretation," 632–36. The eventual products of this work were the *Sixtine Edition* of the Vulgate—published in 1590, but recalled on the pretext that it contained printing errors—and its replacement, the *Clementine Edition*—published in 1592, and remaining the official Vulgate of the Roman Catholic Church until recent times. Some Roman Catholic unease is apparent even in the immediate aftermath of Trent, nevertheless, about a decision "that left the Vulgate isolated from the Hebrew and Greek original texts and only implied a needed work of correcting ... the many inaccuracies of the Vulgate." Wicks, "Catholic Old Testament Interpretation," 628–29.

Gianozzo Manetti (to whom we shall return shortly); and Marsilio Ficino (1433–1499), an important Platonist and Neoplatonist scholar.[28]

Humanism was also favored by fifteenth-century popes in Rome like Pope Nicholas V (1447–1455), to whom we are indebted for the foundation of the Vatican Library—which in the number and value of its recovered manuscripts (particularly Greek manuscripts) surpassed all others. From 1439, when he became a cardinal, Rome was also the residence of Basilius Bessarion (1403–1472), a famous collector of books and manuscripts, whose home became virtually an academy of its own as he welcomed Greek scholars fleeing the sack of Constantinople by the Turks in 1453.

The recovery of classical literature that Renaissance Humanism thus enabled was naturally accompanied in certain quarters by the resurgence of the religious and moral views of pagan antiquity, and Renaissance Italian society was often marked by both immorality and cynicism (as expressed, e.g., in Niccolò Machiavelli's famous work, *The Prince*). Yet at the same time—and perhaps this needs to be emphasized in modern contexts where the terms "Christianity" and "humanism" are often used to designate opposing ideological forces—there was widely to be found in the Renaissance a profound hope for the renewal of a Christian religion that was perceived by many to have become hidebound, stagnant, and lacking sufficient interest in the individual person. From this point of view, Renaissance Humanism was not a new phenomenon, representing a *break* with the past, but a movement connected to a significant history behind it—as represented not only by recent medieval "renewal movements,"[29] but also by the apostles and the Church Fathers. If Christian humanists of the period agreed with their contemporaries on the importance of a renewed study of the humanities (and indeed of the hearty embrace of the sciences), they nevertheless emphasized that the aim of the resulting new and improved education was a deepening of the religious and moral formation of the individual. This was the main point of the retrieval of ancient texts from beneath the deformations (as people saw it) of the centuries that had intervened between their first production and the present. In this quest, "Augustine and Jerome ... were fêted as much as Cicero, Seneca and Livy.... The humanism of this period did not yet draw a sharp distinction between ancient heathen and ancient Christian traditions."[30]

---

[28] For a helpful, brief account of Ficino's life and work, see Reventlow, *Biblical Interpretation*, 3:23–29; and Catto, "Philosophical Context," 117–21.

[29] We may think here, e.g., of the Waldensians and their commitment to living "the apostolic life" in personal imitation of Christ. G. R. Evans, "Scriptural Interpretation in Pre-Reformation Dissident Movements," *HBOT* 2:295–318 (296–305).

[30] Eriksen, "Sociopolitical and Cultural Aspects," 97.

The Renaissance and Biblical Studies

The Renaissance attention to ancient texts and their critical examination that we are now considering inevitably and deeply impacted biblical studies as much as any other discipline, especially as manuscripts were imported from the East as a result of either scholarly migration or entrepreneurial activity within the Ottoman Empire (where they might be purchased from merchants or travelers).[31]

An early and influential biblical text critic was the Italian humanist Lorenzo Valla (1407–1457), who gained notoriety after 1440 because, using manuscript evidence and his knowledge of how the Latin language had developed over time, he exposed as a forgery the so-called *Donation of Constantine*—a document establishing the claims of the papacy to secular power. Perhaps of more importance in the long run, however, was Valla's text-critical work on the NT, in which he set out to compare the Vulgate with the *Graeca veritas* ("the Greek truth/original") and came to the conclusion that what was required was not another revision of a deeply corrupted Vulgate, but a fresh translation directly from the original Greek. The later segments of Valla's work on this project, based on Latin and Greek manuscripts available to him in Rome from 1448 to 1457, were carried out under the patronage mainly of Pope Nicholas V, along with the help of Bessarion. It was on account of Valla's temerity in questioning the Vulgate that Poggio Bracciolini (albeit a humanist) attacked him in his *Invectiva* of 1452 for daring to criticize Jerome, "the saintly and learned man who received the approbation of every century, of all peoples."[32] Valla's response was essentially (but not only) to point out that a translation was only a translation, and that Holy Scripture was the entity that "the saints themselves wrote in Hebrew or Greek."[33] It was not that he wished to criticize Jerome, Valla protested. Nevertheless, fresh attention to the Greek behind the Latin (which, after all, Jerome only revised, and not always very well) was the need of the hour. Valla was in fact far more critical of Thomas Aquinas than of Jerome in his work, precisely because he believed that Aquinas, working only from the Vulgate and "ignorant of the Greek language," often made serious mistakes in biblical interpretation.[34]

---

[31] A good sixteenth-century example of the entrepreneur is Guillaume Postel (1510–1581), who resided for a considerable time in the East and was able to collect many interesting manuscripts, including two Samaritan ones. His scholarship was recognized in his appointment to a chair in Oriental languages (1538–1543) in the Collège de France in Paris, to the founding of which we shall return shortly.

[32] Reventlow, *Biblical Interpretation*, 3:16, citing Poggio.

[33] Reventlow, *Biblical Interpretation*, 3:17, citing Valla.

[34] E.g., Reventlow, *Biblical Interpretation*, 3:21–22. For a fuller account of Valla's contribution to biblical philology, see Jerry H. Bentley, *Humanists and Holy Writ: New Testament Scholarship in the Renaissance* (Princeton: Princeton University Press, 1983), 32–69.

It was a copy of Lorenzo Valla's *Collations* on the NT that Erasmus of Rotterdam found by chance in an abbey near Leuven (in modern Belgium) in 1504, spurring him on to his own work on the biblical text. *His* further research in the available manuscripts also took place in Italy, including Rome, where "[s]everal cardinals gave him a very friendly welcome."[35] This was to result in his famous 1516 Latin edition of the NT, based on the Greek, which appeared in a parallel column alongside the Latin. This work was reissued in revised editions throughout the next twenty years, and the Greek column proved to be enormously influential, as we shall see.[36]

The movement of this same cultural tide with respect to the text of the OT can be traced first through early Italian humanists like Gianozzo Manetti (1396–1459), papal secretary to Pope Nicholas V from 1447 to 1455 and himself the translator of most of the NT from Greek into Latin. Manetti, who had learned Hebrew from Florentine Jews, also began an ambitious project to produce a Latin translation of the OT directly from the MT, with special reference to rabbinical commentaries. Like Valla, he had to fight off challenges to his work on the basis that Jerome had already produced "the" OT translation—the same kind of challenges that Jerome himself had faced when choosing to translate directly from the Hebrew rather than from the "inspired" LXX. Manetti draws on Jerome's own arguments in responding to his critics, questioning the legend of "the Seventy," noting in detail the many divergences between the LXX and the Hebrew, and urging the need for an accurate translation from the Hebrew not least because (again) inaccuracies play into the hands of the Jews. While making sure to praise Jerome, he insists that a fresh translation is necessary.[37]

In the later fifteenth century, the ascending fortunes of the Hebrew language that were necessary if there was to be accurate engagement with the original-language text are well illustrated in the career of the German humanist Johannes Reuchlin (1455–1522). Reuchlin began seriously to learn Hebrew himself, with the help of Jewish teachers, from 1492 onward.[38] In 1505 he published a Hebrew grammar (*On the Fundamentals of Hebrew*)—"a significant moment in the history of biblical exegesis."[39] In his foreword he expresses the fear that the expulsion of Jews from Christian lands would lead to the disappearance of the knowledge of

---

[35] Reventlow, *Biblical Interpretation*, 3:54.

[36] See further on Erasmus' language and translation work, in the context of his Christian humanism more generally, Jenkins and Preston, *Biblical Scholarship*, 27–80.

[37] Reventlow, *Biblical Interpretation*, 3:8–9.

[38] He had apparently been introduced to the language six years previously, however. Sophie Kessler Mesguich, "Early Christian Hebraists," *HBOT* 2:254–75 (257).

[39] R. Gerald Hobbs, "*Hebraica Veritas* and *Traditio Apostolica*: Saint Paul and the Interpretation of the Psalms in the Sixteenth Century," in *The Bible in the Sixteenth Century* (ed. David Steinmetz; Durham, N.C.: Duke University Press, 1990), 83–99 (83).

Hebrew as well—a language "necessary in order to understand the foundations of Christian doctrines."[40] Reuchlin's grammar "shaped the later development of Hebrew study for a long time,"[41] and Luther already had a copy of it in his hands no later than 1509.[42] With such resources now available, Christians in the West could with much greater competence interact with the printed editions of the complete Hebrew text that had begun to appear since the late fifteenth century, including the four-volume edition printed in 1516–1517 in Venice by the Flemish printer Bomberg.

It is the flow of this cultural tide throughout the fourteenth to the early sixteenth centuries that helps to explain why—whereas the first complete printed Bible in the German vernacular (1466) was based entirely on the Vulgate—Luther's vernacular 1534 translation was based on the original Hebrew and Greek texts. For the NT, Luther used as his base text Erasmus' second edition (1519), working in cooperation with his skilled colleague in Greek at the University of Wittenberg, Philipp Melanchthon.[43] For the OT, he may have used the Bomberg edition just mentioned,[44] working in cooperation with Melanchthon (who also knew Hebrew), Matthaeus Aurogallus (who had been teaching Hebrew at the university since 1521), and others—an early Hebrew "think-tank."[45] In the meantime, a Dutch translation of the whole Bible, based on the earlier portions of Luther's work, had been published in Antwerp in 1526, and the first printed French Bible had also appeared in that city in 1530, presaging the explosion in Europe as a whole, in the succeeding decades and centuries, of vernacular Bibles. An English translation of Erasmus' third edition of the Greek text (1522) by William Tyndale, who had studied at Wittenberg, had already been printed in Worms (also in 1526), and shipped to England. Tyndale's subsequent translation of the OT was cut short by his execution as a heretic in 1536, but it was his work, nevertheless, that became the most important influence on the King James Version (KJV) produced in 1604–1611—a Bible that became as central to English-speaking culture in the seventeenth century and afterward as Luther's Bible did

---

[40] Reventlow, *Biblical Interpretation*, 3:34.

[41] Reventlow, *Biblical Interpretation*, 3:35.

[42] Siegfried Raeder, "The Exegetical and Hermeneutical Work of Martin Luther," *HBOT* 2:363–406 (397).

[43] For a helpful, brief account of Melanchthon's life and work (especially on the OT), see Hobbs, "Pluriformity," 487–511.

[44] Eric W. Gritsch, "Luther as Bible Translator," in McKim, *Cambridge Companion to Martin Luther*, 62–72 (72n3).

[45] For a detailed account of the production of Luther's German Bible in its OT section, see Raeder, "Exegetical and Hermeneutical Work," 395–406.

in Germany.⁴⁶ The KJV was commissioned specifically to counter the influence of the earlier English-language Geneva Bible (1560). This latter translation also relied heavily on Tyndale (and on Erasmus' third Greek edition)—although it was the first English Bible in which the *entire* OT was translated directly from Hebrew—and it was read in its day by notable figures like Shakespeare, Donne, and Bunyan. By the end of the sixteenth century, in fact, the Geneva Bible "stood at the intellectual, devotional, and cultural heart of religion in the English-speaking world."⁴⁷ The "Calvinistic tone" of its study notes, however, was not beloved of either Queen Elizabeth I or her successor, King James I.⁴⁸

By the time that Erasmus' fifth and final edition had been printed in 1535—significantly, now without the Latin column accompanying the Greek—his Greek text in its various forms was already well on its way to being regarded as the *textus receptus* ("received text") of the NT—which is actually what it was named in the course of the following century. The Masoretic Hebrew text was already firmly established as the received OT text. In the minds of some seventeenth-century Protestants,⁴⁹ this included even the "jots and tittles" of the MT's vowel points—the series of marks indicating vowels that the Masoretic scribes added to the consonantal text from the sixth century AD onward. The Reformers themselves (as we shall see) had generally maintained a more relaxed attitude toward them.

These are all Protestant developments,⁵⁰ but the commitment at their core to the biblical text in its original languages was not *distinctively* Protestant in the early sixteenth century. Nor was the emphasis placed by the Reformers on the importance of learning the biblical languages in order to be able to read the biblical text in those languages a distinctively Protestant emphasis. The desirability of doing this was widely recognized, and it continued to be so among humanists

---

⁴⁶ See further, on both English and French Bible translations, Henry Wansbrough, "History and Impact of English Bible Translations," and Bertram E. Schwarzbach, "Three French Bible Translations," *HBOT* 2:536–52 and 553–75. On the history of English Bible translation under kings and queens from Henry VIII to James I, see Roland H. Worth Jr., *Church, Monarch and Bible in Sixteenth Century England: The Political Context of Bible Translation* (London: McFarland, 2000).

⁴⁷ Rex, "Humanism," 513.

⁴⁸ Wansbrough, "History," 549.

⁴⁹ Note, e.g., Francis Turretin, *The Doctrine of Scripture* (ed. and trans. John W. Beardslee III; Grand Rapids: Baker, 1981), 135–46; and *The Helvetic Consensus Formula* (1675), article 2, in *Thy Word Is Still Truth: Essential Writings on the Doctrine of Scripture from the Reformation to Today* (ed. Peter Lillback and Richard B. Gaffin Jr.; Philadelphia: Westminster Theological Seminary, 2013), 460.

⁵⁰ This is not to suggest that all Protestants shared exactly the same levels of enthusiasm for new translations of the Bible from primary sources; there were exceptions. Hobbs, "Pluriformity," 484–85.

who remained within what was now to become the Roman Catholic Church rather than joining the Protestant movement.

Notable among these was Erasmus, whose work on the Greek text of the NT we have already noted. Sent by his family at the age of nine to the school of the distinguished humanist Alexander Hegius in Deventer, Erasmus later developed a profound antipathy to many aspects of organized religion while living, of necessity and without enthusiasm, in the monastery of Emmaus, near Gouda. Ordained as a priest in 1492, he journeyed in 1496 to Paris to complete his studies, and added to his list of antipathies the "scholasticism" that he encountered there.

Renaissance Humanists in general, and not just the Reformers, tended to define themselves over against this scholasticism in the sixteenth century. They did not mean by the term "scholasticism" everything about scholastic enquiry as such. "Scholastic" *could* be used simply of what was happening in the "schools" (i.e., of academic method). In that sense someone like Martin Luther was himself a scholastic, and while he frequently railed against scholasticism, he never entirely left it behind.[51] This was also true of others: "It is virtually impossible to identify any Reformation or post-Reformation-era theologian who was not touched in some way by both scholastic and humanistic patterns of thought and education."[52] What was the issue, then? It was that much of the medieval system of education was widely perceived as "invested in academic quibbles," often excessively speculative in nature, "divorced from the needs of the Christian community, arcane . . . and barbaric in its use of language."[53] It was perceived as placing too much emphasis on the power of reason and logic in acquiring knowledge, and as lacking genuine interest in empirical enquiry into originating (including biblical) sources of knowledge. Firsthand knowledge of both the Bible and the Church Fathers could indeed be extraordinarily limited and secondhand in "the schools." Scholasticism was also wedded too closely, in many minds, to inherited dogmatic tradition—tradition provided predominantly in this period by a fusion of Christian and Aristotelian thought.[54] Luther is particularly scathing about Aristotle in his letter in 1520 *To The Christian Nobility of the German Nation*, in which he urges the reformation of the German universities. In these bastions of learning, he proposes,

---

[51] Cummings, *Literary Culture*, 118–27 (118, 121), who points out that Erasmus eventually dismissed Luther as "a Sophist"! Erasmus himself "perhaps only had positive recourse to scholastic themes when their use was absolutely necessary to his defense." Richard A. Muller, *After Calvin: Studies in the Development of a Theological Tradition* (OSHT; Oxford: Oxford University Press, 2003), 89.

[52] Muller, *After Calvin*, 37.

[53] Muller, *After Calvin*, 29.

[54] For a helpful paragraph describing scholasticism along these lines, see Michael C. Legaspi, *The Death of Scripture and the Rise of Biblical Studies* (Oxford: Oxford University Press, 2010), 11.

the blind, heathen teacher Aristotle rules far more than Christ.... In this regard my advice would be that Aristotle's *Physics, Metaphysics, Concerning the Soul,* and *Ethics,* which hitherto have been thought to be his best books, should be completely discarded along with all the rest of his books that boast about nature, although nothing can be learned from them either about nature or the Spirit. Moreover, nobody has yet understood him, and many souls have been burdened with fruitless labor and study, at the cost of much precious time.[55]

In short, then, "[t]he humanist argument, whether posed by Pico della Mirandola, Agrippa von Nettlesheim, Melanchthon, or ... Calvin, saw little value in the approach of the *scholastici* to learning."[56]

This was the "scholasticism" encountered by Erasmus in Paris. A subsequent visit to England (1498–1499) led to a significant friendship with John Colet, later the Dean of St. Paul's Cathedral in London and the founder of St. Paul's School. Colet showed Erasmus how to reconcile his Christian faith with humanism by devoting himself to a thorough study of the Scriptures. Enthused, Erasmus returned to Paris and then to Leuven and to the further study of Greek. His subsequent writings are full of stinging commentary on contemporary Church practice. It was a Church that had lost its evangelical simplicity and become the victim of hairsplitting metaphysical speculations, marked both by a Pharisaic approach that based righteousness on good works and monastic sanctity, and by a ritualism beneath whose weight the truly Christian spirit could be crushed. Among his many targets are teachings and practices relating to the Eucharist (his views resemble those of Huldrych Zwingli), confession, fasts, pilgrimages, the veneration of saints and their relics, and celibacy. Over against such a view of the religious life Erasmus sets simply what he calls "the philosophy of Christ," derived from the simple words of the Scriptures.

Erasmus sounds like a Protestant, and he has often been considered to be one of the intellectual fathers of the Reformation. In its early years, indeed, he and Luther were on friendly terms, and many thought that the latter was simply carrying out the Erasmian reform program. Erasmus himself came under pressure for his "Protestant" views, including his views about the importance of learning biblical languages. He was forced to defend against critics, for example, the teaching of Hebrew, Greek, and Latin in a college he had played an important

---

[55] Martin Luther, *To the Christian Nobility of the German Nation Concerning the Reform of the Christian Estate* (1520), LW 44:200. These books disappeared from the curriculum at the University of Wittenberg around the same time. Melanchthon continued to teach Aristotle's logic and rhetoric, however, and the *Ethics* made a curricular comeback in 1529. Muller, *After Calvin,* 122–23.

[56] Muller, *After Calvin,* 89.

part in founding in Leuven.⁵⁷ Although their friendship markedly cooled as time passed, Erasmus for some time refused to be recruited to any anti-Luther sentiment or action.⁵⁸ Eventually, however, he gave in to pressure, and in 1524 he wrote against Luther and in defense of the freedom of the human will. Luther's *Bondage of the Will* is a response to that essay. Their relationship deteriorated rapidly from that point.

Erasmus did not become a Protestant, then, but he continued to insist on the need for reform while working for peace and indeed reunion within the Church; moreover, his commitment to reading Scripture in its original languages never wavered. His college in Leuven subsequently provided the inspiration for the Roman Catholic humanist monarch Francis I of France in founding in Paris (1530) what later became the Collège de France. His royal aim was to offer free public instruction in Hebrew and Greek.⁵⁹ This was a venture that also attracted criticism, but he carried it through nonetheless.⁶⁰ He was not the only Roman Catholic humanist to display such commitments in this period. Like Francis, "Pope Leo X [d. 1521, and] Duke Georg of Saxony [d. 1539] ... [also] opposed the Reformation throughout their lives, but they also supported Hebrew and Greek learning."⁶¹

Yet it cannot be doubted that it was the Reformation, much more than the patronage of even powerful Roman Catholic rulers and leaders with humanist leanings, which in the succeeding centuries established the biblical languages as permanent fixtures in university curricula. This was precisely because, for Protestants, the learning of these languages was a theological necessity in a way that could never be true for those who remained committed to the "old faith"

---

⁵⁷ Already in the fifteenth century Manetti had needed to defend the usefulness of learning and using Hebrew (Reventlow, *Biblical Interpretation*, 3:11, 55), and similar attacks on the biblical languages continued in the sixteenth century.

⁵⁸ Brecht, *Luther: His Road*, 1:284–86.

⁵⁹ James Veazie Skalnik, *Ramus and Reform: University and Church at the End of the Renaissance* (SCES 60; Kirksville, Mo.: Truman State University Press, 2002), 63–87 (esp. 71–73).

⁶⁰ Responding to Francis' idea, Noel Beda of the University of Paris asked what the point of learning Greek and Hebrew might be, when the Church had for so long used the Vulgate Latin. Arjo Vanderjagt, "Ad Fontes! The Early Humanist Concern for the *Hebraica veritas*," HBOT 2:154–89 (184).

⁶¹ Burnett, *Christian Hebraism*, 29. See also Rex's comments on the embodiment of Erasmus' "trilingual ideal" in the founding of both St. John's College, Cambridge (1511), and Corpus Christi College, Oxford (1515–1516). Rex, "Humanism," 520. For the progress of Catholic biblical scholarship in Leuven itself in the century following Erasmus, see Wim François, "Augustine and the Golden Age of Biblical Scholarship in Louvain (1550–1650)," in *Shaping the Bible in the Reformation: Books, Scholars and Their Readers in the Sixteenth Century* (ed. Bruce Gordon and Matthew McLean; LWW 20; Leiden: Brill, 2012), 235–89.

(whether humanists or not) and its Latin Vulgate.⁶² So committed were early Strasbourg Reformers like Martin Bucer and Wolfgang Capito in their advocacy of the learning of biblical languages, indeed, that Bucer (1491–1551), writing in 1529, could even foresee a future in which Hebrew would be universally spoken in every Christian city. Huldrych Zwingli is also on record as stating that Bible translations are only for beginners: they function like flotation devices for those who are learning to swim.⁶³

THE REFORMERS, THE TRADITION, AND THE FUTURE

We may now weave together the threads of chapters 10 and 11 as we have pursued them to this point in answering the following question: Were the Reformers right to insist that the foundational scriptural texts against which articulations of Christian doctrine and ethics should be measured, and in light of which all translations should be made, are texts in the original biblical languages, which must be learned in pursuit of competent Christian biblical interpretation? Yes, they were quite right, and in so insisting they took their stand in the mainstream of the Christian tradition that lay behind them. This tradition had always recognized the primacy of the original-language texts vis-à-vis their translations into Greek and Latin, even as many had often wrongly assumed, lacking the knowledge in any case to check, that their Greek and Latin translations were perfect (or at least entirely adequate) representations of the originals—a problem that could only ever be solved by sufficient language learning.

Right Paths Before the Reformation

In an age long before the Reformation, Jerome was quite right—having acquired the knowledge that made clear to him at least a substantial part of the truth—to insist on abandoning the attempt to reconstruct the LXX, and instead to base his OT translations on the Hebrew text available to him. The consequence was that "he granted the Western church for the first time a reliable text that was incomparably closer to the original text than the old translations based on the Septuagint."⁶⁴ Augustine, on the other hand—a man possessing "logical power" and "passionate devotion" but neither "critical sagacity" nor "historical learning"⁶⁵—set a bad example for the future, and was indeed out of step with the tradition (although pastorally well motivated), in grasping some of the truth, with Jerome's

---

⁶² Burnett, *Christian Hebraism*, 30–39.
⁶³ Hobbs, "Pluriformity," 462–63. For the extent of the Strasbourgers' commitment to Hebrew, see 455–72. Other Reformers noted for their facility in biblical languages include John Oecolampadius of Basel. Opitz, "Exegetical and Hermeneutical Work," 407–13.
⁶⁴ Reventlow, *Biblical Interpretation*, 2:45.
⁶⁵ Westcott, *Bible*, 184.

help, and then refusing to follow him. An even worse example was set by those who simply rejected Jerome's work, insisting against all the evidence that the LXX was not only accurate but inspired—on the basis of a view of the past that ultimately derived (in the form in which they and Augustine appropriated it) from Philo, and not even from the Christian tradition to which they appealed.

Those Renaissance scholars were also quite right who in their own age, having gradually accumulated the knowledge that revealed to them a more substantial part of the truth than Jerome possessed, insisted on turning aside from the Vulgate and attempting fresh translations, whether into Latin or into other languages, based on the Hebrew and Greek texts available to *them*. Their intention in so doing was simply to provide for their contemporaries what Jerome had provided for his—a "reliable text that was incomparably closer to the original text" than an older translation. Those who rejected their work, on the other hand, insisting that a flawed Vulgate should be retained simply because of its traditionally important role in the Church—thus repeating an argument in favor of the Vulgate that Jerome himself had rejected in respect of the LXX—were wrong to do so. Their posture, which once again (as in Augustine's time) threatened the Church's ability to engage in public discourse about the reliability of its texts, is in fact exemplary of a more general commitment to obscurantism in the face of Renaissance scholarship that was rightly pilloried by some even at the time. This is most famously illustrated by "the Pfefferkorn Affair" in Germany in the years just prior to (and then the early years of) the Reformation, in the course of which the converted Jew Johannes Pfefferkorn attempted to engineer a general imperial confiscation of Jewish literature because it allegedly insulted the Christian faith. Johannes Reuchlin was centrally involved in this business as an advocate for just process. In response to serious attacks on Reuchlin by his opponents for his advocacy on behalf of "the Jews," some of his humanistic supporters in Erfurt issued a biting satire (1515–1516), mocking his enemies as "obscure men and enemies of true scholarship"[66] and ridiculing them for their obsolete methods of instruction and study and their pedantry.

Right Paths During and Since the Reformation

It was in the following year (1517) that Luther pinned his theses to the church door in Wittenberg. The Reformers were right (and in line with Christian tradition) to follow the logic of Renaissance scholarly opinion on the matter of the biblical text. Indeed, over the course of time, their judgment on this point has come to be shared by the Roman Catholic Church itself. The papal encyclical *Divino afflante Spiritu* (1943), mentioned already in chapter 9, makes for fascinating reading in

---

[66] Reventlow, *Biblical Interpretation*, 3:33.

this respect. It affirms that the Bible reader's attention ought to be focused on "the original text, which having been written by the inspired author himself, has more authority and greater weight than any of even the very best translations, whether ancient or modern."[67] It further maintains that textual criticism, "which is used with great and praiseworthy results in the editions of profane writings, is also quite rightly employed in the case of the sacred Books."[68] The "authority of the Vulgate in matters of doctrine" demands

> either the corroboration and confirmation of this same doctrine by the original texts or the recourse on any and every occasion to the aid of these same texts, by which the correct meaning of the Sacred Letters is everywhere daily made more clear and evident. Nor is it forbidden by the decree of the Council of Trent to make translations into the vulgar tongue, even directly from the original texts themselves, for the use and benefit of the faithful and for the better understanding of the Divine Word.[69]

The Vulgate is, after all, only one translation among many that have been and are to be made from "the original texts" and "for the use and benefit of the faithful."

It follows that the Reformers were also quite right to embrace the imperative to learn the biblical languages, already articulated back in the thirteenth century by scholars like Roger Bacon, so as to be able to read and interact with the biblical texts in Hebrew and Greek. Reformation scholars like Calvin

> accepted without hesitation the humanist belief that the understanding of an ancient text depended in the first instance on the mastery of the language in which it was written. Calvin therefore preferred to read the Bible in its Greek and Hebrew originals, going so far as to take the Hebrew and Greek text into the pulpit with him.[70]

In so doing, they were also following the example of Jerome (and the advice of Augustine), and indeed of all those others throughout the subsequent Middle Ages and into the Renaissance who had made attempts in this direction against what must have often seemed insuperable odds. Those who declared "for Jerome," but who then refused to avail themselves of all the linguistic resources emerging by the beginning of the sixteenth century that facilitated the improvement of his work—those who opposed, indeed, the very idea of *anyone* availing himself of these resources—were not, in fact "for Jerome" at all. For it is one thing to make assumptions about the Vulgate's correspondence to the Hebrew and Greek texts

---

[67] *Divino afflante Spiritu*, 122–23.
[68] *Divino afflante Spiritu*, 122–23.
[69] *Divino afflante Spiritu*, 124–25.
[70] Steinmetz, "Calvin as an Interpreter," 287–88.

when one does not have much knowledge of those languages to bring to bear on the question. It is another thing entirely to be robustly "for" linguistic ignorance, decrying the very facility in biblical languages that had enabled Jerome first to do his own work, and now enabled contemporary scholars to do theirs. *Of course* the Reformers were right to insist on the learning of Hebrew and Greek as primary languages for the Christian reader of Scripture—although they were, at the same time, not "against" the learning of Latin or (for that matter) any other language either.[71]

Once again, *Divino afflante Spiritu* makes for interesting reading on this topic. It notes that few among the Church Fathers knew Hebrew, and that in the Middle Ages "the knowledge of even the Greek language had long since become . . . rare in the West." So it was that "even the greatest Doctors of that time, in their exposition of the Sacred Text, had recourse only to the Latin version, known as the Vulgate."[72] Since the time of the Renaissance, however, "the Greek language . . . has been, as it were, restored to new life" and is "familiar to almost all students of antiquity and letters," and "the knowledge of Hebrew . . . has spread far and wide among literary men." What is more, "there are now such abundant aids to the study of these languages that the biblical scholar who by neglecting them would deprive himself of access to the original texts could in no wise escape *the stigma of levity and sloth.*"[73]

> Wherefore, let him diligently apply himself so as to acquire daily a greater facility in biblical as well as in other oriental languages and to support his interpretation by the aids that all branches of philology supply. This indeed St. Jerome strove earnestly to achieve, as far as the science of his time permitted.[74]

The later *Dei Verbum* (1965), also mentioned in chapter 9, further emphasizes the importance of searching out the meaning of the biblical authors in their original historical and linguistic contexts, not least so that "suitable and accurate translations [can be] made into various languages, especially from the original texts of the sacred Books."[75] The Pontifical Biblical Commission's document, "The Interpretation of the Bible in the Church" (1993), actually characterizes "a tendency to ignore or to deny the problems presented by the biblical text in its original Hebrew, Aramaic or Greek form" as a "fundamentalism" that "is often narrowly bound to one fixed translation, whether old or present-day." It urges Roman Catholic authors to make "meaningful to men and women of today" the "forms of

---

[71] Steinmetz, "Calvin as an Interpreter," 288.
[72] *Divino afflante Spiritu*, 122.
[73] *Divino afflante Spiritu*, 122 (emphasis added).
[74] *Divino afflante Spiritu*, 122.
[75] *Dei Verbum*, 29.

expression and literary genres employed in the Hebrew, Aramaic or Greek text," and it is positive about "ecumenical translations of the Bible."[76]

Right Paths Going Ahead

What does all this mean for Christians in the twenty-first century who wish to adhere to a "reformed" biblical hermeneutic? Are attention to the foundational, original-language scriptural texts and a commitment to serious language learning in order to read them and (as necessary) translate them still to mark our thinking and practice moving forward? It is frankly impossible to see how it could be otherwise. We should still view the Bible as fundamentally composing Hebrew (Aramaic) and Greek texts, refusing to regard *any* translation as just as good as (or better than) they are. We should still regard the learning of biblical languages as centrally important in seeking to understand, translate, or otherwise communicate these Scriptures. The literal sense of the text, about which we reflected at such great length in chapters 4 through 9, is intrinsically bound up with the original historical and linguistic contexts in which biblical texts were composed.

SIGNPOSTS ON THE WAY

However, as we move deeper into the twenty-first century (in these respects, as in those already considered in chapters 4 through 9), a contemporary reading of Scripture that embraces Reformation interpretive principles should not look exactly as it did in the sixteenth century. There are at least four reasons why this is so.

Theory and Practice in the Reformation

The Reformers themselves were certainly committed, not only in theory but in practice, to the reading of Scripture in its original Hebrew and Greek forms, and to the learning of the biblical languages in order to be able to do so. They sought to acquire as much learning as they could in pursuit of these goals, depending on both Christian and Jewish sources.

Luther knew enough about the history of the Hebrew text of the OT, for example, to know what the Jewish scholar Elias Levita himself confirmed in his *Masoreth ha-Masoreth*, published in 1538—that in earlier times (e.g., in the time of Jerome) the vowel points had not yet been inserted into the Hebrew text.[77] He used this knowledge in his commentary writing. Calvin "had at his disposal good

---

[76] Pontifical Biblical Commission, "Interpretation," 45, 76, 94.

[77] This was also true of Zwingli, Calvin, and others; see B. Pick, "The Vowel-Points Controversy in the XVI. and XVII. Centuries," *Hebraica* 8 (1892): 150–73 (162–63). For a more recent summary of the controversy, see Steiger, "Development," 747–53.

texts of the Hebrew, Latin, and Greek Bibles, grammars, lexica and concordances,"[78] and he used *these* to good effect in his own work, in the course of which "no translation, regardless of is authority granted by tradition or humanist scholarship, [was] embraced without scrutiny."[79] He was familiar with a range of classical sources and with patristic literature (two of his favorite authors are Chrysostom and Augustine), but he also "appreciated the rabbis with regard to their philological and lexical expertise."[80] The Reformers recognized the importance of gaining a quality of education that would enable them fully to engage with the original-language biblical texts that must be regarded as the basis for all doctrine and ethics. They recognized, indeed, that doctrinal and ethical statements throughout the ages had to some (or even a large) extent been compromised by dependence on translations like the LXX or the Vulgate. They set out to gain just such a quality of education, and they used it. In these respects they surely represent an example for contemporary Christians to follow.

At the same time, the Reformers could often blur just as unhelpfully as Augustine the lines between questions of text and language, on the one hand, and questions of theology and practice, on the other. That is to say: the question of the correct reading of a text could become, not so much a matter of judiciously weighing the evidence about the history of the text and the likely meaning of the Hebrew and Greek *in order to* establish correct theology and practice, but a matter in which prior traditions or personal beliefs concerning correct theology and practice already played a decisive role. Just as Augustine had defended the LXX, not on the basis that it could be shown empirically to be a perfect translation of the Hebrew, but instead on the basis of its alleged inspiration, so too the Reformers could indulge in special pleading. In this scenario, disputes about evidence were quickly confused with, and indeed misrepresented as, disagreements about faith and practice, and opponents immediately became, not merely mistaken in their understanding, but also perverse and wicked heretics.

It is such elements in Luther's exegetical work, for example, to which Siegfried Raeder draws attention when he states that "linguistic findings are subordinated to the Gospel of Christ."[81] Calvin's approach to the text, likewise, leads Kathryn Greene-McCreight to the view that he sometimes "seems to want to rely on the words of the text themselves, that is, verbal meaning, to do all the 'work'

---

[78] Greene-McCreight, *Ad Litteram*, 107.

[79] Greene-McCreight, *Ad Litteram*, 107.

[80] Greene-McCreight, *Ad Litteram*, 122.

[81] Raeder, "Exegetical and Hermeneutical Work," 377; note also Luther's general resistance to "rabbinical exegesis" and his tendency to "Christianize" in translation (403–6). In these respects Luther is not so different from Origen, whose work he so dislikes but which can often be explained according to the rubric, "what is linguistically responsible is not necessarily theologically fruitful." O'Keefe and Reno, *Sanctified Vision*, 56.

of warranting his arguments about the text without acknowledging that he is engaged in Ruled reading [reading in line with the Rule of Faith] as well."[82] When writers wish to defend Calvin to some extent in this area, they tend to say things like "Calvin had a prior, and to him, higher goal than following out the dictates of humanistic interpretive models," and that for him "scholarship was to be in the service of the Church's search for God's truth."[83] It was precisely in the service of the Church's search for God's truth, of course, that Augustine had also defended the use of the LXX. The opponents of Renaissance Humanism in the sixteenth century were still defending the Vulgate and decrying the learning of biblical languages for the same reason.

It is not clear to me, however, that the Church ever truly derives any benefit, either in herself or in the eyes of the watching world, when what appears to be the truth in any aspect of reality is ignored or even suppressed. Where the Reformers did not follow through consistently on their commitments they are not to be defended—even if it is true that in their time they were not alone in failing to pay sufficient attention to textual and linguistic facts.[84] We should instead recognize their limitations and regret the poor examples that they set those who followed them—acknowledging that, unfortunately, "[t]heology came often to dominate philology [and for that matter textual criticism] in the later sixteenth century,"[85] as it did in the seventeenth through the nineteenth centuries, and in some quarters still does today. It is either true or untrue, for example—as a matter of scholarly fact—that the vowel points are additions to the MT dating from around the sixth century AD. It was a mistake to insist, on theological grounds—as some did in the sixteenth and seventeenth centuries—that they *must* derive from the biblical prophets. The "reformed" reading of Scripture in the twenty-first century should try not to repeat such mistakes.

---

[82] Greene-McCreight, *Ad Litteram*, 245.

[83] Holder, *Grounding*, 89, 135–36. To be fair, Holder also agrees that Calvin's paraphrasing of the biblical text, which is the focus of his interest on 136, represents "a weakness in his efforts at interpretation," leaving him open to the very charge that he leveled at others: twisting textual meaning to find doctrine in texts that is not really there.

[84] The editors of the Complutensian Polyglot, e.g., were not keen to move too far away from traditional readings of the Vulgate even when convinced that the textual evidence supported them in doing so; indeed, they "often chose to employ their philological talents in such a way as to protect the reputation of the Vulgate." Bentley, *Humanists*, 91–111 (101).

[85] Bentley, *Humanists*, 13. I do not mean to suggest, however, that someone like Luther was wrong when he insisted that "one cannot discover the meaning of a passage in scripture using *only* philology and grammar"(emphasis added). John A. Maxfield, *Luther's Lectures on Genesis and the Formation of Evangelical Identity* (Sixteenth Century Essays & Studies 60; Kirksville, Mo.: Truman State University Press, 2008), 53.

Developments in Our Understanding of the Biblical Languages

The second reason why a contemporary "reformed" reading of Scripture with respect to texts and languages should not look exactly as it did in the sixteenth century is precisely that time has moved on, and that we understand much more than our forebears about the biblical languages and how they function.

This is especially true of Hebrew, as a result of both voluminous inductive work throughout the intervening centuries and growing competence in cognate languages, often as a result of new archaeological discoveries. The value of Arabic for the study of Hebrew, for example, was already demonstrated in the eighteenth century by Albert Schultens (1686–1750), "the father of comparative Semitic philology."[86] The nineteenth century then saw the deciphering of Mesopotamian cuneiform, associated most importantly with Edward Hincks and Henry Rawlinson and facilitated (although the significance of this has often been overstated) by the recovery of the trilingual Behistun Inscription in Iran (which enabled scholars to use its Old Persian text to help decipher its Elamite and its Babylonian). Rawlinson "is best remembered for the editing and publication of the five volumes of *Cuneiform Inscriptions of Western Asia* (1861–1884) with considerable help from Edwin Norris and other scholars."[87]

It was such nineteenth-century developments that gave scholars access to Akkadian, the earliest of the Semitic languages, typically referenced as representing an East Semitic branch of the Semitic language tree.[88] The language of the city of Ebla in Syria (Tell Mardikh), excavated from 1964 onward, is related in some degree to Akkadian, although it also shares features with the Northwest Semitic group of languages. About this second group—of which Hebrew and Aramaic are members (as well as Phoenician)—we have also accumulated considerable knowledge in recent times. The most important discovery of the twentieth century bearing on our understanding of Hebrew is no doubt the one at Ras Shamra in Syria, the site of the ancient city of Ugarit that flourished from the fifteenth through the thirteenth centuries BC and was excavated from 1929 onward. Ugaritic texts have cast fresh light on a number of linguistic aspects of the text of the OT, as well as illuminating literary styles, cultural references, and religious concepts within the text. As John Huehnergard notes, "It is indeed difficult to overestimate the impact that the discovery of the Ugaritic texts has had on the study of the Hebrew Bible."[89]

---

[86] Stephen G. Burnett, "Later Christian Hebraists," *HBOT* 2:785–801 (792).

[87] Kevin J. Cathcart, "The Earliest Contributions to the Decipherment of Sumerian and Akkadian," *CDLJ* 1 (2011): 1–12 (9).

[88] See further Holger Gzella, "Expansion of the Linguistic Context of the Hebrew Bible/Old Testament: Hebrew among the Languages of the Ancient Near East," *HBOT* 1/1:134–67.

[89] John Huehnergard, *An Introduction to Ugaritic* (Peabody, Mass.: Hendrickson, 2012), 10.

Developments in Our Understanding of the Biblical Textual Tradition

Third, time has also moved on with respect to our understanding of the development of the biblical textual tradition, and the increase in our knowledge in this area must also be taken seriously. As to the NT, first of all, it is clear in retrospect that Erasmus, for all his erudition, and in a (successful) bid to get his Greek NT published before the Complutensian Polyglot appeared, produced his edition with excessive haste and on the basis of very limited Greek manuscript resources.[90] The Erasmian text was certainly widely "received," and indeed it remained for nearly three hundred years the only form of the Greek NT available in print. In the process it attracted in some quarters an almost sacred status—such that, to this day, there are Protestants who insist on the all-but-inerrant nature of translations like the KJV that were based upon it (even though the 1647 *Westminster Confession of Faith* itself takes no such view). Here, once again, "inspiration" has often been invoked simply as a way of enabling the avoidance of evidence. For the fact is that only a handful of the thousands of manuscripts of the NT now known to us were used in the compilation of Erasmus' text—none of them dating before the tenth century AD.[91] It is clear now that there are no grounds at all for identifying this text, wholesale, with the original text of the NT—not even in Erasmus' revised and definitive fourth edition (1527), from which the fifth hardly differed at all, or in later revisions by other people. Indeed, in a number of passages Erasmus' "reading" is supported by no known Greek witness at all.[92] This is the overwhelming judgment of modern NT scholarship, on the basis of more extensive evidence, more carefully sifted—a process that began in earnest in the late eighteenth century, and is described in the appendix toward the end of this book.

With respect to the OT, second, Reformation scholars (like Jerome before them) encountered a Hebrew text, preserved by the Jews, that seemed astonishingly uniform and stable through time and space. Their admiration for it is well expressed by Martin Bucer: "As often as I consider that incredible care and diligence whereby these [manuscripts] have been preserved by the Jews ... I am compelled to admire and embrace God's immense goodness toward us, despite our lack of gratitude."[93] The Reformers had little doubt, then, about the nature of "the" original Hebrew text; it was the text that lay before them (the MT), albeit

---

[90] Bruce M. Metzger and Bart D. Ehrman, *The Text of the New Testament: Its Transmission, Corruption, and Restoration* (4th ed.; Oxford: Clarendon, 2005), 137–52.

[91] Lee M. McDonald, "Wherein Lies Authority? A Discussion of Books, Texts, and Translations," in Evans and Tov, *Exploring the Origins*, 203–39 (218).

[92] Metzger and Ehrman, *Text*, 145.

[93] Cited in Hobbs, "Pluriformity," 470.

that in earlier times it had not yet been "pointed" (given vowel points). These Reformation scholars had little reason to think that the consonantal Hebrew text had ever been otherwise than the one they encountered, especially since Aquila's Greek translation (which the Fathers considered to be earlier than Theodotion or Symmachus) already witnessed to this same text in the second century AD. It was simply assumed on all sides, then, "that the Hebrew text preserved by the Synagogue was authentic and highly accurate."[94] That was where those who wished to travel *ad fontes* in OT studies should go.

The passage of time has made it clear that matters are a little more complicated than this. Already in the period between 1628 and 1645 the appearance for the first time in print, in the Paris Polyglot Bible, of both the Samaritan Pentateuch (mainly based on a fourteenth-century manuscript purchased in Damascus in 1616) and the Syriac version of the whole OT (the Peshitta) provided a significant impetus to the consideration of variants in the textual tradition.[95] The most complete of all the polyglot Bibles was published in London shortly afterward, between 1653 and 1657: "All texts used by Jews, Samaritans and old Christian Churches (except Coptic, Armenian and Georgian) were presented."[96] The availability of these new resources fueled the question as to how exactly the MT was related to the original Hebrew text—not least because the Paris Polyglot proposed, quite straightforwardly, that both the Samaritan Pentateuch and the Peshitta had deeper roots in history than the MT.

Louis Cappel had already come to the conclusion in his *The Mystery of the Points Unveiled* (1624) that many passages in the LXX represented an interpretation of a consonantal Hebrew text that differed from the one found in the "pointed" MT.[97] His later book, *Critica Sacra* (*Sacred Criticism*, 1650), not only "analyzed textual variations . . . between the Hebrew Bible and the ancient translations (as well as the Samaritan Pentateuch)," but also studied "specific kinds of textual corruption, including those attested to within the masoretic apparatus itself."[98] Building on Cappel's work, Benjamin Kennicott concluded in 1753 (*The State of the Printed Hebrew Considered*) that "the received Hebrew Bible text had suffered significant textual corruption and that a return to the manuscripts was necessary in order to restore the pristine purity of the text."[99] His later *Vetus Tes-*

---

[94] Alexander, "Reflections," 362.

[95] Adrian Schenker, "The Polyglot Bibles of Antwerp, Paris, and London," *HBOT* 2:774–84. The Samaritan Pentateuch is "a recension of the Hebrew text of the Torah transmitted among the Samaritans in isolation from the Jews from the second century BC onwards." Peter J. Gentry, "The Text of the Old Testament," *JETS* 52 (2009) 19–45 (23).

[96] Schenker, "Polyglot Bibles," 782.

[97] Burnett, "Later Christian Hebraists," 790.

[98] Burnett, "Later Christian Hebraists," 790.

[99] Burnett, "Later Christian Hebraists," 797.

tamentum Hebraicum (*Hebrew Old Testament*, 1776–1780) contained an unpointed consonantal text with manuscript variants listed at the foot of each page, and it was followed by Giovanni Bernardo de Rossi's attempted improvement on his work in his *Variant Readings of the Old Testament* (1784–1793).[100] Scholars like Cappel and Kennicott in the seventeenth and eighteenth centuries—"would-be improvers of the holy text," as many of their opponents unappreciatively considered them[101]—laid the groundwork for later text-critical scholarship with respect to the OT, the story of which is also briefly told in the appendix to this book.

CONCLUSION

Contemporary Christians should still view the Bible as fundamentally comprising Hebrew (Aramaic) and Greek texts, and they should still regard the learning of biblical languages as centrally important in seeking to understand, translate, and communicate these texts. This involves at the same time a rejection of both "second" and "fourth way" perspectives on biblical literature that diminish the importance of reading the texts in their original languages. However, the "reformed" reading of Scripture as we move deeper into the twenty-first century should not look exactly as it did in the sixteenth. We do not honor the past by remaining more faithful to its *conclusions* than to the commitments that *led* to those conclusions, refusing to acknowledge the truth and value of what has been discovered in the meantime. To insist on ignoring what has been discovered about biblical languages in the five hundred years since the Wittenberg Affair, for example, is not to honor the Reformation, but to discredit it. To imitate even the Reformers in their mistakes and inconsistencies is, likewise, not the best way of standing in line with Reformation thinking and practice.

---

[100] Burnett, "Later Christian Hebraists," 796–801.
[101] Burnett, "Later Christian Hebraists," 801.

II

Now There Are Protestants
Scripture in a Changing World

In each of the areas of biblical interpretation discussed in part 1 the magisterial Reformers were joining long-standing conversations within the Church, and the positions they adopted were far from novel. In part 2 we turn our attention in the first instance to Reformation perspectives that *have* been considered more novel. We attempt to get to the bottom of what the Reformers thought about *sola Scriptura* and the perspicuity of Scripture (chapter 12), and about the nature and scope of Scripture's authority (chapter 13). I shall argue that the novelty has been greatly exaggerated. The Reformers possessed ample warrant in both Scripture and tradition for their insistence on "the perspicuity of Scripture alone." The same is true of their belief that God-inspired Scripture unerringly guides the Church as its authority with respect to right Christian belief and practice. We ourselves should hold to this same Reformation teaching about the authority and perspicuity of Scripture alone. However, since there is currently significant confusion about what this teaching really was, we need to ensure that we have a firm grasp of it.

The importance of this becomes particularly clear as we transition in chapters 14 through 16 into a discussion of modernity. The Reformation occurred toward the end of a long period in Europe, from the fourth to the sixteenth centuries, in which the entire civilization had been Christian. Not everyone who lived in it was a Christian, but for the civilization as a whole, nevertheless, the biblical Story as mediated by the Church—and even as people may have disagreed about precisely what this Story "authorized" in terms of belief and practice—had come to define the reality in which people lived. They inhabited what has often been referred to as a "culture of the Book," in which the Bible as an overarching narrative in which were embedded all sorts of other genres (e.g., wisdom literature, psalms) was, at root, the defining document for private *and* for public life. By the end of the nineteenth century, however, the situation was quite different. The premodern world defined by and organized in terms of the biblical narrative had largely disappeared, and a new, modern world had emerged. The Great Story had lost its place as *the* narrative that framed public discourse; the Bible had been dethroned as the predominant, authoritative source of human knowledge and understanding when it came to a great number of important questions. What had been a Story that fundamentally interpreted the reader and her world had become instead only one object to be analyzed in the pursuit of a larger understanding of the human self and the world that increasingly drew only on nonbiblical sources. These were tumultuous times for biblical hermeneutics, then, and if we are to engage well as Bible readers with modernity (and now postmodernity)—and in particular with the modern and postmodern ("first" and "second" way) proposals about reading the Bible that we shall discuss in part 3—then we need to understand what happened. The emphasis of the narrative that I shall relate about what happened will lie on the role played by poor Christian answers to highly pertinent modern questions, often based (within the Protestant Church) on an only quasi-"reformed" approach to Bible reading. This will clear the ground for my particular proposal about how Protestant Bible readers *ought* to have responded to modernity, and how "reformed" people still ought to respond to its contemporary forms—which will involve an extended critique in chapters 14 (briefly) and 16 of "third" and "fourth" way approaches to biblical interpretation.

12

THE PERSPICUITY OF SCRIPTURE ALONE
A Lamp unto My Feet

> *The meaning of Scripture is, in and of itself, so certain, accessible, and clear that Scripture interprets itself and tests, judges and illuminates everything else.*
>
> —Martin Luther[1]

> *... those ancient Councils of Nice [i.e., Nicea], Constantinople, the first of Ephesus, Chalcedon, and the like ... we willingly embrace, and reverence as sacred, in so far as relates to doctrines of faith, for they contain nothing but the pure and genuine interpretation of Scripture, which the holy Fathers with spiritual prudence adopted to crush the enemies of religion.*
>
> —John Calvin[2]

At the heart of the Protestant Reformation stood a man who, at a crucial and highly dangerous moment in his life (at the Diet of Worms in 1521), famously affirmed that unless he were "convinced by the testimony of the Scriptures or by clear reason," he was "bound by the Scriptures," his "conscience ... captive to the Word of God."[3] It might well be "the pope and not the Scriptures that counted" in Rome,[4] but for Luther Scripture alone (*sola Scriptura*) was the final authority in matters of faith and life. It was perfectly capable of functioning as such because it was *perspicuous*—that is, "plain to the understanding especially because of clarity and precision of presentation" (*Merriam-Webster*). It could be understood without the guidance of the church hierarchy (often called the "magisterium"). Were people to possess both the Bible in its original languages (or, at least, in

---

[1] Martin Luther, *Assertio omnium articulorum* (*Assertion of All the Articles*, 1520), as cited in Bernhard Lohse, *Martin Luther: An Introduction to His Life and Work* (Philadelphia: Fortress, 1986), 157 (referencing WA 7:97).

[2] Calvin, *Institutes* 4.9.8.

[3] Brecht, *Luther: His Road*, 1:460.

[4] Brecht, *Luther: His Road*, 1:283, referring to a letter to Luther in 1519 from his former Erfurt fellow-student, Crotus Rubianus.

an accurate, vernacular translation) and some rudimentary rules of reading, the Reformers believed, no one should have undue difficulty in understanding what Scripture had to say.

These two ideas, then—*sola Scriptura* and perspicuity—lie at the core of the Reformation approach to Christian faith and life. As such they were subjected to intense scrutiny and criticism in the sixteenth century, and they have continued to be so ever since. Their rootedness in Scripture and tradition, their coherence, and their viability have all been questioned. As to coherence and viability, appeals to "Scripture alone" by individuals and groups over against the teaching of the Church have often been associated with heresy (it has been claimed),[5] or at a lower level with multiple differing emphases when it comes to the truth. These appeals have resulted, then, in the fragmentation of the Church, as each denomination or individual congregation sees rather different truths and virtues recommended in "Scripture alone" and separates itself from other groups who read Scripture differently. This was already a problem in sixteenth-century Protestantism. How, and how often, should the Eucharist or the Lord's Supper be celebrated, and exactly how were the bread and wine to be understood?[6] Which persons should be baptized, and when?[7] It has not become less severe with the passing of time. The contemporary Protestant Church is characterized by many denominations and sects, and even by quite individualistic opinions; *sola Scriptura* and perspicuity are primarily responsible (it is claimed). Much of the blame for the entire, secularized, fragmented condition of the modern world has also been laid at their door.[8]

Does this not make a nonsense, then, of the claim that Scripture is perspicuous—a claim that, by way of strenuous attempts to undermine its credibility, already fueled the engine of Roman Catholic scholarship in the sixteenth and seventeenth centuries on a range of issues?[9] Scripture seems far from a per-

---

[5] Von der Eck took exactly this line in his interactions with Luther at the Diet of Worms. Atkinson, *Trial*, 159–60.

[6] See, e.g., Amy N. Burnett, "Hermeneutics and Exegesis in the Early Eucharistic Controversy," in Goran and McLean, *Shaping the Bible*, 85–105.

[7] The Reformers of the magisterial Reformation retained from the long Church tradition (while also arguing for its scriptural basis) the practice of infant baptism. Anabaptists like Balthasar Hubmaier (1480–1528), on the other hand, held that Scripture simply read, in all its perspicuity, did not support infant baptism. Hans-Jürgen Goertz, "Scriptural Interpretation among Radical Reformers," *HBOT* 2:576–601 (590–91).

[8] Gregory, *Unintended Reformation*, 109–12.

[9] The newly founded Society of Jesus (1540), e.g., deployed considerable erudition in the course of a "Jesuitical offensive in Germany" that was in part devoted to demonstrating "that Scripture was obscure and therefore insufficient as the only source of revelation"—in turn provoking Protestant scholars like Martin Chemnitz to still greater efforts to defend Scripture's perspicuity. Bernt T. Oftestad, "Further Development of Reformation Hermeneutics," *HBOT* 2:602–16

spicuous body of literature that "interprets itself and tests, judges and illuminates everything else" (Luther, in the first epigraph above). It seems rather to require an arbiter who is capable of resolving the interpretative disputes that create the disagreements, schisms, and divisions in the first place—what one contemporary author has termed our "pervasive interpretive pluralism."[10]

The question of "arbitration," then, lies at the heart of the matter—its necessity, and also its nature—and the theologians of the magisterial Reformation found themselves having to defend their position on two fronts. On the one side, notable Roman Catholic scholars questioned "both the reliability of the received biblical text when compared to the Vulgate and also its perspicuity, arguing that without the church hierarchy's guidance the unbridled interpretation of these texts would only lead to heresy."[11] The Church could provide this guidance not least because it possessed alongside Scripture (according to the Council of Trent) oral traditions "concerning both faith and conduct, as either directly spoken by Christ or dictated by the holy Spirit, which have been preserved in unbroken sequence in the catholic church"—traditions that the Church "accepts and venerates with a like feeling of piety and reverence."[12] The Church, with the bishop of Rome at its heart, should remain the arbiter. The insufficiency of Scripture alone to reveal the Truth required it.[13] The Reformers rejected this view.

(612–16). More broadly, with respect to the correct text of the OT, "Catholic scholars were keen to establish the *uncertainty* of the originals, so that they could argue for the need for an external agent—the Church—to promulgate the authoritative text. Often regarded as products of progressive humanism, the great Catholic polyglot Bibles were actually important instruments of the Counter Reformation." Alexander, "Reflections," 363.

[10] Smith, *Bible Made Impossible*, 27, and often throughout the book. "Why and how," he asks, "would the Bible be so easily misread by so many believers if, as biblicism believes, it is ... perspicuous?" (39).

[11] Burnett, *Christian Hebraism*, 271. For Robert Bellarmine, e.g., Scripture itself testifies to its own obscurity, and to be true to Scripture is to recognize this truth. It is certainly "not sufficiently clear in itself to 'terminate' controversies over teaching." Wicks, "Catholic Old Testament Interpretation," 647.

[12] Tanner, *Decrees*, 2:663.

[13] A deep sense of this insufficiency still marks contemporary Roman Catholic scholarship, as well as Protestant scholarship that is influenced by it—especially as Scripture is engaged in its "ordinary," literal sense. Note, e.g., Matthew Levering's rhetorical question (*Exegesis*, 64): "Can humanly authored texts, written in particular historical contexts by authors whose understanding of reality did not possess comprehensiveness, communicate the wisdom that is God's providential love?" Apparently not. Even the truth of the central events of Jesus' life, death, and resurrection is only dimly available to us in Scripture, since "[t]he mystery to be believed is never ... even ... tapped by the materiality of the fact that incarnates it" (quoting de Lubac, who is citing Aquinas); "the mystery of the death and Resurrection of the Savior ... goes *infinitely* beyond what an exegete, assuming that he is both perspicacious and firm in his unbelief, would be able to learn about the death and resurrection of the man Jesus." Levering, *Exegesis*, 144 (emphasis added). Exegesis

On the other side, supporters of the Radical Reformation—who could regard leaders like Luther and Calvin themselves as new "popes" still ruling over an only partially reformed Church—argued strongly for a different arbiter, namely the Holy Spirit in the heart of the believing Christian. For Andreas Bodenstein von Karlstadt (1486–1541), for example, the Spirit-filled reader is the proper judge in the exegesis of Scripture. His younger contemporary Melchior Hoffman (c. 1500–1543) writes about the hidden meaning that lies beneath the letter of Scripture, disclosed to those who are led by the Spirit. The Reformers (although they, too, thought the role of the Holy Spirit in interpretation to be crucially important) also rejected *this* view. "Neither custom nor experience determines the Bible's meaning," they affirmed, "for each is too fickle."[14]

These various questions go right to the heart of the question of the viability of Reformation hermeneutics for contemporary Christian faith, and we shall need to ponder them at some length. *My argument will be that the Reformers had ample warrant in both Scripture and tradition for their position, for all that it inevitably entailed in their time, and still entails in ours, an interpretative pluralism that "reformed" Christians must handle with carefulness and integrity.*

THE REFORMERS AND TRADITION

One of the first requirements of any kind of reading of a person, a book, or a movement is to ensure that one has understood what the other is really saying. This is no less true of the Reformation, when it comes to the language of *sola Scriptura*. This language has often been understood (and with good reason, given the way that it has often been used) as representing "a diatribe against tradition and a rebuke to the very idea of catholicity."[15] This being so, it is not surprising that the Reformers' emphasis on *sola Scriptura* has made them seem quite out of step with the prior history of biblical interpretation. Yet the fact is—and my second epigraph above bears this out—that "*sola Scriptura* was not intended by its original advocates in the time of the Reformation as an absolute rebuke to tradition or a denial of genuine ecclesial authority."[16] Neither Luther nor Calvin was simply "against tradition." Indeed, each makes a point of arguing that he stands *within* tradition, referencing the Church Fathers and ancient conciliar Church decisions to demonstrate that this is the case. Yves Congar generalizes the point as follows:

---

gets at only a fragment of what is true, it seems. Scripture is massively insufficient to deliver the whole truth.

[14] Vanhoozer, *Biblical Authority*, 116.

[15] Michael Allen and Scott R. Swain, *Reformed Catholicity: The Promise of Retrieval for Theology and Biblical Interpretation* (Grand Rapids: Baker, 2015), 49.

[16] Allen and Swain, *Reformed Catholicity*, 49.

All [the Reformers] retained the early councils, at least the first four and, possibly, the sixth also ... Zwingli, Calvin, Theodore Beza, as well as Melanchthon after 1527 ... quote the Fathers. Calvin did so more and more after 1534. The Calvinists do the same.... They even produce editions of the Fathers.... For more than a century after the rupture of the Reformation, the consensus of the first five centuries was accepted by many as the empirical criterion of authenticity, and a possible basis for the restoration of Christian unity.[17]

Luther, Calvin, and the Past

Martin Luther, for example, in *The Councils and the Church* (1539), points out that the most fundamental problem faced by the Church in his day lies not in what "the councils and the fathers" had to say (although he will get to that discussion later), but in the fact that the present state of affairs under the papacy "disagrees shamefully with the ways of the councils and fathers," and that "the pope and his people ... would rather let councils and fathers perish" than be reformed in accordance with their teaching.[18] It is not Luther but the pope and his predecessors who are the innovators,[19] and have carried the true Church away into a "Babylonian Captivity."[20] Luther challenges his readers to bring the pope (along with the Reformers) "under the councils and fathers"; if that ever happens, he promises, "we ... will straightway be there" to pursue the reformation of the Church along with our erstwhile opponents. These opponents, warns Luther, should not imagine that his own knowledge of what the Church Fathers have to say is negligible. To the contrary, "I [once] read them more diligently than they who now quote them so defiantly and proudly against me." This claim is more than adequately borne out by Luther's other writings: "his works throughout his career reveal his respect for the Fathers," even as he also "frequently exercised critical judgment" in respect of their exegesis and theology and could at times treat them quite unfairly and sometimes say extraordinarily dismissive things about them.[21]

Calvin, similarly, displays throughout his work an "openness to the weight of tradition," finding "great value in the historical traditions of interpretation of the Church" and generally being "unwilling to depart from the exegetical choices

---

[17] Congar, *Tradition*, 143–44.
[18] Martin Luther, *The Councils and the Church* (1539), *LW* 41:14.
[19] "We are not teaching anything novel," he asserts in another place; "we are repeating and confirming old doctrines." Martin Luther, *Lectures on Galatians Chapters 1–4* (1535), *LW* 26:39.
[20] Martin Luther, *The Babylonian Captivity of the Church* (1520), *LW* 36:11–18.
[21] Robert Kolb, *Martin Luther: Confessor of the Faith* (CTC; Oxford: Oxford University Press, 2009), 36. The Wittenberg theologians in general "neither canonized [the Fathers'] work nor rejected it entirely ... [they] sought to glean from them what testified to the truth and leave aside, sometimes with sharp criticism, what might be used to undermine the church's proper teaching, as they understood it" (37).

made by his favorite patristic exegetes, unless moved by a clarifying motive."²² His reading of Scripture takes place within the bounds of what the Church taught in its early ecumenical councils about the fundamentals of the Christian faith, in continuity with Scripture. That is, his commitment to *sola Scriptura* is not of the kind that allows appeal to Scripture over the head of long-established, orthodox Christian doctrine as ratified by the councils on the basis of scriptural teaching. A good example of the way in which this is true is provided by the case of Michael Servetus (1511–1553). A gifted language student who had read the entire Bible in its original languages, Servetus came to believe that the doctrine of the Trinity is based not on biblical teachings but on Greek philosophy.²³ He advocated a return to the alleged simplicity and authenticity of the Gospels and the early Church in the time before the creeds. He was consequently condemned by both Roman Catholic and Protestant theologians, including Calvin; ultimately he was put on trial in Calvin's Geneva, and executed. I do not mean by mentioning this example to endorse Calvin's stringent response in this case to an "interpretative enemy"—a response that already in sixteenth-century Europe fueled the flames of a lively debate about the best ways of dealing with interpretative pluralism and in the long run did nothing to help the cause of the Gospel in public European culture (see my chapters 14 and 15). I cite the example only to illustrate how Calvin's Scripture reading was conducted within the bounds set by what he regarded as nonnegotiable, orthodox Christian doctrine.²⁴ As to the Church Fathers in particular, Calvin has this to say in the preface to his *Institutes*, concerning the controversy between the Reformers and their Roman Catholic opponents:

> It is a calumny to represent us as opposed to the Fathers.... Were the contest to be decided by such authority (to speak in the most moderate terms), the better part of the victory would be ours.... So far are we from despising them, that if this were the proper place, it would give us no trouble to support the greater part of the doctrines which we now hold by their suffrages.²⁵

---

²² Holder, *Grounding*, 17, 19. On Calvin's liking for all sorts of things about the Fathers, see Thompson, "Calvin as a Biblical Interpreter," 62–63.

²³ Michael Servetus, *De trinitatis erroribus* (*On the Errors of the Trinity*) (1531), and *Dialogorum de Trinitate* (*Dialogues on the Trinity*) (1532).

²⁴ This did not mean, however, that Calvin went looking for just any text in order to defend a particular doctrine—even one as important as the Trinity: "doctrinal shaping of exegesis is inadmissible where it is understood to violate the verbal sense" (e.g., if it is argued that Gen 3:22 speaks of the Trinity). Greene-McCreight, *Ad Litteram*, 143.

²⁵ Calvin, *Institutes*, preface, 10. On Calvin and councils, see Vanhoozer, *Biblical Authority*, 134–35. For a helpful seventeenth-century summation of the Calvinist view of the Fathers, see Turretin, *Scripture*, 227–34.

Tradition and Traditions

"Modern readers must be careful [then] not to mistake the customary denunciation of tradition by Reformation theologians for a renunciation of tradition as such."[26] The magisterial Reformers were certainly opposed to what they regarded as merely human traditions (plural) in the Church—traditions opposed to Holy Scripture. For as the *Ten Theses of Berne* (1528) puts it, "all human traditions ... are binding upon us only in so far as they are based on and commanded by God's Word."[27] However, where the Church Fathers genuinely took their stand within the stream of apostolic tradition, they were widely recognized among the Reformers (in the words of article three of the *First Helvetic Confession*, 1536) "as elect instruments through whom God has spoken and operated."[28] It is "all *other* human doctrines and articles which lead us away from God and true faith" that are "vain and ineffectual, no matter how attractive, fine, esteemed and of long usage they may be" (article 4).[29] In other words, the Reformers affirmed *sola Scriptura* in order "to engage more deeply the catholic fulness of the church's past rather than to hold tradition at bay."[30] Many of those who came afterward did the same: "The theologians working in the wake of the Reformation were concerned to show the far-reaching agreement of their theology with that of early Christianity and the ancient Church."[31] Our message, claims Luther,

> is not a novel invention of ours but the very ancient, approved teaching of the apostles brought to light again. Neither have we invented a new Baptism, Sacrament of the Altar, Lord's Prayer, and Creed; nor do we desire to know or to have anything new in Christendom. We only contend for, and hold to, the ancient.[32]

Pre-Reformation Christian tradition, as such, was not regarded as "bad"; much of it was in reality maintained in different ways and to differing degrees in the

---

[26] Jens Zimmermann, *Recovering Theological Hermeneutics: An Incarnational-Trinitarian Theory of Interpretation* (Grand Rapids: Baker, 2004), 114.

[27] Arthur C. Cochrane, ed., *Reformed Confessions of the Sixteenth Century* (Louisville, Ky.: Westminster John Knox, 2003), 49 (article 2). This Swiss proclamation proceeded, then, to question contemporary Church teaching concerning such matters as the Mass, purgatory, and marriage.

[28] Cochrane, *Reformed Confessions*, 101.

[29] Cochrane, *Reformed Confessions*, 101 (emphasis added). Note also the earlier *Tetrapolitan Confession*, 14 (1530), whose originators "reckon no traditions among human traditions (such, namely, as are condemned in the Scriptures) except those that conflict with the law of God." Cochrane, *Reformed Confessions*, 71.

[30] Allen and Swain, *Reformed Catholicity*, 63, writing specifically about Martin Bucer.

[31] Steiger, "Development," 701.

[32] Martin Luther, *Sermons on the Gospel of St. John Chapters 14–16* (1537–1538), LW 24:368.

churches of the Reformation.³³ It was simply that all traditions, as to both belief and practice, had to be measured against the canon that is Scripture in order to ensure that they possessed biblical warrant.³⁴ It was this canon—as Scripture interpreted Scripture (for "[s]ola scriptura is not simply a principle but a *practice*: the practice of using Scripture to interpret Scripture")³⁵—that must necessarily have the final say.

THE REFORMERS AND INDIVIDUAL JUDGMENT

What becomes especially clear in the course of this exploration of Protestant thinking about tradition is that the charge of individualism often laid at the Reformers' door is difficult to substantiate—at least in the case of magisterial Reformers like Luther and Calvin.

UNLESS I AM CONVINCED...

Perhaps we are so impressed by the actions of Luther, the courageous individual, in standing up to be counted for his convictions in Worms, that we do not pay full attention to his famous words. He does not say at the Diet of Worms, "I have a right to my individual opinion about what the Bible says, so go away and leave me alone"—as if he were a modern individualist and the true paternal ancestor of Descartes, Voltaire, and their ilk.³⁶ What he says is, "unless I am convinced by the testimony of the Scriptures or by clear reason . . . I cannot and I will not recant anything." This "unless" or "if" (German *wenn*) by no means closes down the possibility of further, reasoned conversation with the wider Church about

---

[33] Allen and Swain, *Reformed Catholicity*, 67–70. This was because they regarded this tradition as good. Note, e.g., Luther's view that "there is much that is Christian and good under the papacy . . . true baptism, the true sacrament of the altar, the true keys to the forgiveness of sins, the true office of the ministry, the true catechism in the form of the Lord's Prayer, the Ten Commandments, and the articles of the Creed." Martin Luther, *Concerning Rebaptism: A Letter of Martin Luther to Two Pastors*, LW 40:231–32.

[34] Steiger, "Development," 699, 702. We see in the preface ("epitome") to the Lutheran *Formula of Concord* (1577), e.g., exactly this kind of dual commitment to Scripture and tradition. Scripture is "the only rule and norm" by which doctrines and teachers are to be evaluated, but the authors of the *Formula* clearly wish to stand at the same time in the tradition represented by the Apostles' Creed, the Nicene Creed, and the Athanasian Creed: "We pledge ourselves to these and we hereby reject all heresies and teachings which have been introduced into the church of God contrary to them." These "are not judges like Holy Scripture"; they are, nevertheless, not to be despised, but honored. Theodore G. Tappert, ed., *The Book of Concord: The Confessions of the Evangelical Lutheran Church* (Philadelphia: Fortress, 1959), 464–65.

[35] Vanhoozer, *Biblical Authority*, 127.

[36] "Descartes and Voltaire only extended the reach of individualism and rationalism beyond the narrow confines of Luther's initial endeavors." Allen and Swain, *Reformed Catholicity*, 55–56, reflecting on some words of Alexis de Tocqueville (1805–59). Yet the extension is surely marked.

what Scripture really says. What is refused in these words is capitulation merely on the basis of claimed authority. It was already Luther's complaint with respect to his meetings with Cardinal Cajetan in Augsburg in 1518 that argument was being met merely with power:

> Luther later remembered this meeting as a turning point that led to his final break with Rome. If Cajetan had heard him out, he later recalled, had he been willing to consider scriptural proof rather than simply demanding blind obedience to papal fiat, things might have turned out differently.[37]

Indeed, throughout the early years of the Reformation prior to Worms the historical record is replete with Luther's appeals to be *shown* where he is in error, accompanied by promises to recant if genuine heresy can be demonstrated. Luther is not an individualist (for all that some of his more bombastic statements about himself in his various writings can certainly make him sound like one).[38] He is an individual, appealing to the wider community of Christians and Bible readers to exercise their own individual and corporate judgment as to whether what he is claiming about Scripture and Christian faith is, in fact, true. This is the same posture struck by his Strasbourg contemporary, Wolfgang Capito (1478–1541). Acknowledging the damage done by genuinely arrogant individualism in the course of the Reformation, Capito appeals to 1 Corinthians 14:29-32 as offering a biblical model for handling questions of individual judgment constructively and communally. In this context he invites his interlocutor, Jacob Sturm, to offer criticisms of his own (Capito's) work.[39] Individualism is dangerous, Capito agrees; there must be accountability to a larger community. That community includes (foundationally) the apostles, but for the magisterial Reformers it also includes the Church Fathers—not least when gathered together in councils and articulating creeds—as well as the contemporary Christian community. It is to this community that Luther characteristically appeals: "Whatever argument is better" in this court of appeal "is the one that should prevail in the church."[40]

What is also striking in the historical record prior to Worms—in an era when people had more and more access to primary scriptural and patristic sources

---

[37] Timothy George, *Reading Scripture with the Reformers* (Downers Grove, Ill.: InterVarsity, 2011), 111–12. "Luther was offended by Cajetan's repeated withdrawal into authoritarian behavior." Brecht, *Luther: His Road*, 1:253.

[38] So also Vanhoozer, *Biblical Authority*, 36: "I disagree with critics who blame individual autonomy on the Reformers, even if the blood trail seems to lead back to Luther's 'Here I stand'" (see also 96).

[39] Hobbs, "Pluriformity," 465–66. Erasmus in his *Paraclesis* (*Exhortation*, 1516) had appealed to his contemporaries' own judgment using this same biblical text, as had Luther in his letter *To the Christian Nobility* (1520).

[40] Brecht, *Luther: His Road*, 1:372.

against which the teaching of the medieval Church could be measured—is just how often those who heard and read Luther became convinced by his arguments, even if they had begun by resolutely opposing him on the basis of their own immersion in medieval scholastic theology (on which see my chapter 11). In 1516 Luther's Wittenberg colleague Karlstadt, for example, "who did not even own a Bible when he earned the doctor of theology degree or for many years afterward," appears in the record "as an opponent of Luther's interpretation of Augustine" and some of his other opinions. Yet very shortly thereafter Karlstadt "became convinced of Luther's views," not least because he had bought Augustine's works and actually read them for himself, finding as he did so that "the scholastic edifice collapsed."[41] Another Wittenberg opponent, Thomas Doelsch, describes his own bondage to medieval scholasticism before Luther—impressing him in debates about Scripture—persuaded him to turn instead to the study of the Church Fathers and the Bible.[42] Faced for the first time with Luther's provocative tract *The Babylonian Captivity of the Church* (1520), Johannes Bugenhagen "felt that Luther was the wickedest heretic; however, after examining it thoroughly he believed that Luther was the only man who had recognized the truth in the prevailing blindness and darkness."[43] Luther's arguments did "prevail" for many people in the Church of his time—including many who ultimately chose not to join the Protestant movement—and the hierarchy of the Church was *widely* perceived on the other hand as resorting to power in the place of cogent argument. It was this fact that led John Eck to lament that even the papal bull of 1520 threatening Luther with excommunication "lacked a refutation of Luther's errors on the basis of the Bible, the church fathers, and the decisions of church councils."[44]

Conviction in the Radical Reformation

It is this emphasis on the need for reasoned argument in the context of community that partly explains why the magisterial Reformers were so critical of those who participated in the Radical Reformation. Within this movement individual judgments about the meaning of "Scripture alone" could be valued very highly in relation to tradition (including what was regarded as *Protestant* tradition).[45] Moreover, the community (if any) to which such judgments were submitted

---

[41] Brecht, *Luther: His Road*, 1:84, 121, 168–70.
[42] Brecht, *Luther: His Road*, 1:340–41.
[43] Brecht, *Luther: His Road*, 1:384.
[44] Brecht, *Luther: His Road*, 1:394.
[45] Radicals could perceive the magisterial Reformers, indeed, as "damnable 'scribes' or 'new popes,'" suppressing the truth of Scripture in much the same way that the Catholics did. Goertz, "Scriptural Interpretation," 577.

could be a very small subsection of the Christian Church.[46] So the hermeneutical community to which the Spirit-filled reader was accountable, in theory comprising "the priesthood of all believers," in practice amounted to something much less substantial.[47] The "Scripture alone" with which the Bible reader was wrestling was also, typically, much smaller than the one that Reformation theory demanded. For the most part in the Radical Reformation it was the NT alone that functioned authoritatively. The OT was much less important and tended to be read allegorically in much the same way as prior to the Reformation.

For some Radical Reformers, indeed, even NT Scripture was not finally of great importance for the Christian life. Augustine had proposed in *On Christian Doctrine* (although he is not the only Church Father to touch on this theme) that the person perfectly shaped by the Christian virtues of faith, hope, and love no longer needed Scripture.[48] This was an influential opinion in what is sometimes referred to as the "late medieval spiritualism" of the eleventh through the fourteenth centuries, with its marked dichotomies between spirit and matter, the outer and the inner, institutions and personal faith, mediated salvation and an immediate relationship with God. It was common in this multifaceted movement for all "external" forms of religion to be dismissed as useless for salvation; the fundamentally important thing was to live a simple Christian life. Already in some of its streams in the early eleventh century we find the Scriptures themselves being classed as "external," with a pronounced emphasis being placed on the Spirit who is given to the individual believer and brings that believer personal, internal illumination and knowledge. It is this illumination and knowledge that then opens up the "external" Scriptures to him. In the twelfth century, Joachim of Fiore (1132–1202) anticipates a "time of the Spirit," shortly to arrive, in which a perfect knowledge of reality becomes generally available—an inner illumination, contrasted with scholastic, rationally derived knowledge, which renders Scripture (as well as sacraments and clergy) entirely unnecessary. This collection of "spiritualist" ideas—high regard for the individual or group filled with the Spirit; belief in a higher form of knowledge bestowed on the Spirit-filled person that makes superfluous the "letter" of Scripture; suspicion of external forms of religion, including Scripture; an emphasis on Christian living rather than on dogma—often appears in the literature of Christian humanism in the Renaissance period, where the explicit goal of scholarship is ultimately mystical communion with the

---

[46] This had a lot to do, of course, with the political and social circumstances in which adherents of the Radical Reformation found themselves—a heavily persecuted minority trying to make their way within larger Christian states that viewed the Church and the world quite differently.

[47] For a proper "reformed" account of the priesthood of all believers, see Vanhoozer, *Biblical Authority*, 147–78.

[48] Augustine, *On Christian Doctrine*, 1.39.43 (NPNF 1, 2:534).

divine. It reflects an increasing swing more generally in the fourteenth century toward personal rather than institutional religion. We may note in this connection, for example, the mysticism of Johann Tauler (1300–1361)—a pupil of the German Dominican Johannes (Meister) Eckhardt (1260–1327) who greatly influenced Luther.

In line with this "spiritualism," some Radical Reformers regarded all Scripture as dead "letter" in relation to "spirit." Caspar von Schwenckfeld (1489–1561), for example, sharply distinguishes the letter of Scripture from the divine word.[49] Sebastian Franck (1499–1542) claims that Scripture is not divine revelation but only a witness for the conscience.[50] For Thomas Müntzer (c. 1489–1525) Scripture is a dead thing in the hands of priests; the Spirit of Christ is needed to bring it to life. This kind of approach to hermeneutics in the course of the Reformation was not at all reluctant to call into question even firmly established, creedal, Christian doctrine, including the doctrine of the Trinity. In this kind of radical Pietism, after all, the true Church was not found in the externally organized institution *called* the Church. It was not found even among those holding to orthodox Christian doctrine. So long as their way of life was "Christlike," even heretics could belong to this Church. How people *lived* was much more important than what they *believed*. Indeed, the "inner illumination" upon which this kind of Pietism was founded soon led many of its adherents into quite different religious systems like Deism and Unitarianism—"humanisms" quite cut off from their roots in Christian doctrine.[51]

SOLA SCRIPTURA AND THE RULE OF FAITH

The magisterial Reformers were at pains to distance themselves from all such approaches to individual judgment when it came to the reading of Scripture, the formation of doctrine, and the delineation of Christian practice. None of this was what they meant by invoking *sola Scriptura*. Of Müntzer, in fact, Melanchthon simply notes, sadly, that "he did not remain on the Scriptural path."[52] In the thinking of the magisterial Reformers it was a great mistake to place a higher epistemological value on the work of the Holy Spirit in the believer's heart than on God's revelation of himself through Scripture, and to insist that only the inner endowment of the Spirit, at the individual level, allowed Scripture to be properly,

---

[49] Goertz, "Scriptural Interpretation," 597.
[50] Goertz, "Scriptural Interpretation," 598.
[51] Goertz, "Scriptural Interpretation," 600–601.
[52] Goertz, "Scriptural Interpretation," 580, 583. For a brief essay on Luther's attitude toward the various radical Christian groups of his time (whom he labeled "*Schwärmer*"), see Amy Nelson Burnett, "Luther and the Schwärmer," in *The Oxford Handbook of Martin Luther's Theology* (ed. Robert Kolb et al.; Oxford: Oxford University Press, 2014), 511–24.

"charismatically" interpreted. For Luther and Calvin, the mind of the Holy Spirit could be recognized only *through* Scripture, as it was carefully and diligently (and prayerfully) read within the community of the Church stretching back through the ages and down to the present time.[53] "The Spirit is [certainly] required for the understanding of Scripture, both as a whole and in any part of it," writes Luther, in *Bondage of the Will*. However, the Spirit's work of *interior* illumination is intrinsically bound up with his work of *exterior* illumination, whereby "everything there is in the Scriptures has been brought out by the Word into the most definite light, and published to all the world."[54] For Calvin, likewise, "the inner witness of the Spirit" meant that "what was plain in the text was also true in experience. The idea that the inner witness might somehow lead to a private (and off-beat) interpretation of the Bible was the farthest thing from his mind."[55]

It now becomes possible to see, then, that in the Reformers' articulation of *sola Scriptura* we are not dealing with a novelty at all. This Reformation view of Scripture as the rule of faith or the rule of truth—reflected, for example, in the statements in the French Confession of 1559 that Scripture is "the sure rule of our faith" and "the rule of all truth" (articles 4 and 5)[56]—is deeply rooted in ancient perspectives concerning Scripture such as those of Irenaeus and Tertullian (my chapter 2). "This is ... the purpose of the ancient Rule of Faith ... to encourage canon-conscious and Christ-centered reading.... [It] summarizes the basic biblical story line and shows how the story is fulfilled in the death and resurrection of Jesus."[57] These same perspectives are clearly present in other Church Fathers as well.

In the mid-fourth century, for example, Cyril of Jerusalem's *Catechetical Lectures*, delivered to new believers to explain to them the principal doctrines of the Christian faith, advise them explicitly that if he (Bishop Cyril) presents them

---

[53] This was also true of the Swiss Reformer Huldrych Zwingli, although early in the Reformation years (1522) he published a famous sermon that turned out to be capable of misconstruction on the point. "God's word can be understood by us without any human instruction," he affirmed therein, "owing not to our understanding but to the light or Spirit of God, shining and breathing through the words in such a way that in the Spirit's own light we perceive the rays of divine teaching." His point was that understanding was dependent not on the pope or the tradition of the Church but on the guidance of the Holy Spirit as authorized preachers communicated God's Word. In subsequent years he found it necessary to emphasize that the Spirit speaks through and interprets Scripture and does not speak apart from Scripture—precisely because of the assertions of the Radical Reformation to the contrary. Huldrych Zwingli, *The Clarity and Certainty of the Word of God*, in *Early Protestant Spirituality* (ed. Scott H. Hendrix; New York: Paulist Press, 2009), 43–48 (44–45).
[54] Luther, *Bondage*, LW 33:28.
[55] Bray, *Biblical Interpretation*, 193.
[56] Cochrane, *Reformed Confessions*, 145.
[57] Vanhoozer, *Biblical Authority*, 128.

with any teaching that cannot be validated from Scripture, they should reject it. His authority as a bishop depends upon the conformity of his teachings to the Bible.[58] Gregory of Nyssa (c. 335–395) affirms that "we make the Holy Scriptures the rule and the measure of every tenet; we necessarily fix our eyes upon that, and approve that alone which may be made to harmonize with the intention of those writings."[59] John Chrysostom (c. 347–407) likewise strongly advocates the embrace of the OT *kanōn* shared with the Jews as the standard against which to measure doctrine and practice.[60] He refers to "the norm of Sacred Scripture" in which we should display more confidence than in our own reason.[61] In the course of writing about the doctrine of the Trinity, finally, Augustine grounds his teaching in "the canonical rule, as it is both *disseminated* through the Scriptures, and has been *demonstrated* by learned and Catholic handlers of the same Scriptures."[62] It is Scripture as the rule of faith that provides the context in which readers must wrestle with difficult passages.[63] Like other Church Fathers, Augustine could refer to *summaries* of the Great Story using this language of "rule of faith/truth," but these were indeed summaries of *Scripture*, and not an "external" rule being brought to bear *upon* Scripture: "nowhere is there even a hint [in Augustine] that the *regula fidei* is based, not on God's written Word, but on the active faith of the Church."[64]

It is in this ancient tradition of Scripture as the "final authority for faith and practice"[65] (i.e., the norm that cannot be normed) that Reformers like Luther and

---

[58] "Even to me, who tell thee these things, give no absolute credence, unless thou receive the proof of the things which I announce from the Divine Scriptures. For this salvation which we believe depends not on ingenious reasoning, but on demonstration of the Holy Scriptures." Cyril of Jerusalem, *Catechetical Lectures*, 4.17 (NPNF 2, 7:23); see also 5.12 (NPNF 2, 7:32).

[59] Gregory of Nyssa, *De anima et resurrectione* (*The Soul and the Resurrection*) (NPNF 2, 5:439).

[60] "We ... should obey the teaching of Sacred Scripture; let us follow its canon, place its wholesome doctrines in our mind, and with protection from it take good care of our own welfare." John Chrysostom, *Homilies on Genesis*, 5.15, in *Homilies on Genesis 1–17*, 74.

[61] "Do you see into what absurdity ... people fall who are unwilling to take their cue from the norm of Sacred Scripture but rather have complete confidence in their own reasoning?" Chrysostom, *Homilies on Genesis*, 58.13, in *Saint John Chrysostom: Homilies on Genesis 46–67* (ed. Thomas P. Halton et al.; trans. Robert C. Hill; FC 87; Washington, D.C.: Catholic University of America Press, 1992), 160. His particular topic in this instance is the necessity of the incarnation as a historical fact.

[62] Augustine, *De trinitate* (*The Trinity*), 2.1.2 (NPNF 1, 3:37) (emphasis added).

[63] Augustine, *City of God*, 15.7, 26 (NPNF 1, 2:288, 306).

[64] Andries D. R. Polman, *The Word of God According to St. Augustine* (Grand Rapids: Eerdmans, 1961), 211, who distinguishes Augustine in his "summarizing" use of this language from Church Fathers like Clement of Alexandria, Athanasius, Origen, Chrysostom, and Hilary of Poitiers, who "*fully* equated Scripture with the rule of faith" (209; emphasis added).

[65] Allen and Swain, *Reformed Catholicity*, 83.

Calvin root themselves. They agree with the Swiss Reformer Heinrich Bullinger (successor to Huldrych Zwingli in Zurich, 1504–1575), that "the Church does not judge according to its own pleasure, but according to the sentence of the Holy Spirit and the order and rule of the Holy Scriptures."[66] Nevertheless, it is from *within* the ongoing life of the Church—the Church since its inception and down to its present—that this judgment is to be exercised. The doctrine of *sola Scriptura* was not developed by the Reformers in order to allow the Bible to function essentially as a weapon that could be deployed against the Church by those holding quite alien worldviews and ideologies (even while perhaps asserting them to be Christian). This doctrine was developed in order to protect and enhance the ability of the Church to discriminate, in the context of its own community life together, between beliefs and practices that are truly apostolic and biblical and beliefs and practices that are not—in Bullinger's words, the ability "to give judgment on doctrines."[67] As is often said nowadays, *sola Scriptura* was not for them, and should not be for us, *solo Scriptura*—the latter memorably described by Michael Allen and Scott Swain as that "bastard child nursed at the breast [not of the Reformation, but] of modern rationalism and individualism."[68] If a synonym is sought for *sola Scriptura*, it would better be *prima Scriptura*. Scripture is the rule of faith that guides the Church, as it passes on Christian tradition, concerning what is valid tradition and what is not:

> [I]t is not that Scripture is alone in the sense that it is the sole source of theology; rather, Scripture "alone" is the *primary* or *supreme* authority in theology. "Scripture alone" excludes rivals such as the teaching office of the church and church tradition when it comes to the role of *infallible* (magisterial) authority. It does not eliminate other sources and resources of theology altogether. The challenge for those who wish to maintain *sola scriptura* is to locate it rightly in the broader pattern or economy as the *primal* and *final*, but not the sole, authority.[69]

SCRIPTURE AGAINST TRADITIONS

Did, and does, the Church *require* such an ability to discriminate between beliefs and practices that are truly apostolic and biblical and those that are not? The Reformers, like the Church Fathers before them, certainly thought so. As they

---

[66] Heinrich Bullinger, "Of the Holy Catholic Church," in *Zwingli and Bullinger* (ed. G. W. Bromiley; LCC 24; London: SCM Press, 1953), 283–325 (323).

[67] Bullinger, "Holy Catholic Church," 323.

[68] Allen and Swain, *Reformed Catholicity*, 85. "*Solo scriptura* is something altogether different from *sola scriptura*: the latter affirms 'that our final authority is Scripture alone, but not a Scripture that is alone.'" Vanhoozer, *Biblical Authority*, 121, quoting Keith Mathison. Again, "[i]t is a grievous mistake to think that *sola scriptura* entails *nulla traditio* [no tradition]" (137).

[69] Vanhoozer, *Biblical Authority*, 111.

looked soberly at the Church of their own time they considered it to have been substantially corrupted by merely human traditions. As they looked back into history, moreover—taking the Church Fathers at their own word[70]—they found good reason to think that at least some of the blame lay with those Fathers themselves and not only with the medieval popes. The Reformers were not shy about criticizing any aspect of past understanding, recent or ancient, that was implicated in the problem.

Measured Distance

Calvin, for example, may have been "unwilling to depart from the exegetical choices made by his favorite patristic exegetes," but at the same time he had less favorite patristic exegetes, and in general—regarding exegesis more than doctrine—the Fathers were for Calvin "debating partners with whom he is just as likely to disagree" as agree.[71] With respect to Augustine, for example, Calvin adopts what Ward Holder has described as "a measured distancing of himself" from that great bishop's interpretative practice, depending on him for hermeneutics but not for exegesis.[72] We have seen indeed throughout the present book the way that both Calvin and Luther (as well as others) excoriate the Fathers more generally for the "spiritual" way in which they approach the reading of Scripture in a wide range of their writings, opening up thereby all sorts of opportunity for error. These comments by no means exhaust the Reformers' critique of their ancestors. Luther, in particular, can sometimes express himself very strongly concerning the Fathers. Of Jerome, for example, he can say, "I know no doctor [of the Church] whom I hate so much, although I once loved him ardently and read him voraciously. Surely, there's more learning in Aesop than in all of Jerome."[73] The Reformers were certainly not of the view, then (to put it mildly), that the

---

[70] "[W]e do not despise the interpretations of the holy Greek and Latin fathers ... but we modestly dissent from them when they are found to set down things differing from, or altogether contrary to, the Scriptures. Neither do we think that we do them any wrong in this matter; seeing that they all, with one consent, will not have their writings equated with the canonical Scriptures, but command us to prove how far they agree or disagree with them, and to accept what is in agreement and to reject what is in disagreement." *The Second Helvetic Confession* (1566), 2. Cochrane, *Reformed Confessions*, 226–27.

[71] Thompson, "Calvin as a Biblical Interpreter," 65. Tony Lane puts the matter in this way: "Calvin's use of the fathers (especially in the *Institutio* and in the treatises) is primarily a polemical appeal to authorities. ... He also, less often, criticizes them," often preferring simply to ignore them when they do not agree with him. On exegetical matters in the *commentaries*, though, "Calvin cites others more often to disagree with them." Anthony N. S. Lane, *John Calvin: Student of the Church Fathers* (Grand Rapids: Baker, 1999), 3.

[72] Holder, *Grounding*, 186.

[73] Luther, *Table Talk*, LW 54:72. As a child Luther had developed a fondness for the fables of Aesop and others, and as an adult he still valued their wisdom highly. Brecht, *Luther: His Road*, 1:14.

Church Fathers arrive on the doorstep of later Christian interpreters as a kind of take-it-or-leave-it package mailed to them by God. They did not believe, for instance, that one could only accept their doctrinal teaching as articulated in the creeds if one could at the same time accept the way they read Scripture in defending this doctrine. To the contrary, the Reformers were quite happy to rummage through the patristic package to discover what was good and what was not.

Indeed, in the very same work (*The Councils and the Church*) in which Luther compares the state of the Church under the pope unfavorably with "the ways of the councils and fathers," he goes on to refer to Bernard of Clairvaux's opinion that one should not heed everything that the Fathers say, preferring rather to "drink from the spring itself [i.e., the Scriptures] than from the brook [i.e., the patristic writings flowing from the spring]." If we follow the brooks of the Fathers too much, Luther proposes, "they lead us too far away from the spring, and lose both their taste and nourishment, until they lose themselves in the salty sea, as happened under the papacy."[74] In any case, following the Fathers, *simpliciter*, is impossible, because "they are not only unequal, but often contradictory," and "[i]f we should try to bring them into accord with one another, far greater discord and disputes would ensue than we have at present, and we would never get out of it."[75] The councils of the Church are of no greater help—as Luther devotes an exhausting amount of space to demonstrating. In sum (and this is just the end of the long prologue to his treatise, as he pauses for breath!): "If it had not been for Holy Scripture, the church, had it depended on the councils and fathers, would not have lasted long."[76] Calvin is not of a different mind. In the very same preface to the *Institutes* in which he claims substantially to stand in line with the Fathers, he nevertheless points out that "those holy men were ignorant of many things, are often opposed to each other, and are sometimes at variance with themselves."[77]

NECESSARY DISCRIMINATION

For the Reformers, then, the contemporary Christian community really did require to exercise discrimination in respect of the tradition of the Church—including patristic tradition—holding it all accountable to the standard of apostolic and biblical belief and practice. They saw in their own time, just as clearly as we have seen in this book (in chapters 8 and 9), that even Christians throughout the ages who have made enormously important contributions to our understanding of Christian faith and life have made mistakes. Even "pious people" have been "subject to error," Luther was once disconcerted to discover (particularly with

---

[74] Luther, *Councils and the Church*, LW 41:20.
[75] Luther, *Councils and the Church*, LW 41:20.
[76] Luther, *Councils and the Church*, LW 41:52.
[77] Calvin, *Institutes*, preface, 4.

respect to Augustine).⁷⁸ We need to understand these errors so as not to repeat them, and the question of biblical warrant is central to that quest for understanding. It has been this way for Christians all through the ages, it was so for the Reformers, and it must surely remain so for us.

When some of the Church Fathers, for example, advocate as a true belief the natural immortality of the human soul, this is problematic. There is no scriptural support for this idea, and indeed 1 Timothy 6:15-16 explicitly tells us that "God ... alone is immortal." Nor is there any support for this doctrine among most of the early post-apostolic Christian writers, such as Clement of Rome, Ignatius of Antioch, Justin Martyr, and Irenaeus. Whence, then, does it arise? Athenagorus (c. AD 127–190) is apparently the first to assert its truth, and then Tertullian, who explicitly tells us—even with all his disdain for "mottled Christianity of Stoic, Platonic, and dialectic composition"—that he borrows it from Plato.⁷⁹ It is by way of Origen, then, and later (and decisively) by way of the early Augustine—in his heavily Platonically influenced treatise *The Immortality of the Soul* (387)—that the doctrine becomes entrenched in medieval theology. This is the case even though in his later *Reconsiderations* (426–427) Augustine expresses regret that *Immortality* had been published against his will and confesses that he himself can scarcely any longer follow its argument.⁸⁰

This is not a doctrine that should be believed; it has entered the Christian faith from an alien source, and it possesses no biblical warrant. In biblical faith, immortality comes to humanity as a gift from God in Christ that is not intrinsic to our created nature. We require to be "clothed" with it (1 Cor 15:50-57).

CONTINUING ATTENTIVENESS

Continuing attentiveness to such unfortunate influences on Christian faith and practice from other faiths and philosophies is exactly what an ongoing

---

⁷⁸ Martin Luther, *Sermons on the Gospel of St. John Chapters 1–4* (1537–1539), LW 22:258, 267–68. Athanasius, e.g. (c. AD 296–373), so crucially important to the establishing of orthodox Christology in the fourth century over against the serious errors of Arianism, nevertheless could not bring himself (because of prior philosophical commitments) to accept what Scripture plainly tells us about Jesus thirsting on the cross and being ignorant of the date of the Second Coming. Bray, *Biblical Interpretation*, 85.

⁷⁹ "For some things are known even by nature: the immortality of the soul, for instance, is held by many; the knowledge of our God is possessed by all. I may use, therefore, the opinion of a Plato, when he declares, 'Every soul is immortal.'" Tertullian, *De resurrectione carnis* (*The Resurrection of the Flesh*), 3 (ANF 3:547). Cf. also Tertullian, *The Soul*, 22 (ANF 3:202), even while proceeding to distance himself from Plato.

⁸⁰ Augustine, *Retractionum* (*Reconsiderations*) 1.5.1, in *Saint Augustine: The Retractions* (ed. Roy Joseph Deferrari et al.; trans. Mary Inez Bogan; FC 60; Washington, D.C.: Catholic University of America Press, 1968), 20.

commitment to *sola Scriptura* requires of us, as we sift the Christian tradition for what is true and helpful and what is not. It is not just Platonism that requires our attention in such respects, although Platonism clearly does, not least because the Christian faith of both Augustine and then Gregory the Great—two huge influences on the medieval Church—was so heavily influenced by Platonic perspectives.[81] However, it should equally be a matter of concern to us when Ambrose introduces Stoic ethics into Christian faith through "the back door" of the edifice of Christian ethics by way of allegorical reading[82]—since Stoicism is not biblical faith either. Thomas Aquinas later clearly understood this point about both Platonism and Stoicism because his own Aristotelian commitments gave him sufficient distance from both of them to be able to see more clearly than most of his predecessors just how problematic some of their influences on Christian faith had been.[83] Of course, the influence of Aristotle on Thomas and those who came after him must then also be scrutinized; the light of Scripture must also shine on the "medieval synthesis" between faith and philosophy that Thomas himself produced. So must it shine on subsequent biblical and theological endeavor of every kind, as we seek to remain attentive to the question of whether we still hold to "the faith that was once for all entrusted to the saints" (Jude 3). This includes Protestant endeavor—since *sola Scriptura* cannot with integrity be invoked by Protestants simply to attack the practices of others (indulgences in the sixteenth century, say, or papal infallibility in the present) of which they happen to disapprove. Many Protestants have in fact believed in the natural immortality of the soul, just like their Roman Catholic counterparts. If it is to be of any value, a canon must be *used* actually to measure things. All too often, in Protestant churches as in others, it is not:

> One might think that "canonization" would imply that the texts being canonized took on a regulative function which they formerly lacked. Such is, perhaps, the Protestant theory of the subordination of the Church to the canon of Scripture, so that the Church's beliefs must be adjusted to bring them into line with Scripture. But this does not usually seem to be how matters turn out in practice—not even in Protestant churches with a high doctrine of Scripture. For the most part religious communities interpret their Scriptures in the light of the doctrine and practice they have come, by custom and usage, to regard as correct. Thus any

---

[81] Reventlow, *Biblical Interpretation*, 2:100, 105.

[82] Reventlow, *Biblical Interpretation*, 2:55–56.

[83] Note, e.g., Aquinas' refusal, in his commentary on Romans, to interpret Sir 30:22 in a Stoic manner as advocating the avoidance of sorrow—largely on biblical grounds. Reventlow, *Biblical Interpretation*, 2:199.

conflict there may be between Scripture and doctrine is masked, and is deprived of its power to threaten.[84]

We are all capable of making mistakes. All must look to Scripture to see whether we have—even as we recognize that "conceptions of *sola scriptura* that serve to marginalize or eclipse the significance of Christian tradition in the life of the church ... must be abandoned."[85]

THE PERSPICUITY OF SCRIPTURE

To sum up the argument of chapter 12 to this point, then: the magisterial Reformation makes a point of showing that it stands *within* tradition—in continuity with the ancient teaching of the Church, as disseminated by the apostles, summarized in the early councils and creeds, and demonstrated by the teaching and practice of the Church in all sorts of fundamentally right ways throughout history. At the same time, the teaching of the prophets and the apostles that provides the very foundation of Christian faith, as contained in the Holy Scriptures, remains the rule of faith by which all that is claimed to be Christian doctrine and practice—whether by Church Fathers, popes, bishops, or magisterial and other Reformers—must ultimately be measured. To stand in line with the Reformers involves this same commitment to standing *within* Christian Tradition (capital T) while being willing, where necessary, to criticize Christian traditions (plural) on the basis of scriptural teaching.

This brings us, inevitably, to the question of the perspicuity of Scripture. For if Scripture is to function in this canonical manner, it must necessarily be clear in what it says. This is in fact what the Reformers believed about it. Here again, however, we must pause to consider what they meant by what they said, given that we live in a world where

> the Reformational doctrine of perspicuity has been transformed in much popular Christianity and some scholarly reflection as well to function as the theological equivalent of philosophical objectivity, namely, the belief that any honest observer can, by the use of appropriate measures, always gain the appropriate interpretation of a biblical text.[86]

---

[84] Barton, "Significance," 77–78.

[85] John R. Franke, "Scripture, Tradition and Authority: Reconstructing the Evangelical Conception of *Sola Scriptura*," in *Evangelicals and Scripture: Tradition, Authority and Hermeneutics* (ed. Vincent E. Bacote, Laura Miguelez Quay, and Dennis L. Okholm; Downers Grove, Ill.: InterVarsity, 2004), 192–210 (210).

[86] Allen and Swain, *Reformed Catholicity*, 85.

Indeed, it often appears that when modern Bible readers refer to the "literal" sense of Scripture they are working with just this kind of view of the text. Their opinion seems to be that the text is (or should be) immediately and unproblematically accessible to them such that the literal sense is also the "obvious" or the "plain" sense. This is language to which I promised in chapter 4 eventually to return, and in the interests of clarity I need to do so now.

PERSPICUITY AND THE PLAIN SENSE

Although it is natural to assume that when modern writers refer to the "plain sense" of a biblical text they are indeed referring to the "obvious" meaning of the words on the page—the literal sense—this is not necessarily so. For a significant number of modern authors "the plain sense of Scripture is not an obvious meaning inscribed in the text but the religious community's witness to scripture's authoritative meaning." The plain sense is in fact to be *distinguished* from the literal sense.[87] This has the potential to be confusing to the uninitiated, and I do not consider it to be a helpful development. The point to which such authors hope to draw our attention, nevertheless, is an important one. The literal sense of a text does not arise in some kind of self-evident, objective way from the literality of the text itself, as a set of marks or signs on the page. Their significance, in fact, "often lies beyond the comprehension of the one who encounters them,"[88] as the story of the Ethiopian eunuch in Acts 8 reminds us. Here was a man reading a biblical text with seriousness, but he did not yet have much idea about its meaning. As interpreters we always come to a text from *"somewhere"*—and this "somewhere" will already have predisposed us to look at the text in certain ways, to ask certain questions of it, and even to make judgments about what is "obvious" in it.

This is important when we come to consider what "perspicuity" as applied to Scripture may reasonably be supposed to mean. It cannot mean that what every biblical text is truly saying is immediately and objectively obvious to every reader. Scripture itself forbids us from holding such a view. Nor is this what the Reformers thought that "perspicuity" meant. Consider again a quotation from Martin Luther that we first came across in chapter 1: "The subject matter of the Scriptures . . . is all quite accessible, even though some texts are still obscure owing to our ignorance of their terms. . . . If the words are obscure in one place, yet they are plain in another."[89] Even in a Scripture that is "perfect," some biblical texts remain obscure—at least at the moment when we first encounter them. However, the subject matter of Scripture overall is clear enough; it "offers a clear account of the

---

[87] John E. Thiel, *Senses of Tradition: Continuity and Development in Catholic Faith* (Oxford: Oxford University Press, 2000), 36.
[88] Thiel, *Senses of Tradition*, 32.
[89] Luther, *Bondage*, LW 33:26.

truth it is intended to convey" when it is "interpreted according to the public rules of language."[90] It is certainly *sufficiently* clear "that one need not rely on the official magisterium of the church to mediate its meaning."[91] The *Westminster Confession of Faith* (1647), along similar lines, will later say this:

> All things in Scripture are not alike plain in themselves, nor alike clear unto all; yet those things which are necessary to be known, believed, and observed, for salvation are so clearly propounded and opened in some place of scripture or other, that not only the learned, but the unlearned, in a due use of ordinary means, may attain unto a sufficient understanding of them.[92]

Note that the clarity about which *Westminster* speaks is *sufficient*, not *entire* clarity. Scripture is sufficiently clear that it can accomplish the purposes for which God has providentially designed it, namely, to function as the rule of faith and life for the Church. As Isaiah 55:11 puts it, "[My word] will not return to me empty, but will accomplish what I desire, and achieve the purpose for which I sent it." It is, we note in *Westminster*, "those things which are necessary to be known, believed, and observed, for salvation" that are "clearly propounded and opened in some place of scripture or other" and may be sufficiently understood by the reader. Scripture has a purpose, which is not to teach us everything but only to provide us with necessary guidance in gaining a true faith and living a pious life. We shall return to this point in the next chapter; for the moment we should simply note that Scripture provides a *sufficient* amount of information of which we can gain a *sufficient* understanding.[93] In the words of John Webster,

> Holy Scripture is *sufficient* for the instruction of the saints as they are conveyed by God towards eternal fellowship with himself. The prophets and apostles are not one element in a larger canvas, or even the most important element. Rather, in

---

[90] Kathryn Greene-McCreight, "Scripture, Clarity of," *DTIB*, 727–30 (728). So, too, Matthias Flacius Illyricus (1520–1575), who studied in Wittenberg and then in 1544 became a professor in Hebrew there: "Although there are great impediments to an adequate understanding of the biblical texts, partly in the text itself and partly in our own spirit ... [b]y means of general philological and hermeneutical methods its content can be evidently outlined for everyone." Oftestad, "Development," 611.

[91] Greene-McCreight, "Scripture," 728.

[92] *Westminster Confession of Faith*, 1.7, in *The Creeds of Christendom, with a History and Critical Notes* (vol. 3; ed. Philip Schaff; Grand Rapids: Baker, 1977), 604.

[93] See already in 1560 *The Scottish Confession of Faith*, 19: "we believe and confess the Scriptures of God sufficient to instruct and make perfect the man of God." Cochrane, *Reformed Confessions*, 177. The *Belgic Confession of Faith* (1561) says much the same, at greater length, in its seventh article, and *The Second Helvetic Confession* (1566) in its first article. Cochrane, *Reformed Confessions*, 192, 224.

their words we have the fullness of what for now the Spirit says to the churches. Scripture is *enough*.[94]

Note too that in *Westminster*, while both "the learned" and "the unlearned" may gain sufficient understanding of biblical truth, access to it *requires* something of both groups. It requires that they "use . . . means." They are "ordinary" means, for sure—they do not involve esoteric, "gnostic" knowledge, for example. Nevertheless, the use of "means" is required. *Westminster* does not tell us exactly what they are, but it is not difficult to construct a list on the basis of what we know about common Reformation emphases concerning Scripture. The "due use of ordinary means" involves, among other things, applying oneself to the serious reading of the Scriptures—preferably in Hebrew and Greek, but at least in a reliable translation—with the aid of documentary and personal resources (e.g., commentaries and lexicons, pastor and elders) where they are available. It involves seeking to understand the individual texts within the whole sweep of the canonical story, and refusing to read any text in ways that lead to belief or practice inconsistent with the wider biblical context. All of this is to be carried out in a prayerful attitude and in dependence upon the Holy Spirit. It is to these kinds of "means" that Francis Turretin (1623–1687) refers in the late seventeenth century when explaining what the perspicuity of Scripture does and does not involve. We are not to think of perspicuity as excluding

> necessary means for interpretation, such as the inner light of the Spirit, the attention of the mind, the voice and ministry of the church, lectures and commentaries, prayers and vigils. We acknowledge such means are not only useful but also normally are necessary, but we want to deny any obscurity that keeps the common people from reading Scripture, as if it were harmful or dangerous, or that leads to a falling back on traditions when one should have taken a stand on Scripture alone.[95]

In other words, the perspicuity of Scripture in "reformed" thinking does not obviate the need for determined application and hard work, undertaken in the correct frame of mind and with the right posture.

Perspicuity and Perspiration

That is to say: in the thinking of the Reformers, Scripture is not perspicuous to the ungodly who pay it no attention,[96] nor to all Bible readers across the whole

---

[94] John Webster, *The Domain of the Word: Scripture and Theological Reason* (London: Bloomsbury T&T Clark, 2012), 18.
[95] Turretin, *Scripture*, 187–88.
[96] "[N]o one denies that Scripture is obscure to unbelievers and unregenerate people . . . the question is of the obscurity or perspicuity of the object, or Scripture; is it so obscure that a believing

breadth of what it teaches and irrespective of how much time and effort has been invested in comprehending it.[97] Scripture does not become comprehensible, for example, by way of the immediate illumination of the individual believer, as a Radical Reformer might well have believed. Perspicuity "occurs," rather, in the course of reading, meditating on, and searching Scripture itself, which is broadly accessible in its basic message to those who, relative to each other, are unlearned and learned. Yet the path of learning is, nevertheless, the path of understanding, and in the end "[i]ntensive hermeneutical work and philological competence are necessary in order to be able to experience the self-interpreting dynamism of Scripture."[98] The ideal "reformed" reader is, ultimately, the hermeneutical polymath

> who has profound knowledge of languages, but is also at home in the remaining *artes* [liberal arts], especially in rhetoric and logic. Knowledge of the *disciplinae reales* must be added, that is, in metaphysics, physics, ethics, politics, geography, chronology and history.[99]

Increasing competence in Scripture reading requires increasing erudition and piety; our ability to comprehend Scripture does not arrive in a sudden and blinding flash of light. Indeed, for premodern hermeneutics in general, "*misunderstanding* the biblical text is the norm, while only the combination of painstaking exegetical work and reading in relation with God can lead to an understanding of the word."[100]

Only this explains why the very Protestant movement that insisted so strongly on the perspicuity of Scripture alone was exactly the same movement under whose aegis the learning of biblical languages so dramatically flourished in sixteenth- and seventeenth-century Europe. Restricting ourselves just to the Hebrew language for the sake of establishing the point, "[t]he logic of *sola scriptura* impelled Protestants to pursue Hebrew learning in unprecedented numbers."[101] As Stephen Burnett notes, "[t]he sheer number of Christian Hebrew

---

person cannot comprehend it for salvation without the authority and decision of the church? This we deny." Turretin, *Scripture*, 185.

[97] "It is true that for many people much remains abstruse; but this is not due to the obscurity of Scripture, but to the blindness of indolence of those who will not take the trouble to look at the very clearest truth." Luther, *Bondage*, LW 33:27.

[98] Steiger, "Development," 716–18. For Calvin, e.g., Scripture's perspicuity "is rooted in the accessibility of [the] single, literal sense," discovered through knowing Greek and Hebrew, paying "attention to the historical context of any given passage, separation of doctrinal discussions from exposition of the text ... and a christocentric narrative/historical framework for the whole of the Bible." Greene-McCreight, "Scripture," 729.

[99] Steiger, "Development," 723.

[100] Zimmermann, *Theological Hermeneutics*, 128.

[101] Burnett, *Christian Hebraism*, 271. In response, "the apologetic and theological needs of Catholicism did the same for Catholic scholars."

books produced between 1501 and 1660 reflects the vibrancy of the new market and its perceived importance for supporting the new confessional churches."[102] If it was Scripture in its original languages that was perspicuous, then those original languages had to be learned. In Protestant Europe, therefore,

> Hebrew learning sank deep roots, becoming part not only of university learning but also not infrequently of Latin school instruction as well. The enormous numbers of beginning grammars, readers, anthologies, manuals, and even polyglot catechisms produced there point to strong customer demand among beginning and intermediate Hebrew students for textbooks.[103]

In order to get to the marrow of the matter, moreover, "[b]oth Anglican and Reformed scholars pursued Near Eastern language studies, and they employed the Semitic languages as tools for comparative biblical philology."[104]

In sum, the Reformers opposed, with their doctrine of the perspicuity of Scripture, "the authority of interpretative traditions or élites" in respect of Bible reading, defending "the priority of 'original' reading over reading which [was] merely customary or derivative."[105] They opposed the elitism of the medieval monks, for example, who believed that they alone could grasp the spiritual teaching that was concealed in Scripture, because they alone had acquired the esoteric knowledge that allowed them to unlock its secrets—an elitism that left even the average parish priest outside the circle of the wise, just as ignorant of Scripture as his flock.[106] However, the Reformers did not intend, in opposing this kind of elitism, to baptize anti-intellectualism and ignorance. They did not intend to create a *new* elite whose members prided themselves—on the ground that Scripture is "perspicuous" to all—in being able to read the Bible accurately and wisely without expending any thought or effort on the project, or listening to any advice about it, or accepting any leadership with respect to it. Scripture is *indeed* perspicuous to all who are intent on engaging with it rightly. It is not Scripture's fault, in the end, if we do not comprehend it. Yet comprehending Scripture requires among other things commitment and hard work.

Perspicuity in the Teaching of Jesus

Such is the Reformers' doctrine of the perspicuity of Scripture. Is it to be accepted? Just as the idea that Scripture is the final court of appeal with respect to doctrine

---

[102] Burnett, *Christian Hebraism*, 272.
[103] Burnett, *Christian Hebraism*, 275.
[104] Burnett, *Christian Hebraism*, 275.
[105] John Webster, *Holy Scripture: A Dogmatic Sketch* (CIT; Cambridge: Cambridge University Press, 2003), 93.
[106] Bray, *Biblical Interpretation*, 145–56.

and practice is deeply rooted both in Scripture and tradition, so too is the idea—the associated, necessary idea—that Scripture is perspicuous. This is not a doctrine that a German monk thought up during a quiet moment somewhere in northeastern Germany around the year 1517. Of course we ought to accept it.

As to Scripture, Jesus himself constantly appeals to the OT as the measure of what is true and right, and he evidently does so "not only with the expectation that this testimony will be accepted by faithful Jewish men and women, but that it will be intelligible to them. What use would there be in quoting texts no-one was able to understand?"[107] When he quotes Hosea 10:8 in Luke 23:28, for example, he appears to believe that "the images of this Old Testament text would be both recognizable and intelligible" to his hearers.[108] More generally, as we have already seen in my chapters 5 and 6, Jesus blames the two disciples on the Emmaus Road in Luke 24 for being "foolish" and "slow of heart to believe" with respect to "all that the prophets have spoken." He acknowledges that the meaning of Scripture has previously been obscured *from them*. However, the fault does not lie with Scripture, which is clear enough in the way that it prophesies of Christ; the meaning of its prophetic words is not difficult to discern. The fault lies with the *disciples* for failing to comprehend Scripture's perspicuous words—for failing to take steps ("use . . . ordinary means") to grasp its true meaning.

Jesus' opponents in John's Gospel, likewise, possess the Scriptures and indeed "diligently study" them (John 5:39). Because these holy texts are perspicuous and "testify about" Jesus, his opponents ought to become his disciples, yet "you refuse to come to me to have life" (John 5:40). The truth of Scripture is often described in the Gospels as being hidden from people along these lines. It is not that there is any deficiency in the "lamp" that God has given his people for their "feet"—the "light" that is provided for their "path" (Ps 119:105, KJV). The lamp shines brightly enough. Yet there is darkness in the human heart and mind, and people do not come into the light "because their deeds [are] evil" (John 3:19).

Beyond spiritual darkness, there is also just plain ignorance. People want to know what the Scriptures say, but they lack the necessary knowledge to make much progress. The Ethiopian eunuch in Acts 8 is sufficiently committed that, with an open and curious mind, he is already struggling with the biblical text, and he has made some progress; he knows that in this text a "prophet" is "talking" about someone (Acts 8:34). Significantly, God himself immediately acts to enlarge his understanding (Acts 8:26); he sends an angel with a message to Philip that he should travel in a direction that will intersect with the Ethiopian's path. Philip then takes this baffled reader deeper in his understanding of Scripture.

---

[107] Mark D. Thompson, *A Clear and Present Word: The Clarity of Scripture* (NSBT 21; Downers Grove, Ill.: InterVarsity, 2006), 83, with examples throughout 82–87.

[108] Thompson, *Clear and Present Word*, 84.

This is the kind of thing we would expect of a God who promises "seek, and you will find" (Matt 7:7). Those who desire to understand Scripture will be able to do so in the course of their journey with God; lack of understanding will give way to understanding.

Perspicuity in Apostolic Teaching

The apostles appeal to the OT Scriptures in the same way as Jesus, and what is initially striking here is that "the appeal is not reserved for Jewish audiences where some familiarity with the Scriptures ... might fairly be assumed."[109] It is also made in respect of Gentile audiences. Paul, for example, displays "general confidence in the accessible meaning of the Old Testament" so far as the church in Rome is concerned. This "does not preclude the possibility of difficulty with certain texts or indeed the reality of misunderstanding.... The text [however] is not surrounded by impenetrable darkness."[110] Those who are willing to make the effort to engage with it carefully will make progress in understanding, just like those who persevered in questioning Jesus further about his parables (e.g., Matt 13:36)—for the "secrets of the kingdom of heaven" (Matt 13:11) are available to all who pursue Jesus in this way. Even in Paul's own letters there are "some things that are hard to understand," admits Peter (2 Pet 3:16)—yet they, too, do not make the texts impenetrable. If they did, then it would make no sense for Peter to blame "ignorant and unstable people" for distorting Paul's letters "as they do the other Scriptures, to their own destruction." In other words, the Scriptures, in themselves, are clear enough—"a light shining in a dark place" (2 Pet 1:19). The apostles certainly did not regard them as possessing, in Mark Thompson's words, "any fundamental ambiguity or obscurity."[111]

Perspicuity in Tradition

As to Christian tradition, we have already encountered this same kind of emphasis on the perspicuity of Scripture in Irenaeus (my chapter 7): "the entire Scriptures, the prophets, and the Gospels, can be clearly, unambiguously, and harmoniously understood by all," he asserts in *Against Heresies*, "although all do not believe them."[112] It is also found among the Antiochenes, who were in general (chapter 8) highly critical of Origen's claim that Scripture as a whole is characterized by obscurity—deliberately so, in his view, in order to force the wise elites to search

---

[109] Thompson, *Clear and Present Word*, 88.
[110] Thompson, *Clear and Present Word*, 91, and generally throughout 87–92.
[111] Thompson, *Clear and Present Word*, 93.
[112] Irenaeus, *Against Heresies*, 2.27.2 (*ANF* 1:398).

out the deepest and truest meaning that is not "apparent at first sight."[113] The Antiochenes, conversely, worked on the assumption of general clarity in Scripture while acknowledging a degree of obscurity (especially in the OT) that had identifiable causes. One of these causes was the inexperience of Bible readers; another was that they were not reading the biblical texts in their original languages.[114] Augustine, as we have seen (my chapter 8), also presupposes the clarity of Scripture in general and provides all sorts of advice to its reader for dealing with its apparent unclarity. Much of this comes down to acquiring a good education. Scripture is perspicuous especially with respect to "all things needful for obtaining salvation and for living a godly life,"[115] but this does not necessarily make it easy always to interpret.[116] Moving beyond the patristic period, the same emphasis on perspicuity is also found in medieval writers like Aquinas and Bonaventure, among others.[117]

It is in this tradition of the Church concerning the clarity of Scripture, rooted in Scripture, that the Reformers take their stand. They do not espouse "a plenary perspicuity: the belief that the Scripture is in its entirety perspicuous." They do hold firmly, however, to a *genuine* perspicuity.[118] They do not believe that to read Scripture is to be "led through the thickets and brambles of seeming contradiction, blank oceans and dry deserts of obscure and uncertain material,"[119] in need of special reading methods to find our way. They believe instead that God means to reveal himself clearly to people through "ordinary means" as they read his Word, which is a lamp unto their feet. Scripture is not a puzzle to be solved by the wise, the Reformers assert, but a clear proclamation to be embraced by the poor in spirit and the pure of heart. All readers, to some extent, fail to "get it" as they read the Bible; many fail substantially, and some entirely. The problem does

---

[113] Origen, *First Principles*, Preface, 8 (ANF 4:241).
[114] Hill, *Antioch*, 30, 36, 42–43.
[115] Polman, *Word of God*, 67.
[116] Greene-McCreight, "Scripture," 728.
[117] For Aquinas, "Holy Writ ought to be able to state the truth without any fallacy." *Summa* 1.1.10. For Bonaventure, "all decisive theological statements are contained in the Bible," which "gives sufficient knowledge of first principles ... insofar as it is necessary for salvation"; obscure passages "should be explained by other passages that are clearer." Reventlow, *Biblical Interpretation*, 2:206, 212, 213, partially citing Bonaventure's *Brief Discourse*, 1.1.
[118] Richard M. Edwards, *Scriptural Perspicuity in the Early English Reformation in Historical Theology* (StBibLit 65; New York: Peter Lang, 2009), 89.
[119] O'Keefe and Reno, *Sanctified Vision*, 44. Their predominant view concerning Scripture's fundamental nature throughout this book is that it is a puzzle or a problem to be solved. Scripture represents "a complex and diverse set of data" (125), and the Fathers were engaged in assembling out of all its bits and pieces "a full and complete picture" (45). Only believing this could O'Keefe and Reno possibly find in the writings of Martin Heidegger an appropriate analogy to Scripture (46–47)!

not lie with the Bible, however. It lies with readers who are not yet sufficiently virtuous or educated to grasp it perfectly. It is such deficiencies that explain the gap between what we must believe to be the objective perspicuity of Scripture, on the one hand (since this is how we are instructed by Jesus and the apostles to think of it), and our subjective experiences of nonperspicuity, on the other. That is, we should not make the mistake of thinking that just because Scripture is currently obscure to *us*, it must be intrinsically and essentially obscure. Jesus and his apostles teach us otherwise.

ON INTERPRETATIVE PLURALISM

We are warranted, then, by both Scripture and tradition, in holding to the doctrines of *sola Scriptura* and the perspicuity of Scripture. We cannot and should not abandon these doctrines, even in the knowledge—and here we are circling back to the beginning of the chapter—that versions of them have indeed led some people into incorrect belief and practice. That is undoubtedly so; yet if the argument of this book is correct, the *absence* of these doctrines has also led many into incorrect belief and practice, which have survived in the Church precisely because of a refusal to submit them to prophetic and apostolic norms. We shall not solve the problem of incorrect belief and practice in the Church, then, by diminishing the importance of, or even abolishing, the very measuring stick or canon by which such things *become* "incorrect" in the first place.

Instead, a "reformed" approach to Scripture must insist on the maintenance of these doctrines even though we know that one of their consequences will inevitably be different opinions, even among substantially orthodox Christians, about exactly what to believe and how to practice this. This is inevitable because, on this side of the consummation of all things, there will always be something of a gap between what Scripture teaches, on the one hand, and what individuals and groups *believe* it to teach, on the other. There will always be a lack of complete consensus on such matters. This is because each one of us individually, in differing measure, is lacking in both virtue and knowledge, and because we are integrated into communities and cultures that are corporately lacking in the same. All of this inhibits us—peer pressure being a palpable reality—from making progress in virtue and knowledge. In such circumstances, while Scripture remains always perspicuous, it is inevitable that there will be plural interpretations about exactly what it requires of us. It is therefore inevitable—assuming that followers of Christ do take Scripture sufficiently seriously to allow it to shape their actions as well as their beliefs—that there are going to be different, if overlapping, visions of truly Christian belief and practice, and that there will be different churches and denominations created to support people pursuing these visions. Yet the inevitability of all this occurring in our fallen world, before the consummation of all things, did not prevent the prophets and the apostles from articulating the very ideas we are currently discussing; it was precisely into this darkened world that Scripture came as a lamp and a light. It does not justify us, either, in abandoning these same ideas. We need to affirm them, and then deal with the resultant interpretative pluralism as best we can. Central to this business of "doing the best we can," I profoundly believe, is a renewed commitment in the Church to robust Christian education—a topic to which we shall return in chapter 16.

CONCLUSION

The question of "arbitration" lies at the heart of the matter that the magisterial Reformers addressed in insisting on the perspicuity of Scripture alone. As we have seen, they did not believe in an "unbridled interpretation" of Scripture that would inevitably (as the Council of Trent proclaimed) "only lead to heresy." Nor, however, did they believe that the teaching of the Church in any given age could or should be immune from scrutiny on the basis of Scripture—Scripture that was certainly sufficiently clear in its teaching to be able to function as a "rule" by which doctrine and practice could be measured. The Reformers had ample warrant in both Scripture and tradition for their position, for all that it inevitably entailed in their time, and still entails in ours, interpretative pluralism. "Reformed" Christians must handle this ongoing pluralism with carefulness and integrity—even while believing that it arises, not from any lack of perspicuity on Scripture's part, but only from a lack of virtue and knowledge on ours.

13

The Authority of Scripture
Thy Word Is Truth

I have learned to ascribe honor only to those books that are called canonical, such that I strongly believe that none of their authors has erred.

—Martin Luther[1]

... the Law and the Prophecies are not a doctrine delivered according to the will and pleasure of men, but dictated by the Holy Spirit.... Moses and the prophets did not utter at random what we have received from their hand, but, speaking at the suggestion of God, they boldly and fearlessly testified ... that it was the mouth of the Lord that spake.

—John Calvin[2]

If we grant that Holy Scripture, in its original languages, is given to the Church as the God-inspired, sufficiently perspicuous, canonical rule of truth—by which alone we should ultimately measure (as we read it literally, with "due use of ordinary means") the rightness of both our doctrine and our practice—what is the *scope* of this rule? What, exactly, does Scripture mean to teach us *about*? Does it mean to school us in physics, chemistry, and biology, for example; or in cosmology, geography, or politics? If we can assume that our biblical authors like other ancient writers possessed opinions about some or all of these matters, and that we encounter these opinions from time to time in Scripture, does this mean that contemporary Scripture readers are required to share their opinions, along with their views concerning the significance of Jesus' crucifixion, resurrection, and ascension? How far does the authority of Scripture extend, and how completely, indeed—how *infallibly* or *inerrantly* (as scholars often put it)—does it communicate its teaching about the subjects at the center (or the periphery) of its concern?

---

[1] Martin Luther, *Contra malignum Iohannis Eccii iudicium* (*Against the Malignant Indictment of John Eck, 1519*), WA 2.626 (my own translation from the Latin).

[2] Calvin, *Timothy, Titus, and Philemon*, 249.

Questions like these were already addressed by the sixteenth-century Reformers. Convinced that a Scripture inspired by God so that it could function as a canonical rule could not err in its teaching, they wrestled with what exactly this meant. Like their Roman Catholic opponents they were the inheritors of received knowledge from the past not only about God and his salvation, but also about the nature of the world in which they lived, and how it did (and should) function. This knowledge was typically already associated with certain readings of Scripture that had long been granted the imprimatur of various Church Fathers. How much of this knowledge was still to be received now—in the changing world in which the Church found itself—as emanating from "the mouth of the Lord" (Calvin's words, in the second epigraph to the present chapter)? In which areas should Christians still maintain that the biblical writers (and indeed the Fathers) had not "erred" (Luther's words, in the first epigraph)?

The Church had already faced this issue in the late fifteenth century. The Bible had been widely interpreted in preceding centuries as supporting the idea that all the land in the world comprised one, more or less continuous and already-known landmass. Everything else was ocean.[3] Genesis, it was thought, presupposes that all human beings, descended from Adam and Eve, are distributed throughout adjacent territories in the known world; the Gospels and Acts inform us that the apostles, instructed to preach throughout the world, have already done so. Yet in the fifteenth century, "the possibility of the existence of the Antipodes"—a second landmass in the midst of the Atlantic Ocean, parallel to the one on which Europeans and others lived—"was increasingly widely canvassed."[4] In his promotional campaign for his own projected Atlantic exploration, Christopher Columbus (1451–1506) was apparently open to this idea, mentioning the Antipodes as a possible destination.[5] His opinion was curtly dismissed by one of the committees set up to investigate his plans: "St. Augustine doubts it."[6] According to Columbus' son and biographer Fernando, this was a "Spanish saying commonly used of any doubtful statement."[7] Yet as a result of Columbus' first Atlantic crossing in

---

[3] The idea itself did not necessarily require biblical support for its plausibility. It is also reflected in documents such as the *Tabula Rogeriana*, a world map composed in 1154 for King Roger of Sicily by the Muslim Spanish geographer Muhammed al-Idrisi on the basis of *empirical* evidence (the reports of sailors and so on).

[4] Felipe Fernández-Armesto, *Columbus* (Oxford: Oxford University Press, 1991), 28.

[5] On the three possible destinations Columbus had in mind when planning his voyage and seeking patronage for it—Asia, the Antipodes, and undiscovered islands—see Fernández-Armesto, *Columbus*, 26–33. "The objective evidence ... suggests that he considered all three destinations at different times, or sometimes simultaneously, and advocated them severally in addressing different audiences" (32).

[6] Fernández-Armesto, *Columbus*, 29.

[7] Nancy Rubin, *Isabella of Castile: The First Renaissance Queen* (New York: ASJA, 2004), 255.

1492–1493—even though *he* maintained that he had sailed to Asia as planned—"most Italian commentators seem to have assumed that his discoveries were Antipodean in character."[8] Saint Augustine's doubts were revealed by this and other, later journeys of exploration to be without foundation, and it was not long before the worldview based upon them was abandoned and the associated interpretation of Scripture was revised. Scripture (it was realized) need not be read in the manner previously commended.

In the sixteenth century the same issue arose in a rather different form, pertaining not to geography but cosmology. Was the traditional, pre-Christian, Ptolemaic worldview correct—the idea that the earth stands still at the center of the universe, and that other objects travel around it? In the Christian era this opinion—based, in part, upon the simple fact that the earth appears to be at rest while the stars, sun, and planets appear to revolve around it each day—had also come to be attached to particular interpretations of biblical texts. In Joshua 10:12-13, it was noted, it is the sun and the moon (and not the earth) that are commanded to stand still in order to lengthen the day. In Psalm 93:1 "the world is firmly established; it cannot be moved." In Ecclesiastes 1:4-5 "generations come and generations go, but the earth remains forever. The sun rises and the sun sets, and hurries back to where it rises." However, this reading of Scripture began to become problematic around the middle of the sixteenth century when Nicolaus Copernicus, in a book published in the year of his death (1543), articulated a very different view of things.[9] This book did not provoke much immediate controversy, although Copernican ideas as they seeped out into the culture *were* considered somewhat suspect by many Protestants and Roman Catholics. By the opening decades of the seventeenth century, however, the question had gained a much higher profile. Should the Church now reconsider some of its traditional positions on cosmology—as it had on geography—and revisit the interpretations of Scripture that were integral to these positions? Or should it, on this issue, stand firm?[10]

The underlying question at the heart of the matter in both cases is, what does it really *mean* that Scripture is "inspired"? Which kinds of truth are being communicated to the Church through these God-breathed texts, and how are they to

---

[8] Fernández-Armesto, *Columbus*, 29 (see also 96–97).

[9] Nicolaus Copernicus, *De revolutionibus orbium coelestium* (1543). He had earlier communicated his ideas (in 1514) to close friends, and in 1533 they had been disseminated to a wider audience in Rome (which included Pope Clement VII and several Roman Catholic cardinals) in lectures delivered by a third party. Georg Joachim Rheticus had also outlined them in a book published in 1540.

[10] A brief and readable account of the rise of Copernican cosmology and its reception in the Church can be found in Kyle Greenwood, *Scripture and Cosmology: Reading the Bible between the Ancient World and Modern Science* (Downers Grove, Ill.: InterVarsity, 2015), 159–85.

be received? These were important questions for Protestant Bible readers already in the sixteenth century, and they remain important questions in the twenty-first. Disagreement about their correct answers is in fact one of the main reasons for the continuing contemporary fragmentation of the Protestant Church in spite of widespread commitment to "Scripture alone." It is important, then, to grapple with these questions to the very best of our abilities. My argument in this chapter will be that a "reformed" understanding of Holy Scripture as the Church's God-inspired, sufficiently perspicuous, canonical rule of truth must continue to take account of the mediated, accommodated nature of the guidance that Scripture gives us in pursuing its circumscribed (although crucially important) goals.

SCRIPTURAL AUTHORITY IN THE CHURCH FATHERS

Since patristic understandings of the Bible were so often invoked in the debates that I have just described, it is appropriate that we begin by exploring what the Church Fathers believed about the nature and the scope of biblical authority and indeed about the *manner* in which the authoritative Word addresses us.

The Nature of the Authority

In line with apostolic teaching—and the apostles themselves were developing only concepts and language already found in the OT[11]—the Church Fathers believed that "no prophecy of Scripture came about by the prophet's own interpretation ... but men spoke from God as they were carried along by the Holy Spirit" (2 Pet 1:20-21), and more generally that "all Scripture is God-breathed" (2 Tim 3:16-17). Clement of Rome, for example, exhorts his Christian readers in Corinth to "look carefully into the Scriptures, which are the true utterances of the Holy Spirit."[12] Justin Martyr advises the readers of his *First Apology* that "when you hear the utterances of the prophets spoken as it were personally, you must not suppose that they are spoken by the inspired themselves, but by the Divine Word who moves them."[13] Irenaeus concurs: "the Scriptures are ... perfect, since they were spoken by the Word of God and His Spirit."[14] Later, in the fourth century, John Chrysostom tells us that "[t]he mouths of the inspired authors are the mouth of God."[15] In the fifth century Augustine teaches that in the OT "we behold nothing else in these Scriptures than what the Spirit of God has spoken

---

[11] Note, e.g., the idea that the Ten Commandments came via Moses from God (Exod 20), and the frequent use of the formula "thus says the LORD" in prophetic writings like Isa 18:4, 21:6.
[12] Clement of Rome, *Epistula I ad Corinthios (First Clement)*, 45.2 (*ANF* 1:17).
[13] Justin, *First Apology*, 36.1 (*ANF* 1:175).
[14] Irenaeus, *Against Heresies*, 2.28.2 (*ANF* 1:399).
[15] Cited in Hill, *Antioch*, 30.

through men,"[16] and further that "Sacred Scripture was written under the inspiration of the one Spirit of truth."[17]

Why is Scripture inspired by God in this way? The Fathers followed the teaching of the latter part of 2 Timothy 3:16 in emphasizing the *usefulness* of Scripture: it is God-breathed and "useful for teaching, rebuking, correcting and training in righteousness, so that the man of God may be thoroughly equipped for every good work." As Michael Graves affirms, "[f]or most Church Fathers . . . it was axiomatic that God intended whatever scriptural text they encountered to benefit them and their readers."[18] They generally perceived "a strong connection between the inspiration of Scripture and its usefulness for God's purposes."[19] For Augustine, for example, Scripture possesses "paramount authority," and to it "we yield assent in all matters of which we ought not to be ignorant, and yet cannot know of ourselves."[20] God addresses us therein about important matters, and we "profit" from listening to this address and conforming our beliefs and practices to its God-breathed norms.

Bound up with these convictions in patristic thought, unsurprisingly, is the conviction that the Scriptures do not mislead us in the matters about which God wishes to address us. Otherwise, we could not depend on Scripture for guidance, and it would cease to be "useful" to us. The Scriptures unerringly point us in the right direction; they are a reliable guide. They do not tell us everything that we might wish to know, Irenaeus concedes, but they are nevertheless "perfect, since they were spoken by the Word of God and His Spirit," and they remain so even when we do not fully comprehend their meaning and might be tempted to believe that they contain contradictions.[21] Augustine, similarly, advises:

> If we are perplexed by an apparent contradiction in Scripture, it is not allowable to say, The author of this book is mistaken; but either the manuscript is faulty, or the translation is wrong, or you have not understood . . . we are bound to receive as true whatever the canon shows to have been said by even one prophet, or apostle, or evangelist. Otherwise, not a single page will be left for the guidance of human fallibility, if contempt for the wholesome authority of the canonical books either puts an end to that authority altogether, or involves it in hopeless confusion.[22]

---

[16] Augustine, *City of God*, 18.43 (NPNF 1, 2:387).
[17] Augustine, *Literal Meaning*, 4.34.53 (ACW 41:143).
[18] Graves, *Inspiration*, 20.
[19] Graves, *Inspiration*, 21.
[20] Augustine, *City of God*, 11.3 (NPNF 1, 2:206).
[21] Irenaeus, *Against Heresies*, 2.28.2 (ANF 1:399).
[22] Augustine, *Reply to Faustus*, 11.5 (NPNF 1, 4:180).

The Scriptures are to be regarded as "sacred and infallible"—when they teach, for example, "that in the beginning God created the heavens and the earth."[23]

The Mediation of God's Words

How has God chosen to communicate in Scripture? As some of the above quotes already indicate, it is through "prophets ... authors ... men." That is, it is a *mediated* set of words that we receive from God. How are we to understand this mediation? Some of the Church Fathers can give the impression on occasion that divine inspiration completely overwhelms the human mediator, to such an extent that he does not possess any real freedom or agency in the whole business and does not even comprehend the words that he is writing down. They *can* draw an analogy between the biblical prophets and pagan seers, who were understood by the ancients to be "possessed by a demon who supersedes the human faculties."[24] The words of the author are in this case akin to "belching," and as John Chrysostom notes, "[w]e do not belch when we choose to."[25] At times, the Fathers can use the Latin verb *dictare* ("dictate") of the process of inspiration, implying an analogy with a master dictating a letter to a servant; Augustine uses this verb, for example, in his *Harmony of the Gospels*.[26] We might easily take such language as indicating a high degree of passivity on the part of our biblical authors. The secretary, in such an analogy, has no freedom concerning how a letter is written; therefore, the letter should not and will not reflect his own style or ideas, nor perhaps any aspect of his own circumstances (with the exception of the language chosen for the communication). One can even imagine situations in which such a secretary would not *understand* much about the communication—for example, where the letter involved matters beyond his knowledge.

Yet it should be transparently clear from what we have discovered in earlier chapters about patristic views of Scripture that this is certainly not the kind of mediation of God's word through the human authors of Scripture that the Church Fathers generally presuppose—especially when it comes to the foundationally important literal sense. Throughout the patristic writings, to the contrary, we find a governing assumption that the words of Scripture, albeit truly inspired by God, are nevertheless truly human words as well. They reflect the time and place in which they were uttered and written, including the linguistic

---

[23] Augustine, *City of God*, 11.6 (*NPNF* 1, 2:208).

[24] Hill, *Antioch*, 33.

[25] Cited in Hill, *Antioch*, 34. Chrysostom is drawing here on the opening lines of Psalm 45 in the LXX.

[26] "[Christ's] members have accomplished only what they became acquainted with by the repeated [*dictis*] statements of the Head." Augustine, *De consensu evangeliorum* (*Harmony of the Gospels*), 1.35.54 (*NPNF* 1, 6:101).

and rhetorical forms available to the authors, who clearly wrote each in their own distinctive style. This is certainly what Augustine assumed (my chapter 8)—his occasional use of *dictare* notwithstanding. "St. Augustine clearly rejected the idea of a purely mechanical inspiration," Andries Polman affirms, quoting and agreeing with Paul Schanz: "While divine inspiration is often stressed [in Augustine] so much that the human factor seems to have disappeared completely, the human factor is elsewhere given such prominence that there seems little room left for inspiration."[27] *Both* elements are stressed. To discover the will of God in Scripture we must discover the thought and will of the human authors who wrote it. John Chrysostom, likewise, having briefly toyed with the idea that the inspiration of Scripture involves "belching" (and thus "compulsion and lack of control under the influence of the Spirit"),[28] immediately distances himself from this view: "The Holy Spirit ... does not act like that ... [he] reveals the things that are said with the understanding of the authors."[29] Here he follows his teacher Diodore of Tarsus, who speaks of inspiration in terms of adjusting the tongue "to respond to the movement of grace in the way a pen responds to the leading thought of a fluent writer."[30] Theodore of Mopsuestia also follows Diodore: he writes of the Spirit filling the human heart with "perceptions of revelation," and then allowing "the tongue to speak loud and clear and to formulate the sayings in letters and articulate them distinctly."[31] It may well be true, then, that "few, if any, of the fathers seem to have tried to probe the deeper problems raised by their doctrine of inspiration"[32]—in the sense of trying to work out *how*, dogmatically and precisely, the divine and the human word coexist in Scripture. However, the Fathers did not doubt *that* they coexist: "The majority were content to accept the fact of the inspiration of the sacred writers, without examining further the manner or degree of its impact upon them."[33] What they certainly did not believe is that the one is present *rather than* the other.

One implication of this coexistence of the divine and human word in Scripture is the reality of divine accommodation. The Word of God in Scripture comes to us "clothed in the human limitations which the Word [also] assumed in the Incarnation" (John 1:1).[34] This theme is explored in some depth by John Chrysostom, whose view can be summarized as follows: "The Bible owes its very

[27] Polman, *Word of God*, 50–51.
[28] Hill, *Antioch*, 33, with reference to Basil of Caesarea.
[29] Cited in Hill, *Antioch*, 34.
[30] Diodore of Tarsus, *Commentary on Psalms 1–51* (trans. with an introduction and notes by Robert C. Hill; WGRW 9; Atlanta: Society of Biblical Literature, 2005), 143.
[31] Theodore, *Psalms 1–81*, 565.
[32] John N. D. Kelly, *Early Christian Doctrines* (4th ed.; London: A&C Black, 1968), 63.
[33] Kelly, *Doctrines*, 64.
[34] Hill, *Antioch*, 36.

existence to the condescension of God.... As in the historical Incarnation the Eternal Word became flesh, so in the Bible the glory of God veils itself in the fleshly garments of human thought and human language."[35] Theodoret writes similarly of the way in which God's words "are adjusted to our capacity to receive."[36] Scripture often speaks of God in human terms because only thus can we begin to form an accurate impression (for example) of the kind of being that God is (i.e., personal). We should not be led to believe by such statements, however, that God truly possesses a soul (Jer 9:9, LXX) or indeed legs (Gen 3:8). It was the Antiochenes above all who pressed this point about accommodation, marked as they were in their theology by an overall "emphasis on the human—without denial of the divine—as if to offset a real danger of its being minimized and obliterated. The human author ... and his factual situation cannot be bypassed" in one's reading of Scripture.[37] Just as a truly historical Jesus must be regarded as a nonnegotiable of orthodox Christian faith—as Irenaeus clearly understood in his battle with the Gnostics—so, too, must a truly historical Scripture.

The Extent of Revelation

If the Church Fathers generally perceived "a strong connection between the inspiration of Scripture and its usefulness for God's purposes," how did they conceive of these purposes? If they believed that in the matters about which God wishes to address us Scripture does not mislead us—which matters *are* these?

Their most fundamental answer to this question is that Scripture has been gifted to us so that "we men [humans], each and all of us, as if in a general hospital for souls, may select the remedy for his own condition. For, it says, 'the remedy will make the greatest sin to cease' [referring to Eccl 10:4]."[38] We are spiritually sick and require to be healed; Scripture is medicine to aid us in our desperate need. This is how Scripture is "useful" to us. For Gregory of Nyssa, then, the purpose of the story of Moses in the book of Exodus is "to show Christians how they might leave wickedness and 'the passions' behind, advance toward virtue and purity of soul, and eventually ascend toward the ineffable knowledge of God."[39] It is most especially information on such matters that Scripture is intent on communicating—"matters of which we ought not to be ignorant, and yet cannot know of ourselves" (Augustine). For whereas we

---

[35] Frederic H. Chase, *Chrysostom: A Study in the History of Biblical Interpretation* (Cambridge: Deighton, Bell and Co., 1887), 41–42.

[36] Theodoret of Cyrus, *Commentary on the Prophet Jeremiah* (trans. with an introduction by Robert C. Hill; CP 1; Brooklyn, Mass.: Holy Cross Orthodox Press, 2006), 58.

[37] Hill, *Antioch*, 200.

[38] Basil of Caesarea, *Exegetic Homilies* (trans. A. C. Way; FC; Washington, D.C.: Catholic University of America Press, 1963), 151.

[39] Graves, *Inspiration*, 19–20.

attain the knowledge of present objects by the testimony of our own senses, ... regarding objects remote from our own senses, we need others to bring their testimony, since we cannot know them by our own.... Accordingly ... in the case of things which are perceived by the mind and spirit, *i.e.*, which are remote from our own interior sense, it behoves us to trust those who have seen them set in that incorporeal light, or abidingly contemplate them.[40]

It is this kind of knowledge that Scripture is designed to deliver, and the Church Fathers can be strongly critical of Christians who do not attend to it but "are fond of contention ... and full of zeal about things which do not pertain to salvation."[41] They can be critical, indeed, of Christians who read Scripture, not to discover that which pertains to salvation, but to *subvert* "the knowledge of present objects" that we already possess on account of "the testimony of our own senses." Augustine complains about exactly this kind of reading in his *Literal Meaning of Genesis*, in a famous passage worth quoting at length:

> Usually, even a non-Christian knows something about the earth, the heavens, and the other elements of this world, about the motion and orbit of the stars and even their size and relative positions, about the predictable eclipses of the sun and moon, the cycles of the years and the seasons, about the kinds of animals, shrubs, stones, and so forth, and this knowledge he holds to as being certain from reason and experience. Now, it is a disgraceful and dangerous thing for an infidel to hear a Christian, presumably giving the meaning of Holy Scripture, talking nonsense on these topics; and we should take all means to prevent such an embarrassing situation, in which people show up vast ignorance in a Christian and laugh it to scorn. The shame is not so much that an ignorant individual is derided, but that people outside the household of the faith think our sacred writers held such opinions, and, to the great loss of those for whose salvation we toil, the writers of our Scripture are criticized and rejected as unlearned men. If they find a Christian mistaken in a field which they themselves know well and hear him maintaining his foolish opinions about our books, how are they going to believe those books in matters concerning the resurrection of the dead, the hope of eternal life, and the kingdom of heaven ... ?[42]

There is such a thing as knowledge that is common to all educated people, Christian and non-Christian, and it is known by way of "reason and experience." Augustine does not believe that anyone should cite "the sacred authors of Scripture" in order to overturn such empirically and rationally grounded knowledge, not least because it will undermine the credibility of what the biblical authors say about their matters of central concern—namely, "the resurrection of the dead, the

---

[40] Augustine, *City of God*, 11.3 (*NPNF* 1, 2:206).
[41] Clement of Rome, *First Clement*, 45 (*ANF* 1:17).
[42] Augustine, *Literal Meaning*, 1.19.39 (*ACW* 41:42–43).

hope of eternal life, and the kingdom of heaven." Indeed, Augustine goes on to refer to Bible readers who *fail* to observe the important distinction between what we can and cannot know "of ourselves" as "[r]eckless and incompetent expounders of Holy Scripture [who] bring untold trouble and sorrow on their wiser brethren," because they seek "to defend their utterly foolish and obviously untrue statements" by calling "upon Holy Scripture for proof." Among the matters to which *competent* expositors pay attention, by contrast, is contemporary "science" (as we would nowadays call it—although most people before us have referred to it as "philosophy").[43] Augustine was not the only Church Father who considered this to be important. Various patristic writers develop the same theme, using the language of God's "two books"—Scripture and creation—in doing so. Both books must be carefully read in order to get at the whole truth of things.[44]

Augustine's words just cited reveal, of course, that by no means all Christians in the patristic era agreed with him about what Scripture is designed in the purposes of God infallibly to teach. Some believed that a "perfect" Scripture must constitute a repository of answers to every kind of question that they might wish to ask—that Scripture is a kind of God-breathed encyclopedia of all knowledge. They cited Scripture, therefore, to dismiss and even to deride the kind of commonly shared scientific knowledge of their time that Augustine mentions in *Literal Meaning*. For example, it was generally accepted in Late Antiquity that the earth is spherical, and not flat. The Christian apologist Lactantius (c. AD 240–320), however, ridicules this idea in his *Divine Institutes*. He places the notion that "the world is round like a ball . . . like a globe" among the "marvellous fictions" created by those who "discuss philosophy for the sake of a jest, or purposely and knowingly undertake to defend falsehoods, as if to exercise or display their talents on false subjects."[45] Just after Augustine's time the Alexandrian traveler and (later) monk Cosmas Indicopleustes (sixth century AD)—"the one medieval writer explicitly to deny the sphericity of the earth"[46]—argues in the same way. He appears to view the earth as a flat rectangle surrounded by four seas, with the

---

[43] See further Kenneth J. Howell, "Natural Knowledge and Textual Meaning in Augustine's Interpretation of Genesis: The Three Functions of Natural Philosophy," in *Nature and Scripture in the Abrahamic Religions: Up to 1700* (2 vols.; ed. Jitse M. van der Meer and Scott Mandelbrote; BSCH 36; 2 vols.; Leiden: Brill, 2008), 1:117–45.

[44] See further Pamela Bright, "Nature and Scripture: The Two Witnesses to the Creator," and Paul M. Blowers, "Entering 'This Sublime and Blessed Amphitheatre': Contemplation of Nature and Interpretation of the Bible in the Patristic Period," in van der Meer and Mandelbrote, *Nature and Scripture in the Abrahamic Religions: Up to 1700*, 1:85–115, 147–76.

[45] Lactantius, *Divinae institutiones* (*The Divine Institutes*), 3.24 (ANF 7:94–95).

[46] Lesley B. Cormack, "Myth 3: That Medieval Christians Taught That the Earth was Flat," in *Galileo Goes to Jail, and Other Myths about Science and Religion* (ed. Ronald L. Numbers; Cambridge, Mass.: Harvard University Press, 2009), 28–34 (32).

heavens and the earth together being modeled on the biblical tabernacle. He criticizes "those who, while wishing to profess Christianity, think and imagine like the pagans that the heaven is spherical."[47]

Yet on the whole writers of the patristic age did not take this all-encompassing view of what Scripture is intended to reveal:

> People in antiquity wrote cookbooks, medical manuals, and instructions on how to assemble buildings. By and large, Christians did not stop using books such as these and try to learn this information strictly from the Bible. But they did believe that Scripture could be used to answer any important question about religion, morals, or anything touching on the ultimate questions of life.[48]

By and large the Church Fathers acknowledged that inspired Scripture was designed only to answer infallibly certain kinds of questions—and not others. This was certainly true of Augustine, who cautioned that while the Scriptures "are true and that truth ought to be defended against the cavils of false philosophy … one must not claim more for the Scriptures than they really teach," and claimed specifically that "the sacred authors did not have the construction of a natural philosophy as their aim, even when they spoke about nature."[49]

It is therefore somewhat ironic that later Christian thinkers routinely cited predecessors like Augustine as authorities when it came to scientific questions like the existence or the nonexistence of the Antipodes. It is certainly true that Augustine himself, in *City of God*, calls the Antipodes a "fable."[50] It is important to note, however, the significant difference between Augustine and Lactantius (who also denied the existence of the Antipodes) on this matter. Lactantius begins by characterizing simply as false the widely accepted as demonstrated idea of the earth as a globe, and then he blames this idea for giving rise to the equally false idea of the Antipodes: "the rotundity of the earth leads, in addition, to the invention of those suspended antipodes."[51] This does not imply any openness to evidence that the Antipodes might after all exist, and one can well imagine Lactantius discouraging as futile any idea of trying to accumulate such evidence. Augustine's first objection in *City of God* to the idea of the Antipodes, on the other hand, is that "it is not affirmed that this has been learned by historical knowledge, but by scientific conjecture."[52] For Augustine, this is what *differentiates* belief in the Antipodes from belief in the rotundity of the earth, the latter having been

---

[47] Cosmas Indicopleustes, *The Christian Topography of Cosmas, an Egyptian Monk* (trans. and ed. J. W. McCrindle; London: Hakluyt Society, 1897), 7.
[48] Graves, *Inspiration*, 27.
[49] Howell, "Natural Knowledge," 128, 144.
[50] Augustine, *City of God*, 16.9 (*NPNF* 1, 2:315).
[51] Lactantius, *Divine Institutes*, 3.24 (*ANF* 7:94).
[52] Augustine, *City of God*, 16.9 (*NPNF* 1, 2:315).

"scientifically demonstrated."[53] It does not seem likely, then, given what he says here and in the passage mentioned above from *Literal Meaning of Genesis*—and what he also says and does, generally and exegetically, in that book—that Augustine's "doubts" about the Antipodes would have led *him* to discourage a voyage of discovery designed to look and see whether they were actually there. Rather, Augustine gives every impression in his writings of possessing significant openness to evidence beyond the pages of Scripture in arriving at conclusions about what is true—including evidence bearing on what might be the truest and best way of reading Scripture itself. When commenting on the phrase "let there be light" in Genesis 1, for example, he envisages a scenario in which it might become clear, in the future, that this is not a statement about "material light"—in which case, he proposes, "this teaching was never in Holy Scripture but was an opinion proposed by man in his ignorance."[54] We would discover, in such a case, that this reading of Genesis 1 had always been mistaken.

This important difference in approach between Augustine and Lactantius was noted in later centuries by important players in the "scientific revolution" like Copernicus and Kepler, who lived in a time when, although many were "happy to anathematize Lactantius, many tried to save Augustine."[55] What was important to these later writers was not so much what Augustine as an ancient authority believed, in a whole range of matters—indeed, various of his specific beliefs had turned out to be poorly grounded. What was important was how Augustine went about his business, especially in reading Scripture—the principles that he espoused and to a great extent also followed. It was these Augustinian principles, in fact, that ultimately led later Bible readers to assessments rather different from Augustine's—even on the big question concerning which smaller questions inspired Scripture was probably designed infallibly to answer. Augustine's own particular views concerning the truth about the world were inevitably bound up, like every Bible reader's, with commonly accepted nonscriptural knowledge. He cannot reasonably be "blamed" for this, as if he ought somehow to have known what people standing much further down the historical timeline came to know.

---

[53] Augustine, *City of God*, 16.9 (*NPNF* 1, 2:315). Some have perceived doubt in Augustine's mind concerning the sphericity of the earth because he says this opinion has been "*supposed* or scientifically demonstrated" (emphasis added). This is to overread the text. As the starting point for his immediate argument (about the Antipodes) Augustine accepts what is commonly believed about the earth no matter how people have come to believe it—whether it has been "supposed" or "scientifically demonstrated." *He* accepts, however, that it has been scientifically demonstrated in the same way that many others truths have been—and thus his strictures in *Literal Meaning of Genesis*.

[54] Augustine, *Literal Meaning*, 1.19.38 (ACW 41:42).

[55] Pablo de Felipe, "The Antipodeans and Science-Faith Relations," in *Augustine Beyond the Book: Intermediality, Transmediality and Reception* (ed. Karla Pollmann and Meredith J. Gill; BSCH 58; Leiden: Brill, 2012), 281–311 (309).

It is only exceedingly foolish moderns who characterize ancient people as foolish just because they happen to be ancient. Nevertheless, some of Augustine's particular views did inevitably begin to be questioned by many as time passed and as knowledge about certain matters increased. If consistent with his own principles, Augustine would surely have welcomed these developments.

SCRIPTURAL AUTHORITY IN THE REFORMERS

The magisterial Reformers certainly agreed with the Church Fathers and with those who followed them in the Middle Ages when it came to the authoritative nature of Scripture as a God-inspired text. Writing about the words of David in 2 Samuel 23:1-4, for example, Luther affirms that "these words of David are also those of the Holy Spirit."[56] Prophets, he once said, "preach solely by inspiration of the Holy Spirit."[57] When Paul writes in strong language to the Galatians it is "the Holy Spirit [who] wrests such passionate words out of him."[58] For Calvin, likewise, "it was the mouth of the Lord that spoke" when Moses and the prophets spoke (in the second epigraph to the present chapter). The prophets "did not speak at their own suggestion, but ... being organs of the Holy Spirit, they only uttered what they had been commissioned from heaven to declare."[59] The apostles, likewise, are "sure and authentic amanuenses of the Holy Spirit; and, therefore, their writings are to be regarded as the oracles of God."[60]

The Reformers also agreed with the Church Fathers in closely connecting Scripture's inspiration with its *usefulness*. The same Spirit who inspired Scripture is present with the one who reads it. "When the Word is read," affirms Luther, "the Holy Spirit is present; and thus it is impossible either to listen to or to read Scripture without profit."[61] Calvin writes in his commentary on Romans that "there is nothing ... in Scripture which may not contribute to your instruction and the training of your life ... the oracles of God contain nothing vain or unprofitable."[62]

If Scripture is to be useful along such lines then it must obviously be a *reliable* guide; this, too, was a conviction that the Reformers shared with the Fathers. The Scriptures unerringly point us in the right direction; "none of their writers has erred," as Luther puts it (in the first epigraph to the present chapter). Scripture is

---

[56] Martin Luther, *Treatise on the Last Words of David*, LW 15:276.
[57] Martin Luther, *The Gospel for St. Stephen's Day, Matthew 23[:34–39]* (1522), LW 52:89.
[58] Martin Luther, *Lectures on Galatians Chapters 5–6* (1535), LW 27:9.
[59] Calvin, *2 Timothy*, 248–49.
[60] Calvin, *Institutes* 4.8.9.
[61] Martin Luther, *Lectures on the First Epistle of St. John*, LW 30:321.
[62] John Calvin, *Epistle of Paul the Apostle to the Romans and to the Thessalonians* (CalC 8; trans. Ross Mackenzie; ed. David W. Torrance and Thomas F. Torrance; Edinburgh: Oliver & Boyd, 1961), 304–5.

"the very sure and infallible Word of God"; "the Holy Spirit neither lies nor errs."[63] Calvin describes in his *Institutes* the process by which God revealed himself to people of old, and the way in which

> the certainty of what he taught them was firmly engraven on their hearts, so that they felt assured and knew that the things which they learnt came forth from God, who invariably accompanied his word with a sure testimony, infinitely superior to mere opinion.

In due course this truth in the heart was enlarged upon and written down in Scripture. Therefore, "the first step in true knowledge is taken, when we reverently embrace the testimony which God has been pleased therein to give of himself." It is to this "law of the Lord [that] ... is perfect"—this "testimony of the Lord [that] is sure"—that we must go (Ps 19). We must attend "the proper school for training the children of God," if we are not to continue "labouring under vanity and error" like our ancestors before us.[64]

The Mediation of God's Words

When it comes to the question of *how* God has chosen to communicate his words to us, we find in the writings of the Reformers a spectrum of commentary notably similar to that of their patristic predecessors. The Reformers too can sometimes give the impression that divine inspiration completely overwhelms the human mediator, to such an extent that the latter does not possess any real agency in the whole business and does not even comprehend the words that he is writing down. We saw in the second epigraph to the present chapter, in fact, one instance of Calvin himself referring to the "dictation" of the Holy Spirit, and this is not an isolated instance. God, he writes on another occasion, "dictated to the four Evangelists what they should write, so that, while each had his own part assigned to him, the whole might be collected into one body."[65] Luther can also make strong statements about the authorship of Scripture that might be taken to imply a merely scribal role for the human participants. "The Holy Spirit Himself ... is the Author of this book [of Genesis]," he affirms;[66] a story in the Gospel of John "was

---

[63] Martin Luther, *Lectures on 1 Timothy* (1528), LW 28:239; *Confession Concerning Christ's Supper* (1528), LW 37:279.

[64] Calvin, *Institutes* 1.6.2–4.

[65] John Calvin, "Argument to the Gospel of John," in *Commentary on the Gospel According to John, Volume First* (CalC 17; trans. William Pringle; Grand Rapids: Baker, 1981), 22. See also *Institutes* 4.8.6, where historical details added to prophetic oracles "are also the composition of prophets, but dictated by the Holy Spirit"; and 4.8.8, where "the Spirit of Christ went before, and in a manner dictated words to," the apostles.

[66] Martin Luther, *Lectures on Genesis Chapters 26–30* (1541–1542?), LW 5:275.

recorded by the Holy Spirit."[67] The human author of Scripture, Luther proposes in one famous passage, is nothing but the pen of the Holy Spirit.[68] It is all too easy to read such statements in isolation against the background of those many visual representations from the ninth to the twelfth centuries of authors dictating their works to scribes—God portrayed as whispering in the ear of the prophet, or "dictating to the evangelists serving as secretaries taking down the written word," and the Church Fathers "drawn either as scribes recording divine dictation or as authors in their own right dictating to secretaries."[69] It is all too easy, then, to make mistaken assumptions about the Reformers.

However: we have already seen in earlier chapters the manifold ways in which the Reformers presupposed that the human authors of Scripture were thoroughly and actively involved in the processes by which Scripture came into being. We have noted their conviction, for example, that the language and rhetoric of our biblical texts deeply reflect the times and the places in which they were written. Even in his earlier works, Luther can describe the apostle Paul as "one learned in the Scriptures," and as making a choice about whether he follows the Hebrew text or the LXX.[70] A little later he can refer to Moses' thought and teaching without referencing the Holy Spirit at all, and to Moses himself as "the foremost and chief among the authors of all the sacred books."[71] The author of Job, Luther claims, "was a great theologian" who "wished to paint a picture of patience."[72] Paul, in writing to the Galatians, is dealing with an "issue," and he "wants to establish" something.[73] Some of those who now read this epistle misunderstand it, Luther complains, and they "suppress the true and genuine meaning of Paul."[74] In all of this Luther recognizes that "the human writers made *decisions* about vocabulary,

---

[67] Luther, *Sermons on the Gospel of St. John Chapters 1–4* (1537–1540), LW 22:415.

[68] Martin Luther, *First Psalm Lectures*, LW 10:212.

[69] Mark Vessey, "From *Cursus* to *Ductus*: Figures of Writing in Western Late Antiquity (Augustine, Jerome, Cassiodorus, Bede)," in *European Literary Careers: The Author from Antiquity to the Renaissance* (ed. Patrick Cheney and Alfred De Armas; Toronto: University of Toronto Press, 2002), 47–103 (61, quoting Saenger).

[70] Martin Luther, *Lectures on Hebrews* (1517), LW 29:174, 222–23. I am grateful for guidance in identifying this and the following examples from Luther's writings to Mark D. Thompson, *A Sure Ground on Which to Stand: The Relation of Authority and Interpretive Method in Luther's Approach to Scripture* (PBTM; Carlisle: Paternoster, 2004), 61–67.

[71] Martin Luther, *Avoiding the Doctrines of Men and A Reply to the Texts Cited in Defence of the Doctrines of Men* (1522), LW 35:132; *The Deuteronomy of Moses with Notes* (1525), LW 9:3.

[72] Luther, *Table Talk*, LW 54:80.

[73] Luther, *Lectures on Galatians Chapters 1–4*, LW 26:4.

[74] Luther, *Lectures on Galatians Chapters 5–6*, LW 27:28–29.

expression, and style."[75] For Luther, as Mark Thompson summarizes, "the Scriptures have been 'written by men' *and* they are 'from God.'"[76]

The same is true of Calvin: "the inspiration of scripture did not occur at the expense of the personalities of the human writers. The inspiration process he envisions is far from mechanical."[77] He writes about the authors of the Psalms "laying open all their inmost thoughts and affections,"[78] and about stylistic differences among the apostolic writings.[79] He is also intrigued by differences in prophetic styles, and he offers explanations for these; for example, "Ezekiel's coarse style was appropriate to the slowness and stupidity of the people."[80] Sometimes the very human sentiments of a biblical text disquiet Calvin, as when he refers to Psalm 39:13 in terms of "sinful emotions which [David] had experienced according to the flesh."[81] He often refers to the intention of the Holy Spirit in the biblical text, but at the same time he is deeply interested in the intention of the human author. "Throughout his Old Testament commentaries," for example, "he affirms that the role of an interpreter is to expound the intention of the prophet."[82] He rejects a Christological reading of Genesis 28 because he doubts whether any such thought "entered the mind of Moses or of Jacob," and he dismisses a particular interpretation of Psalm 89:11 because it "seems too much removed from the mind of the prophet."[83] As David Puckett observes, Calvin "is reluctant to allow any division between human and divine intentionality."[84] He works hard (as John Thompson notes) at comprehending the latter by way of the former, employing

> the best tools of his day—establishing historical contexts and background, searching for the precise meaning of terms in the original Hebrew or Greek, worrying

---

[75] Thompson, *Sure Ground*, 66 (emphasis added).

[76] Thompson, *Sure Ground*, 68.

[77] David L. Puckett, *John Calvin's Exegesis of the Old Testament* (CSRT; Louisville, Ky.: Westminster John Knox, 1995), 27. See also Holder, *Grounding*, 58–68, who notes that although Calvin can write of God "dictating" words to the authors of Scripture, for him these authors certainly "maintained their own marks of style, and the peculiarities of their textual manner" (60), being deeply rooted in differing historical contexts.

[78] John Calvin, "Author's Preface," in *Commentary on the Book of Psalms, Volume 1* (CalC 4; trans. James Anderson; Grand Rapids: Baker, 1981), xxxvii.

[79] John Calvin, *The Epistle of Paul the Apostle to the Hebrews and the First and Second Epistles of St. Peter* (CalC 12; trans. William B. Johnston; ed. David W. Torrance and Thomas F. Torrance; Edinburgh: Oliver & Boyd, 1963), 1–2, 325.

[80] Puckett, *John Calvin's Exegesis*, 28.

[81] Calvin, *Psalms*, 2:88.

[82] Puckett, *John Calvin's Exegesis*, 33.

[83] Calvin, *Psalms*, 2:427.

[84] Puckett, *John Calvin's Exegesis*, 35.

over geography and chronology, and so on—to make his case for what the biblical authors intended.[85]

How, exactly, the divine and the human word coexist in Scripture Calvin never works out in any sustained manner—he "never articulates precisely how he conceives of the process of inspiration."[86] This is also true of Luther, whose comments on the dual authorship of Scripture are mostly "incidental" in nature; he "does not develop them into a detailed and coherent doctrine of Scripture."[87] Like the Church Fathers, however, neither Reformer was in any doubt *that* the divine and the human coexist and that the presence of the one in Scripture does not exclude the presence of the other.

As in the Church Fathers, also, one of the implications of this coexistence for the Reformers is the reality of divine accommodation. We came across an example of this just a moment ago in Calvin's opinion that Ezekiel's coarse style was "appropriate" to the condition of the people he (and God through him) was addressing. There are truths that must be communicated, but the communication must attend to the capacities of the recipients. So it is that "[p]atiently God, through our history, accommodates his ways of revelation to our condition";[88] he is to be found "adapting his message to limited human understanding."[89] This is an important theme in Calvin's thought, such that "[a]ny study of Calvin as scriptural exegete would be incomplete which failed to examine his frequent appeal to the principle of accommodation."[90] He appeals to this principle, for example, to explain the whole course of history, including that of the Israelites; even if "a nation was harsh, or barbaric, God did not turn away from them, but accommodated the divine revelation to what can be understood by those people at that time."[91] He appeals to it again with respect to particular biblical texts like Genesis 1:5. Here he proposes that Moses "accommodated his discourse to the

---

[85] Thompson, "Calvin as a Biblical Interpreter," 61.

[86] Puckett, *John Calvin's Exegesis*, 27.

[87] Thompson, *Sure Ground*, 67.

[88] Ford L. Battles, "God Was Accommodating Himself to Human Capacity," *Int* 31 (1977): 19–38 (34). See further David F. Wright, "Calvin's Pentateuchal Criticism: Equity, Hardness of Heart and Divine Accommodation in the Mosaic Harmony Commentary," *CTJ* 21 (1986): 33–50; and Arnold Huijgen, *Divine Accommodation in John Calvin's Theology: Analysis and Assessment* (Göttingen: Vandenhoeck & Ruprecht, 2011). "Central to Calvin's understanding of the self-revelation of God was the principle of accommodation." Steinmetz, "Calvin as an Interpreter," 290.

[89] Puckett, *John Calvin's Exegesis*, 11.

[90] Battles, "God Was Accommodating," 19. With respect to his use of this principle, Calvin was "the closest Christian rival to Chrysostom, who uses the idea of accommodation 'seemingly without end.'" Paul Helm, *John Calvin's Ideas* (Oxford: Oxford University Press, 2004), 185 (partially quoting Benin).

[91] Holder, *Grounding*, 47.

received custom" of his time that reckoned each day as beginning with sundown.[92] That is why the text says that "there was evening, and there was morning—the first day." An even more interesting example is Calvin's reading of Genesis 1:16. Acknowledging that astronomers understand very well that Saturn is larger than the moon, he explains that when Genesis 1:16 speaks of sun and the moon as the two "great lights" in the sky we must understand Moses as speaking of the heavens as they appear to ordinary people and not as they really are:

> Moses does not here subtitely descant, as a philosopher, on the secrets of nature, as may be seen in these words. First, he assigns a place in the expanse of heaven to the planets and stars; but astronomers make a distinction of spheres, and, at the same time, teach that the fixed stars have their proper place in the firmament. Moses makes two great luminaries; but astronomers prove, by conclusive reasons, that the star of Saturn, which, on account of its great distance, appears the least of all, is greater than the moon. Here lies the difference; Moses wrote in a popular style things which, without instruction, all ordinary persons, endued with common sense, are able to understand; but astronomers investigate with great labour whatever the sagacity of the human mind can comprehend.[93]

Luther could write in very similar terms about divine accommodation. Exegeting Matthew 23:37, for example, he notes that Scripture "speaks of God, for the sake of the simplest people, as if he were a human being.... These passages are all written in accordance with our understanding and ability and not in accordance with the essential propensity of the divine nature."[94] In addressing us, Luther believes, God uses "anthropomorphisms and phenomenological language." There is "no other way by which we could know or speak of God, except by this divine condescension."[95] Elsewhere he writes of God lowering himself "to the level of our weak comprehension" and presenting himself to us "in images, in coverings, as it were, in simplicity adapted to a child."[96]

It is because God's address is mediated and accommodated in such ways that the same Scripture that addresses us infallibly about everything that God wishes to say contains at the same time what we might consider as errors—*if* we were expecting Scripture to be perfect in all respects in some abstract way unconnected with God's saving purposes in inspiring it. As we have seen, Luther is profoundly

---

[92] Calvin, *Genesis*, 77–78—in a comment on Gen 1:5. His comments on Zech 1:7-10 in his Zechariah commentary provide another example: "Calvin intends the reader to understand that ... God is accommodating his teaching to limited capacities of human beings." Puckett, *John Calvin's Exegesis*, 80n106.
[93] Calvin, *Genesis*, 86.
[94] Luther, *The Gospel for St. Stephen's Day*, LW 52:95.
[95] Thompson, *Sure Ground*, 107.
[96] Martin Luther, *Lectures on Genesis Chapters 6–14*, LW 2:45.

convinced that none of the biblical writers has erred; yet when considering the tension between Genesis 11 and Acts 7 with respect to the birth of Abraham, he characterizes the speech of Stephen in the latter as not "a formally correct statement, but a story told on the basis of common speech, which is often confused and unclear." He points out in addition the "clear error" in Acts 7 "when it says that God appeared to Abraham 'in Mesopotamia, before he lived in Haran'... for it was in fact in Haran that God had thus appeared to him." The book of Acts often speaks in such "careless and popular terms."[97] Calvin, likewise, writes of Scripture being "dictated by the Holy Spirit,"[98] yet he notes that "in quoting Scripture the apostles often used freer language than the original... they were not over-careful in their use of words."[99] Commenting on Matthew 27:9, he says: "How the name of Jeremiah crept in I cannot confess to know nor do I make much of it: obviously Jeremiah's name is put in error for Zechariah (13.7). Nothing of this sort is said in Jeremiah, or anything like it."[100]

In summation, then: for the Reformers, as for the Church Fathers, Scripture is God-inspired and useful to us in shaping right belief and practice—an infallible, unerring guide that will not let us down. At the same time, God's Word is genuinely mediated to us by human beings who are actively involved in its articulation, such that we must attend carefully to their human words in our pursuit of understanding God's Word. The divine Word is communicated in consideration of their limitations and weaknesses, and of ours.

THE EXTENT OF THE REVELATION

If Reformers like Calvin could inform his readers that "there is nothing in Scripture which is not useful for your instruction," what did they believe that it was useful *for*? Granted that, as Luther proposes, "the Holy Spirit neither lies nor errs," what does the Spirit, through Scripture, truthfully and reliably wish to teach us *about*?

It should already be clear that the Reformers' answer to this question is not "everything." Calvin does not believe, for example, that Scripture is useful for understanding many aspects of the heavens. Commenting on Genesis 1:6-7, for example, he explicitly advises: "He who would learn astronomy, and other

---

[97] James Barr, "Luther and Biblical Chronology," in *Bible and Interpretation: The Collected Essays of James Barr, Volume II: Biblical Studies* (ed. John Barton; Oxford: Oxford University Press, 2013), 423–39 (426–27).
[98] Calvin, *2 Timothy*, 249.
[99] Calvin, *Romans*, 61.
[100] Calvin, *Harmony of the Gospels*, 3:177.

recondite arts, let him go elsewhere."[101] Genesis treats only "the visible form of the world" and not its essential reality, and to believe otherwise (about the waters above the heaven, in this case) would create a conflict with what Calvin believes is already known.[102] Like Augustine, then, Calvin believes that there is such a thing as knowledge common to all educated people—Christian and non-Christian alike—and acquired through reason and experience. For example, astronomers have proved, "by conclusive reasons, that the star of Saturn, which, on account of its great distance, appears the least of all, is greater than the moon." Like other Christian thinkers before him Calvin pays serious attention to contemporary knowledge as he engages in his exegetical and theological work; he is "extremely appreciative of scientific work."[103] He knows (as Augustine knew) that by no means all his contemporaries take the same approach—indeed, some condemn the science of astronomy. Calvin addresses these "others" obliquely in the passage that follows immediately after the one I cited in the previous section. "Moses wrote in a popular style," he has already proposed, "but astronomers investigate with great labour whatever the sagacity of the human mind can comprehend":

> Nevertheless, this study is not to be reprobated, nor this science to be condemned, because some frantic persons are wont boldly to reject whatever is unknown to them. For astronomy is not only pleasant, but also very useful to be known: it cannot be denied that this art unfolds the admirable wisdom of God. Wherefore, as ingenious men are to be honoured who have expended useful labour on this subject, so they who have leisure and capacity ought not to neglect this kind of exercise.[104]

"Reading the heavens" counts as "useful labour," and it "unfolds the admirable wisdom of God" within its own sphere, which pertains to the physical universe. Reading the Bible is also useful labor, and it too unfolds the wisdom of God in its own sphere, which pertains much more centrally to metaphysical matters like sin, repentance, and salvation. "It would have been lost time for David to have attempted to teach the secrets of astronomy to the rude and unlearned," Calvin comments on Psalm 19:4; "therefore he reckoned it sufficient to speak in a homely style, that he might reprove the whole world of ingratitude, if, in beholding the sun, they are not taught the fear and the knowledge of God."[105] This is what really

---

[101] Calvin, *Genesis*, 79. See further Calvin, *Psalms*, 2:184–85: "The Holy Spirit had no intention to teach astronomy; and, in proposing instruction meant to be common to the simplest and most uneducated persons, he made use by Moses and the other Prophets of popular language ... the Holy Spirit would rather speak childishly than unintelligibly to the humble and unlearned."

[102] Calvin, *Genesis*, 79–80.

[103] Davis A. Young, *John Calvin and the Natural World* (Lanham, Md.: University Press of America, 2007), 2.

[104] Calvin, *Genesis*, 86–87.

[105] Calvin, *Psalms*, 1:315.

concerns the psalmist: to teach the fear and the knowledge of God. Elsewhere, then, Calvin identifies the primary function of Scripture as directing sinful people to Christ:

> we ought to read the Scriptures with the express design of finding Christ in them. Whoever shall turn aside from this object, though he may weary himself throughout his whole life in learning, will never attain the knowledge of the truth; for what wisdom can we have without the wisdom of God?[106]

The two spheres of knowledge must not be collapsed into one; indeed, "the Bible should not be considered as the sole source of all knowledge and truth, infallible though it might be."[107] As the contemporary English *Edwardian Homilies* puts it, "the perfection of holy scripture" consists in its containing every truth "necessary for our justification and everlasting salvation," yet "other sciences be good, and [are] to be learned."[108]

Calvin is equally clear that Scripture does not necessarily wish to teach us about historical chronology, nor even about the precise details of some events referred to in the biblical timeline. "In Scripture," he observes, "it is well known that things are not always stated according to the strict order of time in which they occurred."[109] He comments on one of the temptations of Jesus, for example, in this way:

> There is nothing very remarkable in Luke putting in second place the temptation which Matthew places last, for the Evangelists had no intention of so putting their narrative together as always to keep an exact order of events, but to bring the whole pattern together to produce a kind of mirror or screen image of those features most useful for the understanding of Christ. It is quite enough to grasp that Christ was put to three temptations. Which test came second or third, is not a matter for anxious debate.[110]

Then again, the difference in number in Acts 7:14 when compared with Genesis 46:27 in no way detracts from the point of the passage, which is to emphasize the power and the providence of God.[111] It may well *seem* at first sight that the various passages just cited intend to speak about the heavens, historical chronology,

---

[106] Calvin, *Commentary on John*, 1:218.
[107] Young, *Natural World*, 3.
[108] Lillback and Gaffin, *Word*, 283–89 (284, 287).
[109] Calvin, *Psalms*, 2:296.
[110] John Calvin, *A Harmony of the Gospels Matthew, Mark, and Luke, Volume 1* (CalC; trans. A. W. Morrison; Edinburgh: Saint Andrew, 1972), 139.
[111] John Calvin, *The Acts of the Apostles 1–13* (CalC 6; trans. John W. Fraser and W. J. G. McDonald; ed. David W. Torrance and Thomas F. Torrance; Edinburgh: Oliver & Boyd, 1965), 181–82.

or precise numbers, but this is only because we do not understand just how God in his love for us "condescends to our ignorance; and . . . prattles to us in Scripture in a rough and popular style."[112]

Martin Luther also addresses in various places the question of the kind of truth Scripture means to communicate. His most fundamental emphasis is (like Calvin's) Christological. In Scripture "we come across nothing other than Christ."[113] It contains "nothing but Christ and the Christian faith."[114] "If you would interpret well and confidently, set Christ before you," he proposes, "for he is the man to whom it all applies, every bit of it."[115] It is Christ that Scripture is most fundamentally "about." As the *First Helvetic Confession of Faith* (1536) puts it in its fifth article, "[t]he entire Biblical Scripture is solely concerned that man understand that God is kind . . . and [has] demonstrated this His kindness to the whole human race through Christ His Son."[116] Precision in numbers, then, is not necessarily what Scripture is after:

> When one reads [in the Bible] that great numbers of people were slain—for example, eighty thousand—I believe that hardly one thousand were actually killed. What is meant is the whole people. Whoever strikes the king strikes everything he possesses.[117]

Nor is every aspect of chronology of interest to the biblical writers. Writing about the cleansing of the Jerusalem temple in John 2, for example, Luther notes that the same episode is found in Matthew 21, and he asks: "How do we harmonize the accounts of the two evangelists?" The question is not important, he proposes, unless the reader is one of those "who are fond of bringing up all sorts of subtle questions and demanding definite and precise answers":

> But if we understand Scripture properly and have the genuine articles of our faith—that Jesus Christ, God's Son, suffered and died for us—then our inability to answer all such questions will be of little consequence. The evangelists do not all observe the same chronological order. The one may place an event at an earlier, the other at a later time. . . . It may also be that the Lord did this more than once, and that John reports the first, Matthew, the second event. Be that as it may, whether it happened sooner or later, whether it happened once or twice, this will not prejudice our faith. . . . All the evangelists agree on this, that Christ died for our sins.

---

[112] Calvin, *Commentary on John*, 1:119.

[113] Martin Luther, *Predigt am Stephanstage* (Sermon on St. Stephen's Day, 1523), WA 11:223 (my own translation from the Latin).

[114] Martin Luther, *Der 36. (37.) Psalm Davids* (*The 36th [37th] Psalm of David*, 1521), WA 8:236 (my own translation from the German).

[115] Martin Luther, *Preface to the Pentateuch* (1523), LW 35:247.

[116] Cochrane, *Reformed Confessions*, 101.

[117] Luther, *Table Talk*, LW 54:452.

But in their accounts of Christ's deeds and miracles they do not observe a uniform order and often ignore the proper chronological sequence.[118]

As to the heavens above, Luther's view is similar to Calvin's in its overall thrust. He had studied astronomy in Erfurt, and he fully accepted it as a science that was to be sharply distinguished from astrology precisely because the latter could not be confirmed by demonstration.[119] With respect to the sun and the moon, then, Luther already knows that "astronomers debate about the size of these bodies," and he accepts what they say, just as he also defers to "astronomers [when they] say ... that the moon derives its light from the sun."[120] This is "really well proved," he affirms, "at an eclipse of the moon, when the earth, intervening in a direct line between the sun and moon, does not permit the light of the sun to pass to the moon."[121] What astronomers say about the magnitude of the heavenly bodies, however, "really has nothing to do with [Genesis 1].... Scripture so designates these bodies, not on the basis of the magnitude of their masses but on the basis of the magnitude of their light."[122] While the moon does borrow light from the sun, moreover, the important point is that

> it is by divine might that such power has been given to the sun that through its own light it also lights up the moon and the stars; likewise, that the moon and the stars were so created that they are receptive to the light which is sent out by the sun.[123]

We should learn "what may be discussed about these subjects" from astronomers who "are the experts." The theologian's proper task is to discern the *theological* themes in such a passage, which "have power to instill confidence in our hearts."[124]

Clearly Scripture is not designed to be "useful for ... instruction" in all matters. The *Second Helvetic Confession* (1566), written by Heinrich Bullinger and

---

[118] Luther, *Gospel of John 1–4*, LW 22:218–19. Luther's relaxed attitude on this point contrasts sharply with that of fellow Lutheran Andreas Osiander (1498–1552), the rather controversial author of the misleading preface to Copernicus' *On the Revolutions of the Heavenly Spheres* (1543). Osiander was very concerned about chronological "discrepancies" in the Gospels and sought to harmonize them by proposing that "similar events occurred as often as was necessary" to resolve the problems. "Luther," Gerald Bray drily informs us, "was unimpressed by this effort" (Bray, *Biblical Interpretation*, 174).

[119] This was a point of contention between Luther and Melanchthon. John Dillenberger, *Protestant Thought and Natural Science: A Historical Interpretation* (Notre Dame: University of Notre Dame Press, 1960), 33.

[120] Martin Luther, *Lectures on Genesis Chapters 1–5*, LW 1:40–41.

[121] Luther, *Genesis 1–5*, LW 1:41.

[122] Luther, *Genesis 1–5*, LW 1:40.

[123] Luther, *Genesis 1–5*, LW 1:41.

[124] Luther, *Genesis 1–5*, LW 1:41.

destined to become "the most widely received" of all the sixteenth-century Protestant confessions, does tell us that Scripture *is* a "complete exposition" of some important subject matter.[125] Scripture expounds "all that pertains to a saving faith, and also to the framing of a life acceptable to God."[126] But the Holy Spirit has not set out through Scripture truthfully and reliably to teach us about *everything*. Empirical study of Scripture and of the world—of God's two "books"—has already led the sixteenth-century Reformers to understand this, even as it had led Augustine and others before them to the same conclusion.

The one kind of empirical enquiry is in fact feeding the other, because both "books" *are* God's books and must be taken seriously in what they have to say. To this point I have emphasized only one of the two directions of influence—the evident reality that the Reformers factored into their reading of Scripture what they knew about the world on the basis of "philosophy" (science). The influence running in the other direction is, however, equally important. It is not just that the Protestant reading of Scripture incorporated particular insights from modern science; it is also true that what we call "modern science," as an entire project, became possible only because of the deeper grasp of an authentic Christian worldview that the Reformation helped to promote through its insistence on a biblically based Christian theology and its rejection of a medieval scholasticism that was profoundly influenced by Greek philosophy. A fuller discussion of this reality, however, must await my chapter 14.

For the moment we need register only the way in which Martin Luther's own outlook already hints at this outcome. He was notably open to many of the scientific advances of his day—mechanical, medical, and others.[127] Looking ahead, he believed that the reform of religion, and in particular the retrieval of truer versions of the doctrines both of creation and incarnation, would lead people to take nature more seriously and appreciate it more fully than had been possible under the "rule" of either the scholastics or the (unreformed) humanists:

---

[125] Cochrane, *Reformed Confessions*, 220, 224.

[126] Cochrane, *Reformed Confessions*, 224. See also Bullinger's comments on the "end" to which Scripture is revealed in a sermon now reproduced in Lillback and Gaffin, *Word*, 65–73 (66–69). The *Thirty-Nine Articles of Religion of the Church of England* (1571) likewise affirm that "Holy Scripture containeth all things necessary to salvation" (article 6). Lillback and Gaffin, *Word*, 172.

[127] Lewis W. Spitz, *The Renaissance and Reformation Movements, Volume 2: The Reformation* (Chicago: Rand McNally, 1971), 583. E.g., responding on one occasion to a question about whether it was acceptable to use medicine in treating disease, Luther said: "It is our Lord God who created all things and they are good. Wherefore it is permissible to use medicine, for it is a creature of God." Luther, *Table Talk*, LW 54:54. Although he is generally anxious to portray religion and science as perennial enemies, Andrew White acknowledges Luther's "sturdy common sense" in this case and connects with it the fact that Protestant cities in Germany were more ready than others to permit anatomical investigation by way of dissection. Andrew D. White, *A History of the Warfare of Science with Theology in Christendom* (2 vols.; repr.; New York: George Braziller, 1955), 2:46.

We are at the dawn of a new era, for we are beginning to recover the knowledge of the external world that was lost through the fall of Adam. We now observe creatures properly, and not as formerly under the papacy. Erasmus is indifferent, and does not care to know how fruit is developed from the germ. But by the grace of God we already recognize in the most delicate flower the wonders of divine goodness and omnipotence. We see in His creatures the power of His word. . . . Erasmus passes by all that and takes no account of it, and looks upon external objects as cows look at a new gate.[128]

Reformation thinking, Luther believed, enabled Protestants to see the world of "external objects" more clearly, and to comprehend them more fully, than even a very distinguished Roman Catholic humanist.

Recovery of true knowledge about "the external world" was indeed an important aspect of what the Reformation would accomplish, and in a Protestant environment where it was emphasized that specifically religious vocations were not superior to secular ones, but that all should work to the glory of God, an enthusiastic band of "priests" soon emerged who dedicated themselves to the acquisition of this knowledge. The famous Johannes Kepler regarded himself in exactly this priestly way in the late sixteenth century (in a letter dated to 1595): "I wanted to become a theologian, and for a long time I was restless. Now, however, observe how through my [scientific] effort God is being celebrated in astronomy."[129] There was in all of this an *openness* to the world that God had made and what it had to offer humanity in terms of teaching and blessing.

The Reformers and Copernicus

It is particularly important that we grasp the nature and the extent of all this evidence about the Reformers' approach to Scripture and to enquiry into the natural world, for many twenty-first-century people, including a substantial number of Protestant Christians, appear to believe that Christian faith and science are inevitably at war. This opinion has arisen for a number of different reasons, but certainly some influential books have played an important role—books like John Draper's *History of the Conflict between Religion and Science* (1875) and Andrew White's *A History of the Warfare of Science with Theology in Christendom* (1896).[130] In this "warfare model" (and depending on which "side" one takes) the Reformers alternately play the role of heroes of the faith who insisted on the inerrancy

---

[128] Cited by Spitz, *Renaissance*, 582.

[129] Cited in Gerald Holton, "Johannes Kepler's Universe: Its Physics and Metaphysics," *AJP* 24 (1956): 340–51 (351), who goes on to say that "more than a few times in his later writings [Kepler] referred to astronomers as priests of the Deity in the book of nature."

[130] John W. Draper, *History of the Conflict between Religion and Science* (New York: Appleton, 1875). See above for the full White reference.

of Scripture over against a nascent, secular "modernism," and then obscurantist opponents of scientific progress who prevented for as long as they could human enlightenment. How is it that both sets of protagonists have apparently failed to grasp both the openness of the Reformers to science as they read their Scriptures, and the important ways in which what they taught provided the platform upon which modern science was built? One reason is that both groups have looked at particular statements that the Reformers made (or were alleged to have made) on particular topics and have misunderstood their significance. They have taken these statements as representing the Reformers' *principled position* with respect to emerging scientific discovery (i.e., resistance), when in fact they only represent the extent to which the Reformers were (like all of us are) people of their time. They were, therefore, people who held *particular beliefs* about the world that were not yet widely regarded as mistaken. Chief among these misunderstood (and in one case, invented!) statements are a number relating to Nicolaus Copernicus and Copernican cosmology.

It is reported, for example, that at Martin Luther's dinner table once, in 1539, "[t]here was mention of a certain astrologer who wanted to prove that the earth moves and not the sky, the sun, and the moon."[131] This topic may have been of particular interest in Wittenberg in that year because the mathematics professor, Georg Joachim Rheticus, had just been granted leave to go and work with Copernicus.[132] Luther dismissed the Copernican idea as presented at this dinner party not only as contrary to both common sense and Scripture but also as lacking broad intellectual support, and as illustrating a prevailing individualism that brought only disorder to society: "So it goes now. Whoever wants to be clever must agree with nothing that others esteem. He must do something of his own." Luther would rather stick with Scripture: "I believe the Holy Scriptures, for Joshua commanded the sun to stand still and not the earth."[133] This response has often been cited as a parade example of religious obscurantism in the face of scientific evidence. Philipp Melanchthon is then frequently introduced as further evidence for this obscurantism since, in his *Elements of Physics* (1549), he complains about those who contend, "either because of the love of novelties or in order to appear ingenious, that the earth moves." It is "not decent to defend such absurd opinions publicly," he states, "nor is it honest or a good example."[134] "So

[131] Luther, *Table Talk*, LW 54:358–59.

[132] See further on Rheticus Dennis Danielson, *The First Copernican: Georg Joachim Rheticus and the Rise of the Copernican Revolution* (New York: Walker, 2006).

[133] Luther, *Table Talk*, LW 54:359. His words are often quoted in the version passed on by John Aurifaber, which refers to Copernicus as a "fool" (German *Narr*); but the version I have cited is generally regarded as more reliable.

[134] Bruce T. Moran, "The Universe of Philip Melanchthon: Criticism and Use of the Copernican Theory," *CJMRS* 4 (1973): 1–23 (13–14).

earnest does this mildest of the Reformers become," writes Andrew White, "that he suggests severe measures to restrain such impious teachings."[135] John Calvin is then easily drawn into the obscurantist circle, since he has often been quoted as asking, "Who will venture to place the authority of Copernicus above that of the Holy Spirit?"[136] Certainly Calvin does warn in a sermon against those who say "that the sun does not move and that it is the earth that moves";[137] those who hold this view, he proposes, are possessed by the devil.

That all three Reformers believed strongly in geocentricity seems clear enough. It appeared self-evident to them that the earth stood still at the center of the cosmos and that everything else moved around it. To question this truth was to give evidence, at first sight at least, of being mad, or bad, or both. This belief was then naturally integrated with others, such that abandoning it would have knock-on effects.[138] However, the impression given by White that Melanchthon sought the repression of the Copernican view of the cosmos at the University of Wittenberg is unfortunate. Rheticus returned to teach in Wittenberg in the spring of 1542 and became dean of the Faculty of Arts before moving on to the chair in mathematics in Leipzig. He did so with the support of Melanchthon, who wrote him letters of recommendation and was generally very positive about him in other correspondence throughout the next decade and a half.[139] The other professor of mathematics in Wittenberg, Erasmus Reinhold, did not take a clear position on the question of geocentrism or heliocentrism, but he appreciated the elegant simplicity of the Copernican theory. He was therefore attracted to work further on it and published (with Melanchthon's assistance) "a volume of a definitely Copernican nature."[140] If indeed we were rightly to regard Melanchthon as an obscurantist, at least we could not say (it seems) that he was intolerant. Copernicus' book was in fact used in the University of Wittenberg "as an advanced text in astronomy courses, and mention of his work crept into more elementary books,"[141] even while his central ideas were still under dispute.

---

[135] White, *Warfare*, 1:127.

[136] White, *Warfare*, 1:127.

[137] Cited in David F. Wright and Jon Balserak, "Science," in *The Calvin Handbook* (ed. Herman J. Selderhuis; Grand Rapids: Eerdmans, 2009), 448–55 (452).

[138] "Melanchthon and his followers routinely invoked the laws of astronomy as the clearest evidence that the world has a providential design, and hence that the entire structure including the moral law is an objective feature of the cosmos." Peter Barker, "Kepler and Melanchthon on the Biblical Arguments against Copernicanism," in van der Meer and Mandelbrote, *Nature and Scripture in the Abrahamic Religions: Up to 1700*, 2:584–603 (587). See also Dillenberger, *Protestant Thought*, 39–41.

[139] Dillenberger, *Protestant Thought*, 47–48.

[140] Dillenberger, *Protestant Thought*, 48.

[141] Barker, "Kepler and Melanchthon," 589.

It is, however, simply a mistake to interpret the Protestant response to Copernicus as *evidence* of antiscientific obscurantism—even though clever people like White have apparently desired so much to advance this interpretation that they have been prepared to attribute to Calvin, without adequate research, words that he never wrote ("Who will venture ... etc.").[142] The world in which Luther ate his dinner in 1539 was one in which ancient Ptolemy's cosmology (and behind it, Aristotle's) still reigned—even though various aspects of Aristotle's thought were ill regarded by the Reformers. Indeed, Luther had already claimed in 1517 that "a man cannot become a theologian unless he become one without Aristotle."[143] Although Copernicus' theory had been discussed in certain scholarly circles (but not widely) during the preceding decade, the first publication advertising his ideas (written by Rheticus) did not appear until the following year (1540). Copernicus' full manuscript, *On the Revolutions of the Heavenly Spheres*, was not published until 1543. Even when the book became available, and leaving aside for the moment the scholarly population at large, the theory took a long time to be embraced even by Copernicus' fellow *astronomers*, precisely because it lacked a solid empirical foundation. "Widespread acceptance of the Copernican universe," Davis Young tells us

> came only after discoveries made by Galileo Galilei (1564–1642) ... ; [the] formulation of the laws of planetary motion by Johannes Kepler (1571–1630) ... ; and the physical explanation of planetary motion in terms of inertia and gravitation by Isaac Newton (1642–1727).[144]

---

[142] This is a great illustration of the fact that it is not just contemporary users of the Internet who are apt to repeat false information, and specifically false quotations, ad nauseam. On how the quotation came to be attributed to Calvin in the first place, see Young, *Natural World*, 43–49.

[143] Martin Luther, *Disputation against Scholastic Theology*, in *Luther: Early Theological Works* (trans. and ed. James Atkinson; LCC 16; Philadelphia: Westminster, 1962), 269. In general, "Luther believed that the use of Greek concepts ... had clouded rather than aided our knowledge of God. Luther clearly distinguishes Hebrew from Hellenistic thought and argues that through Greek philosophical conceptuality, theology had been turned into an abstract theology of glory." Zimmermann, *Theological Hermeneutics*, 48. The "Hellenization Thesis" with respect to authentic Christian theology is not merely an idea in the head of Adolf von Harnack in the nineteenth century, as some appear to think; it already lies at the heart of the Reformation.

[144] Young, *Natural World*, 28. For six decades after the publication of the Copernican theory, before it "was confirmed in more empirical fashion, practically all those who ventured to stand with him were accomplished mathematicians," for whom mathematical demonstrations were indeed a more reliable path to knowledge than scholastic logic, but whose method of reaching truth was still much more a priori than empirical. Edwin A. Burtt, *The Metaphysical Foundations of Modern Physical Science: A Historical and Critical Essay* (2nd ed.; London: Routledge & Kegan Paul, 1932), 39. See further, on the history of mathematics leading up to the Copernican thesis, 29–44; and Volker R. Remmert, "'Our Mathematicians Have Learned and Verified This': Jesuits, Biblical Exegesis, and the Mathematical Sciences in the Late Sixteenth and Early Seventeenth Centuries," in van der Meer and Mandelbrote, *Nature and Scripture in the Abrahamic Religions: Up to 1700*, 2:665–90.

Even in the middle of the seventeenth century "those opposed to Copernicanism had some quite respectable, coherent, observationally based science on their side. They were eventually proved wrong, but that did not make them bad scientists."[145]

It follows that we cannot expect of Luther in 1539, or of Melanchthon in 1545 (when the words published in 1549 were probably written), or of Calvin around 1556, that they should simply have accepted the new Copernican theory without demur. To do so is to fall prey to the "tendency among some historians and philosophers of science to treat a later, well-supported version of a theory as though it were the same account available to its earliest recipients."[146] In reality Melanchthon is evidently ahead of the intellectual and cultural curve already by 1550, when in the new edition of his *Elements of Physics* he is much more open than beforehand to heliocentrism as a mathematical hypothesis—moderating his opinion, no doubt, under the influence of both Rheticus and Reinhold.[147] The fact is that during the lifetimes of the magisterial Reformers, Copernicus' ideas were simply not accepted as the kind of "common knowledge" of the world that they otherwise allowed to influence their reading of Scripture. This was by no means intellectually irresponsible in their context, for

> it is safe to say that even had there been no religious scruples whatever against the Copernican astronomy, sensible men all over Europe, especially the most empirically minded, would have pronounced it a wild appeal to accept the premature fruits of an uncontrolled imagination, in preference to the solid inductions, built up gradually through the ages, of men's confirmed sense experience.... Contemporary empiricists, had they lived in the sixteenth century, would have been first to scoff out of court the new philosophy of the universe.[148]

This is not least the case because "there were [at that time] no known celestial phenomena which were not accounted for by the Ptolemaic method with as great accuracy as could be expected without more modern instruments."[149] For most of the *seventeenth* century, indeed, the Copernican theory still competed with alternatives, including that of Tycho Brahe, who was an avid collector of empirical astronomical data—"the first competent mind in modern astronomy to feel

---

[145] Dennis Danielson and Christopher M. Graney, "The Case against Copernicus," *Scientific American* 310 (2014): 72–77 (77).

[146] Robert S. Westman, "The Melanchthon Circle, Rheticus, and the Wittenberg Interpretation of the Copernican Theory," *Isis* 66 (1975): 164–93 (164).

[147] Moran, "Universe," 14.

[148] Burtt, *Foundations*, 25. See also Dillenberger, *Protestant Thought*, 48, who writes that "there was no compelling reason for accepting Copernicus in this period."

[149] Burtt, *Foundations*, 23. See 24–25 for further reasons why intelligent sixteenth-century people would have found the Copernican theory problematic.

ardently the passion for exact empirical facts."[150] It was only after Newton published his results concerning gravity and mechanics in 1687 that the heliocentric view began generally to prevail, and this was almost one and a half centuries after Luther's dinner party. Earlier, Kepler had already proposed a way to deal with the passage in Joshua about the sun standing still, very much along the lines of the Reformers' way of dealing with other scriptural passages that seemed to conflict with what was definitely known from science. It only appeared that the sun stood still, Kepler suggested; in reality, it was the earth.[151]

The sixteenth-century Reformation's response to Copernicus, then, by no means undermines the case that I have been making in the latter part of the present chapter in favor of their openness to science as they read their Scriptures.[152] It only illustrates that their judgments about the *content* of the scientific truth that should be brought into conversation with Scripture in pursuit of an integrated reading of God's two "books" were sixteenth-century, and not contemporary, judgments. This was inevitably true in all sorts of areas besides cosmology.[153] The Reformers may have found good reason to believe, for example, that the Gospel writers did not always record the events of Jesus' life in strict chronological order; they still shared the prevailing view of their time, however, that we should read the biblical chronology overall in a fairly straightforward manner, setting the date for the creation of the cosmos approximately four thousand years before Christ.[154] Furthermore, in their understanding of how creation *works* they also attributed to the Fall many aspects of the created order that a modern person possessing knowledge of how ecosystems function would not find at all plausible. Luther lists among the consequences of the Fall, for example, "[u]seless trees and herbs, thorns and thistles, lice, bedbugs, fleas [and] destructive powers of water and

---

[150] Burtt, *Foundations*, 50. Although Brahe "accepted a certain degree of divine accommodation" in Scripture, he remained "convinced that biblical statements in accordance with geocentric cosmology are to be read literally and not as an accommodation to common and primitive human ignorance." Miguel A. Granada, "Tycho Brahe, Caspar Peucer, and Christoph Rothmann on Cosmology and the Bible," in van der Meer and Mandelbrote, *Nature and Scripture in the Abrahamic Religions: Up to 1700*, 2:563–583 (581).

[151] Dillenberger, *Protestant Thought*, 84. In general, Kepler "was prepared to interpret [Scripture] in a flexible manner through the widely held notion of accommodation." See also Klaus Scholder, *The Birth of Modern Critical Theology: Origins and Problems of Biblical Criticism in the Seventeenth Century* (trans. John Bowman; Philadelphia: SCM Press, 1990), 53–58.

[152] Donald H. Kobe, "Copernicus and Martin Luther: An Encounter between Science and Religion," *AJP* 66 (1998): 190–96.

[153] Young, *Natural World*, 55–190, helpfully describes all the ways in which Calvin, e.g., was an (intelligent) man of his time when it came to subjects like sublunary physics, the nature of the Earth and its creatures, and the human body.

[154] E.g., Barr, "Luther and Biblical Chronology," 423–26.

fire,"¹⁵⁵ and Calvin adds "[t]he inclemency of the air, frost, thunders, unseasonable rains, drought, hail," as well as "briers and noxious plants."¹⁵⁶

None of this demonstrates however that after all, and in spite of everything noted above, the Reformers were intent only on paying attention to *Scripture* when it came to God's revelation of truth—that they were determined to ignore what had been learned by other means.¹⁵⁷ It demonstrates only that the Reformers lived in a time and a place in which the culture at large had not yet come to understand everything that would later be understood about the world—in these cases, specifically, about its geology and biology. It is not inconsistent with "reformed" principles of biblical interpretation to decline to abandon a particular reading before other truth has challenged it, or while the status of that truth remains uncertain. It is only inconsistent to cling doggedly to this reading when there is good evidence that one is mistaken.

As to the "warfare model" of the relationship between Christian faith and science in general, this is now widely questioned by scholars who are up to date with the research, and it is agreed to have done violence to a much more complicated historical reality. "While conflicts between science and religion have occurred in the past," Deborah Haarsma concedes, "warfare is not the primary interaction between religion and science."¹⁵⁸ For Lisa Stenmark, "this model simply does not bear up under scrutiny."¹⁵⁹ We should not perpetuate it.

CONCLUSION

Holy Scripture is given to the Church as the God-inspired, sufficiently perspicuous, canonical rule of truth—by which alone we should ultimately measure the rightness of both Christian doctrine and practice. In the present chapter we have wrestled with questions concerning its reliability in guiding us in both these areas. We have reflected on the mediated, accommodated nature of the guidance and on the question of what exactly comes under the heading "doctrine and practice." The magisterial Reformers, standing in line (once again) with the Church Fathers, held that Scripture unerringly guides us when it comes to those matters of belief and practice about which God wishes to address us. They did not

---

[155] Bornkamm, *Luther and the Old Testament*, 60; cf. Luther, *Genesis 1–5*, LW 1:206–9.

[156] Calvin, *Genesis*, 174, 177.

[157] Rheticus himself addressed the hermeneutical issues arising from taking both seriously in a work published posthumously that was discovered to be his only in the late twentieth century. Reijer Hooykaas, *G. J. Rheticus' Treatise on Holy Scripture and the Motion of the Earth* (Amsterdam: North-Holland, 1984).

[158] Deborah B. Haarsma, "Science and Religion in Harmony," in *Science and Religion in Dialogue* (2 vols.; ed. Melville Y. Stewart; Oxford: Wiley-Blackwell, 2010), 1:107–19 (108).

[159] Lisa L. Stenmark, *Religion, Science, and Democracy: A Disputational Friendship* (Lanham, Md.: Lexington, 2013), 13.

believe, however, that God wishes to address us through Scripture about *all* matters. Discrimination is required on this point, not least so that we do not end up using Scripture to promote and defend wrong ideas—among them, ideas that contradict what is known from sources other than the Bible. We must understand that God's Word comes to us through human beings who stand like ourselves within the stream of history and who speak to their contemporaries and to us in accordance with the language, thought forms, and conventions of their time. We must attend to such human realities in seeking to hear the Word of God, correcting mistaken interpretations of God's address to us even if they possess great antiquity and may have previously attracted widespread agreement. For not everything that God has been understood in the past to say through Scripture is, in fact, what God wishes to say through Scripture. This is not because *Scripture* errs; it is only because *interpretation* has erred, sometimes misapprehending both the intended extent of God's revelation and the significance of its detail. As Augustine proposed all those centuries ago, some aspects of what Christians have believed the Great Story to say do not (and did not) represent what it really says. Such interpretations turn out to be merely opinions "proposed by man in his ignorance."

To stand in line with the Reformers when it comes to the authority of Scripture is to stand in line with everything just mentioned. It is important to say so, given that so many Protestants during subsequent centuries, as we shall see in upcoming chapters, have failed in one way or another to follow their example. All too often they have departed from the Reformers' emphasis on the genuine historicality and humanity of Scripture, moving closer to a dictation model in their view of divine inspiration. They have consequently struck a resolutely skeptical posture in respect of modern (and especially scientific) developments, unwilling even to consider the possibility of their fallibility in certain facets of their biblical interpretation. Indeed, it is one of the great ironies of the contemporary scene in biblical hermeneutics that the official Roman Catholic position on Scripture at the present time (leaving aside its beliefs on parallel, oral Christian tradition) is more "reformed" than that of many Protestants.

Long gone are the days of Vatican I (1870), with its assertion that the Scriptures "contain revelation, with no admixture of error" because they were written under the "dictation of the Holy Spirit,"[160] and its warning that "all faithful Christians are ... forbidden to defend, as legitimate conclusions of science, such opinions as are known to be contrary to the doctrines of the faith."[161] Long gone is its anathema against those who maintain "it to be possible that sometimes, according

---

[160] First Vatican Council, *The Dogmatic Decrees of the Vatican Council Concerning the Catholic Faith and the Church of Christ* (1870), 3.2, in Schaff, *Creeds of Christendom*, 2:241–42.

[161] First Vatican Council, *Dogmatic Decrees*, 3.4, in Schaff, *Creeds of Christendom*, 2:249.

to the progress of science, a sense is to be given to doctrines propounded by the Church different from that which the Church has understood and understands."[162] Already by 1893 Leo XIII's encyclical *Providentissimus Deus* is "aware of the advantages of scientific linguistic and exegetical studies" and is "attuned to the fact that the views of the biblical authors in questions of science were not invested with scriptural infallibility."[163] Later, *Divino afflante Spiritu* (1943) acknowledges the value of modern scholarship that has "examined and explained the nature and effects of biblical inspiration more exactly and more fully" than was previously the case. This encyclical affirms that "the inspired writer, in composing the sacred book, is the living and reasonable instrument of the Holy Spirit," and that the aim of the interpreter is first and foremost to comprehend "what he wishes to express by his writings" as a person of his own time and culture.[164] It quotes Thomas Aquinas—"In Scripture divine things are presented to us in the manner which is in common use amongst men"—and agrees with John Chrysostom's emphasis on divine accommodation.[165] In the course of "demonstrating and proving [Scripture's] immunity from all error," then, the Roman Catholic exegete must "determine . . . to what extent the manner of expression or the literary mode adopted by the sacred writer may lead to a correct and genuine interpretation."[166] *Dei Verbum* (1965) later clarifies the term "inerrancy" in this context: "the Books of Scripture [must be acknowledged] as teaching firmly, faithfully, and without error the truth that God wished to be recorded in the sacred writings for the sake of our salvation."[167] All of this is very sensible and patristic. It is also entirely "reformed."

---

[162] First Vatican Council, *Dogmatic Decrees*, 3.4, in Schaff, *Creeds of Christendom*, 2:255.
[163] Cited in Brown and Collins, "Church Pronouncements," 1167.
[164] *Divino afflante Spiritu*, 128.
[165] *Divino afflante Spiritu*, 129.
[166] *Divino afflante Spiritu*, 129.
[167] *Dei Verbum*, 24.

14

The Bible, the Heavens, and the Earth
The Beginnings of an Eclipse

> *The men of the Middle Ages lived in the Bible and by the Bible. . . . There was a desire, not merely to bring all . . . together into a single work of knowledge, expression and praise . . . but also regulate everything according to the sacred text.*
>
> —Yves Congar[1]

> *[A]ll across the theological spectrum the great reversal had taken place; interpretation [from the late eighteenth century onward] was a matter of fitting the biblical story into another world with another story rather than incorporating that world into the biblical story.*
>
> —Hans Frei[2]

As we noted in the introduction to part 2, the Reformation occurred toward the end of a long period in Europe during which the entire civilization had been Christian. Its citizens inhabited a "culture of the Book" in which the Bible was the defining document for both private and public life. They may not personally have read the Bible much; to a very great extent, they may have depended on others to tell them what it said, in the conviction that its true meaning was articulated in the current teaching of Mother Church.[3] Even so, it was widely assumed that it was the Bible, at root, that provided the authoritative reference point when

---

[1] Congar, *Tradition*, 86.
[2] Frei, *Eclipse*, 130.
[3] This would have been especially true for those who were illiterate, of course. Yet we should not underestimate the extent to which people (including nonclergy), at least by the late Middle Ages, "not only had access to the text of the Scriptures, through the production and the dissemination of vernacular Bible translations, but [were also] . . . active agents in the diffusion of texts." Sabrina Corbellini, "Instructing the Soul, Feeding the Spirit and Awakening the Passion: Holy Writ and Lay Readers in Late Medieval Europe," in Gordon and McLean, *Shaping the Bible*, 15–39 (38). Medieval religion was highly "textual," whether in official, orthodox or unofficial, unorthodox ways—"medieval heresy was closely related to a lay culture of literacy in opposition to, although sometimes closely bound up with, clerical literary practice." Cummings, *Literary Culture*, 19.

it came to all human knowledge—albeit that philosophy had its own important role to play, especially when it came to questions about the natural world.

By the time we reach the end of the sixteenth century in Europe, this had been the case for a millennium or more. Science, politics, art, architecture, literature, and music—all reflected the Great Story, as Christian thinkers attempted to unite in one domain, in various medieval syntheses, all human knowledge. This synthetic approach is often described nowadays as bringing together "Jerusalem and Athens"—reflecting Tertullian's famous question, "What has Jerusalem to do with Athens?" In premodern Europe the prevailing answer to this question was: "everything." The central figure representing "Athens" might change from time to time—now Plato or Plotinus, now Aristotle. Athens might sometimes have more of the upper hand than Jerusalem (as in third-century Egypt), and sometimes Jerusalem might be more predominant (as in certain respects in sixteenth-century Protestant Germany). No matter exactly which kind of synthesis was attempted, however, the overarching biblical narrative provided the frame within which the attempt was (at least allegedly) being made.

A mere three centuries later the same cannot be said. By the end of the nineteenth century the biblical Story still remained the defining narrative for many *Christians*, at least in terms of doctrine and morals, and they were exporting it in its various confessional and cultural expressions, through emigration and mission, to the rest of the world. This was when the period of the global expansion of Christian faith that we are still experiencing today really began. Perhaps paradoxically, however, the seventeenth through the nineteenth centuries were also those in which the long, slow death of Christendom in Europe began—a decline that Europeans and those living in their former colonies *are* also still experiencing today. An entire premodern world defined by and organized in terms of the Great Story began to disappear, and a new, modern world began to emerge. There occurred, in the words of the title of Hans Frei's well-known book, *The Eclipse of Biblical Narrative*. The Bible gradually lost its cultural authority, and fewer and fewer people looked to synthesize with it the knowledge they were acquiring from other sources.

The present and the following two chapters will explore the reasons for this "eclipse" and make the beginnings of a proposal about how contemporary Christian Bible readers ought to respond to it. I shall argue that one of the more important reasons for the eclipse of biblical narrative was that the Great Story came to be regarded by many as incapable of embracing all the newly discovered truths about the world (truths scientific, historical, and so on), and at the same time as a major cause of violence, war, and intolerance and a major obstacle to human rights, freedoms, and ultimately well-being. Our contemporary response must include, among other things, repentance and a renewed commitment to robust Christian education.

THE ANALYSIS OF THE PROBLEM

We begin, then, with this: how exactly did the displacement of biblical narrative occur? This is an interesting historical question even if one is quite relaxed about the answer. Of the four "ways" of approaching Protestant biblical hermeneutics outlined in my brief typology in chapter 1, it is not likely that many who embrace the first (historical critics) or the second (postmodern readers) will be too concerned about the displacement, unless their commitment to their "way" is only one aspect of a much larger and more traditional set of commitments. They will almost certainly put it all down in an uncomplicated manner to "progress," and leave it at that. For those who still believe, however—with or without the various caveats entered in my chapter 13—that the biblical narrative still tells us the true story of the cosmos, its eclipse cannot possibly be a matter merely of historical interest. They (we) need to understand as best we can exactly why the Great Story became implausible and unwelcome to so many people in Europe and its (ex-)colonies during the time period in question and why this is still true in contemporary cultures deeply influenced by the thinking of that time. We need to understand this both for our own sakes and also for others'—since if we lack comprehension, it will be difficult to respond well in our present moment to modern and postmodern culture.

The very character of our response will indeed be fundamentally *shaped* by our understanding of the history. We shall explore in chapter 16 how this is true of those following the fourth "way" (counter-Reformational Protestants). For the moment I wish to illustrate the point by way of a brief engagement only with the third "way" Chicago constituency, to which we shall also return at greater length in chapter 16. This popular contemporary way of describing the eclipse of biblical narrative, reflected clearly in *CSBH*, paints it largely as a picture of unjustifiable apostasy. Once there was a Protestant Christian culture founded on the inerrant Word of God. Then there arose "an inductive scientific method [that] was assumed to be a means of obtaining all truth" and a materialism and a naturalism that were antithetical to orthodox Christian faith.[4] After this came an "Age of Enlightenment"—the period that saw "humanity's release from self-imposed tutelage to external authority and readiness to use its independent reason"

---

[4] Norman L. Geisler, "Inductivism, Materialism, and Rationalism: Bacon, Hobbes, and Spinoza," in *Biblical Errancy: An Analysis of its Philosophical Roots* (ed. Norman L. Geisler; Grand Rapids: Zondervan, 1981), 9–22 (10).

(Immanuel Kant, *What Is Enlightenment?* 1784).[5] In the course of this Enlightenment a modern alternative to orthodox faith, often referred to as Deism, was developed, and then other problematic philosophies followed, such as Darwinian evolutionism. The eclipse of biblical narrative, on this view, is the simple consequence of sinful people turning away from God and his inerrant Word for no defensible reason in order to embrace very wrong ideas and attendant practices. It "did not result from a discovery of factual evidence that made belief in an inerrant Scripture untenable. Rather, it resulted from the unnecessary acceptance of philosophical premises that undermined the historic belief in an infallible and inerrant Bible."[6] The Church contributed to the eclipse only insofar as theologians themselves "capitulated to alien philosophical presuppositions."[7]

If this is our view, then it stands to reason that our response to modernity and postmodernity will be resolutely negative. An eclipse of biblical narrative has occurred, and this is not good; we must work to reestablish the authority of the Bible in both Church and society. This involves identifying all the problematic "isms" that have wreaked havoc on biblical authority in the course of the past few centuries. We must reject these "isms," return to our Protestant roots, and try to persuade our neighbors to do the same. *CSBH* and the accompanying commentary by Norman Geisler list a number of these "isms": relativism, subjectivism, naturalism, evolutionism, scientism, and secular humanism.[8] A particular understanding of the history results in a particular response to it, which includes an action-plan for the future. On this view, Christian faith has essentially been at war with both modernity and postmodernity for some time—and not least with modern science. The nature of solution offered—which is essentially to go on fighting the good fight—is bound up directly with the analysis of the nature of the problem.

There are important elements of truth in this Chicago story. No orthodox Christian will wish to dispute that many aspects of modern philosophy are problematic from the point of view of Christian faith; that among the motivations that have driven modern people to choose their philosophies is certainly a desire to oppose at least certain versions of Christian faith; and that, in general, "all have sinned and fall short of the glory of God" (Rom 3:23), and that this reality impacts all aspects of modern (and other) culture. However, I do not believe that

---

[5] Perez Zagorin, *How the Idea of Religious Toleration Came to the West* (Princeton: Princeton University Press, 2003), 290. For a sketch of Kant's life and thought, see John C. O'Neill, *The Bible's Authority: A Portrait Gallery of Thinkers from Lessing to Bultmann* (Edinburgh: T&T Clark, 1991), 54–65.

[6] Geisler, "Inductivism," 10.

[7] Geisler, "Inductivism," 10.

[8] *CSBH*, articles 6 and 19.

the Chicago story provides an adequate account of historical reality in the seventeenth through the nineteenth centuries (or even in the sixteenth), especially when it comes to understanding the modern relationship between Christian faith and science. The generalized "warfare model" of this relationship, I proposed in my chapter 13, should not be perpetuated—by *anyone*. It simply does not help us to see clearly the complex, historical reality. One of the most glaring weaknesses of the Chicago version of this warfare model, in particular—although it is certainly not the only one—is that it sees no role for the Church itself, other than "capitulating" to falsehood, in causing the eclipse of biblical narrative in the modern period. Surrender, in this Chicago "fight," is always a negative. My own view, on the other hand, is that Christian "capitulation" to falsehood has only ever been *part* of the problem; also important has been a Christian refusal to surrender to truth and virtue (including "factual evidence") when surrender was required. This aspect of the story of the eclipse, at least, CSBH neglects, and it is this aspect that I shall emphasize in my own fuller and more accurate analysis in chapters 14 and 15.

The consequence of the flawed Chicago analysis is inevitably an entirely unhelpful and wrongheaded response. It is a response that among other things is not nearly as "reformed" as the responders believe—because its understanding of the true nature of Reformation thinking about "an infallible and inerrant Bible" and its implications is confused. I shall have a lot more to say about this in chapter 16. For the moment it is sufficient to alert the reader to the obvious: that my own very different analysis will lead me (also in that chapter) to a very different and I believe better response. This is the fifth "way" described in my chapter 1—an unabashedly "reformed" way of Bible reading that nevertheless stands in continuity with much of our pre-Reformation Christian heritage and is appreciative of both modern and postmodern contributions to biblical hermeneutics (and to life in general). That is to say: the fifth "way" eschews unnecessary warfare.

THE SIXTEENTH-CENTURY BACKGROUND

Our first steps on this "way" necessarily involve a review of what we have learned so far about the character of the period immediately prior to the seventeenth century in Europe—beyond and beneath the overarching reality of its Christian nature. For although it is true that the notion of a Christian civilization was still alive and well in this period, and that attempts to integrate all knowledge within the bounds of the Christian story were still proceeding apace, it is also the case that in a fast-changing world some significant stresses and strains were already beginning to emerge that were threatening to destabilize the entire project.

On Reading Creation

We recall from my chapter 11 that already in the thirteenth century the English Franciscan monk Roger Bacon, who certainly lived within the "culture of the Book" and wished that it should be better read, was nevertheless also passionately interested in God's other "book"—the book of creation. He himself was an experimental scientist. What can be learned from creation that is true, good, and useful? Indeed, what can be learned from others who have observed and thought about creation, whether they be French Christians, Spanish Jews and Muslims, or (still) ancient Greek pagans? These are some of his questions. His emphasis lies on the gaining of wisdom not through custom, tradition, or even Bible reading, but through empirical enquiry into the natural world. In this Bacon anticipates an important cultural trend in the centuries that lie immediately ahead of him—a trend toward ever-greater dependence upon empirical enquiry in the process of acquiring knowledge.

It was deeply rooted in its European form in a particular version of the Christian worldview that, already in the Renaissance and then certainly in the Reformation, was in the process of freeing itself from the undue influence of the dominant streams of Greek philosophy. For Plato, as for the preceding, non-Israelite ancient Near Eastern cultures that exerted such significant influence on Greek thought,[9] the main importance of the physical world lay in the access that it provided to a "real" world beyond it—the world of the gods (in ancient Near Eastern thought) or the Forms (in Plato). There was a kind of "sacramental" connection between the material and the immaterial worlds, it was believed. The former functioned primarily as a (rather dirty) window through which to apprehend the latter, and it lacked any value in itself—what Tom Torrance once described as "the age-old Hellenistic and Oriental assumption that the real is reached only by transcending the contingent."[10] The purpose of philosophy was to get beyond the dim reflections of reality available to us by way of our senses in the visible world of phenomena and to push on to true knowledge of the reality *beyond* the grasp of our senses by way of contemplative reason. The Greek philosophy of nature that developed out of this worldview via Aristotle held that every object in the cosmos—an all-encompassing, beautiful organism comprising "all beings, material and immaterial, inorganic and living, earthly and heavenly, human and divine"[11]—possesses two elements: form and matter. Neither is created; both are simply "there." The *form* of an object is its essence—the reality that makes the

---

[9] Provan, *Seriously Dangerous Religion*, passim.

[10] Cited in Alister E. McGrath, *The Science of God: An Introduction to Scientific Theology* (Grand Rapids: Eerdmans, 2004), 51.

[11] Michael B. Foster, "Man's Idea of Nature," CS 41 (1958): 361–66 (362).

object what it is. The *matter* is the source only of the imperfection with which the form is realized. As Michael Foster puts it, "the form alone makes the thing to be what it is, whereas the matter contributes no positive element to its being."[12] The point of natural philosophy on this view is to penetrate to the essence of things—to what is "eternal, unchangeable, uncreated, self-regenerating and rational."[13] It is to get at what is "intelligible" about an object as opposed to what is merely "sensible" (i.e., discovered by the senses). On this view, then, reason is crucial to the pursuit of reality, as the philosopher seeks above all *definitions* of natural objects: "All the peculiarities of Greek natural science are derived from the assumption that the essence of a natural object [its form] is definable, as the essence of a geometrical object is [e.g., a triangle]."[14] Intelligent (rational) comprehension of the form is sufficient for an understanding of what an object is. What is learned by sense experience with respect to the object's *matter* contributes nothing to this goal, but results only in a defective understanding of the object.

It follows, then, that the Greek science of nature as it developed in line with the canons of Aristotelian logic did not possess any truly empirical element, even though observation played some role in the process of gaining knowledge. Sense experience "supplied the illustration but not the evidence of the conclusions of science." It helped the philosopher to grasp "by an act of intuitive reason" an understanding "of something which is not itself sensible at all."[15] What nature *must* be like was clarified, a priori, by way of logical and dialectical argument; what remained was only the observation of examples reflecting (however dimly) the rational, necessary truth of the matter. The planets *must* travel in circular orbits, for example, because they are heavenly, immortal bodies and the circle is the perfect figure—that is the way that heavenly (as opposed to earthly) physics must necessarily work.[16] If one turned one's attention to the earth, and wished to know (say) what the purpose of male testicles might be, one necessarily began with observation, asking the question, "what do testicles resemble?" Aristotle's memorable and influential answer was that they resembled the weights that hang down from a weaving loom to guarantee the tension required to enable the loom to function. Therefore, the purpose of testicles (reason suggested) is to ensure a

---

[12] Michael B. Foster, "The Christian Doctrine of Creation and the Rise of Modern Natural Science," *Mind* 43 (1934): 446–68 (455).

[13] Reijer Hooykaas, *Religion and the Rise of Modern Science* (Grand Rapids: Eerdmans, 1972), 6.

[14] Foster, "Christian Doctrine of Creation," 454.

[15] Foster, "Christian Doctrine of Creation," 454, 460. Aristotle and Plato differed on this point "only in estimating differently the importance to be assigned to what is sensible *as illustration*" (454n2).

[16] Charlotte Methuen, "On the Threshold of a New Age: Expanding Horizons as the Broader Context of Scriptural Interpretation," *HBOT* 2:665–90 (666).

healthy tension in the male body without which the interior connections that maintain it in a harmonious and balanced state would get "loosened" and stop functioning in an optimal manner.[17] The very last thing a Greek philosopher (scientist) in this tradition would think of doing was to pursue genuine empirical enquiry in order actually to "discover" what male testicles are "for"—truly to *test* the hypothesis, as it were. The ancient Greeks certainly *knew* about genuine empirical enquiry and valued it in the acquisition of knowledge in certain limited "zones" of reality.[18] However, they did not believe that it provided reliable knowledge about anything outside of these zones.[19]

It was this Aristotelian philosophy of nature that was maintained and developed in medieval Christian scholastic philosophy. It was this same Aristotelian philosophy that was self-consciously rejected by early modern science as it began to emerge in the late sixteenth and then the seventeenth century. This *modern* science depended on the idea that God had created both the heavens and the earth, no part of which is divine and all of which should be expected to share a common physics. Possessing an order imprinted upon it by God (and therefore obeying "laws"), creation is nevertheless distinct from God and represents a legitimate object of enquiry *in itself*. We do not explore material creation merely in order to gain knowledge about an allegedly "real" world elsewhere; material entities are not (merely) symbols pointing to eternal spiritual realities, but (more importantly) creatures in relationship (including causal relationship) with each other.[20] This God is, moreover, not bound by necessity (since he stands outside the cosmos,

---

[17] Aristotle, *Generation of Animals*, 5.7 (trans. A. L. Peck; Cambridge, Mass.: Harvard University Press, 1942), 548–51.

[18] Empirical method was appropriate, e.g., to the work of the *histōr*, whose job was to arbitrate disputes. To succeed in this work he needed to gain knowledge of narrow particularities (*historia*) by way of receiving testimony and testing its claims. Ancient Greek historians such as Thucydides (as well as Roman successors such as Tacitus) proceeded in a similar manner, "convinced that true history could be written only while events were still within living memory, and they valued as their sources the oral reports of direct experience of the events by involved participants in them." Richard Bauckham, *Jesus and the Eyewitnesses: The Gospels as Eyewitness Testimony* (Grand Rapids: Eerdmans, 2006), 8–9.

[19] When it came to acquiring knowledge about matters of medical science, e.g., empirical method was widely regarded as deficient. Galen of Pergamon (c. AD 129–216), e.g., whose medical theories deeply influenced Western medicine well into the modern period, flirted with such method, but was also deeply suspicious of it on the ground that it was not logical.

[20] In the symbolic way of thinking "two things are linked not by cause and effect, but because they share an essential property." E.g., the lion symbolizes Christ "because they share the property of kingship," but also Satan "because both are predators." Jitse M. van der Meer and Richard J. Oosterhoff, "God, Scripture, and the Rise of Modern Science (1200–1700): Notes in the Margins of Harrison's Hypothesis," in van der Meer and Mandelbrote, *Nature and Scripture in the Abrahamic Religions: Up to 1700*, 2:363–96 (378). Wherever this kind of thinking about the cosmos predominates, interest in other kinds of relationships will inevitably be limited.

and is not part *of* it), and his actions in creating the cosmos cannot be predicted rationally—as if his will were subordinate to his reason (and therefore not free). Therefore, one has to look and see what God has actually done: "moderns know that there is in this sense no 'must' about nature and that the only way to find out is to go and see and abide by what you find."[21] Spatial and temporal relationships rather than logical connections come to the fore in this kind of modern enquiry; the fundamental importance of movement and change, over against stasis and permanence, is recognized. It was only as this understanding of reality at the level of metaphysics gained significant ground in the course of the succeeding centuries, and genuine empirical enquiry came to be highly valued by many educated people in European society as a path to knowledge, that what we call modern science became possible.

Where did these "un-Greek" ideas originate? They originated in the biblical, Christian doctrine of creation:

> The medieval philosopher had of course believed the Christian doctrine that nature is created. But the belief had been efficacious only in his theology. In his science of nature he had continued to seek for final causes, to define essences and to deduce properties: in a word—he had continued to employ the methods of Aristotelian science, entirely oblivious of the fact that Aristotle's science was based upon the presupposition that nature is not created.[22]

It is one thing, as Foster notes, "to adopt a faith but quite a different thing to let that faith permeate all departments of thought and action."[23] What we see in the gradual cultural shift from a medieval scholastic to an early modern philosophy of nature is an example of this greater "permeation":

> The modern investigators of nature were the first to take seriously *in their science* the Christian doctrine that nature is created, and the main differences between the methods of ancient and the methods of modern natural science may be reduced to this: that these are and those are not methods proper to the investigation of a created nature.[24]

The Reformation played a crucial role in this cultural shift[25]—only one of its contributions to the dethronement of Aristotle as "'the pope in philosophy'...

---

[21] Foster, "Nature," 365.
[22] Foster, "Christian Doctrine of Creation," 453.
[23] Foster, "Nature," 365.
[24] Foster, "Christian Doctrine of Creation," 453.
[25] This is consciously *not* to claim simplistically that "Christianity led to modern science"—the "myth" that Ronald Numbers is so keen to lay to rest in a recent essay. Ronald L. Numbers, "Myth 9: That Christianity Gave Birth to Modern Science," in Numbers, *Galileo Goes to Jail*, 79–89 (80).

along with the other Pope."[26] We recall from my chapter 11 Luther's judgment that "nothing can be learned [from Aristotle's writings] either about nature or the Spirit."[27] It should come as no surprise to learn, then, that as the new science emerged it was promoted most enthusiastically in those parts of Europe where the old medieval scholastic ideas had become the most marginalized—that is, in Protestant rather than in Roman Catholic areas. For in "an age in which religious sanction was necessary for something to become socially acceptable, it made a great difference whether science was distrusted, merely tolerated, or positively encouraged by the prevalent religion."[28] One small illustration of this truth is that already in sixteenth-century Europe the majority of the notable botanists were Protestants.[29]

The question that soon faced thoughtful Christians, of course, was how far to integrate into their Bible reading and their theology the claimed results of empirical enquiry that Protestant theological perspectives had played such a part in encouraging. What was to be done when the new science unearthed evidence that was, or appeared to be, inconsistent with settled, traditional interpretations of Scripture? How far could this be allowed to go? In the sixteenth century the stresses and strains caused to the contemporary Christian worldview by empirical enquiry were not yet great. New knowledge could be integrated by way of rereading a relatively small number of biblical texts that could be understood without great difficulty (in line with Augustine's thinking as described in my chapter 13) as never having truly implied what they had commonly been taken to imply. The Great Story did not begin to lose its credibility in Europe just because Columbus sailed to the Americas and back. In the case of Copernicus, as we also saw in the previous chapter, the weight of the empirical evidence itself was not yet

---

[26] Peter Harrison, *The Bible, Protestantism, and the Rise of Natural Science* (Cambridge: Cambridge University Press, 1998), 104, referencing Thomas Culpeper (1626–1697) in his *Morall discourses and essayes upon severall select subjects* (1655). For the undermining of Aristotle's authority on a range of subjects already in the late sixteenth century, see Methuen, "Threshold," 668–70.

[27] Luther, *To the Christian Nobility*, LW 44:200.

[28] Hooykaas, *Religion*, 101. This is *not* to dispute, of course, that many Roman Catholics contributed to the scientific revolution. Lawrence M. Principe, "Myth 11: That Catholics Did Not Contribute to the Scientific Revolution," in Numbers, *Galileo Goes to Jail*, 99–106.

[29] Hooykaas, *Religion*, 99; for a Roman Catholic exception in Levinus Lemnius, see Kathleen M. Crowther, "Sacred Philosophy, Secular Theology: The Mosaic Physics of Levinus Lemnius (1505–1568) and Francisco Valles (1524–1592)," in van der Meer and Mandelbrote, *Nature and Scripture in the Abrahamic Religions: Up to 1700*, 2:397–428. In the seventeenth century (and contrary to how the situation has often been represented) Puritanism in particular "and ascetic Protestantism generally ... played no small part in arousing a sustained interest in science.... Puritanism was a basic component of the scientific education of this period." Robert K. Merton, "Science, Technology and Society in Seventeenth Century England," *Osiris* 4 (1938): 360–632 (494–95); and for a brief summary on the general theme, see Hooykaas, *Religion*, 144–49.

sufficiently strong to cause any great angst with respect to medieval cosmology overall, nor any great problem for the standard interpretations of biblical texts that provided support for it. Moreover, because the Copernican proposal was broadly understood as merely a mathematical theory presented for discussion and useful for prediction, rather than a set of dogmatic claims about physical reality, it managed in any case not to ruffle too many sixteenth-century feathers.[30] In the succeeding centuries, however—as we shall soon see—the situation became more challenging. Many would react, then, by denigrating the fruits of empirical enquiry. They would react indeed with the kind of opposition to the whole empirical project that Columbus had previously endured while planning his voyage of exploration. Since the correct answers to so many of the questions now being explored were already known (many would argue), it was impious even to wish to "look and see" what was true. Just so have the natural sciences in the modern period "been considerably inhibited [in general] by those who insisted that they already knew the deep structuring of the world on the basis of *a priori* concepts."[31] It was this kind of commitment to ignorance as a way of "saving" the Christian faith that was to have such devastating consequences for the credibility of the faith in the public square as time passed.

On Reading the Bible

In the *sixteenth* century, however, the significant threat to the coherence of the Great Story did not arise from reading creation and then asking questions of the Bible. It arose from people reading the Bible itself—more people than ever before, reading more Bibles than had hitherto been available. The sixteenth century was marked—as we saw in my chapter 12—by an unprecedented interpretative pluralism with respect to Bible reading. Questions about what Scripture really teaches were generating markedly different answers even on quite central issues of doctrine and practice. This was not just a matter of Protestant disagreement with Roman Catholics; it was also a matter of disagreement *among* Protestants— for example, between Lutherans and Anabaptists, or between Lutherans and Calvinists. Different groups, each claiming to interpret the one Great Story correctly, disagreed about important matters like the proper relationship between Church and state, or baptism, or the Eucharist. Some groups, like the Socinians, even objected conscientiously to core Christian doctrines on the ground that they were not biblical.

---

[30] Kenneth J. Howell, "The Hermeneutics of Nature and Scripture in Early Modern Science and Theology," in van der Meer and Mandelbrote, *Nature and Scripture in the Abrahamic Religions: Up to 1700*, 1:275–98 (280–87).

[31] McGrath, *Science of God*, 159. On the folly of such a priori approaches to knowledge, see further 240–45.

It is not so much the extent as the nature of this pluralism that was the issue. If Bible readers had themselves believed that the Christian stories (in the plural) that they were now telling were simply acceptable variants of the same Story, and if they had consistently conducted themselves accordingly, things might have turned out differently. Even if they had not believed this, but had nevertheless treated dissenters from their cause generously, the problem might not have become as serious as it did. It became really serious because of the readiness with which dissenters of all kinds in sixteenth-century Europe were pronounced to be heretics, and because of the legitimacy that this provided to others, as circumstances allowed, to inflict extreme violence upon them.

To treat dissenters in this way was not of course a novelty of the sixteenth century. However, the number of dissenters (viewed from differing perspectives) was now vastly greater than before, they were often organized in groups of significant size, and they were frequently sanctioned by political and military power (as in the Protestant principalities in Germany, for example). Repression of dissent under these circumstances was always going to be a more bloody affair than it had typically been in the past, involving both attempts to remove whole minority populations *within* states as well as outright war *between* states. It was above all the violence resulting directly from the various dogmatic claims to be telling "the true" Christian story over against counterfeits that began, in the aftermath of the Reformation, to destabilize the very notion of there existing one Christian Story at all that could function as the basis for life in society—for law, government, and public discourse. It was the violence directed against individuals like Michael Servetus in Calvin's Geneva, for example (my chapter 12), and against entire groups (or collections of groups) like the Anabaptists. It was also the violence arising from wars between Protestant and Roman Catholic cities, principalities, and regions, such as the Second War of Kappel of 1531, in the course of which Huldrych Zwingli was killed; or the Schmalkaldic War of 1546–1547, between the forces of Emperor Charles V of the Holy Roman Empire and the Lutheran "Schmalkaldic League." Surely there must be another way of proceeding—some people began to ask—such that society could remain functional and cohesive while allowing individuals and groups within it to hold in good conscience dissenting religious views?

On Dealing with Heretics

In the sixteenth century we have not yet arrived at the point in my account of the eclipse of biblical narrative when this question will be put in its starkest form by a *significant* number of people. We do find precursors, however. Sebastian Castellio (1515–1563) had been the rector of the College of Geneva and an admirer of Calvin until a quarrel led him to leave Geneva and take up an appointment as a professor of Greek at the University of Basle.[32] Reflecting on the Servetus affair in an important pamphlet published in 1554 (*Defense of the Orthodox Faith*), Castellio argues that we do not all have to agree on matters of doctrine in order to be saved; the important thing is that we follow in the way of Christ. This alone can bring salvation. For this reason persecution is wicked and in any case futile, because to kill a person is not to defend a doctrine. People should be permitted to read their Bibles and accept the truth that they find therein as their hearts and minds dictate. When Servetus fought with reasons and writings, Castellio affirms, he should have been repulsed with reasons and writings—not with violence. In this assault on John Calvin we understand that, for Castellio, it is not what one believes that is the most important thing; it is how one lives and the sincerity that one brings to the task. That is what society should be concerned about. As to *ideas*, diversity of opinion should be tolerated.

A similar solution to the problem of interpretative pluralism had already been proposed a few decades earlier by Erasmus of Rotterdam, who stood very much in the stream of the late medieval spiritualism that I described in my chapter 12. For Erasmus, too, human morality and piety were the most important things about religion. He was impatient of aspects of the religious life that appeared to have no substantive relationship to the desired outcome, which was the *imitatio Christi* (the imitation of Christ). The merely visible trappings of religion could at best be tolerated only as an aid to immature piety. They were certainly not essential to the Christian faith—they were not doctrines or practices by which the Church stands and falls. This distinction between the essential and inessential principles of faith then leads Erasmus to argue that heretics should be tolerated insofar as their dissent from the Church's teaching does not touch on what is essential. We do not have to agree on (all) matters of doctrine in order to be saved; the important thing (again) is that we follow in Christ's way. That is the core commitment around which public society should be organized.

These are interesting developments, and they foreshadow momentous ones. For we see here an emerging argument that the moral usefulness of an article of Christian faith should be the decisive factor in distinguishing fundamental doctrines—the ones that should dominate public discourse and where necessary attract public sanctions—from doctrines that do not and should not divide the faith (or lead to executions or wars). In the sixteenth century it is still a distinctively Christian argument, with spiritualist overtones. Yet it is a short step from this kind of position, in which the inner witness of the *Spirit* is a *decisive* factor in discerning the truly important aspects of biblical teaching, to what will become the governing view of the immediately succeeding centuries in many

---

[32] Zagorin, *Toleration*, 93–144.

quarters—as we shall presently see—in which the "inner light of *reason*" (or common sense) becomes the *determining* factor in assessing the value of biblical teaching altogether. Erasmus would no doubt have disapproved of aspects of this later "program," but he would have been happy that it was often conducted in defense of the toleration of religious and political difference and dissent. In the end the distance between the kind of Bible reading that Erasmus and these later thinkers are doing in pursuit of their respective humanist goals is not great. It is only a matter of judgment about which (further) doctrines are "inessential" in respect of the good life. If Erasmus is one of the fathers of the Reformation, then, from a different point of view he can also be understood as one of the fathers of the Enlightenment.

Review

As we review the Europe of the sixteenth century, then, we discover that the notion of a Christian civilization is still alive and well and that the attempt to integrate all knowledge within the bounds of the Great Story is still proceeding. However, there are some stresses and strains in terms of how exactly to integrate new knowledge with the old and how exactly to read Scripture and creation together as the two books of God. There is a particular problem with respect to the *unity* of Christian civilization, which has fractured in the Reformation. This leads on to questions about how diversity of opinion and dissent should be handled in the emerging new world. What is to be done about the fact that people now espouse rather different *readings* of the biblical narrative that has for so long unified Christian Europe?

THE SEVENTEENTH-CENTURY INFORMATION EXPLOSION

We are accustomed to think of "information explosions" and the stresses and strains that they impose on traditional ways of thinking and living as thoroughly contemporary phenomena. The seventeenth century, however, experienced its own kind of information explosion, and this raised new (or renewed) questions about biblical interpretation. What was known, moreover, was increasingly widely disseminated, as the number of printers and their output increased throughout Europe. Holland, in particular, became a haven of tolerance (and not just for Christians) with respect to new ideas, and books could be published there that were prohibited elsewhere. These in turn fed debate not only in the Dutch universities but also in the salons of Paris, the learned societies of England (like the Royal Society, founded in 1660), and elsewhere. Academic journals appeared, and collections of scholarly works from the past were also published.

For increasing numbers of people in such a context—in which "in the eyes of the leaders of thought, the enchanted world of the medieval church dissolved right away"[33]—the old Christian syntheses that for previous generations had succeeded in holding together what was known from the Bible and what was known from other sources now became increasingly problematic. It was difficult any longer to believe, for example, that a Christian account of the cosmos that embraced Ptolemaic cosmology could possibly be true. This raised in turn more pressing questions than ever before about whether Scripture should any longer be assumed to speak truly about *other* important matters—questions that were also increasingly addressed to the Aristotelian natural philosophy with which particular interpretations of Scripture were identified. This was the century of Robert Boyle (1627–1691), for example, who—rejecting the authority of Aristotle—"laid the foundations for modern chemistry."[34]

The Defense of Old Ideas

It did not help Christians to process these questions that to a significant degree the Church of the seventeenth century, both Protestant and Roman Catholic, tended to respond to the information explosion simply by defending older understandings—clinging desperately to a "rigid Aristotelianism . . . which seriously held up advances in the fields of mechanics and astronomy" and other disciplines[35]—and by attempting to suppress the new knowledge that undermined these understandings. The example probably best known to most people involves Galileo Galilei.

As I noted in chapter 13, Copernicus' work did not provoke much immediate controversy when it was published. By the opening decades of the seventeenth century, however, it had evolved from an interesting mathematical theory that was certainly more simple and elegant than Ptolemy's into something else. Johannes Kepler—whose "thinking was genuinely empirical in the modern sense of the term"[36]—had by this point greatly simplified the Copernican thesis by showing that the planetary orbits form ellipses around the sun (thereby departing once and for all from the Greek idea of "necessary" *circular* motion). His friend

---

[33] Richard S. Westfall, "The Rise of Science and the Decline of Orthodox Christianity: A Study of Kepler, Descartes, and Newton," in *God and Nature: Historical Essays on the Encounter between Christianity and Science* (ed. David C. Lindberg and Ronald N. Numbers; Berkeley: University of California Press, 1986), 218–37 (235).

[34] Dillenberger, *Protestant Thought*, 112–17 (112).

[35] McGrath, *Science of God*, 159.

[36] Burtt, *Foundations*, 50. This is not, of course, to suggest that empiricism was all that drove him or contributed to his convictions about the nature of the cosmos (44–60). Yet his "solid and forward-looking achievement as a philosopher of science, is his insistence that valid mathematical hypotheses must be exactly verifiable in the observed world" (71).

Galileo who, for all that he believed that mathematics could deliver a priori truth not available to the senses, also held that experience was the "true mistress of astronomy,"[37] systematically used his telescope (between 1609 and 1613) to provide a great deal of additional evidence in favor of Copernicus and against Ptolemy.[38] The matter was now a serious one for those who wished to defend Ptolemy, but there were many who did.

Within the Roman Catholic Church the opposition to the Copernican thesis crystallized in March 1616 in a decree of the Congregation of the Holy Office that criticized and temporarily banned Copernicus' book while "corrections" were made. The Congregation additionally prohibited any other work defending the mobility of the earth or the immobility of the sun, or attempting to reconcile these assertions with the Bible. In the previous month it had been made clear by the advisers to the Congregation that the second proposal about the immobility of the sun in particular was "foolish and absurd in philosophy and formally heretical," since it explicitly contradicted Scripture "according to the proper meaning of the words, and . . . the common interpretation . . . of the Holy Fathers and of learned theologians."[39] The cardinal tasked with breaking the news to Galileo that the pope had banned the teaching of Copernican-type theory was none other than Robert Bellarmine, whom we have already encountered on numerous occasions in this book. The new proposal was to Bellarmine simply "contrary to the Church Fathers' interpretation of Scripture"; that was all that really needed to be said.[40] On such a view, what was true was already known on the basis of Scripture as mediated through the Church Fathers, and it did not matter what observation now revealed in relation to the recent mathematical theorizing, nor what one's reason might lead one to make of observation. Even the not-unsympathetic Pope Urban VIII took just such a line with Galileo in his discussions with him in Rome in 1624. God can create the universe to *appear* to human beings in any way he likes, the pope suggested to Galileo. However, we cannot move infallibly from appearances to reality; the Bible must be taken as the ultimate guide to that reality. It was the acceptance of this still Plato-inspired claim that led many people in the early seventeenth century to disbelieve the evidence of their own eyes, whether naked or attached to a telescope, when it came to cosmology. The fact that one could see something, they knew, did not mean that it was ultimately *real*.

---

[37] Cited in Burtt, *Foundations*, 66.

[38] Dillenberger, *Protestant Thought*, 77–78.

[39] Richard J. Blackwell, *Behind the Scenes at Galileo's Trial* (Notre Dame: University of Notre Dame Press, 2006), 59.

[40] Wicks, "Catholic Old Testament Interpretation," 648. For a good discussion of the *various* approaches taken to biblical interpretation with respect to the Copernican hypothesis, see Kenneth J. Howell, *God's Two Books: Copernican Cosmology and Biblical Interpretation in Early Modern Science* (Notre Dame: University of Notre Dame Press, 2002).

So it was that Galileo could describe in a letter to Kepler in 1610 a well-educated professor of philosophy at the University of Padua, "whom I have repeatedly and urgently requested to look at the moon and planets through my glass, which he pertinaciously refuses to do," and a philosophy professor at the University of Pisa "laboring... with logical arguments, as if with magical incantations, to charm the new planets out of the sky."[41] Aristotle himself would already have changed his opinions, Galileo proposed, had he observed what was now there to be observed—but not these philosophical colleagues. Galileo believed exactly the opposite of what the pope believed, in fact—at least insofar as "natural problems" were concerned. In discussing creation, he proposes,

> we ought not to begin at the authority of places of scripture, but at sensible experiments and necessary demonstrations... that which either sensible experience sets before our eyes, or necessary demonstrations do prove unto us, ought not, upon any account, to be called into question, much less condemned upon the testimony of texts of scripture, which may, under their words, couch senses contrary thereto.... Nor does God less admirably discover himself to us in Nature's actions, than in the Scripture's sacred dictions.[42]

That is, the new, emergent science—involving mathematics, reason, and empirical enquiry—enables us in various ways to discover what is true. Where it does so we must consider the possibility that it is *Scripture* that actually provides us with the "appearance" of things. God has accommodated his speech in the Bible to limited human understanding, and we must dig deeper into it in order to understand what it is really saying: "scripture is indubitably free from error, but only on the presupposition [in Galileo's own words] 'that we have penetrated to its true meaning.'"[43]

Other Roman Catholics agreed with Galileo,[44] but at the same time, "Roman Catholic theologians in general had to take up a position opposed to Copernicus," no matter what their personal convictions might be, for fear of deviating from the official line taken by their church.[45]

---

[41] Cited in Burtt, *Foundations*, 66–67.
[42] Cited in Burtt, *Foundations*, 72–73.
[43] Scholder, *Birth*, 59.
[44] Maurice A. Finocchiaro, "The Biblical Argument against Copernicanism and the Limitation of Biblical Authority: Ingoli, Foscarini, Galileo, Campanella," in van der Meer and Mandelbrote, *Nature and Scripture in the Abrahamic Religions: Up to 1700*, 2:627–64. For easy access to some primary text from Campanella, see Dennis R. Danielson, ed., *The Book of the Cosmos: Imagining the Universe from Heraclitus to Hawking* (Cambridge, Mass.: Perseus, 2000), 173–77.
[45] Hooykaas, *Religion*, 135.

The Two Books of God?

Some seventeenth-century Protestants were also deeply suspicious of those who argued the Galileo line. "The first anti-Copernican monograph to appear in the Lutheran sphere," Klaus Scholder reminds us, "was that of Danish mathematician and theologian Peter Bartolinus... published in 1632."[46] The Utrecht professor Gisbert Voetius (1588–1676) specifically rejected the arguments both that Scripture does not set out to teach science and that the Holy Spirit accommodates himself to the common people—in which case the Spirit, Voetius proposed, is simply lying on their behalf. The Copernican theory lay "in flat contradiction to the text and the intention of the Bible."[47] His successor Peter van Mastricht (1589–1676) insisted that "'utterances of reason about natural matters' are to be subordinated to the 'dictates of scripture on the same matters.'"[48] God says that the sun rises and sets, noted the Franeker professor Nicolaus Arnoldus (1618–1680), and in so doing he does not conform himself to "a false human view."[49] The Leiden pastor Jacob du Bois complained, finally, that "if we are allowed in matters of physics and astronomy to represent at will words which are in themselves easily understandable and appropriate as tropes or phrases accommodated to our terminology, why not in theological matters and in things of the faith?"[50]

Many seventeenth-century Protestants agreed with Galileo, however, about divine accommodation in Scripture in general and its relevance to the Copernican issue, in particular.[51] The idea that the correct way of proceeding was to set aside the emergent natural science with respect to cosmology and instead to follow a "Mosaic" or "biblical" version "found no general acceptance among the adherents of the Reformation" in the seventeenth century (e.g., Kepler)—just as it had not been accepted by influential writers in the sixteenth like Peter Ramus (1515–1572) and Francis Bacon (1561–1626).[52] In fact, Ramus' criticisms of Aristo-

---

[46] Scholder, *Birth*, 53.

[47] Hooykaas, *Religion*, 130–31, with further examples of anti-Copernican Protestants on 131–38 (e.g., Alexander Ross and John Owen); see also Rienk H. Vermij, "The Debate on the Motion of the Earth in the Dutch Republic in the 1650s," in van der Meer and Mandelbrote, *Nature and Scripture in the Abrahamic Religions: Up to 1700*, 2:605–25.

[48] Cited in Scholder, *Birth*, 120.

[49] Cited in Scholder, *Birth*, 120.

[50] Cited in Scholder, *Birth*, 125.

[51] Stephen D. Snobelen, "'In the Language of Men': The Hermeneutics of Accommodation in the Scientific Revolution," in van der Meer and Mandelbrote, *Nature and Scripture in the Abrahamic Religions: Up to 1700*, 2:691–732.

[52] Hooykaas, *Religion*, 116–17, and see further 122–24, 126–30. For Newton's use of the concept of accommodation as a way of keeping science and Scripture in appropriate conversation with each other, see Stephen D. Snobelen, "'Not in the Language of Astronomers': Isaac Newton, the Scriptures, and the Hermeneutics of Accommodation," in van der Meer and Mandelbrote, *Nature and Scripture in the Abrahamic Religions: Up to 1700*, 2:491–530.

telian thought made a particularly strong impact on seventeenth-century English Calvinists who were confronted by the Aristotelian-Thomistic scholastic theology of their Anglo-Catholic colleagues in the Church of England. Just a few years after Galileo's trial in 1640, for example, John Wilkins (1614–1672)—one of the founders of the Royal Society—insisted on the importance of allowing creation to speak in its own terms alongside Scripture, recognizing that the latter is not intended to provide us with the kinds of information in which science is interested:

> It were happy for us, if we could exempt Scripture from philosophical controversies; if we could be content to let it be perfect for that end unto which it was intended, for a rule of our faith and obedience, and not stretch it also to be a judge of such natural truths as are to be found out by our own industry and experience.[53]

This illustrates the way in which Wilkins and other seventeenth-century Protestants like him had come to discard Scripture "not as a directive for scientific research, but ... as a source of factual information for it."[54] Scripture does not set out to teach of "natural things ... in accordance with the exact truth," affirms the Dutch theologian Christoph Wittich (1625–1687), but "often speaks ... according to the view of the people."[55]

This same acceptance of a legitimate place for the new natural philosophy in the life and faith of the Church is also hinted at in what the *Westminster Confession of Faith* (1647) does and does not say about Scripture and knowledge. The knowledge that Scripture is said to teach in its infallible nature is "the whole counsel of God, concerning all things necessary for his own glory, man's salvation, faith, and life"—what is "either expressly set down in Scripture" or deducible from Scripture. There are various matters, however, which although they might be expected to fall within this remit, in fact do not. Here "the light of nature" must help us arriving at right judgments: "there are some circumstances concerning the worship of God, and government of the church, common to human actions and

---

[53] Cited in Hooykaas, *Religion*, 116. William Ames (1563–1633) expresses sentiments consistent with these in *The Marrow of Sacred Divinity* (1627). "All things which are necessary for salvation are contained in the Scriptures," which represent "a perfect rule of Faith, and manners." Yet there are also such realities as "universal, and scientific rules." Scripture "does not explain the will of God" in this kind of language, but in other ways consistent with its intended "common use" by "all kinds of men." Lillback and Gaffin, *Word*, 333.

[54] Hooykaas, *Religion*, 116.

[55] Cited in Scholder, *Birth*, 125. Early Lutheran Pietists like Philipp Jakob Spener (1635–1705) agreed that with respect to the biblical authors "the Holy Spirit adapted himself to the confines of their capacities." Johannes Wallman, "Scriptural Understanding and Interpretation in Pietism," *HBOT* 2:902–25 (905). This view was shared by Johann Jakob Rambach (1693–1735): the Holy Spirit accommodated not only to the language but also to the emotional state of biblical authors. Steiger, "Development," 707.

societies, which are to be ordered by the light of nature, and Christian prudence, according to the general rules of the Word, which are always to be observed."[56] Unsurprisingly given the positive attitude toward science often evidenced in the Puritan context,[57] *Westminster* says nothing at all about how we should read Scripture in relation to the questions raised by natural philosophy.[58] However, individual participants in the Westminster assembly such as Samuel Rutherford are quite explicit on the matter. Scripture is *not* our rule, he affirms, "in things of Art and Science, as to speak Latine, to *demonstrate conclusions of Astronomie*. . . . But it is our Rule . . . in fundamentalls of salvation . . . [and] in all morals of both first and second table [i.e., the Ten Commandments]," as well as in Church government and worship.[59]

The Question of Lineage

Two quite distinct approaches emerged in the seventeenth-century Protestant Church, then, in response to new scientific ideas. The first involved the attempt to integrate new knowledge into the framework of Christian truth claims, revisiting older interpretations of the Bible that were problematic in this pursuit and appealing as necessary to the ancient idea of divine "accommodation" in communication. Those who took this approach could be appropriately cautious about new ideas—for example, Blaise Pascal (1623–1662), concerning the motion of the earth[60]—until they at least crossed the threshold between "a most probable theory" and "the theory that is likely on the basis of accumulating evidence to be true." Once convinced that they were dealing with genuine knowledge, however, they were committed to integrating it into their understanding of the Great Story of Scripture. The second approach, conversely, involved a determination to dismiss new knowledge in order to avoid any disturbance either to older ways of understanding Christian truth claims or to the interpretations of the Bible that supported them. Were both approaches truly "reformed"?

---

[56] *Westminster Confession of Faith*, 1.6.

[57] It is worth noting in this context that "among the group of ten scientists who during the Commonwealth formed the nucleus of the body that was to become the Royal Society, seven were strongly Puritan." Hooykaas, *Religion*, 98.

[58] Nor do the earlier *Irish Articles of Religion* (1615) or the *Canons of the Synod of Dort* (1618–1619). Lillback and Gaffin, *Word*, 189–215.

[59] Samuel Rutherford, *The Divine Right of Church-Government and Excommunication* (1646), 99, cited in Jack B. Rogers, *Scripture in the Westminster Confession: A Problem of Historical Interpretation for American Presbyterianism* (Grand Rapids: Eerdmans, 1967), 366–67. Note also Rogers' summary comment on 442: "The Westminster Divines were open to the results of empirical science in its own realm . . . the Bible was a book to teach man of salvation, not, e.g., astronomy."

[60] Hooykaas, *Religion*, 134.

It is not clear that the second approach has much to say for itself in this regard. For the Reformers, as we saw in my chapter 13, Scripture is certainly a God-inspired, unerring guide to belief and practice with respect to what God wishes centrally to communicate to Christians and others. Yet we must be careful (they believed) to distinguish between what it *is* that God wishes to communicate and what he does not, remembering that his Word is communicated in Scripture through human words that must be taken deeply seriously and in consideration of our human limitation and weakness. Scripture is centrally concerned to give us the knowledge needed for the attainment of salvation. Its perfection must be understood in terms of its soteriological (saving) purpose, which it is "perfectly equipped to accomplish."[61]

Among the seventeenth-century Protestants we are now considering, conversely, we begin to find—in a marked development of certain tendencies already evident in some late sixteenth-century Protestant writers who also still cite Aristotle as an authority on many matters[62]—an appeal to an "abstract *perfectio* [perfection] and inerrancy of Scripture *in every respect.*"[63] Divine accommodation in Scripture on matters like cosmology is rejected as the Trojan horse of biblical interpretation that will lead to the eventual defeat of orthodoxy. "No error even in unimportant matters" affirms Abraham Calovius, "no defect of memory, not to say untruth, can have any place in all the Sacred Scriptures."[64] We shall explore further, later in the present chapter, the most important underlying reason why people took this approach. For the moment it is important only to note that in doing so its advocates significantly departed from earlier Reformation ideas about what the perfection of Scripture entails—just as they departed, too, from the humanistic and Reformation emphasis on the importance of taking Scripture seriously as genuinely human as well as divine words. What is obscured in their approach is the truth that Scripture is not an "inspired *product*" that may be separated from and "given priority over the revelatory, sanctifying and inspiring activities of the divine agent."[65] Instead, Scripture is a communication from this Person that is intrinsically bound up with his other activities—a communication whose nature we have not always understood very well. One cannot imagine John Calvin, had he lived in the seventeenth century, offering any support for the second approach. Having paid careful attention in his Bible reading in the

---

[61] Scott R. Swain, *Trinity, Revelation, and Reading: A Theological Introduction to the Bible and Its Interpretation* (London: T&T Clark, 2011), 72, who goes on to remark that "Holy Scripture is a sufficient deposit of *special revelation*, but not of *general revelation*" (84–85).
[62] Dillenberger, *Protestant Thought*, 50–74.
[63] Steiger, "Development," 722 (emphasis added).
[64] Cited in Dillenberger, *Protestant Thought*, 97.
[65] Webster, *Holy Scripture*, 33.

sixteenth century to what astronomers had proved "by conclusive reasons," he would certainly have been interested in what people in the seventeenth century had proved in the same way. He would surely not have changed his opinion about the character of Genesis 1, suddenly converting to the idea that it was designed to teach us after all a divine, Mosaic science. Calvin would not have misused the doctrine of the inspiration of Scripture, in the way that these later Calvinists did, to avoid the implications of what science appeared to demonstrate. He would have understood this move, in fact (as we should), as only the latest in a series of unfortunate deployments of the doctrine of inspiration in the course of Christian history—from ancient discussions of the LXX onward (my chapter 10)—that have been designed simply to justify the ignoring of unwelcome evidence.

The Credibility Gap

Beyond the issue of "reformed lineage," of course, the problem with this second approach lies in the signals that it sent, along with its Roman Catholic counterpart, to the wider, watching, seventeenth-century world. Here was a Europe in which, increasingly, many influential people were impressed by what the new natural philosophy was capable of delivering. What it asserted to be true about the world, by way of mathematical calculation, empirical enquiry, and reasoned deduction—combined at their zenith in Isaac Newton, "as thoroughgoing an empiricist as he was a consummate mathematician"[66]—possessed increasing credibility in educated European society at large. With regard to Copernican cosmology, for example, by the late seventeenth century many would have agreed with Lewis Spitz' acid comment that "after Kepler and Galileo, no informed man could continue to support the 'common-sense' observation of the rising sun, and it took a dedicated obscurantist to carry on opposition to the new theory."[67]

If the Christian Story could not be shown to be capable of absorbing this and other new truth and making sense of it—what then? Then, it seemed, a choice had to be made. One could adhere to the official teaching the Church, either Protestant or Roman Catholic, and ignore the science, *or* one could embrace the science and detach oneself from the official teaching of the Church—perhaps not overtly, at this time (since overt detachment was typically not truly possible, culturally and politically), but at least quietly, within the privacy of one's own mind. So it was that a gap began to open in the seventeenth century between those who believed the Great Story and those who believed the science—and indeed, the idea began to arise that faith and science are fundamentally at war

---

[66] Burtt, *Foundations*, 208.
[67] Spitz, *Renaissance*, 587. Even in 1624 the pope was warned by one of his cardinals to be careful about his decision on Copernican cosmology because "all heretics [i.e., Protestants] adhered to [Galileo's] opinion and held it for certain." Hooykaas, *Religion*, 133.

with each other. There can be no doubt that Christians who took the "second approach" greatly contributed to this development. It was their view of faith, hostile to science, which helped to produce its mirror-image—a science that was hostile to faith, pursued by people whose experience had convinced them that many religious persons were "obscurantists" standing in the line of succession from the medieval, scholastic theologians to whom that label was first attached by (largely Christian) Renaissance Humanists. Now, in the seventeenth century, this label was all too easily reattached to Christians by those who were often gradually ceasing to be Christian at all and becoming something else. Isaac Newton himself, it should be remembered, was not a Trinitarian Christian, but an Arian.[68]

This is still how many modern people think of science and faith—in terms of the "warfare model." They no longer remember that the majority of educated Christians in the seventeenth century were not in fact opposed to science at all and did not believe that there needed to be two "sides" in a "war"—any more than they remember the deeper historical truth concerning the Reformation's role in the birth of modern science in the first place. All of this has been forgotten, in part because of the powerful impression made on the European (and now the global) consciousness by the "second approach," especially as illustrated by what happened to Galileo. It was not long, of course, before most Christians themselves came to believe (and now continue to believe)—in common with most non-Christians—in a Copernican-style cosmology. Nowadays there are only a few who continue to think that faithful adherence to Scripture requires that they reject this view of the universe. Most people have conceded the point, just as the majority after Columbus quickly came to affirm the existence of an inhabited Antipodes. Connected with this embrace of the "new" cosmology, interpretations of the Bible once offered so vehemently in support of an older, very different view of the universe were soon abandoned. However, the damage by that point had already been done, and as we shall see (in chapter 15), other examples of "obscurantism" in the face of science had additionally arisen to confirm in the minds of many their original diagnosis of the problem. The problem lay with Bible-based religion.

REASON, RELIGION, AND SOCIETY IN THE SEVENTEENTH CENTURY

The broader context in which the seventeenth-century information explosion occurred involved, in the first half of the century, terrible, devastating war. The Schmalkaldic War of 1546–1547 had been closely followed in 1555 by the Peace of Augsburg, which had attempted to address the question of religiously inspired

---

[68] Dillenberger, *Protestant Thought*, 125.

violence in Europe—insofar as it involved Lutheran and Roman Catholic rulers warring with each other—by dividing Europe into Roman Catholic and Lutheran zones. Each ruler, it was hoped, could now pursue his own vision of Christian civilization within his own domain and within the overarching Holy Roman Empire without their differences spilling over into military conflict. Residents who did not wish to conform to their ruler's choice between Lutheranism and Roman Catholicism were given time to emigrate to another region in which their particular version of Christian faith had been accepted. This did not much help Calvinists and Anabaptists, for whom no provision was made, but it did help to keep religiously inspired violence under some degree of restraint in the succeeding decades. The omission of Calvinism from the settlement, however, ultimately contributed to the unravelling of this uneasy truce, which by the early seventeenth century was also inconvenient to a number of European rulers with territorial ambitions. In 1608 the threatened Calvinist minority in Germany banded together under the leadership of the Elector Palatine Frederick IV (1583–1610) to form the League of Evangelical Union. This provoked the Roman Catholics to form the Catholic League (1609) under the leadership of Duke Maximilian of Bavaria (1573–1651). These renewed tensions ultimately spiraled out of control and into the Thirty Years' War (1618–1648)—one of the longest and most appallingly destructive wars in European history. By its end, millions had been killed by sword, plague, or famine, and millions more had been displaced. The Peace of Westphalia (1648) came as welcome relief to all.

England was involved in the early phases of the Thirty Years' War both directly and indirectly. From 1642 until 1651, however, it was embroiled in its own internal conflict, which also had religious dimensions. King Charles I was a "high Anglican," not a Roman Catholic, but for many of his subjects of Calvinist persuasion (including the Scots) he was certainly too *close* to being a Catholic. Desiring uniformity in Church life throughout Great Britain, Charles' various moves to achieve this end—as someone convinced of his divine right to rule in accordance with biblical and Christian teaching—aroused great hostility both in Scotland and England. Having provoked a rebellion in the former, in 1640 he sought money from the English Parliament to suppress it, thereby entering a period of prolonged conflict with Parliament that ultimately led to the English Civil War. In the end this war cost Charles his life; he was beheaded for treason in 1649. Many others lost their lives as well, both before and after Charles and sometimes under notorious circumstances. In the aftermath of his execution the monarchy was replaced by a republican Commonwealth (1649–1653 and 1659–1660), at least in those periods when Oliver Cromwell was not exercising his own personal rule (1653–1658). It is Cromwell who is still remembered in Ireland, where the civil war continued to be fought after Charles' death, as the man who oversaw the siege of Drogheda in 1649 and the subsequent massacre of nearly 3,500 people, including civilians, prisoners, and priests. For Cromwell and his associates the invasion of Ireland was akin to the invasion of Canaan by the Israelites. His troops were informed of this on more than one occasion during the campaign: their destiny was to annihilate the idolatrous Canaanites.[69] It was not long afterward (1660), in the face of imminent anarchy, that the Calvinist republican experiment in England came to an end with the restoration of King Charles II. Many were relieved by this outcome, too.

With the end of war in Europe around the middle of the century—for although religiously inspired European violence was not confined to Europe,[70] this was the great reality by which almost everyone living in Europe had been directly affected—came a deep desire never to go that way again. The question of "toleration" was now found, therefore, higher up the cultural agenda; it had become an even more important issue, for more people, than ever before. The role of the Bible in feeding intolerance was also now a matter of increased interest. How was fractured, Christian, European civilization to move ahead in a peaceable and just manner? There was significant skepticism in many quarters that more Bible reading in pursuit of more religious dogma would help in this pursuit. Many Bible readers had hitherto not shown themselves capable of loving their interpretative enemies, preferring instead to try and crush them. There had been little evidence among them of any commitment toward maintaining in Christian Europe the tension created by interpretative pluralism rather than trying to resolve it violently. More Bible and religion would not help; what, then, was the answer?

For significant numbers of educated, seventeenth-century Europeans, including many devout Protestants, the answer was simple: the emergent natural philosophy. In the case of cosmology, the new mathematics had predicted accurately what empirical observation, using new technology, had now confirmed. Great progress had been made in understanding the heavens; perhaps the new

---

[69] Denis Murphy, S.J., *Cromwell in Ireland: A History of Cromwell's Irish Campaign* (Dublin: Gill & Son, 1883), 72, 78–79n2.

[70] It had also been exported to the European colonies overseas. Illustrative of the mind-set that produced it are the writings of Cotton Mather. In his case it was the New England colonists whom he regarded as "Israel"; the Native Americans were the "Canaanites" who were to be exterminated in the course of the conquest of the land. The colonists were fighting God's war and God was with them, bringing epidemics, famine, and dissension in fulfillment of the promise of God to Israel to send a hornet among their enemies (Exod 23:27-28). For their own part the colonists must only be careful to remain pure (free of such sins as swearing, drinking, and gaming), so that God could continue to reside in their camp. See, e.g., Cotton Mather, *The Great Works of Christ in America* (2 vols.; Edinburgh: Banner of Truth, 1979), 2:552–55.

science could now foster progress also, not only in *understanding* the earth, but also in learning how to *live* more effectively on it.

René Descartes

One of the key figures guiding European intellectuals as they explored this path, looking for a secure foundation for knowledge and thereby for a better world, was the French Roman Catholic philosopher René Descartes (1596–1650).[71] Educated at a Jesuit college in a curriculum still heavily influenced by Aristotle, Descartes subsequently set out self-consciously to reform philosophy, grounding himself initially in mathematical method and emphasizing the roles of intellect, imagination, sense perception, and memory in gaining knowledge. Rejecting the scholastic, Aristotelian understanding of natural objects as possessing "form" (essential reality) and "matter," Descartes proposed that the entire visible universe is a single, physical entity comprising material objects that possess shape and structure and interact through laws of motion that are overseen by God. Out of this "tree-trunk" that is Cartesian physics then grow all the other sciences, which are principally three: medicine, mechanics, and morals (i.e., the highest moral system). Under these three headings the philosopher/scientist explores such diverse topics as astronomical phenomena, the properties of minerals, the origins of plants and animals, human physiology, and mind-body interaction. All natural objects are known by a combination of pure intellect and sensory observation—such that "looking to see" is necessary for knowledge. The emphasis lies on deductive reasoning, however, rather than upon empirical method; mathematics is the foundation of Descartes' new science, rather than experimentation.

The importance of Descartes' contributions to philosophy consists not so much in their particularities but in the fact that together they provided seventeenth-century intellectuals with a comprehensive alternative to the dominant Aristotelian worldview. Here was a new and exciting world picture in which what is true on earth is also true in the heavens (and vice versa) and everything that is material works "mechanically," according to "laws" of cause and effect. Beyond matter there is mind, possessing chiefly intellect and will, which Descartes equated with the soul. It is mind that differentiates us from the animals even as we share many "bodily" realities with them (instinctive reaction, for example). Descartes quickly gathered disciples who sought to develop various aspects of his thought. Beyond these immediate circles he significantly influenced many

---

[71] Descartes provides an excellent example, therefore, of what is often described as a "foundationalist" approach to knowledge—"the attempt to find an unshakeable foundation ... an indubitable, certain bedrock of truth on which one could then pile, Lego-style, knowledge upon knowledge." Jens Zimmermann, *Hermeneutics: A Very Short Introduction* (Oxford: Oxford University Press, 2015), 21.

others, contributing mightily to what soon became "an almost boundless confidence [in Europe] in the capacities and possibilities of reason" when it came to comprehending the material world.[72] This "Cartesian" confidence is nicely illustrated by Hermann Roëll's description in 1686 of the "power of understanding . . . [that is] divine":

> It can move miraculously and without wings . . . it can see through human customs and even improve nature by art; it can discern justice and injustice, the limits of good and evil . . . [this power] embraces and encompasses the whole universe and all the powers of the world . . . within its own bosom.[73]

There is tremendous optimism in all of this about the future that is to be shaped by the new science—optimism that all the secrets of the world would open up before Cartesian method and that and a new and wonderful age would quickly emerge as a result.

An important aspect of this wonderful age would be religious harmony. Two years before Roëll's comment, Ludwig Meyer had written of Descartes in glowing terms as "our greatest innovator and pioneer," in the light of whose work "the church of Christ, hitherto divided and torn apart by incessant dispute will come together in love."[74] Descartes' work was important on this view not only for understanding and making progress in subjects like human physiology but also for the quest to build a functional human society. In the sixteenth century Nicholas Machiavelli had already urged upon his readers the wisdom of abandoning the goal of building an *ideal* society (the kingdom of God)—this had only ever led to trouble—and embracing instead the more pragmatic goal of building a society that *worked*. The fundamental thing in achieving this goal, he suggested, was to pay attention to the way that things *are* in the world, and not to how they *should or might be*. This Machiavellian pathway was essentially the one that many took in the second half of the seventeenth century. They used the new science (albeit often with much more emphasis than Descartes on empirical method rather than simply deductive reasoning) to discover what *is*, and they proceeded to base their politics and much else besides on this "natural" reality rather than on the Bible or the teaching of the Church.

Thomas Hobbes and John Locke

The Englishman Thomas Hobbes (1588–1679) provides an excellent example of this kind of scientific approach to questions of politics and society. Hobbes was a

---

[72] Scholder, *Birth*, 115.
[73] Cited in Scholder, *Birth*, 116.
[74] Cited in Scholder, *Birth*, 116–17.

rationalistic Anglican who had lived through the English Civil War—a supporter of the absolutist monarchy and of the system of the state church under Charles I. The question lying at the foundation of his famous book *Leviathan* (1651) is, how can a political state retain stability and avoid internal chaos when faced with competing religious claims? In attempting to answer this question Hobbes applies to human beings and to the state that they create exactly the kind of contemporary scientific theory about "bodies in movement" and their influence on each other that we find in Descartes.[75] In the natural way of things, Hobbes proposes—where "all struggle with all"—human survival is threatened. Survival requires peace, and peace is ensured only when everyone transfers their natural rights and powers to a sovereign political state, which then makes possible the social development of the individual. It makes individual freedom possible, albeit only in the private (not the public) sphere. Implicit in Hobbes' approach is a theory of natural law, in line with which the Bible itself must function—since natural law, as Hobbes often says, is the command of God. The Bible itself cannot function as the foundational authority for the state, not least because the very extent of the canon of Scripture is a matter of disagreement among Christians and must be decided by the sovereign of a given Christian nation. It is this sovereign who is authorized (limited only by natural law) to regulate all external forms of religion, and to regulate, too, all those dogmatic statements that lie outside the basic confession of faith necessary for salvation. For Hobbes this creed "necessary for salvation" is limited to the statement that Jesus is the Christ, the king announced by the OT prophets. This is of course a particular form of the old spiritualist distinction between inessential and essential matters of faith, defining the space within which toleration is permitted in personal and private terms that have nothing to do with the "outward forms" of religion. For Hobbes, then, the public realm must be governed by reason based on natural law—by science—and not by particular interpretations of Scripture. "The Scripture was written to show unto men the kingdom of God, and to prepare their minds to become his obedient subjects," he affirms, "leaving the world and the philosophy thereof to the disputation of men for the exercising of their natural reason."[76] Natural reason suggests that only an absolutist monarchy, which people have no right ever to overthrow, can hold in check human selfishness and cruelty of the kind that he himself has witnessed during the Civil War.

---

[75] "Hobbes and Descartes did not disagree fundamentally in their approach to questions in natural science," although they did disagree in their overall *philosophies* of science. Tom Sorell, "Descartes, Hobbes and the Body of Natural Science," *Monist* 71 (1988): 515–25 (515).

[76] Thomas Hobbes, *Leviathan; or The Matter, Forme and Power of a Commonwealth Ecclesiastical and Civil* (New York: Collier Books, 1962), 67.

The Liberal Anglicans known as Latitudinarians who gained a dominant public position in England in the second half of the seventeenth century—people like Edward Stillingfleet (1635–1699)—followed a similar line, at least in distinguishing faith and reason, the private and the public. Like Hobbes they saw no necessary conflict between religious belief and rational scientific enquiry provided that their legitimate "domains" were identified. The Latitudinarians, too, sought harmony within the Church precisely by the kind of reduction in demands for public liturgical and doctrinal unity that Hobbes had advocated. Forms of church government, argued Stillingfleet, are not binding just because they appear in the Bible. They are only binding insofar as they are based on the law of nature and are embraced by consensus among those admitted to a particular community.

An influential thinker who held views similar to the Latitudinarians was John Locke (1632–1704), who argues that government is not legitimated by nature but created by society, and that it remains legitimate only insofar as it governs in the interests of those who first created it. Otherwise it ought to be overthrown. There is in Locke's thinking, then, no absolute Hobbesian state, and certainly not one that involves hereditary monarchy and the divine right of kings—such realities do not in fact belong to the natural order of things, in which men are born free and equal. Government is appointed by the people, in Locke's view, to do a job—to protect life, liberty, and property—and it had better pay attention to these things. Among the things that government should *not* do, he argues, is to interfere with an individual's private religious life. The state must indeed respect private opinions about the meaning of Holy Scripture, leaving people alone as far as possible voluntarily to join such churches as they wish—Holy Scripture that for Locke himself (as he writes to Stillingfleet in 1697) is "and always will be, the constant guide of my assent." The state, then, should attend to the preservation of "external" existence. It should have no interest in a person's views on the Trinity, hellfire, or transubstantiation, or on the right place, time, and guidelines for worshipping God. These are matters "internal" to the individual, or to be settled by consensus in a religious community—unless the individual or community becomes dangerous to the state for some reason. Perhaps individual religious conviction conflicts with the common good (for the preservation of which the state is responsible); or perhaps a church transforms itself into a political party. Granting general tolerance, Locke argues,[77] will bring an end to religious wars by turning "sectarian" adherents into faithful subjects of the realm.

The politics of Locke are not those of Hobbes. The significant point in the present context is, nevertheless, how they both *approach the question* of politics.

---

[77] Roman Catholics are not to be tolerated, though, because they owe allegiance to a foreign ruler (the pope); nor are atheists, since human society is impossible once God is removed as the guarantor of oaths.

Neither argues his case on the basis of biblical revelation, holding that God's will in Scripture broadly regulates everything in a binding way. Locke specifically denies that the OT, rooted in the conditions experienced by the ancient Israelites, can provide any kind of model for the construction of the modern state. Both philosophers illustrate in different ways how in the aftermath of religious war and persecution in the seventeenth century people were trying to identify as a starting point for political discourse an objective reality about which it was not possible to dispute or fight and from which dispassionate reason could then proceed to build an argument that might gain widespread support among reasonable people. The emergent, new natural philosophy provided them with a plausible method for making progress on this project.

Gottfried Leibniz

This was also true of intellectuals in continental Europe like the German philosopher and mathematician Gottfried Leibniz (1646–1716)—although it is immediately necessary to clarify that he was certainly not representative of his homeland in this period (which was dominated by both Lutheran orthodoxy and Pietism)[78] and therefore that he "predominantly sought conversation partners from outside Germany." When he died in 1716, indeed, "he had no worthy obituary in his homeland."[79] In various ways, however, Leibniz sums up the emerging Enlightenment spirit of the age in late seventeenth-century Protestant Europe as a whole. In 1674 he began working on what would quickly become known as calculus: differential and integral calculus. Calculating was important to Leibniz, and it was not a purely theoretical matter. For him it was the very way of avoiding the kind of conflict represented by the Thirty Years' War. Leibniz hoped for a day when human beings would be able to reduce *all* ideas to symbols and thus gain precision in their thinking:

> if we could find characters or signs appropriate for expressing all our thoughts as definitely and as exactly as arithmetic expresses numbers or geometric analysis expresses lines, we could in all subjects *in so far as they are amenable to reasoning* accomplish what is done in Arithmetic and Geometry.[80]

Once matters of fact had been agreed upon in this new world, disputes ranging from those in metaphysics through those in the sciences and then on to those in jurisprudence would all be settled. They would not be resolved by fruitless

---

[78] On the rise of Lutheran Pietism in Germany and its huge influence between 1670 and 1740, see Wallman, "Scriptural Understanding."

[79] Scholder, *Birth*, 4.

[80] Gottfried Leibniz, *Preface to the General Science* (1677), in Philip P. Wiener, *Leibniz: Selections* (New York: Charles Scribner's Sons, 1951), 12–17 (15).

and often acrimonious debates concerning texts with their inevitably indeterminate meanings—about the futility of which many seventeenth-century natural philosophers agreed[81]—and certainly not by violence. Calculation would solve all problems: "if someone would doubt my results, I should say to him, 'Let us calculate, Sir,' and thus by taking to pen and ink, we should soon settle the question."[82] Leibniz' hope, in short, was that human beings might be able to gain access to naked, unvarnished reality. They would no longer need to argue or fight about the truth because there would no longer be any uncertainty about it. Everything obscuring it from our gaze would have been removed—all perspective, all testimony, and all faith. Reason would have penetrated to the self-evident reality of things. The development of this new symbolic language, then—"the highest effort of the human mind"—was much to be desired, "and when the project will be accomplished it will simply be up to men to be happy since they will have an instrument which will exalt reason no less than what the Telescope does to perfect our vision."[83]

Reason, Religion, and the Word of God

So it was, then, that in a seventeenth-century Europe that had come to doubt that a confessionally divided Christian faith could any longer provide a secure foundation for a peaceful, prosperous, and happy societal future, a viable alternative emerged. It was the new, Reformation-inspired science with its promise to deliver, at least in the natural realm, truth that was accessible to all—irrespective of religious belief. Particularly for Protestants who had begun to think that "[f]or a supposedly perspicuous set of scriptures, there was very little that was clear" in the Bible,[84] this science appeared to offer great potential for progress. Just as it had delivered understanding in the realm of cosmology, so would it deliver the same in the realm of politics. The new politics, indeed, eschewing the exegesis of Scripture as its primary task and arguing instead from nature, quickly produced results—at least in the England of John Locke. In 1688 a limited or constitutional form of monarchy had emerged in England. In this new context the English parliament moved in 1689 to adopt an Act of Toleration that allowed freedom of worship under certain circumstances—at least to Protestants who

---

[81] van der Meer and Oosterhoff, "Rise of Modern Science," 382–87.

[82] Leibniz, *Preface*, 15. See also *The Art of Discovery* (1685): "The only way to rectify our reasonings is to make them as tangible as those of the Mathematicians, so that we can find our error at a glance, and when there are disputes among persons, we can simply say: Let us calculate, without further ado, to see who is right." Wiener, *Leibniz*, 50–58 (51).

[83] Wiener, *Leibniz*, 16.

[84] Keith D. Stanglin, "The Rise and Fall of Biblical Perspicuity: Remonstrants and the Transition toward Modern Exegesis," *CH* 83 (2014): 38–59 (57).

dissented from the Church of England, although not yet to others (e.g., Roman Catholics or Unitarians).[85] It seems likely that Locke's publications played some part in this development. It represents the beginnings of a manner of separation between Church and state in England that in the ensuing centuries would contribute much to the internal stability and peaceableness of that country and its colonies, as religiously "sectarian" adherents were indeed found to be capable, to a great extent, of being faithful subjects of the Crown.

Not everyone, of course, welcomed the contributions of the new science to the realm of politics, any more than to the realm of cosmology. In fact, "Cartesianism" and all that was perceived as flowing from it provoked strong reactions in both Roman Catholic and Protestant circles. In 1663 indeed the Roman Catholic Church did to Descartes what they had previously done to Galileo and others: it placed his writings on the Index of Prohibited Books. His was a dangerous philosophy, and not just for political reasons—although the politics were certainly part of it, since Rome continued to believe that confessional Christianity was the correct foundation for the state. That this Roman view prevailed in France helps to explain among other things the rather different course of its history over the next century when compared to England's. In 1685, just before the established English Protestants passed their Act of Toleration to the benefit of other Protestants, a previous policy of limited toleration of Protestants by a Roman Catholic state (embodied in the Edict of Nantes, 1598) was reversed by the absolutist monarch Louis XIV. The serious consequence was that dissent in France was to a significant extent secularized in the course of the eighteenth century, ultimately to explode in the French Revolution. A new intolerance emerged, bred by the old.

Within the Protestant domain, resistance to "Cartesianism" was just as strong in many quarters, and particularly so among "second approach" Protestants of the kind described earlier in the present chapter. Much of this resistance is entirely understandable. "Cartesians" could write with great arrogance about the ability of the new science ultimately to deliver truth unmarked by "prejudice" (as they often called it) in all areas of life—perfect truth, in which there was no error. There was often a marked imperialistic tone to these claims about the ability of the unaided power of reason to comprehend the entire cosmos and to create a utopia. Many devout people understandably reacted negatively to this hubris, which seemed to elevate the philosopher to the status of an all-knowing, all-seeing god. The very nature of Christian religion itself could be redefined within this Enlightenment context so as to make it conform completely to the emergent, thoroughly

---

[85] Toleration for Roman Catholics had nevertheless already been advocated by some English Puritans as early as the 1640s. Norah Carlin, "Toleration for Catholics in the Puritan Revolution," in *Tolerance and Intolerance in the European Reformation* (ed. Ole Peter Grell and Bob Scribner; Cambridge: Cambridge University Press, 1996), 216–30.

rationalist outlook. The character of this "Deism" is well articulated in the writings of one of its early, leading advocates: Edward, Lord Herbert of Cherbury (1582–1648). There is one natural religion, valid for all people, he proposes, the goal of which is morality (which leads to eternal life). It is accessible through reason and the direct experience of God without any help from religious "externals." We read sacred books (including the Bible) only in order to decide where God's word is to be found in them, "searching the Scriptures" (as it were) in line with a prior conception of what God is really like that is deduced by reason. In this way of looking at the world we see again the old Erasmian distinction between the essential and inessential principles of faith in pursuit of a commitment to toleration that Herbert certainly shares with Erasmus—but it is taken to a whole new level.[86] A genuine Christian humanism is replaced by a humanism that has begun to squeeze Christian faith into a different mold. In this new way of thinking, in fact, what is "essential"—the "real message" of the Bible—is very little marked by *any* recognizable Christian doctrine at all. Only those aspects of traditional Christian teaching are retained that are compatible with rationalist, universal religion—the religion that all people of good sense and virtue agree should be believed and practiced, at least in public. There is still a supreme Deity who ought to be worshipped, albeit that this "worship" predominantly involves virtue combined with piety. People ought still to repent of their sins in the belief that there is reward and punishment both in this life and afterward. However, to the extent that the Bible says more than this or diverges from it, it is to be regarded as reflecting a lower stage of religion than the "enlightened" kind now advocated.

Much of the Protestant resistance to "Cartesianism" is understandable, then. The response of "second approach" Protestants, however, was a very particular one. Over against the claimed perfection of a science that could make no error in any subject-matter with which it dealt—and at the same time, over against a Roman Catholic Church that, on quite different grounds, claimed infallibility in all that it taught—"second approach" Protestants now began to appeal to an abstractly perfect, inerrant Scripture. They appealed to a Scripture, we recall for our earlier discussion, which was inerrant *in every respect*—in the realm of nature, as much as in the realm of theology: "[w]hatever reason brings out of its stinking heaps must be subordinate to the word of God and be measured by it as its touchstone" (Arnoldus).[87] Everything! The perfect Scripture stands above all as the measuring stick of all that is claimed to be known. If reason held an absolute and inerrant status on one side, with Scripture subordinated beneath it, then "second-approach" Protestants believed that they must assert the opposite. Some

---

[86] Ronald D. Bedford, *The Defence of Truth: Herbert of Cherbury and the Seventeenth Century* (Manchester: Manchester University Press, 1979), 211–38.

[87] Cited in Scholder, *Birth*, 119.

of them believed that this scriptural perfection extended even to the Hebrew vowel points (my chapter 11): "[w]hereas Luther, Calvin, and their contemporaries viewed the question of the origin of the vowel points as a minor issue to be treated at the level of textual analysis," these Protestants "raised the question to doctrinal status."[88] In the opinion of the eminent philologist Johannes Buxtorf the elder (1564–1629), for example, if the vowel points were indeed the invention of the Masoretes, then Scripture was "of an uncertain authority."[89] It is Elias Levita and not Copernicus who is Buxtorf's opponent in this case—but the approach to the "presenting issue" is just the same.

Few Protestants nowadays believe that we should consider the perfection of Scripture as extending to its vowel points. They are comfortable enough with the sensible view of Brian Walton (1600–1661), that although these points are indeed a Masoretic product they represent "in the main an authentic representation of the oral tradition of pronunciation and a valid guide to meaning" and careful textual work can correct any errors.[90] Probably just as few Protestants believe that defending the inerrancy of Scripture requires defending Ptolemaic cosmology or objecting to the notion of a spherical earth. When it comes to politics, moreover, many Protestant nowadays value tolerance even as they may well possess deep religious convictions. For this reason many would regard the separation of Church and state as a beneficial and a necessary move. That the state should be constructed around the common good and on rational principles, serving a plurality of citizens—this would indeed be regarded by many Christians nowadays as a *self-evident* good, and one that is to be actively pursued where it has not yet been realized. They would not believe, conversely, that the state should be run along confessional, religious lines (Christian or otherwise), because they recognize the inevitability that this leads to the oppression of minorities and ultimately to (other kinds of) violence. It is not just that we have *adjusted* ourselves to these ideas that are rooted in the seventeenth-century European (largely Christian) development of a worldview in which mathematics, reason, and empirical enquiry play important roles in getting at the truth of the cosmos. We actually *welcome* these ideas, recognizing that they have produced much that is good. We may not be "Hobbesian," but we are certainly "Lockean," to a man and a woman. Indeed, we stand with Locke (and Descartes) in many ways *rather than* with those Christians in the seventeenth century who opposed them.

Yet as with cosmology, so too with politics: many contemporary, modern people outside the Church do not associate such a "liberal" approach to politics with the Christian faith. They are convinced that Christian faith has allied itself

---

[88] Muller, *After Calvin*, 151.
[89] Muller, *After Calvin*, 149.
[90] Muller, *After Calvin*, 152–53.

naturally throughout history and down to the present moment with the forces of illiberalism. How are we to account for this belief? The answer is: in just the same way as the contemporary belief that science and Christian faith have always been at war. Once again we cannot underestimate the powerful impression made on the European (and now global) consciousness by "second approach" Protestants in the seventeenth century, along with their Roman Catholic counterparts. In their posture with respect to politics, too—not even asking to what extent "Cartesianism" had important things to say about this topic, but simply knowing in advance that it was the enemy—it was just too easy for their contemporaries to label them as obscurantists. This particular obscurantism, however, did not just affect one's view of what happened in the heavens; it affected one's view of what *should* happen on earth. *This* obscurantism stood in the way of peace and progress—unable and unwilling as it was to explain convincingly how people's legitimate aspirations for both these "goods" in a confessionally divided Europe could be grounded within the Great Story of Scripture. It is not surprising that this obscurantism attracted such antagonistic attention from its critics in the seventeenth century, nor that the antagonism continued down through the succeeding centuries as examples of Christians standing against politically liberal ideals just because they were liberal multiplied over time. Indeed, the antagonism is still with us now partly because the "second approach" is still with us now. It may no longer argue for Ptolemaic cosmology—but it still wishes to found the modern state "on the Bible," and it remains decidedly uncomfortable with a politics that is about "liberty, equality, and fraternity."[91] Thus it remains self-evident to many that "Bible-based religion"—again—is a serious problem. The broader truth is actually, of course, that

> [i]n the battles over religious toleration ... in the sixteenth and seventeenth centuries, the idea of toleration was itself very largely inspired by religious values and was fundamentally religious in character. The proponents of toleration ... might have been seen by their Catholic and orthodox Protestant adversaries as either dangerous heretics or doctrinally deviant, but there could be no question that they were nevertheless profoundly Christian in their thought and ideals ... persecution was contrary to the mind of Christ.[92]

Yet this broader truth has been largely forgotten—and unfortunately, Christians themselves have contributed to the loss of the memory.

---

[91] This second approach is commonly referred to nowadays as "Christian Reconstructionism" or "Theonomy." Its leading proponent before his death in 2001 was Rousas John Rushdoony, for whom (e.g.) democracy was "one of the great heresies of our day." "The Heresy of Democracy with God," http://ensignmessage.com/articles/the-heresy-of-democracy-with-god/ (accessed March 28, 2016).

[92] Zagorin, *Toleration*, 289.

CONCLUSION

To sum up: the seventeenth century was one of growing doubt in Europe about the nature and role of the Christian Story with respect to public life—doubt that was fueled by expanding mathematical and empirical knowledge in the context of weariness with religious war. Christian Bible readers responded in a variety of ways to this developing situation.

There were certainly many who welcomed what the new natural philosophy was discovering about the world and recognized its potential for fostering public discourse that was not entirely confessionally based. They also welcomed the emerging emphasis on toleration and the kind of separation between Church and state that facilitated toleration. They remained comfortable with the idea that Scripture was a genuinely human as well as a divine entity, and they were prepared to acknowledge that previous interpretations of Scripture touching on certain matters—like science and politics—might need to be revised as new knowledge emerged. Indeed, philology itself, pursued as a science, could help people toward more accurate, objective readings of scriptural texts, which in turn would promote harmony rather than discord. To the extent that they believed this they would certainly have agreed with the noted Protestant philologist Joseph Scaliger (1540–1609): "I wish to be a good grammarian. Religious discord depends on nothing except ignorance of grammar."[93]

At the same time there were also many who were suspicious of the new natural philosophy—dismissive both of its intrinsic claims about what human reason could achieve and of the idea that it should play an important role either in the interpretation of Scripture or in shaping the future of society. Their suspicion of empirical enquiry, in particular, extended to enquiry into the nature of Scripture as genuinely human literature. With respect both to Scripture and creation they displayed a tendency to commit strongly to the defense of older interpretations of these "texts" in conscious opposition to newer ones. This only encouraged other people's doubts—already multiplying in the seventeenth century as a result of the grim reality of religiously inspired violence—about the wisdom of placing Bible-based religion at the heart of public, European life.

This second approach to biblical hermeneutics contributed significantly to the eclipse of biblical narrative in western Christendom between the seventeenth and nineteenth centuries. The fuller dimensions of the way in which this is true, however, will become clear only in the course of the next chapter.

---

[93] Cited in Legaspi, *Death of Scripture*, 22.

15

THE EMERGENCE OF SECULAR HISTORY
The Way We (Really) Were

> *God willed for history to be written for us through the fathers and prophets in the best order and with careful transmission of the dates . . . nowhere else in the whole history of the human race is there an older enumeration of kingdoms or times.*
>
> —*Philipp Melanchthon*[1]

> *Turning and turning in the widening gyre*
> *The falcon cannot hear the falconer;*
> *Things fall apart; the centre cannot hold.*
>
> —*William B. Yeats*[2]

William Yeats (1865–1939) wrote his famous lament over the decline of European civilization not within the time period we are examining in chapters 14 and 15 (the seventeenth through the nineteenth centuries), but in the early twentieth century just after the end of the First World War (1919). His words provide us nevertheless with a helpful image of the fate of the Great Story of Scripture in these centuries. For it was in the eighteenth century that the synthesis between Jerusalem and Athens that had provided the basis for public discourse in Europe since the time of the Church Fathers finally began completely to unravel, at least in *Protestant* Europe. By the end of the nineteenth century the eclipse of biblical narrative was largely complete. Things fell apart; the center could not hold.

It is not that Protestant Christian civilization simply evaporated everywhere and all at the same time. To the contrary (and for example), early eighteenth-century Scotland was still a country deeply shaped intellectually and culturally

---

[1] Philipp Melanchthon, *Chronicon Carionis* (*Carion's Chronicle*, 1532), cited in Scholder, *Birth*, 68. This work by Johann Carion (in collaboration with Melanchthon) describes the history of the world from the creation up to the sixteenth century, and was widely read among Protestants.

[2] William B. Yeats, "The Second Coming," in *The New Oxford Book of English Verse: 1250–1950* (ed. Helen Gardner; New York: Oxford University Press, 1972), 820.

by Calvinism, and Lutheranism still exerted a hugely integrative influence on a Germany that was rising again from the ashes of the Thirty Years' War. This was the century, after all, of that Christian "Renaissance man" par excellence Johann Sebastian Bach (1685–1750), and we can easily discern the impact of the biblical narrative on other aspects of Protestant German culture too—theater, fine arts, and architecture.[3] Many people in the eighteenth century still sought to interpret the entirety of life, personally and culturally, in the light of Christian faith, and their heirs were still making the attempt in the nineteenth.

Even so, these were the centuries in which as a result of fervent intellectual attacks, and even as it was in certain ways fervently defended, the Bible finally lost its significance for philosophical thought and for the theoretical constitutional foundations of political ideals in England and subsequently elsewhere. The principles of the humanist worldview—a child that was now beginning along with its sibling science resolutely to leave behind its Christian mother—increasingly took over in the public realm as the measurement of the truth and relevance of the Bible. Secular history now provided the frame within which biblical history—or story, or myth, as it was now often called—was read, and the ethical rationalism that emerged in public life in this context proved to be one of the forces that shaped not only Britain (where it first began truly to flourish) but the entire modern world, including the emerging United States of America. This is the narrative that we must now pursue in the present chapter. We begin by picking up an important thread from the seventeenth century.

THE SEVENTEENTH CENTURY

As we saw in chapter 14, the credibility of certain versions of Christian truth claims, already in doubt because of religiously inspired violence, suffered further in the seventeenth century as a result of Christian opposition to the new science and especially the new cosmology. Significant questions arose about what the Bible apparently had to say about what was happening in the heavens and whether it should remain as a guide for what *should* happen politically on earth. At that same time questions were also multiplying about at least some of what the Bible apparently had to say about *history*—about what *had* already happened on earth. The assumption of many Christian Bible readers prior to the fifteenth century was that Scripture told an older, more complete, and more accurate story about the past than any other sources. Melanchthon, in the first epigraph to the present chapter, reflects this same view in the sixteenth century. On this view the Bible provides the overall framework within which all particular, more local histories should be located. This is still the opinion of the German Calvinist Johann Alsted

---

[3] Steiger, "Development," 702.

(1588–1638) in his *Thesaurus chronologiae* (1628): "Holy Scripture provides a complete chronology from the foundation of the world to its end."[4] This chronology allowed scholars roughly four thousand years from the beginning of the world to the birth of Christ (it was reckoned) into which all pre-Christian history must be fitted. It was a more precise version of this same figure that appeared in the page margin beside Genesis 1 in many versions of the King James Version of the Bible from the late seventeenth century onward, as a result of the meticulous work on biblical chronology of James Ussher (1581–1656).

Isaac de La Peyrère

As soon as the great voyages of discovery began in the fifteenth century, however, and with the growing recognition of the value of empirical enquiry into chronological as well as geographical matters, the idea that Scripture offers us a comprehensive framework for world history began to come under pressure. A summation and critical evaluation of the accumulated evidence up to the middle of the seventeenth century was provided in 1655 by the conservative French Protestant Isaac de La Peyrère (1596–1676) in his *Praeadamitae* (*Men before Adam*).[5] Referencing Chinese, Egyptian, Babylonian, and Greek histories, as well as Mexican and Eskimo data and classical sources, "La Peyrère showed that the ancient chronologies, no matter how they are computed, go back to a time before Adam."[6] There were clearly "pre-Adamites." The Bible, he proposed, does not discuss the whole history of the world, nor of humanity. It is indeed not possible that all the peoples of the earth are the descendants of Noah and his family. The Bible is interested only in describing the history of the Jews. The story of the great flood in Genesis, for example, is the story only of a local flood affecting the area around Palestine; other cultures possess flood stories of a similar kind. In this way La Peyrère set out "to reconcile Genesis and the gospel with the astronomy of the men of old, the history and philosophy of the most ancient of peoples"—to reconcile faith with natural reason.[7] Both science and Scripture, properly understood, are true—but each does need to be properly understood. This same idea of multiple, independent points of origin for modern humans ("polygenesis") as

---

[4] Scholder, *Birth*, 76.

[5] Eric Jorink, "'Horrible and Blasphemous': Isaac La Peyrère, Isaac Vossius and the Emergence of Radical Biblical Criticism in the Dutch Republic," in van der Meer and Mandelbrote, *Nature and Scripture in the Abrahamic Religions: Up to 1700*, 2:429–50.

[6] Richard H. Popkin, *Isaac La Peyrère (1596–1676): His Life, Work, and Influence* (Leiden: Brill, 1987), 47.

[7] Scholder, *Birth*, 83.

opposed to one, common point ("monogenesis") was still popular in many circles in the nineteenth century, prior to the ascendancy of Darwinian biological theory.[8]

In the seventeenth century these ideas landed La Peyrère in considerable trouble across the confessional spectrum—with Roman Catholics, Lutherans, and Calvinists. The Lutheran poet, philosopher, and historian Johannes Micraelius (1597–1658), for example, said of the pre-Adamite theory, "I declare that no more pernicious heresy has ever been circulated in the church than this doctrine."[9] So it was that in 1656—even though the mighty Augustine himself, more than a millennium beforehand, had affirmed that any knowledge of "the chronology of past times assists us very much in understanding the Scriptures"[10]—La Peyrère was arrested in Brussels (in the Roman Catholic Spanish Netherlands) and carried off to Rome for interrogation. He was arrested not because many of his ideas were very different from those of contemporary scholars, but because his book gained immediate notoriety. After his arrest, of course, the question still remained: what was to be done with all the accumulating data to which he had attempted to do justice? The data still existed, and carrying this single author off to Rome, where he recanted his views and converted to Roman Catholicism, did not make them disappear. Here was more information, then, that could not easily be integrated into the Great Story as it was widely understood in the seventeenth century. If La Peyrère was wrong—what then? "Anyone who disputed La Peyrère's theory without replacing it with a new and better one was cutting the last tie which still held criticism back,"[11] suggests Klaus Scholder—anticipating in these words the criticism, specifically, of Baruch (Benedict) Spinoza (1632–1677).

Baruch Spinoza

In the world shaped by Descartes, in which "[w]hat is true is primarily no longer what is guaranteed but what is evident; no longer what is handed down but what is demonstrated and proven,"[12] La Peyrère's work made a significant impact. It was not his own intention to open up Scripture to hostile criticism. He wrote however at a time when many people looking to build a different kind of world in Europe possessed a growing sense that Bible-based religion was the great obstacle to progress, and that progress therefore required a reassessment of the Bible and its role in society. It was all but inevitable, then, that La Peyrère's insights and arguments

---

[8] G. Blair Nelson, "Ethnology and the 'Two Books': Some Nineteenth-Century Americans on Preadamist Polygenism," in *Nature and Scripture in the Abrahamic Religions: 1700–Present* (ed. Jitse M. van der Meer and Scott Mandelbrote; BSCH 37; 2 vols.; Leiden: Brill, 2008), 1:145–79.

[9] Cited in Scholder, *Birth*, 87.

[10] Augustine, *On Christian Doctrine*, 2.28 (*NPNF* 1, 2:549).

[11] Scholder, *Birth*, 87.

[12] Scholder, *Birth*, 112.

would be deployed and developed with this goal in mind. The most influential of those who took this step in the late seventeenth century was Spinoza.

Spinoza was the son of "Maranno" Jews—Jews compelled to convert to Christianity in order to save their lives, but constantly under suspicion of continuing to practice Judaism in secret—who had emigrated to a relatively tolerant Holland in order the escape the Inquisition in an increasingly intolerant Portugal. He grew up in the Jewish community in Amsterdam, but in adulthood—particularly as a result of exposure through his commercial activities to the broader intellectual and political ferment of the seventeenth-century world—he developed unorthodox views and was ultimately excommunicated from the synagogue. He went on to become an influential writer, not least in his *Theological-Political Treatise* (*TPP*), published anonymously in 1670.[13] The central argument of *TPP* is that the stability and security of society is not undermined but enhanced by freedom of thought and expression. These ought to be guaranteed to subjects by a sovereign power that possesses authority in respect of the practice of religion but requires adherence only to a minimalist "creed." His argument is in significant ways broadly similar to Hobbes', then, albeit that for Hobbes the "sovereign power" is a monarchy while for Spinoza it is a democracy. Hobbes also conceives of the state as exercising much more control than Spinoza over both speech and religion. *TPP* was an exceedingly controversial work even in the Dutch context of its time, and one year after Spinoza's death in 1677 this and all his works were banned throughout Holland.

It is in support of the central argument of *TPP* that Spinoza deploys his various arguments concerning Scripture, to which he looks for the doctrines of "true religion" over against religion as typically encountered in contemporary society. It is in the Bible's moral message alone (associated with a basic monotheism), he asserts, that its sacredness lies; otherwise it is merely a human document and not to be depended upon for knowledge, which is attained by way of philosophy. The prophets were not philosophers but merely pious men, and it is only piety that we can learn from them. We can learn nothing else from the ancient Israelites that is relevant to the present—nothing (for example) from their social and political organization or their ritual practices. We must also dismiss their accounts of miracles as contrary to natural law. The biblical documents that tell us of such things were in any case written long after the events that they describe and not by those to whom they have traditionally been ascribed. Most of the Pentateuch does not derive from Moses, and the later historical books are likewise misattributed. Probably it was only the postexilic Ezra who first took all the many sources that had come down to him and began to construct out of them a single narrative

---

[13] Benedict de Spinoza, *Theological-Political Treatise* (ed. Jonathan Israel; trans. Michael Silverthorne and Jonathan Israel; *CTHP*; Cambridge: Cambridge University Press, 2007).

about the history of Israel, which was later completed by others. The prophetic books are the productions of a still later time.

For Spinoza the end result of this process of composition, ultimately resulting in a fairly arbitrary canonization of various texts in the second century BC, is a biblical tradition that is messy, incoherent, and substantially corrupt—so much so that it even defies any attempt to reconstruct the stages of the process. We often find ourselves substantially in the dark, then, about what the biblical text means, for "we do not know its author or when and under what circumstances he wrote it ... [and] if all this is unknown, we cannot ascertain what the author intended or might have intended."[14] Mercifully, however, the clarity of the universal, moral message conveyed by Scripture—the only important one, in the end—is not affected by these defects. It shines through from beneath the murky, corrupt human text. What Scripture requires is simply that we love God, and our neighbor as ourselves. We do not need to know the Bible to know that these are our duties, since our rational faculties already inform us about them. The Bible provides us with only a particular example of what the natural light of reason makes accessible to everyone, regardless of their confession or creed.

The kind of biblical criticism that Spinoza's work represents was not a marked feature of the preceding centuries. Its purpose is not only to note problems with previous interpretations of God's Word in the light of what is now known. Rather, it is to deploy this knowledge in order to reveal the Bible's "true" nature as a flawed and very human set of ancient documents *rather than* God's Word. The biblical critic in this mode wishes to demonstrate emphatically not just that the Bible cannot any longer function as the central authority in European culture on some matters (like cosmology), or merely for pragmatic reasons (that people disagree about its interpretation), but that *in itself* the Bible is not worthy of a position of cultural preeminence in the first place. Reasonable people should understand that in reality the Bible only dimly reflects much more universal and important truths that are revealed in nature and may be grasped by reason. The reader will recall my comment in chapter 1 about the people walking the "first way" of Protestant hermeneutics forming to a significant degree an "anti-perspicuity" movement with respect to the Bible—which has a lot to do, I noted there, with its point of origin. We have just encountered what is arguably that point of origin.

The Humanity of Scripture

It was Spinoza's belief that he had "secularized the Bible as an historical document," rendering it "of interest only in human terms, and to be explained in human

---

[14] Spinoza, *Theological-Political Treatise*, 109.

terms."[15] Yet the fact is that many of the data he deploys in *TPP* are retrieved from earlier Renaissance and Reformation contexts where they had originally been interpreted as speaking to the genuine humanity of Scripture *without* any implication being drawn as to its (consequent) nondivinity. At the heart of the Renaissance project, we recall, lay the idea of going back to the biblical sources in their original languages and subjecting them to close scrutiny, as one would any other ancient text. This led Renaissance and Reformation Bible readers to ask the same questions of biblical as of other texts in pursuit of fully understanding them. Who wrote this text, and when; what was the context in which it was written; how did the author deploy rhetoric in pursuit of his communicative goals; how are we best to appropriate these ancient texts in our present situation, given that "then" is not "now"? The consequence was the development already of some ideas about biblical texts that sound rather "modern" and indeed anticipate modern biblical scholarship.

On the question of the authorship of the Pentateuch, for example—which both La Peyrère and Spinoza discuss—the majority view prior to the seventeenth century was that it was largely, if not entirely, the work of the biblical Moses. Yet Second Esdras 14:1-48 already tells of Ezra dictating under divine inspiration the lost Torah to the scribes. Jerome vacillates between Moses and Ezra in his discussion of authorship; later medieval Jewish scholars, noting certain textual glosses indicating an interval of time between the periods of the writer and of Moses (e.g., Gen 12:6, 13:7), question at least the Mosaic authorship of the whole. It is such ideas that are picked up in the sixteenth century as the attempt to read the Pentateuch in a historical context raises the question of authorship in the minds of Protestant and Roman Catholic scholars alike.[16] The Renaissance also saw early discussion of puzzles in the text of Genesis, such as the differing names for God in Genesis 1-2, which would play into later discussions about the possible sources out of which such a book might have been constructed (see my chapter 17). It was this inheritance of ideas bearing upon the composition of the Pentateuch and other matters that was then mediated to many in the seventeenth century through the writings of people like the Spanish Jesuit theologian Benedict Pererius (1535–1610)—and inheritance now combined with newer ideas arising out of the reading of creation and Scripture (such as those articulated in

---

[15] Richard H. Popkin, "Spinoza and Bible Scholarship," in *The Books of Nature and Scripture: Recent Essays on Natural Philosophy, Theology, and Biblical Criticism in the Netherlands of Spinoza's Time and the British Isles of Newton's Time* (ed. James E. Force and Richard H. Popkin; IAHI; Dordrecht: Kluwer, 1994), 1–20 (16–17).

[16] On the Roman Catholic side, e.g., Andreas Masius (1514–1573) believed that the Pentateuch received its final form from Ezra or some other religious leader. On the Protestant side, Martin Luther accepted the presence of post-Mosaica in the Pentateuch and was not very concerned even about larger questions concerning Mosaic authorship.

La Peyrère's work) to form the basis for the kind of attack launched on the Bible by Spinoza.[17]

RICHARD SIMON

It was no more necessary in the seventeenth than in the sixteenth century, of course, to interpret the genuinely human historicality of the Bible in such a rationalistic manner and to its detriment as an authoritative text. The option still remained to draw on that long stream of Christian interpretation from the Church Fathers down to the Reformation that held human historicality and divine authority together. This alternative option was the one chosen, for example, by the French Roman Catholic scholar Richard Simon (1638–1712) in his *Critical History of the Old Testament* (1678). Simon responds to Spinoza's mainly *rationalist* approach to Scripture with an even more thoroughgoing *historical* approach, precisely along the lines I have just described. If internal evidence suggests that Moses did not write all of the Pentateuch, he proposes, this does not mean that the Pentateuch is diminished in importance—it speaks only to the question of how it was composed. The *status* of the biblical text as inspired and authoritative Scripture is not affected by the *process* of its composition, which no doubt took place over an extended period of time and involved the later editing and transmission of earlier, Mosaic documents. Simon is one of the first in the aftermath of Reformation and Counter-Reformation to carry out this kind of historical investigation in a systematic manner, and it is important to note that it arises not out of hostility to Christian faith but out of a desire to offer an apologetic for it in the face of rationalist criticism. Simon realized, however, "that this could only be done intelligently, by meeting objections half way, and by showing that valid points made by detractors of the Bible could be interpreted differently."[18] He defended Scripture, then, precisely on the basis of understanding its nature as a text from the past that was subject to the normal human processes involved in the transmission of any tradition.

It is unfortunate that in the seriousness with which he took the evidence concerning a question like the authorship of the Pentateuch Simon did not serve as a

---

[17] This same approach is well represented in England by Charles Blount (1654–1693), a resolute defender of the sufficiency of natural religion and a positive skeptic about belief in special revelation (questioning, e.g., the Virgin Birth, and asserting that the religious institutions and ceremonies of the OT are derivative of Egyptian customs, so that what is biblical has not been "revealed" in a special way, but is an evolution from something earlier); and the third Earl of Shaftesbury (1671–1713), for whom, since it is natural for human beings to act well, there is now no need for divine revelation at all, nor for grace or forgiveness.

[18] John W. Rogerson, "Early Old Testament Critics in the Roman Catholic Church—Focusing on the Pentateuch," *HBOT* 2:837–50 (841).

model for more Bible readers of his time than he did. To the contrary, and like so many before him, he was condemned on all sides. I do not mean in pointing this out to endorse everything that he had to say about the OT and how it should be read. I only mean to suggest that as orthodox Christian Bible readers responded to the Enlightenment rationalism of the seventeenth and eighteenth centuries there were better options available to them than the mere anti-rationalism they sometimes adopted—which essentially represented a refusal to engage with the data advanced by rationalist biblical critics in pursuit of their cause. That is to say, they did *not* approach the questions being raised "intelligently, by meeting objections half way, and by showing that valid points made by detractors of the Bible could be interpreted differently." As a matter of fact, Spinoza's declaration of the *imperfectio* of Scripture did not *require*—any more than Galileo's articulation of a Copernican-style cosmology—the resolutely defensive Protestant assertion of its abstract *perfectio* in the sense already described in my chapter 14. That this was nevertheless often the response—for example, among the radical Lutheran Pietists of the early eighteenth century[19]—did not help to allay, unfortunately, the growing perception in these centuries of a certain Christian obscurantism in the face of "facts."

THE EIGHTEENTH CENTURY

It is the eighteenth century above all that is associated with the title "the Age of Enlightenment." Among its most famous names we must include Voltaire (François-Marie Arouet, 1694–1778), David Hume (1711–1776), Jean-Jacques Rousseau (1712–1778), Adam Smith (1723–1790), and Immanuel Kant (1724–1804)—"the heir of [earlier English] rationalism and the executor of its heritage."[20] Its most notable publication, summarizing Enlightenment thought, was the French *Encyclopédie*, chiefly edited by Denis Diderot (1713–1784); its most famous documents include the American Declaration of Independence and the Constitution of the United States. The push for societies based on reason rather than religious confession continued apace in this century, although along varying political lines (both radically democratic and more conservatively reformist). Scientific method continued to produce impressive results, not least in new technological achievements such as James Watt's steam engine. Great progress was made in the course of this century in disciplines like physics, chemistry,

---

[19] Johannes Wallman notes, e.g., the *Berleburg Bible*'s commitment (1726–1742) both to Mosaic authorship of the whole Pentateuch and to the proposition that "all reckoning of time must also begin with Moses." Wallman, "Scriptural Understanding," 916.

[20] Henning G. Reventlow, "Towards the End of the 'Century of Enlightenment': Established Shift from *Sacra Scriptura* to Literary Documents and Religion of the People of Israel," *HBOT* 2:1024–63 (1040).

mathematics, and medicine; it also saw the birth of economics, the appearance of the antecedents of modern anthropology and sociology, and the beginnings of modern geology (to which we shall return later).

It was in this new world that organized religion now had to find its way as much Enlightenment scholarship continued to attempt to curtail its political power. It was in this new context that Bible reading now took place. It was the world of the Scottish Enlightenment, for example, which followed fast on the heels of the last execution in Britain for blasphemy (in Edinburgh on January 8, 1697)—a sign of the changing times.[21] It was a world increasingly marked by John Locke's ideas about the legitimacy of the state as rooted in the will of the people rather than the will of God—a world marked by foundational political documents characterized by claims about self-evident human rights rather than prescribed human duties (and certainly not duties grounded in Scripture). It was a world in which notions of a principled separation between Church and state gained ever more traction, greatly influencing (for example) the way in which the U.S. constitution was written. It was a world, too, of growing freedom for people to believe and to speak as they wished, so long as they did not disturb the peace of society—to express their views about the *Bible* freely and without fear of punishment, precisely because the Bible's interpretation no longer impacted so directly the survival and shape of the state itself. One's views of the Bible were increasingly regarded as "private," therefore, even where they were published.

Jonathan Edwards

It seems appropriate as we begin our review of how Christian Bible readers responded to this new situation to begin with a rather famous Christian leader of the time who, although he held conservative and orthodox theological views, responded in a much more positive way than the radical Lutheran Pietists to what was happening around him. Jonathan Edwards was born in Connecticut in 1703 in what would soon be the United States; he died in 1758. He is probably best remembered as a Puritan pastor in the religious revival known as the (First) Great Awakening (c. 1730–1755). More important for our present purposes, however, is his upbringing among New Englanders who (as George Marsden reminds us) "had long been friendly to scientific advances and were confident that discoveries of God's ways of governing the natural world would only confirm what they knew from Scripture."[22] Newton, Locke, and others were all known there, and

---

[21] Arthur Herman, *How the Scots Invented the Modern World: The True Story of How Western Europe's Poorest Nation Created Our World and Everything in It* (New York: Three Rivers, 2002), 2–10.

[22] George M. Marsden, *Jonathan Edwards: A Life* (New Haven: Yale University Press, 2003), 60.

"[e]ducated New Englanders took a Copernican viewpoint and the new science for granted."[23] At a young age Edwards himself became familiar with Locke's *Essay Concerning Human Understanding*, which greatly influenced him, and he was also fascinated and profoundly influenced by the work of Newton. He was a keen observer of the natural world and wrote on various topics in natural philosophy, including spiders, light, and optics. All of this he integrated with his Christian faith, as someone with "a lifelong interest in the religious significance of nature, as well as an abiding interest in modern science."[24] The world that was progressively becoming more deeply understood Edwards still viewed as creation; its laws, for him, demonstrated God's wisdom and care. "Only an all-wise Governor of the universe could account for such marvels. There was no other way to explain them";[25] and "[a] God of this magnitude ... could, of course, easily plan for miracles and arrange for any number of coincidences that would have special providential meanings."[26] The universe represented the complex language of God. "Everything pointed to a higher meaning."[27] All in all, Edwards'

> fundamental outlook was strikingly akin to that group of late seventeenth- and early-eighteenth-century thinkers who have been characterized as "theocentric metaphysicians" ... [who] asserted that the new science was fully compatible with God's most intimate involvement with every moment of existence.[28]

In Jonathan Edwards, then, we see the continuation of the Puritan stream of scholarship already described in my chapter 14, with its openness toward considering how the reading of creation might inform the reading of Scripture and vice versa.

In all of this Edwards was above all concerned to "answer the new rationalistic interpretive thrust of Deism." He understood clearly "that the Deist insistence on understanding nature according to 'mere reason' would never lead to a conclusion of the religious significance of nature, or creation, as this was portrayed in the Bible and explicated by Christian theology."[29] In answering Deism, however, Edwards was quite "willing to acknowledge the epistemological and perceptual

---

[23] Marsden, *Jonathan Edwards*, 60.
[24] Robert E. Brown, "Jonathan Edwards and the Discourses of Nature," in van der Meer and Mandelbrote, *Nature and Scripture in the Abrahamic Religions: 1700–Present*, 1:83–114 (83).
[25] Marsden, *Jonathan Edwards*, 66.
[26] Marsden, *Jonathan Edwards*, 70.
[27] Marsden, *Jonathan Edwards*, 77.
[28] Marsden, *Jonathan Edwards*, 73–74. For a discussion of the rather more ambivalent attitude toward science of Edward's close English contemporary John Wesley (1703–1791), see Randy L. Maddox, "John Wesley's Precedent for Theological Engagement with the Natural Sciences," *WesTJ* 44 (2009): 23–54.
[29] Brown, "Jonathan Edwards," 109–10.

limitations of the biblical narratives and to transform his interpretation of them accordingly."[30] Such appropriate reinterpretation was indeed an important aspect of resolving the problem of "the growing conflict between Scripture texts and science," and he set about the task with optimism and enthusiasm. In this he was by no means alone in the English-speaking world, as the closing decades of the eighteenth century gave way to the opening decades of the nineteenth. English-speaking scholarship in this period remained broadly convinced that "the truths discovered in the empirical study of the natural world would tend to confirm the theological truths revealed in the study of Scripture" that was responsibly conducted with due attention to the latter's "time-conditioned features."[31] Leading figures of the English evangelical movement of the eighteenth century, for example, while suspicious of pure (and as they saw it, speculative) Cartesianism, certainly accepted and worked within the broad parameters of the Newtonian science of their time with its commitment to empirical method and its delivery of practical, beneficial results. From their point of view—whether they were theologians, hymn writers, poets, or artists—what modern science revealed about the natural world simply confirmed the truths of special revelation, and provided one further set of good reasons to praise and worship the Creator.[32]

It was by no means a problem in the eighteenth century, then, to combine heartfelt religious devotion and orthodox Protestant belief with intellectual openness to the world around about. Unfortunately, as we shall see, the kind of revivalism that Jonathan Edwards himself supported in the Great Awakening ultimately contributed greatly to a view in North America (and elsewhere) of what it meant to be a Christian and a faithful Bible reader that had little place for integrated Christian thinking in engagement with the outside world.

GERMAN RATIONALISM

One of the most significant developments in Enlightenment Europe was the way in which Germany, "from the Thirty Years' War until well into the eighteenth century . . . closed to the great questions of the time in a remarkable way,"[33] opened up to these questions and rose to intellectual and cultural prominence in its embrace of modern answers to them. The intellectual center of European philosophy (and theology) now moved increasingly from Holland, Britain, and

---

[30] Brown, "Jonathan Edwards," 110.

[31] William Yarchin, "Biblical Interpretation in the Light of the Interpretation of Nature: 1650–1900," in van der Meer and Mandelbrote, *Nature and Scripture in the Abrahamic Religions: 1700–Present*, 1:41–82 (63–64).

[32] See further Bruce Hindmarsh, *The Spirit of Early Evangelicalism* (New York: Oxford University Press, forthcoming, 2017), chs. 4 and 5.

[33] Scholder, *Birth*, 4.

France to Germany and, once rooted in German soil, the new ideas that had lately been fermenting elsewhere quickly developed and flourished in a vibrant, decentralized political environment in which "censorship of new ideas was virtually impossible."[34] If one got into trouble in one German principality it was generally a simple matter (depending on exactly what had caused the trouble) to find a more welcoming environment in a neighboring one. By the end of the century, Germany "was beginning to dominate the scholarly world, and to set an agenda which still remains influential today."[35]

The story of biblical interpretation here in the eighteenth century played out in a rather different way than elsewhere, albeit that it did so also against the background of rationalistic Deism. The earlier part of the century was dominated by the teaching of both Lutheran orthodoxy on the one hand and revivalist Lutheran Pietism on the other. I have already mentioned the more radical stream of Pietism—sectarian, and critical of mainstream institutions and churches—but this was not the only kind. There was also the Pietist renewal movement *within* mainstream German society, with its institutional focal point in the University of Halle. Here, under the leadership of August Hermann Francke (1663–1726), the study of the Bible remained for a time central to the quest for knowledge, and in its pursuit philology—that which was historical and grammatical—remained much more important than philosophy. The tide was now swiftly flowing in a different direction, however, and that direction is well exemplified in the person and work of Hermann Samuel Reimarus (1694–1768). Reimarus was an Enlightenment rationalist par excellence, deeply committed to "toleration and equal rights for those who were and those who were not able to overcome their doubts regarding the truth of the biblical revelation"[36] and personally convinced that the Bible was not in fact a *source* of divine revelation. The real, historical Jesus, he believed, was only "a teacher of the universal and rational principles of a moral religion."[37] In pursuit of his own vision of reality Reimarus enthusiastically endorsed the many writings of the English Deists that were being published in German in his day.[38]

It was these writings that "inspired the growth of the critical scholarship of the Bible and of Christian theology, first at Halle and then at Tübingen."[39]

---

[34] Bray, *Biblical Interpretation*, 227.

[35] Bray, *Biblical Interpretation*, 227.

[36] Christoph Bultmann, "Early Rationalism and Biblical Criticism on the Continent," *HBOT* 2:875–901 (881).

[37] Bultmann, "Early Rationalism," 881.

[38] "Between 1745 and 1782, some twenty works by English deist writers were published in German translation." Scott Mandelbrote, "Biblical Hermeneutics and the Sciences, 1700–1900: An Overview," in van der Meer and Mandelbrote, *Nature and Scripture in the Abrahamic Religions: 1700–Present*, 1:3–37 (22).

[39] Mandelbrote, "Biblical Hermeneutics," 22.

In Halle the turning of the tide is illustrated by the changing fortunes of the rationalist philosopher Christian Wolff (1679–1754). Wolff had been appointed at the university in 1707 as a professor of mathematics and natural philosophy on the recommendation of none other than Leibniz. In 1723 he was exiled from Prussia by King Frederick-Wilhelm I because of criticism by the Pietists. In 1740, however, he was asked to return by Frederick-Wilhelm's son, Frederick the Great. The "old Christian synthesis, despite its new Pietist form," had come to be seen by many as "incapable of unifying intellectual life."[40] It now appeared, "by the light of the new *Aufklärung* [Enlightenment] breaking over the German lands, to be unworkable, implausible, and outworn."[41]

The founding of the University of Göttingen in 1737 reveals the extent to which, by the fourth decade of the century, this perception was already changing the understanding of the nature and purpose of the university in Germany— with significant consequences for the study of the Bible thereafter. In general German universities in this period "were created or remade expressly to serve the interests of the state" as part of the Enlightenment "cultural enterprise aimed at overcoming confessional loyalties while preserving Christian intellectual and religious forms."[42] Halle was remade; Göttingen was created, with a view to providing "cutting-edge higher education for bureaucratically oriented small-state nobility" who would emerge "competent, public-minded, knowledgeable, and, above all, socially adept," and ready to play a leadership role in a newly enlightened society.[43] Göttingen did possess a theological faculty, but its founders "stripped [it] . . . of its traditional powers and preeminence and thrust theology into the lowest position that the discipline, to that point, had ever occupied at a European university."[44] One could hardly ask for a better illustration of the "eclipse of biblical narrative" in eighteenth-century Europe than this. In Enlightenment Germany this narrative must now somehow find its way as a substory within a larger secularized history as it was understood by intellectuals like the writer and philosopher Gotthold Lessing (1729–1781) and the poet Friedrich Schiller (1759–1805)—as "a process of an advancing stabilization of a culture of reason."[45] This was a culture that was now invulnerable, in Lessing's opinion, to the merely individual and rather weak "accidental truths of history," which could not get across "the ugly broad ditch"

---

[40] Legaspi, *Death of Scripture*, 54.
[41] Legaspi, *Death of Scripture*, 53.
[42] Legaspi, *Death of Scripture*, 9.
[43] Legaspi, *Death of Scripture*, 43.
[44] Legaspi, *Death of Scripture*, 33.
[45] Jan Rohls, "Historical, Cultural and Philosophical Aspects of the Nineteenth Century with Special Regard to Biblical Interpretation," *HBOT* 3/1:31–63 (32). On Spinoza's influence on Lessing, see O'Neill, *Bible's Authority*, 14.

that divided them from the strong and "necessary truths of reason."⁴⁶ The very justification for bothering with the Bible at all would now need to be articulated in terms of the overall purpose of the university in "turning out moral, rational, and useful citizens."⁴⁷

JOHANN DAVID MICHAELIS

If Bible reading were to survive in the long term in such a self-consciously post-confessional environment, it was clear to many that it could not do so as a confessional activity. The Bible could not be the Bible of any particular confession; it needed to become the Bible of the university and indeed the state—a Bible that was simply part of the "common cultural inheritance" that helped to hold the state together and contributed to its well-being and peaceableness.⁴⁸ It is at this point that we must reckon with Johann David Michaelis (1717–1791), who "exemplified a conservative progressivism that took the cultural obsolescence of confessional Christianity for granted and aimed at the creation of an irenic social order based on reason, morality, and the growing power of the state."⁴⁹ Michaelis played an important role in "saving" the Bible for posterity with respect to its role in public discourse in eighteenth-century Germany, and in so doing he also greatly influenced the future direction of biblical studies in Europe.

Michaelis was clearheaded about the purpose of the German Enlightenment university. It was not primarily to advance the Christian faith, nor was it to advance knowledge in general; rather, it was to aid the state in achieving its economic and social goals—"to educate students broadly so that they would possess a modest understanding of scholarship and enough theoretical knowledge to succeed in a professional career."⁵⁰ Theology had an important role to play in inducting these future leaders into reasonable religion and in helping to marginalize religious extremism. The stability of the state would be greatly enhanced if the theology taught to these university students possessed "sufficient linguistic competence and if it [were] enlightened by philosophy";⁵¹ such theology might even enrich their understanding of politics, literature, and life. In just such a way was Michaelis able to carve out an important ongoing role for Bible reading in the university, and indeed for the study of the original languages in which the Bible was written—especially the OT and its Hebrew. The OT was to be read as the literary remains of an important ancient civilization, in a period in which many

---

⁴⁶ O'Neill, *Bible's Authority*, 17–18 (citing Lessing's *The Proof of the Spirit and of Power*, 1777).
⁴⁷ Legaspi, *Death of Scripture*, 44.
⁴⁸ Legaspi, *Death of Scripture*, 5.
⁴⁹ Legaspi, *Death of Scripture*, ix–x.
⁵⁰ Legaspi, *Death of Scripture*, 35.
⁵¹ Cited in Legaspi, *Death of Scripture*, 35.

German intellectuals were turning to ancient Greece and not to ancient Israel in order "to recover an integrative vision of life."[52] A significant figure in the development of this "philhellenism" was Johann Winckelmann (1717–1768), who influenced other important intellectuals like Lessing,[53] Schiller, the leading German Romantics August and Friedrich Schlegel (1767–1845 and 1772–1829), and the author and statesman Johann Wolfgang von Goethe (1749–1832). For Michaelis, much of the literature of the OT, read with careful attention to Hebrew language and ancient historical context,[54] and most especially to aesthetics—where he depended greatly on the work of the Englishman Robert Lowth (1710–1787) on Hebrew poetry[55]—could be experienced by the educated reader in a new and inspiring way as "sublime." A Moses could be encountered, in fact, who was a paradigm for contemporary European leaders, working as he did "in a pragmatic, conservative way to make ancient Israel a rational, tolerant, and happy society."[56] This was how space could be created for Israel and its literature in Enlightenment scholarship "on a landscape already crowded with ancient exemplars."[57]

There can be no question but that Michaelis, a lifelong Lutheran and the explicit defender of core Christian doctrines in the face of the attacks of critics like Reimarus,[58] believed that in pursuing this project within the German university context he was defending Protestant Christian faith against its rationalistic despisers. If Spinoza used historical and textual investigation of the Bible only to show that it was largely irrelevant to modern life, Michaelis set out in a determined fashion to demonstrate that serious historical and textual work revealed its direct and substantial relevance even apart from any theological and confessional context. Like other German scholars of similar persuasion he "did not follow many English Deists, French *philosophes* [such as Voltaire], or Enlightenment radicals in scorning or minimizing the Bible."[59] His strategy was in fact

> to maximize the Bible, to renegotiate its relation to modern life on as large a scale as possible.... [Michaelis and his colleagues] read the Bible in order to understand

---

[52] Legaspi, *Death of Scripture*, 54. On the importance of both Greece and Rome more broadly in the European Enlightenment, see 105–6.

[53] Aside from his oft-repeated dictum concerning the great gulf fixed between historical truth on the one hand and religious truth on the other, Lessing is perhaps best known nowadays for his play *Nathan the Wise* (1779)—"a forceful exhortation to tolerance between Islam, Judaism, and Christianity." Bultmann, "Early Rationalism," 894.

[54] On Michaelis' "recovery" of Hebrew in pursuit of his project, see Legaspi, *Death of Scripture*, 79–104.

[55] Legaspi, *Death of Scripture*, 105–28.

[56] Legaspi, *Death of Scripture*, 146.

[57] Legaspi, *Death of Scripture*, 106.

[58] Legaspi, *Death of Scripture*, 49–50.

[59] Legaspi, *Death of Scripture*, 31.

its aesthetic power and to harvest political insights ... [as] a resource for moral philosophy and the study of language."[60]

However, they chose to try to accomplish this maximization in ways that substantially departed not only from particular confessional understandings of the Bible but also from historic Christian ones in general. This was no longer a Bible that provided an overarching, unified narrative, typologically integrated and centered on Christ and interpreting all of human existence. That this idea should be abandoned had already been conceded to the rationalists. The materials in *this* Bible were not to be read as part of a "canon"—a structure that was often viewed as an imposition by the post-apostolic Church on the biblical materials and was dismissed by the Halle rationalist Johann Salomo Semler (1725–1791) in *A Free Enquiry into the Canon* (1771–1775) as something that "reflects and was conditioned by historical and local conditions ... [and] cannot be identified with the 'Word of God.'"[61] In the case of the OT the biblical materials were to be read instead against the background of a reconstructed ancient and classical Israelite civilization. In this new context, then, the psalms were important not as liturgy, nor the prophets as foretellers of Christ, but both predominantly as examples of beautiful Hebrew poetry. The great figures of Hebrew narrative were no longer the carriers of the redemptive story, but "classical artists [now] of the imagination."[62]

Many of Michaelis' specific ideas have not stood the test of time, and his own pupil and successor in Göttingen, Johann Gottfried Eichhorn (1752–1827), regarded his reconstructed Israel as only a figment of his own imagination.[63] The important literary critic Johann Gottfried von Herder (1744–1803) also emphasized his deficiencies: "Michaelis's knowledge of the ancient world allowed him, perhaps, to see something of the ancient Moses, but it did not illuminate the Israelite *people*."[64] In retrospect it is easy to see that Michaelis' particular version of Moses as a pragmatic conservative is in fact about as convincing as Spinoza's portrait of him as the promoter of republican democracy.[65] Michaelis' real achievement, nevertheless, was to lay the foundation for the university-based discipline

---

[60] Legaspi, *Death of Scripture*, 31.

[61] John H. Hayes, "Historical Criticism of the Old Testament Canon," *HBOT* 2:985–1005 (1003), who reports Semler's belief that "different writings in the Bible reflected in different degrees the 'Word of God,' if at all." Semler distinguished Scripture, then, from a true "Word of God" that was only *contained* in Scripture, here and there—a Word that was not historically conditioned, but addressed to everyone, in all times and places. For a sketch of Semler's life and thought, see O'Neill, *Bible's Authority*, 39–53.

[62] Legaspi, *Death of Scripture*, 128.

[63] For a sketch of Eichhorn's life and thought, see O'Neill, *Bible's Authority*, 78–94.

[64] Legaspi, *Death of Scripture*, 157.

[65] Legaspi, *Death of Scripture*, 132–34.

of biblical studies that flourished in much of Europe after his time—even as the surrounding academic culture grew less and less welcoming to it[66]—with its strong philological and historical focus and its often avowedly nontheological or (in various ways) anti-theological posture. The birth of this discipline with its newly conceived Bible, we now understand, was a direct consequence of the death of Scripture as conceived by Christians for seventeen hundred years beforehand—and indeed, it was part of a concerted ongoing effort to make sure that Scripture stayed in its grave and did not climb back out again. This is not in the least degree to suggest that we should diminish the importance of all that has been discovered about the Bible and its background since the creation of this discipline, nor that we should be anything less than appreciative of the commitment that has given us access to this information.[67] If Robert Lowth is correct, for example, "that poetry does not simply delight and instruct; it delights in order to instruct," and if this is as true of Hebrew poetry as of any other kind, then that is an important piece of information.[68] Such data are no less important than any of the remainder that modern empirical enquiry into either Scripture or creation has placed before us for our consideration (see further part 3 of the present book), and it was Michaelis more than anyone in the eighteenth century who generated interest in their pursuit as part of "a compelling interpretive program" of the kind that to some extent still drives modern university departments of biblical studies.[69] It is a very good thing that since the eighteenth century "[a] rational, irenic study of the Bible supported by state resources and disciplined by academic standards cultivated across a range of fields has produced, in a relatively short time, an astonishing amount of useful information."[70] I do not wish to diminish or fail to appreciate such an achievement. I wish simply to point out that the work of scholars like Michaelis was not truly designed to prevent the eclipse of biblical narrative; it was in fact already premised upon this eclipse. Nor has much of the work within the discipline of biblical studies since his time been undertaken in the hope that the now-dead Scriptures can be resurrected. This discipline has mainly been concerned, carefully and methodically, to dissect the corpse, focusing on parcels of

---

[66] For a brief description of the trajectory of the surrounding German academic culture already in the late eighteenth and nineteenth centuries, influenced by both philhellenism and a new Orientalism, see Legaspi, *Death of Scripture*, 157–59.

[67] Michaelis himself invested significant effort, e.g., in planning an admittedly disastrous scientific expedition to the Near East that would "gather background material for the study of the Bible in a systematic, scientific way" so that it could be read much more fully in its ancient historical and cultural context. John Sandys-Wunsch, "Early Old Testament Critics on the Continent," *HBOT* 2:971–84 (983).

[68] Legaspi, *Death of Scripture*, 108.

[69] Legaspi, *Death of Scripture*, 165.

[70] Legaspi, *Death of Scripture*, 169.

flesh that have over time become ever-decreasing in size such that more and more is known about less and less, and why most of it matters any longer has become (within the discipline itself, at least) unclear.

Conclusion

In the middle of the seventeenth century it was still possible for the Dutch clergyman and astronomer Jacob du Bois to write a book on cosmology in which part of his argument in favor of a pre-Copernican cosmology was that it is biblical, and that his opponents represented merely "a sect of new philosophers."[71] The eighteenth century, however, saw the Bible largely lose this kind of cultural preeminence in Europe. For many people the Bible ceased to be the one document in which all knowledge could be assumed to be rooted, even where it retained some residual authority for religious faith and morals. The Bible became, even more clearly than in any preceding period, a document from the past that must be studied according to the normal procedures employed in studying any ancient text *in order to see* how much knowledge it might contribute to the modern knowledge pool. Its truthfulness and its usefulness must now be determined. They were no longer presupposed.

The importance of this "historical criticism," now resolutely divorced in principle from any confessional, theological context, is already illustrated in two important documents from the closing decades of the century. The first is (Michaelis' student) Johann Friedrich Eichhorn's *Introduction to the Old Testament* (1780–1783), with its pronounced emphasis on the historical circumstances behind a biblical passage, chapter, or book as the key to understanding the Bible's historical development. The second is the 1787 inaugural lecture of (Eichhorn's student) Johann Philipp Gabler (1753–1826) as a professor of theology at the University of Altdorf, which sharply distinguishes biblical and dogmatic theology, characterizing the former in terms of historical investigation into and description of the beliefs of the biblical authors. It is this historical-critical program that would dominate the discipline of biblical studies in the nineteenth-century universities of Europe, with significant impact on the culture of both Church and society in general.

THE NINETEENTH CENTURY

If the work of La Peyrère and Spinoza had already begun in the late seventeenth century to open up serious questions about reading Scripture in order to frame all of world history, various developments in the nineteenth century all but "eliminated [for many people] Scripture's relevance for understanding the history of

---

[71] Vermij, "Debate," 612.

Earth."⁷² Important here already in the late eighteenth century was the work of James Hutton (1726–1797), who came to the conclusion through observation and reasoned deduction that the earth had arrived at its present form over a long period of time as a result of processes like erosion, volcanism, and sedimentation (*Theory of the Earth*, 1795). Here lie the beginnings of modern geology. Within a few decades—by the time that Charles Lyell (1797–1875) had published his three-volume *Principles of Geology* (1830–1833) and his *Elements of Geology* (1838)—the idea was becoming widely accepted that the pre-Christian history of the earth was extensive and that in those ancient times it had been subject to natural processes of the kind still observed in the present.⁷³ Charles Darwin (1809–1882) read the *Principles of Geology* while sailing on the HMS *Beagle* during his scientific expedition of 1831–1836. He made further geological discoveries that supported Lyell's thesis, and used it as a grid upon which to plot his own developing ideas about biological evolution over long periods of time. These ideas, too, gradually began to command a broad consensus with respect to the history of life in general and of humanity in particular.

In the nineteenth-century European mind in general, then, and across the world in Europe's contemporary and previous colonies, scientific method continued to "produce the goods," not least in ongoing, spectacular technological breakthroughs. Knowledge of all of this was disseminated at ever-increasing speeds as steam-powered presses produced more and more books more cheaply, then newspapers became widely affordable. Transportation and communications by rail and sea improved and regular mail services took off, allowing greater scholarly contact than ever before.

The credibility of any version of Christian faith that could or would not reckon with this impressive modern world and its ideas diminished—although "reason" was not having everything its own way, and other realities were giving people pause for thought. Even as reason seemingly prevailed when it came to subjects like geology and biology, the nineteenth century saw the loosening of the grip of Enlightenment rationalism on European culture in other respects—not least because the French Revolution and its aftermath appeared to confirm the critique of many of its eighteenth-century detractors that reason was naively

---

⁷² Yarchin, "Biblical Interpretation," 41.

⁷³ For a comprehensive account of the developments between 1776 and 1848 that led to this result, see Martin J. S. Rudwick, *Bursting the Limits of Time: The Reconstruction of Geohistory in the Age of Revolution* (Chicago: University of Chicago Press, 2005); for a shorter, earlier book on the entire nineteenth century, see Mott T. Greene, *Geology in the Nineteenth Century: Changing Views of a Changing World* (Ithaca, N.Y.: Cornell University Press, 1982). Modern geology, however, while still holding that all past geological processes are like all present ones, builds elements of "catastrophism" (occasional natural catastrophic events) into Lyell's "uniformitarian" framework (whereby the Earth becomes what it now is as a result of a gradual, lengthy process).

optimistic about what human beings once emancipated from tradition (including religious tradition) could achieve. The Revolution demonstrated that in reality, reason unshackled from tradition, and freedom unconstrained by ancient law and custom, did not necessarily usher in the anticipated, glorious new age—and certainly not an age of tolerance. Now that reason had produced chaotic violence, followed by Napoleon's despotic imperialism—what now, for a European culture that had invested so much hope in reason's capacity to quell violence and oppression? For many in what was a period of growing national consciousness all over Europe the answer lay in renewed attention to the myth and the history—the tradition—that held *particular* groups together (rather than *all* human beings, rationally and universally).

This meant different things to different people. There were certainly those who interpreted it in a more subjective manner. An influential eighteenth-century precursor here is the "proto-Romantic" German author Herder, with his emphasis on the need for the interpreter, in interpreting a text from the remote past, to enter into "the mental state of its author, his public, his nation.... Feeling is the way of understanding."[74] The Romanticism that flowed out from such wellsprings in the first half of the nineteenth century in Europe paid attention, then, to questions of national origin as well as to native folklore, ballads, poetry, dance, and music, in pursuit of the retrieval of each nation's unique historical and cultural inheritance. It did not always produce accounts of the past that were very attentive to facts, and in due course it produced a great deal of its own ugliness in the world, as uncritically absorbed myths fed the nationalisms that in turn produced the devastating persecutions and wars of the twentieth century.[75]

At the other end of the spectrum we find the self-consciously objective and scientific approach to history proposed by Leopold von Ranke (1795–1886), which involved at its core *rigorous attention* to "facts." Ranke's goal was simply to present the past, after exhaustive examination of the available sources, *wie es eigentlich gewesen*: "the way it actually was." He was not much interested in questions of contemporary relevance. As we shall see, it was Ranke's approach to history much more than Herder's that influenced the development of the discipline of biblical studies in the nineteenth century as it became even more avowedly "historical" than in the eighteenth, although the kind of Romanticism that emerged out of

---

[74] Reventlow, "Enlightenment," 1045. Study of the OT, then (e.g.) would be about empathetically accessing "the particular genius of the Israelite *Volk* [people]" with the goal of imitating in one's own specific and contemporary culture the Israelites as an authentic embodiment of a specific culture back then. Legaspi, *Death of Scripture*, 147. For a sketch of Herder's life and thought, see O'Neill, *Bible's Authority*, 66–77.

[75] See, e.g., George L. Mosse, *The Crisis of German Ideology: Intellectual Origins of the Third Reich* (New York: Grosset & Dunlap, 1964).

Herder's perspectives is certainly also mirrored in some Christian responses to nineteenth-century developments among Bible readers more generally. Whether on the "revivalist," evangelical wing of the Church, or in the more liberal circles influenced by Friedrich Schleiermacher (1768–1834), insulating theology from the advance of scientific method by grounding religion in the inner world of the individual's feelings or sensibility about spiritual matters where criticism could not reach it became a popular option.

World History and the Bible

In the sixteenth century, during the time of the Reformation, "very few people were engaged in systematic study of the Earth. Geology as a science did not yet exist.... Significant developments in the scientific investigation of the Earth lay ... in most cases, at least two centuries in the future."[76] At the beginning of the nineteenth century, however, "old-earth cosmology" was widely perceived as credible,[77] and by the middle of the century we find ourselves well on the way to the contemporary situation in which for two further centuries

> thousands of geologists from around the globe have examined in astounding detail dozens of lines of evidence that bear on the antiquity of the Earth ... the fact that the Earth is extremely old with an age that is measurable in hundreds of millions to billions of years has been established.[78]

As to the relevance of the Bible to this question, already by the end of the nineteenth century it was widely understood that the earth was "the product of an historical process that could no longer be described in the terms and by the data available from Scripture."[79] How did educated Protestant Bible readers in the nineteenth century respond to this changing situation?

The range of these responses is similar to that in the case of Copernican cosmological theory in the seventeenth century. Especially as the new ideas first begin to impinge on people's consciousness, we find significant resistance to them in many quarters—strong affirmations of traditional "young-earth" cosmology. Unsurprisingly, many people needed to be convinced that the new ideas were valid and that fresh adjustments really did require to be made to the way in which they read Scripture. For much of the nineteenth century, then, there was lively debate in Britain and in the United States on this question of the age of the earth, and how it had reached its present condition—about the correct way in

---

[76] Young, *Natural World*, 77–78.
[77] Ralph O'Connor, "Young-Earth Creationists in Early Nineteenth-Century Britain? Towards a Reassessment of 'Scriptural Geology,'" *HS* 45 (2007): 357–403.
[78] Young, *Natural World*, 199.
[79] Yarchin, "Biblical Interpretation," 51.

which to read both creation and Scripture. As the strength of the new scientific evidence then became more widely accepted and the wisdom of continuing to argue for "Mosaic geology" was questioned, we find more and more recourse to popular proposals for reading Genesis 1 in new ways—since "most old-earth geologists before 1850 . . . believed in the inspiration and authority of Scripture" and taking Genesis seriously remained important to them.[80] One of these proposals was to read a huge, unmentioned chronological "gap" into Genesis 1:1-3 at some point, most often between verses 1 and 2. Another was to interpret the Hebrew word *yōm* ("day") throughout Genesis 1 as referring to an "age" rather than a twenty-four-hour day.[81] The latter idea in particular was often presented in an "accommodationist" manner; for example, the six-day creation reflects "the perspective of an Earth-bound observer because it was presented to Moses in a series of visionary images that captured the primary characteristics of each geological period."[82] Either because they accepted such specific proposals or simply because they had now come to recognize "that Scripture was not the sort of literature that spoke reliably of geological or natural history" but "more authentically an historical witness to ancient faith and religious ideas,"[83] many Protestant Bible interpreters by the century's end—including the noted Princeton theologian Benjamin Warfield[84]—had come to accept the great age of the earth. As in the earlier case of Copernicus, however, many had not. They steadfastly held to a young-earth cosmology in the teeth of accumulating evidence to the contrary. Once again this was widely perceived in society at large as obscurantism in the face of the facts.

Close on the heels of Lyell's work came the publication of Darwin's *On the Origin of Species by Means of Natural Selection* (1859). In this book Darwin presented the biological theory upon which he had been working ever since returning from his great sea journey. The idea of evolution itself was not new. The eighteenth- and early nineteenth-century study of fossils when combined with the perspectives of the emerging science of geology on the successive nature of geological strata had already suggested to many that creation had changed markedly over time and that its history involved extinctions. Already at the beginning of the nineteenth century Jean-Baptiste Lamarck (1744–1829) had proposed

---

[80] O'Connor, "Young-Earth Creationists," 365. For a detailed account of developments in England in particular between the publication of Lyell's *Principles* in 1830–1833 and Darwin's *Origin of Species* in 1859, see J. M. I. Klaver, *Geology and Religious Sentiment: The Effect of Geological Discourse on English Society and Literature between 1829 and 1859* (BSIH 80; Leiden: Brill, 1997).

[81] August Ludwig von Schlözer had proposed this idea in 1772. Yarchin, "Biblical Interpretation," 49.

[82] This was the view Scottish geologist Hugh Miller (1802–1856). Yarchin, "Biblical Interpretation," 63n61.

[83] Yarchin, "Biblical Interpretation," 51, 59.

[84] Yarchin, "Biblical Interpretation," 67n71.

adaptation as the mechanism that accounted for change; for example, giraffes are tall because they continually stretch to reach their food. However, Darwin now not only provided vast amounts of evidence for the reality of evolutionary change but also proposed a different mechanism.

All organisms, he suggested, share common ancestors with other organisms. These include human beings. It is this shared ancestry that explains the similarities that organisms share with each other. The *differences* primarily result from "natural selection" over long periods of time. As traits are passed on, with variation, from parents to offspring, some organisms will be more likely to flourish than others in a given environment. In the struggle for resources they will do better, and they will therefore contribute more offspring to the next generation. Over time these beneficial adaptations will radically alter the world, as species diverge from each other and indeed some die out. The giraffe is with us now not because his neck gradually grew so that he could reach the highest leaves but because variations among his predecessors resulted over time in a longer neck, thereby giving him a competitive advantage over other proto-giraffes.

Nineteenth-century responses to Darwin's work among Protestant Bible readers were mixed, as they wrestled once again, first of all, with the particular issue of what to do with traditional readings of Scripture, but second and more broadly with two questions: "could the idea of God as creator be reconciled with naturalistic explanations of design in nature? And if humans had evolved, what did that do to the claim that there was a unique relationship between God and man?"[85] Against a background in nineteenth-century Britain in which Christians—including the great majority of evangelical Protestants—were generally interested in and open to new scientific ideas,[86] many in that country took the new evolutionary ideas very seriously and sought to account for the data in ways that were congruent with a Christian worldview. They "acknowledged that humans might have evolved, but [they argued] that this did not require change in the essential features of Christian anthropology." Since "evolution was shot

---

[85] Richard England, "Interpreting Scripture, Assimilating Science: Four British and American Christian Evolutionists on the Relationship between Science, the Bible, and Doctrine," in van der Meer and Mandelbrote, *Nature and Scripture in the Abrahamic Religions: 1700–Present*, 1:183–223 (183). More broadly, see James R. Moore, *The Post-Darwinian Controversies: A Study of the Protestant Struggle to Come to Terms with Darwin in Great Britain and America 1870–1900* (Cambridge: Cambridge University Press, 1979).

[86] Aileen Fyfe, *Science and Salvation: Evangelical Popular Science Publishing in Victorian Britain* (Chicago: University of Chicago Press, 2004), 3–9. Fyfe argues in this book that British evangelicals "were not opposed to the sciences but did worry about the manner in which the sciences were presented and interpreted" (14)—which is why they committed such huge resources to popular publishing on faith and science.

through with divine intention, it was not functionally different from creation: therefore human evolution did not challenge fundamental Christian doctrines."[87]

For some of these authors there was no expectation that Scripture should be making scientific claims that could directly contribute to the science of biology. Charged by an interlocutor with "giving up Genesis" because of his accommodationist views, for example, Aubrey Moore (1848–1890) responds by saying that he has no problem with adopting this language if his opponent means by it "refusing to claim for [Genesis] what it never claims for itself—that it is a prophetic anticipation of nineteenth-century science."[88] At the same time, however, these authors were robust in insisting that the moral and spiritual truths taught by Scripture remained authoritative, and they strongly opposed the reductionistic materialism of some versions of evolutionary theory.[89] Here is Aubrey Moore again: "we are as little prepared to consult Genesis on the order of the palaeontological series as to ask the high priests of modern science to solve for us the difficulties of our moral and spiritual life."[90] The interest of Scripture lay in the formation of the "moral and spiritual life," and science did not directly address this question. Nevertheless, the theory of biological evolution was a welcome development in the world of science, for its "organicist paradigm" was more congruent with Christian faith than the mechanistic one that had dominated the immediately preceding centuries; evolution *could* be interpreted in terms of growth toward the fulfillment of a divine purpose.[91] Such a view was not only opposed to reductionistic materialism but also to the monism of someone like the German zoologist Ernst Haeckel (1834–1919), for whom "[a]ll natural events pointed to an everlasting order of a steadily improving nature, guaranteed by necessity"—with "necessity" being equivalent in this system to "God."[92] Among Darwin's more "forgotten defenders" in this time period were many Protestants of evangelical persuasion in different parts of the world—"forgotten" now because the popular contemporary "warfare

---

[87] England, "Interpreting Scripture," 185. He is thinking specifically of Aubrey Moore (1848–1890), James Iverach (1839–1922), George F. Wright (1838–1921), and John Gulick (1832–1932).

[88] England, "Interpreting Scripture," 189.

[89] An example is provided, e.g., by the work of the German radical Carl Vogt (1817–1895), for whom God had been replaced in the cosmos by "blind, unconscious necessity." Berhard Kleeberg, "The Will to Meaning: Protestant Reactions to Darwinism in Nineteenth-Century Germany," in van der Meer and Mandelbrote, *Nature and Scripture in the Abrahamic Religions: 1700–Present*, 1:257–91 (258).

[90] England, "Interpreting Scripture," 193.

[91] England, "Interpreting Scripture," 188.

[92] Kleeberg, "Will to Meaning," 261, and passim, for the various attempts of German Protestant scholarship to deal with Darwinism within the context of ongoing Christian belief in (at least) divine providence and purpose, "defending the concept of teleology against chance and necessity" (287).

model" of science and faith discussed in my chapters 13 and 14 can find no place for them.[93]

Other nineteenth-century Bible readers, while comfortable with the general idea "that the Bible was written in terms accommodated to human understanding" and while generally seeking "to reconcile apparent discrepancies between science and Scripture by the careful reinterpretation of one or the other,"[94] were nevertheless uncomfortable with recourse to the idea of divine accommodation in Scripture when it came to the new biology. Scholars like Edward Pusey (1800–1882), Charles Hodge (1797–1878), and John Dawson (1820–1899) accepted the reinterpretations of Scripture that had arisen as a result of Copernicus' work on cosmology, and even the more recent discoveries of the new geology—at least insofar as these established an ancient age for the earth.[95] Hodge is on record, for example (in 1863), as insisting that although the Bible is infallible its interpretation is not, and must be aided by science. This was the lesson to be learned from the earlier reaction of the Church to Copernicus: "With the advent of better scientific knowledge, later readers came to see that scriptural statements about the Sun's motion were matters of common experience, not astronomical teaching."[96] With respect to Darwinian biology, however, these same scholars were generally opposed to making a similar move—at least given the present state of scientific knowledge. On this point they firmly maintained that Scripture stated "the facts," and they contrasted these facts with what they characterized as merely scientific "theories," which (in the words of Hodge) "are human speculations, and can have no higher authority than their own probability."[97] For Hodge, Darwin's idea that natural selection could produce new species was just such a mere hypothesis, and "no man under the guidance of reason will renounce the teachings of a

---

[93] David N. Livingstone, *Darwin's Forgotten Defenders: The Encounter between Evangelical Theology and Evolutionary Thought* (Grand Rapids: Eerdmans, 1987), for whom "the old warfare thesis ... has turned out to be sterile" (185).

[94] Richard England, "Scriptural Facts and Scientific Theories: Epistemological Concerns of Three Leading English-Speaking Anti-Darwinians (Pusey, Hodge, and Dawson)," in van der Meer and Mandelbrote, *Nature and Scripture in the Abrahamic Religions: 1700–Present*, 1:225–56 (227).

[95] There was more disagreement about the usefulness of modern geology for settling those earlier, seventeenth-century questions about the (non)universality of the Genesis flood, but "men like Pusey ... could see a role for science in helping to settle the matter." Richard England, "Scriptural Facts," 229. In general his view was that "[t]he claims of geology do not even touch upon theology" (234).

[96] England, "Scriptural Facts," 239.

[97] Charles Hodge, *Systematic Theology, Volume 1: Theology* (New York: Scribner, 1871), 57. Cited in England, "Scriptural Facts," 229. Pusey, nevertheless, concedes that "evolution, unproven though it be, would not contradict the Bible claim that God created all life" (236).

well-authenticated revelation, in obedience to human speculation."[98] For Dawson, "the scriptural account of human and geological history better fitted the facts than evolutionary theories,"[99] albeit that he too agreed that scientific knowledge could improve Bible reading and he demonstrated this in numerous ways (e.g., in his treatment of a [local] Genesis flood).[100] These English-language opponents of Darwinism had their counterparts in Germany, such as the Lutheran theologian Otto Zöckler (1833–1906) who characterized the Darwinist hypothesis "as a 'chain of pseudo-arguments,' 'scientifically untenable,' and 'pathological,' since it lacked the support of *observed evidence.*"[101] In the Netherlands of the nineteenth century, too, the Calvinist churches were marked by "unanimous disagreement with every aspect of the theory, which was considered a direct attack on essential elements of the orthodox protestant religion."[102]

In a European context in which the Darwinian hypothesis increasingly came to be seen as explaining coherently a very large number of data—and doing so much more successfully than the competing theory of special creation[103]—and therefore steadily gained support in public discourse as a true hypothesis, Pusey's work in England on science and faith was destined to have little lasting impact there: "To the next generation of Anglo-Catholics, evolution was an established theory which could be shown to be compatible with the right reading of Scripture."[104] Dawson's thoughts on science and faith were likewise generally discounted in his native Canada after his death, and views like Zöckler's in Germany commanded little ongoing support. Even in the Netherlands, where in the early part of the twentieth century the neo-Calvinist successors of Abraham Kuyper (1837–1920) and Herman Bavinck (1854–1921) displayed a renewed "opposition to every aspect of the theory of evolution,"[105] by the 1960s more and more Calvinist scholars were paying attention to it, perhaps more cognizant than before of the earlier warning of the scientist Julius Pieter de Gaay Fortman "that the theory of evolution ... was accepted almost everywhere in the international scientific community,

---

[98] Charles Hodge, *Systematic Theology, Volume 2: Anthropology* (New York: Scribner, 1872), 22. Cited in England, "Scriptural Facts," 241. Common sense itself stood against Darwin's theory: "It shocks the common sense of unsophisticated men to be told that the whale and the humming-bird, man and the mosquito, are derived from the same source." Cited from the *Systematic Theology*, unfortunately without a reference, in Bradley J. Gundlach, *Process and Providence: The Evolution Question at Princeton, 1845–1929* (Grand Rapids: Eerdmans, 2013), 123.

[99] England, "Scriptural Facts," 244.

[100] England, "Scriptural Facts," 247.

[101] Kleeberg, "Will to Meaning," 270.

[102] Rob P. W. Visser, "Dutch Calvinists and Darwinism, 1900–1960," in van der Meer and Mandelbrote, *Nature and Scripture in the Abrahamic Religions: 1700–Present*, 2:293–315 (293).

[103] McGrath, *Science of God*, 215–16.

[104] England, "Scriptural Facts," 238.

[105] Visser, "Dutch Calvinists," 297.

and that Calvinists could no longer neglect it unless they were willing to become intellectually isolated."[106] It is Charles Hodge, not only in his opposition to the atheism that he understood to be integral to Darwin's work, but also in his insistence that evolution had not in any case occurred, who has had the greatest ongoing influence in his own country (the United States) down to the present time.[107] That part of the story, however, must await chapter 16.

The History of Israel and the Bible

As science continued to reveal the truth about the history of the world in general to its nineteenth-century audience, it is not surprising that we should find an ever-increasing conviction that scientific method could deliver similar truth if applied rigorously to the history of regions and nations in particular. The rigorous study of "facts," in written and other sources as much as in nature, would reveal—if handled with the correct scientific method—"the way it actually was." As Ranke put it, the historian is interested only in "naked truth without any ornament"— the truth that lies deeper than rhetoric and therefore lies beneath written sources from the past rather than *in* them.[108] It is against this background that we must understand the astonishing extent of the historical analysis to which the Bible was subject in the nineteenth century as exciting new discoveries cast fresh light on its background. This was the century in which the Holy Land was first mapped in detail and the ancient Near East extensively explored. Egyptian hieroglyphics were deciphered in the wake of the discovery of the famous Rosetta Stone (by Napoleon's troops in Egypt in 1799); Mesopotamian cuneiform was also deciphered as described in my chapter 11. Important inscriptions of particular interest to Bible readers were discovered, such as the Moabite Stone and the "Israel stela"

---

[106] Visser, "Dutch Calvinists," 301. Although denying "that natural selection was the driving force of evolutionary change," Kuyper himself accepted that the mutability of species "must be accepted as a serious possibility" and that "Scripture did not contradict" the idea. Both he and Bavinck "incorporated organic mutability into divine providence" (295, 297). See further George Harinck, "Twin Sisters with a Changing Character: How Neo Calvinists Dealt with the Modern Discrepancy between the Bible and Natural Sciences," in van der Meer and Mandelbrote, *Nature and Scripture in the Abrahamic Religions: 1700–Present*, 2:317–70.

[107] The interesting question, of course (to which the answer is unknowable), is whether the passing of time would ultimately have led Hodge to revise his judgment concerning the facts, as "a working hypothesis which is at present on its probation" (Benjamin Warfield) in due course and increasingly came to be regarded as true. Gundlach, *Process*, 129. It is a good question, since the most important issue for the Old Princeton theologians was not whether creation involved a process but whether God was "transcendent and sovereign over, as well as immanent in, the world process." Gundlach, *Process*, 315.

[108] Cited in Gunter Scholtz, "The Phenomenon of Historicism as a Backcloth of Biblical Scholarship," *HBOT* 3/1:64–89 (75).

of Pharaoh Merneptah.[109] A greater understanding arose of the broader anthropological, sociological, and mythological contexts within which the OT should be understood—of the lives of other "primitive peoples" around the world and of some of their texts (like the ancient Babylonian stories of creation and flood).[110]

Inevitably, however—especially given its points of origin in the preceding centuries as described earlier in the present chapter—the historical analysis of the Bible that emerged in the nineteenth century often took a quite particular form. It reflected a broadly shared conviction that to a greater or lesser extent the "real" history of Israel lies beneath our rhetorically or poetically constructed biblical texts (if indeed they reflect history at all) and must be rescued from its plight by modern scientist-historians who now understood much more clearly both the general laws that govern history and religion and the overall shape that history objectively possesses. The quest for the historical Israel, conceived along these lines, now began in earnest—just as in NT studies there emerged a similar quest for the historical Jesus, most famously associated in the first half of the nineteenth century with the name of David Friedrich Strauss (1808–1874). For Strauss (in *The Life of Jesus, Critically Examined*, 1835), the NT Gospels are not themselves historical, although they remain symbolically important because they provide access to the religious consciousness of the earliest Christians.[111]

A good example of someone who approached the history of Israel in such a manner is Strauss' friend Wilhelm Vatke (1806–1882). Vatke had studied in Berlin with Wilhelm Martin Leberecht de Wette (1780–1849), who had in turn been influenced by Herder ("Feeling is the way of understanding"). De Wette had proposed in his doctoral thesis (1805) that Deuteronomy was not known in Israel as Moses' law book prior to the reign of King Josiah of Judah (2 Kgs 22–23). This was part of his argument that the Pentateuch as a whole is the composition of a much later time than Moses' and an unreliable source for the history of earliest Israel. It is religious poetry, valuable in reflecting Israel's "spirit and patriotism, its philosophy and religion"—but not for telling us anything about her distant past.[112] Vatke develops de Wette's ideas, viewing "the entire Moses tradition as an unhistorical projection of later processes"—as the product, in fact, of the Babylonian exile.[113] It is "contradictory to all laws of the history of religion that an entire nation should have been raised by one lone individual, and in one single act from a lower

---

[109] See further Steven W. Holloway, "Expansion of the Historical Context of the Hebrew Bible/Old Testament," *HBOT* 3/1:90–118.

[110] See further John W. Rogerson, "Expansion of the Anthropological, Sociological and Mythological Context of the Hebrew Bible/Old Testament," *HBOT* 3/1:119–33.

[111] For a sketch of Strauss' life and thought, see O'Neill, *Bible's Authority*, 108–16.

[112] Rohls, "Aspects," 40.

[113] Rohls, "Aspects," 49.

religious developmental stage to a far superior one of faith in Yahweh."[114] Vatke already knows the "laws" that govern the history of religion, we note—and he therefore "knows" that "Moses neither introduced the pure Yahweh faith nor the political or cultic law, and he did not found a theocracy."[115] It is quite impossible.

Other nineteenth-century scholars were generally reluctant to adopt such a radical position on the entirety of the Pentateuch, but their overall *approach* was not very different. In an environment in which scientific method was now so highly regarded, the study of history too must necessarily be scientific—no longer based on tradition, and especially not on artistically constructed tradition, but only on "the facts" understood within the context of a matrix of "laws." All reference to the Bible now had to be justified, in principle, in terms of this received scientific model. So it is that another famous German biblical scholar, Heinrich Ewald (1803–1875), can write in typically Rankean fashion in the middle of the nineteenth century (1843) that his ultimate aim as a historian of Israel is "the knowledge of what really happened—not what was only related and handed down by tradition, but what was actual fact."[116] This project inevitably involved historians in the attempt to *demonstrate* that particular biblical traditions in their current form could function at least in part as reliable sources for the historian. Their usefulness could no longer be assumed—it had to be proved. Ewald himself, for example, thought that the patriarchal traditions in Genesis were of questionable reliability. Tradition, he believed, is a pliable entity that can be molded as time passes by religious interests, etiological concerns, and mythological perspectives. Even the substitution of writing for memory only checks this process rather than stopping it. The value of the patriarchal traditions, then, dating (as he believed) from the period of Israel's early monarchy, must be doubted.

So it is that as we move toward the end of the nineteenth century the eclipse of biblical narrative becomes more complete. The *storied* account of ancient Israel in the Bible—and indeed of Jesus—increasingly seems for many people to have little to do with the *real* world of ancient history as it has been discovered by science.

CONCLUSION

Looking back on chapters 14 and 15, then: why was there an "eclipse of biblical narrative" in the course of the seventeenth through the nineteenth centuries in those parts of the world deeply impacted historically by Christian truth claims?

---

[114] Rohls, "Aspects," 49.
[115] Rohls, "Aspects," 40.
[116] Georg Heinrich August Ewald, *The History of Israel* (trans. R. Martineau and J. E. Carpenter; 6 vols.; London: Longmans, Green, 1869), 1:13. For a sketch of Ewald's life and thought, see O'Neill, *Bible's Authority*, 135–49.

Among the various causes we have identified a number of important ones. The Christian narrative came to be suspected of being, and then "known" by many to be, incapable of embracing all the truths discovered about the world in the course of these centuries—truths scientific, historical, and so on. It also came to be understood as a major cause of violence, war, and intolerance, and as a major obstacle to legitimate human rights, freedoms, and ultimately well-being, and happiness. These same suspicions—this same "knowledge"—marks the contemporary moment of those who are heirs to the narrative of modernity. It is common knowledge among these heirs that the Bible is untrue and moreover wicked. It is common knowledge that the Bible cannot help us build the New Jerusalem. Only Reason, working with empirically established facts, can be our guide.

16

On Engaging with a Changing World
Fight, Flight, and the Fifth Way

> ... "the intention of the Holy Ghost is to teach us how one goes to heaven, not how heaven goes" ... I should think it would be the part of prudence not to permit anyone to usurp scriptural texts and force them in some way to maintain any physical conclusion to be true, when at some future time the senses and demonstrative or necessary reasons may show the contrary.
>
> —Galileo Galilei[1]

> Back in the seventeenth century Sir Thomas Browne could remark ... "Time we may comprehend, 'tis but five days elder than ourselves." ... But we, unlike Browne and his contemporaries, now take it for granted that even our most remote ancestors were long preceded by ... deep or prehuman history.
>
> —Martin Rudwick[2]

For the reasons noted near the beginning of my chapter 14, we should not imagine that every kind of contemporary Protestant Bible reader regards the eclipse of biblical narrative as a problem. It is not likely that many "first way" (historical critical) or "second way" (postmodern) readers do. It is not likely, then, that many of them will feel too exercised about articulating a coherent response to the problem. For the rest of us, however, the question of coherent response is much more pressing—not least because we need to work out how to engage, consistently with that response, both historical critics and postmodern readers. What are we to say, then, about this widespread abandonment in erstwhile Western Christendom of Christian Scripture as the all-encompassing metanarrative that makes sense of human existence? And what are we to *do* about it?

---

[1] Galileo Galilei, *Discoveries and Opinions of Galileo* (trans. Stillman Drake; Garden City, N.Y.: Doubleday, 1957), 186–87.

[2] Rudwick, *Bursting the Limits of Time*, 2.

ON THE IMPOSSIBILITY OF FLIGHT

For some contemporary Protestants who care about these questions—the "fourth way" counter-Reformational Protestants of chapter 1—the important lesson to be learned from the fact that "[t]he men of the Middle Ages lived in the Bible and by the Bible"[3] whereas the majority of Westerners currently do not is first and foremost that we need to *go back*. We have lost something that needs to be retrieved. This position is well represented by my Regent College colleague Hans Boersma in his book *Heavenly Participation* (2011).[4] Boersma calls "for a reevaluation of the Reformation," which he sees as a tragedy whose occurrence we should lament.[5] We need to get back behind it to recover "the Great Tradition" that is the "broad consensus of the church fathers and medieval theologians" who sought to perceive "the eternal mystery of the Word of God" in the data available to our senses.[6] In particular, we need to recover its "sacramental ontology," which, while insisting on the infinite difference between creation and God, understood the former as participating through Christ in God.[7] This is to move well beyond biblical covenantal categories for describing God's relationship with the world.[8] It is essentially to recover an ancient "Platonist-Christian synthesis" that preceded the rediscovery of Aristotle in the West and then his rise to dominance in high medieval theology.[9] Precisely his rediscovery contributed in due course to what Boersma understands as the inappropriate detachment of nature from God, of the natural from the supernatural, of nature from grace—and to the rise of secular modernity, which is focused on the natural and *not* on the spiritual.[10] We must recover this "Platonist-Christian synthesis," getting back behind a period in Church history when the authority of Scripture unfortunately came to be set against the authority of the Church in order to recover an integrated, spiritually focused Bible *for* the Church, which will allow us "to retain the centrality of the Bible [while rediscovering] its hidden spiritual depths."[11] We must reject, then, the Protestant dismissal—a *fateful* one, which led ultimately to the development of a secular hermeneutic—of much of the pre-Reformation biblical hermeneutic that was practiced in a still-enchanted medieval world. We must instead attempt the recovery of a sacramental approach in which the literal meaning of Scripture

---

[3] Congar, *Tradition*, 86.
[4] See my chapter 1 for the full reference.
[5] Boersma, *Heavenly Participation*, 85, 104.
[6] Boersma, *Heavenly Participation*, xi.
[7] Boersma, *Heavenly Participation*, 9–11, 19–39.
[8] Boersma, *Heavenly Participation*, 24.
[9] Boersma, *Heavenly Participation*, 33–39.
[10] Boersma, *Heavenly Participation*, 52–83.
[11] Boersma, *Heavenly Participation*, 153.

points to (rather than "is") a spiritual meaning.¹² This is the broader context for the work of someone like Craig Allert on canon, introduced first in my chapter 1 and then discussed at length in chapter 2. Both scholars are looking to reconnect Protestant hermeneutics with a more distant past than they believe the Reformation represents—a more unified past, in which (to reference the second epigraph to my chapter 15) the center *did* hold and things had not yet begun to fall apart. On this view the answer to the problem of the eclipse of biblical narrative is to get back behind the Reformation, which was in fact one of its significant causes. We must learn to reinhabit an older and better (more orthodox) worldview, reunifying a divided Church in the process and putting it in a stronger position to deal effectively with a secular age.

The Great Tradition, Plato, and Reading Scripture

It will not surprise the reader of this book to learn that I do not regard this as a viable response to the situation in which we find ourselves. Among some of my initial difficulties, the first is that I agree with the Reformers that there never was such a thing as a "broad consensus of the church fathers and medieval theologians." As we have seen, what we discover in the history of the Christian Church once we get beyond the earliest ecumenical creeds (the "Great Tradition" that the Reformers and I certainly *do* affirm) is a range of Christian leaders possessing a range of views on a range of topics—not all of which views are consistent with the teaching of Scripture. We find in this context not one ancient "Platonist-Christian synthesis" but many. Early "Protestant theologians had no trouble showing that a monolithic patristic tradition [in particular] simply did not exist,"¹³ and I know of no reason to depart from their judgment.

This leads me to my second difficulty. When a particular patristic writer goes astray in his thinking on a path that leads away from scriptural teaching, it is often (as we have seen) precisely a particular Platonist-Christian synthesis that is the root cause of the problem. Plato does not help; he hinders. It is simply not true, in my view, that ancient Christians (in Boersma's words) "generally knew when to say no to the Platonic worldview"—that "by and large Christians did reject the excesses of Platonism."¹⁴ The problem is far more severe than that, and it is well illustrated in the fact that Boersma's words here are embedded in an account of a number of Platonist-Christian doctrinal "fusions" that are in my view highly questionable—for example, the notion that the world returns to God "by means of the deification of human beings"¹⁵ and indeed that our ultimate

---

[12] Boersma, *Heavenly Participation*, 21–24, 137–53.
[13] Zimmermann, *Theological Hermeneutics*, 82.
[14] Boersma, *Heavenly Participation*, 35.
[15] Boersma, *Heavenly Participation*, 36.

destiny is to penetrate in a beatific vision to the heart of who God essentially is.[16] Whether Boersma himself finds some or all of these fusions questionable is not entirely clear in his text.[17] For my own part, anyway, I am really only interested—like the Reformers—in lenses for reading Scripture that actually help me to understand what *Scripture* is saying, by way of both affirmation and negation of Plato (or anyone else). As one aspect of this endeavor I am interested—like the Reformers—in what authoritative Scripture sometimes has to say over *against* the authority of the Church. I do not need a "sacramental hermeneutic" that will make these things more difficult to perceive and may indeed lead me far astray even in centrally important matters of faith and life.[18] The hermeneutical task is challenging enough as it is.

My third initial difficulty is that for all the reasons enunciated in my chapters 4 through 9 I believe that the last thing we need to recover in this post-Reformational world of ours is any kind of "spiritual reading" that departs from the literal sense of the text. As I argued in chapter 9, "spiritual reading" is exactly what deprives Scripture of its ability truly to function authoritatively. It is exactly what destroys our capacity to perceive when the teaching of Plato or anyone else conflicts with scriptural teaching. It is precisely what has always allowed the unnoticed introduction into Christian theology of ideas that should have been

---

[16] Boersma, *Heavenly Participation*, 37.

[17] This lack of clarity then unfortunately permits the reader who has followed my discussion of Origen's eschatology in chapter 8 to form the impression later (*Heavenly Participation*, 186–87) that Boersma considers the resurrection of the physical body to be problematic when considered in the light of the traditional doctrine of the beatific vision. The (Platonic) implication here, that our ultimate destiny does not essentially involve ongoing material physicality, is certainly marked in Radical Orthodoxy where "the beatific vision ... is an event of nondiscursive immediacy; the need for material mediation, [Milbank and Pickstock] conclude, is something that we shall 'outgrow' ... our end is to somehow escape embodiment." Smith, *Radical Orthodoxy*, 200, 203. As a matter of fact, however (as I happen to know), Boersma does *not* believe that we shall one day see the essence of God in the beatific vision, nor does he doubt the bodily resurrection.

[18] Consider, e.g., the way in which the Platonic perspectives that are central to both Roman Catholic and counter-Reformational Protestant scholarship routinely lead to a strong emphasis both that God is Wholly Other and that the human capacity to understand him and to speak about him—even in Scripture—is extraordinarily limited. Who God really is lies well beyond the grasp of our senses and even our language (e.g., Boersma, *Heavenly Participation*, 70–76, even while distancing Christian faith from some aspects of Neoplatonism). To this kind of theologizing about God Martin Luther already and rightly responded by emphasizing that, scripturally, "this wholly other God is also personal and present, eager to communicate with his creation," seeking "communion with his creatures through speech." Zimmermann, *Theological Hermeneutics*, 53. The word that God speaks both in Scripture and especially in the incarnation is perspicuous, entirely reliable, and genuinely revelatory of God: "anyone who has seen me has seen the Father" (John 14:9). God is distant from us not because we are *creatures* (as in a considerable amount of Platonically inspired theology) but because we are *fallen* creatures. Vanhoozer, *Biblical Authority*, 48–49, in the course of his retrieval of a properly understood "reformed" idea of *sola gratia* (grace alone).

rejected. Martin Luther worried "that allegorizing could easily become a Trojan horse with which one could smuggle all sorts of mischief into the Scriptures,"[19] and he was right to be worried. Literal reading, on the other hand, can at least ask questions like, "is the notion even of a sacramental ontology itself a biblical one?" Boersma himself does not satisfactorily address this question. He simply appears to assume both that our task is to "*search* for an ontology that is compatible with the Christian faith" and that such an entity is not found in Scripture itself.[20] No argument is entered on either point. His later citation of a tiny number of biblical texts appears perfunctory in this context, and it is certainly unpersuasive in respect of establishing the ontology for which he advocates.[21] Scripture does not visibly teach a "sacramental ontology" in respect of God's relationship with creation—and this is especially clear in the OT texts. In fact, it was the ancient Near Eastern cultures in the midst of which the ancient Mosaic Yahwists lived—the cultures whose essentially shared worldview they rejected—that more obviously possessed a sacramental ontology.[22] So should we embrace this Platonist-Christian view of the cosmos as true? Or should we not rather insist with James Smith that our task as Christians is "to take seriously the integrity of a biblically (i.e., revelationally) informed ontology and its uniqueness vis-à-vis the ultimately pagan ontology of Plato"?[23] From this point of view what is wrong with counter-Reformational Protestantism is not that it wishes to "go back," but that it does not wish to go back *far enough* (i.e., to Scripture), in order then to move forward.

---

[19] Vanhoozer, *Biblical Authority*, 79.

[20] Boersma, *Heavenly Participation*, 20 (emphasis added). (The text clearly gives this impression, although Boersma assures me that he does in fact believe that an ontology is to be found in Scripture.) Radical Orthodoxy appears essentially to proceed from the same kinds of assumptions, simply *asserting* in the first instance that "participation [is] the only proper metaphysical model for understanding creation" (Smith, *Radical Orthodoxy*, 74). The "participation" in question is the Greek *methexis*, which derives directly from Plato's attempt to describe the relationship between the real world of the Forms and the world merely of the phenomena that are accessible to our senses—and does not once appear in Scripture. The consequence, predictably, is further statements about creation that are certainly also out of joint with Scripture: e.g., Catherine Pickstock's remark that "every created reality is absolutely nothing in itself" (cited in Smith, *Radical Orthodoxy*, 75; see also 103–4 for the direct connection with Plato, and 204–23 for Smith's critique). The attempts that are then made after the fact to find scriptural texts that are consistent with the Platonic view are, like Boersma's, unconvincing. Smith, *Radical Orthodoxy*, 191n18. Contrast Vanhoozer's substantial engagement with Scripture in the course of his attempt to differentiate his "communicative ontology" from "a sacramental ontology." Vanhoozer, *Biblical Authority*, 53–58.

[21] Boersma, *Heavenly Participation*, 24.

[22] John H. Walton, *Ancient Near Eastern Thought and the Old Testament: Introducing the Conceptual World of the Hebrew Bible* (Grand Rapids: Baker, 2006), 87–112.

[23] Smith, *Radical Orthodoxy*, 199.

Plato, Aristotle, and Science

It is not only Scripture that raises this question of truth; it is modernity itself. As we saw in my chapter 14, modern science was not built on the foundation of the Platonist-Christian synthesis. In fact, it was Plato's view that the main importance of the physical world lay in the access that it provided to a "real" world elsewhere along with his conviction that philosophy needed to get beyond sense perception in order to apprehend this reality that initially made science in the modern sense of the word impossible, even in the Christian West. Not even the addition of Aristotle to the mix, as we saw, produced modern, empirical science. Before it could fully emerge, the whole Greek philosophy of nature had to be set aside; philosophers needed to allow far more deeply Christian ideas about the world as genuinely *created* to impact the medieval science of nature.

The modern science that did ultimately emerge has proceeded then to confirm again and again all the many ways in which the Greek philosophy of nature, and the Christian understandings of physical, created reality that have been grounded in it, are not true. Modern science has certainly demonstrated *that*, whatever its own inadequacies may be in terms of comprehending everything that creation is. The cosmos physically described, it turns out, really does comprise a network of creatures in relationship (including causal relationship) with one another—a network that has been granted its own freedom to operate in accordance with "laws," including laws that govern growth and change, such that it can successfully be treated as a legitimate object of enquiry *in itself* and independently of its Creator. If this were not so, then (among other things) modern science could not have produced modern technology. It is a view of the world that *works*, only because it taps into cosmological truth. This is fundamentally why most modern people accept the modern scientific worldview; it has a tremendous track record of penetrating to some fundamental realities of the physical universe, and as an ultimate consequence it makes our lives (oftentimes and in various ways) better. Even medieval Aristotelian Christians, it turns out, were much closer to the truth than Platonic ones—in the midst of the multiple errors that both shared—when it came to some important aspects of cosmology. We really *should* think of nature as appropriately "detached" from God and possessing its own integrity. As one perceptive reviewer of *Heavenly Participation* has noted this is indeed what our Christian creeds, when they touch on the two natures of Christ, would (by analogy) imply:

> Boersma's retrieval of sacramental ontology needs to pass through and be measured by the Chalcedonian confession that the one Person of Christ is to be acknowledged in two natures without confusion or separation. A sustained reflection on the distinct integrity of Christ's human nature would require a rethinking

of Boersma's criticism that Aquinas was wrong in affirming *a relatively autonomous natural order.*[24]

To the contrary, Aquinas was surely quite *correct* in affirming the existence of "a relatively autonomous natural order," granting as he did "a great degree of integrity to nature and creatures."[25] It is not a "brute autonomy," to be sure, but a "graced autonomy."[26] Yet autonomy it certainly is, and one for which God has evidently created substantial space in the cosmos.

We can if we wish ignore this reality, just as Galileo's detractors ignored the reality of the heavens they would have encountered had they peered through his telescope. We can if we wish go on believing that cats are cats not *fundamentally* because of their biological relationships with each other but because of their sacramental participation in the Platonic Form of the Cat—their participation "in a common 'felineness.'"[27] But why would we wish to do this? In order to solve the problem of the eclipse of biblical narrative? But how will this problem be solved by reintroducing into Christian thinking a Platonist-Christian ontology that is demonstrably unable to account for many important facts—including the evolutionary history of cats? "Everyone is entitled to his own opinion," someone once said, "but not his own facts";[28] the facts remain, and need to be accounted for. Is it not much more likely that a renewed commitment to sacramental ontology will simply confirm in many minds that Christian faith represents a *flight* from the facts? If it is clear that one of our problems historically is that we have known with certainty "so much that ain't so,"[29] is it not likely that this contemporary "Platonic" move will simply look like continuing commitment to obscurantism in the face of empirical reality? A reunited Western Church might well result, *if* one could persuade a sufficient number of Christians to join it. It would be a unified

---

[24] Nicholas J. Healy Jr., "Evangelical *Ressourcement*," *First Things*, May 2011, http://www.firstthings.com/article/2011/05/evangelical-ressourcement (accessed March 21, 2016) (emphasis added). I must again acknowledge here, however, that Boersma has insisted in a personal communication that although most of *Heavenly Participation* argues against the modern "autonomy of nature," he *does* himself believe in a relatively autonomous order. He references on this point his larger book *Nouvelle Théologie and Sacramental Ontology: A Return to Mystery* (Oxford: Oxford University Press, 2009).

[25] Smith, *Radical Orthodoxy*, 162–63.

[26] Smith, *Radical Orthodoxy*, 162–63.

[27] Boersma, *Heavenly Participation*, 80.

[28] This saying is sometimes attributed to the modern U.S. politician Daniel Patrick Moynihan (1927–2003).

[29] "The trouble with people is not that they don't know but that they know so much that ain't so." *The Oxford Dictionary of Quotations* (3rd ed.; Oxford: Oxford University Press, 1979), 491. This is often attributed wrongly and in various forms to Mark Twain and others, but Josh Billings (Henry Wheeler Shaw, 1818–1885) appears to have been the first to popularize it.

Church, however, with little ability to speak to the modern world, except with an invitation to turn its back, wholesale, on modernity.

However, the "if" in this case is surely an enormous one. It does not seem at all likely in reality that most modern Western Christians, Protestant *or* Roman Catholic, would be capable of dealing with the unbearable tension that would inevitably arise in the Christian mind from this attempt to "go back"—the tension between the part of the mind that understands only too well the multifaceted superiority of the modern scientific over the medieval worldview and the part that nevertheless yearns, nostalgically, to retrieve the latter. After all, the truth of the former is every day reinforced, not least by the benefits that come the way of the "haves" in modern society. This truth is acknowledged also by the "have-nots," who do not despise but deeply desire a share in those same benefits. Few appear to be pining for a bygone age in which these benefits simply did not exist—and certainly there is no generalized pining for the European Middle Ages in particular. Most of us—including theologians—enjoy living in the modern world with all its benefits such as excellent sanitary systems, widely available clean water, and antibiotics. The Middle Ages did not produce these benefits, and we all understand that we possess them now because we live in an age when we know more than our ancestors about the nature of the world and how it works. We typically celebrate our progress in these respects—although it is significant that the tone of counter-Reformational Protestantism when pondering such matters typically appears distinctly less celebratory than is customary.[30] How is it possible at the same time, really, to believe in one part of our mind that a medieval understanding of the world is better after all? Such a flight from modernity is surely impossible.

Conclusion

To repeat, I do not consider viable this kind of Protestant counter-Reformational response to the eclipse of biblical narrative. The problems raised for many traditional renderings of the Christian metanarrative by modernity are far more serious than can possibly be addressed by swapping one problematic ancient Greek philosopher for another in a modern context where the truthfulness of both is one of the main issues in question among modern orthodox Christians *and* their critics. In such a context it will not do to play off "spiritual pre-modernity" against "secular modernity," or a "sacramental hermeneutic" against a "secular" one, as if

---

[30] We note, e.g., that having plotted the lamentable unraveling and then cutting of the medieval sacramental tapestry in his chapters 3 and 4, Hans Boersma goes on to note that "[t]he achievements of mathematics and the scientific method would have been unthinkable without [those] developments." *Heavenly Participation*, 155. Surely he is not saying that we should turn our back on these achievements? But how are we to respond to his opinion on the same page, then, that "[t]he recovery of truth as sacramental reality seems to me particularly urgent today"?

it were obvious that the second in each pair represents a fateful declension in respect of the first. All that this does is to beg the question of truth and indeed of virtue: is what came later truer, and better, than what came earlier—or not? Granted that there is much to be critiqued in modern and postmodern rhetoric about "progress," did not modernity uncover truth unknown in earlier ages? Did not life in this world improve in many ways as a result? What are the facts? It is in part because so many people nowadays believe that the obvious answer to the first two questions is "yes" that the Christian narrative has suffered its impressive "eclipse." This situation will not be improved by diminishing the importance of the truth and virtue that modernity has discovered while advocating for failed, earlier ideas—blithely ignoring the fact that the main reason why the Platonist-Christian synthesis collapsed was that it actually ceased to be able any longer to *synthesize*.[31] By adopting such a retrograde approach, indeed, we lessen our capacity effectively to subject modernity to a necessary, measured, and important Christian critique. To this final point we shall return shortly.

Did Reformation ideas play an important role, then, in producing modernity as we know it, with the somewhat grim face that Roman Catholicism (e.g., Charles Taylor, Brad Gregory, and Christian Smith), Radical Orthodoxy (e.g., John Milbank and Catherine Pickstock), and "fourth way" Protestantism (e.g., Hans Boersma) typically paint upon it? Yes, they did play a role—although we must be careful not to overemphasize it, as these authors often appear to do. No doubt the Protestant emphasis on the perspicuity of Scripture alone (Gregory), for example, did play some role in producing the post-Reformation "pervasive interpretive pluralism" that Smith is so concerned about (and even if "[n]either individualism nor pluralism was *inherent* in *sola scriptura*")[32]—but surely the invention of the printing press prior to the Reformation already offered the promise (or the threat) of that outcome, as more and more books got into more and more European hands. As assiduous as the Roman Catholic Church became in the sixteenth century and afterward in attempting to ban and burn "unwelcome" books it was always going to fall short. New ideas would have spread anyway, under the new political arrangements in Europe that were already in the process of emerging even before the Reformation.[33]

---

[31] Radical Orthodoxy shares in this tendency to regard the rejection of the Platonist-Christian synthesis as arising merely from an apostate mind engaged in "the *invention* of the secular"—as if *discovery* had no part to play. Smith, *Radical Orthodoxy*, 46, 88 (emphasis added).

[32] Vanhoozer, *Biblical Authority*, 110, with the argument following (emphasis added).

[33] "Given human nature and the lust for power, it was only a matter of time before the written word would be used to challenge centralized institutional authorities." Vanhoozer, *Biblical Authority*, 36.

But granted that the Reformation did play *a* role in producing modernity as we know it, is it to be lamented—as a *tragedy*? I cannot agree with those who say so. While frequently concurring with them about what is wrong with modernity in its current manifestations I am strongly of the opinion that there has been and remains much that is good about it, beyond scientific and technological progress—much that is consistent with Ephraim Radner's claims that "[t]he story of modernity is a story of Christian love's ongoing embodiment, and this often in spite of and against official Christian practice."[34] After all:

> Most of those who contributed to the emergence of a distinctively modern and secular culture in Europe... were Christians themselves, often devout (even Hobbes was that!), even if they had usually given up on their own churches' ability to abandon their mutual hostilities and predatory instincts, and increasingly worked apart from their ecclesial traditions.[35]

Just as importantly, my view of *pre-Reformation* reality is far less rosy than those who are inclined to lament the passing of its ideas (and even practices). Brad Gregory himself draws attention to the many "real, pervasive, and undeniable problems" of the pre-Reformation Church,[36] focusing on the moral aspects (what Radner calls "failures of love")[37]—among which we would have to include (already) significant division and dissension within the Church. I have additionally drawn attention throughout the present book to many intellectual and theological problems. However, it is just as important to consider the political aspects of the matter.

It has long been a tendency in the kind of narrative about modernity we are currently considering to regard Protestantism as having disrupted "the integral march of Catholic civilization by introducing socially disintegrative ideas into the habits of European life, weakening the otherwise powerful sway of a unified religious political power"[38]—as if this were a negative development. I regard the collapse of this civilization, on the other hand, as a positive development that opened up the way for new forms of the *polis* (and indeed the Church) to emerge. Power became progressively more widely distributed, human rights came to be more robustly protected, and individual agency came to be taken much more seriously than before. The eventual abolition of slavery in the West, for example, was a result of such liberalization, and it cannot be dissociated from strongly Christian impulses arising in part from "evangelical missionary attitudes and

---

[34] Radner, "Reformation," 50.
[35] Radner, "Reformation," 51.
[36] Gregory, *Unintended Reformation*, 85.
[37] Radner, "Reformation," 49.
[38] Radner, "Reformation," 50.

discoveries."³⁹ These in turn were the product of the loss of monolithic Church control over Western Protestant Christians and the rise of diverse, energetic missionary groups that were the very embodiment of "pervasive interpretive pluralism" but managed to spread the Gospel effectively nevertheless! A better world, in many ways, emerged after the Reformation than existed before it—that is the truth of the matter; and I find it disturbing when the lamenters will not acknowledge this, or when they give the impression that it does not matter.⁴⁰ I am not *surprised*, however, that scholars who hold Plato in such high regard would find it difficult to think of change through time as involving anything other than a declension from what is perfect, rather than viewing it as progress toward a divinely ordained goal.

We should not lament the Reformation. We should celebrate it, even as we also retrieve it from beneath numerous misunderstandings of it—as I have been attempting to do in this book. We should do so in the conviction that the Reformation itself was "a missiological retrieval of the gospel as set forth in the original languages of the Bible."⁴¹ Celebration with retrieval—that is what we need, as we attempt to formulate a properly "reformed" response to both modernity and postmodernity.⁴²

ON PICKING THE WRONG FIGHTS

Some kind of retrieval is also very much on the minds of another group of contemporary Protestants—the "third way" Chicago constituency last encountered near the beginning of chapter 14—for whom the appropriate response to the modern eclipse of biblical narrative is not so much *flight* as *fight*. According to this

---

³⁹ Radner, "Reformation," 51.

⁴⁰ E.g., in various places in his book—and not just on the pages where he discusses mathematics and scientific method (above)—Hans Boersma gives the strong impression that he himself believes either that the world has *not* become a better place in the course of modernity or that it does not matter that it has. He is not particularly impressed with modern liberal democracy; he notes without comment the roots of the Platonist-Christian synthesis in medieval feudalism (no one who has read Plato's *Republic* would be surprised!); and he appears to approve of Radical Orthodoxy's negative appraisal of modernity's "new social arrangements, new political ideals, [and] new economic models." Boersma, *Heavenly Participation*, 19–20, 64, 82–83. Interestingly, Graham Ward at least is careful to distinguish Radical Orthodoxy from this kind of (apparently) comprehensive critique of modernity (Smith, *Radical Orthodoxy*, 126)—although whether its overall approach really *permits* his qualifications is an interesting question. *Can* one consistently truly advocate for the recovery of Plato *and* accept the good in even *some* of the "fruits of modernity" that grew out of his marginalization?

⁴¹ Vanhoozer, *Biblical Authority*, 25.

⁴² So also Vanhoozer, *Biblical Authority*, 23–24—contrasting the Roman Catholic "Henri de Lubac's *ressourcement* [retrieval] of patristic theology" with "a properly Protestant *ressourcement*—i.e., a retrieval of distinctly Reformation insights" (23).

view, however, nothing was lost in the Reformation that now needs to be retrieved *from the Middle Ages or the Church Fathers*; the Reformation was certainly no tragedy. The Reformers essentially got it right in their "back to the Bible" rejection of much medieval theology, transmitting to us and building on what was already sound in the Church Fathers. We need no Platonist-Christian synthesis, nor for that matter a synthesis between the Christian faith and *any* human philosophy; we need no "spiritual reading" of Scripture. What we need is the courage to fight for our Protestant heritage. We are embroiled in a battle for the Bible,[43] and we must man the barricades, rejecting the search for any other kind of meaning in the Bible than the single, definite, and fixed meaning expressed in each biblical text. The Bible in its original languages remains the Holy Scripture that is given to the Church as the God-inspired, sufficiently perspicuous, canonical rule of truth, infallible in all that it teaches. Indeed, it is completely inerrant with respect to whatever subject it touches upon (all science included), representing all such matters as they actually are and never misrepresenting the facts. On this view that is what orthodox Christians, including the Reformers, have always believed. The eclipse of biblical narrative is merely a consequence of apostasy from this true faith. We need do nothing except ensure that we ourselves do not capitulate to apostasy. An important aspect of what this means is that we should only bring to Scripture (as *CSBH* puts it) "preunderstandings ... in harmony with scriptural teaching and subject to correction by it," avoiding the temptation to adjust Scripture "to fit alien preunderstandings, inconsistent with itself" (article 19).

This is indeed fighting talk, but it is unfortunately uttered in defense of a second indefensible position. We must continue to stand in line with the Protestant Reformers, we are told, in our understanding of the Bible. However, we are then offered (first) an understanding of Scripture's infallibility (and inerrancy) that stands in serious tension with how the Reformers themselves understood these matters—*not* a retrieval after all but a misunderstanding of that position. This leads on (second) to a posture with respect to natural science in particular that is greatly at odds with a substantial body of Protestant literature throughout the centuries since the Reformation. This posture is just as deeply unhelpful as the counter-Reformational one when it comes to dealing well with the eclipse of biblical narrative, and for the same reason: it simply ignores all the challenges to traditional representations of the Christian metanarrative that have arisen in recent centuries and refuses to engage with the question of what is true and good about modernity along *with* what we might consider not so good. Once again it is

---

[43] The allusion here to Harold Lindsell's *The Battle for the Bible* (Grand Rapids: Zondervan, 1976) is not accidental, since it provides an important context for the Chicago Statements on both Inerrancy (*CSBI*, 1978) and Hermeneutics (*CSBH*, 1982). Stephen R. Holmes, "Evangelical Doctrines of Scripture in Transatlantic Perspective," *EvQ* 81 (2009): 38–63 (40).

as if we could deal with the "problem" of modernity without really paying serious attention to the complexity of what has happened and why, but merely by getting the philosophical ducks inside our heads in a suitable row. This looks, again, like obscurantism, especially when it leads to attempts to create a new "science" that fits better with what Chicago claims to be true. It is moreover largely a *selective* obscurantism. This does not encourage observers to revise their developing opinion about the intellectual dishonesty of the position. We shall discuss each of these points more fully in turn, using *CSBH* and Norman Geisler's commentary on it as the basis for our discussion.[44]

CHICAGO ON BIBLICAL INERRANCY

CSBH first addresses the question of Scripture's inerrancy in article 2. It affirms "that as Christ is God and Man in one Person, so Scripture is, indivisibly, God's Word in human language"; it denies "that the humble, human form of Scripture entails errancy any more than the humanity of Christ, even in His humiliation, entails sin." This is a curious beginning. Sin is always moral fault, but errors in texts are not always a matter of moral fault, and can arise for other reasons such as limitations of knowledge on the part of the author. What is it about Scripture in particular, then, that inevitably leads to the equation of "error" with "sin"? The assumption appears to be that there is no other possible explanation for what *CSBH* regards as an error in a God-inspired text than that God has lied—since God is not limited in knowledge.[45] But are we really to regard Scripture as being just as unfettered as God by limitations of knowledge, whether these belong to its authors or to its readers?

As we saw in my chapters 13 and 14, the Reformers and the majority of the Protestants who came after them in the sixteenth and seventeenth centuries certainly did not believe so. They believed in the genuine historicality of divine revelation. God's Word comes to us through human beings who stand within the stream of history and speak in accordance with the language, thought forms, and conventions of their time. As people of their time and culture the biblical authors

---

[44] I recognize, of course, that not everyone who has "signed off" on *CSBH* in the past several decades agrees with Geisler's interpretation of it in every respect, but a great many do appear to regard this interpretation as "official" and "authoritative," and it does typically appear to be very much in line with *CSBH*'s plain sense. I leave it to others to explain how they are able to interpret *CSBH* otherwise and to affirm the *Statement* even while their own hermeneutical approaches, as demonstrated in their own published works, appear to place them in significant conflict with it.

[45] This is certainly the view of Chicago participant John S. Feinberg, "Truth: Relationship of Theories of Truth to Hermeneutics," in Radmacher and Preus, *Hermeneutics*, 1–50 (15): "If the Holy Spirit refuses to deceive us in regard to whatever he knows, and if He knows everything ... then His participation in the production of Scripture as co-author eliminates both willful deception, factual error, and doctrinal error of any kind."

were certainly limited in knowledge as well as in expression—exactly like God as he enters the world in Christ, in fact. It could not be otherwise. The Reformers then also believed that God graciously accommodated his revelation to the circumstances of time, place, and human condition, such that Scripture *reflects* previous (and present) limitations in human knowledge. Scholars such as Calvin did not worry about these limitations, since they were convinced that *even in their midst* the truth that God wishes to communicate to us through Scripture is sufficiently clear. They were more worried that Bible readers, in failing to attend to the limitations, would make interpretive mistakes. Scripture, they believed, unerringly guides us into all manner of truth about correct belief and practice—but only as we attend to its human form and its attendant limitations.

CSBH will have none of this: "error" is impossible in Scripture, just as sin is impossible in Christ. And what is an error? In a Bible that allegedly "expresses God's truth in propositional statements," providing us with "biblical truth [that] is both objective and absolute," an error is a statement that "misrepresents the facts," as opposed to one that "represents matters as they actually are" (article 6). There is no genuine space here for biblical texts marked by time- and culture-bound limitations. Either they represent "matters as they actually are"—and they are true—or they do not—and they are in error. Such a view of "error" compels us, then, to hold that it is *absolutely* true that "as the cloud fades and vanishes, so those who go down to Sheol do not come up; they return no more to their houses, nor do their places know them any more" (Job 7:9)—or, that this is simply an error. The latter must in reality be the case, since other parts of Scripture know about a bodily resurrection. The *CSBH* position on "error" compels us likewise to hold that it is *absolutely* true that "a slack hand causes poverty, but the hand of the diligent makes rich" (Prov 10:4)—or, that this too is an error (as the book of Job would imply). In both cases we are forbidden from adopting what is surely the very sensible view that these statements only express limited perspectives on the whole truth about the afterlife and the causes of poverty.

An impossible burden is thereby placed on the person who actually reads Scripture, rather than simply theorizing about it, and this is the direct consequence of abandoning a "reformed" perspective on the nature of Scripture and replacing it with something else. The Reformers understood Scripture as truly human literature that is inspired by God. They read it literally (see my chapter 4), seeking to understand the communicative intentions of the historically located human authors in their rhetorically shaped texts of diverse genre throughout the Bible, and—with and in all of that—the communicative intention of God. *CSBH*, on the other hand, while giving some weight to the importance of that fact "that Scripture communicates God's truth to us verbally through a wide variety of literary forms" (article 10), much more decisively insists that "the Bible expresses

God's truth in propositional statements" that sit on the page as "objective and absolute" truths in singular independence of their historically located human authors and their communicative intentions. This is *not* to read the biblical literature literally, but in reality to do so "literalistically" (my chapter 4), focusing only on the words of the texts in themselves and failing to pay attention to the "speech acts" of its authors (and Author). Indeed, given that it is manifestly untrue as a general proposition that "the Bible expresses God's truth in propositional statements," to read Scripture in a *CSBH* way is in a very real sense not to read it at all but to set off instead in pursuit of the Bible that we might have *preferred* to possess, defining in an Aristotelian manner what it *must* necessarily be rather than looking to see what it *is*. The doctrine of inerrancy ceases to be in the process the "reformed" guarantee that God in Scripture, for all its human diversity and limitations, personally communicates his reliable truth to us. It becomes the quite different guarantee that Scripture, objectively speaking, is free of all factual mistakes according to the definition provided by *CSBH*'s authors. The question of communicative intent is patently irrelevant.[46]

Chicago on Modern Science

What this means for *CSBH*'s engagement with modernity becomes particularly clear—as does its problematic relationship with the "reformed" tradition—when we consider its attitude toward modern science. We must approach this question, first of all, by way not only of article 10 ("Scripture communicates God's truth to us verbally through a wide variety of literary forms") but also article 13 (which commends to the exegete "awareness of the literary categories, formal and stylistic, of the various parts of Scripture"). Both articles apparently wish to give some weight to genre recognition as an indispensable aspect of biblical hermeneutics—and thus, we at first assume, to the rhetoric of the authors who produced our biblical texts. What kind of text did they set out to write? What were the ancient literary conventions governing their work? What did they and what did they not wish to say?

The denial that accompanies the affirmation in article 13, however, is our first sign that our assumption is not correct. It is a denial "that generic categories which negate historicity may rightly be imposed on biblical narratives which present themselves as factual." This is a very strange thing to say. It ought to be obvious that no interpreter should *impose* a generic category on any text to which it is not suited—whether it is a cooking book, a car maintenance manual, or a

---

[46] Geisler, comment on article 6: "in common parlance a statement is in error if it is a factual mistake, even if there was no intention to mislead anyone by it. So to suggest that the Bible contains mistakes, but that these are not errors so long as they do not mislead, is contrary to both Scripture and ordinary usage."

text in Holy Scripture. This would be an entirely counterproductive move by anyone genuinely seeking to understand a text. It is still more curious that the interest of *CSBH* at this point has narrowed to "biblical narratives which present themselves as factual"—as if this were the only kind of unfortunate genre labeling that should concern the Bible interpreter. Why have "narratives" that are "factual" been singled out here? This becomes clear when we arrive at article 23, which affirms "that Genesis 1–11 is factual, as is the rest of the book," proceeding to deny "that the teachings of Genesis 1–11 are mythical and that scientific hypotheses about earth history or the origin of humanity may be invoked to overthrow what Scripture teaches about creation." *CSBH* is deeply concerned that no one should read Genesis 1–11 as anything other than a factual account of, offering inerrant propositions about, the early history of the earth. Geisler's commentary on article 23 underscores the importance of recognizing "the factual nature of the account of the creation of the universe, all living things, the special creation of man, the Fall, and the Flood." He continues later: "the use of the term 'creation' [in article 23] was meant to exclude the belief in macro-evolution, whether of the atheistic or theistic varieties."

The first important point to notice here is that no consideration has been given to the question of *how* the "facts" in Genesis 1–11 are presented. This is not very surprising in the light of my comments earlier about the kind of inerrancy that *CSBH* espouses, but it does underline the lack of seriousness with which *CSBH* actually takes the question of genre. I do not doubt that Genesis 1–11 intends to provide us with facts—facts about God (e.g., that God is one and not many), human beings (we are both male and female and made in the image of God), and the world in which we live (it is not divine, although it is inhabited and blessed by God). Yet the question remains, "In what *form* are these facts given to us?" This is connected to the question, "How many facts *are* there?" Perhaps it is all "factual," and in just the same way; yet most Christians before us have not interpreted Genesis 1:1 ("In the beginning God created the heavens and the earth") in quite the same way as Genesis 3:8 ("the man and his wife heard the sound of the Lord God as he was walking in the garden"). Most Christians before us have not, therefore, proceeded to attribute legs and feet to divinity. Which *kinds* of facts are there in Genesis 1–11, and how does the rhetoric of these chapters relate to these facts? This is simply not the kind of question with whose complexity the Chicago mind-set typically deals satisfactorily. It prides itself on the syllogistic logic that can move deftly enough from "God cannot lie" to "the Word of God cannot lie" to "the Bible which is the Word of God cannot lie," but it all too often fails to comprehend that once we have established that this is so we are still only a small part of the way along the road to understanding what God in Scripture *is saying*.

This brings us, second, to the question of the limitations under which the author of Genesis 1–11 is operating. He is evidently a person of his time and place, using the language and categories available to him—which are not those of black holes, red dwarves, or quantum physics. At all points he is in dialogue not with our contemporary science but with the governing presuppositions about reality expressed in ancient Near Eastern literature outside the Bible and in various non-literary aspects of ancient Near Eastern culture such as architecture. He is, evidently, working within such limitations. He is proclaiming new and radical truth within this context, to be sure; yet his limitations are real and must be taken seriously. Inevitably they must include limitations of knowledge; it is not at all likely that he *knew* about black holes, red dwarves, or quantum physics. Even if we were to imagine that he (somehow) did it is clear that what he *writes* is accommodated to the kind of knowledge about the world that people of his time possessed. Even where he says something new he uses existing language and categories to do so—inevitably so, since he wishes to be understood in his own time and place.

What does this mean, though, for *our* reading of Genesis 1–11 in *our* time and place? This is another question that *CSBH* does not consider. It simply asserts that Genesis 1–11 provides us with "facts." Without reflecting further on their number and nature, the nature of the context in which they were first articulated, and by whom and following which literary and cultural conventions, *CSBH* simply assumes that it is obvious "what Scripture teaches about creation" and that this is incompatible with modern "scientific hypotheses about earth history or the origin of humanity." Its composers do not appear to consider even for a moment (and in spite of all the lip service in *CSBH* to the "wide variety of literary forms" in Scripture) that our biblical authors might inevitably have had to embed their radical propositions about reality in a narrative that *truly* reflects the time and culture of its origin and *truly* speaks the language of its day—and that this matters.

The Reformers and the majority of the Protestants who followed them in the sixteenth and seventeenth centuries were far more astute (my chapters 13 and 14) in their approach to matters of Scripture and science. They agree with *CSBH* in denying "that any genuine scientific facts are inconsistent with the true meaning of any passage of Scripture" and in affirming "the harmony of special with general revelation and therefore of biblical teaching with the facts of nature" (article 21)—"that since God is the author of all truth, all truths, biblical and extrabiblical, are consistent and cohere" (article 20). However, in seeking "the true meaning of any passage of Scripture" the Reformers are interested in exploring the *kinds* of information that Scripture offers us and in reflecting on the limitations of human knowledge to which its various statements are accommodated. As we have seen, these interests are particularly evident in their reading of Genesis 1–11. Here, as elsewhere, Calvin (for instance) understands that "God, through our history, accommodates his ways of revelation to our condition";[47] God is to be found "adapting his message to limited human understanding."[48] We must be careful, then, about apparently "factual" statements that might be understood by the undiscerning as "matters pertaining to nature, history, or anything else," about which "the Bible speaks truth when it touches on" them (*CSBH*, article 20). Genesis 1:6-7, for example, *might* be thought to "touch on" astronomy—yet for Calvin, the person "who would learn astronomy, and other recondite arts, let him go elsewhere."[49] At all points in our Bible reading we must remain attentive to this crucially important question of how the various "facts" on the page (the textual data) are meant to relate to "facts" outside the page in "nature, history, or anything else." And for the Reformers one way of determining this was to read God's "other" book of creation and discover what it had to say. Genesis 1:16, for example, *might* be thought to "touch on" the question of which are the largest of the heavenly bodies, but this cannot be the case since astronomers have demonstrated that Saturn is larger than the moon. Calvin *could* have dealt with the "problem" here simply by denying, with Geisler (in his commentary on article 21) "that we should accept scientific views that contradict Scripture" and by insisting that "Genesis 1–11 is factual, as is the rest of the book." Instead, he offered a rereading of Scripture: "Moses wrote in a popular style things which, without instruction, all ordinary persons, endued with common sense, are able to understand."[50] On Calvin's view we should therefore not read Genesis 1:16 as "factual," in the *CSBH* sense, at all.

Chicago and Double-Think

It was in these ways that mainstream Protestant tradition attempted to respond in the sixteenth and seventeenth centuries to modern scientific discoveries that challenged traditional interpretations of Scripture. How does *CSBH* propose, on the other hand, that we should deal with this challenge? Some very strong affirmations and denials in *CSBH* and in the Geisler commentary encourage us simply to ignore the challenge and to "trust the Bible" rather than a science that is "based on naturalistic presuppositions" (his commentary on article 21). Article 20 denies, in fact, "that extrabiblical views ever disprove the teaching of Scripture or hold priority over it," and in his commentary on *this* article Geisler underlines the "priority of the teaching of God's scriptural revelation over anything outside it." When its propositions conflict with those of Scripture, modern science must be rejected. A veritable industry has in fact now arisen within the Chicago constituency that is committed to the creation of a new "science" that is not based

---

[47] Battles, "God Was Accommodating," 34.
[48] Puckett, *John Calvin's Exegesis*, 11.
[49] Calvin, *Genesis*, 79.
[50] Calvin, *Genesis*, 86.

on "naturalistic presuppositions" but on the Bible. Like *CSBH*, this industry is particularly interested in persuading us that is impossible for the Bible-believing Christian to embrace a "belief in macro-evolution, whether of the atheistic or theistic varieties" (Geisler's commentary on article 22). Contemporary "creationists" therefore seek entirely to remodel modern science so that it corresponds more closely to the "facts" of the Bible as they understand them.

Yet how committed is *CSBH*, really, to this confrontation with modernity? Here we must recognize some deep tensions within the *Statement*. Scripture holds "priority... over anything outside it," proposes Geisler. Yet "in some cases extra-biblical data have value for clarifying what Scripture teaches, and for prompting correction of faulty interpretations" (*CSBH*, article 20). Which cases are these? Geisler's commentary helps us with one of them: "some have taught the world to be square because the Bible refers to 'the four corners of the earth' (Isa 11:12). But scientific knowledge of the spherical nature of the globe leads to a correction of this faulty interpretation." It is acceptable for contemporary Christians to hold to a modern scientific understanding on this matter in spite of what Scripture appeared to some of our ancestors to teach. Then again, even though article 22 denies "that scientific hypotheses about earth history or the origin of humanity may be invoked to overthrow what Scripture teaches about creation" it is apparently acceptable (in Geisler's commentary) to hold *either* a young-earth *or* an old-earth view of the antiquity of our planet. A traditional, young-earth interpretation of Scripture that was only widely questioned historically because of modern scientific discovery *may* now rightly be revised. There are presumably other "cases" in which "extra-biblical data have value" in the same way; for example, I am not aware of widespread support in the Chicago constituency for geocentric cosmology.

So let us assume for the sake of argument that at least these three are instances in which ancient, "faulty interpretations" of Scripture have rightly been revised (in respect of the shape and age of the planet and of the relationship between the sun and the earth). The obvious question follows: if *these* traditional interpretations of the Bible are capable of revision, on the basis of modern cosmology and geology, why is it out of the question to revise *other* traditional interpretations, on the basis of *other* kinds of modern knowledge? If in general it is acceptable to believe, as Bernard Ramm once put it, that "the Bible does not theorize as to the actual nature of things," and that it specifically "does not contain a theory of astronomy or geology or chemistry"[51]—then what is the problem with believing, for example, that it does not contain a theory of biology either?

---

[51] Bernard Ramm, *Protestant Biblical Interpretation: A Textbook of Hermeneutics* (Grand Rapids: Baker, 1970), 210.

There is no good answer to this question. It appears that *CSBH* has simply chosen quite arbitrarily to draw a line in the sand between the matters that it is prepared to allow its predominantly antimodern posture truly to impact, hermeneutically, and the matters that it is not. Its position is, fundamentally, intellectually incoherent. For either it is true, or it is not, that "in some cases extra-biblical data have value for clarifying what Scripture teaches."

If it is true then one must necessarily be open to the possibility that extra-biblical data have value for clarifying what Scripture teaches not just about the age of the earth but also about other aspects of "the account of the creation of the universe, all living things, the special creation of man, the Fall, and the Flood" (Geisler's commentary on article 22). Even while wishing to deny (with article 22) "that scientific hypotheses . . . may be invoked to overthrow what Scripture teaches about creation," one should absolutely not dismiss, therefore, the possibility that these hypotheses will contribute to our *understanding* of what Scripture (really) teaches about creation.

If on the other hand it is *not* true that "in some cases extra-biblical data have value for clarifying what Scripture teaches," then Christians should never have changed their interpretations of Scripture in the first place on the basis of what developing modern science had to say about reality. They should now repent of doing so. If this is the case, however, then the Chicago constituency should comprise only those who continue to believe (among other things) in a very young earth ("young-earthers") and in a Ptolemaic cosmology ("geocentrists"). Indeed, since it is not just *modern* science that we should forbid from "clarifying what Scripture teaches," Chicago people should not allow for a moment "scientific knowledge of the spherical nature of the globe" to influence their reading of Isaiah 11:12 and its "four corners of the earth," which should presumably be understood in a "factual" manner (as "flat-earthers" do).

The point is that one cannot have Chicago's epistemological cake and eat it too. It is in fact precisely because of the clarity with which some have grasped this point that there do *remain* in the modern world not only young-earthers, who regard old-earthers as "unbiblical," but also geocentrists and flat-earthers, who regard everyone to *their* "left" (including both old- and young-earthers) in the same way—as dangerously liberal in their approach to Scripture. The Bible, these Christians insist, must trump *in all cases* what unbelieving scientists say; we cannot pick and choose. Those who no longer believe in geocentrism (or flat-earthism), they allege, have capitulated to science even while pretending that they have not. They no longer adhere to what the Bible clearly teaches—in passages like Joshua 10, for example, where the sun indisputably stands still.

Clearly, most Chicago people do not wish to concede this point. Their attempts to defeat it, however, are routinely unconvincing, for the arguments they wish to deploy in doing so are the very arguments whose validity they need to *deny* in order to avoid challenges to their own favored positions from people who embrace modernity more than they do.[52] They have made their own stand in order to avoid sliding down what they perceive as the slippery slope of taking modern science seriously in their Bible reading. Unfortunately they often seem unaware that *where* they stand is already a considerable way down the slope, making them vulnerable to attack from all those still positioned above them. Even while striving to be "biblical" they have already unconsciously inherited the compromises of their predecessors with modern and indeed ancient science.

Conclusion

I do not consider this Chicago response to the situation in which we find ourselves any more viable than the counter-Reformational response. I do not even find it particularly "reformed." In fact it departs markedly from the Reformers' emphasis on the genuine historicality and humanity of Scripture and their genuine openness to considering *both* new scientific knowledge *and* the possibility of their fallibility in certain facets of their biblical interpretation. But what is certainly true in any case is that Chicago cannot help us at all in overcoming the problem of the eclipse of biblical narrative in the modern world.

Most modern people accept that modernity (and centrally, modern science) has discovered much that is true and has delivered much that is good for individuals and for society. They also believe that they know that Christian faith has recurrently throughout the last few centuries opposed modernity, despising what is true and rejecting what is good. To the majority of educated people around the globe, considering the matter in this context, the fighting Chicago response to modernity (and especially to modern science) looks like simply the most extreme evolution of obscurantism in the face of real "facts" that the Christian Church has ever yet embraced. Indeed, its high profile as "the correct" evangelical, Protestant Christian approach to matters of science and Scripture in many parts of the world—successfully hiding from view the fact that a large number of evangelical, Protestant Christians profoundly disagree with it—has confirmed in many minds that the "warfare" model of science and faith is the correct model. All of this is the inevitable consequence of contemporary Christians following, not the Reformers, but different predecessors in claiming "that the science that contradicted [their current interpretation of] Scripture was no science at all."[53] It is only

---

[52] For a description of contemporary geocentrism and some of the responses it has evoked, see Edward B. Davis and Elizabeth Chmielewski, "Galileo and the Garden of Eden: Historical Reflections on Creationist Hermeneutics," in van der Meer and Mandelbrote, *Nature and Scripture in the Abrahamic Religions: 1700–Present*, 2:437–64 (448–55).

[53] England, "Scriptural Facts," 251.

a contemporary variation on this same theme to claim that nonscience ("creation science") is actually science because it agrees with a particular, traditional interpretation of Scripture. It is surely no coincidence that this fundamentally new, modern progeny of earlier pseudo-Protestant rivals to the Reformers' approach to Scripture has taken deepest root in an American culture deeply shaped by a "revival tradition"—ironically owing much to Jonathan Edwards—that has come "to compromise the life of the mind."[54] "Revivalism and disestablishment [of religion] together," Mark Noll tells us,

> set up a style of faith with scant use for patient, comprehensive thinking about the world and life as a whole. So it was that the *context* for evangelical life in America, though that context had been promoted by America's greatest Christian thinker [Edwards], was working against the development of a Christian mind.[55]

To many contemporary critics of the Church it is above all the existence of "creation science" in significant segments of the Protestant Church that has convinced them that "Christian" and "mind" do not rightly belong in the same sentence.[56] How can anyone simply ignore the empirical evidence amassed by geologists for the great age of the earth?[57] Surely the evidence in favor of biological evolution by way of natural selection, now that the discoveries of the science of genetics have been added to all the rest, has become overwhelming?[58] These Christians, they declare, are simply not interested in truth.

To the majority of educated people around the globe, then, the Chicago response to modernity is not credible. It does just the kind of damage to the Christian faith that Augustine worried about all those centuries ago when he wrote about people outside the Church finding "a Christian mistaken in a field which they themselves know well and [hearing] him maintaining his foolish opinions about our [scriptural] books," and he asked: "how are they [then] going to believe those books in matters concerning the resurrection of the dead, the hope

---

[54] Mark A. Noll, *The Scandal of the Evangelical Mind* (Grand Rapids: Eerdmans, 1994), 80.

[55] Noll, *Scandal*, 80.

[56] For a readable introduction to the entire phenomenon, see Ronald L. Numbers, *The Creationists: From Scientific Creationism to Intelligent Design* (Cambridge, Mass.: Harvard University Press, 2006).

[57] This is a question also asked by Christian geologists like Davis Young, in the midst of a general plea for decent Christian education in science and the reintegration of faith and science. Young, *Natural World*, 191–230.

[58] This science is helpfully explained for the layperson by top geneticist (and Christian) Francis S. Collins in *The Language of God: A Scientist Presents Evidence for Belief* (New York: Free Press, 2006). Genetics has clarified that Darwin's variations arise by mutation in part of the genetic code for a particular trait. These mutations occur prior to any situation in which they provide an organism with an advantage or a disadvantage; they do not occur because they are visibly "needed."

of eternal life, and the kingdom of heaven?"[59] Others do not find this Chicago response credible; I do not find it credible. I wish that more of my fellow North American Protestants agreed. The eclipse of biblical narrative was *not* as a matter of fact only a consequence of apostasy from true Christian faith. It was at least in part the consequence of large numbers of people coming to believe that the Great Story could not account for much that they now believed to be true and did not promote various agendas that they considered to be good. The eclipse, then, was not merely the consequence of a Deist rejection of orthodox faith during the Enlightenment. It was also a consequence (during and after the Enlightenment) of a stubbornly obscurantist and indeed quasi-Gnostic retreat on the part of people who were at least in many respects creedally orthodox Christians from the world of public discourse and into an intellectual black hole from which no light could emerge that might enlighten society in its way ahead. It does not help us to deal with this same eclipse in the present that the framers and disciples of *CSBH* have opted to follow this same, negative, and desperately inadequate path, attacking modernity without showing any willingness to praise it and even to learn from it. Among other things, to opt for a *fight* of this nature in our present context is just as likely as opting for counter-Reformational *flight* to diminish our capacity to subject modernity to any kind of more balanced Christian critique.

ATHENS AND JERUSALEM REVISITED

I do not believe that the correct response to the eclipse of the biblical narrative is either fight or flight. Both are of course understandable responses to the marital estrangement of Athens and Jerusalem in the modern (and now postmodern) period. They mirror the preferences among children for one or other parent, and the hopes they might hold in their hearts for a happier parental future, which one often finds in such circumstances. The counter-Reformational children favor Athens, conceived in a quite literalistic way—that is, they look for their future to Plato, in synthetic relationship with biblical faith as it was in the good old days. The Chicago children favor Jerusalem. They are glad to see the back of Plato and all the other Greek suitors, and they are generally minded to discourage further liaisons. Jerusalem does better alone, in their view—barricaded in a castle where no one can speak to her and lead her astray, surrounded by warriors who will defend her honor until their dying breath. Both responses are understandable—but they are both wrongheaded.

The "fifth way" that I am advocating in this book is rather different. I do not believe that Jerusalem should be locked away in a castle and defended against all those who want a relationship with her; I do not regard this as being her calling.

---

[59] Augustine, *Literal Meaning*, 1.19.39 (ACW 41:43).

I believe that "Athens" and Jerusalem should get remarried, although I agree that there should be no Greeks in prominent positions at the wedding. I agree, in fact, that the good old days were not necessarily so very good, and that in any case that Plato has done his job and cannot help us further; ancient Athens is, literally, a ruin. We live in a different world and Jerusalem needs a new partner. So "Athens," in my scenario, is simply "nonbiblical truth of all kinds," including modern and postmodern truth. This is the kind of marriage that contemporary "reformed" Christians should continue to encourage and support, as others before us have done right back to the Reformation. We should in fact enlist the help of all these righteous forebears in our quest and make them central to our project, while sending Jerusalem's fierce warriors back to the barracks for a long rest. This is the correct way to respond to the eclipse of biblical narrative: by creating the circumstances in which the sun can once again shine. We should respond by doing an even better job than before of showing how the Great Story of Scripture can after all make space and account for all that is true and good in the world, providing thereby a reliable map for our journey through life. We should respond by creating a new, compelling, and quintessentially "reformed" synthesis in which it is once again clear how and in which respects the biblical narrative does in fact tell the true story of the cosmos.

The Need for Repentance

What will this involve? It will involve, first of all, a frank assessment of past Christian mistakes and a determination not to repeat them nor anything the least bit like them. No doubt the mistakes have been many, and it is not possible or necessary to name them all in this chapter. As I retrace my steps back through the story told from the beginning of chapter 14 to this point, however, and as I attempt to draw its various threads together here, I believe that it is possible to identify some important ones.

To pick up the threads of my previous section, first of all: to the extent that our post-Reformation Christian forebears continued to insist that ancient Greek philosophy must remain the primary or only dialogue partner for Christian faith—and indeed, that *only* a Christian faith involved in such a dialogue was authentic—that was a mistake. The particular articulations of Christian truth arising from this dialogue ought to have been held more lightly, such that it was possible to reexamine them when questions were raised about their veracity. No one need have entered commitments in advance to abandon any one of them, if any turned out on further inspection to be true after all. Yet the possibility that they might need to be adjusted or even abandoned in the light of older truth found in Scripture or newer truth emerging from other quarters ought to have been entertained—as indeed should the possibility that Greek philosophical perspectives might turn out more generally to be false and that much of the dialogue would need to be severely curtailed. The ability to imagine these possibilities would greatly have aided Christian thinkers from the sixteenth century onward in dealing with reality. It would have helped them to avoid being wedded to Athens in one generation only to find themselves widowed in various respects in the next.

Related to the above, second: to the extent that our post-Reformation Christian forebears continued to insist that traditional interpretations of Scripture must be retained in the face of mounting scientific evidence that this would mean that Scripture was speaking falsely, that was a mistake. Those interpretations, too, should have been held more lightly, in line with Thomas Aquinas' advice that

> one should adhere to a particular explanation, only in such measure as to be ready to abandon it, if it be proved with certainty to be false; lest Holy Scripture be exposed to the ridicule of unbelievers, and obstacles be placed to their believing.[60]

No commitments need have been entered in advance to abandon any one of the traditional interpretations of Scripture if any of *them* turned out on further inspection to be true after all. Yet there should have been more openness to the possibility that they might be mistaken and might need to be adjusted or abandoned. Already in the seventeenth century it was clear just how problematic some of them had become, with respect to the natural world. Galileo was right in what he said about this reality (in the first epigraph to the present chapter): it was imprudent for anyone in his time to insist that scriptural texts compelled Christians to maintain "any physical conclusion to be true, when at some future time the senses and demonstrative or necessary reasons may show the contrary." The imprudence of such a stance has only become clearer with the passing of time.

Related to this, third: to the extent that our Christian forebears from the sixteenth century onward failed to respond positively both to new articulations of truth and (often-related) proposals for societal change, but instead suppressed, opposed, and obstructed the same, that was a mistake. This was not just a matter of failing to respond well to modern science. We must recognize more generally that the modern period has been marked to a significant degree by a wrongheaded kind of Christian conservatism that has simply opposed new articulations of truth because they are new and change because it is change. It has tended simply to be "against" the Enlightenment, "secular humanism" (*CSBH*, article 19) or whatever, rather than seeking to make a judicious assessment of what such movements have contributed positively to the world. Yet it is surely the case that *much* has been contributed, and it is important to recognize this.

---

[60] Aquinas, *Summa*, 1.68.1.

For example: was it not a good idea in an early modern Western world where confessional Christianity was bound up with significant violence to propose some degree of separation between Church and state? Was democracy not a good idea, given that it is "the worst form of government, except for all the others"?[61] To the extent that modernity has increased our grasp of the full extent of the pool of truth and has produced at times less violent, less prejudiced, and more open and caring societies than before, this is surely a good thing. Yet at every turn along with Christians who have contributed mightily to this progress we find Christians who have fiercely opposed it. This has been true both of issues that retain a very high profile in the modern mind, such as the European and North American slave trade, and of a myriad of issues that do not. It was a mistake, we must confess, when some of our Christian forebears embraced such a "principled" (but actually often deeply unprincipled) conservatism—looking always backward, as if that was the only place in which truth and virtue could be found, and never forward. No Christian should ever have been simply "against" the Enlightenment, or even against secular humanism, which in various respects only arose to fill the vacancy left by the departure of the Christian variety. We have paid dearly for such mistakes, because of the tendency of secular modernity (and postmodernity) to remember and highlight (often in quite a calculating manner) the Christians who obstructed the progress that led to human flourishing while ignoring those who contributed to it. Who remembers now, for example, the way in which the Puritan New England pastor Cotton Mather (1663–1728), much influenced by Robert Boyle's *The Usefulness of Experimental Natural Philosophy* (1663), supported the practice of inoculation against smallpox during the outbreak of 1721 in Boston—in the face of fierce opposition that easily found support in theological and biblical sources? I suspect that more people recall (and exaggerate) the opposition in Britain and Ireland two centuries later (1847) when James Simpson (1811–1870)—a devout Presbyterian—advocated the use of ether-based anesthesia in childbirth in defiance of the "clear teaching" of Genesis 3 that women were cursed to experience pain in childbirth.[62] The cultural memory of what used to be Christendom has become highly selective and indeed twisted—both inside and outside the Church—and we now require entire books designed to reconfigure

---

[61] This quote is often attributed to Winston Churchill, but in using it he himself depended on an unknown source. C. S. Lewis supported democracy precisely because he believed that no fallen human being "can be trusted with unchecked power over his fellows." C. S. Lewis, *Present Concerns* (ed. Walter Hooper; San Diego: Harcourt Brace Jovanovich, 1986), 17.

[62] See further Linda S. Schearing, "Parturition (Childbirth), Pain, and Piety: Physicians and Genesis 3:16a," in *Mother Goose, Mother Jones and Mommie Dearest: Biblical Mothers and Their Children* (ed. Cheryl Kirk-Duggan and Tina Pippin; SemeiaSt 61; Atlanta: Society of Biblical Literature, 2009), 85–96; and Rennie B. Schoepflin, "Myth 14: That the Church Denounced Anesthesia in Childbirth on Biblical Grounds," in Numbers, *Galileo Goes to Jail*, 123–30.

it.⁶³ So much of what we think we know about Christianity and modernity—both within and without the Church—is simply not true.

Related to the above, finally: to the extent that the Christians who preceded us in the modern period advocated or failed to oppose coercion and violence in pursuit of their various agendas, that was a shameful mistake. Orthodox Christian faith abides always under the imperative to love, even where it holds another person to be terribly misguided and perhaps even wicked. It is, I believe, true that "[s]ola scriptura is not [itself] a recipe for sectarianism, much less an excuse for schism, but rather a call to listen for the Holy Spirit speaking in the history of Scripture's interpretation in the church."⁶⁴ Yet even so our forebears should have recognized the inevitability of interpretive pluralism with respect to Scripture—of the inevitable gap, on this side of the consummation of all things, between what the Bible teaches on the one hand and what individuals and groups *believe* it to teach on the other (my chapter 12)—and they ought to have been enthusiastic advocates for the creation of legitimate space in society for dissent from majorities. They ought to have advocated for dialogue rather than repression, premised on the Christian virtues of humility (it is possible that I, as well as you, may be mistaken) and hope (the Holy Spirit will help us to see which of these is true). They ought to have understood that a commitment to dialogue is not a (foolish) commitment to abandoning a proper Christian belief in the authority, perspicuity, and infallibility of Scripture. It is in fact a (sensible) commitment to deepening our grasp of the truths we already rightly believe while revising our opinions when we discover on reflection that these truths are not quite accurately held. To the extent that our modern forebears failed to understand this, and coercion and violence ensued that resulted in considerable harm, they made a huge mistake. The unity of the Church itself does not need to be conceived of—and this is just as well, given the on-the-ground reality—as "monological institutional unity" focused on Rome or on any other city. It can be conceived of instead as "a dialogical or 'plural' unity," focused around the core truths and ethical commitments that orthodox, biblical, Nicene Christians hold in common.⁶⁵ Protestant Christianity itself can be understood in terms of "*a kind of Pentecostal plurality*":

> [E]ach Protestant church seeks to be faithful to the gospel, but no one form of Protestantism exhausts the gospel's meaning. Rather, it takes the discussion ("conference") between the many Protestant churches to appreciate fully the richness of the one gospel. The particularity of each Protestant tradition is thus not a source of conflict but a servant of unity—the unity of the truth of the

---

⁶³ E.g., Jonathan Hill, *What Has Christianity Ever Done for Us? How It Shaped the Modern World* (Downers Grove, Ill.: InterVarsity, 2005).

⁶⁴ Vanhoozer, *Biblical Authority*, 145.

⁶⁵ Vanhoozer, *Biblical Authority*, 30.

gospel ... evangelicalism offers a transdenominational denominator that makes of Protestantism not a pervasive interpretive pluralism but a unitive interpretive plurality—a mere Protestant Christianity.[66]

Outside this kingdom realm, Christians are supposed to love even their enemies. This is as true of *interpretive* enemies as of any other kind. Whether dealing with enemies, then, or simply with confused friends who cannot presently be in full communion with us, we are bound by a divine imperative toward charity.

On Becoming Our Best Selves

Possessing clarity about our past mistakes and a determination not to repeat them we shall then find it possible, second, to move ahead along a much better path, identifying the many "reformed" ancestors in the faith who have tried to walk this path before us and seeking to follow their example. As I have often pointed out in this book, this does not mean trying to become sixteenth- or seventeenth-century Protestants. It means identifying the ancestral line in which we believe it right to stand and then thinking and living consistently with that identity in our own time as "reformed" people. It means retrieving a particular family history (with the help of good books) on the way to finding our best selves.

As our best selves, I propose, we certainly ought to continue to believe that Scripture in its original languages constitutes our God-inspired, sufficiently perspicuous, canonical rule of truth, infallible in all that it teaches—the rule by which alone we should ultimately measure the rightness of both our doctrine and our practice. As people standing in line with the magisterial Reformers (and indeed with the Church Fathers) we need to affirm that Scripture unerringly guides us when it comes to those matters of belief and practice about which God wishes to address us therein. However, we need to state clearly in the midst of that affirmation, as they did, that God does not wish to address us through Scripture about *all* matters but only a certain number, and that we require the help of sources of knowledge other than the Bible to help us discern which these matters might be. It is possible to make mistakes on this point precisely because God's Word comes to us through human beings who stand like ourselves within the stream of history and speak to their contemporaries and to us in accordance with the language, thought forms, and literary conventions of their time. In seeking to hear the Word of God, then, we *must* attend to such human realities, sometimes judiciously correcting previous understandings of what God is addressing us about even if they possess great antiquity and have previously attracted widespread agreement. For not everything that God has been understood in the past to say through Scripture is in fact what we should believe that God wishes to say.

---

[66] Vanhoozer, *Biblical Authority*, 223–24.

This is even clearer to us than it was to predecessors like Augustine, Calvin, and Edwards, because we know more than they did about important areas of human knowledge like ancient history, physics, chemistry, and biology.

Attending to such realities, I propose that it is by no means clear that Galileo is correct when he agrees with his unnamed source in the first epigraph to the present chapter that "the intention of the Holy Ghost [in Scripture] is to teach us how one goes to heaven, not how heaven goes." This is cute, but inadequate. Scripture is not designed merely as a manual on how to gain safe access to the afterlife, which is not in turn about "going to heaven."[67] Scripture evidently paints a much more expansive picture of the nature and character of God, the nature and destiny of the world and its creatures, and the history of God's dealings with his particular and special people (among other things)—as well as advising us about the afterlife.

I propose at the same time, however, that we can see much more clearly than historical figures like Calvin (or Augustine) the *variety of ways* in which this picture has been painted and what this means in terms of the kinds of questions we may sensibly ask of the biblical text. For example, it is particularly clear at this point in time that Genesis 1–11 may not sensibly be interrogated about the physical history of the earth prior to the time of Abraham. Indeed, there is little reason to think that answering such questions was ever the intention of its author. The case is different in Genesis 12–50 where—although it is not the sole or main purpose of the narrative to recount what modern people might call "history," but rather to teach its readers a number of important truths about God, ourselves, and so on—interrogation about historical questions at least makes sense. Still, it has been clear for centuries that we cannot use the numbers in any part of Genesis, as many previously thought, to reconstruct a chronology even of the patriarchs, much less of the world in general. The Genesis story communicates many important truths, we should still affirm—but not all the kinds of truth that people previously imagined.

We must accept, I propose, that the same has turned out to be true of the remainder of Scripture in some degree and in different ways. All sorts of data have been discovered in the past several centuries that bear on the interpretation of our biblical texts. The historical analysis of the Bible that became so prolific in the nineteenth century (my chapter 15), and continued in the twentieth has been most helpful in this respect. Not everything that biblical scholars have *said* about the Bible on the basis of this analysis has been helpful (see further my part 3). Yet where there are data and accurate analysis they must be taken seriously and

---

[67] In the book of Revelation, e.g., it appears that heaven comes to earth, just as the Lord's Prayer might also be taken to suggest.

accounted for as we continue to affirm the truth that is revealed throughout Genesis to Revelation and seek to understand what kind of truth it is.

For the Life of the World

It is only as we do this that we shall by degrees begin to deal effectively with significant underlying causes of the eclipse of biblical narrative. It is particularly important that we commit to this task because, as much as the eclipse has hurt the Church, it has also hurt the rest of creation.

Let me illustrate this point with respect to the development of modern science. As we saw in chapter 14, modern science arose in the context of distinctively Christian thought. Already in the writings of the English philosopher Francis Bacon (1561–1626) in the early seventeenth century,[68] however, we find science beginning to slip its moorings and sail off in a different direction. For Bacon, "reason exploring nature," unencumbered by any previous form of tradition, philosophy, or religion, was everything. Rigorous empirical enquiry into the nature of this world, with experimentation at its heart, was the method; total knowledge of nature—not in order to live in *agreement* with it, but in order to *master* it— was the goal. It is an approach to "nature" that was inevitably (in the seventeenth century) still influenced by some biblical ideas. They were now recontextualized, however, within a thoroughly this-worldly, utopian story about reality that justified (as biblical faith does not) the bending of everything in nature to human ends and was exceedingly optimistic about the ability of human power to reach these ends.[69]

In Francis Bacon, then, we see foreshadowed the development of science as a totalizing worldview in principle independent of the doctrinal and ethical constraints of Christian religion. We are still dealing today with the consequences of the birth of this autonomous, modern, scientific monster.[70] How did it gain so much traction? Part of the answer lies precisely in the seventeenth-century failure or refusal of Christians to stand in the line of succession of many of their Christians forebears in seeking an integrative approach to knowledge and in the ongoing popularity of this kind of obscurantism with respect to science in the succeeding centuries. We shall never know how differently the modern world

---

[68] John Channing Briggs, "Bacon's Science and Religion," in *The Cambridge Companion to Bacon* (ed. Markku Peltonen; Cambridge: Cambridge University Press, 1996), 172–99.

[69] For the ways in which Bacon's utopianism played out among the radical English Puritans, see Hooykaas, *Religion*, 139–44.

[70] At the broadest level, the consequences pertain to the entire planet: "It was Francis Bacon . . . who hijacked the Genesis text to authorize the project of scientific knowledge and technological exploitation whose excesses have given us the ecological crisis." Richard Bauckham, *Bible and Ecology: Rediscovering the Community of Creation* (London: Darton, Longman & Todd, 2010), 6.

might have turned out had emerging, modern scientific knowledge been fully integrated as it arose (and much more than it was) into an authentically biblical and Christian worldview. All we do know is that it was not, and that part of the reason was that Christian faith came to be seen as incapable of the integration.

The more-than-unfortunate consequence has been the substantive, modern bifurcation of Protestant Christianity and science, the latter slowly sinking into reductionistic scientism that has lost its metaphysical and ethical bearings, often in overt reaction to an antiscientific Protestant fundamentalism that is quite unable to accept scientific progress. To a significant extent this is our corporate, Protestant fault. We cannot expect to be taken seriously when we object to this or that particular aspect of "progress" as a negative step, if in general we are "known" always to be against progress. It is a little like a politician expecting a speech opposing a particular war to be taken seriously when it is known that he is a principled, lifelong pacifist. The consequence is that the Church has not been able to offer as much guidance in the development of science in modern societies as it should have. To that extent the world of science has been deprived of crucially important input and guidance on matters that cannot be decided within its own parameters of operation—questions, for example, about what to do and not do with scientific discoveries, and why. "The natural sciences ... have been an extraordinary success," notes Brad Gregory, "but because of the self-imposed limitations that have *made* them so successful, by definition they can offer no answers to any [what he describes as] ... Life Questions."[71] Modern and postmodern people, oblivious to the reductionism involved, have often *believed* that they *can* offer such answers—that by establishing what *is* the case they have thereby established how we *ought* to live (e.g., drawing conclusions from Darwinian biology or genetics about how we ought to treat the weak in society or how we ought to think about and conduct our sexual lives). This is a significant mistake. By *definition* "the natural sciences ... can offer no answers to any ... Life Questions."

Yet the continuing eclipse of biblical narrative means that the contemporary Christian ability to supply such much-needed answers remains compromised—assuming, of course, that Christians are even interested any longer in offering this kind of guidance. We all too often appear frankly oblivious to the really important questions of the moment, scientifically—such as what is to be done or not done about robotics and genetic engineering—distracted still by quite old and trivial questions that do not really matter very much in the whole scheme of things, such as the age of the earth and the processes by which life came to be the way it is now. And when we do engage from the perspective of the Great Story of Scripture with Life Questions of particular interest to the devotees of scientism

---

[71] Gregory, *Unintended Reformation*, 377.

around us, all too often our own confusion about the best ways of understanding the relationship between science and Christian faith inhibits our ability to engage well—for example, when we fall into the trap of agreeing with others that what is "natural" to us, sexually, is relevant to the question of how we ought to define our sexual "identities" and conduct ourselves in that part of our lives.[72]

It would be easy if space allowed to provide further examples to illustrate the importance of retrieving biblical narrative "for the life of the world."[73] Modernity is not doing as well in adulthood as it might have expected when it first began to make off with its Christian parents' wealth in its prodigal adolescence back in the seventeenth century, and it needs some ongoing family support (and rebuke).[74] But space does not, in fact, allow.

ON LEVITY, SLOTH, AND LEARNING

If the project I have been describing in this present chapter is to succeed, it will need to be widely owned. If it is to be widely owned, however, it must involve a renewed commitment in the orthodox Protestant community to education. Both the internal disarray in which we presently find ourselves and our inability coherently to address the world outside stem in large measure from a lack thereof.[75] All too often, internally, we do not agree with other Protestants about what Scripture alone perspicuously teaches simply because we or they lack knowledge. The

---

[72] This appears to be the implicit assumption shared by many people on both sides of the contemporary debate in the Church about sexuality and sexual ethics. It is perhaps more obvious on the "liberal" side in the frequent assertion that what is "natural" is God-ordained and right. Yet it is evident, too, in the frequently voiced "conservative" fear that if we "give up" on something like belief in a six-day creation because of what modern science has to say we shall inevitably slide down a slippery slope that leads in the end to the abandonment of traditional Christian sexual ethics. This presupposes precisely that science, if it is capable of describing what *is*, can also inform us about how we *ought* to live. However, Scripture does not premise its sexual ethic on what is "natural" to us (for whatever reason it may be so). To the contrary, we are constantly urged in this and in all areas of life to put aside what is "natural" and to follow Christ, reading *our* story in the context of *God's* Story, and finding our fundamental identity in *Christ* and not in our gender, race, or anything else of lesser importance. Sexual ethics in Scripture are premised not on what is "natural" to us, but on our calling in Christ; they are eschatologically, and not creationally, driven.

[73] I have borrowed this header from Alexander Schmemann, *For the Life of the World* (2nd ed.; Crestwood, N.Y.: St. Vladimir's Seminary Press, 2002).

[74] See, e.g., Gregory, *Unintended Reformation*, 365–87; and Mark Lilla, *The Stillborn God: Religion, Politics, and the Modern West* (New York: Knopf, 2007).

[75] I do not mean to imply that a lack of education is the only issue we need to address in the contemporary Church—as if right thinking by itself would resolve all our problems, irrespective of whether our desires and wills were rightly directed. Right thinking remains, however, of enormous importance. On the broader issues, see e.g., James K. A. Smith, *Desiring the Kingdom: Worship, Worldview, and Cultural Formation* (Grand Rapids: Baker, 2009); and *You Are What You Love: The Spiritual Power of Habit* (Grand Rapids: Brazos, 2016).

pursuit of such knowledge is indeed discouraged by certain views of both *sola Scriptura* and the perspicuity of Scripture within the Protestant community—as is depending on others who already possess it.[76] The inevitable result of this is deficient Bible reading. The blind lead the blind while deliberately refusing the help of those—including "secular scholars"—who can see at least a little more clearly on this or that topic. In truth, as we saw in my chapter 12, this is a perverse way of understanding the implications of both "reformed" doctrines. Rightly understood both actually *require* that all Christians should aim to become as educated as they can so that they can enter into discussions about the correct meaning of Scripture as intelligently and helpfully as they can. Not everyone has the same capacities, of course—yet each person should press to the limits of his or her capacity. Not everyone is provided with the same opportunities—yet each should respond to every opportunity provided, creating opportunity where none exists.

On Opportunity

In truth, the opportunities for ongoing education that are available to many people in the modern world, including education in biblical languages, are vastly greater than they were when Martin Luther (as noted in the second epigraph to my chapter 10) told his own contemporaries what "a sin and a shame" it would be not to "study languages, especially in these days when God is offering and giving us men and books and every facility and inducement to this study, and desires his Bible to be an open book." Our opportunities are also greater than in the succeeding period, when the Pietist August Hermann Francke founded alongside his orphanage in Halle (1694) the *Collegium Orientale Theologicum* (1702), "as an institution primarily devoted to a more thoroughly academic study of the Bible."[77] They are vastly greater than in the period just *prior* to the Reformation, when in Holland Geert de Groote (1340–1384), a missionary preacher in the diocese of Utrecht, founded the movement known as *devotio moderna* ("modern devotion") that became especially prominent in Dutch cities during the fourteenth and fifteenth centuries. Here, gathered groups of laypeople and clergy known as "Brethren of the Common Life" would learn Greek (for example) because of their commitment to understanding what the Bible really had to say. Our opportunities are greater still than when Augustine was writing *On Christian Doctrine* and so strongly emphasized the importance of a broad and deep Christian

---

[76] It is therefore a great pity that following the twenty-third article of *CSBH*, which affirms the essential clarity of Scripture albeit acknowledging that not all passages are equally clear, we find the twenty-fourth proposing that "a person is not dependent for understanding of Scripture on the expertise of biblical scholars." This is unhelpful in what is all too often already a contemporary, conservative, evangelical environment in which anti-intellectualism is rife.

[77] Wallman, "Scriptural Understanding," 910.

education. They are also greater than when John Chrysostom (who was fond of discussing scriptural textual variants in his homilies) would exhort congregants upon returning home from church services, in a Roman Empire where the literacy rate among Christians was probably not very high,[78] to take "the Scriptures in our hands and gain benefit from them and provide spiritual nourishment for our soul" and to read commentaries.[79]

Our problem lies not in lack of opportunity, nor indeed in our capacity (did people in general back in these prior generations possess *greater* capacity?). Especially in the Western Church the problem lies largely in what *Divino afflante Spiritu* so memorably describes as "levity and sloth." We have the capacity to become better educated, and we also have plenty of opportunity. What we lack is the correct attitude and a strong enough will. In an age in which it has become all too common for Christians—in a staggering departure from the "reformed" tradition that lies behind them—to believe that a robust Christian education (including an education in challenging subjects like biblical languages) is something of an optional extra in the Christian life, we would rather spend our time and our money on other pursuits.

On Adequacy

How have we come to believe that this is acceptable? No doubt there are many causes—aside from promoting versions of the doctrines of *sola Scriptura* and perspicuity that themselves encourage sloth—and some of them are not so much under the control of the Church at large as others. That the Church at large is nevertheless culpable to an important extent is clear enough. Educational programs in individual churches are typically of a low level; not much is expected of church members, and they in turn rise only to the level of the expectations. Beyond the individual church, however—where in modern times it has become routine not to expect much in terms of commitment to a robust Christian education—what is truly disturbing is what is happening in many of our colleges and seminaries, where this commitment used to be central. All too often now, at least in North America, it has been replaced with a commitment only to "an education of some kind"—shorter in length, shallower in depth, and (importantly)

---

[78] The number of Christians who could read "probably never exceeded 15–20 percent in the first few centuries." Harry Y. Gamble, *Books and Readers in the Early Church: A History of Early Christian Texts* (New Haven: Yale University Press, 1995), 231. See also Elizabeth A. Clark, *Reading Renunciation: Asceticism and Scripture in Early Christianity* (Princeton: Princeton University Press, 1999), 45–61.

[79] Chrysostom, *Homilies on Genesis*, 10:20, in *Homilies on Genesis 1–17*, 141. The Alexandrian scholar Didymus the Blind also reveals in one passage an expectation that some of his readers will have read his previous works (Hill, *Antioch*, 48n2).

cheaper, designed to provide the Church not so much with highly educated pastors and teachers but only with ones that are (allegedly) "adequately" trained.

What "adequate" means in this context depends on the convictions (and the motivations) of those who have the power to define it. What it increasingly signifies, unfortunately, is a marked lowering of the expectations placed upon students in our colleges and seminaries, relative to what was expected of their predecessors. This is particularly true when it comes to the learning of biblical languages in the context of serious, scholarly biblical studies—on the ground (all too often) that "the average pastor" does not need such a high level of education in order to run a church. This being so, the average pastor will no doubt find his or her average church, and life will go on as usual. What about the average graduate pursuing a different vocation, who—"choice" being everything in the consumer society, including curricular matters—may never have been compelled to learn biblical languages (or to engage much with serious biblical scholarship) at all? He or she will find his or her own niche in church and society, and life will go on as usual there as well.

On Betrayal

What all this represents, however—and let us be clear about this—is a betrayal of the Reformation. In Reformation thinking it was the responsibility and the privilege of *all* God's people, as capacity and opportunity allowed, to engage with the Holy Scriptures deeply and personally and (even if only through the media of good translations) always with respect to its original languages. This is why one of the immediate consequences of the Reformation was an increased effort at the education of ordinary people (both male and female), beginning with the children. Lewis Spitz tells us that in general, in Protestant lands, "60 to 80 percent of the income from secularized [i.e., expropriated] monastic and church lands was subsequently devoted to education, hospitals, and charity."[80] By way of specific examples, Martin Luther "urged compulsory universal education for both boys and girls.... No labour or expense should be spared in educating the youth."[81] In Reformed Geneva, just prior to Calvin's arrival there in 1536, the citizens committed themselves to universal primary education, which was to be free for the poor. In Calvinist Scotland John Knox published his own plan (in 1560) for "the vertue and godlie upbringing of the youth of this Realm." He envisaged education for rich and poor alike by way of an ambitious plan involving parish primary schools, burgh grammar schools, high schools, and universities. By 1696

---

[80] Spitz, *Renaissance*, 549. For a good description of some of what this meant, especially in Lutheran Germany, but also elsewhere, see Ulrich Köpf, "The Reformation as an Epoch of the History of Theological Education," *HBOT* 2:347–62.

[81] Spitz, *Renaissance*, 558.

the Scottish Parliament had passed an Act for Setting Schools whereby every parish was required to establish a schoolhouse and hire a schoolmaster. By the eighteenth century Scotland possessed the highest standard of literacy of any European nation.[82] It was not only important, however, to educate children; "Theodore Beza believed that in working as a professor of Greek he was performing as great a service in promoting religion as he would have done in the pulpit."[83] For the Reformers generally "higher education was . . . an activity carried on together with God."[84] The point was that each person had to be able to engage with "Scripture alone" in order to be transformed (once due effort had been expended in its pursuit) by its perspicuous truth.

What has happened now to this noble Reformation vision of the human person in all of his or her legitimate autonomy as a Scripture reader? What has happened if even the graduates of our institutions of higher learning, including our pastors and teachers, are no longer expected to embrace this vision and indeed their education has become a paltry affair in comparison to their "reformed" forebears?[85] What has happened to this vision, specifically in its linguistic dimensions, if we apparently no longer agree with the Scottish Reformer Andrew Melville's view that theological study must be based on the study of the Scriptures in Hebrew and Greek, "from which resort to Latin or vernacular editions in controversies is practically foolish and impious"?[86] It was of the ancient heretics that Clement of Alexandria once said: "too indolent to descend to the bottom of things, reading superficially, they have dismissed the Scriptures."[87] What would he say of the modern and postmodern orthodox in these same respects?

CONCLUSION

If the project I have been describing in this chapter is to succeed it must inevitably be accompanied by a renewed Christian commitment to education. Perhaps we smile, now, at Martin Bucer's vision (my chapter 11) of a future in which Hebrew would be universally spoken in every Christian city, or Huldrych Zwingli's notion that a Bible translation is only a flotation device for beginners in the art of swimming in the Scriptures. This has a lot to do, however, with the fact that we have

---

[82] Richard L. Greaves, "The Social Awareness of John Knox: The Problems of Poverty and Educational Reform," *RR* 12 (1976): 36–48.

[83] Spitz, *Renaissance*, 558–59.

[84] Spitz, *Renaissance*, 559.

[85] Leaving aside the first Reformers themselves, to read even a little into the literature that touches on the commitment to learning among their successors in the sixteenth and seventeenth centuries is immediately to understand the gulf that separates them from us in this respect. See, e.g., Steiger, "Development," 700–732, 740–57.

[86] Cited in Rex, "Humanism," 527.

[87] Clement of Alexandria, *Miscellanies*, 7.16.

become content with the average church led by its average pastor, educated at what is fast becoming the average seminary or college. Bucer and his Reformation colleagues, on the other hand, possessed a much larger and richer vision, and they had not yet developed the contempt for the striving for excellence (including intellectual excellence) that has become so characteristic of the Church in our time. It is only by recovering such a vision that we shall even perceive the need to move beyond lament for the modern eclipse of biblical narrative and on to lament for our own complicity in it. It is only in the midst of such lament that we shall then be able to move onward to a renewed, "reformed" commitment to doing better, for our own good and for the good of the world that God so loves—a renewed commitment to the resurrection of the Christian mind, brought back into harmony with the pietistic Christian heart; a renewed commitment to the judicious union of Athens and Jerusalem.

III

STILL PROTESTING
Scripture in the (Post)Modern World

As we discovered in part 2, the Protestant heirs of the Reformers responded in different ways in the course of the sixteenth through the nineteenth centuries to the challenge of remaining hermeneutically Protestant in a fast-changing world. Some were inclined to emphasize Reformation *principles* in interpreting biblical texts, paying ongoing attention to the rhetoric of their original-language forms as they read them in the context of the ancient past out of which they had emerged while also taking seriously new knowledge gained since the Reformers' time about our world and how it works. Others, while affirming these same Reformation principles to a certain extent, were inclined to lay continuing weight on *particular interpretations* of biblical texts offered during the Reformation (and beforehand), irrespective of changes in knowledge. I have offered various reasons why we ought to imitate the first group of Bible readers and not the second—even as we should certainly not adopt, either, the hermeneutical approach of contemporary counter-Reformational Protestants, which undermines the Reformation approach to Scripture altogether. The correct response to the eclipse of the biblical narrative is neither "fight" nor "flight" with respect to the modern (and postmodern) world but faithful *engagement* with it—which requires an earnest recommitment to high-quality Christian education. This is an important facet of a broader commitment to do an even better job than our forebears of demonstrating how the Great Story can still be read as cohering with all that is true and good in the world outside the Bible and how it continues to provide a reliable map for our life journey.

Part of that education (and commitment) will necessarily involve engagement with various modern and postmodern proposals about Bible reading that have been developed since the latter part of the nineteenth century. These "critical" or "higher-critical methods" (as they are often called) have arisen *in the midst of* the eclipse of biblical narrative, and their advocates have often had little genuine interest in deploying them in pursuit of its recovery. Indeed, these methods have regularly been "applied to the Bible with the in-built assumption that God can neither act nor speak" in Scripture or anywhere else.[1] The question before us, nevertheless, is whether and how far they *can* be so deployed, insofar as they represent further new knowledge gained since the Reformers' time about how both the *world* and our biblical *texts* "work." It is to these modern, critical reading methods that we now turn our attention, then, in part 3. In each case I shall offer an informative outline of the method, referring illustratively to early exemplars of the approach (rather than more recent ones), and I shall suggest how it should be integrated (or not) into a "reformed" hermeneutical approach to the Bible. How do these critical methods help us with the "seriously literal interpretation" of Scripture as Christian metanarrative, even as their "underpinnings may require reconfiguration in relation to the epistemic priority" of the Triune God who is revealed in this Story?[2] The footnotes will guide the interested reader to useful bibliography that pertains to each reading method individually and will allow for further in-depth study.

---

[1] Bartholomew, *Biblical Hermeneutics*, 11.
[2] Bartholomew, *Biblical Hermeneutics*, 10.

17

SOURCE AND FORM CRITICISM
Behind the Text

> *Higher Criticism was concerned with going behind the Biblical text, dismantling it into its original sources, dating these, and rewriting Biblical history on the basis of this analysis.*
>
> —*Philip Alexander*[1]
>
> *We must be satisfied with the soup that is set before us, and not desire to see the bones of the ox out of which it has been boiled.*
>
> —*J. R. R. Tolkien*[2]

I noted in part 2 the rise in the eighteenth century of a "historical criticism" of the Bible divorced in principle from any confessional, theological context—the heir of Spinoza's early historical-critical work in the late seventeenth century. This criticism, however—interested as it was in "questions of authorship of books, unity of books, and sources underlying books, without the restraints imposed by traditional opinions on these matters"—had not yet resulted in any presentation of the history of ancient Israel that was "radically different from what is implied in the Old Testament."[3] This is not an accident. The early historical critics certainly found the OT's account of Israel's history problematic in all sorts of ways. It is just that for the most part they had little confidence that they possessed sufficient data to improve upon it.

It is only as the eighteenth gives way to the nineteenth century and we find an increasing conviction in Europe and then beyond that scientific method ought to be able to deliver truth not only about the natural world, but also about the

---

[1] Alexander, "Reflections," 368.

[2] J. R. R. Tolkien, "On Fairy Stories," in *Tree and Leaf* (London: Unwin, 1964), 11–79 (25), quoting George Dasent (but to a very different purpose).

[3] John W. Rogerson, *Old Testament Criticism in the Nineteenth Century: England and Germany* (London: SPCK, 1984), 27, 24.

world of the past, that the situation changes. In chapter 15 we considered the importance of Leopold von Ranke in this context, and how this conviction began to play out first specifically in German OT studies in the work of de Wette and its development by Vatke. It might be possible, many scholars now came to believe, to discover the "real" history of ancient Israel by setting aside the OT story as we have it and focusing instead on its original written sources—whose reconstruction careful, methodical attention to the biblical text itself would make possible.

The Pentateuch attracted particular attention in this regard, and I shall use it initially in this chapter as our main example for consideration. De Wette had already proposed that Deuteronomy should be dated considerably later than the other books of the Pentateuch, which as a whole should not be trusted to be a truthful guide to the history of Israelite religion. Notable other scholars aside from Vatke—Wilhelm Gesenius (1786–1842), Carl Peter Wilhelm Gramberg (1797–1830), and Johann Friedrich Ludwig George (1811–1873)[4]—developed and refined de Wette's ideas. By the middle of the nineteenth century there was general agreement among source critics so far as the Pentateuch and Joshua were concerned

> that Deuteronomy had been composed in the seventh century BC, and that Deuteronomistic editorial work in the seventh or sixth centuries had brought the Pentateuch and Joshua to the form in which we now have them, barring some minor post-exilic additions. The books Genesis to Numbers and the pre-Deuteronomic Joshua were the work of the Yahwist. He had used an even earlier book, the so-called *Grundschrift* or Book of Origins, which was a priestly composition containing the basic narrative of the Pentateuch from Genesis 1, and including the levitical legislation in parts of Exodus, in Leviticus and in parts of Numbers.[5]

Variations in the detail of each scholar's understanding of these reconstructed sources, however, produced "differing reconstructions of Israel's history before the monarchy."[6] One of the most important of the disputed questions was whether the *Grundschrift* was a unified or a composite document. Karl Heinrich Graf (1815–1869) argued in 1865 that it was composite, and that its legislative sections should be dated later than the book of Deuteronomy. Theodor Nöldeke responded in 1869 by reasserting both its unity and its early, preexilic date. August Kayser (1821–1885) defended its unity in 1874 but argued for a *postexilic* date.[7] This brings us to Julius Wellhausen.

---

[4] Rogerson, *Criticism*, 50–68.
[5] Rogerson, *Criticism*, 257. "Deuteronomistic" refers here to editors deeply influenced by and anxious to promote the concerns of Deuteronomy. For the "Yahwist," see further below.
[6] Rogerson, *Criticism*, 257.
[7] Rogerson, *Criticism*, 258–60.

THE DOCUMENTARY AND OTHER HYPOTHESES

Julius Wellhausen was born in 1844 and died in 1918.[8] It was his version of the source-critical analysis of the Pentateuch and Joshua that came to dominate historical-critical biblical scholarship in the twentieth century, along with his associated reconstruction of the history of Israel. Rudolf Smend writes of his work along with that of his Dutch colleague Abraham Kuenen (1828–1891)—an important influence on and conversation partner for Wellhausen—that "in them the previous history of Old Testament studies drew to a certain conclusion, and it is there that the work that came afterward has its inception."[9] A student of Heinrich Ewald in Göttingen, Wellhausen learned early from his teacher to approach his textual work on the OT with careful attention to detail. It was this that led him by stages to his own distinctive opinions about the "Hexateuch" (Genesis through Joshua),[10] which he revealed to the scholarly world in three essays during 1876–1877 in the *Yearbooks for German Theology*. His opinions may be summarized as follows, although the summary inevitably simplifies to a great extent what is in reality a very complicated theory.[11]

First, Wellhausen distinguishes two mainly narrative sources, J and E, which are similar to each other but distinguishable among other things because of their different names for God: J prefers the divine name "Yahweh" (*Jahweh* in German), while E prefers "Elohim" (and thus the authors of these sources are often referred to as the "Yahwist" and the "Elohist"). At some point these two sources were combined by a redactor (i.e., editor) known as the Jehovist (JE), such that it is now often very difficult or impossible to disentangle them. Then came Deuteronomy (D), which was subsequently combined with JE. At a later point still the final form of the *Grundschrift* (now known as P, for "Priestly Code") was combined with JED. So emerged the "classical" twentieth-century understanding of the four large documentary sources that lie behind the Hexateuch and their correct chronological order: JEDP. The J- and E-sources date from the period of the monarchy and were combined at some point before the religious reform of King Josiah (2 Kgs 22–23). The D-source originated as the law book on the basis of which King Josiah carried out his reform and was composed around the same time as the reform (in the seventh century BC). The P-source is connected with the reconstitution of Judaism after the exile. The Pentateuch that resulted from

---

[8] For a sketch of Wellhausen's life and thought, see O'Neill, *Bible's Authority*, 198–213.
[9] Rudolf Smend, "The Work of Abraham Kuenen and Julius Wellhausen," *HBOT* 3/1:424–53 (425).
[10] This term appears to have been coined in the late eighteenth century, but its exact origins are unclear. Thomas Römer, "'Higher Criticism': The Historical and Literary-Critical Approach—With Special Reference to the Pentateuch," *HBOT* 3/1:393–423 (406–7).
[11] See Rogerson, *Criticism*, 260–64, for more detail.

the combination of these sources was publicly accepted as authoritative in conjunction with the postexilic reformation of Ezra.

Examples from Genesis

A couple of examples will help illustrate the way in which this kind of source-critical analysis works. In the biblical flood story in Genesis 6 through 9 the source division rests on two central observations. The first is that we encounter here a considerable number of passages that appear broadly parallel to each other and therefore somewhat redundant and repetitious in relation to each other ("doublets"). Genesis 6:11-13 appears substantially to repeat Genesis 6:5-8 with respect to the corrupt state of the world and the divine intention to bring judgment upon it. Genesis 6:19-22 describes the living creatures that are to be brought into Noah's ark and Genesis 7:1-5 apparently covers the same ground, albeit differing in the numbers of the animals involved (pairs of everything in Genesis 6, but seven pairs of clean and one pair of unclean in Genesis 7). Both Genesis 7:7-10 and Genesis 7:13-15 describe the entry into the ark, and both Genesis 7:18-21 and Genesis 7:22-23 describe the destructive flood. This leads to the hypothesis that two parallel but not exactly similar accounts of the flood have been combined into one. Then, second, each of these reconstructed accounts possesses its own distinctive vocabulary, not least in the names that are used for God ("Yahweh" in the one and "Elohim" in the other). This leads analysts to ascribe one account to the J-source and the other to the P-source (which, like the E-source, prefers "Elohim" in referring to God). To the J-source in the flood story is typically attributed Genesis 7:1-5, 7-10, 12, 16b, 17b, 22-23; 8:2b-3a, 6-12, 13b, 20-22; and 9:18-27. The P-source comprises Genesis 6:9-22; 7:6, 11, 13-16a, 17a, 18-21, 24; 8:1-2a, 3b-5, 13a, 14-19; and 9:1-17, 28-29.[12]

Our second example comes from Genesis 37—the beginning of the Joseph story. Here the distribution of the names for God cannot help the source critic, since "Yahweh" is almost entirely restricted to a cluster of verses in Genesis 39 (39:2-3, 5, 21, 23; the one exception is found in Gen 49:18). Yet typically the J-source is found by source critics in the Joseph story in more places than these, and certainly in Genesis 37. It is identified in this case in part by comparing this chapter to what source critics already believe they know about the style of J and E from passages elsewhere in the Pentateuch. The dreams in Genesis 37 are said to be unlike the dreams in E, for example (they do not function as a means of communication between God and humanity), and when Joseph's father is called "Israel" in Genesis 37:3 and 37:13 but "Jacob" in Genesis 37:34, this corresponds more generally to J and E ways of referring to this patriarch. Moreover, the supposition

---

[12] Samuel R. Driver, *The Book of Genesis* (2nd ed.; London: Methuen, 1904), iv–v.

that J and E have been combined in Genesis 37 helps us clarify what is said to be a somewhat confused storyline, in which we once again find doublets. Reuben (Gen 37:21-24) and Judah (Gen 37:25-27) pursue two different strategies to save Joseph's life: throwing him into an empty water cistern, on the one hand, and selling him for twenty shekels to traders, on the other. The traders are called by two names: Ishmaelites and Midianites (Gen 37:28). These duplications are explicable if we assume that two stories have been combined. The J-source knows Judah as Joseph's protector and the Ishmaelites as the traders who buy the boy from the brothers. The E-source knows Reuben as Joseph's protector and the traders as Midianites, who *find* the boy in the cistern and, unnoticed by the brothers, extract him and take him down to Egypt; Reuben returns to find the boy gone (Gen 37:29-30). The P-source is found in Genesis 37:2, in one of its trademark structuring notices that help the reader to read the finished Joseph story in the context of the whole book of Genesis.

The History of Israel

Wellhausen's source-critical analysis is associated, just like the analyses of his forebears, with a particular reconstruction of the history of ancient Israel, first presented in written form in 1878.[13] When one reads the OT as it now stands, he maintains, it makes no historical sense. One must in this case assume that Israelite life and history were regulated from near the beginning by the legislation of P and indeed of D—but in fact, a straightforward reading of Joshua through Kings makes clear that this was not so.

Deuteronomy 12 demands, for example, that Israel should have only one, central worship sanctuary—but in 1 Kings 18 Elijah rebuilds an altar of Yahweh on top of Mount Carmel, and the rectitude of this action is simply assumed. Neither Joshua through 2 Kings nor the early prophetic books of the OT in fact presuppose or reflect the laws *or* the narratives of P, and D is likewise out of joint with much of their content. When we put the reconstructed sources of the Hexateuch in their correct chronological order, conversely, everything becomes comprehensible. It is possible then to see a logical progression through time in five areas of Israelite worship. With respect to sanctuaries, for example, JE knows of a multiplicity of worship sites in Israel; D then *commands* one place of worship; and P *presupposes* one. With respect to feasts, JE describe the joyous celebration of agricultural festivals, and D is fairly consistent with this, but in P the feasts have lost their connection with the agricultural year.[14]

---

[13] Julius Wellhausen, *Prolegomena to the History of Israel* (1885; repr., Atlanta: Scholars Press, 1994).

[14] For a visual summary of this material and further comment on feasts and offerings, see John H. Hayes, *An Introduction to Old Testament Study* (Nashville: Abingdon, 1979), 161.

Wellhausen's historical reconstruction, then, posits an early period in Israel's history in which (in agreement with de Wette)

> "each meal [was] a sacrifice, each festive and important event a festival, and each prophet, king and father of a household was without further qualification a priest." Josiah's reform began the path to conformity, but it was the destruction of the Temple and the Exile that were really crucial ... the Priestly Code and its back-projection of priestly religion to the time of Moses marked, together with Chronicles, the complete triumph of the priestly.[15]

As soon as we encounter the ancient Israelites in real history, Wellhausen maintains—and he is skeptical about our ability to know very much prior to the period just before the rise of the monarchy—we find them to be a natural kinship group (i.e., not constituted by law or institutions) without any centralized, powerful priesthood or any fully fledged system of sacrifices. Early Israelite religion was much more informal and decentralized than what came later—a "natural" period of their expression of their faith, with spontaneity rather than structure as its hallmark. The ministries of the charismatically endowed eighth-century prophets represented its finest hour. It was only toward the end of the monarchy that these ideals began to be abandoned, as the book of the law "found" in the temple in Jerusalem (but actually just freshly written and deposited there) provided the basis for unfortunate new developments. For Wellhausen, postexilic Judaism represented the end point of the process of decline that set in with Deuteronomy, with natural and spontaneous worship ultimately becoming impossible because of the accumulation of cultic and ritual laws. True religion was crushed under their weight, only to be resurrected in NT times when Jesus liberated it from the shackles that had bound it for so many centuries and revived the earlier prophetic tradition. In articulating this theory Wellhausen was essentially putting substance to an intuition he describes as emerging just over a decade previously (1867) when he first heard about Graf's work: "almost without knowing his reasons for the hypothesis ... I readily acknowledged to myself the possibility of understanding Hebrew antiquity without the book of the Torah."[16]

Beyond Wellhausen

Wellhausen's Documentary Hypothesis quickly established itself as the default source-critical theory about the Hexateuch in Germany and beyond. It was widely regarded as possessing great explanatory power, such that there were even various attempts in subsequent decades to identify "pentateuchal" sources not only

---

[15] Rogerson, *Criticism*, 265.
[16] Wellhausen, *Prolegomena*, 3–4.

in Joshua, but also in Judges, Samuel, and Kings.[17] The source-critical approach was also popular with scholars working in other parts of the Bible, including the Gospels. The quest for the historical Israel found its parallel here in the ongoing quest for the historical Jesus. Might it be possible by way of source-critical method to get back to the earliest possible written sources touching on Jesus' life and ministry, behind even the earliest gospel—which by the late nineteenth century was widely agreed among NT scholars to be the Gospel of Mark? Advocates of Markan priority faced the question of how to account for the material absent from Mark that Matthew and Luke share in common.[18] If Matthew and Luke did not know each other (and this was generally considered likely), then where did this common material come from? One possible answer was that it derived from a common written source, named as Q (from the German *Quelle*, "source").[19] Many felt that only this would explain the exactness of wording in some of the Q parallels in Matthew and Luke as well as the frequent agreement in order between the two Gospels where the parallels appear. The Q hypothesis remains popular to this day in NT studies, at least among "Markan priority" scholars. If one believes in the more traditional view, on the other hand, that Matthew came first, followed by Luke and Mark in that order, then Q becomes unnecessary. In this case we can explain the Matthew/Luke agreements against Mark by positing that Luke sometimes followed Matthew but Mark followed neither.

REFLECTIONS ON SOURCE CRITICISM

From the perspective of "seriously literal interpretation" there is nothing problematic about the idea that the Great Story told in the current form of our biblical text has been put together on the basis of *sources*, including written sources. Various biblical authors explicitly draw our attention to such sources,[20] implying that they themselves have used them, and there are instances where the evidence clearly points to that conclusion even though nothing explicit is stated.[21] All of this comes under the heading of the normal, human compositional processes involved in the formation of Scripture that the Reformation affirmed. As someone once said, "Time is what keeps everything from happening at

---

[17] Karl W. Weyde, "Studies in the Historical Books—Including Their Relationship with the Pentateuch," *HBOT* 3/1:521-55 (525-43).

[18] E.g., Matt 6:24 and Luke 16:13; Matt 7:7-11 and Luke 11:9-13; Matt 11:25-27 and Luke 10:21-22; Matt 23:37-39 and Luke 13:34-35.

[19] For a brief introduction to this Q-source, see Graham N. Stanton, "Q," in *Dictionary of Jesus and the Gospels* (ed. Joel B. Green and Scot McKnight; Downers Grove, Ill.: InterVarsity, 1992), 644-50.

[20] E.g., 2 Sam 1:18; 1 Kgs 14:19.

[21] E.g., it is clear either that 1-2 Chronicles depend in various places (often word for word) on 1-2 Kings (the normal view), or that both use a common source.

once"[22]—and Scripture certainly did not come into existence all at once, but as a result of various processes over time that include some use of sources. Our understanding of the Bible as God's Word must be able to accommodate such realities; otherwise we are not paying attention to the Bible.

It is one thing to acknowledge this reality, of course; it is quite another to agree that there is sufficient evidence to allow us confidently to reconstruct such sources and date them and then proceed to rewrite the history of Israel on this basis. I profoundly doubt that this is the case.

Internal Considerations

Granted the possibility or even the likelihood that our biblical authors often worked from written sources, but also the reality that we do not possess them in extant form, is it possible to reconstruct (and date) them? Or does not the attempt inevitably involve a very high degree of subjectivity? Certainly the Documentary Hypothesis—one of the most carefully worked-over examples of source-critical endeavor within the discipline of biblical studies—gives pause for general thought on this point. It is true that this hypothesis was widely regarded in the decades following its articulation as possessing great explanatory power. It is also true, however, that right from the start there were questions about whether Wellhausen had really described the putative sources entirely accurately.[23] Wellhausen himself soon developed some doubts of his own about at least some (unspecified) aspects of his hypothesis.[24] As time passed a veritable academic industry then arose whose workers were committed to improving on his work while still employing his general method. A plethora of variations on the Wellhausen thesis emerged as a result,[25] including widely variant datings of some of the sources.[26] Inevitably this led many in due course to begin to question the method itself and the assumptions upon which it was built. The *objectivity* of a method so patently capable of producing so many different outcomes came into dispute. "Many rigorous studies on pentateuchal sources have been published," notes Alan Hauser in a critical review of the history of source-critical Pentateuchal studies, "but consensus regarding these sources continues to elude

---

[22] Source unknown—the quote is commonly attributed to Albert Einstein, however.

[23] Rogerson, *Criticism*, 268–71.

[24] Rudolf Smend, "In the Wake of Wellhausen: The Growth of a Literary-Critical School and Its Varied Influence," *HBOT* 3/1:472–93 (476), citing a letter in 1900 to Nöldeke: "I by no means stand by the correctness of everything written there; my confidence has come to be severely shaken."

[25] See, e.g., Smend, "Wake," 478–93, for early examples.

[26] More recently, e.g., John Van Seters has dated the J-source to the exilic and not the early monarchic period. John Van Seters, *Prologue to History: The Yahwist as Historian in Genesis* (Louisville, Ky.: Westminster John Knox, 1992), xi (e.g.).

us"[27]—and the obvious question became, "why?" Could it be that the criteria commonly deployed in distinguishing sources were flawed? Repetition has typically been regarded as indicating different sources, for example—but is this necessarily so? Cannot repetition have a rhetorical purpose in Hebrew prose, as it certainly does in Hebrew poetry?[28] What about variation in style and language, including the naming of either God or human beings? Cannot authors vary their style and language for particular literary purposes?

For example, is it necessary to interpret the "doublets" in the biblical flood story as indicating that two sources have been merged by an editor? As a matter of fact it is not; one can interpret them in terms of Hebrew parallelism, which "is a much more complex phenomenon than it is often thought to be,"[29] and (or) as components of an elaborate chiastic structure or palistrophe that rises and falls with the flood waters and necessitates a certain degree of contrivance on the part of the author in order to accomplish it.[30] If one insists on using the doublets in the flood story to reconstruct two sources, indeed, difficult questions arise. The reconstructed J-source turns out to be a story in which Noah is instructed to go into an ark (Gen 7:1-5) that has not previously been built or even mentioned. It also provides us with no account of Noah leaving this mysteriously appearing ark (Gen 8:6-12, 13b, 20-22). This is a somewhat terse "source" to say the least, and most source critics feel compelled to argue that we no longer possess it all. The editor of the biblical flood story has omitted the parts of J that he did not need, because he already possessed parts of P that could do the job. But if he was prepared to *omit* parts of J for this reason why did he *include* other parts of J that are allegedly duplicates of, and even in conflict with, material in P? Why did he include exactly the "ill-fitting" passages that provide source critics with evidence that J and P are combined in the flood story in the first place? Why are *these* sections of J useful enough to be included when others are left out?

There is no clearly satisfactory answer to such questions. And then we must also note that, if *indeed* our two sources are to be distinguished on the basis of the "doublets," then their separation does not always lead to consistency with respect

---

[27] Alan J. Hauser, "Sources of the Pentateuch: So Many Theories, So Little Consensus," *SBL Forum* (August 2007), http://sbl-site.org/Article.aspx?ArticleID=725 (accessed August 16, 2016).

[28] Hauser, "Sources of the Pentateuch"; Jacob Licht, *Storytelling in the Bible* (Jerusalem: Magnes, 1978), 51–95.

[29] Allan Rosengren, "Why Is There a Documentary Hypothesis, and What Does It Do to You If You Use It? A Response to David Clines," *SBL Forum* (July 2006), http://sbl-site.org/Article.aspx?ArticleID=566 (accessed June 14, 2016).

[30] Gordon J. Wenham, "The Coherence of the Flood Narrative," *VT* 28 (1978): 336–48. Within this context Wenham explicitly addresses the question as to whether the repetitions really *are* mere repetitions. He argues, e.g., that in Gen 6:11-22 God tells Noah what to do when (in the distant future) the flood comes, while in Gen 7:1-5 God is telling him what he must *now* do.

to the "divine name criterion" also used by source critics for this purpose. If Genesis 7:13-15 belong to P, for example, then the doublet passage in Genesis 7:7-10 must belong to J—but the latter passage inconveniently refers to God as "Elohim" in verse 9, and this is a "P-usage." The implausibility of the ways in which source critics attempt to get around such problems in their analysis of the book of Genesis is well illustrated by Ephraim Speiser. The mere occurrence of "Elohim" in a text is not decisive in itself for source-division, Speiser claims, because "Elohim" can be used

> not only for alien gods and idols but also in the broader sense of our Providence, Heaven, Fate, and is actually so attested in the J source, among others. The evidence remains significant, but one-sided: Elohim could well appear in any document, as is only natural in the circumstances; on the other hand, Yahweh is in Genesis the exclusive companion of J (barring occasional lapses in the composite text under the influence of an adjacent passage from another source).[31]

In other words: "Yahweh" and "Elohim" appear in passages assigned by source critics to both J and P, but we shall explain away all the occurrences that are inconvenient to the source theory. This is not very convincing logic.

By the time we get to the closing chapters of Genesis (Gen 37–50) the difficulties have multiplied. Here "Elohim" is *invariably* used in allegedly J-contexts and "Yahweh" is almost entirely restricted to the small number of verses already identified above. Walter Moberly's theory about the divine names here certainly seems much more likely than Wellhausen's to be correct: a narrator selectively added "Yahweh" to a section of Genesis that originally referred to God throughout as "Elohim."[32] Yet this raises profound questions, then, about the viability of the Wellhausen thesis. Of Genesis 37–50 Wellhausen himself said this: "One suspects that this section, like the rest, is a synthesis of J and E; our earlier results impose this solution and would be profoundly affected were it not demonstrable."[33] Yet without the help of the "divine names criterion" source critics have in fact *struggled* to "demonstrate" that Wellhausen's sources continue all the way through this section of Genesis. Certainly the other phenomena cited in favor of the source division can easily be explained in alternative ways. There is no reason for example why Joseph's father cannot be referred to using two names, when the preceding narrative clearly knows that he already possesses both (Gen 32:28) and indeed many people in the OT narrative have more than one (e.g., Solomon/

---

[31] Ephraim A. Speiser, *Genesis* (AB 1; Garden City, N.Y.: Doubleday, 1964), xxii–xxiii.

[32] R. W. L. Moberly, *The Old Testament of the Old Testament: Patriarchal Narratives and Mosaic Yahwism* (OBT; Minneapolis: Fortress, 1992), 70–71.

[33] The translation is taken from Claus Westermann, *Genesis 37–50* (CC; trans. John J. Scullion; Minneapolis: Fortress, 2002), 19.

Jedidiah, 2 Sam 12:24-25; Mattaniah/Zedekiah, 2 Kgs 24:17). Two different strategies for saving Joseph, moreover, can inhabit the one story if we understand Reuben's intervention as only a temporary respite that in spite of his hopes did not change his brothers' ultimate intentions. And the term "Ishmaelites" *can* be used in the OT in the general sense of "Bedouin" (Judg 8:24; cf. Gen 16:12), in which case we can perhaps understand that the traders in Genesis 37 are first identified (from a distance) as Ishmaelites and only later specifically as Midianites. Clearly the final *editor* of the text regarded these as two terms for the one group of people. There is no good reason to think that his sources ever suggested anything different.

In retrospect it seems clear that strong assumptions have operated among source critics about what ancient Hebrew literature "ought" to look like and that these have driven attempts to *make* it look like that—to restore to it a certain kind of "coherence," as measured by the modern source-critical mind. Yet whether we should rightly expect this kind of coherence is open to question—and whether we may be sure that we have "reconstructed" anything real once we have imposed it on the text has increasingly come to be doubted. So it is that, writing in 1987, Norman Whybray reviewed the Documentary Hypothesis in some depth and concluded that it is fundamentally flawed: it does not provide "a reliable and convincing approach to the question of the composition of the Pentateuch."[34] He opts instead for a relatively integrated central core tradition in the Pentateuch, albeit established in the exilic period, with supplementary material added later. This is merely one of the books from the 1970s and 1980s (along with significant precursors) that have contributed not only to "the collapse of consensus on [the traditional Wellhausen] model and the emergence of a debate surrounding virtually every aspect in it over the last four decades,"[35] but more significantly have led to a situation in which increasing numbers of biblical scholars currently have little confidence that we can get behind the current text to written sources of this kind at all.

External Considerations

This is not least the case because the epigraphic evidence from the ancient Near East more generally provides scant support for many of the redactional models that have been routinely presupposed by source critics. Comparative literature suggests indeed that the kind of goal that source critics have traditionally set themselves is probably impossible to achieve: "documented cases of transmission

---

[34] R. Norman Whybray, *The Making of the Pentateuch: A Methodological Study* (JSOTSup 53; Sheffield: Sheffield Academic, 1987), 221.

[35] David M. Carr, "Changes in Pentateuchal Criticism," *HBOT* 3/2:433–66 (434), with extensive discussion of the literature on the following pages.

history ... show that texts that are the result of textual growth do not consistently preserve enough traces of that growth in their final form for scholars to reconstruct each and every stage of that growth"[36] This is because, as David Carr proposes, "their authors often worked from memory in incorporating earlier texts"—an idea alien to much modern biblical scholarship, which has tended radically to distinguish "orality/memorization" and "writing/literacy."[37] We need to reckon instead with "an oral-written [ancient] context where the masters of literary tradition used texts to memorize certain traditions seen as particularly ancient, holy, and divinely inspired."[38]

If these comparative models represent a reliable guide to what was happening in ancient Israel as well, then all sorts of issues arise for traditional source-critical endeavor. For example, many source critics have envisioned *multiple* stages of redaction in various biblical texts, but comparative enquiry reveals that most texts in the remainder of the ancient Near East "seem to have undergone at most two to three major stages of growth."[39] More generally, "an overview of documented cases of transmission history suggests that—in many cases—it would be virtually impossible for scholars to reconstruct earlier stages if they lacked documentation of such stages" (i.e., did not possess a copy of the earlier version).[40] This implies (for Carr) the necessity of a careful, modest approach, although not complete skepticism, when attempting "to reconstruct transmission history for compositions where we lack a documented prehistory."[41]

The general case is well illustrated by a particular example involving a non-biblical Jewish text from Qumran. Stephen Kaufman asks of the Temple Scroll, "can one—*without peeking into the Bible*—reconstruct the biblical sources upon which the Scroll is based and separate them from the editorial hand of the final author by using the standard methods of literary criticism?"[42] His conclusion is

> that although the Temple Scroll demonstrates the feasibility, indeed perhaps even the high probability, that the Torah, too, was composed primarily of earlier, written sources, it also demonstrates that the attempt to identify and reconstruct those sources in other than their broadest outlines is a consummately fruitless endeavor.[43]

---

[36] David M. Carr, *The Formation of the Hebrew Bible: A New Reconstruction* (New York: Oxford University Press, 2011), 4.

[37] Carr, *Formation*, 4–5.

[38] Carr, *Formation*, 4.

[39] Carr, *Formation*, 145.

[40] Carr, *Formation*, 146.

[41] Carr, *Formation*, 147.

[42] Stephen A. Kaufman, "The Temple Scroll and Higher Criticism," *HUCA* 53 (1982): 29–43 (33).

[43] Kaufman, "Temple Scroll," 29.

There is little external, empirical evidence, then, that can be marshalled in defense of the plausibility of the source-critical enterprise as traditionally conceived— little reason to believe that an accurate, detailed reconstruction of the sources of an ancient Near Eastern text on the basis of inductive study of the text itself is possible. The confidence of the nineteenth and twentieth centuries on this point, as historical criticism was entering its mature years, turns out to have been much less warranted than the greater caution of its youth during the seventeenth and eighteenth centuries.[44]

Internal and external considerations combine, then, to raise serious doubts about the genuine objectivity of proposed source-reconstructions with respect to parts of the Bible like the Pentateuch. In a curious way, in fact, source-critical reading shares in certain respects the weaknesses of allegorical reading (my chapter 9). In both cases there is an evident desire to look behind the text for the real (coherent) truth and a conviction that the truly wise reader will find it there; for Origen, Frances Young reminds us, "[c]oherence lay not in the text or narrative itself, but in what lay behind it."[45] Skeptical observers in both cases are struck, however, by just how lacking in objectivity these readings are—just how little the text is allowed the opportunity to "bite back" against the meaning that is being extracted from (or imposed upon) it. They are struck by just how much of what is claimed to be "really there" appears in reality to be the free creation of the readerly mind. This is how Carr assesses much of the source-critical heritage:

> [T]he documented variety of readable sources that can be produced out of Pentateuchal and other texts militates against the probability that such reconstructed sources ever existed in an earlier time. Instead, given what we know about partial preservation and modification of prior traditions by ancient scribes, it is more likely that most (semi-)readable texts produced by contemporary transmission historians are nothing but the inventions of their creators.[46]

The reconstructed text turns out substantially (and perhaps even simply) to reflect the prejudices and values of the person reconstructing it.

Text and History

So also does the *history* that is reconstructed on the basis of the reconstructed text. Or perhaps we should say: the history that has fueled the source-critical analysis in the first place—since

---

[44] See Legaspi, *Death of Scripture*, 167–69, for some insightful comment on the pessimism about historical reconstruction found in someone like Spinoza over against the optimism of modern historical critics—which from Michaelis onward has proved ill-founded.

[45] Young, *Biblical Exegesis*, 184.

[46] Carr, *Formation*, 114.

[p]roposed pentateuchal sources feed into the reconstruction of ancient Israelite history, which, in turn, feeds back into the study of the sources. Such reconstructions are essentially incestuous, and the opportunity for circular thinking is boundless.[47]

It is "boundless" precisely because the biblical text itself as we have it, read in its ancient Near Eastern context, provides no substantial check on either kind of theorizing—since everyone "knows" that the real truth (both in terms of text and history) lies behind it and not *in* it. So the ultimate "result" of scholarly analysis in terms of historical reconstruction, overtly premised on a particular reconstruction of the alleged sources and a particular dating of these along a timeline, all too often appears *in fact* to be a construal of the past that has much to do with the scholar's own contemporary worldview—and is perhaps only, or mainly, a back projection of that worldview. In the case of Wellhausen's construal of the history of Israel, for example, it is surely no coincidence that he was heir to a German Romanticism that regarded the early period of any people's history as the true expression of that people's spirit; that his generally Protestant context valued spontaneity over ritual; that his particular Lutheran context encouraged a negative view of Law in comparison to Gospel (and indeed a negative view of Judaism); and that he inhabited a political culture that led him to view Israel's monarchic period particularly favorably in contrast to her postexilic period (see further below). This was the nineteenth-century source critic, then, who—striving for "strict rectitude and objectivity" as he did[48]—nevertheless retold the story of Israel so as to make it speak of an early, "natural" period of spontaneous religion that continued late into the monarchic age, of the unfortunate introduction of Law in the seventh century BC, of degenerate postexilic Judaism, and of the later recovery of authenticity in the first century AD.

The way in which Wellhausen himself understood this "story" to cast light on the events of his own life and times is palpable in his writings. The origins of the Church that he encountered in Germany are to be found in ancient Judaism, he maintained. Jesus protested against the scribal multiplication of commandments in Judaism, but the Church did for Jesus what Judaism did for the prophets—"it killed the true spirit of Christianity"[49] and created a religious system that was alien to an authentic, inner life. Both Judaism and the Church were now obstacles to progress—for it is only as supreme individuals like the prophets "sow a seed in the field Time"[50] that history moves forward. As a result of these convictions, shortly after the publication of his *Prolegomena to the History of Israel*, Wellhausen

---

[47] Hauser, "Sources of the Pentateuch."
[48] Smend, "Work," 425.
[49] O'Neill, *Bible's Authority*, 204.
[50] O'Neill, *Bible's Authority*, 204.

attempted to transfer out of his university position in theology in Greifswald and into the philosophical faculty there. "It strikes me as a lie," he wrote, "that I should be educating ministers in an Evangelical Church to which in my heart I do not belong."[51] Unable in fact to transfer within Greifswald, he ultimately moved on to the University of Halle, and afterward to Marburg and then Göttingen.

It is inevitable, of course, that "[a]ll interpreters bring presuppositions to the text"[52]—that "all interpretation [is] always guided by its own prejudice"[53]—and we have certainly seen many examples of this so far in this book. However, if it is the actual text to which we bring our presuppositions and prejudices—a solid entity that is actually there and can challenge us about their propriety—then we are much less likely than otherwise simply to impose them *on* the text. The problem with something as subjective as "reconstruction" in a context where we are operating entirely inductively from the text without external help is that there is always a danger that what we "reconstruct" (both sources and history) will turn out to be substantially (or merely) the externalized figment of our own imaginations—that we shall find in "the past" merely a reflection of and a validation for what is important to us in the present. This is a danger *in any case*; but the "text" is obviously much more malleable in our hands if *we* are in charge of creating it than if we encounter something that is already there. So is history.

For all sorts of reasons, then (and we have not exhausted them), "[t]he Wellhausen paradigm no longer functions as a commonly accepted presupposition for Old Testament exegesis"—and the author of these words wrote them already more than twenty years ago.[54]

THE RISE OF FORM CRITICISM

The Europe of the nineteenth century that produced classical source criticism was a continent in which many profoundly believed in the individual creative genius: the man of destiny who arises from among the masses and who by force of personality imposes himself on the general consciousness, bringing something new to human experience. One of the most notable of these in the realm of politics was Otto von Bismarck (1815–1898), who founded the German Empire in 1871 and of whom Julius Wellhausen was such an admirer—to such an extent

---

[51] Quoted in O'Neill, *Bible's Authority*, 201.

[52] John Barton, "The Legacy of the Literary-Critical School and the Growing Opposition to Historico-Critical Bible Studies: The Concept of 'History' Revisited—*Wirkungsgeschichte* and Reception History," *HBOT* 3/2:96–124 (108).

[53] Craig G. Bartholomew, "Postmodernity and Biblical Interpretation," *DTIB*, 600–607 (602), referencing Gadamer's view.

[54] Rolf Rendtorff, "The Paradigm Is Changing: Hopes—and Fears," *BibInt* 1 (1993): 34–53 (44).

that he ultimately lost Ewald's friendship over it.[55] Bismarck was, to Wellhausen, exactly the prophet-like genius whose unencumbered activity in "sowing a seed in the field of Time" moved history along.

It is this creative individualism that also characterizes Wellhausen's thinking about biblical texts and Israelite history. In his documentary source theory the sources are above all the creations of individual authors. These authors may have used older traditions (myths, songs, stories) in writing their works, but Wellhausen saw these as detached, isolated entities awaiting the poetic or literary genius who would weave them into an artistic whole. It is because these sources were composed by authors who were creatively free of their environment and their community that they reflect their own time much more than they reflect any real past—hence Wellhausen's skepticism about our access to the real history of the patriarchs, for example. It is because individuals are important to Wellhausen that the prophets appear in his thought as the highest pinnacle of Israelite religion: energetic people, directly inspired by God and creatively free of the ritual and ceremonial life of the people, who bring fresh impetus and ethical consciousness to a religion in danger of falling into mere externalism. It is also partly for this reason that Wellhausen regards the period of the monarchy so much more highly than that of the postexilic community. Kings—people like Bismarck—make history; communities only live in it.

The decades around the turn of the twentieth century, however, saw the emergence to prominence of a balancing and perhaps even contradictory emphasis on the larger social matrix within which individuals inevitably operate and within which their freedom of thought and action is inevitably constrained. We see this in political thought in the impressive inroads made by Marxist ideology—the idea that we are all enmeshed in groups, classes, and institutional structures that determine our experience and manner of life, our ways of thinking, and our destiny. We see it also in the rise to prominence of the social sciences (anthropology, sociology, ethnology, psychology) with their stress on individual thought and action as the product of socialization—the shaping of lives either by deep structures common to human beings in general or by specific experiences of groups such as families or tribes. Theorists in these disciplines tended to stress the social dimensions and functions of religion in particular and to play down the significance of the individual in that context. Their emphasis lay on religion as a function of the group—not so much as an *individual* activity, but as participation in *community* activity. Two kinds of scientific discovery in particular fueled this kind of approach to religion in Europe. First, ongoing discovery of hitherto unknown people groups continued to make clear the *intrinsic* nature of customs,

---

[55] Smend, "Work," 444.

ceremonials, and rituals in so-called "primitive" religions. This raised questions about any facile distinction between the "true" religion of the individual and his spirit, on the one hand, and the religion of a community, on the other. Second, a vast literature from ancient Near Eastern cultures other than the Israelite one was in the process of recovery, and this enabled for the first time extensive comparison between ancient Near Eastern and OT texts, which in turn raised questions about any simplistic claims about what was creatively new in the OT.

In due course this shift in emphasis from the creative, autonomous individual who shapes culture to the individual as enmeshed in culture helps to produce a number of new ways of reading the Bible that we shall examine in later chapters: structuralism, and both social-scientific and feminist criticism. In due course, indeed, the focus of critical engagement with biblical literature moves in many quarters away from the authors to the *readers* of texts that are the products of culture, and questions about the autonomy of the author are replaced by questions about the autonomy of the reader. In fact, this whole question of how to think about the relationship between the individual (whether author or reader) and the broader context in which the individual operates lies at the heart of the modern hermeneutical debate.

In the present chapter we are still far away from these later developments. For the moment all that needs to be noted is that already among those who by the turn of the twentieth century are pondering the solidarity of the individual Israelite with his Israelite community, the solidarity of Israel with the ancient Near East as a whole, and the solidarity of human beings overall—that is, elaborating theories about "humanness" and human religiosity in general—it was inevitable that the Wellhausen approach to Israelite literature and religion was going to be critiqued, even as it was broadly exerting great influence. What arose out of this pondering in the first instance was form criticism—or literary history (*Literaturgeschichte*), or genre research (*Gattungsforschung*), as it was known to its German originator, Hermann Gunkel.

Hermann Gunkel

Gunkel was born in 1862 and died in 1932.[56] The book that made his name was called *Schöpfung und Chaos* (*Creation and Chaos*), and it was published in 1895 while Gunkel was teaching at the University of Berlin (1894–1907). In this book Gunkel sought to demonstrate that neither Genesis 1 in the OT nor Revelation 12 in the NT are free compositions deriving from individual, creative authors.

---

[56] For a sketch of Gunkel's life and thought, see O'Neill, *Bible's Authority*, 236–47; for more detail on his broader context, Erhard S. Gerstenberger, "Albert Eichhorn and Hermann Gunkel: The Emergence of a History of Religion School," *HBOT* 3/1:454–71.

To the contrary, each contains a mythical drama whose originating point lies in ancient Babylonian religion. That is, there is substantial continuity between ancient pagan and biblical religion and literature. Wellhausen's response concerning Revelation 12, published in 1899, illustrates nicely the difference of perspective between himself and Gunkel. Most of what Gunkel has to say is not new, claims Wellhausen; everyone is aware that there are some connections between the book of Revelation and ancient mythology. However, these connections are not important for gaining an understanding of the book, which depends on focusing on its author, his historical circumstances, and the message that he wished to communicate to his contemporaries in those circumstances. Understanding Babylonian religion has nothing to do with that, and to raise its profile in such a context is to be guilty of a failure of method. Where Gunkel stressed the dependence of the author on earlier forms of literature, then, Wellhausen predictably emphasized his independence.

This attack by the influential Wellhausen was not good news for Gunkel's academic career but he persevered, publishing in the same year a spirited defense of his work and continuing for the remainder of his life, carefully but pointedly, to draw attention to the deficiencies of Wellhausen's own approach to the Bible.

The Form-Critical Idea

Gunkel's pressing interest lay, like Wellhausen's, in the original shape of OT tradition prior to the construction of our current biblical text—but from the point of view, now, of the social background of the tradition and its original function, particularly in the oral stage of its development. The necessity of this kind of attention to the oral stage becomes apparent, he suggested, when we read the written forms of our OT traditions and discover in them conventional patterns of *speech*. These are the speech forms of everyday social life in ancient Israel, appropriate to different public occasions (formal and informal) and only making proper sense when considered in those contexts. In order to understand our biblical traditions fully, then, we must attempt to determine the life setting (*Sitz im Leben*) in which each of these conventional forms of speech found their original meaning. It is indeed impossible to understand the literature of the OT properly unless we do this, since *many* of the conventions apparent in the OT are not truly *literary* conventions at all. The biblical authors simply fixed in writing material whose ground rules were partly or wholly those of oral communication. To fail to understand this might well lead to a misreading of the written text, just as might happen if we ourselves were to read a contemporary text in English and fail to take account of the original life setting. Consider the following statements:

- I name this ship *Prince of Denmark*. May God bless her and all who sail in her.
- With this ring I thee wed.
- Not guilty.
- Fire![57]

Each of these statements is connected to a life setting (or more than one life setting) in which it makes sense, and English-speaking readers immediately recognize what each statement communicates in that context. Form critics like Gunkel essentially argued that the OT literature arose out of a far more oral culture than modern European literature did—an oral culture that is quite alien to us in many ways. If we are to understand this ancient literature, then, we must work hard to understand how *its* component parts were understood in *their* original (oral) contexts.

We must work hard precisely because we *are* dealing with an alien culture, and our intuitions about ancient communicative intent may not always be reliable. Kenneth Bailey provides us with a good example from the modern Middle East of the challenge—the report of a fatal shooting in a village during a wedding, when guns were customarily fired into the air in celebration:

> Hanna fired the gun. The gun did not go off. He lowered the gun. The gun fired.... The bullet passed through the stomach of Butrus. He died. He did not cry out, "O my father," nor "O my mother."... When the police came we told them, "A camel stepped on him."[58]

Are we to imagine that the gun fired all by itself—that what Hanna had been doing with his trigger finger in the preceding seconds had nothing to do with it? No, in that life setting, this was simply a conventional way of stating that the shooting was an accident, not a deliberate act (whether or not Hanna had his finger on the trigger at the time—perhaps the gun was simply defective and the bullet in the chamber was only now released). Are we to think, then, that all males in that culture were supposed to cry out in such circumstances, "O my father" and "O my mother," and that it was notable that Butrus did not do so? No, this is simply a conventional way of saying that Butrus died instantly, without crying out. And in introducing the camel, did the villagers lie to the police about what had really happened? If so it was an implausible lie, since there was an obvious bullet hole in Butrus' stomach and everyone could have seen it. But in fact it

---

[57] These exemplary statements are borrowed from John Barton, *Reading the Old Testament* (London: Darton, Longman & Todd, 1984), 32.

[58] Kenneth E. Bailey, "Informal Controlled Oral Tradition and the Synoptic Gospels," *Them* 20 (1995): 4–11 (9).

was not a lie; it was conventional speech, understood by all: "no deception [was] intended or perpetrated."[59] This was an accident, and no further action against anyone was required—either by the police or by the family of the dead man who might otherwise seek blood vengeance.

In the same way we need to understand the conventional speech of the OT literature in its original life setting if we are not to make mistakes in reading it. We must seek such understanding not only at the level of the sentence but also at the level of the story—since on the form-critical view many of the larger units of text in the Bible began life as orally transmitted entities. We must try to grasp the *genre* of these stories. This was "the prime task of a history of Israelite literature," Gunkel believed.[60] Which kinds of truth were they attempting to communicate in their original contexts and as they were subsequently passed down through the generations?

How Gunkel envisaged this process is well illustrated in his 1901 commentary on Genesis.[61] The genre of the Genesis narratives is legend, he asserts, and they must be read as such if they are to be properly appreciated. The individual legends, originally the creations of individuals far in the past, were then retold in families and by professional storytellers, or in worship contexts (each sanctuary and festival had its own cultic legend), and passed on in this way to subsequent generations. They were originally short, oral, self-contained, and independent units. Later they developed either individually into "novellas" (like the Joseph story), or in the context of legend cycles. The novellas and legend cycles were then later collected to form the source documents of the Pentateuch.

We can see from this summary that for Gunkel form-critical work was not antithetical but *complementary* to the work of the source critics like Wellhausen, with whom he in fact shared significant presuppositions.[62] Form criticism simply added a more satisfactory backstory to their story about J and E, compensating for a source-critical method that "was insufficient for answering the most pressing and natural queries of the reader" about the deeper roots of biblical literature in the ancient context.[63] This is interesting because in fact some aspects of

---

[59] Bailey, "Oral Tradition," 9.

[60] Cited in Antony F. Campbell, "The Emergence of the Form-Critical and Traditio-Historical Approaches," *HBOT* 3/2: 125–47 (128).

[61] Hermann Gunkel, *Genesis* (3rd ed., 1910; trans. Mark E. Biddle; repr., Macon, Ga.: Mercer University Press, 1997), vii–lxxxvi.

[62] E.g., whatever Gunkel had to say about "the social dimensions of developing religious ideas" in general, he shared Wellhausen's high estimation of Israel's eighth-century prophets as individuals of special significance. Gerstenberger, "Emergence," 463–65. "What was characteristic of classical prophecy" on this view "was the solitude of the individual." Christopher R. Seitz, "Prophecy in the Nineteenth Century Reception," *HBOT* 3/1:556–81 (563).

[63] James Muilenburg, "Form Criticism and Beyond," *JBL* 88 (1969): 1–18 (2).

Gunkel's proposals about the nature of oral narrative cut against the grain of the source-critical approach. Building on prior work by others on Northern European traditions, for example, Gunkel suggested that one of the general "laws" of oral narrative is "the law of repetition"—that repetition is an intrinsic feature of oral composition. If repetition is already a feature of the narrative artistry of our biblical tradition at a pre-JE stage of the text, however, then it might well be asked how it can function at the same time as an indicator of the *combination* of sources in the text's later stages. This is a particularly pertinent question given that in Gunkel's reconstruction of the tradition history J and E inherit much more from the past than they do in Wellhausen's—they are collectors as much as authors. It is this inherited material that potentially provides much more *access* to the past as well. We are not stuck with J- and E-sources that tell us only about their own time. Units of tradition, larger and smaller, originally preserved orally and then *embedded* in these sources, can be studied as sources themselves for the earlier period to which they relate. Admittedly this cannot be done without difficulty, in Gunkel's view, since the preliterary stages of the traditions cannot be expected to preserve historical memories without significant corruption. Yet we can gain some insight into the religious and other beliefs of those who first shaped and transmitted these traditions. Where Wellhausen engages with his Pentateuchal sources in their particularity, then, asking about their individuality—about what is novel and creative in them—Gunkel stresses the importance of understanding the context out of which J and E emerged and of noting what they transmit from the past that is not genuinely novel or creative at all. We can only understand the particular rhetorical and theological moves they make against this much larger background.

Gunkel himself did not follow through the implications of all this for the source-critical project, and notable figures in German scholarship who followed him—like Gerhard von Rad and Martin Noth (my chapter 18)—continued to treat form and source criticism as allies illuminating different phases of Israel's traditions. Later Scandinavian scholars like Sigmund Mowinckel, on the other hand, would sharply distinguish form and source criticism as methods, arguing that much more of the Israelite tradition was transmitted in oral form than source critics suspected and that there was no need to posit large-scale, written sources behind the Pentateuch at all. They proposed, indeed, that the source critics were guilty of anachronistic thinking both in their emphasis on creative, individualistic authors and in their expectations about the "coherence" of ancient texts. In the ongoing debate about this issue Gunkel's own characterization of Genesis 37–50 as an ancient novella played an important role. If this view was correct, did it not make the JE hypothesis redundant in those chapters—and if in *those* chapters, then what did this do to the entire Documentary Hypothesis?

Rudolf Bultmann

As a young man Rudolf Bultmann (1884–1976) spent two semesters with Gunkel in Berlin in 1904–1905. He famously went on to apply Gunkel's form-critical method to NT studies in his *History of the Synoptic Tradition* (1921), where he classified individual episodes in the Gospels in terms of literary type. His first group comprised "individual sayings," which he subdivided into wisdom or proverbial sayings (e.g., Matt 8:20), prophetic utterances (e.g., Luke 12:54-56), and legal sayings and church rules (Mark 7:6-8). Then, second, there were "pronouncement stories"—short stories about an action of Jesus whose primary purpose was to lead up to a climactic pronouncement on a given topic (e.g., Mark 2:13-17)—and, third, parables (short metaphorical narratives designed to reveal some aspect of the kingdom of God). Bultmann's fourth category comprised speeches (longer connected utterances of Jesus, usually thought to be constructed out of shorter forms; e.g., Matt 5–7). His fifth included miracle stories (healing and nature miracles, as in Luke 7:11-17 and John 2:1-11), and his sixth other historical narratives, myths, or legends (e.g., Luke 2:1-20). He then proposed an original *Sitz im Leben* in the early Church for each genre, before proceeding to reconstruct the history of the entire tradition. For example, pronouncement stories would have been mainly transmitted in popular preaching, miracle stories in Christian apologetic with respect to Greco-Roman beliefs in other "divine" men, and parables during times of popular storytelling. Bultmann judged the historical reliability of certain literary forms with reference to their life setting, especially doubting those genres that seemed colored by the later beliefs of the early Christian community.

One of his foundational presuppositions here was that the teachings of Jesus and the narratives about his life were transmitted orally over a considerable period of time after his death, and independently of each other. Comparison with the oral folk literature of ancient European cultures made it highly likely, then, that the final form in which the Gospels appeared could not be trusted to supply a reliable account of what Jesus actually said and did. In order to recover the historical Jesus one must work backward to the original, pure forms (which he believed to be short, streamlined, unadorned, and strikingly Jewish in style and milieu), recovering in the process an authentic Jesus tradition that had been lost as its oral form was progressively *conformed* to the post-Easter proclamation of the early Church. Bultmann considered parables to be, in the main, well preserved; it was above all here (and in a few eschatological sayings) that the authentic Jesus was to be found. In general, he maintained, a law of increasing distinctness operated in the transmission process. Stories became longer, details were added, and characters identified; they became larger than life as time passed.

REFLECTIONS ON FORM CRITICISM

In discussing in my chapter 4 what it means to read an oral communication or a written text "literally" I already noted the importance of paying attention not only to an author's (or a speaker's) words but also to his or her communicative intent. I illustrated the point with reference to the "Amelia Bedelia" stories of Peggy Parish. What this author is trying to accomplish is not only to teach young children to read the words on the page of a book, but also to encourage them to think about the nature of the language that they are reading. What does it really mean? What are the words trying to accomplish, in terms of description, or command, or whatever? For as Amelia shows us in these books, to misconstrue the communicative intent of words can lead to unfortunate outcomes. It can lead us to believe things that we should not believe, and to do things that we should not do. Parish is engaged in important work, then—the kind of work that parents and schoolteachers do all the way through a child's young life. As we grow up we learn by using our first language and being affirmed or corrected not just what words mean in themselves, but what they mean in sentences, in contexts, and as delivered in particular tones of voice and with accompanying facial expressions. So it is that we gradually become literate people, less and less likely (if our education is adequate) to make mistakes about what other people are really saying to us and what they mean by what they say. And once we are literate we do not even notice that we are, because our ability to "read" what is going on all around us becomes second-nature, just in the way that all of us eventually cease to think about what our fingers are doing when we type on the keyboard of our computer. Reading words well, and understanding what is really being said, becomes an unconscious skill.

So to take an example from near where I currently live in Canada: if Canadians read in a newspaper the headline "Flames Slaughter Oilers," most of us know immediately what is meant and what is not. We do not pause to consider the curiosity of the language: that flames do not typically slaughter but burn. We do not expect as we read on that we shall learn about a fire at an oil refinery. And even though the word "slaughter" implies death, we shall not go looking for dead bodies. We know immediately, without even knowing *how* we know, what this strange text means: that in a recent hockey match a team from Calgary (the Flames) heavily defeated a team from Edmonton (the Oilers). None of this is *said* in the text, but it is nevertheless what the text literally *means*. And we know this because we are literate people. We understand Canadian culture and how communication works within it. We intuitively recognize the *genre*—and therefore we do not misconstrue what we are being told.

The Importance of Genre

Insofar as the form-critical approach to biblical texts is likewise about competent genre-recognition when it comes to communicative acts rooted in ancient Near-Eastern cultural contexts, including the ancient Israelite context, Bible readers committed to "seriously literal interpretation" should warmly embrace it as an important tool in their interpretive toolbox. If not, then we risk category errors in our understanding of biblical communications; we risk making assumptions about what we are reading that have more to do with our expectations on the basis of our own culture and literature than they have to do with any ancient reality. If we wish to estimate the height of a particular mountain peak, Gunkel himself once proposed, then we need to know first the height of the mountain range that it looks down upon.[64] In the same way, understanding a particular text requires that we understand the class of texts of which it forms a part. Comprehending the generic context out of which a text emerges will help us to understand both the conventional constraints under which it operates and the unique elements that it may possess as well. And from the point of view of "reformed" hermeneutics, which holds that God employs fully human language in order to speak to us through Scripture, accurately grasping the genre of particular biblical texts in such a manner helps us in the end to hear the Word of God.

We discern it, for example, as we compare OT *narratives* with analogous literature in the ancient Near East, in terms of both how they were composed and how they "work," and as we deploy these insights as a corrective to any temptation we may face to read Scripture anachronistically. We discern it as we consider what is suggested about the true origin and nature of the Genesis creation and flood stories by their broader literary context in the ancient Near East, and what that means for how we read them. We discern it also as we reflect on what ancient conquest accounts in general tell us about how best to read the conquest account in Joshua—an example already provided in my chapter 4. And it is not just comparison with external literature that is useful as we strive for full comprehension of a particular biblical text. Recognizing patterns *within* OT texts helps us identify those texts as part of the same "set," and in turn the set as a whole aids us in the interpretation of individual examples. In reading our OT *prophetic* books, for example, it is beneficial to understand the different types of prophetic oracles that exist and how they typically begin and end. Identifying segments of text that are formally similar to each other helps us among other things to discover where the boundaries between prophetic oracles within a prophetic book lie. In turn this helps us to make sense of whole sections of prophetic books both against their various historical backgrounds and in their internal

---

[64] O'Neill, *Bible's Authority*, 244.

organization—books that may seem incoherent at first, when their material is simply read consecutively. Great light is cast on the Psalms, likewise, when they are set against the background of similar Babylonian and Egyptian compositions, and it is understood that they fall into categories (e.g., hymns, laments) related in the first instance to the needs of corporate Israelite worship. They represent traditional forms, in other words, even though each possesses its own particular, "creative" elements as well.

In NT studies, too, form criticism helps us to think carefully about the expectations that we bring to the Scriptures, pressing upon us the need to set them in their context when we come to interpret them. With respect to the parables, for example, form criticism has generally strengthened the conviction among scholars that the allegorical reading of such texts that was common in the medieval period—each detail often being compelled to carry great interpretive weight—was wrongheaded. "The parable" as a genre is not intended to be read with such grave attention to its incidental detail; "the parable" is designed only to make one or two central points. Recognizing that the main point of a pronouncement story *is* the pronouncement, likewise, helps the reader to avoid stressing peripheral details. And study of the Gospel miracle stories as a group makes clear that *their* focus is on Christology and the kingdom of God—so that the cursing of the fig tree in Mark 11:12-14 is not primarily a lesson about faith, but rather a symbolic demonstration of impending judgment on Israel. At a larger level form criticism has focused our attention helpfully on what a "Gospel" is—namely, a literary form that is much more similar to the Hellenistic form of "biography" than to anything else (note Luke 1:1-4, in particular), including modern historiography. This helps us to understand the shape of our Gospels. For example, Hellenistic biographers did not feel compelled to describe all the periods of an individual's life, nor to narrate everything about it in chronological order; they selected events in order to teach moral lessons or to promote a particular ideology (or theology). They frequently focused on a person's death, because they believed that the way people died revealed much about their character.

All of this is important. Form criticism can certainly contribute to making us better readers of Scripture—if we take its concerns seriously.

Oral and Written Texts

The reader will have noted, however, that the previous section focuses on *written* texts that we actually possess, whether biblical or extrabiblical. We are no doubt on firm ground in *assuming* that many of these texts are the instantiations of traditions that once circulated in oral form. But is anything to be gained by trying to *reconstruct* these oral traditions and then to reconstruct a history of their development—something that form critics have often wished to accomplish? Is this in the end not just as problematic as source-critical attempts to reconstruct written sources? I believe that it is. In both cases the project is fraught with subjectivism even as objectivity is strongly claimed; it is indeed marked by assumptions that are entirely questionable.

In his Genesis commentary, for example, Gunkel finds various originally separate "legends" about Jacob. At Penuel in Genesis 32 Jacob is the hero who challenges God; in the Jacob-Esau stories he is shrewd, but cowardly; and the Jacob to whom God appears at Bethel is a different person again. However, to demonstrate that Jacob appears in differing *personae* in different parts of Genesis is not to demonstrate that these different parts of the story originally circulated separately—as if the kind of "consistency" for which Gunkel is looking here were demonstrably a feature of ancient (or modern) stories. It is only to draw our attention away—on the basis of unargued assumption—from the interesting, very human portrayal of the complex character Jacob in the present text, who in this moment challenges God and in that moment is shrewd but cowardly. A different example: some early form critics attempted to get all the lament psalms in the OT to conform consistently to the 3+2 (*qinah*) meter that *is* actually often found in these psalms. They did so in the apparent conviction that what they imagined to be the "pure" form of each psalm was also its *original* form. There is, however, no reason to think that ancient Hebrew poets ever felt themselves so narrowly constrained by convention that they would have stuck only to "pure" forms rather than employing convention to suit their own purposes. This case nicely illustrates, in fact, a persistent problem in form-critical research. If source critics have tended to overemphasize the *freedom and creativity* of biblical authors vis-à-vis their environments, form critics have certainly often tended so to stress *convention* that authorial individuality all but disappears. "Pure" forms may never in fact have existed—except in the imagination of the scholars who conceived of them. It may well be better to think of "forms" simply "as a literary 'menu' from which the speaker/author can choose."[65] This is as true of NT as of OT forms. This is no reason to think, with Bultmann, that there were ever short, streamlined, unadorned, and strikingly Jewish pure forms in which the earliest Christian message was communicated[66]—no reason, in fact, to acknowledge a general "law of increasing distinctness" in the transmission process. Studies of oral tradition in analogous cultures close to the time of the NT find no consistent patterns of lengthening or abbreviation as traditions are passed on. And while we are

---

[65] Richard L. Schultz, "Form Criticism and the OT," *DTIB*, 233–37 (234).

[66] "[T]here is no reason why [the Gospel traditions] should not have existed from the beginning in modified or mixed forms." Bauckham, *Jesus and the Eyewitnesses*, 246. For other criticisms of the Bultmann model, see 246–49.

considering Bultmann, there is also no reason to think that the various pericopes now found in our Gospels ever circulated independently of each other.

The reconstructive element of form criticism is not its strongest suit, then, and it is widely regarded nowadays as delivering unconvincing results, often leading to the extreme dissection of the text into a meaningless mass of individual units, each supposedly having its own structure, content, mood, and *Sitz im Leben*—an innately implausible reality, which suggests that there is something deeply wrong with the method at this point. With respect to the NT, for example, "[t]here is no reason to believe that the oral transmission of Jesus traditions in the early church was at all as Bultmann envisaged it."[67] The case is no different, in the end, than in source criticism. A strong suspicion emerges that the "reconstruction" is not a reconstruction at all, but merely a "construction" of the scholar at the heart of the exercise, who evades the text in the course of claiming to discover its more authentic elements. "In the end, the educated and supposedly historically more advanced consciousness rather than the text determines meaning."[68]

Form Criticism and History

To recall Bultmann's work is of course to recall among other things the pronounced historical skepticism that many form critics have combined with their literary analyses, and this brings me to my final comments on the method. It might seem at first sight that form criticism opens up much more possibility of access to the past than Wellhausen's source theory. In reality, however, scholars using the method have often possessed little confidence that the oral traditions now embedded in our biblical literature can deliver real history to us, for at least two reasons: first, many of the traditions were not designed to do so in the first place; and second, even if they once reflected historical events, oral transmission is not reliable when it comes to preserving accounts of the past.

Gunkel understands the genre of the Genesis narratives, for example, to be "legend," and this he differentiates sharply from "history." Legends are passed on orally, history in writing, he maintains; and legends deal with private and family relations, while history deals with public occurrences and matters of political importance. Legend depends on tradition and imagination, history on eyewitnesses and records. Legends frequently report things that are incredible, while history deals with the credible. Finally, legend is poetic, and aims to please, while history is prosaic, and seeks to instruct. Historical memories *can* be preserved in popular tradition of the kind that legend represents, but "uncivilised peoples" are

---

[67] Bauckham, *Jesus and the Eyewitnesses*, 249.
[68] Zimmermann, *Theological Hermeneutics*, 157, on Schleiermacher as anticipating Bultmann.

generally incapable of transmitting reliably the events of their time to posterity. The stories that they tell around the campfire, or hear from professional storytellers during religious festivals, are stories in which experience and imagination intermingle to produce syntheses that are aesthetically pleasing and indeed "true" in a certain sense (i.e., religiously true), but certainly do not represent accurate reflections of the real past. Oral tradition, which cannot remain uncorrupted for any length of time, is simply inadequate to be the vehicle of history. It was this perspective that Bultmann later brought to the NT literature, leading him to confess:

> I do indeed think that we can now know almost nothing concerning the life and personality of Jesus, since the early Christian sources show no interest in either, are moreover fragmentary and often legendary; and other sources about Jesus do not exist.[69]

"What the sources offer us," he goes on to assert, "is first of all the message of the early Christian community, which for the most part the church freely attributed to Jesus."[70]

This kind of approach to text and history is problematic. First of all, Gunkel's attempt to distinguish between legend and history is incoherent, and he managed thereby only to launch his entire form-critical school "on a wild goose chase."[71] History is not always passed on in writing, and many historians have been and still are interested in both public and family/community matters. Does not the historian require imagination, moreover? And how many eyewitnesses does he characteristically use, and why are they more valuable than other kinds of sources? History, for sure, is full of incredible events—incredible at least to those who were first involved in them (e.g., the landing of the first man on the moon). And good history hopes to please as well as to instruct, while legend itself is not without its instructive aspects.

The real distinction between legend and history lies in none of these areas but in communicative intent. Any narrative, *even if* it has formal similarities to a legend, might nevertheless be intended by its author truly to refer to a real past; and there seems little doubt that the author of Genesis in particular so intended his story, at least in Genesis 12–50—along with the great majority of the other biblical narrative's authors.[72] The *form* of a text does not of itself inevitably inform

---

[69] Rudolf Bultmann, *Jesus and the Word* (trans. Louise P. Smith and Erminie H. Lantero; New York: Charles Scribner's Sons, 1958), 8.

[70] Bultmann, *Jesus and the Word*, 12.

[71] Meir Sternberg, *The Poetics of Biblical Narrative: Ideological Literature and the Drama of Reading* (Bloomington: Indiana University Press, 1985), 26.

[72] Provan, Long, and Longman, *Biblical History*, 62–64.

us as to its referential value; the mere fact that, formally speaking, a piece of text is "legend-like" tells us nothing of itself about its historical reference (or nonreference). So with respect to Bultmann's work: it may well be that some of what we find in the Gospels has a formal similarity to a contemporary "myth of the dying and rising god"—but the authors of the Gospel clearly intended to write history, nevertheless, when they described Jesus' death and resurrection.

Second, there are excellent grounds for questioning the frequent form-critical assumption that the process of oral transmission in the case of ancient texts, including biblical texts, inevitably renders them less historical than when they first took shape. Both Gunkel and Bultmann are working in this area with what Kenneth Bailey calls the model of "informal, uncontrolled oral tradition." In this model the community is not very interested in controlling tradition, and consequently there is no formal structure within which it is transmitted from one person to another (e.g., a teacher/student relationship); it is always open to new community creations and additions. But there is also such a thing as "formal, controlled oral tradition"—a model proposed by various Scandinavian scholars in reaction against Gunkel's idea. Here tradition is passed on within formal structures, such as the rabbinic schools of the NT era; each tradition is "partly memorized and partly written down in notebooks and private scrolls."[73] Then there is also Bailey's "informal, controlled oral tradition." This model involves a high degree of formal control, with some fluidity and freedom also possible. In the modern Middle Eastern context in which he lived for a time Bailey saw all three models at work: "rumour transmission," in which small incidents became larger in the retelling; the "memorisation of the entire Qur'an by Muslim sheiks," or of "extensive liturgies in Eastern Orthodoxy";[74] and tradition passed on in villages during evening gatherings where each community consciously preserved its store of tradition.[75]

Here we have two models for the transmission of oral tradition, then, which must be considered (separately, or as two aspects of the same process) alongside the main model employed by Gunkel and Bultmann. Either one, or a mixture of the two,[76] points us in a very different direction with respect to how things might

---

[73] Bailey, "Oral Tradition," 5. See further Bauckham, *Jesus and the Eyewitnesses*, 249–52, for a critically appreciative interaction with "the Scandinavian Alternative."

[74] Bailey, "Oral Tradition," 5.

[75] For a robust response to some unconvincing criticism of Bailey's ideas, see James D. G. Dunn, "Kenneth Bailey's Theory of Oral Tradition: Critiquing Theodore Weeden's Critique," *JSHJ* 7 (2009): 44–62. The "KB thesis," Dunn maintains, explains "better than an exclusively literary model, the enduring character of the Synoptic Jesus tradition—again and again the same event being narrated, the same teaching being passed on, but with diverse detail and differing emphases, in different groupings, sometimes compressed, sometimes extended" (62).

[76] For an extensive discussion, see Bauckham, *Jesus and the Eyewitnesses*, 257–318.

have happened in ancient Israel or in the early Church, and in turn questions the assumption that there is inevitably some great gulf fixed between biblical tradition and the historical events it intends to describe. To put the matter very mildly, there is nothing inevitable about it. There are indeed no strong grounds, even in the case of the very long history of ancient Israel, for doubting the capacity of oral transmission (very likely combined with written transmission; see the comments of Carr earlier in the present chapter) to pass on tradition in a fundamentally reliable manner—retaining what C. S. Lewis once called a story's "particular pattern of events"—even while presenting it in a variety of ways.[77] When it comes to the Gospels—which were composed in written form such a short time (relatively) after the events they describe—the grounds for doubt diminish still further. This is all the more the case when we consider the important role that eyewitnesses had in "controlling" Christian tradition in the period prior to the writing of our current Gospels.[78]

CONCLUSION

Insofar as the original source- and form-critical project was about going "behind the Biblical text" with a view to "dismantling it into its original sources, dating these, and rewriting Biblical history on the basis of this analysis" (the first epigraph to the present chapter), we must conclude that it has not been successful. For all sorts of reasons its diverse "results" do not inspire confidence. This is important news in the context of the hermeneutical project articulated in this book. For if the source and form critics had succeeded, the *storied* account of ancient Israel in the Bible—and indeed of Jesus and his Church—would have been found to have little to do with the *real* world of ancient history "discovered" by scientific method. The eclipse of biblical narrative would be complete, except insofar as even fiction can communicate truth. But it seems that with respect to the biblical literature we must indeed largely "be satisfied with the soup that is set before us, and not desire to see the bones of the ox out of which it has been boiled" (the second epigraph to the present chapter)—even though we are fairly sure that bones once existed, and we can imagine how interesting it might be to contemplate them.

The journey behind the text has not been entirely in vain, however, since it has certainly cast important light on how to eat the soup. It has underlined the reality that our biblical texts do indeed come *from* somewhere (other than from God); that in this "somewhere" people spoke and wrote in particular languages

---

[77] Provan, Long, and Longman, *Biblical History*, 69–83.
[78] Bauckham, *Jesus and the Eyewitnesses*, passim. "One reason Gospels were written was to maintain this accessibility and function of the eyewitnesses beyond their lifetimes" (308).

in accordance with particular conventions, and passed on tradition in particular customary ways; and that we must pay careful attention to these realities as we seek to interpret Scripture well. This is what historical criticism at its best does for "reformed" biblical interpreters—and even if it *is* being practiced outside of a confessional, theological context. Rather than creating the text that the critic would *prefer* to have, it provides us with historical background that illuminates the text that is actually *there*—the text that is of central interest to "reformed" hermeneutics.[79] The fact that historical criticism has quite often not *been* "at its best" is not really the point.

---

[79] Kevin J. Vanhoozer, "Lost in Interpretation: Truth, Scripture, and Hermeneutics," *JETS* 48 (2005): 89–114 (104–5).

18

REDACTION AND RHETORICAL CRITICISM
The Persuasive Text

> *It is now generally recognised that the evangelists were not merely "scissors and paste men." On the contrary the "scissors" were manipulated by a theological hand, and the "paste" was impregnated with a particular theology.*
>
> —Robert Stein[1]

> War and Peace *now has less war, more peace—and significantly fewer words.* . . .
> "This is authentic Tolstoy," [the new edition's publisher] said.
> "To read this text is pure pleasure. I don't understand how we could have kept reading that [conventional] one."
>
> —Vancouver Sun[2]

The middle decades of the twentieth century saw a resurgence of interest among modern historical-critical scholars in the biblical texts as we actually have them, and this is evident in the emergence of redaction criticism. Here the focus shifts away from the oral forms or written sources that lie behind the text (although these are still important) to the later or perhaps even final stages of the formation of tradition. At the center of attention now is what redactors (i.e., editors) did with their sources and why: as they transmitted the earlier material, what were they trying to accomplish? What did they wish to *say*? In redaction criticism, then, the editorial task is taken much more seriously than previously. Over against a tendency in source and form criticism to view the editors of earlier tradition as mindless functionaries, sticking together bits and pieces of inherited material in a thoughtless and rather clumsy way—"scissors and paste men," in the words of the first epigraph above—redaction critics see them as genuinely creative people in their own right, each consciously shaping tradition in order to

---

[1] Robert H. Stein, "What Is Redaktionsgeschichte?," *JBL* 88 (1969): 45–56 (46).
[2] The story was published on February 5, 2000, under the headline: "New Edition of Tolstoy Classic Is Reputed to Be First Draft of Novel."

communicate his own message. Redaction criticism is thus allied to rhetorical criticism, to which we shall turn later in this chapter.³

REDACTION CRITICISM AND GENESIS–KINGS

Like source and form criticism, redaction criticism emerged in the first instance in the context of the study of the Pentateuch (or Hexateuch). The occasion of its emergence is well described in an important work published in 1938 by the German OT scholar Gerhard von Rad (1901–1971): "The Form-Critical Problem of the Hexateuch."

GERHARD VON RAD

The theological study of the Hexateuch, von Rad asserts in the opening pages of this book, has "reached a position of stalemate which many view with considerable anxiety":

> So far as the analysis of source documents is concerned, there are signs that the road has come to a dead end. Some would say that we have already gone too far. On the other hand, in the examination of isolated passages, with regard to both their content and their literary form, we must frankly admit that we have by no means done all that might have been done. But in this field, too, controversy has ceased, and it may be said without exaggeration that scholars, especially the younger ones, are weary of research in hexateuchal studies.⁴

The reason for this weariness is that both source and form criticism lead "inevitably further and further away from the final form of the text as we have it." In fact, "[o]n almost all sides the final form of the Hexateuch has come to be regarded as a starting-point barely worthy of discussion, from which the debate should move away as rapidly as possible in order to reach the real problems underlying it."⁵

Von Rad takes this situation as his own starting point for the development of a fresh approach, which begins with a brief summary of the contents of the Hexateuch and its "statements of belief" (e.g., "God, who created the world, called the first ancestors of Israel and promised them the land of Canaan"). The Hexateuch recounts a "history of redemption." Certainly this history has passed through earlier stages of development—but the essential "creed" that comes to expression

---

³ Nowadays redaction criticism can also be called "composition criticism" in order to emphasize that it is not only what the redactor changed, but also what he retained, that is important for understanding his message. Grant R. Osborne, "Redaction Criticism," *DTIB*, 663–66 (664).

⁴ Gerhard von Rad, "The Form-Critical Problem of the Hexateuch," in *The Problem of the Hexateuch and Other Essays* (trans. E. W. Trueman Dicken; New York: McGraw-Hill, 1966), 1–78 (1).

⁵ Von Rad, "Problem," 1.

in it has not changed. What has changed is only "the external expression, the outward form; and not only this external appearance, but above all the degree of theological penetration and manipulation of the traditional deposit."[6] Von Rad sets out, then, to trace the development of the whole tradition, with this creed at its unchanging heart, from the beginning to "the final and conclusive form of the Hexateuch."[7]

His focus is not so much on the forms and sources themselves but on the redactor who he thinks gives the Hexateuch its foundational shape, which others then build upon. This redactor he identifies as the "source" J. Von Rad tries to trace the origin of the framework that the J-narrative gave to the individual traditions he inherited to show how J used these traditions to his own ends. He argues that the short "creeds" that are found in places like Deuteronomy 6:20-24, 26:5-9, and Joshua 24:2-13, are most likely once to have been early confessions of faith used during acts of worship. The earliest, most basic summaries do not mention the covenant making and law giving at Sinai. These items were woven in later, as the summaries were expanded to include traditions from various tribal and regional sources. Traditions once used in the religious cult were thus desacralized and connected into a great national epic. The traditions are old—J does not invent them, and he indeed is faithful to their fundamental shape. He does however create something new out of them: a coherent account of the history of his people that sets the story line that the later authors E and P follow.

Martin Noth

Von Rad's German colleague Martin Noth (1902–1968) essentially agreed with the main points in this presentation (although he also thought rather different thoughts about the whole nature of Genesis–Kings, to which we shall return in a moment). In his 1948 work *A History of Pentateuchal Traditions*, however, he went further than von Rad in seeking to understand the development of the Pentateuchal material from originally short narrative units and lists, to larger narrative complexes, and eventually to a great national history.[8] In this process Noth argued for the importance of five great themes that he posited had served as "magnets" that attracted other material so as to form the foundational tradition (*Grundlage*). These themes are the promise to the patriarchs, the exodus from Egypt, the wandering in the wilderness, the revelation at Mount Sinai, and the entry into the land. Observing its repeated and often independent appearance in statements of faith scattered throughout the OT, Noth hypothesized that the exodus theme

---

[6] Von Rad, "Problem," 3.
[7] Von Rad, "Problem," 3.
[8] Martin Noth, *A History of Pentateuchal Traditions* (trans. Bernhard W. Anderson; Englewood Cliffs, N.J.: Prentice Hall, 1972).

formed the primary element in Israel's confession of faith; this was the kernel of the whole subsequent tradition. To this was then added the theme of the entry into the land. These two themes were central to the early gatherings of the various tribal groups of Israel at a central sanctuary in the land of Canaan. The promise to the patriarchs was added next, and then the wilderness wandering. Finally, the Sinai theme was incorporated. The traditions were first combined together during the Judges period, and the resulting *Grundlage* formed the basis for both J and E. Noth's work represents a full exploration of the history of the tradition in Genesis through Numbers, taking it all the way from original units of tradition, passed on in various contexts, to the epic history that we now see before us.[9]

Noth stops in Numbers because, unlike von Rad and much German scholarship prior to him, he did not believe in a Hexateuch. Noth saw Wellhausen's documentary sources as only underlying a "Tetrateuch" (i.e., the first four books of the Bible); he did not believe that JE and P ran all the way into the book of Joshua, nor (as some did) that they ran even further into Judges, Samuel, and Kings. He understood Deuteronomy–Kings, rather, as a self-standing "work" of its own. Others had already laid the groundwork for his view—scholars like Hugo Gressmann (1877–1927), who had published a short commentary on Samuel and Kings in 1910 arguing that we must interpret the individual narratives in these books by themselves, in accordance with Gunkel's form-critical method; and Leonhard Rost (1896–1979), who had published in 1926 a detailed study of the literary structure and purpose of 2 Samuel 9–20 and 1 Kings 1–2, arguing that it forms a unified story (a "succession narrative") explaining why Solomon succeeded to the throne of Israel. Here we see a growing awareness that in 1–2 Samuel at least we possess extended collections of stories formed into a connected history at a comparatively early period and connected and shaped *with intent* so that they could serve particular religious or political ends. The form-critical work of Albrecht Alt (1883–1956) on the book of Joshua was also decisive for Noth, who published a commentary on the same book in 1938. Noth became convinced that Joshua comprises a number of originally quite independent traditions: lists of tribal boundaries and cities, for example (Josh 13–19, following Alt), and stories (Joshua 3–9) that have local reference and are etiological in character (that is, they arose in order to explain certain features of topography and local cultic practice). There was in fact no evidence of J and E in Joshua at all, Noth argued; Alt had already questioned in a series of articles the presence of P.

In due course this led Noth to articulate his famous hypothesis of the Deuteronomistic History.[10] Joshua through Kings, he proposed, had first been composed out of individual "pockets" of tradition (like Rost's Succession Narrative)

---

[9] See especially his summary in Noth, *Pentateuchal Traditions*, 228–51.
[10] Martin Noth, *The Deuteronomistic History* (Sheffield: JSOT Press, 1981).

that had not previously been combined into one piece of work; there was no single continuous source underlying these books. The person responsible for the combination, then (the Deuteronomist), was not merely the editor of a history that already existed from Genesis onward; he was the *author* of a history that began with Deuteronomy and was linked to the first four books of the Bible only at a later stage. This is a *Deuteronomistic* History because its language and style and indeed its outlook are those of Deuteronomy. For example, Deuteronomy threatens that disobedience to its laws will lead to the eventual loss of the land by the Israelites, and this theme recurs in Joshua 23, 1 Samuel 12, and 2 Kings 17 (to name but three passages).

Why was the history composed at all? Noth hypothesized that it was put together during the exile by someone who shared Deuteronomy's outlook on the world and God's relation to it and wanted to explain Israel's eventual downfall in those terms. At some later stage, various other bits and pieces of tradition (e.g., Judg 1 and 17–21, which are clearly very different in style from the remainder) were added to the Deuteronomistic History to bring it to its present state, and the whole entity was divided into the separate books that we encounter now.

INITIAL REFLECTIONS: FIRST AND SECOND CHRONICLES

From the perspective of "seriously literal interpretation" there is nothing problematic about the idea that many of the biblical texts as we find them now have been redacted. Redaction is an intrinsic feature of textual life generally, especially where texts have a long life over time and it becomes necessary to explain some aspects of them to new readers, or to update them in certain ways, or even to revise them in the light of new information. The *Sitz im Leben* of the reader or the reading community changes in some way, and changes are made in the text that take account of this reality—second thoughts, clarifications, corrections, amplifications, and so on.

Redaction is also an inevitable feature of the composition of texts, whether ancient or modern, where the author is working from sources. Burnett Streeter provides a good example of the dynamics involved in describing a time when he was asked to write with a friend a biographical sketch of the "Indian St. Francis" Sadhu Sundar Singh.[11] The authors, he reports, "had to rely upon a collection of printed and manuscript material"[12] as well as their own recollections and the recollections of others about the great man. That is, they had to rely on written sources and oral tradition. As to written sources they had before them two brief,

---

[11] Burnett H. Streeter, *The Four Gospels: A Study of Origins* (London: Macmillan, 1927), 191–95.

[12] Streeter, *Four Gospels*, 192.

overlapping biographies written in India, as well as three different collections of the Sadhu's talks delivered in different countries and various newspaper reports. Because the Sadhu repeated the same content on different occasions they often found parallel versions of the same material. Their challenge, then, was to combine into a single work materials deriving "from a number of disconnected, independent, but to a large extent overlapping, sources."[13] After the book had been completed Streeter realized "that circumstances had forced us [the authors] to devise ways of dealing with our materials having the closest analogy to those which criticism suggests were habitually employed by editors in antiquity."[14] They began by identifying "the central ideas and leading topics to which the Sadhu most frequently recurred"[15] and arranging the materials from the different sources under headings corresponding to these main ideas so as to present in the Sadhu's own words a coherent account of his teaching on particular topics. Faced with differing versions of the same story or saying they typically selected "what seemed the freshest and most original version"[16]—but sometimes they worked other details or phrases into the selected version, conflating two and sometimes three parallel accounts. Inevitably, particularly given the costs of book production, they omitted a lot of material. They also amended the Sadhu's grammar and style wherever it seemed necessary, since his knowledge of English was limited. As this example illustrates, composition often involves editing. In this kind of project, indeed, "some such editorial methods are forced upon an author who wishes to present the reader with a biographical portrait rather than a chaotic mass of disconnected *obiter dicta*."[17]

Redaction is an intrinsic feature of textual life generally—and there is every reason to think that it was also an intrinsic feature of the life of many biblical texts right from the beginning. Certainly it is clearly evident in a number of them, including 1–2 Chronicles.

Chronicles Compared with Samuel–Kings

Readers of 1–2 Chronicles who have the books of Samuel and Kings open at the same time will notice a strong similarity between much of the material as to content and often wording. This has led the great majority of modern scholars to the view (and I concur in this) that 1–2 Chronicles depend on Samuel–Kings as their primary source. The author of Chronicles ("the Chronicler"), however, is evidently not interested in reproducing the entirety of this source. Having opened

---

[13] Streeter, *Four Gospels*, 192.
[14] Streeter, *Four Gospels*, 192–93.
[15] Streeter, *Four Gospels*, 193.
[16] Streeter, *Four Gospels*, 193.
[17] Streeter, *Four Gospels*, 194.

with multiple genealogical lists (in 1 Chr 1–9) that track the history of Israel in the briefest possible form from the beginning of the world down to the period of the return from exile (note, e.g., 1 Chr 3:1-24, which brings the Davidic line well down into the postexilic period beyond Zerubbabel), the Chronicler dives into the story of the monarchy only where 1 Samuel reports the death of King Saul (cf. 1 Sam 31 and 1 Chr 10). The remainder of 1 Chronicles is given over to an account of the reign of David, much of which parallels material in 2 Samuel.

First Chronicles differs from 2 Samuel, however, in *adding* certain things (e.g., new material in chapters 22–29 describing various worship arrangements made by King David), and in *omitting* other things (e.g., all the ground covered by 2 Sam 1–4 describing David's reign over Judah alone). The careful reader will further note various alterations in the *ordering* of the material when compared with 2 Samuel, and many small changes to the wording. First Chronicles 20 illustrates nicely a number of these features as we compare it with 2 Samuel 11–21—and it also begins to press upon us the question of editorial rationale. Here we immediately notice some huge omissions. The David/Bathsheba incident is entirely omitted, as is all of Absalom's revolt and its aftermath and the story at the beginning of 2 Samuel 21 about the death of Saul's relatives. Why should the Chronicler have done this? Is this an attempt to absolve David of blame? Or is it that he simply has no interest in these political or personal stories within the context of what he is trying to do? Then there are some interesting small differences in the material that *does* parallel 2 Samuel. The Samuel account emphasizes, for example, that David did what kings were not supposed to do: he sent everyone away to war while he stayed at home (in order to bed Bathsheba?). The Chronicler's account does not stress that everyone left Jerusalem except David (since he is not going to tell us the story of Bathsheba; cf. 2 Sam 11:1 and 1 Chr 20:1). Later, "Gob" in 2 Samuel 21:18 is replaced in 1 Chronicles 20:4 with "Gezer." This may either be a deliberate change for reasons of clarity, or a result of textual corruption (the words are very similar in Hebrew). Later again, "Goliath" in 2 Samuel 21:19 has been replaced by "the brother of Goliath" in 1 Chronicles 20:5—possibly another example of textual corruption,[18] but possibly also an attempt to resolve the apparent contradiction between 1 Samuel 17:7 and 2 Samuel 21:19. Finally, the Chronicler omits in 1 Chronicles 20:8 the reference to the "four" giants in 2 Samuel 21:22. This is because he has omitted the battle story found in 2 Samuel 21:15-17 in which a Philistine giant by the name of Ishbibenob attacks a tired David, who escapes only because Abishai rescues him. So there are not "four" giants in the Chronicler's account—there are only three.

---

[18] Provan, Long, and Longman, *Biblical History*, 293–97.

The Chronicler as Redactor

As we ponder this kind of evidence throughout 1–2 Chronicles it is clear that the Chronicler is editing his source in order to tell his own story; he is not simply adding some information to it (as the LXX title for Chronicles implies: *Paraleipomenon*, "the things omitted"). Partly he seems intent on making the earlier tradition intelligible to his readers, and partly he wants to draw out what he considers to be its most important meaning for them. He assumes *knowledge* of the prior tradition, but he passes it on in a fresh way to his contemporaries. What was he trying to say? What was his agenda? Working from the data that we have, we deduce first that he was very interested in the unity of the people of Israel as a twelve-tribe entity; he passes over hints of the later division between north and south in his accounts of David and Solomon, for example, stressing the participation of "all Israel" in the major events of the time. Second, he emphasizes the theme of the kingdom of God, connecting it closely with kingship in Israel. He emphasizes, third, the temple and its worship; the temple stands at the center of the Israelite community, which is as much a single community of faith as it is two ancient political states. Finally, the Chronicler draws attention even more than the "Deuteronomist" to the way in which the justice of God works out in the world, such that the righteous are blessed and the wicked punished within their own lifetimes.[19] These interests make perfect sense in a work dating from the postexilic period, when the whole issue of "who is now a true Israelite?" was very much a live one in a context where the Israelites no longer possessed either a king or a state and where many were apparently asking whether they still carried a burden of guilt on behalf of their ancestors or were now capable of being blessed by God if they obeyed his will. The Chronicler retells the story of Israel in order to address his contemporaries in this new situation, editing older source texts with particular purposes in mind. The perspective of 1–2 Chronicles differs from that of 1–2 Samuel and 1–2 Kings precisely because the *Sitz im Leben* is different.[20]

FURTHER THOUGHTS

Redaction is certainly a reality in 1–2 Chronicles, then, and the redaction-critical approach illuminates their reading. In other texts, too, it is fairly evident that redaction has occurred (even though we do not actually possess the extant sources), and the hypothesis that (as in Chronicles) there was a *point* to the exercise also illuminates the content of the text. Isaiah 2:2-5, for example, is a famously hopeful oracle about the future of Jerusalem and indeed the world. It

---

[19] H. G. M. Williamson, *1 and 2 Chronicles* (NCB; London: Marshall, Morgan & Scott, 1982), 24–33.

[20] Williamson, *1 and 2 Chronicles*, 15–17.

is followed by a series of judgment oracles in Isaiah 2:6–4:1 that are uniformly negative in tone; yet Isaiah 4:2-6 is once again a positive, hopeful prophecy. In other words, the two prophecies of hope appear to function as "bookends" to the oracles of judgment. This is apparently one aspect of a larger strategy in Isaiah 2–12 overall—the first main section of the book (signaled by the opening words of chapters 2 and 13). The redactor wishes us to read the fierce judgment oracles throughout this section of Isaiah in the context of optimistic oracles about ultimate outcomes. Read this material on the judgment of Israel, he suggests, in the context of these promises of hope not just for Israel but also for the world. This is his construal of the significance of the ministry of Isaiah as a whole. So if we want to know what Isaiah himself said, in particular places and at particular times back in the eighth century BC, form criticism will help us get at this reality (my chapter 17). But if we want some overall feel for the message of Isaiah in toto— the significance of what Isaiah was about *in general*—then we shall have to turn to redaction criticism, which asks intelligent questions about why certain oracles in our prophetic books are grouped together in the way they are, and what the overall intention is.

Redaction, Perspective, and Agenda

It is obvious, of course, that when we are operating inductively like this our level of confidence in our redaction-critical reading will correlate directly with the level of confidence we have in the objective reality of the traditions to which (we are proposing) the redactor had access. Not every particular redactional hypothesis inspires confidence in this regard; some of them are at the very least debatable, and some of them are positively unlikely. Quite a few are vulnerable to the criticism that their starting points in the process of textual composition they claim to be describing are in fact quite beyond demonstration. This is true for example of von Rad's hypothesis about the Pentateuch and its "creeds." We simply cannot know if the short historical creeds at the heart of his theory are truly as old as he claims, originally functioned in the way he suggests, or can be hung along a developmental timeline of the kind that he has in mind. I noted already in chapter 17 the general problem with the form-critical idea that "shorter is earlier." In the von Rad (and Noth) case it is worth asking in particular whether summaries necessarily always refer to everything that their authors know about. Does the *prominence* of the Exodus "confession," for example, have anything at all to say about its *chronological priority* in terms of Israelite tradition? More generally, if the Documentary Hypothesis rests on weak foundations (my chapter 17 again) then what von Rad has to say about J as redactor is undermined, since the existence of J comes into question. Similar difficulties arise in the case of Noth's Deuteronomistic History. He builds on preexisting theories such as Rost's idea of a self-standing Succession Narrative; but it is not at all clear that such an entity ever existed.[21]

However, we need not endorse every particular redactional theory in order to recognize the value of the approach in general, especially in the way that it underlines the importance of the question of *perspective* and *agenda* in our reading of biblical texts—the question of *why* the text is shaped in just this way and not another, and what that has to do with its meaning. Form criticism invites us to consider the genre of a text: what sort of text it is, and what we may expect from it. Redaction criticism goes beyond this, inviting us to consider the particular orientation of a text: what is it trying to say in construing the tradition it inherits in *this* particular way? Pre-Reformation biblical interpretation often failed to engage these questions of perspective and agenda, since it was not very interested in the particularity of the biblical texts as human productions: it was enough to know that the inspired text came from God. Interestingly, modern historical-critical biblical scholars ("first way" Protestants) have also often shown scant regard for these questions, at least when it comes to the *redaction* of biblical texts, because they have so often believed that editorial perspective (and agenda) is part of what corrupts the original purity of texts as witnesses to historical or sociological reality. Their goal has been to get behind perspective and agenda to "reality" (to real sources giving us access to real history). Here the perceived insufficiency of the inspired text prompts reconstruction. Even more interestingly, modern "third way" Protestants, who have typically strongly rejected "first way" reconstructionist approaches, have nevertheless often agreed with them that human "perspective" and "agenda" in the text are a problem. They have taken this view, however, because their particular ideas about the divine inspiration of Scripture make little space for such realities.[22] One consequence has been quite implausible attempts to harmonize the Gospels, aimed at removing what are considered to be "discrepancies" between them.[23] The insufficiency of the inspired text in this case prompts *construction*—essentially of a fifth Gospel alongside the other four. The lasting contribution of redaction criticism in the modern period has been to help us to see clearly that biblical texts do indeed possess perspective and agenda—that each is written from a point of view and has a particular message to communicate. And if we cannot reconstruct fully or even partially the sources that biblical redactors

---

[21] See my chapter 20 below.

[22] E.g., Robert L. Thomas, "Redaction Criticism," in *The Jesus Crisis: The Inroads of Historical Criticism into Evangelical Scholarship* (ed. Robert L. Thomas and F. David Farnell; Grand Rapids: Kregel, 1998), 261: "the three synoptists wrote without depending on each other in a literary way. To conclude otherwise raises questions about their integrity and ultimately about the inspiration of the three Synoptic Gospels."

[23] E.g., Lindsell, *Battle for the Bible*, who invents six denials of Jesus by Peter in order to avoid "discrepancies" between the various Gospel accounts (174–76).

used, we must nevertheless take the fact of perspective and agenda seriously in our interpretation of their texts. This is really nothing other than the recovery of a genuinely Reformation approach to Scripture—to the inspiration of Scripture and its entailments and nonentailments, as much as anything—which was itself rooted in the recovery of ancient understandings of rhetoric to which we shall shortly turn. It is on the other hand absolutely not in line with a Reformation approach to fail to take seriously what are clearly some of the intrinsic realities of Scripture on the ground that they "cannot" be there.

Matthew as Redactor

Before we do turn to rhetoric, however, let us consider a further case where redaction criticism clearly illuminates what a biblical text is saying—what God's Word to us in it *is*—precisely because it focuses on the perspective of its human author. Here I want to introduce a classic little essay by the German NT scholar Günther Bornkamm (1905–1990), first published in 1948, that is commonly regarded as launching the redaction-critical movement in NT studies.[24]

Bornkamm's interest in this essay lies in the story of the stilling of the storm in Matthew's Gospel (8:23-27) in comparison to Mark (4:35-41) and Luke (8:22-25), who both report the story in the same context, and in more or less the same form. Matthew, however, handles the pericope very differently from his two colleagues. First of all, he connects the miracle stories in Mark 1-2 and 4-5 (Bornkamm assumes Markan priority) with the Sermon on the Mount, taking "the nature miracle of the stilling of the storm ... out of a biographical context" and inserting it into a series of texts consisting predominantly of healing miracles.[25] Matthew does this in order to present to the reader the "Messiah of the deed" after the "Messiah of the word" (Matt 5–7).[26] Second, he places before the storm story (uniquely) two sayings about discipleship (Matt 8:19-22): a warning against an "unconsidered decision" to follow, and a summons to "radical decisiveness" in following (Gk. *akolouthein*).[27] He follows these sayings with a statement unparalleled in the other two gospels (Matt 8:23): "[Jesus] got into the boat and his disciples *followed* him" (same verb, *akolouthein*). Matthew thus interprets the journey of the disciples with Jesus in the storm, and the stilling of the storm itself, as an episode in the life of discipleship.[28]

---

[24] Günther Bornkamm, "The Stilling of the Storm in Matthew," in *Tradition and Interpretation in Matthew* (ed. Günther Bornkamm, Gerhard Barth, and Heinz Joachim Held; Philadelphia: Westminster, 1963), 52–57.

[25] Bornkamm, "Storm," 53.

[26] Bornkamm, "Storm," 53.

[27] Bornkamm, "Storm," 54.

[28] Bornkamm, "Storm," 55.

Various other details in Matthew's version of the story, third, agree with this interpretation. Only in Matthew's Gospel is the disciples' cry for help a prayer (Matt 8:25): "Lord (Gk. *kurie*), save us!" Bornkamm shows from elsewhere in Matthew that *kurie* has a divine sense—it indicates here in Matthew 8 "a confession of discipleship."[29] In Matthew, moreover, the miracle of the stilling of the storm comes *after* the rebuke to the disciples (Matt 8:26) rather than *before* it (as in Mark and Luke). It is in the midst of danger that Jesus draws attention to their lack of faith. Matthew uses for this lack of faith the Greek word *holigopistia*, which is a favorite of his: "apart from Luke 12:28, he is the only evangelist to use it."[30] This *holigopistia* denotes faith that is too weak, too paralyzed by anxiety, to withstand the pressure of demonic powers. The storm for Matthew is therefore representative of the life of discipleship as a whole. This reality is underlined by the choice of language for the storm itself in Matthew 8:24. "A great earthquake (Gk. *seismos*) happened on the sea," he tells us—unusual Greek for a storm at sea, but language that often occurs in Scripture when apocalyptic events are described (e.g., Matt 24:7; Rev 6:12). The need of the disciples in the midst of the storm is symbolic of the distresses involved in discipleship overall. Finally, we should note that in Matthew 8:27 it is the "men" who are "amazed" by all this—not (explicitly) the disciples (represented simply by "they" in Mark and Luke). Bornkamm suggests that this is intended to broaden the significance of the story still further, inviting other people to "imitation and discipleship."[31]

Bornkamm moves toward the conclusion of his essay by reminding his readers about the results of form-critical research, and advocating a movement beyond them while not abandoning them:

> In more recent Synoptic investigation we have learned to look upon the single pericope, the single saying and the single deed of Jesus as the primary data of tradition and to regard context and framework of the single pericopes on the other hand as secondary. We do not propose to attack these conclusions. It will be necessary to be more careful, however, than has generally been the case up to the present, to enquire also about the motives in the composition of the individual Gospels.[32]

It is beyond question, he concedes, that "the evangelists worked to a large extent simply as collectors and often arranged the individual portions of the tradition according to relatively superficial points of view."[33] However, sometimes we see evi-

---

[29] Bornkamm, "Storm," 55.
[30] Bornkamm, "Storm," 56.
[31] Bornkamm, "Storm," 56.
[32] Bornkamm, "Storm," 56–57.
[33] Bornkamm, "Storm," 57.

dence of definite theological intentionality. This story, in Matthew's Gospel, is one such place.

More recent NT scholarship has found even more reason than Bornkamm to dispute the contention that "the evangelists worked ... simply as collectors." On the contrary, they are clearly exegetes and theologians as well, and if we are to understand the distinctive message of each we must work in the first instance within the individual Gospels themselves, discerning how their authors used their material and for what purpose. Only thus can we arrive at an overall view of what "the Gospels" testify about Jesus' life, death, and resurrection—a properly multiperspectival view that honors God's decision to inspire four Gospels *rather than* just one. Clearly, four are needed. It is *profoundly* to miss the point, then, if we simply collapse these various perspectives into one in pursuit of a text that conforms better to some predigested doctrine of Scripture that we happen to hold—a doctrine of Scripture that obviously cannot have been drawn from Scripture itself. In "reformed" hermeneutics it is the Gospels in their particularity that are to be regarded as inspired, trustworthy testimony to the past that has the function of guiding Bible readers in matters of faith and life. All four need to be read, with due attention to their similarity to *and* their difference from each other. We do not need to hold a particular view of their chronological order (Markan priority or not) in order to understand this necessity.

THE RECOVERY OF RHETORIC

If we have learned from modern source criticism to think about biblical literature in terms of the *processes* of composition that produced it, and if form criticism has both enlarged the scope of our thinking about these processes and reminded us of the need to take *genre* seriously in biblical interpretation, then redaction criticism has urged us also to consider the processes' end point. It is indeed most interested in the text that we actually have, and not primarily in reconstructions. Rhetorical criticism shares the same interest. What are authors doing with the tradition that they inherit in order to communicate their particular message to their audience? At one end of the spectrum of rhetorical critical work, in fact, this approach to the text tends to become somewhat uninterested in "process issues" altogether. It wants to know simply "how texts work." What is distinctive about rhetorical criticism in any case is its self-conscious retrieval, at least in the case of our NT literature, of classical rhetorical resources from the past to help it do its job.

Rhetoric and Its Enemies

The use and the study of rhetoric is of course something that predates by many, many centuries the modern interest in rhetoric that is evident in the discipline of biblical studies.[34] It first flourished (so far as we know) in ancient Greece—in the Homeric tradition, and then among the great rhetoricians of fifth- and fourth-century Athens. The Romans inherited the mantle of Greece in this respect as in many others and produced great orators like Cicero and Quintilian. The Church Fathers everywhere demonstrate their own rhetorical skills and interests, from Tertullian to Augustine (see especially my chapter 8 on Augustine). Later, in a European Renaissance marked so greatly by a general revival of interest in the classical era, we find intense preoccupation with rhetoric, as illustrated (for example) in the writings of Shakespeare and (in biblical studies) Erasmus, who published rhetorical analyses of 1–2 Corinthians. As we have seen, the magisterial Reformers also took rhetoric very seriously in their own study of Scripture (see especially my chapter 4); Melanchthon, for example, offered rhetorical analyses of Romans and Galatians.

Even as the importance of rhetoric has long been recognized, however, its potential downside has also been noted. Throughout Western history since classical times we can indeed trace a consistent line of thinking that considers rhetoric to be an instrument of dubious morality. It is mere bombast, high-sounding words without content that serve falsification. At best it is only literary ornamentation, minimally related to content. We find such sentiments expressed already in Socrates and Plato, who stress truth and logic over against rhetorical flourish and thereby define themselves over against the Sophists of their own time whom they represent as divorcing art from truth. These Sophists were in the business of training people in the verbal skills at the heart of effective public speaking. They were apparently not especially interested in the use that their disciples made of this education—whether they told the truth, or promoted virtue. Indeed, the Sophists appear to have held a cynical view of any claims to objective truth and virtue at all, presenting these as relating only to social conventions within given societies. The purpose of rhetoric was simply to win people over to whichever point of view the rhetorician wished to promote. Questions of right and wrong, good and bad, were irrelevant.

It stands to reason that anyone who believes that truth and virtue are grounded in objective reality would necessarily reject this approach to rhetoric—whether in ancient times or in the present. For on this view, art is essentially manipulation. Rhetoric is not about *representing* the world truthfully to other people, but about *distracting* them from it, often with an ulterior motive. People seeking truth and virtue must therefore resist its powerful effects and keep their eye on the ball, as it were. For whether back then or now we encounter all around us rhetorical art designed to manipulate in the pursuit of power (e.g., political

---

[34] Phyllis Trible, *Rhetorical Criticism: Context, Method and the Book of Jonah* (Minneapolis: Fortress, 1994), 5–24.

rhetoric), or profit (e.g., advertising), or prestige (e.g., self-advertising), or simply to transport us out of the world for a while and help us forget what it is really like (e.g., Hollywood, anticipated in Longinus' ancient work *On the Sublime*, which is all about taking the audience out of themselves by affecting their feelings).[35] Much of this art is evidently at odds with truth and virtue. A politician both misrepresents contemporary reality and misleads us as to the benefits of his plan to improve on it; an advertisement tries to overwhelm us with attractive images so that we will not listen to the voiceover telling us the hundred ways in which the advertised drug can kill us; and the latest famous narcissist tries to sell us a thoroughly distorted image of herself so that she will garner the admiration that she craves. In short, suspicion of rhetoric is often thoroughly justified. We often need to try to penetrate behind it in order to get at the True and the Good, if it is there to be found at all.

When it comes to the reading of the Bible, much of the academic biblical scholarship of the late nineteenth and the early twentieth centuries was of course driven by a conviction that *in the biblical text itself* as we now have it, rhetorical art likewise obscures the True and the Good. Art gets in the way of science, and of history or theology conceived as science, and the artfully constructed literary forms in which our biblical texts now appear must therefore be disregarded. The point was to get behind the text to the real history of Israel and the Church and to the real message of the Bible—not to pay attention to the distorting rhetoric of the current text, which was close cousin to the distorting effects of redaction more generally. This greatly helps to explain the decline of interest in rhetoric in biblical studies in the early period of modern biblical scholarship after so much attention to it in the preceding centuries. It is not an accident, in other words, that rhetorical criticism was such a relative latecomer to the modern biblical-critical party (as we shall see below). It is a direct consequence of the fact that in the minds of many late nineteenth- and early twentieth-century biblical scholars "truth" and "rhetoric" were to be found in different compartments. The felt need in many quarters to make a clear distinction between the two even as late as the 1960s is evident in these words from an influential Bible dictionary of the time: "[Paul] positively rejected the artful literary and rhetorical devices of the 'wise in this age.'.... The same is true of other parts of the NT.... There are echoes of oratory and of orators here and there, but no studied imitation."[36]

---

[35] Trible, *Rhetorical Criticism*, 12.
[36] Frederick C. Grant, "Rhetoric and Oratory," *IDB* 4:75–77 (76–77).

Rhetoric Resurgent

It is just this kind of view, however, that other authors of the same decade began to challenge. Writing in 1964 Amos Wilder analyzed *Early Christian Rhetoric*, emphasizing "not so much ... what the early Christians said as how they said it."[37] Two years later, Robert Funk published *Language, Hermeneutic and Word of God*, applying Wilder's ideas specifically to the forms of "parable" and "epistle" and arguing in each case that the *form* creates a language event in which a fresh experience or understanding of ultimate reality occurs.[38] Both books maintained that a careful analysis of NT rhetoric provides us with an understanding of the social-historical setting and circumstances that produced the various NT texts and of the thought of the biblical author in that context. Edwin Judge added a further essay in 1968 reflecting on "Paul's boasting in relation to contemporary professional practice"; to what extent, he asked, did the apostle Paul receive rhetorical training?[39]

A particularly important moment in the establishment of the new discipline of rhetorical criticism occurred in that same year, when OT scholar James Muilenburg delivered a presidential address to the Society of Biblical Literature titled "Form Criticism and Beyond."[40] Like von Rad before him he presented his new idea as a development grounded in an already-established biblical-critical method: form criticism. As redaction criticism had first focused attention on *what* OT redactors had done with earlier traditions in order to communicate a particular message, now Muilenburg announced his desire to draw attention to *how* biblical authors and redactors had deployed rhetorical art to achieve this end. In the published form of his address Muilenburg quite explicitly does not reject the results of form criticism. In fact he presupposes them, for a primary task in rhetorical criticism is "to define the limits or scope" of the rhetorical unit to be studied, and indeed to examine its rhetorical situation and problem.[41] Nevertheless, he is concerned with the business of understanding more fully "the literary unit in its precise and unique formulation."[42] Form criticism, he maintains—in its focus on "the traditional elements and motifs" of each literary genre—does not offer sufficiently careful inspection of the literary unit in this unique formulation. We

---

[37] Amos N. Wilder, *Early Christian Rhetoric: The Language of the Gospel* (Cambridge, Mass.: Harvard University Press, 1964), 2.

[38] Robert W. Funk, *Language, Hermeneutic and Word of God* (New York: Harper & Row, 1966).

[39] Edwin A. Judge, "Paul's Boasting in Relation to Contemporary Professional Practice," now accessible in *Social Distinctives of the Christians in the First Century: Pivotal Essays* (ed. David M. Scholer; Peabody, Mass.: Hendrickson, 2008), 57–71.

[40] Muilenburg, "Form Criticism."

[41] Muilenburg, "Form Criticism," 8–9.

[42] Muilenburg, "Form Criticism," 7.

need to take "full account of the features" of each biblical text "which lie beyond the spectrum of the genre."[43] Picking up my own language from earlier, we need to examine the "peak" that rises above the mountain range. How does the present text work, rhetorically? How is it arranged in order to achieve its rhetorical purpose? Muilenburg does in fact believe that the authors of Hebrew literature used aesthetics in putting their texts together in a way that would accomplish their purposes, and he details a whole range of rhetorical devices in Hebrew poetry to illustrate the point. His emphasis thus lies on the fluidity of the forms of the biblical literature—the versatility and artistry with which the biblical authors use these forms, and what they add to them that lies beyond the influence of convention and custom on ancient Israelite speech and literary composition. "For after all has been said and done about the forms and types of biblical speech, there still remains the task of discerning the actuality of the particular text."[44]

From this starting point rhetorical-critical endeavor in OT studies quickly developed in such a way that it produced studies not only of Hebrew poetry but also of Hebrew narrative. We shall return to this development in chapter 20 and discuss at the same time NT narrative criticism. For the moment I wish to illustrate only how rhetorical-critical method can illuminate nonnarrative biblical texts—both OT poems and NT letters.

The Rhetoric of Psalm 22

In 1982 John Kselman published a compelling rhetorical-critical reading of Psalm 22 that has the merit of clearly indicating what this kind of approach to the text offers us that form criticism by itself cannot.[45] He begins by noting that verses 1 and 2 serve as an "overture" to the entire psalm, "announcing themes and perspectives that will recur throughout the poem."[46] The fundamental theme of the poem, communicated in the repeated use of the Hebrew word *raḥaq* in verses 1 ("far, distant"), 11, and 19 ("be not far"), is the psalmist's experience of the absence of God—God's distance from the psalmist along two "axes." These are the vertical or cosmological "axis of separation from the transcendent God in a spatial sense" and the horizontal or historical "axis of separation from God as the psalmist moves through time."[47] In the entirety of his experience the psalmist finds only

---

[43] Muilenburg, "Form Criticism," 7.
[44] Muilenburg, "Form Criticism," 18.
[45] John S. Kselman, "'Why Have You Abandoned Me?' A Rhetorical Study of Psalm 22," in *Art and Meaning: Rhetoric in Biblical Literature* (ed. David J. A. Clines, David M. Gunn, and Allan J. Hauser; Sheffield: JSOT Press, 1982), 172–98.
[46] Kselman, "Psalm 22," 183. He himself refers throughout to the Hebrew verse numbering; I have "translated" this into English Bible verse numbering.
[47] Kselman, "Psalm 22," 183.

that God is "far." The spatial and temporal dimensions introduced in verses 1 and 2 are then elaborated in verses 3-5 and 9-10. In verse 3 ("But you among the holy ones sit enthroned, amid Israel's praises"), in a scene that reminds us of Isaiah 6, the transcendent God sits "enthroned among the members of his heavenly court," and as in Isaiah 6 "the psalmist's sense of distance, alienation, and separation is profound."[48] Verse 3 considers the spatial dimension, then. Verses 4-5 and 9-10 consider the dimension of time: the distant past of Israel's tradition (vv. 4-5) and the immediate past of the psalmist's early life (vv. 9-10). "Enclosed by the past-time frame" of verses 4-5 and 9-10 are verses 6-8, dealing with his present circumstances.[49] "Abandoned by the saving God and without human support, his lament answered only by mockery, the psalmist experiences a profound sense of dehumanization."[50] This is strikingly expressed in verse 6: "I am a worm, not a man." The first section of Psalm 22 then ends with two "inclusions"—that is, forms of speech that repeat language from earlier and so "enclose" what lies between, inviting the reader to read the enclosed content in the light of the beginning and the end. Verses 1 and 11 both contain the language of "far," and "you are my God" in verse 10 evokes "My God, my God" in verse 1. The poet has "enveloped" what lies between by the first of these inclusions, surrounding "the psalmist's plea as the psalmist's enemies surround him in the next section."[51] But the second inclusion makes clear that "the psalmist is also enveloped by the care of a God whom the poet can address from beginning to end as '*my* God' even in deepest distress."[52] In sum, Psalm 22:1-11 presents

> a remote God enthroned on high, far from the lament of the psalmist. Time and space are experienced as empty of God, the God in whom the fathers trusted, the saving God of Israel's sacral traditions. The presence of the trustworthy God in the past of the community and of the psalmist makes his absence in the present all the more poignant.[53]

Yet the God in question is still "my God," and this fact is crucial to how the remainder of the poem develops.

Its second section, in verses 12 to 21, connects with its first by way of a number of links. For example, the verb "to roar" is repeated from verse 1, where it is disguised by NIV's "groaning." The "roaring" of the psalmist in prayer at the beginning of section I is in fact "drowned out by the roar ... of his enemies at

---

[48] Kselman, "Psalm 22," 184.
[49] Kselman, "Psalm 22," 184.
[50] Kselman, "Psalm 22," 185.
[51] Kselman, "Psalm 22," 186.
[52] Kselman, "Psalm 22," 186.
[53] Kselman, "Psalm 22," 186.

the beginning of Section II" (v. 13).⁵⁴ These enemies "are described with a variety of animal names that cluster at the beginning and end of the section."⁵⁵ The names are arranged in a "chiasm"—they move inward in a certain order and then out again in reverse order. The enemies are "bulls/lions/dogs" (vv. 12-13, 16) and "dogs, lions, bulls" (NIV's "oxen," vv. 20-21). "This chiastic arrangement is a good example of how structure can mirror and reinforce meaning," since the reversal of the names in verses 20-21 "prepares for the coming reversal of the poet's situation (from lament to thanksgiving)" in verses 22-31.⁵⁶

The final section of Psalm 22 (vv. 22-31), Kselman informs us, "has been the object of considerable study and controversy."⁵⁷ Earlier in the modern period some scholars argued that it represented an originally independent piece of text that was added later to verses 1-21. Kselman dismisses this opinion on form-critical grounds: lament psalms typically include both praise and thanksgiving. Another proposal that has been mooted is that, while verses 22-26 are part of the original Psalm 22, verses 27-31 are a later addition. Kselman attempts to demonstrate, however, that verses 27-31 function "as an integral part of the rhetorical unity that is Psalm 22."⁵⁸ The poem begins in section I with an expression of radical alienation: "on the one hand, the remote, transcendent God; on the other, the psalmist, crying out day and night, with no response from the distant God."⁵⁹ This experience of the God who is absent in space and time is then developed in the following verses. It is space and time, Kselman points out, that also unify section III. Now, however, they are not empty; they "resound with the praise of God who has answered the psalmist's lament."⁶⁰ In verse 22 "the psalmist praises God in the presence of his 'brothers' ... who in this section replace the mocking onlookers [vv. 7-8] and his fierce enemies [vv. 12-13, 16-18]."⁶¹ He is reintegrated into the community and his dehumanizing solitude comes to an end. He can now join "the chorus of Israel's praise" (v. 3), which has become "my praise" (v. 25).⁶² But he goes on from there to invite "an ever-widening circle to join him in praising God, using spatial images: from his brothers [v. 22], the God-fearing descendants of Israel [v. 23], to the ends of the earth and all the families of nations [v. 27]."⁶³ Verses 29-

---

⁵⁴ Kselman, "Psalm 22," 186.
⁵⁵ Kselman, "Psalm 22," 187.
⁵⁶ Kselman, "Psalm 22," 188.
⁵⁷ Kselman, "Psalm 22," 188.
⁵⁸ Kselman, "Psalm 22," 188.
⁵⁹ Kselman, "Psalm 22," 188.
⁶⁰ Kselman, "Psalm 22," 189.
⁶¹ Kselman, "Psalm 22," 189.
⁶² Kselman, "Psalm 22," 189.
⁶³ Kselman, "Psalm 22," 189.

31 focus rather on *time*: "[t]he psalmist who prayed day and night to no avail [v. 2] now invites past, present, and future to join him in praise and worship."⁶⁴

In conclusion, Kselman expresses the hope that he has established that we are dealing in Psalm 22 with a "carefully constructed and developed psalm [that] demonstrates the high degree of artistry of which Hebrew poets are capable."⁶⁵ He closes with some words of William Holladay about the poetry of Jeremiah, noting that they "could apply equally well" to OT poetry more generally:

> Finally, many who have been patient enough to work through the details of the analysis given here respond with the judgment that it is too subtle; that one cannot expect ancient man to have paid so much attention to key words, to the balance of phonemes, or whatever; that no ancient collector could have been conscious of anything so intricate. But surely it is evident that there can be a great gap between structure that is *sensed* by a poet or artist, or by one who enjoys a work of art, on the one hand, and the *systematic analysis* of the structure by a critic, on the other.⁶⁶

In Kselman we have an OT scholar, then, whose careful analysis of what a Hebrew poet is doing in Psalm 22 has among other things led him to question disintegrating approaches to the text from the standpoint of form criticism. Verses 22-31 are not to be regarded as a "later addition" to an earlier, "purer" form of the psalm just because they add praise and thanksgiving to lament, nor are verses 27-31 to be regarded as a "later addition" just because they universalize the praise. Rhetorical-critical analysis has demonstrated this.

The Rhetoric of Galatians

In 1984 George Kennedy published an entire book on *New Testament Interpretation through Rhetorical Criticism*, in which he devotes a section to Paul's letter to the Galatians, analyzing the letter in line with his overall rhetorical-critical method.⁶⁷ This method requires the reader first to determine the rhetorical unit to be studied and then to examine the rhetorical situation and discover the problem that the speaker had to overcome with rhetoric's aid.⁶⁸ In trying to determine the genre of the argument we must among other things note how the author engages the sympathies of the audience (Greek *ethos*), plays on their emotions (*pathos*), and tries to persuade them using logical argument (*logos*)—for not all classical

---

⁶⁴ Kselman, "Psalm 22," 189.
⁶⁵ Kselman, "Psalm 22," 193.
⁶⁶ Kselman, "Psalm 22," 193.
⁶⁷ George A. Kennedy, *New Testament Interpretation through Rhetorical Criticism* (SR; Chapel Hill: University of North Carolina Press, 1984), 144–52.
⁶⁸ This paragraph is based for the most part on Kennedy's own summary of the entire method in *Rhetorical Criticism*, 33–38.

rhetoric is quite the same.⁶⁹ It is possible to distinguish three types: judicial or forensic rhetoric, which is designed to elicit judgment from the hearers (e.g., in a court of law); deliberative rhetoric, aimed at effecting a particular decision (e.g., in a public assembly); and epideictic rhetoric, which intends to produce assent or dissent in respect of a particular stance (e.g., in the course of a public ceremony). Next, we should consider the rhetorical arrangement of the material before us, identifying its various parts and the way in which they are organized for rhetorical effect, and we should analyze the devices of style. Finally, we need to review the entire rhetorical unit "and review its success in meeting the rhetorical exigence."⁷⁰ How successful has the author been in his quest?

Turning to Galatians, then, Kennedy introduces the epistle as one of Paul's "most vigorous and eloquent," possessing "great rhetorical interest."⁷¹ He offers his analysis in conscious distinction to that of Hans Dieter Betz from a decade earlier,⁷² from which (Kennedy says) "much can be learned about the epistle and about rhetoric" but also about "the pitfalls of rhetorical criticism when not practiced in accordance with the method" that Kennedy has outlined.⁷³ Betz regards the epistle as apologetic in nature and thus an example of judicial rhetoric; it is designed as Paul's defense against various charges. Betz "was apparently led to this view, at least in part, by the existence of a narrative section in Galatians 2,"⁷⁴ which he took to be a characteristic of judicial rhetoric. Consequently, he tried to find in Galatians "the traditional parts of a judicial oration" as described by the Roman rhetorician Quintilian (AD 35–100).⁷⁵ Betz "may also have been influenced by his own extensive knowledge of the dispute between parties in the early Church and a desire to bring out that dissension more sharply than may be immediately apparent to many readers of the Bible."⁷⁶ Be that as it may, his approach (Kennedy maintains) is wrongheaded:

> Paul certainly *could* have written a defense of the charges made against him in Galatia or elsewhere; but one of the most important things to notice about Galatians is that he did not choose to do so. Instead, he preached the gospel of Christ. What the Galatians thought of Paul mattered only in that it contributed to or detracted from his authority, and thus influenced their belief and actions.⁷⁷

---

[69] Kennedy, *Rhetorical Criticism*, 15–16.
[70] Kennedy, *Rhetorical Criticism*, 38.
[71] Kennedy, *Rhetorical Criticism*, 144.
[72] Hans Dieter Betz, *Galatians* (Hermeneia; Philadelphia: Fortress, 1979).
[73] Kennedy, *Rhetorical Criticism*, 144.
[74] Kennedy, *Rhetorical Criticism*, 144.
[75] Kennedy, *Rhetorical Criticism*, 144.
[76] Kennedy, *Rhetorical Criticism*, 144.
[77] Kennedy, *Rhetorical Criticism*, 144–45.

What really interested Paul was what the Galatian Christians believed and how they were going to live as a result.

The key point is that *all* species of classical rhetoric "make use of narrative, but they use it for different purposes and in different ways."[78] Judicial narrative sets out the facts at issue (Quintilian 4.2.66–68). However, the narrative in Galatians 1 and 2 is not an account of "the facts at issue." This narrative provides instead "supporting evidence for Paul's claim ... that the gospel he preached was not from man, but from God" (Gal 1:11).[79] The epistle to the Galatians is not judicial but deliberative rhetoric. Paul's exhortation to the Galatians (Gal 5:1–6:10) provides strong evidence in support of this proposal. Exhortation "is not regarded as a part of judicial rhetoric by any of the ancient authorities"[80]—but in this epistle, it is the very thing that Paul is building up to in chapters 1 to 4. "The basic argument of deliberative oratory is that an action is in the self-interest of the audience, or as Quintilian prefers to put it, that it is right (8.3.1–3). That is the pervasive argument of Galatians."[81] The Galatian Christians *should not* observe the Law and *should not* practice circumcision; they *should* love one another and live a holy life. The letter concerns future conduct; it is not asking its readers to render judgment about the past.

With this set of basic contentions in mind Kennedy sets out his own analysis of the epistle, beginning with the opening salutation (Gal 1:1-5). This is followed by a *proem* (Gal 1:6-10) "which by its vigor immediately attracts attention and which ... contains a biting attack on those who would counsel otherwise" than Paul.[82] The core idea is that there is no other gospel than the one preached by Paul, which in verses 11-12 is said to be "not man's gospel." The narrative in Galatians 1:13–2:14 is designed to demonstrate this. Here "the isolation of Paul from the other apostles serves to amplify their ultimate acceptance of him in 2:6-10 and thus to strengthen his ethos, while that of his opponents is undermined in 13-14 and in the following dramatic incident with Peter" (2:15-21).[83]

These closing verses of Galatians 2 provide the conclusion to the material in this first section of the letter, which is all about Paul's authority, and they introduce the specific issue that Paul must now examine—the question of the Jewish law. The second section, beginning in Galatians 3:1,

> may be summarized as [making] the claim that the gospel is true because of the experience of the Galatians.... The Galatians' experience of the gospel has been

---

[78] Kennedy, *Rhetorical Criticism*, 145.
[79] Kennedy, *Rhetorical Criticism*, 145.
[80] Kennedy, *Rhetorical Criticism*, 145.
[81] Kennedy, *Rhetorical Criticism*, 146.
[82] Kennedy, *Rhetorical Criticism*, 148.
[83] Kennedy, *Rhetorical Criticism*, 148.

challenged by those who demand observance of the Law, and it is thus appropriate for Paul to insert here a refutation of their views.[84]

The grounding in Scripture for Paul's view of the law is revealed in Galatians 3:6-18, and what is of immediate importance for the Galatians "is recapitulated in personal terms in 3:23–4:11, with repeated use of the personal pronoun 'you.'"[85] A personal appeal by Paul to his readers follows in Galatians 4:12-20, and then the allegorical interpretation (according to Kennedy—but see my chapter 6) of the story of Sarah and Hagar (Gal 4:21-31). Looking back on his analysis to this point Kennedy then says this:

> The entire section of the proof from 1:11 to 5:1 corresponds to the theological sections seen in most other epistles of Paul and provides the basis for the specific commandments which are the practical purpose of the letter. These begin with the negative injunction against circumcision in 5:2, which is complemented by the positive injunction of love in 5:14.[86]

Paul follows up with a description of the works of the flesh and of the spirit in Galatians 5:19-24 and with additional pastoral exhortations. It is important to notice from the conclusion of the letter (Gal 6:11-17) "that what Paul thinks he has demonstrated to the Galatians is not that they should alter their judgment of him, but that 'neither circumcision counts for anything nor uncircumcision, but a new creation'" (Gal 6:15).[87] A benediction brings the letter to a close.

It is Kennedy's critique of Betz, then, that he is overinfluenced by his reading of the opening chapters of Galatians in judging Paul's argument to be judicial in nature. The genre of the whole epistle is instead deliberative rhetoric. The letter is not a defense of the apostle Paul but rather an articulation of the Gospel and a description of the Christian life, designed to bring the Galatians to a decision about their future. Betz makes a genre mistake. Part of what leads him into this mistake is a fairly typical modern "reconstructive" tendency. Betz "knows" too much about the background to Galatians in intra-Church disputes—another good example of the dangers of reading behind our biblical texts and finding only what one first suspected *must* be there. Kennedy, on the other hand, is resolutely focused on the text as a verbal reality and on its original persuasive power. It is not what *must* be there that interests him—it is what actually does appear to *be* there.

---

[84] Kennedy, *Rhetorical Criticism*, 149.
[85] Kennedy, *Rhetorical Criticism*, 150.
[86] Kennedy, *Rhetorical Criticism*, 150.
[87] Kennedy, *Rhetorical Criticism*, 151.

REFLECTIONS ON RHETORICAL CRITICISM

It is clearly one of the great strengths of rhetorical criticism that it does focus in this way on the biblical texts as we have them, trying to understand the parts in relation to the whole ancient document, rather than engaging in the speculative reconstruction and study of other texts that "ought" to be there instead. Even where the critic is proceeding largely inductively, as in the case of Kselman's study of Psalm 22, there is an objectivity about the exercise that is simply not present when one is "studying" J or P. As always in the literal reading of Scripture, at least when we are working with real texts in this way, they can "bite back" and insist on being heard. They can "object" to particular hypotheses about them. Hypothetical texts, whether allegedly and historically or spiritually "behind" the text on the page, are incapable of doing this. The more good evidence we have in general, moreover, that phenomena like chiasmus and inclusion are some of the "realities" in Hebrew poetry, the more that particular proposals about their presence in this or that text gain plausibility—and external evidence about Semitic poetry more broadly can also function helpfully here.[88]

Scholars working in NT studies have even more external help to draw upon, of course, as my description of Kennedy's work has already implied. Since they possess many Greek and Roman writings on ancient rhetoric, the conventions governing Greco-Roman rhetorical composition are well understood, and there can be little question but that they cast considerable light on the NT literature—as previous generations of Bible readers already understood. It is not *only* Greco-Roman rhetoric that likely influenced our NT authors, of course; their Jewish heritage must be taken just as seriously as the Greco-Roman. Here we must avoid the kind of reductionism that is all too often found among form critics, who can miss what is unique about one biblical text through focusing too much on what it has in common with others. At the heart of the rhetorical-critical version of that fault stand those Bible readers who are so convinced of the impact of Greco-Roman rhetoric on the NT literature that they risk missing features within it that are actually peculiar to early (Jewish-)Christian rhetoric. Still, the influence of Greco-Roman rhetoric on the NT epistles in particular appears to be pronounced, even if they *are* epistles and do not strictly speaking fall under the rubric of "rhetoric" as "officially" understood in the Greco-Roman context.[89] It is unsurprising that rhetorical concerns would have animated someone like Paul

---

[88] Wilfred G. E. Watson, *Traditional Techniques in Classical Hebrew Verse* (JSOTSup 170; Sheffield: Sheffield Academic, 1994).

[89] Duane F. Watson, "Rhetorical Criticism," in *The Blackwell Companion to the New Testament* (ed. David E. Aune; Oxford: Wiley-Blackwell, 2010), 166–76 (172–74), noting the "strong debate about the extent to which Greco-Roman rhetorical theory influenced the epistolary genre in antiquity" (172).

in his letter writing, in particular, given that his letters were clearly designed to be *read out* in public.

THE PERSUASIVE TEXT AND HISTORICAL REALITY

The question that remains to be explored concerning "the persuasive text" is its relationship to any *historical* reality about which it might be held to testify. I put it in exactly this way because (of course) not every biblical text *means* to speak about the past, even in part. The question is important, however, because many do. Arising out of a context in which scholars have often looked for history in the sources or forms that might be reconstructed *behind* the biblical texts, both redaction and rhetorical criticism insist that we pay attention *to* the text as an artfully constructed, perspective-laden entity. Is that also where their advocates believe that we should look for history?

The short answer to this question is, not necessarily! Many redaction and rhetorical critics, even though they disagree with their source- and form-critical colleagues about the kind of work on the biblical text that should be emphasized, retain their skepticism about the ability of the persuasive text—whether it is the poetry of Isaiah or the prose of Matthew—to provide us with reliable access to history (e.g., to the historical Isaiah or the historical Jesus). Perspective and agenda are *still* problematic, in their view, when it comes to *that* issue. So it is that George Kennedy, for example, can sum up the merits of rhetorical criticism in this way:

> Rhetoric cannot describe the historical Jesus or identify Matthew or John; they are probably irretrievably lost to scholarship. But it does study a verbal reality, our text of the Bible, rather than the oral sources standing behind the text, the hypothetical stages of its composition, or the impersonal workings of social forces, and at its best it can reveal the power of those texts as unitary messages.[90]

Rhetorical criticism studies "verbal reality," turning our attention away from the reconstruction of sources and of processes of composition, and when rhetorical critics do their job well clarity emerges about the nature of *this* (verbal) reality. But as to *historical* reality, Kennedy concedes, there is nothing that rhetorical critics can say. They can greatly help us to understand "the biblical text as we have it"—what its message is and how that message is being communicated—but they cannot help us (for example) to "describe the historical Jesus," who is "probably irretrievably lost to scholarship." While it is not difficult to find source and form critics, then, who set aside the persuasive biblical text in their pursuit of "historical truth," it is also not difficult to find redaction and rhetorical critics who,

---

[90] Kennedy, *Rhetorical Criticism*, 158–59.

while focusing on the persuasive biblical text, still believe that historical truth lies elsewhere. Indeed, in the decades since the inception of both ways of reading the Bible the idea has steadily gained ground that the very fact that biblical texts *are* persuasive texts *disqualifies* them as reliable testimony to the real past, even if that is apparently what they are designed (at least in part) to be. The very fact that they are "ideologically loaded"—that they present a particular perspective on the past and possess an intention to persuade others of the truth of that perspective—is problematic. The historian of Israel Gösta Ahlström, for example, writes as follows: "Because the authors of the Bible were historiographers and used stylistic patterns to create a 'dogmatic' and, as such, tendentious literature, one may question the reliability of their product."[91] The critical historian of Israel will give preference instead to accounts of the past that are not "ideological" in nature—for example, to nonwritten archaeological and extrabiblical textual data.

This is not a position that any sensible person should endorse. There is simply no reason to believe, in principle, that a persuasive text cannot also be a trustworthy text, whether concerning the past or anything else. If this were really so then knowledge of the past in general would be difficult to obtain, since there is no account of the past anywhere that is free of ideology. This includes accounts based on nonwritten archaeological and extrabiblical textual data relevant to the history of Israel. I shall pass over this particular point in the present context, however, since I have written about it elsewhere.[92] It also inevitably includes any sources, oral or otherwise, that might underlie our current Gospels. Suppose, for example, that Q really did once exist. If discovered, it would still provide us no less with ideologically loaded *testimony* about Jesus than the earliest of the Gospels—by common consent, Mark—just as Mark provides us no less than Matthew with such testimony. The hope that drove much of the early modern criticism of the Gospels, then, that it would enable the discovery of the oldest *and therefore the best* historical source for investigating the life of Jesus—since we would then possess a source that described reality "as it really was," unalloyed by the ideology (theology) of the early Church—this hope always rested upon an illusion. The quest for the historical Jesus, understood in such terms, was therefore doomed from the start—if it was about finding a Jesus independent of the testimony of the early Church about him. Günther Bornkamm puts this well, arguing that in fact form criticism already

---

[91] Gösta W. Ahlström, "The Role of Archaeological and Literary Remains in Reconstructing Israel's History," in *The Fabric of History: Text, Artifact and Israel's Past* (ed. Diana V. Edelman; JSOTSup 127; Sheffield: JSOT Press, 1991), 116–41 (118).

[92] Provan, Long, and Longman, *Biblical History*, 83–92.

put an end to the fiction which had for so long ruled critical investigation, that it would eventually be possible to distil from the Gospels a so-called life of Jesus, free from and untouched by any kind of "over-painting" through the faith of the Church. Faith in Jesus Christ, the Crucified and Resurrected, is by no means a later stratum of the tradition, but its very foundation, and the place from which it sprang and grew and from which alone it is intelligible. From this faith in Jesus, the Crucified and Exalted, both characteristics of the primitive Christian tradition can be understood—the obvious pains taken to preserve the tradition about Jesus conscientiously and faithfully but at the same time the peculiar freedom with which this tradition is presented in detail.[93]

Perspective and agenda are not realities that corrupt the original purity of the Jesus tradition; they are intrinsic to that tradition.

All texts that speak about the past are "ideologically loaded" in this way—rhetorical in nature and persuasive in intent. Yet we do not routinely assume that *just because* such texts possess perspective and agenda they are to be distrusted as testimony about the past. We routinely make the opposite assumption, in fact—that ideological literature can be in whole or in part at the same time historically accurate literature. We may find it necessary to believe on particular occasions that particular testimony is false, especially when we are faced with what appears to be, after careful consideration, straightforward conflict in testimony. We may well come to believe, in particular cases, that rhetoric has been deployed in the service of falsehood. The mere *presence* of rhetoric in testimony about the past, however, should never lead us to this conclusion. For as Aristotle long ago allowed in his important work, *On Rhetoric*—and I am delighted to affirm his thinking here, when I have so routinely criticized it elsewhere in this book—art *can* imitate reality, and rhetorical art in particular can be a means of *communicating* reality (the so-called "mimetic" view of speech and literature).[94] Therefore any thoroughgoing suspicion of art or rhetoric vis-à-vis truth and virtue is unjustified.

So why is it that "[r]hetoric cannot describe the historical Jesus" (Kennedy)? Why should we not regard each of the Gospels as seeking to do just that—each from its own perspective, of course, and each with its own rhetorical device, but each nevertheless *truly*? What is the problem with taking each one equally seriously as attempting to contribute in its own way to one, multifaceted portrait of the historical Jesus? Readers of the Gospels still influenced even subliminally by the "quest for the historical Jesus" will no doubt balk at least at the word "equally." Surely, they will say, priority in understanding the real Jesus must be given to our earliest source—the "original" Gospel of Mark. My response, however, is simply

---

[93] Bornkamm, "Storm," 52.
[94] Aristotle, *On Rhetoric: A Theory of Civic Discourse* (trans. George A. Kennedy; New York: Oxford University Press, 1991).

to affirm that there is no reason to think that an "original" or "earlier" Gospel brings us closer to the "authentic" Jesus than a later one. And here I return to Streeter's work on the four Gospels to illustrate the point.

Earlier I described his account of his own writing project concerning Sadhu Sundar Singh. I did not disclose his purpose, however, in sharing this story. He tells it in the context of his argument about the Gospels earlier in his book—in the course of which he contends for Markan priority and for the real existence of Q—with the purpose of helping his readers to reflect well on the significance of these judgments. What he wants to impress upon them is that redactional work in the Gospels does not impair an effective presentation of Jesus and his teaching, but rather the contrary:

> Insomuch as the loss of a single syllable which might throw a ray of light on any act or word of our Lord is to be regretted, we must regret that Q, and possibly some other early writings used by Matthew and Luke, have not been preserved unaltered and entire. Yet perhaps the loss is less than we may think. Who does not feel that St. Mark, the oldest of the Gospels we still have, is the one we could best spare? Without him we should miss the exacter details of a scene or two, a touch or two of human limitations in the Master, or of human infirmity in the Twelve, but it is not from him that we get the portrait of the Master which has been the inspiration of Christendom. A mechanical snapshot is for the realist a more reliable and correct copy of the original than a portrait by Rembrandt, but it cannot give the same impression of the personality behind. The presence of a great man, the magic of his voice, the march of his argument, have a mesmeric influence on those who hear, which is lost in the bare transcript of fragmentary sayings and isolated acts such as we find in Mark or Q. Later on, two great, though perhaps unconscious, artists, trained in the movement begun by the Master and saturated by His Spirit, retell the tale, idealise—if you will—the picture, but in so doing make us to realise something of the majesty and tenderness which men knew in Galilee.[95]

Streeter then goes on to provide an example, imagining a "realist" who might object to Matthew's presentation of the Sermon on the Mount on the ground that it comprises "a mosaic of the more striking fragments of perhaps twenty discourses," preferring Mark or Q because "there we have the fragments frankly as fragments."[96] However,

> on the hill or by the lake they were not listened to as scattered fragments but in the illuminating context, and behind the words was ever the speaker's presence. "The multitude marvelled as they heard," says Mark in passages where *his* story leaves

---

[95] Streeter, *Four Gospels*, 194–95.
[96] Streeter, *Four Gospels*, 195.

us cold. We turn to the arresting cadence of the Sermon on the Mount and it is no longer the multitude but *we* that marvel.[97]

The original, earlier Gospel is not more valuable than the later ones that build on it, any more than Tolstoy's "original, earlier" version of *War and Peace* is more "authentic" than his finished work (the second epigraph to my present chapter). Indeed, in certain respects we can see that Mark's Gospel provides a more limited perspective than the others.

CONCLUSION

Redaction is an intrinsic feature of textual life generally, and it is certainly an intrinsic feature of the life of many biblical texts in particular. Redaction criticism illuminates our reading of such texts, focusing our attention on questions of authorial perspective and agenda: what is the text trying to say in construing the tradition it inherits in *this* particular way? Rhetorical criticism emphasizes the same reality with particular attention to the question of *how* biblical authors artfully construct their texts to achieve their communicative goals. Not everything that redaction and rhetorical critics have proposed is equally plausible, and in particular there is no reason to embrace the principled historical skepticism that sometimes accompanies their attention to "the text as we have it." Yet many of their insights are extraordinarily helpful to Bible readers wishing to grasp the meaning of redactionally and rhetorically shaped biblical texts on the way to hearing the Word of God as it comes to expression in the whole canon of Scripture. Both reading methods are therefore indispensable to "reformed" biblical hermeneutics.

---

[97] Streeter, *Four Gospels*, 195.

19

Structuralism and Poststructuralism
Texts and Subtexts

There is nothing outside of the text . . . there has never been anything but writing.

—*Jacques Derrida*[1]

. . . theories, whether scientific or theological, are not free creations of the human mind, but are rather constructed in response to an encounter with an existing reality.

—*Alister McGrath*[2]

In the next chapter we shall discuss narrative criticism, which follows on naturally from our discussion of rhetorical criticism. To engage with narrative criticism fully, however, we first need a working knowledge of structuralism and poststructuralism. It is these two broader movements within literary criticism and their impact on modern biblical studies that we consider in the present chapter.

FORMALISM AND NEW CRITICISM

We begin with "formalism" and "new criticism." "Formalism" has Russian roots, although it was not influential outside Russia until the 1930s and 1940s.[3] "New criticism" arose in the 1920s in English-speaking literary circles and was later influenced by formalism.[4] They flow together in certain respects, by way of general developments in linguistics and anthropology that I shall shortly describe, into the literary-critical stream that is routinely referred to nowadays as

---

[1] Jacques Derrida, *Of Grammatology* (trans. Gayatri Chakravorty Spivak; Baltimore: Johns Hopkins University Press, 1976), 158–59—first published in 1967.

[2] McGrath, *Science of God*, 171.

[3] Victor Erlich, *Russian Formalism: History-Doctrine* (4th ed.; The Hague: Mouton, 1980). For a brief introduction to both formalism and new criticism, see Michael E. Travers, "Formalism," *DTIB*, 230–32, and Jonathan Culler, *Literary Theory: A Very Short Introduction* (Oxford: Oxford University Press, 1997), 122–23.

[4] Art Berman, *From the New Criticism to Deconstruction: The Reception of Structuralism and Post-structuralism* (Chicago: University of Illinois Press, 1988).

"structuralism." What all three approaches have in common is an emphasis on texts *rather than* authors. Hitherto in our survey of modern biblical criticism, from the late nineteenth through to the middle of the twentieth century, we have discovered a marked emphasis on authors and editors and their communicative intent. What did *they mean* in the texts they produced? This concern has continued to dominate the thinking of many biblical scholars about our biblical texts down to the present time. In secular literary criticism, however, this long-standing preoccupation with authorial or editorial intent was abandoned by many literary critics already in the first part of the twentieth century. It was abandoned by some—and this was especially true of formalists—because of the kind of general move away from interest in the individual to interest in his social matrix that we already discussed with respect to the rise of form criticism in chapter 18. For others the concern had more to do with separating *form* and *content* in literature. We should not look behind the text but *at* the text. This perspective is nicely summed up in the famous aphorism of Archibald MacLeish (1892–1982): "a poem should not mean, but be."[5] In other words, a poem (in this case) is not reducible to propositions or general truths; it is not possible to paraphrase it. To steal an example from John Barton, we could not without great loss replace Alfred Lord Tennyson's poem "In Memoriam" by a sentence such as "I am extremely sorry that my friend has died."[6] In particular, in this view of literature, it is not possible to get behind a text to the mind or intentions of any author, and its meaning is not bound up with these intentions. To believe the opposite, in this view, is to become embroiled in the so-called "intentionalist fallacy."

STRUCTURALISM: THE ENCODED TEXT

For one reason or another, then, the focus of interest comes to fall on the structures and forms of a piece of literature in itself. Structuralists are typically little interested in "reconstruction," but they are also not very interested even in the historical background of a text as an aid to its interpretation, including who wrote it, when, and why. Like the rhetorical critics, to be sure, they are convinced that "structure is a key to meaning and interpretation."[7] Whereas rhetorical critics join redaction critics, however, in placing their emphasis on the *individuality* of texts as they build on convention and travel along a historical path toward their final form—Muilenburg, for example, is concerned to know historical facts such as from whom "the poets and prophets of Israel acquire[d] their styles and

---

[5] Susan Ratcliffe, ed., *Oxford Dictionary of Quotations by Subject* (2nd ed.; Oxford: Oxford University Press, 2010), 367.
[6] Barton, *Reading the Old Testament*, 159.
[7] Trible, *Rhetorical Criticism*, 35, citing Jack Lundbom.

literary habits"[8]—structuralists are indifferent to such matters. The reason is that they take the "binding" of the individual author (or editor) of a text even more seriously than form critics do; that is, they are far more consistently determinist than someone like Gunkel in their view of the enduring power of forms. There are "deep structures" of thought in all literature, they believe, and these structures transcend individual authors and determine their writing. Irrespective of any particular author's conscious intentions, there exist universally recurring features in the literatures of all cultures and ages, and it is these that reveal any particular text's most fundamental meaning.

Ferdinand de Saussure

An important book lying at the heart of this way of thinking about literature is Ferdinand de Saussure's *Course in General Linguistics*, written up on the basis of student notes on his lectures at the University of Geneva between 1906 and 1911 and published in 1916.[9] Whereas previous linguistic theory had been preoccupied with the historical development of language and looked to explain language within that historical frame (what is often called a "diachronic" approach to language), de Saussure (1857–1913) argued that language is in fact a system that is complete at every moment, no matter which developments may have taken place. Language should therefore be studied *synchronically*, as a unified field—a self-sufficient system as we actually experience it *now*. In such study the researcher should be looking for the abstract set of rules—the permanent structures or "grammar" of language—that lie at each language's heart. De Saussure called this (in French) *langue*. Each individual, concrete speech utterance is always made in obedience to this "grammar." These individual speech utterances de Saussure called *parole*. *Langue* represents the rules of the language game, *parole* the individual moves—just as there is such a thing as the game chess, with its overarching rules, and then there are individual games of chess, in which various moves are made in accordance with the rules.

Texts comprise language, of course; so de Saussure's structuralist approach was soon applied to literature more broadly. Two scholars in particular are worthy of note, for each stands at the origin of a particular way of approaching literature as a structuralist that in due course will influence biblical studies.

---

[8] Muilenburg, "Form Criticism," 18.
[9] Ferdinand de Saussure, *Course in General Linguistics* (trans. Roy Harris; London: Bloomsbury, 2013).

Vladimir Propp

The first is the Russian folklorist Vladimir Propp (1895–1970), who in 1928 published a book titled *Morphology of the Folktale* (translated into English in 1958).[10] This was an attempt to find the laws that govern the telling of traditional stories. Inspecting around one hundred Russian folktales, Propp began to notice significant recurring features within them. Analyzing these further he believed that he had discovered a "deep structure," or grammar of possible relationships, that all folktales obey. There are within these folktales, he proposed, a limited number of possible actions that their characters perform. For example, a character might present a gift. These actions Propp called "functions," and he insisted that they never change. The range of character types is also limited—the same kinds of characters show up in folktales from very different contexts, performing the same kind of functions, even though the names of the characters performing the functions in each individual tale obviously vary. Propp reckoned that he had discovered thirty-one such functions in his folktales, involving seven types of characters. What is individually distinctive is not the most important aspect of a folktale, then. What matters is to grasp the "invariants." That is the heart of the matter. What is the *function* that a particular event—just because it happens—fulfills in the course of a narrative? The rest is simply packaging—that which makes a story a particular manifestation of its general type.

Algirdas Greimas (1917–1992) later adapted Propp's system to produce a model that he regarded as describing the permanent structures behind *all* narratives.[11] Figure 19.1 below sets out the basic idea, portraying six different character poles of narrative and three functional axes (communication, volition, power).

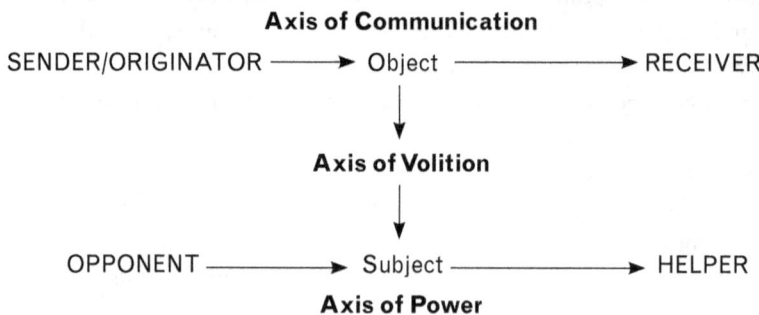

---

[10] Vladimir Propp, *Morphology of the Folktale* (2nd ed.; trans. Laurence Scott; rev. Louis A. Wagner; Austin: University of Texas Press, 1968).

[11] Algirdas J. Greimas, *Structural Semantics: An Attempt at a Method* (trans. Daniele McDowell, Ronald Schleifer, and Alan Velie; Lincoln: University of Nebraska Press, 1983)—first published in 1966.

A story usually begins, Greimas proposed, when a sender tells a receiver (on the communication axis) to undertake some task. The volitional axis represents the quest, and the power axis represent the struggle involved in its execution. Along this power axis we find helpers and opponents. For example, we might imagine a story in which a king sends a prince to find his daughter. The prince is waylaid by orcs before being helped by an eagle to win his prize. Structurally, this could be represented as in Figure 19.2.

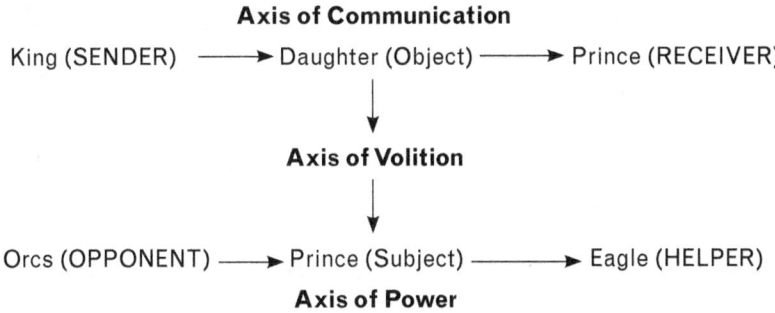

Claude Lévi-Strauss

The second figure of importance to the development of structuralist method is Claude Lévi-Strauss (1908–2009), who used de Saussure's linguistic system in his study of myths.[12] Lévi-Strauss believed that the rules that govern myth and those that govern language emerge from identical unconscious structures of the mind. The unconscious structure behind myth is the tendency to think in oppositions and to resolve them. Lévi-Strauss was therefore interested in the *langue* behind mythical stories. This *langue* is established through the discovery of recurrent combinations of constant features or "mythemes" that obey the rules of a transcendental grammar that is manifested in the resolution of things existing in binary opposition (universal contrasts such as Immortal/Mortal, Male/Female, Parent/Child, etc.). This is one aspect of a larger search for "invariants beyond the empirical diversity of human societies."[13]

STRUCTURALISM AND SCRIPTURE

Structuralism took some time to impact a modern biblical studies discipline still profoundly rooted in what Kevin Vanhoozer has described as "the age of the

---

[12] Claude Lévi-Strauss, *Structural Anthropology* (Garden City, N.Y.: Doubleday, 1967)—first published in 1958.
[13] Claude Lévi-Strauss, *The Savage Mind* (London: Weidenfeld & Nicolson, 1966), 247.

author"[14]—that is, still marked by a belief in the central importance of the communicative intentions of authors—and in that respect (if not in others) holding on to age-old (including Protestant) tradition about how Scripture should be approached. Eventually the impact was felt, however, in the midst of continuing concerns that even a traditional, historically oriented (diachronic) exegetical approach with form-critical perspectives as part of the "package" was not adequate by itself to account for the scriptural reality in which it professed an interest. There was still too much emphasis on the biblical authors as the "creators of significations" (to borrow language from Daniel Patte).[15] In this perspective the individual author is understood as predominantly someone of conscious beliefs, intentions, and motives, creatively and freely responding to situations that confront him. "The author creates new symbols," and uses existing symbols in his own way, "ascribing to them specific meanings which suit *his* argument."[16] He "*uses* the language as a whole as well as literary techniques" in communicating his message, "'making a coherent deformation of the language' in order to express a new thought or idea."[17] History, on this view, "is made up of a succession of 'authors'" and "to reach them is to reach the very fabric of history."[18] For Patte, however, this represents only half the truth, and this is why traditional, historically focused exegesis has found it so difficult to address modern human beings. Getting at the business of what the text once *meant* (exegesis) has not always led to greater (or any) clarity about what the text *means* (hermeneutic). For the *reality* is that human beings are not simply "creators of significations" but also have significations imposed upon them.[19]

According to Patte it is the latter reality that structuralist (synchronic) exegesis takes seriously. It "no longer aims at what the author meant" but at "the linguistic, narrative, or mythical structures of the text under consideration,"[20] whether or not the author was aware of these or intended them. Whether he was or did, the structures are simply and inevitably *there*—since an author in his speech (*parole*) cannot but use the *langue* available to him. Structuralist analysis concerns itself with the text, then, seeking whichever meanings are embedded there *in* the structures. It aims not at what arises from the author's creativity but at what imposes itself upon him.

---

[14] Vanhoozer, *Meaning*, 25–26.
[15] Daniel Patte, *What Is Structural Exegesis?* (Philadelphia: Fortress, 1976), 12.
[16] Patte, *Structural Exegesis*, 12.
[17] Patte, *Structural Exegesis*, 12.
[18] Patte, *Structural Exegesis*, 12.
[19] Patte, *Structural Exegesis*, 13.
[20] Patte, *Structural Exegesis*, 14.

Genesis as Myth, and the Struggle with the Angel

When structuralist exegesis did eventually begin to impact biblical studies it is unsurprising that its first "experiments" were carried out on Genesis—as we have seen, a significant testing-ground for much modern critical method, and a rather obvious place (given prevailing modern opinions about the genre of Genesis) in which to try out theories originally developed in relation to fairy tale and myth. One of the first to apply the method of Lévi-Strauss was Edmund Leach.[21] In Leach's work we find exactly the emphasis on binary oppositions in which Lévi-Strauss was so interested. Just as myth in general routinely sets up opposing categories, so it is that all the way through Genesis we find common opposites: heaven/earth, light/darkness, and so on. Genesis is a particular example of the general case: "every myth is one of a complex [of myths]" in this way, and "any pattern which occurs in *one* myth in the complex will recur, in the same or other variations, in other parts of the complex."[22] Genesis, like other myths, is an observable phenomenon expressive of "unobservable realities."[23]

One of the first scholars to bring the method deriving from *Propp and Greimas* to bear on Scripture was Roland Barthes (1915–1980), who in 1971 wrote a famous essay titled "The Struggle with the Angel."[24] In this essay Barthes discusses Jacob's struggle at Penuel with the man or the angel described, which moves toward its conclusion in this way (Gen 32:25-28):

> When the man saw that he could not overpower him, he touched the socket of Jacob's hip so that his hip was wrenched as he wrestled with the man. Then the man said, "Let me go, for it is daybreak." But Jacob replied, "I will not let you go unless you bless me." The man asked him, "What is your name?" "Jacob," he answered. Then the man said, "Your name will no longer be Jacob, but Israel, because you have struggled with God and with men and have overcome."

In this story we find "actants" (characters) who may be described in terms of recognizable "functions." For example, Jacob is the hero (the "subject") who is on a quest (the "object" is the crossing of the Jabbok so that he can reconcile with Esau). God stands behind the events of the story as the "sender" or the originator of this quest. Yet when we get to the "opponent" and the "helper" not everything is quite so "recognizable." In a way no "helper" appears in the story at all—Jacob provides "help to himself through his own, legendary, strength."[25] This is unusual.

---

[21] Edmund Leach, *Genesis as Myth and Other Essays* (London: Jonathan Cape, 1969).
[22] Leach, *Genesis as Myth*, 22.
[23] Leach, *Genesis as Myth*, 23.
[24] Roland Barthes, *Image, Music, Text: Essays Selected and Translated by Stephen Heath* (London: Fontana, 1977), 125–41.
[25] Barthes, *Image*, 138.

Even more, remarkably, however, in the course of his struggle Jacob recognizes that his "opponent"—the one who waylays the hero in this wrestling match and tries to prevent him from accomplishing his mission—is none other than God himself, who sent him on the quest in the first place. We may represent this reality structurally as in Figure 19.3.

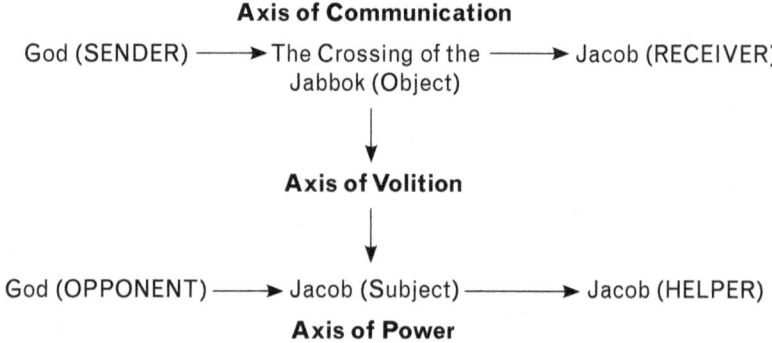

"[T]hat the sender be the opponent," writes Barthes, "is very rare,"[26] and it is bound to surprise. In fact, "there is only one kind of narrative that can present this paradoxical form—narratives relating an act of blackmail."[27] We are thus led to recognize how "extremely audacious" the story is, structurally speaking.[28] It is also audacious—although Barthes himself does not make this point—in its theology, when read against its ancient Near Eastern background. Here the plans of "senders," even if they were gods, were not immune to thwarting by opposing powers. This was the case not least at liminal points like river crossings, which were commonly understood as gateways into the lands to which they gave entry, and as such were believed to be guarded by the gods or their servants. Mosaic Yahwism's monotheism did not make room for opposing power that could ultimately thwart the purposes of the divine Sender; such "power" was always under God's sovereign control.

Further Examples

Most examples of structuralist reading of the Bible resemble one of these examples. Either they are concerned with the resolution of binary oppositions, in the conviction that this is how myth works, or they are interested in plot functions, in the conviction that there is a fundamental narrative grammar that all narratives

---

[26] Barthes, *Image*, 138.
[27] Barthes, *Image*, 138.
[28] Barthes, *Image*, 138.

obey, just as speech obeys the rules of grammar generally. These readings tend to be resolutely ahistorical, taking up de Saussure's emphasis on language as an integrated system rather than on the history of language. They are particularly uninterested in authors, despite Patte's more moderate presentation of structuralism; Barthes himself once wrote a famous essay about "The Death of the Author" (1967).[29] Structuralist readings are a feature of modern study not only of the OT but also of the NT. The NT parables invite such explorations, for example—precisely because they represent the most obvious examples of narrative fiction in this part of the Bible, and the analysis of narrative fiction was where structuralism began. The parable of the Rich Man and Lazarus in Luke 16:19-31, for instance, can be analyzed in terms of characters and functions as in Figure 19.4.

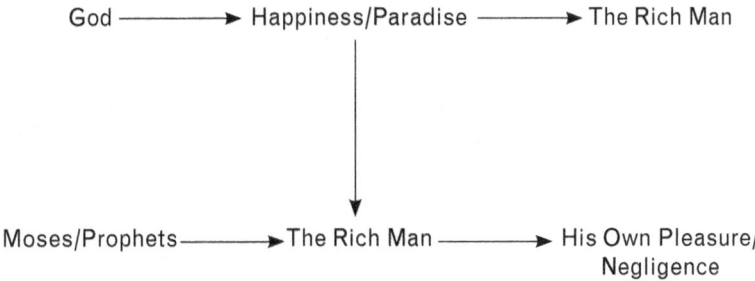

In this passage God the sender wishes to communicate eternal happiness to everyone (the receivers, represented by the would-be receiver, the rich man). However, the rich man (who is also the subject) cannot receive the intended gift because his lifestyle gets in the way. Obedience to Moses and the Prophets could have removed this obstacle. The diagrammatic form quickly enables us to "separate the essential elements of a passage from subordinate details": the parable "is not about the nature of the afterlife, but about the need to exhibit true godliness through stewardship in this life."[30]

REFLECTIONS ON STRUCTURALISM

The textual realities in which structuralists are interested are well illustrated by a short story told by Robert Capon in his book *The Third Peacock*.[31] In this story we encounter a princess who is under a curse and has fallen asleep. She can be awakened only with "an apple from the tree in the middle of the garden at the

---

[29] Barthes, *Image*, 142–48.
[30] Craig L. Blomberg, *Interpreting the Parables* (Downers Grove, Ill.: InterVarsity, 1990), 150. See further Bartholomew, *Biblical Hermeneutics*, 401–7.
[31] Robert F. Capon, *The Third Peacock: The Goodness of God and the Badness of the World* (Garden City, N.Y.: Doubleday, 1971).

Western End of the World."[32] Capon imagines how a king well trained in logistics might approach the problem of acquiring this apple. He would get out his maps, brief his generals, and send "a couple of well-supplied divisions to the garden to fetch the apple."[33] It would be a simple matter, and success would be guaranteed. But "[e]veryone knows, of course, that that is not the way the story goes."[34] The only suitable candidate for the quest turns out to be the Miller's Third Son. He sets off for the garden with strict instructions about what he must and must not do: "after entering the garden, go straight to the tree, pick the apple, and get out. Do not, under any circumstances, engage in conversation with the third peacock on the left."[35] Capon continues as follows:

> Any child worth his root beer can write the rest of the story for you. The boy goes into the garden and gets as far as the third peacock on the left, who asks him whether or not he wouldn't like a stein of the local root beer. Before he knows it, he has had three and falls fast asleep. When he wakes up, he's in a pitch-black cave; a light flickers, a voice calls—and from there on all hell breaks loose. The boy follows an invisible guide wearing a cocked hat and descends into the bowels of the earth; he rows down rivers of fire in an aluminum dinghy, is imprisoned by the Crown Prince of the Salamanders, is finally rescued by a confused eagle who deposits him at the *Eastern* end of the World, works his way back to the Western End in the dead of winter, gets the apple, brings it home, touches it to the princess's lips, arouses her, reveals himself as the long-lost son of the Eagle King, and marries the princess. Then, and only then, do they live happily ever after.[36]

How is it that "[e]veryone knows . . . the way the story goes"? How is it that, halfway through, "any child worth his root beer can write the rest of the story for you"? It is because there are *patterns* to storytelling, and folktales in their individuality nevertheless reflect these patterns—they follow basic *structures*. Therefore, we know how stories *should* go. We know, for example, that although the three little pigs in one ancient children's story are not the three bears who discover Goldilocks' home invasion in another, yet nevertheless the climactic moment in both stories will be found in the third case. The big, bad wolf destroys the first two pigs' houses, made of straw and sticks respectively, but he is not able to blow down the house of the wise third pig, who built his house with bricks. Goldilocks finds ideal the third bowl of porridge, the third chair, and the third bed that she tests, and the fact that she has tested each is successively found out by the bears, whose third discovery leads to the finding of Goldilocks herself. This "rule

---

[32] Capon, *Third Peacock*, 26.
[33] Capon, *Third Peacock*, 26.
[34] Capon, *Third Peacock*, 26.
[35] Capon, *Third Peacock*, 27.
[36] Capon, *Third Peacock*, 27–28.

of three" is a marked feature of ancient storytelling—a *structural* feature of such storytelling, underlying all sorts of narratives that are very different from each other in their individual detail.

OF MOTHERS- AND DAUGHTERS-IN-LAW

A different example begins to bring us even closer to the relevance of such insights to the reading of Scripture. This story begins with a mother-in-law and her daughter-in-law, both of whose husbands have died:

> Because the father-in-law and husband had died, the mother-in-law said to the daughter-in-law, "I am old. Because you are still young you get married again. How about it?" The daughter-in-law replied, "Although I am young I will truly not marry another. I will certainly live with my old mother-in-law." The mother-in-law again exhorted her thus, "Young people must not be deceived in this way. Won't it be all right to marry another?" The daughter-in-law said, "I cannot marry anyone like that."[37]

Hitherto the story is rather similar to the beginning of the biblical story of Ruth, and it would be natural, in fact, for biblically literate readers encountering it for the first time to assume that it *is* a version of Ruth that they are reading—and to have certain expectations about where it is going next. However, these expectations are soon confounded:

> Later the mother-in-law again said, "Because you will not marry away, I can get another to be my son (and your husband). Will that be all right?" The daughter-in-law also said, "According to this, I request mother to be very careful." When the mother-in-law heard these words, she could hardly think out a plan. So when on that day she saw a beggar standing in a cave, she returned home and told her daughter-in-law. The daughter-in-law said, "That is good." The mother-in-law asked, "Why is a beggar good?" She replied. "Because he is a poor man, on the one hand I can live with my mother (in-law) and on the other hand I can assist a poor person without relatives. This is my mind." Her mother-in-law said, "Tomorrow I will bring him here."[38]

The story concludes with the mother-in-law giving the new husband a piece of silver to buy rice for breakfast. This leads to the discovery that his erstwhile home in the cave is full of what he now understands to be the valuable commodity "silver." The family becomes extremely rich.[39]

---

[37] J. Dominic Crossan, "Perspectives and Methods in Contemporary Biblical Criticism," *BR* 32 (1977): 39–49 (46).
[38] Crossan, "Perspectives," 46.
[39] Crossan, "Perspectives," 47.

This story has certain structural similarities, then, to the biblical story of Ruth. It is unlikely, however, that there is any *historical* connection between the two, since the former is one among about seven hundred and fifty stories collected in the period 1921–1934 in midwestern China. A number of these stories were also about mothers-in-law and daughters-in-law and shared structural similarities among *themselves*—although most were about *cruel* mothers-in-law and only one other concerned a *loving* daughter-in-law. The similarities between the story of Ruth and the Chinese story just recounted do not arise from direct influence from one to the other. They are rooted in a much wider experience of the life of extended families in a world in which mother-in-law/daughter-in-law relationships have often been fraught and yet consideration and loyalty can be realities and everyone hopes for a more secure and a happier future—for a happy ending.

Structuralism and Reformation Hermeneutics

All of this speaks to the truth in the structuralist perspective, and in the form-critical perspective preceding it. We can indeed speak and write about reality only according to the categories available to us for doing so. As noted by the German philosopher Martin Heidegger (1889–1976), "language is what makes the world a home to us, providing the symbolic web of meaning relations that make up the conceptual map by which we interpret the world."[40] With the help of form criticism we have already seen what this looks like in terms of the ancient Near Eastern and Mediterranean cultural context of biblical literature, considering the conventions of speech and writing that necessarily shaped our biblical texts. Structuralism now invites us to consider the broader context of humanity in general. The writing of biblical narrative was part of a wider human activity, reflecting and addressing important human questions that are not specific to particular cultures; for example, what is the world, who are the gods, why is there suffering, and what am I to hope for? Sometimes extrabiblical literature reflects and addresses such important questions in strikingly similar ways to the Bible—just because (it seems) there are only so many stories that can be told and only so many different kinds of characters, performing their important "functions," who can inhabit them. This remains just as true in our contemporary world as in any previous one. As modern literature and film continue to explore the enduring "big questions" of human existence they inevitably "structure" their treatments of these questions—whether or not they are conscious of doing so—in ways that make the treatments recognizable to readers and viewers as new evolutions of past genres. It is not only ancient Chinese folktales that resemble parts of the

---

[40] Zimmermann, *Short Introduction*, 37.

biblical narrative in certain ways, therefore, but also contemporary popular movie epics like *Star Wars*, which draw on old ideas about the promised hero who saves the day, against all the odds, in spite of great adversity and through significant suffering.

None of this is in the least degree problematic for Bible readers committed to "seriously literal interpretation." From a Christian point of view it is quite to be expected that human beings who are made in the image of the one God will ask big questions about their existence—including questions about God—and that, when they do, their resultant literature will reflect in various ways the fact that they *are* all image-bearers created (and indeed "structured") by this one God. The structure of their literature will mirror the structure of their humanity. When we encounter the realities of literature in which structuralists are interested, then, we should not be surprised. Indeed, we should pay serious attention to them, for at least two reasons. First, they can help to clarify aspects of the biblical text itself. Roland Barthes' essay about Jacob and the angel, for example, helps us understand why we might experience such a powerful sense of disorientation in reading the story. It is rather like discovering at the end of a murder mystery that the detective is the murderer, or perhaps even that the *narrator* is the murderer (as in a novel I once read—title withheld out of respect for future readers). Second, these same textual realities provide an effective means of communicating the biblical message, drawing attention to the ways in which other stories sometimes address similar questions in similar ways, but often end up with very different (and from a Christian point of view, inadequate) answers.

Structural Flaws

It is of course important to *note* the differences along with the similarities, and this brings me to my first point of criticism of some structuralist treatments of biblical texts. For like form criticism, with its own emphasis on what is *imposed* on the author rather than on what the author *creates*, there is a tendency in structuralist criticism to obscure what is different between texts in the pursuit of what is similar. There is an arbitrariness and subjectivity about some structural classifications, indeed—as in some "formal" classifications—such that individual texts can be pressed much farther than is sensible in order to "find" the "deep, structural truth" beneath them. In this kind of deployment of the structuralist approach we arrive all too quickly at the same kinds of implausible outcome as in allegorical exegesis. The "death of the author" in such cases—an impressive piece of hyperbole that in all honesty should not be taken very seriously, since someone still needs to have composed the structured text—has been engineered precisely to allow imaginative readers full scope to have their way with the text without the possibility of authorial revenge: the author's death is necessary for "the birth of the reader," as Barthes puts it.[41] Much of Edmund Leach's reading of Genesis, for example, is wildly implausible in just such ways. To be fair, he does not single Genesis out for such treatment; he is equally loose with his cannons (or canons) elsewhere in his writings on ancient narrative. When dealing with the Greek story of Orpheus and Eurydice, for example, his obsession with binary oppositions leads him to claim that Orpheus rescues Eurydice from Hades "by means of music, but loses her because of silence."[42] This is ingenious, but also somewhat of a stretch. The reader of the actual story will quickly discover that Orpheus loses Eurydice, not because of silence, but because he turns around to look at her. Structuralist analysis is a fine tool for gaining understanding of some aspects of the biblical text; we must certainly take the structural as well as the formal aspects of texts seriously. However, we also need to take texts in their *individuality* seriously, considering the mountain as well as the mountain range. Otherwise we risk missing the point. For the fact that every author is inevitably *shaped* by language and tradition does not mean that each is a *slave* to that language and tradition. Authors (like readers) also possess "freedom to appropriate creatively our cultural heritage in light of our own present situation" (Heidegger again).[43]

Like many redaction and rhetorical critics, second, structuralists in their focus on "the text as we have it" often adopt a skeptical attitude with respect to our ability to access any reality of a *historical* kind outside the text by way of a *reading* of the text. Even where the structured text appears to wish to speak about the real past, it allegedly cannot do so. There is, however, no good reason to accept this view. Texts can surely tell us *both* about the deep structures of human thought *and* about the past. Even modern historical narratives can be subjected to structural analysis, since each one is (after all) literature—but no one argues that, because of this, modern historical narratives do not truly reflect the past.[44] Structuralism certainly contributes to our understanding of *how* and *why* people tell stories in the way that they do—but it is working above its hermeneutical pay grade when it seeks to forbid us in advance from believing that structured stories purporting to speak truthfully about the past are in fact able to do so.

Conclusion

We need not and we should not buy everything in the standard structuralist package. Yet much of what structuralists offer in their literary criticism is valuable, and "it is possible to select certain structuralist methods judiciously, without

---

[41] Barthes, *Image*, 148.
[42] Edmund Leach, *Claude Lévi-Strauss* (Harmondsworth: Penguin, 1976), 74.
[43] Zimmermann, *Short Introduction*, 38.
[44] See the excellent section on "Fiction and History" in Sternberg, *Poetics*, 23–35.

subscribing to a structuralist ideology."[45] As an ideology structuralism is of course resolutely determinist; authors become merely channels through which "deeper meanings," unintended by them, flow onward to the reader. No person of common sense should accept this deterministic account of writing, and indeed, structuralists themselves do not—or they would not bother writing books that they expect to be taken seriously as new and important contributions to their discipline. Yet there can be no question but that structuralist biblical criticism has an important role to play in helping us to understand Scripture in its *connectedness* to other human intellectual and religious literary endeavor, globally and through time.

POSTSTRUCTURALISM: THE CREATIVE READER

Structuralism represents one step away from the world of methods like redaction criticism, because it is not particularly interested in authors at all but much more in texts as we find them. In a fundamental way, however, structuralism is still rooted in the modern rather than the postmodern world. It arises out of a world that still believes in "metanarratives"—in overarching stories about reality, including human reality. It may have given up to a very great extent on the "eclipsed" biblical narrative, but it still holds that other true and comprehensive stories can be told about the world. This is the world in which the social sciences are establishing themselves, for example (anthropology, sociology, psychology), with their often-generalizing accounts about what is true about human culture or the human mind. It is a world greatly impacted by Marxism, with its historical-materialist account of reality in all of its epic, biblical proportions. Structuralism in literature breathes this same modernist air. It takes linguistics as a model and attempts to develop "grammars" that account for the form and meaning of literary works. Structuralists, too, have often given up on *the biblical narrative* as their overarching account of reality. They remain convinced, however, that systematic knowledge of reality is possible, as scientific method brings the biblical literature under its scrutiny—knowledge, for example, of what makes human beings fundamentally "tick," as indicated by what their stories share in common.

Postmodernity, conversely, has famously declared itself to be incredulous toward metanarratives.[46] It greets claims about Truth outside ourselves with suspicion or derision, and it reasserts the ability of individuals or groups to

---

[45] Anthony C. Thiselton, *The Two Horizons: New Testament Hermeneutics and Philosophical Description* (Exeter: Paternoster, 1980), 431.

[46] "I define *postmodern* as incredulity toward metanarratives. This incredulity is undoubtedly a product of progress in the sciences: but that progress in turn presupposes it." Jean-François Lyotard, *The Postmodern Condition: A Report on Knowledge* (trans. Geoff Bennington and Brian Massumi; Minneapolis: University of Minnesota Press, 1993), xxiv. For a brief introduction to postmodernity, especially as it affects biblical interpretation, see Bartholomew, "Postmodernity."

create meaning—often doing this so vigorously that there remains little place for notions of meaning and reality beyond the individual or group experience or mind at all. In literature this paradigm shift in Western and now global culture is reflected in the shift from structuralism to poststructuralism. For what marks out poststructuralists is that they are much less interested in *texts* than they are in *readers* and the act of reading. Structuralism has killed the author; poststructuralism now wishes to consider the implications of his death. "There is nothing outside of the text," maintains Jacques Derrida (1930–2004), in the first epigraph to the present chapter—and he sounds like a structuralist. But as *he* means it (as we shall see) this is actually "a markedly 'poststructuralist' claim."[47]

This interest in the reader takes milder and stronger forms. At the milder end of the poststructuralist spectrum are to be found critics interested in "reader-response" criticism (related to "reception theory," which emphasizes the role of past interpretations in shaping the response). Poststructuralists in this mode ask: is it mainly the text that directs the act of reading, or is it more the reader or the community of readers that determine the meaning of a text? They tend to ask at their most radical: does the text direct the act of reading *at all*, or is it the reader or the community of readers that *entirely determine* the meaning of a text? Wherever they find themselves at this milder end of the spectrum, poststructuralists are certainly interested in the reader who *to some extent* creates meaning by deciphering words and sentences, filling in the gaps in the story, relating parts to the whole, selecting and organizing, anticipating and modifying expectations.

At the stronger end of the poststructuralist spectrum we find *deconstructionists*. These tend to be among the more pessimistic of poststructuralist readers, standing furthest away from their Jewish and Christian forebears as a consequence not only of their incredulity toward metanarratives but also their lack of any eschatology that allows readers to "live happily ever after" in a world they can comprehend. In deconstructionism the pilgrim reader does not merely find the path to knowledge challenging but in the last analysis fruitful; she finds it instead to be a dead end. There is no confidence as to what reading can achieve. All texts—indeed, all human communications—ultimately deconstruct or undermine themselves, falling to pieces (at least as objective entities) in the reader's hands and failing to provide the information that might enable that reader to adjudicate between competing interpretations. Modern optimism about recovering "the meaning" of a text through the application of scientific method has completely evaporated; "[t]he very possibility of determinate and true readings of texts has been called into question."[48]

---

[47] For a brief introduction, see Bruce E. Benson, "Poststructuralism," *DTIB*, 607–9 (607).
[48] Bartholomew, "Postmodernity," 603.

In both cases—reader-response criticism and deconstruction—we have now resolutely left behind Vanhoozer's "age of the author," and we have also passed beyond "the age of the text." We find ourselves now in "the age of the reader."[49]

READER-RESPONSE CRITICISM

Jonathan Culler provides a helpful introduction to reader-response criticism in his book *On Deconstruction*.[50] Culler notes that structuralism, in killing the author, has already raised the reader to a prominent position; indeed, he is unconvinced in general that we can make sharp distinctions between structuralism and poststructuralism as actually practiced.[51] Who is it, after all, who makes sense of the text in all its deep structuredness if it is not the author—and it is assuredly not the author? It *must* be the reader. This awareness is already found in structuralist writing, Culler claims—even though structuralists are much more interested in "the codes and conventions responsible for . . . [a text's] intelligibility"[52] than in the business of who *perceives* that intelligibility. Others have pursued much further, however, this question of the role of the reader in creating meaning. Some of them have come to view the interpretation of a literary work in fact as *nothing other* than an account of what happens to the reader while reading. On this view "[t]o speak of the meaning of the work is to tell a story of reading."[53] In other words, the structure and meaning of a literary work are not just "there": "they emerge through an account of the reader's activity."[54] Therefore, the reader of the work is no longer the *consumer* but actually the *producer* of the text.[55] This means among other things that there is no such thing as a *wrong* reading of a text. There are only *different* readings, each of which is a "species of production."[56] The meaning of any particular literary work *is* its reader's experience. This is the pluralism of postmodernity, over against the monism of modernity and its obsession with single meanings and single readings. On this view "there is no single way of reading that is correct or natural, only 'ways of reading' that are extensions of community perspectives."[57]

---

[49] Vanhoozer, *Meaning*, 27–29.
[50] Jonathan Culler, *On Deconstruction: Theory and Criticism after Structuralism* (Ithaca, N.Y.: Cornell University Press, 1982).
[51] Culler, *Deconstruction*, 22–30.
[52] Culler, *Deconstruction*, 33.
[53] Culler, *Deconstruction*, 35.
[54] Culler, *Deconstruction*, 35.
[55] Culler, *Deconstruction*, 38, quoting Barthes.
[56] Culler, *Deconstruction*, 38.
[57] Stanley Fish, *Is There a Text in This Class? The Authority of Interpretive Communities* (Cambridge, Mass.: Harvard University Press, 1980), 16.

Active Reading

Reader-response literary critics are thus interested in the reader not as a passive but as an active and constructive person[58]—otherwise the text could not elicit a "response" in the reader. "What unites all reader-response critics is a belief that reading is an active process, not simply the passive registration of meaning."[59] The text is at least to some extent a puzzle that readers must solve in order to gain understanding. It consists of "signs" that they must interpret correctly in order to break the code—just as someone observing another person using the "semaphore" method of communication would need to know how those various signs should be read.[60] The science underlying this interpretation of "signs" is known as "semiotics." It treats *language* as a "sign" in relation to the reality that it evokes—for example, the "signifier" F-I-S-H and the signified animal "fish." Semiotics "seeks to identify the conventions and operations by which any signifying practice (such as literature) produces its observable effects of meaning."[61] Thus the chief aim of semioticians in reading texts is to discover the conventions and operations through which the reader understands what is signified. Structuralists tend to emphasize the operations and conventions as they are embedded in the text itself. Poststructuralists tend to emphasize the reader and his or her ability to render the text intelligible—the reader who can read the signs of the times (if it is *The Times* that she is reading).

Different kinds of readers emerge as attention is fixed in this way on the reading process. Peter Rabinowitz, for example, distinguishes four textual audiences:

- The actual audience—"the flesh-and-blood people who read the book"[62]—which combines the following three roles to varying degrees:
- The authorial audience, which takes the work as a communication from an author.[63]
- The narrative audience, which takes the work as a communication from the narrator.[64]

---

[58] Robin Parry, "Reader-Response Criticism," *DTIB*, 658–61 (658–59).

[59] Barton, "Legacy," 116.

[60] "A system of visual signaling by two flags held one in each hand." "Semaphor," *Webster's Learner's Dictionary*, http://www.merriam-webster.com/dictionary/semaphore.

[61] Jonathan Culler, *The Pursuit of Signs: Semiotics, Literature, Deconstruction* (Ithaca, N.Y.: Cornell University Press, 1981), 48.

[62] Peter J. Rabinowitz, "Truth in Fiction: A Reexamination of Audiences," *CI* 4 (1977): 121–41 (126).

[63] Rabinowitz, "Truth in Fiction," 126–27, 130–34.

[64] Rabinowitz, "Truth in Fiction," 127–34.

- The ideal narrative audience—"the audience for which the narrator wishes he were writing."[65]

The last of these interprets the narrator's communication in line with her apparent wishes. In its individual form the ideal narrative audience is often referred to as the "implied reader"—the reader as he or she *should* respond to the text.

Reader-Response and Rhetorical Criticism

In some ways of approaching reader-response criticism the method is similar to some forms of rhetorical criticism. There is an interest still in the text as an objective entity, even though readers have a part to play in interpreting it and making decisions about what to do with it. Before the rise of rhetorical criticism, "new critics" were already writing about "gaps" in narratives that readers were required to "fill" in order to make sense of them (e.g., supplying motivations for the actions of characters where they are not explicitly described). I already noted in my chapter 18, in addition, the importance of not always simply conceding to the rhetoric of a text; once we recognize it as a rhetoric we should also recognize that we have a choice about how to respond. To the extent that reader-response critics consider the readerly filling of gaps as a determinate task set by the boundaries of the text itself, then, we are not really in new territory here.

It is only when they begin to view readers not so much as respondents at all but as *free creators* of meaning that they begin to slip away from their moorings in prior literary-critical endeavor and to enter uncharted critical waters. Some of the work of Stanley Fish—appropriately enough, in such waters—illustrates this move. Readers read the poem that they themselves have created: "[p]rior to such a response there is no meaning and there is no text."[66] So does the work of Norman Holland, who argues that readers use texts merely "to replicate themselves." "The individual can accept the literary work only to the extent he exactly re-creates with it a verbal form of his particular pattern of defense mechanisms."[67] For Holland, reading is essentially defensive warfare. Gianni Vattimo exemplifies the trend, finally, with his emphasis on the virtue of "weak thought":

> there are no "strong" objective essential, timeless meanings. Hence interpretation does not represent pre-existent meaning but *generates* meaning. We don't discover the world through interpretation, but we create our world by describing and thus by interpreting it.[68]

---

[65] Rabinowitz, "Truth in Fiction," 134–36.
[66] Parry, "Reader-Response Criticism," 659.
[67] Culler, *Deconstruction*, 69.
[68] Zimmermann, *Short Introduction*, 140.

Culler decisively demonstrates, however, the self-contradiction and incoherence entailed in these kinds of moves, pointing out that it is simply impossible to maintain this kind of view of the reader as a free creator of meaning for any length of time. He notes, for example, how "Fish's stories" about literary theory "switch back and forth between a reader who actively takes charge and a hapless reader buffeted by fierce sentences. Fish sets out to challenge the formalist notion of the text as a structure that determines meaning,"[69] but he inevitably falls back upon this idea even as he challenges it. Readers, like authors (it turns out), are no more *unconstrained* by structure than they are *determined* by it. As Culler rightly points out, "[t]he reemergence of the text's control, in stories that sought to recount just the opposite, is a powerful illustration of the constraints discursive structures impose on theories that claim to master or describe them."[70] It is really only an account of reading that takes seriously both text and reader, recognizing the important place of each in the process that leads to understanding, which corresponds to the reality of the way in which reading operates. "There must always be dualisms: an interpreter and something to interpret, a subject and an object, an actor and something he acts upon or that acts on him."[71]

This is the kind of account of reading that Culler attributes to Wolfgang Iser, for example—a theorist who nicely combines "the creative, participatory activity of readers" with "determinate texts which require and induce a certain response."[72] Culler also mentions Eric Hirsch's attempt to get at the same balance by distinguishing between the meaning of a text (embedded in it) and its significance (drawn out of it by the reader).[73] Alister McGrath is very much on the same page in *The Science of God* with respect to God's *other* "book" of creation (see the second epigraph to the present chapter). He dismisses the postmodern attempt to see the natural sciences merely as "culturally or socially constructed entities" that do not reflect objective reality in their "text" as "quite untenable."[74] To the contrary,

> [t]he development of these constructs represents a principled exercise in attempting to understand the world as best as possible, and to develop for this purpose whatever tools or conceptualities are best suited to the tasks of the individual natural science in question, and the level of reality it engages. Within the natural sciences, such constructs are empirically based, and represent legitimate and warranted means of gaining a tighter grasp on the reality being studied.[75]

---

[69] Culler, *Deconstruction*, 71.
[70] Culler, *Deconstruction*, 72.
[71] Culler, *Deconstruction*, 75.
[72] Culler, *Deconstruction*, 75.
[73] Culler, *Deconstruction*, 76–77.
[74] McGrath, *Science of God*, 135.
[75] McGrath, *Science of God*, 136.

It may be a matter of debate in individual instances which aspects of any interpretation belong to the text (of Scripture or creation) and which to the reader. However, a principled distinction between text and reader, as between the perceiving individual and perceived reality in general, is nevertheless important and necessary, and to give it up produces theory that is radically out of line with common sense and observable human behavior. McGrath's "critical realism," conversely, finds an appropriate place for both.[76]

The Value of Reader-Response Criticism

The great value of reader-response criticism is that it makes us conscious of the fact that we *are* indeed responding in reading texts—that we are actively *doing* things as we read. It further presses upon us the question, then: are those things that we are doing in reading a particular text *justifiable*—even *asked for*? Or are we imposing ourselves inappropriately on it? Reader-response criticism makes us think hard in such ways about our readings and about the kinds of realities that influence them. It gets us reflecting, for example, on how far we do *indeed* merely engage in a "defensive" reading that is designed to absorb texts into our own world rather than have them absorb us. It gets us thinking about how far our readings are dictated or at least heavily influenced by our community of readers (and whether this is a good thing), and how far they are genuinely *our* readings. To what extent, reader-response criticism asks, are we predisposed to one interpretation rather than another by the readerly community of which we form a part? It makes us aware that we are in fact filling gaps in narratives in certain ways, whereas we may not ever before have noticed that there *are* gaps because we have never before had an alternative reading held in front of us.

In focusing on the role of readers in such ways, and in showing how we do participate in the construction of meaning as we read, reader-response criticism makes us more self-aware—aware, not least, of our ethical responsibility in adopting particular interpretations that have particular consequences. Given what is at stake, it urges us no longer simply to assume in advance that our favorite reading is the only possible one—that just because it is our favorite, it is also self-evidently correct. It urges us to consider whether as real readers of a text we are also its *ideal* readers.

---

[76] McGrath, *Science of God*, 139–69.

LET THE READER UNDERSTAND: THE GOSPEL OF MARK

Robert Fowler's book *Let the Reader Understand* provides us with a fine example from the 1990s of how reader-response criticism can illuminate a biblical text.[77] The introduction explains his project:

> This book intends to hasten the metamorphosis of my critical guild. This guild is still predominantly philological-historical in its presuppositions and practices, although in recent years significant movements into a formalist-structuralist phase and in some quarters to a poststructuralist-deconstructive phase have occurred. Here I take up the enduring legacy of philological-historical biblical criticism and more recent formalist literary criticism of the Bible to demonstrate one way we can move on from there.[78]

Although readers may assume otherwise, Fowler assures us that his book is not about the Gospel of Mark. It is rather "about the experience of reading the Gospel of Mark."[79] The "critical comments made by generations of biblical critics" about this gospel are indeed only "disguised reports of the critics' own experience of reading" it:

> Analogous to what [Stanley] Fish used to say about the legacy of criticism associated with texts such as *Paradise Lost*, I claim that we have always talked about our experience of reading Mark's Gospel but have usually done so under the guise of talking about the intentions of the evangelist, the historical events or theological ideas toward which the Gospel points, or the literary structure of the Gospel, in short, in terms of almost everything except our own encounter with the text in the act of reading.[80]

Fowler wishes to redirect our gaze. Whereas many modern readers of Mark have sought the world that lies behind our biblical texts, he wants to explore "the world that lies in front ... the world I live in and the world in which readers have always lived, the world of the reception of the Gospels—rather than the world of their production."[81] Part I of his book then goes on to give us a helpful introduction to reader-response criticism generally and its application to the Gospel of Mark in particular.

---

[77] Robert M. Fowler, *Let the Reader Understand: Reader-Response Criticism and the Gospel of Mark* (Minneapolis: Fortress, 1991).
[78] Fowler, *Let the Reader Understand*, 1.
[79] Fowler, *Let the Reader Understand*, 1.
[80] Fowler, *Let the Reader Understand*, 1.
[81] Fowler, *Let the Reader Understand*, 2.

The Storyteller's Craft and Commentary

Part II concerns the reading of the gospel itself. Fowler discusses first "the storyteller's craft" in general,[82] noting the way that Mark consistently invites the real reader of the story to play the role of implied (ideal) reader by moving as close as possible to the narrator and Jesus and adopting their point of view. The author of Mark is eager to secure the reader's adherence to the Jesus of the story, Fowler claims, even at the expense of the disciples, who typically stand at an "ironic distance" from Jesus.[83] The author's real concern in fact is not so much with the fate of either Jesus or the disciples but with the fate of the reader. This is illustrated by the way in which the Gospel ends—without resolution, pressing the reader to a decision.

Fowler next discusses "explicit commentary by the narrator"—clear guidance for readers concerning how they should read.[84] The clearest example of this explicit commentary is found in Mark 13:14 with its parenthetical "let the reader understand"—"pay attention here, O reader!" We should also see such commentary, however, in many of the words of Jesus himself (e.g., "He who has ears to hear let him hear"), as well as in clauses beginning with the Greek word *gar* ("for," as in Mark 1:16) and *hoti* ("because," as in Mark 1:34), in statements of purpose (with the conjunction *hina*, such as in Mark 14:10), and in other aspects of the Gospel that Fowler explores. Such statements provide the reader with "inside knowledge," making clear how certain events and sayings are to be interpreted. This *explicit* commentary is to be distinguished from *implicit* commentary,[85] which directs our reading without explicitly invoking the narrator's voice—by way of statements uttered by characters, for example (most prominently by Jesus), or through the particular arrangement of episodes in the story (e.g., Mark 16:1-8, 3:2, 14:10).

The Rhetoric of Indirection

Although Mark's Gospel thus gives its readers substantial guidance in reading it—much that is "clear, determinate, and direct"[86]—we also encounter a significant amount of what Fowler calls "the rhetoric of indirection."[87] It is this that gives Mark's narrative its distinctiveness and power as a work of literature. Consider the way, for example, that "hardly a word is spoken by any character" in the entirety of Mark's Passion Narrative "that the reader can take up in a

---

[82] Fowler, *Let the Reader Understand*, 61–80.
[83] Fowler, *Let the Reader Understand*, 80.
[84] Fowler, *Let the Reader Understand*, 81–126.
[85] Fowler, *Let the Reader Understand*, 127–54.
[86] Fowler, *Let the Reader Understand*, 154.
[87] Fowler, *Let the Reader Understand*, 155–94.

straightforward fashion."[88] Irony is everywhere to be found. The entire Gospel is indeed marked by "irony, metaphor, paradox, ambiguity, and opacity."[89] Werner Kelber summarizes the situation in this way:

> Jesus announces the Kingdom but opts for the cross; he is King of the Jews but condemned by the Jewish establishment; he asks for followers but speaks in riddles; he is identified as Nazarene but rejected in Nazareth; he makes public pronouncements but also hides behind a screen of secrecy; he saves others but not himself; he promises return but has not returned; he performs miracles but suffers a non-miraculous death; he is a successful exorciser but dies overcome by demonic forces; he is appointed by God in power but dies abandoned by God in powerlessness; he dies but rises from death. His beginning is nebulous and his future status is indefinite, and at the moment of Messianic disclosure he still speaks enigmatically of himself in the third person ... [as Son of Man]. If there is one single feature which characterizes the [Markan] Jesus it is contradiction or paradox.[90]

We recognize Mark's Gospel in this description of it. Yet Fowler interestingly notes that with the exception of "he saves others but not himself" and "he dies but rises from death" Kelber "borrows none of these paradoxical statements directly from the Gospel itself."[91] What he offers us is

> a catalogue of one reader's insights into moments of extended or dramatic paradox in his experience of reading Mark's Gospel. Kelber has articulated clearly and explicitly moments of paradoxical insight that came to him in his encounter with a discourse that is typically implicit and indirect. This report is a model of one reader's response to a paradoxical narrative.[92]

Moves of Greater Uncertainty

This rhetoric of indirection then bleeds into what Fowler calls "moves of greater uncertainty"—places in Mark where "clarity is intentionally avoided."[93] Consider Mark 8:11-13, for example:

> Reading Mark 8:11-13 is an instructive encounter with uncertainty.... Modern readers tend to regard this passage as a brief sketch of the Pharisees' opposition to Jesus at story level or as a throwaway transition in the narrator's discourse, an interlude in which the narrator can catch his breath. However, considering the passage more seriously, primarily at the level of discourse, is worthwhile. Mark

---

[88] Fowler, *Let the Reader Understand*, 159.
[89] Fowler, *Let the Reader Understand*, 163.
[90] Cited in Fowler, *Let the Reader Understand*, 193.
[91] Fowler, *Let the Reader Understand*, 193.
[92] Fowler, *Let the Reader Understand*, 194.
[93] Fowler, *Let the Reader Understand*, 195–227 (195).

8:11 is a request for certainty, resolution, and clear referential ("sign") meaning. The Pharisees ask Jesus for an escape from uncertainty, and he turns them down. This passage demonstrates clearly to the reader that this narrative will not strive for clarity at any price. Clarity is not always its highest priority.[94]

The end of the Gospel is, again, "a masterpiece of indirection."[95] We do not know where to turn, and we receive no "clear guidance from either the narrator or the characters" in the story.[96] The truth is veiled, the narrative opaque.

This focus on the reader's experience, particularly as it distinguishes different kinds of readers, can often lead us to see things in our biblical text that we would otherwise not have seen—and yet, upon further consideration, we come to believe that they represent justifiable understandings of the text.

DECONSTRUCTION

With deconstruction we move into a slightly different realm than reader-response criticism, and Jonathan Culler helpfully distinguishes the two.[97] He points out that what unites even reader-response criticism with its critical forebears is the belief that in the end, "the outcome of reading ... is always knowledge."[98] It is true that "[r]eaders may be manipulated and misled" as they read.[99] The pilgrim reader may well discover on the journey that texts are devious, and the traveler may well fall into many traps on the road and become "frustrated and dismayed."[100] He will certainly have discovered by the end that reading is a more complex business than he had anticipated. At the end of the hermeneutical road, however, wisdom emerges—even if it is only the wisdom that arises from "the loss of illusions."[101] There may not be any substantial notion of a metanarrative in much reader-response criticism, then, but there is certainly an eschatology: the story of reading has a happy ending in comprehension. It is similar to the hermeneutical eschatology that we observed in Origen in my chapter 8. The text resists our attempts at coherent reading, at least in its literal sense. Yet ultimately we gain knowledge—in Origen's view because it is God who has *ensured* that the text is initially incapable of coherent reading, and it is God who also guides us to knowledge by way of its spiritual sense.

---

[94] Fowler, *Let the Reader Understand*, 195–96.
[95] Fowler, *Let the Reader Understand*, 219.
[96] Fowler, *Let the Reader Understand*, 219.
[97] Culler, *Deconstruction*, 78–83.
[98] Culler, *Deconstruction*, 79.
[99] Culler, *Deconstruction*, 79.
[100] Culler, *Deconstruction*, 79.
[101] Culler, *Deconstruction*, 79.

The Impossibility of Knowledge

It is this kind of optimism that deconstructionists suspect and attack. They are much more pessimistic about what reading can achieve, partly because they eschew discussion of the "ideal reader" and prefer to look at what real readers have actually done. Here they claim to find readers who have only ever "failed to understand what they were doing, were influenced by assumptions they did not control, [and] were generally misled in ways which we can describe but they cannot."[102] Deconstructionists are the literary heirs of the nihilist philosophy of Friedrich Nietzsche (1844–1900), then, particularly as developed by Derrida. If "[s]tructuralists are convinced that systematic knowledge is possible," these poststructuralists "claim to know only the impossibility of this knowledge."[103] There is, in this sense, "nothing outside of the text" itself (Derrida, in the first epigraph again)—that is, no "determinate reality outside the play of signs ... nothing beyond particular and contingent language systems, and therefore nothing to keep meaning centered, stable, and determinate."[104] As Culler puts it, "when you think you are getting outside signs and text, to 'reality itself,' what you find is more text, more signs."[105] Deconstruction is indeed "the negation, reversal, and contradiction of all methodological attempts to achieve knowledge or truth" as a result of reading literary works.[106] If structuralists attempt to develop "'grammars' ... that would account for [their] form and meaning," these poststructuralists "investigate the way in which this project is subverted by the workings of the texts themselves."[107] On this view "the particulars swallow up any attempt to unify them or to domesticate their sheer plurality."[108] If reading is, as Culler claims, "an attempt to understand writing by determining the referential and rhetorical modes of the text ... removing obstacles in the quest for a coherent result," then deconstructionists argue that "the construction of texts" themselves "may block this process of understanding."[109] Coherent reading is impossible—and in Nietzsche's world, as opposed to Origen's, *ultimately* impossible. Mastery of any text is quite beyond us. Every text—indeed all human communication—ultimately deconstructs or undermines itself in this way.

It is such realities that deconstructionists set out to demonstrate, generating conflicting meanings from the same text and playing those meanings off against

---

[102] Culler, *Deconstruction*, 80.
[103] Culler, *Deconstruction*, 22.
[104] Vanhoozer, *Meaning*, 63.
[105] Culler, *Literary Theory*, 15.
[106] Vanhoozer, *Meaning*, 39.
[107] Culler, *Deconstruction*, 22.
[108] Vanhoozer, *Meaning*, 39–40.
[109] Culler, *Deconstruction*, 81.

one another. They search out ideological inconsistencies or ambiguities that prevent interpreters from ever saying that the text has a fixed meaning. They revel, in fact, "in the play of endlessly deferred meaning."[110] As Kevin Vanhoozer puts it, "[d]econstruction is a strategy for resisting closure";[111] interpretation just goes on and on. Readings multiply as "products" for consumption by those who find them attractive, discarded later for new and more pleasing models in a postmodern (ultramodern) culture whose great characteristic *is* consumption.[112] In resisting closure in this way it is intriguing to note that deconstructionists often point to features of the text that have been noted by older historical critics but interpreted as evidence of sources and redaction. Deconstruction in this sense is the heir of reconstruction, as a historically focused method is now replaced by a textually focused one. However, the new method has a consciously ethical edge to it that the older ones have not:

> [D]econstruction is oriented toward radical hospitality that allows another to disrupt one's expectations and does not seek to interpret another's communication in order to assimilate his views to the framework of my own interpretive horizon.[113]

Derrida once famously "described the hermeneutic impulse to understand another as [itself] a form of violence that seeks to overcome the other's particularity and unique difference... Hermeneutics' quest for meaning is... really a quest for domination."[114] Deconstruction, conversely, is about making space for "the other"—that is what its "disruption of sense" seeks to achieve.[115]

Deconstruction and the "Second Way"

It is this kind of deconstructionist thinking about communication and literature, allied to the thinking of the "free-creation" reader-response critics, that provides the basis for the "second way" Protestant approaches to biblical hermeneutics introduced in my first chapter. Here, too, the emphasis lies on the independence of texts from their authors as well as the role of readers in *constructing* meaning out of texts. Here, too, we find Vattimo's "weak thought," now in the form of John Caputo's "weak theology." Now it is God himself who does not oppress "the other"—not even by personally existing, in some ways of thinking, and certainly

---

[110] Zimmermann, *Short Introduction*, 138.
[111] Vanhoozer, *Meaning*, 40. Vanhoozer's engagement throughout the book with Derrida in particular is extensive and will repay the careful attention of the reader who wishes to delve further into the latter's thought.
[112] Bartholomew, "Postmodernity," 600–601, 605.
[113] Zimmermann, *Short Introduction*, 138.
[114] Zimmermann, *Short Introduction*, 137.
[115] Zimmermann, *Short Introduction*, 138.

not by speaking authoritatively about anything. God, like the author in general, is dead, unless he is resurrected by his readers: "God is what God does, and what God does is what is done in the name of God, which is the birth of God in the world. The death of God means that God's call goes unheard, is stillborn."[116] It is readers who are the really important persons in the world, and among these readers dogma should be "out" and radical hospitality and openness must be "in." Dogma *must* be out because it inevitably breeds violence *rather than* hospitality: "I do not see," writes Caputo

> how any religious tradition or theological language can take shape *without* violence ... whether institutionally or in the readings it makes of texts which differ from its point of view, unless it is through and through marked by thinking and acting in deconstructive style.[117]

Among these texts are certainly the *biblical* ones—texts that just as resolutely as any others resist our attempts to understand their true meaning. As Peter Rollins puts it, introducing to the public his book *The Fidelity of Betrayal*,

> the Judeo-Christian narrative pushes back on [our] desire [for a master we can dominate], inviting us to take responsibility for our own thoughts rather than placing them onto another. In short, every time we attempt to master the master (e.g. understand the true meaning of the text), the master pushes back on us (slipping out of our attempts to reduce its truth to some set of facts).[118]

For Rollins, understanding the true meaning of the biblical text is *mastery*, and that is something that we should not and cannot possess. The biblical narrative continually slips out of our grasp. It is indeed a manifestation of unbelief that the Church has constructed out of Scripture and offered to the world "yet another grand narrative that tells us why we are here, where we are going, and what we ought to be doing."[119] In the event that birthed Christianity (the crucifixion), claims Rollins, we find "something far more powerful than one more master mythology designed to cover over our unknowing and anxiety"—not "another

---

[116] John D. Caputo, *The Insistence of God: A Theology of Perhaps* (ISPR; Bloomington: Indiana University Press, 2013), 36.

[117] John D. Caputo, "What Do I Love When I Love My God? Deconstruction and Radical Orthodoxy," in *Questioning God* (ed. John D. Caputo, Mark Dooley, and Michael J. Scanlon; Bloomington: Indiana University Press, 2001), 291–317 (307). It is Radical Orthodoxy that he particularly has in his sights in this quotation.

[118] Peter Rollins, "The Fidelity of Betrayal: Give Me a Master I Can Dominate," http://peterrollins.net/the-fidelity-of-betrayal-give-me-a-master-i-can-dominate/ (accessed September 15, 2016).

[119] Rollins, *Idolatry of God*, 98.

system of meaning to place alongside all the others but a type of splinter that disturbs all meaning systems and calls them into question."[120]

The Incoherence of Deconstruction

If truth be told, there is little in the deconstructionist approach to either communication in general or literature in particular that is worthwhile, beyond its reminder that all interpreters are language-bound beings, constantly tempted to idolatry (including the idolatry of the self) who should remember their limitations and love their interpretive neighbors, listening to what they have to say and not subjecting them to violence. This is all well and good. It is simply a reality, however, that although we may well understand that communication can be flawed and partial—can indeed involve puzzlement and self-contradiction—we do not hold that because of this true knowledge (of persons or texts) cannot be communicated. We do not and we *cannot* live as if meaningful communication were ultimately beyond our reach. Deconstructionists *themselves* do not live or write as if they themselves really believe this. They deliver lectures and write books, after all; one imagines that they mostly have a serious purpose in doing so, and that it is to *refer* reliably to reality outside their text. If so, then the kind of position they theoretically hold is simply incoherent.

I remember an exchange at a conference a number of years ago between myself and another biblical scholar that illustrates this incoherence only too well. He had taken exception to remarks about his work that I had made in a presentation on OT historiography. His first objection was that I had misrepresented what he had written in his books. His second was that on a number of occasions I had referred in my presentation to "the plain sense" of the biblical text. Did I not understand how naïve this was, he enquired, in these poststructuralist times? My response was to ask him how, if he really did not believe in such a thing as the plain sense of a text, he could reasonably claim that I had misrepresented what he had written in his books. This response did not please him, because if there is one thing that poststructuralist scholars in deconstructionist mode do not appreciate it is the application of their own method to their own work. *Their* books, it seems, are quite capable of communicating true, stable knowledge, even if other people's are not.

The fact is that all deconstruction inevitably deconstructs itself in this way, disappearing up its own hermeneutical back passage even as it births the interpretive chaos that it seems so keen—for whichever noble or ignoble ends—to set loose upon the rest of the world. This is as true of quasi-Christian versions of the approach as of other kinds. Peter Rollins wishes us to believe, for example,

---

[120] Rollins, *Idolatry of God*, 98–99.

that authentic Christian faith involves the continual "disturbing" of "all meaning systems." If this is true, then it already fatally undermines his own attempts in his various books to provide us with one of these—and he does appear to wish to do so. He has his own "grand narrative" that he wants to relate, which involves at its heart "the crucifixion that splinters" all grand narratives—except his own, we assume. Or, if his own is included, why should we spend time reading his books? It is exactly the same kind of question that arises with respect to the plays written by predominantly European playwrights in the middle of the twentieth century that are often referred to under the general heading "the Theatre of the Absurd" (e.g., the plays of Samuel Beckett). How can one really take seriously plays in which the audience is addressed as a community and with meaning about the alleged truth that humans beings find themselves alone in a meaningless world?

If we are only interested in playing intellectual games that reveal how sophisticated we are then of course the charge of incoherence is one that can easily be brushed aside. But although deconstructionists do indeed often claim to be interested only in "play," it always turns out in reality that their play is selective. It is designed to disable competing worldviews—to render implausible competing ideologies. Their own worldviews and ideologies are always kept safely at home, out of risk of being mugged by someone else's deconstructive gangster. This quickly becomes apparent when their own sacred cows (to change the metaphor) are threatened with deconstruction. There are very few, then, who are prepared simply to laugh everything off—including the real or imagined misinterpretation of their own texts. It may well be, then, that the stated postmodern objective is to some extent to "celebrate and play amid our limitations and finitude, in a sort of cheerful nihilism"[121]—but the extent to which this is the actual reality is limited.

CONCLUSION

Both structuralist and poststructuralist perspectives are capable of helping us with the right reading of Scripture, if they are deployed with discrimination. The first focuses our attention on the way in which the telling of the biblical Story is related to storytelling more generally, in terms of both the *manner* in which it is told and the *themes* that it addresses. This helps Christian Bible readers understand more clearly both the similarity and the difference between stories in general and the Story that they hold to be ultimately True in particular. The second focuses our attention on the act of reading Scripture. It can help us to be more conscious of what we are doing when we read the Bible as Christian Scripture and to be more determined not to impose ourselves inappropriately upon it. Discrimination *is* necessary, however, because a considerable amount of structuralist

---

[121] Bartholomew, "Postmodernity," 601.

and poststructuralist thought has been developed not so much to aid the understanding of particular texts (including biblical texts) as to obstruct it. And while the rhetoric has often involved respect for the voice of "the other," the reality has often involved the silencing of at least the *textual* "other"—just as effectively as in the allegorical or historical-critical reading of earlier times. Love of such textual "others," and indeed of the dead neighbors who wrote them, has quite often been in short supply.

20

Narrative Criticism
Getting the Story Straight

Beyond the desert of criticism, we wish to be called again.

—*Paul Ricoeur*[1]

Story refers to the content of the narrative, what it is about. A story consists of such elements as events, characters, and settings, and the interaction of these elements comprises what we call the plot. Discourse refers to the rhetoric of the narrative, how the story is told.

—*Mark Powell*[2]

The modern critical developments described in chapters 18 and 19, each in its own way, flow into what is typically described in contemporary biblical scholarship as "narrative criticism"—a broad "movement" among academic readers of the biblical narrative literature who, in the aftermath of a prolonged period of dominance by "behind the text" scholarship in biblical studies, have turned their attention once again to the text in its present form. Recognizing that something valuable has been lost in the eclipse of biblical narrative, while often also appreciating many of the insights of modern criticism about it, narrative critics do not necessarily wish to return to premodern ways of reading the Bible (although they often value these much more than do their modern critical forebears). They do not wish to take modern Bible readers back, as it were, to a hermeneutical Egypt. Neither are they content, however, to leave them thirsty in a "desert of criticism" (the first epigraph above) where the Bible has been disabled by modern scholarship from speaking to contemporary readers in meaningful ways. The point of leaving Egypt was never to die in the desert, but rather to journey on to the Promised Land. So it is that Paul Ricoeur, for example, aims at what he calls "a

---

[1] Paul Ricoeur, *The Symbolism of Evil* (trans. Emerson Buchanan; New York: Harper & Row, 1967), 349.

[2] Mark A. Powell, *What Is Narrative Criticism?* (Minneapolis: Fortress, 1990), 23.

second naïveté" in his reading of Scripture. We cannot go back, he proposes, to "a primitive naïveté": "But if we can no longer live the great symbolisms of the sacred in accordance with the original belief in them, we can, we modern men, aim at a second naïveté in and through criticism. In short, it is by *interpreting* that we can *hear* again."[3] We can reappropriate the biblical narrative even as modern, critically aware readers.

The scholars interested in this narrative-critical project are diverse in other respects. What unites them is that they are influenced less by the insights of "behind the text" modern criticism—source, form, and to some extent redaction criticism—than by those of formalism and new criticism as they have impinged on biblical studies in association with redaction criticism (from a different point of view), rhetorical criticism, structuralism, reader-response criticism, and deconstruction. Some of them self-identify under one of these very headings,[4] and the way in which each of them combines prior methods in his or her particular narrative-critical approach varies. There is widespread disagreement, further, on questions we have touched upon in previous chapters: for example, about the extent to which biblical narrative as an artistically constructed entity is capable of historical or theological reference. The term "narrative critics," then, does not describe a tightly bound-together "school of thought." It describes a diverse group of scholars whose approach to biblical narrative texts *prioritizes*, at the very least, questions of how these texts are fashioned in terms of plot, point of view, characterization, and rhetorical structure; how authors, readers, narrators, and implied readers are involved in the appropriation of the text; and how the texts "work" to achieve their ends as tools of persuasion. They attend, in Mark Powell's words (in the second epigraph above), both to biblical "story" and to biblical "discourse."

THE ART OF THE BOOK OF GENESIS

When the honor list is drawn up of those who have been most influential in establishing a modern narrative approach to biblical texts, Robert Alter's name is always among those at the top—so we shall begin by looking at part of one of his books, *The Art of Biblical Narrative*.[5] What role does literary art play in the shaping of biblical narrative, he asks? In affirming that its role is crucial, he takes as his example chapter 38 from the book of Genesis and explores its place within the story of Joseph and his family that is told in Genesis 37–50.

---

[3] Ricoeur, *Symbolism*, 351.
[4] E.g., Phyllis Trible's 1994 narrative-critical study of the book of Jonah is actually titled *Rhetorical Criticism: Context, Method, and the Book of Jonah*.
[5] Robert Alter, *The Art of Biblical Narrative* (New York: Basic Books, 1981), 3–22.

Genesis 38 and Criticism

Genesis 38 is an interesting example to choose, precisely because of the difficulty that readers have often had in reading it as part of the Joseph story at all—at least in its present context. Already in the closing centuries BC, for example, the author of the *Book of Jubilees*, in his retelling of the Genesis story, delays the account of Judah and Tamar until he has reported the Joseph story up to the point of Joseph's gathering of food in preparation for the famine in Egypt (Gen 41). *Jubilees* is one of the ancient Jewish Pseudepigrapha (writings where the stated author is not the true author), and it sets out to recapitulate the contents of the OT, sometimes staying fairly close to the biblical narrative but sometimes adding or deleting material or giving new reasons for what is happening in the story.[6] It probably dates from around 104 BC. Clearly its author thinks that the content of Genesis 38 finds a more "natural" position just where he places it.

Modern source critics have unsurprisingly emphasized the tensions between Genesis 38 and its surrounding context in pursuit of a historical explanation of the *development* of the text. They have generally attributed Genesis 38 to the J-source (note the divine name "Yahweh" in vv. 7 and 10), but they have unanimously agreed that the story does not "fit" in its current location. For whereas it presupposes a prolonged interval in Judah's life in which he is away from his family long enough to accumulate both sons and grandsons (Gen 46:12), no such interval is assumed in the remainder of the Joseph story. Judah is throughout a member of Jacob's household, unseparated from his family. Form critics have looked at the matter no differently, even though Gunkel's entire treatment of Genesis 37–50 as a traditional *novella* departs from the standard source-critical view. This *novella*, nevertheless, also finds no place for Genesis 38 in its current location. How is the chapter to be explained, then? The standard "behind the text" explanation of this kind of problem has been deployed: a redactor inserted it in this inappropriate position. He did so either because he was incompetent or because he had no choice—he understood himself as the custodian of diverse traditions that he could not attempt to coordinate and harmonize. One way or another, Genesis 38 is regarded as "a completely independent unit" without any "connection with the drama of Joseph."[7]

---

[6] C. T. R. Hayward, "Genesis and Its Reception in Jubilees," in *The Book of Genesis: Composition, Reception, and Interpretation* (ed. C. A. Evans, J. N. Lohr, and D. L. Petersen; VTSup 152; Leiden: Brill, 2012), 375–404.

[7] Speiser, *Genesis*, 299.

The Insufficiency of Criticism

Alter brilliantly parodies this insufficient explanation for the existence of Genesis 38, arguing that it involves the implausible belief that "the redactors were in the grip of a kind of manic tribal compulsion, driven again and again to include units of traditional material that made no connective sense, for reasons they themselves could not have explained."[8] Seeking a more satisfactory understanding of the text, he draws attention to a number of interesting connections between Genesis 38 and its immediate context that suggest conscious artistry in the redactor who put the Joseph story together.[9] For example, there are two "goings down" described in Genesis 37–39 (38:1, "Judah went down from his brothers"; 39:1, "Joseph was brought down to Egypt"), both concerning the "death" of sons (Joseph, allegedly, and Er and Onan, actually). "Recognition" is a recurrent motif not just in Genesis 37–38 but also in chapters 42 and 45. In Genesis 37:32-33 Jacob recognizes the garment shown to him by his sons as Joseph's garment, and in chapter 38 Judah recognizes the seal, cord, and staff as his own (38:25-26). In both stories we also find the common symbol of the kid goat (the brothers slaughter one in order to deceive in Gen 37:31; Judah sends one to "the woman" in Gen 38:20 in order to redeem a pledge). And finally, Genesis 38 is a tale of exposure through a lack of sexual restraint, while chapter 39 is a tale of seeming defeat and ultimate triumph through sexual self-discipline.

In reading Genesis 37–39 in this integrated manner Alter notes that various of these insights are found in early Jewish commentary on Genesis, from both the early and the medieval periods. The common symbol of the young goat and the common speech of recognition are already noted in *Genesis Rabbah*, for example—a fifth-century AD Palestinian midrash that provides a running, detailed commentary on Genesis.[10] Alter does not recommend that we seek to become once again premodern people like such ancient readers or that we adopt every perspective of theirs on the sacred text. He does believe that Genesis 37–39 are the product of a redactor, who has shaped traditions that have come down to him over a long period of time. To this extent Alter reflects a modern view of the text. The point he is making, however, is that the ancient redaction is *intelligent*. The redactor is a conscious, literary artist who has placed the story in Genesis 38 where it now stands quite deliberately and with rhetorical purpose.

Art and Meaning

What Alter advocates for, then, is a truly literary approach to the biblical texts—approaching them as serious literature and reading them closely as such. This

---

[8] Alter, *Art of Biblical Narrative*, 20.
[9] Alter, *Art of Biblical Narrative*, 6–10.
[10] Alter, *Art of Biblical Narrative*, 10–12.

close reading leads to a greater depth of understanding in the case of Genesis 38 as to how the biblical text works as a piece of art. "Behind the text" approaches to Genesis 37–39 are at the same time undercut in two ways. They are undercut, first, in their claims about the importance of understanding the *process* by which a text came into being. Alter believes that such a process occurred, and he does not wish to argue with people of antiquarian interest on this point. At the same time it is no longer clear what the *importance* of reflecting very much on this process might be. It certainly *cannot* be that we are unable to read the text coherently in its present form. "Behind the text" approaches are undercut, second, in their typical prejudice that only "enlightened" people can read biblical texts properly— that "pre-critical" exegesis offers little of value. If one thinks that Alter's reading of Genesis 37–39 is plausible, then one is also compelled to the conclusion that at least in certain respects some ancient readers have read these passages better than some modern ones. They have perceived the art in these chapters much more clearly than their successors—and have therefore grasped their true meaning with greater clarity as well.

Building on Alter's insights, it is indeed possible to find our way to a better understanding of the meaning of the whole of Genesis 37–50 than has often been managed, especially in the modern period. The gateway to this understanding is the obvious question (one would have thought), *why* place a story about *Judah*, in particular, in Genesis 38? The most plausible answer to this question is that our redactor means to introduce Judah as the other major player in the drama of Genesis 37–50, providing us with some important facts about him that are important for understanding the story that follows. Genesis 38 is indeed a story that expands on the preceding chapter in revealing more about Judah's character (in unflattering terms) while informing us also about his line—in danger of extinction as Genesis 38 opens, but saved in the end by the actions of the resourceful Tamar. Genesis 39–50 then paint an interesting picture of the positive development of Judah's character, and toward the end they reveal the fundamental importance of Judah's line (Gen 49:8-12): "your father's sons will bow down to you" (49:8). It was Joseph who dreamed the dream about his brothers bowing down to him in Genesis 37, but it is Judah who ultimately inherits this dream. Genesis 37–50 carefully considered as narrative literature turns out to be as much a Judah story as a Joseph story.[11]

THE ART OF THE BOOKS OF SAMUEL

The obsession with "behind the text" issues that contributes to modern commentators missing both the art and the meaning of Genesis 37–50 as we find them

---

[11] For more details, see Provan, *Discovering Genesis*, 185–88.

now on the page is also responsible for deficient readings of other OT narrative texts. A great example is the story of the reign of King David as recounted in 2 Samuel.

The Depths Beneath

In chapter 18 I noted the way in which Martin Noth's hypothesis about a once-existing "Deuteronomistic History" posited the incorporation into this entity of a preexisting "Succession Narrative" as envisaged by Leonhard Rost (2 Sam 9 through 1 Kgs 2). "Behind the text" scholarship has disagreed somewhat since Rost's time about the extent of this Succession Narrative, not least on the question of where it *begins*. Second Samuel 9 is in reality an implausible suggestion, since David's request therein for survivors from the house of Saul presupposes the account of the death of Ishbosheth in the opening chapters of 2 Samuel. A proposed alternative in 2 Samuel 2 involves similar difficulties, because other aspects of the story in chapters 9 to 20 presuppose not only the stories of Ishbosheth and Abner but also the story of David as far back as 1 Samuel 18–20. Then again, are we really dealing with a "Succession" Narrative at all, or simply a "Court History" beginning perhaps in 2 Samuel 13?[12] Typically for much of the scholarship that is obsessed with hypothetical prebiblical sources, the fact that the same texts produce such widely varying historical reconstructions of the Succession Narrative did not for a long time after Rost disturb the consensus that the Narrative really did once exist. There was little general appetite for a more holistic approach in which 2 Samuel 9–20 and 1 Kings 1–2 were treated once again simply as an integral part of the story of David (and Solomon).

An Unwise Angel

The consequence of this general belief about a Succession Narrative has been readings of 2 Samuel that have missed important aspects of the story. As Peter Ackroyd once put it, commentators have been "hindered by restrictions imposed by artificial and hypothetical categorizing of the text," and this has resulted in a "too narrow reading [of the text]."[13] In particular, in focusing on the theme of Davidic succession, which is not obviously a leading concern of 2 Samuel 9–20, they have failed to do justice to what clearly *is* one of the main themes of these chapters—the possession (or not) of wisdom. Right at their heart lie the

---

[12] For an introduction to the theorizing around these issues up until the early 1990s, see Gillian Keys, *The Wages of Sin: A Reappraisal of the "Succession Narrative"* (JSOTSup 221; Sheffield: Sheffield Academic, 1996), 14–42.

[13] Peter R. Ackroyd, "The Succession Narrative (So-Called)," *Interpretation* 35 (1981): 383–96 (396).

questions, "what is wisdom, and who possesses it?"[14] David is *said* to possess it in 2 Samuel 14:20—to display "wisdom like that of the angel of God [to know] everything that happens in the land/on the earth." This is what the wise woman of Tekoa indicates. Yet the story of David told in 2 Samuel 9–20 casts doubt on this claim. Certainly after 2 Samuel 11–12 David is a divided man with a divided family who fosters division in his kingdom in pursuit of power, foreshadowing in his own person the divided kingdom of his grandson Rehoboam's day. What kind of wisdom is it, then, that produces the results that are the story of David in 2 Samuel 13–20? Is David *truly* a wise man? Or are the words of the wise woman merely flattery? Is it *she* who is truly wise (along with her sponsor Joab), as she manipulates the king through her rhetoric to persuade him to do as she wishes?

If so, she is not the only wise person to appear in the story as a foil to David. In 2 Samuel 13 we have previously met Jonadab, Amnon's friend: a wise man anxious to help this son of the king who, like his father, desires to possess a woman. Jonadab also contrives a story for David, knowing only too well how to manipulate the allegedly all-knowing king—and his plan to facilitate the rape of Tamar duly succeeds. At the end of that chapter Jonadab reappears as someone who again knows vastly more than David about what is going on in the king's own domain. David simply believes what he is told: Absalom has killed all the king's sons. Jonadab knows differently: only Amnon is dead. How he knows is never made clear: perhaps his wisdom partly resides in knowing when to stick with his friends and when to keep quiet about plots to have them murdered. The main point is this, however: that David knows nowhere near as much in these stories as the wise people around him.

Wisdom under a Cloud

Jan Fokkelman has summed up nicely the movement of the narrative in 2 Samuel 13–14. A combination of illusion and reality holds the texts in this section of the book together:

> The illusion: David thinks that he is visiting an ailing Amnon, that he is sending his sons to a feast, and that he is hearing a widow pleading for her son. The reality:

---

[14] What follows is substantially based on an earlier essay of mine, "On 'Seeing' the Trees while Missing the Forest: The Wisdom of Characters and Readers in 2 Samuel and 1 Kings," in *In Search of True Wisdom: Essays in Old Testament Interpretation in Honour of Ronald E. Clements* (ed. Edward Ball; JSOTSup 300; Sheffield: Sheffield Academic, 2000), 153–73, to which the reader is referred for the detailed argument and supporting references. This essay is now conveniently available also in Provan, *Against the Grain*, 247–71.

Amnon, full of energy, is on the way to gratifying his sexual appetite, Absalom kills his brother, and Joab tries to arrange a reconciliation.[15]

As Fokkelman goes on to suggest, David, blinded by his ego, repudiates the unity of life and people, dividing Bathsheba from Uriah, divorcing himself from God, and dividing his family against itself. From that point onward the world presented to him becomes steadily less reliable, fragmented, and difficult to put together. As David has abused people around him mercilessly, now he is abused. His sons manipulate him, using him for their own crimes.[16] Yet David knows little throughout of what is really happening.

This play on the nature of wisdom and who possesses it does not cease with 2 Samuel 13–14; it continues into 2 Samuel 15–20. David is "wise," allegedly—but in the narrative reality that contextualizes this claim he appears anything *but* wise. A close reading of the text reveals the manifold ways in which this is so. It is not that we are to think that the wisdom of the other characters in the story is necessarily beyond question either. The wisdom that in 2 Samuel 13 facilitates rape, or in chapter 14 eases Absalom's return and rebellion, or in chapters 16 and 17 advocates the humiliation or execution of David—this is not wisdom of which the reader should think well. It is not just Davidic wisdom that is under a cloud in 2 Samuel, therefore, but the very notion of human wisdom *at all* as it seeks to function in independence of the divine will. The point is, though, that one way or another the nature of wisdom is one of the main things that 2 Samuel is *about*. Yet modern readers have often been oblivious to this reality.

THE ART OF THE BOOKS OF KINGS

The reading mistakes in 2 Samuel that follow from a critical focus on the hypothetical Succession Narrative are matched by further errors when it comes to 1 Kings. Here the modern critic already "knows" as he begins that there is a major disjunction in the text between 1 Kings 2 and 1 Kings 3. One story ends and something different begins just at this point. The Succession Narrative ends—and the historian who incorporated this source into his Deuteronomistic History begins to take on a more active authorial role. Here is another ancient literary "work" of whose existence much "behind the text" modern scholarship has been certain, even as it has not been able to agree on its original extent (did it once reach only as far as Hezekiah or Josiah or was it always longer?), its

---

[15] Jan P. Fokkelman, *Narrative Art and Poetry in the Books of Samuel: A Full Interpretation Based on Stylistic and Structural Analyses. I. King David (2 Sam. 9–20 & 2 Kings 1–2)* (SSN 20; Assen: Van Gorcum, 1981), 156–57.

[16] Fokkelman, *Narrative Art*, 158–61.

original date (preexilic or exilic, or even postexilic?), or the number and nature of its authors and editors.[17]

SIMPLE SOLOMON

The existence of both works is simply assumed, for example, in Gwilym Jones' 1984 commentary on 1 Kings.[18] Leonhard Rost is said to have "established" that 2 Samuel 9–20 and 1 Kings 1–2 originally formed an unbroken narrative, and a detailed discussion of this narrative follows.[19] This leads Jones then to propose that "these first two chapters [of Kings] are to be separated from the account of Solomon's reign in 3:1–11:43."[20] The fact that we so obviously have a source in 1 Kings 1–2 means that there must be "separation" between chapters 1–2 and 3–11 in the reading of 1 Kings 1–11. First Kings 3 no longer follows 1 Kings 1–2, as it were (and certainly does not follow 2 Samuel). And indeed, later in the commentary it is 1 Kings 3–11 only, treated as a block that is quite independent of 1 Kings 1–2, that are included under the heading "The Reign of Solomon."[21] The consequences for the interpretation of the Solomon story of this kind of "separation" in the critical mind have been significant. What follows from this reconstruction of the history of the text is typically an account of Solomon's reign that is divided into two fairly self-contained parts: an earlier period in which a wise Solomon is obedient to God and is blessed by God (1 Kgs 3–10), followed by a later period (1 Kgs 11) in which an unwise Solomon is disobedient to God and divine judgment falls upon him.

A MORE INTERESTING SOLOMON

What is obvious to the reader of the present Hebrew text of 1 Kings, on the other hand, is that its author (or redactor) presents Solomon's reign as beginning not in 1 Kings 3, but in 1 Kings 2:12. It is in chapter 2 that we read of the early days of his reign during which he enacts the advice of his father, David, and rids himself of his enemies—and it is here that we first encounter a reference to his wisdom. David urges his son to "act according to [his] wisdom" in getting rid of Joab son of Zeruiah (1 Kgs 2:6) and Shimei son of Gera (1 Kgs 2:9). The emphasis lies on subtlety: Solomon must not act rashly but use his brain and find some justification for removing these troublesome characters from his kingdom. The word

---

[17] For a review of the scholarship at least up until the early 1990s, see Steven L. McKenzie, *The Trouble with Kings: The Composition of the Book of Kings in the Deuteronomistic History* (VTSup 42; Leiden: Brill, 1991).

[18] Gwilym H. Jones, *1 and 2 Kings* (NCB; 2 vols.; Grand Rapids: Eerdmans, 1984).

[19] Jones, *1 and 2 Kings*, 1:48–57.

[20] Jones, *1 and 2 Kings*, 1:88.

[21] Jones, *1 and 2 Kings*, 1:119–247.

behind "wisdom" is however the Hebrew *ḥokmāh*, exactly as it is elsewhere in the Solomon story—and its use in 1 Kings 2, in a chapter that is highly ambiguous about the rights and wrongs of the executions and banishments it portrays, and thus raises questions both about the quality of the wisdom described and the character of David and his successor,[22] must surely influence our understanding of its later deployment.

Read in this context 1 Kings 3 clearly presents Solomon as a king aware of the deficiency of his previous wisdom and addressing God about this fact. The emphasis of the whole section 1 Kings 3:4-15 falls, we note, on wisdom as a supernatural gift from God rather than as something innate (as it is implicitly in 1 Kings 2). This is wisdom from above, not below. A "wise and discerning heart" is given to Solomon by God in 1 Kings 3, which enables Solomon for a while to govern his people well and to distinguish between right and wrong (1 Kgs 3:9)—a veiled allusion to the events of 1 Kings 2 by a God who expresses pleasure that the king has not sought long life, wealth, nor *the death of his enemies* (1 Kgs 3:10-11) and then *grants* him long life and wealth but specifically *not* the death of his enemies (1 Kgs 3:13-14). The glory of Solomon's newly acquired wisdom is then further celebrated in 1 Kings 4, with questions posed about it in chapters 9 and 10, just before the king's collapse into apostasy in chapter 11.

On Reading Chapters One after Another

Ultimately the Solomon story from 1 Kings 2 through 11 is exploring just the same questions as the preceding 2 Samuel: what is the nature of true wisdom, and who possesses it? The various chapters compose part of the same narrative, organized around the same theme. Close narrative-critical reading reveals that this is so, and in the process reveals that the simplistic "good Solomon/bad Solomon" dichotomy of much modern reading of 1 Kings, premised on certain modern, settled, and detailed convictions about the processes of composition that lie behind the text, is much more a figment of the scholarly imagination than anything else. "Behind the text" theorizing has actually *disabled* the reader from understanding the text rather than contributing anything of value to it. And the two-dimensional Solomon that ultimately emerges from this theorizing—the Solomon of the modern scholar, rather than the Solomon of the ancient artist—is vastly less interesting and colorful than the Solomon who actually inhabits the text, in all his complexity and ambiguity.

---

[22] Provan, *Kings*, 31–36.

THE ART OF THE BOOK OF JONAH

In the aftermath of to-be-expected "behind the text" attention to the book of Jonah among earlier generations of modern biblical scholars, narrative critics have also turned their attention to this text. In doing so they have not encountered any thoroughgoing source-critical analysis of the book, not least because the distribution of the divine names therein is not helpful to that project. "Yahweh" appears in Jonah 1:1–2:2; "Elohim" in Jonah 3:5-10; "Yahweh" again in Jonah 4:1-4; the combination "Yahweh Elohim" in Jonah 4:6; "Elohim" in Jonah 4:7-9; and "Yahweh" finally in Jonah 4:10. This distribution has not only inhibited even the most enthusiastic advocate of the divine name criterion from appealing to it in the case of Jonah, but also contributed to doubts about its overall validity among those already less than enthusiastic about it in the first place (because, e.g., it obviously does not "work" in the Joseph story). The variation in divine name that we find in the book of Jonah appears to have as much to do with *theme* as anything else. "Yahweh" predominates where the story concerns God's pursuit of the Israelite Jonah and Jonah's conversation with God. "Elohim" predominates where God's role as the creator of everything is in view; "Yahweh Elohim" in Jonah 4:6, where God provides the prophet with a vine, is in fact the name of God in Genesis 2:4, where the creation of the garden in Eden with all its plants is described.

Source criticism *has* found other data of interest to its practitioners, however —in Jonah's prayer to God in the belly of the great fish that rescues him (Jonah 2:2-9), and in the story of Jonah's shelter as he waits to see what is going to happen to Nineveh (4:5-10).

The Psalm in Jonah 2

The psalm in Jonah 2 has strong points of contact with other biblical psalms, and it has often been regarded in the modern period as a secondary addition to the book. Like Genesis 38, in fact, we find some evidence of *premodern* concern about its current nature and position. Retelling the story, Philo replaces the current psalm of praise and thanksgiving with a plea for deliverance—arguably, a more appropriate response to Jonah's predicament. Josephus apparently views the psalm as having been uttered *after* Jonah arrived safe on dry land.[23] Source critics have agreed with this ancient, implicit judgment that the psalm does not "fit" in its current position, observing that in the remainder of the book Jonah is depicted negatively as a rebellious, self-pitying character. The psalm of praise and thanksgiving therefore seems incongruous. What is more, the story in Jonah 1 suggests that the prophet would rather die than do what God has instructed—he asks the ship's crew to throw him overboard, presumably believing that this would finish

---

[23] Robin B. Salters, *Jonah and Lamentations* (OT Guides; Sheffield: JSOT Press, 1994), 31.

the business. It is strange, then, to find him praising God for his rescue. Further, idolatry is condemned in the psalm (Jonah 2:8), but elsewhere in the book both the pagan sailors and the pagan Ninevites receive sympathetic treatment. Finally, the psalm contains vocabulary that is not found in the remainder of the book, and it lacks characteristic language that *is* found there. The Hebrew word *gādôl* ("great"), for example, often appears in the Jonah narrative—it is one of the author's favorite words. Yet it is absent from the psalm.

Narrative criticism raises a skeptical eyebrow concerning this assessment of the data. Granted that we might have *expected* a prayer of confession and repentance from Jonah in the belly of the fish, why should we change the text to give us the psalm that is expected rather than the one that we have? Should we not rather consider whether the author might have intended to *confound* our expectations? And come to that, what *are* our expectations of Jonah on the basis of the first chapter of the book in any case? Should we expect consistency of thought and action from a man who has just tried to escape from God on the sea that he confesses that God has made (Jonah 1:9)? I do not think so.

Further to this point, it is true that when we examine the scenes in which Jonah appears in the rest of the book we find a character who is rebellious and given to self-pity. The psalm does indeed seem incongruous. What are we to make of this, though? Perhaps when in deep trouble Jonah strikes a posture toward God different from the one he assumes when he is not—a deeply human reaction, we might well think. Perhaps his piety is selective. It is after all easier for people to *say* that they would rather die than carry out a divine commission than actually to *do* it. This brings us to the third point. Idolatry *is* condemned in the psalm and the pagans in the narrative *are* given sympathetic treatment—but is it not possible that this is designed precisely to suggest that Jonah who condemns idolatry is by no means as pious as the pagans he encounters in the surrounding chapters? The final source-critical point is scarcely worth bothering about. The Hebrew poetry of the psalm does contain vocabulary that is not found in the prose part of the book. It *is* a psalm, after all, and not a narrative. One would not normally expect much overlap in vocabulary between a narrative and a psalm. In any case, the differences do not indicate that the psalm was not part of the book of Jonah from the beginning. At most they *perhaps* suggest that the author incorporated into his story a preexisting composition that suited his rhetorical purposes.

The Shelter in Jonah 4

The narrative in Jonah 4:5-10 displays some initially puzzling features. In Jonah 4:5 we are told that "Jonah went out and sat down at a place east of the city. There he made himself a shelter, sat in its shade and waited to see what would happen to the city." Two questions arise. First, "did Jonah not already know that Nineveh had repented and that God was not going to carry out his threat" against the city (Jonah 3:10)?²⁴ This was surely the reason for Jonah's anger in Jonah 3:10 through 4.3. So why should he now go out to see what would happen to the city—and for that matter, why is it that from Jonah 4:6 until the end of the book we hear nothing more about what happens *in* the city or *to* the city? Second, just after we are told about the shelter that Jonah builds for shade (in verse 5), we learn about a plant designed for the same purpose (in verse 6). By verse 8 Jonah has *only* the plant, and no further mention is made of the shelter. Why is this?

A common source-critical explanation of these various data is that Jonah 4:5 is in the wrong place. Originally it stood after Jonah 3:4, where it makes perfect sense: Jonah preaches his sermon and then sits down under his shelter to see what will happen next. Later, however, the verse somehow became displaced and ended up in its current position. If we move it out of there then the difficulty in Jonah 4 disappears. In this case Jonah does not wait under a shelter at this later time—which is why the shelter is not mentioned there.

Again, narrative-critical questions lead us to doubt the wisdom and the necessity of this hypothesis. If Jonah 4:5 does not fit where it is currently placed, why did someone put it there (or allow it to remain there, in its "obviously" incoherent position)? *When*, indeed, did this happen—since there is no manuscript or versional support for the proposal that the verse is not original to its current position? For as long as we have had a Jonah textual tradition, its content is found exactly where it now is. Further, does not a close reading of the text suggest a quite simple solution to its puzzles that does not require any textual reengineering? First, while it is certainly true that Jonah *does* already know in chapter 4 that Nineveh has repented, is it not possible that we are meant to understand that he is unwilling to accept this outcome? He "goes out to see" what will happen as a result of his conversation with God about the matter in verses 2-4. His actions can easily be read as a challenge to God: he waits to see whether his ultimatum will change God's mind. In this case the city is not mentioned in the remaining verses of Jonah 4 because it is not the fate of the city that is any longer the issue. It is the fate of *Jonah* that is the issue—the only character in the book, it turns out, who by its closing verses has not repented (and this includes the Assyrian cows, v. 8).²⁵ As to the shelter and the vine, second, what forbids us from understanding Jonah's shelter as a rather feeble structure that is unable to protect the prophet fully from the heat? The vine is then God's provision of real protection. In support

---

²⁴ Salters, *Jonah*, 34.
²⁵ Rob Barrett, "Meaning More Than They Say: The Conflict between YHWH and Jonah," *JSOT* 37 (2012): 237–57. The text is sometimes translated in a way that does not help us to see the point about the cattle. Following the Hebrew closely we get: "they shall be covered with sackcloth, humans and beasts, and they shall cry out mightily to God. Each shall turn from his evil way."

of this interpretation we should note that the text of verse 5 does not refer to the success of Jonah's shelter in protecting his *head*. Verses 6-8, however, clearly imply the success of the vine in this respect. Jonah's attempt at self-protection is inadequate; he does build a shelter, but it is not able to save him from the discomfort caused by the sun. This fits well with the theme of the whole book: *every* attempt that Jonah makes at self-protection in this story fails!

EXPANDING THE CANVAS: HEBREW COMPOSITION

A narrative-critical approach, then, greatly illuminates the Joseph, the David, and the Solomon stories—as indeed contemporary biblical scholars have found it to illuminate many other OT narrative texts, including Jonah. Close reading of such texts, in the light of general literary theory, has then generated overarching proposals about the "poetics" of biblical narrative and what this means for how we approach it.[26] We can think of these as rooted in three general truths about the overall character of OT narrative. It is important to grasp these truths, because our expectations about what we are going to find in particular cases in any literature will inevitably be influenced by our overall understanding of the general nature of the literature in question. With this in mind, we need to be aware that OT narratives are (in the words of Phil Long) scenic, subtle, and succinct.[27]

Scenic, Subtle, Succinct

First of all, OT narratives are scenic—"in the way that a stage play involves scenes."[28] That is, our biblical authors do more *showing* than *telling*. We are seldom explicitly informed by a narrator how to evaluate characters or actions (although *sometimes* we are). Instead, we are shown the characters in action and speech, and encouraged thereby to make our judgments about them: "In other words, the reader comes to know and understand the characters in the narrative in much the same way as in real life, by watching what they do and by listening to what they say."[29]

---

[26] Among the earlier contributions not already mentioned in the footnotes are Shimon Bar-Efrat, *Narrative Art in the Bible* (trans. D. Shefer-Vanson; Sheffield: Almond, 1989); Adele Berlin, *Poetics and Interpretation of Biblical Narrative* (Sheffield: Almond, 1983); and Tremper Longman, *Literary Approaches to Biblical Interpretation* (FCI 3; Grand Rapids: Zondervan, 1987). Among the more recent books devoted to explaining narrative criticism to a general, literate audience are James Resseguie, *Narrative Criticism of the New Testament: An Introduction* (Grand Rapids: Baker, 2005); and Patricia Dutcher-Walls, *Reading the Historical Books: A Student's Guide to Engaging the Biblical Text* (Grand Rapids: Baker, 2014). On the relationship between narrative art and history, see V. Philips Long, *The Art of Biblical History* (FCI 5; Grand Rapids: Zondervan, 1994).

[27] Provan, Long, and Longman, *Biblical History*, 127–30.

[28] Provan, Long, and Longman, *Biblical History*, 128.

[29] Provan, Long, and Longman, *Biblical History*, 128.

This being so, second, OT narratives are subtle. Their authors typically deploy "an array of . . . indirect means in developing the narrative's characterizations and in focusing readers' attention on those aspects of the narrative that contain its persuasive power."[30] They "show" us detail and expect us to pay attention to it: "If we read that Esau is hairy, Ehud left-handed, Eglon fat, and Eli portly and dim-sighted, we should anticipate (though not insist) that such details in some way serve the characterizations or the action of the story."[31] The biblical narrators also indirectly guide us in our reading by using the words or actions of one character in the story as indirect commentary on those of another.

Finally, OT narratives are succinct. Their authors "tend to be economical in their craft," accomplishing (like a portrait painter) "the greatest degree of definition and color with the fewest brushstrokes."[32] They do not belabor their various rhetorical points, but demand that we listen carefully because "[a] nuance, an allusion hangs on nearly every word."[33] We need to be able to track with the ways in which this highly allusive, brief style works, as our authors draw "special attention to key elements in their texts" by means of devices like repetition—repeated words and word stems, for example, or repeated situations ("sometimes called 'type-scenes' or 'stock situations'").[34]

Such is the general character of OT narrative, and if we do not bear this seriously in mind as we read it we shall not read it well—for we shall bring to it the wrong expectations. On more than one occasion in class or outside of it, for example, after I have referred to a particular biblical text, I have been offered by a listener a variation on this comment: "But that is not what the text explicitly says." The assumption is that everything important in biblical texts is always said by their authors explicitly. Yet there is no good reason to believe that this is so. The assumption is indeed inconsistent with the general character of OT narratives. It is actually the fact that they are characteristically scenic, subtle, and succinct, conversely, that makes them so engaging; they require our careful attention as readers as they draw us into dialogue with them. It is the very artistry of the text that engages the reader in this way, and once this kind of process of reading is begun it is borne along by its own momentum and indeed excitement at "making sense" of the story.

---

[30] Provan, Long, and Longman, *Biblical History*, 128.
[31] Provan, Long, and Longman, *Biblical History*, 128.
[32] Provan, Long, and Longman, *Biblical History*, 129.
[33] Provan, Long, and Longman, *Biblical History*, 129. He is quoting here Edward L. Greenstein, "Biblical Narratology," *Proof* 1 (1981): 201–8 (202).
[34] Provan, Long, and Longman, *Biblical History*, 129.

Reading Guidelines

What are the particular questions that we should have in mind as we read OT narrative and indeed biblical narrative more generally? Jan Fokkelman proposes the following,[35] and I have annotated them with my own comments and examples:

1. *Who is the hero? What is your reason for thinking this (remember the criteria of presence, initiative, and the executor of the quest)?* We recognize the form of these questions from our earlier discussion of structuralism in chapter 19. For example, in the story of David's rise to power in 1 Samuel 16–31 David is the "hero." He stands at the center of the story, undertaking the "quest" for the throne (albeit that in a typically Hebrew way he submits to God's will while doing so, scarcely "undertaking" himself at all), and he certainly takes initiative, especially in war (while Saul stays at home).
2. *What does the quest consist of? What is the hero after, that is, what is his object of value? Does he attain his goal, and if not, why not?* At this juncture, too, and under the next point, the structuralist perspective is patent. Here it helps us to see how Jonah is actually an antihero. The "quest" upon which he is sent by the "sender" (God)—the salvation of the people of Nineveh—is actually one that Jonah tries to subvert. The quest succeeds, but Jonah does not—because he is only a man, and not God.
3. *Who are the helpers and opponents? Besides characters, factors, situations, or personality traits also qualify. Are any attributes (objects) present? What do they contribute? Do they have a symbolic added value?* In the story of Moses' "quest" to free the Israelites from Egypt in the book of Exodus, for example, his helpers include Aaron and his antagonists include the Egyptian magicians. Moses' staff makes a mighty contribution all the way through the story.
4. *Can you feel the narrator's presence anywhere in the text? This will apply especially in the case of information, comments, explanations, or value judgments on his part. Can you point to these instances of the writer speaking? Where is the writer less obviously present (for instance in his deliberate arrangement or composition of the material)? Does he usually make his own statements at strategic points in the text?* We encountered good examples of all these phenomena in Fowler's reader-response reading of Mark in my chapter 19.
5. *Does the narrator keep to the chronology of the events and processes themselves? If not, where does he deviate, and why do you think he does that? Try and get an idea of the discourse time/narrated time ratio.* Biblical narrators, like other ancient narrators, do not necessarily tell their stories in strict chronological

---

[35] Jan P. Fokkelman, *Reading Biblical Narrative: An Introductory Guide* (trans. Ineke Smit; Louisville, Ky.: Westminster John Knox, 1999), 208–9.

order, and at times they certainly prioritize meaning over chronology. The NT perhaps provides the best example in this case, in the positioning of the temple-cleansing narrative in John 2:13-22 much earlier in Jesus' ministry than we find it in the other gospels. NT scholars generally agree that this event happened only once, not twice, and during the last week of Jesus' life. However, "the Fourth Evangelist ... set his account at the beginning of the ministry of Jesus to highlight its significance for understanding the course of the ministry."[36]

6. *Where are the gaps where narrated time has been skipped, and are there cases of acceleration, retardation, retrospect, and anticipation? Assuming that the writer inserted them at the right point, why are they where they are? What is their relation with the context?* In 2 Kings 21–23, for example, we notice that the very long reign of King Manasseh is summarized by the narrator in eighteen verses, whereas forty-three verses are devoted to the events of King Josiah's eighteenth year. It seems clear that Josiah's religious reform is particularly important to the author and that Manasseh's reign represents only its backdrop—as well as offering a brief explanation as to why the reform failed to change the course of Judah's history.

7. *Is there a clear plot, or is the unit you are reading more or less without a plot of its own, because it forms part of a greater whole? What, then, is the macroplot there?* For example, the macroplot of the book of Judges concerns the recurrent failure of Israel to worship and obey God, and the long, slow decline of its leadership until we arrive at the barbarism described in Judges 17–21. There are also notable subplots within the macroplot, however, as the lives of famous "judges" of Israel are described.

8. *Where are the speeches? Are there many of them? Have speeches been left out where you would expect them? What factors influence the character who is speaking, what self-interest, background, desires, expectations? Congruence: Do the characters' words match their actions? If not, how come? Does the text contain indications of the writer supporting or approving of his character?* This is a veritable avalanche of questions, but let us consider by way of one example the dialogue between Ahab and Elijah in 1 Kings 18:17-19. Ahab views Elijah as one who has "troubled" an otherwise prosperous kingdom by bringing drought upon it, but Elijah views *Ahab* as the real "troubler of Israel" because he has turned away from the one true God and disobeyed him. That the narrator applauds Elijah and not Ahab is clear enough from

---

[36] Beasley-Murray, *John*, 38–39. He continues: "It provides a vital clue for grasping the nature and the course of our Lord's work, his words and actions, his death and resurrection, and the outcome of it all in a new worship of God, born out of a new relation to God in and through the crucified-risen Christ."

the rest of the story, but it is already hinted at in the very way in which this dialogue is reported: the Israelites had once before found and killed a man who was bringing "trouble" upon them through disobedience to God (Achan in Joshua 6–7, also described using Heb. *'ākar*, "to trouble").[37]

9. *Is there any particular choice of words that strikes you? Any other characteristics of style or structure? Take them seriously, and keep pondering them, guided, for instance, by such questions as "what does this contribute to plot or characterization?"* For example, when Jacob is described as "a smooth man" (Heb. *ḥālāq*) in Genesis 27:11 (KJV), it is intriguing that this adjective is appropriate with respect not only to his skin but also to his character throughout the story—he is a "smooth operator." The adjective already appears in the OT with this sense in Proverbs 5:23 ("For the lips of an adulteress drip honey, and her speech is smoother than oil") and Proverbs 26:28 ("a flattering [smooth] mouth works ruin").

10. *Boundaries: what devices are used to demarcate a unit? (Consider the data regarding time, space, beginning and end of the action, entrances or exits of the characters.) Can you make a division in the text (divide it into smaller units)? By what signals are you guided? Try and find other signals or markers, which may possibly lead to a different structuration. To what extent does the division clarify your view of themes or "content?"* Sometimes these "marks" are easy to spot—for example, the book of Genesis is explicitly divided into sections by the recurring phrase, "these are the generations of" or "this is the account of" (e.g., Gen 11:10). Sometimes, apparently, they are more difficult to spot, as in the marker for the beginning of Solomon's reign in 1 Kings 2:12—"So Solomon sat on the throne of his father David, and his rule was firmly established" (recall the earlier discussion of the art of 1–2 Kings).

ART IN THE GOSPEL OF MARK

Focusing now directly on the NT, the Gospels have attracted considerable attention from narrative critics. An early example is *Mark as Story* (1982) by David Rhoads and Donald Michie, which begins in this way:

> When we enter the story world of the Gospel of Mark, we enter a world full of conflict and suspense, a world of surprising reversals and strange ironies, a world of riddles and hidden meanings. The hero of the story—perhaps the most memorable in all of literature—is most surprising of all.[38]

---

[37] Provan, *Kings*, 136–42.

[38] David Rhoads and Donald Michie, *Mark as Story: An Introduction to the Narrative of a Gospel* (Philadelphia: Fortress, 1982), 1. All the quotes in my introductory paragraph here are from p. 1.

We immediately recognize here an affinity with the language of Fowler's reader-response treatment of Mark a decade later, which is not surprising; both books are interested in Mark as *literature*, and they see in this Gospel *as literature* many similar features:

> The Gospel of Mark deals with the great issues—life and death, good and evil, human triumph and human failure. It is not a simple story in which virtue easily triumphs over vice, nor is it a collection of moralizations on life. What may on a cursory reading appear to be simple answers to many of life's complications are really very tough pronouncements fraught with irony and paradox: to be most important, one must be least; to enter the rule of God, one must become like a little child; nothing is hidden except to become known; whoever wants to save one's life must lose it.

Mark is a story "full of intrigue," then, in which the author "has used sophisticated literary techniques, developed the characters and the conflicts, and built suspense with deliberateness" in order to "generate certain emotions and insights in the reader." The ending of the Gospel in particular "has a surprising twist and leads the reader to rethink much of the drama." So it is that "analyzing the narrative involves understanding not only the world of the story but also the impact which it may have on the reader."

The Rhetoric of the Gospel

With this introduction complete, Rhoads and Michie launch into a fresh translation of Mark (chapter 1) and then into an examination of the *rhetoric* of the Gospel (chapter 2), which discusses the narrator (very much along the lines of Fowler's book), point of view and standards of judgment, style, narrative patterns, and other literary features such as riddles and irony.[39] On style, for example:

> Mark's style is terse. Words are concrete rather than abstract. Descriptions such as "dressed in camel's hair" or "with wild animals" or "like a dove" are pictorial and suggestive, rather than detailed and exhaustive. With a few carefully chosen words, the narrator suggests things and encourages readers to use imagination.[40]

The narrator typically "'shows' the action directly, seldom talking about it indirectly" (see my general discussion of OT narrative just above), and it moves along rapidly; we are "drawn quickly into the story by means of this fast-paced,

---

This book is now available in a third edition, coauthored by Joanna Dewey (Minneapolis: Fortress, 2012).

[39] Rhoads and Michie, *Mark*, 35–62.
[40] Rhoads and Michie, *Mark*, 44.

dramatic movement."[41] Indeed, the "brevity of style and rapidity of motion give the narrative a tone of urgency."[42] Toward the end of Jesus' journey to Jerusalem, however, the narrative

> slows to a day-by-day description of what happens in a single location, Jerusalem, and then an hour-by-hour depiction of the crucifixion. Because the whole narrative moves toward Jerusalem and toward crucifixion, the slowing of the tempo greatly intensifies the experience of this event for the reader.[43]

The Settings in the Gospel

The third chapter of the book deals with the various *settings* in the narrative in Mark's Gospel.[44] The idea of the journey provides the overarching thematic structure:

> The journey is the way of God. Being "on the way" means more than moving through a physical landscape to Jerusalem; it also means that Jesus moves toward the goal God has set for him: death in the service of proclaiming God's rule. For the disciples, this journey is a movement toward an understanding and an acceptance of what Jesus' "way" is.[45]

Just as the "way" operates not only at a physical but also at a metaphorical level, so too do the local settings in which the action takes place. The settings themselves, in other words, communicate meaning as a result of their associations with other parts of Israel's story. When John baptizes at the Jordan River, for example, we recall the way in which this same river once

> provided a threshold experience in Israel's history. After Israel's exodus from Egypt, crossing the Jordan signalled the entrance to "the promised land." Even in the first century, Jewish prophets led followers to re-enact the crossing of the Jordan River in hopes of anticipating Israel's liberation from the Roman Empire. Mark's story opens with people coming out to be baptized at the Jordan River, preparing the way for the lord.[46]

Then again, the desert in Mark's story "has a hostile and threatening atmosphere; it is desolate and barren. It is important to the story as a place of preparation."[47] Among other things, it "has an association with the earlier event in Israel's history

---

[41] Rhoads and Michie, *Mark*, 45.
[42] Rhoads and Michie, *Mark*, 45.
[43] Rhoads and Michie, *Mark*, 45.
[44] Rhoads and Michie, *Mark*, 63–72.
[45] Rhoads and Michie, *Mark*, 64–65.
[46] Rhoads and Michie, *Mark*, 65.
[47] Rhoads and Michie, *Mark*, 65.

when the people wandered forty years in the desert in preparation for entering the land of Israel. Both of these journeys were associated with new beginnings."[48] The theme of "testing" is common to both the OT and NT treatments of the desert:

> Unlike the Israelites who lost faith during the forty years of wandering in the desert, Jesus successfully endures forty days of testing by Satan, and the angels serve him. Later, the desert tests the disciples, twice revealing their lack of faith. Like the ancient Israelites, the disciples do not have faith that God can provide bread in such a barren place. By contrast, Jesus' faith in God enables him to provide for the crowd.[49]

Other settings in the Gospel of Mark discussed by Rhoads and Michie include the sea—"a place of chaos and destruction," inviting "readers to recall the chaos of the waters in Israelite creation stories and the destructiveness of the flood"; and the mountain—"a setting of refuge and safety" and for revelation, recalling the time when God gave the Law to Moses on a mountain, and later Elijah encountered him there.[50] By triggering such associations, the Gospel's settings thus greatly enrich the meaning of the episodes that take place within them.

THE PLOT OF THE GOSPEL

The best way of approaching the plot of Mark's Gospel, Rhoads and Michie propose (their chapter 4), is by way of the analysis of its various conflicts.[51] The "establishment of God's rule provides the larger background for the story. The actions in the foreground focus on the resulting conflicts of the protagonist [Jesus]."[52] Jesus "battles the unclean spirits, overcomes threatening forces of nature, confronts the Jewish and gentile authorities, struggles with the disciples, and agonizes within himself about his death."[53] The narrator builds suspense in his story "by gradually escalating the opposition and by leaving the reader in doubt as to the outcome. Finally, the narrator brings the major conflicts to a dramatic conclusion in Jerusalem."[54] All those who oppose Jesus share similarities:

> The demoniac forces, the authorities, and at times the disciples dominate people, oppose Jesus, put him to the test, are afraid, and are preoccupied with saving themselves. The narrator suggests these similarities by means of verbal threads, parallel actions, and the juxtaposition of episodes. That is, the narrator has interwoven all

---

[48] Rhoads and Michie, *Mark*, 66.
[49] Rhoads and Michie, *Mark*, 66.
[50] Rhoads and Michie, *Mark*, 66–67.
[51] Rhoads and Michie, *Mark*, 73–100.
[52] Rhoads and Michie, *Mark*, 73.
[53] Rhoads and Michie, *Mark*, 73.
[54] Rhoads and Michie, *Mark*, 73–74.

the conflicts into an artistic whole so that one conflict is to be seen in relation to the others.[55]

As these various conflicts reach their dramatic climax in Jerusalem, the main antagonist becomes death itself. The resolution of the conflicts comes to focus, in fact, on the different ways that the characters in the story deal with the reality of death.

The Characters in the Gospel

This leads Rhoads and Michie to a broader analysis *of* the characters in Mark's Gospel (chapter 5), which "inevitably overlaps with the analysis of the conflicts, since the characters are so integrally related to the plot."[56] The dominant character in Mark's story is naturally Jesus. Then,

> the authorities can be treated together as a single character, because the different groups which oppose Jesus share similar traits and carry on a continuing role in the plot in relationship to each other. For the same reasons, the disciples also can be treated as a character. And although Peter, James, and John have individual roles, they typify the disciples as a whole. The minor characters, whom we call the "little people," can also be treated together because of their similar traits.[57]

Once again, the narrator of Mark's Gospel "primarily 'shows' the characters to the reader rather than 'telling' us about them"; for example, he "reveals characters by comparison and contrast with other characters in the story" rather than explicitly providing information about them.[58] We form our overall impression of them much as we do of people we are getting to know in the present—"observing what they say and do and how others react to them" (see my earlier comment on OT narrative), noting how they participate in the events of the story and how they interact with others in it, and so on.[59] It is a measured process: the narrator "reveals the characters gradually so that the readers' perception of the characters changes and develops."[60] As we move toward the end of the story, "the major characters are shown fully for who they are in the face of death."[61]

---

[55] Rhoads and Michie, *Mark*, 100.
[56] Rhoads and Michie, *Mark*, 101–36 (101).
[57] Rhoads and Michie, *Mark*, 101.
[58] Rhoads and Michie, *Mark*, 101–2.
[59] Rhoads and Michie, *Mark*, 102.
[60] Rhoads and Michie, *Mark*, 103.
[61] Rhoads and Michie, *Mark*, 103.

The Implied Reader

Rhoads and Michie conclude their reading of Mark as narrative literature with some reflections both on the first- and twentieth-century readers of the work and on its "implied reader"—the reader that the Gospel appears to desire.[62] An implied reader, we recall, is "an imaginary reader with the ideal responses implied or suggested by the narrative, experiencing suspense or feeling amazement or sympathizing with a character at the appropriate times." The implied reader of the Gospel of Mark is the one who sees "the hidden rule of God in Jesus" and follows him. The characters in Mark's story "are mostly concerned with themselves, their own importance, power, and security, all of which prevent the authorities and the disciples from understanding Jesus' actions and teaching about God's rule." Jesus' conflicts with them "reveal not only the depth of human resistance to renouncing one's life in order to serve others but also the extent of human destruction which results from saving one's life." They are "blind." The story world and its rhetoric together, on the other hand, lead the implied reader "to see God's hidden rule and to accept the true greatness of those who follow God's ways." This "following" is what people who "see" embrace:

> The narrative defines the implied reader as a faithful follower of Jesus. The implied reader travels the journey with Jesus, like a disciple who understands the ways of God when others do not, accepts Jesus' teaching when his disciples resist, and arrives in Jerusalem prepared to go through death with Jesus. In a sense, by staying with the story, the reader remains faithful to the end, staying awake at Gethsemane, being present at the trial and crucifixion, and afterward following the women to the grave. . . . [In fact, the] reader alone has remained faithful to the last and is now left with a decision, whether to flee in silence like the women or to proclaim boldly in spite of fear and death. The implied reader will choose to proclaim.[63]

REFLECTIONS ON NARRATIVE CRITICISM

Bible readers committed to the "seriously literal interpretation" of Scripture should warmly welcome the explosion of interest and expertise in narrative-critical reading of Scripture in the modern biblical scholarship of the past forty years or so. From the perspective of "reformed" hermeneutics, the more we understand about the narrative art and the rhetoric of biblical literature, the better—for the more we understand the Bible as literature, the better we understand it also as the Word of God.

---

[62] Rhoads and Michie, *Mark*, 137–42. All the quotes following in this paragraph come from 137–39.

[63] Rhoads and Michie, *Mark*, 140.

The main concern that arises from this renewed attention to biblical narrative as we find it, considered in the context of literary studies more generally, lies in the *assumption* that has often accompanied it. It is exactly the assumption that I noted in my chapters 18 and 19 with respect to other modes of reading the Bible that focus on the text that we have rather than with entities that allegedly lie behind it. It is that there *is* no "behind"—or at least, that the artistically constructed text does not allow us to *access* what is "behind." Many of our biblical narrative texts clearly mean to *refer* to reality outside the text, and not least to history. However, in a modern scholarly world in which an obsession with history has often led to inattention to the biblical text as literature, renewed interest in this topic has often led in the course of a marked intellectual pendulum swing to skepticism about the text's ability to refer truthfully to history—and indeed to anything else "outside" it, including God. God is in fact often regarded simply as a character in the story, and the relationship between that character and any Person *outside* the story is entirely unclear. The text is *fiction*—powerful, wonderful fiction, to be sure, that in its own way tells us various kinds of truth. Yet it *is* fiction, and its connection with history in particular is opaque. In the opinion of OT scholars like Keith Whitelam, for example, there was never any such entity as the ancient Israel described in the Bible; "[a]ccording to Whitelam, little evidence exists that this 'Israel' is anything other than a literary fiction."[64]

Robert Alter on Fiction

It is this language of "fiction" that we already encounter in the work of Robert Alter, with whom we began the present chapter. Yet Alter handles this term in a far more nuanced way than many others do, and consideration of his approach begins helpfully to set us in the right direction in thinking about it—for he does not propose a radical dichotomy between "fiction" and "history." Even the book of Genesis, in his mind, is not merely "fiction" but "*historicized* prose fiction."[65] By this designation he means to refer to fiction that sets human beings in a historical rather than a mythological framework—which moves "away from the stable closure of the mythological world and toward the indeterminacy, the shifting causal concatenations, the ambiguities of a fiction made to resemble the uncertainties of life in history."[66] As we consider the OT more broadly we discover (in Alter's view) "an uneven continuum and a constant interweaving of factual historical detail" with fictions of various kinds.[67] There is a spectrum in the OT

---

[64] Provan, Long, and Longman, *Biblical History*, 4, referring to Keith W. Whitelam, *The Invention of Ancient Israel: The Silencing of Palestinian History* (London: Routledge, 1996).
[65] Alter, *Art of Biblical Narrative*, 24.
[66] Alter, *Art of Biblical Narrative*, 27.
[67] Alter, *Art of Biblical Narrative*, 33.

with respect to this question of fiction and history. Fiction is "historicized," and history is "fictionalized"—but both are present. What Alter wishes to *emphasize* in his own work is that in telling their story the biblical authors certainly "exercised a good deal of shaping power over their materials as they articulated them."[68] This means that if "we fail to see that the creators of biblical narrative were writers who ... took pleasure in exploring the formal and imaginative resources of their fictional medium ... we shall miss much that biblical stories are meant to convey."[69] Yet it is also true that "history is far more intimately related to fiction than we have been accustomed to assume."[70]

FICTION AND HISTORY

Indeed this is so. There is storytelling in general, and then there is storytelling about the past in particular, and both involve art and rhetoric. *Both* involve "fiction," if that term is properly understood.[71] Consider the analogy of the portrait, which has already appeared on several occasions throughout chapters 17 to 20 in relation to the "art" of narrative representation:

> In one sense, a portrait is all history, since its essential purpose is to represent a historical subject. Ideally, every brushstroke in the portrait serves that purpose. In another sense, however, a portrait is all fiction—that is, it is all "fabrication," just paint on canvas. No brushstroke or combination of brushstrokes exactly *duplicates* the historical subject. Taken together, however, the brushstrokes *depict*, or represent, the historical subject.[72]

When we are thinking about the narrative representation of the past in Scripture, the same considerations apply, for

> a biblical narrative, as verbal representation, also does not duplicate but, rather, depicts the past. Like a portrait, a biblical narrative is in one sense a fabrication, because it consists of words on paper and not the actual past. Nevertheless, these words on paper, like paint on canvas, can accurately represent the historical past.... All this discussion would almost seem inane were it not for the fact that some biblical scholars and even historians appear to miss the distinction between fictionality in the sense of artistry, or craft, and fiction in the sense of genre. The former is about *how* a representation is achieved, the latter is about *what* is

---

[68] Alter, *Art of Biblical Narrative*, 41.
[69] Alter, *Art of Biblical Narrative*, 46.
[70] Alter, *Art of Biblical Narrative*, 24.
[71] Sternberg, *Poetics*, 23–35.
[72] Provan, Long, and Longman, *Biblical History*, 114–15.

represented. Both portraiture and narrative historiography involve "fabrication" (better "artistry"), but neither is art for art's sake.[73]

The art of biblical narrative does not disqualify it as historiography (where that is what it seemingly intends to be); we should dismiss the common idea "that a natural law decrees hostility between good literature and serious history, between literary effects and factual accuracy."[74] It may well be that the constant use of "immediately" in the Gospel of Mark, for example, is not so much meant to inform us about the speed with which Jesus moved around first-century Israel as to catch us up in the breathless excitement of the story that Mark is telling. Yet Mark's is a story told about a real past, and its art is intended to connect us with and not disbar us from that past. The main point to be taken from Alter's discussion is in fact that grasping the biblical art is *crucial* to grasping the biblical past. This is generally true of narrative about the past: "One of the first contributions that the critic of history can make is to serve as an intelligent reader who is willing to understand and discuss the rhetoric in which history is written."[75]

Art and History in Genesis 38

We conclude by returning to the example of Genesis 38 with which we began, using it now to illustrate the point about art and history. If we have grasped the art involved in the telling of this story in the context of Genesis 37–50, is there any problem with the history? We recall the perceived problem with the chronology raised by source critics as a prelude to their remodeling of the text: that the Joseph story as a whole presents Judah throughout as a member of Jacob's household and does not know of any "gap" in which he lives away from his family long enough to accumulate both sons and grandsons (already born by the time the whole extended family goes down to Egypt in Genesis 46).

Yet it is unclear why we should expect the remainder of the Joseph story to reiterate the separation of Judah from his family when Genesis 38 has already described it and when it is not directly relevant to the story that follows. As to the sons and grandsons, there are at least thirteen years between Joseph going down to Egypt and his entering Pharaoh's household (compare Gen 37:2 and 41:46), at least another seven years of abundance before Judah himself goes down to Egypt, and approximately another two after that before the family goes down to Egypt (Gen 45:6). So *if* the events of Genesis 38 occurred in *real* time where they are

---

[73] Provan, Long, and Longman, *Biblical History*, 115; see also Long, *Art of Biblical History*, 60–63.

[74] David Levin, *In Defense of Historical Literature: Essays on American History, Autobiography, Drama, and Fiction* (New York: Hill and Wang, 1967), 3.

[75] Levin, *Defense*, 23.

now located in *narrative* time, then there are *at least* twenty-two years for Judah to father all his sons and for his son Perez to have his own sons—and if the number "thirty" in Genesis 41:46 (Joseph's age when he entered the service of Pharaoh) is a round number, this would allow for a few more years still.

It is also entirely possible, on the other hand, that the events described in Genesis 38 actually occurred earlier in real time, and that they have been narrated in their present position on the principle already articulated above: that in ancient historiography, meaning can trump chronology. The Genesis author has in this case deliberately moved this story about Judah out of its strictly chronological location in order to make the kind of connections between Judah and Joseph to which Alter has already drawn our attention. This also has the interesting effect of giving Joseph (unnarrated) time to get down to Egypt—he essentially disappears for a time from the *reader* as well as from his *father*. With Joseph in temporary eclipse, Genesis 38 takes up the slack with a different story. We noted earlier the way in which John makes a similar kind of move in his Gospel in the case of the temple-cleansing narrative, and this is not the only other biblical example. The Gospel of Luke (for example) also transfers to an earlier point in the story of Jesus the account of his visit to Nazareth at the beginning of his Galilean ministry (Luke 4:16-30)—because "what then took place presaged the outcome of the entire ministry of our Lord in the Jewish rejection of him and his acceptance among the Gentiles, so preparing for volume 2 of Luke's story of Jesus and his Church [in the Acts of the Apostles]."[76]

In none of this is there any reason to doubt the historical roots of the events described—*however* they may be described using narrative artistry and rhetoric. We encounter here not the irreconcilability of art and history, but simply the inevitable fusion of the two.

CONCLUSION

The Reformers and many of their immediate heirs in biblical interpretation paid scrupulous attention to the rhetoric of the original-language forms of the biblical texts as they read them in the context of the ancient past out of which they once emerged. If we are committed to embracing the same Reformation principles in interpreting biblical texts in the present, then narrative-critical tools must be among those in our own hermeneutical toolbox—not so that we can fly away into ahistorical aestheticism in our Bible reading, but so that (among other things) we can do justice to its historical truth claims. This is something that "reformed" biblical hermeneutics will certainly wish to do.

---

[76] Beasley-Murray, *John*, 39.

21

SOCIAL-SCIENTIFIC AND FEMINIST CRITICISM
Texts as Social Constructs

> ... scientific enquiry has entered the realms of culture, of behavior, of morals and of the causes of religion. In none of these cases do scientists speak the language of the Bible. Each in turn is (re)defined as one of the works of nature, subject only to its own laws, and unrelated to human or biblical concerns.
>
> —Rienk Vermij[1]

> ... if you please, no reference to examples in books. Men have had every advantage of us in telling their own story. Education has been theirs in so much higher a degree; the pen has been in their hands. I will not allow books to prove any thing.
>
> —Anne Elliott, in Jane Austen's Persuasion[2]

Throughout chapters 17 to 20 we have been tracking the evolution of modern (and postmodern) biblical criticism through the lenses of both art and science and exploring their interplay. In chapter 21 we focus on two approaches to Bible reading, rising to prominence in the closing decades of the twentieth century, that further illustrate the way in which modern biblical scholarship has sought to employ these two lenses to clarify what the Bible is really about and what we should and should not do with it. In social-scientific criticism we encounter in a fresh form the confidence of earlier modern times that scientific enquiry can unlock all the secrets of the universe and tell us the truth about it all—whether in the realms of physics, chemistry, and biology, or (now) in "the realms of culture, of behavior, of morals [or] of the causes of religion" (the first epigraph above). In feminist criticism we encounter a particular "take" on the rhetoric of our biblical texts that leads on to questions about whether some or all of it should be resisted. "Men have had every advantage of [women] in telling their own story"

---

[1] Vermij, "Debate," 623.
[2] Jane Austen, *Persuasion*, chapter 23, in *The Penguin Complete Novels of Jane Austen* (London: Penguin, 1983), 1143–1290 (1279; the context is Anne's conversation with Captain Harville about Captain Benwick).

(the second epigraph above), including the biblical story. We should therefore not "allow books to prove anything." As we shall see, there is an important *connection* between these two critical reading methods, in that they both invite us to focus on biblical texts as social constructs designed to promote certain "ideologies" (or theologies) and to oppose others in pursuit of particular visions of society. We could in fact classify much of what scholars using these methods have been doing as "ideological criticism": "the task of uncovering the hidden ideologies at work in social practices, structures, and texts."[3] Ideological criticism, in turn, has many more aspects than we can possibly cover in the space available in this chapter. I hope that the subjects we do discuss, however, will help the reader to think well about the ones that we do not.[4]

THE RISE OF SOCIAL-SCIENTIFIC CRITICISM

We already noted in chapters 18 and 19 the broad change of focus in many quarters at the beginning of the twentieth century away from the individual and onto the broader social matrix in which he or she lives, and both its indirect and direct effects on biblical criticism. The emergence of form criticism and structuralism provides obvious examples. This is the context in which we must also understand the earliest, limited attempts to bring social-scientific theory and method to bear on biblical studies.[5]

Early Studies

In OT studies, for example, we see the publication of *From the Prophets to Jesus* (1935) by Adolphe Lods (1867–1948),[6] and of *From Ethnic Group to Religious Community* (1937) by Antonin Causse (1877–1947).[7] Both books develop the insights of the founder of the modern sociological study of religion Max Weber (1864–1920).[8] Particularly interesting is their view of the OT prophets, under-

---

[3] Robin Parry, "Ideological Criticism," *DTIB*, 314–16 (314).

[4] Parry, "Ideological Criticism," provides a helpful initial introduction with a brief bibliography and links to related articles. For a longer introduction and voluminous bibliographies, focused on the OT, see David J. A. Clines, "Contemporary Methods in Hebrew Bible Criticism," *HBOT* 3/2:148–69 (160–69).

[5] For a brief introduction to the whole topic, see Stephen C. Barton, "Social-Scientific Criticism," *DTIB*, 753–55.

[6] This book appears in English translation as *The Prophets and the Rise of Judaism* (trans. S. H. Hooke; New York: Routledge, 1996).

[7] Antonin Causse, *Du groupe ethnique à la communauté religieuse. Le problème sociologique de la religion d'Israël* (Paris: Alcan, 1937).

[8] Max Weber, *Ancient Judaism* (trans. and ed. Hans H. Gerth and Don Martindale; Glencoe, Ill.: Free Press, 1952). For a brief summary of his work, see Anselm C. Hagedorn, "Institutions and Social Life in Ancient Israel: Sociological Aspects," *HBOT* 3/2:58–95 (67–74).

stood as both representing the interests of the peasant farmers in their resistance to urbanization in ancient Israel and developing a personal morality that moved beyond the previous collective consciousness. Here we see a synthesis between emerging sociological theory and prior scholarly convictions about the importance of the individual prophetic genius (e.g., in Wellhausen). A few decades later (in his *History of Israel*, 1960), looking for a secure starting point for the "real" history of Israel, Martin Noth appealed to the societal organization of adjacent cultures in Greece and Italy to ground his contention that there was an ancient, twelve-tribe Israelite "amphictyony" (a sacred society centered around a particular shrine) in Canaan in the "judges" period.[9] In NT studies Shirley Jackson Case (1872–1947) drew attention in the early decades of the century to the necessity of looking to social factors in the history of religious movements (e.g., in *The Evolution of Early Christianity*, 1914). Frederick Grant (1891–1974) published *The Economic Background of the Gospels* (1926), which remained the standard work on first-century Palestinian economics for almost the next fifty years.[10]

OVERARCHING APPROACHES

On the whole these represent fairly modest uses of sociological method, however—the selective use of social-scientific perspectives to fill in the background to the Bible. Not until the 1970s do we begin to find the wholesale application of social-scientific theory and method to biblical studies, as increasing numbers of scholars transition from what they have come to regard as the mere "social description" of the world behind the Bible (in the older studies) to the exploration, using models from the social sciences, of the social world of the Bible as a comprehensive world of meaning.[11] This phenomenon coincides, naturally enough, with the significant secularization of biblical studies as a discipline that occurred in the same time period.

So long as the Bible was mainly regarded as a theological document, studied by people interested in it as Scripture—no matter how "liberal" or "conservative" they might be—and held to be a special set of texts that speak of God and of the individual life lived out before God, there was bound to be resistance to any approach challenging these assumptions. Even structuralist perspectives

---

[9] Martin Noth, *The History of Israel* (2nd ed.; rev. trans. Peter R. Ackroyd; London: A&C Black, 1960), 85–109.

[10] Shirley Jackson Case, *The Evolution of Early Christianity: A Genetic Study of First-Century Christianity in Relation to Its Religious Environment* (Chicago: University of Chicago Press, 1914); Frederick C. Grant, *The Economic Background of the Gospels* (Oxford: Oxford University Press, 1926).

[11] For a discussion of the distinction, see Jerome H. Neyrey, S.J., "Social-Scientific Criticism," in Aune, *Blackwell Companion to the New Testament*, 177–91 (177–81).

began to impact biblical studies significantly only a considerable time after their appearance in literary studies more generally. Only as biblical studies began to get "liberated" (as some saw it) from its bondage to theology did the social-scientific approach to the Bible begin to proliferate. Only as the grip of a theological worldview loosened, which had at its center a personal God and his relationship with his personal (and other) creatures, could Bible readers conceive of embracing the kind of view of the social sciences held by Claude Lévi-Strauss (for example): "I believe the ultimate goal of the human sciences to be not to constitute, but to dissolve man."[12] In this reductionistic way of thinking, as we saw it expressed in fullblown structuralism, human beings are not essentially thinking persons ("I think therefore I am") who are importantly involved in endowing objects around them with meaning. Nor is God. Meaning in this way of thinking is explained instead in terms of systems of signs that impose themselves upon and work their way out through minds and bodies. The personal self is thereby dissolved in social-scientific acid, as its various functions are ascribed to impersonal systems that allegedly operate through it. As Michel Foucault once put it, "the researches of psychoanalysis, linguistics, and ethnology have decentred the subject in relation to the laws of his desire, the forms of his language, the rules of his action, or the games of his mythical or fabulous discourse."[13] They have decentered human persons, and they have decentered the personal God.

THE CLASH OF WORLDVIEWS

It is unsurprising, then, that many theologically interested, twentieth-century readers of the Bible did not welcome the entry of the social sciences into the world of biblical studies—for a serious threat is implied in the thoroughgoing application of "science" to realms of human enquiry that have traditionally belonged to the domain of the humanities in general and of theology in particular. It was really only as significant numbers of scholars became involved in biblical studies, then, who either did not care very much about protecting the Bible from a degree of reductionism or were positively hostile to any attempts to privilege the Bible in this way that social-scientific criticism of the Bible began to proliferate, often representing a parallel track in biblical scholarship to the kind of narrative criticism that is also very little interested in theology. Narrative criticism in this mode picks up that stream of critical tradition that stresses that human beings are thinking subjects who produce creative art. Social-scientific criticism, by contrast, picks up that stream of critical tradition that stresses the locatedness of human beings

---

[12] Lévi-Strauss, *Savage Mind*, 247.
[13] Michel Foucault, *The Archaeology of Knowledge* (trans. A. M. Sheridan Smith; New York: Pantheon, 1972), 13.

in contexts. Neither is necessarily interested in the testimony of the text about God or about divine action in history, nor about how human beings should think and live before God. Narrative criticism in this mode does not take questions of reference seriously. Social-scientific criticism does take them seriously, but often holds that what the text really testifies about is something quite other than what is found in its surface meaning.

All of this notwithstanding, I argued in chapter 20 that there is much to be learned from narrative criticism by the person interested in the "seriously literal interpretation" of Scripture—even if we do not warm to its frequent flights into antireferential aestheticism. Is this also true of social-scientific criticism, even though much of it is marked by antitheological reductionism?

BINDING THE STRONG MAN

Ched Myers' book *Binding the Strong Man* provides us with a good example of the value of the social-scientific approach to Scripture when judiciously employed.[14]

A Political Reading

Myers begins this book by asking the question, "Why a political reading?" His answer is that texts are vulnerable to interpreters and dependent upon them to restore their voice. Texts produced in times, places, and cultures distantly removed from those of the interpreter are "all the more vulnerable,"[15] given that each interpreter is embroiled in a particular *Sitz im Leben* that determines the questions brought to the text and influences how it is understood. Therefore, the Gospel of Mark is vulnerable to Myers and to all readers who live at the center of "empire" in positions of privilege and power—since this Gospel was written from the *periphery* of empire. A conscious effort is required by such readers not to miss the point.[16] Unfortunately many have done so, offering readings of the Gospel that are insufficiently political and suppressing "the fully human, concretely sociohistorical character of the Gospel" in a way that is "nothing less than a perpetuation of the docetic heresy."[17] Myers' reading, we learn, will summon readers to practice, helping them to grasp in a new way why the Gospel was written: "to help imperial subjects learn the hard truth about their world and themselves"[18] and call them to discipleship. He recognizes that Mark is *more* than political, involving spiritual and personal dimensions too, but he is convinced that it is not *less* than

---

[14] Ched Myers, *Binding the Strong Man: A Political Reading of Mark's Story of Jesus* (Maryknoll, N.Y.: Orbis, 1988).
[15] Myers, *Binding the Strong Man*, 4.
[16] Myers, *Binding the Strong Man*, 5–7.
[17] Myers, *Binding the Strong Man*, 9.
[18] Myers, *Binding the Strong Man*, 11.

political. Personally oriented readings of Scripture are part of the picture, but all reading in the end must be understood also "in terms of the socio-political practices it justifies."[19]

The War of Myths

Having laid this foundation for his commentary Myers proceeds to a discussion of the "war of myths" in which we are all involved, particularly as prosecuted in the symbolic actions we perform.[20] Our reflections on structuralism help us here, since Myers' discussion involves "signs"—whether words or narratives or actions—and their use in social and political struggle. This "symbolic discourse about social realities and conflicts" Myers labels "ideology," referring to Karl Marx's dictum: "Life is not determined by consciousness, but consciousness by life"[21] (note the similarity to the comment of Lévi-Strauss cited earlier). Ideas are social and political products; they do not fall from the sky, but arise from social and political practice. *Ideology* either legitimates the current social and political order or subverts it, and we must examine each of its forms to find out what it seeks to accomplish. *Theology* Myers considers to be "the practice of 'ideological literacy'" in the service of promoting liberating ideologies and subverting oppressive ones from the standpoint of the Gospel.[22] This is *how* we participate in the "war of myths" in our time, affirming the helpful and deconstructing the unhelpful.

The question of how we read Mark's Gospel naturally follows on from this. Myers' opinion is that

> neither of the two contemporary "routes" in biblical criticism—literary and sociological analysis—are alone adequate for a political reading.... The former leave us with free-floating texts which move toward gratuity and fantasy. The latter evacuate the recitals of their full import in the quest for facts and thematics.[23]

We must hold the concerns of "art" and "science," convention and creativity, together in our reading, taking the rhetorically sophisticated biblical story seriously while recognizing that like other texts it already encodes "social relationships, tensions, and strategies" in representing a world extrinsic to the text.[24] Myers will read the Gospel of Mark along such lines: as "the manifesto of an early Christian discipleship community in its war of myths with the dominant social

---

[19] Myers, *Binding the Strong Man*, 14.
[20] Myers, *Binding the Strong Man*, 14–21.
[21] Myers, *Binding the Strong Man*, 17.
[22] Myers, *Binding the Strong Man*, 21.
[23] Myers, *Binding the Strong Man*, 26, partially quoting Amos Wilder.
[24] Myers, *Binding the Strong Man*, 29, with 35.

order and its political adversaries."[25] This will involve combining narrative-critical analysis with an examination of "the historical and ideological setting and prevailing social strategies of Mark's 'world'" in his time.[26]

Mark's World

Myers proceeds next to discuss the sociohistorical site of Mark's story of Jesus.[27] He begins with the striking observation that "Mark's story of Jesus stands virtually alone among the literary achievements of antiquity" precisely because it is already socially located in a very particular way: "it is a narrative for and about the common people."[28] There follows a description of the world of late second-temple Jewish Palestine under Roman occupation.

In this description Myers self-consciously employs a Marxist model of analysis in which "social formations are defined by the competition among class, race, and gender interests."[29] He chooses this model because of the questions he is interested in asking, although he also insists on the need not to allow modern perspectives to dominate our reading agenda; he agrees, for example, that the notion of "class struggle" involving "proletarian consciousness" is "hopelessly anachronistic" as applied to first-century Palestine.[30] He is simply using this model in order to see how far it illuminates the data. However we frame our questions, he maintains, "the Jesus story is always more radical when understood first in its own socio-historical terms."[31]

A discussion of the economics of first-century Palestine follows, emphasizing the social location of the poor, tensions between city and village, and tensions between Galilee and Judea. The sociopolitical tensions that led up to the Jewish War in AD 66–70 are then discussed, bringing us to the "historical moment of Mark"[32]—for Myers holds that the Gospel was written during that war from the perspective of the poor in Galilee. He then explores the socio*cultural* tensions, arguing that the symbolic order of Palestine was centered on the "mutually reinforcing systems of debt and pollution (purity)."[33] These systems "operated in three basic social spheres"[34]—land and table, village and house, synagogue and sanctuary. "The two main institutional 'vehicles' in which the symbolic order was

---

[25] Myers, *Binding the Strong Man*, 31.
[26] Myers, *Binding the Strong Man*, 31.
[27] Myers, *Binding the Strong Man*, 39–87.
[28] Myers, *Binding the Strong Man*, 39.
[29] Myers, *Binding the Strong Man*, 44.
[30] Myers, *Binding the Strong Man*, 47.
[31] Myers, *Binding the Strong Man*, 47.
[32] Myers, *Binding the Strong Man*, 64–69.
[33] Myers, *Binding the Strong Man*, 73.
[34] Myers, *Binding the Strong Man*, 74.

objectified and in which its authority was invested were the law (Torah) and the temple," representing respectively "the covenant and presence of Israel's God."[35] They defined and controlled debt and impurity.

Finally, Myers discusses the ideological and social strategies adopted by the main groups in Palestine in their contemporary war of myths.[36] Some accommodated to the dominant order (employing legitimating strategies), and some did not (employing subversive strategies). The ruling classes were cooperatively nationalistic (the Sadducees) or adopted the quieter or more escapist strategies of reform (the Pharisees and the Essenes). The Zealots were "loyalistically radical," looking to replace the "collaborationist priestly leadership ... with a patriotic one."[37] Jesus "disdained the collaborationist aristocracy *and* Romans equally," yet he also repudiated withdrawal (the option chosen by the Qumran community) and Pharisaic activism "on the grounds that neither addressed the roots of oppression in the dominant symbolic order."[38] He invoked "the Deuteronomic vision of a just redistribution system ... appealing to the subversive tradition" of the prophets in unmasking "the oppressive economic self-interest of the Jerusalem hierarchy, their tithing structure, Sabbath regulations and temple."[39] This is the Jesus that Mark's Gospel describes when read in its social context.

FIRST REFLECTIONS

We have already been alerted by redaction criticism to the inevitability of point of view and perspective in biblical texts (as in all texts). Rhetorical criticism, in addition, recognizes that no discourse is objectively neutral: texts participate in the construction of a social reality, just as "speech [is] a means and source of power."[40] When we set these insights within the framework of social-scientific criticism it is inevitable that the emphasis will fall upon the *social context* out of which different readings arise and the purpose for which they are generated. What does the embeddedness of texts in social contexts signify in terms of the vision of society that they are defending, promoting, or subverting? What kinds of perspectives do we have in our *biblical* texts, and in support of which ideology—whose vision of the world? On what grounds should we embrace the rhetoric of any text as it seeks to persuade us of its reality? On what grounds should we resist? Implicit in all these questions is the adoption to some extent of a thoroughgoing Platonic suspicion of rhetoric—a hermeneutic of suspicion. We should *expect* texts of all

---

[35] Myers, *Binding the Strong Man*, 74.
[36] Myers, *Binding the Strong Man*, 80–87.
[37] Myers, *Binding the Strong Man*, 85.
[38] Myers, *Binding the Strong Man*, 86.
[39] Myers, *Binding the Strong Man*, 86.
[40] Walter Brueggemann, cited in Trible, *Rhetorical Criticism*, 52.

kinds to be seeking to impose a vision upon us that is not necessarily in our own interests; we should *suspect* that this is so. And we should be suspicious of readers as well. Why have particular readers produced their particular readings? For what end? In defense of which interests? These are the kinds of questions often raised in the context of the social-scientific criticism of literature in general and, by extension, the social-scientific criticism of the Bible in particular.

Religion and Politics

As we can see from *Binding the Strong Man*, such an approach is not necessarily hostile to Scripture in itself, nor indeed to its theological appropriation, although it is often very hostile to certain *readings* of the Bible and to certain theological frameworks—particularly as they are used to legitimate particular visions of the world. Myers himself is especially interested in what Mark's Gospel has to say over against the myths of his own American culture—which, from the standpoint of "seriously literal interpretation," is a commendable goal. Mark's Gospel is after all part of that body of literature that God has provided for the Church to be useful "for teaching, rebuking, correcting and training in righteousness" (2 Tim 3:16)—not least in respect of our idolatrous attachments to contemporary political mythology. The biblical prophets bring the Word of God to bear on the national myths of their own time in just such a manner. One of the great merits of Myers' approach, indeed, is that it reminds us of the interconnectedness of religion and politics in the ancient world in general, and of the inevitable social and political implications of Jesus' teaching and actions in the real flesh and blood world of first-century Palestine in particular. Jesus' words both reflect a set of convictions about the shape of righteous social and political life and urge us to live in this way. Myers' treatment of Mark's Gospel makes it less easy than is often the case, then, to engage in Bible reading that does not immediately lead on to the embrace or rejection of particular *practices*. Stories always mean *something* for how we live, and we need to be critically aware of the connections so that we do in fact inhabit the biblical Story well and live as we should, rather than telling a twisted version of it that simply legitimates our own interests.

On Avoiding Savage Criticism

Writing from a very different *Sitz im Leben* in the developing world, Vinoth Ramachandra perhaps sees more clearly than most what such a self-interested reading involves. "The Good News is packaged and marketed," he writes, "as a religious product: offering 'peace of mind,' 'how to get to heaven,' 'health and prosperity,' 'inner healing,' 'the answer to all your problems' etc."[41] Faith in God "often

---

[41] This and all of the quotes in this section come from Vinoth Ramachandra, *Gods That Fail: Modern Idolatry and Christian Mission* (Carlisle: Paternoster, 1996), 40–42.

turns out, on closer inspection, to be a means for obtaining emotional security or material blessing in this life and an insurance policy for the next." This kind of reading of the biblical Story, and the preaching that follows from it, cannot change the world:

> It does not raise fundamental and disturbing questions about the assumptions on which people build their lives. It does not threaten the false gods in whose name the creation of God has been taken over; indeed, it actually reinforces their hold on their worshippers. This kind of "gospel" is essentially escapist, the direct descendent of the pseudo-gospels of the false prophets of the Old Testament. It is simply a religious image of the secular consumerist culture in which modern men and women live.

As such, "[i]t lays itself wide open to the full blast of the savage criticism of Marx and Freud." It is a manifestation of idolatry—"the attempt to manipulate 'God' or the unseen 'spiritual world' in order to obtain security and well-being for oneself and one's 'group' (whether family, business corporation, ethnic community or nation-state)." This is not what *biblical faith* is about, claims Ramachandra. Biblical faith involves

> the radical abandonment of our whole being in grateful trust and love to the God disclosed in the life, death and resurrection of Jesus Christ: so that we become his willing agents in a costly confrontation with every form of evil and unjust suffering in the world.

Myers' use of social-scientific method to flesh out the social world implicit in Mark's Gospel and connect the Gospel in this way with our own world, embroiled in its own war of myths, helps us to avoid this justified, savage criticism—in the first instance simply by raising our consciousness about the inevitable connection between the stories we tell and the vision of the world that we are striving to make (or maintain as) a reality.

THE TRIBES OF YAHWEH

This deep connection between ideas and social reality is also explored by Norman Gottwald in his slightly earlier book *The Tribes of Yahweh* (1979), which offers a social-scientific approach to ancient Israel. Gottwald explicitly references the connection I mentioned earlier between structuralism and a "sociohistorical approach" to the biblical text:

> There appears to be a measure of conjunction, as yet largely unexplored, between the linguistic context isolated by structuralism and the sociohistorical context, in

the sense that each points to a larger structure of regularities that finds expression in particular texts.[42]

This quotation highlights Gottwald's priorities in his analysis. He is interested not so much in the particularities of the biblical texts as in the deep structures underlying them—the broader Israelite *Sitz im Leben* out of which they emerge. However, the *Sitz im Leben* is not now understood (as it was in form criticism) as the life setting of individual pieces or collections of tradition, but rather as the whole social matrix out of which Israelite literature emerged and in respect of which it must be understood. The form-critical and structuralist lesson about the need to understand the "mountain" against the background of the "mountain range" has been well taken, and deeper clarification of the *Sitz im Leben* of ancient Israelite literature is now sought using social-scientific categories and methods.

Comprehensive Understanding

Gottwald begins his massive work with some reflections on "obstacles to a comprehensive understanding of ancient Israel."[43] Despite all the historical interest in ancient Israel in preceding generations, he claims, "premonarchic Israel continues to escape our efforts to visualise it as a totality, to locate its deepest roots, and to account for its cohesion and vitality."[44] Academic overspecialization lies at the heart of the problem: "the enslaving hold of hyperspecialization disconnected from a larger framework which could relate means and ends, parts and wholes."[45] This discourages attempts at large-scale interpretative models, with the result that "the larger possible designs of Israel as an historic phenomenon of the first magnitude are increasingly lost to the workaday mentality and method of biblical scholarship."[46] A particular obstacle is that a "humanities perspective on ancient Israel," while getting at "important dimensions of the phenomenon," is *not in any case up to the task* of providing such a large-scale interpretative model:

> The Israelites wrote engrossing literature. The Israelites experienced an eventful history. The Israelites developed a novel and consequential religion. . . . [But w]hy are some events remembered by a people and not others? And how are the newly discovered events and factors of Israel's world, uncovered by modern research, to be related to those events and factors which Israel identified and proclaimed in an overarching cultural schema?[47]

---

[42] Norman K. Gottwald, *The Tribes of Yahweh: A Sociology of the Religion of Liberated Israel, 1250–1050 BCE* (BibSem 66; Sheffield: Sheffield Academic. 1999), 720n43.
[43] Gottwald, *Tribes*, 3–7.
[44] Gottwald, *Tribes*, 3.
[45] Gottwald, *Tribes*, 5.
[46] Gottwald, *Tribes*, 6.
[47] Gottwald, *Tribes*, 7.

Are people always able to identify "the significant events and forces at work" in their history, and if they are, "do they always choose to give direct expression to them?"[48] And now we get to the heart of the matter:

> [W]hat are the transactions by which the events through which a people pass, especially in their beginnings, are transmuted into symbolic structures of collective identity and meaning? What are the forms of living together and thinking about the communal life which take ever-changing shapes and orientations in the course of historical experience? And how are the social interaction patterns and the thought patterns of a people related? How can a student of ancient Israel take its total existence as a social system of interacting doers and thinkers into account and still give the inquiry a boundable controlled form? The humanities as such give very little help in answering such questions.[49]

Unfortunately most biblical scholars are trained in the humanities, so it is unsurprising that these questions do not get asked, much less answered. Gottwald wishes to redress the balance by bringing social theory to bear on the history of Israel. Therefore, he looks at Israelite religion not so much in terms of particular institutions and practices created by historical individuals for distinctively religious reasons but as only one "aspect of a wider network of social relations in which it has intelligible functions to perform."[50] Any "changes in religious behaviour and thought are best viewed as aspects of change in the wider network of social and economic relations."[51]

Religion as Societal Instrument

We cannot do more than summarize the major conclusions at which Gottwald arrives by the end of his extremely large book; fortunately he too summarizes them near the beginning.[52] Early Israel, he proposes, comprised a complicated mixture of marginalized Canaanites, including peasants living in a "feudalized" political and economic situation, mercenaries and adventurers, pastoralists moving seasonally between different pastures, and tribally organized farmers. The Israelites did not enter the land of Canaan from outside; "Israel" emerged from within, as a result of a deliberate and highly conscious "retribalization" process—this new social structure being *chosen* rather than simply carrying over from previous forms of existence. The religion of Yahweh was crucial to this whole enterprise—a necessary "societal instrument" that held the new people together,

---

[48] Gottwald, *Tribes*, 7.
[49] Gottwald, *Tribes*, 7.
[50] Gottwald, *Tribes*, xxiii.
[51] Gottwald, *Tribes*, xxiii.
[52] Gottwald, *Tribes*, xxiii.

allowed their new society to flourish, and in extreme need ensured its survival. This was a distinctive ancient society, whose religion both reflected and reinforced its values and its practices.

These conclusions represent a major shift away from previous understandings of the emergence of early Israel. Prior to Gottwald in the modern period two main models had dominated the scene: the conquest model and the immigration model, both largely grounded in the biblical text but also utilizing various forms of archaeological evidence.[53] Gottwald essentially rejects these two earlier models in favor of his "revolt" model, claiming the support of the earlier work of George Mendenhall. Fundamentally, the people of Israel emerged out of Canaanite disaffection with respect to their lives inside Canaan—and not as a result of events in Egypt or in the wilderness.

Gottwald's concluding comments in his final chapter are important to the understanding of his entire argument.[54] Here he firmly binds together the "radical social experiment" that was ancient Israel with the radical theology that it birthed and that sustained it. What is evident from his study, Gottwald proposes, is that "efforts to draw 'religious inspiration' or 'biblical values' from the early Israelite heritage will be romantic and utopian" unless they are grounded in cultural-material reality.[55] Social-scientific analysis of ancient Israel undermines

> the idealist and supernaturalist illusions still permeating and bedeviling our religious outlook. Yahweh and "his" people Israel must be demystified, deromanticized, dedogmatized and deidolized. Only as we carry through this sociological demythologization of Yahwistic faith, and of its Jewish and Christian derivatives, will those of us who have been formed and nurtured by those curiously ambiguous Jewish and Christian symbols be able to align heart and head, to combine theory and practice.[56]

Ideas and practice must be kept together, and "[s]ymbol systems claiming to be based on 'biblical faith'" must be judged on how well they achieve this. Symbol systems that obscure this necessary connection

> by talking fuzzy nonsense, by isolating us in our private souls, by positing "unseen" worlds to compensate for the actual world we fear to see ... by persuading us to accept the humanly unacceptable and to desist from changing what is manifestly changeable ... by decrying power while feasting on its benefits.[57]

---

[53] Provan, Long, and Longman, *Biblical History*, 191–201.
[54] Gottwald, *Tribes*, 700–709.
[55] Gottwald, *Tribes*, 706.
[56] Gottwald, *Tribes*, 708.
[57] Gottwald, *Tribes*, 708.

—all such systems must be cast off. "They are, in a word, the Canaanite idols that Israel smashed when it smashed the Canaanite kings."[58]

SECOND THOUGHTS

There is much that is deeply insightful in Gottwald's work, as he seeks to show how deeply and intimately connected are the social organization and the theology promoted in the OT literature, and how distinctive these are when compared with the prevailing norms of the surrounding culture. His understanding of early Israelite history immediately clarifies the message of the prophets in a new way, for example, as well as helping us to see clearly that the business of "being biblical" is not quite as simple as quoting biblical texts in support of a particular position we have already decided to adopt. Texts always mean things in relation to other things (the parts in relation to the whole), and if what they mean is at least partly bound up with the larger social matrix out of which they emerge, then we shall need to grapple with that matrix in order fully to understand them.

At the same time Gottwald is much more antitheological in his approach to Scripture than Myers, at least as theology has traditionally been understood. In his desire to show that we cannot divorce the transcendental from the material, ideas from practices, he often writes as if the former depend almost entirely on the latter—which is surely a reductionistic overstatement, and a dangerous one if he does not wish his readers simply to dismiss his own book with, "Well, he *would* say that, wouldn't he?" It is important to note here, however, that in response to criticism of the first publication of his ideas Gottwald much more carefully maintains in the later reissue that religion and society are "functions *of one another,*" giving ideas a proper place in the dialectic and arguing only that "ideologies and religions [never] stand apart from and prior to socially bonded and conflicting persons."[59] This more nuanced statement is far closer to the mark. "Gods" ("idols") do arise in human society (e.g., "Mammon") in order to legitimate or subvert ways of living in it. To describe their societal function, however, is neither to prove nor disprove their reality. Nor does it necessarily follow that social practice came first and ideas about God only second.

Gottwald is also much more "suspicious" of the biblical text than Myers, and he allows its narrative much less control over his results. Indeed, he holds resolutely to his "revolt model" of the emergence of ancient Israel in Canaan in the face of the claims of the biblical text and of other evidence as well—and he has been much criticized for doing so. We cannot say for certain that some element of revolt within the Canaanite city-states was not involved in the formation of

---

[58] Gottwald, *Tribes*, 708.
[59] Gottwald, *Tribes*, 903 (emphasis added).

the people of Israel. Certainly the Bible itself does not straightforwardly suggest that conquest of the land by outsiders was all there was to it. Yet our biblical texts place enormous emphasis on the significance of the exodus and what happened subsequently to the people who participated in it, and it is simply arbitrary to set this testimony aside in favor of another way of thinking about the emergence of Israel in Canaan that is in any case problematic for other reasons.[60] That Mosaic Yahwism was distinctive as to belief and practice in comparison to the prevailing Canaanite culture of its time is true—but it should be obvious that this does not prove that Mosaic Yahwism originated within that culture.

In sum, there is much of value to be learned from the social-scientific criticism of the Bible, as we explore the question of the broad *Sitz im Leben* of our biblical literature. A "seriously literal interpretation" committed to deploying all the insights it can in pursuit of the best reading of this literature should certainly embrace this learning. It will of course resist (as the reading of all literature should) any foolish and incoherent reductionism that tries to claim that what is "really" going on in a text is what lies *behind* it rather than *in* it and regards generalizing models about reality as providing us with better access to it than the rhetoric of particular texts. Yet we cannot (and which orthodox Christian would wish to?) escape the reality that a human being belongs to a particular society, and that it is within the context of that society that the kingdom of God is experienced and expressed. This is as true of the NT as of the OT:

> As with any human being or reality, the soul is not to be had without the body, i.e., we are not going to see the meaning of early Christianity unless we see the social embodiment of this meaning and the dialectic process between belief and social structure this entails.[61]

FEMINIST CRITICISM

Jonathan Culler helpfully introduces the feminist reading of literature in the book on poststructuralism first discussed in my chapter 19. What difference does it make, he asks, if the reader of a literary work experiences it "as a woman" rather than "as a man"?[62] "Women's experience, many feminist critics claim, will lead them to value [literary] works differently from their male counterparts"[63]—if they are truly reading as women. Unfortunately many women have been taught to identify with *male* experience and perspective, presented to them from a young age as

---

[60] Provan, Long, and Longman, *Biblical History*, 190–201.
[61] Bengt Holmberg, *Sociology and the New Testament: An Appraisal* (Minneapolis: Fortress, 1990), 3.
[62] Culler, *Deconstruction*, 43–64.
[63] Culler, *Deconstruction*, 45.

if they were simply *human* experience and perspective. For this reason "women can read, and have read, as men."⁶⁴ The effort to read "not as a man," conversely, demonstrates that male readings of literature are not inevitable—that there is nothing self-evident about them. It only appears so because the prejudices of male *authors* typically correspond so deeply with the prejudices of male *readers*. Other readings are entirely possible, and we should generate such readings in pursuit of the feminist agenda. They might be based on the text itself, or they might arise out of resistance to the text. They might well challenge as "male" *the very way in which reading has traditionally been carried out*, in the belief that literary criticism itself has been complicit in attempts to preserve male authority. On this third way of approaching the matter, feminists propose that males in criticism, as in life, tend to focus on *authorship* as tied up with meaning, and are greatly concerned with "controlling intercourse with texts so as to prevent the proliferation of illegitimate interpretations."⁶⁵ The feminist assault at this level, then, is on the entire enterprise of traditional reading as corruptly male—an attack on male attempts to suppress the fertility of the text. We must substitute for this corrupt model a less rational, more intuitive, and empathetic approach.

The Maleness of Criticism?

Culler identifies three models for the feminist reading of literature, then, and I shall proceed on the same basis.⁶⁶ The first thing to be said, however, is that it is difficult to know what to do with the third model, if one believes (as I do) that rational argument has an important role to play in arriving at sound judgments concerning the right ways of reading texts. If proposals about legitimate as opposed to illegitimate interpretations of a text, premised on arguments about the likely communicative intentions of its author, are to be dismissed at the outset as reflecting a "merely male" concern, where do we go next? Feminists themselves typically wish to assert that there are legitimate and illegitimate ways of reading texts, and that the "fertility" of the text is not boundless. Yet if a particular assertion, based on intuition and empathy, is not at the same time a rational *argument*, what is one supposed to do with it in the realm of public discourse? Are we to see the assertion as reflecting "merely female" concern, and dismiss it as such? If not, why not? In the absence of a credible answer, this devolution of the reading of literature into what is "merely male" and "merely female" takes us well down the way, it seems, toward a situation in which the meaning of a text cannot be discussed at all across "tribal" boundaries and indeed the text itself "disappears."

---

⁶⁴ Culler, *Deconstruction*, 49.

⁶⁵ Culler, *Deconstruction*, 61.

⁶⁶ For a different way of parsing the various approaches at least as they pertain to Scripture, see Cherith Fee Nordling, "Feminist Biblical Interpretation," *DTIB*, 228–30.

It becomes merely a useful tool in an ideological power-struggle between men and women, "meaning" whatever it *must* mean in order to promote the interests of each "group," as each maintains of the other, "you only say that because...." In fact, the text becomes the victim in the end of the *individual* will to power—since *members* of each "group" can no longer gather around it as an objective entity that might somehow "speak" to them with its own distinctive voice. The purpose of reading literature *at all* then comes into question—which is why, in the contemporary postmodern West, it is indeed not actually *being* read in many university departments of literature. The teaching of the politics of gender, race, and a host of other realities has all too often replaced the teaching of "great books." Interest in the text is much less pressing than the interests of the readers in the classroom as persons of a particular color, gender, sexuality, or "privilege." The remarkable thing about this "education" is that student fees are still capable of being collected in order to fund it—fees paid for classes that quite apart from anything else are typically crushingly dull and predictable. Every student knows after the first week, if they did not know before, which questions "ought" to be asked of every text and which are the "right" answers.

I do not believe that the entire model of traditional literary criticism should be regarded as "male." It has been developed, to the contrary, precisely to allow texts and their authors the possibility of being heard by *all* readers, by way of setting constraints around each reader's ability to co-opt the text immediately for his or her own agenda. It has not always succeeded in this goal—but simply removing the constraints does not help anyone, male or female. It simply puts the text under the control of the most powerful voice in the room, with no possibility remaining for dissent from the party line on the basis that the text itself does not support that reading of it. The abandonment of rational discourse about such important matters helps no one in the end—any more than radical poststructuralism in general does so (see my chapter 19). In particular, it does not seem at all likely that any improvement in the lot of women in the world will be achieved by this route.

Two Models

This leaves two models of feminist critical engagement with literature for further consideration, both of which recognize that texts communicate in a determinate manner. In the first model, feminist reading works *with* the text, trying to show that traditional (typically male) readings are mistaken or only partially correct, and that there are better readings that are far more positive about and beneficial in respect of women. These new readings either complement earlier readings, making up something that is lacking in them, or they subvert them, demonstrating how they are flawed, erroneous, and bound up with male prejudice. In the second model of critical engagement, feminist reading works *against* the text, viewing it as irredeemably compromised by male interests and detrimental in various ways to women's well-being. Here the feminist critique is not merely of other readers but of the text itself. The text is problematic, and its rhetoric must be resisted.

At the center of the exercise of reading in both cases stands a woman who is self-consciously reading as a woman and valuing the female perspective and approach to the text as highly as, if not more highly than, a male perspective or approach. This is the distinctive of the feminist approach, for if a woman were reading "as a man," subordinating her perspective and approach to the man's, she would not qualify as a feminist reader (we shall come back to this point later in reflecting on the matter of "women's experience"). Whether in one camp or the other, then, it is likely that all feminist literary critics would agree with Judith Fetterley's definition of the overall enterprise: "[F]eminist criticism is a political act whose aim is not simply to interpret the world but to change it by changing the consciousness of those who read and their relation to what they read."[67] Perhaps one of the more significant disagreements among feminists at this point concerns the question: who *are* "those who read"? For feminists do vary according to whether they see feminism as a redemptive force for all humanity, male and female, or only as a redemptive force for women. They differ, therefore, on the question of whether they wish to change everyone's consciousness, or only women's.

The Virtue of the Project

As we have already established in various sections of part 3 of this book, texts are always written from a particular point of view. Indeed, whether in their deep structures or in their explicit intentionality, they promote a certain vision of the world. Sometimes the vision ought to be resisted, and therefore the texts that promote it ought to be resisted (e.g., Adolf Hitler's *Mein Kampf*). Yet readers who have not had their consciousness raised about such matters will not necessarily realize that a particular vision is being promoted by a particular text and may not recognize the need for (or the possibility of) resistance—even if the vision does not include them, and may not even value them as persons.

Among such persons are undoubtedly many women—and for the sake of their own well-being they need to comprehend like every human being what is going on around them. They need to understand the war of myths in which they are embroiled, and to learn to be resisting as well as accepting readers of the

---

[67] Judith Fetterley, *The Resisting Reader: A Feminist Approach to American Fiction* (Bloomington: Indiana University Press, 1978), viii.

various "texts" (whether literary or not) that promote the views of this or that faction in the struggle. It is this empowering of women by way of reading skills in the first instance that feminist criticism in the two forms just described fundamentally sets out to achieve, and it is a worthy goal. We all need our consciousness raised about the war of myths that rages around us so that we can become active participants in it rather than just cannon fodder. As the father of two (now adult) women I certainly wanted them as they were growing up to become resisting readers (for example) of the earlier Walt Disney movies and others of a similar kind, with all the stereotyping of women that such movies have often involved. I wanted them to become resisting readers of television advertising, with its implicit and explicit commentary on what it means to be "a real woman." I also wanted them to become resisting readers of the kind of classical literature that Culler himself describes in his book as he draws attention to all the assumptions about women both implicit and explicit in much of it. I considered it not merely *desirable* but rather *essential for their well-being* that my daughters should learn to read literature "as women." For it was (I believed) only by reading self-consciously as women that they would learn to discriminate in their reading of both literature and culture between what is really true, on the one hand, and what some men (and indeed some other women) would like them to *believe* is true, on the other—whichever political, cultural, or commercial agenda might be driving the rhetoric.

Insofar as the feminist critical project concerns such matters it is a virtuous project, and all right-thinking people, including Christian people, ought to support it. It is right to draw attention to the ways in which texts often legitimate a world in which women are not taken as seriously, valued as highly, or dealt with as justly as men—a world in which, in fact, they have often been treated atrociously by men. To participate in such a project is simply one aspect of what it means to obey the biblical imperative to love one's neighbor—to take active steps, indeed, to ensure that we are not part of our neighbor's problem rather than part of the solution to their problem. The feminist agenda can of course be pursued in ways that are problematic for Christian faith—when its pursuit is motivated by anger or by a desire for revenge, for example, rather than by love for neighbor, or when it involves redressing past wrongs against women by discriminating now against men instead. This does not mean, however, that the agenda itself is problematic.

FEMINIST REJECTION OF THE BIBLE

The two models of the feminist criticism of literature in general just described are both represented when it comes to the feminist criticism of *biblical* literature in particular. Taking them in reverse order, we can identify first of all "rejectionist" biblical critics. These are critics who find not only the Bible itself but also Judaism and Christianity in toto to be so corrupted by patriarchy, reflecting and promoting a social reality in which men hold the power and women are largely excluded from it, that it is irredeemable.

The Male as God

Already Elizabeth Cady Stanton (1815–1902), the inspiration behind *The Woman's Bible* (1895–1898), was significantly of this view.[68] For Stanton the Bible stood at the core of the problem facing people with women's interests at heart, particularly since the Bible formed the bedrock of Western law. Western law in turn routinely held women to be unequal to men—subordinate to their male counterparts. Her response was very much in line with others before her (like Spinoza) who since the Enlightenment had sought social and political change in Europe and beyond: she used contemporary critical thinking to undermine the authority of the Bible on the issue she cared about. In the second half of the nineteenth century the new historical criticism was helpful to her in this quest, and its presence is everywhere to be seen in her and her colleagues' work in *The Woman's Bible*.

One of the better known of the more recent "rejectionists" was Mary Daly (1928–2010). Daly began her writing life as a member of the Roman Catholic Church. Her first book was *The Church and the Second Sex* (1968),[69] and it examined the oppression of women by the Church as understood by the French feminist Simone de Beauvoir in *The Second Sex* (1949). Daly is critical in her book of de Beauvoir's disillusionment with the Church, and she regards the Second Vatican Council as a sign of hope for the liberation of women. By 1973, however, Daly had published *Beyond God the Father*.[70] This book was an attack on both the Bible and Christianity. Here Daly's central concern is with Mariolatry, and particularly with how male theologians have manipulated this seemingly positive feminist aspect of Catholicism so as to make it a means of subjugation for ordinary women. The whole Judeo-Christian tradition is in fact a male structure designed by men and for men: "when god is male the male is god." Radical feminism must reject this tradition in favor of an exclusively female articulation of female religious experience based on ancient female counterparts to the ancient Israelite male cult. In her still later books Daly becomes even more radical, attacking not only Christianity but also Christian feminists—"robotized tokens" who play into the hands of male supremacists.[71] Only radical lesbian feminists, she maintains, can rise above the normal experience of male patriarchy.

---

[68] Elizabeth Cady Stanton, *The Woman's Bible* (Seattle: Pacific, 2010).

[69] Mary Daly, *The Church and the Second Sex* (New York: Harper & Row, 1968).

[70] Mary Daly, *Beyond God the Father: Toward a Philosophy of Women's Liberation* (Boston: Beacon, 1973).

[71] E.g., Mary Daly, *Gyn/Ecology: The Metaethics of Radical Feminism* (Boston: Beacon, 1978), and *Pure Lust: Elemental Feminist Philosophy* (Boston: Beacon, 1984).

Initial Questions

There are clearly some questions arising from Mary Daly's work that require further discussion. One of them is of a broader philosophical kind: granted that all sorts of women no doubt have all sorts of experiences, including religious ones, *is* there such an entity as a "female religious experience" that can be the subject of "exclusively female articulation," or indeed *any* articulation? Is the notion of "women's experience" coherent? I shall return to this matter later in the chapter. Another question is of a particularly Christian and theological kind, but is related more generally to the question of "tribalism" that I raised earlier: is it acceptable from any sort of Christian perspective to promote a vision of the world in which redemption involves only one half of the human race and not the other? Daly herself was apparently unconcerned about this issue. "I don't think about men," she once stated; "I really don't care about them. I'm concerned with women's capacities, which have been infinitely diminished under patriarchy."[72] She said this in the aftermath of a legal challenge by a male student in 1998 to her long-term policy since 1973 of banning men from her seminars at Boston College on the ground that women can realize the truths of feminism only among themselves—without men in the room.

These are not the only questions we can ask, however. Is Daly not *correct* that Christian Bible readers throughout the ages have often tended to think of God as male? Is this not what terms like "Father" and "Son" are often taken to imply even nowadays—in modern discussion about the ordination of women, for example, when it is claimed that only men can truly represent Father and Son as priests? Again, is there not abundant evidence throughout Church history that supports Daly's contention that "when god is male the male is god"—evidence of females being regarded precisely as "second-class," inferior human beings? Consider the effortlessness, for example, with which John Chrysostom can in this homily assume the superiority of the male over the female:

> If the more important, most beneficial concerns were turned over to the woman, she would go quite mad. Therefore God did not apportion both duties to one sex.... Nor did God assign both to be equal in every way.... But taking precautions at one and the same time for peace and for decency, God maintained the order of each sex by dividing the business of human life into two parts and assigned the more necessary and beneficial aspects to the man and the less important, inferior matters to the woman. God's plan was extremely desirable for us ...

---

[72] Julie Bindel, "Mary Daly Obituary," https://www.theguardian.com/world/2010/jan/27/mary-daly-obituary (accessed November 14, 2016).

so that a woman would not rebel against the husband due to the inferiority of her service.[73]

Consider, second, Augustine's prejudice on the same topic when considering that human beings fell for the lie of the serpent in the garden in Eden:

> It is surely strange if a man endowed with a spiritual mind could have believed this. Was it because the man would not have been able to believe this that the woman was employed on the supposition that she had limited understanding, and also perhaps that she was living according to the spirit of the flesh and not according to the spirit of the mind?[74]

Consider that Thomas Aquinas in the thirteenth century also believed that women were (in David Scholer's words) "inferior, dependent, dominated by sexual appetites, and unfit for any important role in society or in the church," and thus believed (along with all medieval male theologians) "that women should be subordinate and submissive to men in virtually all matters."[75] Consider by way of example, finally, the assumptions made about the proper place of women in Church and society in this nineteenth-century sermon, in which the preacher worries about the way in which the principles of biblical interpretation espoused by those arguing for the abolition of slavery must inevitably lead to the emancipation of women:

> Let these principles be carried out, and there is an end to all social subordination, to all security for life and property, to all guarantee for public or domestic virtue. If our women are to be emancipated from subjection to the law which God has imposed upon them, if they are to quit the retirement of domestic life, where they preside in stillness over the character and destiny of society; if they are to come forth in the liberty of men, to be our agents, our public lecturers, our committeemen, our rulers, if, in studied insult to the authority of God, we are to renounce in the marriage contract all claim to obedience, we shall soon have a country ... from which all order and all virtue would speedily be banished.... It would not be fair to object to the abolitionists [in this way] ... were not these opinions the legitimate consequences of their own principles. Their women do but apply their own method of dealing with Scripture to another case.[76]

---

[73] John Chrysostom, *The Kind of Women Who Ought to Be Taken as Wives*, 4, cited in David M. Scholer, "The Evangelical Debate over Biblical 'Headship,'" in *Women, Abuse and the Bible: How Scripture Can Be Used to Hurt or to Heal* (ed. Catherine Clark Kroeger and James R. Beck; Grand Rapids: Baker, 1996), 28–57 (35).

[74] Augustine, *Literal Meaning*, 2.11.42 (ACW 41:175).

[75] Scholer, "Headship," 35.

[76] Willard M. Swartley, *Slavery, Sabbath, War, and Women: Case Issues in Biblical Interpretation* (Scottdale, Pa.: Herald, 1983), 49–50.

If God is male, the male is god—and that is why it is only very recently, within the past hundred years or so, that women in many Christianized countries have begun to be viewed as other than their husband's property, have acquired equal rights before the law, have had some degree of access to political power, and have begun (in some circles) to be paid equal salaries for equal work. "Biblically based" societies do look as if they have been set up for the benefit of males, using a male god to legitimate the enterprise.

The Bible Implicated

One possible response to these questions and observations is to concede that men have indeed often *used* the Bible as one of the tools by which to construct and maintain their dominance, but that they were not justified in doing so—that the biblical text itself does not justify their reading and use of it. What marks out "rejectionist" feminists from their "revisionist" colleagues, however, is their belief that *the Bible itself* is steeped in patriarchy and responsible for the oppression of women. It is not simply a matter of poor biblical interpretation.

Consider biblical law, for example. In the Ten Commandments as articulated in Exodus 20 the wife is evidently the property of the husband: "You shall not covet your neighbor's house. You shall not covet your neighbor's wife, or his male or female servant, his ox or donkey, or anything that belongs to your neighbor" (Exod 20:17). In Deuteronomy 22:13-21, moreover, we read of the case of a man "taking" a woman as his wife and subsequently hating and slandering her. The woman in this case does have some protection under the law, but the implication throughout the passage is that she is not a legal "person"—she has no legal role. She is defended by her previous owners (her father and mother), the father being the one who initially "gave" her to the husband and to whom the fine is ultimately paid if the case is won (vv. 17, 19). What we have in this passage is essentially a business or property dispute: did the father sell "damaged goods" to the husband? The language throughout is thoroughly patriarchal—"her father's house," "the men of her town" (vv. 20-21)—and the interest is resolutely male: can men be sure that their children are really theirs? There is no good outcome for the woman in this situation. If guilty she is put to death; if innocent she is condemned to live with a man who has publicly humiliated her. There is certainly no equality under the law: the penalty for the woman if guilty is death, but the penalty for the man—even though he threatened the life of his wife—is only a monetary fine. Leviticus 27:1-7 underlines the reality of male-female relations under OT law in terms of the value attached to persons. When it comes to compensation, females in this passage are worth half as much as males.

Consider, next, the biblical wisdom literature, as illustrated by the book of Proverbs—a book written by men and for men. The opening chapters are addressed, in fact, by a "father" to a "son," who is exhorted to embrace the female figure of Wisdom and to avoid the "adulterous" or "wayward woman" who might seduce him and lead him off the right path. The wayward woman is one of two main types in the book, in fact. The other is the ideal wife—the one who brings wealth to her husband and should receive a reward because of it (Prov 31:31). That is to say: women are described in Proverbs from a male point of view and function only in relation to the men.

Consider, finally, biblical narrative as illustrated by Judges 11:29-40. This passage tells the story of the daughter of Jephthah the Gileadite, who is killed because Jephthah makes a vow to sacrifice to God whatever and whoever comes out to meet him after his victory over the Ammonites. It is a tragic story that serves to illustrate the kind of patriarchal society in action that we have already encountered in theory in the law. Jephthah makes a vow that might turn out to apply to any of his possessions, a daughter as well as a goat or an ox; he does not appear to be very concerned to differentiate among them. When his daughter turns out to be the first of his possessions to greet him, Jephthah does not blame himself for the evil he has brought on *her* but instead blames *her* for the evil that she has brought on *him* (Judg 11:35). The victim is blamed for her own plight. Nor does Jephthah offer himself in her place, or simply refuse to fulfill the vow and suffer the consequences. The daughter simply serves the needs of the father. The only solace she finds in this story comes from her female friends who weep with her (v. 38)—and even the permission for this mourning has to come from the father. The only remembrance she finds is also in the company of women, as they lament her passing each year (v. 40). The canon of Scripture itself does not remember Jephthah's daughter, although it does remember and glorify her father. In Judges 12 Jephthah the mighty warrior prevails over the Ephraimites uncensured. His military victories enhance his name in the years that follow, such that Samuel later mentions him among those who delivered Israel (1 Sam 12:11)—again without criticism. The author of Hebrews explicitly names him as one who through faith conquered kingdoms, enforced justice, and so on (Heb 11:32-34). Jephthah is remembered in Scripture, his daughter forgotten.

The Challenge to Faith

It is not difficult to see, then, why feminists like Mary Daly have decided to part company with both the Bible and the Church. From their point of view the Bible legitimates a world in which women are subservient to men. The Church for whom the Bible functions authoritatively as Scripture has also historically legitimated that world. The only path for those who care about women's issues is therefore the path of rejection. The question for those who do still hold the Bible to be authoritative Scripture is how best to respond to the substantive points that Daly and others have raised about it.

THE REVISIONIST RESPONSE

This is the background against which "revisionist" feminist critics have been doing their work. These are feminists who neither wish to relinquish the label "Christian" nor indeed to distance themselves entirely from the biblical tradition as divine revelation. They employ a number of strategies in the attempt to hold Bible, faith, and feminism together, and they make differing judgments on important questions in the course of this quest concerning such matters as the nature of biblical authority and the role of experience vis-à-vis the authority of the Bible. For this reason "revisionist" feminists represent a mixed multitude, theologically speaking. Their numbers include both avowedly evangelical scholars like Elaine Storkey (*What's Right with Feminism?*, 1985) and more radical scholars like Elisabeth Schüssler Fiorenza (*In Memory of Her*, 1983).[77]

A Compendium of Opinions

What both unites and divides them is helpfully illustrated in a 1985 compendium of essays edited by Letty Russell and titled *Feminist Interpretation of the Bible*.[78] Almost everywhere we turn in these essays we come across some discussion of the issue of authority, and particularly the sort of authority that the Bible can be held to possess as a book that seems to legitimate patriarchy. The essayists raise questions about the very nature of authority (is it domination or partnership?) and whether each and every part of the Bible is authoritative or only Scripture as a whole. They also assess the roles of reason and experience in our assessment of *which* parts of the Bible are specifically the Word of God to us and which are not. There is a general view throughout the essays that feminist consciousness must have an important part to play in the task of biblical interpretation, in which certain core convictions operate—the most fundamental of which is "that women are fully human and are to be valued as such."[79] There must be a determined effort to unmask patriarchy in the biblical texts and not to shirk that task because of any particular view of authority. There is a keen recognition, in fact, that "[t]he Bible was shaped by males [living] in a patriarchal culture," the "revelatory experiences" at its heart being "interpreted by men from a patriarchal perspective." These men eliminated "traces of female experience" or interpreted them "in an

---

[77] Elaine Storkey, *What's Right with Feminism?* (London: SPCK, 1985); Elisabeth Schüssler Fiorenza, *In Memory of Her: A Feminist Theological Reconstruction of Christian Origins* (New York: Crossroad, 1983).

[78] Letty M. Russell, ed., *Feminist Interpretation of the Bible* (Philadelphia: Westminster, 1985).

[79] Margaret A. Farley, "Feminist Consciousness and the Interpretation of Scripture," in Russell, *Feminist Interpretation*, 41–51 (44).

androcentric way."[80] Inevitably, therefore, the Bible justifies patriarchy in ongoing Jewish and Christian society, and simply to give in to its "authority" is not going to lead to the different world that feminists envision. Thus far these writers are entirely with Mary Daly.

They disagree with Daly, however, in her view that the Bible is *irredeemably* male. Fiorenza concedes that if Daly is correct on this point then "self-identified women struggling for survival should avoid it like the plague."[81] But she thinks that Daly is mistaken, and so do all "revisionist" feminists to one extent or another. Each of them believes that in reality the Bible in places or even in its overall shape *subverts* patriarchy. Margaret Farley writes about "the biblical witness as a whole" and about the way in which, if "experienced as authentic" by women, this witness overall provides them with a context in which its different parts can be assessed.[82] Rosemary Radford Ruether refers to a "prophetic-messianic tradition"—"a critical perspective and process through which biblical tradition constantly reevaluates, in new contexts, what is truly the liberating Word of God."[83] The critique is limited and partial, but it may be used as a model: "The feminist interpretation of prophetic critique as feminist critique ... continues the process of scriptural hermeneutic itself, whereby the text is reinterpreted in the context of new communities of critical consciousness."[84] Russell takes a similar view.[85] Fiorenza is critical of this view but nevertheless agrees that the Bible is a force for liberation *as well as* for oppression.[86] Women have found help in Scripture in the past in the midst of their struggles, and they will do so also in the future. A pervasive theme in all this material is that many of the essayists have themselves found the Bible to be a liberating force in their own lives. That is why in the end they cannot adopt Daly's position. Their experience itself, as part of female experience more generally, leads them to affirm the authority of at least parts of the Bible even while questioning some of the remainder.

FEMALE EXPERIENCE

Earlier I said that I would return to this notion of "women's experience." Evidently this is an important concept for many feminist biblical critics, but as we

---

[80] Rosemary Radford Ruether, "Feminist Interpretation: A Method of Correlation," in Russell, *Feminist Interpretation*, 111–24 (116).

[81] Elisabeth Schüssler Fiorenza, "The Will to Choose or to Reject: Continuing Our Critical Work," in Russell, *Feminist Interpretation*, 125–36 (130).

[82] Farley, "Consciousness," 50.

[83] Ruether, "Correlation," 117.

[84] Ruether, "Correlation," 122.

[85] Letty M. Russell, "Authority and the Challenge of Feminist Interpretation," in Russell, *Feminist Interpretation*, 137–46.

[86] Fiorenza, "Will to Choose," 131–32.

begin to move toward some concluding reflections on the value of feminist criticism for the overall approach to biblical interpretation that I am commending in this volume, it is important to recognize that there is a problem here. The essays in *Feminist Interpretation* acknowledge in numerous places that in reality the experience of women is *varied*.[87] Yet again and again we find the grounding for feminist interpretation of the Bible nevertheless *rooted* in claims about "women's experience." Farley tells us, for example, that "a careful listening to women's own experience" leads on to certain conclusions, one of which is that "all efforts to justify the inferiority of women to men falsify women's experience."[88] This is a bold claim, and it could surely be substantiated empirically only if one were very careful about which women one asked. I am reasonably confident that many readers will have known women personally who certainly believed themselves to be inferior to men. In a similar vein Ruether claims that

> if the cross of Jesus would be experienced by women as pointing them only toward continued victimization and not redemption, it would be perceived as false and demonic in this way, and women could no longer identify themselves as Christians.[89]

The reality is, however, that throughout history crucifixion has *often* been taken as informing female piety in the church, particularly in terms of how women should deal with violence and abuse at the hands of their husbands. It is exactly the woman's "victimization" that validates her claim to be a Christian—to be one who follows the victim Christ. As Carolyn Osiek notes:

> It has been to women and other oppressed groups that the message of the cross has been particularly directed. Women have been exhorted to enter into the destiny and vocation that belong to them through their superior capacity for self-sacrifice, self-denial, and suffering that has been thought ... to belong to their "proper nature" ... women have been invited to participate in and conform themselves to the suffering of Christ by remaining passive and powerless because it is these qualities that will humanize the children they raise and the men for whom they provide a home.... This persistent portrayal of women as demonstrating heroic but fitting sacrifice by submitting passively and silently to pain and abuse ... leads directly to the image of the battered woman. She is the victim not only of the rage of her abuser but the blindness of a whole society that in the name of the sanctity of home and family will do nothing to rescue her.... [W]omen are to imitate the victim Christ while at the same time they are denied any possibility of fully

---

[87] E.g., "Surely all women do not have the same experiences. There are many variations in the consciousness of women, shaped by different cultural contexts and life experiences. How then can one generalize about women's experience?" Ruether, "Correlation," 113.

[88] Farley, "Consciousness," 45–46.

[89] Ruether, "Correlation," 112.

identifying with him. Doomed to be like him in suffering and humiliation, they are equally doomed to be unlike him in power, authority, or exaltation.[90]

The point is not only that the message of the cross has been *directed* at women in this way, however, but that many have *embraced* it. Consider this comment from a battered Christian wife: "If my gentle spirit in the midst of his violence finally causes him to see the face of Jesus in me, every blow I have sustained throughout our marriage will have been worth it."[91]

The appeal to "women's experience" that so often appears in feminist writing about the Bible, then, is weak—*if* it is indeed an appeal to *general* experience, which in the above cases it surely must be if the argument is to be persuasive.[92] What feminists like Ruether and Farley really want to do is to make claims about what is true and right. They do not wish merely to tell us how they and like-minded feminists feel about the world, or how each one of them personally prefers to read the Bible. That would be an insufficient ground from which to challenge the status quo. They require an "authority" to which they can appeal in support of their position—a unified, stable authority. But in reality "women's experience" cannot provide such an authority, since there is no such one, stable thing. It can exist only as a generalized abstraction, immediately vulnerable to empirical enquiry—at which point, however, it becomes clear that it really *is* only the experience of women like the writers in question that is being described over against other, "falsifying" experiences:

> By women's experience as a key to hermeneutics or theory of interpretation, we mean precisely that experience which arises when women become critically aware of these falsifying and alienating experiences imposed upon them as women by a male-dominated culture. Women's experience, in this sense, is . . . an infusion of liberating empowerment from beyond the patriarchal cultural context.[93]

So "women's experience" is really not "women's experience" after all. It is instead an ideal state of being (from these authors' perspective) for which all right-thinking women should be striving and which some enlightened ones have already achieved. This is the way that women *ought* to experience the world, and *would* experience it if only their consciousness were entirely raised to the appropriate level. Thus

---

[90] Cited in Scholer, "Headship," 32.

[91] Carolyn Holderread Heggen, "Religious Beliefs and Abuse," in Kroeger and Beck, *Women, Abuse and the Bible*, 15–27 (23).

[92] Amy-Jill Levine notes this tendency "to universalize their own experiences and concerns" as a feature of "second-wave" feminism in particular (in the 1960s and 1970s)—yet it appears to be more prevalent than that. Amy-Jill Levine, "Feminist Criticism," in Aune, *Blackwell Companion to the New Testament*, 156–65 (159).

[93] Ruether, "Correlation," 114.

do we find in a particular form in this kind of feminist criticism the ambiguity and indeed incoherence that is present in much reader-response criticism more generally. Jonathan Culler notices it, for example, in the work of Stanley Fish: "On the one hand, experience is a given to which one appeals; on the other hand, the experience one proposes to use is to be produced by particular operations."[94]

No generalized "experience" of any kind—whether "female," "male," or simply "human"—can fulfill the kind of role as a viable foundation for theology and ethics that some feminist statements about "women's experience" appear to claim for it. It is simply impossible to root great claims about what is true and right in "experience" globally described. Even if we could establish what *is* the case universally regarding experience (and we cannot), it would remain entirely unclear what bearing this had on how we *ought* to think and live—or, indeed, how we *ought* to read Scripture. And as to claims that "women's experience" itself *ought* to be of a certain kind—such claims only raise the question, "why *ought* it to be so?" Why is that the right way of thinking?

THE SUBVERSION OF PATRIARCHY

Feminist thinking on such matters rests, then, on insubstantial foundations. When it comes to concrete proposals, on the other hand, about fresh readings of the Bible that demonstrate that Scripture itself subverts patriarchy in different ways and provides liberating perspectives vis-à-vis women, "revisionist" feminists stand on much firmer ground. Now we are dealing with suggestions about textual meaning that are not grounded in claims about experience (whether global or local) but in close attention to the text itself as a canonical whole, informed by feminist concerns (and experiences). Now, however, the female reader can be regarded as essentially no different from any other reader of the Bible who takes it seriously (and literally) as his or her guide to faith and life. We all bring ourselves as readers to the biblical text with our various questions and experiences, and we each engage with it in dialogue looking to understand its various parts in relation to the whole. In this process we do not prioritize our experience, since then we could find nothing new in the text—nothing that could disorientate and challenge us. Nor do we pretend, however, that our experience does not contribute to the act of interpretation, enabling us to see perhaps what others have missed. Perhaps they have missed the point, for example, that OT law must necessarily be read in the context of what Genesis 1 has to say about every man and woman being made in the image of God—which raises all sorts of important questions about what is of lasting relevance in the law and what is not. Perhaps they have failed to notice that the book of Proverbs looks at the world from only the male

[94] Culler, *Deconstruction*, 41.

point of view and that its reading must involve intelligent generalizations if it is to speak to female as well as to male image bearers. Feminist-critical reading is capable of raising the consciousness of all readers of biblical texts (including men's) in just such ways, and thus has an important role to play in biblical hermeneutics. It represents another of the tools that can provide Bible readers with fresh distance from the text so that we can consider whether our settled interpretation of it is truly justified or not—whether this is indeed the best reading we can offer, or whether we can do better. As such, feminist-critical reading can make an important contribution to the "seriously literal interpretation" of Scripture—so long as it agrees that whatever the text in its biblical context is ultimately heard to say, whether pleasing to us or not, should be taken as authoritative. Otherwise feminist critics put themselves beyond Scripture's correction and criticism, which is not something that followers of Jesus should wish to do. It is for Scripture to "rebuke" readers (2 Tim 3:16); it is not for its readers to rebuke Scripture. Yet sometimes even feminist critics with quite a high regard for Scripture seem overly relaxed about some of their conclusions in this respect.

TEXTS OF TERROR

Phyllis Trible, in *Texts of Terror*, provides a good example on this point in her treatment of the Jephthah story in Judges 11[95]—the reading upon which I based my description of the feminist approach to this passage earlier. She helpfully raises our consciousness about the troubling nature of this story, and does so as a scholar possessing a strong commitment to Scripture, which she contends in her postscript to the Russell volume must provide feminism "with a needed critique of itself"—since even "[p]rophetic movements are not exempt from sin."[96] Yet in *Texts of Terror* Trible is not only prepared to accuse the collectors of the Jephthah cycle of stories of "patriarchal hermeneutics"[97] in their failure to acknowledge the horror of Jephthah's deed, but she also holds the (male) canonizers of Scripture responsible for sweeping under the carpet of history his act of brutality against his innocent daughter. In Trible's view Scripture has "violated the ancient story."[98] Her own response is to make up for the lack in Scripture by composing a lament over Jephthah's daughter, patterned after the model of David's lament for Saul and Jonathan in 2 Samuel 1.

---

[95] Phyllis Trible, *Texts of Terror: Literary-Feminist Readings of Biblical Narratives* (Philadelphia: Fortress, 1984), 93–116.
[96] Phyllis Trible, "Postscript: Jottings on the Journey," in Russell, *Feminist Interpretation*, 147–49 (149).
[97] Trible, *Texts of Terror*, 107.
[98] Trible, *Texts of Terror*, 108.

This is not the kind of conclusion about Scripture about which we *should* feel relaxed. Nor is it a necessary conclusion, however. In the first place, I do not believe that it can be deduced from Judges 12 (as Trible thinks) that the collectors of the Jephthah traditions did not care about his daughter. Biblical narrative, as we have seen, tends to be extraordinarily understated. It leaves gaps in many places, inviting the reader to form *judgments* about what is happening in the story. The absence of explicit editorial comment on Jephthah's daughter in Judges 12, then, proves little about the collectors' thinking on the matter. With regard to the Samuel and Hebrews passages, second, they simply focus elsewhere (as all texts need to focus *somewhere*)—on Jephthah's role in carrying through God's plan of redemption. They do not ask us to think of him as an entirely exemplary figure in thus participating in God's plan, and there are many other examples where less than exemplary characters do this. The absence of Jephthah's daughter from these later texts is no more significant than the absence of all sorts of other people, both male and female. I do not believe, then, that one can deduce from these passages very much at all about the "bias" in the collectors and canonizers of Scripture, whether in an allegedly "androcentric" direction or not.

Certainly the Bible taken as a canonical whole does not encourage us to *read* them in an androcentric manner. On the contrary, given the overall vision of the kingdom of God that it presents, in which God cares for all human beings equally and brings justice to all equally, Scripture surely leads us to precisely the penetrating analysis of Judges 11 that Trible largely offers. Explicit evidence that she herself cites, indeed, indicates that early Jewish readers already understood this as they read the Jephthah story within their broader canonical context. *Pseudo-Philo*, one of the Jewish Pseudepigrapha, has God criticizing Jephthah severely for his wicked vow and praising his daughter for being "wiser than both her father and 'the wise men of the people.'"[99] Jewish legend further records "that in death Jephthah was punished [for his crime] by dismemberment."[100] These early readers, at least, did not believe that Judges 11 should be understood as suggesting that Jephthah was blameless, or as encouraging the obliteration of his daughter's memory. Nor did many later readers.[101] And Tikva Frymer-Kensky proposes that

---

[99] Trible, *Texts of Terror*, 115n59.
[100] Trible, *Texts of Terror*, 115n59.
[101] After an extensive discussion, John Thompson concludes that many of the treatments of the story in Judges 11 in postbiblical literature may be read as "means whereby minds both theological and pious attempted to identify with Jephthah's daughter, reading their own lives and concerns and ecclesial contexts into her story in order to recall the witness of her truncated life—in mourning, warning, and grace." Thompson, *Writing the Wrongs*, 178. That this is not commonly understood is a result of "the stereotyping, neglect, and wholesale dismissal with which precritical [male] commentators have been treated" in much feminist writing about the "texts of terror" in general (253). The critics "find" the readers and the biblical text that they expect to find.

we should not think of the collectors of the Judges traditions or the canonizers of Scripture as reading in such ways either: "The idea of a great savior of Israel offering his daughter in sacrifice would have been as horrible to the ancient Israelite as it is to the modern reader."[102] Of the OT "texts of terror" in general she says this:

> These biblical tales of terror portray the horrible things that happen to women under patriarchy; they serve as a warning to us to prevent such happenings, and they were probably included in the Bible to show how things went wrong in Israel.... This is not misogynist storytelling but something far more complex, in which the treatment of women becomes the clue to the morality of the social order.[103]

CONCLUSION

Both social-scientific and feminist criticism have much to offer the Bible reader committed to "seriously literal interpretation." Not everything in either reading method is valuable, and the theory and practice of each can indeed be marked by considerable intellectual incoherence, implausibility, and self-defeating futility. Yet both help us to think hard about the worldviews that the biblical texts and their readings reflect and endorse, and to examine with a strenuous critical eye not only the biblical text but also ourselves as we interpret it. To this extent both aid "reformed" biblical interpretation.

---

[102] Tikva Frymer-Kensky, *Studies in Bible and Feminist Criticism* (JPSSDS; Philadelphia: Jewish Publication Society, 2006), 172.
[103] Frymer-Kensky, *Studies*, 174.

22

THE CANONICAL READING OF SCRIPTURE
The End of Criticism

> *Biblical authority on Protestant terms . . . exists only where one is free, on the ground of scripture, to question, to adjust, and if necessary to abandon the prevailing doctrinal traditions. Where this freedom does not exist, however much the Bible is celebrated, its authority is in fact submitted to the power of a tradition of doctrine and interpretation.*
>
> —James Barr[1]

> *The whole intention in the formation of an authoritative canon was to pass theological judgments on the form and scope of the literature.*
>
> —Brevard Childs[2]

We began our explorations in biblical hermeneutics (in chapters 2 and 3) by considering the canon of Scripture, and we complete them now in chapter 22 by doing the same. Modern biblical criticism finds its roots, we recall, in the context of debate in the post-Reformation centuries about the proper relationship between the Bible, the Church, and European society. With the "eclipse of biblical narrative" the study of the Bible in the public realm had to adapt to an increasingly postconfessional environment. The Bible of the Church needed to become the Bible of the university and the state. This was no longer a Scripture, then, that provided an overarching, unified narrative typologically integrated and centered on Christ and interpreting human existence in an authoritative way. That is, the materials in *this* Bible were no longer to be read as part of a canon. We noted in chapter 15 the late eighteenth-century work of Semler on this point in *A Free Enquiry into the Canon* (1771–1775). "Canon" had been imposed on the biblical materials by the post-apostolic Church, he argued, and as one aspect of the "dogma" of the Church it must be set aside by a biblical scholarship now in the

---

[1] Barr, *Holy Scripture*, 31–32.
[2] Brevard S. Childs, "A Response," *HBT* 2 (1980): 199–211 (210).

process of freeing itself from confessional constraint. Biblical materials must be read in their true historical rather than in their canonical context and according to the normal procedures employed in the study of any ancient text. Here lie the beginnings of the modern, historical-critical, biblical scholarship already considered in my chapters 17 and 18, with its evident lack of interest in reading individual texts and parts of texts in the context of the canon of Scripture. However, this lack of interest is also a marked feature of much modern biblical criticism more generally. Biblical texts can be read in the light of what we know about ancient rhetoric or about how literature generally works, or against the background of how societies generally function or should function. The great majority of contemporary biblical scholars working in such areas, however, are not interested in reflecting on the significance of their work for a canonical reading of Scripture. They do not understand their job description as requiring it.

It is this long-term neglect of canonical reading that was addressed by Brevard Childs (1923–2007) in a number of writings dating from the latter half of the twentieth century, including his *Introduction to the Old Testament as Scripture* (1979) and his *Biblical Theology of the Old and New Testaments* (1993). A summary and critique of Childs' work will lead us to concluding reflections on the modern period of biblical hermeneutical endeavor, and in due course to the conclusion of my entire argument.

THE INTRINSIC NATURE OF CANON

Childs' leading idea is that the concept of canon, pushed to one side in the Enlightenment in the name of academic and religious freedom, must be brought back to the center of the agenda in biblical studies. For in reality canon is *not* (as Semler proposed) an arbitrary and late imposition on the biblical texts by ancient religious authorities that distorts the "real truth" of the Bible. It does not represent the suppression of history by dogma. To the contrary, canon is itself a complex historical process within ancient Israel and then the Church that entailed the collecting, selecting, and ordering of what are now our biblical texts so as to serve a normative function as Scripture within the continuing religious community. Therefore, canon must be regarded as possessing hermeneutical significance; biblical interpreters cannot and should not simply ignore it. The biblical texts *as we have them now*, Childs maintains, should be the focus of our interpretive concern—the final form of Scripture recognized as authoritative by Jews and then Christians. For this and not earlier stages that may or may not be plausibly recovered by the historical critic is the form of the biblical tradition that "alone bears witness to the full history" of God's revelation.[3] It is, therefore, the final

---

[3] Childs, *Introduction*, 76.

canonical shape of Scripture that must guide our interpretation of the various biblical books as we reflect upon them theologically.

In making this proposal Childs does not intend to dismiss the importance of modern historical-critical research. As we shall see, he can be quite dismissive of *other* aspects of contemporary criticism (e.g., narrative criticism). Historical-critical tools, however, have an important role to play in illuminating what Childs considers to be the "depth dimension" of the biblical tradition—precisely the prior forms of the tradition that source and form critics set out to reconstruct. Nevertheless, these tools should be used to *illuminate* the canonical text as we have it, and not for other purposes: "features within the tradition that have been subordinated, modified or placed in the distant background of the text," Childs argues, cannot be interpreted "apart from the role assigned them in the final form."[4] The tradition has not been passed down to us through the process of canonical shaping for that purpose. The task of biblical theology is to reflect theologically on the final form of the Christian canon, exploring the relation between the OT and NT witnesses in serious dialogue with the traditions of dogmatic theology. Biblical theology on this view, we note, is not antagonistic to dogmatic theology, but functions as its conversation-partner.

THE AKEDAH

A good example of what Childs' approach looks like in practice is provided by his treatment in the *Biblical Theology* of the story about Abraham and Isaac in Genesis 22:1-19—"the Akedah," in Jewish tradition.[5]

The Modern Debate

Childs begins his discussion with some commentary on the modern exegetical debate about the passage. He reminds the reader that source critics of the nineteenth century "largely agreed" in assigning the story to the E-source, "but also frequently allocated some smaller fragments" to the J-source.[6] Many believed that verses 15-18 represent "a secondary redactional addition, not necessarily connected with the literary sources."[7] Gunkel's form-critical approach then attempted to reconstruct from the story "an early aetiological cult-saga" that "addressed the question of why Israel no longer sacrificed children as did the Canaanites."[8] Von Rad's great contribution was to offer "sensitive analysis of the synchronic

---

[4] Brevard S. Childs, *Old Testament Theology in a Canonical Context* (Philadelphia: Fortress, 1986), 11.
[5] Childs, *Biblical Theology*, 325–36.
[6] Childs, *Biblical Theology*, 325.
[7] Childs, *Biblical Theology*, 325.
[8] Childs, *Biblical Theology*, 325.

dimension of the text as a narrative"—not denying "the growth of the story from a cult-saga," but demonstrating how these early features "had been consigned to the text's background."⁹ What the redactor really wanted to draw his reader's attention to was the divine promise in the story. After mentioning a few other modern interpretations Childs goes on to describe the modern consensus that has emerged concerning some features of the text, but then expresses his own concern about the entire discussion:

> Within the modern debate there seems to be little direction or even concern on how one moves exegetically to include the whole Christian Bible. Often the interpreter feels constrained to move into existential categories, citing from Kierkegaard or recalling a verse from Paul, before then suggesting some loose connection with the New Testament. The implication underlying the uncertainty is that at best the New Testament is linked charismatically with the Old.¹⁰

Canonical Shaping

This is the context in which Childs sets out to demonstrate that Genesis itself "has been shaped throughout its lengthy development in such a way as to provide important hermeneutical guidelines for its theological use by a community which treasured it as scripture."¹¹ Those who passed it on (the tradents) *guide* us in our reading of it as part of a wider Scripture—among other things by introducing verses 15-18, which (even if they are "judged form-critically to be secondary") now play "a significant role in developing the message of the divine promise."¹² These Genesis tradents also tell us that what happened to Abraham was a "test" (Gen 22:1), which "allows the reader from the outset to experience the events in a way different from Abraham for whom no motivation [for the divine command] is given."¹³ Finally by way of example, they employ vocabulary—"ram," "burnt offering," and "appear"—that is only found in association elsewhere in the OT in Leviticus 8–9 and 16, which concern the Israelite tabernacle:

> The effect for the informed reader is that the story of Abraham's uniquely private experience is thus linked to Israel's collective public worship, and conversely Israel's sacrifice is drawn into the theological orbit of Abraham's offering: "God will provide his own sacrifice." In terms of the Old Testament canon, these two witnesses are not conflicting historical ideologies, but diverse witnesses within the cult to the same gracious ways of God with Israel. It is not surprising when the

---

⁹ Childs, *Biblical Theology*, 325.
¹⁰ Childs, *Biblical Theology*, 326.
¹¹ Childs, *Biblical Theology*, 326.
¹² Childs, *Biblical Theology*, 327.
¹³ Childs, *Biblical Theology*, 327.

rabbis held that the sacrifices and festivals of Israel were efficacious by virtue of the "binding of Isaac."[14]

Later Exegesis

Childs next considers the NT appropriation of the Akedah, noting "a variety of different echoes and allusions lying often just below the surface of the text which show that the Jewish traditions were widely known."[15] Then there are clearer examples:

> The strongest case for a direct dependency on the Akedah tradition occurs in Rom. 8.32 where the phraseology "God did not spare his own son," is almost identical to that of Gen. 22.16 according to the LXX ... Heb. 11.17f makes an explicit mention of Abraham's offering of Isaac. The reference is set within the larger context of the theme of faith which is first defined and then illustrated by biblical examples.... The most striking feature of the New Testament interpretation is in attributing to Abraham a belief in the resurrection of the dead, obviously missing in the Genesis passage, by which to explain the patriarch's faith. Abraham held on to the divine promise even in the face of Isaac's death because of his confidence in the creative power of God to overcome the humanly impossible.[16]

These reflections lead on next to a consideration of the history of ancient exegesis more generally, with particular attention to how the two testaments have been linked together in regard to Genesis 22.[17] Childs mentions among others Melito of Sardis, who understood the sacrifice of Isaac as a type of the crucifixion of Christ; Origen, who focused attention on the nature of Abraham's temptation (test), envisioning it "as a struggle between love of God and love of the flesh";[18] and the Reformers, who resisted this "allegorical legacy" and emphasized "faith in relation to the promise of God. Abraham was challenged to hold on to the truth of God's word of promise even though the divine command seemed flatly to contradict it."[19]

Canonical Reading

How should contemporary readers engage in theological reflection on the Akedah, then, within the entire context of Scripture? Childs proposes that we must recognize, first, the features of the story that should *not* occupy our main

---

[14] Childs, *Biblical Theology*, 327–28.
[15] Childs, *Biblical Theology*, 329.
[16] Childs, *Biblical Theology*, 329–30.
[17] Childs, *Biblical Theology*, 330–33.
[18] Childs, *Biblical Theology*, 331.
[19] Childs, *Biblical Theology*, 332.

attention. The story testifies, for example, "to a particular incident in the life of Abraham. It is a 'patriarchal temptation' and as such viewed as non-repeatable within the Bible."[20] Then again,

> the nature of the divine command to sacrifice one's own child as an offering to the deity arose from within an Ancient Near Eastern setting. Nevertheless, the point has to be made energetically that these history-of-religions features have been subordinated by being placed into the distant background of the Old Testament witness and do not function in the text as the bearers of the essential testimony.[21]

So what *is* the story essentially about? "The theological issue at stake," Childs suggests, "is that God's command to slay the heir stands in direct conflict with his promise of salvation through this very child, and therefore Abraham's relation to God is under attack."[22] The OT bears witness "that God was faithful to his promise and confirmed his word by providing his own sacrifice instead of the child."[23] Moreover,

> the editors of this chapter—in my language, the canonical shapers—did not allow this witness to become simply tied to the historical past, but actualized the witness for the sake of every successive generation of Israel. God not only saw to his own sacrifice, rather he still "sees" in the present and future. In Israel's public worship this same God "lets himself be known" today (v. 14).[24]

The NT picks up this same theme: "God demonstrated his faithfulness to the selfsame promise by not 'sparing his own son but gave him up for us all'" (Rom 8.32).[25] Both testaments

> bear testimony to the faithfulness of God, first demonstrated to Abraham, but understood as applying also to "us." The major focus of the Genesis text lies in its witness to the test of Abraham's faith, but, as we have seen, faith turns on the belief in God's promise even when it seemed contradicted by God himself. The issue is above all theological in nature stemming from the relationship between God and Abraham. The text emphasizes the radical nature of Abraham's faith in God. Hebrews 11 attributes anachronistically a full-flown doctrine of the resurrection of the dead to Abraham, but correctly witnesses thereby to the radical discontinuity between a faith which looks to God and one which sees in the empirical evidence only the contradiction of death.[26]

---

[20] Childs, *Biblical Theology*, 334.
[21] Childs, *Biblical Theology*, 334.
[22] Childs, *Biblical Theology*, 334.
[23] Childs, *Biblical Theology*, 334.
[24] Childs, *Biblical Theology*, 334.
[25] Childs, *Biblical Theology*, 334.
[26] Childs, *Biblical Theology*, 334–35.

It is "the canonical guidelines for interpretation which have been structured into the biblical text" in such ways that should guide us in our reading of the Bible. Childs refers to this guidance more strongly, in fact, as "coercion."[27] Appropriate "reader response" to Scripture pays serious attention to such coercion:

> [I]t is crucial to theological reflection that canonical restraints be used and that reader response be critically tested in the light of different witnesses of the whole Bible.... The point is to recognize the legitimate role of the reader's response in the activity of both exegesis and subsequent theological reflection without compromising the uniqueness of the witness by assigning an autonomous role to human imagination. Once the task of discerning the kerygmatic content of the witness has been pursued, it is fully in order to offer an analogical extension of this kerygmatic message by means of a modern reader response.[28]

In such ways, then, does Brevard Childs seek to take seriously all the history of modern historical-critical scholarship that lies behind him, but also the witness of the text itself and the interpretation of the text through the ages, while insisting that our final reading of Scripture must always be a canonical reading. Canonical reading is "the end of criticism," in the sense of being its final destination and purpose.

FIRST REFLECTIONS ON CANONICAL READING

The canonical approach to the Bible that Childs has proposed has raised many questions in the minds of modern biblical scholars, and we need to consider some of these in the course of arriving at a judgment on the viability of the approach.[29]

Canon-Consciousness and Final Form

Is Childs correct, first of all, in his claim that canon-consciousness lies deep within the biblical literature itself, and that "canon" is not a late and arbitrary imposition on this literature? Some have pushed back strongly against this idea, among them James Barr. Yet as I have demonstrated already in my chapter 2, Barr's argument for the lateness of both Scripture- and canon-consciousness in ancient Israel is unconvincing, as are other arguments of a similar kind with respect to the early Church. Our biblical literature was indeed formed in the midst of both Scripture and canon-consciousness on the part of both Mosaic Yahwists in the centuries BC and disciples of Jesus in the early centuries AD, none of whom can rightly

---

[27] Childs, *Biblical Theology*, 335.
[28] Childs, *Biblical Theology*, 335–36.
[29] See further Iain Provan, "Canons to the Left of Him: Brevard Childs, His Critics, and the Future of Old Testament Theology," *SJT* 50 (1997): 1–38. This essay is now conveniently reproduced in Provan, *Against the Grain*, 108–43.

be said to have *imposed* "canon" on anything. This argument having already been made, we need not dwell on it any longer at this point.

Which canon, and which text, should form the basis for the kind of theological reflection that Childs has in mind? This is another question that Childs' readers have asked—mainly regarding the OT, where the matter of "the final form of the text" has been viewed as particularly problematic. Childs has answered this question in different ways in different books. In his *Introduction* he first expresses the view that the final limits of the *Jewish* canon should be observed even by Christian interpreters of the OT, and that the MT should be regarded as the vehicle both for recovering and for understanding the canonical text of the OT.[30] In the face of criticism, however, Childs later modified this opinion (in his *Biblical Theology*) and began to refer to the search for the Christian Bible.[31] There has always been diversity within the Church regarding the form of the Christian Bible, he concedes in this later book, and "this diversity should be respected," although it should not be exaggerated. The Church "has not functioned without a scripture or in deep confusion" just because "the outer limits of the Christian canon" have remained unsettled throughout its history, or because different groups of Christians assessed "the role of translations" (like the LXX) differently.[32] These areas of disagreement have made little theological or practical difference, he suggests, and a Christian biblical theology in which canon plays a central role does not need to resolve the disagreements before it begins. Biblical theology should work theologically "within the narrow and wider forms of the canon in search for both the truth and the catholicity of the biblical witness to the church and the world."[33]

I happen to agree with Childs on the relative lack of importance of the question of the canon's *extent* for a canonical approach to biblical theology (see the close of my chapter 3)—even though there is no doubt in my mind that we should adopt the shorter canon. As to the *text*, however, I strongly believe (for the reasons outlined in my chapters 10 and 11) that the position adopted by Childs in his *Introduction* is far more coherent than his later, modified position.

THE COERCIVE TEXT

If we grant that the expression "the OT texts as we have them" makes sense as referring to the books of the canon in their final Hebrew, Aramaic (OT), and Greek (NT) forms, what next? For Childs our exegetical activity should concentrate on the final canonical shape of the tradition since this "alone bears witness

---

[30] Childs, *Introduction*, 84–106.
[31] Childs, *Biblical Theology*, 55–94.
[32] Childs, *Biblical Theology*, 65–66.
[33] Childs, *Biblical Theology*, 67.

to the full history" of divine revelation. As useful as the prehistory (and indeed the post-history) of the biblical literature may be for interpreting the final form, it is the latter that has been received as authoritative Scripture. This is where we should focus our attention, rather than on the earlier stages of the process of textual formation. In response to one of his critics, therefore, who contends that every stage in the history of the literature has as much right to its own integrity as the final form, Childs replies that "this scholarly conviction was not shared by the editors of the biblical literature, nor by the subsequent Jewish and Christian communities of faith," proceeding to assert (in the words of the second epigraph to my present chapter) that "[t]he whole intention in the formation of an authoritative canon was to pass theological judgments on the form and scope of the literature."[34] This is connected in Childs' thinking with the fact that the mode of divine revelation in Christ was not a *process* but an *incarnation* within a historical moment. Childs further notes concerning the post-history of the text that the early Church distinguished sharply between apostolic and post-apostolic tradition precisely because it regarded both the period of Christ's incarnation and the apostolic witness about it as unique.[35]

How, exactly, does this canonical text "coerce" its readers? It is as we grasp its communicative intentions and respond to them as ideal readers. Yet what kind of intentions are these? Here Childs has been criticized for imprecision in framing his argument. In the *Introduction* he writes of a "canonical intentionality" that is "coextensive with the meaning of the biblical text," making the tradition accessible to future generations.[36] He explicitly resists the idea that the main focus of research should lie on pursuing the motivations and biases of redactors. Logical and literary rules, to which the interpreter must pay attention, are clearly operative *within the text itself* as it has emerged out of the canonical process. To this extent Childs chooses not to live in Vanhoozer's "age of the author."

Yet he certainly does not live in "the age of the reader" either. He resists any hermeneutical theory that appears to him to underplay the importance of the intention of the text *as an authoritative witness located in history* and to overemphasize the importance of the modern-day interpreter or interpretive community in the construction of meaning. That is the basis of his critique of Paul Ricoeur in the *Introduction*, for example (see further below), and it resurfaces in his comments in the *Biblical Theology* on Walter Brueggemann's emphasis on the canonical interpreter.[37] The way in which Childs argues this out, however, makes it clear that he does not simply live in "the age of the text" either—although he has

---

[34] Childs, "Response," 210.
[35] Childs, "Response," 202.
[36] Childs, *Introduction*, 79.
[37] Childs, *Biblical Theology*, 72–73.

sometimes been described as a structuralist. Nothing—and this must include much structuralist theorizing, with its resolutely ahistorical emphases—must be allowed to compromise "[t]he theological appeal to an authoritative canonical text which has been shaped by Israel's witness to a history of divine, redemptive intervention."[38]

Can texts have communicative intentions that are not wholly related to the intentions of the human authors or editors who first produced them? Charles Scalise (drawing on Ricoeur), Mark Brett (on Gadamer), and others have argued in relation to Childs' work that they can, and their arguments are persuasive.[39] His thesis is coherent, even if it cannot easily be allocated to one of Vanhoozer's categories. As they are drawn together through the canonical process by those responsible for supervising it, texts can "gather" meaning that probably exceeds the meaning that earlier authors or editors ascribed to them. We saw good examples of this phenomenon in respect of both the Psalms and Isaiah in my chapters 4 and 5.

THE FREEDOM TO CHOOSE?

The biblical text coerces us—leads us to read it in the right way—as we grasp its canonical communicative intention. But why should we submit to its coercion? Even if Scripture possesses communicative intent at the canonical level, are we not free to examine earlier stages in the tradition and indeed to find theological value there? Are we not free to resist the rhetoric of the final form of the text? Is it not our *responsibility*, in fact, to subject it to criticism in terms of its relationship to the reality that lies both behind and in front of it—that is, our own reality in the modern world? Childs is unapologetic on this point. The final canonical shape of the Bible "alone bears witness to the full history" of divine revelation. Therefore, it is this text and not others upon which theologians should reflect theologically. The task of the critic is not in the end to criticize—although plenty of critical thinking will take place along the way. The task of the critic is in the end to discern the will of God for the present through the Scriptures, in dependence on the Holy Spirit.

It would be fair to say that this proposal has not been well received within modern and postmodern biblical-critical circles, and it is not difficult to understand why. It has been an integral aspect of the self-understanding of biblical

---

[38] Childs, *Biblical Theology*, 73. See further on this point Dennis Olson, "Types of a Recent 'Canonical Approach,'" *HBOT* 3/2:196–218 (210–12).

[39] Charles J. Scalise, *Hermeneutics as Theological Prolegomena: A Canonical Approach* (StABH 8; Macon, Ga.: Mercer University Press, 1994), 68–71; Mark G. Brett, *Biblical Criticism in Crisis? The Impact of the Canonical Approach on Old Testament Studies* (Cambridge: Cambridge University Press, 1991), 135–67.

scholars in the modern and postmodern periods that "freedom" lies right at the heart of their vocation (note the first epigraph to the present chapter)—the freedom to follow critical methods wherever they lead, independently of Church and confession, and indeed the freedom to construe the meaning of biblical texts in any way that its readers choose, consistent with their own "stories." Childs now proposes that freedom exists so that in the end it may serve a higher purpose: the illumination of the communicative intent that Scripture possesses at the canonical level, and thus of the communicative intent of God. From an Enlightenment perspective this is counterrevolution; from a postmodern perspective, anti-pluralistic oppression.

In response, however—focusing on modernity for the moment (since this is Childs' own concern)—it is surely the case that the scholarly freedom to enquire, where it exists, is always the servant of a higher purpose, whether explicitly stated or not. It is never a matter merely following critical methods wherever they lead—as if the scholar had never been born into and educated in a particular time and place, shaped in terms of imagination and desire, and formed by particular philosophies and political ideologies; as if this scholar possessed no larger agendas and pursued no larger goals that impinged upon his or her research. As Childs himself points out, all the "great giants of biblical study" in the modern period "have worked within certain dogmatic and philosophical traditions."[40] Equally clearly, even the OT and NT theologies within this period that have explicitly aimed merely at description rather than offering explicitly constructive ideas have been thoroughly undergirded by dogma and tradition. Likewise, readers need only engage briefly with a selection of modern commentaries on the same biblical book in order to gain a clear impression of the relative weight therein of dogma and tradition, on the one hand, and the free exercise of critical reason, on the other. To assert that this "freedom to follow critical methods wherever they lead" actually exists in any absolute sense, then, is to display signs of self-delusion—or, to betray a conscious ideological move designed to draw a line by sleight of hand around those whom one regards as the scholarly sheep and thereby to separate them off from those who are self-evidently the obscurantist goats. Of *course* such "freedom" does not exist.

It is, then, only a question of which master freedom will serve. Childs' proposal—that modern criticism's engagement with Scripture should have as its ultimate goal the illumination of the communicative intent of the canonical biblical text, with a view to obedience—is perfectly reasonable. The same proposal can be put with equal reasonableness to postmodern critics. From an orthodox Christian perspective it is a very good thing to listen to everyone's stories; this is

---

[40] Childs, *Biblical Theology*, 12.

simply one aspect of loving one's neighbor (see my chapter 21). Yet the ultimate purpose of listening is to help us help each other the better to read our various individual and group stories accurately and fruitfully in the context of the Great Story. The stories do not trump the Story; the Story contextualizes (and indeed must to some extent criticize) the stories.

CANONICAL READING DEVELOPED

As may already be apparent, my own approach to modern biblical-critical method is itself indebted to Brevard Childs' canonical approach. Yet while his various proposals represent a good starting point for a canonical reading of Scripture—and thus a valuable contribution toward rescuing the Church from the eclipse of biblical narrative—I do not find them entirely adequate. My main concern is that Childs is too concerned with validating and applying the results of earlier "behind the text," historical-critical scholarship, and so fails to do justice to other forms of modern and postmodern biblical interpretation. And in various ways this neglect works to the detriment of his canonical project overall.

An Unhelpful Obsession

That Childs typically accepts historical-critical theories about the development of the biblical text as nonnegotiable starting points for his canonical reading that must be accommodated by the canonical critic will be immediately evident to anyone who reads his work. Indeed, Childs is often so preoccupied with the detailed rehearsal and evaluation of the historical-critical state of the question against which his canonical proposal is set—especially in his *Introduction*—that this aspect of his work even outweighs his efforts to specify both the canonical shape of the biblical book in question and its larger theological and hermeneutical implications. Canonical reading as such gets short shrift, and can appear almost as a footnote to the scholarly enterprise delivering "results" that are frankly disappointing in the light of the effort taken to arrive at them. His treatment of the book of Jonah in the *Introduction* is a case in point; his canonical reading here is extraordinarily "thin."[41] He simply notes how Jonah is drawn into connection with the book of Psalms by way of the psalm in Jonah 2 and with Israel's preexilic heritage through the setting of the story in Jeroboam's day. He does not get far beyond this. Yet there is more to be said even about these connections, as we shall see, and there is much more to be said about other connections that Childs does not even mention.

It is all the more surprising that older historical-critical theorizing should attract so much of Childs' attention in his canonical reading when we remember

---

[41] Childs, *Introduction*, 421–27.

that he lived and worked in a time when so many critical questions were being raised about this theorizing by biblical scholars, particularly with respect to biblical narrative. One might have expected, then, that Childs would have begun his reading by considering and evaluating the older proposals—and indeed pondering the ways in which all the other developments in biblical hermeneutics in the closing decades of the twentieth century should impact the way in which canonical reading must be carried out. However, when Childs mentions narrative criticism (for example) in his writings, he does so typically only to note its existence and move on, or even to diminish its significance for his project. It does not *inform* his canonical reading of the biblical text. For example, Paul Ricoeur's approach to the Bible is dismissed in the *Introduction* as simply "incompatible with the canonical approach," since it "fails to take seriously the essential function of the canon in grounding the biblical metaphors within the context of historic Israel."[42] In the *Biblical Theology* Ricoeur's work is now "fruitful," yet the consideration of it in the broader context of what "narrative theology" has to offer the biblical theologian leads in the end to the apparent conclusion that it is one aspect of the *problem* that biblical theology must overcome.[43] Again, in the *Introduction* Childs mentions the emergence of rhetorical/narrative criticism over the preceding two decades with respect to Genesis, but simply notes a few critical questions about this development before abandoning the topic.[44] Even in the *Biblical Theology* Robert Alter only shows up twice—once in a bibliography and once so that Childs can refer in passing to a "devastating review" of Alter and Kermode's *Literary Guide to the Bible*.[45] His engagement with other emerging aspects of biblical-critical interpretation is likewise scant. By the time he is writing the *Biblical Theology*, for example, he already knows about a number of Phyllis Trible's writings—yet these (and feminist writings more generally) play little observable role in his canonical reading.

An Unhelpful Reading

This focus on older historical-critical theorizing is no small matter, because Childs' inherited convictions about the historical process through which the final form of a text came to exist directly impact his view of its correct canonical reading. His work on Jonah, for example, builds firmly on what he describes as the

---

[42] Childs, *Introduction*, 77.
[43] Childs, *Biblical Theology*, 18–20, 204–6. Contrast Bartholomew, *Biblical Hermeneutics*, 315: "Ricoeur's metacritical hermeneutic phenomenology is of great significance for biblical hermeneutics."
[44] Childs, *Introduction*, 143–44.
[45] Childs, *Biblical Theology*, 12, 684, referencing Robert Alter and Frank Kermode, eds., *The Literary Guide to the Bible* (Cambridge, Mass.: Belknap, 1987).

majority view among critical scholars that the prayer in Jonah 2 is a later interpolation into the original (reconstructed) story. In the original,

> Jonah never changes in voicing his opposition to his mission. He first flees, but is compelled to return by God's direct intervention. He then carries out his commission, but is angry at its success. His explanation (4.2) indicates his consistent resistance from the beginning. He knows in advance that God will not carry through with his threat. The issue turns on the fulfilment of the prophet's word. Jonah resisted because he did not want to be a false prophet. In his response God defends his right as Creator to let his mercy to his creation override the prophetic word. By the removal of chapter 2 the sharp lines of the original story emerge, thus confirming the interpretation which related the purpose of the book to the issue of unfulfilled prophecy.[46]

What is the effect, then, when in the final form of the book the psalm is added? The structure of the book, Childs proposes, is thereby substantially altered. Chapter 2 now functions as a parallel to chapter 4, and the meaning of the latter is now strongly influenced by the former. The contrast between what are now *two* prayers of Jonah refocuses the narrative. The central issue is not, now, unfulfilled prophecy, but the scope of the divine mercy:

> Jonah is thankful for his own deliverance, but resentful of Nineveh's inclusion within the mercy which had always been restricted to Israel. This interpretation is further supported by the prayer of the king. His response: "who knows, God may yet repent and turn from his fierce anger," is a citation from Joel 2.14, and a continuation of the same covenant formula which Jonah uses in 4.2. Clearly the issue is now on the recipient of the divine mercy.[47]

Not only is the narrative refocused but, in addition, the reader is now given a way of connecting with the faith of the prophet:

> Jonah is portrayed as a typical Jew who shares Israel's traditional faith. In his trouble he renders thanksgiving to God and is confident of divine rescue. In sum, the effect of the prayer from a canonical perspective is to typify Jonah! The lesson which was directed to Jonah now also serves a larger audience. The book addresses those other faithful Jews who have been set apart from the nations by the Mosaic covenant, and who were sustained by the sacred traditions of their Psalter.[48]

Childs then turns, finally, to the question of how we are to relate to each other what he calls the "two different interpretations found in the book"—the book of Jonah without, and then including, the psalm of chapter 2:

---

[46] Childs, *Introduction*, 423.
[47] Childs, *Introduction*, 424.
[48] Childs, *Introduction*, 424.

If the above analysis is at all correct, the final form of the story does seek to address the issue of God's salvation being extended to the nations as well as to Israel. Moreover, this redactional stamp has not obliterated the earlier form of the story, but refocused it. In my judgment, the final reworking of the story simply extended the original point. In the "first edition," the theological point turned on God's right as Creator to override his prophetic word for the sake of his entire creation. The "second edition" merely amplified the point respecting the whole creation in terms of the nations, but it did not alter the basic creation theology by substituting one of election.[49]

This is all well and good; but of course the entire canonical reading here depends on the premise that there *are* two "editions" of Jonah in the first place—and a narrative-critical reading of Jonah calls into question the necessity of such a hypothesis (see my chapter 20). It is, as George Landes puts it, "by no means a foregone conclusion."[50] This is important, because taking a *narrative-critical* analysis of Jonah as the starting point for our canonical reading leads (as Landes briefly shows) to a rather different understanding of its message.[51] In the latter case the theme of repentance stands out as centrally important throughout the book—a theme that Childs underemphasizes because of his overall approach.

A DIFFERENT DIRECTION

Clearly, then, the kind of contemporary canonical reading of Scripture we produce will have a lot to do with our prior decisions about the strengths and weaknesses of the modern critical reading methods already described in my preceding chapters. My own proposals about how and to what degree these methods should and should not inform the "seriously literal interpretation" of Scripture lead me to a canonical reading of the book of Jonah that is not only somewhat different from Childs', but in my view also much richer and more comprehensive.

THE CANONICAL READING OF JONAH: PROLEGOMENA

We have already examined the source-critical reading of Jonah in chapter 20. There I dismissed as implausible source-critical theorizing about the book's "original form." Even where its "behind the text" theorizing fails to convince, however, source-critical analysis is often valuable—because source critics tend to be "detail people"—in drawing our attention to aspects of the text to which we need to pay attention in our reading.

---

[49] Childs, *Introduction*, 425.
[50] George M. Landes, "The Canonical Approach to Introducing the Old Testament: Prodigy and Problems," *JSOT* 16 (1980): 32–39 (38).
[51] Landes, "Canonical Approach," 38–39.

The Contribution of Source Criticism

We may well find unnecessary, for example, the hypothesis that the psalm in Jonah 2 is a secondary addition to the book. Yet the phenomena of the text that lead source critics to that opinion still need to be accounted for in our reading of it, and in seeking to explain them we already begin to form an opinion about the communicative intent of the text. Jonah himself, we understand, is someone from whom we should not expect consistency of thought and action—he is at the least confused, and perhaps even lacking in integrity, as well as rebellious, prone to self-pity, and not particularly pious. This is not a "hero" in any normal sense of the word. Jonah 4 continues to form our impression of this strange prophet with his contrary ways. He is someone who challenges God, rather than doing his will—someone who is apparently incapable of the repentance that others of God's creatures display. He is additionally a man strongly committed to, but poor at achieving, self-protection. Jonah is an antihero. The source-critical enterprise contributes to our comprehension of these realities (even though many source critics themselves never noticed them) and begins to form in our minds the idea that the author of Jonah is indulging in considerable ironic humor. This leads us directly to the question of the genre of the book, which is a form-critical concern.

The Contribution of Form Criticism

Much ink has been spilled throughout the history of biblical interpretation on the question of whether the book of Jonah is a historical or a fictional work. It is generally agreed that it is a *didactic* work—that it means to teach the reader something. But is it a historical didactic or a fictional didactic work? In the absence of help from its immediate literary context, various data both inside and outside the book have been appealed to in support of each view, although the arguments advanced on their basis have often proved inconclusive.

For example, we know from 2 Kings 14:23-27 that Jonah really existed. This has led many readers to the immediate conclusion that *this particular story* about the prophet in the book of Jonah is intended as historical. This does not logically follow, of course. Then again, the narrative in the book of Jonah looks similar to historical narratives elsewhere in the Bible—compare, for example, the wording of 1 Kings 17:8-9 and Jonah 1:1. However, it also looks similar to other kinds of biblical literature, like the NT parable about the Good Samaritan (Luke 10:30-35). This parable taken by itself *looks* like a historical narrative, but is not. Third, there are various extraordinary features in the text of Jonah that have led many modern readers to dismiss it as a historical account:

At almost every step the reader who takes the story as a record of actual happenings must ask questions. How was it possible that a true prophet should disobey a direct divine command? Is it likely that God should send a storm simply in order to pursue a single person and thus cause many others to suffer too? Do such things happen in a world like ours? ... What an exaggerated idea of the greatness of Nineveh the author had! What language did Jonah speak in Nineveh? How could the people understand him? And what a wonderful result followed his preaching! The greatest prophets in Israel had not been able to accomplish anything like this.[52]

Yet these features do not necessarily indicate that the *author* of Jonah did not intend the story as historical—and that is the crucial question when questions of genre are being discussed.

Fourth, attention has been drawn to elements of the Jonah narrative that could be construed as allegorical in nature. The Hebrew for "Jonah" means "dove," and there is evidence that "dove" was a symbolic name for Israel (e.g., Hos 7:11). Jeremiah 51 moreover, speaks first of Israel (v. 34) and then of God (v. 44) in language that reminds us of Jonah: "Nebuchadnezzar ... has swallowed us like a sea-monster. He has filled his belly with our delicacies, and then has spewed us out.... I will punish Bel in Babylon, and make him spew out what he has swallowed." Is Jonah an allegory, then, concerning an Israel swallowed up in the Babylonian exile, turning to God in prayer, liberated, yet continuingly unfaithful to God? Yet a few allegorical elements, if that is what they are, do not an allegory make.

Over against claims that the book of Jonah is fiction, fifth, some have appealed to data outside the text. Can we find a king in the Assyrian records, for example, whom we can correlate with the king in Jonah 3? Douglas Stuart settles on Asshur-dan III because this king's reign was apparently marked by natural disasters, meaning that he would have been "the sort of king (among others) who might well have been predisposed to receive Jonah's message sincerely as a chance for respite from his troubles."[53] Can we find a large fish in the biological record capable of swallowing a person whole and regurgitating him alive, or even a historical account of someone other than Jonah who had such an experience? Yet searching for "likely" royal and piscine candidates is a strange thing to do when everything in the story of Jonah seems to turn on the *unlikelihood* of the events described,[54] while the examples typically given of "likely" candidates are in any

---

[52] J. A. Bewer, *A Critical and Exegetical Commentary on Jonah* (Edinburgh: T&T Clark, 1912), 3, cited in T. Desmond Alexander, "Jonah and Genre," *TynBul* 36 (1985): 35–59 (44–45).

[53] Douglas Stuart, *Hosea–Jonah* (WBC 31; Waco, Tex.: Word, 1987), 492.

[54] It is interesting to note in this regard John Calvin's careful handling of the question of "plausibility" when it comes to the fish: "either a whale, or a Lamia, or a fish unknown to us, may be

case unconvincing.⁵⁵ Moreover, it is not clear what difference it would make to our assessment of the genre of the book if we *were* able to uncover such external data. Fictional stories can be told about real kings just as readily as about real prophets, and for that matter, real fish.

Finally, some have appealed to Matthew 12:39-41 (paralleling Luke 11:29-32) to settle the question of genre:

> A wicked and adulterous generation asks for a miraculous sign! But none will be given it except the sign of the prophet Jonah. For as Jonah was three days and three nights in the belly of a huge fish, so the Son of Man will be three days and three nights in the heart of the earth. The men of Nineveh will stand up at the judgment with this generation and condemn it; for they repented at the preaching of Jonah, and now one greater than Jonah is here.

Jesus confirms, it is claimed, that the Jonah story is historical narrative. Yet in truth he "confirms" no such thing; rather, he assumes common ground in Scripture with his hearers in order to teach them important lessons about looking for miraculous signs, about repentance, and about himself. In general, if we do not distinguish between some of what Jesus *assumes* as a first-century Palestinian Jew and what he *teaches* we run into all sorts of problems (e.g., what to do with his "teaching" in Mark 4:31 that the mustard seed is the smallest of all seeds; see further the general discussion about divine accommodation in my part 2).

If much of this argument is indeed inconclusive, this does not mean that engaging in it has been futile. To the contrary, we have uncovered a whole host of further data that are important to an integrated, canonical reading of Jonah as we connect the book with other parts of the canon. We have noted, for example, how 2 Kings 14:23-27 illuminates the context in which the prophet operated, and how the wording of 1 Kings 17:8-9 and Jonah 1:1 invites us to make a connection between Jonah and Elijah. We have also noted the way in which connections with Hosea and Jeremiah lead us to reflect on the message of the book of Jonah in the

---

able to swallow up a man whole and entire; but he who is thus devoured cannot live in the inside of a fish. Hence Jonah, that he might mark it out as a miracle, says that the fish was prepared by the Lord." John Calvin, *Commentaries on the Twelve Minor Prophets*, vol. 3 (CalC 14; trans. John Owen; repr., Grand Rapids: Baker, 1980), 73.

⁵⁵ The Assyrian records that we possess (for what this is worth, which may not be very much, given the nature of the records—see Provan, Long, and Longman, *Biblical History*, 85–91) describe no change of religious allegiance by either Ashur-dan III or his son Ashur-nirari V. Large fish exist that could swallow a man; but whether that man could possibly survive for three days and nights in the belly of the fish is questionable. The most famous historical analogy offered by commentators involves the alleged loss overboard in 1891 from a boat of the whaling ship *Star of the East* of a certain James Bartley, who, it is claimed, was swallowed by the whale he was pursuing and subsequently fell out of its stomach alive when it was cut open. The story is however almost certainly untrue; see Edward B. Davis, "A Whale of a Tale: Fundamentalist Fish Stories," *PSCF* 43 (1991): 224–37.

context of Israel's exile to and return from Babylon. Finally, the importance of the repentance theme in Jonah (noted by Landes) has been underlined by the connection between Jonah and the Gospels of Matthew and Luke. We shall return to these connections shortly.

NARRATIVE-CRITICAL READING

Passing over the redaction-critical analysis of Jonah, which we have already adequately addressed above, and leaving structuralism aside until near the end of our reflections in this section, we turn next to narrative-critical reading, which also draws in contributions from rhetorical and poststructuralist (reader-response) criticism. Phyllis Trible's book on rhetorical criticism, which deploys the book of Jonah as its extended example, is a great resource here.[56] However, I want to concentrate on a shorter essay written by Mona West about irony in the story—picking up a thread from my comments earlier on the source-critical contribution, and expanding now on the discussion of the art of Jonah in my chapter 20.[57]

West begins by addressing the genre question. "Jonah is a short story characterized by irony," she proposes.[58] Jonah is not a typical prophet:

> Instead of "arising" and "crying" as the Lord commands, he "arises" and "flees" from the presence of the Lord. The audience would have recognized immediately the conflict between a "normal response" to a prophetic call and the flight of Jonah.[59]

This is because Jonah begins like most other prophetic books: "Now the word of the LORD ...."—so the opening words are familiar to the audience. However, the normal prophetic response to the word of the LORD is obedience, whereas Jonah flees:

> This incongruity may have seemed a bit humorous to the audience since they realized (and Jonah soon found out) that one cannot flee from the presence of the God who made both the sea and dry land. It also must have seemed humorous to the hearers that Jonah would take to sailing the seas in his "escape" since the Hebrews were not known for their love of the water.[60]

Throughout the book of Jonah, in fact, the prophet's actions are inconsistent with his speech about God; they also contrast with the actions of others: "The city of

---

[56] Trible, *Rhetorical Criticism*—see chapter 18 for the full reference.
[57] Mona West, "Irony in the Book of Jonah: Audience Identification with the Hero," *PRSt* 11 (1984): 233–42.
[58] West, "Irony," 235.
[59] West, "Irony," 237.
[60] West, "Irony," 237.

Nineveh repents of their evil and believes God; all the reluctant prophet can do is sulk over what he knew was bound to happen anyway."[61] The very means by which the repentance comes about is awash with irony: "It must have seemed ironic to the audience that so great a repentance could take place in response to such a small oracle, 'Yet forty days, and Nineveh shall be overthrown!'"[62] Jonah's anger in chapter 4 is also "drawn out into ironic proportions. Who would be angry enough to want to die for a plant, but not concerned enough for the life of a whole city?"[63]

Another level of irony is found in the contrast that often exists in the book between appearance and reality:

> Jonah "misreads" the role of the great fish and the plant. The fish is a threat—his sheol (2:2)—when in reality God had appointed the fish for his deliverance. The plant, on the other hand, Jonah saw as a welcome relief, although God had provided it only to take it away in order to teach Jonah a lesson.[64]

The exaggerations in the book of Jonah are also important. As noted in my chapter 20, the Hebrew word *gādôl* ("great") is one of the author's favorite words: it is indeed

> used fourteen times in the book with reference to Nineveh, the wind, and Jonah's anger. Other points of exaggeration are the repentance of Nineveh (even the cattle!) and the size of the fish that swallowed Jonah when he was thrown overboard by the sailors at his request.[65]

Even Jonah's name comes into play when exploring irony in the book. Jonah means "dove," and "son of Amittai" means "son of faithfulness." "Jonah by no means fulfills the expectations of his name."[66]

Such insights into the narrative art of the book of Jonah lead West, then, to the following conclusion:

> The incongruities and opposition draw the audience into a dynamic encounter with the message of the book.... What sort of "undisturbed attentiveness" did the author of Jonah want to jolt his hearers out of? Whether the irony was intended specifically to criticize prophetic hypocrisy, blatant nationalism, jealousy over the repentance of such great evil, or to expound on the love of God, it is evident that the post-exilic audience of Israelites were not living up to the expectations that God had for a people that were to be a "light unto the nations" (Isa 42:6).... By

---

[61] West, "Irony," 237.
[62] West, "Irony," 237.
[63] West, "Irony," 237.
[64] West, "Irony," 237–38.
[65] West, "Irony," 238.
[66] West, "Irony," 238.

means of ironic identification of the audience with Jonah, the author seeks to draw post-exilic Israel's attention away from pitying herself to a greater pity: the love and concern of God for all of humankind.[67]

We are now beginning to build on the rudimentary insights first gained in our reflections on the source- and form-critical contributions to a reading of Jonah and to give them more substance. This further narrative-critical analysis suggests that we have in Jonah a satirical tale designed to show that prophets do not always behave as prophets preach and, more generally, to reveal how the people of God characteristically fail in their vocation to further the kingdom of God in the world. They have a narrow vision, being far less gracious than the God whom they worship and preferring judgment to redemption.

SOCIAL-SCIENTIFIC AND FEMINIST CRITICISM

A canonical reading looks to the social-scientific approach to literature to illuminate the sociological background against which the book and its parts are to be understood—in this case, the phenomenon of prophecy in ancient Israel and indeed the remainder of the ancient Near East. Robert Wilson's book on *Prophecy and Society in Ancient Israel*, for example, provides its readers with suggestions about the origins of Israelite prophecy, the development of its prophetic traditions, the mixing of Judean and Israelite traditions after the fall of Jerusalem in the early sixth century, and the decline of prophecy and the rise of apocalyptic afterward.[68] Within that context he briefly discusses Jonah—briefly, because in this case there is not much for the social-scientific critic to say. Second Kings 14:25-27

> implies that Jonah was active in Ephraim, where he is said to have delivered an oracle to Jeroboam II. Nothing can be said about the prophet's characteristic behavior or about his social location. In spite of the fact that he delivers a positive oracle to the king, there are no grounds for assuming that Jonah was part of the royal court. The Deuteronomic Historian recounts the fulfillment of Jonah's oracle concerning the restoration of Israel's borders, and by this means the writer may intend to link Jonah with earlier Ephraimite prophets whose words were fulfilled by Yahweh, but Jonah is not explicitly portrayed as a Mosaic prophet. The link with other Ephraimite prophets may be strengthened by the fact that Jonah's Judahite contemporary, Amos, condemns the same border expansion that Jonah here supports (Amos 6:13-14). An oblique reference to Amos's prophecies of the destruction of Samaria may also be found in 2 Kgs 14:27, where the Deuteronomic Historian comments that Yahweh *did not* threaten to destroy Ephraim. If 2 Kgs 14:25-27 is to

---

[67] West, "Irony," 240–41.
[68] Robert R. Wilson, *Prophecy and Society in Ancient Israel* (Philadelphia: Fortress, 1980).

be understood as a subtle polemic against the activities of Amos, then Jonah may have been involved in a prophetic conflict with the Jerusalemite establishment, but no conflict of this sort is actually mentioned in the text.[69]

On this occasion, then, social-scientific criticism does not help us very much—although we shall not know this in any given case, of course, unless we look and see. But certainly the broad social context that Wilson describes—a time of national resurgence and expansion in the face of Israel's enemies—illuminates the choice of Jonah for the satire in the book that bears his name. A prophet associated with the national interest—as many prophets in the ancient Near East were—is presented to us here in a story that aims to remind the Israelites that they are called to represent interests that are broader.

Ideological criticism more generally asks about a book like Jonah, "Whose vision is this?" The feminist reading of the book asks, in particular, about whether the vision includes women and furthers their well-being. Along these lines Elizabeth Harper notes in the *IVP Women's Bible Commentary* that

> Jonah seems to be the ultimate patriarchal book in which women never appear, the main characters are one man and his God, and even the backdrop is masculine—sailors on the high seas, a king and his court. Yet for all its masculine characteristics this story transcends gender and implicitly attacks racism, sexism, ageism and any -ism that questions God's full acceptance of all human beings and God's freedom to bestow good gifts on anyone.[70]

She signals in this way that perhaps in this case the contribution of feminist criticism to our understanding of the book is going to be as limited as that of social-scientific criticism. Certainly one could not say that there has even been an abundance of specifically feminist writing on Jonah; not even the original *Women's Bible* discusses it. Since the male hero is so heavily satirized already, perhaps it makes little difference to read Jonah "as a woman."

Yet it does make *some* difference. The following insight, for example, appears to arise directly out of a reading-perspective that is consciously aware of gender questions:

> In Jonah 1:17 ... Jonah is swallowed into the inner parts or belly (*m'h*, a masculine noun) of a masculine fish (*dāg*), while in Jonah 2:1 he prays from the belly (*m'h*) of a very feminine fish (*dāgāh*).... In Jonah 2:3 ... Jonah cries out again from the belly of Sheol, but this time the word for belly is the feminine *beten*, a synonym with the added possible translation "womb." The image is incongruous. Sheol is the

---

[69] Wilson, *Prophecy*, 213.
[70] Elizabeth Harper, "Jonah," in *The IVP Women's Bible Commentary* (ed. Catherine C. Kroeger and Mary J. Evans; Downers Grove, Ill.: InterVarsity, 2002), 458–63 (458).

place of death, not birth, a barren womb (Prov 30:16) from which no one comes up (Job 7:9) and from whence none can praise Yahweh (Ps 6:5). Yet always in Jonah the impossible and the improbable are the reality. Jonah, who has sought death to escape God, discovers that death is his place of capture, his womb of rebirth.[71]

Similarly, we note the following comment on Jonah 3: "God is not oblivious to the evil of the world. The cries of the oppressed (so often feminine!) rise up to Yahweh ... and this story holds out for everyone hope of justice in this world."[72] The parenthesis reminds us of our need when exegeting or preaching a text dealing only with men (or indeed only with women)—and this should be obvious, but it is all too often not—to generalize the message of the Bible and not even accidentally to give the impression that we believe Scripture to be more interested in addressing one gender than the other.

JONAH IN CANONICAL PERSPECTIVE

A canonical reading of the book of Jonah should draw together all the insights about the text that we have generated so far—and indeed others that have not been explicitly mentioned—and clarify what they all ultimately signify when understood in the wider canonical context. Brevard Childs takes some initial steps in this direction, noting the connections between Jonah and the Psalms and Jonah and 2 Kings 14. I believe, however, that we can do a much better job.

Jonah among the Prophets

Beginning with the most immediate context of the book of Jonah in the Minor Prophets (see my chapter 2),[73] we notice first that the book appears more or less at the mid-point of this collection. Right in the midst of multiple series of oracles *from* prophets has been inserted this narrative *about* a prophet—and as we have seen, he is not a very impressive prophet. We are entitled to ask whether this is significant. In the biblical *narrative* tradition, certainly, there is an evident determination to show that all the human characters in Israel's story were very much *human* characters, whether they be prophets, priests, or kings. Biblical narrative does not shrink from revealing the dark side of even the best of them. It is intriguing, then, that after a series of books that contain mainly prophetic oracles, and to a great extent shield from view the embodied, on-the-ground prophetic reality, we should encounter a narrative about a prophet that is so satirical in nature.

---

[71] Harper, "Jonah," 461.
[72] Harper, "Jonah," 461.
[73] This is itself a specifically "canonical-critical" move, over against the modernist tendency to treat the books of the Minor Prophets only individually and self-consciously to ignore their literary context. Seitz, "Prophecy in the Nineteenth Century," 564–70.

It is a narrative that deconstructs any pretensions that prophets might have to standing above the flow of embodied history in some "pure" realm of thought and speech, as well as dispelling any romantic notions that we as readers might have about these exalted figures. Prophets, we are reminded, are just like us. They readily give in to wrong thinking and to disobedient action. They forget that they are called to represent a God who desires that all should be saved, even as he also warns everyone of the judgment that is coming if they do not repent. Readers of the Minor Prophets themselves might make this mistake if they did not possess Jonah in close proximity to Nahum—that excoriating oracle against Nineveh on account of all her sins. Of course, they would additionally have to ignore the ending of the also-proximate Micah, with its picture of the incomparable God who pardons sin and forgives transgression—"You do not stay angry forever but delight to show mercy" (v. 18)—as well as other more distant prophetic passages like Isaiah 19, which ends by foreseeing a time when "Israel will be the third, along with Egypt and Assyria, a blessing on the earth" (v. 24).

Jonah, Narrative, and Worship

At this point it becomes natural, next, to refer to the connections between Jonah and the broader narrative and worship traditions of Israel to which Childs draws attention. As we have seen, the human character at the center of the book of Jonah is already known *from* the narrative tradition—a prophet whose historical ministry was conducted during a time of national prosperity and self-confidence in Israel, when the Israelites were taking great pride in their status as the chosen people of God. We learn from other proximate texts in the Minor Prophets (Hosea and Amos, in addition to Micah) that in fact their theology had lost touch with reality—had lost touch with God. They were not living faithfully as the people of God inside the Promised Land, but they possessed confidence, nevertheless, that their election—and particularly the choice of Zion as the place where the temple and Davidic dynasty were centered—would protect them from divine judgment. This becomes even clearer when we transition into the reading of the Major Prophets and we encounter Isaiah. The book of Jonah enters this ongoing prophetic conversation by emphasizing that God's people (in the person of Jonah) were not living as the people of God, either, in their God-given calling as it related to the world *outside* the Promised Land—the calling to be a blessing to the Gentiles (Gen 12:2-3), a kingdom of priests mediating blessing to other kingdoms (Exod 19:6), and "a light for the Gentiles, that my salvation may reach to the ends of the earth" (Isa 49:6). They were well able (like Jonah) to sing psalms about God's deliverance without really believing that it had anything much to do with the world at large that God had created. It is the *representative* role of Jonah in these respects that is suggested both by the Hosea 7:11 passage, with its reference to Israel as a dove (Heb. *yōnāh*) —which readers of the Minor Prophets collection have already encountered before they get to the book of Jonah— and (more distantly) by Jeremiah 51 as well, with its allusions to Nebuchadnezzar and Bel in Babylon as sea-monsters. As the suffering servant in the book of Isaiah stands for Israel in her *faithfulness* to her vocation as a light to the Gentiles, then, so Jonah stands for Israel in her *unfaithfulness* and indeed her hypocrisy.

JONAH AND ELIJAH

If the wording of 1 Kings 17:8-9 and Jonah 1:1 invites us to make an initial connection between Jonah and Elijah in terms of their contrasting responses to the divine word, then further study of the entire Elijah story in 1 Kings certainly encourages us to pursue the comparison. For there comes a point in *this* story when the relationship between the prophet and the word of God *also* comes into question. Throughout the narrative prior to 1 Kings 19 Elijah only moves in response to the divine word (1 Kgs 17:2, 8; 18:1). In 1 Kings 19:1-9, however, it is a word from Queen Jezebel that he receives: "May the gods deal with me, be it ever so severely, if by this time tomorrow I do not make your life like that of one of them" (v. 2). Receiving *this* word, Elijah turns tail and flees. The great hero of 1 Kings 18 becomes in chapter 19 a man on the run, from God (it seems) as well as from Jezebel. The "word of the LORD" does not in fact reappear until 1 Kings 19:9, where it takes the form of a question: "What are you doing here, Elijah?" This makes it clear that although God has helped Elijah along the way, his journey was not initially part of the divine plan. Like Jonah, then, Elijah travels to a far-flung place without a divine travel permit (Jonah 1), attempting to write his own contract for the job of prophet (Jonah 4:8; 1 Kgs 19:4). Yet in neither case is the disobedient prophet rejected. God makes every effort in both stories to get him back on track.[74]

JONAH AND THE NEW TESTAMENT

The NT draws on the story of Jonah both explicitly and implicitly, and we noted the explicit example earlier. In Matthew 12:39-41 Jesus rails against those who look for signs before they will believe in him. The only sign that will be given is the "sign" of Jesus' death and (implied) resurrection—a sign akin to Jonah's "death" and "resurrection" with respect to the fish. Even this sign will not be sufficient for the people of God in Jesus' time, however, for they are a much harder case than the Gentiles of Jonah's time. *Those* Gentiles were open to God in a way that God's own first-century people are not. The evident theme of Jonah, that "outsiders" are

---

[74] See further Provan, *Kings*, 143–50.

more prepared to repent than "insiders" like Jonah himself, is thus brought to bear on the people of God of later times and indeed our time as well.

The tenth chapter of Acts, using the book of Jonah in a more implicit way, develops the same theme. Here we read about the conversion of the Roman centurion Cornelius, who lives in Caesarea. A devout and God-fearing man, Cornelius has a vision telling him to seek out the apostle Peter. Meanwhile, Peter is having a vision of his own: "Do not call anything impure that God has made clean," a voice tells him, just as Cornelius' messengers arrive. Peter goes with them, having worked out from the vision that, even though it is against Jewish law for Jews to associate with Gentiles, the law on *this* point no longer applies. So he goes to Caesarea and speaks with Cornelius. "I now realize," says Peter, "how true it is that God does not show favoritism, but accepts men from every nation who fear him and do what is right." The Holy Spirit falls on all the Gentiles present and they are baptized. The outsiders become insiders. They do so because Peter understands the missional heart of God. Even though he is initially reluctant to see it, he overcomes his reluctance—and we find that the Gentiles are just as receptive of God's word in Acts 10 as they are in the story of Jonah. But Peter himself is very different from Jonah in his response to God. The one story illuminates the other in laying bare both the character of God and the characters of his servants. A small detail makes their interconnectedness especially clear. Where is Peter, when Cornelius summons him to Caesarea? He is in Joppa—the very port from which Jonah sailed when he was trying to avoid being a missionary. Joppa is the point of departure in both stories—the starting point both in Jonah's journey *away* from the Gentiles he is called to serve and in Peter's journey *toward* them. It is intriguing in this respect that one of the ways that Simon Peter's full name is rendered in the Gospels is "Simon son of Jonah" (Matt 16:17)—just after Peter confesses that Jesus is the Christ, thereby "getting" what the missional God is up to in the world. It is Peter from the family of Jonah who comes from Joppa to preach the Gospel to the Gentiles. He does what a prophet *should* do, just as Jonah does not.[75]

THE CONTRIBUTION OF STRUCTURALISM

No doubt this is not everything that can be said about reading the book of Jonah canonically, but it represents a substantial beginning—certainly more substantial than Childs'. The greater substance is substantially due to the greater embrace of everything insightful about the biblical literature that modern, critical, biblical interpretation across its entire range can offer. I am strongly convinced, as I have

---

[75] See further Robert W. Wall, "Peter, 'Son' of Jonah: The Conversion of Cornelius in the Context of Canon," *JSNT* 29 (1987): 79–90.

revealed in the preceding chapters in part 3, that this is the right way of approaching the modern interpretive endeavor—just as it is the right way (I proposed in part 2) of approaching other features of modernity such as modern science. All truth being God's truth, the truth that modernity (and postmodernity) has uncovered, whoever has uncovered it and whatever *they* want to do with it, must be taken seriously—truth about our biblical texts, as well as other kinds of truth. It must all find its place in a canonical rendition of the True Story.

What structuralist reading contributes to this project is a much wider literary background against which we can understand more clearly both the connections between what our biblical texts have to say, and how they say it, and the disconnections—and what this means for communicating the Great Story to culture at large. Northrop Frye's book *The Great Code*, for example, makes for interesting reading in relation to the book of Jonah.[76] "The central expression of human energy," claims Frye,

> is the creative work that transforms the amorphous natural environment into the pastoral, cultivated, civilized world of human shape and meaning. The other side of this is the struggle against the enemy, who has two aspects. The enemy is, first, the human enemy encountered in warfare, and, second, the unshaped and chaotic element in nature, usually symbolized as some kind of monster or beast of prey, and identified with drought, floods, and natural sterility of all kinds.[77]

In the context of this struggle heroes emerge. With respect to the human enemy it is the military leader; with respect to nature it is someone like Theseus, who in Greek tradition descends into the Cretan labyrinth and kills the Minotaur, which until that time had been propitiated with human sacrifice:

> The general form of the myth connected with such rites is given us in the legend we know as that of St. George and the dragon, associated in Classical myth with the story of Perseus. In this legend an old and impotent king rules over a wasteland oppressed by a sea monster who demands human victims. Already we see a cluster of metaphorical identifications. The land is waste because the king is impotent, the fertility of the land and the virility of the king being linked by sympathetic magic. The monster from the sea inevitably turns up when the land and the king have lost their power, because he is another aspect of sterility. The victims provided for his dinner are chosen by lot, and eventually the lot falls on the king's daughter. At that point the hero arrives, also from over the sea; he kills the dragon, releases the daughter, and becomes the next king by marrying her.[78]

---

[76] Northrop Frye, *The Great Code: The Bible and Literature* (London: Penguin, 1990), 187–93.
[77] Frye, *Code*, 187.
[78] Frye, *Code*, 187–88.

In this form the myth is about renewal: "the hero is the reviving power of spring and the monster and old king the outgrown forces of apathy and impotence in a symbolic winter."[79] We also find *creation* myths, however, that involve the killing of a monster or dark power—the myth of Marduk and Tiamat in Babylon is one such example. Such creation myths, Frye proposes, "are incorporated into the Old Testament as a form of poetic imagery" and "identified with the heathen empires."[80] He continues:

> Now if Leviathan and Rahab are also Babylon and Egypt, it follows that Israel in Egypt, or the Jews in captivity in Babylon, have already been swallowed by the monster, and are living inside his belly.... But what is true of Israel in Egypt is typologically true of the human situation generally. All of us are born, and live our natural lives, within the leviathan's belly.[81]

Politically we live in the midst of empire, "in subjection to secular powers that may become at any time actively hostile to everything except their own aggressiveness."[82] Cosmologically "the leviathan is the element of chaos within creation," which, as we now experience it, consists in "the limitless expanse that is the most secure and impregnable of all prisons":

> This suggests a modulation of the St. George-Perseus story, in which the heroine (Andromeda in the Perseus version) is already inside her leviathan, and the hero has to go down the brute's throat to rescue her. Here we have the structural pattern behind any number of displaced versions in romance, in which a hero has to make a perilous journey into a place of great danger where the heroine is held.[83]

It is in this context that Frye refers to Jonah, "swallowed by a great fish [the Great Cod, perhaps], who eventually disgorges him on dry land." He relates the Jonah story not only to the remainder of the biblical narrative but to the wider world of literary tradition as well:

> Jesus accepted the Jonah story as a type of his own Passion (Matthew 12:40), and in medieval paintings of the descent to hell he is shown walking into the throat of a large toothy monster representing hell ... metaphorically, his redemption ("harrowing") of the subterranean world is identical with his redemption of the world above it, the latter being symbolically subterranean as well. The heroine, or Andromeda, of the gospel story is the "bride" Jerusalem, the total body of redeemed souls who are symbolically a single female.[84]

---

[79] Frye, *Code*, 188.
[80] Frye, *Code*, 188, 189.
[81] Frye, *Code*, 190.
[82] Frye, *Code*, 190.
[83] Frye, *Code*, 190.
[84] Frye, *Code*, 191.

Frye continues:

> We can now, perhaps, understand why there should be so much about fishing in the Gospels, and why Jesus himself should be so often associated in later legend with a fish or dolphin. The identification of Jesus with a fish has been traditionally assisted by an acronym: the initial letters of "Jesus Christ, Son of God, Saviour" in Greek spell out the word *ichthys*, fish. In any case the theme of redemption out of water follows in the sequence that includes the story of Noah's ark, the crossing of the Red Sea by the Israelites, the symbolism of baptism in which the person baptized is separated into a mortal part that symbolically drowns and an immortal part that escapes, and such occasional uses of the image as the cry to God from the depths of the waters in Psalm 69.[85]

Furthermore, "if the monster that swallows us is metaphorically death, then the hero who comes to deliver us from the body of this death ... has to be absorbed in the world of death—that is, he has to die."[86] The St. George plays grasp this point, typically having the hero die along with the dragon before being brought back to life by a doctor.

This is a fascinating set of reflections on both the inner connections of biblical literature and how it relates to literature more generally—on the ways in which the Jonah story reflects the larger picture of human storytelling, even as it proclaims by itself and as part of the Christian canon a distinctive message. Indeed, with the help of Frye's analysis we can perceive further internal biblical connections between the story of Jonah and a story about Jesus in the NT that we saw illuminated already in my chapter 18 by redaction criticism. In Matthew 8:23-27 (paralleled in Mark 4:35-41 and Luke 8:22-25) we find Jesus asleep like Jonah in a boat (Jonah 1:5; Matt 8:24). A storm blows up (Jonah 1:4; Matt 8:24). When awakened, Jonah's "solution" to the problem is to have himself thrown overboard in order to appease God (Jonah 1:12). Jesus' solution is to still the storm (Matt 8:26). "What kind of man is this?" ask the disciples; "Even the winds and the waves obey him!" (Matt 8:27)—and now we recognize with particular clarity that the question is rhetorical. They already know that no *man* can calm the winds and the waves, but only the creator God (Gen 1:1-9): "You rule over the surging sea; when its waves mount up, you still them" (Ps 89:9). The sailors in the boat in Jonah chapter 1 find in their midst a man *running away from God*, reluctant to participate in his great mission to save the lost. The sailors in the boat in Matthew 8 find in their midst *God himself*, shortly to disembark and save two lost souls in the region of the Gadarenes (Matt 8:28-34).

---

[85] Frye, *Code*, 192.
[86] Frye, *Code*, 192.

CONCLUSION

"First" and "second way" Protestants in the modern and postmodern periods of biblical interpretation typically insist on pursuing their chosen biblical-critical method (or clusters of methods) of reading "wherever they may lead," convinced of their general utility while often lacking in perception of (and remarkably uncritical about) their weaknesses. They are generally unwilling or unable to integrate their insights into a holistic reading of the Great Biblical Story as a canon governing belief and practice. Holy Scripture may still be "a source of inspiration" for many of them, but it has "ceased to be the absolute norm of faith and morals."[87] "Third" and "fourth way" Protestants are each in their own way committed to reading the Story, but they are dismissive about what modern and postmodern reading can contribute to our understanding of it. My own "fifth way" is different. On the one hand it recognizes *both* strengths and weaknesses in modern and postmodern reading methods and insists on affirming their genuine insights where they exist. It is entirely unsympathetic to the "third" and "fourth way" refusal to engage properly with these insights into important aspects of the humanity of Scripture. The "fifth way" also insists on the other hand, however—with Brevard Childs and over against much "first" and "second way" interpretive endeavor—that the proper "end" of criticism is *precisely* the illumination of the Great Biblical Story as a canonical whole. Its end is to cast light on the multifaceted ways in which this God-breathed Story remains "useful for teaching, rebuking, correcting and training in righteousness, so that the servant of God may be thoroughly equipped for every good work" (2 Tim 3:16-17)—the ways in which it summons us to be the ideal readers that we ought to be. The end of criticism is to cast light, indeed, on the way that Scripture does this *sufficiently* as it is read *literally* and *historically* in line with Reformation thinking. "Fourth way" Protestantism claims that in order for Scripture to function as the Church's canonical guide its historical and literal reading must function only as a prelude to its "spiritual" (allegorical) reading. The "fifth way" insists, to the contrary, that a truly literal and historical reading is *already* a canonical and a spiritual reading—the narrative biblical theology that it produces being precisely "a contemporary explication of the Rule of Faith."[88] The "spiritual depths" of biblical texts are not "hidden" in them.[89] They are patent to all who with patient attentiveness (ideally informed by some knowledge of Hebrew and Greek), employing ordinary reading skills and with the help of the

---

[87] Gerstenberger, "Emergence," 465—in its original context referring specifically to the German "History of Religion School."

[88] Bartholomew, *Biblical Hermeneutics*, 59.

[89] Boersma, *Heavenly Participation*, 153.

Holy Spirit,[90] read what they find before them in the context of the Great Story as a whole. The spiritual depths of Scripture are evident to all those who engage with growing understanding in its "seriously literal interpretation."

---

[90] "Men may have a knowledge of *words*, and the *meaning* of propositions in the Scripture, who have no knowledge of the *things themselves* designed in them." The Puritan John Owen, cited in Vanhoozer, *Biblical Authority*, 68.

23

Postscript

> *The preceding lines, rightly understood, express an entire system of philosophy. It is mine. I resume.*
>
> —Count Isidore Ottavio Baldassore Fosco, *in* The Woman in White[1]

I first read these lines in November 2015, in an Indonesian restaurant in the center of Erfurt in Germany, as I was coming toward the end of both Wilkie Collins' epic novel and my sabbatical leave. Erfurt, "the commercial center of the fruitful Thuringian basin" and "a sort of outpost of humanism in northern Germany,"[2] was really where it all began for Martin Luther—not Wittenberg. It was to Erfurt that he moved from Eisenach in 1501 in order to attend university for the first time, here that he completed his initial studies in the liberal arts between 1501 and 1505.[3] It was also in Erfurt that he began his studies in law in the summer of 1505—already a troubled young man, by all accounts, "not sure about his future course," and already "devoted . . . to much reading of the Bible" in the midst of his spiritual angst.[4] It was just to the northeast of Erfurt, near Stotternheim, returning from a visit to his parents in Mansfeld on July 2, 1505, that Luther found himself in fear for his life in the midst of a thunderstorm, and promised St. Anne, in return for her help, that he would become a monk. This vow he immediately fulfilled, entering the monastery of the Augustinian Hermits in Erfurt on July 17, 1505.[5] It was while living in this monastery, in the course of striving to become the perfect monk and Christian and devoting himself ever more to his Bible reading,

---

[1] Wilkie Collins, *The Woman in White* (London: Penguin, 1974), 619.
[2] Brecht, *Luther: His Road*, 1:23, 40.
[3] For a good description of this period in Luther's life, see Brecht, *Luther: His Road*, 1:29–45.
[4] Brecht, *Luther: His Road*, 1:46, 47.
[5] For a description of Luther's "crisis" and the order and the monastery that he entered, see Brecht, *Luther: His Road*, 1:46–57.

that Luther's thinking about right theology and practice began to diverge from what was commonly affirmed around him:

> The monk Luther brought the questions which troubled him to the Scriptures, expecting an answer. In the hearing, new perceptions and insights were brought forth. The theological theory was altered thereby, and this had simultaneous consequences for the determination of the situation of the man, i.e. the embattled monk. In this way something new started.[6]

It was in Erfurt, finally, that Luther began his formal study of theology in the summer of 1507 after being ordained a priest in the impressive cathedral that still dominates the town square, ultimately taking his doctor of theology degree in Wittenberg in October 1512 after his transfer to the Augustinian monastery there late in 1511.[7] If we wish to understand Luther in Wittenberg, we cannot do so without understanding Luther in Erfurt.

My own purpose in Erfurt during the fall semester of 2015 was to research for and to begin writing this book—a book whose central question would be redundant if Luther's revolution had never begun. Are "reformed" biblical hermeneutics still viable in the twenty-first century, fully five hundred years after Luther first penned his ninety-five theses? I have sought to demonstrate in the preceding chapters that they are. The Reformers' confidence about our ability to read Scripture "rightly" was well grounded, even if not every particular of Protestant Bible interpretation has been right. And their fundamental proposals about what "right reading" involves are still to be accepted, even if there are dimensions to this that contemporary interpreters must inevitably add to the reading tradition that precedes them.

For myself, as for Martin Luther, this is not merely an academic matter. It has profound implications for what I believe and how I live. The preceding lines that are the whole of this book, then, rightly understood—by which I mean, of course, *literally* understood—express an entire system of philosophy (and ethics). It is mine. It is not Luther's (or, for that matter, Calvin's, or Zwingli's); yet it stands in continuity with his (and theirs), and intentionally so—because I believe that these Christian ancestors of mine were much more right than they were wrong. I hope that others may find this philosophy coherent and compelling, and embrace it. For myself, like Count Fosco, I resume. Here I stand, as Martin Luther might have said in Worms but probably did not; I can do no other than engage with all the means at my disposal in the "seriously literal interpretation"—the right reading—of Holy Scripture.

---

[6] Brecht, *Luther: His Road*, 1:58–90 (quote on 90).
[7] Brecht, *Luther: His Road*, 1:90–128.

Appendix
Modern Developments in Our Understanding of the Biblical Text

The origins of the modern approach to the text of the NT lie in the late eighteenth century with the various editions of Johann Jakob Griesbach, who "laid foundations for all subsequent work on the Greek text of the New Testament."[1] Bruce Metzger identifies another German scholar, Karl Lachmann (1793–1851), as the first "to break totally with the Textus Receptus," and Samuel Prideaux Tregelles (1813–1875) as the scholar "most successful in drawing British preference" away from it in the period just prior to the publication in 1881 of Westcott and Hort's important new critical edition.[2] Westcott and Hort's view was that the "Neutral" family of biblical manuscripts, best represented by the codices Vaticanus and Sinaiticus (and nowadays typically referred to as the "Alexandrian" text type), was earlier than the Byzantine family and that its textual tradition was a more accurate representation of the original NT writings.[3] The readings of Vaticanus and Sinaiticus, they therefore believed, should be taken as the true readings until strong internal evidence suggested otherwise.[4]

Westcott and Hort's edition played an important role in the work on the NT text that followed, not least because it was one of the editions consulted by Eberhard Nestle in producing his *Novum Testamentum Graece* at the turn of the twentieth century. Nestle adopted for his Greek text the majority opinion about the best readings among Westcott and Hort, Tischendorff, and (beginning with the third edition) Weiss, placing the variant preferred by the dissenting voice of the three on each occasion in the apparatus. In the 1960s, with the publication of the

---

[1] Metzger and Ehrman, *Text*, 165.
[2] Metzger and Ehrman, *Text*, 170, 173.
[3] This was so, they proposed, even though the Neutral family is smaller in size than the Byzantine—which is often referred to as the "Majority" text type precisely because it is encountered in NT manuscripts most frequently.
[4] Metzger and Ehrman, *Text*, 174–81.

twenty-fifth edition, "Nestle" then became "Nestle-Aland" (NA)—the standard for academic work in the NT since that time. The text of NA[26], published in 1979, is identical to the text of the third edition of the United Bible Societies' Greek NT (1975), by way of which the modern, critically established text—in one modern scholar's view "about as close to the original text of the New Testament as we can get"—has been made available to many Bible translators and others.[5] The latest edition of Nestle-Aland is NA[28] (providing the text for UBS[5]).[6]

Time has moved on again since Westcott and Hort's day. Further manuscripts have been discovered, and the manner of approaching text-critical work on the NT has changed. Most NT scholars continue to believe, nevertheless, that the Alexandrian text type offers us the best starting point in reconstructing the original NT text in the relatively small number of (often trivial) cases where our various manuscripts disagree. This is because the Alexandrian manuscripts are the oldest known and their readings often best explain the variants found in other text types. There remain advocates, however, of other views.[7]

Our contemporary understanding of the text of the OT has been significantly impacted since 1947 by the discovery and analysis of the Qumran manuscripts.[8] These manuscripts demonstrate that in the three centuries before the destruction of the Jerusalem temple in AD 70, after which time "the sole texts to be used by Jewish communities were the proto-Masoretic texts ... [because] no Jewish communities had survived [the Roman onslaught] which carried a rival biblical text," there was a significant degree of textual diversity in Judaism.[9]

The (proto-)MT is certainly represented at Qumran and is in fact reflected in the majority (about 60 percent) of the texts discovered. The actual copies of the MT found there (and this is true of other early manuscripts from sites like Masada) "differ little from each other and from the medieval text of MT with

---

[5] McDonald, "Wherein Lies Authority?," 229.

[6] For an introduction to this edition and advice on how best to use it, see David Trobisch, *A User's Guide to the Nestle-Aland 28 Greek New Testament* (SBLTCS 9; Atlanta: Society of Biblical Literature, 2013).

[7] For ongoing resistance in the West to the idea that the Byzantine text type is inferior and secondary in relation to the Alexandrian, e.g. (and for a critique of this resistance), see Daniel B. Wallace, "The Majority Text Theory: History, Methods, and Critique," in *The Text of the New Testament in Contemporary Research: Essays in the Status Quaestionis* (FS B. M. Metzger; ed. Bart D. Ehrman and Michael W. Holmes; Grand Rapids: Eerdmans, 1995), 297–320.

[8] "It is not too much to say that the entire discipline [of OT studies] has been revolutionized by these finds, since they have given scholars access to scores of manuscripts (or the fragmentary remains thereof) that are more than a thousand years older than any that had been available before." Al Wolters, "The Text of the Old Testament," in *The Face of Old Testament Studies: A Survey of Contemporary Approaches* (ed. David W. Baker and Bill T. Arnold; Grand Rapids: Baker, 1999), 19–37 (20).

[9] Tov, "History and Significance," 66.

regard to the latter's consonantal text."[10] This suggests widespread distribution of a text that was marked by careful and very conservative scribal transmission.[11] In all probability, "since it is reflected in the rabbinic literature as well as in the Targumim and many of the Jewish-Greek revisions," it originated "in the spiritual and authoritative center of Judaism (that of the Pharisees?), possibly in the temple circles," where it was also copied and preserved.[12] To this extent it is clear that the confidence shown by sixteenth-century scholars that the consonantal text that lay before them reflected accurately an ancient and authoritative Hebrew text was not misplaced.

At the same time textual pluriformity in the early period is also evidenced at Qumran. In particular, it has been confirmed that both the Samaritan Pentateuch and the LXX (unlike ancient translations and paraphrases)[13] depend to some extent on ancient, non-MT Hebrew texts.[14] That is to say, the differences between the MT and the Samaritan Pentateuch or the LXX did not only arise from realities like distinctive interpretative tendencies or translation styles in respect of the Hebrew texts being transmitted. These differences were to some extent (and sometimes to a significant extent) already found among ancient Hebrew texts themselves. For example, the LXX text of Jeremiah is approximately one-seventh shorter than the MT, and "two fragmentary Hebrew manuscripts that reflect the shorter text ... have turned up among the Dead Sea Scrolls (4QJer^{b,d})."[15]

How best to interpret the Qumran finds overall remains a matter of ongoing discussion, not least on the question of how many groups of texts exist.[16] Their most important consequence for the text-critical study of the OT is that they potentially provide direct access to earlier readings of some Hebrew texts than we find in the MT—although measuring "earlier" is by no means always a simple matter. More generally, and especially because of the overlap that exists between

---

[10] Tov, "History and Significance," 63.

[11] "As a rule, the scribes treated MT with reverence, and they did not alter its orthography and morphology as did the scribes of the Sam. Pent. and of many of the Qumran scrolls." Tov, "History and Significance," 64.

[12] Tov, "History and Significance," 64.

[13] The "Three" (kaige/Theodotion, Aquila, and Symmachus—see my chapter 10) are of course revisions of the LXX back in the direction of the MT; the Targums with the exception of Job reflect a text very close to the MT; and the parent text of both the Syriac Peshitta in its earliest form and also the Vulgate is substantially that of the MT. For a brief summary, see Wolters, "Text," 25–28; for an extensive discussion of all the ancient translations, see Emanuel Tov, *Textual Criticism of the Hebrew Bible* (3rd ed.; Minneapolis: Fortress, 2012), 127–54.

[14] However, "many differences" between the Samaritan Pentateuch and MT "represent a modernizing of the former in terms of grammar and spelling." Gentry, "Text," 24.

[15] Wolters, "Text," 21. The initial number in the designation of the manuscripts indicates that they were found in Cave 4 at Qumran.

[16] Wolters, "Text," 21–23.

some of the Qumran manuscripts and the LXX, the Qumran discoveries open up the possibility of accessing by way of the LXX early Hebrew readings that are not actually reflected at Qumran. At the very least, "[i]t should not be assumed that the Hebrew *Vorlage* [parent text] of (any form of) the LXX is identical with that of the Masoretic text commonly in use in exegesis classes today."[17]

Of course, there are practical difficulties involved in "reading back" from the LXX to a supposed Hebrew *Vorlage*. Translations are translations (and also interpretations), and determining what a translator is doing with any particular *Vorlage* is not a simple matter.[18] Are we dealing in a particular case with a free (and perhaps even ideological) rendering of a Hebrew text that in its essentials is not very different from the MT, or with a more conservative rendering of a substantially different Hebrew text?[19] On the whole, reflection on such questions has tended to reduce scholarly conviction about the number of occasions upon which the latter is the more likely solution, and has tended to encourage the view that in many cases differences between the LXX and the MT have translational and interpretative rather than textual roots.[20] These are not only questions that arise at the micro-level of the text. When we find that the LXX of a whole book is shorter than its MT counterpart—what then? Does this mean that the MT reflects an expansion of an early version of the Hebrew text, or that the LXX reflects an abbreviation of it?[21]

The extent to which as text critics we are going to find readings from Qumran texts or from the LXX (or elsewhere) compelling rather than merely historically interesting—even if we think that they might be earlier than the MT—is going to depend very much on what the ultimate purpose of our text-critical endeavors might be. Is it to reconstruct as best we can the earliest possible version

---

[17] Hill, *Antioch*, 64.

[18] Dines, *Septuagint*, 131–35, 151–52.

[19] See, e.g., John W. Wevers, *Textual History of the Greek Exodus* (MSU 21; Göttingen: Vandenhoeck & Ruprecht, 1991). For a brief discussion with other examples, see Gentry, "Text," 26–30.

[20] Note, e.g., the examples cited in Gentry, "Text," 38–39. For a general discussion of the whole issue, see John W. Wevers, "The Interpretative Character and Significance of the Septuagint Version," *HBOT* 1/1:84–107. For the interpretative character of other ancient translations, see e.g., Levine, "Targums"; Schulz-Flügel, "Latin Old Testament," 652–57; and Michael Weitzman, "The Interpretative Character of the Syriac Old Testament," *HBOT* 1/1:587–611 ("an idiomatic, though faithful, translation," 609).

[21] Tov accepts, e.g., that the MT version of Jeremiah, which he calculates is one-sixth longer than the LXX version, represents an expansion; but he also states that the LXX of Job, which is one-sixth shorter than the MT, represents an abbreviation. Emanuel Tov, "The Septuagint as a Source for the Literary Analysis of Hebrew Scripture," in Evans and Tov, *Exploring the Origins*, 31–56.

of a Hebrew text (e.g., the book of Joshua),[22] or is it to reconstruct the original version of that text as received as canonical by mainstream (rather than sectarian) Palestinian Judaism prior to the first century AD,[23] and then by the Church in the first century AD (as described in my chapters 2 and 3)? Both are entirely legitimate scholarly endeavors, but if the argument of chapters 2 through 11 is fundamentally correct, the "reformed" biblical scholar is certainly not going to neglect the second in pursuit of the first. For it is not (for example) the shorter and probably earlier book of Jeremiah reflected in the LXX (any more than the *longer* LXX versions of books like Daniel) that is then to be regarded as canonical, but its longer Hebrew version (along with the shorter Hebrew/Aramaic Daniel) as represented in the Masoretic tradition. These are the "original texts" in which we shall be primarily interested.[24] It is just such a text-critical project in respect of the (proto)-Masoretic tradition that is represented by the Hebrew Old Testament Text Project, with its analysis of the divergences from the MT that have been accepted in modern commentaries and Bible translations—about which the Project, in its conclusions, is incidentally not very affirming.[25]

As the description of this last study itself suggests, it is indeed the MT as represented in modern critical editions like *Biblica Hebraica Stuttgartensia* (*BHS*) that continues to provide the basis for both modern scholarly work on the OT text and modern Protestant (and more recently Roman Catholic) Bible translations of the OT. The *BHS* edition (the fourth in a series of *Biblia Hebraica* going back to 1906), which remains at present the standard edition used in classrooms, is based on the early eleventh-century Leningrad Codex of the whole OT. Along with the pointed Hebrew text it contains at the foot of each page a textual apparatus that displays textual variations and includes editorial suggestions

---

[22] Kristin de Troyer proposes, e.g., that the "Old Greek text of Joshua reflects what the Hebrew text of Joshua looked like in its penultimate, pre-Masoretic stage" (second century BC), albeit that the differences she discusses are small. Kristin de Troyer, *Rewriting the Sacred Text* (SBLTCS 4; Leiden: Brill, 2003), 29–58 (quote on 127).

[23] I.e., the text at the point when "literary alterations and supplements in the manuscript-transmission were no longer regarded as part and parcel of a canonical book's essential form but as departures from it." Ellis, *Old Testament*, 49.

[24] It is because I do think that the argument of my chapters 2 through 11 is fundamentally correct, then, that I disagree with Daniel Hays that the Protestant Church (or any Church) should use the LXX as its best guide to the "original autograph" of the book of Jeremiah—as if there were any good scriptural or theological reason at all to think that "earlier" is necessarily "better" with respect to OT texts. Jeremiah himself is described in his own book as initiating an expansion of it in the direction of its current canonical form (Jer 36:32). J. Daniel Hays, "Jeremiah, the Septuagint, the Dead Sea Scrolls and Inerrancy: What Exactly Do We Mean by the 'Original Autographs'?," in Bacote, Quay, and Okholm, *Evangelicals and Scripture*, 133–49.

[25] "In volume 2, out of eight hundred emendations that were examined, only seventy-eight were found to be probable, and most of these do not materially affect the sense." Wolters, "Text," 36.

for emendations. The fifth and significantly updated edition, *Biblica Hebraica Quinta* (*BHQ*), is currently in the process of appearing, fascicle by fascicle (2004 until the present). At the same time, the Hebrew University Bible Project, established in 1956, is working on a new critical edition based on the earlier Aleppo Codex (tenth century). This project aims at a "comprehensive critical edition of the Hebrew Bible providing the entire range of textual evidence collated from all extant sources."[26] Fascicles have slowly been appearing since 1975. In this edition there are four separate textual apparatuses that are entirely descriptive rather than partially evaluative.[27]

---

[26] The wording is taken from their website, http://www.hum.huji.ac.il/english/units.php?cat=4981&incat=4980 (accessed March 28, 2016).

[27] For a readable, helpful introduction to the modern critical editions of the Hebrew text, see Paul D. Wegner, *A Student's Guide to Textual Criticism of the Bible: Its History, Methods and Results* (Downers Grove, Ill.: IVP Academic, 2006), 100–117. See also, on *BHS* specifically, William R. Scott, *A Simplified Guide to Biblia Hebraica Stuttgartensia* (3rd ed.; North Richland Hills, Tex.: Bibal, 1995).

Bibliography

Ackroyd, Peter R. *Continuity: A Contribution to the Study of the Old Testament Religious Tradition.* Oxford: Blackwell, 1962.
———. *Studies in the Religious Tradition of the Old Testament.* London: SCM Press, 1987.
———. "The Succession Narrative (So-Called)." *Interpretation* 35 (1981): 383–96.
Adams, Douglas. *The Hitchhiker's Guide to the Galaxy.* London: Pan Books, 1979.
Africanus, Julius. *Epistula ad Origenem (Letter to Origen). ANF* 4:385
Ahlström, Gösta W. "The Role of Archaeological and Literary Remains in Reconstructing Israel's History." In *The Fabric of History: Text, Artifact and Israel's Past*, edited by Diana V. Edelman, 116–41. JSOTSup 127. Sheffield: JSOT Press, 1991.
Alexander, Philip S. "Midrash and the Gospels." In *Synoptic Studies: The Ampleforth Conferences of 1982 and 1983*, edited by C. M. Tuckett, 1–18. JSNTSup 7. Sheffield: JSOT Press, 1984.
———. "Reflections on the Christian Turn to the *Hebraica Veritas* and Its Implications." In *Studies on the Text and Versions of the Hebrew Bible in Honour of Robert Gordon*, edited by Geoffrey Khan and Diana Lipton, 353–72. VTSup 149. Leiden: Brill, 2012.
Alexander, T. Desmond. "Jonah and Genre." *TynBul* 36 (1985): 35–59.
Allen, Michael, and Scott R. Swain. *Reformed Catholicity: The Promise of Retrieval for Theology and Biblical Interpretation.* Grand Rapids: Baker, 2015.
Allert, Craig D. *A High View of Scripture? The Authority of the Bible and the Formation of the New Testament Canon.* Grand Rapids: Baker, 2007.
Alter, Robert. *The Art of Biblical Narrative.* New York: Basic Books, 1981.
Alter, Robert, and Frank Kermode, eds. *The Literary Guide to the Bible.* Cambridge, Mass.: Belknap, 1987.
Ambrose. *De Jacob et vita beata (Jacob and the Happy Life).* In *St. Ambrose: Seven Exegetical Works*, edited by Bernard M. Peebles et al., translated by Michael P. McHugh. FC 65. Washington, D.C.: Catholic University of America Press, 1985.

Aquinas, Thomas. *Summa theologiae*. Translated by Fathers of the English Dominican Province. New York: Benziger Brothers, 1947.
Aristotle. *Generation of Animals*, 5.7. Translated by A. L. Peck. Cambridge, Mass.: Harvard University Press, 1942.
———. *On Rhetoric: A Theory of Civic Discourse*. Translated by George A. Kennedy. New York: Oxford University Press, 1991.
Athanasius. *Epistulae Festalis (Festal Letters)*. NPNF 2, 4:552.
Atkinson, James. *The Trial of Luther*. New York: Stein & Day, 1971.
Augustine. *City of God*, 15.23, 18.36. NPNF 1, 2:305, 382.
———. *Contra Adimantum (Against Adimantus)* 3.4. Translated in David F. Wright, "Augustine: His Exegesis and Hermeneutics." *HBOT* 1/1 (1996):701–30.
———. *Contra Faustum (Reply to Faustus)*, 11.5. NPNF 1, 4:180.
———. *De bono conjugali (On the Good of Marriage)*, 8. NPNF 1, 3:403.
———. *De civitate Dei (City of God)*, 15.23.4. NPNF 1, 2:305.
———. *De consensu evangeliorum (Harmony of the Gospels)*, 1.35.54. NPNF 1, 6:101.
———. *De doctrina christiana (On Christian Doctrine)*, 2.8.12. NPNF 1, 2:538.
———. *De Genesi ad litteram (The Literal Meaning of Genesis)*. 2 vols. Translated by John H. Taylor. ACW 41–42. New York: Newman, 1982.
———. *De Genesi contra Manichaeos (On Genesis against the Manicheans)*, 2.2.3. In *Saint Augustine on Genesis*, edited by Thomas P. Halton et al., translated by Roland J. Teske. FC 84. Washington, D.C.: Catholic University of America Press, 1991.
———. *De trinitate (The Trinity)*, 2.1.2. NPNF 1, 3:37.
———. *Letters*, 28, 71, 82. NPNF 1, 1:251–53, 326–28, 349–61.
———. *Quaestiones Evangeliorum (Questions on the Gospels)*, 2.19. In *New Testament I and II*, edited by Boniface Ramsey. Vols. 15–16 of *The Works of Saint Augustine: A Translation for the 21st Century*, 388–89. New York: New City, 2014.
———. *Retractionum (Reconsiderations)*. In *Saint Augustine: The Retractions*, edited by Roy Joseph Deferrari et al., translated by Mary Inez Bogan. FC 60. Washington, D.C.: Catholic University of America Press, 1968.
———. "Sermon 171." In *Sermons 148–183*, edited by John E. Rotelle, translated by Edmund Hill. Vol. 5 of *Sermons*, pt. III of *The Works of Saint Augustine: A Translation for the 21st Century*. New York: New City, 1992.
Aune, David E., ed. *The Blackwell Companion to the New Testament*. Oxford: Wiley-Blackwell, 2010.
Austen, Jane. *Persuasion*. In *The Penguin Complete Novels of Jane Austen*, 1143–1290. London: Penguin, 1983.
Auwers, J. M., and H. J. De Jonge, eds. *The Biblical Canons*. BETL 163. Leuven: Leuven University Press, 2003.
Bacon, Roger. *The Opus Majus of Roger Bacon*. Translated by R. B. Burke. Philadelphia: University of Pennsylvania Press, 1928.

Bacote, Vincent E., Laura Miguelez Quay, and Dennis L. Okholm, eds. *Evangelicals and Scripture: Tradition, Authority and Hermeneutics*. Downers Grove, Ill.: InterVarsity, 2004.

Bailey, Kenneth E. "Informal Controlled Oral Tradition and the Synoptic Gospels." *Them* 20 (1995): 4–11.

Bar-Efrat, Shimon. *Narrative Art in the Bible*. Translated by D. Shefer-Vanson. Sheffield: Almond, 1989.

Barker, Peter. "Kepler and Melanchthon on the Biblical Arguments against Copernicanism." In van der Meer and Mandelbrote, *Nature and Scripture in the Abrahamic Religions: Up to 1700*, 2:584–603.

Barnes, Julian. *Flaubert's Parrot*. London: Bloomsbury, 1992.

Barr, James. "Childs' Introduction to the Old Testament as Scripture." *JSOT* 16 (1980): 12–23.

———. *Holy Scripture: Canon, Authority, Criticism*. Philadelphia: Westminster, 1983, 31–32.

———. "Literality." *FP* 6 (1989): 412–28.

———. "Luther and Biblical Chronology." In *Bible and Interpretation: The Collected Essays of James Barr, Volume II: Biblical Studies*, edited by John Barton, 423–39. Oxford: Oxford University Press, 2013.

———. *Old and New in Interpretation: A Study of the Two Testaments*. London: SCM Press, 1982.

Barrett, Rob. "Meaning More Than They Say: The Conflict between YHWH and Jonah." *JSOT* 37 (2012): 237–57.

Barthes, Roland. *Image, Music, Text: Essays Selected and Translated by Stephen Heath*. London: Fontana, 1977.

———. "An Introduction to the Structural Analysis of Narrative." *NLH* 6 (1975): 256.

Bartholomew, Craig G. *Introducing Biblical Hermeneutics: A Comprehensive Framework for Hearing God in Scripture*. Grand Rapids: Baker, 2015.

———. "Postmodernity and Biblical Interpretation." *DTIB*, 600–607.

Bartholomew, Craig G., and David J. H. Beldman, eds. *Hearing the Old Testament: Listening for God's Address*. Grand Rapids: Eerdmans, 2012.

Barton, John. "The Legacy of the Literary-Critical School and the Growing Opposition to Historico-Critical Bible Studies: The Concept of 'History' Revisited—*Wirkungsgeschichte* and Reception History." *HBOT* 3/2 (2015): 96–124.

———. *Oracles of God: Perceptions of Ancient Prophecy in Israel after the Exile*. London: Darton, Longman & Todd, 1986.

———. *Reading the Old Testament*. London: Darton, Longman & Todd, 1984.

———. "The Significance of a Fixed Canon of the Hebrew Bible." *HBOT* 1/1 (1996): 67–83.

Barton, Stephen C. "Social-Scientific Criticism." *DTIB*, 753–55.

Basil of Caesarea. *Exegetic Homilies*. Translated by A. C. Way. FC. Washington, D.C.: Catholic University of America Press, 1963.

———. *Hexaemeron (Six Days)*, 9.1. *NPNF* 2, 8:101.

———. Letters. In *Basil: Letters and Works*. Vol. 8 of *Nicene and Post-Nicene Fathers, Second Series*, edited by Philip Schaff and Henry Wace. Peabody, Mass.: Hendrickson, 1999.

Battles, Ford L. "God Was Accommodating Himself to Human Capacity." *Int* 31 (1977): 19–38.

Bauckham, Richard. *Bible and Ecology: Rediscovering the Community of Creation*. London: Darton, Longman & Todd, 2010.

———. *Jesus and the Eyewitnesses: The Gospels as Eyewitness Testimony*. Grand Rapids: Eerdmans, 2006.

Bavinck, Herman. *Gereformeerde Dogmatiek*. 4 vols. Kampen: J. H. Bos, 1895–1901.

Beasley-Murray, George R. *John*. WBC 36. Dallas: Word, 1987.

Béchard S.J., Dean P., ed. and trans. *The Scripture Documents: An Anthology of Official Catholic Teachings*. Collegeville, Minnesota. The Order of St. Benedict, 2002.

Beckwith, Roger. *The Old Testament Canon of the New Testament Church, and Its Background in Early Judaism*. Grand Rapids: Eerdmans, 1985.

Bedford, Ronald D. *The Defence of Truth: Herbert of Cherbury and the Seventeenth Century*. Manchester: Manchester University Press, 1979.

Beentjes, Pancratius C. "Canon and Scripture in the Book of Ben Sira (Jesus Sirach/Ecclesiasticus)." *HBOT* 1/2 (2000): 591–605.

Bellarmine, Robert. *Disputations about the Controversies of the Christian Faith against the Heretics of This Time*. Ingolstadt, 1586–1593.

Benson, Bruce E. "Poststructuralism." *DTIB*, 607–9.

Bentley, Jerry H. *Humanists and Holy Writ: New Testament Scholarship in the Renaissance*. Princeton: Princeton University Press, 1983.

Berchman, Robert M. *From Philo to Origen: Middle Platonism in Transition*. BJS 69. Chico, Calif.: Scholars Press, 1984.

Berlin, Adele. *Poetics and Interpretation of Biblical Narrative*. Sheffield: Almond, 1983.

Berman, Art. *From the New Criticism to Deconstruction: The Reception of Structuralism and Post-structuralism*. Chicago: University of Illinois Press, 1988.

Berndt, Rainer. "The School of St. Victor in Paris." *HBOT* 1/2 (2000): 467–95.

Betz, Hans Dieter. *Galatians*. Hermeneia. Philadelphia: Fortress, 1979.

Bewer, J. A. *A Critical and Exegetical Commentary on Jonah*. Edinburgh: T&T Clark, 1912.

Bindel, Julie. "Mary Daly Obituary." https://www.theguardian.com/world/2010/jan/27/mary-daly-obituary. Accessed November 14, 2016.

Blackwell, Richard J. *Behind the Scenes at Galileo's Trial*. Notre Dame: University of Notre Dame Press, 2006.

Blair, Peter Hunter. *The World of Bede*. 2nd ed. Cambridge: Cambridge University Press, 1990.

Blenkinsopp, Joseph. *Prophecy and Canon: A Contribution to the Study of Jewish Origins*. Notre Dame: University of Notre Dame Press, 1977.

Blomberg, Craig L. *Interpreting the Parables.* Downers Grove, Ill.: InterVarsity, 1990.
Blowers, Paul M. "Entering 'This Sublime and Blessed Amphitheatre': Contemplation of Nature and Interpretation of the Bible in the Patristic Period." In van der Meer and Mandelbrote, *Nature and Scripture in the Abrahamic Religions: Up to 1700*, 1:147–76.
Boersma, Hans. *Heavenly Participation: The Weaving of a Sacramental Tapestry.* Grand Rapids: Eerdmans, 2011.
———. *Nouvelle Théologie and Sacramental Ontology: A Return to Mystery.* Oxford: Oxford University Press, 2009.
Böhmer, Heinrich. *Road to Reformation: Martin Luther to the Year 1521.* Translated by John W. Doberstein and Theodore G. Tappert. Philadelphia: Muhlenberg, 1946.
Borchert, Gerald L. *John 1–11.* NAC 25A. Nashville: Broadman & Holman, 1996.
Bornkamm, Günther. "The Stilling of the Storm in Matthew." In *Tradition and Interpretation in Matthew*, edited by Günther Bornkamm, Gerhard Barth, and Heinz Joachim Held, 52–57. Philadelphia: Westminster, 1963.
Bornkamm, Heinrich. *Luther and the Old Testament.* Translated by E. W. and R. C. Gritsch. Edited by V. I. Gruhn. Mifflintown, Pa.: Sigler, 1997.
Bouwsma, William J. *John Calvin: A Sixteenth-Century Portrait.* Oxford: Oxford University Press, 1988.
Bray, Gerald. "Allegory." *DTIB*, 34–36.
———. *Biblical Interpretation: Past and Present.* Leicester: Apollos, 1996.
Brecht, Martin. *Martin Luther: His Road to Reformation 1483–1521.* Vol. 1 of *Martin Luther.* Translated by James L. Schaaf. Philadelphia: Fortress, 1985.
———. *Martin Luther: Shaping and Defining the Reformation 1521–1532.* Vol. 2 of *Martin Luther.* Translated by James L. Schaaf. Minneapolis: Fortress, 1990.
Brett, Mark G. *Biblical Criticism in Crisis? The Impact of the Canonical Approach on Old Testament Studies.* Cambridge: Cambridge University Press, 1991.
Briggs, John Channing. "Bacon's Science and Religion." In *The Cambridge Companion to Bacon*, edited by Markku Peltonen, 172–99. Cambridge: Cambridge University Press, 1996.
Bright, Pamela. "Nature and Scripture: The Two Witnesses to the Creator." In van der Meer and Mandelbrote, *Nature and Scripture in the Abrahamic Religions: Up to 1700*, 1:85–115.
Brock, Sebastian P. "The Phenomenon of the Septuagint." *OtSt* 17 (1972): 23–77.
Brown, Raymond E., and Thomas A. Collins, O.P. "Church Pronouncements." *NJBC*, 1166–74.
Brown, Robert E. "Jonathan Edwards and the Discourses of Nature." In van der Meer and Mandelbrote, *Nature and Scripture in the Abrahamic Religions: 1700–Present*, 1:83–114.
Bruce, F. F. *Commentary on the Epistle to the Hebrews.* London: Marshall, Morgan & Scott, 1964.
Bucer, Martin. *Quomodo S. Literae pro Concionibus tractandae sint Instructio.* 1531.

Bullinger, Heinrich. "Of the Holy Catholic Church." In *Zwingli and Bullinger*, edited by G. W. Bromiley, 283–325. LCC 24. London: SCM Press, 1953.

Bultmann, Christoph. "Early Rationalism and Biblical Criticism on the Continent." *HBOT* 2 (2008): 875–901.

———. "Wider 'Ein feste Burg' als faktisches Motto des Reformationsgedenkens 2017." *Pastoral-Theologie* 102 (2013): 219–38.

Bultmann, Rudolf. *Jesus and the Word*. Translated by Louise P. Smith and Erminie H. Lantero. New York: Charles Scribner's Sons, 1958.

Burnett, Amy Nelson. "Hermeneutics and Exegesis in the Early Eucharistic Controversy." In Gordon and McLean, *Shaping the Bible*, 85–105.

———. "Luther and the Schwärmer." In *The Oxford Handbook of Martin Luther's Theology*, edited by Robert Kolb et al., 511–24. Oxford: Oxford University Press, 2014.

Burnett, Stephen G. *Christian Hebraism in the Reformation Era (1500–1660): Authors, Books, and the Transmission of Jewish Learning*. LWW 19. Leiden: Brill, 2012.

———. "Later Christian Hebraists." *HBOT* 2 (2008): 785–801.

Burrus, Virginia. *Begotten Not Made: Conceiving Manhood in Late Antiquity*. FRMC. Stanford: Stanford University Press, 2000.

Burtt, Edwin A. *The Metaphysical Foundations of Modern Physical Science: A Historical and Critical Essay*. 2nd ed. London: Routledge & Kegan Paul, 1932.

Calvin, John. *The Acts of the Apostles 1–13*. Translated by John W. Fraser and W. J. G. McDonald. Edited by David W. Torrance and Thomas F. Torrance. CalC 6. Edinburgh: Oliver & Boyd, 1965.

———. "Argument to the Gospel of John." In *Commentary on the Gospel According to John, Volume First*, translated by William Pringle, 22. CalC 17. Grand Rapids: Baker, 1981.

———. "Author's Preface." In *Commentary on the Book of Psalms, Volume 1*, translated by James Anderson, xxxvii. CalC 4. Grand Rapids: Baker, 1981.

———. *Commentaries on the Epistles of Paul to the Galatians and Ephesians*. Translated by William Pringle. Grand Rapids: Eerdmans, 1948.

———. *Commentaries on the Epistles to Timothy, Titus, and Philemon, Galatians, Ephesians, Philippians, Colossians, I & II Thessalonians*. Edited and translated by William Pringle. CalC 21; GSC. London: Calvin Translation Society, 1847. Reprint, Grand Rapids: Baker, 1981.

———. *Commentaries on the First Book of Moses Called Genesis*. Edited and translated by John King. CalC 1. London: Calvin Translation Society, 1847. Reprint, Grand Rapids: Baker, 1981.

———. *Commentaries on the Twelve Minor Prophets*, vol. 3. Translated by John Owen. CalC 14. 1847. Reprint, Grand Rapids: Baker, 1980.

———. *Commentary on the Book of the Prophet Isaiah*, vol. 1. Translated by William Pringle. Grand Rapids: Eerdmans, 1958.

———. *Commentary on the Book of Psalms*, vol. 2. Translated by James McLean. CalC 5. London: Calvin Translation Society, 1847. Reprint, Grand Rapids: Baker, 1996.

———. *Commentary on the Epistles of Paul the Apostle to the Corinthians*. Edited and translated by John Pringle. CalC 20; GSC. London: Calvin Translation Society, 1847. Reprint, Grand Rapids: Baker, 1981.

———. *Commentary on the Gospel According to John, Volume First*. Translated by William Pringle, 22. CalC 17. Grand Rapids: Baker, 1981.

———. *The Epistle of Paul the Apostle to the Hebrews and the First and Second Epistles of St. Peter*. Translated by William B. Johnston. Edited by David W. Torrance and Thomas F. Torrance. CalC 12. Edinburgh: Oliver & Boyd, 1963.

———. *Epistle of Paul the Apostle to the Romans and to the Thessalonians*. Translated by Ross Mackenzie. Edited by David W. Torrance and Thomas F. Torrance. CalC 8. Edinburgh: Oliver & Boyd, 1961.

———. *The First Epistle of Paul the Apostle to the Corinthians*. Translated by John W. Fraser. Edinburgh: Saint Andrew Press, 1960.

———. *A Harmony of the Gospels Matthew, Mark, and Luke, Volume 1*. Translated by A. W. Morrison. CalC. Edinburgh: Saint Andrew, 1972.

———. *A Harmony of the Gospels Matthew, Mark, and Luke, Volume 3, and the Epistles of James and Jude*. Translated by A. W. Morrison. CalC. Edinburgh: Saint Andrew, 1972.

———. *Institutes of the Christian Religion*. 2 vols. Translated by Henry Beveridge. Grand Rapids: Eerdmans, 1989.

Campbell, Antony F. "The Emergence of the Form-Critical and Traditio-historical Approaches." *HBOT* 3/2 (2015): 125–47.

Capon, Robert F. *The Third Peacock: The Goodness of God and the Badness of the World*. Garden City, N.Y.: Doubleday, 1971.

Caputo, John D. *The Insistence of God: A Theology of Perhaps*. ISPR. Bloomington: Indiana University Press, 2013.

———. *The Weakness of God: A Theology of the Event*. ISPR. Bloomington: Indiana University Press, 2006.

———. "What Do I Love When I Love My God? Deconstruction and Radical Orthodoxy." In *Questioning God*, edited by John D. Caputo, Mark Dooley, and Michael J. Scanlon, 291–317. Bloomington: Indiana University Press, 2001.

———. *What Would Jesus Deconstruct? The Good News of Postmodernism for the Church*. CPC. Grand Rapids: Baker, 2007.

Carleton Paget, J. N. B. "The Christian Exegesis of the Old Testament in the Alexandrian Tradition." *HBOT* 1/1 (1996): 478–542.

Carlin, Norah. "Toleration for Catholics in the Puritan Revolution." In *Tolerance and Intolerance in the European Reformation*, edited by Ole Peter Grell and Bob Scribner, 216–30. Cambridge: Cambridge University Press, 1996.

Carr, David M. "Changes in Pentateuchal Criticism." *HBOT* 3/2 (2015): 433–66.

———. *The Formation of the Hebrew Bible: A New Reconstruction.* New York: Oxford University Press, 2011.

Case, Shirley Jackson. *The Evolution of Early Christianity: A Genetic Study of First-Century Christianity in Relation to Its Religious Environment.* Chicago: University of Chicago Press, 1914.

Cathcart, Kevin J. "The Earliest Contributions to the Decipherment of Sumerian and Akkadian." *CDLJ* 1 (2011): 1–12.

Catto, Jeremy. "The Philosophical Context of the Renaissance Interpretation of the Bible." *HBOT* 2 (2008): 106–22.

Causse, Antonin. *Du groupe ethnique à la communauté religieuse. Le problème sociologique de la religion d'Israël.* Paris: Alcan, 1937.

Chapman, Stephen B. "The Canon Debate: What It Is and Why It Matters." *JTI* 4 (2010): 273–94.

———. *The Law and the Prophets: A Study in Old Testament Canon Formation.* FAT 27. Tübingen: Mohr Siebeck, 2000.

———. "Second Temple Jewish Hermeneutics: How Canon Is Not an Anachronism." In *Invention, Rewriting, Usurpation: Discursive Fights over Religious Traditions in Antiquity*, edited by Jörg Ulrich, Anders-Christian Jacobsen, and David Brakke, 281–96. ECCA 11. Frankfurt am Main: Peter Lang, 2012.

———. "'A Threefold Cord Is Not Quickly Broken': Interpretation by Canonical Division in Early Judaism and Christianity." In *The Shape of the Writings*, edited by Julius Steinberg and Timothy J. Stone, 281–309. Winona Lake, Ind.: Eisenbrauns, 2015.

Chase, Frederic H. *Chrysostom: A Study in the History of Biblical Interpretation.* Cambridge: Deighton, Bell, 1887.

Childs, Brevard S. *Biblical Theology of the Old and New Testaments: Theological Reflection on the Christian Bible.* Minneapolis: Fortress, 1993.

———. *Introduction to the Old Testament as Scripture.* London: SCM Press, 1979.

———. *Isaiah.* OTL. Louisville, Ky.: Westminster John Knox, 2001.

———. *Old Testament Theology in a Canonical Context.* Philadelphia: Fortress, 1986.

———. "A Response." *HBT* 2 (1980): 199–211.

Chrysostom, John. *Ad Theodorum lapsum* (*Letters to the Fallen Theodore*). NPNF 1, 9:92–93.

———. *Commentary on Galatians.* NPNF 1, 13:34.

———. *Homiliae in Genesim* (*Homilies on Genesis*). In *Saint John Chrysostom: Homilies on Genesis 1–17*, edited by Thomas P. Halton et al., translated by Robert C. Hill, 56. FC 74. Washington, D.C.: Catholic University of America Press, 1986.

———. *Homilies on Genesis.* In *Saint John Chrysostom: Homilies on Genesis 46–67*, edited by Thomas P. Halton et al., translated by Robert C. Hill. FC 87. Washington, D.C.: Catholic University of America, 1992.

———. *Homily 47.* NPNF 1, 10:292.

Clark, Elizabeth A. *Reading Renunciation: Asceticism and Scripture in Early Christianity*. Princeton: Princeton University Press, 1999.
Clement of Alexandria. *Stromata (Miscellanies)*, 7.16. ANF 2:550–54.
Clement of Rome. *Epistula I ad Corinthios (1 Clement)*, 45.2. ANF 1:17.
Clines, David J. A. "Contemporary Methods in Hebrew Bible Criticism." *HBOT* 3/2 (2015): 148–69.
Cochrane, Arthur C., ed. *Reformed Confessions of the Sixteenth Century*. Louisville, Ky.: Westminster John Knox, 2003.
Cohen, Shaye J. D. *The Beginnings of Jewishness: Boundaries, Varieties, Uncertainties*. Berkeley: University of California Press, 1999.
Collins, Francis S. *The Language of God: A Scientist Presents Evidence for Belief*. New York: Free Press, 2006.
Collins, Wilkie. *The Woman in White*. London: Penguin, 1974.
Congar, Yves M.-J., O.P. *Tradition and Traditions: An Historical and a Theological Essay*. Translated by Michael Naseby and Thomas Rainborough. London: Burns & Oates, 1966.
Copeland, Rita, and Peter T. Struck, eds. *The Cambridge Companion to Allegory*. Cambridge: Cambridge University Press, 2010.
Corbellini, Sabrina. "Instructing the Soul, Feeding the Spirit and Awakening the Passion: Holy Writ and Lay Readers in Late Medieval Europe." In Gordon and McLean, *Shaping the Bible*, 15–39.
Cormack, Lesley B. "Myth 3: That Medieval Christians Taught That the Earth Was Flat." In Numbers, *Galileo Goes to Jail*, 28–34.
Cosmas Indicopleustes. *The Christian Topography of Cosmas, an Egyptian Monk*. Translated and edited by J. W. McCrindle. London: Hakluyt Society, 1897.
Cranfield, C. E. B. *The Epistle to the Romans*. ICC. 2 vols. Edinburgh: T&T Clark, 1975.
Cross, Frank M. *From Epic to Canon: History and Literature in Ancient Israel*. Baltimore: Johns Hopkins University Press, 1998.
Crossan, J. Dominic. "Perspectives and Methods in Contemporary Biblical Criticism." *BR* 32 (1977): 39–49.
Crowther, Kathleen M. "Sacred Philosophy, Secular Theology: The Mosaic Physics of Levinus Lemnius (1505–1568) and Francisco Valles (1524–1592)." In van der Meer and Mandelbrote, *Nature and Scripture in the Abrahamic Religions: Up to 1700*, 2:397–428.
Culler, Jonathan. *Literary Theory: A Very Short Introduction*. Oxford: Oxford University Press, 1997.
———. *On Deconstruction: Theory and Criticism after Structuralism*. Ithaca, N.Y.: Cornell University Press, 1982.
———. *The Pursuit of Signs: Semiotics, Literature, Deconstruction*. Ithaca, N.Y.: Cornell University Press, 1981.
Cummings, Brian. *The Literary Culture of the Reformation: Grammar and Grace*. Oxford: Oxford University Press, 2002.

Cyril of Jerusalem. *Katēchēseis (Catechetical Lectures)*, 4.17. NPNF 2, 7:23.

Dahan, Gilbert. "Genres, Forms and Various Methods in Christian Exegesis of the Middle Ages." *HBOT* 1/2 (2000): 198–236.

Daley, Brian E., S.J. "Is Patristic Exegesis Still Usable? Some Reflections on Early Christian Interpretation of the Psalms." In *The Art of Reading Scripture*, edited by Ellen F. Davis and Richard B. Hays, 69–88. Grand Rapids: Eerdmans, 2003.

Daly, Mary. *Beyond God the Father: Toward a Philosophy of Women's Liberation*. Boston: Beacon, 1973.

———. *The Church and the Second Sex*. New York: Harper & Row, 1968.

———. *Gyn/Ecology: The Metaethics of Radical Feminism*. Boston: Beacon, 1978.

———. *Pure Lust: Elemental Feminist Philosophy*. Boston: Beacon, 1984.

Danielson, Dennis R., ed. *The Book of the Cosmos: Imagining the Universe from Heraclitus to Hawking*. Cambridge, Mass.: Perseus, 2000.

———. *The First Copernican: Georg Joachim Rheticus and the Rise of the Copernican Revolution*. New York: Walker, 2006.

Danielson, Dennis, and Christopher M. Graney. "The Case against Copernicus." *Scientific American* 310 (2014): 72–77.

Davis, Edward B. "A Whale of a Tale: Fundamentalist Fish Stories." *PSCF* 43 (1991): 224–37.

Davis, Edward B., and Elizabeth Chmielewski. "Galileo and the Garden of Eden: Historical Reflections on Creationist Hermeneutics." In van der Meer and Mandelbrote, *Nature and Scripture in the Abrahamic Religions: 1700–Present*, 2:437–64.

Dawson, David. *Allegorical Readers and Cultural Revision in Ancient Alexandria*. Berkeley: University of California Press, 1992.

de Felipe, Pablo. "The Antipodeans and Science-Faith Relations." In *Augustine Beyond the Book: Intermediality, Transmediality and Reception*, edited by Karla Pollmann and Meredith J. Gill, 281–311. BSCH 58. Leiden: Brill, 2012.

de Lubac, Henri. *History and Spirit: The Understanding of Scripture According to Origen*. 1950. Reprint, San Francisco: Ignatius Press, 2007.

de Margerie, Bertrand, S.J. *An Introduction to the History of Exegesis, Volume 1: The Greek Fathers*. Translated by Leonard Maluf. Petersham, Mass.: St. Bede's Publications, 1993.

de Saussure, Ferdinand. *Course in General Linguistics*. Translated by Roy Harris. London: Bloomsbury, 2013.

de Spinoza, Benedict. *Theological-Political Treatise*. Edited by Jonathan Israel. Translated by Michael Silverthorne and Jonathan Israel. Cambridge: Cambridge University Press, 2007.

de Troyer, Kristin. *Rewriting the Sacred Text*. SBLTCS 4. Leiden: Brill, 2003.

Dempster, Stephen G. "Canon and Old Testament Interpretation." In Bartholomew and Beldman, *Hearing the Old Testament*, 154–79.

———. *Dominion and Dynasty: A Theology of the Hebrew Bible*. NSBT 15. Downers Grove, Ill.: InterVarsity, 2003.

———. "Torah, Torah, Torah: The Emergence of the Tripartite Canon." In Evans and Tov, *Exploring the Origins of the Bible*, 87–127.
Derrida, Jacques. *Of Grammatology*. Translated by Gayatri Chakravorty Spivak. Baltimore: Johns Hopkins University Press, 1976.
Dillenberger, John. *Protestant Thought and Natural Science: A Historical Interpretation*. Notre Dame: University of Notre Dame Press, 1960.
Di Mattei, Steven. "Paul's Allegory of the Two Covenants (Gal 4.21-31) in Light of First-Century Hellenistic Rhetoric and Jewish Hermeneutics." *NTS* 52 (2006): 102–22.
Dines, Jennifer M. *The Septuagint*. UBW. London: T&T Clark, 2004.
Diodore of Tarsus. *Commentary on Psalms 1–51*. Translated by Robert C. Hill. WGRW 9. Atlanta: Society of Biblical Literature, 2005.
D. Martin Luthers Werke. Kritische Gesamtausgabe. Tischreden. 6 vols. Weimar: Hermann Böhlaus Nachfolger, 1912–1921.
Dodd, Charles H. *According to the Scriptures: The Sub-structure of New Testament Theology*. Welwyn: James Nisbet, 1952.
———. *The Epistle of Paul to the Romans*. London: Fontana, 1959.
Draper, John W. *History of the Conflict between Religion and Science*. New York: Appleton, 1875.
Driver, Samuel R. *The Book of Genesis*. 2nd ed. London: Methuen, 1904.
Dunn, James D. G. "Kenneth Bailey's Theory of Oral Tradition: Critiquing Theodore Weeden's Critique." *JSHJ* 7 (2009): 44–62.
———. *Romans 1–8*. WBC 38A. Dallas: Word, 1988.
Dutcher-Walls, Patricia. *Reading the Historical Books: A Student's Guide to Engaging the Biblical Text*. Grand Rapids: Baker, 2014.
Edgecomb, Kevin P., ed. *The Tertullian Project*. http://www.tertullian.org/fathers/. Accessed March 23, 2016.
Edwards, Mark J. "Origen." In *The Stanford Encyclopedia of Philosophy*, Spring 2014 ed., edited by Edward N. Zalta. https://plato.stanford.edu. Accessed February 23, 2016.
———. *Origen against Plato*. ASPTLA. Aldershot: Ashgate, 2002.
Edwards, Richard M. *Scriptural Perspicuity in the Early English Reformation in Historical Theology*. StBibLit 65. New York: Peter Lang, 2009.
Ekserdjian, David. *Parmigianino*. New Haven: Yale University Press, 2006.
Ellis, E. Earle. *The Old Testament in Early Christianity: Canon and Interpretation in the Light of Modern Research*. Grand Rapids: Baker, 1991.
England, Richard. "Interpreting Scripture, Assimilating Science: Four British and American Christian Evolutionists on the Relationship between Science, the Bible, and Doctrine." In van der Meer and Mandelbrote, *Nature and Scripture in the Abrahamic Religions: 1700–Present*, 1:183–223.
———. "Scriptural Facts and Scientific Theories: Epistemological Concerns of Three Leading English-Speaking Anti-Darwinians (Pusey, Hodge, and Dawson)." In

van der Meer and Mandelbrote, *Nature and Scripture in the Abrahamic Religions: 1700–Present*, 1:225–56.

Eriksen, Trond Berg. "Some Sociopolitical and Cultural Aspects of the Renaissance." *HBOT* 2 (2008): 94–105.

Erlich, Victor. *Russian Formalism: History-Doctrine*. 4th ed. The Hague: Mouton, 1980.

Eusebius. *Historia ecclesiastica (Church History)*, 6.25. *NPNF* 2, 1:272.

Eusebius. *Praeparatio evangelica (Preparation for the Gospel)*. Translated by Edwin H. Gifford. Grand Rapids: Baker, 1981.

Evans, Craig A. "Introduction." In Evans and Tov, *Exploring the Origins of the Bible*, 15–29.

Evans, Craig A., and Emanuel Tov, eds. *Exploring the Origins of the Bible: Canon Formation in Historical, Literary, and Theological Perspective*. Grand Rapids: Baker, 2008.

Evans, G. R. "Masters and Disciples: Aspects of Christian Interpretation of the Old Testament in the Eleventh and Twelfth Centuries." *HBOT* 1/2 (2000): 237–60.

———. "Scriptural Interpretation in Pre-Reformation Dissident Movements." *HBOT* 2 (2008): 295–318.

Ewald, Georg Heinrich August. *The History of Israel*. Translated by R. Martineau and J. E. Carpenter. 6 vols. London: Longmans, Green, 1869.

Farley, Margaret A. "Feminist Consciousness and the Interpretation of Scripture." In Russell, *Feminist Interpretation of the Bible*, 41–51.

Feinberg, John S. "Truth: Relationship of Theories of Truth to Hermeneutics." In Radmacher and Preus, *Hermeneutics*, 1–50.

Fernández-Armesto, Felipe. *Columbus*. Oxford: Oxford University Press, 1991.

Fetterley, Judith. *The Resisting Reader: A Feminist Approach to American Fiction*. Bloomington: Indiana University Press, 1978.

Fiddes, Paul S., and Günter Bader, eds. *The Spirit and the Letter: A Tradition and a Reversal*. London: Bloomsbury T&T Clark, 2013.

Finn, Leonard G. "Reflections on the Rule of Faith." In *The Bible as Christian Scripture: The Work of Brevard S. Childs*, edited by Christopher R. Seitz and Kent H. Richards, 221–42. Atlanta: Society of Biblical Literature, 2013.

Finocchiaro, Maurice A. "The Biblical Argument against Copernicanism and the Limitation of Biblical Authority: Ingoli, Foscarini, Galileo, Campanella." In van der Meer and Mandelbrote, *Nature and Scripture in the Abrahamic Religions: Up to 1700*, 2:627–64.

Fiorenza, Elisabeth Schüssler. *In Memory of Her: A Feminist Theological Reconstruction of Christian Origins*. New York: Crossroad, 1983.

———. "The Will to Choose or to Reject: Continuing Our Critical Work." In Russell, *Feminist Interpretation of the Bible*, 125–36.

First Vatican Council. *The Dogmatic Decrees of the Vatican Council Concerning the Catholic Faith and the Church of Christ* (1870). In Schaff, *Creeds of Christendom*, 2:241–42.

Fish, Stanley. *Is There a Text in This Class? The Authority of Interpretive Communities*. Cambridge, Mass.: Harvard University Press, 1980.

Flesseman-van Leer, Ellen. *Tradition and Scripture in the Early Church*. Assen: Van Gorcum, 1954.

Flood, John L. "Martin Luther's Bible Translation in Its German and European Context." In Griffiths, *Bible in the Renaissance*, 45–70.

Fokkelman, Jan P. *Narrative Art and Poetry in the Books of Samuel: A Full Interpretation Based on Stylistic and Structural Analyses. I. King David (2 Sam. 9–20 & 2 Kings 1–2)*. SSN 20. Assen: Van Gorcum, 1981.

———. *Reading Biblical Narrative: An Introductory Guide*. Translated by Ineke Smit. Louisville, Ky.: Westminster John Knox, 1999.

Foster, Michael B. "The Christian Doctrine of Creation and the Rise of Modern Natural Science." *Mind* 43 (1934): 446–68.

———. "Man's Idea of Nature." *CS* 41 (1958): 361–66.

Foucault, Michel. *The Archaeology of Knowledge*. Translated by A. M. Sheridan Smith. New York: Pantheon, 1972.

Fowler, Robert M. *Let the Reader Understand: Reader-Response Criticism and the Gospel of Mark*. Minneapolis: Fortress, 1991.

France, Richard T. *The Gospel of Matthew*. Grand Rapids: Eerdmans, 2007.

François, Wim. "Augustine and the Golden Age of Biblical Scholarship in Louvain (1550–1650)." In Gordon and McLean, *Shaping the Bible*, 235–89.

Franke, John R. "Scripture, Tradition and Authority: Reconstructing the Evangelical Conception of Sola Scriptura." In Bacote, Quay, and Okholm, *Evangelicals and Scripture*, 192–210.

Frei, Hans W. *The Eclipse of Biblical Narrative: A Study in Eighteenth and Nineteenth Century Hermeneutics*. New Haven: Yale University Press, 1974.

Froelich, Karlfried. "Christian Interpretation of the Old Testament in the High Middle Ages." *HBOT* 1/2 (2000): 496–558.

Frye, Northrop. *The Great Code: The Bible and Literature*. London: Penguin, 1990.

Frye, R. M. "Calvin's Theological Use of Figurative Language." In *John Calvin and the Church: A Prism of Reform*, edited by Timothy George, 172–94. Louisville, Ky.: Westminster John Knox, 1990.

Frymer-Kensky, Tikva. *Studies in Bible and Feminist Criticism*. JPSSDS. Philadelphia: Jewish Publication Society, 2006.

Funk, Robert W. *Language, Hermeneutic and Word of God*. New York: Harper & Row, 1966.

Fyfe, Aileen. *Science and Salvation: Evangelical Popular Science Publishing in Victorian Britain*. Chicago: University of Chicago Press, 2004.

Galilei, Galileo. *Discoveries and Opinions of Galileo*. Translated by Stillman Drake. Garden City, N.Y.: Doubleday, 1957.

Gallagher, Edmon L. *Hebrew Scripture in Patristic Biblical Theory: Canon, Language, Text*. VCSup 114. Leiden: Brill, 2012.

———. "Why Did Jerome Translate Tobit and Judith?" *HTR* 108 (2015): 356–75.

Gamble, Harry Y. *Books and Readers in the Early Church: A History of Early Christian Texts*. New Haven: Yale University Press, 1995.

Gamble, Richard C. "Brevitas et Facilitas: Toward an Understanding of Calvin's Hermeneutic." *WTJ* 47 (1985): 1–17.

Garland, David E. *1 Corinthians*. BECNT. Grand Rapids: Baker, 2003.

———. *2 Corinthians*. NAC 29. Nashville: Broadman & Holman, 1999.

Geisler, Norman L. "Inductivism, Materialism, and Rationalism: Bacon, Hobbes, and Spinoza." In *Biblical Errancy: An Analysis of Its Philosophical Roots*, edited by Norman L. Geisler, 9–22. Grand Rapids: Zondervan, 1981.

Gentry, Peter J. "The Text of the Old Testament." *JETS* 52 (2009): 19–45.

George, Timothy. *Galatians*. NAC 30. Nashville: Broadman & Holman, 1994.

———. *Reading Scripture with the Reformers*. Downers Grove, Ill.: InterVarsity, 2011.

Gerstenberger, Erhard S. "Albert Eichhorn and Hermann Gunkel: The Emergence of a History of Religion School." *HBOT* 3/1 (2013): 454–71.

Gilbert, George H. "Interpretation of the Bible by the Fathers." *BW* 38 (1911): 151–58.

Goertz, Hans-Jürgen. "Scriptural Interpretation among Radical Reformers." *HBOT* 2 (2008): 576–601.

Goethe, Johann Wolfgang. *Faust: Erster und Zweiter Teil*. Munich: Deutscher Taschenbuch Verlag, 1997.

Goldhill, Simon. *Aeschylus: The Orestia*. 2nd ed. Cambridge: Cambridge University Press, 2004.

Gordon, Bruce, and Matthew McLean, eds. *Shaping the Bible in the Reformation: Books, Scholars and Their Readers in the Sixteenth Century*. LWW 20. Leiden: Brill, 2012.

Gottwald, Norman K. *The Tribes of Yahweh: A Sociology of the Religion of Liberated Israel, 1250–1050 BCE*. BibSem 66. Sheffield: Sheffield Academic, 1999.

Grabois, Aryeh. "Political and Cultural Changes from the Fifth to the Eleventh Century." *HBOT* 1/2 (2000): 28–55.

Granada, Miguel A. "Tycho Brahe, Caspar Peucer, and Christoph Rothmann on Cosmology and the Bible." In van der Meer and Mandelbrote, *Nature and Scripture in the Abrahamic Religions: Up to 1700*, 2:563–83.

Grant, Frederick C. *The Economic Background of the Gospels*. Oxford: Oxford University Press, 1926.

———. "Rhetoric and Oratory." *IDB* 4:75–77.

Graves, Michael. *The Inspiration and Interpretation of Scripture: What the Early Church Can Teach Us*. Grand Rapids: Eerdmans, 2014.

Greaves, Richard L. "The Social Awareness of John Knox: The Problems of Poverty and Educational Reform." *RR* 12 (1976): 36–48.

Greene, Mott T. *Geology in the Nineteenth Century: Changing Views of a Changing World.* Ithaca, N.Y.: Cornell University Press, 1982.

Greene-McCreight, Kathryn E. *Ad Litteram: How Augustine, Calvin, and Barth Read the "Plain Sense" of Genesis 1–3.* IST 5. New York: Peter Lang, 1999.

———. "Rule of Faith." *DTIB*, 703–4.

———. "Scripture, Clarity of." *DTIB*, 727–30.

Greenstein, Edward L. "Biblical Narratology." *Proof* 1 (1981): 201–8.

Greenwood, Kyle. *Scripture and Cosmology: Reading the Bible between the Ancient World and Modern Science.* Downers Grove, Ill.: InterVarsity, 2015.

Greer, Rowan A. *Theodore of Mopsuestia: Exegete and Theologian.* London: Faith Press, 1961.

Gregory, Brad S. *The Unintended Reformation: How a Religious Revolution Secularized Society.* Cambridge, Mass.: Belknap, 2012.

Gregory of Nyssa. *De anima et resurrectione* (*The Soul and the Resurrection*). NPNF 2, 5:439.

Greimas, Algirdas J. *Structural Semantics: An Attempt at a Method.* Translated by Daniele McDowell, Ronald Schleifer, and Alan Velie. Lincoln: University of Nebraska Press, 1983.

Griffiths, Richard, ed. *The Bible in the Renaissance: Essays on Biblical Commentary and Translation in the Fifteen and Sixteenth Centuries.* SASRH. Aldershot: Ashgate, 2001.

Gritsch, Eric W. "Luther as Bible Translator." In McKim, *Cambridge Companion to Martin Luther*, 62–72.

Grossman, Avraham. "The School of Literal Jewish Exegesis in Northern France." *HBOT* 1/2 (2000): 321–71.

Gundlach, Bradley J. *Process and Providence: The Evolution Question at Princeton, 1845–1929.* Grand Rapids: Eerdmans, 2013.

Gunkel, Hermann. *Genesis.* 3rd ed. Translated by Mark E. Biddle. 1910. Reprint, Macon, Ga.: Mercer University Press, 1997.

Gzella, Holger. "Expansion of the Linguistic Context of the Hebrew Bible/Old Testament: Hebrew among the Languages of the Ancient Near East." *HBOT* 1/1 (1996): 134–67.

Haarsma, Deborah B. "Science and Religion in Harmony." In *Science and Religion in Dialogue*, 2 vols., edited by Melville Y. Stewart, 1:107–19. Oxford: Wiley-Blackwell, 2010.

Hackett, Conrad, et al. *The Global Religious Landscape: A Report on the Size and Distribution of the World's Major Religious Groups as of 2010.* PTGRFP. Washington, D.C.: Pew Research Center, December 2012.

Hagedorn, Anselm C. "Institutions and Social Life in Ancient Israel: Sociological Aspects." *HBOT* 3/2 (2015): 58–95.

Hagner, Donald A. *Matthew 1–13*. WBC 33A. Dallas: Word, 1993.
Hankins, James. *Plato in the Italian Renaissance*. CSCT 17; 3rd impression. Leiden: Brill, 1994.
Hansen, G. Walter. *Galatians*. IVPNTC. Downers Grove, Ill.: InterVarsity, 1994.
Hanson, Richard P. C. *Allegory and Event: A Study of the Sources and Significance of Origen's Interpretation of Scripture*. Louisville, Ky.: Westminster John Knox, 2002.
———. "Notes on Tertullian's Interpretation of Scripture." *JTS* 12 (1961): 273–79.
Harinck, George. "Twin Sisters with a Changing Character: How Neo Calvinists Dealt with the Modern Discrepancy between the Bible and Natural Sciences." In van der Meer and Mandelbrote, *Nature and Scripture in the Abrahamic Religions: 1700–Present*, 2:317–70.
Harper, Elizabeth. "Jonah." In *The IVP Women's Bible Commentary*, edited by Catherine C. Kroeger and Mary J. Evans, 458–63. Downers Grove, Ill.: InterVarsity, 2002.
Harris, Jay M. "From Inner-Biblical Interpretation to Early Rabbinic Exegesis." *HBOT* 1/1 (1996): 256–69.
Harrison, Peter. *The Bible, Protestantism, and the Rise of Natural Science*. Cambridge: Cambridge University Press, 1998.
Hauser, Alan J. "Sources of the Pentateuch: So Many Theories, So Little Consensus." *SBL Forum*, August 2007. http://sbl-site.org/Article.aspx?ArticleID=725. Accessed August 16, 2016.
Hayes, John H. "Historical Criticism of the Old Testament Canon." *HBOT* 2 (2008): 985–1005.
———. *An Introduction to Old Testament Study*. Nashville: Abingdon, 1979.
Hays, J. Daniel. "Jeremiah, the Septuagint, the Dead Sea Scrolls and Inerrancy: What Exactly Do We Mean by the 'Original Autographs'?" In Bacote, Quay, and Okholm, *Evangelicals and Scripture*, 133–49.
Hays, Richard B. *First Corinthians*. Interpretation. Louisville, Ky.: Westminster John Knox, 1997.
———. *Reading Backwards: Figural Christology and the Fourfold Gospel Witness*. Waco, Tex.: Baylor University Press, 2014.
Hayward, C. T. R. "Genesis and Its Reception in Jubilees." In *The Book of Genesis: Composition, Reception, and Interpretation*, edited by C. A. Evans, J. N. Lohr, and D. L. Petersen, 375–404. VTSup 152. Leiden: Brill, 2012.
Healy, Nicholas J., Jr. "Evangelical *Ressourcement*." *First Things*, May 2011. http://www.firstthings.com/article/2011/05/evangelical-ressourcement. Accessed March 21, 2016.
Healy, Nicholas M. "Introduction." In *Aquinas on Scripture: An Introduction to His Biblical Commentaries*, edited by Thomas G. Weinandy et al., 1–20. London: T&T Clark, 2005.
Heggen, Carolyn Holderread. "Religious Beliefs and Abuse." In Kroeger and Beck, *Women, Abuse and the Bible*, 15–27.

Heide, Gale. *Timeless Truth in the Hands of History: A Short History of System in Theology*. PTMS 178. Eugene, Ore.: Pickwick, 2012.
Heine, Ronald E. "The Beginnings of Latin Christian Literature." In Young, Ayres, and Louth, *Cambridge History of Early Christian Literature*, 131–41.
Helm, Paul. *John Calvin's Ideas*. Oxford: Oxford University Press, 2004.
Heraclitus. *Homeric Problems*, 1.1–3. Edited by Donald A. Russell and David Konstan. WGRW 14. Leiden: Brill, 2005.
Herman, Arthur. *How the Scots Invented the Modern World: The True Story of How Western Europe's Poorest Nation Created Our World and Everything in It*. New York: Three Rivers, 2002.
Hidal, Sten. "Exegesis of the Old Testament in the Antiochene School with Its Prevalent Literal and Historical Method." *HBOT* 1/1 (1996): 543–68.
Hill, Jonathan. *What Has Christianity Ever Done for Us? How It Shaped the Modern World*. Downers Grove, Ill.: InterVarsity, 2005.
Hill, Robert C. *Reading the Old Testament in Antioch*. BAC 5. Leiden: Brill, 2005.
Hillerbrand, Hans J. "The Legacy of Martin Luther." In McKim, *Cambridge Companion to Martin Luther*, 227–39.
Hindmarsh, Bruce. *The Spirit of Early Evangelicalism*. New York: Oxford University Press, forthcoming, 2017.
Hippolytus. *Contra haeresin Noeti (Against the Heresy of One Noetus)*. ANF 5:227.
Hobbes, Thomas. *Leviathan; or The Matter, Forme and Power of a Commonwealth Ecclesiastical and Civil*. New York: Collier Books, 1962.
Hobbs, R. Gerald. "*Hebraica Veritas* and *Traditio Apostolica*: Saint Paul and the Interpretation of the Psalms in the Sixteenth Century." In *The Bible in the Sixteenth Century*, edited by David Steinmetz, 83–99. Durham, N.C.: Duke University Press, 1990.
———. "Pluriformity of Early Reformation Scriptural Interpretation." *HBOT* 2 (2008): 452–511.
———. "Translation of the Bible." In *The Oxford Encyclopedia of the Reformation*, 4 vols., edited by Hans J. Hillerbrand, 1:164. Oxford: Oxford University Press, 1996.
Hodge, Charles. *Systematic Theology, Volume 1: Theology*. New York: Scribner, 1871.
———. *Systematic Theology, Volume 2: Anthropology*. New York: Scribner, 1872.
Holder, R. Ward. *John Calvin and the Grounding of Interpretation: Calvin's First Commentaries*. SHCT. Leiden: Brill, 2006.
Holloway, Steven W. "Expansion of the Historical Context of the Hebrew Bible/Old Testament." *HBOT* 3/1 (2013): 90–118.
Holmberg, Bengt. *Sociology and the New Testament: An Appraisal*. Minneapolis: Fortress, 1990.
Holmes, Stephen R. "Evangelical Doctrines of Scripture in Transatlantic Perspective." *EvQ* 81 (2009): 38–63.
Holton, Gerald. "Johannes Kepler's Universe: Its Physics and Metaphysics." *AJP* 24 (1956): 340–51.

Honigman, Sylvie. *The Septuagint and Homeric Scholarship in Alexandria: A Study in the Narrative of the Letter of Aristeas*. London: Routledge, 2003.

Hooykaas, Reijer. *G. J. Rheticus' Treatise on Holy Scripture and the Motion of the Earth* Amsterdam: North-Holland, 1984.

———. *Religion and the Rise of Modern Science*. Grand Rapids: Eerdmans, 1972.

Howell, Kenneth J. *God's Two Books: Copernican Cosmology and Biblical Interpretation in Early Modern Science*. Notre Dame: University of Notre Dame Press, 2002.

———. "The Hermeneutics of Nature and Scripture in Early Modern Science and Theology." In van der Meer and Mandelbrote, *Nature and Scripture in the Abrahamic Religions: Up to 1700*, 1:275–98.

———. "Natural Knowledge and Textual Meaning in Augustine's Interpretation of Genesis: The Three Functions of Natural Philosophy." In van der Meer and Mandelbrote, *Nature and Scripture in the Abrahamic Religions: Up to 1700*, 1:117–45.

Huehnergard, John. *An Introduction to Ugaritic*. Peabody, Mass.: Hendrickson, 2012.

Huijgen, Arnold. *Divine Accommodation in John Calvin's Theology: Analysis and Assessment*. Göttingen: Vandenhoeck & Ruprecht, 2011.

Instone-Brewer, David. "Rabbinic Writings in New Testament Research." In *The Handbook of the Study of the Historical Jesus*, 4 vols., edited by Tom Holmén and Stanley E. Porter, 2:1687–1721. Leiden: Brill, 2011.

———. *Traditions of the Rabbis from the Era of the New Testament, Volume 1: Prayer and Agriculture*. Grand Rapids: Eerdmans, 2004.

Irenaeus. *Adversus haereses* (*Against Heresies*) 1.10.1. ANF 1:330.

———. *Epideixis tou apostolikou kērygmatos* (*Proof of the Apostolic Preaching*). Translated by Joseph P. Smith. ACW 16. New York: Newman, 1952.

Irwin, Robert. *For Lust of Knowing: The Orientalists and Their Enemies*. London: Allen Lane, 2006.

Isidore of Seville. *Etymologies*. Translated by Stephen A. Barney et al. Cambridge: Cambridge University Press, 2006.

Jacob, Christoph. "The Reception of the Origenist Tradition in Latin Exegesis." *HBOT* 1/1 (1996): 682–700.

Jenkins, Allan K., and Patrick Preston, eds. *Biblical Scholarship and the Church: A Sixteenth-Century Crisis of Authority*. ANCTRTB. Aldershot: Ashgate, 2007.

Jerome. *Adversus Rufinum* (*Apology*). NPNF 2, 3:515–16.

———. *De viris illustribus* (*Illustrious Men*), 4. NPNF 2, 3:362.

———. *Jerome's Commentary on Daniel*. Translated by Gleason L. Archer Jr. Grand Rapids: Baker, 1977.

———. *Prologus galeatus* (*Helmeted Preface to Samuel and Kings*). In Leiman, *Canonization*, 45–47.

———. *Prologus* (*Preface*) *to Daniel*. NPNF 2, 6:493.

———. *Prologus* (*Preface*) *to Ezekiel*. In Edgecomb, *Tertullian Project*. http://www.tertullian.org/fathers/jerome_preface_isaiah.htm. Accessed March 23, 2016.

———. *Prologus* (*Preface*) *to Genesis*. NPNF 2, 3:515–16.

———. *Prologus (Preface) to the Gospels*, 4. NPNF 2, 6:487.
———. *Prologus (Preface) to Isaiah*. In Edgecomb, *Tertullian Project*.
———. *Prologus (Preface) to Job*. NPNF 2, 6:491.
———. *Prologus (Preface) to Proverbs, Ecclesiastes, and Song of Songs*. NPNF 2, 6:492.
———. "To Pammachius on the Best Method of Translating." In *Epistulae* (*Letters*), 57.11. NPNF 2, 6:118.
Johnson, H. Wayne. "The 'Analogy of Faith' and Exegetical Methodology: A Preliminary Discussion on Relationships." *JETS* 31 (1988): 69–80.
Johnson, Luke T. *The Acts of the Apostles*. SP 5. Collegeville, Minn.: Liturgical Press, 1992.
Johnson, Timothy J. *Bonaventure: Mystic of God's Word*. New York: New City, 1999.
Jones, Gwilym H. *1 and 2 Kings*. NCB. 2 vols. Grand Rapids: Eerdmans, 1984.
Jorink, Eric. "'Horrible and Blasphemous': Isaac La Peyrère, Isaac Vossius and the Emergence of Radical Biblical Criticism in the Dutch Republic." In van der Meer and Mandelbrote, *Nature and Scripture in the Abrahamic Religions: Up to 1700*, 2:429–50.
Josephus. *Contra Apionem* (*Against Apion*), 1.38–42. In *Josephus, Volume 1*. Translated by Henry St. John Thackeray, 179, 181. LCL 186. London: Heinemann, 1926.
Judge, Edwin A. "Paul's Boasting in Relation to Contemporary Professional Practice." In *Social Distinctives of the Christians in the First Century: Pivotal Essays*, edited by David M. Scholer, 57–71. Peabody, Mass.: Hendrickson, 2008.
Junghans, Helmar. "Luther's Wittenberg." In McKim, *Cambridge Companion to Martin Luther*, 20–35.
Justin Marytr. *Apologia I* (*First Apology*), 31. ANF 1:173.
———. *Dialogus cum Tryphone* (*Dialogue with Trypho*). ANF 1:234–35.
Kamesar, Adam. *Jerome, Greek Scholarship, and the Hebrew Bible: A Study of the Quaestiones Hebraicae in Genesim*. Oxford: Clarendon, 1993.
Kaufman, Stephen A. "The Temple Scroll and Higher Criticism." *HUCA* 53 (1982): 29–43.
Keel, Othmar. *The Song of Songs*. Translated by Frederick J. Gaiser. CC. Minneapolis: Fortress, 1994.
Kelly, John N. D. *Early Christian Doctrines*. 4th ed. London: A&C Black, 1968.
Kennedy, George A. *New Testament Interpretation through Rhetorical Criticism*. SR. Chapel Hill: University of North Carolina Press, 1984.
Kenyon, Frederic. *Our Bible and the Ancient Manuscripts*. 5th ed. London: Eyre & Spottiswoode, 1958.
Kessler, Stephan Ch. "Gregory the Great: A Figure of Tradition and Transition in Church Exegesis." *HBOT* 1/2 (2000): 135–47.
Keys, Gillian. *The Wages of Sin: A Reappraisal of the "Succession Narrative."* JSOTSup 221. Sheffield: Sheffield Academic, 1996.
Kirk, K. E. *The Epistle to the Romans in the Revised Version with Introduction and Commentary*. CB. Oxford: Clarendon, 1950.

Klaver, J. M. I. *Geology and Religious Sentiment: The Effect of Geological Discourse on English Society and Literature between 1829 and 1859.* BSIH 80. Leiden: Brill, 1997.

Kleeberg, Berhard. "The Will to Meaning: Protestant Reactions to Darwinism in Nineteenth-Century Germany." In van der Meer and Mandelbrote, *Nature and Scripture in the Abrahamic Religions: 1700–Present,* 1:257–91.

Knapp, Henry M. "Protestant Biblical Interpretation." *DTIB,* 633–38.

Kobe, Donald H. "Copernicus and Martin Luther: An Encounter between Science and Religion." *AJP* 66 (1998): 190–96.

Kofsky, Aryeh. *Eusebius of Caesarea against Paganism.* Leiden: Brill, 2002.

Kolb, Robert. *Martin Luther: Confessor of the Faith.* CTC. Oxford: Oxford University Press, 2009.

Köpf, Ulrich. "The Institutional Framework of Christian Exegesis in the Middle Ages." *HBOT* 1/2 (2000): 148–79.

———. "The Institutional Framework of Theological Studies in the Late Middle Ages." *HBOT* 2 (2008): 123–53.

———. "The Reformation as an Epoch of the History of Theological Education." *HBOT* 2 (2008): 347–62.

Kotzé, Annemaré. "Augustine, Jerome and the Septuagint." In *Septuagint and Reception: Essays Prepared for the Association for the Study of the Septuagint in South Africa,* edited by Johann Cook, 245–60. Leiden: Brill, 2009.

Kraemer, David. "Local Conditions for a Developing Rabbinic Tradition." *HBOT* 1/1 (1996): 270–84.

Kraus, Hans-Joachim. "Calvin's Exegetical Principles." *Int* 31 (1977): 8–18.

Kroeger, Catherine Clark, and James R. Beck, eds. *Women, Abuse and the Bible: How Scripture Can Be Used to Hurt or to Heal.* Grand Rapids: Baker, 1996.

Kselman, John S. "'Why Have You Abandoned Me?' A Rhetorical Study of Psalm 22." In *Art and Meaning: Rhetoric in Biblical Literature,* edited by David J. A. Clines, David M. Gunn, and Allan J. Hauser, 172–98. Sheffield: JSOT Press, 1982.

Lactantius. *Divinae institutiones (The Divine Institutes),* 3.24. *ANF* 7:94–95.

Lamberton, Robert. *Homer the Theologian: Neoplatonist Allegorical Reading and the Growth of the Epic Tradition.* TCH 9. Berkeley: University of California Press, 1986.

Landes, George M. "The Canonical Approach to Introducing the Old Testament: Prodigy and Problems." *JSOT* 16 (1980): 32–39.

Lane, Anthony N. S. *John Calvin: Student of the Church Fathers.* Grand Rapids: Baker, 1999.

Leach, Edmund. *Claude Lévi-Strauss.* Harmondsworth: Penguin, 1976.

———. *Genesis as Myth and Other Essays.* London: Jonathan Cape, 1969.

Legaspi, Michael C. *The Death of Scripture and the Rise of Biblical Studies.* Oxford: Oxford University Press, 2010.

Leibniz, Gottfried. *Preface to the General Science* (1677). In Weiner, *Leibniz: Selections,* 12–17.

Leiman, Sid Z. *The Canonization of the Hebrew Scripture: The Talmudic and Midrashic Evidence*. Hamden, Conn.: Archon, 1976.
Leonardi, Claudio. "Aspects of Old Testament Interpretation in the Church from the Seventh to the Tenth Century." *HBOT* 1/2 (2000): 180–95.
Levering, Matthew. *Participatory Biblical Exegesis: A Theology of Biblical Interpretation*. Notre Dame: University of Notre Dame Press, 2008.
Levin, David. *In Defense of Historical Literature: Essays on American History, Autobiography, Drama, and Fiction*. New York: Hill & Wang, 1967.
Levine, Amy-Jill. "Feminist Criticism." In Aune, *Blackwell Companion to the New Testament*, 156–65.
Levine, Étan. "The Targums: Their Interpretative Character and Their Place in Jewish Text Tradition." *HBOT* 1/1 (1996): 323–31.
Lévi-Strauss, Claude. *The Savage Mind*. London: Weidenfeld & Nicolson, 1966.
———. *Structural Anthropology*. Garden City, N.Y.: Doubleday, 1967.
Lewis, C. S. *Present Concerns*. Edited by Walter Hooper. San Diego: Harcourt Brace Jovanovich, 1986.
Licht, Jacob. *Storytelling in the Bible*. Jerusalem: Magnes, 1978.
Lilla, Mark. *The Stillborn God: Religion, Politics, and the Modern West*. New York: Knopf, 2007.
Lillback, Peter, and Richard B. Gaffin Jr. *Thy Word Is Still Truth: Essential Writings on the Doctrine of Scripture from the Reformation to Today*. Philadelphia: Westminster Theological Seminary, 2013.
Lim, Timothy H. *The Formation of the Jewish Canon*. AYBRL. New Haven: Yale University Press, 2013.
Lincoln, Andrew T. *Ephesians*. WBC 42. Dallas: Word, 1990.
Lindsell, Harold. *The Battle for the Bible*. Grand Rapids: Zondervan, 1976.
Livingstone, David N. *Darwin's Forgotten Defenders: The Encounter between Evangelical Theology and Evolutionary Thought*. Grand Rapids: Eerdmans, 1987.
Lods, Adolphe. *The Prophets and the Rise of Judaism*. Translated by S. H. Hooke. New York: Routledge, 1996.
Lohse, Bernhard. *Martin Luther: An Introduction to His Life and Work*. Philadelphia: Fortress, 1986.
Long, V. Philips. *The Art of Biblical History*. FCI 5. Grand Rapids: Zondervan, 1994.
Longenecker, Richard N. *Biblical Exegesis in the Apostolic Period*. 2nd ed. Grand Rapids: Eerdmans, 1999.
———. *Galatians*. WBC 41. Dallas: Word, 1990.
Longman, Tremper. *Literary Approaches to Biblical Interpretation*. FCI 3. Grand Rapids: Zondervan, 1987.
Louth, Andrew. "Eusebius and the Birth of Church History." In Young, Ayres, and Louth, *Cambridge History of Early Christian Literature*, 266–74.

Louw, Johannes P., and Eugene A. Nida, eds. *Greek-English Lexicon of the New Testament: Based on Semantic Domains*. 2nd ed., 2 vols. New York: United Bible Societies, 1989.

Lust, Johan L. "Quotation Formulae and Canon in Qumran." In *Canonization and Decanonization*, edited by Arie van der Kooij and Karel van der Toorn, 67–77. SHR 82. Leiden: Brill, 1998.

———. "Septuagint and Canon." In Auwers and De Jonge, *Biblical Canons*, 39–55.

Luther, Martin. *Answer to the Hyperchristian, Hyperspiritual, and Hyper-learned Book by Goat Emser in Leipzig—Including Some Thoughts Regarding His Companion, the Fool Murner* (1521). LW 39:178.

———. *Avoiding the Doctrines of Men and A Reply to the Texts Cited in Defence of the Doctrines of Men* (1522). LW 35:132.

———. *The Babylonian Captivity of the Church* (1520). LW 36:11–18.

———. *The Bondage of the Will* (1525). LW 33:26.

———. *Concerning Rebaptism: A Letter of Martin Luther to Two Pastors*. LW 40:231–32.

———. *Confession Concerning Christ's Supper* (1528). LW 37:279.

———. *Contra malignum Iohannis Eccii iudicium (Against the Malignant Indictment of John Eck)* (1519). WA 2.626.

———. *The Councils and the Church* (1539). LW 41:14.

———. *Der 36. (37.) Psalm Davids (The 36 [37] Psalm of David)* (1521). WA 8:236.

———. *The Deuteronomy of Moses with Notes* (1525). LW 9:3.

———. *Disputation against Scholastic Theology*. In *Luther: Early Theological Works*, translated and edited by James Atkinson, 269. LCC 16. Philadelphia: Westminster, 1962.

———. *First Lectures on the Psalms II*. LW 11:195–207.

———. *First Psalms Lectures*. LW 10:212.

———. *The Gospel for St. Stephen's Day, Matthew 23[:34–39]* (1522). LW 52:89.

———. *Lectures on the First Epistle of St. John*. LW 30:321.

———. *Lectures on Galatians Chapters 1–4* (1535). LW 26:39.

———. *Lectures on Galatians Chapters 5–6* (1535). LW 27:9.

———. *Lectures on Genesis* (1535–1536). LW 1:232–33.

———. *Lecture on Genesis Chapters 1–5*. LW 1:40–41.

———. *Lectures on Genesis Chapters 6–14*. LW 2:45.

———. *Lectures on Genesis Chapters 26–30* (1541–1542?). LW 5:275.

———. *Lectures on Hebrews* (1517). LW 29:174, 222–23.

———. *Lectures on Isaiah Chapters 1–39*. LW 16:78–87.

———. *Lectures on 1 Timothy* (1528). LW 28:239.

———. *Ninety-Five Theses or Disputation on the Power and Efficacy of Indulgences* (1517). LW 31:25.

———. *On the Papacy in Rome against the Most Celebrated Romanist in Leipzig* (1520). LW 39:83.

———. *Predigt am Stephanstage (Sermon on St. Stephen's Day)* (1523). *WA* 11:223.
———. *Preface to the Pentateuch* (1523). *LW* 35:247.
———. *Selected Psalms III. LW* 14:243.
———. *Sermons on the Gospel of St. John Chapters 1–4* (1537–1539). *LW* 22:258, 267–68.
———. *Sermons on the Gospel of St. John Chapters 14–16* (1537–1538). *LW* 24:368.
———. "Sunday after Christmas." In *Sermons of Martin Luther*, vol. 1, edited by John Nicholas Lenker, translated by John Nicholas Lenker et al., 255–307. Grand Rapids: Baker, 1983.
———. *Table Talk. LW* 54.
———. *To the Christian Nobility of the German Nation Concerning the Reform of the Christian Estate* (1520). *LW* 44:200.
———. *To the Councilmen of All Cities in Germany That They Establish and Maintain Christian Schools* (1524). *LW* 45:360.
———. *Treatise on the Last Words of David. LW* 15:276.
Lyell, James P. R. *Cardinal Ximenes: Statesman, Ecclesiastic, Soldier and Man of Letters with an Account of the Complutensian Polyglot Bible*. London: Grafton, 1917.
Lyotard, Jean-François. *The Postmodern Condition: A Report on Knowledge*. Translated by Geoff Bennington and Brian Massumi. Minneapolis: University of Minnesota Press, 1993.
Maddox, Randy L. "John Wesley's Precedent for Theological Engagement with the Natural Sciences." *WesTJ* 44 (2009): 23–54.
Mandelbrote, Scott. "Biblical Hermeneutics and the Sciences, 1700–1900: An Overview." In van der Meer and Mandelbrote, *Nature and Scripture in the Abrahamic Religions: 1700–Present*, 1:3–37.
Marcos, N. Fernández. *The Septuagint in Context: Introduction to the Greek Versions of the Bible*. Leiden: Brill, 2001.
Marsden, George M. *Jonathan Edwards: A Life*. New Haven: Yale University Press, 2003.
Marshall, I. Howard. "An Assessment of Recent Developments." In *It Is Written: Scripture Citing Scripture. Essays in Honour of Barnabas Lindars SSF*, edited by Don A. Carson and H. G. M. Williamson, 1–21. Cambridge: Cambridge University Press, 1988.
Martens, Peter W. *Origen and Scripture: The Contours of the Exegetical Life*. OECS. Oxford: Oxford University Press, 2012.
Martial. *Epigrams*. Translated by Walter C. A. Ker. London: William Heinemann, 1968.
Martin, Ralph P. *James*. WBC 48. Waco, Tex.: Word, 1988.
Mason, Steve. "Josephus on Canon and Scriptures." *HBOT* 1/1 (1996): 217–35.
Mather, Cotton. *The Great Works of Christ in America*. 2 vols. Edinburgh: Banner of Truth, 1979.

Maurus, Hrabanus. *De institutione clericorum (On the Institution of the Clergy).* In *De institutione clericorum libri tres: Studien und Edition von Detlev Zimpel.* Frankfurt: Peter Lang, 1996.
Maxfield, John A. *Luther's Lectures on Genesis and the Formation of Evangelical Identity.* Sixteenth Century Essays & Studies 60. Kirksville, Mo.: Truman State University Press, 2008.
McDonald, Lee M. *The Biblical Canon: Its Origin, Transmission, and Authority.* Rev. ed. Peabody, Mass.: Hendrickson, 2007.
———. "Wherein Lies Authority? A Discussion of Books, Texts, and Translations." In Evans and Tov, *Exploring the Origins of the Bible,* 203–39.
McGrath, Alister E. *The Science of God: An Introduction to Scientific Theology.* Grand Rapids: Eerdmans, 2004.
McKenzie, Steven L. *The Trouble with Kings: The Composition of the Book of Kings in the Deuteronomistic History.* VTSup 42. Leiden: Brill, 1991.
McKim, Donald, ed. *The Cambridge Companion to Martin Luther.* Cambridge: Cambridge University Press, 2003.
McLeod, Frederick G. *The Roles of Christ's Humanity in Salvation: Insights from Theodore of Mopsuestia.* Washington, D.C.: Catholic University of America Press, 2005.
Melanchthon, Philipp. *Erotematum Dialectices,* book 1. 1520.
Melugin, Roy F. *The Formation of Isaiah 40–55.* BZAW 141. Berlin: de Gruyter, 1976.
Merton, Robert K. "Science, Technology and Society in Seventeenth Century England." *Osiris* 4 (1938): 360–632.
Mesguich, Sophie Kessler. "Early Christian Hebraists." *HBOT* 2 (2008): 254–75.
Methuen, Charlotte. "On the Threshold of a New Age: Expanding Horizons as the Broader Context of Scriptural Interpretation." *HBOT* 2 (2008): 665–90.
Metzger, Bruce M. *The Canon of the New Testament: Its Origin, Significance and Development.* Oxford: Clarendon, 1997.
Metzger, Bruce M., and Bart D. Ehrman. *The Text of the New Testament: Its Transmission, Corruption, and Restoration.* 4th ed. Oxford: Clarendon, 2005.
Mitchell, David C. *The Message of the Psalter: An Eschatological Programme in the Book of Psalms.* JSOTSup 252. Sheffield: Sheffield Academic, 1997.
Moberly, R. W. L. *The Old Testament of the Old Testament: Patriarchal Narratives and Mosaic Yahwism.* OBT. Minneapolis: Fortress, 1992.
Moore, James R. *The Post-Darwinian Controversies: A Study of the Protestant Struggle to Come to Terms with Darwin in Great Britain and America 1870–1900.* Cambridge: Cambridge University Press, 1979.
Moran, Bruce T. "The Universe of Philip Melanchthon: Criticism and Use of the Copernican Theory." *CJMRS* 4 (1973): 1–23.
Mosse, George L. *The Crisis of German Ideology: Intellectual Origins of the Third Reich.* New York: Grosset & Dunlap, 1964.
Muilenburg, James. "Form Criticism and Beyond." *JBL* 88 (1969): 1–18.

Muller, Richard A. *After Calvin: Studies in the Development of a Theological Tradition.* OSHT. Oxford: Oxford University Press, 2003.
Murphy, Denis, S.J. *Cromwell in Ireland: A History of Cromwell's Irish Campaign.* Dublin: Gill & Son, 1883.
Myers, Ched. *Binding the Strong Man: A Political Reading of Mark's Story of Jesus.* Maryknoll, N.Y.: Orbis, 1988.
Nelson, G. Blair. "Ethnology and the 'Two Books': Some Nineteenth-Century Americans on Preadamist Polygenism." In van der Meer and Mandelbrote, *Nature and Scripture in the Abrahamic Religions: 1700–Present,* 1:145–79.
Newman, Carey C. "Jude 22, Apostolic Theology, and the Canonical Role of the Catholic Epistles." *PRSt* 41 (2014): 367–78.
Neyrey, Jerome H., S.J. "Social-Scientific Criticism." In Aune, *Blackwell Companion to the New Testament,* 177–91.
Nienhuis, David R., and Robert W. Wall. *Reading the Epistles of James, Peter, John and Jude as Scripture: The Shaping and Shape of a Canonical Collection.* Grand Rapids: Eerdmans, 2013.
Nogalski, James D. *The Book of the Twelve: Hosea–Jonah.* SHBC. Macon, Ga.: Smyth & Helwys, 2011.
———. *The Book of the Twelve: Micah–Malachi.* SHBC. Macon, Ga.: Smyth & Helwys, 2011.
Noll, Mark A. *The Scandal of the Evangelical Mind.* Grand Rapids: Eerdmans, 1994.
Nolland, John. *The Gospel of Matthew: A Commentary on the Greek Text.* Grand Rapids: Eerdmans, 2005.
Nordling, Cherith Fee. "Feminist Biblical Interpretation." *DTIB,* 228–30.
Norris, Richard A., Jr. "The Apologists." In Young, Ayres, and Louth, *Cambridge History of Early Christian Literature,* 36–44.
———. "Irenaeus." In Young, Ayres, and Louth, *Cambridge History of Early Christian Literature,* 45–52.
Noth, Martin. *The Deuteronomistic History.* Sheffield: JSOT Press, 1981.
———. *The History of Israel.* 2nd ed. Translated by Peter R. Ackroyd. London: A&C Black, 1960.
———. *A History of Pentateuchal Traditions.* Translated by Bernhard W. Anderson. Englewood Cliffs, N.J.: Prentice Hall, 1972.
Numbers, Ronald L. *The Creationists: From Scientific Creationism to Intelligent Design.* Cambridge, Mass.: Harvard University Press, 2006.
———, ed. *Galileo Goes to Jail, and Other Myths about Science and Religion.* Cambridge, Mass.: Harvard University Press, 2009.
———. "Myth 9: That Christianity Gave Birth to Modern Science." In Numbers, *Galileo Goes to Jail,* 79–89.
O'Connor, Michael. "A Neglected Facet of Cardinal Cajetan: Biblical Reform in High Renaissance Rome." In Griffiths, *Bible in the Renaissance,* 71–94.

O'Connor, Ralph. "Young-Earth Creationists in Early Nineteenth-Century Britain? Towards a Reassessment of 'Scriptural Geology.'" *HS* 45 (2007): 357–403.
Oftestad, Bernt T. "Further Development of Reformation Hermeneutics." *HBOT* 2 (2008): 602–16.
O'Keefe, John J., and Russell R. Reno. *Sanctified Vision: An Introduction to Early Christian Interpretation of the Bible*. Baltimore: Johns Hopkins University Press, 2005.
Olson, Dennis. "Types of a Recent 'Canonical Approach.'" *HBOT* 3/2 (2015): 196–218.
O'Neill, John C. *The Bible's Authority: A Portrait Gallery of Thinkers from Lessing to Bultmann*. Edinburgh: T&T Clark, 1991.
Opitz, Peter. "The Exegetical and Hermeneutical Work of John Oecolampadius, Huldrych Zwingli and John Calvin." *HBOT* 2 (2008): 407–51.
Origen. *Commentarius in Canticum (Commentary on the Song of Songs)*. Translated by R. P. Lawson. ACW 26. New York: Newman, 1957.
———. *Commentarii in evangelium Joannis (Commentary on John)*, 6.25. ANF 9:371.
———. *Commentary on Matthew*, 14.25. ANF 9:512.
———. *Contra Celsum (Against Celsus)*, 5.54. ANF 4:567.
———. *De Principiis (First Principles)*. ANF 4:380.
———. *Epistula ad Africanum (Letter to Africanus)*. ANF 4:391.
———. *Homiliae in Numeros (Homilies on Numbers)*. Edited by Christopher A. Hall. Translated by Thomas P. Scheck. Downers Grove, Ill.: IVP Academic, 2009.
Osborne, Grant R. "Redaction Criticism." *DTIB*, 663–66.
The Oxford Dictionary of Quotations. 3rd ed. Oxford: Oxford University Press, 1979.
Pak, G. Sujin. *The Judaizing Calvin: Sixteenth-Century Debates over the Messianic Psalms*. Oxford: Oxford University Press, 2010.
Parry, Robin. "Ideological Criticism." *DTIB*, 314–16.
———. "Reader-Response Criticism." *DTIB*, 658–61.
Patte, Daniel. *What Is Structural Exegesis?* Philadelphia: Fortress, 1976.
Perhai, Richard J. *Antiochene Theōria in the Writings of Theodore of Mopsuestia and Theodoret of Cyrus*. Minneapolis: Fortress, 2015.
Petersen, David L. *Zechariah 9–14 and Malachi*. OTL. Louisville, Ky.: Westminster John Knox, 1995.
Philo. *De Abrahamo (On the Life of Abraham)*, 58. WP, 416.
———. *De cherubim (On the Cherubim)*, 3–8. WP, 80.
———. *De congressu eruditionis gratia (On the Preliminary Studies)*. WP, 320.
———. *De decalogo (On the Decalogue)*, 81. WP, 525.
———. *De gigantibus (On Giants)*. WP, 153.
———. *De opificio mundi (On Creation)*, 67–69. WP, 10–11.
———. *De posteritate Caini (On the Posterity of Cain)*, 12. WP, 133.
———. *De vita contemplativa (The Contemplative Life)*, 3.25, 28, 29.
———. *De vita Mosis (On the Life of Moses)*, 2.40. WP, 494.
———. *Legum allegoriae (Allegorical Interpretation)*. WP, 58.

Pick, B. "The Vowel-Points Controversy in the XVI. and XVII. Centuries." *Hebraica* 8 (1892): 150–73.
Polhill, John B. *Acts*. NAC 26. Nashville: Broadman & Holman, 1992.
Polman, Andries D. R. *The Word of God According to St. Augustine*. Grand Rapids: Eerdmans, 1961.
Polycarp. *Epistula ad Philippenses (Letter to the Philippians)*. ANF 1:34.
Pontifical Bible Commission. "The Interpretation of the Bible in the Church." In *The Interpretation of the Bible in the Church*, edited by J. Leslie Houlden, 3–98. London: SCM Press, 1995.
Pope Pius XII. "Encyclical Letter Promoting Biblical Studies, *Divino afflante Spiritu*." In *The Scripture Documents: An Anthology of Official Catholic Teachings*, edited by Dean P. Béchard, 115–39. Collegeville, Minn.: Liturgical Press, 2002.
Popkin, Richard H. *Isaac La Peyrère (1596–1676): His Life, Work, and Influence*. Leiden: Brill, 1987.
———. "Spinoza and Bible Scholarship." In *The Books of Nature and Scripture: Recent Essays on Natural Philosophy, Theology, and Biblical Criticism in the Netherlands of Spinoza's Time and the British Isles of Newton's Time*, edited by James E. Force and Richard H. Popkin, 1–20. IAHI. Dordrecht: Kluwer, 1994.
Powell, Mark A. *What Is Narrative Criticism?* Minneapolis: Fortress, 1990.
Principe, Lawrence M. "Myth 11: That Catholics Did Not Contribute to the Scientific Revolution." In Numbers, *Galileo Goes to Jail*, 99–106.
Procopé, J. F. "Greek Philosophy, Hermeneutics and Alexandrian Understandings of the Old Testament." *HBOT* 1/1 (1996): 451–77.
Propp, Vladimir. *Morphology of the Folktale*. 2nd ed. Translated by Laurence Scott. Revised by Louis A. Wagner. Austin: University of Texas Press, 1968.
Provan, Iain. *1 and 2 Kings*. UB. Grand Rapids: Baker, 1995.
———. *Against the Grain: Selected Essays*. Edited by Stacey L. Van Dyk. Vancouver: Regent, 2015.
———. "Canons to the Left of Him: Brevard Childs, His Critics, and the Future of Old Testament Theology." *SJT* 50 (1997): 1–38.
———. *Discovering Genesis: Content, Interpretation, Reception*. London: SPCK, 2015.
———. "Hearing the Historical Books." In Bartholomew and Beldman, *Hearing the Old Testament*, 254–76.
———. "The Messiah in the Book of Kings." In *The Lord's Anointed: Interpretation of Old Testament Messianic Texts*, edited by Philip E. Satterthwaite, Rick S. Hess, and Gordon J. Wenham, 67–85. Carlisle: Paternoster, 1995.
———. "On 'Seeing' the Trees while Missing the Forest: The Wisdom of Characters and Readers in 2 Samuel and 1 Kings." In *In Search of True Wisdom: Essays in Old Testament Interpretation in Honour of Ronald E. Clements*, edited by Edward Ball, 153–73. JSOTSup 300. Sheffield: Sheffield Academic, 2000.
———. "Pain in Childbirth? Further Thoughts on 'An Attractive Fragment' (1 Chronicles 4:9-10)." In *Let Us Go Up to Zion: Essays In Honour of H. G. M.*

Williamson on the Occasion of His Sixty-Fifth Birthday, edited by Iain Provan and Mark Boda, 285–96. VTSup 153. Leiden: Brill, 2012.

———. *Seriously Dangerous Religion*. Waco, Tex.: Baylor University Press, 2014.

Provan, Iain, V. Philips Long, and Tremper Longman III. *A Biblical History of Israel*. 2nd ed. Louisville, Ky.: Westminster John Knox, 2015.

Provence, Thomas E. "'Who Is Sufficient for These Things?' An Exegesis of 2 Corinthians 2:15–3:18." *NovT* 24 (1982): 54–81.

Puckett, David L. *John Calvin's Exegesis of the Old Testament*. CSRT. Louisville, Ky.: Westminster John Knox, 1995.

Rabinowitz, Peter J. "Truth in Fiction: A Reexamination of Audiences." *CI* 4 (1977): 121–41.

Radmacher, E. D., and R. D. Preus, eds. *Hermeneutics, Inerrancy, and the Bible: Papers from ICBI Summit II*. Grand Rapids: Zondervan, 1984.

Radner, Ephraim. "The Reformation Wrongly Blamed." *First Things*, June/July 2012, 47–52.

Raeder, Siegfried. "The Exegetical and Hermeneutical Work of Martin Luther." *HBOT* 2 (2008): 363–406.

Ramachandra, Vinoth. *Gods That Fail: Modern Idolatry and Christian Mission*. Carlisle: Paternoster, 1996.

Ramm, Bernard. *Protestant Biblical Interpretation: A Textbook of Hermeneutics*. Grand Rapids: Baker, 1970.

Ratcliffe, Susan, ed. *Oxford Dictionary of Quotations by Subject*. 2nd ed. Oxford: Oxford University Press, 2010.

Remmert, Volker R. "'Our Mathematicians Have Learned and Verified This': Jesuits, Biblical Exegesis, and the Mathematical Sciences in the Late Sixteenth and Early Seventeenth Centuries." In van der Meer and Mandelbrote, *Nature and Scripture in the Abrahamic Religions: Up to 1700*, 2:665–90.

Rendtorff, Rolf. "The Paradigm Is Changing: Hopes—and Fears." *BibInt* 1 (1993): 34–53.

Resseguie, James. *Narrative Criticism of the New Testament: An Introduction*. Grand Rapids: Baker, 2005.

Reventlow, Henning G. *History of Biblical Interpretation, Volume 1: From the Old Testament to Origen*. Translated by Leo Perdue. RBS 50. Atlanta: Society of Biblical Literature, 2009.

———. *History of Biblical Interpretation, Volume 2: From Late Antiquity to the End of the Middle Ages*. Translated by James O. Duke. RBS 61. Atlanta: Society of Biblical Literature, 2009.

———. *History of Biblical Interpretation, Volume 3: Renaissance, Reformation, Humanism*. Translated by James O. Duke. RBS 62. Atlanta: Society of Biblical Literature, 2010.

———. "Towards the End of the 'Century of Enlightenment': Established Shift from *Sacra Scriptura* to Literary Documents and Religion of the People of Israel." *HBOT* 2 (2008): 1024–63.
Rex, Richard. "Humanism and Reformation in England and Scotland." *HBOT* 2 (2008): 512–35.
Rhoads, David, and Donald Michie. *Mark as Story: An Introduction to the Narrative of a Gospel.* Philadelphia: Fortress, 1982.
Ricoeur, Paul. *The Symbolism of Evil.* Translated by Emerson Buchanan. New York: Harper & Row, 1967.
Roberts, Alexander, and James Donaldson, eds. *The Apostolic Fathers with Justin Martyr and Irenaeus.* Vol. 1 of *Ante-Nicene Fathers.* Peabody, Mass.: Hendrickson, 1999.
Roberts, Robert E. *The Theology of Tertullian.* London: Epworth Press, 1924.
Robinson, James H., ed. *From the Opening of the Protestant Revolt to the Present Day.* Vol. 2 of *Readings in European History: A Collection of Extracts from the Sources Chosen with the Purpose of Illustrating the Progress of Culture in Western Europe since the German Invasions.* Boston: Ginn, 1906.
Rogers, Jack B. *Scripture in the Westminster Confession: A Problem of Historical Interpretation for American Presbyterianism.* Grand Rapids: Eerdmans, 1967.
Rogerson, John W. "Early Old Testament Critics in the Roman Catholic Church—Focussing on the Pentateuch." *HBOT* 2 (2008): 837–50.
———. "Expansion of the Anthropological, Sociological and Mythological Context of the Hebrew Bible/Old Testament." *HBOT* 3/1 (2013): 119–33.
———. *Old Testament Criticism in the Nineteenth Century: England and Germany.* London: SPCK, 1984.
Rohls, Jan. "Historical, Cultural and Philosophical Aspects of the Nineteenth Century with Special Regard to Biblical Interpretation." *HBOT* 3/1 (2013): 31–63.
Rollins, Peter. "The Fidelity of Betrayal: Give Me a Master I Can Dominate." http://peterrollins.net/the-fidelity-of-betrayal-give-me-a-master-i-can-dominate/. Accessed September 15, 2016.
———. *The Fidelity of Betrayal: Towards a Church Beyond Belief.* Brewster, Mass.: Paraclete, 2008.
———. *The Idolatry of God: Breaking Our Addiction to Certainty and Satisfaction.* New York: Howard, 2012.
Römer, Thomas. "'Higher Criticism': The Historical and Literary-Critical Approach—With Special Reference to the Pentateuch." *HBOT* 3/1 (2013): 393–423.
Rosengren, Allan. "Why Is There a Documentary Hypothesis, and What Does It Do to You If You Use It? A Response to David Clines." *SBL Forum,* July 2006. http://sbl-site.org/Article.aspx?ArticleID=566. Accessed June 14, 2016.
Rubin, Nancy. *Isabella of Castile: The First Renaissance Queen.* New York: ASJA, 2004.

Rudwick, Martin J. S. *Bursting the Limits of Time: The Reconstruction of Geohistory in the Age of Revolution*. Chicago: University of Chicago Press, 2005.

Ruether, Rosemary Radford. "Feminist Interpretation: A Method of Correlation." In Russell, *Feminist Interpretation of the Bible*, 111–24.

Rummel, Erika. "The Textual and Hermeneutic Work of Desiderius Erasmus of Rotterdam." *HBOT* 2 (2008): 215–30.

Runia, David T. *Philo and the Church Fathers: A Collection of Papers*. Leiden: Brill, 1995.

Rushdoony, Rousas John. "The Heresy of Democracy with God." http://ensignmessage.com/articles/the-heresy-of-democracy-with-god/ (accessed March 28, 2016).

Russell, Letty M. "Authority and the Challenge of Feminist Interpretation." In Russell, *Feminist Interpretation of the Bible*, 137–46.

———, ed. *Feminist Interpretation of the Bible*. Philadelphia: Westminster John Knox, 1985.

Russell, S. H. "Calvin and the Messianic Interpretation of the Psalms." *SJT* 21 (1968): 37–47.

Sæbø, Magne. "The Problem of Periodization of 'the Middle Ages': Some Introductory Remarks." *HBOT* 1/2 (2000): 19–27.

Salters, Robin B. *Jonah and Lamentations*. OT Guides. Sheffield: JSOT Press, 1994.

Sanders, James A. *Torah and Canon*. Philadelphia: Fortress, 1972.

Sandys-Wunsch, John. "Early Old Testament Critics on the Continent." *HBOT* 2 (2008): 971–84.

Scalise, Charles J. *Hermeneutics as Theological Prolegomena: A Canonical Approach*. StABH 8. Macon, Ga.: Mercer University Press, 1994.

Schaff, Philip, ed. *The Creeds of Christendom, with a History and Critical Notes*. 3 vols. Grand Rapids: Baker, 1977.

Schaper, Joachim. *Eschatology in the Greek Psalter*. WUNT 2/76. Tübingen: Mohr Siebeck, 1995.

Schearing, Linda S. "Parturition (Childbirth), Pain, and Piety: Physicians and Genesis 3:16a." In *Mother Goose, Mother Jones and Mommie Dearest: Biblical Mothers and Their Children*, edited by Cheryl Kirk-Duggan and Tina Pippin, 85–96. SemeiaSt 61. Atlanta: Society of Biblical Literature, 2009.

Schenker, Adrian. "The Polyglot Bibles of Antwerp, Paris, and London." *HBOT* 2 (2008): 774–84.

Schmemann, Alexander. *For the Life of the World*. 2nd ed. Crestwood, N.Y.: St. Vladimir's Seminary Press, 2002.

Schoepflin, Rennie B. "Myth 14: That the Church Denounced Anesthesia in Childbirth on Biblical Grounds." In Numbers, *Galileo Goes to Jail*, 123–30.

Scholder, Klaus. *The Birth of Modern Critical Theology: Origins and Problems of Biblical Criticism in the Seventeenth Century*. Translated by John Bowman. Philadelphia: SCM Press, 1990.

Scholer, David M. "The Evangelical Debate over Biblical 'Headship.'" In Kroeger and Beck, *Women, Abuse and the Bible*, 28–57.

Scholtz, Gunter. "The Phenomenon of Historicism as a Backcloth of Biblical Scholarship." *HBOT* 3/1 (2013): 64–89.
Schultz, Richard L. "Form Criticism and the OT." *DTIB*, 233–37.
Schulz-Flügel, Eva. "The Latin Old Testament Tradition." *HBOT* 1/1 (1996): 642–62.
Schwarzbach, Bertram E. "Three French Bible Translations." *HBOT* 2 (2008): 553–75.
Schweibert, Ernest G. *Luther and His Times: The Reformation from a New Perspective.* St. Louis: Concordia, 1950.
Scott, Mark S. M. *Journey Back to God: Origen on the Problem of Evil.* AAR Academy Series. Oxford: Oxford University Press, 2012.
Scott, William R. *A Simplified Guide to Biblia Hebraica Stuttgartensia.* 3rd ed. North Richland Hills, Tex.: Bibal, 1995.
Second Vatican Council. "Dogmatic Constitution on Divine Revelation, *Dei Verbum*." in Béchard et al., *Scripture Documents*, 24.
Seitz, Christopher R. *The Character of Christian Scripture: The Significance of a Two-Testament Bible.* STI. Grand Rapids: Baker, 2011.
———. *Figured Out: Typology and Providence in Christian Scripture.* Louisville, Ky.: Westminster John Knox, 2001.
———. *The Goodly Fellowship of the Prophets: The Achievement of Association in Canon Formation.* Grand Rapids: Baker, 2009.
———. "Prophecy in the Nineteenth Century Reception." *HBOT* 3/1 (2013): 556–81.
Semler, Johann. *Treatise on the Free Investigation of the Canon.* 4 vols. Halle: Carl Hermann Hemmerde, 1771–1776.
Servetus, Michael. *De trinitatis erroribus (On the Errors of the Trinity).* 1531.
———. *Dialogorum de Trinitate (Dialogues on the Trinity).* 1532.
Shakespeare, William. *Romeo and Juliet.* In *The Plays and Sonnets of William Shakespeare*, edited by William G. Clarke and William A. Wright. Great Books 26. Chicago: Encyclopedia Britannica, 1952.
Siegert, Folker. "Early Jewish Interpretation in a Hellenistic Style." *HBOT* 1/1 (1996): 130–98.
Silva, Moisés. "Old Testament in Paul." In *Dictionary of Paul and His Letters*, edited by Gerald F. Hawthorne, Ralph P. Martin, and Daniel G. Reid, 630–42. Downers Grove, Ill.: InterVarsity, 1993.
Skalnik, James Veazie. *Ramus and Reform: University and Church at the End of the Renaissance.* SCES 60. Kirksville, Mo.: Truman State University Press, 2002.
Skarsaune, Oskar. "The Question of Old Testament Canon and Text in the Early Greek Church." *HBOT* 1/1 (1996): 443–50.
———. "Scriptural Interpretation in the Second and Third Centuries." *HBOT* 1/1 (1996): 373–442.
Smalley, Beryl. *The Study of the Bible in the Middle Ages.* Notre Dame: University of Notre Dame Press, 1964.
Smend, Rudolf. "In the Wake of Wellhausen: The Growth of a Literary-Critical School and Its Varied Influence." *HBOT* 3/1 (2013): 472–93.

———. "Questions about the Importance of the Canon in an Old Testament Introduction." *JSOT* 16 (1980): 45–51.
———. "The Work of Abraham Kuenen and Julius Wellhausen." *HBOT* 3/1 (2013): 424–53.
Smith, Christian. *The Bible Made Impossible: Why Biblicism Is Not a Truly Evangelical Reading of Scripture*. Grand Rapids: Brazos, 2011.
Smith, James K. A. *Desiring the Kingdom: Worship, Worldview, and Cultural Formation*. Grand Rapids: Baker, 2009.
———. *Introducing Radical Orthodoxy: Mapping a Post-Secular Theology*. Grand Rapids: Baker, 2004.
———. *You Are What You Love: The Spiritual Power of Habit*. Grand Rapids: Brazos, 2016.
Smith, Lesley. "Nicholas of Lyra and Old Testament Interpretation." *HBOT* 2 (2008): 49–63.
Smith, Rachel H. "Parmigianino." In *Renaissance and Reformation, 1500–1620: A Biographical Dictionary*, edited by Jo E. Carney, 279–80. London: Greenwood, 2001.
Snider, Phil, and Emily Bowen. *Toward a Hopeful Future: Why the Emergent Church Is Good News for Mainline Congregations*. Cleveland: Pilgrim Press, 2010.
Snobelen, Stephen D. "'In the Language of Men': The Hermeneutics of Accommodation in the Scientific Revolution." In van der Meer and Mandelbrote, *Nature and Scripture in the Abrahamic Religions: Up to 1700*, 2:691–732.
———. "'Not in the Language of Astronomers': Isaac Newton, the Scriptures, and the Hermeneutics of Accommodation." In van der Meer and Mandelbrote, *Nature and Scripture in the Abrahamic Religions: Up to 1700*, 2:491–530.
Sorell, Tom. "Descartes, Hobbes and the Body of Natural Science." *Monist* 71 (1988): 515–25.
Speiser, Ephraim A. *Genesis*. AB 1. Garden City, N.Y.: Doubleday, 1964.
Spitz, Lewis W. *The Renaissance and Reformation Movements, Volume 2: The Reformation*. Chicago: Rand McNally, 1971.
Stanglin, Keith D. "The Rise and Fall of Biblical Perspicuity: Remonstrants and the Transition toward Modern Exegesis." *CH* 83 (2014): 38–59.
Stanton, Elizabeth Cady. *The Woman's Bible*. Seattle: Pacific, 2010.
Stanton, Graham N. "Q." In *Dictionary of Jesus and the Gospels*, edited by Joel B. Green and Scot McKnight, 644–50. Downers Grove, Ill.: InterVarsity, 1992.
Steiger, Johann A. "The Development of the Reformation Legacy: Hermeneutics and Interpretation of the Sacred Scripture in the Age of Orthodoxy." *HBOT* 2 (2008): 691–757.
Stein, Robert H. "What Is Redaktionsgeschichte?" *JBL* 88 (1969): 45–56.
Steinmetz, David C. "John Calvin as an Interpreter of the Bible." In *Calvin and the Bible*, edited by Donald K. McKim, 282–91. Cambridge: Cambridge University Press, 2006.

———. "The Superiority of Pre-critical Exegesis." *ThTo* 37 (1980): 27–38.
Stemberger, Günter. "Exegetical Contacts between Christians and Jews in the Roman Empire." *HBOT* 1/1 (1996): 569–86.
Stenmark, Lisa L. *Religion, Science, and Democracy: A Disputational Friendship*. Lanham, Md.: Lexington, 2013.
Sternberg, Meir. *The Poetics of Biblical Narrative: Ideological Literature and the Drama of Reading*. Bloomington: Indiana University Press, 1985.
Stofanik, Stefan. "Introduction to the Thinking of John Caputo: Religion without Religion Is the Way out of Religion." In *Between Philosophy and Theology: Contemporary Interpretations of Christianity*, edited by Lieven Boeve and Christophe Brabant, 19–25. Farnham: Ashgate, 2010.
Storkey, Elaine. *What's Right with Feminism?* London: SPCK, 1985.
Streeter, Burnett H. *The Four Gospels: A Study of Origins*. London: Macmillan, 1927.
Stuart, Douglas. *Hosea–Jonah*. WBC 31. Waco, Tex.: Word, 1987.
Studzinski, Raymond. *Reading to Live: The Evolving Practice of Lectio Divina*. Collegeville, Minn.: Liturgical Press, 2009.
Sundberg, Albert C. *The Old Testament of the Early Church*. Cambridge, Mass.: Harvard University Press, 1964.
Swain, Scott R. *Trinity, Revelation, and Reading: A Theological Introduction to the Bible and Its Interpretation*. London: T&T Clark, 2011.
Swartley, Willard M. *Slavery, Sabbath, War, and Women: Case Issues in Biblical Interpretation*. Scottdale, Pa.: Herald, 1983.
Tanner, Norman P., S.J., ed. *Decrees of the Ecumenical Councils*. 2 vols. London: Sheed & Ward, 1990.
Tappert, Theodore G., ed. *The Book of Concord: The Confessions of the Evangelical Lutheran Church*. Philadelphia: Fortress, 1959.
Taylor, Charles. *A Secular Age*. Cambridge, Mass.: Belknap, 2007.
Tertullian. *Apologeticus* (*Apology*), 18. ANF 3:32.
———. *Adversus Hermogenem* (*Against Hermogenes*). ANF 3:490.
———. *Adversus Marcionem* (*Against Marcion*). ANF 3:285–86.
———. *De anima* (*The Soul*), 3. ANF 3:184.
———. *De carne Christi* (*The Flesh of Christ*). ANF 3:523.
———. *De cultu feminarum* (*The Apparel of Women*), 1.3. ANF 4:15–16.
———. *De praescriptione haereticorum* (*Prescription against Heretics*). ANF 3:249.
———. *De resurrectione carnis* (*The Resurrection of the Flesh*). ANF 3:547.
———. *De virginibus velandis* (*The Veiling of Virgins*). ANF 4:27.
———. *The Soul*. ANF 3:202.
Theodore of Mopsuestia. *The Commentaries on the Minor Epistles of Paul*. Edited by John C. Cavadini and John T. Fitzgerald. Translated by Rowan A. Greer. WGRW 26. Atlanta: Society of Biblical Literature, 2010.
———. *Commentary on Psalms 1–81*. Edited by Rowan A. Greer. Translated by Robert C. Hill. WGRW 5. Atlanta: Society of Biblical Literature, 2006.

———. *Commentary on the Twelve Prophets*. Translated by Robert C. Hill. FC 108. Washington, D.C.: Catholic University of America Press, 2004.

Theodoret of Cyrus. *Commentary on the Prophet Jeremiah*. Translated with an introduction by Robert C. Hill. CP 1. Brooklyn, Mass.: Holy Cross Orthodox Press, 2006.

Thiel, John E. *Senses of Tradition: Continuity and Development in Catholic Faith*. Oxford: Oxford University Press, 2000.

Thiselton, Anthony C. *Hermeneutics: An Introduction*. Grand Rapids: Eerdmans, 2009.

———. *The Two Horizons: New Testament Hermeneutics and Philosophical Description*. Exeter: Paternoster, 1980.

Thomas, Günter. "The Temptation of Religious Nostalgia: Protestant Readings of *A Secular Age*." In *Working with A Secular Age: Interdisciplinary Perspectives on Charles Taylor's Master Narrative*, edited by Florian Zemmin, Colin Jager, and Guido Vanheeswijck, 49–70. Berlin: de Gruyter, 2016.

Thomas, Robert L. "Redaction Criticism." In *The Jesus Crisis: The Inroads of Historical Criticism into Evangelical Scholarship*, edited by Robert L. Thomas and F. David Farnell. Grand Rapids: Kregel, 1998.

Thompson, John L. "Calvin as a Biblical Interpreter." In *The Cambridge Companion to John Calvin*, edited by Donald McKim, 58–73. Cambridge: Cambridge University Press, 2004.

———. "The Immoralities of the Patriarchs in the History of Exegesis: A Reappraisal of Calvin's Position." *CTJ* 26 (1991): 9–46.

———. *Writing the Wrongs: Women of the Old Testament among Biblical Commentators from Philo through the Reformation*. Oxford: Oxford University Press, 2001.

Thompson, Mark D. *A Clear and Present Word: The Clarity of Scripture*. NSBT 21. Downers Grove, Ill.: InterVarsity, 2006.

———. *A Sure Ground on Which to Stand: The Relation of Authority and Interpretive Method in Luther's Approach to Scripture*. PBTM. Carlisle: Paternoster, 2004.

Tolkien, J. R. R. "On Fairy Stories." In *Tree and Leaf*, 11–79. London: Unwin, 1964.

Torjesen, Karen Jo. *Hermeneutical Procedure and Theological Method in Origen's Exegesis*. PTS 28. Berlin: de Gruyter, 1986.

Tov, Emanuel. "The History and Significance of a Standard Text of the Hebrew Bible." *HBOT* 1/1 (1996): 49–66.

———. "The Septuagint as a Source for the Literary Analysis of Hebrew Scripture." In Evans and Tov, *Exploring the Origins of the Bible*, 31–56.

———. *Textual Criticism of the Hebrew Bible*. 3rd ed. Minneapolis: Fortress, 2012.

Travers, Michael E. "Formalism." *DTIB*, 230–32.

Treier, Daniel J. "Typology." *DTIB*, 823–27.

Trible, Phyllis. "Postscript: Jottings on the Journey." In Russell, *Feminist Interpretation of the Bible*, 147–49.

———. *Rhetorical Criticism: Context, Method and the Book of Jonah.* Minneapolis: Fortress, 1994.
———. *Texts of Terror: Literary-Feminist Readings of Biblical Narratives.* Philadelphia: Fortress, 1984.
Trigg, Joseph W. *Origen: The Bible and Philosophy in the Third-Century Church.* 1998. Reprint, London: Routledge, 2012.
Trobisch, David. *A User's Guide to the Nestle-Aland 28 Greek New Testament.* SBLTCS 9. Atlanta: Society of Biblical Literature, 2013.
Turretin, Francis. *The Doctrine of Scripture.* Edited and translated by John W. Beardslee III. Grand Rapids: Baker, 1981.
———. *The Helvetic Consensus Formula* (1675). In Lillback and Gaffin, *Thy Word Is Still Truth,* 60.
Ulrich, Eugene. "Qumran and the Canon of the Old Testament." In Auwers and De Jonge, *Biblical Canons,* 57–80.
Vanderjagt, Arjo. "*Ad Fontes!* The Early Humanist Concern for the *Hebraica veritas.*" *HBOT* 2 (2008): 154–89.
van der Meer, Jitse M., and Scott Mandelbrote, eds. *Nature and Scripture in the Abrahamic Religions: Up to 1700.* BSCH 36. 2 vols. Leiden: Brill, 2008.
———, eds. *Nature and Scripture in the Abrahamic Religions: 1700–Present.* BSCH 37. 2 vols. Leiden: Brill, 2008.
van der Meer, Jitse M., and Richard J. Oosterhoff. "God, Scripture, and the Rise of Modern Science (1200–1700): Notes in the Margins of Harrison's Hypothesis." In van der Meer and Mandelbrote, *Nature and Scripture in the Abrahamic Religions: Up to 1700,* 2:363–96.
Vanhoozer, Kevin J. *Biblical Authority after Babel: Retrieving the Solas in the Spirit of Mere Protestant Christianity.* Grand Rapids: Brazos, 2016.
———. *Is There a Meaning in This Text? The Bible, the Reader, and the Morality of Literary Knowledge.* Grand Rapids: Zondervan, 1998.
———. "Lost in Interpretation: Truth, Scripture, and Hermeneutics." *JETS* 48 (2005): 89–114.
van Liere, Frans. *An Introduction to the Medieval Bible.* Cambridge: Cambridge University Press, 2014.
Van Seters, John. *Prologue to History: The Yahwist as Historian in Genesis.* Louisville, Ky.: Westminster John Knox, 1992.
Vermij, Rienk H. "The Debate on the Motion of the Earth in the Dutch Republic in the 1650s." In van der Meer and Mandelbrote, *Nature and Scripture in the Abrahamic Religions: Up to 1700,* 2:605–25.
Vessey, Mark. "From *Cursus* to *Ductus*: Figures of Writing in Western Late Antiquity (Augustine, Jerome, Cassiodorus, Bede)." In *European Literary Careers: The Author from Antiquity to the Renaissance,* edited by Patrick Cheney and Alfred De Armas, 47–103. Toronto: University of Toronto Press, 2002.

Visser, Rob P. W. "Dutch Calvinists and Darwinism, 1900–1960." In van der Meer and Mandelbrote, *Nature and Scripture in the Abrahamic Religions: 1700–Present*, 2:293–315.

von Rad, Gerhard. "The Form-Critical Problem of the Hexateuch." In *The Problem of the Hexateuch and Other Essays*, translated by E. W. Trueman Dicken, 1–78. New York: McGraw-Hill, 1966.

Wall, Robert W. "Peter, 'Son' of Jonah: The Conversion of Cornelius in the Context of Canon." *JSNT* 29 (1987): 79–90.

Wallace, Daniel B. "The Majority Text Theory: History, Methods, and Critique." In *The Text of the New Testament in Contemporary Research: Essays in the Status Quaestionis*, FS B. M. Metzger, edited by Bart D. Ehrman and Michael W. Holmes, 297–320. Grand Rapids: Eerdmans, 1995.

Wallace-Hadrill, David S. *Christian Antioch: The Study of Christian Thought in the East*. Cambridge: Cambridge University Press, 1982.

———. *The Greek Patristic View of Nature*. Manchester: Manchester University Press, 1968.

Wallman, Johannes. "Scriptural Understanding and Interpretation in Pietism." *HBOT* 2 (2008): 902–25.

Walton, John H. *Ancient Near Eastern Thought and the Old Testament: Introducing the Conceptual World of the Hebrew Bible*. Grand Rapids: Baker, 2006.

Wansbrough, Henry. "History and Impact of English Bible Translations." *HBOT* 2 (2008): 536–52.

Watson, Duane F. "Rhetorical Criticism." In Aune, *Blackwell Companion to the New Testament*, 166–76.

Watson, Wilfred G. E. *Traditional Techniques in Classical Hebrew Verse*. JSOTSup 170. Sheffield: Sheffield Academic, 1994.

Watts, John D. W. *Isaiah 1–33*. WBC 24. Waco, Tex.: Word, 1985.

Watts, Rikk E. "How Do You Read? God's Faithful Character as the Primary Lens for the New Testament Use of Israel's Scriptures." In *From Creation to New Creation: Biblical Theology and Exegesis*, edited by D. M. Gurtner and B. L. Gladd, 199–220. Peabody, Mass.: Hendrickson, 2013.

Weber, Max. *Ancient Judaism*. Translated and edited by Hans H. Gerth and Don Martindale. Glencoe, Ill.: Free Press, 1952.

Webster, John. *The Domain of the Word: Scripture and Theological Reason*. London: Bloomsbury T&T Clark, 2012.

———. *Holy Scripture: A Dogmatic Sketch*. CIT. Cambridge: Cambridge University Press, 2003.

Wegner, Paul D. *A Student's Guide to Textual Criticism of the Bible: Its History, Methods and Results*. Downers Grove, Ill.: IVP Academic, 2006.

Weitzman, Michael. "The Interpretative Character of the Syriac Old Testament." *HBOT* 1/1 (1996): 587–611.

Wellhausen, Julius. *Prolegomena to the History of Israel*. 1885. Reprint, Atlanta: Scholars Press, 1994.
Wenham, Gordon J. "The Coherence of the Flood Narrative." *VT* 28 (1978): 336–48.
———. *Genesis 16–50*. WBC 2. Dallas: Word, 1994.
West, Mona. "Irony in the Book of Jonah: Audience Identification with the Hero." *PRSt* 11 (1984): 233–42.
Westcott, Brooke F. *The Bible in the Church*. London: Macmillan, 1877.
Westermann, Claus. *Genesis 37–50*. CC. Translated by John J. Scullion. Minneapolis: Fortress, 2002.
Westfall, Richard S. "The Rise of Science and the Decline of Orthodox Christianity: A Study of Kepler, Descartes, and Newton." In *God and Nature: Historical Essays on the Encounter between Christianity and Science*, edited by David C. Lindberg and Ronald N. Numbers, 218–37. Berkeley: University of California Press, 1986.
Westman, Robert S. "The Melanchthon Circle, Rheticus, and the Wittenberg Interpretation of the Copernican Theory." *Isis* 66 (1975): 164–93.
Westminster Confession of Faith. In Schaff, *Creeds of Christendom*, 3:604.
Wevers, John W. "The Interpretative Character and Significance of the Septuagint Version." *HBOT* 1/1 (1996): 84–107.
———. *Textual History of the Greek Exodus*. MSU 21. Göttingen: Vandenhoeck & Ruprecht, 1991.
Weyde, Karl W. "Studies in the Historical Books—Including Their Relationship with the Pentateuch." *HBOT* 3/1 (2013): 521–55.
Whitaker, William. *A Disputation on Holy Scripture: Against the Papists Especially Bellarmine and Stapleton*. Translated by William Fitzgerald. Cambridge: Parker Society, 1849. Reprint, Morgan, Pa.: Soli Deo Gloria, 2000.
White, Andrew D. *A History of the Warfare of Science with Theology in Christendom*. 2 vols. Reprint, New York: George Braziller, 1955.
Whitelam, Keith W. *The Invention of Ancient Israel: The Silencing of Palestinian History*. London: Routledge, 1996.
Whybray, R. Norman. *The Making of the Pentateuch: A Methodological Study*. JSOTSup 53. Sheffield: Sheffield Academic, 1987.
Wicks, Jared. "Catholic Old Testament Interpretation in the Reformation and Early Confessional Eras." *HBOT* 2 (2008): 617–48.
Wiener, Philip P., ed. *Leibniz: Selections*. New York: Charles Scribner's Sons, 1951.
Wilder, Amos N. *Early Christian Rhetoric: The Language of the Gospel*. Cambridge, Mass.: Harvard University Press, 1964.
Williams, Daniel H. *Evangelicals and Tradition: The Formative Influence of the Early Church*. Grand Rapids: Baker, 2005.
Williamson, H. G. M. *1 and 2 Chronicles*. NCB. London: Marshall, Morgan & Scott, 1982.
Wilson, Derek. *Out of the Storm: The Life and Legacy of Martin Luther*. New York: St. Martin's, 2007.

Wilson, Robert R. *Prophecy and Society in Ancient Israel*. Philadelphia: Fortress, 1980.
Wolters, Al. "The Text of the Old Testament." In *The Face of Old Testament Studies: A Survey of Contemporary Approaches*, edited by David W. Baker and Bill T. Arnold, 19–37. Grand Rapids: Baker, 1999.
Worth, Roland H., Jr. *Church, Monarch and Bible in Sixteenth Century England: The Political Context of Bible Translation*. London: McFarland, 2000.
Wright, David F. "Augustine: His Exegesis and Hermeneutics." *HBOT* 1/1 (1996): 701–30.
———. "Calvin's Pentateuchal Criticism: Equity, Hardness of Heart and Divine Accommodation in the Mosaic Harmony Commentary." *CTJ* 21 (1986): 33–50.
Wright, David F., and Jon Balserak. "Science." In *The Calvin Handbook*, edited by Herman J. Selderhuis, 448–55. Grand Rapids: Eerdmans, 2009.
Wright, J. Robert, ed. *Proverbs, Ecclesiastes, Song of Solomon*. ACCS [OT] 9. Downers Grove, Ill.: InterVarsity, 2005.
Wright, N. T. *Jesus and the Victory of God*. Minneapolis: Fortress, 1996.
Yarchin, William. "Biblical Interpretation in the Light of the Interpretation of Nature: 1650–1900." In van der Meer and Mandelbrote, *Nature and Scripture in the Abrahamic Religions: 1700–Present*, 1:41–82.
Yeats, William B. "The Second Coming." In *The New Oxford Book of English Verse: 1250–1950*, edited by Helen Gardner, 820. New York: Oxford University Press, 1972.
Yeroulanos, Marinos, ed. *Dictionary of Classical Greek Quotations*. London: I. B. Tauris, 2016.
Young, Davis A. *John Calvin and the Natural World*. Lanham, Md.: University Press of America, 2007.
Young, Frances M. *Biblical Exegesis and the Formation of Christian Culture*. Cambridge: Cambridge University Press, 1997.
Young, Frances, Lewis Ayres, and Andrew Louth, eds. *The Cambridge History of Early Christian Literature*. Cambridge: Cambridge University Press, 2004.
Younger, K. Lawson, Jr. *Ancient Conquest Accounts: A Study in Ancient Near Eastern and Biblical History Writing*. JSOTSup 98. Sheffield: JSOT Press, 1990.
Zagorin, Perez. *How the Idea of Religious Toleration Came to the West*. Princeton: Princeton University Press, 2003.
Zimmermann, Jens. *Hermeneutics: A Very Short Introduction*. Oxford: Oxford University Press, 2015.
———. *Recovering Theological Hermeneutics: An Incarnational-Trinitarian Theory of Interpretation*. Grand Rapids: Baker, 2004.
Zwingli, Huldrych. *The Clarity and Certainty of the Word of God*. In *Early Protestant Spirituality*, edited by Scott H. Hendrix, 43–48. New York: Paulist Press, 2009.

Index of Biblical References and Ancient Jewish Sources

Old Testament

Genesis

1–11	16, 222, 430, 431, 432, 443
1–2	389
1	10, 125, 324, 368, 385, 405, 456, 471, 605
1:1	10, 430
1:1-3	405
1:1-9	637
1:5	329, 330
1:6-7	331, 432
1:6	10
1:16	330, 432
1:28	167, 222
2–3	222, 223
2	196, 222
2:4	10
2:7	167, 196, 212
2:8	222
2:18	10
2:24	132
3	105, 143, 440
3:7	196
3:8	320, 430
3:16	223, 440
3:22	288
6	458
6:5-8, 9-22	458
6:11-22	463
6:11-13	458
6:19-22	458
7	458
7:1-5	458, 463
7:6	458
7:7-10	458, 464
7:11, 12	458
7:13-16, 17, 18-21, 22-23, 24	458
7:13-15	458, 464
8:1-5	458
8:6-12, 13	458, 463
8:14-19	458
8:20-22	458, 463
9:1-17, 18-27	458
9:20-27	213
9:28-29	458
11	222, 331
11:10	566
12:2-3	632
12:2	146
12:3	132
12:6	389
12:7	136
12–50	443, 482
13:7	389
13:15	136
14:14	155
15	128
15:1-20	146
15:6	128, 132
16	146
16:10	146
16:12	465
17:5	132
17:20	146
17:23	155

19	165	19:6	632
21:1-20	102	20	115, 316, 599
21:10, 18	146	20:4	101
22	128	20:10	134
22:1-19	611	20:12-16	116
22:1	612	20:13, 14	115
22:10-13	126	20:17	115, 599
24:7	136	21:24	116
24:43	118	23:27-28	371
27:11	566	28:4	156
28	126, 328	32	168
28:12	126	32:1-35	101
32	480	32:4, 5, 26	101
32:25-28	523	33–34	125
32:28	464	33:3-5	111
37–50	464, 475, 550, 551, 553, 574		
37–39	552, 553	Leviticus	
37	458, 459, 465, 553	8–9	612
37:2	459, 574	11	164
37:3, 13	458	11:44	128
37:21-24, 25-27, 28, 29-30	459	16	156, 169, 206
37:31	552	19:12	116
37:32-33	552	19:18	116, 128
37:34	458	19:33	116
38	114, 551, 552, 553, 559, 574, 575	24:20	116
38:20	552	25:6-7	134
39–50	553	26:41	111
41	551	27:1-7	599
41:46	574, 575		
45:6	574	Numbers	
46	574	20:2-13	135
46:12	551	21:8-9	168
46:27	333	29:4-9	126
49	200		
49:8-12	553	Deuteronomy	
49:10	153	6:13, 16	114
49:18	458	6:20-24	489
		8:3	114
Exodus		10:16-20	132
1:14	101	10:16	111
2:8	118	15:7-11	116
2:23	101	18:15, 18, 19	112
4:1-17, 21	101	19:15	132
5:1-21	101	19:21	116
7:3-4, 13	101	21:23	132
17:5-7	135	22:13-21	599
17:8-13	155	24–25	134
		24:1	115

25:4	134	13–14	555, 556
26:5-9	489	13	554, 555, 556
27:26	132	14:20	555
30	133	15–20	556
30:6	132	21	493
30:12-14	133	21:15-17, 18, 19, 22	493
32	135	23:1-4	324

Joshua
2	128, 156	1 Kings	
3–9	490	1–11	114, 557
10	95, 434	1–2	490, 554, 557
10:12-13	315	2	554, 556, 558
10:13	57	2:6, 9	557
10:40	94	2:12	557, 566
13–19	490	3–11	557
23	491	3	556, 557, 558
24:2-13	489	3:4-15	558
		3:9, 10-11, 13-14	558
		12	101

Judges
1	491	12:8-11, 15, 28	101
8:24	465	14:19	461
11	607	17:2	633
11:29-40	600	17:8-9	624, 626, 633
12	600, 607	17:8	633
17–21	565	18	459, 557, 633
		18:1	633
		18:17-19	565

1 Samuel
12	491	19	633
12:11	600	19:1-9	633
16–31	564	2 Kings	
17:7	493	14	631
18–20	554	14:23-27	624, 626
31	493	14:25-27	629
		17	491

2 Samuel
1–4	493	20	120
1	606	21–23	565
1:18	461	22–23	114, 411, 457
2	554	24:17	465
9–20	490, 554, 555, 556, 557	25:27-30	38
9	554	1 Chronicles	
11–21	493	1–9	493
11–12	555	3:1-24	493
11:1	493	4:9-10	223
11:2-4	115	10	493
12:24-25	465	16:8-36	70
13–20	555	20:1, 4, 5, 8	493

2 Chronicles
- 24:20-21 — 70

Job
- 7:9 — 428
- 31:1-4 — 115
- 31:29 — 116

Psalms
- 1 — 95, 127
- 2 — 95, 96, 113, 114, 126
- 2:6-8 — 95
- 3 — 95
- 4:4 — 115
- 5:5 — 116
- 6:5 — 631
- 11:4 — 116
- 14:1-3 — 132
- 16 — 113, 188
- 19 — 326
- 19:4 — 332
- 22 — 503, 504, 506, 510
- 22:1-11 — 504
- 22:18 — 127
- 22:22-31 — 505
- 23:1-4 — 126
- 31:6 — 116
- 33:6 — 125
- 34 — 187
- 34:12-16 — 128
- 34:19-20 — 127
- 37:8 — 115
- 39:13 — 328
- 41 — 222
- 41:9 — 60, 127
- 45 — 97, 318
- 68 — 137
- 68:18 — 137
- 68:25 — 118
- 69 — 126, 637
- 69:9 — 126
- 78 — 135
- 80:1 — 126
- 80:9-17 — 127
- 82:7 — 127
- 89:9 — 637
- 89:11 — 328
- 90 — 97
- 93:1 — 315
- 94 — 97
- 95:7 — 126
- 96 — 157
- 103:15-16 — 128
- 106:47-48 — 70
- 110 — 110, 113, 114
- 110:1 — 109, 110
- 118 — 113
- 118:22 — 113
- 119:105 — 308
- 119:113 — 116
- 137 — 47, 95
- 139:21 — 116

Proverbs
- 2:12, 16 — 116
- 3:34 — 128
- 5:23 — 566
- 7:21 — 116
- 8 — 125
- 8:30 — 125
- 10:4 — 428
- 10:19 — 116, 128
- 10:31 — 128
- 11:12 — 128
- 12:6 — 116
- 12:10 — 134
- 12:18-19 — 116, 128
- 15:2, 4 — 128
- 16:7 — 116
- 17:20 — 128
- 17:27 — 116
- 18:4 — 126
- 18:6-8 — 116
- 18:21 — 128
- 21:6, 23 — 128
- 24:17, 21 — 116
- 25:23 — 128
- 26:28 — 128, 566
- 29:11 — 115
- 30:16 — 631
- 30:19 — 118
- 31:31 — 600

Ecclesiastes
- 1:4–5 — 315
- 7:9 — 115

10:4	320	53:1	127
11:5	126	53:7-8	112
		53:7	125

Song of Songs

1:3	118	53:9	128
6:8	118	53:12	126
		54	127

Isaiah

2–12	495	54:1	127
2:2-5	494	54:13	126
2:3	153	55:3	113
2:6–4:1	495	55:11	304
4:2-6	495	58:1-7	134
6–9	119	63:10	111
6:1–9:7	119	66:1-2	111
6	11, 504		
7	97	Jeremiah	
7:3	97	4:4	132
7:14	118, 119, 120, 153, 154, 156, 158, 168, 235	9:9 [LXX]	320
8	169	9:25-26	132
8:4	156, 157, 158, 159	18:18	72
8:8	118	31	121
8:14	168	31:12-14, 15, 17	121
8:23–9:6	120	36:32	647
9:5-6	120	51	625, 663
9:6	153		
11:12	433, 434	Ezekiel	
18:4	316	7:26	72
19:23-25	136	15:1-8	127
19:24	632	28	167
21:6	316	34	126
28:16	128	36:25-27	126
36–39	118, 119, 120	37:24-28	126
39:5-8	119	37:24-27	125
39:8	120	44:9	132
40–55	120		
40:1-5	127	Daniel	
40:1	119	2:34-35	164
40:3	125	Hosea	
40:6-8	128	7:11	625, 632
40:5	125	10:8	308
42:6	628	11:1	121, 124
44:7	166		
45:7	166, 167	Joel	
49:6	632	2:14	622
49:14	147	2:28-32	112
52:5	132	Amos	
53	125, 126	5:22-24	116
		5:25-27	111

6:13-14	629
9:11-12 [LXX]	112

Jonah

1:1–2:2	559
1	559, 633
1:1	624, 626, 633
1:4, 5	637
1:9	560
1:12	637
1:17	630
2	559, 620, 622, 624
2:1	630
2:2-9	559
2:3	630
2:8	560
3	625, 631
3:4	247, 561
3:5-10	559
3:10–4:3	561
4	560, 561, 624
4:1-4	559
4:5-10	560
4:5	560, 561
4:6	559, 561
4:7-9	559
4:8	633
4:10	559

Micah

3:9-12	128
5:2	114, 153, 155, 187, 188
7:18	116
7:20	136

Zechariah

1:7-10	330
7:12	38
9:9	127
13:7	331

Apocrypha and Septuagint

2 Esdras

14:1-48	389
14:44-48	63

1 Maccabees

1:54	70
6:7	70

2 Maccabees

2:13-14	72

Sirach

30:22	301

Psalms (LXX)

151	58

New Testament

Matthew

1:1-17	120
1:1, 3, 5, 6, 10-11	114
1:22-23	118
1:22	115, 121
2:6	114
2:15	121, 124
2:16, 17-18, 23	121
4	114
4:3-11	114
4:14	121
4:17	70, 90
5–7	115, 476, 497
5	115, 116
5:17-20	39
5:17	115, 117, 121
5:20	117
5:21-24, 27-30, 31-32	115
5:33-37, 38-48	116
5:48	166
6:24	461
7:7-11	461
7:7	309
7:12	39
8	498, 637
8:17	121
8:19-22	497
8:20	476
8:23-27	637
8:23	497
8:24	498, 637
8:25	498
8:26, 27	498, 637
8:28-34	637
11:10	40
11:25-27	461

INDEX OF BIBLICAL REFERENCES AND ANCIENT JEWISH SOURCES 693

12:11	134	4:10-11	70			
12:17	121	4:16-30	575			
12:39-41	626, 633	7:11-17	476			
12:40	636	8:22-25	637			
13:11	309	10	197			
13:34	185	10:21-22	461			
13:35	121	10:30-35	624			
13:36	309	11:9-13	461			
13:48	115	11:29-32	626			
16:17	634	12:28	498			
16:18	7	12:54-56	476			
19	116	13:34-35	461			
19:3-9	115	16:13	461			
19:12	174	16:16	37			
21	334	16:19-31	525			
21:4	121	20:41-44	109			
22:41-46	109	23:28	308			
23	70	24	123, 124, 308			
23:16-22, 23	116	24:13-35	123, 150			
23:37-39	461	24:44	40, 60			
23:37	330	24:25-27	40			
24:7	498					
27:9	121, 331	John				
		1:1-3	125			
Mark		1:1	319			
1-2	497	1:14, 23, 29	125			
1:16, 34	539	1:41	126			
2:13-17	476	1:46	3			
3:2	539	1:49, 51	126			
4-5	497	2	334			
4:31	626	2:1-11	476			
4:35-41	637	2:13-25	126			
7:6-8	476	2:13-22	565			
8:11-13	540	3	126			
8:11	541	3:8, 14	126			
11:12-14	479	3:19	308			
12:35-37	109	5:39, 40	308			
12:36	70	6	126			
13:14	70, 539	6:10	127			
14:10	539	6:45	126			
14:27	40	7:38	126			
14:62	70	8	126			
16:1-8	539	8:17, 18	126			
		10:1-21	126			
Luke		10:22-39	127			
1:1-4	479	10:34	60			
2:1-20	476	10:36	127			

12:15, 37-40	127	3:10-18	132
13:18	60	3:21	132
14–15	127	3:23	350
14:9	418	4:3, 10	132
15:25	60, 127	4:13-18	136
19:22-24, 33-35	127	4:16-17	132
		5	162

Acts

2		5:14	98
2:4-6	113	7:6	181
2:14-39	249	7:7	40
2:16-21, 24	112	7:14	182
2:25-31, 32-35	112	8:4	115
3	113	8:32	613, 614
3:13-15	112	9–11	132
3:13, 22-23, 25	107	9:4, 5	132
4	112	9:7, 10	136
4: , 25-28	113	9:13	70
7	113	10:6-9	133
7:11, 13	111–12, 331, 333	13:9	40
7:14	111		
7:42-43	333	1 Corinthians	
7:44	111	2:6	46
7:49-50, 51, 52	98	3:19-20	70
8	111	6:12-20	132
8:26	112, 303, 308	7:29	167
8:32-35	308	9:8-9	84
8:34	126	9:9-10	133, 134
10	308	9:9	133
11:19-30	634	9:10	133, 134
13	184	10:1-4	134
13:15	112	10:4	133, 136
13:22	40	10:5	136
13:32-37	112	10:6	98
15	113	10:11	98, 100
15:15-18	112	10:18	176
17:23	112	11:14	90
17:28	249	14:29-32	291
21:37–22:2	56, 249	15:33	249
24:14	249	15:50-57	300
26:14	40	15:50	46
	249		
		2 Corinthians	

Romans

1:1-3	131	3:6	10, 85, 181
2:21, 24, 28-29	132	3:12-18	181
2:29	181	13:1	132
3:2	39		
3:4	70	Galatians	
		1	508

1:1-5, 6-10	508
1:11—5:1	509
1:11	508
1:13—2:14	508
2	507, 508
2:6-10, 15-21	508
3:1	508
3:6-18	509
3:6-8	132
3:7	146
3:8	60
3:10, 13	132
3:16	133, 136
3:23—4:11	509
3:24	163
3:25	147
3:29	136
4	103, 131, 138, 147, 148, 149, 150, 168, 186
4:12-20	509
4:21-31	102, 133, 137, 138, 140, 145, 169, 509
4:21	137
4:22	83, 173
4:24	85, 146, 147
4:27	147
4:28	136, 146
4:29	145
4:30, 31	146
5:1—6:10	508
5:2, 14, 19-24	509
6:11-17	509

Ephesians

4:7-10	137
4:8	70, 133
6:2-3	40

Philippians

3:17	98
4:18	115

Colossians

2:16-17	99

1 Thessalonians

1:7	98

2 Thessalonians

3:9	98

1 Timothy

4:12	98
5:18	134
6:15-16	300

2 Timothy

3:16-17	210, 316, 638
3:16	24, 40, 585, 317, 606

Titus

1:12	56, 249
2:7	98

Hebrews

1:1	158
1:5	114
8:5	98, 99
9:24	98
10:1	99
11	614
11:17	613
11:32-34	600

James

2:8, 21-23, 25	128
4:6	70
4:14	128
5:1-6, 10-11, 17-18	128

1 Peter

1:15-16, 24-25	128
2:4-8, 9, 22	128
3:5, 9-12	128
3:18-20	71
3:21	98
5:3	98

2 Peter

1:19	309
1:20-21	40, 316
1:21	158
3:16	309

Jude

3	301
9	71

14–15	70, 71	2.40	227, 233
		De opificio mundi (On Creation)	
Revelation		8, 67–69	142
6:12	498	*De posteritate Caini (On the Posterity of Cain)*	
12	471	12	142

Ancient Jewish Sources

Dead Sea Scrolls

1QHa 11.9-10	120

Philo

De Abrahamo (On the Life of Abraham)	
58	142
De cherubim (On the Cherubim)	
3-8	145
De vita contemplativa (On the Contemplative Life)	
3.25, 28, 29	61
De congressu eruditionis gratia (On the Preliminary Studies)	
180	145
De decalogo (On the Decalogue)	
81	142
De gigantibus (On Giants)	
12–15	142
15	142
157–59	142
Hypothetica	62
Legum allegoriae (Allegorical Interpretation)	
1.108	142
3.69, 72–74	142
3.244	145
De vita Mosis (On the Life of Moses)	
2.34, 37	233

Josephus

Contra Apionem (Against Apion)	
1.37–43	61
1.38–42	55
1.42–43	62
Antiquitates judaicae (Jewish Antiquities)	
10.5.1	70
10.78	70

Mishnah, Talmud, and Related Literature

B. Bava Batra 14b–15a	63, 66
Berakhot 28b	120
M. Eduyyot 5.3	67
B. Hagigah 13a	67
B. Megillah 7a	66, 67, 68
Sanhedrin 94a	120
M. Sanhedrin 10.1	58
J. Sanhedrin 28a	58
B. Shabbat 13b, 30b	67
T. Sotah 13.2	58
T. Yadayim 2.13	58
M. Yadayim 3.5	68

Other Rabbinic Works

B. Abot of Rabbi Nathan 1:4	67

Index of Authors

Ancient Classical and Christian Writers

Ambrose: *Jacob and the Happy Life*, 213
Aristotle: *Generation of Animals*, 354; *Rhetoric*, 513
Athanasius: *Festal Letters*, 55, 76
Augustine: *Against Adimantus*, 44; *Answer to the Letters of Petilian*, 44; *Christian Doctrine*, 77, 190–97, 199, 200, 209, 245–47, 251, 293, 386, 447; *City of God*, 71, 77, 246–47, 296, 317–18, 321, 323–24; *Genesis against the Manicheans*, 85, 196; *Good of Marriage*, 211; *Harmony of the Gospels*, 318; *Letters*, 245–46; *Literal Meaning of Genesis*, 195–97, 321, 324; *Questions on the Gospels*, 197; *Reconsiderations*, 300; *Reply to Faustus*, 45, 317; "Sermon 171," 197; *Trinity*, 296

Basil of Caesarea: *Exegetic Homilies*, 320; *Letters*, 44; *Six Days*, 189

Clement of Alexandria: *Miscellanies*, 50, 178, 450
Clement of Rome, 31, 41, 73, 316, 321; *Clementine Homilies*, 52
Cosmas Indicopleustes: *Christian Topography*, 323
Cyril of Jerusalem: *Catechetical Lectures*, 76, 295–96

Diodore of Tarsus: *Commentary on Psalms 1–51*, 319; *Epistle of Barnabas*, 41

Eusebius: *Church History*, 58, 61, 73–74, 76, 125, 174, 214

Gregory of Nyssa: *The Soul and the Resurrection*, 296

Heraclitus: *Homeric Problems*, 131, 140
Hippolytus: *Against the Heresy of One Noetus*, 51

Irenaeus: *Against Heresies*, 17, 33, 43, 45–47, 160–65, 235, 309, 316–17; *Apostolic Preaching*, 43
Isidore of Pelusium: *Letter 195*, 159
Isidore of Seville: *Etymologies*, 254

Jerome: *Apology*, 243–44; *Helmeted Preface to Samuel and Kings*, 59, 61, 63; *Illustrious Men*, 71; *Preface to Daniel*, 240; *Preface to Ezekiel*, 243; *Preface to Genesis*, 243–44; *Preface to the Gospels*, 255; *Preface to Isaiah*, 243; *Preface to Job*, 243; *Preface to Judith*, 240; *Preface to Proverbs, Ecclesiastes, and Song of Songs*, 59; *Preface to Tobit*, 240
John Chrysostom: *Commentary on Galatians*, 131; *Homilies on Genesis*, 240, 296, 448; *Homily 47*, 185; *Letters to the Fallen Theodore*, 211; *Women Taken as Wives*, 598
Julius Africanus: *Letter to Origen*, 239
Justin Martyr: *Dialogue*, 42, 151–52, 154, 156–57, 235; *First Apology*, 42, 152–54, 157–58, 316; *Second Apology*, 152

Index of Authors

Lactantius: *Divine Institutes*, 322–24

Martial: *Epigrams*, 31

Origen: *Against Celsus*, 76, 179; *Commentary on John*, 76; *Commentary on Matthew*, 174, 237; *Commentary on the Song of Songs*, 212; *First Principles*, 59, 173–76, 179–80, 182–83, 211, 310; *Genesis Homilies*, 213; *Homilies on Numbers*, 76; *Letter to Africanus*, 58, 237, 240, 250; *Miscellanies*, 239

Plato: *Apology*, 233; *Phaedo*, 179; *Phaedrus*, 179; *Republic*, 91, 139, 179, 425; *Timaeus*, 179
Polycarp: *Letter to the Philippians*, 48
Porphyry: *Against the Christians*, 214

Tertullian: *Against Hermogenes*, 51; *Against Marcion*, 49, 158, 162, 166–70; *Apparel of Women*, 76; *Apology*, 235; *Flesh of Christ*, 50–51; *Prescription against Heretics*, 49–51, 151; *Resurrection of the Flesh*, 300; *Soul*, 170; *Veiling of Virgins*, 50
Theodore of Mopsuestia: *Commentaries on the Minor Epistles of Paul*, 184; *Commentary on Psalms 1–81*, 187; *Commentary on the Twelve Prophets*, 185
Theodoret of Cyrus: *Commentary on the Prophet Jeremiah*, 320

Modern Authors

Ackroyd, Peter R.: *Continuity*, 38; *Studies in the Religious Tradition*, 119–20; "Succession Narrative," 554
Adams, Douglas: *Hitchhiker's Guide*, 171
Ahlström, Gösta W.: "Archaeological and Literary Remains," 512
Alexander, Philip S.: "*Hebraica Veritas*," 256, 278, 285, 455; "Midrash and the Gospels," 109
Alexander, T. Desmond: "Jonah and Genre," 625
Allen, Michael, and Scott R. Swain: *Reformed Catholicity*, 286, 289–90, 296–97, 302
Allert, Craig D.: *High View of Scripture?*, 17, 27–28, 32–34, 37, 41, 43–45, 52, 55, 417

Alter, Robert: *Art of Biblical Narrative*, 550, 552, 572–73
Alter, Robert, and Frank Kermode: *Literary Guide to the Bible*, 621
Ames, William: *Marrow of Sacred Divinity*, 365
Atkinson, James: *Trial of Luther*, 7, 284
Austen, Jane: *Persuasion*, 577

Bacon, Roger: *Opus Majus*, 256–58, 271, 352
Bailey, Kenneth E.: "Oral Tradition," 473–74, 483
Bar-Efrat, Shimon: *Narrative Art in the Bible*, 562
Barker, Peter: "Kepler and Melanchthon," 339
Barnes, Julian: *Flaubert's Parrot*, 207
Barr, James: "Childs' Introduction," 34; *Holy Scripture*, 13, 34–37, 80, 609; "Literality," 86; "Luther and Biblical Chronology," 331, 342; *Old and New in Interpretation*, 103
Barrett, Rob: "Meaning More than They Say," 561
Barthes, Roland: *Image, Music, Text*, 523–25, 530; "Structural Analysis of Narrative," 94
Bartholomew, Craig G.: *Introducing Biblical Hermeneutics*, 45, 79, 104, 454, 525, 621, 638; "Postmodernity and Biblical Interpretation," 469
Barton, John: "Fixed Canon," 36–37, 302; "Legacy of the Literary-Critical School," 469, 534; *Oracles of God*, 35; *Reading the Old Testament*, 473, 518
Barton, Stephen C.: "Social-Scientific Criticism," 578
Battles, Ford L.: "God Was Accommodating Himself," 329, 432
Bauckham, Richard: *Jesus and the Eyewitnesses*, 354, 480–81, 483–84
Bavinck, Herman: *Gereformeerde Dogmatiek*, 52
Beasley-Murray, George R.: *John*, 126, 565, 575
Beckwith, Roger: *Old Testament Canon*, 29–31, 61, 63–65, 68–72, 76, 78
Bedford, Ronald D.: *Defence of Truth*, 379

Beentjes, Pancratius C.: "Canon and Scripture in the Book of Ben Sira," 61
Bellarmine, Robert: *Disputations about the Controversies of the Christian Faith*, 84
Benson, Bruce E.: "Poststructuralism," 532
Bentley, Jerry H.: *Humanists and Holy Writ*, 262, 275
Berchman, Robert M.: *From Philo to Origen*, 179
Berlin, Adele: *Poetics and Interpretation of Biblical Narrative*, 562
Berman, Art: *From the New Criticism to Deconstruction*, 517
Berndt, Rainer: "St. Victor," 258
Betz, Hans Dieter: *Galatians*, 507, 509
Bewer, J. A.: *Jonah*, 625
Bindel, Julie: "Mary Daly Obituary," 597
Blackwell, Richard J.: *Behind the Scenes at Galileo's Trial*, 362
Blair, Peter Hunter: *World of Bede*, 254
Blenkinsopp, Joseph: *Prophecy and Canon*, 36
Blomberg, Craig L.: *Interpreting the Parables*, 525
Blowers, Paul M.: "Sublime and Blessed Amphitheatre," 322
Boersma, Hans: *Heavenly Participation*, 17–18, 416–23, 425, 638
Böhmer, Heinrich: *Road to Reformation*, 1–3
Bonaventure: *Breviloquium*, 310
Borchert, Gerald L: *John 1–11*, 125
Bornkamm, Günther: "Stilling of the Storm," 497–99
Bornkamm, Heinrich: *Luther and the Old Testament*, 41, 83, 88, 90, 99, 213–14, 217–19, 222, 343
Bouwsma, William J.: *John Calvin*, 88
Bray, Gerald: "Allegory," 215; *Biblical Interpretation*, 8–9, 114, 133, 177, 200–201, 203, 215, 218, 253, 295, 300, 307, 335, 395
Brecht, Martin: *Martin Luther: His Road to Reformation 1483–1521*, 3–8, 48, 268, 283, 291–92, 298, 641–42; *Martin Luther: Shaping and Defining the Reformation 1521–1532*, 9
Brett, Mark G.: *Biblical Criticism in Crisis?*, 618

Briggs, John Channing: "Bacon's Science and Religion," 444
Bright, Pamela: "Nature and Scripture," 322
Brock, Sebastian P.: "Phenomenon of the Septuagint," 141
Brown, Raymond E., and Thomas A. Collins: "Church Pronouncements," 204, 345
Brown, Robert E.: "Jonathan Edwards," 393–94
Bruce, F. F.: *Commentary on the Epistle to the Hebrews*, 114
Bucer, Martin: *Quomodo S. Literae pro Concionibus tractandae sint Instructio*, 82
Bullinger, Heinrich: *Of the Holy Catholic Church*, 297, 335
Bultmann, Christoph: "Early Rationalism and Biblical Criticism," 395, 398; "Wider 'Ein feste Burg,'" 2
Bultmann, Rudolf: *Jesus and the Word*, 482
Burnett, Amy N.: "Hermeneutics and Exegesis," 284; "Luther and the Schwärmer," 294
Burnett, Stephen G.: *Christian Hebraism*, 259, 268–69, 285, 306–7; "Later Christian Hebraists," 276, 278–79
Burrus, Virginia: *Begotten Not Made*, 208
Burtt, Edwin A.: *Metaphysical Foundations*, 340–42, 361–63, 368

Calvin, John: *Acts of the Apostles 1–13*, 333; "Argument to the Gospel of John," 326; "Author's Preface," to *Commentary on the Book of Psalms, Volume 1*, 328; *Commentaries on the Epistles of Paul to the Galatians and Ephesians*, 83, 102–3, 173, 217; *Commentaries on the Epistles to Timothy, Titus, and Philemon*, 12, 313; *Commentaries on the First Book of Moses Called Genesis*, 9–10, 90, 102, 222, 224, 330, 332, 343, 432; *Commentary on the Book of Psalms*, 97, 328, 332–33; *Commentary on the Book of the Prophet Isaiah*, 97; *Commentary on the Epistles of Paul the Apostle to the Corinthians*, 10; *Epistle of Paul the Apostle to the Hebrews and the First and Second Epistles of St. Peter*, 328; *Epistle of Paul the Apostle to the Romans and to the*

Thessalonians, 325, 331; *First Epistle of Paul the Apostle to the Corinthians*, 84; *Harmony of the Gospels*, 92, 331, 333; *Institutes of the Christian Religion*, 27, 88–89, 283, 288, 299, 325–26

Campbell, Antony F.: "Form-Critical and Traditio-Historical Approaches," 474

Capon, Robert F.: *Third Peacock*, 525–26

Caputo, John D.: *Insistence of God*, 544; *Weakness of God*, 14–15; "What Do I Love When I Love My God?" 544; *What Would Jesus Deconstruct?*, 15

Carleton Paget, J. N. B.: "Alexandrian Tradition," 149, 174–75, 177–78, 183, 212, 237

Carlin, Norah: "Toleration for Catholics," 378

Carr, David M.: "Changes in Pentateuchal Criticism," 465; *Formation of the Hebrew Bible*, 466–67, 484

Case, Shirley Jackson: *Evolution of Early Christianity*, 579

Cathcart, Kevin J.: "Decipherment of Sumerian and Akkadian," 276

Catto, Jeremy: "Renaissance Interpretation of the Bible," 202, 261

Causse, Antonin: *From Ethnic Group to Religious Community*, 578

Chapman, Stephen B.: "Canon Debate," 79; *Law*, 36, 38–39, 41, 61–62, 70; "Second Temple Jewish Hermeneutics," 35–36, 94; "Threefold Cord," 65

Chase, Frederic H.: *Chrysostom*, 320

Childs, Brevard S.: *Biblical Theology*, 34, 610–21; *Introduction to the Old Testament*, 34, 36, 96, 119, 610, 616–17, 620–23; *Isaiah*, 120; *Old Testament Theology*, 611; "Response," 609, 617

Clark, Elizabeth A.: *Reading Renunciation*, 448

Clines, David J. A.: "Contemporary Methods," 578

Cochrane, Arthur C.: *Reformed Confessions of the Sixteenth Century*, 289, 295, 298, 304, 334, 336

Cohen, Shaye J. D.: *Beginnings of Jewishness*, 189–90

Collins, Francis S.: *Language of God*, 436

Collins, Wilkie: *Woman in White*, 641

Congar, Yves M.-J.: *Tradition and Traditions*, 45, 47, 286–87, 347, 416

Copeland, R., and P. T. Struck: *Cambridge Companion to Allegory*, 139, 150

Copernicus, Nicolaus: *De revolutionibus orbium coelestium*, 315

Corbellini, Sabrina: "Instructing the Soul," 347

Cormack, Lesley B.: "Myth 3," 322

Cranfield, C. E. B.: *Epistle to the Romans*, 181

Cross, Frank M.: *From Epic to Canon*, 69

Crossan, J. Dominic: "Contemporary Biblical Criticism," 527

Crowther, Kathleen M.: "Sacred Philosophy, Secular Theology," 356

Culler, Jonathan: *Literary Theory*, 517, 542; *On Deconstruction*, 533, 535–36, 541–42, 591–92, 605; *Pursuit of Signs*, 534

Culpeper, Thomas: *Morall discourses and essayes upon severall select subjects*, 356

Cummings, Brian: *Literary Culture of the Reformation*, 4, 214, 266, 347

Dahan, Gilbert: "Christian Exegesis," 257

Daley, Brian E.: "Is Patristic Exegesis Still Usable?", 216

Daly, Mary: *Beyond God the Father*, 596; *Gyn/Ecology*, 596; *Pure Lust*, 596; *Second Sex*, 596

Danielson, Dennis: *Book of the Cosmos*, 363; *First Copernican*, 338

Danielson, Dennis, and Christopher M. Graney: "Case against Copernicus," 341

Davis, Edward B.: "Whale of a Tale," 626

Davis, Edward B., and Elizabeth Chmielewski: "Galileo and the Garden of Eden," 435

Dawson, David: *Allegorical Readers*, 142, 178, 208

De Felipe, Pablo: "Antipodeans," 324

De Lubac, Henri: *History and Spirit*, 173

De Margerie, Bertrand: *History of Exegesis*, 157, 159, 171, 178–79, 182

De Troyer, Kristin: *Rewriting the Sacred Text*, 647

Dempster, Stephen G.: "Canon and Old Testament Interpretation," 52; *Dominion and Dynasty*, 96; "Torah, Torah, Torah," 52
Derrida, Jacques: *Of Grammatology*, 517, 532, 542–43
Di Mattei, Steven: "Paul's Allegory," 140, 144–45, 147–48, 150
Dillenberger, John: *Protestant Thought and Natural Science*, 335, 339, 341, 342, 361–62, 367, 369
Dines, Jennifer M.: *Septuagint*, 30, 228, 230–34, 236–38, 241–42, 248, 646
Dodd, Charles H.: *According to the Scriptures*, 155–56; *Epistle of Paul to the Romans*, 133
Draper, John W.: *Religion and Science*, 337
Driver, Samuel R.: *Genesis*, 458
Dunn, James D. G.: "Kenneth Bailey's Theory of Oral Tradition," 483; *Romans 1–8*, 182
Dutcher-Walls, Patricia: *Reading the Historical Books*, 562

Edwards, Mark J.: "Origen," 178–79; *Origen against Plato*, 180
Edwards, Richard M.: *Scriptural Perspicuity*, 310
Ekserdjian, David: *Parmigianino*, 198
Ellis, E. Earle: *Old Testament in Early Christianity*, 58–60, 62–66, 75–77, 80, 99, 647
England, Richard: "Interpreting Scripture," 406–9; "Scriptural Facts and Scientific Theories," 408–9, 435
Eriksen, Trond Berg: "Sociopolitical and Cultural Aspects," 202, 259, 261
Erlich, Victor: *Russian Formalism*, 517
Evans, Craig A.: "Introduction," 30
Evans, G. R.: "Masters and Disciples," 257–58; "Scriptural Interpretation," 261
Ewald, Georg Heinrich August: *History of Israel*, 412

Farley, Margaret A.: "Feminist Consciousness and the Interpretation of Scripture," 601–4
Feinberg, John S.: "Truth," 427
Fernández-Armesto, Felipe: *Columbus*, 314
Fee Nordling, Cherith: "Feminist Biblical Interpretation," 592
Fetterley, Judith: *Resisting Reader*, 594
Fiddes, Paul S., and Günter Bader: *Spirit*, 181
Finn, Leonard G.: "Rule of Faith," 48, 52
Finocchiaro, Maurice A.: "Biblical Argument against Copernicanism," 363
Fiorenza, Elisabeth Schüssler: *In Memory of Her*, 601; "Will to Choose," 602
First Vatican Council: *Dogmatic Decrees of the Vatican Council*, 344–45
Fish, Stanley: *Is There a Text in This Class?*, 533
Flesseman–van Leer, Ellen: *Tradition and Scripture*, 48, 50, 52
Flood, John L.: "Martin Luther's Bible Translation," 9
Fokkelman, Jan P.: *Narrative Art and Poetry in the Books of Samuel*, 555–56; *Reading Biblical Narrative*, 564–66
Foster, Michael B.: "Christian Doctrine of Creation," 353, 355; "Man's Idea of Nature," 352, 355
Foucault, Michel: *Archaeology of Knowledge*, 580
Fowler, Robert M.: *Let the Reader Understand*, 538–41, 564, 567
France, Richard T.: *Gospel of Matthew*, 115, 117, 121–22, 124
François, Wim: "Augustine and the Golden Age," 268
Franke, John R.: "Scripture, Tradition and Authority," 302
Frei, Hans W.: *Eclipse of Biblical Narrative*, 98, 100, 347
Froelich, Karlfried: "Christian Interpretation," 82, 208, 257
Frye, R. M.: "Figurative Language," 89
Frye, Northrop: *Great Code*, 635–37
Frymer-Kensky, Tikva: *Studies in Bible and Feminist Criticism*, 607–8
Funk, Robert W.: *Language, Hermeneutic and Word of God*, 502
Fyfe, Aileen: *Science and Salvation*, 406

Galilei, Galileo: *Discoveries and Opinions of Galileo*, 415
Gallagher, Edmon L.: *Hebrew Scripture in Patristic Biblical Theory*, 236–42, 244, 248–51; "Jerome," 240
Gamble, Harry Y.: *Books and Readers in the Early Church*, 448
Gamble, Richard C.: "Brevitas et Facilitas," 83
Garland, D. E.: *1 Corinthians*, 134; *2 Corinthians*, 181
Geisler, Norman L.: "Inductivism, Materialism, and Rationalism," 349–50
Gentry, Peter J.: "Text of the Old Testament," 278, 645–46
George, Timothy: *Galatians*, 136; *Reading Scripture with the Reformers*, 291
Gerstenberger, Erhard S.: "Albert Eichhorn and Hermann Gunkel," 471, 474, 638
Gilbert, George H.: "Interpretation of the Bible," 155, 158
Goertz, Hans-Jürgen: "Scriptural Interpretation," 284, 292, 294
Goethe, Johann Wolfgang: *Faust*, 209
Goldhill, Simon: *Aeschylus*, 139
Gottwald, Norman K.: *Tribes of Yahweh*, 586–90
Grabois, Aryeh: "Political and Cultural Changes," 254
Granada, Miguel A.: "Tycho Brahe, Caspar Peucer, and Christoph Rothmann," 342
Grant, Frederick C.: *Economic Background of the Gospels*, 579; "Rhetoric and Oratory," 501
Graves, Michael: *Inspiration and Interpretation of Scripture*, 93, 317, 320, 323
Greaves, Richard L.: "Social Awareness of John Knox," 450
Greene, Mott T.: *Geology in the Nineteenth Century*, 402
Greene-McCreight, Kathryn E.: *Ad Litteram*, 45, 84, 89, 102, 105, 190, 196–97, 220, 222–23, 274–75, 288; "Rule of Faith," 52; "Scripture, Clarity of," 304, 306, 310
Greenwood, Kyle: *Scripture and Cosmology*, 315
Greenstein, Edward L.: "Biblical Narratology," 563
Greer, Rowan A.: *Theodore of Mopsuestia*, 250
Gregory, Brad S.: *Unintended Reformation*, 16, 19, 284, 424, 445–46
Greimas, Algirdas J.: *Structural Semantics*, 520–21
Gritsch, Eric W.: "Luther as Bible Translator," 264
Grossman, Avraham: "Literal Jewish Exegesis," 201
Gundlach, Bradley J.: *Process and Providence*, 409–10
Gunkel, Hermann: *Genesis*, 474
Gzella, Holger: "Linguistic Context," 276

Haarsma, Deborah B.: "Science and Religion in Harmony," 343
Hackett, Conrad: *Global Religious Landscape*, 12
Hagedorn, Anselm C.: "Institutions and Social Life," 578
Hagner, Donald A.: *Matthew 1–13*, 116
Hankins, James: *Plato in the Italian Renaissance*, 208
Hansen, G. Walter: *Galatians*, 147–48
Hanson, R. P. C.: *Allegory and Event*, 104, 148–49, 180, 198; "Notes on Tertullian's Interpretation of Scripture," 170
Harinck, George: "Twin Sisters with a Changing Character," 410
Harris, Jay M.: "Inner-Biblical Interpretation," 108
Harrison, Peter: *Bible, Protestantism*, 356
Harper, Elizabeth: "Jonah," 630–31
Hauser, Alan J.: "Sources of the Pentateuch," 462–63, 468
Hayes, John H.: "Historical Criticism," 399; *Introduction to Old Testament Study*, 459
Hays, J. Daniel: "Jeremiah," 647
Hays, Richard B.: *First Corinthians*, 134; *Reading Backwards*, 107, 121–25, 215
Hayward, C. T. R.: "Genesis and Its Reception in Jubilees," 551
Healy, Nicholas J., Jr.: "Evangelical Ressourcement," 421; "Introduction," 201

Heggen, Carolyn Holderread: "Religious Beliefs and Abuse," 604
Heide, Gale: *Timeless Truth*, 174
Heine, Ronald E.: "Latin Christian Literature," 152
Helm, Paul: *John Calvin's Ideas*, 329
Herman, Arthur: *How the Scots Invented the Modern World*, 392
Hill, Jonathan: *What Has Christianity Ever Done for Us?*, 441
Hill, Robert C.: *Reading the Old Testament in Antioch*, 11, 43–44, 66, 183–88, 203, 210, 221–22, 228, 238–39, 242, 250, 310, 316, 318–20, 448, 646
Hillerbrand, Hans J.: "The Legacy of Martin Luther," 83
Hindmarsh, Bruce: *The Spirit of Early Evangelicalism*, 394
Hobbes, Thomas: *Leviathan*, 373–74
Hobbs, R. Gerald: "Early Reformation Scriptural Interpretation," 84, 206, 215, 264–65, 269, 277, 291; "Hebraica Veritas," 263; "Translation of the Bible," 229
Hodge, Charles: *Systematic Theology*, 408–10
Holder, R. Ward: *John Calvin*, 90–91, 98, 102, 275, 288, 298, 328–29
Holloway, Steven W.: "Expansion of the Historical Context," 411
Holmberg, Bengt: *Sociology and the New Testament*, 591
Holmes, Stephen R.: "Evangelical Doctrines of Scripture," 426
Holton, Gerald: "Johannes Kepler's Universe," 337
Honigman, Sylvie: *Septuagint*, 230–32
Hooykaas, Reijer: *G. J. Rheticus' Treatise on Holy Scripture*, 343; *Religion and the Rise of Modern Science*, 353, 356, 363–66, 368, 444
Howell, Kenneth J.: *God's Two Books*, 362; "Hermeneutics of Nature and Scripture," 357; "Natural Knowledge and Textual Meaning," 322–23
Huehnergard, John: *Introduction to Ugaritic*, 276
Huijgen, Arnold: *Divine Accommodation*, 329

Instone-Brewer, David: "Rabbinic Writings," 109; *Traditions of the Rabbis*, 109
Irwin, Robert: *For Lust of Knowing*, 259

Jenkins, Allan K., and Patrick Preston: *Biblical Scholarship and the Church*, 203, 263
Johnson, H. Wayne: "Analogy of Faith," 11
Johnson, Luke T.: *Acts of the Apostles*, 113
Johnson, Timothy J.: *Bonaventure*, 81–82
Jones, Gwilym H.: *1 and 2 Kings*, 557
Jorink, Eric: "'Horrible and Blasphemous,'" 385
Judge, Edwin A.: "Paul's Boasting," 502
Junghans, Helmar: "Luther's Wittenberg," 2

Kamesar, Adam: *Jerome*, 241
Kaufman, Stephen A.: "Temple Scroll," 466
Keel, Othmar: *Song of Songs*, 188
Kelly, John N. D.: *Early Christian Doctrines*, 319
Kennedy, George A.: *Rhetorical Criticism*, 506–9, 511
Kenyon, Frederic: *Our Bible and the Ancient Manuscripts*, 255
Kessler Mesguich, Sophie: "Early Christian Hebraists," 263
Kessler, Stephan Ch.: "Gregory the Great," 190
Keys, Gillian: *Wages of Sin*, 554
Kirk, K. E.: *Epistle to the Romans*, 133
Klaver, J. M. I.: *Geology and Religious Sentiment*, 405
Kleeberg, Berhard: "Will to Meaning," 407, 409
Knapp, Henry M.: "Protestant Biblical Interpretation," 11
Kobe, Donald H.: "Copernicus and Martin Luther," 342
Kofsky, Aryeh: *Eusebius of Caesarea against Paganism*, 215
Kolb, Robert: *Martin Luther*, 287
Köpf, Ulrich: "Christian Exegesis in the Middle Ages," 257; "Reformation," 449; "Theological Studies in the Late Middle Ages," 257
Kotzé, Annemaré: "Augustine, Jerome and the Septuagint," 246

Kraemer, David: "Local Conditions," 108
Kraus, Hans-Joachim: "Calvin's Exegetical Principles," 83
Kselman, John S.: "Why Have You Abandoned Me?," 503–6, 510

Lamberton, Robert: *Homer the Theologian*, 139, 142
Landes, George M.: "Canonical Approach," 623, 627
Lane, Anthony N. S.: *John Calvin*, 298
Leach, Edmund: *Claude Lévi-Strauss*, 530; *Genesis as Myth*, 523
Legaspi, Michael C.: *Death of Scripture*, 266, 382, 396–400, 403, 467
Leibniz, Gottfried: *Art of Discovery*, 377; *Preface to the General Science*, 376–77
Leiman, Sid Z.: *Canonization of the Hebrew Scripture*, 27, 38, 57–59, 62, 64–71, 75
Leonardi, Claudio: "Aspects of Old Testament Interpretation," 254
Lessing, Gotthold E.: *Proof of the Spirit*, 397
Levering, Matthew: *Participatory Biblical Exegesis*, 18, 285
Lévi-Strauss, Claude: *Savage Mind*, 521, 580; *Structural Anthropology*, 521
Levin, David: *In Defense of Historical Literature*, 574
Levine, Amy-Jill: "Feminist Criticism," 604
Levine, Étan: "Targums," 31
Lewis, C. S.: *Present Concerns*, 440
Licht, Jacob: *Storytelling in the Bible*, 463
Lilla, Mark: *Stillborn God*, 446
Lillback, Peter, and Richard B. Gaffin Jr.: *Thy Word Is Still Truth*, 265, 333, 336, 365–66
Lim, Timothy H.: *Formation of the Jewish Canon*, 37, 61–62, 69, 71, 234
Lincoln, Andrew T.: *Ephesians*, 137
Lindsell, Harold: *Battle for the Bible*, 426, 496
Livingstone, David N.: *Darwin's Forgotten Defenders*, 408
Lods, Adolphe: *Prophets*, 578
Lohse, Bernhard: *Martin Luther*, 283
Long, V. Philips: *Art of Biblical History*, 562
Longenecker, Richard N.: *Biblical Exegesis*, 108–10, 114, 137, 148; *Galatians*, 146

Longman, Tremper : *Literary Approaches*, 562
Louth, Andrew: "Eusebius and the Birth of Church History," 58
Louw, Johannes P., and Eugene A. Nida: *Greek-English Lexicon of the New Testament*, 149
Lust, Johan L.: "Quotation Formulae and Canon," 69–70; "Septuagint and Canon," 69
Luther, Martin: *36th [37th] Psalm of David*, 334; *Against John Eck*, 313; *Answer to the Goat Emser*, 10, 83; *Assertion of All the Articles*, 283; *Avoiding the Doctrines of Men*, 327; *Babylonian Captivity of the Church*, 287, 292; *Bondage of the Will*, 10–12, 90, 268, 295, 303, 306; *Christ's Supper*, 326; *Concerning Rebaptism*, 290; *Councils*, 287, 299; *Deuteronomy*, 327; *Disputation against Scholastic Theology*, 340; *First Psalm Lectures*, 97, 327; *Gospel for St. Stephen's Day*, 325, 330; *Lectures on 1 Timothy*, 326; *Lectures on the First Epistle of St. John*, 325; *Lectures on Galatians*, 287, 325, 327; *Lectures on Genesis*, 81, 326, 330, 335, 343; *Lectures on Hebrews*, 327; *Lectures on Isaiah*, 97, 217; *Ninety-Five Theses*, 1, 5, 90; *On the Papacy in Rome*, 83; *Sermon on St. Stephen's Day*, 334; *Preface to the Pentateuch*, 334; *Selected Psalms III*, 97; *Sermons on the Gospel of St. John*, 289, 300, 327; *Song of Songs*, 9; "Sunday after Christmas," 99; *Table Talk*, 95, 298, 327, 334, 336, 338; *To the Christian Nobility*, 266–67, 291, 356; *To the Councilmen of All Cities in Germany*, 9, 227, 253; *Treatise on the Last Words of David*, 325
Lyell, James P. R.: *Cardinal Ximenes*, 260
Lyotard, Jean-François: *Postmodern Condition*, 531

Maddox, Randy L.: "John Wesley's Precedent," 393
Mandelbrote, Scott: "Biblical Hermeneutics," 395
Marcos, N. Fernández: *Septuagint in Context*, 239

Marsden, George M.: *Jonathan Edwards*, 392–93
Marshall, I. Howard: "Recent Developments," 155
Martens, Peter W.: *Origen and Scripture*, 85, 179–80, 236–37, 242
Martin, Ralph P.: *James*, 128
Mason, Steve: "Josephus on Canon and Scriptures," 31, 62–64
Mather, Cotton: *Great Works of Christ*, 371
Maurus, Hrabanus: *On the Institution of the Clergy*, 254–55
Maxfield, John A.: *Luther's Lectures on Genesis*, 275
McDonald, Lee M.: *Biblical Canon*, 29–30, 32, 69; "Wherein Lies Authority?," 277, 644
McGrath, Alister E.: *Science of God*, 352, 357, 361, 409, 517, 536–37
McKenzie, Steven L.: *Trouble with Kings*, 557
McLeod, Frederick G.: *Roles of Christ's Humanity*, 188
Melanchthon, Philipp: *Carion's Chronicle*, 383; *Erotematum Dialectices*, 82
Melugin, Roy F.: *Formation of Isaiah 40–55*, 119
Merton, Robert K.: *Science, Technology and Society*, 356
Methuen, Charlotte: "On the Threshold of a New Age," 353, 356
Metzger, Bruce M.: *Canon of the New Testament*, 42–43, 73
Metzger, Bruce M., and Bart D. Ehrman: *Text of the New Testament*, 277, 643
Mitchell, David C.: *Message of the Psalter*, 96
Moberly, R. W. L.: *Old Testament of the Old Testament*, 464
Moore, James R.: *Post-Darwinian Controversies*, 406
Moran, Bruce T.: "Philip Melanchthon," 338, 341
Mosse, George L.: *Crisis of German Ideology*, 403
Muilenburg, James: "Form Criticism and Beyond," 474, 502–3, 518–19
Muller, Richard A.: *After Calvin*, 266–67, 380

Murphy, Denis: *Cromwell in Ireland*, 371
Myers, Ched: *Binding the Strong Man*, 581–86, 590

Nelson, G. Blair: "Ethnology," 386
Newman, Carey C.: "Jude 22," 73
Neyrey, Jerome H.: "Social-Scientific Criticism," 579
Nienhuis, David R., and Robert W. Wall: *Reading the Epistles of James, Peter, John and Jude*, 73
Nogalski, James D.: *Book of the Twelve: Hosea–Jonah*, 39; *Book of the Twelve: Micah–Malachi*, 39
Noll, Mark A.: *Scandal of the Evangelical Mind*, 436
Nolland, John: *Gospel of Matthew*, 117–18
Norris, Richard A., Jr.: "Apologists," 152; "Irenaeus," 152
Noth, Martin: *Deuteronomistic History*, 490; *History of Israel*, 579; *History of Pentateuchal Traditions*, 489–90
Numbers, Ronald L.: *Creationists*, 436; "Myth 9," 355

O'Connor, Michael: "Neglected Facet," 203
O'Connor, Ralph: "Young-Earth Creationists," 404–5
Oftestad, Bernt T.: "Reformation Hermeneutics," 284, 304
O'Keefe, John J., and Russell R. Reno: *Sanctified Vision*, 49, 103–4, 162, 163, 207, 208, 274, 310
Olson, Dennis: "Canonical Approach," 284, 304
O'Neill, John C.: *Bible's Authority*, 350, 396–97, 399, 403, 411–12, 457, 468–69, 471, 478
Opitz, Peter: "John Oecolampadius, Huldrych Zwingli and John Calvin," 218, 269
Osborne, Grant R.: "Redaction Criticism," 488

Pak, G. Sujin: *Judaizing Calvin*, 97, 190
Parry, Robin: "Ideological Criticism," 578; "Reader-Response Criticism," 534–35
Patte, Daniel: *Structural Exegesis*, 522
Perhai, Richard J.: *Antiochene Theōria*, 146

Petersen, David L.: *Zechariah 9–14 and Malachi*, 38
Pick, B.: "Vowel-Points," 273
Polhill, John B.: *Acts*, 111
Polman, Andries D. R.: *Word of God According to St. Augustine*, 296, 310, 319
Pontifical Bible Commission: "Interpretation of the Bible," 205, 272–73
Pope Pius XII: *Divino afflante Spiritu*, 203–4, 216, 224, 270–72, 345, 448
Popkin, Richard H.: *Isaac La Peyrère*, 385; "Spinoza and Bible Scholarship," 389
Powell, Mark A.: *Narrative Criticism*, 549–50
Principe, Lawrence M.: "Myth 11," 356
Procopé, J. F.: "Greek Philosophy," 140, 179, 215
Propp, Vladimir: *Morphology of the Folktale*, 520
Provan, Iain: *1 and 2 Kings*, 101; *Against the Grain*, 120, 555, 615; "Canons to the Left," 615; *Discovering Genesis*, 108, 213, 553; "Hearing the Historical Books," 92; "Messiah in the Book of Kings," 120; "Pain in Childbirth," 223; "Missing the Forest," 555; *Seriously Dangerous Religion*, 160, 221, 223, 352
Provan, Iain, V. Philips Long, and Tremper Longman III: *Biblical History of Israel*, 482, 484, 493, 512, 562–63, 572–74, 589, 591, 626
Provence, Thomas E.: "Who Is Sufficient for These Things?," 181
Puckett, David L.: *John Calvin's Exegesis*, 328–30, 432

Rabinowitz, Peter J.: "Truth in Fiction," 534–35
Radmacher, E. D., and R. D. Preus: *Hermeneutics, Inerrancy, and the Bible*, 15, 427
Radner, Ephraim: "The Reformation Wrongly Blamed," 17, 424–25
Raeder, Siegfried: "Martin Luther," 264, 274
Ramachandra, Vinoth: *Gods That Fail*, 585–86
Ramm, Bernard: *Protestant Biblical Interpretation*, 433

Ratcliffe, Susan: *Oxford Dictionary of Quotations*, 518
Remmert, Volker R.: "Mathematicians," 340
Rendtorff, Rolf: "Paradigm," 469
Resseguie, James: *Narrative Criticism*, 562
Reventlow, Henning G.: *History of Biblical Interpretation*, 41–43, 47, 97, 140, 154–55, 158–60, 163–64, 177–80, 182, 185, 188, 190, 200–202, 209–10, 212, 214, 228, 242–44, 250, 254–55, 258–59, 261–64, 268–70, 301, 310; "Century of Enlightenment," 391, 403
Rex, Richard: "Humanism and Reformation," 248, 265, 268, 450
Rhoads, David, and Donald Michie: *Mark as Story*, 566–71
Ricoeur, Paul: *Symbolism of Evil*, 549–50
Roberts, Robert E.: *Theology of Tertullian*, 183
Robinson, James H.: *Protestant Revolt*, 8
Rogers, Jack B.: *Scripture in the Westminster Confession*, 366
Rogerson, John W.: "Early Old Testament Critics," 390; "Expansion," 411; *Old Testament Criticism*, 455–57, 460, 462
Rohls, Jan: "Historical, Cultural and Philosophical Aspects," 396, 411–12
Rollins, Peter: *Fidelity of Betrayal*, 15, 544; *Idolatry of God*, 15, 54–55
Römer, Thomas: "Higher Criticism," 457
Rosengren, Allan: "Documentary Hypothesis," 463
Rubin, Nancy: *Isabella of Castile*, 314
Rudwick, Martin J. S.: *Bursting the Limits of Time*, 402, 415
Ruether, Rosemary Radford: "Correlation," 602–4
Rummel, Erika: "Desiderius Erasmus," 214
Runia, David T.: *Philo and the Church Fathers*, 177
Rushdoony, Rousas John: "The Heresy of Democracy with God," 381
Russell, Letty M.: "Feminist Interpretation," 602; *Feminist Interpretation of the Bible*, 601–2, 606
Russell, S. H.: "Calvin and the Messianic Interpretation of the Psalms," 96
Rutherford, Samuel: *Divine Right*, 366

Sæbø, Magne: "Problem of Periodization," 22
Salters, Robin B.: *Jonah and Lamentations*, 559, 561
Sanders, James A.: *Torah and Canon*, 36
Sandys-Wunsch, John: "Early Old Testament Critics," 400
Saussure, Ferdinand de: *Course in General Linguistics*, 519
Scalise, Charles J.: *Hermeneutics as Theological Prolegomena*, 618
Schaper, Joachim: *Eschatology in the Greek Psalter*, 96
Schearing, Linda S.: "Parturition (Childbirth)," 440
Schenker, Adrian: "Polyglot Bibles," 278
Schmemann, Alexander: *For the Life of the World*, 446
Schoepflin, Rennie B.: "Myth 14," 440
Scholder, Klaus: *Birth of Modern Critical Theology*, 342, 363–65, 373, 376, 379, 383, 383–86, 394
Scholer, David M.: "Headship," 598, 604
Scholtz, Gunter: "Historicism," 410
Schultz, Richard L.: "Form Criticism," 480
Schulz-Flügel, Eva: "Latin Old Testament Tradition," 242–43, 646
Schwarzbach, Bertram E.: "Three French Bible Translations," 265
Schweibert, Ernest G.: *Luther and His Times*, 2
Scott, Mark S. M.: *Journey Back to God*, 179–80
Second Vatican Council: *Dei Verbum*, 204–5, 272, 345
Semler, Johann: *Free Investigation of the Canon*, 399, 609–10
Seitz, Christopher R.: *Character of Christian Scripture*, 41; *Figured Out*, 105, 174; *Goodly Fellowship of the Prophets*, 39, 45, 72–73; "Prophecy in the Nineteenth Century Reception," 474, 631
Servetus, Michael: *Dialogues on the Trinity*, 288; *On the Errors of the Trinity*, 288
Shakespeare, William: *Hamlet*, 1; *Romeo and Juliet*, 138

Siegert, Folker: "Early Jewish Interpretation," 30–31, 139–40, 142, 149, 177
Silva, Moisés: "Old Testament in Paul," 234
Skalnik, James Veazie: *Ramus and Reform*, 268
Skarsaune, Oskar: "Old Testament Canon," 70, 75; "Scriptural Interpretation," 152, 155, 160, 166
Smalley, Beryl: *Bible in the Middle Ages*, 185, 195, 258
Smend, Rudolf: "Questions about the Importance of the Canon," 36; "In the Wake of Wellhausen," 462; "The Work of Abraham Kuenen and Julius Wellhausen," 457, 468, 470
Smith, Christian: *Bible Made Impossible*, 18–19, 87, 285
Smith, James K. A.: *Desiring the Kingdom*, 446; *Introducing Radical Orthodoxy*, 14, 18, 419, 421, 423, 425; *You Are What You Love*, 446
Smith, Lesley: "Nicholas Lyra," 82, 258
Smith, Rachel H.: "Parmigianino," 198
Snider, Phil, and Emily Bowen: *Toward A Hopeful Future*, 15
Snobelen, Stephen D.: "In the Language of Men," 364; "'Not in the Language of Astronomers,'" 364
Sorell, Tom: "Descartes, Hobbes and the Body of Natural Science," 374
Speiser, Ephraim A.: *Genesis*, 464, 551
Spinoza, Benedict de: *Theological-Political Treatise*, 386–88
Spitz, Lewis W.: *Renaissance and Reformation Movements*, 336–38, 449–50
Stanglin, Keith D.: "Biblical Perspicuity," 377
Stanton, Elizabeth Cady: *Woman's Bible*, 596
Stanton, Graham N.: "Q," 461
Steiger, Johann A.: "Reformation Legacy," 218, 273, 289–90, 306, 365, 367, 384, 450
Stein, Robert H.: "Redaktionsgeschichte," 487
Steinmetz, David C.: "John Calvin as an Interpreter of the Bible," 83, 271–72, 329; "The Superiority of Pre-Critical Exegesis," 18

Stemberger, Günter: "Exegetical Contacts," 250
Stenmark, Lisa L.: *Religion, Science, and Democracy*, 343
Sternberg, Meir: *Poetics of Biblical Narrative*, 482, 530, 573
Stofanik, Stefan: "John Caputo," 15
Storkey, Elaine: *What's Right with Feminism?*, 601
Streeter, Burnett H.: *Four Gospels*, 491–92, 514–15
Stuart, Douglas: *Hosea–Jonah*, 625
Studzinski, Raymond: *Reading to Live*, 205
Sundberg, Albert C.: *Old Testament of the Early Church*, 32–33, 35–36, 55, 71
Swain, Scott R.: *Trinity, Revelation, and Reading*, 367
Swartley, Willard M.: *Slavery, Sabbath, War, and Women*, 598

Tanner, Norman P.: *Decrees of the Ecumenical Councils*, 28, 85, 189, 253, 259, 285
Tappert, Theodore G.: *Book of Concord*, 290
Taylor, Charles: *Secular Age*, 16
Thiel, John E.: *Senses of Tradition*, 303
Thiselton, Anthony: *Hermeneutics*, 184; *Two Horizons*, 531
Thomas Aquinas: *Summa theologiae*, 82, 199, 210, 310, 439
Thomas, Günter: "Religious Nostalgia," 16
Thomas, Robert L.: "Redaction Criticism," 496
Thompson, John L.: "Calvin as a Biblical Interpreter," 84, 208, 219–20, 288, 298, 329; "The Immoralities of the Patriarchs," 213; *Writing the Wrongs*, 607
Thompson, Mark D.: *Clear and Present Word*, 308–9; *Sure Ground*, 327–30
Tolkien, J. R. R.: "On Fairy Stories," 455
Torjesen, Karen Jo: *Hermeneutical Procedure*, 173
Tov, Emanuel: "Septuagint," 646; "Standard Text," 232, 644–45; *Textual Criticism of the Hebrew Bible*, 645
Travers, Michael E.: "Formalism," 517
Treier, Daniel J.: "Typology," 99, 104
Trible, Phyllis: "Postscript," 606; *Rhetorical Criticism*, 500–501, 518, 550, 584, 627; *Texts of Terror*, 606–7
Trigg, Joseph W.: *Origen*, 173
Trobisch, David: *User's Guide*, 644
Turretin, Francis: *Doctrine of Scripture*, 265, 288, 305–6

Ulrich, Eugene: "Qumran and the Canon of the Old Testament," 69–70

van der Meer, Jitse M., and Richard J. Oosterhoff: "God, Scripture, and the Rise of Modern Science," 354
van Liere, Frans: *Introduction to the Medieval Bible*, 255
Van Seters, John: *Prologue to History*, 462
Vanderjagt, Arjo: "Ad Fontes!," 268
Vanhoozer, Kevin J.: *Biblical Authority*, 17, 286, 288, 290–91, 293, 295, 297, 418–19, 423, 425, 441–42, 639; *Is There a Meaning in This Text?*, 87–89, 91, 104, 213, 522, 533, 542–43; "Lost in Interpretation," 485
Vermij, Rienk H.: "Motion of the Earth," 364, 401, 577
Vessey, Mark: "From *Cursus* to *Ductus*," 327
Visser, Rob P. W.: "Dutch Calvinists and Darwinism," 409–10
Von Rad, Gerhard: "Form-Critical Problem of the Hexateuch," 488–89

Wall, Robert W.: "Peter, 'Son' of Jonah," 634
Wallace, Daniel B.: "Majority Text Theory," 644
Wallace-Hadrill, David S.: *Christian Antioch*, 179, 186; *Greek Patristic View of Nature*, 210
Wallman, Johannes: "Scriptural Understanding and Interpretation in Pietism," 365, 376, 391, 447
Walton, John H.: *Ancient Near Eastern Thought*, 419
Wansbrough, Henry: "History and Impact of English Bible Translations," 265
Watson, Duane F.: "Rhetorical Criticism," 510
Watson, Wilfred G. E.: *Traditional Techniques in Classical Hebrew Verse*, 510

Watts, John D. W.: *Isaiah 1–33*, 119, 124–25
Watts, Rikk E.: "How Do You Read?", 121, 135, 137
Weber, Max: *Ancient Judaism*, 578
Webster, John: *Domain of the Word*, 305; *Holy Scripture*, 307, 367
Wegner, Paul D.: *Student's Guide to Textual Criticism*, 648
Weitzman, Michael: "Syriac Old Testament," 646
Wellhausen, Julius: *Prolegomena to the History of Israel*, 459–60
Wenham, Gordon J.: "Coherence of the Flood Narrative," 463; *Genesis 16–50*, 146
West, Mona: "Irony in the Book of Jonah," 627–29
Westcott, Brooke F.: *Bible in the Church*, 77–78, 269
Westermann, Claus: *Genesis 37–50*, 464
Westfall, Richard S.: "Rise of Science," 361
Westman, Robert S.: "Melanchthon Circle," 341
Weyde, Karl W.: "Studies in the Historical Books," 461
Wevers, John W.: "Septuagint Version," 646; *Textual History of the Greek Exodus*, 646
Whitaker, William: *Disputation on Holy Scripture*, 78
White, Andrew D.: *History of the Warfare of Science with Theology*, 336–37, 339
Whitelam, Keith W.: *Invention of Ancient Israel*, 572
Whybray, R. Norman: *Making of the Pentateuch*, 465
Wicks, Jared: "Catholic Old Testament Interpretation," 203, 229, 260, 285, 362
Wiener, Philip P.: *Leibniz: Selections*, 376–77
Wilder, Amos N.: *Early Christian Rhetoric*, 502

Williams, Daniel H.: *Evangelicals and Tradition*, 18, 45
Williamson, H. G. M.: *1 and 2 Chronicles*, 494
Wilson, Derek: *Out of the Storm*, 6
Wilson, Robert R.: *Prophecy and Society in Ancient Israel*, 629–30
Wolters, Al: "The Text of the Old Testament," 644–45, 647
Worth, Roland H., Jr.: *Church, Monarch and Bible in Sixteenth Century England*, 265
Wright, David F.: "Augustine: His Exegesis and Hermeneutics," 44, 190, 248; "Calvin's Pentateuchal Criticism," 329
Wright, David F., and Jon Balserak: "Science," 339
Wright, J. Robert: *Proverbs, Ecclesiastes, Song of Solomon*, 189
Wright, N. T.: *Jesus and the Victory of God*, 123

Yarchin, William: "Biblical Interpretation," 394, 402, 404–5
Yeats, William B.: *Second Coming*, 383
Young, Davis A.: *John Calvin and the Natural World*, 332–33, 340, 342, 404, 436
Young, Frances M.: *Biblical Exegesis*, 104, 158, 186, 467
Younger, K. Lawson, Jr.: *Ancient Conquest Accounts*, 95

Zagorin, Perez: *Idea of Religious Toleration*, 350, 359, 381
Zimmermann, Jens: *Recovering Theological Hermeneutics*, 289, 306, 340, 417–18, 481; *Short Introduction*, 372, 528, 530, 535, 543
Zwingli, Huldrych: *Clarity and Certainty*, 295

Index of Subjects

allegory, allegorical reading, 81–225
Alexandria, Alexandrian exegesis/school, 131–225
Antioch, Antiochene exegesis/school, 131–225
authority of Scripture, 205–25, 313–45

biblicism, 18, 87, 285

canon: and Scripture-consciousness, 34–37; formation of, 55–80
canonical criticism, 609–39
communicative intent, 81–225
Chicago Statement on Biblical Hermeneutics (1982), 349–51, 425–37

deconstruction, 541–47

eclipse of biblical narrative, 347–49
Enlightenment, 391–401
feminist criticism, 591–608

form criticism, 469–85

Gnosticism, 42–43, 46–47, 52, 160, 164–65, 171, 178, 182–83, 190, 211, 305, 320, 437

humanism, 202, 260–61, 267, 275, 285, 293–94, 350, 379, 439–40, 641

inerrancy of Scripture, 16, 19, 337, 345, 367, 380, 426, 427, 429–30

inspiration of Scripture, 11–12, 40, 79, 158, 176, 181–82, 185, 233, 247, 248, 274, 277, 317–20, 325–26, 328–29, 344–45, 368, 389, 405, 496–97

literal sense, literal reading, 81–106

narrative criticism, 549–75
New Testament reading of Scripture, 107–50

original texts and languages, importance of, 260–79, 643–48

patristic reading of Scripture (major discussions): in Augustine, 190–97; in Irenaeus, 159–65; in Justin Martyr, 152–59; in Origen, 173–83; in Tertullian, 165–70; in Theodore, 184–90
perspicuity of Scripture, 302–12
poststructuralism, 531–47
Protestant hermeneutics: "first way" (historical-critical), 13–14, 93–94, 388, 415, 496; "second way" (postmodern), 14–15, 63, 105, 217, 224, 282, 415, 543, 638; "third way" (Chicago), 15–16, 18, 21, 93, 105, 425, 496; "fourth way" (counter-Reformational), 16–18, 21, 52, 93, 105–6, 216, 225, 279, 282, 416, 423, 638

reader-response criticism, 533–47
redaction criticism, 488–99
rhetorical criticism, 499–515

scholasticism, 266–67, 292–93, 336, 340, 354–56, 365, 369, 372
science: Copernican cosmology, 315–43, 361–69; Darwinian evolution, 401–46
secular history, emergence of, 383–413
Septuagint (as Christian Scripture), 227–51
social scientific criticism, 578–91
source criticism, 455–69
sola scriptura (Scripture alone), 283–302

spiritual sense/reading, 10, 18, 82–84, 93, 103, 114, 125, 127, 129, 131, 150, 165, 176, 181–82, 186, 196, 199, 201, 205, 209–10, 214, 215–16, 220, 225, 246, 258, 418, 426, 541, 638
structuralism, 517–31

textual criticism, 236–48, 260–79, 643–48

Vulgate (as Christian Scripture), 252–60

www.ingramcontent.com/pod-product-compliance
Lightning Source LLC
Chambersburg PA
CBHW031536091125
35182CB00030B/644